Business
Research Methods

D1509237

Canadian Edition

Business
Research Methods

Alan Bryman | Emma Bell | Albert J. Mills | Anthony R. Yue

OXFORD

UNIVERSITY PRESS

8 Sampson Mews, Suite 204, Don Mills, Ontario M3C 0H5
www.oupcanada.com

Oxford University Press is a department of the University of Oxford.
It furthers the University's objective of excellence in research, scholarship,
and education by publishing worldwide in

Oxford   New York

Auckland   Cape Town   Dar es Salaam   Hong Kong   Karachi
Kuala Lumpur   Madrid   Melbourne   Mexico City   Nairobi
New Delhi   Shanghai   Taipei   Toronto

With offices in

Argentina   Austria   Brazil   Chile   Czech Republic   France   Greece
Guatemala   Hungary   Italy   Japan   Poland   Portugal   Singapore
South Korea   Switzerland   Thailand   Turkey   Ukraine   Vietnam

Oxford is a trade mark of Oxford University Press
in the UK and in certain other countries

Published in Canada
by Oxford University Press

Copyright © Oxford University Press Canada 2011

The moral rights of the author have been asserted

Database right Oxford University Press (maker)

First Published 2011

Original edition published by Oxford University Press, Inc.,
Great Clarendon Street, Oxford, England 0X2 6DP
Copyright © 2003 Oxford University Press, Inc.

All rights reserved. No part of this publication may be reproduced,
stored in a retrieval system, or transmitted, in any form or by any means,
without the prior permission in writing of Oxford University Press,
or as expressly permitted by law, or under terms agreed with the appropriate
reprographics rights organization. Enquiries concerning reproduction
outside the scope of the above should be sent to the Permissions Department
at the address above or through the following url:
www.oupcanada.com/permission/permission_request.php

You must not circulate this book in any other binding or cover
and you must impose this same condition on any acquirer.

Every effort has been made to determine and contact copyright holders. In the case of any omissions,
the publisher will be pleased to make suitable acknowledgement in future editions.

Library and Archives Canada Cataloguing in Publication
Business research methods / Alan
Bryman ... [et al.].—1st Canadian ed.

Includes bibliographical references and index.

ISBN 978-0-19-543029-5

1. Business—Research—Methodology.

I. Bryman, Alan

HD30.4.B88 2011   658.0072   C2010-906625-1

Cover image: Ocean Photography/Veer

Oxford University Press is committed to our environment. This book is printed on permanent (acid-free) paper ∞.
Printed and bound in Canada

1 2 3 4 — 14 13 12 11

Brief Contents

Detailed Contents

Abbreviations

AACSB	Association to Advance Colleges and Schools of Business
ABA	American Bar Association
ABTA	Association of British Travel Agents
AES	Annual Employment Survey
ALS	average leadership style
ANT	Actor-network Theory
AOM	Academy of Management
ASA	American Sociological Association
ASAC	Administrative Sciences Association of Canada
ASB	Atlantic Schools of Business
ASQ	Administrative Sciences Quarterly
BHPS	British Household Panel Study
BMRB	British Market Research Bureau
BSA	British Social Attitudes
BSA	British Sociological Association
CA	conversation analysis
CAPI	computer-assisted personal interviewing
CAQDAS	computer-assisted qualitative data analysis software
CASS	Centre for Applied Social Surveys
CATI	computer-assisted telephone interviewing
CBC	Canadian Broadcasting Corporation
CDA	Critical Discourse Analysis
CIHR	Canadian Institutes of Health Research
CJAS	Canadian Journal of Administrative Sciences
CMS	Critical Management Studies
CPA	Canadian Psychological Association
CRSP	Centre for Research in Security Prices
CSAA	Canadian Sociology and Anthropological Association
CSRA	Canadian Society and Anthropology Association
CV	curriculum vitae
DA	discourse analysis
DEFRA	Department for Environment, Food and Rural Affairs
EBSCO	(online academic research database service)
ECA	ethnographic content analysis
EFQM	European Foundation for Quality Management
EFS	Expenditure and Food Survey
EGOS	European Group for Organization Studies
ERIC	Education Resources Education Center
ESRC	Economic and Social Research Council
FES	Family Expenditure Survey
FDA	foreign direct investment
FTSE	Financial Times (London) Stock Exchange
GESS-R	Revised Generalized Expectancy of Success Scale
GHS	General Household Survey
GMID	General Market Information Database
GM	General Motors
HMO	health maintenance organization
HR	human resources
HRM	Human Resource Management
HRT	Hormone Replacement Therapy
IBSS	International Bibliography of the Social Sciences
ICI	Imperial Chemical Industries
IFSAM	International Federation of Scholarly Associations of Management
IiP	Investors in People
IS	Information Systems
ISP	Internet Service Provider
ISSP	International Social Survey Programme
JDS	Job Diagnostic Survey
LFS	Labour Force Survey
LOT-R	Life Orientation Test-Revised
LPC	least-preferred co-worker
MDPS	multidisciplinary partnerships
MIT	Massachusetts Institute of Technology
MPS	Motivating Potential Score
MRS	Market Research Society
MUD	multi-user domain

NAICS	North American Industrial Classification System	REB	Research Ethics Board
NFS	National Food Survey	REPONSE	Relations professionnelles et négociations d'enterprise
NGO	non-government organization	RI	Rotary International
NHS	National Health Service	SAM	Society for the Advancement of Management
NIT	New Instititutional Theory (also known as new institutionalism or neoinstitutionalism)	SCELI	Social Change and Economic Life Initiative
NSP	Nova Scotia Power	SIC	Standard Industrial Classification
NSERC	Natural Sciences and Engineering Research Council of Canada	SME	small- or medium-sized enterprise
		SOGI	society, organization, group, and individual
NTSB	(U.S.) National Transportation and Safety Board	SPSS	Statistical Package for the Social Sciences
		SSCI	Social Sciences Citation Index
OCS	Organizational Culture Scale	SSHRC	Social Science & Humanities Research Council
OD	organizational development		
OECD	Organisation for Economic Co-operation and Development	SYMLOG	Systematic Multiple Level Observation of Groups
OISE	Ontario Institute for Studies in Education	SRA	Social Research Association
OMS	Outcomes Management System	TDM	Total Design Method
ONS	Office for National Statistics	TGI	Target Group Index
ORACLE	Observational Research and Classroom Learning Evaluation	TQM	Total Quality Management
		TSX	Toronto Stock Exchange
PAA	Pan American Airways	VDL	vertical dyadic linkage
PIPED	Personal Information Protection and Electronic Documents Act	WERS	Workplace Employee Relations Survey
		WES	Workplace and Employment Survey
POB	positive organizational behaviour	WOS	Web of Science
PWC	PricewaterhouseCoopers (Canada) (see also PwC)	WIRS	Workplace Industrial Relations Survey
		WLU	Wilfrid Laurier University

About the Authors

Alan Bryman was appointed Professor of Organizational and Social Research at the University of Leicester in August 2005. Prior to this he was Professor of Social Research at Loughborough University for 31 years.

His main research interests are in leadership especially in higher education, research methods (particularly mixed methods research), and the 'Disneyization' and 'McDonaldization' of modern society. In 2003–04 he completed a project on the issue of how quantitative and qualitative research are combined in the social sciences, as part of the Economic and Social Research Council's Research Methods Programme.

He has published widely in the field of Social Research, including: *Quantitative Data Analysis with SPSS 14, 15 and 16: A Guide for Social Scientists* (Routledge, 2009) with Duncan Cramer; *Social Research Methods* (Oxford University Press, 2008); *The SAGE Encyclopedia of Social Science Research Methods* (Sage, 2004) with Michael Lewis-Beck and Tim Futing Liao; *The Disneyization of Society* (Sage 2004); *Handbook of Data Analysis* (Sage, 2004) with Melissa Hardy; *Understanding Research for Social Policy and Practice* (Policy Press, 2004) with Saul Becker; and the *SAGE Handbook of Organizational Research Methods* with David Buchanan (Sage, 2009) as well as editing the *Understanding Social Research* series for Open University Press.

He has contributed articles to a range of academic journals including *Journal of Management Studies*; *Human Relations*; *International Journal of Social Research Methodology*; *Leadership Quarterly*, and *American Behavioral Scientist*. He is also on the editorial board of *Leadership*; *Qualitative Research in Organizations and Management: An International Journal*, and the *Journal of Mixed Methods Research*. He was a member of the ESRC's Research Grants Board and has recently completed research into effective leadership in higher education, a project funded by the Leadership Foundation for Higher Education.

Emma Bell is Senior Lecturer in Organisation Studies at University of Exeter Business School. Prior to this she held senior lecturing posts at the University of Bath, School of Management and the School of Business and Management at Queen Mary University of London. She graduated with a PH.D. from Manchester Metropolitan University in 2000 before becoming a lecturer at Warwick University Business School.

Her main research interests relate to the critical study of managerial discourses and modern organization. A substantial aspect of her work at the moment involves exploration of the relationship between religion, spirituality and organization and focuses on the role of belief-led business in providing alternatives to globalised capitalism. She has also recently completed a book which analyses how management and organization are represented in film. She is a founding member of *invisio* the *International Network of Visual Studies in Organization* and is currently working on an ESRC *Researcher Development Initiative* project that promotes the development of visual analysis among management researchers. Prior to this she conducted research into the social construction of meaning around payment systems and an evaluation of the impact of the 'Investors in People' initiative.

Her research has been published in journals including the *British Journal of Management*; the *British Journal of Industrial Relations*; *Human Relations*; *Organization*; the *Journal of Management Studies*; *Management Learning*, and *Time & Society*. She has written a number of articles and book chapters relating to management research methods on topics such as research ethics, visual methods, ethnography and the politics of management research.

Emma is committed to the development of innovative approaches to learning and has been awarded prizes for her teaching at Queen Mary and Bath.

Albert J. Mills is Professor of Management and Director of the PH.D. (Management) program at the Sobey School of Management at Saint Mary's University, in Halifax, Nova Scotia.

Albert Mills's research interests centre on the impact of organizational power, knowledge, and practice on human potential, focusing on organizational change and liberation. This focus was shaped by his experience of leaving school at age fifteen and his early images of organization—of frustration, power disparities, conflict, and sexually segregated work—mediated through a series of unskilled jobs and given broader meaning through campaigns for peace, social justice, and human liberation in the 1960s. He eventually went on to Ruskin College, Oxford and a career in academia.

He has taught at various levels of higher education (from undergraduate to PH.D.), in different modes (including classroom and distance education settings), varying class size and in various countries, including Canada, Denmark, Finland, Hungary, Kuwait, Macedonia, the Netherlands, Slovenia, the United Kingdom, the United States, and Vietnam.

His research interests include gender and organization; management and organizational history; historiography and business studies; research methods; identity; existentialism and the workplace; and management knowledge and education. These varied, but interrelated, interests have been pursued through active involvement in scholarly associations and through over 300 scholarly publications and conference presentations. He has served as President of the Administrative Sciences Association of Canada; Divisional Chair of the Critical Management Studies Division of the Academy of Management; Executive Member of the International Federation of Scholarly Associations of Management; and currently serves on the Executive of the Atlantic Schools of Business. His twenty or so books include the *Sage Encyclopedia of Case Study Research* (Sage, 2010); *The Dark Side: Critical Cases on the Downside of Business* (Greenleaf, 2009); *Understanding Organizational Change* (Routledge, 2008*); Organizational Behaviour in a Global Context* (University of Toronto Press, 2007); and *Sex, Strategy, and the Stratosphere: the Gendering of Airline Cultures* (Palgrave MacMillan, 2006). He is an Associate Editor of *Qualitative Research in*

Organizations and Management; *Gender, Work & Organization*; *the Canadian Journal of Administrative Sciences*; and is on the editorial board of several other journals, including *Management & Organizational History.*

Anthony R. Yue is an assistant professor in the Department of Communication Studies at Mount Saint Vincent University, in Halifax, Nova Scotia. Anthony came to academic life after an extensive practitioner career working in a variety of entrepreneurial organizations. He has managed in the retail sector; created a financial services company; contributed to family business in the import/export arena; and trained petroleum workers and military personnel in helicopter egress/sea and survival skills. He holds an Executive MBA from Saint Mary's University and is preparing to defend a PH.D. thesis concerning gossip in organizations.

Anthony is broadly interested in how individuals navigate their organized world. His research spans diverse topics such as gossip and storytelling in organizations; occupational health and safety issues; disability and workers; and existentialist thought. These various topics of interest link together such that they offer nuanced understandings of how individuals are simultaneously both free-acting and yet contextually constrained. This fascination further extends to the use of wide ranging varieties of research methods, perspectives, and tools. He has written a book chapter concerning a micro organizational behaviour view of industrial relations for *The Sage Handbook of Organizational Behaviour* and encyclopedia entries concerning existentialism, Sartre, validity and fiction analysis for *The Sage Encyclopedia of Case Studies.* He has published both sole authored and collaborative works in a variety of peer-reviewed journals. His teaching includes the areas of public relations, management, business, and research methods.

Anthony continues to consult with industry concerning evidence-based approaches to HR practices and leadership. Aside from his work, both he and his spouse have ample opportunities to practice mental and physical agility with their one-year-old daughter on their outdoor sporting adventures.

About the Students

Ten undergraduate and 32 postgraduate students—from several countries studying in Canada, Finland, the United Kingdom, and other countries—have provided valuable input that has informed our writing of the Student Experience feature of this text. We are extremely grateful to them for being willing to share their experiences of doing a research project and we hope that sharing what they have learned from this process with the readers of this book will enable others to benefit from their experience.

Studying in Canada

We are grateful to Mark Desjardine, who was completing his Honour's thesis in the School of Business at Acadia University when we interviewed him in a local coffee shop in Wolfville, Nova Scotia. We were also very fortunate to spend time interviewing Cindy Dean, Amanda Rafuse, and Melissa Van Der Voort—all graduates of the Research Methods course of Mount Saint Vincent University's ('the Mount') Public Relations degree. It was instructive and fun to learn how they had conducted research projects at 'the Mount' but also, in Amanda and Cindy's case, their experiences of Honours projects in, respectively, Anthropology and History.

Our sincere thanks go out to the current students and graduates of the Sobey Ph.D. in Management program at Saint Mary's University (in Halifax, NS). All in all 18 people responded to our incessant calls for helpful examples: this included our current students: Marcelle Allen (PH.D. Entry, 2008), Salvador Barragan (2007), Shelagh Campbell (2006), Janet Bell Crawford (2005), Brad Long (2005), Doreen MacAulay (2007), Bill Murray (2006), and Donna Boone Parsons (2007)—and graduates—Drs Wendy Carroll (University of Prince Edward Island), Patricia Genoe McLaren (Wilfrid Laurier University), James D. Grant (Acadia University), Scott MacMillan (Mount Saint Vincent Univercity), Margaret McKee (Saint Mary's University), Mary Runté (Lethbridge University), Amy Thurlow (Mount Saint Vincent University), Peggy Wallace (Trent University), Amy Warren (Memorial University of Newfoundland), and Terrance G. Weatherbee (Acadia University).

From Finland

We are deeply appreciative of the time and energy that the following students and graduates of the Department of Management and Organization of Hanken University (Helsinki) gave to us: Eric Breit, Tricia Cleland, Charlotta Niemisto, Beata Segercrnatz, Jonna Louvrier, Anne Rindell, and Mikeal Laakso.

From the United Kingdom

We are grateful for the time and insights provided by Lisa Mellors (who studied at Lancaster University Management School for a Bachelor's degree in Business Administration in Management); Chris Phillips (who was doing an undergraduate degree in Commerce at Birmingham Business School); Nirwanthi De Vaz (who was an undergraduate on a three-year course studying for a BA Management Studies at the University of Leicester); Tom Easterling (who took an M.SC. in occupational psychology at Birkbeck College, University of London); Karen Moore (who studied a four-year Business Administration in Management degree at Lancaster University); Lucie Banham (who had completed an MA in Organization Studies at Warwick Business School); and Angharad Jones (who studies for an undergraduate degree in Commerce at the University of Birmingham).

Anonimia

Finally, our thanks go to Jennifer and Karla who have asked us to anonymize their identities and the research sites of their doctoral studies.

Publisher's Preface

Important features of this edition

Business Research Methods gives students essential guidance on how to carry out their own research projects while introducing them to the core concepts, methods, and values involved in doing research. The book provides a valuable learning resource through its comprehensive coverage of methods that are used by experienced researchers investigating the world of business as well as introducing some of the philosophical issues and ethical controversies that these researchers face.

A Canadian focus

It might be asked 'why a Canadian edition?' 'What can be peculiarly Canadian about research methods?' 'Aren't research methods universality applicable?' Our answer is twofold: first, language and the meanings associated with it are very much contextual. This means that the theory and application of research methods can be better understood where language use is geared to the reader. Second, research depends on a number of factors such as sampling, interviewing, ethnography, and ethical concerns. The successful use of such factors depends to some extent on knowledge of specific national conditions, practices, organizations, associations, statistics, and media.

Throughout the book students will find references to Canadian media, institutions, practices and conditions such as bilingualism, the impact of the Employment Equity Act, the Nova Scotia Power Corporation, the Social Sciences and Humanities Research Council, and Statistics Canada. There are also numerous discussions and findings drawn from Canadian researchers. Nonetheless, to reflect Canada's international and global interests we have retained, as far as possible, international examples, UK student experiences, and student experiences from other countries, including Finland.

Why is it important to study research methods?

To some students, there does not seem to be a compelling reason to study research methods. Their reasoning might be that if they have to conduct an investigation, they would be better off just looking into how to do research once they are on the verge of carrying out the investigation. Aside from the fact that this is an extremely risky approach to take, it neglects the following opportunities that training in research methods offers:

- An awareness of the range of research methods that can be used to collect data and the variety of approaches to the analysis of data. Such an awareness will help you to make appropriate choices for your project, since you need to be aware of when it is appropriate or inappropriate to employ particular techniques.
- An awareness of the 'dos' and 'don'ts' when taking a particular approach to collecting or analyzing data. Once you have made your choice of research method (for example, a questionnaire), you need to be aware of the practices you need to follow in order to implement that method properly.
- Insights into the overall research process. You will gain a general vantage point for understanding how research is done. This illuminates the various stages of research, so that you can plan your research and think about such issues as how your research methods will connect with your research questions.
- An awareness of what constitutes good and poor research. You will develop a critical awareness of the limits and limitations of research that you read. This can be helpful in providing a critical appraisal of research that you read for courses in fields like organizational behaviour and HR.
- Transferable skills: Knowing how to sample, how to design a questionnaire, how to conduct semi-structured interviewing or focus groups, analyzing a variety of texts, and so on requires skills that are relevant to

research in other spheres (such as firms, public sector organizations, and so on).

 # The structure of the book

In structuring the book we have tried to reflect the process that a student goes through in conducting a research project and the choices of method available based on the cognitive abilities utilized. The book is divided into four parts.

Part One takes you through the initial process of planning your research project.

Chapter 1 takes you through the main steps that are involved in planning and designing a research project and offers advice on how to manage the process. It includes a discussion of research questions—what they are, why they are important, and how they come to be formulated.

Chapter 2 takes you through the first important part of that process: the literature review, which will help you to develop and refine your research question as well as identify key readings in your field of study.

Part Two introduces research strategy and design, and takes you through the process of developing each. In particular it focuses on key philosophical differences within social science research and the generation of six research strategies for developing a research project.

Chapter 3 outlines a variety of considerations that impinge on the practice of business and management research and relates these to the issue of research strategy. Six research strategies are identified based on the use of quantitative, qualitative, and mixed methods in either positivist or postpositivist approaches.

Chapter 4 introduces the idea of a *research design*. This chapter allows an introduction to the basic frameworks within which social research is carried out, such as social survey research, case study research, and experimental research.

Chapter 5 explores the nature of quantitative research and as such provides a context for the later chapters.

Chapter 6 provides an overview of the nature of qualitative research and as such supplies the context for many later chapters.

Chapter 7 presents some ways in which quantitative and qualitative research can be combined to produce what is referred to as mixed methods research.

Chapter 8 examines the issue of ethics in research and the need to ensure not only that you meet the criteria but also the spirit of the ethical standards in research.

Part Three takes you through various research methods, roughly grouped—in four sections consisting of 14 chapters—according to the cognitive abilities that need to be utilized to undertake a research project. Those abilities include the reasoning, talking, observing, and reading that we use to make sense of a research problem. Naturally many research strategies involve all four processes, but we have tried to group each according to the primary one used. The first section is largely rooted in a positivist approach that privileges a certain form of rational thinking, seeking to answer research questions through a process that is convincing through its objectivity and generalizability. All other sections include approaches that can be rooted in either positivist or postpositivist strategies. The second section focuses on how research data is generated through asking questions of people. The third section moves us to observation and the fourth section deals with the generation of data through the reading of a variety of materials, including newspapers, the Internet, and those collected in designated archives. These various sections and chapters will provide you with a feel for the different ways of doing research, whether from a positivist or postpositivist approach, and their connection to the thought processes and senses that are primarily involved.

Part 3a: Surveying

Chapter 9 deals with sampling issues: how to select a sample and the considerations that are involved in assessing what can be inferred from different kinds of sample.

Chapter 10 covers the design of questionnaires. This involves a discussion of how to devise self-completion questionnaires, such as postal questionnaires.

Chapter 11 examines the issue of how to ask questions for questionnaires and structured interviews.

Chapter 12 shows you how to use computer software in the form of SPSS, the most widely used software for analyzing quantitative data. This will be useful for the techniques learned in Chapter 5 and their application in Chapter 23.

Part 3b: Questioning/Discussing

Chapter 13 is concerned with the kind of interviewing that takes place in survey research, that is, structured interviewing.

Chapter 14 deals with the kinds of interview that (positivist and postpositivist) qualitative researchers conduct, which is typically semi-structured interviewing or unstructured interviewing.

Chapter 15 explores the focus group method, whereby groups of individuals are interviewed on a specific topic.

Part 3c: Observing

Chapter 16 covers structured observation, which is a method that has been developed for the systematic observation of behaviour. It has been especially influential in the areas of business and management research.

Chapter 17 is concerned with ethnography and participant observation, which is the source of some of the best-known studies in business and management research. The two terms are often used interchangeably and refer to the immersion of the researcher in a social setting.

Part 3d: Reading

Chapter 18 presents content analysis, a method that provides a rigorous framework for the analysis of a wide range of documents.

Chapter 19 deals with the analysis of data collected by other researchers and by official bodies. The emphasis then switches to the ways in which we can analyze quantitative data.

Chapter 20 examines two ways in which qualitative researchers analyze language: conversation analysis and discourse analysis.

Chapter 21 moves us to historiography as a method for dealing with history and the past, and deals with the examination of documents in qualitative research.

Chapter 22 is concerned with the use of the Internet as a context or platform for conducting research.

Part Four shows you how to undertake quantitative analysis, qualitative analysis and, importantly, how to write up and publish your research project.

We feel that a training in research methods has much to offer and that readers of this book will recognize the opportunities and advantages that it provides.

Chapter features

Chapter guide

A 'route map' of the chapter material that summarizes the goals of each chapter so you know what you should be learning as you read.

ⓘ *Chapter guide*

Questionnaires that are completed by respondents themselves are one of the main instruments for gathering data using a **social survey** design, along with the **structured interview**, which is covered in chapter 13. Probably the most common form is the **mail or postal questionnaire**. The term **self-completion questionnaire** is often used because it is somewhat more inclusive than *mail questionnaire*. This chapter explores:

* The advantages and disadvantages of the questionnaire in comparison to the structured interview.
* How to address the potential problem of poor response rates, which is often a feature of the mail questionnaire.
* How questionnaires should be designed in order to make answering easier for respondents and less prone to error.
* The use of diaries as a form of self-completion questionnaire.

Checklists

Many chapters end with a checklist of issues that you should keep in mind when undertaking research activities such as writing a literature review or conducting a focus group and progress in your research project .

✓ *Checklist*

Planning a research project:

☐ Do you know what the requirements for your dissertation are, as set out by your university or department?

☐ Have you made contact with your supervisor?

☐ Have you left enough time for planning, doing, and write-up your research project?

☐ Do you have a clear timetable for your research project with clearly identifiable milestones for the achievement of specific tasks?

☐ Have you got sufficient financial and practical resources (e.g. money to enable travel to a research site, to buy a tape recorder) to enable you to carry out your research project?

☐ Have you formulated some research questions and discussed these with your supervisor?

☐ Are the research questions you have identified able to be answered through your research project?

☐ Do you have the access that you require in order to carry out your research?

☐ Are you familiar with the data analysis software that you may be using to analyze your data?

Key points
A short, bulleted summary of crucial themes covered in each chapter, this feature serves as a spotlight that reinforces important issues.

Key points
- Follow the dissertation guidelines provided by your institution.
- Thinking about your research subject can be time consuming, so allow plenty of time for this aspect of the dissertation process.
- Use your supervisor to the fullest extent allowed and follow the advice offered by them.
- Plan your time carefully and be realistic about what you can achieve in the time available.
- Formulate some research questions to express what it is about your area of interest that you want to know.
- Writing a research proposal is a good way of getting started on your research project and encouraging you to set realistic objectives.
- Consider access and sampling issues at an early stage and consider testing your research methods by conducting a pilot study.
- Keep good records of what you do in your research as you go along and don't wait until all of your data have been collected before you start coding.

Questions for review

Reviewing the existing literature and engaging with what others have written:
- What are the main reasons for writing a literature review?
- How can you ensure that you get the most from your reading?
- What are the main advantages and disadvantages associated with systematic review?
- What type of research questions is systematic review most suited to addressing?
- What are the main reasons for conducting a narrative literature review?
- In what type of research is narrative review most appropriate?

Searching the existing literature and looking for business information:
- What are the main ways of finding existing literature on your subject?
- What is a keyword and how is it useful in searching the literature?

Review questions
Up to 20 review questions at the end of every chapter test your grasp of ideas and concepts and assist in test preparation.

Key concept margin definitions
The world of research has its own language. To help you build your research vocabulary, key terms have been defined in key concept boxes that appear in the margins.

Key concept 2.1:
Meta-analysis:

involves summarizing the results of a large number of quantitative studies and conducting various analytical tests to show whether or not a particular variable has an effect.

A full Glossary supports the margin notes and enhances understanding of key concepts.

More boxes online
This easily recognizable icon identifies topics or references in the text which are discussed in greater detail online. Follow the icon and discover over 200 boxes, including 'Web: Thinking Deeper,' 'Web: Student Experiences,' 'Web: Key Concepts' and 'Web: Research in Focus' boxes.

Glossary

Abduction or Abductive analysis The process of forming a possible explanation involving an imaginative effort to understand on the past of beings acting and learning in the world. It is a practical reasoning mode whose purpose is to invent and propose ideas and explanations that account for surprises and unmet expectations' (Locke, 2010, p. 1).

Action research An approach in which the action researcher and a client collaborate in the diagnosis of a problem and in the development of a solution based on the diagnosis.

Ad libitum **sampling** A sampling approach in structured observation whereby whatever is happening at the moment that observation is due to occur is recorded.

Adjacency pair The tendency for certain kinds of activity in talk to be characterized by linked phases.

Analytic induction An approach to the analysis of qualitative data in which the researcher seeks universal explanations of phenomena by pursuing the collection of data until no cases that are inconsistent with a hypothetical explanation (deviant or negative cases) of a phenomenon are found.

ANT **i-History** An approach to the study of the past and of history in the production and dissemination of knowledge. Developed by Durepos and Mills, ANTi-History draws on Actor Network Theory, poststructuralist historiography and the Sociology of Knowledge, to simultaneously represent and destabilize selected past events with the ultimate aim of pluralizing history.

Archaeological approach to the past An approach which characterizes an earlier phase of the work of Foucault and involves exploration 'in language the sedimented evidence of the assumptions; the values; the common sense through which, for instance, a phenomenon such as madness could have one set of meanings in one era and a contradictory set of meanings in another' (Jacques, 2010, p. 305).

Arithmetic mean Also known simply as the *mean*, this is the everyday average—namely, the total of a distribution of values divided by the number of values.

in real time, so that there may be long spaces of time between interviewers' questions and participants' replies, and in the case of focus groups, between participants' contributions to the discussion.

Attached email survey A survey in which respondents are sent a questionnaire, which is received as an email attachment. Compare with *embedded email survey*.

Behaviour sampling A sampling approach in *structured observation* whereby an entire group is watched and the observer records who was involved in a particular kind of behaviour.

Behaviouralism A methodological approach modelled after the natural sciences that focuses on the behaviour of individuals and the way it can be shaped to achieve more efficient (organizational) outcomes.

Biographical method See *life history method*.

Bivariate analysis The examination of the relationship between two variables, as in *contingency tables* or correlation.

Boolean search Is a search which makes use of one or more of the four common Boolean operators (AND, OR, NOT, ADJ). These connectors allow for a narrowed and specified search requiring:
- All the terms specified through the use of the operator AND (e.g. internal AND reliability).
- Either or both terms or phrases through the use of the operator OR (e.g. firm OR company).
- The elimination of results through the use of the operator NOT (e.g. research NOT medical).
- The specified sequence in order through the operator ADJ (e.g. focus ADJ group).\

CAQDAS An abbreviation of *computer-assisted (or -aided) qualitative data analysis software*.

Case study A *research design* that entails the detailed and intensive analysis of a single case. The term is sometimes extended to include the study of just two or three cases for comparative purposes.

7.2   Research in Focus

Combining survey research and qualitative interviewing in a study of managers

Wajcman and Martin (2002) conducted survey research using a questionnaire on male and female managers (470 in total) in six Australian companies. The authors were interested in career orientations and attitudes. They also conducted semi-structured interviews with 136 managers in each company. The survey evidence showed that male and female managers were generally more similar than different in terms of most variables. Thus, contrary to what many people might have anticipated, women's career experiences and orientations were not distinctive. They then examined the qualitative interviews in terms of narratives of identity. Wajcman and Martin found that both male and female managers depicted their careers in 'market' terms (as needing to respond to the requirements of the managerial labour market to develop their skills, experience, and hence career). But, whereas, for men, narratives of career meshed seamlessly with narratives of domestic life, for women there was a disjuncture. Female managers found it much harder to reconcile managerial identities with domestic ones. They needed to opt for one. Thus, choices about career and family are still gendered. This research shows how a mixed methods research approach was able to reveal much more than could have been gleaned through one approach alone by collecting evidence on both career patterns and expectations and identities using research methods suited to each issue area.

Research in Focus boxes
are designed to provide a sense of place for the theories and concepts being discussed in the chapter text, by providing real examples of published research.

Tips and Skills boxes
help you avoid the common research mistakes and equip you with the necessary skills to become a successful researcher.

Tips and Skills

Sample size and probability sampling

As we have said in the text, the issue of sample size is the matter that most often concerns students and others. Basically, this is an area where size really does matter (!) as the bigger the sample the more representative it is likely to be (provided the sample is randomly selected), regardless of the size of the population from which it is drawn. However, when doing projects, students clearly need to do their research with very limited resources. You should try to find out from your department or business school if there are any guidelines about whether or not samples of a minimum size are expected. If there are no such guidelines, you will need to conduct your survey in such a way as to maximize the number of interviews you can manage or the number of postal questionnaires you can send out given the amount of time and resources available to you. Also, in many, if not most cases, a truly random approach to sample selection may not be open to you. The crucial point is to be clear about and to justify what you have done. Explain the difficulties that you would have encountered in generating a random sample. Explain why you really could not include any more in your sample of respondents. But, above all, do not make claims about your sample that are not sustainable. Do not claim that it is representative or that you have a random sample when it is clearly not the case that either of these is true. In other words, be frank about what you have done. People will be much more inclined to accept an awareness of the limits of your sample design than claims about a sample that are inherently false. Also, it may be that there are lots of good features about your sample such as the range of people included, the good response rate, and the high level of cooperation you received from the firm. Make sure you play up these positive features at the same time as being honest about its limitations.

3.1   Student Experience

Personality, experience, and research strategy

It is clear that a number of things influence a person's choice of research strategy. Sometimes the choice is limited by the requirements of a course or course instructor. Cindy, Melissa, and Amanda, for example, were given a choice of focus groups, interviews, or surveys. Sometimes it can depend on past experience. Cindy had already gained experience of interviews and a survey so was drawn to focus groups as a new learning challenge. Research choices can also be influenced by type of research question you are interested in. Mark, for example, was interested in gaining a general understanding of the relationship between age, technology use, and performance while Tricia was interested in an in-depth study of the institutional contexts in which nurses work. And research decisions can be based on how you 'feel' about different approaches; whether they make sense to you or not; whether you are more or less comfortable with a focus on numbers or words, etc. Beata sums this up well in an interesting turn of phrase when she says 'I think the perspective chooses.' After exposure to a number of methods within a 'positivist research' framework she studied social constructionism and 'really enjoyed it. It really helped me understand my work when I did HR too. . . . I was just drawn to that perspective and really started looking at that and that was my starting point for some reason I just liked it and starting developing [it].'

Student Experience boxes
draw on interviews with real research students from a variety of business schools around Canada, Finland, and the UK.

Extensive ancillary package
www.oupcanada.com/BrymanBusiness

Online Resources for Instructors
- Figures and screenshots from the text are available for downloading into presentation software or for use in assignments and exam material
- Extensive lecturer's guide containing teaching notes and many other features to assist teaching
- A set of customizable PowerPoint slides for every chapter

COMPANION WEBSITE

Alan Bryman
Business Research Methods
First Canadian Edition
ISBN 13: 9780195430295

About the Book

The only research methods text that marries a Canadian perspective with a management focus, Business Research Methods is a core text that introduces upper-level undergraduates to the most prominent methods of business research in use today. The text will also be a useful reference for MBA and PhD business students. The first text to offer balanced coverage of both qualitative as well as quantitative research methods, Bryman/Bell /Mills/Yue reflects contemporary practice, which draws upon both methods.

Inspection copy request
Ordering information
Contact & Comments

Sample Material

Get Adobe PDF reader [US | UK]

Instructor Resources

You need a password to access these resources. Please contact your local Sales and Editorial Representative for more information.

Student Resources

Online Resources for Students
- Self-grading multiple choice questions
- Downloadable data sets
- Interviews with students who have completed their own research project
- Research Project Guide takes students through each of the key research phases
- Helpful suggestions for using Excel in data analysis
- Over 200 valuable boxes available online, including 'Thinking Deeper,' 'Student Experiences,' 'Key Concepts,' and 'Research in Focus' boxes
- Web links

Instructors should contact their Oxford University Press sales representative for details on the supplements and for login and password information.

Acknowledgements

Again, we would like to thank the undergraduate and postgraduate students who provided valuable input that has informed our writing of the Student Experience feature of this text. We are extremely grateful to them for being willing to share their experiences of doing a research project and we hope that sharing what they have learned from this process with the readers of this book will enable others to benefit from their experience. We would like to thank Katja Seitz for bringing a student's perspective and her own dedication to this project. Katja developed self-test multiple choice questions for the companion website and it is the richer for it.

We would like to thank the 2007 cohort of the Sobey PH.D. for their patience, enthusiasm, and advice as we used them as our test group for the early drafts of the book.

In addition, we are grateful for the suggestions and constructive criticism from the following three reviewers of the manuscript: Linda Dyer, Concordia University; Judith Holton, Mount Allison University; and Tanya Mark, University of Guelph. We are also indebted to Christopher Adams, University of Manitoba, and Anja-Lina Wamser, University of Lethbridge, as well as one anonymous reviewer for their feedback on the project proposal.

Our thanks to Stephen Kotowych, Andrea Kennedy, and Mary Wat of Oxford University Press for their commitment to the project and their guidance in moving it towards completion.

To Drs Mary Runté, Peggy Wallace, Kelly Dye, Scott Macmillan, and Gabie Durepos who, as my PH.D. students, taught me so much about qualitative methods.

— Albert J. Mills

To my research mentors, Dr E. Kevin Kelloway and Dr Albert J. Mills, who taught by example the personal commitment required to do good social science research. To my wife Patricia and daughter Sienna for reminding me of both pragmatic considerations and the wonders that unfettered curiosity reveals. Finally, to my father, whose profound will to live has been a renewed inspiration to me.

—Anthony R. Yue

Part One

Getting Started

Part One of this book is about the types of thing you need to know about starting to undertake a research project. In Chapter 1 we assume that you are starting a research project—whether at the undergraduate or graduate level—with little or no idea of where to start, except the idea that you need to undertake a dissertation of some kind to complete your degree. With that in mind we take you through the steps of planning a research project and formulating questions. Mindful of the kinds of time and other constraints involved we also discuss such things as time management skills and how to develop a Gantt chart to help you think through the process. By the end of the chapter you should have a good initial grasp of the process you need to go through to develop your research question (or thesis). In Chapter 2 we then take you through the first important part of that process—the literature review, which will help you to develop and refine your research question as well as identify key readings in your field of study.

1

Planning a Research Project and Formulating Research Questions

Chapter guide

The goal of this chapter is to provide advice to students on how to develop a research focus, and specifically some of the issues that they need to consider if they have to prepare a dissertation based upon a research project. Increasingly, business and management students are required to produce such a dissertation as part of the requirements for their degrees. In addition to needing help with the conduct of research, which will be the aim of the chapters that come later in this book, more specific advice on tactics in doing and writing-up research for a dissertation can be useful. It is against this background that this chapter has been written. The chapter explores a wide variety of issues such as:

- Advice on timing.
- Advice on generating research questions.
- Advice on writing to help you produce compelling findings.
- Understanding the requirements of a dissertation project.
- Advice on what makes a good dissertation.

Chapter 2 will then focus on how to get started with your research project by conducting a literature review.

Introduction

This chapter is designed to get you started on a program of research by taking you through the process of picking a research topic, formulating research questions, and planning a research project. The chapters that follow in Parts Two, Three, and Four of this book will then provide more detailed information about the choices available to you and how to implement them. Although, as we shall discuss below, research is generated from a number of sources, this chapter is specifically geared to undergraduate and graduate students of business and management programs who are required to write a research dissertation. The chapter is especially geared to assist students who are conducting projects with a component of empirical research in which they collect new data or conduct a secondary analysis of existing data.

The importance of research

Research involves the systematic investigation of a particular phenomenon in order to develop or increase knowledge of that phenomenon. The phenomenon to be investigated could, for example, be the relationship between lung cancer and smoking (http://info.cancerresearchuk.org/cancerstats/types/lung/smoking/); the effect of job loss on the careers of business professionals (Zikic & Richardson, 2007); the impact of organizational culture on workplace discrimination (Abella, 1984); or numerous other issues on which social agencies and communities base their decision making.

It is because of its contribution to knowledge that research is so valued at various levels of social life. Throughout society we rely heavily on the outcome of research to form judgements, make decisions, and take action that can involve people's lives and the expenditure of valuable resources. As such we need to be sure that we can trust the processes through which the knowledge was created. Simply put, in matters where we are required to make important and far-reaching decisions we are less likely to accept something that is the result of hearsay, gossip, uninformed opinion or guesswork, and more likely to accept something that is the outcome of rigorous and systematic investigation. Arguably, our preference for research-based knowledge is linked to an underlying belief in rationality that pervades modern society and encourages us to trust that which follows an acceptable series of rules of investigation (Weber, 1947, 1967). We shall return to this point at various parts of the book as we examine different methods.

To base decisions on research outcomes requires that people have some understanding of the nature of research, either from the perspective of researchers, policy makers, or other users of research. To that end, the university system strongly focuses on how to read and evaluate the outcomes of research and also, in a number of institutions, on how to undertake a program of research. It is in the latter regard that students get an important opportunity to develop the research skills that are essential for decision making at all levels of social life. Business students, no less than other students, need to gain an intimate knowledge of the research process in other to contribute to the functioning of a range of organizations. They need to be able to make evaluations of such things as Canadian hedging practices (Al Zaman & Lightstone, 2008), ownership concentration and corporate governance (Bozec & Bozec, 2007), the value of household life cycle variables in consumer expenditure research (Putler et al., 2007), and gender identity and consumer behaviour (Fischer & Arnold, 1994).

Starting the research process

To return to our definition of research as a systematic investigation, systematic refers to the processes used to conduct an investigation. Those processes include identifying an area of research; formulating research questions; developing a clear research strategy, research design, and choice of methods; and coming up with detailed explanations of the overall process of research and the results.

Many factors encourage the development of a research project but importantly they begin with some kind of questioning (see Web Thinking deeper 1.1). For example, have you ever wondered what was the cause of the 2008 economic downturn? Maybe you have speculated why it is that there are fewer women than men in Canada's corporate boardrooms (Long & Morris, 2008)? Perhaps you have thought about how and why industrial accidents occur (Mullen, 2004)? Or maybe you have felt that there was a need for a more relevant introductory business course in your program (Skipton & Furey, 2008). These types of thoughts form the basis of research questions. However, these thoughts are not enough. They need to be turned into research questions before the research project can begin. You need to know what it is that you are trying to find out. Whether the questions are narrowly or more broadly focused will depend on the research strategy you adopt, and we will we be looking at that more closely in Chapter 3.

Thinking about your research area

Many students want to conduct research into areas that are of personal interest to them. However, it is wise to start to think about your project well in advance so that you are not scrambling for ideas when the time comes to develop a term project or thesis topic. For example, as you work your way through different courses, begin to think about what specifically grabs your interest and could provide you with an area of research. Make notes on your various thoughts and talk them through with other students and professors to help you hone in on a specific area of research. In the process you will find that some areas are too vague (e.g., 'a study of organizational culture and leadership'), too trivial (e.g., 'do women who wear dresses make better co-workers?'), too large (e.g., 'what are the causes of worldwide economic depression?'), or too narrow (e.g., 'is unemployment higher this year compared with last year?') for a research project.

Formulating suitable research questions

Having identified an area of research you need to develop research questions that will provide your dissertation with a clear focus. Your research questions will serve as the basis of your investigation. For example, a vague question about organizational culture and leadership can be turned into an investigation that asks 'How do managers make sense of organizational change and what are the implications? A case study of a North American

1.1   Student Experience

Why do a research project?

For some students, doing a research project is an optional part of their degree program or dissertation requirement. In this case the decision whether or not to do research becomes more personal. For Amanda her choice was based on her interest in learning new techniques.

In Amanda's research methods course for her Public Relations degree at Mount Saint Vincent University, students were required to undertake a small research project as part of the course requirements. Students were broken into groups of five and given a choice of research methods to utilize for their research project. Those methods were limited to the ones that had been taught on the course, and included surveys, interviews, focus groups, and participant observation. As a graduate in Anthropology from Dalhousie University, Amanda had been exposed to a few research methods already and wanted to learn something different. She heeded the advice of the course professor that participant observation could be very time consuming (see Chapter 17) but in any event was keen on learning more about the focus group method: 'I really wanted to do a focus group because I hadn't done one before. I'd done interviews, surveys, other things so was pretty interested in doing a focus group'. To make the focus group relevant and interesting to both the participants and the members of Amanda's research team they chose to ask about student responses about the impact of the (then) economic downturn on perceptions of future job opportunities.

In Cindy's case 'the most valuable thing' about a research project was that '[as students] we would be conducting the research ourselves and actually seeing the findings, and analyzing the findings'. It was exciting to find out 'that the further that you dig, the more that you're going to find out and the more that your initial thought may have changed'.

For Chris, doing a research project was an opportunity 'to find things out from the horse's mouth' by investigating how things worked in the 'real world' after three years of studying theories of business and management: 'I thought it would be interesting to actually find out what people really think about [a] subject. When you read these textbooks you read theories, you know, papers and you get told things in lectures . . . newspapers or whatever—and you think "Right, great. That's interesting and I'm sure that must be right." I mean sometimes I used to question. "Well, I don't agree with that . . . ." [and] I thought "Well, [now] I've got this really good opportunity to find out things . . . ." within an organization'.

In his opinion this meant that a research-based dissertation stood apart from dissertations, which didn't include a research project. '[Some of my friends for their dissertations] took a load of information . . . commented on it and came up with a conclusion and essentially, you know, that's an essay [like any other] essay that we've been doing throughout the three years at [university], just a bit longer . . . it was . . . worth putting the extra effort in because it was [an entire] module. And it was fun. It was enjoyable and I got exposure to people that I [wouldn't otherwise have had] . . . which has helped me recently in my graduate scheme . . . [And] maybe it's just me, but it's nice to question theories . . . that you don't necessarily believe and it's very easy to say "Oh well, I don't believe it, but there we go." The way I [saw] it was "Well, I don't believe it, so [let's] see if I can find out anything to back that up"'.

Utility Company' (Helms Mills, 2003). Developing research questions applies to **qualitative** research as well as **quantitative** research. As we explain in Chapter 5, qualitative research is more *open-ended* than quantitative research, and in Chapters 6 and 17 we will mention some notable studies that appear not to have been driven by specific research questions. However, very open-ended research is problematic where the student does not have a sufficient grasp or understanding of the type of **research strategy** needed (see chapter 3). The result can be the collection of too much data and lack of clarity about the focus of the study. This can lead to confusion when attempting to write up the results. So, unless your supervisor advises you to the contrary, we would advise you to formulate some research questions, even if they turn out to be less specific than the kinds we often find in quantitative research. In other words, what is it about your area of interest that you want to know?

Research questions are, therefore, important. A lack of research questions or poorly formulated research questions will lead to poor (i.e., unclear, unusable) research. If you do not specify clear research questions, there is a great risk that your research will be unfocused and that you will be unsure about what your research is about and what you are collecting the data for. It does not matter how well you design a questionnaire or how skilled an interviewer you are; you must be clear about your research questions. Equally, it does not matter whether your research is for a research contract for $200,000, a doctoral thesis, or a class research project. Research questions are crucial because they will:

- Guide your literature search.
- Guide your decisions about the kind of research design to employ.
- Guide your decisions about what data to collect and from whom.
- Guide your analysis of your data.
- Guide your write-up of your data.
- Stop you from going off in unnecessary directions.

 Marx (1997) has suggested a wide range of sources of research questions (see Web Thinking deeper 1.1) and

outlines some of the features that your research questions should exhibit. Figure 1.1 indicates the main steps in developing research questions. As you will see in Chapters 3 and 4, research questions in quantitative research are sometimes more specific than in qualitative research. However, there is a growing tendency for qualitative researchers to advocate a more focused approach to their research strategy (e.g., Hammersley & Atkinson, 1995, pp. 24–9). Nonetheless, some qualitative researchers advocate a very open approach with no research questions. For students this is a very risky approach unless they have a good grasp of the appropriate methodology (see Chapter 3).

We usually start out with a general research area that interests us. It may derive from any of several sources:

- *Personal interest or experience.* As we will discuss in Chapter 3, Bryman's interest in theme parks can be traced back to a visit to Disney World in Orlando in 1991. In turn, Bell's interest in 'Investors in People' (IIP) stems from her involvement in managing the implementation of this quality standard in a National Health Service (NHS) trust hospital. Additionally, Mills's interest in the impact of an organization on people's sense of worth is rooted in his experiences in a series of unskilled jobs after leaving school at the age of 15. Finally, Yue's previous experience as a survival instructor informs his present interest in how people adapt and thrive in organizational settings.
- *Theory.* Someone might be interested in testing aspects of motivation theory or the contingency perspective on organization structure.
- *The research literature.* Studies relating to a research area like downsizing in Canadian companies could be an example of research literature to be reviewed that might stimulate interest in what happens to the motivation and morale of those employees who are retained.
- *Puzzles.* How are team and individual empowerment compatible?
- *New developments in society.* Examples might include the rise of the Internet or the diffusion of new models of organization, e.g., Total Quality Management (TQM), customer service programs, call centres.

Figure 1.1

Steps in selecting research questions

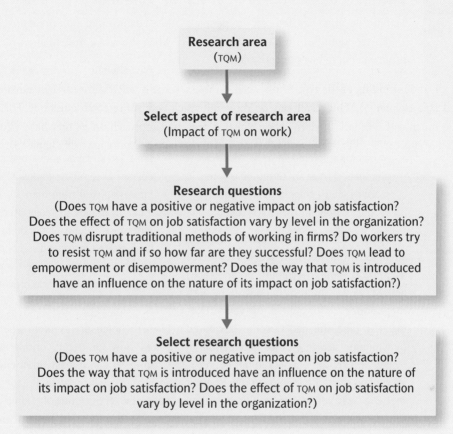

• *Social problem*. An example might be how staff in call centres should handle consumer rage when consumers are interrupted by unwanted telephone calls.

As these types of source suggest, in research we often start out with a general research area which has to be narrowed down so that we can develop a tighter focus out of which research questions can be developed. We can depict the process of generating research questions as a series of steps that are suggested in Figure 1.1. The series of stages is meant to suggest that, when developing research questions, the researcher is involved in a process of progressive focusing down, moving from a general research area down to specific research questions. In making this movement, we have to recognize the following restrictions.

• We cannot answer all the research questions that occur to us. This is not just to do with issues of time and the cost of doing research. It is very much to do with the fact that we must keep a clear focus so that our research questions must relate to each other to form a coherent set of issues.

• We, therefore, have to select from the possible research questions that we arrive at.

1.2 | Student Experience

Choosing a research area based on personal experience

Jennifer locates her interest in people's workplace identities (in international companies) in her family's experiences:

> when I was in high school I went . . . to Germany [for a year] and after I graduated . . . I first moved to Sweden and then I moved to Spain and so it kind of made me interested in . . . cultural identities. [Thus, in terms of my research topic] I think that it definitely . . . comes from my own background.

Karla's focus on work-family balance stemmed from her past work experience as 'an NGO [non-government organization] activist' where she had 'been working with these issues . . . for quite a few years'. During that time she had become fascinated by what she saw as clashes between 'family law and gender equality in her country'. When she started her Ph.D. studies she felt that she 'was young and ambitious and so on and so on . . . and [had] my own children, and then I noticed how my thinking changed, and that was sort of already quite funny, and then it drew me to [issues of] family politics and gender equality. So when I came here [to my University], I actually just thought that this was too interesting a topic not to look into. Yeah, that was a long process. That was long and painful actually'.

Lucie's choice of research subject reflected her personal experience of having been exposed to entrepreneurial discourses while she was a student at university.

> As a student . . . I was being exposed to kind of these enterprise courses . . . kind of . . . bombarded [with messages] like 'Join this course', 'Join this course', and I was . . . quite interested in enterprise . . . so I'd attended one of these courses as an undergraduate, so I was interested in it from then . . . Also, a lot of my friends are really interested in enterprise . . . and a lot of them kind of have started to try and run businesses while at university . . . So I was interested in what kind of was provoking . . . students to do this.

Lucie's choice of research area also illustrates how practical considerations (see Chapter 1) can impact upon choice of research area, since Lucie already had social contact with the kinds of people who might become the focus of her research, in this case university students, and had already had contact with the research setting that she was intending to base her study on. In some senses, Lucie could be seen as engaged in studying her own social grouping, i.e. students. This is interesting because it raises particular considerations about the nature of the relationship between the researcher and research subjects; this is an issue that we will return to in Chapter 6.

- In making our selection, we should be guided by the principle that the research questions we choose should be related to one another. If they are not, our research will probably lack focus and we may not make as clear a contribution to research in that field as would be the case if research questions were connected. Thus, in the example in Figure 1.1, the research questions relating to TQM are closely connected.

Tips and Skills

Criteria for evaluating research questions

Research questions for a dissertation or project should:

- *Be clear.* They must be understandable to you and to others.
- *Be researchable.* They should be capable of development into a research design, so that relevant data may be collected. This means that extremely abstract terms are unlikely to be suitable.
- *Connect with established theory and research.* This means that there should be research literature on which you can draw to help illuminate how your research questions should be approached. Even if you find a topic that has been scarcely addressed by social scientists, it is unlikely that there will be no relevant literature (for example, on related or parallel topics). Making connections with theory and research will also allow you to show how your research has made a contribution to knowledge and understanding.
- *Be linked to each other.* Unrelated research questions are unlikely to be acceptable, since you should be de-veloping an argument in your dissertation. You could not very readily construct a single argument in connection with unrelated research questions.
- *Have potential for making a contribution to knowledge.* They should at the very least hold out the prospect of being able to make a contribution—however small—to the topic.
- *Be neither too broad nor too narrow.* The research questions should be neither too large (so that you would need a massive grant to study them) nor too small (so that you cannot make a reasonably signifi-cant contribution to your area of study).

If you are stuck about how to formulate research questions (or indeed other phases of your research), it is always a good idea to look at journal articles or research monographs to see how other researchers have formulated them. Also, look at past dissertations for ideas as well.

Tips and skills '*Criteria for evaluating research questions*' gives some suggestions about the kinds of considerations that should be taken into account when developing your own research questions.

Research in focus 1.1 describes some considerations that went into Helms Mills (2003) exploration of how managers made sense of organizational change in Nova Scotia Power, a Canadian utility company.

Helms Mills' reflections on the overall process are instructive. As she undertook her research different meth-odological issues confronted her. At the beginning she had to confront the issue of whether to conduct a clinical or **ethnographic** (Schein, 1985) study of NSP. The former, with its emphasis on client-based problems and concerns, was shaped by the needs of access, which required her to take a 'snap shot' of NSP's culture program to judge its success and reveal the weak links. This approach allowed unlimited access to the company but meant that the data collected was problematic if she also wanted to conduct an ethnographic study, designed to contribute to our broader understanding of organizational culture and change. This latter approach informed her research for her Master's thesis and latter PH.D. work. She was also confronted with the issue of employing a qualitative, quantitative, or **mixed methods** approach to her study. She eventually opted for mixed methods but with a primary reliance on qualitative research. She argued that: 'of the methodological questions before me the issue of qualitative research was the least problematic. As a study of *processes* of organisational change I felt that it was more appropriate to use techniques that could identify socio-psychological patterns associated with those processes rather than a frequency count of outcomes'. But she concludes that while the research process did little to change her 'opinion on the value of a qualitative approach [she conceded] that counts of the frequency of some expressed opinions may have been valu-able in the overall findings' (2000, p. 81). Finally, she was faced with the choice of **positivist** or **postpositivist** strate-gies— sticking closely to a more natural science model of research (positivist) or choosing techniques that empha-

1.1   Research in Focus

Developing research questions

Helms Mills (2000, 2003) provides a useful account of the research **strategies** that she adopted in her study of organizational change in Nova Scotia Power (NSP), and reveals how the process of research can go through various developments. She was drawn to the study of NSP because of the various changes that it went through, including a company-wide attitude survey (1987), culture change (1988–93), privatization (1992), downsizing (1993, 1995), reengineering (1993–95), key leadership changes (1983, 1996), strategic business units (1996), and a balanced scorecard strategic plan (1999–2000) (Helms Mills, 2003, p. 4). However, the initial impetus for Helms Mills's study began in 1991 and came from two disparate sources. The first was the thesis requirement of her Lancaster University (UK) Master's program. The second was a chance meeting with an old acquaintance at a bus stop in Halifax, Nova Scotia, where she was offered the opportunity to study culture change at NSP. In exchange for access to the company, NSP required Helms Mills to undertake an audit of the culture change that it introduced in 1988. Between 1991 and 1993 she was given 'almost unlimited access to the company to study the "success" of its "Culture Change program"' (2003, p. 4).

To meet the company's requirements she interviewed 176 employees at 15 different locations across the company (2000, p. 79), asking a series of **semi-structured** questions to find out what they knew about the culture change and how they felt about it. This stage of the research was linked to a report that was provided to the company at the conclusion of the research (2000, Appendix E). For her Master's thesis she used the answers to the structured questions and observations at a series of meetings of senior managers to investigate whether organizational culture could be manipulated and changed. On completion of her Master's thesis Helms Mills was given more limited access to NSP to develop her Ph.D. thesis on how these managers made sense of organizational change and what were the implications of their '**sensemaking**' (2003, p. 4). In this phase of the study she conducted more interviews, observed various management meetings, and undertook extensive **content analysis** of corporate documents. Eventually, she used a sensemaking framework (adapted from the work of Weick, 1995) to analyze various data and assess the role of sensemaking in organizational change. Her study has encouraged further research into the role of the psychological properties of sensemaking in organizational change (Weick, Sutcliffe, & Obstfeld, 2005).

size the socially constructed nature of social reality (for a discussion of postpositivism see Prasad, 2005). Eventually she settled on a postpositivist framework of sensemaking (Weick, 1995), which allowed her to treat even data that was gathered using positivist techniques as sensemaking data, i.e. data that was useful for its plausibility rather than its accuracy (Weick, 1995). Helms Mills's work suggests that while the establishment of specific methodological guidelines may be established in advance the researcher needs to be open to, or at least aware of, the various methodological problems, contentions, and debates that occur during the research process and can shape the final outcome (2000, p. 79).

Writing your research proposal

You may be required as part of your research project or thesis to write a short proposal or plan outlining what your research project will be about and how you intend

1.3 | Student Experience

Narrowing down your research questions

Mark went through several different ideas before narrowing his honours thesis topic down to:

a study of technology differences in the workplace between younger and older workers and how they perceive it and how they use it and how it affects their performance.

He began with a totally different study but his ideas were 'transformed from talking to professors'.

'My problem was everyone was telling me I was thinking too big . . . [because] I was thinking that I want to look at all these different things but everyone said just narrow it down'. Nonetheless, as Mark explains, the process was never that simple. Indeed, he describes narrowing down his topic as his 'biggest struggle and it was kind of discouraging'. He adds that: 'I was in the beginning of my third year, I had these ideas but I didn't know what to [do with them or how to] narrow it down. . . . So I talked to a whole bunch of professors and they slowly guided me down to where I was going wrong and I was told to do a lot more reading'.

The literature review also helped Mark to narrow things down, but, again, there were a number of questions he had to ask

of himself and his project before he found a way forward. A lot was involved in 'just the reading on my topic . . . then just trying to narrow it down, reading the texts, reading past examples of what does a research question ask. It might not be specific enough'. From his professors Mark 'got recommendations . . . to look in specific areas and . . . specific articles . . . and [answers] really came with reading more theses and journal articles . . . .'

Like Mark, Tom found it was common for students in his course to be too ambitious in forming their research questions: 'We all came up with really big questions like "How does leadership impact on the NHS?" Some huge question like that—you know, not the sort of thing that's very easy to test in an M.SC. research project . . . we were encouraged to . . . knock [these] ideas around. Most of [them] . . . were pretty impractical because they were sort of like five-year research projects needing thousands and thousands of hours to be operationalized, whereas we only had very limited time. So we were encouraged to kind of focus down'. This echoes our own experience as dissertation project supervisors, which suggests that it is much more common for students to be too broad in designing their research questions than to be too narrow.

to go about it. This is a useful way of preparing for your research and it will encourage you to think about many of the issues that are covered in the next section. You need to outline the research design and methods that you intend to use, the topic area in which your study is going to be located, and the research questions that you intend to address. Your proposal should demonstrate some knowledge of the literature in your chosen field, including identifying several key authors or important research studies. This information may be used as the basis for choosing a supervisor who is knowledgeable in your area of research interest. The proposal is also a useful basis

Figure 1.2

A 'what, why, and how' framework for crafting research

What?	**Why?**
What puzzles/intrigues me! What do I want to know more about/understand better? What are my key research questions?	Why will this be of enough interest to others to be published as a thesis, book, paper, guide to practitioners or policy-makers? Can the research be justified as a 'contribution to knowledge'?
How—conceptually?	**How—practically?**
What models, concepts, and theories can I draw on/develop to answer my research questions? How can these be brought together into a basic conceptual framework to guide my investigation?	What investigative styles and techniques shall I use to apply my conceptual framework (both to gather material and analyse it)? How shall I gain and maintain access to information sources?

Source: Watson (1994b: S80). Reprinted with permission of Wiley Publishing.

for discussion of your research project with your supervisor. If it includes a timetable for the project, this can provide a basis for planning regular meetings with your supervisor to review your progress. Writing a proposal is, therefore, useful in getting you started on your research project and encouraging you to set realistic objectives for your research project. However, the important thing to remember about the research proposal is that it is a working document and the ideas that you set out in it can be refined and developed as your research progresses.

 ## Preparing for your research

Do not begin your data collection until you have identified your research questions. Decide on your data collection methods with your research questions at the forefront of your thinking. If you do not do this, there is the risk that your results will not allow you to illuminate the research questions. If possible, conduct a small pilot study to determine how well your research methods work.

You will also need to think about access, **sampling** or **interpretive** issues, and ethical approval. If your research requires you to gain access to, or the cooperation of, an organization, you need to confirm, at the earliest opportunity, that you have the necessary permission to conduct your research. You also need to consider how you will go about gaining access to people. These issues lead you into sampling considerations, such as the following:

- Who do you need to study in order to investigate your research questions?
- How easily can you gain access to a sampling frame?

1.4 | Student Experience

The importance of having a plan

When researching work-family balance Lotta listed a number of things she would need to know and understand before starting to survey people and conduct follow-up interviews:

> The legal frame, I had to know that. And then I had to have some idea of what companies additionally had. For example, what labour agreements [they] might have and so on . . . and so I had to look into that and there wasn't a lot of material from Finland . . . [so] I've been reading the international [material] all the time. [But work-family policies] differ so much from different legal contexts, so I always have to read it with that in mind. . . . So I had to find out all these [things].

To assist her in the process she developed a 'research plan'. She had an initial research plan at the beginning of her studies but this was changed and amended as she did more reading and more thinking. 'Initially I was thinking of looking for some gender equality family policies and [legal cases] on family leaves . . . but that's actually changed more to see . . . why companies are doing what they're doing . . .'. Lotta submitted a research plan when she applied to do her

PH.D. and has updated it regularly. '[The] longest version isn't that updated, but sort of shorter summaries are updated, so I'm sort of doing that all the time also in order to keep [up] . . .. When I apply for grants, these people want to know what I'm doing and then when I report I have to tell what I've sort of done so in that sense, [the] system is good because then you also check what you have [done] and how you've planned to do [it]'.

Karen found one of the things she had learned from the experience of doing a research project was the importance of planning: 'For our dissertation we actually had to do a plan and submit it . . . and get that approved by our dissertation tutor before we started the actual writing. And I think that's really important just for them to check that you're on the right lines and just to clarify for you because I think when you first start you think "Oh, it's such a lot of pages or a lot of words" and you have . . . the desire to . . . do so much, but then once you start writing you realize that it's much better to be a lot more focused and then you can go a lot deeper into things. So I think having that plan right at the beginning is really important'.

- What kind of sampling strategy will you employ (e.g., **probability sampling**, **quota sampling**, **theoretical sampling**, **convenience sampling**)?
- Can you justify your choice of sampling method?

Also, at this stage, if you are using a **case study** design, you will almost certainly need to find out more about the organization that you intend to investigate. Consider the following questions: What is its financial position? Has

it been in the news recently? Where is it located? What market conditions does it face? There are a wide variety of sources available on the Web that can provide this kind of background information to inform your research. One of several sources of company financial and business news in Canada, for example, can be found at: http://www.financialpost.com/. In addition, the largest multinational corporations often make their annual reports and accounts available through their homepages. Although this is often primarily a marketing exercise, you can usually obtain the full text as it appears in hard copy free of charge. The best way to find these pages is by using a search engine and entering the full company name as a phrase.

Newspapers such as the *Financial Post* are also accessible on the Web, although there are some limitations on the amount of information that you can obtain free of charge. Newslink is a collection of links to newspapers all over the world. It can be found at: www.newslink.org.

Qualitative research strategies also need some advanced thinking about such things as the following:

- What will be the best source of data? Interviews, observation, content analysis, or some combination of all three?
- Will access be sufficient to allow the tracking of a phenomenon (e.g., gossip) across an organization? Is data best collected through overt or covert means as in, for example, the study of corporate theft or attitudes towards outsiders?

Last, but not least, is the question of ethics and ethics approval. The two are linked but are not exactly the same. To think about the ethics of your research means that you need to consider whether people can ultimately be harmed by your research and/or the methods used (see Chapter 8). In any event you will be required to seek 'ethical approval' from your university before you are allowed to proceed. This consists of an application form that requires you to spell out your research and answer a series of structured and semi-structured questions. The form has to have the approval of your supervisor and is then submitted to the council or committee, for example, at your university that is responsible for ethics in research (see chapter 8).

 ## Doing your research and analyzing your results

Here are some useful reminders of the practicalities involved:

- Keep good records of what you do. A research diary can be helpful, but there are several other things to bear in mind. For example, if you are doing a mail-out survey, keep good records of who has replied, so that you know who should be sent reminders. If participant observation is a component of your research, remember to keep good field notes and not to rely on your memory.
- Make sure that you are thoroughly familiar with any hardware you are using in collecting your data, such as tape recorders for interviewing, and check that it is in good working order (for example, that the batteries are not dead or are low).
- Do not wait until all your data have been collected to begin coding. This recommendation applies to both quantitative and qualitative research. If you are conducting a questionnaire survey, begin coding your data and entering them into SPSS or whatever computer software package you are using after you have put together a reasonably sized batch of completed questionnaires. In the case of qualitative data, such as interview transcripts, the same point applies, and, indeed, it is a specific recommendation of the proponents of **grounded theory** that data collection and analysis should be intertwined.
- Remember that the **transcription** of tapes with recorded interviews takes a long time. Allow at least six hours' transcription for every one hour of recorded interview talk, at least in the early stages of transcription.
- Become familiar with any data analysis packages as soon as possible. This familiarity will help you to establish whether or not you need them and will ensure that you do not need to learn everything about them at the very time you need to use them for your analysis.
- Finally, undertaking a successful research project will also depend on your overall preparation, adaptation, and organizing skills. You will need to take into account such things as your university requirements, working effectively and cooperatively with your supervisor, and managing your time and resources.

 ## Get to know what is expected of you by your institution

Your institution or department will have specific requirements concerning the development of a research project or thesis. Those requirements will include a range of things, including whether your dissertation should be bound or not and, if so, the form of binding to be used; how the project or thesis is to be presented; whether or not an abstract is required; how wide the page margins should be; the format for referencing; the maximum (and sometimes minimum) number of words; and sometimes the structure of the thesis (e.g., an introduction, followed by a literature review, a methods chapter, research and findings chapters and a concluding chapter); whether or not a thesis proposal is required; policies on plagiarism; deadlines; etc. This information is likely to be found in your university's calendar and website. For example, Saint Mary's University's regulations for Honour's, Master's, and ph.d. dissertations and other major research projects can be found at: http://www.smu.ca/administration/archives/theses.html.

The advice here is simple: follow the requirements, instructions, and information you are given.

 ## Working with your supervisor

Most institutions that require a dissertation or similar research project also require that students work with a supervisor. There are two main processes and considerations here.

First, in a number of cases, you may be assigned a supervisor. This is more likely at the undergraduate and Master's levels but may in some cases occur at the ph.d. level. In such cases you can expect that the supervisor is well versed in the research process and will be able to provide you with help and feedback at all stages of your research.

Second, you may have some freedom in your choice of supervisor. In such cases you should develop a preliminary outline of your proposed research that you can show to potential supervisors. In some ph.d. programs, for instance, the submission of a research proposal is an entry requirement so that the school can assess whether they have potential supervisors for the applicant's area of interest. Having developed your outline, do some background research to see who is likely available at your institution, the type of research they are engaged in and their preferred research strategies (e.g., qualitative or quantita-

tive research). To some extent you can find this out from their university faculty web pages. You can also follow-up by reading some of their research papers. You should then make an appointment to talk with them, in person where possible, but failing that by telephone or email. You will need to get a feel for whether you can work with this person and whether he or she can work with you. Undertaking a research project can involve a relatively long process based on trust and consideration on both sides. This is especially the case with a ph.d., which can take a few years to complete. Thus, you need to take into account the potential supervisor's areas of interest, whether they are more interested in and comfortable with supervising a quantitative, qualitative, or mixed methods approach (see Chapters 5–7), and if your personalities are compatible.

Universities vary quite a lot in what can be expected of supervisors in terms of what kinds of assistance and how much they can give to students. Equally, students may vary a great deal in how frequently they see their supervisor and in their work with them. Our advice here is simple: use your supervisor to the fullest extent that you are allowed and follow the advice and insights you are given by him or her.

Understand and prepare for the fact that your supervisor will almost certainly see his or her role as providing you with the best advice that they can give; that they will be working to ensure that you acquire and/or develop the required research skills; and they will want you to produce the best possible work. Inevitably this will involve at least some critique of your work and suggestions for improvements. This is to be expected. Try to deal with critique in a positive way, treat it as a learning experience. Do your best to be clear about what is being asked of you. If you don't understand, ask questions, make notes, paraphrase what is being asked of you and ask for clarification. Above all ensure that you maintain an open atmosphere of trust and consideration.

 ## Managing time and resources

All research is constrained by time and resources. There is no point in working on research questions and plans that cannot be seen through because of time pressure or because of the costs involved. Two points are relevant here.

1. Work out a timetable—preferably in conjunction with your supervisor—detailing the different stages of your research (including the review of the literature and write-up). This is particularly important if you are a part-time student combining your studies with full-time work. The timetable should specify the different stages and the calendar points at which you should start and finish. Some stages of the research are likely to be ongoing such as searching the literature for new references, but that should not prove an obstacle to developing a timetable.

2. Find out what, if any, resources can be put at your disposal for carrying out your research. For example, will you receive help from your university with such things as travel costs, photocopying, secretarial assistance, postage, stationery, and so on? Will the institution be able to loan you hardware such as tape recorders and transcription machines if you need to record and transcribe your interviews? Has it got the software you need, such as SPSS or a qualitative data analysis package like NVivo? This kind of information will help you to establish how far your research design and methods are financially feasible and practical.

As the research project progresses, the chart may be amended to indicate the portions of tasks that have been completed. However, one of the limitations of Gantt charts is that they do not indicate task dependencies, so you cannot tell, for example, how falling behind with your literature review will affect the timing of other tasks in your research project. This is a particular problem for undergraduate and some Master's student research projects where you will almost certainly be working to a fixed and immovable deadline for completion of the dissertation, so falling behind in your timetable will necessarily reduce the amount of time that you have to devote to other stages of the project. A further difficulty with Gantt charts is that, even though they allow for overlaps between different tasks, they do encourage you to see the research process as a linear, sequential activity. This may be inappropriate particularly for qualitative research projects where many of the tasks are iterative. Such a project might produce a Gantt chart where tasks overlap to such an extent that the graph becomes impossible to follow.

1.5 | Student Experience

Finding time to do a research project alongside a full-time job and family commitments

When Tricia began her Master's in Health Care Quality Improvement and Leadership Development at the University of Helsinki she was relatively new to Finland. In the two-year program the first year involved 'really intense coursework, we were there five days a week, eight-hour days. And then it was a different way of studying for me. And then the thesis took about eight months to write'. She found the work 'a really great experience . . . and a different way of thinking for me that's for sure'. Despite the fact Tricia also held down a full-time job: 'I was surprised I didn't go crazy, because when I was writing my thesis, I was waking up every day at four thirty in the morning to go to the hotel and I was told that I was only going to be working six . . . seven hour shifts. Well it doesn't work that way in a hotel restaurant. Like sometimes they would keep you for eight, ten hours. I don't know how I did it, but I got through. And I'm actually . . . grateful for the experience because it really . . . made me more aware of what, for instance, immigrants go through for making money and establishing their daily routines'. She basically survived by 'sheer perseverance, but … also [through] a great social network. Like I have a lot of support here in Finland and I have a lot of support in Canada too, so I think that that's really important. I think that as an immigrant, you can come here and not know anyone, but establishing a good network of friends helps you a lot, because a lot of people are experiencing the same thing and just to know that someone else is feeling the same way as you are, it helps out a lot'.

For part-time MBA, undergraduate, and postgraduate students, doing a research project sometimes has to be combined with the intense demands of work and family, which in themselves may constitute more than a full-time job. From our experience of supervising such students we have observed that they develop many different and creative ways of managing the time pressures associated with doing a dissertation project, but this can often involve an element of personal sacrifice for them. Female MBA students from Warwick Business School interviewed by Bell (2004) described some of the effects of these time pressures, for example causing them to temporarily give up social activities or family time in order to work on their dissertation at weekends or during holidays. Students also highlighted the importance of partners and other family members in helping to enable them to find time and giving them emotional and practical support in doing their research project.

Students who don't fully take these time pressures into account can sometimes find that they are unable to meet the deadlines for submitting their dissertation and have to repeatedly postpone this final stage of their degree study. One female MBA student working full time with two young children interviewed by Bell (2004, pp. 69–70) summarized the pressures associated with these conflicting demands: '[My son is] growing up really quickly and . . . yes, [people] can take him off [so I can work on my MBA dissertation] but I'm [at] work all week [and] I actually quite like seeing him at the weekend . . . I'm just conscious that as the gap . . . between the [MBA] course and the project [gets bigger] the project gets harder because . . . you can't remember anything that you've done'.

Tom, the part-time student at Birkbeck College at the University of London, took a different approach, cutting down on his work time in order to create time for his research project: '[This] isn't going to be any help to people that are working full time [but] I . . . reduced my hours to work four days a week for the second half of the course so I had a day a week to do [my] studies . . . that was a big help . . . . A lot of people . . . did extend their studies over a third year because it was just really difficult to fit it all in.' Even so, Tom found the pressures of doing a research project daunting at times. 'It's very easy to feel like it's this huge mountain that you'll never get to the top of and just feel like you can never do . . . . You know, you can never sit down and watch telly or relax because this thing's always there . . . living with this thing can be annoying at times as well and obviously there are times when you are stuck and it doesn't feel great'.

Tips and Skills

Constructing a Gantt chart for your research project

One way of keeping track of your research project is through the use of a *Gantt chart*. This is a horizontal bar chart that was originally developed as a production control tool in 1917 by Henry L. Gantt, an American engineer and social scientist. Although Gantt charts are more commonly used in project management, they can also help you to plan, coordinate, and track specific tasks in your research project by providing a graphical illustration of your timetable and the key tasks involved in it. Simple Gantt charts may be designed on graph paper or as a table in Microsoft Word. More complex automated versions can be created using project management applications such as Microsoft Project or Microsoft Excel.

The horizontal axis of the chart represents the total time span of the project divided into units such as weeks or months. The vertical axis represents the tasks involved in the project. An example of a Gantt chart for a student research project is provided in Figure 1.3. As Figure 1.3 shows, you would put 'conduct literature review' at the top of the vertical axis and fill in the squares on the graph to represent the amount of time you expect to spend on this task. The filled-in squares may overlap, to reflect the fact, for example, that you may continue to review the literature in the same time span as starting to collect your data.

Figure 1.3

An example of a Gantt chart for a student research project

	Sept	Oct	Nov	Dec	Jan	Feb	Mar	April
Identify research area	▓							
Formulate research questions		▓						
Formulate research strategy, research design and select methods		▓	▓					
Write research proposal			15th					
Negotiate access								
Literature review			▓	▓				
Data collection				▓				
Data analysis						▓		
Write first draft						▓		
Write second draft							▓	
Write final draft								▓
Dissertation due								21st

Checklist

Planning a research project:

- [ ] Do you know what the requirements for your dissertation are, as set out by your university or department?
- [ ] Have you made contact with your supervisor?
- [ ] Have you left enough time for planning, doing, and writing up your research project?
- [ ] Do you have a clear timetable for your research project with clearly identifiable milestones for the achievement of specific tasks?
- [ ] Have you got sufficient financial and practical resources (e.g., money to enable travel to a research site, to buy a tape recorder) to enable you to carry out your research project?
- [ ] Have you formulated some research questions and discussed these with your supervisor?
- [ ] Are the research questions you have identified able to be answered through your research project?
- [ ] Do you have the access that you require in order to carry out your research?
- [ ] Are you familiar with the data analysis software that you may be using to analyze your data?

Key points

- Follow the dissertation guidelines provided by your institution.
- Thinking about your research subject can be time consuming, so allow plenty of time for this aspect of the dissertation process.
- Use your supervisor to the fullest extent allowed and follow the advice offered by them.
- Plan your time carefully and be realistic about what you can achieve in the time available.
- Formulate some research questions to express what it is about your area of interest that you want to know.
- Writing a research proposal is a good way of getting started on your research project and encouraging you to set realistic objectives.
- Consider access and sampling issues at an early stage and consider testing your research methods by conducting a pilot study.
- Keep good records of what you do in your research as you go along and don't wait until all of your data have been collected before you start coding.

Questions for review

The importance of research

- What types of evidence do people prefer? What types of evidence are people less likely to accept?

Starting the research process

- What qualities does a good research question have?
- What are the main sources of research questions?
- What are the main steps involved in developing research questions?
- What criteria can be used to evaluate research questions?

Writing your research proposal

- What is the purpose of the research proposal and how can it be useful?

Preparing for your research

- What are the most important steps when preparing to start a research project?

Doing your research and analyzing your results

- What are some useful habits to follow when doing your research and analyzing the results?

Managing time and resources

- What are the main advantages/disadvantages associated with using a *Gantt chart* to plan your research?

2

Getting Started: Reviewing the Literature

Chapter guide

The goal of this chapter is to provide guidance on how to get started on and how to refine a research project. Once you have identified your research questions (see Chapter 1), the next step in any research project is to search the existing literature and write a literature review. The principal task at this early stage involves reviewing the main ideas and research relating to your chosen area of interest. This provides the basis for the writing of a literature review, which forms an important part of the dissertation. This chapter explores:

- How to go about searching the literature and engaging critically with the ideas of other writers.
- What is expected in a literature review and the criteria that are used to evaluate it.
- How to assess the quality of existing research in your subject area.
- The role of the bibliography and the importance of referencing the work of others.
- The importance of understanding what constitutes plagiarism and the penalties that are associated with it.

Introduction

This chapter is intended to help you to get started on one of the most important tasks in carrying out a research project of your own—reviewing the literature in your chosen subject area. The literature review is a crucial part of an undergraduate or postgraduate thesis, often constituting a separate chapter or substantial section that is usually positioned towards the beginning of the finished document. It provides the basis on which you justify your research questions and build your research design. The literature review also informs how you collect and analyze data in an informed way. However, doing a literature review can initially feel quite daunting, either because so many other researchers have written numerous books and articles about your chosen subject, or because your subject area does not seem to have a clearly defined boundary. Hence there are various literatures that you could review and you are not sure how to choose between or combine them. The process of reviewing the literature, therefore, involves making judgements about what to include and exclude from your literature review and then reading what other researchers have written about your subject and writing about it in a way that demonstrates your understanding. The advice we give in this chapter is designed to assist in this process.

As we stated in Chapter 1, a literature review is a useful way to identify a research area by finding out what ar-eas interest you the most and what gaps may exist in the existing literature. A 'gap' refers to an area of knowledge that has yet to be explored or more fully explored. For example, you may be interested in finding out about the impact of the Internet on business communications and feel that very little research has been done on the area. By undertaking a review of the literature you will almost certainly find that there is considerable research on the subject. However, in the process you may come to find that there is very little research on forms of aggression or 'cyber aggression', in which case you may have found a research gap that you can help to fill by your study. Once you have identified an area of research you will then need to return to your review of relevant literature to begin to further refine your research.

Reviewing the existing literature and engaging with what others have written

Why do you need to review the existing literature? The most obvious reason is that you want to know what is already known about your area of interest so that you do not simply 'reinvent the wheel'. Your literature review is where you demonstrate that you are able to engage in scholarly review based on your reading and understanding of the work of others in the same field as you. Beyond this, using the existing literature on a topic is a means of developing an argument about the significance of your research and where it leads. For example, if you think of your research as a story then the aim of the literature review is to help you develop your story line (see Thinking deeper 2.1 on the website).

Alternatively, it might help you to develop your research if you think of it in terms of a court case in which you have to develop an argument (e.g., the impact of organizational culture on discrimination), defend it to an audience that is ultimately judging you (i.e., using appropriate methods and evidence to make your case), and anticipate and answer potential criticisms of your cases (e.g., by outlining the strengths and limitations of your research). Nonetheless, however you approach a literature review it is important to be clear about the goal that the process is directed towards achieving. A competent review of the literature is at least in part a means of affirming your credibility as someone who is knowledgeable in your chosen area. This is not simply a matter of reproducing the theories and opinions of other scholars, but also being able to interpret what they have written, possibly by using their ideas to support a particular viewpoint or argument. The purpose of exploring the existing literature should be to identify the following issues:

1. What is already known about this area?
2. What concepts and theories are relevant to this area?
3. What research methods and research strategies have been employed in studying this area?
4. Are there any significant controversies?
5. Are there any inconsistencies in findings relating to this area?
6. Are there any unanswered research questions in this area?

This last issue points to the possibility that you will be able to revise and refine your research questions in the process of reviewing the literature. The gap that we referred to above can involve developing new theories and concepts, applying research methods and strategies to the problem that have as yet not been used or have been under-utilized, helping to resolve controversies or inconsistencies, and/or answering unanswered questions.

Getting the most from your reading

Since a great deal of time during the early stages of your research project will be taken up with reading the existing literature in order to write your review, it is important to make sure that the process of reading is also preparing you for this. Getting the most from your reading involves developing your skills in being able to read actively and critically. When you are reading the existing literature try to do the following:

- Take good notes. It is important to carry a notebook with you at all times to jot down any ideas that occur to you during the reading process. For example, you may read an article that references some of the key works in the field, you may find some key theories or concepts you want to explore further, and you will likely have insights and ideas that you want to remember. Bear in mind that you will want to return to much of the literature that you examine in the discussion of your findings and conclusion.
- Keep detailed references of the full publication information of anything that you read. This is important information that will be required for your bibliography (see Tips and skills '*Using bibliographic software*').
- Develop critical reading skills. In other words, don't just take what you read at face value, ask questions. For example, has the author clearly followed a particular research strategy? If not, why not and how might it affect the research findings? Is the argument and associated references convincing? If not, what is wrong or missing? It is worth developing these skills and recording relevant critical points in the course of taking notes. Developing a critical approach is not necessarily one of simply criticizing the work of others. It entails moving beyond mere description and asking questions about the significance of the work. It entails attending to such issues as: How does the item relate to others you have read? Are there any apparent strengths

and deficiencies—perhaps in terms of methodology or in terms of the credibility of the conclusions drawn? What theoretical ideas have influenced the item?

- Use your review of the literature as a means of showing why your research questions are important. For example, if one of your arguments in arriving at your research questions is that, although a lot of research has been done on X (a general topic or area, such as the psychological contract, female entrepreneurship, or employee absenteeism), little or no research has been done on $X1$ (an aspect of X), the literature review is the point where you can justify this assertion. Alternatively, it might be that there are two competing positions with regard to $X1$ and you are going to investigate which one provides a better understanding. In the literature review, you should outline the nature of the differences between the competing positions. The literature review, then, allows you to locate your own research within a tradition of research in an area. Indeed, reading the literature is itself often an important source of research questions.

- Do not try to get everything you read into a literature review. Trying to force everything you have read into your review (because of all the hard work involved in uncovering and reading the material) is not going to help you. As a rule of thumb only reference those arguments that help you build your case. A literature review needs to be understood as a review of relevant literature to the research case you are developing, rather than a general review of everything in a particular area of study. Generally speaking you will be examined not on how much you know in terms of volume of references but rather how well you have understood the literature in order to develop a specific argument.

- You should continue your search for and reading of relevant literature more or less throughout your research. This means that, if you have written a literature review before beginning your data collection, you will need to regard it as provisional. Indeed, you may want to make quite substantial revisions of your review towards the end of writing up your work.

 - Further useful thoughts about how to develop the literature can be found in Web Thinking deeper 2.1

In Chapter 3 we will be reviewing some of the debates concerning the nature of business and management research. As you will see, there is considerable difference between those who argue for a positivist approach and the need for a systematic and scientific approach to research (Donaldson, 1985), and those who argue for a postpositivist approach and the need to question 'social reality and knowledge production [. . . by] emphasizing the constructed nature of social reality, the constitutive role of language, and the value of research as critique' (Prasad, 2005). These differences in research strategy influence all aspects of the research process, including the literature review. Thus, in the next two sections we will highlight the differences by contrasting a systematic with a narrative approach.

Systematic review

Tranfield et al. (2003) use the phrase 'systematic review' to describe the method that they recommend for improving the quality of literature review in management research, which they argue tends to 'lack thoroughness' and reflects the bias of the researcher. The systematic review process is an approach developed in the medical sciences over the last 20 years to try to improve the evidence base of health care delivery, particularly in UK and Canadian (see, for example, Chaudhry et al, 2006; Roine et al. , 2001) contexts. Drawing on this model, Tranfield et al. contrast systematic review with what they describe as 'traditional narrative reviews' (the subject of the following section). They describe systematic review as 'a replicable, scientific and transparent process, in other words a detailed technology, that aims to minimize bias through exhaustive literature searches of published and unpublished studies and by providing an audit trail of the reviewer's decisions, procedures and conclusions' (2003, p. 209). An example of systematic review can be found in Research in focus 2.2 on our website. However, they acknowledge that unlike medical science, management research is a relatively young field that stems from the social, rather than the biological, sciences and is characterized by low consensus concerning key research questions. Also, medical science is often concerned with research questions to do with whether or not particular interventions (such as a medicine or a therapy) are effective. Such issues are well suited to systematic review, but are not often encountered in business and management research. So how can a review process developed in a discipline that is largely based on a quantitative research strategy inform development of a more systematic literature review process in management research?

Tranfield et al. (2003) suggest that certain key characteristics of the systematic review method can be transferred to the management field. The key stages of this process are:

- *Planning the review*. This involves setting up a review panel of experts in the subject area who will meet at regular intervals, first to define and clarify the boundaries of the review and, later, to monitor its progress. The result of their deliberations is then captured through a formal document called a review protocol, which provides a plan for the review and includes criteria for identification of relevant studies and for the inclusion and exclusion of studies in the review. Any modifications made to these criteria as the review progresses must be fully justified.
- *Conducting a review*. This involves carrying out 'a comprehensive, unbiased search' (Tranfield et al., 2003, p. 215) based on keywords and search terms generated as a result of the review panel meetings. The search strategy must be described in terms that allow it to be replicated and searches should be carried out in unpublished (e.g., conference proceedings) as well as published sources. Based on the strict application of the inclusion criteria formulated at the planning stage, the information search will lead to the production of a list of all the articles and books on which the review will be based. Once the items to be included in the review have been identified, the analysis begins. The aim of this is to achieve a cumulative understanding of what is known about the subject through applying techniques of research synthesis, which may include **meta-analysis** (see Key concept 2.1 and Research in focus 2.3 on our website) or **meta-ethnography**, which is one approach to the systematic review of qualitative studies (see Key concept 2.2).
- *Reporting and dissemination*. This involves reporting in a way that provides a descriptive map of the re-

search on the subject, including who the contributors are, where they are based, and when the main temporal periods of research activity on the subject occurred. A further criterion for reporting is accessibility and readability. The review process should make it easier for the practitioner to understand the research, so that it is more likely that it will be translated into practice.

Tranfield et al. (2003) suggest that the systematic review process provides a more reliable foundation on which to design research, because it is based on a more comprehensive understanding of what we know about a subject. Research that involves systematic literature review is argued to be more strongly evidence-based because it is concerned with seeking to understand the effects of a particular variable or intervention that have been found in previous studies. This is particularly useful in subjecting certain widely held assumptions about a subject to empirical scrutiny. For example, it is widely assumed that workplace stress produces ill health effects in employees. Systematic review provides a way for the researcher who is interested in this subject to find out whether or not previous studies have found this to be the case. This can be helpful in encouraging researchers to think critically about their subject. Proponents of systematic review also commend the approach for its transparency; in other words, the grounds on which studies were selected and how they were analyzed are clearly articulated and are potentially replicable.

However, one of the limitations of systematic

> **Key concept 2.1**
> **Meta-analysis:**
>
> involves summarizing the results of a large number of quantitative studies and conducting various analytical tests to show whether or not a particular variable has an effect.

> **Key concept 2.2:**
> **Meta-ethnography**
>
> is a method that is used to achieve interpretive synthesis of qualitative research and other secondary sources, thus providing a counterpart to meta-analysis in quantitative research (Noblit & Hare, 1988). For an example of meta-ethnography in use see Research in focus 2.3 on our website.

2.1   Research in Focus

A meta-analysis on predictors of workplace aggression

A meta-analysis conducted by Herschcovis et al. (2007) set out to develop predictors of workplace aggression. Their approach was a meta-analysis of 57 empirical studies, designed to determine individual and organizational predictors of aggression, potential differences between supervisor and co-worker targeted aggression at the individual level, and the relative contributions of individual and situational factors in explanations of interpersonal and organizational aggression. The results of the meta-analysis indicated that both individual and situational factors predict aggression and 'that the pattern of predictors' (p. 228) of workplace aggression is target specific.

The authors began by identifying those studies (published and unpublished) that focused on 'enacted workplace aggression' (pp. 228–38). In the first stage they searched various databases, including PsycINFO, Sociological Abstracts, ERIC, and ABI-INFORM. They used the following keywords: aggress*, counterproductive work behavio*, deviance, antisocial behavio*, assault, bully*, incivility, mistreatment, mobbing, retaliat*, tyranny, and violen* [NOTE: the use of the asterisk was designed to generate words with different letters and spellings that might otherwise have been missed such as behaviour and behavior; violent and violence].

The research team then manually searched the bibliographies of recently published studies on workplace aggression, spoke to researchers in the field, and searched the proceedings of appropriate scholarly conferences for further published but also unpublished work.

The various searches yielded 191 articles that examined some form of workplace aggression. This was further reduced to 57 studies consisting of 59 samples, through a detailed search for only those that (a) measured enacted as opposed to experienced aggression and which (b) included some measure of association.

This stage of identifying the relevant studies in the field constituted an attempt to integrate the existing literature on workplace aggression. In the process two initial problems were identified: the first was definition, and the research team addressed the issue by developing a definition of workplace aggression that focused on 'target specificity' (p. 228) by which they refer to aggression aimed at the organization or specific individuals at work; the second, was focus, with studies placing different emphasis on individual and situational variables. In this latter case the research team set out to weigh the relative contributions of each and their possible interrelationship. The two issues were addressed through analysis of the various studies using three interrelated questions:

1. 'What are the individual and situational correlates of interpersonal and organizational aggression?'
2. 'Within interpersonal aggression, are there differential predictors of supervisor- and coworker-targeted aggression?'
3. 'What are the relative contributions of individual and situational predictors in explaining interpersonal and organizational aggression?'
4. The findings of this meta-analysis indicated that 'trait anger and interpersonal conflict [are] the strongest predictors of individual aggression', that interpersonal conflict, situational constraints, and job dissatisfaction are the strongest predictors of organizational aggression, that 'interpersonal conflict was a stronger predictor of interpersonal aggression than of organizational aggression', and that 'situational constraints were stronger predictors of organizational aggression than of interpersonal aggression' (p. 232).

The results also showed that the strongest predictors of aggression targeted at supervisors were 'poor leadership and interpersonal injustice' and that 'sex and trait anger predicted both interpersonal [and] and organizational aggression' (p. 232).

The researchers concluded that their meta-study 'lends support to the importance of an integrationist approach' to the study of workplace aggression (p. 234) and that it 'provides evidence for the need to clearly separate the targets of workplace aggression and to examine both individual and situational predictors of workplace aggression' (p. 235).

review stems from situations where research questions are not capable of being defined in terms of the effect of a particular variable, or when the subject boundaries are more fluid and open or subject to change. Since business is an applied field of study that borrows theory from a range of social science and other disciplines, this is more common than it might first seem. Another criticism of the approach is that it can lead to a bureaucratization of the process of reviewing the literature because it is more concerned with the technical aspects of how it is done than with the analytical interpretations generated by it. A third potential limitation of the approach relates to its application to qualitative research studies and in particular the methodological judgements that inform decisions about quality that determine the inclusion or exclusion of an article from a literature review. These stem from differences between qualitative and quantitative research in relation to the criteria used to assess their methodological quality (see Chapters 5 and 6). The systematic approach assumes that an objective judgement about the quality of an article can be made. It is interesting to note that this is something that many management researchers have spent a great deal of time and energy debating in relation to the practice of management, and they are by no means in agreement about it. Moreover, some researchers would say that they measure the quality of published research in terms of what they find interesting. This may or may not include empirical study, but such a view is not compatible with the systematic approach, which requires articles to be evaluated in terms of methodological criteria. In addition, researchers in the medical sciences have found the process of identifying relevant qualitative studies is quite time consuming and cannot be done on the basis of the abstract or summary in the way that quantitative research studies can (Jones, 2004). Finally, whether or not the systematic review approach makes sense to you depends somewhat on your epistemological position (see Chapter 3). As Noblit and Hare (1988, p. 15) state: 'Positivists have had more interest in knowledge synthesis than postpositivists. For them, knowledge accumulates. The problem has been how best to accomplish that accumulation.' For these reasons, researchers who adopt a postpositivist approach to understanding the social sciences and use qualitative methods

may find the systematic review approach more problematic. Similar concerns have been expressed by educational researchers about the suitability of systematic review in an area of study that is quite different from the medical field where it was developed (see Web Thinking deeper 2.7).

RESEARCH NOTE: You should note that the summary of our understanding of systematic review is an example of critical reading.

Narrative review

Rather than reviewing the literature to find out what their research project can add to existing knowledge about a subject, postpositivist researchers (see Chapter 3 for an explanation of postpositivism) can have quite different reasons for reviewing the literature on a particular subject. Postpositivists' purpose is to enrich human discourse (Geertz, 1973) by generating *understanding* rather than by accumulating knowledge. The literature review is for them a means of gaining an initial impression of the topic area that they intend to understand through their research. Narrative reviews, therefore, tend to be less focused and more wide-ranging in scope than systematic reviews. They are also less explicit about the criteria for exclusion or inclusion of studies (see Research in focus 2.2).:

If your approach to the relationship between theory and research is **inductive** rather than **deductive** (see Chapter 3), setting out all the main theoretical and conceptual terms that define your area of study prior to data collection is extremely problematic because theory is the outcome of the study, rather than the basis for it. Hence in the process of researching a topic, a researcher may discover issues that they did not previously anticipate as likely to be important to their area of study. As a result, they become aware of the limitations of the topic area that they originally intended to inform, and this can lead them towards an unanticipated understanding of it (Noblit & Hare, 1988). **Postpositivist** researchers are thus more likely than deductive researchers to change their view of the theory or literature as a result of the analysis of collected data, and so they require greater flexibility to modify the boundaries of their subject of study as they go along. This means that narrative review may be more suitable for **qualitative** researchers whose research strat-

2.2 Research in Focus

A narrative review of narrative research

Rhodes and Brown (2004) conducted a review of the business and management literature on narrative analysis (see Chapter 20 for an explanation of narrative analysis). Their use of narrative review is consistent with the focus of their review, which was on a qualitative research method. They identify five principal research areas that narrative analysis has explored, assessing the theoretical value each has added:

1. *Sensemaking* – focuses on the role of stories as a device through which people make sense of organizational events;
2. *Communication* – explores how narratives are used to create and maintain organizational culture and power structure;
3. *Learning/change* – analyzes how stories help people to learn and subjectively make sense of change;
4. *Politics and power* – considers the role of shared narratives in the control of organizational meaning;
5. *Identity and identification* – focuses on the role of stories in creating and maintaining organizational identity.

While they do not make explicit their criteria for inclusion or exclusion of certain studies, the authors assess the main contributions, implications, and limitations of **narrative analysis**. They also cite a number of their own publications in this subject area. This helps to convince the reader of the credibility of the authors' evaluations of other people's research on the subject from the 1970s to date.

egy is based on an interpretive **epistemology**, and systematic review should not be automatically accepted as a better way of dealing with the literature. However, there have been recent attempts to combine strategic and narrative approaches to meta-analysis (see Research in focus 2.3).

Searching the existing literature and looking for business information

Usually, students will have in mind a few initial references when they begin work on a project. These will probably come from recommended reading in courses. The bibliographies provided at the end of textbook chapters, journal articles, books, and book chapters will usually provide you with a number of further relevant references that can also be followed up. A literature search relies on careful reading of books, journals, and reports in the first instance. After identifying a few keywords that help to define the boundaries of your chosen area of research (see below), electronic databases of published literature can be searched for previously published work in the field.

Electronic databases

Online bibliographical databases accessible on the Internet are an invaluable source of journal references. An increasing number of these will also provide access to the full text of an article in electronic format and are usually referred to as e-journals. Many universities, if not all, have access to these responses in varying degree. Usually a simple check on the university's library website will indicate what resources are available. Let us look at some examples by visiting the libraries of the universities of Calgary (Alberta), Toronto (Ontario), and Saint Mary's (Nova Scotia).

University of Calgary (U of C). To access the library of the U of C click on http://library.ucalgary.ca/. At the top (right-hand side) of the screen you will see a menu. Choose 'Online Resources'. This will take you to a page at: http://library.ucalgary.ca/resources. Go to the bottom of the page to 'Browse Resources by Subject' and from the list click on 'Business'. This will take you to: http://library.ucalgary.ca/rdd/business. Now, from the list click on 'Business—General' and you will be taken to: http://library.ucalgary.ca/rdd?s=3. You have arrived at the on-

2.3 Research in Focus

Combining systematic and narrative reviews in meta-analysis?

In an analysis of the **European Foundation for Quality Management** (EFQM) business excellence model studies Dong-Young, Kumar, and Murphy (2008) set out to assess fit between research topics and methodologies.

EFQM is a not-for-profit organization that has developed a model for implementing high-quality performance strategies. Dong-Young et al. were interested in the extent to which the EFQM model utilized a range of compatible research topics and methodologies. In particular they were interested the processes through which theory was generated by the EFQM.

In approaching analysis of EFQM generated studies the authors undertook an 'integrative literature review methodology' (p. 34), which combined systematic and narrative reviews. The integrative approach was justified in terms of the strengths and limitations of each individual review strategy. Thus, while narrative review facilitates 'in-depth analysis,' it is, according to Dong-Young et al., limited by 'researchers' subjective judgments' (p. 34). Systematic reviews, on the other hand, are useful for re-examining 'prior statistical results of empirical research' but limited by such things as disagreement over 'which study characteristics are important,' 'equally weighted papers,' and analysis of 'all empirical papers without considering their quality' (p. 35). Thus, an integrative method is called for to deal with the fact that there is 'no single method to analyze [published and unpublished] papers' (p. 35). Nonetheless, Dong-Young et al. proceeded to collect data that retained some elements of a systematic review but was largely based on a narrative review approach. In other words, they included a focus on gathering data on a number of statistical analyses and well as qualitative studies but they did so using a narrative review process and analysis. Their findings suggest that the majority of EFQM papers pay too much attention to a single research strategy, that is to say **quantitative** case studies focusing on performance measures. They conclude that this is very limiting in the kind of topic and data that can be generated and is due, in large part, to an over-reliance on one form of methodological approach. Dong-Young et al. argue that a way forward—across research projects—is to encourage plural methodological approaches and the use of combinations of **qualitative** and quantitative methods.

Mazutis and Crossan (2008), like Dong-Young et al. (2008), also argue for an integrated approach to meta-analysis. However, a difference in topic and motivation— an interest in the impact of strategic leadership on innovation, and an extant literature dominated by narrative reviews—led Mazutis and Cannon to begin with a narrative review, which they then subjected to a systematic review. They used this 'meta synthesis' to generate a 'conceptual model and an evidence-based theoretical model of the relationship between strategic leadership and innovation' (p. 108). They conclude that the resultant 'multi-level, mixed effect model answers the call for a multi-level theory of organizational movitation' (p. 108).

line 'Research Databases' for business and will see a large list of resources, including ABI/INFORM and Web of Science (WOS). Below we will deal with which databases to use and how to use them.

University of Toronto (U of T): To access the U of T library click on: http://main.library.utoronto.ca/index.shtml. Now look for the blue menu in the middle of the screen and click on 'Article and Research Databases'. This takes you to: http://main.library.utoronto.ca/eir/resources.cfm?T=I. In the middle of the screen you will find a pop-up window under the heading 'Find the best article and research databases'. Scroll down the window to 'Business and Management' and then click on 'go' at the side of the window. This will take you to: http://main.

library.utoronto.ca/eir/articlesbytopic.cfm?subject=20. You should now see a list of databases including the popular ABI/INFORM.

Saint Mary's University (SMU): The SMU website is found at http://www.smu.ca. Then at the bottom of the screen you click on 'library'. You are now at: http://www.smu.ca/administration/library/index.html. At the top left-hand side of the screen is a section in yellow and the heading 'Finding It'. Click on 'journal articles and databases'. You are now at: http://www.smu.ca/administration/library/journals.html and you will see a large list of databases, including once again ABI/INFORM and Web of Science, but also EBSCO and Wiley Interscience. The databases you use will depend to some extent on your specific research project but we will look at ABI/INFORM, EBSCO, Web of Science, and Wiley Interscience to illustrate the research value of such sites. For this exercise you should log in to your own university library site because you will need a password to access the library's online resources.

1. ABI/INFORM provides business information from a wide range of periodicals and reports, coverage is international, and it is possible to search by keyword or to *browse by topic* to search for relevant articles by subject. Once you have accessed your university library's list of databases, click on ABI/INFORM. You will likely see a window for a 'Basic Search', in the window below type in 'Albert Mills'; the other windows should read as follows:

    'Database: Business — ABI/INFORM Global'

    'Date Range: all dates' 'Limit results to. [Click] 'Full text documents only'

    Now, click 'Search' and you should get at least nine articles by Albert Mills, from at least six different journals. You should be able to download the complete version of any of these articles on to your computer. Now return to the search and, without changing any of the other windows, write in 'Woman at Work', hit 'Search' and you should see close to 1500 articles listed. (Note: if you go back and limit your search to the last 12 months you will get closer to 600 articles.)

2. EBSCO Business Source Premier and EBSCO Business Source Elite are increasingly widely used business periodical databases that now rival ABI/INFORM in scope and coverage. EBSCO's databases are popular in part due to the provision of extremely comprehensive full-text access to certain key business and management journals, including *Harvard Business Review* and *Academy of Management Review*. In addition, these two EBSCO databases provide indexing and abstracts for over 3000 business journals. In addition, they provide access to some company and market reports.

3. Web of Science: This database 'consists of three large multidisciplinary databases', (SMU website) that consist of the Science Citation Index, the Arts and Humanities Citation Index, and Social Sciences Citation Index (SSCI). The latter includes over 1700 major social science journals covering all social science disciplines dating back to 1970.

    The SSCI database is a little less easy to use than the others. However, it does provide references and abstracts, and some libraries add full-text links for articles from some 120 of the most important business and management journals published worldwide. The database also covers related fields such as accountancy and finance, economics, and public administration. It is, therefore, very useful as an initial source in your literature search because, if you search the database effectively, you can be relatively confident that you have covered the majority of recent academic journals that may have published articles on your topic of interest. Here are some introductory guidelines for searching SSCI:

    Click on GO beside Web of Science.

    Choose Social Science Citation Index by unticking the Science and Arts sections.

    Click on GENERAL SEARCH. Note that the default is to search 1970 to date. You can change this by using the pull-down menus.

    You can then search by TOPIC or by AUTHOR.

    A feature of SSCI is its complete coverage of journal contents, so in addition to research and scholarly articles it also contains book reviews and editorial material, which invariably can be identified through keyword searches. You will need to experiment with the use of keywords, because this is usually the way in which databases like these are searched, though author searches are also possible. Finally, a feature that is often useful is the 'Times cited' link. If you find an article that is relevant to your dissertation then you can click to see which other articles have cited it. This does two things: first it allows you to see how an article has been used in more recent research, and in particular whether it has been challenged; second, it also gives an impression of whether the article and the ideas in it have been developed with new data. For example, go to the Web of Science homepage, enter the name 'Bryman A' (and click in 'author'). In the next section enter 'Sociological Review' (and click in 'publication name'). Now move down the screen and under 'current limits' choose from 1999 to 1999. Uncheck the Science and the Arts & Humanities boxes. Now click 'Search'. You will see that Alan's article on the Disneyization of society has been cited by at least 24 people. If you click on 'Times Cited' it provides a full list of the citing journal articles, consisting of papers about related subjects, such as emotional labour and retailing.

You can also use the CITED REF SEARCH to search for articles that cite an article you know about already. This can help you find other related research and also see what other authors thought of your original article. This is particularly useful if your article is a few years old.

4. Wiley InterScience: provides full-text articles from over 300 journals in science, social science, and the humanities. Of interest to Canadian researchers is the fact that Wiley InterScience publishes the *Canadian Journal of Administrative Sciences* (CJAS) in conjunction with the Administrative Sciences Association of Canada (ASAC). In 2009 Wiley InterScience completed a project to develop and make available all issues of CJAS from the first issue in 1983 to current issues in electronic form.

Other academic publishers have also begun to offer their journals for full text through their own websites, Cambridge University Press (Cambridge Journals Online) and SAGE Publications (HighWire Press) are the two most prominent examples. You will need to check with your librarian to find out which of these resources you can use and how to access them. The IngentaConnect website offers full text from various publishers, but you will be able to access full text only to titles to which your library subscribes.

The Proceedings of the Administrative Sciences Association of Canada (ASAC): recently ASAC has made available online most of its annual conference proceedings from 1979 to the present. The collection is not complete and there are some missing articles but the collection currently consists of literally hundreds of conference papers, from over 20 different disciplines and research areas from accounting to business history, and from technology and information management to gender and diversity in organizations. The material is proving a valuable resource for Canadian research and researchers and can be easily accessed for free at the ASAC website: http://www.asac.ca.

Other interesting websites

PsycINFO: This is an abstract database of psychological literature from the 1800s to the present. It contains bibliographic citations, abstracts, cited references, and descriptive information from across a wide variety of scholarly publications in the behavioural and social sciences. It can be accessed at: http://www.apa.org/psycinfo/.

PsycARTICLES: is a database of full-text articles from journals published by the American Psychological Association, the APA Educational Publishing Foundation, the Canadian Psychological Association, and Hogrefe Publishing Group. It can be accessed at: http://www.apa.org/psycarticles/.

Other sources: In addition to scholarly books and journals, newspaper archives can provide a valuable supplementary resource through which to review the emergence of new topics in business and management. Most newspapers require subscription to be able to search their online databases (e.g., *The Globe and Mail*, *National Post*, *Financial Post*). However, most academic libraries will have a subscription to some individual newspapers or to a service

Tips and Skills

Using information on the Web

The Internet provides an enormous and richly varied source of freely available information about business and management that can be quickly and easily accessed without the need for university agreements to gain access to it. However, there is a difficulty in relying on this because the strength of the Internet in providing access to huge amounts of information is also its weakness, in that it can be very difficult to differentiate what is useful and reliable from that which is too simplistic, too commercially oriented, too highly opinionated or just not sufficiently academic. The worst thing that can happen is that you end up quoting from sources from the Web that are quite simply misleading and incorrect. Therefore, it is important to be selective in your use of information on the Internet and to build up a list of favourite websites that you can check regularly for information. Here is a list of some sites you might want to try, compiled with the help of some of our students:

Concepts and definitions

The following sites were recommended for providing clear and easily understood definitions of important business and management concepts, and basic explanations of theories:

http://www.answers.com/
http://en.wikipedia.org/wiki/Main_Page
http://management.about.com/

Scholarly articles and business and management research

Google has a really useful product called 'Google Scholar' which can be accessed from the Google homepage. This product provides a simple way to broadly search for academic literature. Searches are focused on peer-reviewed papers, theses, books, abstracts and articles, from academic publishers, professional societies, pre-print repositories, universities, and other scholarly organizations. Google Scholar also enables you to see how often an item has been cited by other people. This can be very useful in assessing the importance of an idea or a particular scholarly writer:

http://scholar.google.ca/

Also worth exploring, especially for information about current research, are sites that support the development of management research, such as the Advanced Institute of Management, the Academy of Management, the Administrative Sciences Association of Canada, the Atlantic Schools of Business, and the International Federation of Scholarly Associations of Management:

http://www.aimresearch.org
http://www.aomonline.org
http:// http://www.asac.ca/
http://asb.acadiau.ca/
http://www.ifsam.org/

Case studies and current affairs

For case study analyses and keeping up to date on current business issues, the CBC News website is reasonably well balanced and analytical:

http://www.cbc.ca

Also useful for business-related articles, and company and industry profiles are the news magazines *The Economist* and *Canadian Business*. However, full access will require subscription fees:

http://www.economist.com/
http://www.canadianbusiness.com/

Finally, there are a few websites and business magazines that take a look at the top 100 companies in Canada. These provide information of an introductory nature but may be useful as background information and insights into the companies' positions and standing in Canada.

For information on companies that are judged 'Canada's Top 100 Employers':

http://www.canadastop100.com/
http://www.macleans.ca/business/companies/
    article.jsp?content=20081001_99175_99175
http://www.canadianbusiness.com/
    managing/employees/article.jsp?content
    =20060410_76004_76004
http://working.canada.com/top100/fp/story.
    html?id=98305edb-c868-4628-a6d0-5196786e538d

For information on Canada's 'Top 100' fastest growing companies:

> http://list.canadianbusiness.com/rankings/
>   profit100/2008/intro/Default.
>   aspx?sp2=1&d1=d&sc1=9

On the 'Top 1000' companies in Canada across different financial indicators:

> http://business.theglobeandmail.com/top1000/

The main message for Internet searches is the importance of thoroughly looking through each website and ensuring that the information is relevant to your studies. You will note that many websites only provide a small amount of what you are looking for and the rest of the information may be irrelevant. So be cautious about the material you have gathered.

such as ProQuest or LexisNexis, which allow you to search several newspapers at once. You may need a password to access them. Newspapers and periodicals can be a rich source of information about certain topics that make good stories for journalists, such as financial scandals, discrimination, or trade union disputes. The level of analysis can also be high; however, for an academic dissertation they should always be seen as secondary to published literature in books and journals. Also, it takes some time for academic articles to be published, so for recent events, newspapers can be the only source of information.

Another valuable resource to supplement your literature searching is provided by the various non-academic institutions that publish policy-oriented research on issues related to business and management, such as the Canadian Human Rights Commission, the Social Science and Humanities Research Council (SSHRC), the C.D. Howe Institute, the Canadian Centre for Policy Alternatives, the Canadian Race Relations Foundation, Catalyst, and many others (see http://www.irpp.org/links/index.htm for a list of policy generating research organizations). Reports are often published via the Web in Portable Document Format (PDF) and they can usually be downloaded free, thereby providing a faster route to publication than more academic routes. This is particularly useful when researching a currently emerging topic in management and business, or a government-led initiative.

A word of warning about using Google and other search engines for research. Internet search engines are very useful for researching all sorts of things. However, they merely

find sites, they do not evaluate them, so be prepared to look critically at what you've found. Remember that anyone can put information on the Web, so when looking at websites you need to evaluate whether the information you have found is useful. The following points are worth considering:

- Who is the author of the site and what is their motive for publishing?
- Where is the site located? The URL can help you here. Is it an academic site (.ac in the UK and .edu in the US) or a government site (.gov in the UK and United States, and .gc in Canada), a non-commercial organization (.org) or a commercial one (.com or .co)?
- How recently was the site updated? Many sites will give you a last updated date, but you can get clues as to whether a page is being well maintained by whether or not the links are up to date and by its general appearance.

Try to confine your literature search to reliable websites, such as those mentioned in this chapter.

The library catalogue of your own university is an obvious route to finding books, but so too are the catalogues of other universities, and many universities have reciprocal agreements with other universities that allows searches across university libraries. Saint Mary's University, for example, is part of a system called Novanet that allows readers to search the library holdings of a number of universities and colleges throughout the province, including the Nova Scotia Community College libraries and university libraries from the University of Cape Breton

2.1 # Student Experience

Learning from other students

One of the biggest things that Amanda found useful in her research endeavours was the support of other students. When she was completing her Anthropology degree at Dalhousie University, Amanda felt that she was making a whole number of errors: 'I remember telling the prof that I could have written an entire book on what I did wrong. Because it's really not until you start doing it, that's when you get the grasp of what you should be doing'. The problems could have derailed Amanda's efforts but the advice and support of her course professor and her fellow students stopped her from 'freaking out'. Others told her that 'it happens to everyone' . . . and 'don't worry, you can do [it]' and 'you won't fail based on this'. This helped her to gain some perspective on the problems she was encountering: 'Well just recounting several stories of the same thing happening to other people basically is what really made me feel ok I'm not the only one, it happens. Yeah, and because our class was so small, it was just me and four other girls in the Honour's program, and we all became quite close so I had that support structure as well. We all knew quite intimately what was going on each other's research and our experiences, so that was a big help as well having not only your supervisor, but your peers as well going through the same thing.' Amanda used this to her advantage when she enrolled in Mount Saint Vincent University's Public Relations (PR) undergraduate degree,

which she found to be 'highly competitive' in comparison to her Anthropology studies at Dalhousie University. In contrast to her previous studies, 'where you kind of do your own thing' the PR degree involved a lot of group work, which was 'totally foreign to her.' When it came to forming groups for a research methods project she was relieved that students could pick their own group members, and thus, drawing on her experience of supportiveness from her previous degree program, Amanda sought out friends to join with: 'Two of my good friends . . . were in that class so we were together and then another girl she asked if she could work with us and we formed our group.'

Similarly, Lisa found other students in her degree course provided a valuable source of support in addition to the feedback she gained from her supervisor. Her advice to others was to communicate 'with other people on your degree that are doing dissertations, [find] out how they're doing it, what their stance is . . . perhaps people that are doing similar subjects to you.' Lisa discussed her ideas with another student who was also doing a research project in the field of human resource management that related to the same subject as her project looking at performance management. By talking about what literature they had read they were able to point each other towards articles and books they had each found interesting or useful, and in this way to make the process of reviewing the literature easier.

to Dalhousie University. Some bibliographic software will also allow you to search for different books from libraries across the globe. You won't be able to access those books unless you have specific borrowing rights but you could access them through interlibrary loan. On its own, however, the search can be used as a research tool to find out the extent to which a subject has been researched (see Tips and skills '*Using bibliographic software*').

You may also need to find out background information about the markets or companies in which you are interested. There are numerous database sources that can provide you with this kind of company and market research data, including the General Market Information Database (GMID), which contains marketing profiles, consumer market sizing for 52 countries, consumer lifestyle reports, data for over 200 countries, market forecasts to 2012, and information about 100,000 brands and 12,000 companies. Industry Canada provides access to databases of a range of Canadian companies, and Reuters Business Insights provides access to hundreds of market research reports focused on energy, consumer goods, finance, health care, and technology. Depending on the library you belong to, you might also be able to access Infor Datastream, Amadeus, or INVESTEXT, all of which contain company-specific information. Others such as Creative Club are more subject specific; it provides an archive of advertisements in all media from 1997 on. Also an increasing number of companies are putting their annual reports online and can often be accessed quite easily, but there may be a change in some cases.

Again, you will need to check with your library to find out which of these is available to you.

Finally, the Statistics Canada website offers a wide range of statistics about Canada, including such things as business performance and ownership; business, consumer, and property services; economic accounts; ethnic diversity and immigration; education, training, and learning, and many other categories:

http://w ww.statcan.gc.ca/

European statistics relating to specific countries, industries, and sectors can be found on Europa, the portal to the European Union website:

http://europa.eu/index_en.htm

Statistics on UK society and business can be found at:

http://www.statistics.gov.uk

All three sites are freely available.

Keywords and defining search parameters

For all of these online databases, you will need to work out some suitable keywords that can be entered into the search engines and that will allow you to identify suitable references. There are a number of business dictionaries that can help you to define your area of research and to identify changes in the language used to describe the subject. For example, the term 'personnel management' has now been largely superseded by 'HRM', and 'payment systems' are now more widely referred to under the umbrella of 'reward management'. You will also need to think of synonyms and try to match your language to that of the source you are searching. For example, performance management may be more usually referred to in practitioner publications as 'employee evaluation' or 'appraisal'. Sometimes opposites are useful, e.g., employment/unemployment. You also need to think about alternative spellings, e.g., organization/organisation, labor/labour. Be prepared to experiment and to amend your keywords as your research progresses. You may find that as you search the literature there are other ways of describing your subject.

Tips and Skills

Using industrial classification codes to search an electronic database

When searching for literature related to a particular service or industry it can be useful to refine your search strategy by using the appropriate code for the sector from an industrial classification system such as SIC or NAICS (see Tips and skills '*A guide to industry classification systems*' in Chapter 9). For example, if you are interested in researching the shoe industry it may not be enough to simple use the search word 'shoe'. The

North American industry classification uses the term 'footwear', with 31,620 as the industry code. The latter is particularly useful when using search engines such as Business Source Premier run by the EBSCO host, which indexes journal content using the NAICS and SIC systems. By typing the relevant code into your search string you can obtain articles that relate to the particular service or sector that you are interested in.

Figure 2.1

One way of searching the literature

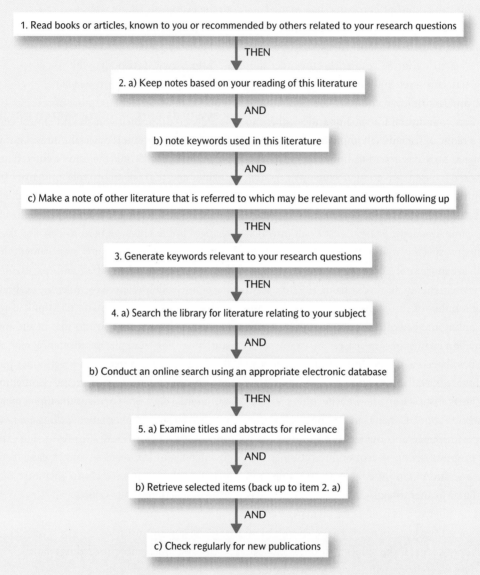

Note: At each stage, keep a record of what you have done and your reasons for certain decisions. This will be useful to you for remembering how you proceeded and for writing up a description and justification of your literature search strategy, which can form part of your methods section. When making notes on literature that you read, make notes on content and method, as well as relevance and keep thinking about how each item will contribute to your critical review of the literature.

In most databases, typing in the title of your project, or a sentence or long phrase as your search term is not advisable as unless someone has written something with the same title you are unlikely to find very much. You need to think in terms of keywords. For example, if you are interested in 'the role of women in the management of banks' your keywords would be WOMEN and MANAGE-MENT and BANKS.

Use the HELP provided in the databases themselves, to find out how to use your keywords to best effect.

In some areas of research, there are very many references. Try to identify the major ones and work outwards from there. Move on to the next stage of your research at the point that you identified in your timetable (see Chapter 1) so that you can dig yourself out of the library. This is not to say that your search for the literature will cease, but that you need to force yourself to move on.

Seek out your supervisor's advice on whether or not you need to search the literature much more. Figure 2.1 outlines one way of searching the literature. The most important thing to remember is to keep a record of the process so that you can keep track of what you have done.

 ## Referencing your work

Referencing the work of others is an important academic convention for two main reasons: (1) it is important to acknowledge the work of others as the source of your information and associated ideas. To use and reproduce the works of others without referencing, especially where you represent the work or associated ideas as your own, is viewed as plagiarism (see the section on Avoiding plagiarism); (2) through acknowledgement of your various sources you are demonstrating an awareness of the theoretical and/or empirical work that has contributed to your subject area, and a recognition that your own research builds on the work of others. Referencing in your literature review is thus a way of emphasizing your understanding and knowledge of the subject. In other parts of your dissertation referencing will serve somewhat different purposes. For example, it will show your understanding of methodological considerations or help to reinforce your argument. A reference is also sometimes described as a citation and the act of referencing as citing.

A key skill in writing your literature review is to keep a record of what you have read, including all the bibliographic details about the articles or books that will go into your bibliography or references. If you are writing an (undergraduate) Honour's thesis or other kind of under-graduate student project it may be sufficient to keep an electronic record of all the items that you have read in a Word document, although you should bear in mind that you may not include all of these in your final bibliography. The main thing to make sure of is that you keep your bibliographic records up to date and don't leave this until the very end of the writing-up process. If, however, you are intending to go onto graduate study, where you will be required to undertake a number of research papers as well as a dissertation, then you should almost certainly buy a software package that is especially designed for referencing (see Tips and skills '*Using bibliographic software*').

When you keep records of the things you have read you should make sure that you note down the following details:

1. The full names of each author involved, e.g., Alan Bryman, Emma Bell, Albert J. Mills, Anthony R. Yue.
2. The full names of each editor involved (e.g., Barbara Austin) where you are citing a chapter in an edited book.
3. The full title of the book (e.g., *Business Research Methods*), book chapter (e.g., 'The Administrative Sciences Association of Canada, 1957–1999'), journal article (e.g., 'Making Sense Out of Bad Faith: Sartre, Weick and Existential Sensemaking in Organizational Analysis'), or paper (e.g., 'Typologie de la Filiére de l'environnment au Québec').
4. The name of the publisher (e.g., Oxford University Press).
5. The name of the city where the book was published (e.g., Toronto).
6. The page numbers of the book chapter, journal article, or conference proceedings paper.
7. The year of publication.
8. The volume and issue number of the journal article and conference proceedings where they appear.
9. The edition of the book where it appears. This may be the 'Canadian edition' as in the case of this book or it may be a reference to a second or third edition (e.g., Greenberg et al., 1996, Canadian edition; Griffin et al., 2002, second Canadian edition).
10. The url when you are citing a source from the website (e.g., Statistics Canada, 2003).

If you use a bibliographic software package there are electronic cards into which you enter all this information in separate spaces. The information is findable in the first two or three pages of a book, or usually on the front of a journal article.

Collecting the information is one important part of the process. Formatting the references is the next important step because your university may well have a required referencing style. At the very least they will require you to use a recognized reference style. To give you some idea of the range of referencing styles available the 2008 version of EndNote X2 lists 3657 different styles. The good news is that very few are used in business writing (75 are listed as business referencing styles) and even fewer are popularly used. For example, most of the 75 styles used in business are based on a version of APA (American Psychological Association), Chicago (Manual of Style), and Harvard (Style).

Regardless of the style you use, whenever you paraphrase the argument or ideas of an author or authors in your writing, you add in brackets immediately afterwards the surname of the author(s) and the year of publication. If you are quoting the author(s), you put quotation marks around the quote and after the year of publication you include the page number where the quote is from. For example, you may want to reference Sexty's (2008) recollections of the origins and challenges of the *Canadian Journal of Administrative Sciences* (CJAS). Or you may want to say that 'the early years of the Cold War within the United States is often seen as a watershed in terms of political anxiety, repression, and fear of outsiders' (Spector, 2008). The latter case uses an APA citation but this will vary slightly according to the referencing style used. Thus, in the Harvard style the citation would read (Spector, 2008: 121).

All books, articles, and other sources that you have cited in the text are then listed in a bibliography at the end of the dissertation in alphabetical order by author surname.

Footnoting: The use of footnotes is a common feature of published work but it is not always encouraged by supervisors and certain journals. One view on this is that 'if it is not worth saying in the main body of the text then don't say it at all'. However, there are various reasons for footnoting. As well as being used to refer to sources, footnotes are often used to provide additional detail, including comments from the writer about the source being cited. This is a particular feature of historical writing. One of the advantages of the numeric or footnote method is that it can be less distracting to the reader in terms of the flow of the text, where sometimes particularly long strings of references can make a sentence or a paragraph difficult for the reader to follow. Furthermore, software packages like Microsoft Word make the insertion of footnotes relatively simple and many students find that this is a convenient way of referencing their work. In some referencing styles, such as in history for example, footnotes replace the list of references (or bibliography). However, many referencing styles include footnoting conventions so it is important to ensure that your use of footnoting is consistent with the reference style used. APA and Chicago footnoting follows in-text citations, while Harvard follows the bibliography. In the following example we show how the work of how Robert Sexty's 2008 article is cited at all three levels:

APA

In-text citation = (Sexty, 2008)

Footnote = (Sexty, 2008)

Bibliography = Sexty, R. (2008). CJAS: Recollections of its origins and challenges. *Canadian Journal of Administrative Sciences / Revue Canadienne des Sciences de l'Administration, 25*(4), 269–270.

CHICAGO

In-text citation = (Sexty 2008)

Footnote = (Sexty, 2008)

Bibliography = Sexty, Robert. 2008. CJAS: Recollections of its origins and challenges. *Canadian Journal of Administrative Sciences / Revue Canadienne des Sciences de l'Administration* 25 (4):269–270.

HARVARD

In-text citation = (Sexty, 2008)

Footnote = (Sexty, 2008)

Bibliography = SEXTY, R. (2008) CJAS: Recollections of its origins and challenges. *Canadian Journal of Ad-*

Tips and Skills

Using bibliographic software

ProCite, EndNote, and Reference Manager are three of the leading software tools used for publishing and managing bibliographies. Your university may have a site licence for one of these packages. The packages are used by academic researchers, information specialists, and students to create bibliographic records equivalent to the manual form of index cards. They allow you to compile your own personal reference database. These records can then be automatically formatted to suit different requirements, for example to comply with the referencing requirements of a particular scholarly journal. A further advantage to the software is that it can enable you to export references directly from databases such as the Social Sciences Citation Index (ssci). The software also has search options that help you to locate a particular reference, although the extent of these features varies from one package to another.

We will use EndNote X2 as an example of the potential value of such software programs but would encourage exploration of various products to see what suits you best and what potential problems as well as strengths there may be with each program.

At the time of writing, EndNote X2 is the latest version of the software. Some of its central features include the use of reference cards on which to enter the details of each thing you read. When you open a Word Document an Endnote X2 menu appears at the top. You can then open EndNote X2 and find one of your references (e.g., Sexty, 2008). By clicking on the entry and hitting 'insert' the entry will not only appear in the text as (Sexty, 2008) but also the full reference will appear at the end of your document. In other words, you won't have to spend time at the end of your thesis in constructing a bibliography. EndNote X2 has already done it for you. However, you may need your bibliography to conform to a particular style. Simple. All you have to do it to choose the style you want and hit the 'format bibliography' button and the style will change to the one you have chosen. Other useful feature of EndNote X2 is that you can conduct an online search for book titles and their full bibliographic details and download the results into your EndNote X2 library. This system allows you to search such libraries as the National Library of Canada and the Library of Congress as well as hundreds of university libraries across the English-speaking world.

The following website provide information on EndNote as well as two other popular citation tools:

http://www.endnote.com/
http://www.procite.com/
http://www.refman.com/

However, if you do not have access to one of these packages, similar software is offered free to students and can be downloaded from the Internet. One of these is BiblioExpress, a simplified version of the package Biblioscape. This package offers the main features associated with bibliographic referencing software and provides extensive user support from its website, which includes a free downloadable user manual. BiblioExpress enables you to do most of the main things that would be needed for a student research project and does not require very much computing memory. For more details go to:

http://www.biblioscape.com/biblioexpress.htm

---

ministrative Sciences / Revue Canadienne des Sciences de l'Administration, 25, 269–270.

You will notice that the punctuation of references—such as where to place a comma, whether to capitalize a title in full or just the first word varies considerably from style to style. The year of publication, for example, is in brackets in the APA and Harvard styles but not in the Chicago style. If your university supervisor does not specify a particular style find a consistent style and stick to it. University libraries will usually provide you with an outline of a recognized style, but Procite, EndNote or Reference Manager users can use one of the main business styles on these software programs.

Select a format for punctuating your references, such as the one adopted by a leading journal in your subject area, and then stick to it.

The role of the bibliography

What makes a good bibliography? You might initially think that length is a good measure, since a longer bibliography containing more references might imply that the author has been comprehensive in their search of the existing literature. This is undoubtedly true, but only up to a point, since it is also important for the bibliography to be selectively focused, i.e., not to try to include everything that has ever been written about a subject but instead to reflect the author's informed judgement of the importance and suitability of sources. This incorporates some of the judgements about quality that were discussed earlier in this chapter. One common proxy for quality is the reputation of the journal in which an article is published. However, although this is a useful indicator, we recommend that it is not one you should rely on exclusively, since there might be articles in lesser-status journals, for instance those targeted at practitioners, which have relevance to your subject, but it is important to be aware of these judgements of quality and to seek the advice of your supervisor when making them. Another important feature of a good bibliography relates to secondary referencing. This is when you refer to an article or book that has been cited in another source such as a textbook and you do not, or cannot, access the original article or book from which it was taken. However, relying heavily on secondary references can be problematic because you are dependent upon the interpretation of the original text that is offered by the authors of the secondary text. This may be adequate for some parts of your literature review but there is always the potential for different interpretations of the original text and this increases the further removed you are from the original source. So it is a good idea to be cautious in the use of secondary references and to go back to the original source if you can, particularly if the reference is an important one for your subject. A further feature of a good bibliography stems from the relationship between the list of references at the end and the way they are used in the main body of the text. It should go without saying that it is not very helpful to include references in the bibliography that are not even mentioned in the text. If references are integrated into the text in a way that shows that you have read them in detail and understood the theoretical perspective from which they are written, this is much more impressive than if a reference is inserted into the text in a way that does not closely relate to what is being said in

the text. Finally, Barnett (1994) argues that a good bibliography gives no indication of the quality of a piece of work, pointing out that some of the most influential academic books ever written do not even include one. Indeed, some of the early business textbooks published in the United States did not have bibliographies, nor did some articles in early editions of the Academy of Management Journal, and a relative lack of references characterized some of the earlier work of management guru Peter Drucker.

 # Plagiarism

An issue to bear in mind when writing up your literature review (and other aspects of your research) is the need to avoid plagiarism. But what is it? How can you find out about it? Why is it important to know about it? And, how can it be avoided?

What is plagiarism?

Plagiarism is a form of cheating. According to the definition in *The Canadian Oxford Dictionary*, to plagiarize something is to 'take and use (the thoughts, writings, inventions, etc., of another person) as one's own' (Barber, 2004, p. 1186). Thus, you need to be careful to reference any ideas, thought, and writings that you use to develop your dissertation.

There is also something called self plagiarism where a person attempts to pass off his or her work as new when in fact they have used all or most of the argument elsewhere. Universities usually discourage this to avoid situations where students hand in the same piece of work for different courses, but also to ensure that dissertations involve a serious attempt to contribute something new to knowledge (however small). Journals discourage self plagiarism because they largely seek to publish material that has not been published elsewhere. The same is true of presentations at conferences where the expectation is that you are presenting new material. In the case of conferences and journals it is normally understood that authors will need to cover some ground that has been discussed elsewhere and that is acceptable so long as (a) this is acknowledged by the author(s), and (b) constitutes a minority of the paper and its central ideas.

How can you find out about plagiarism?

University policy on plagiarism is usually available through its library and on its website. Wilfrid Laurier University (WLU), for example, posts its definition of plagiarism on its website: it is 'the unacknowledged presentation, in whole or in part, of the work of others as one's own, whether in written, oral or other form, in an examination, report, assignment, thesis or dissertation . . . ' (http://www.wlu.ca/page.php?grp_id=1865&p=6206). Similarly, Concordia University's website defines plagiarism as 'the presentation of the work of another person as one's own or without proper acknowledgement'. It goes on to give a detailed account of what types of action constitute plagiarism:

> This could be material copied word for word from books, journals, internet sites, professor's course notes, etc. It could be material that is paraphrased but closely resembles the original source. It could be the work of a fellow student, for example, an answer on a quiz, data for a lab report, a paper or assignment completed by another student. It might be a paper purchased through one of the many available sources. Plagiarism does not refer to words alone—it can also refer to copying images, graphs, tables, and ideas. 'Presentation' is not limited to written work. It also includes oral presentations, computer assignments and artistic works. Finally, if you translate the work of another person into French or English and do not cite the source, this is also plagiarism (http://provost.concordia.ca/academicintegrity/plagiarism/).

In addition to universities, journals and scholarly conferences also have policies on plagiarism. The Academy of Management, for example, deals with plagiarism on its website under a section called 'Academy of Management Code of Ethics' (http://www.aomonline.org/aom.asp?ID=268&page_ID=240). Similarly, the Administrative Sciences Association of Canada (ASAC), posts its 'Code of Ethics' on its website, which it notes is 'adapted with permission from the Academy of Management' (http://www.asac.ca/en/governance/code-of-ethics). ASAC's ethics code defines plagiarism as:

The failure to give sufficient attribution to the words, ideas, or data of others that have been incorporated into a work, which an author submits for academic credit or other benefit. Attribution is sufficient if it adequately informs and, therefore, does not materially mislead a reasonable reader as to the source of the words, ideas, or data. Attribution (or the lack thereof) is materially misleading *if it could cause a reasonable reader to be mistaken as to the source of the words, ideas, or data in a way that could benefit the author submitting the work* (emphasis added).

The code then goes on to deal with the submission of papers to ASAC conferences, stating, 'furthermore, submitted papers must not be currently under consideration or have been previously presented or scheduled for presentation, published, accepted for publication and if under review, must not appear in print before ASAC meetings (http://www.asac.ca/en/governance/code-of-ethics).

Most journals make a similar point in their submission guidelines. CJAS, for example, states, 'submission of a manuscript will be held to imply that it contains original unpublished work and is not being submitted for publication elsewhere at the same time' (http://www3.interscience.wiley.com/journal/114269012/home/ForAuthors.html).

Why is it important to know about plagiarism?

Plagiarism is about research ethics. Although it is usually discussed in terms of the penalties against it, plagiarism draws attention to the importance of giving full credit to people's ideas, theories, writing, and other academic work. We all know how it feels when people thank us for our ideas and suggestions and we all know how it feels when someone else is thanked for our ideas and suggestions, especially when they allow people to think that it was their idea in the first place. Our feelings are hurt. In academia the outcomes can be more serious. Ideas, models, theories, key concepts, ways of expressing ideas, new methods, inventions, and specific findings can have important implications for a researcher in terms of reputation, career, job tenure, and promotion, and, on rare occasion, fame and fortune.

On the other hand, even if plagiarism does not directly affect those whose ideas have been misappropriated it is a form of cheating to claim the ideas of others as your own. You are basically trying to deceive your examiners into thinking that you have done the important work of developing ideas, concepts, theories, models, or inventions that contribute to knowledge, and should be awarded a degree on the basis of the work.

Thus, on the positive side, we all want to encourage people to give due credit to the ideas of others. On the negative side we want to avoid the penalties that are associated with plagiarism, that range from the loss of grade points through to expulsion where the cases is deemed serious enough. Both WLU and Concordia, for example, point out that plagiarism is considered an academic offense that will incur penalties. Concordia warns that plagiarism is an 'offense under the Code of Conduct (Academic)', and WLU refers to it as 'academic misconduct'. ASAC asks its members to 'notify appropriate division chairs or committees regarding the practices or actions of members they believe may violate ASAC regulations or general standards of ethical conduct' (http://www.asac.ca/en/about-asac/code-of-ethics). For active scholars, journalists, inventors, and others engaged in forms of writing, creative expression, and research, plagiarism can lead to dismissal, disgrace, and a loss of reputation.

An increasing number of universities are now employing plagiarism detection software, such as Turnitin.com, which requires the electronic submission of a student's work that is then compared with a wide variety of Internet sources, including previously submitted student work. Although not nearly as effective it is often possible to detect plagiarism by running a search for a unique string of words on Google.com.

How can plagiarism be avoided?

Although there are some grey areas in what constitutes plagiarism (see grey areas below) it is mostly common sense. It helps if you gain an understanding not so much of the penalties involved but the reason behind the penalties, namely, that the ethical thing to do is to credit others ideas. Put yourself in the mindset of a person who has a breakthrough idea in her or his thesis but cannot now use

that idea because someone has stolen the idea and used it in their own work. It is now seen as their idea, not yours. How would you feel?

Nonetheless, stuff happens. Mistakes can be made and it is the genuine mistakes that you need to avoid (see below). To avoid such mistakes here are a few pointers:

1. Make careful notes of all your sources, and indicate where you have copied the wording. For example, you may be interested in strategic thinking and make extensive notes on Alfred Sloan's (1963) biography on his years with General Motors. Mostly your notes consist of your opinions on what Sloan says and where (page numbers) he said it. But, for various reasons, you may want to copy out one of Sloan's statements, e.g., 'some kind of rational policy was called for . . .' In such a case you should put the statement in quotes and note the page number so that you will not later mistake it for your own thoughts. In fact, this is how Henry Mintzberg uses that actual passage from Sloan:

> Alfred Sloan notes in his memoirs a justification of the consolidated product Line strategy developed at General Motors under his leadership: 'some kind of rational policy was called for . . . it was necessary to know what one was trying to do', especially with regard to duplication across certain product lines.[4] (Mintzberg, 1987, p. 26)

> [4]A.P. Sloan, *My Years with General Motors* (New York, NY: Doubleday, 1963), p.267

Here you will note not only how Mintzberg cites Sloan but how we cite the larger passage from Mintzberg by indenting the paragraph and ending with the reference to Mintzberg and the page number. You may also note that the footnoting that Mintzberg is using is that of the Chicago Manual of Style.

2. When inserting large sections of text from another source make very clear that the text in question is not your own work but that you are making a point by quoting someone. Relatively small quotes can be signified by the use of quotation marks (e.g., as Mintzberg does with the reference from Sloan). Larger passages

can be indented to indicate that it is a quote (e.g., like the Mintzberg statement that we reproduced above).

It is easy to get this wrong. In June 2006, it was reported that a plagiarism expert at the London School of Economics had been accused of plagiarism in a paper he published on plagiarism! A paragraph was found that copied verbatim a published source by someone else and that had not been acknowledged properly as from another source. The accused person defended himself by saying that this was due to a formatting error.

The lack of indentation meant that the paragraph in question looked like it was his own work. While it may be that this is a case of 'unintentional plagiarism' (Park, 2003), distinguishing the intentional from the unintentional is by no means easy. Either way the credibility and possibly integrity of the author may be undermined.

3. It is also important to realize that for many if not most institutions, simply copying large portions of text and changing a few words will also be regarded as plagiarism. The message here is that language is rich and varied so use it rather than simply recycling the phrases, sentences, and even paragraphs of others.

4. One of the main ideas of a literature search is to find out if your ideas have already been explored. If they have, you can either build *on* them or develop a different idea. Sadly, some of our best ideas turn out to have been thought of (and published) by someone else. In a strange way you can console yourself with the thought that at least you did have a good idea, but it is not an excuse to act as if it is still your idea and you can ignore the fact that someone else beat you to the punch.

5. Get as much information on avoiding plagiarism as you can. Many university libraries, including WLU and Concordia, not only define plagiarism but provide useful information on how to avoid it. Libraries often also have written versions on this information. The Vaughan Memorial Library of Acadia University (Nova Scotia) goes so far as to provide a useful slide show on the issue, titled: 'You Quote It, You Note It' (see http://library.acadiau.ca/tutorials/plagiarism/).

For an example, of plagiarism in publishing see Web Thinking deeper 2.8.

Student rights, human rights, and plagiarism: The grey areas

One final point to note is that plagiarism is like a moving target. What it is, how it should be defined, how it can be detected, how it should be penalized: all of these issues and others are in a state of flux as we write this chapter (Gulli et al., 2007). In the process of dealing with plagiarism universities, scholarly journals, and academic associations have struggled with the issue because there are potential grey areas (much like the problem of the London student discussed above). One area that has caused concern is the use of plagiarism detection software. In some universities students have successfully challenged the use of such technology. At Mount Saint Vincent University, for example, the use of Turnitin.com was banned in 2006 after students complained over the issue of intellectual property and its use. In the words of the student union president, Chantal Brushett: 'Students should not have to wonder if their paper is going to become part of the profit company of Turnitin.com' (http://www.gazette.uwo.ca/article.cfm?section=news&articleID=632, accessed March 13, 2009). Similar concerns were raised by McGill students two years earlier in 2004 (http://media.www.mcgilltribune.com/media/storage/paper234/news/2004/03/23/News/Senate.Hears.Silent.Protest.Sends.Turnitin.Policy-638555.shtml, accessed March 13, 2009).

Finally in recent years we have seen the potential for the political use of plagiarism in a high profile case at the University of Colorado at Boulder (see Web Thinking deeper 2.9, '*The case of Ward Churchill*').

In summary, we need to uphold the ethics of research and the dissemination of ideas by need properly citing the ideas of others. However, while we need to find ways to reduce the incidence of plagiarism—most of which is obvious and easily detectable—we need to also always keep to the fore broader issues of human rights to ensure that prevention and/or detection methods do not outweigh those rights.

Checklist

Questions to ask yourself when reviewing the literature:

- ☐ Is your list of references up to date in your current areas of interest? Are there new areas of interest that you need to search for?
- ☐ What literature searching have you done recently?
- ☐ What have you read recently? Have you found time to read?
- ☐ What have you learned from the literature? Has this changed in any way your understanding of the subject in which you are working?
- ☐ Is what you have read going to influence your research design in any way? Has it given you ideas about what you need to consider and incorporate?
- ☐ Have you been writing notes on what you have read? Do you need to reconsider how what you have read fits into your research?

Adapted from Bruce (1994).

Key points

- Writing a literature review is a means of reviewing the main ideas and research relating to your chosen area of interest.
- A competent literature review confirms you as someone who is competent in the subject area.
- A great deal of the work of writing a literature review is based upon reading the work of other researchers in your subject area; key skills can be acquired to help you get the most from your reading.
- Systematic review is a method that is gaining in popularity in business research as a way of enhancing the reliability of literature searching and review.
- Narrative review is a more traditional approach, which has the advantage of flexibility that can make it more appropriate for inductive research and qualitative research designs.

Questions for review

Reviewing the existing literature and engaging with what others have written:
- What are the main reasons for writing a literature review?
- How can you ensure that you get the most from your reading?
- What are the main advantages and disadvantages associated with systematic review?
- What type of research questions is systematic review most suited to addressing?
- What are the main reasons for conducting a narrative literature review?
- In what type of research is narrative review most appropriate?

Searching the existing literature and looking for business information:
- What are the main ways of finding existing literature on your subject?
- What is a keyword and how is it useful in searching the literature?

Referencing your work:
- Why is it important to reference your work?
- What are the three main referencing styles used in academic work and which of these is preferred by your institution?
- What is the role of the bibliography and what makes a good one?

Plagiarism:
- What is plagiarism?
- Why is it taken so seriously by researchers?

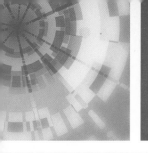

Part Two

Research Strategies

Part Two of this book is concerned with two ideas that will recur again and again during the course of this book: research strategy and research design. Chapter 3 outlines a variety of considerations that impinge on the practice of business and management research and relates these to the issue of research strategy. Six research strategies are identified based on the use of quantitative, qualitative, and mixed methods in either positivist or postpositivist approaches. Chapter 4 identifies the different kinds of research design that are employed in business research. In Chapters 5, 6, and 7, respectively, we take a closer look at the nature of quantitative, qualitative, and mixed methods. Finally, in Chapter 8 we examine the issue of ethics in research and the need to ensure not only that you meet the criteria but also the spirit of the ethical standards in research.

These chapters move you from the formulation of a research project to consideration of the types of research strategies, associated methods, and ethical considerations needed to develop a thesis. You will come to see that research strategies and their associated methods are not simply technical means to achieve a certain end (i.e., the empirical demonstration of a particular set of ideas or theory) but are an essential part of that end; like tinted glasses that influence not only 'what' but 'how' you see things.

3

Business Research Strategies

Chapter guide

The chief aim of this chapter is to show that a variety of considerations enter into the process of doing business research and how they shape research strategies. In the process we will look at two main distinctions that occur in business research. One is the more common discussion of the relative merits of **quantitative** and **qualitative** methods. The other is the less discussed but nonetheless fundamental distinction between **positivist** and **postpositivist** research strategies. We shall use the term research strategies to refer to a framework of methods, research design, and the theory that informs a particular approach to a selected area of study. This chapter explores:

* The nature of the relationship between theory and research, in particular whether theory guides research (known as a **deductive** approach) or whether theory is an outcome of research (known as an **inductive** approach).
* *Epistemological* issues. That is, questions about what is appropriate knowledge about the social world; focusing on the difference between a natural science (positivist) approach and a socially **constructivist** (postpositivist) approach to the study of the social world.
* *Ontological issues*. That is, questions about whether the social world is viewed as something external to social actors (as in a positivist approach) or as something that people socially construct and interpret (as in a postpostivist approach).
* The ways in which these issues relate to the widely used distinction in the social sciences between two types of **research strategy**—positivism and postpositivism—and their relationship to quantitative, qualitative, and **mixed methods**.
* The ways in which *values* and *practical issues* also impinge on the business research process.

Introduction

In the previous two chapters we took you through the process of thinking about your research question and how to conduct a review of the literature. Although it is not as simple as it seems, let us assume that you have a research question that you want to study. In a nutshell, you know *what* you want to study and hopefully *why* you want to study it. Now you need to know *how* to study it. Later you will need to know how to *analyze* (see Chapters 23 and 24) and *write up* (see Chapter 25) the collected data but for now this chapter deals with the question of methods, methodologies, and research strategies that constitute the 'how' of the research process.

To be clear, the term *methods* is often used to mean techniques for data collection (e.g., interviews, observation, surveys, etc.). It is the thing you use to gather information on your area of research. While not all researchers use the term methods in this way, for the sake of clarity, it

is the definition we shall use throughout the book to refer to *techniques* of data collection. However, some researchers prefer to use the term *methodology* to capture the relationship between the method of study (e.g., observation) and the theory that informs the method (e.g., **objectivism**; **interpretivism**). For example, while an objectivist researcher would use observation as a way of seeing data, an interpretivist would see observation as part of a broad process involving the interpretation of the researcher as well as those observed. Thus, again for clarity, we shall use the term methodology to refer to a relationship of theory to methods. In addition to making decisions about theory and method, researchers need to make a number of research design decisions about the level and type of data to be collected (e.g., **case study** design—see Chapter 4). The combination of theory, method, and research design constitute a research strategy.

By understanding the different elements of a **research strategy** you will gain insights into the thinking behind the choice of different methods—how they are applied; how they are analyzed; and how they relate to different theories and research designs. This will help you with your research project in two important ways: it will give you insights into (1) how, where, and why certain methods are used; and (2) the range of research choices available to you.

Before we examine research strategies in some depth we will look at the socio-economic and intellectual influences on business research.

The nature of business research

Business research does not exist in a vacuum. It is shaped by what is going on in the world of business and management, and by many of the intellectual traditions that shape the social sciences at large. Both influence the research questions that get asked and how those questions are studied.

Historically, business research developed out of managerial concerns with productivity, profitability, stability, and growth (Rose, 1978; Burrell & Morgan, 1979), and these concerns continue to play a major role in business studies today (Khoury et al., 2006, Schweitzer & Duxbury, 2006). Over time, however, business research has also come to include broader social concerns about the impact of business on various aspects of social life, including such things as business ethics (Lightstone & Driscoll, 2008), workplace discrimination (McKay, 2001), organizational disasters (O'Connell & Mills, 2003), and the problems of private enterprise and capitalism (Mills et al., 2005). In short, business research ranges from studies designed to affect improvement within and for companies, through to challenges to the notion of private enterprise and its broader impact on society. The types of questions asked influence and are influenced by the choice of research strategy and the intellectual traditions that inform them.

Business research developed within the social sciences (e.g., sociology, psychology, anthropology, economics) and humanities (e.g., history, literary criticism, philosophy), and was influenced to a greater or lesser degree by the intellectual traditions involved. This chapter explores some of the intellectual traditions that influence business research. By discussing the underlying philosophies (or world views) behind different research strategies we can understand not only how to undertake business research but also the processes involved in developing legitimate and accepted research outcomes. In this way the reader will come to understand how business research methods are closely tied to different visions of organizational reality, and how those different visions influence the choice and use of certain methods to form a research strategy. In the process we will see that methods are not simply neutral tools or techniques but are linked to the ways in which social scientists think about social reality and how it should be examined. Thus, methods are not a bunch of tools waiting to be used by any and all researchers. Most postpositivist researchers, for example, will not use a *survey* as a means of collecting data. Positivist researchers, on the other hand, are unlikely to engage in **ethnomethodology** (i.e., observational studies of people's strategies for making sense of a situation). The underlying philosophies of positivist and postpositivist research draw them to some methods but not others. To draw an analogy, methods are not like vehicles that, regardless of make, colour or speed, take everyone to the same destination. They are more like prescription glasses that vary in strength and tint that influence what the wearer sees through the lenses.

Questions within research paradigms

Within different theoretical approaches to business studies researchers are influenced by a variety of factors that shape the types of questions they ask. Research questions can arise directly out of an organization's needs as, for example, where the senior management of a company become concerned with their corporate culture and seek research advice (Helms Mills, 2003). This type of approach has been called 'clinical research' (Schein, 1992) or 'action research' (Argyris et al., 1985) where the research questions are generated by a client group. As we shall see later (Chapter 6), action research can be a useful way to gain access to a research site.

Research questions also arise out of such things as major events or disasters that capture national or international attention such as the Bhopal gas leak disaster of 1984 (Shrivastava, 1987), the Westray Mine disaster (O'Connell & Mills, 2003), the Walkerton tainted water scandal (McLeod & Helms Mills, 2009), and the Hurricane Katrina disaster (Rostis & Helms Mills, 2009). Such events can also include high-profile cases of corporate failure (Miller, 1990) or success (Mintzberg et al., 1986).

Yet another stimulus for research can arise out of personal experiences. Lofland and Lofland (1995) note that many research publications emerge out of the researcher's personal biography. Alan Bryman, for example, traces his interest in Disney theme parks back to a visit to Disney World in Florida in 1991 (Bryman, 1995, 1999), while his interest in the representation of social science research in the mass media (Fenton, Bryman, & Deacon 1998) can almost certainly be attributed to a difficult experience with the press reported in Haslam and Bryman (1994). Similarly, the experience of having been involved in the implementation of a quality management initiative in an National Health Service (NHS) hospital trust prompted Emma Bell to explore the meaning of badging in an organizational context (Bell et al., 2002).

Finally, research data are also collected in relation to social scientific theory where researchers are encouraged to address issues that are current topics in the field. This can arise out of a perceived gap in a particular field of interest; an interest in replicating a study to see if the findings hold across certain situations; a challenge to received wisdom; or, more often, a desire to build of existing research. Student research projects may take any of these forms but it is far more likely for Ph.D. research to focus on gaps in the literature and for undergraduate work to do small incremental or replication studies.

 ## Evaluating business research

The diverse nature of management and business scholarship has led to considerable disagreement about how its research claims ought to be evaluated. Hence, some writers have suggested that management research can be understood only as an applied field because it is concerned not only with understanding the nature of organizations but also with solving problems that are related to managerial practice. Tranfield and Starkey (1998) argue that much management research has lost touch with the concerns and interests of practitioners and that management and business researchers must relearn how to be responsive to them in order for their research to retain a value and a purpose.

However, other writers would suggest that management and business research is too concerned with lengthy 'fact-finding' exercises and is insufficiently guided by theoretical concerns. They would argue that application is not a primary purpose to which management research should be directed (Burrell, 1997). For these scholars, making research relevant to managerial practice ought not to be the main aim of academic study (Clegg, 2002; Hinings & Greenwood, 2002). They believe that research should not be dictated by non-academic interests, such as professional associations and government agencies, who may seek to influence its focus and guide its development in a way that is 'useful' to current practice but susceptible to the whim of current management fads and fashions. Others suggest that the applied nature of management and business research has influenced the development of the field in a manner that has made it overly pragmatic and susceptible to users' agendas.

A further debate that has influenced our understanding of the role of management and business research stems from the thesis developed by Gibbons et al. (1994) concerning the way that scientific knowledge is produced. Gibbons et al. suggest that the process of knowledge production in contemporary society falls into two contrasting categories or types, which they describe as 'mode 1' and 'mode 2' knowledge production. These are summarized as follows:

- *Mode 1.* Within this traditional, university-based model, knowledge production is driven primarily by an academic agenda. Discoveries tend to build upon existing knowledge in a linear fashion. The model makes a distinction between theoretically pure and applied knowledge, the latter being where theoretical insights are translated into practice. However, only limited emphasis is placed on the practical dissemination of knowledge because the academic community is defined as the most important audience or consumer of 'mode 1' knowledge.

- *Mode 2*. This model draws attention to the role of *trans-disciplinarity* in research, which it assumes is driven by a process that causes the boundaries of single contributing disciplines to be exceeded. Findings are closely related to context and may not easily be replicated, so knowledge production is less of a linear process. Moreover, the production of knowledge is not confined to academic institutions. Instead, it involves academics, policy makers, and practitioners who apply a broad set of skills and experiences in order to tackle a shared problem. This means that knowledge is disseminated more rapidly and findings are more readily exploited in order to achieve practical advantage.

Although 'mode 2' research is intended to exist alongside mode 1, rather than to replace it, some researchers have suggested that management and business research is more suited to a mode 2 model of knowledge production (Tranfield & Starkey, 1998).

These debates frame a series of questions about the nature and purpose of management and business research, which any new researcher in this field must deal with. For example:

What is the aim or function of business research?

Is it conducted primarily in order to find ways of improving organizational performance through increased effectiveness and efficiency?

Or is it mainly about increasing our understanding of how organizations work, and their impact on individuals and on society?

Who are the audiences of business research?

Is business research conducted primarily for managers and, if not, for who else in organizations is it conducted?

Or is it done in order to further the academic development of business and management as a field or even as a discipline?

These questions are the subject of considerable ongoing academic debate about the nature and status of business research. Being aware of them is important in understanding what influences your choice of research topic and how you address it. Another way of understanding this issue is by thinking about the practices of scholars who do business and management research. There are four points that can be made in relation to this:

1. In order to evaluate the quality of management and business research it is necessary to know as much as possible about researchers' own role in this process—including how they collected and analyzed the data and the theoretical perspective that informed their interpretation of it. This understanding relies on examination of methods used by business researchers, which is why, throughout this book, we have used real examples of published research to illustrate how researchers deal with and justify these methodological choices.

2. This leads to a second point in relation to the use of examples. Business research methods tend, on the whole, to be more eclectically used and explained in less detail than in some other social sciences such as sociology. Perhaps this is due to the emergent nature of the field or because it draws from such a diverse range of disciplines, but in practice it means that novice researchers can sometimes find it difficult to identify examples of existing research that can be used to inform their own practice. One of the purposes of our use of examples in this book is, therefore, to draw attention to the range of methodological approaches that business researchers have taken in a way that can be understood by those who are new to this field of study.

3. The third point relates to the kinds of methods used in business research. In some instances, it is hard to identify examples of the use of particular research methods, while in others, such as the case study method, there are numerous studies to choose from. We believe, however, that this can provide an opportunity for new researchers to make use of less popular or less commonly used methods in order to gain insight into a research problem. In other words, we hope that, through reading this book, business students will possibly be encouraged to use research

methods that are less commonly used, as well as those that have a more established reputation.

4. Finally, despite some of the limitations of business research, in terms of the availability of examples that illustrate the use of various research methods, we have tried to confine our choice of examples to the field of business and management. This is partly because by getting to know how other researchers have approached the study of business it is possible to build up an understanding of how the use of research methods in this field might be improved and developed in the future.

Theory and research

Characterizing the nature of the link between theory and research is by no means a straightforward matter. There are several issues at stake here, but two stand out in particular. First, there is the question of what form of theory one is talking about. Secondly, there is the matter of whether data are collected to test or to build theories.

What type of theory?

The term *theory* is used in a variety of ways, but its most common meaning is as an explanation of observed regularities, to explain, for example, why women and ethnic minorities are under-represented in higher-paid managerial positions, or why the degree of alienation caused by the introduction of new technology varies according to the methods of production that are involved. However, such theories do not in themselves constitute a theoretical *perspective*, which is characterized by a higher level of abstraction in relation to research findings. Examples of this kind of theory include *structural-functionalism*, **symbolic interactionism**, *critical theory*, *poststructuralism*, *structuration theory*, and so on. What we see here is a distinction between theories of the former type, which are often called *theories of the middle range* (Merton, 1967), and *grand theories*, which operate at a more abstract and general level.

According to Merton, grand theories offer few indications to researchers as to how they might guide or influence the collection of empirical evidence. So, if someone

wanted to test a theory or to draw an inference from it that could be tested, the level of abstractness is likely to be so great that the researcher would find it difficult to make the necessary links with the real world. For research purposes, then, Merton argued that grand theories are of limited use in connection with social research (see Web Research in focus 3.1 that suggests that an abstract theory like structuration theory can have some payoff in research terms).

Instead, middle-range theories are 'intermediate to general theories of social systems which are too remote from particular classes of social behaviour, organization, and change to account for what is observed and to those detailed orderly descriptions of particulars that are not generalized at all' (Merton, 1967, p. 39).

By and large, then, it is not grand theory that typically guides management and business research. Middle-range theories are much more likely to be the focus of empirical enquiry. In fact, Merton formulated the idea as a means of bridging what he saw as a growing gulf between theory (in the sense of grand theory) and empirical findings. This is not to say that there were no middle-range theories before he wrote, there definitely were, but what Merton did was to seek to clarify what is meant by 'theory' when social scientists write about the relationship between theory and research.

Middle-range theories, unlike grand ones, operate in a limited domain. Whether it is a perspective on strategic choice or labour process theory (see Web Research in focus 3.2), they vary somewhat in the purpose of their application. In other words, they fall somewhere between grand theories and empirical findings. They represent attempts to understand and explain a limited aspect of social life. For example, contingency theory has been used widely in management and business research to explain the interrelationships among subsystems, as well as the relationship between the organization and its environment. The theory relies on a number of assumptions that guide research: first, there is no one best way to organize; second, any particular way of organizing is not equally effective under all conditions; and, third, in order to be most effective, organizational structures should be appropriate to the type of work and the environmental conditions faced by the organization (Schoonhoven, 1981). However, contingency theory has been applied in different ways and for different purposes, by different writers. Some, like Lawrence and Lorsch (1967), have used it descriptively to show that factors within the environment must be taken into account. Others, for example in the field of leadership, have applied the theory in a normative sense, adopting a solution-seeking focus and providing a guide to managerial action based on 'best fit' in a particular situation (e.g., Fiedler, 1967). A normative stance suggests that, although factors within the environment should be taken into account, it is up to managers to make decisions about how they respond to these in order to achieve the impact on organizational performance that they want.

However, even the grand/middle-range distinction does not entirely clarify the issues involved in asking the deceptively simple question of 'What is theory?'. This is because the term *theory* is frequently used in a manner that means little more than the background literature in an area of social enquiry. To a certain extent, this point can be taken to apply to contingency theory mentioned above. For example, Schoonhoven (1981) suggests that it is not a theory at all, in the sense of being a well-developed set of interrelated propositions. Willmott (1990) suggests that *contingency theory* is based on empirical evidence without any acknowledgement of the social theories that affect the political realities of organizations, and so it is unable to deal with complex organizational problems.

In many cases, the relevant background literature relating to a topic fuels the focus of an article or book and thereby acts as the equivalent of a theory. In Ghobadian and Gallear's (1997) article on Total Quality Management (TQM) and the competitive position of small- or medium-sized enterprises (SMEs), there are virtually no allusions to theories. Instead, the literature informs the generation of research questions in rela-

tion to what the authors perceive to be a neglected topic, as the majority of TQM literature tends to focus on large companies. The researchers are then able to seek to resolve inconsistencies between different findings in relation to small and large companies in terms of the impact of TQM on competitive position. Other ways in which background literature influences the focus of research include: the researcher may spot a neglected aspect of a topic, certain ideas may not previously have been tested, the researcher may feel that existing approaches being used for research on a topic are deficient, and so on.

Social scientists are sometimes prone to being somewhat dismissive of research that has no obvious connections with theory—in either the grand or middle-range senses of the term. Such research is often dismissed as naive **empiricism** (see Key concept 3.1). It would be harsh, not to say inaccurate, to brand as naive empiricism the numerous studies in which the publications-as-theory strategy is employed, simply because their authors have not been preoccupied with theory. Such research is conditioned by and directed towards research questions that arise out of an interrogation of the literature. The data collection and analysis are subsequently geared to the illumination or resolution of the research issue or problem that has been identified at the outset. The literature acts as a proxy for theory. In many instances, theory is latent or implicit in the literature.

Indeed, research that appears to have the characteristics of the 'fact-finding exercise' should not be prematurely dismissed as naive empiricism either. For example, research in the field of industrial relations that focuses on the detail of current employment practices in a variety of sectors or cultural contexts has sometimes been criticized for its attention to facts, which is suggested to be accompanied by a lack of theoretical development (Marsden, 1982; Godard, 1994). The problem with this, according to Marsden (1982), is that 'empiricists tend to assume that theory will somehow arise from the facts "like steam from a kettle". But facts are never given, they are selected or produced by theory' (Marsden, 1982, p. 234) and consequently industrial relations has not managed to develop sufficient theory to establish its status as a discipline distinct from economics and sociology. To explore the accu-

---

Key concept 3.1: Empiricism

denotes (1) a general approach to the study of reality that suggests that only kn owledge gained through experience and the senses is acceptable; and (2) a belief that the accumulation of 'facts' is a legitimate goal in its own right. It is this second meaning that is sometimes referred to as 'naive empiricism'.

racy of such claims in contemporary context, Frege (2005) looked at patterns of publication within the field of industrial relations in leading American, German, and British journals between 1970 and 1973, and 1994 and 2000. She found that empirical publications were much more common in the United States (72% in the 1970s and 91% in the 1990s) than in Germany (41% over both time periods), with Britain in between (72% over both periods). Similar results were found in recent Canadian studies of the proceedings of the Administrative Sciences Association of Canada for the period 1974–2007 (Serenko et al., 2008; Hartt et al., 2009).

However, looking more closely at the nature of these empirical papers reveals differences in the type of empirical work that was carried out in different countries. Specifically, Frege detects a shift away from empirical-descriptive articles towards empirical-deductive and empirical-inductive papers in the American journals. She concludes 'the notion of what is empirical research shifted over time away from purely descriptive towards more sophisticated analytical work' (Frege, 2005, p. 194). However, while the scale of empirical work also increased in Britain over the time period, although at a slower rate, the empirical articles in these journals were less analytical and the number of descriptive pieces published actually increased rather than decreased.

Raising the question of what is empiricism invites consideration of another question: in so far as any piece of research is linked to theory, what was the role of that theory? Up to this point, we have tended to write as though theory is something that guides and influences the collection and analysis of data. In other words, research is done in order to answer questions posed by theoretical considerations. But an alternative position is to view theory as something that occurs after the collection and analysis of some or all the data associated with a project. We begin to see here the significance of a second factor in considering the relationship between theory and research—whether we are referring to deductive or inductive theory.

Deductive and inductive theory

Deductive theory represents the commonest view of the nature of the relationship between theory and research.

The researcher, on the basis of what is known about a particular domain and of theoretical considerations in relation to that domain, deduces a **hypothesis** (or hypotheses) that must then be subjected to empirical scrutiny.

Embedded within the hypothesis will be concepts that will need to be translated into researchable entities. The social scientist must both skilfully deduce a hypothesis and then translate it into operational terms. This means that the social scientist needs to specify how data can be collected in relation to the concepts that make up the hypothesis.

This view of the role of theory in relation to research is very much the kind of role that Merton had in mind in connection with middle-range theory, which, he argued, 'is principally used in sociology to guide empirical inquiry' (Merton, 1967, p. 39). Theory and the hypothesis deduced from it come first and drive the process of gathering data (see Web Research in focus 3.3 for an example of a deductive approach to the relationship between theory and data). The sequence can be depicted as one in which the steps outlined in Figure 3.1 take place.

The last step involves a movement that is in the opposite direction from deduction—it involves *induction*, as the researcher infers the implications of his or her findings for the theory that prompted the whole exercise. The findings are fed back into the stock of theory and the research findings associated with a certain domain of enquiry. This can be seen in the case of Whittington's (1989) case study research into strategic choice within the domestic appliance and office furniture industries. Whittington's approach is primarily deductive, since it is based on the contention that a critical realist approach to strategic choice enables recognition of the importance of plural and contradictory social structures for human agency and thus avoids determinism. However, as he points out towards the end of his book, 'after the empirical interlude of the last four chapters, it is time now to return to the theoretical fray' (1989, p. 244) to assess how well deterministic and realist approaches to strategic choice account for the behaviour within the eight case study firms. At this stage he claims that, although dominant actors within the firms 'began from their structural positions within the capitalist enterprise, this starting point was neither unambiguous

Figure 3.1

The process of deduction

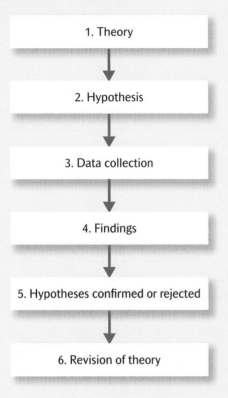

1. Theory

2. Hypothesis

3. Data collection

4. Findings

5. Hypotheses confirmed or rejected

6. Revision of theory

or exhaustive' (1989, p. 282). This finding thus confirms his central proposition that these organizational structures could be converted into 'the effective instruments of private agency'.

A further point to bear in mind is that the deductive process appears very linear—one step follows the other in a clear, logical sequence. However, there are many instances where this is not the case. There are several reasons why a researcher's view of the theory or literature may change as a result of the analysis of the collected data:

- New theoretical ideas or findings may be published by others before the researcher has generated his or her findings.
- The relevance of a set of data for a theory may become apparent only *after* the data have been collected.
- The data may not fit with the original hypotheses.

The Hawthorne studies, undertaken at the Western Electric Company's Hawthorne plant between 1927 and 1932, aptly illustrate how deductive research can sometimes produce unexpected findings. In the early stages of this research, which explored the human effects of work and working conditions (Roethlisberger & Dickson, 1939), the aim was to explore the relationship between conditions of work and the incidence of fatigue and monotony among employees. In order to test this relationship, a series of experiments were undertaken to establish the effects of **variables** such as lighting, temperature, humidity, and hours of sleep that could be isolated and measured separately. These early experiments involved adjusting the level of artificial illumination in departments at stated intervals in order to see if this had any effect on efficiency of production. However, researchers were not able to make sense of the changes in productivity of workers, which increased and remained high despite manipulation of a range of variables such as temperature and lighting. This led researchers to move away from the 'test room method' and to adopt a more qualitative strategy based on interview and observation. By modifying their approach towards this more inductive position, researchers were able to make sense of the data through generation of an alternative hypothesis that focused on the importance of informal social relationships. Eventually, this led to the development of an alternative method for the study of the informal work group. In the Bank Wiring Observation Room investigators spent a total of six months observing informal social relationships within a group of male operators. The Hawthorne research thus made an important methodological contribution to the study of work organizations by allowing research questions and methods to evolve and change during the course of the investigation (Schwartzman, 1993).

Similarly, in a study of the impact of Total Quality Management (TQM) on the competitive position of small- and medium-sized enterprises (SMEs), Ghobadian and Gallear (1997) examine the differences between SMEs and large organizations and explore the relationship between organizational size and the implementation of TQM. A series of research questions about this relationship were developed through analysis of the TQM literature. Although

3.1 | # Student Experience

Personality, experience, and research strategy

It is clear that a number of things influence a person's choice of research strategy. Sometimes the choice is limited by the requirements of a course or course instructor. Cindy, Melissa, and Amanda, for example, were given a choice of focus groups, interviews, or surveys. Sometimes it can depend on past experience. Cindy had already gained experience of interviews and a survey so was drawn to focus groups as a new learning challenge. Research choices can also be influenced by type of research question you are interested in. Mark, for example, was interested in gaining a general understanding of the relationship between age, technology use, and performance while Tricia was interested in an in-depth study of the institu-

tional contexts in which nurses work. And research decisions can be based on how you 'feel' about different approaches; whether they make sense to you or not; whether you are more or less comfortable with a focus on numbers or words, etc. Beata sums this up well in an interesting turn of phrase when she says 'I think the perspective chooses.' After exposure to a number of methods within a 'positivist research' framework she studied social constructionism and 'really enjoyed it. It really helped me understand my work when I did HR too. . . . I was just drawn to that perspective and really started looking at that and that was my starting point for some reason I just liked it and starting developing [it].'

Ghobadian and Gallear describe their research as deductive, they also point out that classic hypotheses were not easily formulated, because the variables and issues identified were mainly contextual and, therefore, did not translate into simple constructs. They, therefore, shift towards a more inductive approach in the later stage of the study, using four case studies to explore the relevance of the research questions and to develop a 10-step framework for the implementation of TQM in SMEs.

This may all seem rather surprising and confusing. There is a certain logic to the idea of developing theories and then testing them. In everyday contexts, we commonly think of theories as things that are quite illuminating but that need to be tested before they can be considered valid or useful. In point of fact, however, while the process of deduction outlined in Figure 3.1 does undoubtedly occur, it is better considered as a general orientation to the link between theory and research. As a general orientation, its broad outlines may frequently be found in business research, but it is also the case that we often find departures from it.

However, in some research *no* attempt is made to follow the sequence outlined in Figure 3.1. Some researchers prefer an approach to the relationship between theory and research that is primarily *inductive*. With an inductive stance, theory is the *outcome* of research. In other words, the process of induction involves drawing generalizable inferences out of observations. To put it simply, whereas deduction entails a process in which:

theory → observations/findings,

with induction the connection is reversed:

observations/findings → theory.

However, just as deduction entails an element of induction, the inductive process is likely to entail a modicum of deduction. Once the phase of theoretical reflection on a set of data has been carried out, the researcher may want to collect further data in order to establish the conditions in which a theory will and will not hold. Such a general strategy is often called *iterative*: it involves a weaving back and forth between data and theory. It is particularly evident in **grounded theory**, which will be examined in Chapter 24, but in the meantime the basic point is to note that induction represents an alternative strategy for linking theory and research, although it contains a deductive element too.

However, as with *theory* in connection with the deductive approach to the relationship between theory and research, we have to be cautious about the use of the term in the context of the inductive strategy too. While some researchers undoubtedly develop theories, it is equally necessary to be aware that very often what one ends up with can be little more than empirical generalizations of the kind Merton (1967) wrote about. Inductive researchers often use a grounded theory approach to the analysis of data and to the generation of theory. This approach, which was first outlined by Glaser and Strauss (1967), is frequently regarded as especially strong in terms of generating theories out of data. This contrasts with the nature of many supposedly inductive studies, which generate interesting and illuminating findings but whose theoretical significance is not entirely clear. They provide insightful empirical generalizations, but little theory. Secondly, in much the same way that the deductive strategy is associated with a quantitative research approach, an inductive strategy of linking data and theory is typically associated with a qualitative research approach (see Web Research in focus 3.4 is an example of research that can be classified as inductive) in the sense that it develops a hypothesis out of interview data about innovation and change and the formation of organizational subcultures. However, the analytic strategy adopted by Sackmann (1992) in Web Research in focus 3.4 was more complex and multifaceted, combining **ethnographic**, **phenomenological**, and clinical methods and relying on **qualitative** (thematic) **content analysis** (see Chapter 18). It thus illustrates how research methods can be combined within a broadly inductive approach. In addition, it is not a coincidence that Sackmann's research is based on in-depth, semi-structured interviews that produced qualitative data in the form of respondents' detailed answers to her questions. However, this characterization of the inductive strategy as associated with qualitative research is not entirely straightforward: not only does much qualitative research *not* generate theory, but also theory is often used at the very least as a background to qualitative investigations.

Epistemological considerations

An epistemological issue concerns the question of what is (or should be) regarded as acceptable knowledge in a discipline. A particularly central issue in this context is the question of whether or not the social world can be studied according to the same principles, procedures, and ethos as the natural sciences. This approach is usually associated in the social sciences with **positivism** (see Key concept 3.2), an approach in which:

1. Only phenomena confirmed by the senses can genuinely be warranted as knowledge.
2. The purpose of theory is to generate hypotheses that can be tested and that will thereby allow explanations of laws to be assessed (the principle of deductivism).
3. Knowledge is arrived at through the gathering of facts that provide the basis for laws (the principle of inductivism).
4. Science must (and presumably can) be conducted in a way that is value free (that is, objective).
5. There is a clear distinction between scientific statements and normative statements and a belief that the former are the true domain of the scientist.

Postpositivism, on the other hand, questions the relationship between social reality and knowledge production and the viability of any approximating a natural sciences approach to the study of human behaviour (see Key concept 3.3).

A natural science epistemology: Positivism

As we can see from the five principles above, positivism is an approach to research that attempts to conform as closely as possible to that in the natural sciences, by: (1) relying on observations of the empirical world, (2) avoiding the use of subjective or metaphysical speculation, (3) attempting to be objective, neutral, and value free, (4) requiring empirical verification of theories through empirical testing, and (5) focusing on the production of knowledge that enables the prediction and control of social events (Johnson & Duberley, 2000).

Students will likely be more familiar with positivist research than its name. That is because positivism has been the dominant underlying philosophy in Western society since the Enlightenment and influences how we judge the truthfulness of things (Johnson & Duberley, 2000). Ironically the very dominance of positivist thinking in much of the social sciences, especially business studies, has provided a context in which many, if not most, researchers doing positivist informed research do not refer to themselves as positivists. What they do is so normal that it is often just referred to as normal, rigorous, and/or scientific research. Indeed, some business research methods do not even reference positivism (Hair et al., 2003, see for example Cooper & Schindler, 2006). There are a few exceptions, where researchers—such as Derek Pugh (see Web Research in focus 3.5)—feel the need to state their underlying epistemological assumptions or, on rare occasions, to defend them (Donaldson, 1985, 1996).

The term positivism is more usually invoked by critics who offer a contrasting approach. Sometimes that alternative approach is referred to as interpretivism (Brewerton & Millward, 2001); sometimes **constructionism** (Easterby-Smith et al., 1993); and sometimes **postpositivism** (Prasad, 2005).

Returning to the five principles we can see a link with some of the points that have already been raised about the relationship between theory and research. For example, positivism entails elements of both a deductive approach (point 2) and an inductive strategy (point 3). Also, a fairly sharp distinction is drawn between theory and research. The role of research is to test theories and to provide material for the development of laws. Pugh (1983), for example, describes the research task as entailing the collection of data upon which to base generalizable propositions that can be tested (see Web Research in focus 3.5). But both of these connections between theory and research carry with them the implication that it is possible to collect observations in a manner that is not influenced by pre-existing theories. Moreover, theoretical terms that are not directly amenable to observation are not considered genuinely scientific; they must be susceptible to the rigours of observation. All this carries with it the implication of greater epistemological status being given to observation than to theory.

You might now be asking why do you need to be concerned with understanding positivism when it constitutes the dominant, or 'normal' approach in business studies? There are three main reasons. First, by the very fact that it is the dominant approach in business studies makes it important to study (see Web Research in focus 3.5). Second, it is important to understand the roots of any approach to knowledge. This way you are better able to judge the strengths and limitations of any given study or research outcome. Positivism has been critiqued from several perspectives in recent years (Burrell & Morgan, 1979; Corman & Poole, 2000; Johnson & Duberley, 2000; Piekkari et al., 2009), and thus raises a number of interesting points that are worth considering. Third, alternative—postpositivist—approaches are in large part a reaction to positivism and are best understood in contrast to positivism.

Easterby-Smith et al. (1993, p. 23) list eight elements of positivism that characterize research in business studies: (1) independence; (2) value-freedom; (3) causality; (4) hypothetico-deductive; (5) operationalization; (6) reductionism; (7) generalization; and (8) cross-sectional analysis. Easterby-Smith et al. (1993, p. 27) make the following contrast between positivism and phenomenology:

Postpositivism

Definitions of postpositivism vary sharply. Definitions range from those who respond in 'a limited way' to the critiques of positivism 'while remaining within essentially the same set of beliefs' (Guba & Lincoln, 1994, p. 109), through to those who view postpositivism, not as a 'single invariant tradition' but rather 'a number of diverse genres' (Prasad, 2005, p. 9). The latter include such approaches as interpretivism, feminism, critical realism, and poststructuralism—'all of which are primarily united in their rejection of prominent positivist assumptions' (Prasad, 2005, p. 9). Arguably these different genres, more the most part, share a common reaction to positivism in questioning 'social reality and knowledge production from a more problematized

> **Key concept 3.2: Positivism**
>
> is an epistemological position that advocates the application of the methods of the natural sciences to the study of social reality.

Table 3.1 Contrast Between Positivism and Phenomenology

	Positivist Paradigm	Phenomenological Paradigm
Basic beliefs	The world is external and objective	The world is socially constructed and subjective
	Observer is independent	Observer is part of what is observed
	Science is value-free	Science is driven by human interests
Researcher should:	focus on facts	focus on meaning
	look for causality and fundamental laws	try to understand what is happening
	reduce phenomena to simplest elements	look at the totality of each situation
	formulate hypotheses and test them	develop ideas through induction from data
Preferred methods include:	operationalising concepts so that they can be measured	using multiple methods to establish different views of phenomena
	taking large samples	small samples investigated in depth over time

From: *Management Research: An Introduction*, (p. 27), by M. Easterby-Smith, R. Thorpe, and A. Lowe, 1993, London: Sage. Copyright by M. Easterby-Smith, R. Thorpe, and A. Lowe. Reprinted with permission.

vantage point, emphasizing the constructed nature of social reality, the constitutive role of language, and the value of research as critique' (Prasad, 2005, p. 9).

Here we need to note two important points: (1) we shall draw on Prasad's (2005) notion of postpositivism throughout this book but readers should be aware that there are other different definitions and understandings of the term. When encountering the terms positivism and postpositivism (and indeed many other key terms) the student should always attempt to ascertain how each particular author is defining and using the term. (2) For simplicity of argument we shall be discussing postpositivism as if a singular approach in comparison with positivism. However, as Prasad (2005) counsels, postpositivism consists of several traditions and it is important to be aware of the differences between the different traditions. Thus, beyond the issue of comparisons with positivism we shall be examining selected strands from within postpositivism to show the range of research strategies available (see Chapters 6, 14–16, 18–20, 22–24).

Prasad (2005) makes three points in her definition of postpositivism. First, theories are not disconnected from people; they reflect not only the ideas of theorists but the context in which they live and operate. The theories are thus influenced by a number of scholars who interact with each others' ideas (challenging and/or building on those ideas), in a specific socio-political context. To that extent the theories and their adherents are not just representatives of a particular **paradigm** or world view (Burrell & Morgan, 1979) but rather an 'intellectual tradition' that changes over time, depending on context.

For example, a case has been made that the development of management theory in the United States owed much to the Cold War context in which those theories developed (Cooke, 1999; Kelley et al., 2006) but changed over time as a reaction to new socio-political realities. Second, positivism is itself not just a powerful rationalization for undertaking a scientific approach to social and business studies but is itself an 'intellectual tradition', and one that, in practice, does not conform to the scientific processes it lays claim to (Latour, 1987). Third, postpositivism consists of various 'intellectual traditions' that include 'interpretive traditions', 'traditions of deep

Key concept 3.3: Postpositivism

is a disparate number of 'intellectual traditions' that share a common rejection of fundamental tenets of positivism—especially the insistence on emulating the natural sciences in the study of human society, and its characterization as a unified scientific community or practice.

structure', 'critical traditions', and 'traditions of the 'Post' (i.e., postmodernism, poststructuralism, postcolonialism) (Prasad, 2005, contents page). Similarly, although not classifying them as postpositivist, Esterberg (2002) includes as alternatives to positivism 'social constructionist and interpretivist approaches', 'feminist and other critical approaches', and 'postmodernism'.

However, before we move on, we want to provide a couple of important contrasts between positivism and postpositivism through an examination of two postpositivist approaches—critical realism and interpretivism.

Critical realism is mentioned here as a special case in that it shares an **ontological realism** with positivism, and to that extent it differs from other postpositivist approaches. On the other hand, its adherents set out to be anti-positivists in their claim that 'things that cannot be measured or observed via our senses may still be real' (Johnson & Duberley, 2000, pp. 151–52) (see Key concept 3.4c).

Critical realism implies two things. First, it implies that, whereas positivists take the view that the scientist's conceptualization of reality actually directly reflects that reality, realists argue that the scientist's conceptualization is simply a way of knowing that reality. As Bhaskar (1975, p. 250) has put it: 'Science, then, is the systematic attempt to express in thought the structures and ways of acting of things that exist and act independently of thought'. Second, by implication, critical realists, unlike positivists, are perfectly content to admit into their explanations theoretical terms that are not directly amenable to observation. As a result, hypothetical entities to account for regularities in the natural or social orders (the 'generative mechanisms' to which Bhaskar refers) are perfectly admissible for realists, but not for positivists. What makes critical realism *critical* is that the identification of generative mechanisms offers the prospect of introducing changes that can transform the status quo.

Thus, critical realism differs from positivism in at least four major ways, including the view that: (1) social and natural reality are not wholly constituted as directly observable entities but need to be understood through a process of theorization; (2) the language that we use to make sense of observations is not theory-neutral (it is influenced by our sociopolitical *situatedness*) nor is there a correspondence theory of truth (language does not reflect reality so much as serve as an interpretive lens); (3) 'science' is not the outcome of scientific practices but rather a legitimation of practices that are referred to as 'scientific'; and (4) causation 'is not wholly expressed through a constant conjunction of events as in positivism' but can '*underlie* regular events' (our emphasis). The latter are studied through a process of 'retroductive argument' involving the description of the phenomenon, a description of the assumed underlying mechanism or structure that causes the phenomenon and a testing of the assumed relationship between the two (Johnson & Duberley, 2000, pp. 154–55).

Interpretivism provides a different contrasting epistemology to positivism (see Key concept 3.5). The term subsumes the views of writers who have been critical of the application of the scientific model to the study of the social world and who have been influenced by different intellectual traditions, which are outlined below. They share a view that the subject matter of the social sciences—people and their institutions—is fundamentally different

Key concept 3.4a: Realism

shares two features with positivism: A belief that the natural and the social sciences can and should apply the same kinds of approach to the collection of data and to explanation, and a commitment to the view that there is an external reality to which scientists direct their attention (in other words, there is a reality that is separate from our descriptions of it).

Key concept 3.4b: Empirical realism

is the view that through the use of appropriate methods, reality can be understood.

Key concept 3.4c: Critical realism

is a specific form of realism that (i) recognizes the reality of the natural order and the events and discourses of the social world while (ii) arguing that there 'are enduring structures and generative mechanisms' (Bhaskar, 1989, p. 2) (as influencing views of the world) that need to be made sense of (identified) 'through the practical and theoretical work of the social sciences' (Bhaskar, 1989, p. 2).

Key concept 3.5: Interpretivism

views the social world as the outcome of the interpretations of actors through a series of interactions.

from that of the natural sciences. The study of the social world, therefore, requires a different logic of research procedure, one that reflects the distinctiveness of humans as against the natural order. Von Wright (1971) has depicted the epistemological clash as being between positivism and **hermeneutics** (a term that is drawn from theology and that, when imported into the social sciences, is concerned with the theory and method of the interpretation of human action). This clash reflects a division between an emphasis on the *explanation* of human behaviour that is the chief ingredient of the positivist approach to the social sciences and the *understanding* of human behaviour. The latter is concerned with the empathic understanding of human action rather than with the forces that are deemed to act on it. This contrast reflects long-standing debates that precede the emergence of the modern social sciences but find their expression in such notions as the advocacy by Max Weber (1864–1920) of a *Verstehen* approach. Weber described sociology as a 'science which attempts the interpretive understanding of social action in order to arrive at a causal explanation of its course and effects' (1947, p. 88). Weber's definition seems to embrace both explanation *and* understanding here, but the crucial point is that the task of 'causal explanation' is undertaken with reference to the 'interpretive understanding of social action' rather than to external forces that have no meaning for those involved in that social action.

An example of an interpretative understanding of leadership is given in Web Research in focus 3.6. Grint (2000) claims that the concept of leadership can be understood only through understanding the meaning of the concept for those involved in this form of social action. His approach to this subject is thus broadly interpretative.

Phenomenology, one of the main intellectual strands within the interpretivist tradition, is a philosophy that is concerned with the question of how individuals make sense of the world around them and how, in particular, the philosopher should bracket out preconceptions in

his or her grasp of that world (see Web Research in focus 3.6). As such, it is useful for drawing out some of the key features of the interpretivist approach. The initial application of phenomenological ideas to the social sciences is attributed to the work of Alfred Schutz (1899–1959), whose work did not come to the notice of most English-speaking social scientists until the translation from German of his major writings in the 1960s, some 20 or more years after they had been written. His work was profoundly influenced by Weber's concept of Verstehen, as well as by phenomenological philosophers, like Husserl. Schutz's position is well captured in the following passage, which has been quoted on numerous occasions:

> The world of nature as explored by the natural scientist does not 'mean' anything to molecules, atoms, and electrons. But the observational field of the social scientist— social reality—has a specific meaning and relevance structure for the beings living, acting, and thinking within it. By a series of common-sense constructs they have preselected and pre-interpreted this world, which they experience as the reality of their daily lives. It is these thought objects of theirs, which determine their behaviour by motivating it. The thought objects constructed by the social scientist, in order to grasp this social reality, have to be founded upon the thought objects constructed by the common-sense thinking of men [and women!], living their daily life within the social world. (Schutz, 1962, p. 59)

Two points are particularly noteworthy in this quotation. First, it asserts that there is a fundamental difference between the subject matter of the natural sciences and the social sciences and that an epistemology is required that will reflect and capitalize upon that difference. The fundamental difference lies in the fact that social reality has a meaning for human beings and, therefore, human action is meaningful—that is, it has a meaning for them and they act on the basis of the meanings that they attribute to their acts and to the acts of others. This leads to the second point—namely, that it is the job of the social scientist to gain access to people's 'common-sense thinking' and hence to interpret their actions and their social world from their point of view. It is this particular feature that social scientists claiming allegiance to phenomenology have typically emphasized: 'The phenomenologist views human behavior . . . as a product of how people interpret the world . . . . In order to grasp the meanings of a person's behavior, *the phenomenologist attempts to see things from that person's point of view*' (Bogdan & Taylor, 1975, pp. 13–14, emphasis in original).

Verstehen and the hermeneutic-phenomenological tradition do not exhaust the intellectual influences on interpretivism. The theoretical tradition in sociology known as **symbolic interactionism** has also been regarded by many writers as a further influence. It is an approach that is rooted in the work of George Herbert Mead (1863–1931), whose discussion of the way in which our notion of self emerges through an appreciation of how others see us. Over the years this approach has been hotly debated and developed in two different directions: one that is positivist in tone (Meltzer, Petras, & Reynolds, 1975; McPhail & Rexroat, 1979), and one that exemplifies interpretivist research. In the latter case symbolic interactionism can be seen as occupying similar intellectual space to the hermeneutic-phenomenological tradition and so broadly interpretative in approach. This tendency is largely the product of the writings of Herbert Blumer, a student of Mead's who acted as his mentor's spokesman and interpreter, and his followers (Hammersley, 1989; Collins, 1994). Symbolic interactionists argue that interaction takes place in such a way that the individual is continually interpreting the symbolic meaning of his or her environment (which includes the actions of others) and acts on the basis of this imputed meaning. In research terms, according to Blumer (1962, p. 188), 'the position of symbolic interaction requires the student to catch the process of interpretation through which [actors] construct their actions', a statement that brings out clearly his views of the research implications of symbolic interactionism and of Mead's thought.

Taking an interpretative stance can mean that the researcher may come up with surprising findings, or at least findings that appear surprising if a largely external stance is taken—that is, a position from outside the particular social context being studied. The Hawthorne studies, referred to earlier in this chapter, provide an interesting example of

this, particularly as it was the failure of the investigation to come up with answers that related to the original research questions that stimulated the researchers to change their approach and methods and to adopt a more interpretative epistemological position. Of course, when the social scientist adopts an interpretative stance, he or she is not simply laying bare how members of a social group interpret the world around them. The social scientist will almost certainly be aiming to place the interpretations that have been elicited into a social scientific frame. As the example in Web Research in focus 3.6 illustrates, there is a double interpretation going on, whereby the researcher is providing an interpretation of others' interpretations of effective leadership. Indeed, there is a third level of interpretation going on, because the researcher's interpretations have to be further interpreted in terms of the concepts, theories, and literature of a discipline.

The aim of this section has been to outline how epistemological considerations—especially those relating to the question of whether a natural science, and in particular a positivist, approach, can supply legitimate knowledge of the social world—are related to research practice. There is a link with the earlier discussion in this chapter about the relationship between theory and research, in that a deductive approach is typically associated with a positivist position. Key concept 3.2 suggests that inductivism is also a feature of positivism (see third principle above), but, in the working through of its implementation in the practice of research, it is the deductive element (second principle) that tends to be emphasized. Similarly, the third level of interpretation that a researcher engaged in interpretative research must bring into operation is very much part of the kind of inductive strategy described in the previous section. However, while such interconnections between epistemological issues and research practice exist, it is important not to overstate them, since they represent tendencies rather than definitive points of correspondence. Thus, particular epistemological principles and research practices do not necessarily go hand in hand in a neat unambiguous manner. For example, although inductive approaches tend to rely on qualitative methods, Hofstede's research study of cultural differences (see Web Research in focus 3.7) provides an example where this is not the case.

Ontological considerations

Questions of social ontology are concerned with the nature of social entities. The central point of orientation here is the question of whether social entities can and should be considered objective entities that have a reality external to social actors, or whether they can and should be considered social constructions built up from the perceptions and actions of social actors. These positions are frequently referred to respectively as **objectivism** and **constructionism**. Their differences can be illustrated by reference to two of the most common and central terms in social science—organization and culture.

Objectivism

Objectivism is an ontological position that implies that social phenomena confront us as external facts that are beyond our reach or influence (see Web Key concept 3.6). We can discuss organization or *an* organization as a tangible object. It has rules and regulations. It adopts standardized procedures for getting things done. People are appointed to different jobs within a division of labour. There is a hierarchy. It has a mission statement, and so on. The degree to which these features exist from organization to organization is variable, but in thinking in these terms we are tending to the view that an organization has a reality that is external to the individuals who inhabit it. Moreover, the organization represents a social order in that it exerts pressure on individuals to conform to the requirements of the organization. People learn and apply the rules and regulations. They follow the standardized procedures. They do the jobs to which they are appointed. People tell them what to do and they tell others what to do. They learn and apply the values in the mission statement. If they do not do these things, they may be reprimanded or even fired. The organization is, therefore, a constraining force that acts on and inhibits its members.

The same can be said of culture. Cultures and subcultures can be viewed as repositories of widely shared values and customs into which people are socialized so that they can function as good citizens or as full participants. Cultures and subcultures constrain us because we internalize their beliefs and values. In the case of both organization and culture, the social entity in question comes across as something external to the actor and as having an almost tangible reality of its own. It has the characteristics of an object and hence of having an objective reality. To a very large extent, these are the 'classic' ways of conceptualizing organization and culture.

Constructionism

However, we can consider an alternative ontological position—constructionism (see Web Key concept 3.7). This position challenges the suggestion that categories such as organization and culture are pre-given and, therefore, confront social actors as external realities that they have no role in fashioning.

In recent years, the term has also come to include the notion that researchers' own accounts of the social world are constructions. In other words, the researcher always presents a specific version of social reality, rather than one that can be regarded as definitive. Knowledge is viewed as indeterminate. The discussion of postmodernism in Chapters 24 and 25 further examines this viewpoint. This sense of constructionism is usually allied to the ontological version of the term. In other words, these are linked meanings. Both meanings are antithetical to *objectivism* (see Web Key concept 3.6), but the second meaning is also antithetical to **realism** (see Web Key concept 3.4). The first meaning might be thought of usefully as constructionism in relation to the social world; the second as constructionism in relation to the nature of knowledge of the social world (and indeed the natural world).

Increasingly, the notion of constructionism in relation to the nature of knowledge of the social world is being incorporated into notions of constructionism, but in this book we will be using the term in relation to the first meaning, whereby constructionism is presented as an on-

---

Key concept 3.6: Objectivism

is an ontological position that asserts that social phenomena and their meanings have an existence that is independent of social actors. It implies that social phenomena and the categories that we use in everyday discourse have an existence that is independent or separate from actors.

**Key concept 3.7:
Constructionism**

is an ontological position (often also referred to as constructivism), which asserts that social phenomena and their meanings are continually being accomplished by social actors. It implies that social phenomena and categories are not only produced through social interaction but that they are in a constant state of revision.

tological position in relating to social objects and categories—that is, one that views them as socially constructed.

Let us take organization first. Strauss et al. (1973), drawing on insights from symbolic interactionism, carried out research in a psychiatric hospital and proposed that it was best conceptualized as a 'negotiated order'. Instead of taking the view that order in organizations is a pre-existing characteristic, they argue that it is worked at. Rules were far less extensive and less rigorously imposed than might be supposed from the classic account of organization. Indeed, Strauss et al. prefer to refer to them as 'much less like commands, and much more like general understandings' (1973, p. 308). Precisely because relatively little of the spheres of action of doctors, nurses, and other personnel was prescribed, the social order of the hospital was an outcome of agreed-upon patterns of action that were themselves the products of negotiations between the different parties involved. The social order is in a constant state of change because the hospital is 'a place where numerous agreements are continually being terminated or forgotten, but also as continually being established, renewed, reviewed, revoked, revised . . . . In any pragmatic sense, this is the hospital at the moment: this is its social order' (Strauss et al., 1973, pp. 316–17). The authors argue that a preoccupation with the formal properties of organizations (rules, organizational charts, regulations, roles) tends to neglect the degree to which order in organizations has to be accomplished in everyday interaction, though this is not to say that the formal properties have *no* element of constraint on individual action.

Much the same kind of point can be made about the idea of culture. Instead of culture being seen as an external reality that acts on and constrains people, it can be taken to be an emergent reality in a continuous state of construction and reconstruction. Becker (1982, p. 521), for example, has suggested 'people create culture

continuously. . . . No set of cultural understandings . . . provides a perfectly applicable solution to any problem people have to solve in the course of their day, and they, therefore, must remake those solutions, adapt their understandings to the new situation in the light of what is different about it'. Like Strauss et al., Becker recognizes that the constructionist position cannot be pushed to the extreme: it is necessary to appreciate that culture has a reality that 'persists and antedates the participation of particular people' and shapes their perspectives, but it is not an inert objective reality that possesses only a sense of constraint: it acts as a point of reference but is always in the process of being formed.

Neither the work of Strauss et al. nor that of Becker pushes the constructionist argument to the extreme. Each admits to the pre-existence of their objects of interest (organization and culture respectively). However, in each case we see an intellectual predilection for stressing the active role of individuals in the social construction of social reality. Not all writers adopting a constructionist position are similarly prepared to acknowledge the existence or at least importance of an objective reality. Walsh, for example, has written that 'we cannot take for granted, as the natural scientist does, the availability of a preconstituted world of phenomena for investigation' and must instead 'examine the processes by which the social world is constructed' (1972, p. 19). It is precisely this apparent split between viewing the social world as an objective reality and as a subjective reality in a continuous state of flux that Giddens sought to straddle in formulating his idea of structuration (see Web Research in focus 3.1).

Constructionism also suggests that the categories that people employ in helping them to understand the natural and social world are in fact social products. The categories do not have built-in essences; instead, their meaning is constructed in and through interaction. Thus, a category like 'masculinity' might be treated as a social construction. This notion implies that, rather than being treated as a distinct inert entity, masculinity is construed as something in which meaning is built up during interaction (see for example the study of masculinity in the making of Air Canada in Mills and Helms Mills, 2006). That meaning is likely to be a highly ephemeral one, in that it will vary according to both time and place. This kind of stance frequently displays a concern with the language that is employed to present categories in particular ways. It suggests that the social world and its categories are not external to us, but are built-up and constituted in and through interaction. This tendency can be seen particularly in discourse analysis, which is examined in Chapter 20. As Potter (1996, p. 98) observes: 'The world . . . is *constituted* in one way or another as people talk it, write it and argue it'. This sense of constructionism is highly antithetical to realism (see Key concept 3.7). Constructionism frequently results in an interest in the representation of social phenomena (Web Research in focus 3.10 provides an illustration of this idea in relation to the representation of the position of middle managers during the late 1990s).

Constructionism is also frequently used as a term reflects the indeterminacy of our knowledge of the social world (see Key concept 3.7). However, in this book we will be using the term in connection with the notion that social phenomena and categories are social constructions.

Relationship of epistemology and ontology to business research

As we saw in Web Research in focus 3.6, questions of social ontology cannot be divorced from issues concerning the conduct of business research. Ontological assumptions and commitments will feed into the ways in which research questions are formulated and research is carried out. If a research question is formulated in such a way as to suggest that organizations and cultures are objective social entities that act on individuals, the researcher is likely to emphasize the formal properties of organizations or the beliefs and values of members of the culture. Alternatively, if the researcher formulates a research problem so that the tenuousness of organization and culture as objective categories is stressed, it is likely that an emphasis will be placed on the active involvement of people in reality construction. In either case, it might be supposed that different approaches to the design of research and the collection of data will be required.

Competing paradigms

A key influence on understanding the epistemological and ontological foundations of business research has been Burrell and Morgan's (1979) exposition of the four paradigms that they suggest reflect the assumptions that researchers make about the nature of organizations and how we find out about them. Their use of the notion of paradigm draws on the work of Kuhn (1970; see Key concept 3.8). Burrell and Morgan suggest that each paradigm contains assumptions that can be represented as either:

> **Key concept 3.8: Paradigm**
>
> is 'a cluster of beliefs and dictates which for scientists in a particular discipline influence what should be studied, how research should be done, [and] how results should be interpreted' (Bryman, 1988a, p. 4).

- *objectivist*—there is an external viewpoint from which it is possible to view the organization, which is comprised of consistently real processes and structures; or
- *subjectivist*—an organization is a socially constructed product, a label used by individuals to make sense of their social experience, so it can be understood only from the point of view of individuals who are directly involved in its activities.

Each paradigm also makes assumptions about the function and purpose of scientific research in investigating the world of business as either:

- *regulatory*—the purpose of business research is to describe what goes on in organizations, possibly to suggest minor changes that might improve it but not to make any judgement of it; or
- *radical*—the point of management and business research is to make judgements about the way that organizations ought to be and to make suggestions about how this could be achieved.

Plotting the assumptions of researchers along these two axes provides a framework for the identification of four possible paradigmatic positions for the study of organizations:

- *Functionalist.* The dominant framework for the study of organizations, based on problem-solving orientation which leads to rational explanation.
- *Interpretative.* Questions whether organizations exist in any real sense beyond the conceptions of social actors, so understanding must be based on the experience of those who work within them.
- *Radical humanist.* Sees an organization as a social arrangement from which individuals need to be emancipated and research as guided by the need for change.
- *Radical structuralist.* Views an organization as a product of structural power relationships, which result in conflict.

They suggest that each paradigm results in the generation of a quite different type of organizational analysis as each seeks to address specific organizational 'problems' in a different way. Web Research in focus 3.8 illustrates the different organizational insights that each paradigm can produce.

However, one of the most significant areas of controversy to have arisen in relation to this model relates to the issue of commensurability or otherwise of the four paradigms. Burrell and Morgan were quite specific in arguing that 'a synthesis between paradigms cannot be achieved' (Jackson Carter, 1991, p. 110), as they are founded upon a commitment to fundamentally opposing beliefs, in other words they are incommensurate with each other. Each paradigm must, therefore, develop independently of the others. Jackson and Carter argue that paradigm incommensurability is important because it protects the diversity of scientific thought, resisting the hegemony of functionalist approaches, which have tended to dominate business research, particularly in North American-based journals. Reed (1985), on the other hand, suggests that the boundaries between paradigms are not as clear as Burrell and Morgan suggest and that overstatement of the differences between them leads to isolationism and reduces 'the potential for creative theoretical development' (1985, p. 205). However, Willmott (1993) takes a different tack. He suggests that, although the four-paradigm model challenges the intellectual hegemony of functionalism and opens up possibilities for alternative forms of analysis

within management, its central thesis is, therefore, distinctly double edged. In particular, the division between subjectivist and objectivist forms of analysis leads to a polarization of methodological approaches. Instead, he suggests that paradigms arise through critical reflection upon the limitations of competing approaches. For example, labour process theory has sought to incorporate an appreciation of the subjective dimension of work while at the same time retaining a commitment to structural analysis of the dynamics involved in capitalist production. Willmott argues that this example draws attention to the 'practical indivisibility' of subjective and objective dimensions of organization.

Whatever view is held in relation to the relative commensurability of the four paradigms, it is clear that this model has significantly influenced business researchers by encouraging them to explore the assumptions that they make about the nature of the social world and the way it can be studied. Building on this approach, Mills, Helms Mills, Bratton, and Foreshaw (2007) argue that while there is still evidence of a radical structuralist approach to organization studies, radical humanism never really moved beyond Burrell and Morgan's imagination, but other paradigms have emerged, including feminism, racio-ethnicity, and postmodernism.

The paradigm debate thus draws attention to the relationship between epistemology and ontology in business and management research. It can also reasonably be supposed that the choice of which paradigm to adopt has implications for the design of the research and the data collection approach that will be taken; it is to this question that we will now turn in the following section.

 ## Research strategies and the quantitative and qualitative debate

On the surface quantitative and qualitative research offers two distinguishable strategies based on the observation that quantitative researchers employ measurement and qualitative researchers do not. Certainly that would be a good starting point. Can/should what you intend to study be measured? How you answer that question will depend on a number of things, not least of which is your ontological and epistemological ways of viewing the world. If you are a positivist you may not trust any other 'evidence' than the 'scientific' outcome (i.e., significance) of what has or can be measured. However, not all positivists rely solely on quantification. There are those who utilize non-qualitative methods—such as interviews and observation—to collect data that is then analyzed 'within conventional positivist assumptions about the nature of social reality and the production of knowledge' (Prasad, 2005, p. 4). Prasad and Prasad (2002) refer to this as qualitative positivism in its adoption of a 'relatively commonsensical and realist approach to ontological and epistemological issues. Reality is assumed to be concrete, separate from the researcher, and understandable through the accurate use of 'objective' methods of data collection' (Prasad, 2005, p. 4). This characterizes some forms of ethnography, case study and, as we saw above, some forms of symbolic interactionism. Thus, a qualitative positivist may argue that measurement and quantification may be useful for understanding a range of phenomena but qualitative methods are more useful for in-depth studies (see for example McCracken, 1988). There also has been a growing use of qualitative studies as an exploratory stage of a large quantitative study. Ouadahi (2008), for example, was interested in discovering what factors lead employees to accept or resist the introduction of new information systems. Instead of using a deductive approach aimed at verifying a priori the factors involved, he used an inductive approach to 'explore' the issue (see Web Research in focus 3.4)

Returning to our question of how or why to use quantitative research methods we have already indicated that postpositivist researchers are more likely to use qualitative methods to 'surface' people's meanings and understandings in the construction of their social world. To that end, quantification and measurement might be seen as obscuring meaning and understanding through a process of aggregating a series of individual responses (e.g., as in an attitude survey). As noted above, an important exception to this is critical realism that is accepting of some forms of realism in research but argues that qualitative research is needed to understand the non observable patterns of events through 'retroductive argument' (Johnson & Duberley, 2000, p. 155).

 ## Six research strategies

From our discussion of epistemology, ontology, paradigms, and qualitative and quantitative methods we can generate six research strategies—three positivist and three postpositivist strategies (see Figure 3.2). In both cases this involves a research strategy that is primarily quantitative, qualitative, or a combination of the two—the latter case is usually referred to as mixed methods or triangulation (see Table 3.2). As you will see from Table 3.2, not all strategies are adopted equally by researchers but that should not inhibit students and other researchers from considering different approaches to research. In positivist research the more common approach is through some form of quantitative study but there is a growing use of qualitative studies and mixed methods as witnessed in the relative popularity of the case study method (Serenko et al., 2008; Hartt et al., 2009; Mills et al., 2009;Piekkari et al., 2009). In postpositivist research the more common approach is qualitative studies but within one or two traditions—particularly liberal feminism and critical realism—it is not uncommon to find some form of quantification in use. Outside of liberal feminism (commonly referred to Women in Management research in business studies) the *term* 'mixed methods' or 'triangulation' is rarely used although there have been some attempts to define how it would/should look as a postpositivist research strategy (Wolfram Cox & Hassard, 2009). Missing from our list of strategies is the mixed methods approach, which combines some aspects of positivist (usually quantification) and postpositivist (usually qualitative methods) approaches. This constitutes a potential seventh research strategy but because of confusion around its use and the limited number of available examples we have left it out of account. Kitchenham (2010), for example, refers to mixed methods as 'a research paradigm that combines specific positivistic elements of quantitative research methods with specific constructivist elements of qualitative research methods'. However, the examples he gives of this approach in action

3.1 Research in Focus

An example of qualitative positivism in action

Ouadahi (2008) was interested in finding out what influenced employees in their decision to accept or resist the introduction of new information systems (IS). His starting point for the study was research suggesting that attitudes to the adoption of IS is influenced by psychological characteristics, including open-mindedness, self efficacy, interest in IS and related technology, and closeness to retirement age. Nonetheless, rather than a deductive (quantitative) approach focused on verifying a priori 'the importance of factors thought to influence the success of IS adoption' (p. 203), Ouadahi used an inductive (qualitative) approach to explore the issue.

Through the establishment of two case studies—a social welfare public organization and a ministerial department of the Government of Quebec—Ouadahi conducted a series of two-hour interviews with 10 employees in each case. The aim was to assess employees' perceptions of a new IS in their workplace, and to identify the personal characteristics and management practices that may have influenced employee perceptions. The end result was the generation of an emerging conceptual 'model of receptivity to IS' (p. 211).

Semi-structured questions were used throughout the interviews and reflected the existing literature on receptivity to change and IS. Thus, the questions were built around issues of psychological factors (e.g., personality traits), perceptions of IS (e.g., reliability), effects of IS on workplace performance and health, and organizational factors (e.g., culture). The responses were coded and transcribed using NVivo 6 software (see Chapter 24).

The research indicates that addressing some of the factors strongly associated with employee rejection of IS will serve to lessen the opposition but will not necessarily lead to endorsement. Similarly the absence of factors that encourage endorsement (e.g., open-mindedness, perceived usefulness of IS, leader competence) will not necessarily lead to resistance.

This led Ouadahi to develop an 'emerging model of receptivity to new IS' (p. 211) and a recommendation that it 'must be empirically tested using different and larger samples' (p. 212).

In reviewing Ouadahi's approach we can note the following. First, it involved qualitative research, drawing primarily on interviews and case study research, and second, it was initially inductive. However, in a number of ways it was framed within a positivist worldview. Thus, third, the starting point was an established literature rooted in quantitative research (i.e., the specific literature on 'adaptation to technological change'), which, fourth, was used to semi-structure the interview questions. Fifth, the research was not focused on the respondents' interpretations of reality but rather on their representation of reality. Six, the research outcome was cast as an 'exploratory' (p. 203) stage or contribution to a broader quantitative study.

---

look remarkably like positivist qualitative methods combined with positivist quantitative methods. An interesting but fairly rare example of an attempt to mix quantitative methods with postpostitivist qualitative methods can be found in Wicks and Bradshaw, 2002. This account involved an empirical study of the gendered nature of organizational culture. To that end, they surveyed a group of participants attending a seminar on organizational change. The survey instrument they used was SYMLOG (Systematic Multiple Level Observation of Groups) but ultimately the data was analyzed from a feminist, social constructionist perspective. The issue of mixed methods is explored in more depth in Chapter 7.

Influences on the conduct of business research

We are beginning to get a picture now that business research is influenced by a variety of factors. Figure 3.3 summarizes the influences that have been examined so

Table 3.2   Fundamental Differences Between Positivist and Postpositivist Research Strategies

	Quantitative Research	Qualitative Research	Mixed Methods
P O S I T I V I S M	• Primary mode of research within the positivist tradition; • Emphasizes quantification in the collection and analysis of data; • Deductive approach to the relationship between theory and research; • Accent placed on the testing of theories; • Incorporates the practices and norms of the natural science model; • Embodies a view of social reality as an external, objective reality.	• Secondary (but growing) mode of research within the positivist tradition; • Usually emphasizes words rather than quantification in the collection and analysis of data; • Views language as representational in its relationship to reality; • Inductive approach to the relationship between theory and research; • Emphasis on the generation of theories; • Subscribes to a view of social reality as rooted in a realist ontology.	• Combination of quantitative and qualitative methods; • Usually designed as an exploratory qualitative study to identify potential constructs for a quantitative research project; • Analysis of both qualitative and quantitative data from a realist perspective; • To quote Wolfram, Cox, and Hassard (2009): The idea of mixed methods 'is based on the logic that researchers can move closer to obtaining a "true" picture if they take multiple measurements, use multiple methods, or examine a phenomenon at multiple levels of analysis. In social research, the term is associated with . . . measures of an empirical phenomenon in order to reduce bias and improve *convergent validity*, which is the substantiation of an empirical phenomenon through the use of multiple sources of evidence'.
P O S T P O S I T I V I S M	• Mostly used by liberal and some materialist feminists, and critical realist researchers; • Quantification in the collection and analysis of data often seen as an aspect of study to accompany qualitative accounts of reality (see, for example, Konrad et al., 2005); • Tends to draw on metatheory—Feminism and/or materialism—in which quantification is confirmatory or testing of theory; • Embodies a view of social reality as an external, objective reality that is mediated (understood) through human cognition and structures of thought.	• Primary mode of research within the postpositivist traditions; • Emphasizes meaning rather than quantification in the collection and analysis of 'data'; • Overwhelmingly rejects the practices and norms of the natural scientific model and of positivism in particular for an emphasis on the way in which individuals interpret their social world; • In limited instances—(e.g., Grounded Theory—see Chapter 17)—focuses on an inductive approach to the relationship between theory and research in which the emphasis is placed on the generation of theories; • Embodies a view of social reality as a constantly shifting emergent property of individuals' creation.	• A mix of quantitative and qualitative methods is more often found in Liberal feminist accounts (often called 'Women in Management' accounts in business research). It is rare within other postpositivist traditions. However, Wolfram, Cox, and Hassard (2009) argue for a 'postpositivist perspective on triangulation [which, in contrast to positivist approaches] gives emphasis to questioning the organizing and ordering practices that stabilize situated knowledge: to understanding researcher stance rather than reducing or removing the effect of research distance from objective truth'.

far, but has added two more—the impact of *values* and of *practical considerations*.

Values

Values reflect either the personal beliefs or the feelings of a researcher. On the face of it, we would expect that social scientists should be value free and objective in their research.

We might want to argue that research that simply reflected the personal biases of its practitioners could not be considered valid and scientific because it was bound up with the subjectivities of its practitioners. Such a view

Figure 3.2

Six research strategies

is held with less and less frequency among social scientists nowadays. Émile Durkheim (1858–1917) argued that to treat social facts as things all 'preconceptions must be eradicated' (1938, p. 31). Since values are a form of preconception, his exhortation was at least implicitly to do with suppressing them when conducting research. His position is unlikely to be regarded as credible nowadays, because there is a growing recognition that it is not feasible to keep the values that a researcher holds totally in check. These can intrude at any or all of a number of points in the process of business research:

- Choice of research area.
- Formulation of research question.
- Choice of method.
- Formulation of research design and data collection techniques.
- Implementation of data collection.
- Analysis of data.
- Interpretation of data.
- Conclusions.

There are, therefore, numerous points at which bias and the intrusion of values can occur. Values can materialize at any point during the course of research. The researcher may develop an affection or sympathy, which was not necessarily present at the outset of an investigation, for the people being studied. It is quite common, for example, for

researchers working within a qualitative research strategy, and in particular when they use participant observation or very intensive interviewing, to develop a close affinity with the people that they study to the extent that they find it difficult to disentangle their stance as social scientists from their subjects' perspective. This possibility may be exacerbated by the tendency of some researchers to be very sympathetic to underdog groups. For example, following publication of his classic study of the Ford factory in Dagenham, Beynon (1975) was criticized by the press for having become too emotionally involved in the lives of workers. Equally, social scientists may feel unsympathetic towards the people they study. Although business and management researchers generally tend to emphasize their interest in understanding the problems and issues that affect practitioners, their value systems, particularly if they

Figure 3.3

Influences on business research

Theory   Practical considerations   Epistemology

Business research

Values   Ontology

are working within a radical structuralist paradigm, are very likely to be antithetical to those of many managers working within a profit-making industry.

Another position in relation to the whole question of values and bias is to recognize and acknowledge that research cannot be value free, but to ensure that there is no untrammelled incursion of values into the research process, and to be self reflective and so exhibit **reflexivity** about the part played by such factors. This view is borne of the assumption that the prior knowledge, experience, and attitudes of the researcher will influence not only how the researcher sees things but also *what* he or she sees (Web Research in focus 3.9 considers some of these issues in relation to organization research). Researchers are increasingly prepared to forewarn readers of their biases and assumptions and how these may have influenced the subsequent findings. There has been a growth since the mid-1970s of collections of inside reports of what doing a piece of research was really like, as against the generalities presented in business research methods textbooks (like this one!). These collections frequently function as 'confessions', an element of which is often the writer's preparedness to be open about his or her personal biases. This point will be taken up further in chapter 25.

Still another approach is to argue for consciously value-laden research. This is a position taken by some feminist writers who have argued that only research on women that is intended *for* women will be consistent with the wider political needs of women. Mies (1993, p. 68) has argued that in feminist research the 'postulate of *value free research*, of neutrality and indifference towards the research objects, has to be replaced by *conscious partiality*, which is achieved through partial identification with the research objects' (emphases in original).

The significance of feminism in relation to values goes further than this, however. In particular, several feminist researchers around the early 1980s proposed that the principles and practices associated with quantitative research were incompatible with feminist research on women. For writers like Oakley (1981), quantitative research was bound up with male values of control that can be seen in the general orientation of the research strategy—control of the research subject/respondent and control of the research

context and situation. Moreover, the research process was seen as 'one-way traffic' in which researchers extract information from the people being studied and give little, or more usually, nothing in return. For many feminists, such a strategy bordered on exploitation and was incompatible with feminism's values of sisterhood and non-hierarchical relationships between women. The antipathy towards quantitative research resulted in a preference for qualitative research among feminists. Not only was qualitative research seen as more consistent with the values of feminism; it was seen as more adaptable to those values. Thus, feminist qualitative research came to be associated with an approach in which the investigator eschewed a value-neutral approach and engaged with the people being studied as people and not simply as respondents to research instruments. The stance of feminism in relation to both quantitative and qualitative approaches demonstrates the ways in which values have implications for the process of social investigation. In more recent years, there has been a softening of the attitudes of feminists towards quantitative research. Several writers have acknowledged a viable and acceptable role for quantitative research, particularly when it is employed in conjunction with qualitative research (Jayaratne & Stewart 1991; Oakley, 1998). This issue will be picked up in Chapters 6, 7, and 25.

There are, then, different positions that can be taken up in relation to values and value freedom. Far fewer writers overtly subscribe to the position that the principle of objectivity can be put into practice than in the past. Quantitative researchers sometimes seem to be writing in a way that suggests an aura of objectivity (Mies, 1993), but we simply do not know how far they subscribe to such a position. There is a greater awareness today of the limits to objectivity, so that some of the highly confident, not to say naive, pronouncements on the subject, like Durkheim's, have fallen into disfavour. A further way in which values are relevant to the conduct of business research is through the following of ethical principles or standards. This issue will be followed up in Chapter 8.

Practical considerations

Nor should we neglect the importance and significance of *practical issues* in decisions about how business research

| 3.2 | **Student Experience** |

Gaining research access through workplace contacts

Jennifer was interested in studying the identify work of employees in the context of organizational change, such as a merger or takeover. When she shared with fellow students her interest and concern about finding and gaining access to such a company one of those students suggested talking to a person she knew in such a company: 'I got to know about this case through [Agnes, another Ph.D. student who] knew somebody there who . . . she suggested [I] contact.' Agnes offered to telephone the contact person to gain advice on who Jennifer needed to contact in the company for access. Jennifer eventually went on to meet with a senior person in the company who agreed to allow her access to conduct in-depth interviews with staff members.

Beata's research actually started long before she entered the Ph.D. program: 'I worked with HR in an IT company . . . for nine months, but during that time I got the experience [of a] period of rapid growth and the downsizing process, and I thought it was quite interesting to see how people reacted. [So] when I began working there, I interviewed all employees, all those who agreed to do that which was pretty much everyone.' Her initial motives for the interviews were two-fold, as an HR person it was 'a way of getting to know people' but it was also a way to 'ask about the HR issues, about recruitment, about their background and all sorts of things'. It was also a time when the company began downsizing. 'The IT bubble started to burst and the company had got these problems and we started this downsizing process, and I asked the management team if I could, you know, help the people in any way because it was of course stressful to them. [But] they didn't want me really to do that because they were sort of still ignoring or hoping that we would overcome all the problems. So I said, "What if I would interview people and ask them about their experiences", and that was okay.' As Beata went on to observe: 'Saying that I want to help you, they [management] didn't want me to do that, but interviewing [employees] to produce a report was okay!' By the time she had completed the project and started at Hanken University as a Ph.D. student she already had 50 to 60 interviews completed, varying in length from 30 minutes to one hour. Not surprisingly Beata decided to build her thesis topic around her interviews and the issue of IT developers in periods of change. To that end she went back and conducted interviews with a group of people from her former (now bankrupt) company who were now working in various other companies.

should be carried out. There are a number of dimensions to this issue. For one thing, choices of **research strategy**, **design**, or method have to be dovetailed with the specific research question being investigated. If we are interested in teasing out the relative importance of a number of causes of a social phenomenon, it is quite likely that a quantitative strategy will fit our needs, because, as will be shown in Chapter 5, the assessment of cause is one of its keynotes. Alternatively, if we are interested in the world views of members of a certain social group, a **qualitative research** strategy that is sensitive to how participants interpret their social world may be the direction to choose. If a researcher is interested in a topic on which no or virtually no research has been done in the past, the **quantitative strategy** may be difficult to employ because there is little prior literature from which to draw leads. A more exploratory stance may be preferable and, in this connection, qualitative research may serve the researcher's

Practical reasons not to research your own organization

There may, however, be situations when it is more practical not to carry out your research in the place where you work or study. Mark, for example, wanted to study, 'technology differences in the workplace between . . . younger and older workers and how they perceive it and how they use it and how it affects their performance'. He wanted his study to be relevant and interesting to employers. To that end, he drew on his friendship with a fellow student to gain access to a local Halifax-based company—Clearwater—and 'asked them what kind of technologies [they are] using and how prominent it [is] in the organization? And I got the response back that everyone uses it and it's a major part of the company'. The answer convinced him to move forward (with permission) with a survey of Clearwater employees. In the process he rejected the idea of surveying his fellow Acadia University students, which 'everyone's been saying . . . [is] the easiest way to do [surveys] because you know [the students], and all the professors. [You] know them and you're right here. And then another part of the ethics component [is easier to deal with] 'cause it's going through Acadia. There's an easy corner to cut there if you want to'. However, for Mark the problem with using students was that this limited (1) the number of potential responses he would likely get due to interest and relevance to the respondents (he got 400 responses from his Clearwater survey); (2) the age range of respondents [the Clearwater survey got responses from people from a range of ages]; (3) the study of technology use (Acadia University students were largely experienced on learning technology]; and (4) relevance to anyone outside of a university. By focusing on a non-university group Mark found that it gave him 'the motivation to really analyze and make something of [the data]' because he felt that there was a useable 'pay off' at the end.

In Tom's case, he explained that this stemmed from the risks associated with the lack of continuity in his current work environment: 'When I started the course I was doing a job which was on a fixed-term basis and I knew I was going to be moving on, so I wasn't in a sort of settled work environment so I knew that it might be tricky kind of to get access and keep access . . . negotiated . . . where I was working. So it wasn't like I'd been working in one organization for a long time and had kind of things that I could sort of explore in that environment'. Researching your own workplace also introduces particular ethical and analytical considerations that stem from having to maintain the dual roles of being a colleague and a researcher. These issues will be discussed in more detail in Chapter 17.

needs better, since it is typically associated with the generation rather than the testing of theory (see Table 3.2) and with a relatively unstructured approach to the research process (see Chapter 6). Another dimension may have to do with the nature of the topic and of the people being investigated. For example, if the researcher needs to engage with individuals or groups involved in illicit activities, such as industrial sabotage (Sprouse, 1992) or pilferage (Ditton, 1977), it is unlikely that a social survey would gain the confidence of the subjects involved or achieve the necessary rapport. It is not surprising, therefore, that researchers in these areas have tended to use a qualitative strategy.

While practical considerations may seem rather mundane and uninteresting compared with the lofty realm inhabited by the philosophical debates surrounding such discussions about epistemology and ontology, they are important ones. All business research is a coming together of the ideal and the feasible. Because of this, there will be many circumstances in which the nature of the topic or of the subjects of an investigation and the constraints on a researcher loom large in decisions about how best to proceed (see Web Thinking deeper 3.19, which considers the extent to which opportunism is, or indeed should be, a basis for doing research in a particular setting or focusing on a certain subject).

Key points

- Business research is subject to considerable debate concerning its relevance to practitioners and its fundamental purpose.
- Quantitative and qualitative research constitute different approaches to social investigation and carry with them important epistemological and ontological considerations.
- Theory can be depicted as something that precedes research (as in quantitative research) or as something that emerges out of it (as in qualitative research).
- Epistemological considerations loom large in considerations of research strategy. To a large extent, these revolve around the desirability of employing a natural science model (and in particular positivism) versus interpretivism.
- Ontological considerations, concerning objectivism versus constructionism, also constitute important dimensions of the quantitative/qualitative contrast.
- These considerations have informed the four-paradigm model that has been an important influence on business research.
- Values may impinge on the research process at different times.
- Practical considerations in decisions about research methods are also important.
- Feminist researchers have tended to prefer a qualitative approach, though there is some evidence of a change of viewpoint in this regard.

Questions for review

The nature of business research
- How did business research develop?

Questions within research paradigms
- How might research questions arise and how might researchers attempt to answer these questions?

Evaluating business research
- What, in your view, is the function or purpose of business and management research?
- What are the differences between mode 1 and mode 2 forms of knowledge production, as proposed by Gibbons et al., and why is this distinction important?

Theory and research
- If you had to conduct some business research now, what would the topic be and what factors would have influenced your choice? How important was addressing theory in your consideration?
- Outline, using examples of your own, the difference between grand- and middle-range theory.
- What are the differences between inductive and deductive theory and why is the distinction important?

Epistemological considerations

- What is meant by each of the following terms: positivism, realism, and interpretivism? Why is it important to understand each of them?
- What are the implications of epistemological considerations for research practice?

Ontological considerations

- What are the main differences between epistemological and ontological considerations?
- What is meant by objectivism and constructionism?
- Which theoretical ideas have been particularly instrumental in the growth of interest in qualitative research?
- What are the main arguments for and against paradigm commensurability within management and business research?

Relationship of epistemology and ontology to business research

- What are the four main paradigms in business research and how do they influence the insights that are gained?

Research strategies and the quantitative and qualitative debate

- Outline the main differences between quantitative and qualitative research in terms of: the relationship between theory and data; epistemological considerations; and ontological considerations.
- To what extent is quantitative research solely concerned with testing theories and qualitative research with generating theories?

Six research strategies

- What are the six research strategies?
- What are the strengths and weaknesses of each of the six research strategies?

Influences on the conduct of business research

- What are some of the main influences on business research?

4

Research Designs

Chapter guide

In focusing on the different kinds of research design, we are paying attention to the different frameworks for the collection and analysis of data. A research design relates to the criteria that are employed when evaluating business research. It is, therefore, a framework for the generation of evidence that is suited both to a certain set of criteria and to the research question in which the investigator is interested. This chapter is structured as follows:

- Reliability, replication, and validity are presented as criteria for assessing the quality of business research. The latter entails an assessment in terms of several criteria covered in the chapter: *measurement validity*, *internal validity*, *external validity*, and *ecological validity*.

- The suggestion that such criteria are mainly relevant to positivist research is examined, along with the proposition that an alternative but related set of criteria should be employed in relation to **postpositivist** research. This alternative set of criteria, which is concerned with the issue of **trustworthiness**, is outlined briefly.

- Five prominent research designs are then outlined:
  - **Experimental** and related designs (such as the quasi-experiment).
  - **Cross-sectional design**, the most common form of which is social survey research.
  - **Longitudinal** design and its various forms, such as the panel study and the cohort study.
  - **Case study design.**
  - **Comparative design.**

Each research design is considered in terms of the criteria for evaluating research findings.

Introduction

In the previous chapter, the idea of research strategy was introduced as a broad orientation to business and management research. The specific context for its introduction was the distinction between positivist and postpositivist research as different research strategies. However, the decision to adopt one or the other strategy will not get you far along the road of doing a piece of research. Two other key decisions will have to be made (along with a host of tactical decisions about the way in which the research will be carried out and the data analyzed). These decisions concern choices about **research design** and **research method**. On the face of it, these two terms would seem to mean the same thing, but it is crucial to draw a distinction between them (see Key concepts 4.1 and 4.2).

Research methods can be and are associated with different kinds of research design. The latter represents a structure that guides the execution of a research method and the analysis of the subsequent data. The two terms are often confused. For example, one of the research designs to be covered in this chapter—the **case study**—is very often referred to as a method. As we will see, a case study entails the detailed exploration of a specific case, which could be a community, an organization, or a person. But, once a case has been selected, a research method or research methods are needed to collect data. Simply selecting an organization and deciding to study it intensively are not going to provide data. Do you observe? Do you conduct interviews? Do you examine documents? Do you administer **questionnaires**? You may in fact use any or

---

Key concept 4.1: What is a research design?

A research design provides a framework for the collection and analysis of data. A choice of research design reflects decisions about the priority being given to a range of dimensions of the research process.

Key concept 4.2: What is a research method?

A research method is simply a technique for collecting data.

all of these research methods, but the crucial point is that deciding to choose a case study approach will not in its own right provide you with data. This choice is further complicated by the fact that what counts as data is not an entirely straightforward matter. Bartunek, Bobko, and Venkatraman (1993) acknowledge the diversity in the way that management researchers define the concept of data to include responses to questionnaire items, transcripts of public inquiry hearings, case studies, and advertisements.

In this chapter, five different research designs will be examined: experimental design and its variants, including quasi-experiments, **cross-sectional** or **social survey design**, **longitudinal design**, **case study design**, and **comparative design**. However, before embarking on the nature of and differences between these designs, it is useful to consider some recurring issues in business and management research that cut across some or all of these designs.

 ## Criteria in business research

Three of the most prominent criteria for the evaluation of business and management research are reliability, replication, and validity. All of these terms will be treated in much greater detail in later chapters, but in the meantime a fairly basic treatment of them can be helpful.

Reliability

Reliability is concerned with the question of whether the results of a study are repeatable. The term is commonly used in relation to the question of whether or not the measures that are devised for concepts in business and management (such as teamwork, employee motivation, organizational effectiveness) are consistent. In Chapter 5, we will look at the idea of reliability in greater detail, in particular the different ways in which it can be conceptualized. Reliability is particularly at issue in connection with quantitative data. In this case, the researcher is likely to be concerned with the question of whether a measure is stable or

not. After all, if we found that IQ tests, which were designed as measures of intelligence, were found to fluctuate, so that people's IQ scores were often wildly different when administered on two or more occasions, we would be concerned about it as a measure. We would consider it an unreliable measure—we could not have faith in its consistency.

Replication

The idea of reliability is very close to another criterion of research—replication (and more specifically, replicability). It sometimes happens that researchers choose to replicate the findings of others. There may be a host of different reasons for doing so, such as a feeling that the original results do not match other evidence that is relevant to the domain in question. In order for replication to take place, a study must be capable of replication—it must be replicable. This is a very obvious point: if a researcher does not spell out his or her procedures in great detail, replication is impossible. Similarly, in order for us to assess the reliability of a measure of a concept, the procedures that constitute that measure must be replicable by someone else.

Validity

A further, and in many ways the most important criterion of research, is validity. Validity is concerned with the integrity of the conclusions that are generated from a piece of research. Like reliability, we will be examining the idea of validity in greater detail in later chapters, but in the meantime it is important to be aware of the main types of validity that are typically referred to:

- *Measurement validity*. This primarily applies to positivist research using quantitative data and to the search for measures of social scientific concepts. Measurement validity is also often referred to as construct validity. Essentially, it concerns the question of whether or not a measure that is devised of a concept really does reflect the concept that it is supposed to be denoting. Does the IQ test really measure variations in intelligence? If we take the study reported in Web Research in focus 4.1, there are two issue-related concepts that need to be measured in order to test the hypotheses: 'magnitude of consequences' and 'issue framing', and two context-related concepts that also need to be measured: 'perceived social consensus' and 'competitive context'. The question then is: do the measures really represent the concepts they are supposed to be tapping? If they do not, the study's findings will be questionable. We may thus appreciate that measurement validity is related to reliability: if a measure of a concept is unstable in that it fluctuates and hence is unreliable, it simply cannot be providing a valid measure of the concept in question. In other words, the assessment of measurement validity presupposes that a measure is reliable.

- *Internal validity*. This form of validity relates mainly to the issue of **causality**, which will be dealt with in greater detail in Chapter 5. Internal validity is concerned with the question of whether a conclusion that incorporates a causal relationship between two or more **variables** holds water. If we suggest that *x* causes *y*, can we be sure that it is *x* that is responsible for variation in *y* and not something else that is producing an apparent causal relationship? In the study examined in Web Research in focus 4.1, the authors conclude that moral awareness is more likely when an individual perceives the issue to have significant harmful consequences, such as putting a competitor out of business ('magnitude of consequences'), and when the individual perceives a social consensus within the organization that the activity in question is ethically problematic ('perceived social consensus'). Internal validity raises the question: can we be sure that 'magnitude of consequences' and 'perceived social consensus' really do cause variation in moral awareness and that this apparent causal relationship is genuine and not produced by something else? In discussing issues of causality, it is common to refer to the factor that has a causal impact as the **independent variable** and the effect as the **dependent variable**. In the case of the research of Butterfield, Treviño, and Weaver (2000) in Web Research in focus 4.1, the 'magnitude of consequences' was an independent variable and moral awareness the dependent variable. Thus, internal validity raises the question: how confident are we that the independent variable really is at least in part responsible for the variation that has been identified in the dependent variable?

- *External validity*. This issue is concerned with the question of whether the results of a study can be generalized beyond the specific research context. It is in this context that the issue of how people or organizations are selected to participate in research becomes crucial. This is why Scase and Goffee (1989) go to such great lengths to detail the process whereby their sample of UK managers was generated (see Web Research in focus 4.1). External validity is one of the main reasons why quantitative researchers are so keen to generate **representative samples** (see Chapter 9).

- *Ecological validity*. This criterion is concerned with the question of whether or not social scientific findings are applicable to people's every day, natural social settings. As Cicourel (1982, p. 15) has put it: 'Do our instruments capture the daily life conditions, opinions, values, attitudes, and knowledge base of those we study as expressed in their natural habitat?' This criterion is concerned with the question of whether business research sometimes produces findings that may be technically valid but have little to do with what happens in people's everyday lives. If research findings are ecologically invalid, they are in a sense artefacts of the social scientist's arsenal of data collection and analytic tools. The more the social scientist intervenes in natural settings or creates unnatural ones, such as a laboratory or even a special room to carry out interviews, the more likely it is that findings will be ecologically invalid. This was an important finding to have emerged from the Hawthorne studies (see Web Research in focus 4.2). Furthermore, the conclusions deriving from a study using questionnaires may have measurement validity and a reasonable level of internal validity, and they may be externally valid, in the sense that the findings can be generalized to other samples confronted by the same questionnaire, but the unnaturalness of the fact of having to answer a questionnaire may mean that the findings have limited ecological validity.

One feature that is striking about most of the discussion so far is that it seems to be geared mainly to positivist quantitative research rather than to postpositivist research. Both reliability and measurement validity are essentially concerned with the adequacy of measures, which are most obviously a concern in positivist quantitative research. Internal validity is concerned with the soundness of findings that specify a causal connection, an issue that is most commonly of concern to positivist **quantitative** researchers. **External validity** may be relevant to both **positivist** and **postpositivist** research, but the whole question of *representativeness* of research subjects with which the issue is concerned has a more obvious application to the realm of positivist quantitative research with its focus upon sampling procedures that maximize the opportunity for generating a **representative sample**. The issue of ecological validity relates to the naturalness of the research approach and seems to have considerable relevance to both streams of research strategy.

Some writers have sought to apply positivist concepts of reliability and validity to the practice of postpositivist **qualitative research** (e.g., LeCompte & Goetz, 1982; Kirk & Miller, 1986; Peräkylä, 1997), largely reflecting the common practice of dividing research strategies and design along the lines of the type of data rather than fundamental **epistemological** concerns. This reasoning is extended when others argue that the grounding of these ideas in **quantitative research** renders them inapplicable to or inappropriate for qualitative research. Writers like Kirk and Miller (1986) have applied concepts of validity and reliability to qualitative research but have changed the sense in which the terms are used very slightly. Some qualitative researchers sometimes propose that the studies they produce should be judged or evaluated according to different criteria from those used in relation to quantitative research. Lincoln and Guba (1985) usefully propose that alternative terms and ways of assessing qualitative research are required, in part offering a way to see broad based utility of the concepts in both positivist and postpositivist strategies. For example, they propose trustworthiness as a criterion of how good a qualitative study is. Each aspect of trustworthiness has a parallel with the previous quantitative research criteria:

- *Credibility*. Which parallels internal validity, i.e., how believable are the findings?
- *Transferability*. Which parallels external validity, i.e., do the findings apply to other contexts?

- *Dependability*. Which parallels reliability, i.e., are the findings likely to apply at other times?
- *Confirmability*. Which parallels objectivity, i.e., has the investigator allowed his or her values to intrude to a high degree?

We will revisit these criteria again in Chapter 6.

Hammersley (1992*a*) occupies a kind of middle position here in that, while he proposes validity as an important criterion (in the sense that an empirical account must be plausible and credible and should take into account the amount and kind of evidence used in relation to an account), he also proposes relevance as a criterion. Relevance is assessed from the vantage point of the importance of a topic within its substantive field or the contribution it makes to the literature on that field. The issues in these different views have to do with the different objectives that many postpositivist researchers argue are distinctive about their craft. The distinctive features of postpositivist research will be examined in later chapters.

However, it should also be kept in mind that one of the criteria previously cited—ecological validity—may have been formulated largely in the context of positivist quantitative research, but is actually an aspect of research in which qualitative research (both positivist and postpositivist) fares quite well. Qualitative research often involves a naturalistic stance (see Key concept 4.3). This means that the researcher seeks to collect data in naturally occurring situations and environments, as opposed to fabricated, artificial ones. This characteristic probably applies particularly well to **ethnographic research**, in which participant observation is a prominent element of data collection. However, it is sometimes suggested that it also applies to the sort of interview approach typically used by in qualitative research, which is less directive than the kind used in quantitative research. This leads us to expect that much qualitative research might be stronger than quantitative investigations in terms of ecological validity.

By and large, these issues in business research have been presented because some of them will emerge in the context of the discussion of research designs in the section on research designs (below), but in a number of ways they also represent background considerations for some of the issues to be examined. We will return to these issues later in the book.

 # Research designs

In this discussion of research designs, five different types will be examined: **experimental design**, **cross-sectional** or **social survey design**, **longitudinal design**, **case study design**, and **comparative design**. Variations on these designs will be examined in their relevant subsections.

Experimental design

True field experiments are rare in business and management research, mainly because of the problems of achieving the requisite level of control when dealing with organizational behaviour. Why, then, bother to introduce experimental designs at all in the context of a book written for business and management researchers? The chief reason, quite aside from the fact that they are sometimes employed, is that a true **experiment** is often used as a measure against which non-experimental research is assessed. Experimental research is frequently held up as a touchstone because it offers considerable confidence in the robustness and trustworthiness of causal findings. In other words, true experiments tend to be very strong in terms of internal validity.

Manipulation

If experiments are so strong in this respect, why do business researchers not make far greater use of them? The reason is simple: in order to conduct a true experiment, it is necessary to manipulate the independent variable in order to determine whether it does in fact have an influence on the dependent variable. Experimental subjects are likely to be allocated to one of two or more experimental groups, each of which represents different types or levels of the independent variable. It is then possible to establish how far differences between the groups are responsible for variations in the level of the dependent variable. Manipulation, then, entails intervening in a situation to determine which of two or more things happens to subjects. However, the vast majority of independent variables with which business researchers are concerned

cannot be manipulated. If we are interested in the effects of gender on work experiences, we cannot manipulate gender so that some people are made male and others female. If we are interested in the effects of variations in the economic environment on organizational performance, we cannot alter share prices or interest rates. As with the huge majority of such variables, the levels of social engineering that would be required are beyond serious consideration.

Before moving on to a more complete discussion of experimental design, it is important to introduce a basic distinction between the *laboratory experiment* and the *field experiment*. As its name implies, the laboratory experiment takes place in a laboratory or in a contrived setting, whereas field experiments occur in real-life settings, such as in classrooms and organizations, or as a result of the implementation of reforms or new policies. It is experiments of the latter type that are most likely to touch on areas of interest to business and management researchers. However, in business and management research it is more common to find field experiments in which a scenario is employed as a substitute for a real-life setting, as the example in Web Research in focus 4.1 illustrates. Furthermore, and somewhat confusingly, researchers will sometimes refer to their research as a field study. This simply means that the research was conducted in a real-life setting; it need not imply that a field experiment was involved.

Classic experimental design

In what is known as the classical experimental design, two groups are established and this forms the basis for experimental manipulation of the independent variable. The *experimental group*, or *treatment group*, receives the treatment and it is compared against the *control group*, which does not. The dependent variable is measured before and after the experimental manipulation, so that a

Key concept 4.3: What is Naturalism?

Naturalism has three different meanings: a commitment to adopting the principles of natural scientific method; being true to the nature of the phenomenon being investigated; a style of research that seeks to minimize the intrusion of artificial methods of data collection.

before-and-after analysis can be conducted. Moreover, the groups are assigned randomly to their respective groups. This enables the researcher(s) to feel confident that any difference between the two groups is attributable to manipulation of the independent variable.

In order to capture the essence of this design, the following simple notation is employed:

Obs An observation made in relation to the dependent variable; there may well be two or more observations, before (the pre-test) and after (the post-test) the experimental manipulation.

Exp The experimental treatment (manipulation of the independent variable). No Exp refers to the absence of an experimental treatment and represents the experience of the control group.

T The timing of the observations made in relation to the dependent variable.

Thus, the classical experimental design is comprised of the following elements: **random assignment** to the experimental and control groups; pre-testing of both groups at T1; manipulation of the experimental treatment so that the experimental group receives it (Exp) but the control group does not (No Exp); and post-testing of the two groups at T2. The difference between each group's pre- and post-test scores is then computed to establish whether or not Exp has made a difference. See Figure 4.1 for an outline of these elements.

Classic experimental design and validity

The purpose of the control group in a true experiment is to control (in other words, eliminate) the possible effects of rival explanations of a causal findings. We might

Figure 4.1

Classical experimental design

T_1		T_2
Obs_1	Exp	Obs_2
Obs_3	No Exp	Obs_4

then be in a position to take the view that the study is internally valid. The presence of a control group and the random assignment of subjects to the experimental and control groups enable us to eliminate rival explanations and eliminate threats to internal validity. These threats include the following:

- *Testing.* This threat refers to the possibility that subjects may become sensitized to the aims of the experiment. The presence of a control group, which presumably also experience the same 'experimenter effect', allows us to discount this possibility if there is no difference between the experimental and control groups.
- *History.* This threat refers to the possibility that events in the experimental environment, unrelated to manipulation of the independent variable, may have caused the changes. If there is no control group, we would be less sure that changes to the independent variable are producing the change. If there is a control group, differences between the control and experimental groups can be more confidently attributed to manipulation of the independent variable.
- *Maturation.* Quite simply, people change and the ways in which they change may have implications for the dependent variable. Since maturation should affect the control group subjects as well, the control group allows us to discount the possibility that changes would have occurred anyway, with or without manipulation of the independent variable.
- *Selection.* If there are differences between the two groups, which would arise if they had been selected by a non-random process, variations between the experimental and control groups could be attributed to pre-existing differences in their membership. However, if a random process of assignment to the experimental and control groups is employed, this possibility can be discounted.
- *Ambiguity about the direction of causal influence.* The very notion of an independent variable and dependent variable presupposes a direction of **causality**. However, there may be occasions when the temporal sequence is unclear, so that it is not possible to establish which variable affects the other. The existence of a control group can help to make this clear.

A field experiment in business ethics

In a study of moral awareness in business organizations, Butterfield, Treviño, and Weaver (2000) wanted to understand the factors that influenced whether or not an individual in an organization was able to recognize the moral nature of an ethically ambiguous situation. They hypothesized that respondents would be influenced by two kinds of factors, those that were:

1. Issue related—the degree of harm that may be caused by an action or decision and the kind of language used to frame the issue.
2. Social context related—the degree of social consensus that exists in the organization about whether an issue is ethically problematic and the extent to which the business context is characterized by aggressive competition.

The field experiment was conducted on 'competitive intelligence (CI) practitioners', whose job it is to collect information about a business's competitors. They suggest that CI practitioners 'represent a unique, and in some ways ideal, sample for research on moral awareness', because CI is a new field 'in which ethical guidelines, norms concerning ethical and unethical practices and legal guidelines are still emerging' (2000, p. 992).

A random sample of 1000 practitioners was generated from a membership list of a CI professional association. The researchers constructed scenarios that presented realistic and ethically ambiguous situations that would be relevant to people working in the CI field. Scenario methodology, which is commonly used in business ethics research, was suggested to enable the study of basic cognitive processes and to provide a stimulus to which individuals can respond.

The scenarios formed the basis for a postal questionnaire, which was sent to each individual to be completed anonymously. Two different scenarios were constructed and respondents were randomly assigned to each one. This formed the basis for qualitative and quantitative analysis of responses to each scenario in order to make comparisons between them. The scenarios were written from the point of view of a protagonist and respondents were encouraged to take on this role. This research strategy, combined with an assurance of anonymity, was designed to ensure against social desirability bias (see Chapter 13), which is a particular problem in researching ethical issues.

Immediately after having read the scenario, the respondent was asked to write down a list of issues that the protagonist would view as important in the scenario. The researchers then coded this list according to whether it might reasonably involve ethical concerns. Adding the number of ethical issues together produced a single number, representing the respondent's overall level of moral awareness in response to the scenario, and this was treated as a dependent variable.

The scenarios were constructed to manipulate two of the independent variables: 'magnitude of consequences' (how much harm may be caused by the decision), and 'issue framing' (the amount of moral language used to describe the issue). The research found that 'magnitude of consequences' was indeed significant in influencing moral awareness, but that 'issue framing' appeared to be significant only in certain scenario conditions. In addition, the social context was also found to influence moral awareness, but not always in the way that was anticipated. The prediction that aggressive competition would be negatively associated with moral awareness was disconfirmed. The authors speculate that working in a highly competitive context may actually make people more, rather than less, sensitive to moral concerns.

Although the authors describe their research as a 'field experiment', and it does involve manipulation of independent variables, this is achieved by way of the scenarios, which act as a substitute for real-life organizational settings, so in this sense the study relies on an artificially created field.

These threats are taken from Campbell (1957), and Cook and Campbell (1979), but not all the threats to internal validity they refer to are included. The presence of a control group coupled with random assignment allows us to eliminate these threats. As a result, our confidence in the causal finding is greatly enhanced.

Simply because research is deemed to be internally valid does not mean that it is beyond reproach or that questions cannot be raised about it. When a positivist research strategy has been employed, other criteria can be applied to evaluate a study. In the case of the Bunce and West (1996) study, for example (see Web Research in focus 4.3), there is a potential question of measurement validity. Even though measures of intrinsic job motivation and intrinsic job satisfaction may appear to exhibit a correspondence with work-related stress—that is, to possess face validity—in the sense that they appear to exhibit a correspondence with what they are measuring, we might feel somewhat uneasy about how far increases in job motivation and satisfaction can be regarded as indicative of improvements in psychological well-being and an individual's ability to manage occupational strain. Does it really measure what it is supposed to measure? The second question relating to measurement validity is whether or not the experimental manipulation really worked. In other words, did the stress management program and the innovation promotion program create the conditions for improvements in psychological well-being and reductions in occupational strain to be examined?

Secondly, is the research externally valid? Campbell (1957) and Cook and Campbell (1979) identify five major threats to the external validity and hence the **generalizability** of an investigation. These can be summarized as follows:

- *Interaction of selection and treatment.* This threat raises the question: to what social and psychological groups can a finding be generalized? Can it be generalized to a wide variety of individuals who might be differentiated by gender, ethnicity, social class, and personality? For instance, many influential studies of leadership, conducted on samples comprising a majority of men, rarely treat gender as a significant variable (Wilson, 1995). It is possible that the findings of these studies simply reflect the characteristics of the predominantly male samples and,

therefore, cannot provide a theory of effective leadership that is generalizable across both men and women.

- *Interaction of setting and treatment.* This threat relates to the issue of how confident we can be that the results of a study can be applied to other settings. For example, in Powell's (1995) research (see Web Research in focus 3.3), the postal questionnaire was sent to 143 companies in the north-eastern United States. Can his findings about TQM be generalized beyond this geographical area to companies in other countries where TQM programs are also used? In other words, if this research was not externally valid, it would apply to north-eastern United States and to no other geographical area. If it was externally valid, we would expect it to apply more generally to companies with TQM programs in other countries and other geographical regions in the United States.

- *Interaction of history and treatment.* This raises the question of whether or not the findings can be generalized to the past and to the future. The original Aston studies, for example, were conducted over 40 years ago. How confident can we be that these findings would apply today?

- *Interaction effects of pre-testing.* As a result of being pre-tested, subjects in an experiment may become sensitized to the experimental treatment. Consequently, the findings may not be generalizable to groups that have *not* been pre-tested and, of course, in the real world people are rarely tested in this way. The findings may, therefore, be partly determined by the experimental treatment as such and partly by how pre-test sensitization has influenced the way in which subjects respond to the treatment. This may have occurred in Bunce and West's research (see Web Research in focus 4.3).

- *Reactive effects of experimental arrangements.* People are frequently, if not invariably, aware that they are participating in an experiment. Their awareness may influence how they respond to the experimental treatment and, therefore, affect the generalizability of the findings. This was a major finding of the Hawthorne studies (see Web Research in focus 4.2).

Thirdly, are the findings ecologically valid? The fact that the research is a field experiment rather than a laboratory experiment seems to enhance this aspect of the Bunce and West (1996) research. The fact that Bunce and West made intensive use of various instruments to measure psychological well-being and job strain might be considered a source of concerns about ecological validity, though this is an area in which most if not all quantitative research is likely to be implicated.

A fourth issue that we might want to raise relates to the question of **replicability**. For example, Pugh et al. (1968) lay out very clearly the procedures and measures that were employed in the Aston studies and these have been used by several other researchers seeking to carry out replication of this research, both in business and non-business organizations, including trade unions, churches, schools, and public bureaucracies. Consequently, the research is replicable. However, analysis of the same data by Aldrich (1972) and Hilton (1972) using a different statistical technique showed other possible patterns of relationships between the variables in the Aston studies (see Web Research in focus 4.4). This failure to replicate casts doubt on the external validity of the original research and suggests that the first three threats referred to above may have played an important part in the differences between the two sets of results.

The laboratory experiment

Many experiments in fields like social psychology are laboratory experiments rather than field experiments. Some of the most well known of these, such as Milgram's (1974) electric shock experiments or Zimbardo's prison experiments (see Web Research in focus 8.1), have informed our understanding of how individuals and groups behave within modern work organizations to such an extent that they have inspired the development of television programs based on them (see Web Research in focus 4.5 and 8.4). One of the main advantages of laboratory experiments is that the researcher has far greater influence over the experimental arrangements. For example, it is easier to randomly assign subjects to different experimental conditions in the laboratory than to do the same in an ongoing, real-life organization. The researcher, therefore, has a higher level of control and this is likely to enhance the internal validity of the study. It is also likely that laboratory experiments will be more straightforward

to replicate because they are less bound up with a certain milieu that is difficult to reproduce.

However, laboratory experiments like the one de- scribed in Web Research in focus 4.6 suffer from a number of limitations. First, the external validity is likely to be difficult to establish. There is the interaction of setting and treatment, since the setting of the laboratory is likely to be unrelated to real world experiences and contexts. Also, there is likely to be an interaction of selection and treatment. In the case of Howell and Frost's (1989) study described in Web Research in focus 4.6, there are a number of difficulties: the subjects were students who are unlikely to be representative of the general population, so that their responses to the experimental treatment may be distinctive; they were volunteers and it is known that volunteers differ from non-volunteers (Rosnow & Rosenthal, 1997, Chapter 8); and they were given incentives to participate, which may further demarcate them from others, since not everyone is equally responsive to inducements. There will have been no problem of interaction effects of pre-testing, because, like many experiments, there was no pre-testing. However, it is quite feasible that reactive effects may have been set in motion by the experimental arrangements. As Web Research in focus 4.2 illustrates, reactive effects associated with an experiment can have a profound effect on the outcomes of the research. Secondly, the ecological validity of the study may be poor because we do not know how well the findings are applicable to the real world and everyday life. However, while the study may lack what is often called mundane realism, it may nonetheless enjoy experimental realism (Aronson & Carlsmith, 1968). The latter means that the subjects are very involved in the experiment and take it very seriously.

Quasi-experiments

A number of writers have drawn attention to the possibilities offered by **quasi-experiments**—that is, studies that have certain characteristics of experimental designs but that do not fulfill all the internal validity requirements. A large number of types of quasi-experiment have been identified (Cook & Campbell, 1979) and it is not proposed to cover them here. A particularly interesting form of quasi-experiment occurs in the case of 'natural experiments'.

These are 'experiments' in the sense of entailing manipulation of a social setting, but as part of a naturally occurring attempt to alter social arrangements. In such circumstances, it is invariably not possible to randomly assign subjects to experimental and control groups. An example is provided in Web Research in focus 4.3.

The absence of random assignment in Web Research in focus 4.3 casts a certain amount of doubt on the study's internal validity, since the groups may not have been equivalent. However, the results of such studies are still compelling, because they are not artificial interventions in social life and, therefore, their ecological validity is very strong. Hofstede's (1984) study of cultural differences (see Web Research in focus 3.7) falls into this category, because the research design enabled some degree of control to be maintained over variables—all employees belonged to the same multinational organization, even though the research took place in a natural setting. This meant that corporate culture constituted the dependent variable and differences in national cultures and mentalities of employees constituted independent variables, where Hofstede (1984) anticipated the main differences would be seen. In addition, some requirements of internal validity were managed through replication of the questionnaire survey on two separate occasions, once during 1967–9 and again during 1971–3.

Most writers on quasi-experimentation discount experiments in which there is no control group or basis for comparison (Cook & Campbell, 1979). However, some experiments do involve manipulation of the independent variable within experimental groups without a control group as the basis for comparison. For example, in an experimental study of electronic brainstorming, Gallupe et al. (1992) wanted to test the effect of group size on performance. The researchers wanted to find out if electronic brainstorming could more effectively support the generation of ideas within large groups (six and twelve persons), as well as small groups (two, four, and six persons)—unlike the traditional, verbal brainstorming technique. In this study, both the large and the small groups received the experimental treatment—that is, electronic brainstorming—and both received the control treatment—that is, verbal brainstorming. It was anticipated that large and small groups would show similar levels of productivity in

the verbal brainstorming experiment, but that large groups would outperform small groups in the electronic brainstorming experiment. Because there was no control group, where no manipulation of the independent variable occurs, this study cannot be seen as a classic experimental design. However, the internal validity of the findings was reinforced by the fact that both the experiments were also carried out on small groups, where it was found that electronic brainstorming made no difference to group performance. Comparison between large and small experimental groups helped to reduce threats to the internal validity of the findings. The study thus exhibited some of the characteristics of an experimental design, even though no control group was used.

Finally, **experimental** designs, and more especially **quasi-experimental** designs, have been particularly prominent in **evaluation research** studies (see Key concept 4.4 and Web Research in focus 4.7).

Significance of experimental design

As was stated at the outset, the chief reason for introducing the experiment as a research design is because it is frequently considered to be a measure against which positivist research is judged. This occurs largely because of the fact that a true experiment will allow doubts about internal validity to be put aside and reflects the considerable emphasis placed on the determination of causality in positivist research. As we will see in the next section, **cross-sectional designs** of the kind associated with social survey research are frequently regarded as limited, because of the problems of unambiguously imputing causality when using such designs.

Logic of comparison

However, before exploring such issues, it is important to draw attention to an important general lesson that an

> **Key concept 4.4: What is evaluation research?**
>
> Evaluation research, as the name implies, is concerned with the evaluation of such occurrences as organizational programs or interventions. The essential question that is typically asked by such studies is: has the intervention (for example, a new policy initiative or an organizational change) achieved its anticipated goals?

examination of experiments teaches us. A central feature of any experiment is the fact that it entails a *comparison*: at the very least it entails a comparison of results obtained by an experimental group with those engendered by a control group. In the case of the Howell and Frost (1989) experiment in Web Research in focus 4.6 there is no control group: the research entails a comparison of the effects of three different forms of leadership. The advantage of carrying out any kind of comparison like this is that we understand the phenomenon that we are interested in better when we compare it with something else that is similar to it. The case for arguing that charismatic leadership is an effective, performance-enhancing form of leadership is much more persuasive when we view it in relation to other forms of leadership. Thus, while the specific considerations concerning experimental design are typically associated with positivist research using quantitative data, the potential of comparison in business research represents a more general lesson that transcends matters of both research strategy and research design. In other words, while the experimental design is typically associated with a positivist quantitative research strategy, the specific logic of comparison provides lessons of broad applicability and relevance. This issue is given more specific attention below in relation to the comparative design.

Cross-sectional design

The **cross-sectional design** is often called a **social survey** design, but the idea of the social survey is so closely connected in most people's minds with **questionnaires** and **structured interviewing** that the more generic-sounding term **cross-sectional design** is preferable. While the research methods associated with social surveys are certainly frequently employed within the context of cross-sectional research, so too are many other research methods, including structured observation, **content analysis**, and **official statistics**. All these research methods will be covered in later chapters, but in the meantime the basic structure of the cross-sectional design will be outlined.

The cross-sectional design is defined in Key concept 4.5. A number of elements of this definition have been emphasized.

- *More than one case.* Researchers employing a cross-sectional design are interested in variation. That variation can be in respect of people, organizations, nation states, or whatever. Variation can be established only when more than one case is being examined. Usually, researchers employing this design will select a lot more than two cases for a variety of reasons: they are more likely to encounter variation in all the variables in which they are interested; they can make fine distinctions between cases; and the requirements of sampling procedure are likely to necessitate larger numbers (see Chapter 9).

- *At a single point in time.* In cross-sectional design research, data on the variables of interest are collected more or less simultaneously. When an individual completes a questionnaire, which may contain 50 or more variables, the answers are supplied at essentially the same time. This contrasts with an experimental design. Thus, in the classical experimental design, someone in the experimental group is pre-tested, then exposed to the experimental treatment, and then post-tested. Days, weeks, months, or even years may separate the different phases.

- *Quantitative or quantifiable data.* In order to establish variation between cases (and then to examine associations between variables—see next point), it is necessary to have a systematic and standardized method for gauging variation. One of the most important advantages of quantification is that it provides the researcher with a consistent benchmark. The advantages of quantification and of measurement will be addressed in greater detail in Chapter 5.

- *Patterns of association.* With a cross-sectional design it is only possible to examine relationships between variables. There is no time ordering to the variables, because the data on them are collected more or less simultaneously, and the researcher does not (because

Key concept 4.5: What is a cross-sectional research design?

A cross-sectional design entails the collection of data on more than one case and at a single point in time in order to collect a body of quantitative or quantifiable data in connection with two or more variables that are then examined to detect patterns of association.

he or she cannot) manipulate any of the variables. This creates the problem referred to in Web Research in focus 4.4 in establishing the direction of causal influence. If the researcher discovers a relationship between two variables, he or she cannot be certain whether this denotes a causal relationship, because the features of an experimental design are not present. All that can be said is the variables are related. This is not to say that it is not possible to draw causal inferences from research based on a cross-sectional design. As will be shown in Chapter 23, there are a number of ways in which the researcher is able to draw certain inferences about **causality**, however these inferences rarely have the credibility of causal findings deriving from an experimental design. As a result, cross-sectional research lacks the internal validity that one finds in most experimental research.

In this book, the term *survey* will be reserved for research that employs a **cross-sectional research design** and in which data are collected by **questionnaire** or by **structured interview** (see Key concept 4.6). This will allow us to retain the conventional understanding of what a survey is while recognizing that the cross-sectional research design has a wider relevance—that is, one that is not necessarily associated with the collection of data by questionnaire or by structured interview. An example of a survey that is widely used and cited in the study of UK human resource management and industrial relations is given in Web Research in focus 4.1.

Reliability, replicability, and validity

How does cross-sectional research measure up in terms of the previously outlined criteria for evaluating quantitative research: reliability, replicability, and validity?

- The issues of **reliability** and **measurement validity** are primarily matters relating to the quality of the measures that are employed to examine the concepts in which the researcher is interested, rather than matters to do with a research design. In order to address questions of the quality of measures, some of the issues outlined in Chapter 5 must be considered.

- *Replicability* is likely to be present in most cross-sectional research to the extent that the researcher spells out procedures they used for selecting respondents, designing measures of concepts, administration of research instruments (such as structured interview or **self-completion questionnaire**), and the analysis of data. Most positivist quantitative research based on cross-sectional research designs identifies such procedures.

- *Internal validity* is typically weak. As has just been suggested above, it is difficult to establish causal direction from the resulting data. Cross-sectional research designs produce associations rather than findings from which causal inferences can be clearly made. However, procedures for making causal inferences from cross-sectional data will be referred to in Chapter 23, though most researchers feel that the resulting causal findings rarely have the internal validity of those deriving from experimental designs.

- *External validity* is strong when, as in the case of research like the 2004 Workplace Employee Relations Survey (see Web Research in focus 4.1), the sample from which data are collected has been randomly selected. When non-random methods of sampling are employed, external validity becomes questionable. Sampling issues will be specifically addressed in Chapter 9.

- Since much cross-sectional research makes a great deal of use of research instruments, such as self-completion questionnaires and structured observation schedules, **ecological validity** may be jeopardized because these very instruments disrupt the 'natural habitat', as Cicourel (1982) put it (see quotation on p. 78).

> **Key concept 4.6: What is survey research?**
>
> Survey research comprises a cross-sectional design in relation to which data are collected predominantly by questionnaire or by structured interview on more than one case.

Non-manipulable variables

As was noted at the beginning of the section on experimental design, in much, if not most, business research it is not possible to manipulate the variables, which we find interesting. This is why most positivist quantitative business research employs a cross-sectional research design rather than an experimental one. Moreover, some of the variables in which social scientists are interested, and which are often viewed as potentially significant independent variables, simply cannot be manipulated, other than by extreme measures. At the individual level of analysis, age, ethnicity, gender, and social backgrounds are 'givens' that are not really amenable to the kind of manipulation that is necessary for a true experimental design. To a lesser extent this also applies at the organizational level of analysis to variables such as size, structure, technology, and culture. On the other hand, the very fact that we can regard certain variables as givens provides us with a clue as to how we can make causal inferences in cross-sectional research. Many of the variables in which we are interested can be *assumed* to be temporally prior to other variables. For example, we can assume that, if we find a relationship between gender and entrepreneurial behaviour, then the former is more likely to be the independent variable because it is likely to be temporally prior to entrepreneurial behaviour. In other words, while we may not be able to manipulate the gender variable, we can draw some causal inferences from cross-sectional data.

Structure of the cross-sectional design

The cross-sectional research design is not easy to depict in terms of the notation previously introduced, but Figure 4.2 captures its main features, except that in this case Obs simply represents an observation made in relation to a variable.

Figure 4.2 implies that a cross-sectional design comprises the collection of data on a series of variables (Obs_1, Obs_2, Obs_3, Obs_4, Obs_5, ... Obs_n) at a single point in time, T_1. The effect is to create what Marsh (1982) referred to as a 'rectangle' of data that comprises variables Obs_1 to Obs_n and cases $case_1$ to $case_n$, as in Figure 4.3. For each case (which may be a person, household, city, nation, etc.) data are available for each of the variables, Obs_1 to Obs_n, all of which will have been collected at T_1. Each cell in the matrix will have data in it.

Cross-sectional design and research strategy

This discussion of the cross-sectional design has placed it firmly in the context of positivist quantitative research. It

should also be noted, however, that qualitative research often entails a form of cross-sectional design. A fairly typical form of such research is when the researcher employs unstructured interviewing or semi-structured interviewing with a number of people. Web Research in focus 4.1 provides an illustration of such a study.

While not typical of the qualitative research tradition, the study described in Web Research in focus 4.8 bears some research design similarities with cross-sectional studies within a predominantly quantitative research tradition, like the WERS (see Web Research in focus 4.1), while retaining some research design features more typi-

Figure 4.2

A cross-sectional design

T_1
Obs_1
Obs_2
Obs_3
Obs_4
Obs_5
. . .
Obs_n

Figure 4.3

The data rectangle in cross-sectional research

	Obs_1	Obs_2	Obs_3	Obs_4	. . .	Obs_n
$Case_1$						
$Case_2$						
$Case_3$						
$Case_4$						
$Case_5$						
. . .						
$Case_n$						

cal of qualitative studies. The research was not directly preoccupied with such criteria of positivist quantitative research as internal and external validity, replicability, measurement validity, and so on, but it is clear that the researchers took considerable care to ensure the *representativeness* of their sample of managers in relation to the overall population. In fact, it could be argued that the use of interview as a follow-up method after the initial questionnaire survey made the study more ecologically valid than research that just uses more formal instruments of data collection. It is common within business and management research to see such a *triangulated* approach, where attempts are made to cancel out the limitations of one method by the use of another in order to cross-check the findings. Hence, cross-sectional studies in business and management tend not to be so clearly divided into those that use either quantitative or qualitative data.

Longitudinal design(s)

The **longitudinal** design represents a distinct form of research design that is typically used to map change in business and management research. Pettigrew (1990) has emphasized the importance of longitudinal study in understanding organizations as a way of providing data on the mechanisms and processes through which changes are created. Such a 'contextualist' research design involves drawing on 'phenomena at vertical and horizontal levels of analysis and the interconnections between those levels through time' (1990, p. 269). However, partly because of the time and cost involved, longitudinal design is relatively little used in business and management research. In the form in which it is typically found, it is usually an extension of social survey research based on **self-completion questionnaire** or **structured interview** research within a cross-sectional design. Consequently, in terms of reliability, replication, and validity, the longitudinal design is little different from cross-sectional research. However, a longitudinal design can allow some insight into the time order of variables and, therefore, may be more able to allow causal inferences to be made. This was one of the aims of the WERS series (see Web Research in focus 4.1).

With a longitudinal design a sample is surveyed and is surveyed again on at least one further occasion. It is common to distinguish two types of longitudinal design: the *panel study* and the *cohort study*. With the former type, a sample, often a randomly selected national one, is the focus of data collection on at least two (and often more) occasions. Data may be collected from different types of case within a panel study framework: individuals, organizations, and so on. An illustration of this kind of study is incorporated into the 2004 WERS (see Web Research in focus 4.1).

The cohort study selects either an entire cohort of people or a randomly selected sample of them as the focus of data collection. The *cohort* is made up of people who share a certain characteristic, such as all being born in the same week or having a certain experience, such as being unemployed or getting married on a certain day or in the same week. However, this design is rarely used in business and management research.

Panel and cohort studies share similar features. They have a similar design structure: Figure 4.4 portrays this structure and implies that data are collected in at least two waves on the same variables on the same people or organizations. They are both concerned with illuminating social change and improving the understanding of causal influences over time. The latter means that longitudinal designs are somewhat better able to deal with the problem of ambiguity about the direction of causal influence that plagues cross-sectional designs. Because certain potentially independent variables can be identified at T_1, the researcher is in a better position to infer that purported effects that are identified at T_2 or later have occurred *after* the independent variables. This does not deal with the entire problem about the ambiguity of causal influence, but it at least addresses the problem of knowing which variable came first. In all other respects, the points made above about cross-sectional designs are the same as those for longitudinal designs.

Panel and cohort studies share similar problems. First, there is the problem of sample attrition through employee job changes, companies going out of business, and so on, and through subjects choosing to withdraw at later stages of the research. The 1998 WERS panel survey, for example, traced a random selection of workplaces from the 1990 sur-

Figure 4.4

The longitudinal design

$$
\begin{array}{ccc}
T_1 & \ldots & T_n \\
Obs_1 & & Obs_1 \\
Obs_2 & & Obs_2 \\
Obs_3 & & Obs_3 \\
Obs_4 & & Obs_4 \\
Obs_5 & & Obs_5 \\
\ldots & & \ldots \\
Obs_n & & Obs_n \\
\end{array}
$$

vey for re-interview. This yielded a sample of 846 'continuing workplaces', a response rate of 82%, which effectively minimized potential bias through attrition. A continuing workplace was defined as one that employed 25 or more people and had continued to operate between 1990 and 1998. However, changes in activity, ownership, or location were not considered critically to impair this concept of continuity. The problem with attrition is largely that those who leave the study may differ in some important respects from those who remain, so that the latter do not form a representative group. In order to account even more fully for this possibility, the WERS panel survey was accompanied by a short telephone survey of all remaining workplaces from the 1990 cross-section not included in the panel survey. The researchers wanted to know how many of the 1990 cross-section sample workplaces had survived, whether they had expanded, moved premises, changed ownership, or amalgamated with or split from another establishment since the time of the 1990 study. This enabled them to build up a more general picture of the survival status of workplaces, which helped to enhance the internal validity of the panel study. Secondly, there are few guidelines as to when is the best juncture to conduct further waves of data collection. Thirdly, it is often suggested that many longitudinal studies are poorly thought out and that they result in the collection of large amounts of data with little apparent planning. Fourthly, there is evidence that a *panel conditioning* effect can occur whereby continued participation in a longitudinal study affects how respondents behave.

Case study design

The basic case study entails the detailed and intensive analysis of a single case. As Stake (1995) observes, case study research is concerned with the complexity and particular nature of the case in question. Some of the best-known studies in business and management research are based on this kind of design. A case can be:

- *A single organization*, such as Pettigrew's (1985; see Web Research in focus 4.9) research at Imperial Chemical Industries (ICI), Joanne Martin's (1992) study of organizational culture at 'OzCo', a high-technology industry company based in California, or Durepos's (2009) study of the creation of an interest driven corporate history of Pan American Airlines.
- *A single location*, such as a factory, production site, or office building—for example, Pollert's (1981; see Web Research in focus 17.6) research in a tobacco factory, or Linstead's (1985) study of humour in a bakery.
- *A person*, like in Marshall's (1995) study of women managers where each woman constitutes a separate case—such studies are characterized as using the life history or biographical approach.
- *A single event*, such as the NASA space shuttle *Challenger* disaster in 1986 (Vaughan, 1990; see Chapter 21) or the events surrounding a pipeline accident in Canada (Gephart 1993).

What is a case?

The most common use of the term associates the case study with a location, such as a workplace or organization. The emphasis tends to be upon an intensive examination of the setting. There is a tendency to associate case studies with qualitative research, but such an identification is not appropriate. It is certainly true that exponents of the case study design often favour qualitative methods, such as participant observation and **unstructured interviewing**, because these methods are viewed as particularly helpful in the generation of an intensive, detailed examination of a case. For example, Knights and McCabe (1997) suggest that the case study provides a vehicle through which several qualitative methods can be combined, thereby avoiding too great a reliance on one single approach. In their study of quality management in a UK retail bank, they were able to combine participant observation with semi-structured interviewing and documentary data collection of company reports, TQM management guides, and newsletters. Knights and McCabe (1997) suggest that the findings from the case study can be used to identify insights into why so many quality management programs have failed. However, case studies are frequently sites for the employment of both quantitative and qualitative research, an approach that will receive attention in Chapter 7. Indeed, in some instances, when an investigation is based exclusively upon quantitative research, it can be difficult to determine whether it is better described as a case study or as a cross-sectional research design. The same point can often be made about case studies based upon qualitative research.

With a case study, the case is an object of interest in its own right and the researcher aims to provide an in-depth elucidation of it. Unless a distinction of this or some other kind is drawn, it becomes impossible to distinguish the case study as a special research design, because almost any kind of research can be construed as a case study. However, it also needs to be appreciated that, when specific research illustrations are examined, they can exhibit features of more than one research design. What distinguishes a case study is that the researcher is usually concerned to uncover the unique features of the case. This is known as an *idiographic* approach. Research designs like the cross-sectional design are known as *nomothetic* in that they are concerned with generating statements that apply regardless of time and place.

With experimental and cross-sectional designs, the typical orientation to the relationship between theory and research is a **deductive** one. The research design and the collection of data are guided by specific research questions that derive from theoretical concerns. However, when a qualitative research strategy is employed within a cross-sectional design, the approach tends to be **inductive**. In other words, whether a cross-sectional design is inductive or deductive tends to be affected by which type of research strategy is employed. The same point can be made of case study research. When the predominant re-

search strategy is qualitative, a case study tends to take an inductive approach to the relationship between theory and research. If a predominantly quantitative strategy is taken, it tends to be deductive.

Reliability, replicability, and validity

The question of how well the case study fares in the context of the research design criteria cited early on in this chapter—measurement validity, internal validity, external validity, ecological validity, reliability, and replicability—depends in large part on how far the researcher feels that these are appropriate for the evaluation of case study research. Some writers on case study research, like Yin (1984), consider that they are appropriate criteria and suggest ways in which case study research can be developed to enhance its ability to meet the criteria; for others, like Stake (1995), they are barely mentioned if at all. A third category of authors, such as Yue (2009), take the approach that the concerns which underlay the criteria are important, but their specific application to any given case study is determined largely by the epistemological stance of the researcher. Traditionally, writers on case study research, whose point of orientation lies primarily with a qualitative research strategy, tend to play down or ignore the salience of these factors, whereas those writers who have been strongly influenced by the quantitative research strategy tend to depict them as more significant.

However, one question on which a great deal of discussion has centered concerns the **external validity** or **generalizability** of case study research. How can a single case possibly be representative so that it might yield findings that can be applied more generally to other cases? For example, how could the findings from Pettigrew's (1985) research into ICI (see Web Research in focus 4.8), be generalizable to all large multinational pharmaceutical corporations? The answer, of course, is that they cannot. It is important to appreciate that case study researchers do not delude themselves that it is possible to identify typical cases that can be used to represent a certain class of objects, whether it is factories, managers, or critical events. In other words, they do not think that a case study is a sample of one.

However, although many researchers emphasize that they are interested in the detail of a single case, they do sometimes claim a degree of theoretical generalizability on the basis of it. For example, in her study of Indsco Supply Corporation, Kanter (1977) explains that the case enabled her to generate concepts and give meaning to abstract propositions, which she then sought to test in three other large corporations. It is, therefore, clear that she is seeking to achieve a degree of theoretical generalizability from this case.

Types of case

Following on from the issue of external validity, it is useful to consider a distinction between different types of case that is sometimes made by writers. Yin (2003) distinguishes five types:

- The *critical case*. Here the researcher has a clearly specified hypothesis, and a case is chosen on the grounds that it will allow a better understanding of the circumstances in which the hypothesis will and will not hold.
- The *unique case*. The unique or extreme case is, as Yin observes, a common focus in clinical studies.
- The *revelatory case*. The basis for the revelatory case exists 'when an investigator has an opportunity to observe and analyze a phenomenon previously inaccessible to scientific investigation' (Yin, 1984, p. 44). While the idea of the revelatory case is interesting, it seems unnecessary to restrict it solely to situations in which something has not previously been studied. Much qualitative case study research that is carried out with a predominantly inductive approach to theory treats single case studies as broadly 'revelatory'.
- The *representative* or *typical case*. This type seeks to explore a case that exemplifies an everyday situation or form of organization.
- The *longitudinal case*. This type of case is concerned with how a situation changes over time.

Any particular study can involve a combination of these elements, which can be viewed as rationales for choosing particular cases.

Exponents of case study research counter suggestions that the evidence they present is limited because it has restricted external validity by arguing that it is not the purpose of this research design to generalize to other cases or to populations beyond the case. This position is very different from that taken by practitioners of **survey research**. Survey researchers are invariably concerned about being able to generalize their findings to larger populations and frequently use random sampling to enhance the representativeness of the samples on which they conduct their investigations and, therefore, the external validity of their findings. Case study researchers argue strenuously that this is not the purpose of their craft.

Case study as intensive analysis

Instead, case study researchers tend to argue that they aim to generate an intensive examination of a single case, in relation to which they then engage in a theoretical analysis. The central issue of concern is the quality of the theoretical reasoning in which the case study researcher engages. How well do the data support the theoretical arguments that are generated? Is the theoretical analysis incisive? For example, does it demonstrate connections between different conceptual ideas that are developed out of the data? The crucial question is not whether or not the findings can be generalized to a wider universe, but how well the researcher generates theory out of the findings (Mitchell, 1983; Yin, 1984). Such a view places case study research firmly in the inductive tradition of the relationship between theory and research. However, a case study design is not necessarily associated with an inductive approach, as can be seen in the research by Whittington (1989), which was referred to in Chapter 3. Thus, case studies can be associated with both theory generation and theory testing.

More than one case

Case study research is not restricted to the study of a single case. Multiple-case study designs have become increasingly common in business and management research. They are extensions of the case study design. The multiple-case study design is considered in the section on 'Comparative design' because multiple-case studies are largely undertaken for the purpose of comparing the cases that are included. As such, they allow the researcher to compare and contrast the findings deriving from each of the cases. This, in turn, encourages researchers to consider what is unique and what is common across cases, and frequently promotes theoretical reflection on the findings.

It might be asked what the difference is between a multiple-case study involving several cases and a cross-sectional design. After all, if an investigation involved, say, eight cases, it could be viewed as either a multiple-case study involving several cases or as a cross-sectional design. A simple rule of thumb is to ask: 'What is the focus?' If the focus is on the cases and their unique contexts, it is a multiple-case study and, as such, is an extension of the case study approach. If the emphasis is on producing general findings, with little regard for the unique contexts of each of the eight cases, it is better viewed as a cross-sectional design. In other words, with a multiple-case study design the emphasis is on the individual case; with a cross-sectional design, it is on the sample of cases.

Longitudinal research and the case study

Case study research frequently includes a longitudinal element. The researcher is often a participant of an organization for many months or years. Alternatively, he or she may conduct interviews with individuals over a lengthy period. Moreover, the researcher may be able to inject an additional longitudinal element by analyzing archival information and by retrospective interviewing. Web Research in focus 4.9 provides an illustration of longitudinal case study research.

Another way in which a longitudinal element occurs is when a case that has been studied is returned to at a later stage. An interesting instance of this is Burawoy's (1979) study of a factory in Chicago, which he claims was the same one as originally studied by Roy in the 1950s. This is a somewhat loose connection, however, as the theoretical focus adopted by the two researchers was markedly different, although their research methods, based on participant observation, were quite similar. A further example of longitudinal research carried out by different researchers is given in Web Research in focus 4.10. This study is interesting because it relies on social survey methods in addition to preliminary interviews with managers, union officials, and employees. Generally speaking, however, it is difficult for the researcher to establish how far change is the result of real differences over the two time periods or of other factors, such as different people in the organization, different ownership of the company between the two time periods, and the possible influence of the initial study itself.

Comparative design

It is worth distinguishing one further kind of design: comparative design. Put simply, this design entails the study using more or less identical methods of two or more contrasting cases. It embodies the logic of comparison in that it implies that we can understand social phenomena better when they are compared in relation to two or more meaningfully contrasting cases or situations. The **comparative design** may be realized in the context of either quantitative or qualitative research. Within the former, the data collection strategy will take the form outlined in Figure 4.5. This figure implies that there are at least two cases (which may be organizations, nations, people, etc.) and that data are collected from each usually within a cross-sectional design format.

One of the more obvious forms of such research is in cross-cultural or cross-national research (see Key concept 4.7). In a useful definition, Hantrais (1996) has suggested that such research occurs when individuals or teams set out to examine particular issues or phenomena in two or more countries with the express intention of comparing their manifestations in different socio-cultural settings (institutions, customs, traditions, value systems, life-styles, language, thought patterns), using the same research instruments either to carry out secondary analysis of national data or to conduct new empirical work. The aim may be to seek explanations for similarities and differences or to gain a greater awareness and a deeper understanding of social reality in different national contexts.

Cross-cultural research in business and management tends to presuppose that culture is a major explanatory variable that exerts a profound influence on organizational behaviour. In business and management research there has been a tendency in recent years to question the adaptability of many management theories and practices to other, particularly non-Western, cultural contexts. There has also been mounting criticism of the universalist vision that business and management research has promoted, based predominantly on unacknowledged Anglo-Saxon values. These pressures have led to greater interest in cross-cultural research. Within this overall category, however, there are some important distinctions. International management research concerns itself with how and why companies internation-

Figure 4.5

A comparative design

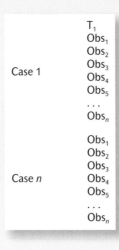

ize, it may focus on a specific country or make cross-cultural comparisons between several countries. Usunier (1998) distinguishes between:

- *cross-cultural approaches* —which compare national management systems and local business customs in various countries; and
- *intercultural approaches*—which focus on the study of interaction between people and organizations with different national/cultural backgrounds.

Comparative research should not be treated as solely concerned with comparisons between nations. The logic of comparison can be applied to a variety of situations to inform a number of levels of analysis. For example, Hofstede's (1984) research on cultural differences has informed a generation of studies that have explored cultural differences in organizations other than IBM and the framework has also been applied to understanding specific organizational behaviours, such as ethical decision making.

Key concept 4.7: What is cross-cultural and international research?

As its name implies, cross-cultural research entails the collection and/or analysis of data from two or more nations.

Cross-cultural research is not without problems such as: managing and gaining the funding for such research (see Key concept 4.7); ensuring when existing data, such as official statistics or survey evidence, are submitted to a secondary analysis, that the data are comparable in terms of categories and data-collection methods; and ensuring, when new data are being collected, that the need to translate data-collection instruments (for example, interview schedules) does not undermine genuine comparability. This raises the further difficulty that, even when translation is carried out competently, there is still the potential problem of an insensitivity to specific national and cultural contexts. On the other hand, cross-cultural research helps to reduce the risk of failing to appreciate that social science findings are often, if not invariably, culturally specific. Cross-cultural research also creates particular issues in achieving equivalence between the samples, variables, and methods that are used (McDonald, 2000). For example, in many cases nationality is used as a surrogate for culture; differences may thus be attributed to culture even if they could be more readily attributed to national situation. Equally, people inhabiting a country under the same government may belong to quite different cultures that reflect historical or religious affiliations. Further issues are raised by language differences, which can cause translation problems. Adler (1983) claims that many comparative cross-cultural studies in business and management do not adequately acknowledge these distinctions.

In terms of issues of reliability, validity, replicability, and generalizability, the comparative study is no different from the cross-sectional design. The comparative design is essentially two or more cross-sectional studies carried out at more or less the same point in time.

The comparative design can also be applied in relation to a research strategy employing qualitative data. When this occurs, it takes the form of a multiple-case study (see Web Research in focus 4.11). Essentially, a multiple-case (or multi-case) study occurs whenever the number of cases examined exceeds one. In business research this is a popular research design that usually takes two or more organizations as cases for comparison, but occasionally a number of people are used as cases. For example, MacMillan (2009) adopts a multiple-case study approach in his study of individuals' existential sense of meaning in work and life. He retains a focus on intensive examination of each case but there is qualitative comparison of each individual's situation with that of other individuals. The main argument in favour of the multiple-case study is that it improves theory building. By comparing two or more cases, the researcher is in a better position to establish the circumstances in which a theory will or will not hold (Yin, 1984; Eisenhardt, 1989). Moreover, the comparison may itself suggest concepts that are relevant to an emerging theory.

Web Research in focus 4.11 describes one approach to selecting cases for a multiple-case study that involved researchers in each country selecting two workplaces from retail and financial service sectors. Another example is found in the study of TQM by Edwards, Collinson, and Rees (1998) (see Web Research in focus 7.2), where the researchers selected two case studies from three main sectors of the UK economy: private services, public sector, and manufacturing. Their selection of two cases in each sector, rather than just one, was intended to allow for variation; the limitation to two cases, rather than three, was due to time and resource constraints. To identify their cases the researchers searched press reports and listings of leading quality institutes such as the National Society for Quality through Teamwork. However, they were also keen to avoid companies that had a high profile as 'success stories', instead choosing cases that 'had made significant moves' in quality management but 'were not among the leading edge examples' (1998, p. 454). From this they identified 25 potential cases and on the basis of interviews with quality or HR managers in each one, narrowed their sample down to just six. With a case selection approach such as this, the findings that are common to the firms can be just as interesting and important as those that differentiate them.

However, not all writers are convinced about the merits of multiple-case study research. Dyer and Wilkins (1991), for example, argue that a multiple-case study approach tends to mean that the researcher pays less attention to the specific context and more to the ways in which the cases can be contrasted. Moreover, the need to forge comparisons tends to mean that the researcher needs to develop an explicit focus at the outset, whereas it may be advantageous to adopt a more open-ended approach in many instances. These concerns about retaining contextual insight and a rather more unstructured research approach are very much associated with the goals of the qualitative research strategy (see Chapter 6).

The key to the comparative design is its ability to allow the distinguishing characteristics of two or more cases to act as a springboard for theoretical reflections about contrasting findings. It is something of a hybrid, in that in quantitative research it is frequently an extension of a cross-sectional design and in qualitative research it is frequently an extension of a case study design. It even exhibits certain features that are similar to experiments and **quasi-experiments**, which also rely on the capacity to forge a comparison.

Level of analysis

A further consideration for business researchers that applies to the research designs covered in this chapter relates to the concept of level; in other words, what is the primary unit of measurement and analysis? Hence, research might focus on:

- *Individuals*—this would include studies that focus on specific kinds of individuals such as managers or employees;
- *Groups*—this would include research that considered certain types of groupings for example, HR departments or boards of directors;
- *Organizations*—in addition to studies that focused on companies, this would include surveys, such as WERS (see Web Research in focus 4.1) which treat the workplace as the principal unit of analysis;
- *Societies*—the main focus of this kind of analysis would be on the national, political, social, environmental, and economic contexts in which business organizations are located.

Differences in level of analysis are commonly referred to in terms of the SOGI model (societies, organizations, groups, and individuals). However, some research designs draw on samples that combine different levels of analysis—for example, organizations and departments. This begs the question as to whether it is possible to combine data from different levels to produce a meaningful analysis. The complexity of organizational types can make the issue of level particularly difficult to determine. Rousseau (1985) suggests that it is important to make explicit the problems of using data derived from one level to represent something at another level in order to avoid misinterpretation. For example, processes of individual and organizational learning may be constructed quite differently at different levels. If researchers make inferences about organizational learning on the basis of data about individuals, they are at risk of making a cross-level misattribution. Since the phenomenon of learning is an essentially human characteristic, and being that organizations don't behave but people do, this leads to the attribution of human characteristics to a higher-level system. Misattribution can also occur when metaphors are used to interpret organizational behaviour. It is, therefore, good practice to identify and make clear in your research design the level of analysis that is being used and then to switch to another level only after having made this clear (Rousseau, 1985).

Another illustration of mixed-level research cited by Rousseau (1985) is found in the area of leadership studies. The average leadership style (ALS) approach assumes that leaders display the same behavioural style towards all subordinates. Research, therefore, relies on eliciting subordinate perceptions of the leader, which are averaged and treated as group-level characteristics. In contrast, the vertical dyadic linkage (VDL) model assumes that a leader's style may be different with each subordinate, thereby treating leadership as an individual-level phenomenon rather than as a group one. Each model thus conceptualizes leadership at a different level.

Bringing research strategy and research design together

Finally, we can bring together the six research strategies covered in Chapter 3 with the research designs outlined in this chapter. Table 4.1 shows the typical form associated with each combination of type of data (i.e., qualitative or quantitative) and research design as well as a number of examples that either have been encountered so far or will be covered in later chapters. Table 4.1 refers also to research methods that will be encountered in later chapters, but which have not been referred to so far. The Glossary will give you a quick reference to terms used that are not yet familiar to you.

When Table 4.1 is examined in conjunction with the fundamental differences between positivist and postpositivist research strategies (see Table 3.2) we can now understand that both the researcher's foundational assumptions about the world around them combined with the type of data and research design offers many possible combinations. Indeed the distinctions between such intersections are not always perfect. In particular, in some qualitative and quantitative research it is not obvious whether a study is an example of a longitudinal design or a case study design. **Life history** studies, research that concentrates on a specific issue over time,

Table 4.1   Research strategy and research design

Research design	Research strategy	
	Quantitative	Qualitative
Experimental	*Typical form.* Most researchers using an experimental design employ quantitative comparisons between experimental and control groups with regard to the dependent variable. See, for example, the study of leadership by Howell and Frost (1989).	*No typical form.* However, the Hawthorne experiments provide an example of experimental research design that gradually moved away from the 'test room method' towards use of qualitative methods. Howell and Frost (1989).
Cross-sectional	*Typical form.* Social survey research or structured observation on a sample at a single point in time. See, for example, the Aston studies of organizational size, technology, and structure; Powell's research into TQM programmes in US firms; and Berg and Frost's (2005) telephone survey of low-skill, low-wage workers. This can also include content analysis on a sample of documents such as in Kabanoff, Waldersee, and Cohen's (1995) study of organizational values.	*Typical form.* Qualitative interviews or focus groups at a single point in time. For example, Scase and Goffee's (1989) research into managers in large UK organizations; or Blackburn and Stokes' (2000) study of small business owner-managers. Can also be based upon qualitative content analysis of a set of documents relating to a single event or a specific period in time such as in Gephart's (1993) study of an organizational disaster.

Table 4.1 *Continued*

Research design	Research strategy	
	Quantitative	Qualitative
Longitudinal	*Typical form.* Social survey research on a sample on more than one occasion, as in the five Workplace Employee Relations Surveys; the 1997 and 2001 Skills Survey; or may involve content analysis of documents relating to different time periods such as in Boyce and Lepper's (2002) study of information in a joint venture involving two shipping firms between 1904 and 1975.	*Typical form.* Ethnographic research over a long period, qualitative interviewing on more than one occasion, or qualitative content analysis of documents relating to different time periods. Such research warrants being dubbed longitudinal when there is a concern to map change, such as in Pettigrew's study of ICI or in the Work Foundation's study of what happened to workers following the closure of the MG Rover plant in Longbridge.
Case study	*Typical form.* Social survey research on a single case with a view to revealing important features about its nature. Examples include Hofstede's study of cultural differences based on a survey study of a large multinational business organization; and Sørensen's (2004) study of the racial composition of workplaces based on a large multidivisional financial services institution.	*Typical form.* The intensive study by ethnography or qualitative interviewing of a single case, which may be an organization—such as Sackmann's (1992) study of organizational subculture in a medium-sized US conglomerate; a group of employees within an organization—as in Perlow's (1999) study of software engineers in a high-tech organization; or an individual—as in Marshall's (1995) study of women managers.
Comparative	*Typical form.* Social survey research in which there is a direct comparison between two or more cases, including cross-cultural research. Examples include Brengman et al.'s (2005) study of Internet shoppers in the United States and Belgium; and Tüselmann, McDonald, and Heise's (2002) study of German multinational companies operating in an Anglo-Saxon setting.	*Typical form.* Ethnographic or qualitative interview research on two or more cases where some comparison is sought between them, such as in Hyde et al.'s (2006) evaluation study of role redesign in the NHS; and Collins and Wickham's (2004) panel study of patterns of female employment across Europe.

and ethnography, in which the researcher charts change in a single case, are examples of studies that cross the two types. Such studies are perhaps better conceptualized as longitudinal case studies rather than as belonging to one category of research design or another. A further point to note is that there is no typical form in the qualitative research strategy/ experimental research design cell. Qualitative research in the context of true experiments is very unusual. However, as noted in the table, the Hawthorne studies (Roethlisberger & Dickson, 1939) provide an interesting example of the way that a quasi-experimental research design can change over

time. What you will also notice as you encounter many of the examples in this book is that business research designs often use a combination of quantitative and qualitative methods, so the distinction between quantitative and qualitative research strategies that is suggested in Table 4.1 is rarely as clear as this table suggests. In Chapter 7 of the book we will consider the implications of this and discuss the implications of research that combines quantitative and qualitative methods. Increasingly, research that combines quantitative and qualitative research, whether positivist or postpositivist in nature, is referred to as mixed methods research.

Key points

- There is an important distinction between a research method and a research design.
- It is necessary to become thoroughly familiar with the meaning of the technical terms used as criteria for evaluating research: reliability; validity; replicability; and the types of validity (measurement, internal, external, ecological).

- It is also necessary to be familiar with the differences between the five major research designs covered (experimental, cross-sectional, longitudinal, case study, and comparative) and to consider the level of analysis (individual, group, organization, and market) that research may focus on. In this context, it is important to realize that the term 'experiment', which is often used somewhat loosely in everyday speech, has a specific technical meaning.
- There are various potential threats to validity in non-experimental research.
- Although the case study is often thought to be a single type of research design it, in fact, has several forms. It is also important to be aware of the key issues concerned with the nature of case study evidence in relation to issues like external validity (generalizability).

Questions for review

- In terms of the definitions used in this book, what are the chief differences between each of the following: a research method; a research strategy; and a research design?

Criteria in business research

- What are the differences between reliability and validity and why are these important criteria for the evaluation of business research?
- Outline the meaning of each of the following: measurement validity; internal validity; external validity; and ecological validity.
- Why have some qualitative researchers sought to devise alternative criteria from reliability and validity when assessing the quality of investigations?
- What is the 'experimenter effect' and how might it contribute towards bias?
- What is social desirability bias and how might its effects be reduced?

Research designs

- What are the main research designs that have been outlined in this chapter?
- Why is level of analysis a particular consideration in business and management research?
- 'The main importance of the experimental design for the business researcher is that it represents a model of how to infer causal connections between variables.' Discuss.
- Following on from the last question, if it is so useful and important, why is it not used more?
- What is a quasi-experiment?

Cross-sectional design

- What is meant by a cross-sectional research design?
- In what ways does the social survey exemplify the cross-sectional research design?
- Assess the degree to which the survey researcher can achieve internally valid findings.
- To what extent is the survey design exclusive to quantitative research?

Longitudinal design(s)

- Why might a longitudinal research design be superior to a cross-sectional one?
- What are the main differences between panel and cohort designs in longitudinal research?

Case study design

- What is a case study?
- Is case study research exclusive to qualitative research?
- What are some of the principles by which cases might be selected?

Comparative design

- What are the chief strengths of a comparative research design?
- Why might comparative research yield important insights?

Bringing research strategy and research design together

- What are the main characteristics of the research designs and research strategies outlined in Table 4.1?

5

The Nature of Quantitative Research

Chapter guide

This chapter is concerned with the characteristics of **quantitative research**, an approach that has been the dominant strategy for conducting business research, although its influence has waned slightly since the mid-1980s when **qualitative research** became more common. Nevertheless, quantitative research continues to exert a powerful influence in business research. The emphasis in this chapter is very much on what quantitative research typically entails, although at a later point in the chapter the ways in which there are frequent departures from this ideal are outlined. This chapter explores:

- The main steps of quantitative research, which are presented as a linear series of stages.
- The importance of concepts in quantitative research and the ways in which measures may be devised for concepts; this discussion includes a discussion of the important idea of an *indicator*, which is devised as a way of measuring a concept for which there is no direct measure.
- The procedures for checking the **reliability** and **validity** of the measurement process.
- The main preoccupations of quantitative research, which are described in terms of four features: **measurement**, **causality**, **generalization**, and **replication**.
- Some criticisms that are frequently leveled at quantitative research.

Introduction

In Chapter 3 quantitative research was outlined as a distinctive research strategy. In very broad terms, it was described as:

- Entailing the collection of numerical data.
- Viewing of the relationship between theory and research as deductive.
- Having affinity for a natural science approach (and of positivism in particular).
- Having an objectivist conception of social reality.

A number of other features of quantitative research were outlined, but in this chapter we will be examining the strategy in much more detail.

It should be quite clear by now that the description of a research strategy as 'quantitative research' should not be taken to mean that the quantification of aspects of social life is all that distinguishes it from a qualitative research strategy. The very fact that it has a distinctive **epistemological** and **ontological** position suggests that there is a good deal more to it than just the presence of numbers. In this chapter, the main steps in quantitative research will be outlined. We will also examine some of the principal preoccupations of the strategy and how certain issues of concern among practitioners are addressed, like the concerns about measurement validity.

The main steps in quantitative research

Figure 5.1 outlines the main steps in quantitative research. This is very much an idealized and typical account of the process: it is probably never or rarely found in this pure form, but it represents a useful starting point for getting to grips with the main ingredients of the approach and the links between them. Research is rarely as linear and as straightforward as the figure implies, but its aim is to do no more than capture the main steps and to provide a rough indication of their interconnections.

Some of the principle steps have been covered in the preceding four chapters. The fact that we start off with theory signifies that a broadly deductive approach to the

Figure 5.1

The process of quantitative research

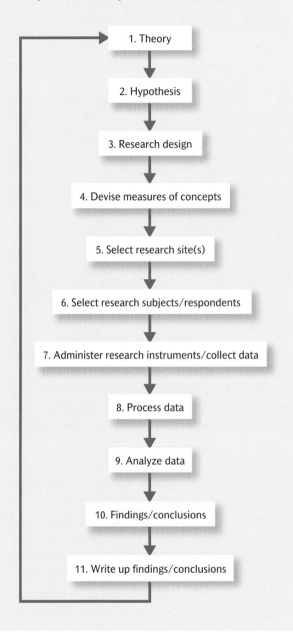

1. Theory

2. Hypothesis

3. Research design

4. Devise measures of concepts

5. Select research site(s)

6. Select research subjects/respondents

7. Administer research instruments/collect data

8. Process data

9. Analyze data

10. Findings/conclusions

11. Write up findings/conclusions

search does not entail the specification of a hypothesis. Instead theory acts, loosely, as a set of concerns in relation to which the business researcher collects data. The specification of a **hypothesis** to be tested is especially likely to be found in **experimental** research. Although other research designs sometimes entail the testing of **hypotheses**, as a general rule, we tend to find that Step 2 is more likely to be found in experimental research.

The next step entails the selection of a **research design**, a topic that was explored in Chapter 4. As we have seen, the selection of research design has implications for a variety of issues, such as the **external validity** of findings and researchers' ability to attribute causality to their findings. Step 4 entails devising measures of the concepts in which the researcher is interested. This process is often referred to as **operationalization**, a term that originally derives from physics to refer to the operations by which a concept (such as temperature or velocity) is measured (Bridgman, 1927). Aspects of this issue will be explored later on in this chapter.

The next two steps entail the selection of a research site or sites and then the selection of subjects/respondents. (Experimental researchers tend to call the people on Figure 5.1 whom they conduct research 'subjects', whereas social survey researchers typically call them 'respondents'.) Thus, in **social survey research** an investigator must first be concerned to establish an appropriate setting for his or her research. A number of decisions may be involved. Research in focus 5.1 provides an example of research that involved specific choices regarding what size of organization and what industry groups of organizations would provide a comprehensive **sample** of medium-large Canadian organizations that were likely to have conducted permanent reductions of the workforce.

Step 7 involves the administration of the research instruments. In experimental research, this is likely to entail pre-testing subjects, manipulating the **independent variable** for the experimental group, and post-testing respondents. In cross-sectional research using social survey research instruments, it will involve interviewing the sample members by **structured interview** schedule or distributing a **self-completion questionnaire**. In research using structured observation, this step will mean an ob-

relationship between theory and research is taken. It is common for outlines of the main steps of quantitative research to suggest that a hypothesis is deduced from the theory and is tested. This notion has been incorporated into Figure 5.1. However, a great deal of quantitative re-

5.1 Research in Focus

Selecting research sites and sampling respondents: Factors affecting Canadian permanent workforce reduction

Wagar's 1997 investigation of factors affecting permanent workforce reduction in medium to large Canadian organizations involved surveying senior human resource managers of organizations of 100 or more employees in the following industry groups: manufacturing, wholesale and retail trade, communication and transportation, finance and insurance, other business services, health, and education. These industry groups were chosen to broadly reflect the Canadian context in terms of the firm size that Wagar was investigating.

The survey was sent out using a mailing list generated by Dun and Bradstreet and asked Human Resource managers or CEO's (or that the survey be forwarded to the appropriate respondent) about the following:

- Permanent workforce reduction in terms of size and strategies.

- Economic conditions based upon market demand for each organization.
- Change in corporate strategy or management.
- Merger or acquisition involvement.
- Introduction of new technology that would impact labour.
- The size and organizational sector grouping.
- The organizational commitment to formal training and job security.
- The presence of a union.

These efforts resulted in a response rate of approximately 35%, or 1282 organizations. This example shows clearly the ways in which researchers make decisions about selecting research site(s) and samples.

server (or possibly more than one) watching the setting and the behaviour of people and then assigning categories to each element of behaviour.

Step 8 simply refers to the fact that, once information has been collected, it must be transformed into 'data'. In the context of quantitative research, this is likely to mean that it must be prepared so that it can be quantified. With some information this can be done in a relatively straightforward way—for example, for information relating to such things as people's ages, incomes, number of years spent at school, and so on. For other **variables**, quantification will entail **coding** the information—that is, transforming it into numbers to facilitate the **quantitative** analysis of the data, particularly if the analysis is going to be carried out by computer. **Codes** act as tags that are placed on data about people to allow the information to be processed by the computer. This consideration leads into Step 9—the analysis of the data. In this step, the researcher uses a number of techniques of quantitative data analysis to reduce the amount of data collected, to test

for relationships between variables, to develop ways of presenting the results of the analysis to others, and so on.

On the basis of the analysis of the data, the researcher must interpret the results of the analysis. It is at this stage that the 'findings' will emerge. The researcher will consider the connections between the findings that emerge out of Step 8 and the various concerns and interests that formed the rationale for the research in the first place. If there is a hypothesis, is it supported? What are the implications of the findings for the theoretical ideas that formed the background to the research?

Then the research must be written up. It cannot take on significance beyond satisfying the researcher's personal curiosity until it enters the public domain in some way by being written up as a paper to be read at a conference or as a report to the agency that funded the research or as a book or journal article for academic business researchers. In writing up the findings and conclusions, the researcher is doing more than simply relaying what has been found to others: readers must be convinced that the research conclusions are important and that the findings are robust. Thus, a significant part of the research process entails convincing others of the significance and validity of one's findings.

Once the findings have been published, others become aware of them and can then refer to them. Thus they become part of the stock of knowledge (or *theory* in the loose sense of the word) in their domain. In this way, there is a feedback loop from Step 11 back up to Step 1. The presence of both an element of **deductivism** (Step 2) and **inductivism** (the feedback loop) is indicative of the positivist foundations of quantitative research. Similarly, the emphasis on the translation of concepts into measures (Step 4) is symptomatic of the principle of *phenomenalism* (see Web Key concept 3.2), which is also a feature of positivism. It is to this important phase of translating concepts into measures that we now turn. As we will see, certain considerations follow on from the stress placed on measurement in quantitative research. By and large, these considerations are concerned with the validity and reliability of the measures devised by social scientists. These considerations are central to the following discussion.

Concepts and their measurement

What is a concept?

Concepts are the building blocks of theory and represent the points around which business research is conducted. For example, just think of the numerous concepts that are mentioned in relation to just some of the research examples cited in this book (e.g., structure, agency, deskilling, organizational size, technology, charismatic leadership, followers, TQM, functional subcultures, knowledge, managerial identity, motivation to work, moral awareness, productivity, stress management, employment relations, organizational development, competitive success). Each represents a label that we give to elements of the social world that seem to have common features and that strike us as significant. As Bulmer succinctly puts it, concepts 'are categories for the organization of ideas and observations' (1984, p. 43). One item mentioned in Chapter 2 but omitted from the list of concepts above is IQ. It has been omitted because it is not a concept! It is a *measure* of a

concept—namely, intelligence. This is a rare case of a social scientific measure that has become so well known that the measure and the concept are almost as synonymous as is temperature and the centigrade or Fahrenheit scales that measure it. The concept of intelligence has arisen as a result of noticing that some people are very clever, some are quite clever, and still others are not at all bright. These variations in what we have come to call the concept of 'intelligence' seem important, because we might try to construct theories to explain these variations. We may try to incorporate the concept of intelligence into theories to explain variations in things like job competence or entrepreneurial success. Similarly, with indicators of organizational performance such as productivity or return on investment, we notice that some organizations improve their performance relative to others, others remain static, and others decline in economic value. Out of such considerations, the concept of organizational performance is reached.

If a concept is to be employed in quantitative research it will have to be measured. Once they are measured concepts can be in the form of **independent** or **dependent variables**. In other words, concepts may provide an explanation of a certain aspect of the social world, or they may stand for things we want to explain. Sometimes a concept like organizational performance may be used in either capacity: for example, as a possible explanation of culture (are there differences between highly commercially successful organizations and others, in terms of the cultural values, norms, and beliefs held by organizational members?) or as something to be explained (what are the causes of variation in organizational performance?). Equally, we might be interested in evidence of changes in organizational performance over time or in variations between comparable nations in levels of organizational performance. When we begin to investigate such issues, we are likely to formulate theories to help us understand why, for example, rates of organizational performance vary between countries or over time. This will in turn generate new concepts, as we try to tackle the explanation of variation in rates.

Why measure?

There are three main reasons for the preoccupation with measurement in quantitative research:

- Measurement allows us to delineate *fine differences* between people in terms of the characteristic in question. This is very useful because, although we can often distinguish between people in terms of extreme categories, finer distinctions are much more difficult to recognize. We can detect clear variations in levels of job satisfaction—people who love their jobs and people who hate their jobs—but smaller differences are much more difficult to detect.

- Measurement gives us a *consistent device* for making such distinctions. A measurement device provides a consistent instrument for gauging differences. This consistency relates to two things: our ability to be consistent over time and our ability to be consistent with other researchers. In other words, a measure should be something that is not influenced by the timing of its administration or by the person who administers it. Obviously, saying that the measure is not influenced by timing is not meant to indicate that measurement readings do not change: they are likely to be influenced by the process of social change. What it means is that the measure should generate consistent results, other than those that occur as a result of natural changes. Whether a measure actually possesses this quality has to do with the issue of **reliability**, which will be examined in detail below.

- Measurement provides the basis for *more precise estimates of the degree of relationship between concepts* (for example, through **correlation** analysis, which will be examined in Chapter 23). Thus, if we measure both job satisfaction and the things with which it might be related, such as stress-related illness, we will be able to produce more precise estimates of how closely they are related than if we had not proceeded in this way.

Indicators

In order to provide a measure of a concept (often referred to as an **operational definition**, a term deriving from the idea of *operationalization*), it is necessary to have an indicator or indicators that will stand for the concept (see Key concept 5.1). There are a number of ways in which indicators can be devised:

- Through a question (or series of questions) that is part of a **structured interview schedule** or **self-completion questionnaire**. The question(s) could be concerned with the respondents' report of an attitude (e.g., job satisfaction) or their employment status (e.g., job title) or a report of their behaviour (e.g., job tasks and responsibilities).

- Through the recording of individuals' behaviour using a **structured observation schedule** (e.g., managerial activity).

- Through official statistics, such as the use of WES (Workplace and Employment Survey) survey data from Statistics Canada to measure Canadian employee and employer responses to changing technology in the competitive workplace.

- Through an examination of mass media content through content analysis—for example, to determine changes in the salience of an issue, such as courage in managerial decision making (Harris, 2001).

Indicators can be derived from a wide variety of sources and methods. Very often the researcher has to consider whether one indicator of a concept will be sufficient. This consideration is frequently a focus for social survey researchers. Rather than have just a single indicator of a concept, the researcher may feel that it may be preferable to ask a number of questions in the course of a structured interview or a self-completion questionnaire that tap that concept (see Web Research in focus 5.1 and 5.2).

> ### Key concept 5.1: What is an indicator?
>
> An indicator is something that is devised or already exists and that is employed as though it were a measure of a concept. We use indicators to tap concepts that are not easily directly quantifiable (e.g., job satisfaction).

Using multiple-indicator measures

What are the advantages of using a multiple-indicator measure of a concept? The main reason for its use is the recognition that there are potential problems with a reliance on just a single indicator:

- It is possible that a single indicator will incorrectly classify many individuals. This may be due to the wording of the question or it may be a product of misunderstanding. But if there are a number of indicators, it is possible to offset the effects of people being wrongly classified through any particular question.
- One indicator may capture only a portion of the underlying concept or be too general. A single question may need to be of an excessively high level of generality and so may not reflect the true state of affairs for the people replying to it. Alternatively, a question may cover only one aspect of the concept in question. For example, if you were interested in job satisfaction, would it be sufficient to ask people how satisfied they were with their pay? Almost certainly not, because most people would argue that there is more to job satisfaction than just satisfaction with pay. A single indicator such as this would be missing out on such things as satisfaction with conditions, with the work itself, and with other aspects of the work environment. By asking a number of questions, the researcher can get access to a wider range of aspects of the concept.
- Likewise, you can make much finer distinctions through using more than one indicator.

Dimensions of concepts

One elaboration of the general approach to measurement is to consider the possibility that the concept in which you are interested has different dimensions. This view is particularly associated with Lazarsfeld (1958). The idea behind this approach is that, when the researcher is seeking to develop a measure of a concept, the different aspects or components of that concept should be considered. This specification of the dimensions of a concept would be undertaken with reference to theory and research associated with that concept. An example of this kind of approach can be discerned in Hofstede's (1984; see Web Research in focus 3.7) delineation of four dimensions of cultural difference (power distance, uncertainty avoidance, individualism, and masculinity). Bryman and Cramer (2004) demonstrate the operation of this approach with reference to the concept of 'professionalism'. The

idea is that people scoring high on one dimension may not necessarily score high on other dimensions, so that for each respondent you end up with a multidimensional 'profile'. Web Research in focus 5.2 demonstrates the use of dimensions in connection with the concept of internal motivation to work.

However, in much if not most quantitative research, there is a tendency to rely on a single indicator of concepts. For many purposes this is quite adequate. It would be a mistake to believe that investigations that use a single indicator of core concepts are somehow deficient. In any case, some studies employ both single- and multiple-indicator measures of concepts. What *is* crucial is whether or not measures are reliable and whether or not they are valid representations of the concepts they are supposed to be tapping. These are the issues that we will now discuss.

Reliability and validity

Although the terms *reliability* and *validity* seem to be almost like synonyms, they have quite different meanings in relation to the evaluation of measures of concepts, as was seen in Chapter 2.

Reliability

As Key concept 5.2 suggests, **reliability** is fundamentally concerned with issues of consistency of measures. There are at least three different meanings or usages of the term. These are outlined in Key concept 5.2 and elaborated upon below.

Stability

The most obvious way of testing for the stability of a measure is the *test–retest* method. This involves administering a test or measure on one occasion and then re-administering it to the same sample on another occasion, i.e.:

$$T_1 \; T_2$$
$$Obs_1 \; Obs_2$$

We should expect to find a high correlation between Obs_1 and Obs_2. **Correlation** is a measure of the strength of the relationship between two variables. This topic will be covered in Chapter 23 in the context of a discussion

Key concept 5.2: What is reliability?

Reliability refers to the consistency of a measure of a concept.

about quantitative data analysis. Let us imagine that we develop a multiple-indicator measure that is supposed to tap a concept that we might call 'designerism' (a preference for buying goods and especially clothing with 'designer' labels). We would administer the measure to a sample of respondents and re-administer it some time later. If the correlation is low, the measure would appear to be unstable over time, implying that respondents' answers cannot be relied upon.

However, there are a number of problems with this approach to evaluating reliability. Respondents' answers at T_1 may influence how they reply at T_2. This may result in greater consistency between Obs_1 and Obs_2 than is in fact the case. Secondly, events may intervene between T_1 and T_2 that influence the degree of consistency. In our example, if a long span of time is involved, changes in the economy or in respondents' personal financial circumstances could influence their views about and desire for designer goods. There are no obvious solutions to these problems, other than to introduce a complex research design and thus turn the investigation of reliability into a major project in its own right. Perhaps for these reasons, many if not most reports of research findings do not appear to carry out tests of stability. Indeed, longitudinal research is often undertaken precisely in order to identify social change and its correlates.

Internal reliability

This meaning of reliability applies to multiple-indicator measures like those examined in Web Research in focus 5.1 and 5.2. When you have a multiple-item measure in which each respondent's answers to each question are aggregated to form an overall score, there is the possibility that the indicators do not relate to the same thing; in other words, they lack coherence. We need to be sure that all our 'designerism' indicators are related to each other. If they are not, some of the items may actually be unrelated to 'designerism' and, therefore, indicative of something else.

One way of testing internal reliability is the *split-half* method. We can take the management ethics measure developed by Jackson (2001) as an example (see Web Research in focus 5.1). The twelve indicators would be divided into two halves with six in each group. The indicators would be allocated on a random or an odd–even basis. The degree of correlation between scores on the two halves would then be calculated. In other words, the aim would be to establish whether respondents scoring high on one of the two groups also scored high on the other group of indicators. The calculation of the correlation will yield a value, known as a coefficient, that varies between 0 (no correlation and, therefore, no internal consistency) and 1 (perfect correlation and, therefore, complete internal consistency). It is usually expected that a result of 0.8 and above implies an acceptable level of internal reliability. Do not worry if these particular values appear somewhat confusing. The meaning of correlation will be explored in much greater detail later on. The main point to take away at this stage is that the correlation establishes how closely respondents' scores on the two groups of indicators are related.

Nowadays, most researchers use a test of internal reliability known as *Cronbach's alpha* (see Key concept 5.3). Its use has grown as a result of its incorporation into computer software for quantitative data analysis.

Key concept 5.3: What is Cronbach's alpha?

Cronbach's alpha is a commonly used test of internal reliability. It essentially calculates the average of all possible split-half reliability coefficients. The correlation establishes how closely respondents' scores on two groups of indicators are related.

Inter-observer consistency

The idea of *inter-observer consistency* is briefly outlined in Key concept 5.1. The issues involved are rather too advanced to be dealt with at this stage and will be briefly touched on in later chapters. Cramer (1998: Chapter 25) provides a very detailed treatment of the issues and appropriate techniques.

Validity

As noted in Chapter 4, the issue of measurement **validity** has to do with whether or not a measure of a concept really measures that concept (see Key concept 5.4). When people argue about whether or not a person's IQ score really measures or reflects that person's level of intelligence, they are raising questions about the measurement validity of the IQ test in relation to the concept of intelligence. Similarly, one often hears people say that they do not believe that the Consumer Price Index really reflects inflation and the rise in the cost of living. Again, a question is being raised in such comments about measurement validity. And whenever students or lecturers debate whether or not formal examinations provide an accurate measure of academic ability, they too are raising questions about measurement validity.

Writers on measurement validity distinguish between varieties of types of validity. These types actually reflect different ways of gauging the validity of a measure of a concept. These different types of **validity** will now be outlined.

Face validity

At the very minimum, a researcher who develops a new measure should establish that it has **face validity**—that is, that the measure apparently reflects the content of the concept in question. Face validity might be established by asking other people whether or not the measure seems to be getting at the concept that is the focus of attention. In other words, people, possibly those with experience or expertise in a field, might be asked to act as judges to determine whether or not, at first glance, the measure seems to reflect the concept concerned. Face validity is, therefore, an essentially intuitive process.

Key concept 5.4: What is validity?

Validity refers to the issue of whether or not an indicator (or set of indicators) that is devised to gauge a concept really measures that concept.

Concurrent validity

The researcher might seek also to gauge the *concurrent validity* of the measure. Here the researcher employs a *criterion* on which cases (for example, people) are known to differ and that is relevant to the concept in question. We can take the creation of a new measure of job satisfaction as an example. A criterion might be absenteeism, because some people are more often absent from work (other than through illness) than others. In order to establish the concurrent validity of a measure of job satisfaction, we might see if people who are satisfied with their jobs are less likely than those who are not satisfied to be *absent* from work. If a lack of correspondence was found, such as there being no difference in levels of job satisfaction among frequent absentees, doubt might be cast on whether or not our measure is really addressing job satisfaction.

Predictive validity

Another possible test for the validity of a new measure is *predictive validity*, whereby the researcher uses a *future* criterion measure, rather than a contemporary one, as in the case of concurrent validity. With predictive validity, the researcher would take future levels of absenteeism as the criterion against which the validity of a new measure of job satisfaction would be examined. The difference from concurrent validity is that a future rather than a simultaneous criterion measure is employed.

Construct validity

Some writers advocate that the researcher should also estimate the *construct validity* of a measure. Here the researcher is encouraged to deduce hypotheses from a theory that is relevant to the concept. For example, drawing upon ideas about the impact of technology on the experience of work, the researcher might anticipate that people who are satisfied with their jobs are less likely to work on routine jobs; those who are not satisfied are more likely to work on routine jobs. Accordingly, we could investigate this theoretical deduction by examining the relationship between job satisfaction and job routine. However, some caution is required in interpreting the absence of a relationship between job satisfaction and job routine in this example. First, either the theory or the deduction that is made from it might be misguided. Secondly, the measure of job routine could be an invalid measure of that concept.

Convergent validity

In the view of some methodologists, the validity of a measure ought to be gauged by comparing it to measures of the same concept developed through other methods. For example, if we develop a questionnaire measure of how much time managers spend on various activities (such as attending meetings, touring their organization, informal discussions, and so on), we might examine its validity by tracking a number of managers and using a structured observation schedule to record how much time is spent in various activities and their frequency. An example of *convergent validity* is described in Web Research in focus 5.3 and an interesting instance of convergent *in*validity is described in Web Research in focus 5.4.

Reflections on reliability and validity

There are, then, a number of ways of investigating the merit of measures that are devised to represent social scientific concepts. However, the discussion of reliability and validity is potentially misleading, because it would be wrong to think that all new measures of concepts are submitted to the rigours described above. In fact, measurement is typically undertaken within a stance that Cicourel (1964) described as 'measurement by fiat'. By the term 'fiat', Cicourel was referring not to a well-known Italian car manufacturer but to the notion of 'decree'. He meant that most measures are simply asserted. Fairly straightforward but minimal steps may be taken to ensure that a measure is reliable and/or valid, such as testing for internal reliability when a multiple-indicator measure has been devised and examining face validity. But in many, if not the majority, of cases in which a concept is measured, no further testing takes place. This point will be further elaborated below.

It should also be borne in mind that, although reliability and validity are analytically distinguishable, they are related because reliability is a precondition of validity. Simply put, if your measure is not reliable, it cannot be valid. This point can be made with respect to each of the three criteria of reliability that have been discussed. If the measure is not stable over time, it simply cannot be providing a valid measure. The measure could not be tapping the concept it is supposed to be related to if the measure fluctuated. If the measure fluctuates, it may be measuring different things on different occasions. If a measure lacks internal reliability, it means that a multiple-indicator measure is actually measuring two or more different things. Therefore, the measure cannot be valid. Finally, if there is a lack of inter-observer consistency, it means that observers cannot agree on the meaning of what they are observing, which in turn means that a valid measure cannot be in operation.

The main preoccupations of quantitative researchers

Both quantitative and qualitative research can be viewed as exhibiting a set of distinctive but contrasting preoccupations. These preoccupations reflect **epistemologically** grounded beliefs about what constitutes acceptable knowledge. In this section, four distinctive preoccupations that can be discerned in quantitative research will be outlined and examined: measurement, causality, generalization, and replication.

Measurement

The most obvious preoccupation is with measurement, a feature that is hardly surprising given much of the discussion in this chapter so far. From the position of quantitative research, measurement carries a number of advantages that were previously outlined. It is not surprising, therefore, that issues of reliability and validity are a concern for quantitative researchers, though this is not always manifested in research practice.

Causality

There is a very strong concern in most quantitative research with explanation. Quantitative researchers are rarely concerned with merely describing how things are, but are keen to say why things are the way they are. This emphasis is also often taken to be a feature of the ways in which the natural sciences proceed. Thus, researchers are often not only interested in a phenomenon like motivation to work as something to be described, for example, in terms of how motivated a certain group of employees are, or what proportion of employees in a sample are highly motivated and what proportion are largely lacking in motivation. Rather, they are likely to want to explain it, which means examining its causes. The researcher may seek to explain motivation to work in terms of personal characteristics (such as 'growth need strength', which refers to an individual's need for personal growth and development—see Web Research in focus 5.2) or in terms of the characteristics of a particular job (such as task interest or degree of supervision). In research articles you will often come across the idea of 'independent' and 'dependent' variables, which reflect the tendency to think in terms of causes and effects. Motivation to work might be regarded as the dependent variable, which is to be explained, and 'growth need strength' as an independent variable, and which, therefore, has a *causal* influence upon motivation.

When an experimental design is being employed, the independent variable is the variable that is manipulated. There is little ambiguity about the direction of causal influence. However, with cross-sectional designs of the kind used in most social survey research, there is ambiguity about the direction of causal influence because data concerning variables are simultaneously collected. Therefore, we cannot say that an independent variable occurs before the dependent one. To refer to independent and dependent variables in the context of cross-sectional designs, we must *infer* that one causes the other, as in the example concerning 'growth need strength' and motivation to work in the previous paragraph. We must draw on common sense or theoretical ideas to infer the likely temporal order of variables. However, there is always the risk that the inference will be wrong.

The concern about causality is reflected in the preoccupation with internal validity that was referred to in Chapter 4. Recall that it was noted that a criterion of good quantitative research is frequently the extent to which there is confidence in the researcher's causal inferences. Research that exhibits the characteristics of an experimental design is often more highly valued than cross-sectional research, because of the greater confidence in declaring causal findings than that associated with the former. For their part, quantitative researchers who employ cross-sectional designs are invariably concerned with developing techniques that will allow causal inferences to be made. Moreover, the emergence of longitudinal research or data collection, such as the WES (Workplace and Employment Survey conducted by Statistics Canada), almost certainly reflects a desire on the part of quantitative researchers to improve their ability to generate data and findings that permit a causal interpretation.

Generalization

In quantitative research the researcher is usually concerned that his or her findings can be generalized beyond the confines of the particular context in which the research was conducted. Thus, if a study of motivation to work is carried out by a questionnaire with a number of people who answer the questions, we often want to say that the results can apply to individuals other than those who responded in the study. This concern reveals itself in **survey research** through the attention that is often given to the question of how one can create a **representative sample**. Given that it is rarely feasible to send questionnaires to or interview whole populations (such as all members of a town, or the whole population of a country, or all members of an organization), we have to sample. However, we will want the sample to be as representative as possible in order to be able to say that the results are not unique to the particular group upon whom the research was conducted; in other words, we want to be able to generalize the findings beyond the cases (for example, the people) that make up the sample. The preoccupation with generalization means some researchers become focused on developing law-like principles about human behaviour that can be used to predict what people will do in certain situations. To further complicate matters, this research is sometimes based on studies of animal rather than human behaviour, thus raising the question of whether or not behaviour can be generalized from one species to another (see Web Research in focus 5.5).

Probability sampling, which will be explored in Chapter 9, is the main way in which researchers seek to generate a representative sample. This procedure largely eliminates bias from the selection of a sample by using a process of **random selection**. The use of a random selection process does not guarantee a representative sample, because, as will be seen in Chapter 9, there are factors that operate over and above the selection system used that can jeopardize the representativeness of a sample. A related consideration here is this: even if we did have a representative sample, what would it be representative *of*? The simple answer is that it will be representative of the population from which it was selected. This is certainly the answer that sampling theory gives us. Strictly speaking, we cannot generalize beyond that population. This means that, if the members of the population from which a sample is taken are all inhabitants of a town, city, or region, or are all members of an organization, we can generalize only to the inhabitants or members of the town, city, region, or organization. Nevertheless, it is very tempting to see the findings as having a more pervasive applicability, so that, even if the sample was selected from a large organization like IBM, the findings are relevant to all similar organizations. We should not make inferences beyond the population from which the sample was selected, yet researchers frequently do so. The concern to be able to generalize is often so deeply ingrained that the limits to the generalizability of findings are frequently forgotten or sidestepped.

The concern with generalizability or external validity is particularly strong among quantitative researchers using cross-sectional and longitudinal designs. There is a concern about generalizability among experimental research, as the discussion of external validity in Chapter 4 suggested, but users of this research design usually give greater attention to internal validity issues.

Replication

The natural sciences are often depicted as wanting to reduce to a bare minimum the contaminating influence of the scientist's biases and values. The results of a piece of research should be unaffected by the researcher's special characteristics or expectations. If biases and lack of objectivity were common, then the claims of the natural sciences to provide a definitive picture of the world would be seriously undermined. As a check upon the influence of these potentially damaging problems, scientists may seek to *replicate*— that is, to reproduce—each other's experiments. If there was a failure to replicate, so that a

scientist's findings repeatedly could not be reproduced, serious questions would be raised about the validity of his or her findings. As a result, scientists often attempt to be highly explicit about their procedures so that an experiment is capable of replication. Likewise, quantitative researchers in the social sciences often regard replication, or more precisely the ability to replicate, as an important ingredient of their activity. It is easy to see why: the possibility of a lack of objectivity and of the intrusion of the researcher's values would appear to be much greater when examining the social world than when the natural scientist investigates the natural order. Consequently, it is often regarded as important that the researcher spells out clearly his or her procedures so that they can be replicated by others, even if the research does not end up being replicated. The study by Schutte et al. (2000) described in Web Research in focus 5.6 relies on replication of the Maslach Burnout Inventory—General Survey, a psychological measure that has been used by the authors to test for emotional exhaustion, depersonalization, and reduced personal accomplishment across a range of occupational groups and nations.

It has been relatively straightforward and, therefore, quite common for researchers to replicate the Job Characteristic Model, developed by Hackman and Oldham (1980, see Web Research in focus 5.2), in order to enhance confidence in the theory and its findings. Several of these have attempted to improve the **generalizability** of the model through its replication in different occupational settings—for example, on teachers, university staff, nursery school teachers, and physical education and sport administrators. However, some criticism has been leveled at the original research for failing to make explicit how the respondent sample was selected, beyond the fact that it involved a diverse variety of manual and non-manual occupations in both manufacturing and service sectors, thus undermining the potential generalizability of the investigation (Bryman, 1989a). A further criticism relates to the emphasis that the model places on particular characteristics of a job, such as feedback from supervisors, which may be less of a feature in today's working context than they were in the late 1970s. A final criticism made of later replications of the initial study is that they fail to test the total model, focusing on the core job characteristics rather than incorporating the effects of the mediating psychological states, which Hackman and Oldham suggest are the 'causal core of the model' (1976, p. 255).

A study by Johns, Xie, and Fang (1992) attempts to address this last criticism by specifically focusing on the mediating and moderating effects of psychological states on the relationship between job characteristics and outcomes. Basing their research on a random sample of 605 first- and second-level managers in a large utility company (response rate approximately 50%), the authors used a slightly modified version of the JDS questionnaire to determine the relationship between job characteristics, psychological states, and outcome variables. Their results provide some support for the mediating role of psychological states in determining outcomes based on core job characteristics. However, not always in the way that is specified by the model. In particular, some personal characteristics, such as educational level, were found to affect psychological states in a reverse manner to that which was expected—those with less education responded more favourably to elevated psychological states.

Another significant interest in replication stems from the original Aston studies (see Web Research in focus 4.5), which stimulated a plethora of replications over a period of more than 30 years following publication of the first generation of research in the early 1960s. Most clearly associated with replication were the 'fourth-generation' Aston researchers, who undertook studies that:

- used a more homogenous sample drawn from a single industry, such as electrical engineering companies, 'to further substantiate the predictive power of the Aston findings' (Grinyer & Yasai-Ardekani, 1980, p. 405); or
- extended the original findings to other forms of organization, such as churches (e.g., Hinings, Ranson, and Bryman, 1976) or educational colleges (Holdaway et al., 1975).

Later proponents of the 'Aston approach' made international comparisons of firms in different countries in order to test the hypothesis that the relationship between the context and the structure of an organization was dependent on the culture of the country in which it operates. Studies conducted in China, Egypt, France, Germany, India, and Japan (e.g., Shenoy, 1981) sought to test the proposition that some of the characteristic differences in organizational structure, originally identified by the Aston researchers, remained constant across these diverse national contexts.

However, replication is not a high-status activity in the natural or the social sciences, partly because it is often regarded as a straightforward and uninspiring pursuit. Moreover, standard replications do not form the basis for attractive articles, as far as many academic journal editors are concerned. Consequently, replications of research appear in print far less frequently than might be supposed. A further reason for the low incidence of published replications is that it is difficult to ensure in business research that the conditions in a replication are precisely the same as those that pertained in an original study. If there is some ambiguity about the degree to which the conditions relating to a replication are the same as those in the initial study, any differences in findings may be attributable to the design of the replication rather than to some deficiency in the original study.

Nonetheless, it is often regarded as crucial that the methods used in generating a set of findings are made explicit, so that it is *possible* to replicate a piece of research. Thus, it is *replicability* that is often regarded as an important quality of quantitative research.

 ## The critique of quantitative research

Over the years, quantitative research along with its epistemological and ontological foundations has been the focus of a great deal of criticism, particularly from those who favour qualitative research. It can be difficult to distinguish between different kinds of criticism when considering the different critical points and argument offered concerning quantitative research methods. These include: criticisms of quantitative research in general as a research strategy; criticisms of the epistemological and ontological foundations of quantitative research; and criticisms of specific methods and research designs with which quantitative research is associated.

Criticisms of quantitative research

To give a flavour of the critique of quantitative research, four criticisms will be covered briefly.

- *Quantitative researchers fail to distinguish people and social institutions from 'the world of nature'.* The phrase 'the world of nature' is from the writings of Schutz (1962, p. 59) and the specific quotation from which it has been taken can be found in Chapter 3. Schutz and other phenomenologists charge social scientists that employ a natural science model with treating the social world as if it were no different from the natural order. In so doing, they draw attention to one of positivism's central tenets—namely, that the principles of the scientific method can and should be applied to all phenomena that are the focus of investigation. As Schutz argues, this tactic essentially implies that this means turning a blind eye to the differences between the social and natural world. More particularly, as was observed in Chapter 3, it means, therefore, ignoring the fact that people interpret the world around them, whereas this capacity for self-reflection cannot be found among the objects of the natural sciences ('molecules, atoms, and electrons', as Schutz put it).

- *The measurement process possesses an artificial and spurious sense of precision and accuracy.* There are a number of aspects to this criticism. For one thing, it has been argued that the connection between the measures developed by social scientists and the concepts they are supposed to be revealing is assumed rather than real; hence, Cicourel's (1964) notion of 'measurement by fiat'. Testing for validity in the ways previously described cannot really address this problem, because the very tests themselves entail measurement by fiat. A further way in which the measurement process is regarded by writers like Cicourel as flawed is that it presumes that when, for example, members of a sample respond to a question on a questionnaire (which is itself taken to be an indicator of a concept), they interpret the key terms in the question similarly. For many writers, respondents simply do not interpret such terms similarly. An often used response to this problem is to use questions with fixed-choice answers, but this approach merely provides 'a solution to the problem of meaning by simply ignoring it' (Cicourel, 1964, p. 108).

- *The reliance on instruments and procedures hinders the connection between research and everyday life.* This issue relates to the question of ecological validity that was raised in Chapter 4. Many methods of quantitative research rely heavily on administering research instruments to subjects (such as structured interviews and self-completion questionnaires) or on controlling situations to determine their effects (such as in experiments). However, as Cicourel (1982) asks, how do we know if survey respondents have the requisite knowledge to answer a question or if they are similar in believing that the topic is important to them in their everyday lives? Thus, if respondents answer a set of questions designed to measure motivation to work, can we be sure that they are equally aware of what it is and its manifestations, and can we be sure that it is of equal concern to them in the ways in which it connects with their everyday working life? One can go even further and ask how well their answers relate to their everyday lives. People may answer a question designed to measure their motivation to work, but respondents' actual behaviour may be at variance with their answers (LaPiere, 1934).

- *The analysis of relationships between variables creates a static view of social life that is independent of people's lives.* Blumer argued that studies that aim to bring out the relationships between variables omit 'the process of interpretation or definition that goes on in human groups' (1956, p. 685). This means that we do not know how what appears to be a relationship between two or more variables has been produced by the people to whom it applies. This criticism incorporates the first and third criticisms that have been referred to— that the meaning of events to individuals is ignored and that we do not know how such findings connect to everyday contexts. But it adds a further element, namely that it creates a sense of a static social world that is separate from the individuals who make up that world. In other words, quantitative research is seen as being grounded in an **objectivist ontology** that *reifies* the social world.

We can see in these criticisms a set of concerns associated with a qualitative research strategy that reveals the combination of an interpretivist epistemological orientation (an emphasis on meaning from the individual's point of view) and a constructionist ontology (an emphasis on viewing the social world as the product of individuals rather than as something beyond them). The criticisms may appear very damning, but, as we will see in Chapter 6, quantitative researchers have a powerful battery of criticisms of qualitative research in their arsenal as well!

 ## Is it always like this?

One of the problems with characterizing any research strategy, research design, or research method is that to a certain extent one is always outlining an ideal-typical approach. In other words, one tends to create something that represents that strategy, design, or method, but that may not be reflected in its entirety in the actual research practice. This gap between the ideal type and actual practice can arise as a result of at least two major considerations. First, it arises because those of us who write about and teach research methods cannot cover every eventuality that can arise in the process of business research, so that we tend to provide accounts of the research process that draw upon common features. Thus, a model of the process of quantitative research, such as that provided in Figure 5.1, should be thought of as a general *tendency* rather than as a definitive description of all quantitative research. A second reason why the gap can arise is that, to a very large extent when writing about and teaching research methods, we are essentially providing an account of *good practice*. The fact of the matter is that these practices are often not followed in the published research that students are likely to encounter in the courses that they will be taking. This failure to follow the procedures associated with good practice is not necessarily due to incompetence on the part of business researchers (though in some cases it can be!), but is much more likely to be associated with matters of time, cost, and feasibility—in other words, the pragmatic concerns that cannot be avoided when one does business research.

Reverse operationism

As an example of the first source of the gap between idealized and actual research practice we can take the case of something that Bryman has referred to as 'reverse operationism' (1988*a*, p. 28). The model of the process of quantitative research in Figure 5.1 implies that concepts are specified and measures are then provided for them. As we have noted, this means that indicators must be devised. This is the basis of the idea of *operationism* or *operationalism*, a term that derives from physics (Bridgman, 1927), and that implies a deductive view of how research should proceed. However, this view of research neglects the fact that measurement can entail much more of an inductive element than Figure 5.1 implies. Sometimes, measures are developed that, in turn, lead to conceptualization. One way in which this can occur is when a statistical technique known as **factor analysis** is employed. In order to measure the concept of 'charismatic leadership', a term that owes a great deal to Weber's (1947) notion of charismatic authority, Conger and Kanungo (1998) generated 25 items to provide a multiple-item measure of the concept. These items derived from their reading of existing theory and research on the subject, particularly in connection with charismatic leadership in organizations. When the items were administered to a sample of respondents and the results were factor analyzed, it was found that the items bunched around six factors, each of which represented a dimension of the concept of charismatic leadership:

- Strategic vision and articulation behaviour.
- Sensitivity to the environment.
- Unconventional behaviour.
- Personal risk.
- Sensitivity to organizational members' needs.
- Action orientation away from the maintenance of the status quo.

The point to note is that these six dimensions were not specified at the outset: the link between conceptualization and measurement was an inductive one. This is not an unusual situation as far as research is concerned (Bryman 1988*a*, pp. 26–8).

Reliability and validity testing

The second reason why the gap between idealized and actual research practices can arise is because researchers do not follow some of the recommended practices. A classic case of this tendency is that, while, as in the present chapter, much time and effort are expended on the articulation of the ways in which the reliability and validity of measures should be determined, a great deal of the time these procedures are not followed. There is evidence from analyses of published quantitative research in organization studies (Podsakoff & Dalton, 1987) that writers rarely report tests of the stability of their measures and even more rarely report evidence of validity (only 3% of articles provided information about measurement validity). A large proportion of articles used *Cronbach's alpha*. However, since this device is relevant only to multiple-item measures, because it gauges internal consistency, the stability and validity of many measures that are employed are unknown. This is not to say that this research is necessarily *un*stable and *in*valid, but that we simply do not know. The reasons why the procedures for determining stability and validity are rarely used are almost certainly the cost and time that are likely to be involved. Researchers tend to be concerned with substantive issues and are less than enthusiastic about engaging in the kind of development work that would be required for a thorough determination of measurement quality. However, what this means is that Cicourel's (1964) previously cited remark about much measurement in sociology being 'measurement by fiat' has considerable weight.

The remarks on the lack of assessment of the quality of measurement should not be taken as a justification for readers to neglect this phase in their work. Our aim is merely to draw attention to some of the ways in which practices described in this book are not always followed and to suggest some reasons why they are not followed.

Sampling

A similar point can be made in relation to sampling, which will be covered in Chapter 9. As we will see, good practice is strongly associated with random or **probability sampling**. However, quite a lot of research is based on non-probability samples—that is, samples that have not been selected in terms of the principles of probability sampling to be discussed in Chapter 9. Sometimes the use of non-probability samples will be due to the impossibility or extreme difficulty of obtaining probability samples. Yet another reason is that the time and cost involved in getting a probability sample are too great given the resources available. And yet a third reason is that sometimes the opportunity to study a certain group presents itself and represents too good an opportunity to miss. Again, such considerations should not be viewed as a justification and hence a set of reasons for ignoring the principles of sampling to be examined in the next chapter, not least because not following the principles of probability sampling carries implications for the kind of statistical analysis that can be employed (see Chapter 23). Instead, our purpose, as before, is to draw attention to the ways in which gaps between recommendations about good practice and actual research practice can arise.

 Key points

- Quantitative research can be characterized as a linear series of steps moving from theory to conclusions, but the process described in Figure 5.1 is an ideal from which there are many departures.
- The measurement process in quantitative research entails the search for indicators.
- Establishing the reliability and validity of measures is important for assessing their quality.
- Quantitative research can be characterized as exhibiting certain preoccupations, the most central of which are: measurement; causality; generalization; and replication.
- Quantitative research has been subjected to many criticisms by qualitative researchers. These criticisms tend to revolve around the view that a natural science model is inappropriate for studying the social world.

Questions for review

The main steps in quantitative research

- What are the main steps in quantitative research?
- To what extent do the main steps follow a strict sequence?
- Do the steps suggest a deductive or inductive approach to the relationship between theory and research?

Concepts and their measurement

- Why is measurement important for the quantitative researcher?
- What is the difference between a measure and an indicator?
- Why might multiple-indicator approaches to the measurement of concepts be preferable to those that rely on a single indicator?

Reliability and validity

- What are the main ways of thinking about the reliability of the measurement process? Is one form of reliability the most important?
- 'Whereas validity presupposes reliability, reliability does not presuppose validity.' Discuss.

Validity

- What is validity?
- What are the main criteria for evaluating measurement validity?

The main preoccupations of quantitative researchers

- Outline the main preoccupations of quantitative researchers. What reasons can you give for their prominence?
- Why might replication be an important preoccupation among quantitative researchers, in spite of the tendency for replications in business research to be fairly rare?

The critique of quantitative research

- 'The crucial problem with quantitative research is the failure of its practitioners to address adequately the issue of meaning.' Discuss.
- How central is the adoption by quantitative researchers of a natural science model of conducting research to the critique by qualitative researchers of quantitative research?

Is it always like this?

- What are the two major considerations that arise as a result of the gap between the ideal type and actual practice?

6

The Nature of Qualitative Research

Chapter guide

Qualitative research is a research strategy that usually emphasizes words rather than quantification in the collection and analysis of data. In this chapter we focus on explaining the differences between qualitative and quantitative methods. However, as we discussed in Chapter 3, qualitative research can be utilized as either a positivist or a postpositivist research strategy (see Figure 3.2). To that end, this chapter will also contrast positivist and postpositivist qualitative methods. For ease of discussion, we will begin with the contrast between qualitative and quantitative methods within the positivist tradition before moving on to a consideration of postpositivist qualitative methods.

Thus, while qualitative and quantitative research methods in the positivist tradition share an ontological belief in realism they differ in their strategies of inductive (qualitative) and deductive (quantitative) forms of theory building (see Table 3.2). Positivist qualitative research differs from postpositivist qualitative methods in their respective philosophical framework.

This chapter is concerned with outlining the main features of (positivist and postpositivist) qualitative research strategies that have become increasingly popular in the study of business. This chapter explores:

- The main steps associated with the postpositivist qualitative research strategy.
- The relationship between theory and research in the two qualitative strategies.
- The nature of concepts in qualitative research and their differences from concepts in quantitative research.
- The role of **reliability** and **validity** in the two different qualitative approaches.
- The main preoccupations of qualitative researchers.
- Some common criticisms of qualitative research.
- The main contrasts between qualitative and quantitative research.

Introduction

In Chapter 3 it was argued that there are at least two main types of qualitative research—positivist and postpositivist. It was also noted that qualitative methods could also be a central part of two further—**mixed methods**—strategies. For ease of discussion this chapter will focus on the former two qualitative strategies and discuss mixed methods in the Chapter 7.

It is important from the beginning to understand the distinction between positivist and postpositivist approaches to qualitative methods. The reason for this is to avoid many of the confusions that occur when qualitative methods are contrasted with quantitative methods.

Confusion number 1: Reducing the difference between qualitative and quantitative research to a respective focus on words and numbers.

While this focus helps to define at least one importance difference between the type of data that are collected in qualitative (largely words) and quantitative (largely numbers) research it oversimplifies the differences. For example, there are a growing number of research projects that use a qualitative study to generate concepts to be tested (usually by way of a survey) at a later stage of the research (see Web Research in focus 3.2). Thus, while a 'focus on words' might be seen as the ultimate focus for some qualitative research strategies, in other qualitative approaches it might be seen as an 'exploratory' stage (Ouadahi, 2008) of a more substantial study 'focused on numbers.' Furthermore, some qualitative approaches, such as **ethnostatistics** and **content analysis**, incorporate words and numbers. Content analysis, for example, often involves the counting of words in a given text or set of texts (see Chapter 18) and ethnostatistics deals with words as rhetorical strategies for making sense of numerical data (Gephart, 1988; Helms Mills et al., 2006). Finally, the inclusion of 'numbers' in a study does not make it a quantitative approach. Researchers, for example, may describe the percentages of men and women that they interviewed in their study to provide *information* rather than evidence per se. Quantitative research methods are usually thought of as techniques of data collection and analysis, involving some form of statistical technique (see Chapters 5, 9, 23, 25) that go well beyond the description of 'numbers' or 'counting'.

Confusion number 2: Reducing the central difference between qualitative and quantitative research to a difference of *technique*, i.e., a focus on either 'words' or 'numbers'.

However, it is not simply the focus on 'words' that makes something distinctive but the underlying ontological and epistemological approach. For example, qualitative methods can be rooted in a range of different philosophical traditions, including interpretivism, feminism, critical realism, poststructuralism, and several other approaches. To talk about a focus on 'words' does not capture the range or nuance of qualitative approaches. For example, the words of an interviewee may be used to document attitudes, beliefs, and/or opinions (see Chapter 14); words used in conversation may be studied for how people shape a given sense of reality (see Chapter 20); and words that are seen as part of a discourse may be studied for their relationship to particular meanings that serve to create knowledge of important aspects of life (see Chapter 24).

Confusion number 3: Viewing qualitative methods as opposite (or in opposition) to quantitative methods.

The difference between qualitative and quantitative methods is often expressed in research methods accounts as 'quantitative *versus* qualitative methods' (Berg, 1989; Cooper & Schindler, 2006). Although there is some truth in this argument, it is confusing because it only works in those cases where qualitative methods are equated with postpositivist traditions and compared with positivist quantitative methods. In such cases, as we shall see throughout this chapter, there are distinct differences between certain qualitative and quantitative methods.

Also, it only works where both approaches are reduced to techniques of analysis; methods rather than methodologies. Postpositivist qualitative methods are very different from positivist quantitative methods but the key is not the *method* of study but rather the *philosophy* behind its use. For example, a realist researcher who wants to find out what people's opinions are of a certain product may use one of several techniques: a survey, to gain an impression of what people generally think (generalizable data); a focus group, to see how group influence affects the way people think of a product; or interviews, to gain an in-depth understanding of the types of factors that influence a person's opinion of a product. In each case a different method is used to explore a similar realist concern with what people *actually* think. On the other hand, interpretivist researchers will not face similar choices of method. They will reject the use of a survey, not because it is a quantitative method but because of the underlying positivist philosophy that assumes that survey data can reveal some type of truth about what people think. The **interpretivist**, with his or her focus on meaning and the process of social construction, will use methods of study capable of accessing those processes. Thus, an interview might be used not as a way of revealing what a person is actually thinking so much as a technique of surfacing how a person's thinking *constructs* the reality of a situation. Similarly, a focus group might be used to surface how people negotiate *a sense* of truth and reality through interaction (Rose-Anderssen et al., 2010). In these cases the method of study is less about technique and more an epistemological view of how a sense of reality comes to be constructed (see Chapter 7).

Confusion number 4: Seeing qualitative and quantitative methods as different ways of accessing or surfacing a common reality.

This is the mirror opposite of confusion number 3. It assumes a positivist worldview in which all reality is discoverable through empirical study and that empirical study can access and represent that reality through either quantitative or qualitative methods— viewing both as dealing with different levels, or depth, of analysis. Hair, Babin, Money, and Samouel (2003), for example, explain that 'qualitative data is usually *captured* in narrative form and is used to *describe* human behavior or business phenomena [while] quantitative data . . . is *captured* through the use of various numeric scales' (p. 142, our emphasis). Hair et al. (2003, p. 142) are then able to reconcile the two by explaining, 'qualitative approaches to data collection are frequently used at the exploratory stage of the research process. Their role is to identify and or refine research problems that may help to formulate and *test* conceptual frameworks' (our emphasis). This can be contrasted with 'quantitative approaches to data collection [which] are often used when we have well defined research problems or theoretical models.'

Notwithstanding the ontological similarities between positivist qualitative and quantitative methods we argue that *in use* qualitative research can be seen as constituting different research strategies from quantitative methods, i.e., that researchers do see a difference between the use of qualitative and quantitative methods and the choices behind their adoption.

Beyond the main ontological differences between positivist and postpositivist qualitative methods, there are various forms of qualitative methods and it is important to understand something about the differences between them as they provide a range of choice when it comes to undertaking a particular project of study (Silverman, 1993).

The following are some of the main research methods associated with qualitative research:

- **Ethnography/participant observation**. While some caution is advisable in treating ethnography and participant observation as synonyms, in many respects they refer to similar, if not identical, approaches to data collection in which the researcher is immersed in a social setting for some time in order to observe and listen with a view to gaining an appreciation of the culture of a social group. It has been employed in such business research classics as Dalton's (1959) study of managerial work in the United States, Lupton's (1963) exploration of shop floor factory life and restriction of output in England, and Mintzberg's (1973) study of the nature of managerial work in Sweden, Britain, and the United States.

- *Qualitative interviewing*. This is a very broad term to describe a wide range of interviewing styles. Moreover, qualitative researchers employing ethnography or participant observation typically engage in a substantial amount of qualitative interviewing.
- ***Focus groups*** (see Key concept 15.1).
- *Language-based approaches to the collection of qualitative data,* such as discourse and conversation analysis.
- *The collection and qualitative analysis of texts and documents.*

Each of these approaches to data collection will be examined in Part Three but can also be explored through a literature review of specialized journals and books, such as *Qualitative Research in Organizations and Management, Qualitative Sociology* and *Qualitative Inquiry*; texts on qualitative research (e.g., Silverman, 1993, 2000, 2005; Seale, 1999); the *Handbook of Qualitative Research* (Denzin & Lincoln, 2000); the Sage Qualitative Research Methods Series, and other qualitative studies that appear in a range of other journals.

The picture with regard to the very different methods and sources that comprise qualitative research is made somewhat more complex by the fact that a mixed-methods approach (see Chapter 7) is frequently employed. As noted above, researchers employing ethnography or participant observation frequently conduct qualitative interviews. However, they also often collect and analyze texts and documents as well. Thus, there is considerable variability in the collection of data among studies that are typically deemed to be qualitative. Of course, quantitative research also subsumes several different methods of data collection (these are covered in Chapters 5 and 7), but the inclusion of methods concerned with the analysis of language as a form of qualitative research implies somewhat greater variability.

A second reason why there is some resistance to a delineation of the nature of qualitative research is that the connection between theory and research is somewhat more ambiguous than in quantitative research. With the latter research strategy, theoretical issues drive the formulation of a research question, which in turn drives the collection and analysis of data. Findings then feed back into the relevant theory. This is rather a caricature, because what counts as 'theory' is sometimes little more than the research literature relating to a certain issue or area (see Chapter 3 for a discussion on types of theory). As Bakker (2009, p. 930) argues, 'the word *theory* has many different meanings in different contexts'. These include:

- *Metatheory*, where the attempt is to create an overarching perspective that provides an understanding of many of the complex influences that construct a given worldview (e.g., Marxism, Christianity, etc.).
- A set of interrelated hypotheses or propositions that form a framework for predicting behaviour and other phenomena.
- A specific hypothesis that speculates about an aspect of behaviour or other phenomena.

Bakker (2009) concludes that 'because of these varied usages, it is difficult to generalize about the role of theory' in social science research (p. 930).

Undertaking qualitative research

We can now attempt to answer the question of when and why should a researcher use qualitative research. There are at least four main reasons for adopting qualitative methods:

- *Philosophical*. Some researchers reject the idea that a natural science model of research can, or should, be applied to the studies of social life. Within the post-positivist traditions, for instance, interpretivists argue that reality is not a concrete entity waiting to be (objectively) discovered but rather a socially constructed phenomenon. As such, we need methods capable of capturing the subjectivism of those processes that contribute to socially constructed realities; this can be a focus on signs (e.g., use of certain words), as in **semiotics** and the study of language, or symbols (e.g., mutually defined meanings), as in **symbolic interactionism**, or text (e.g., a document or defined set of statements) as in hermeneutics. This has led to methods for trying to

surface the meanings and understandings associated with human behaviour and the construction of reality. Kristine Esterberg (2002, p. 17) describes the difference, thus: 'Whereas the goal of positivist research . . . is to "predict and control" . . . the goal of interpretivist research is to understand and interpret. . . .'

- *Level or focus of analysis.* Not all qualitative researchers reject positivism per se and accept the use of quantitative methods as an appropriate technique for accessing data that can reveal the broad or general nature of an aspect of social life. However, they may feel that a qualitative approach is needed to generate rich data on the subject, to understand, for example, not just what people are thinking about something but why or how they have arrived at that viewpoint. Take for example the issue of organizational culture. A positivist qualitative researcher may find the survey of organizational culture an acceptable and legitimate way of gauging how people see, and feel about, their organization, but believe that a qualitative approach is needed to find out more about how and why people have developed those feelings and/or perceptions. Commenting on this Edgar Schein (2000, p. xxix) argues that surveys of organizational culture (sometimes called organizational climate surveys) are useful for identifying the existing climate of opinion at work in an organization but they 'are not enough. One must analyze the underlying cultural assumptions.' To get at the latter Schein (2000, p. xxviii) suggests that an 'ideal research design would measure the present and desired norms, and then check in the underlying assumption set (through group interviews that get at assumptions) why discrepancies exist between the present state and the desired state in the first place'. An example of a survey of workplace culture is the work of Zerbe, Dobni, and Harel (1998), who examined perceptions of service culture in Canadian airlines. Perhaps the most noted qualitative work on cultural assumptions is the work of Schein (1990, 1991, 1992). [It should be noted that postpositivist qualitative researchers tend to begin by rejecting the notion of organizational culture as a concrete entity, whose elements and influences can be revealed but rather view it as a metaphor or heuristic for making sense of organizational life. See, for example, Allaire and Firsirotu (1984), Martin (2002), Smircich (1983).]

- **Triangulation**. As we have discussed in Chapter 3 and will look at in more detail in Chapter 7, some researchers view qualitative research as an elementary or exploratory stage of a **mixed methods** (also called triangulation) approach. Amy Warren (2009), for example, used both qualitative and quantitative methods in her study of mandatory retirement in Canada. Her qualitative study 'explored the contexts in which people make their retirement decisions' while her quantitative study 'tested a model of retirement decisions' (pp. 19–20). The first (qualitative) stage was used to generate themes that would later be tested (at the quantitative stage).

- **Researcher sensibilities.** At the end of the day the choice of research method can come down to what the researcher is most comfortable with. This can be to do with relative abilities (e.g., the researcher feels better at qualitative than quantitative methods); personality (e.g., the researcher may prefer to talk directly with people rather than survey them); and the type of questions asked (e.g., the researcher may be more interested in studying the processes that lead to, rather than a measure of, a given phenomenon).

 ## Doing qualitative research

As you will now appreciate, there are various approaches to qualitative research, both between positivist and postpositivism traditions but within those traditions. While there is no single process to follow in undertaking a qualitative approach there are some broad guidelines to consider (see Figure 6.1) and they differ from the process of quantitative research (see Figure 5.1).

Before we begin: how you begin the research process will depend on a number of factors, including the level of study (from undergraduate to graduate); whether the project is course specific (i.e., is outlined by the course professor or left open to the student) and the extent to which your program, or your supervisor, has certain

ontological requirements or expectations (e.g., whether you are required to do a quantitative rather than a qualitative study; a positivist rather than a postpositivist research project). These factors will influence the methods you choose and the types of research questions you ask. When, for example, Cindy Dean, majored in History as part of her Bachelor of Arts degree (at Mount Saint Vincent University) her choice of research subject was left fairly open but was influenced by an approach to history that was largely positivist in its direction. Later, when she studied research methods as part of her undergraduate degree in Public Relations (also at Mount Saint Vincent University), she was given the choice of focus groups, interviews, or surveys as a method of study for a final class assignment. Mark, on the other hand, was able to make a broad range of decisions on methods when he undertook his Honour's thesis for his Bachelors of Business Administration (at Acadia University). At the Master's level students are more likely to have more leeway in their choice but that will vary from university to university and from department to department. When Albert—one of this book's authors—did his Master's of Arts thesis (at Sheffield University) his thesis topic was open within the limits of Occupational Psychology but constrained by the requirement to use statistical methods of data collection and analysis. At Saint Mary's University students can decide on their direction after exposure to courses on paradigmatic differences in management, quantitative, and qualitative methods. A similar process is adopted by Hanken University in Helsinki, Finland.

1. *Establishing research questions.* As we discussed in Chapter 1, any research project starts off with a key question or set of questions to be answered, e.g., 'how does the meaning we place on our work relate to our existential Being' (Macmillan, 2009). This differs between quantitative and qualitative research and between qualitative traditions.

   Qualitative versus quantitative research. Qualitative research varies from quantitative research in regard to theory. Quantitative researchers tend to view theory as 'a set of interrelated hypothesis or propositions—that form a framework for predicting behaviour and other phenomena' (Bakker, 2009, p. 930) whereas qualitative researchers tend to view theory as 'an attempt to create an overarching perspective that provides an understanding of many of the complex influences that construct a given worldview' (p. 930). Quantitative researchers usually begin with a deductive approach that identifies an existing theory to be tested or built on through a set of hypotheses (see stages 1 and 2 of Figure 5.1). In contrast, qualitative researchers are more likely to adopt an inductive approach whereby concepts and theoretical elaboration emerge out of data collection. Often broad research questions are posed, e.g., 'why do women leave accounting before they reach partner level?' (Wallace, 2009*b*), see stage 1 of Figure 6.1.

Differences within qualitative traditions. The role of theory varies between postpositivist and positivist qualitative approaches, with the latter approximating to the notion of theory in quantitative approaches (but differing in emphasis on the emergent role of theory). Within the postpositivist traditions grounded theory and *actor network theory* (ANT) (see Chapters 20 and 21) differ from other approaches by their emphasis on the emergence of theory and avoidance of preconceived notions and theories of social life. For example, in Durepos, Mills, and Helms Mills's tudy of the corporate history of Pan American Airways (Durepos et al., 2008*b*; Durepos et al., 2008*a*; Durepos et al., 2008*c*) they avoided any assumptions about factors that contribute to a business history of the airline. Instead, they looked for evidence of what the people involved *felt* was of interest in describing a company's history; how they negotiated a sense of history; and how a particular history came to be written over other potential versions.

2. *Selecting relevant site(s) and subjects.* In both qualitative and quantitative research relevant sites and subjects are an important stage, and the choices arise out of the respective theoretical framework and the questions being asked. However, whereas quantitative researchers reach this point after dealing with issues of research design and measures of concepts (see stages 3–4, Figure 5.1), this is the second stage in qualitative research (see Figure 6.1). Although not without its problems, normally the identification of appropriate subjects and a research site is relatively straightforward. Peggy Wallace (2009), for example, was interested in reasons why women left the accounting industry before making partner. In the process she gathered written material from the largest accounting firms in Canada and interviewed a selection of women who had left the industry before making it to partnership. Interested in how dramatic changes in work can affect a person's sense of being, Scott MacMillan (2009) interviewed people who had gone through some dramatic form of job change over their lives.

3. *Collection of relevant data.* What data should be collected and how do they form the central issues in qualitative research. In quantitative research this stage (see stage 7 Figure 5.1) involves administering the research instruments and collecting resultant data (i.e., the outcome of the research instrument). In qualitative research, however, this involves careful choices based on the types of research questions being asked and the theoretical starting point. Peggy Wallace and Scott MacMillan both started with a theoretical framework grounded in existentialist philosophy. This influenced not only the type of data they collected but also how they collected it. For example, with a focus on understanding the existential being of individuals neither Wallace nor MacMillan contemplated surveys (which can only capture broad data about groups or defined categories of people). Instead they chose to interview a number of selected individuals and treat what they had to say as examples of individual reflections. To that end, the interview questions were open ended and related to a respective opening questions that asked respondents to talk about their careers in accounting (Wallace) or how they viewed work (MacMillan).

4. *Interpretation of data.* While quantitative researchers move through stages of data processing and analysis (steps 8–9, Figure 5.1), qualitative researchers recognize the fact that the outcomes of the data collection require some level of *plausible* interpretation.

For example, having interviewed 13 women who had left their accounting firms before making partner Peggy Wallace had to make sense of the interview transcripts. She did this in two ways. First, she drew on her chosen theoretical framework of feminist existentialism and the work of Simone de Beauvoir (de Beauvoir, 1952). Here Wallace focused on the career *decisions* that her interviewees reported. Second, she used narrative analysis (Boje, 1995) to make sense of the interviewees' individual career stories. Using both existentialism and narrative analysis, Wallace assessed each individual stories for patterns of decision making to gauge the extent to which each interviewee had acted according to the dictates of others (called 'bad faith' decisions in existentialism) or had self-consciously made her own decisions in the full knowledge of the risks involved (acting 'authentically'). In this stage the qualitative researcher turns raw data into processed or interpreted data as part of the process of developing theoretical insights.

5. *Conceptual and theoretical work.* Here the qualitative researcher examines the interpreted data for clues that will help him or her make sense of the research questions that grounded the research or which have emerged in the process of the research itself. Through her focus on stories and decision making Wallace was able to add a new understanding to the literature on why it is that women (more so than men) leave the accounting industry at an apparently crucial stage of their career. Commenting on the data itself, Wallace (2009, p. 1) states that the women's 'stories provide us with deeper insights to the previously reported reasons for leaving firms that are often reported as broad categories'. She notes that her reading of the data indicated that 'work-family issues received limited attention in the participants' stories suggesting it is not a key reason for leaving a firm. Two major themes did emerge: the absence of stated aspirations and desire to become a partner; and frustrations with the intrinsic and monetary value of services delivered by public accounting firms' (Wallace, 2009a, p. 180). Wallace concluded that participants originally entered the profession in the absence of information

on the character of the 'work performed by public accounting firms and the role of accountants within those firms. They offered many reasons for pursuing a CA designation, often influenced by institutions such as universities and individuals such as parents [but] did not enter the profession with any explicit goal of becoming a partner in a public accounting firm' (2009a, p. 180). While this finding is not in itself new—other research has identified that males and females enter the profession in the absence of stated goals—Wallace's interviews were able to reveal what impact the lack of stated goals had on career trajectories and the multiple meanings involved. Wallace (2009a) was, in fact, able to show that far from being simple victims of a discriminatory system that saw fewer women reach partnership than men, many of her interviewees had left because they rejected what the system appeared to be offering. Instead her participants emphasized a:

> need for continuous learning and exposure to new challenges [which] led them to question the *value* of the work performed in public accounting firms, particularly in the area of audit services. They did not appear willing to remain in an area or position in which they perceived there was limited or no value, to their clients and to themselves. Consequently they moved when opportunities for new learning and new challenges. (Wallace, 2009a, p. 191)

5a. *Tighter specification of the research question(s)*, and 5b. *Collection of further data.* Qualitative research is often an iterative approach in which the interpretation of data may raise further questions and a need for more data to confirm issues that appear to be emerging. When, for example, Mary Runté (2005) was undertaking a study of the work-family conflict literature she often shared her findings with a group of her female friends who, in turn, would often respond with a supportive anecdote. Runté (2005) increasingly began to feel that the anecdotes, although not part of her original research strategy, were providing

Figure 6.1

An outline of the main steps of qualitative research

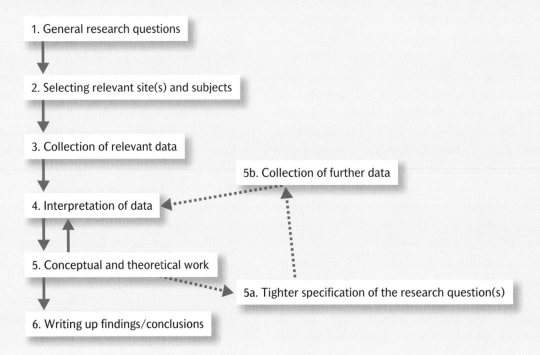

valuable insights into how discourses of work and family influenced people's thinking and understandings of their family and workplace roles. Encouraged by this finding Runté added the collection of anecdotes to her research.

6. *Writing up findings/conclusions*. There is no real difference between the significance of writing up in quantitative research and qualitative research, so that exactly the same points made in relation to step 11 in Figure 5.1 apply here. An audience has to be convinced about the credibility and significance of the interpretations offered. Researchers are not and cannot be simply conduits for the things they see and the words they hear. The salience of what researchers have seen and heard has to be impressed on the audience and the account has to be plausible. Again this is true for both quantitative and qualitative research, but of which ultimately rely on some form of a narrative to convince an audience (Van Maanen,

1988). Whereas in quantitative research the *accuracy* of selected numbers are used to convince an audience, in qualitative research it is the *plausibility* of the narrative itself that is used to convince an audience (Weick, 2001). In both cases the audience needs to be convinced that the data collection techniques were appropriately, properly, and rigorously used. This can mean adequately following the broad steps of a statistical technique or a particular method such as **grounded theory** or critical **discourse analysis**. What this means in practice is that the qualitative researcher needs to make clear his or her research method and explain in some detail why the method was appropriate and useful to the research at hand; how it was used to collect and make sense of the data, and what were the limitations involved. In essence the researcher tries to put the reader in his or her shoes and convince the reader that by following the same process he or she will arrive at similar conclusions.

Thus, when Peggy Wallace set out to find out why women leave the accounting industry she had to convince the reader that it was worthwhile exploring the individual decision making of selected women. Structural analyses suggested that more women left the industry than men because of systemic discrimination. However, according to Wallace (2009*a*) that did not provide any understanding of the different reasons that individuals place on her or his own decisions. Having made that case, Wallace then needed to convince her potential readers that a study of individuals needs an appropriate method that seeks to understand a person's decision making at a profound level. That approach, argues Wallace (2009*a*), is existentialism—or more specifically feminist existentialism—because it is arguably one of the few traditions that has a well-developed theory of the individual. As an added problem Wallace was faced with the problem of having to develop a feminist existentialist method by extracting ideas from the philosophy of Simone de Beauvoir (Wallace, 2009*a*). Finally, Wallace shares with the reader the problems she grappled with in attempting to interpret other people's existential reflections on their lives and careers (Wallace, 2007).

Some contrasts between quantitative and qualitative research

Several writers have explored the contrasts between quantitative and qualitative research by devising tables that allow the differences to be brought out (e.g., Halfpenny, 1979; Bryman, 1988*a*; Hammersley, 1992*b*). Table 6.1 attempts to draw out the chief contrasting features:

- *Numbers vs. Words*. Quantitative researchers are often portrayed as preoccupied with applying measurement procedures to social life, while qualitative researchers are seen as using words in the presentation of analyses of society, although, as we have argued above, this distinction can be problematic if applied too rigidly. Beyond (written and spoken words) qualitative research-

ers are also concerned with the analysis of visual data (see Web Research in focus 6.1).

- *Point of view of researcher vs. Point of view of participants*. In quantitative research, the investigator is in the driving seat. The set of concerns that he or she brings to an investigation structures the investigation. In qualitative research, the perspective of those being studied, what they see as important and significant, provides the point of orientation.

- *Researcher is distant vs. Researcher is close*. In quantitative research, researchers are uninvolved with their subjects and in some cases, as in research based on postal questionnaires or on hired interviewers, may have no contact with them at all. Sometimes, this lack of a relationship with the subjects of an investigation is regarded as desirable by quantitative researchers, because they feel that their objectivity might be compromised if they become too involved with the people they study. The qualitative researcher seeks close involvement with the people being investigated, so that he or she can genuinely understand the world through their eyes.

- *Theory and concepts tested in research vs. Theory and concepts emergent from data*. Quantitative researchers typically bring a set of concepts to bear on the research instruments being employed, so that theoretical work precedes the collection of data, whereas in qualitative research concepts and theoretical elaboration more often emerge out of data collection. This, however, is not always the case as some qualitative approaches begin with key concepts that serve to frame their data collection and analysis. Karl Weick (Weick, 2001; Weick et al., 2005), for example, uses the notion of (7) interrelated sensemaking properties as a 'recipe' to make sense of organizational behaviour. Mills and Helms Mills (Helms Mills, 2003; Mills and Helms Mills, 2004; Mills, 2008) also use Weick's **sensemaking** properties as a framework for analyzing various organizational outcomes. Nonetheless, it is fair to say that qualitative research is more about theory emergence that theory testing.

- *Static vs. Process*. Quantitative research is frequently depicted as presenting a static image of social reality with its emphasis on relationships between variables.

Table 6.1   Some common contrasts between quantitative and qualitative research

Quantitative	Qualitative
Numbers	Words
Point of view of researcher	Points of view of participants
Researcher distant	Researcher close
Theory testing	Theory emergent
Static	Process
Structured	Unstructured
Generalization	Contextual understanding
Hard, reliable data	Rich, deep data
Macro	Micro
Behaviour	Meaning
Artificial settings	Natural settings

- *Structured vs. Unstructured.* Quantitative research is typically highly structured so that the investigator is able to examine the precise concepts and issues that are the focus of the study; in qualitative research the approach is invariably unstructured, so that the possibility of getting at actors' meanings and of concepts emerging out of data collection is enhanced.
- *Generalization vs. Contextual understanding.* Whereas quantitative researchers want their findings to be generalizable to the relevant population, the qualitative researcher seeks an understanding of behaviour, values, beliefs, and so on in terms of the context in which the research is conducted.
- *Hard, reliable data vs. Rich, deep data.* Quantitative data are often depicted as 'hard' in the sense of being robust and unambiguous, owing to the apparent precision offered by measurement. Qualitative researchers claim, by contrast, that their contextual approach and their often prolonged involvement in a setting engender rich data.
- *Macro vs. Micro.* Quantitative researchers are often depicted as involved in uncovering large-scale social

Change and connections between events over time tend not to surface, other than in a mechanistic fashion. Qualitative research is often depicted as being attuned to the unfolding of events over time and to the interconnections between the actions of participants of social settings.

6.1 | Student Experience

Interviews versus ethnography

Although ethnography can and often does involve interviews they play a somewhat different role in the research process than where interviews are the sole means of data collection. Karla provides her particular take on this in regard to a focus on identity: 'I always thought that interviews were good but I thought that the danger of entering into interviews with people is in picturing themselves the way they want to do like I do now. I am giving a picture of myself the way I like to do it whereas if you follow my life you would probably have [a] completely different [view], but you would probably have different perspectives. So I've always had this [view] that alright you tell me this but then I'm sure that there is more, and to get to the more or to get more around the idea, I need to see something, not just talk. And then especially when it comes to work . . . it's such a personal thing for many people, [for] most people's identity. And then it's also sensitive because you have to kind of measure how good [a] person you are based on how you are in your workplace, and if you are good at what you do . . . what you achieve and what you accomplish. So I was thinking that if I want to go in, and if I want to see people's work, it's not enough to talk about it with them. I need to be there. I need to see what happens there'.

trends and connections between variables, whereas qualitative researchers are seen as concerned with small-scale aspects of social reality, such as interaction.

- *Behaviour vs. Meaning.* It is sometimes suggested that the quantitative researcher is concerned with people's behaviour and the qualitative researcher with the meaning of action.
- *Artificial settings vs. Natural settings.* Whereas quantitative researchers conduct research in a contrived context, qualitative researchers investigate people in (so-called) natural environments.

However, as we have attempted to argue throughout, while these contrasts depict reasonably well the differences between quantitative and qualitative research, they should not be viewed as constituting hard and fast distinctions.

Theory and research

As we have noted, broadly speaking qualitative research differs from quantitative research in terms of its understanding of theory (overarching perspective versus sets of interrelated hypotheses) and its role (emergent versus testing). There are exceptions. Some qualitative researchers do engage in theory testing (Silverman, 1993). Nonetheless, when undertaking postpositivist qualitative research it is important to understand the type of theory that underlies any particular approach. Peggy Wallace (2007) and Scott MacMillan (2009), for example, drew on existentialist theory when studying people's decisions; whereas Mary Runté (2005) started from a feminist poststructuralist point of view when analyzing the impact of work and family conflict on people's perceptions of their lives.

Concepts in qualitative research

A central feature of Chapter 5 was the discussion of concepts and their measurement. For most qualitative researchers, developing measures of concepts will not be a significant consideration, but concepts are very much part of the landscape in qualitative research. However, the way in which concepts are developed and employed is often different from that implied in the **quantitative research** strategy. Blumer's (1954) distinction between 'definitive' and 'sensitizing' concepts captures aspects of the different ways in which concepts are thought about.

Blumer (1954) argued against the use of definitive concepts in social research, i.e., those concepts that once developed become fixed through the elaboration of indicators. For Blumer, such an approach entailed the application of a straitjacket on the social world, because the concept in question comes to be seen exclusively in terms of the indicators that have been developed for it. This reduces the possibility of alternative ways of viewing the concept and its manifestations. In other words, definitive concepts are excessively concerned with what is common to the phenomena that the concept is supposed to subsume rather than with variety. Instead, Blumer recommended that social researchers should recognize that the concepts they use are sensitizing concepts in that they provide 'a general sense of reference and guidance in approaching empirical instances' (1954, p. 7). For Blumer, then, concepts should be employed in such a way that they give a very general sense of what to look for and act as a means for uncovering the variety of forms that the phenomena to which they refer can assume. In providing a critique of definitive concepts, it is clear that Blumer had in mind the concept-indicator model described in Chapter 5. Blumer's distinction is not without its problems. It is not at all clear how far a very general formulation of a concept can be regarded as a useful guide to empirical enquiry. If it is too general, it will simply fail to provide a useful starting point, because its guidelines are too broad; if too narrow, it is likely to repeat some of the difficulties Blumer identified in relation to definitive concepts. However, his general view of concepts has attracted some support, because his preference for not imposing preordained schemes on the social world chimes with that of many qualitative researchers. As the example in Research in focus 6.1 suggests, the researcher frequently starts out with a broad outline of a concept, which is revised and narrowed during the course of data collection. For subsequent researchers, the concept may be taken up and revised as it is employed in connection with different social contexts or in relation to somewhat different research questions.

6.1 Research in Focus

An example of the emergence of a concept in qualitative research: 'emotional labour'

Hochschild's (1983) idea of emotional labour, labour that 'requires one to induce or suppress feelings in order to sustain the outward countenance that produces the proper state of mind in others' (1983, p. 7), has become a very influential concept in the sociology of work and in the developing area of the sociology of emotions. Somewhat ironically for a predominantly qualitative study, Hochschild's initial conceptualization appears to have emerged from a questionnaire she distributed to 261 university students. Within the questionnaire were two requests: 'Describe a real situation that was important to you in which you experienced a deep emotion' and 'Describe as fully and concretely as possible a real situation that was important to you in which you either changed the situation to fit your feelings or changed your feelings to fit the situation' (1983, p. 13). Thus, although a self-completion questionnaire was employed, the resulting data were qualitative. The data were analyzed in terms of the idea of emotion work, which is the same as emotional labour but occurs in a private context. Emotional labour is essentially emotion work that is performed as part of one's paid employment. In order to develop the idea of emotional labour, Hochschild looked to the world of work. The main occupation she studied was the flight attendant. Several sources of data on emotional labour among flight attendants were employed. She gained access to Delta Airlines, a large American airline, and in the course of her investigations she:

- Watched sessions for training attendants and had many conversations with both trainees and experienced attendants during the sessions.
- Interviewed various personnel, such as managers in various sections, and advertising agents.
- Examined Delta advertisements spanning 30 years.
- Observed the flight attendant recruitment process at Pan American Airways, since she had not been allowed to do this at Delta.
- Conducted 'open-ended interviews lasting three to five hours each with thirty flight attendants in the San Francisco Bay Area' (1983, p. 15).

As a contrasting occupational group that is nonetheless also involved in emotional labour, she also interviewed five debt collectors. In her book, she explores such topics as the human costs of emotional labour and the issue of gender in relation to it. It is clear that Hochschild's concept of emotional labour began as a somewhat imprecise idea that emerged out of a concern with emotion work and that was gradually developed in order to address its wider significance.

The concept has been picked up by a range of researchers in management and organization studies, including Brotheridge's (1999) quantitative study of the 'effectiveness of personal authenticity in mediating the effects of emotional labour on emotional exhaustion' (p. 11), and Runté and Mills's (2002) study of the relationship between emotionality at home and work.

Reliability and validity in qualitative research

In Chapters 4 and 5 it was noted that reliability and validity are important criteria in establishing and assessing the quality of research for the quantitative researcher. However, there has been some discussion among qualitative researchers concerning their relevance for qualitative research. Moreover, even writers who do take the view that the criteria are relevant have considered the possibility that the meanings of the terms need to be altered. For example, the issue of measurement validity almost by definition seems to carry **connotations** of measurement and, beyond that, issues of realism. Since measurement is not a major preoccupation among qualitative researchers, the issue of validity would seem to have little bearing on such studies. As foreshadowed briefly in Chapter 4, a number of stances have been taken by qualitative researchers in relation to these issues.

Adapting reliability and validity for qualitative research

One stance, particularly with positivist qualitative researchers, is to assimilate reliability and validity into qualitative research with little change of meaning other than playing down the salience of measurement issues. Mason, for example, in her book on qualitative research, argues that reliability, validity, and generalizability (which is the main component of external validity, see Chapter 4) 'are different kinds of measures of the quality, rigour and wider potential of research, which are achieved according to certain methodological and disciplinary conventions and principles' (1996, p. 21). She sticks very closely to the meaning that these criteria have in quantitative research, where they have been largely developed. Thus, validity refers to whether 'you are observing, identifying, or "measuring" what you say you are' (1996, p. 24). LeCompte and Goetz (1982) and Kirk and Miller (1986) also write about reliability and validity in relation to qualitative research but invest the terms with a somewhat different meaning from Mason. LeCompte and Goetz (1982) write about the following.

- *External reliability*, by which they mean the degree to which a study can be replicated. This is a difficult criterion to meet in qualitative research, since, as LeCompte and Goetz recognize, it is impossible to 'freeze' a social setting and the circumstances of an initial study to make it replicable in the sense in which the term is usually employed (see Chapter 5). However, they suggest several strategies that can be introduced in order to approach the requirements of external reliability. For example, they suggest that a qualitative researcher replicating ethnographic research needs to adopt a similar social role to that adopted by the original researcher. Otherwise what a researcher conduct-

ing a replication sees and hears will not be comparable to the original research.

- *Internal reliability*, by which they mean whether or not, when there is more than one observer, members of the research team agree about what they see and hear. This is a similar notion to *inter-observer consistency* (see Web Key concept 5.1).
- *Internal validity*, by which they mean whether or not there is a good match between researchers' observations and the theoretical ideas they develop. LeCompte and Goetz argue that internal validity tends to be a strength of qualitative research, particularly ethnographic research, because the prolonged participation in the social life of a group over a long period of time allows the researcher to ensure a high level of congruence between concepts and observations.
- *External validity*, which refers to the degree to which findings can be generalized across social settings. LeCompte and Goetz argue that, unlike internal validity, external validity represents a problem for qualitative researchers because of their tendency to employ case studies and small samples.

As this brief treatment suggests, qualitative researchers have tended to employ the terms reliability and validity in very similar ways to quantitative researchers when seeking to develop criteria for assessing research.

Alternative criteria for evaluating qualitative research

However, a second position in relation to reliability and validity in qualitative research can be discerned. Some writers have suggested that qualitative studies should be judged or evaluated according to quite different criteria from those used by quantitative researchers. Lincoln and Guba (1985) and Guba and Lincoln (1994) propose that it is necessary to specify terms and ways of establishing and assessing the quality of qualitative research that provides an alternative to reliability and validity. They propose two primary criteria for assessing a qualitative study: **trustworthiness** and *authenticity*.

Trustworthiness is made up of four criteria, each of which has an equivalent criterion in quantitative research:

- *Credibility*, which parallels internal validity.
- *Transferability*, which parallels external validity.
- *Dependability*, which parallels reliability.
- *Confirmability*, which parallels objectivity.

A major reason for Guba and Lincoln's unease about the simple application of reliability and validity standards to qualitative research is that the criteria presuppose that a single absolute account of social reality is feasible. In other words, they are critical of the view (described in Chapter 3 as *realist*) that there are absolute truths about the social world that it is the job of the social scientist to reveal. Instead, they argue that there can be more than one and possibly several accounts.

Credibility

The significance of this stress on multiple accounts of social reality is especially evident in the trustworthiness criterion of *credibility*. After all, if there can be several possible accounts of an aspect of social reality, it is the feasibility or credibility of the account that a researcher arrives at that is going to determine its acceptability to others. The establishment of the credibility of findings entails both ensuring that research is carried out according to the canons of good practice and by submitting research findings to the members of the social world who were studied for confirmation that the investigator has correctly understood that social world. This latter technique is often referred to as **respondent validation** or *member validation* (see Key concept 6.1). Another technique they recommend is **triangulation** (see Web Key concept 6.2).

Transferability

As qualitative research typically entails the intensive study of a small group, or of individuals sharing certain characteristics (that is, depth rather than the breadth that is a preoccupation in quantitative research), qualitative findings tend to be oriented to the contextual uniqueness and significance of the aspect of the social world being studied. As Guba and Lincoln (1985) put it, whether or not findings 'hold in some other context, or even in the same context at some other time, is an empirical issue' (Lincoln and Guba 1985, p. 316). Instead, qualitative researchers

are encouraged to produce what Geertz (1973a) calls **thick description**— that is, rich accounts of the details of a culture. Guba and Lincoln (1985) argue that a thick description provides others with what they refer to as a database for making judgements about the possible transferability of findings to other milieux.

Dependability

As a parallel to reliability in quantitative research, Guba and Lincoln (1985) propose the idea of dependability and argue that, to establish the merit of research in terms of this criterion of trustworthiness, researchers should adopt an 'auditing' approach. This entails ensuring that complete records are kept of all phases of the research process: problem formulation; selection of research participants, fieldwork notes, interview transcripts, data analysis decisions, and so on in an accessible manner. Peers would then act as auditors, possibly during the course of the research and certainly at the end to establish how far proper procedures are being and have been followed. This would include assessing the degree to which theoretical inferences can be justified. Auditing has not become a popular approach to enhancing the dependability of qualitative research within management and business, partly due to some of the problems that are associated with it. One is that it is very demanding for the auditors, bearing in mind that qualitative research frequently generates extremely large data sets, and it may be that this is a major reason why it has not become a pervasive approach to validation.

Confirmability

Confirmability is concerned with ensuring that the researcher can be shown to have acted in good faith; in other words, it should be apparent that he or she has not overtly allowed personal values or theoretical inclinations manifestly to sway the conduct of the research and findings deriving from it. Guba and Lincoln (1985) propose

> **Key concept 6.1: Respondent validation**
>
> sometimes called member validation, is a process whereby a researcher provides the people on whom he or she has conducted research with an account of his or her findings. The aim of the exercise is to seek corroboration or otherwise of the account that the researcher has arrived at.

that establishing confirmability should be one of the objectives of auditors.

Authenticity

In addition to these four trustworthiness criteria, Guba and Lincoln (1985) suggest criteria of *authenticity*. These criteria raise a wider set of issues concerning the wider political impact of research. These are the criteria:

- *Fairness*. Does the research fairly represent different viewpoints among members of the social setting? For example, according to Starbuck (1981) one of the most serious deficiencies of the early (1963–72) Aston studies stems from the fact that the data about contexts and structures were collected primarily through interviews with senior managers. The first wave of interviews (1962–4) was conducted with chief executives and heads of departments, whereas the second set of interviews involved just one (senior) executive in the organization. Starbuck (1981) suggests that the data thus represent managerial perceptions and exclude the perceptions of other stakeholders, including first-line workers, customers, and suppliers.
- *Ontological authenticity*. Does the research help members to arrive at a better understanding of their social milieux?
- *Educative authenticity*. Does the research help members to appreciate better the perspectives of other members of their social setting?
- *Catalytic authenticity*. Has the research acted as an impetus to members to engage in action to change their circumstances?
- *Tactical authenticity*. Has the research empowered members to take the steps necessary for engaging in action?

The authenticity criteria are thought provoking but have not been influential, and their emphasis on the wider impact of research is controversial. However, the main point of discussing Guba and Lincoln's ideas is that they differ from writers like LeCompte and Goetz in seeking criteria for evaluating qualitative research that represent a departure from those employed by quantitative researchers.

The authenticity criteria also have certain points of affinity with **action research**, which became popular as a research method within business and management during the 1980s and 1990s. The emphasis on practical outcomes differentiates action research from other forms of qualitative investigation. We will return to the subject of action research later in this chapter.

Between quantitative and qualitative research criteria

Hammersley (1992a) lies midway between the two positions outlined above. He proposes that validity is an important criterion but reformulates it somewhat. For Hammersley, validity means that an empirical account must be plausible and credible and should take into account the amount and kind of evidence used in relation to an account. In proposing this criterion, Hammersley shares with realism (see Key concept 3.4) the notion that there is an external social reality that can be accessed by the researcher. However, he simultaneously shares with the critics of the empirical realist position the rejection of the notion that such access is direct and in particular that the researcher can act as a mirror on the social world, reflecting its image back to an audience. Instead, the researcher is always engaged in representations or constructions of that world. The plausibility and credibility of a researcher's 'truth claims' then become the main considerations in evaluating qualitative research.

Hammersley also suggests *relevance* as an important criterion of qualitative research. Relevance is taken to be assessed from the vantage point of the importance of a topic within its substantive field or the contribution it makes to the literature on that field. Hammersley also discusses the question of whether or not the concerns of practitioners (that is, people who are part of the social setting being investigated and who are likely to have a vested interest in the research question and the implications of findings deriving from it) might be an aspect of considerations of relevance. In this way, his approach touches on the kinds of consideration that are addressed by Guba and Lincoln's authenticity criteria (Lincoln and Guba, 1985; Guba and Lincoln, 1994). However, he recognizes that the kinds of research questions and findings that might be of interest to practitioners and researchers are likely to be somewhat different. As Hammersley notes, practitioners are likely to be interested in research that helps them to understand or address problems with which they are confronted. These may not be (and perhaps are unlikely to be) at the forefront of a researcher's set of preoccupations. However, there may be occasions when researchers can combine the two and may even be able to use this capability as a means of securing access to organizations in which they wish to conduct research (see Chapter 19 for a further discussion of access issues).

Overview of the issue of criteria

There is a recognition that a simple application of the quantitative researcher's criteria of reliability and validity to qualitative research is not desirable, but writers vary in the degree to which they propose a complete overhaul of those criteria. Nor do the three positions outlined above represent the full range of possible stances on this issue (Hammersley 1992a; Seale, 1999). The differences between the three positions, to a large extent, reflect divergences in the degree to which the realist position is broadly accepted or rejected. Writers on qualitative research who apply the ideas of reliability and validity with little, if any, adaptation broadly position themselves as realists that is, as saying that social reality can be captured by qualitative researchers through their concepts and theories. Lincoln and Guba reject this view, arguing instead that qualitative researchers' concepts and theories are representations and that there may, therefore, be other equally credible representations of the same phenomena. Hammersley's position occupies a middle ground in terms of the axis, with realism at one end and anti-realism at the other, in that, while acknowledging the existence of social phenomena that are part of an external reality, he disavows any suggestion that it is possible to reproduce that reality. Most qualitative researchers nowadays probably operate around the midpoint on this realism axis, though without necessarily endorsing Hammersley's views. Typically, they treat their accounts as one of a number of possible representations rather than as definitive versions of social reality. They also bolster those accounts through some of the strategies advocated by Lincoln and Guba, such as

thick descriptions, respondent validation exercises, and triangulation.

 ## The main preoccupations of qualitative researchers

As was noted in Chapter 5, quantitative and qualitative research can be viewed as exhibiting a set of distinctive but contrasting preoccupations. These preoccupations reflect epistemologically grounded beliefs about what constitutes acceptable knowledge. In Chapter 3 it was suggested that at the level of epistemology, whereas quantitative research is profoundly influenced by a natural science approach of what should count as acceptable knowledge, qualitative researchers are more influenced by postpositivist worldviews, such as interpretivism (see Key concept 3.5), feminism, and poststructuralism. In this section, five distinctive preoccupations among qualitative researchers will be outlined and examined.

Seeing through the eyes of the people being studied

An underlying premise of many qualitative researchers is that the subject matter of the social sciences (that is, people and their social world) differs from the subject matter of the natural sciences. A key difference is that the objects of analysis of the natural sciences (atoms, molecules, gases, chemicals, metals, and so on) cannot attribute meaning to events and to their environment. People, however, *do* (see Chapter 3). Consequently, many qualitative researchers have suggested that a methodology is required for studying people that reflects these differences between people and the objects of the natural sciences. As a result, many qualitative researchers express a commitment to viewing events and the social world through the eyes of the people that they study. The social world must be interpreted from the perspective of the people being studied, rather than as though those subjects were incapable of their own reflections on the social world. The epistemology underlying qualitative research has been expressed by the authors of one widely read text as involving two central tenets: '(1) . . . face-to-face interaction is the fullest condition of participating in the mind of another human being, and (2) . . . you must participate in the mind of another human being (in sociological terms, 'take the role of the other') to acquire social knowledge' (Lofland & Lofland 1995, p. 16).

It is not surprising, therefore, that many researchers make claims in their reports of their investigations about having sought to take the views of the people they studied as the point of departure (see Web Research in focus 6.2). This tendency reveals itself in frequent references to empathy and seeing through others' eyes. For example, in a series of studies of accidents Weick (1990, 1993, 1996) set out to understand how participants made sense of the events involved. He later drew on the lessons from these studies to develop a **sensemaking** framework (consisting of seven sociopsychological properties) for understanding events as the outcomes of people's sensemaking (Weick, 2001). Similarly, albeit drawing on a different notion of sensemaking, Gephart (1997) studied the impact of people's sensemaking on the development of measures of risk. Thurlow (2007) has since drawn on Helms Mills's (2003) notion of **critical sensemaking** and its relationship to organizational change by interviewing a number of people in the education and health fields to understand how language use in context influences how people assess change.

Strategies of 'seeing through the eyes' of the people studied is often accompanied by the closely related goal of seeking to probe beneath surface appearances. By taking the position of the people you are studying, the prospect is raised that they might view things differently from what an outsider with little direct contact might have expected. For example, it is inexplicable for outsiders to understand why firefighters would not drop their tools to outrun a fire or a trained commercial airline pilot would fail to tell his captain that he was clearly taking the wrong course of action. Yet, by getting 'inside the heads' of those involved Weick (1990, 1996) was able to convincingly show that the training of the men involved (they were all men in both cases) shaped their subsequent sensemaking of unfolding events. Through intensive training the identity of the firefighters was closely linked to the tools they used, and that of airline crew members encouraged obedience to the decisions of superior officers. Weick was able to

use this 'insider' perspective to encourage training that allowed for more flexible approaches in unusual situations.

Description and the emphasis on context

Qualitative researchers are much more inclined than quantitative researchers to provide a great deal of descriptive detail when reporting the fruits of their research. This is not to say that they are exclusively concerned with description. They *are* concerned with explanation, and indeed the extent to which qualitative researchers ask 'Why?' questions is frequently understated. In addition, more critical or radical qualitative researchers are often concerned with understanding the political and economic interests that inform organizational actions, in order to enhance the possibilities for changing them. For example, in her critical **ethnography** of a multinational corporation, Casey (1995) describes herself as concerned with understanding dominant social constructions about work, the self, and society, in the hope that this might increase the likelihood of societal transformation.

Many qualitative studies provide a detailed account of what goes on in the setting being investigated. Very often qualitative studies seem to be full of apparently trivial details. However, these details are frequently important for the qualitative researcher, because of their significance for their subjects and also because the details provide an account of the context within which people's behaviour takes place. It was with this point in mind that Geertz (1973a) recommended the provision of thick descriptions of social settings, events, and often individuals. As a result of this emphasis on description, qualitative studies are often full of detailed information about the social worlds being examined. On the surface, some of this detail may appear irrelevant, and, indeed, there is a risk of the researcher becoming too embroiled in descriptive detail. Lofland and Lofland (1995, pp. 164–5), for example, warn against the sin of what they call 'descriptive excess' in qualitative research, whereby the amount of detail overwhelms or inhibits the analysis of data.

One of the main reasons why qualitative researchers are keen to provide considerable descriptive detail is that they typically emphasize the importance of the contextual understanding of social behaviour. This means that behaviour, values, or whatever must be understood in context. This recommendation means that we cannot understand the behaviour of members of a social group other than in terms of the specific environment in which they operate. In this way behaviour, that may appear odd or irrational, can make perfect sense when we understand the particular context within which that behaviour takes place. The emphasis on context in qualitative research goes back to many of the classic studies in social anthropology, which often demonstrated how a particular practice, such as the magical ritual that may accompany the sowing of seeds, made little sense unless we understand the belief systems of that society. One of the chief reasons for the emphasis on descriptive detail is that it is often precisely this detail that provides the mapping of context in terms of which behaviour is understood. The propensity for description can also be interpreted as a manifestation of the naturalism that pervades much qualitative research (see Key concepts 4.3 and Web Key concept 6.1), because it places a premium on detailed, rich descriptions of social settings.

Emphasis on process

Qualitative research tends to view social life in terms of processes. This tendency reveals itself in a number of ways. One of the main ways is that there is often a concern to show how events and patterns unfold over time. As a result, qualitative evidence often conveys a strong sense of change and flux. As Pettigrew (1997, p. 338) usefully puts it, process is 'a sequence of individual and collective events, actions, and activities unfolding over time in context'. Qualitative research that is based in ethnographic methods is particularly associated with this emphasis on process. It is the element of participant observation that is a key feature of ethnography that is especially instrumental in generating this feature. Ethnographers are typically immersed in a social setting for a long time—sometimes years. Consequently, they are able to observe the ways in which events develop over time or the ways in which the different elements of a social system (values, beliefs, behaviour, and so on) interconnect. Such findings can inject a sense of process by seeing social life in terms of streams of interdependent events and elements. Weick (2001), for example, argues that we should focus on the processes of organizing rather than on organizations as fixed entities. According to Weick (2001), by focusing on organizations as concrete entities we shift our attention to rational decision-making and seemingly objective structures that mask the role of people in the life of a given organizational entity. By focusing on the sense-making activities of the people involved Vaughan (1996) was able to provide unique insights into the 1986 American space shuttle *Challenger* disaster, arguing that 'the disaster was an accident, the result of a mistake [but not one simply attributed to individuals, rather due to the fact] that mistakes themselves are socially organized and systematically produced' (p. 394).

This is not to say, however, that ethnographers are the only qualitative researchers who inject a sense of process into our understanding of social life. It can also be achieved through semi-structured and unstructured interviewing, by asking participants to reflect on the processes leading up to or following on from an event. Broussine and Vince (1996), for example, were interested in the way that managers use metaphors in relation to the management of change. Research was undertaken in a public-sector organization in the UK at a time when the public services were experiencing a high level of uncertainty. Broussine and Vince chose a relatively unusual research method within management and organizational research, based on the analysis of managers' drawings. By drawing pictures, managers reflected on their experience of the change process. Analysis of the drawings involved 'listening to the drawing's story', its style, use made of colour, the way that space is represented, and the general atmosphere. A total of 86 managers produced drawings and individually and collectively they reflected on their emotional content. A picture of a ship swamped by a tidal wave was construed as reflecting the emotions of anxiety, fear, and dread, whereas drawings of piles of paperwork and queues of people reflected feelings of powerlessness and debility. The discussions were tape-recorded and comparisons were made between groups of senior and middle managers, to see if there were differences in the use of metaphor between colleagues at different hierarchical levels. Broussine and Vince suggest that on some occasions this process enabled managers to appreciate each other's perspectives; in other cases, it simply made apparent their differences.

Student Experience

Access issues and data collection

In gaining access to her research site Karla got more than she bargained for. She was initially interested in the work of parliamentary administrators and applied to undertake a research project. However, the response was less than enthusiastic and she felt that 'they basically just didn't want me there. It was made explicit [: the] managers of the administration were not keen on this idea at all'. She felt that government officials have this view that 'we're just doing our job here', 'we're just trying to support the main function and there's nothing interesting here', and thus were unwilling to be the focus of a study. Karla, on the other hand, felt that the translation work of those hired to make sense of legislation could be very interesting for what it could say about how things are made sense of and enacted. Around the time of her initial attempt to gain access it was at the end of a parliamentary session and she 'got the permission initially from the speaker of the previous political side'. Just before that person retired from the position he contacted his personal assistant who 'thought that this kind of research would be interesting'. The outgoing speaker then 'emailed his administrative manager and said "this girl needs to come in and do this research, bye" [but] this didn't set me off on very good terms with the administrative manager'. As a result Karla's access was initially very limited: 'they first let me in the parliament library, and then in the library there's this very weird room [for researchers] where you can apply for . . . a desk . . . I don't know why you would ever want to do that, because it's like a dark, uncomfortable, horrible room, but there are people sitting there who are . . . parliamentary researchers. So I was allocated a desk there'.

She was told by an administrator that '"we are letting you in . . . at the outskirts of our camp"'. She was also told that the research library room was a good place to start her research but she felt that the administrator 'was never intending to let me work upstairs, this was downstairs, they sat upstairs'. However, soon after she started at the research library room another administrator—'with her own agenda'—allowed Karla more access. Reflecting on her access problems, Karla gives cautionary advice. While she feels that a researcher should persevere to gain access this has to be weighed against the potential pitfalls: 'in hindsight I would maybe say that if it's problematic, if it's clear to start with that you're not wanted in the organization by the management, then it sets you off in a very sort of odd beginning, because it means that if somebody then wants you in, they have some sort of mission of their own. So you're immediately in a sort of funny relationship to these people and that will effect how you see everything and you need to think about that. So there's this sort of issue of complex reflexivity becomes highly important. And even though I tried to sort of look at myself and look at how things went all the time and write about it, I still think that I was probably used, and very much in the midst of this weird power struggle between these managers as well, and somehow involved myself as well, even though I never meant to be . . . I think that a lesson to learn [is] if you can see to start with that there will be trouble, then you probably should take extra care of yourself and how you position yourself in relation to these people and how you think about [things] before even going in'.

The life history approach is another form of qualitative research, although one that is relatively little used in business and management research. This technique takes as research data accounts of individuals about their lives or specific areas of their social world. Accounts focus on the relationship between the individual and his or her social context. Jones (1983) suggests that the life history approach is useful as a means of researching organizational socialization and career development. This involves leading individuals through an account of their organizational careers and asking them to chart out significant events through which they came to an understanding of their social organizational context. Bell and Nkomo (1992) used a life histories approach to document the problems that Black women face in the United States when attempting to rise up the corporate ladder.

An example relating to experiences of work is provided by Terkel's (1974) anthology of working lives in the United States. Written as a series of first-person narratives detailing the everyday reality of working lives, the accounts link individuals' past and present experiences of employment with their hopes, fears, ambitions, home, and family lives. Although Terkel acknowledges that he used 'no one method or technique' in searching out the feelings of 'ordinary' people, this diverse set of narratives, which covers everyone from factory mechanics to washroom attendants, provides a colourful example of the life history approach.

Other qualitative studies begin with an ethnographic approach in order to gain access to organizational data and then proceed to analyze it using other methods. For example, in his study of a public inquiry concerning a fatal pipeline accident, Gephart (1993) employed what he calls a 'textual approach'. This involved systematically gathering together a set of documents concerning the event, which he subsequently analyzed using a combination of theoretical sampling, computer-assisted qualitative data analysis, and expansion analysis. The documents, including official proceedings of the public inquiry, company documents, field notes, reports, and newspaper articles, enabled a reconstruction of the events leading up to the pipeline disaster. Passages of **text** were selected to illustrate the unfolding sensemaking about key decisions relating to the disaster, highlighting issues such as risk, blame, and responsibility. These quite different approaches to data analysis and collection highlight the diverse nature of qualitative research within management and business.

Flexibility and limited structure

Many qualitative researchers are disdainful of approaches to research that entail the imposition of predetermined formats on the social world. This position is largely to do with the preference for seeing through the eyes of the people being studied. After all, if a structured method of data collection is employed, since this is bound to be the product of an investigator's ruminations about the object of enquiry, certain decisions must have been made about what he or she expects to find and about the nature of the social reality that is to be encountered. Therefore, the researcher is limited in the degree to which he or she can genuinely adopt the worldview of the people being studied. Consequently, most qualitative researchers prefer a research orientation that entails as little prior contamination of the social world as possible. To do otherwise risks imposing an inappropriate frame of reference on people. Keeping structure to a minimum is supposed to enhance the opportunity of genuinely revealing the perspectives of the people you are studying. Also, in the process, aspects of people's social world that are particularly important to them, but that might not even have crossed the mind of a researcher unacquainted with it, are more likely to be forthcoming. As a result, qualitative research tends to be a strategy that tries not to delimit areas of enquiry too much and to ask fairly general rather than specific research questions (see Figure 6.1).

Due to the preference for a loosely structured approach to the collection of data, qualitative researchers adopt methods of research that do not require the investigator to develop highly specific research questions in advance and, therefore, to devise instruments specifically for those questions to be answered. Ethnography, with its emphasis on **participant observation**, is particularly well suited to this orientation. It allows researchers to submerge themselves in a social setting with a fairly general research focus in mind and gradually to formulate a narrower emphasis by making as many observations of that setting as possible. They can then formulate more specific research questions out of their collected data. Similarly, interviewing is an extremely prominent method in the qualitative researcher's armoury, but it is not of the kind we will encounter in the course of most of Chapter 13—namely, the structured interview. Instead, qualitative researchers prefer less structured approaches to interviewing, as we will see in Chapter 14. Blumer's (1954) argument for sensitizing rather than definitive concepts (that is, the kind employed by quantitative researchers) is symptomatic of the preference for a more open-ended, and hence, less structured, approach. Some researchers have argued that this is more likely to lead to research that is interesting, in terms of standing out in some way from other studies and changing the way that we think about the social world (see Thinking deeper 6.4).

An advantage of the unstructured nature of most qualitative enquiry (that is, in addition to the prospect of gaining access to people's world views) is that it offers the prospect of flexibility. The researcher can change direction in the course of his or her investigation much more easily than in quantitative research, which tends to have a built-in momentum once the data collection is under way: if you send out hundreds of postal questionnaires and realize after you have started to get some back that there is an issue that you would have liked to investigate, you are not going to find it easy to retrieve the situation.

Structured interviewing and **structured observation** can involve some flexibility, but the requirement to make interviews as comparable as possible for survey investigations limits the extent to which this can happen. Bryman et al. (1996), for example, carried out a multiple-case-study investigation of strategic responses to deregulation in nine British bus companies. Using semi-structured interviews with senior managers and the examination of documents, the researchers were interested in the significance of organizational culture for types of strategic response. However, from early interviews, it soon became apparent from early that the bus companies—selected to reflect a range of post-deregulation experiences and ownership patterns—were remarkably similar in their response to deregulation, reflecting a concentration on survival at a time of declining passenger numbers. Sensing theoretical saturation for their main concepts and interconnections, Bryman et al. shifted their focus on to the similarities between the companies and started to explore the possibility that organizational culture was far less significant to the nine companies than what the researchers termed 'industry culture'. This shift in focus was important because it helped the researchers to understand the firms and how they were coping with declining patronage, but it was also theoretically significant because of the attention that organizational culture had attracted among scholars in the 1980s and early 1990s. Although the research had been influenced by this stream of thinking, Bryman and his colleagues began to view organizational culture as less significant in this particular study.

Concepts and theory grounded in data

For qualitative researchers, concepts and theories are usually inductively arrived at from the data that are collected (see Research in focus 6.1). When, for example, Parsons and Mills (2008) began to analyze issues of *Rotary International* (*RI*) for the period immediately prior to the admittance of women in the United States in 1986, the period immediately following, and the current era (2005–2006), they were interested in how the journal portrayed women—particularly female members, and whether those images changed over time as increasing numbers of women joined Rotary International clubs in North America. Initially, they found that dominant images of the ideal typical member shifted quite dramatically in *RI* over a 20-year period; moving from focuses on male corporate executive types as an exemplar of the typical Rotarian, to male and female community volunteer types. The focus of rotary work also moved from large-scale, indirect projects, such as 'the War Against Polio', to more direct involvement in small-scale local, and international development projects. On the surface it certainly appeared as if attitudes to gendered relationship had changed in North American clubs but specific textual analysis of some of the recent stories on international projects revealed a surprising reproduction of Rotary's more traditional attitudes to women prior to 1986. What emerged was a concept that Parsons and Mills (2009) call 'the outsourcing of gender' in which a number of stories portrayed white American male members of the Rotary as local heroes to non-white, poor, helpless, Third World women.

 # The critique of qualitative research

In a similar way to the criticisms that have been levelled at quantitative research mainly by qualitative researchers, a parallel critique has been built up of qualitative research. Some of the more common ones follow.

Student Experience

Identifying emerging concepts from experience

Anne's doctorate on 'how consumers construct their images' of products has its roots in a personal experience she had one day outside her apartment building: 'Well, there was a happening that sort of opened my eyes, [although later] I realized I had been interested in the same subject for a long time. It was an occasion when one of our neighbours came to the parking place and unloaded his car and he was behaving very strangely, he was somehow digging into the car, being embarrassed or something strange was going on . . . you know intuition told me that everything was not as it should be . . . I got interested in what was going on and I waited and so forth because we were good friends . . . I wanted to say hello and good morning and then finally, very embarrassed, he excused himself for having shopping bags from a bargain store nearby. [He] said that he "doesn't usually go there, but you know they have opened up a new shop quite nearby and now when he went there, they really had nice stuff", and he suggested that I should go and [tried to] convinced [me] to visit the same shop. [In fact] I hadn't paid attention to the shop . . . I didn't think anything special or specific about the neighbourhood shop, not that it's a bargain store or anything, because it was outside my sort of choices. So I wondered "What is he thinking that I'm thinking?" and "What is he actually referring to?" and "How comes he thinks that we are sharing the same view?" So this interested [me] . . . I thought this was interesting so actually I decided to make an exploratory study. I picked the same company, I interviewed six persons . . . on the subject: "What comes to mind, how do you think about this company?" This later informed her research project and her doctoral thesis.

Qualitative research is too subjective

Quantitative researchers sometimes criticize qualitative research as being too impressionistic and subjective. By these criticisms they usually mean that qualitative findings rely too much on the researcher's often unsystematic views about what is significant and important, and also upon the close personal relationships that the researcher frequently strikes up with the people studied. Precisely because qualitative research often begins in a relatively open-ended way and entails a gradual narrowing down of research questions or problems, the consumer of the writings deriving from the research is given few clues as to why one area was the chosen area upon which attention was focused rather than another. By contrast, quantitative researchers point to the tendency for the problem formulation stage in their work to be more explicitly stated in terms of such matters as the existing literature on that topic and key theoretical ideas.

Difficult to replicate

Quantitative researchers also often argue that these tendencies are even more of a problem because of the difficulty of replicating a qualitative study, although **replication** in business and management research is by no means a straightforward matter regardless of this particular issue (see Chapter 5). Precisely because it is unstructured and often reliant upon the qualitative researcher's ingenuity, it is almost impossible to conduct a true replication, since there are hardly any standard procedures to be followed. In qualitative research, the investigator himself or herself is the main instrument of data collection, so that what is observed and heard and also what the researcher decides to concentrate upon is very much a product of his or her predilections. There are several possible components of this criticism: what qualitative researchers (especially perhaps in ethnography) choose to focus upon while in the field is a product of what strikes them as significant, whereas other researchers are likely to empathize with other issues; the responses of participants (people being observed or interviewed) to qualitative researchers is likely to be affected by the characteristics of the researcher (personality, age, gender, and so on); and, because of the unstructured nature of qualitative data, interpretation will be profoundly influenced by the subjective leanings of a researcher. Because of such factors it is difficult, not to say impossible, to replicate qualitative findings. The difficulties ethnographers experience when they revisit grounds previously trodden by another researcher (often referred to as a 'restudy') do not inspire confidence in the replicability of qualitative research (Bryman, 1994).

Problems of generalization

It is often suggested that the scope of the findings of qualitative investigations is restricted. When participant observation is used or when unstructured interviews are conducted with a small number of individuals in a certain organization or locality, they argue that it is impossible to know how the findings can be generalized to other settings. How can just one or two cases be representative of all cases? In other words, can we really treat Perlow's (1997) research on the time and the work-life balance of software engineers in a high-tech corporation in the United States as representative of all software engineers; or Prasad's (1993) research on computerization in a health management organization as representative of the symbolic effects of implementing new technology in other types of work organization? In the case of research based on interviews rather than participation, can we treat interviewees who have not been selected through a probability procedure or even quota sampling as representative? Are Watson's (1994a) managers typical of all managers working within the telecommunications industry, or are Ram's (1994) small firm case studies in the West Midlands typical of small firms elsewhere?

The answer in all these cases is, of course, emphatically 'no'. A case study is not a sample of one drawn from a known population. Similarly, the people who are interviewed in qualitative research are not meant to be representative of a population and indeed, in some cases, like managers, we may find it more or less impossible to enu-

merate the population in any precise manner. Instead, the findings of qualitative research are to generalize to theory rather than to populations. It is 'the cogency of the theoretical reasoning' (Mitchell, 1983, p. 207), rather than statistical criteria, that is decisive in considering the generalizability of the findings of qualitative research. In other words, it is the quality of the theoretical inferences that are made out of qualitative data that is crucial to the assessment of generalization.

These three criticisms reflect many of the preoccupations of quantitative research that were discussed in Chapter 5. A further criticism that is often made of qualitative research, but that is perhaps less influenced by quantitative research criteria, is the suggestion that qualitative research frequently lacks transparency in how the research was conducted.

Lack of transparency

It is sometimes difficult to establish from qualitative research what the researcher actually *did* and how he or she arrived at the study's conclusions. For example, qualitative research reports are sometimes unclear about such matters as how people were chosen for observation or interview. This deficiency contrasts sharply with the sometimes laborious accounts of sampling procedures in reports of quantitative research. However, it does not seem plausible to suggest that outlining, in some detail, the ways in which research participants are selected constitutes the application of quantitative research criteria. Readers have a right to know how far research participants were selected to correspond to a wide range of people. Also, the process of qualitative data analysis is frequently unclear (Bryman & Burgess, 1994a). It is often not obvious how the analysis was conducted, in other words, what the researcher was actually doing when the data were analyzed and, therefore, how the study's conclusions were arrived at. To a large extent, these areas of a lack of transparency are increasingly being addressed by qualitative researchers.

 ## Is it always like this?

This was a heading that was employed in Chapter 5 in relation to quantitative research, but it is perhaps less easy to answer in relation to qualitative research. To a large extent, this is because qualitative research is less codified than quantitative research, that is, it is less influenced by strict guidelines and directions about how to go about data collection and analysis. For example, Dalton (1964) explains that no explicit hypotheses formed the basis for his participant-observational study of managerial work, for three reasons. First, he was not able to be sure what was relevant until he had gained 'some intimacy with the situation'; secondly, once uttered, a hypothesis becomes somewhat 'obligatory'; and, thirdly, there is a danger that the hypothesis carries a quasi-scientific status. Instead he worked on the basis of 'hunches', which guided him through the research.

As a result, accounts of qualitative research are frequently less prescriptive in tone than those encountered in relation to quantitative research. Instead, they often exhibit more of a descriptive tenor, outlining the different ways qualitative researchers have gone about research or suggesting alternative ways of conducting research or analysis based on the writer's own experiences or those of others. To a large extent, this picture is changing, in that there is a growing number of books that seek to make clear-cut recommendations about how qualitative research should be carried out.

However, if we look at some of the preoccupations of qualitative research that were described above, we can see certain ways in which there are departures from the practices that are implied by these preoccupations. One of the main departures is that qualitative research is sometimes a lot more focused than is implied by the suggestion that the researcher begins with general research questions and narrows it down so that theory and concepts are arrived at during and after the data collection. There is no necessary reason why qualitative research cannot be employed to investigate a specific research problem. For example, Truss (2001) takes as her research problem the relationship between organizational performance and human resource management (HRM). However, instead of devising a list of 'best practice' indicators from the literature and testing their impact on performance, this study looked at a firm that was successful, in this case Hewlett-Packard, and asked what human resources policies and

practices were used and how they were being enacted. Using a variety of methods, including interviews and focus groups, Truss found that many of the company's human resources policies and practices were contradictory, particularly in relation to training and career management, where a large number of employees did not believe they received the training they needed. Yet, even though the company did not achieve a high level of 'fit' within its human resources system, it still managed to achieve high levels of financial performance. Truss concludes that there is a disjuncture between formal policy and informal organization, which quantitative studies of High Performance Work Systems fail to capture. A related way in which qualitative research differs from the standard model is in connection with the notion of a lack of structure in approaches to collecting and analyzing data. As will be seen in Chapter 20, techniques like **conversation analysis** entail the application of a highly codified method for analyzing talk. Moreover, the growing use of **computer-assisted qualitative data analysis software** (CAQDAS) is leading to greater transparency in the procedures used for analyzing qualitative data. This greater transparency may lead to more codification in qualitative data analysis than has previously been the case.

 ## Researcher–subject relationships

A further difference between quantitative and qualitative research arises in relation to the way that qualitative researchers relate to their research subjects. Specifically, qualitative researchers tend to take greater account of the power relations that exist between the researcher himself or herself and the people who are the main subject of study. This has led to the development of several qualitative approaches that enable research subjects to play a more active part in designing the research and influencing the outcomes of the process. Action research, feminism, and collaborative and participative forms of enquiry all fall into this category. In the last section of this chapter we will consider the main features of each of these approaches and explore the implications that they have for researcher–subject relationships.

Action research

There is no single type of action research but broadly it can be defined as an approach in which the action researcher and a client collaborate in the diagnosis of a problem and in the development of a solution based on the diagnosis. A common theme among management and business researchers is that action research output results from 'involvement with members of an organization' over a matter of 'genuine concern to them' (Eden & Huxham, 1996, p. 75). Many writers, therefore, stress the need for **action research** to be useful to the practitioner and suggest it should provide a means of empowering participants.

Action research is defined by Argyris, Putnam, and Smith (1985) as follows:

- Experiments are on real problems within an organization and are designed to assist in their solution.
- This involves an iterative process of problem identification, planning, action, and evaluation.
- Action research leads eventually to re-education, changing patterns of thinking and action. This depends on the participation of research subjects (who are often referred to in action research as clients) in identifying new courses of action.
- It is intended to contribute both to academic theory and practical action.

Eden and Huxham (1996) define the characteristics of action research in terms of outcomes and processes. Good and effective action research should have the following outcomes:

- It should have implications that relate to situations other than the one that is studied.
- As well as being usable in everyday life, action research should also be concerned with theory.
- It leads to the generation of emergent or grounded theory, which emanates from the data in gradual incremental steps.
- Action researchers must recognize that their findings will have practical implications and they should be clear about what they expect participants to take away from the project.

In business and management, action research plays a particular role in bridging the gap between researchers and practitioners (by which it is usually meant managers). Gummesson (1999) stresses the need for business and management researchers to be involved in practice and he suggests that there is actually very little difference between the roles of the academic researcher and the management consultant. Action research is seen as particularly useful in researching processual problems in organizations such as learning and change. Hence, many action research projects are undertaken by part-time students who take their own work organization and problems within it to be their primary focus of study. These individuals are already immersed in the organizations as complete participants and have an understanding of it that is derived from being an actor in the processes being studied. They face three interrelated sets of issues that relate to:

- Their pre-understanding of the setting.
- Role duality.
- Organizational politics (Coghlan, 2001).

Pre-understanding refers to the knowledge, insight, and experience that researchers have about the lived experience of their own organization; for example, they already know the history, key events, and jargon used within the organization and who to turn to for information. Their role duality sets them apart from other organizational members and can affect the data that are generated, particularly when they are engaged in research that may threaten existing organizational norms.

A further source of action research projects is related to organizational consultancy, which is conducted by some business school academics as a way of informing their own practice and as a source of additional income. However, this alternative source of research material can also cause problems. Even though consultancy settings provide access to data, a clear design must be formulated for the action research before the setting is encountered (Eden & Huxham, 1996). In addition, the tendency to refer to research subjects as clients suggests that research participants are employing the services of the researcher. This can create conflicts of interest for the researcher and introduce bias towards those who are financially supporting the research. Action researchers must, therefore, possess a high degree of self-awareness in order to combine the roles of researcher and consultant and be prepared to defend their research in these terms.

The collection of data is likely to be involved in the formulation of the diagnosis of a problem and in the evaluation of a problem. Action research can involve the collection of both quantitative and qualitative data. Data collection methods can include: keeping a diary of subjective impressions, a collection of documents relating to a situation, observation notes of meetings, questionnaire surveys, interviews, tape or video recordings of meetings, and written descriptions of meetings or interviews (which may be given to participants for them to validate or amend). In action research, the investigator becomes part of the field of study, and, as with participant observation, this has its own attendant problems. In their action research study of an outpatient health centre, Ramirez and Bartunek (1989) suggest that they were involved in dilemmas that related to conflicting organizational roles, which led to conflict over researcher loyalties. This affected how the action researcher (who was an internal consultant) was seen, as rumours were spread in order to discredit the action researcher by suggesting that she was using the project to set up a favourable position within the organization for herself.

A further claim of action research is that the research outputs are more readable, relevant, and interesting to practitioner as well as academic audiences. When the research is written up, the action research report is seen primarily as a discussion document, which presents a number of action strategies from which collaborators will jointly select a course to take. The narrative format is recommended as an appropriate way of expressing the sequence of practice and reflection that is entailed in the action research role (Winter, 1989).

Action research is criticized, in a similar way to other qualitative methods, for its lack of repeatability and consequent lack of rigour and for concentrating too much on organizational action at the expense of research findings. In their defence, action researchers claim that involvement with practitioners concerning issues that are important to them provides a richness of insight that cannot be gained in other ways. It is also claimed that theory generated from action research is 'grounded in action' (Eden & Huxham, 1996), thereby overcoming some of the difficulties of relying on talk as a source of data, instead of action or overt behaviour. Cooke (2006), however, critiques the way that action research is often overly viewed in business studies as a method that was developed to assist managers in improving the bottom line. From historical analysis of various texts, Cooke (2006) goes on to argue that an important strand of action research was designed to address social problems, such as racism, with communities—rather then business managers—as clients.

Action research should not be confused with **evaluation research** (see Key concept 4.4), which usually denotes the study of the impact of an intervention, such as a new social policy or a new innovation in organizations.

Cognitive mapping

Cognitive mapping is a predominantly qualitative method that has been used widely by business and management researchers in a variety of contexts (see Web Research in focus 6.3 for an example), particularly in the field of strategy development. Cognitive mapping is seen as complementary to action research because the maps can be used as a problem-solving device by researchers, who work interactively with managers to address a particular organizational issue. Thus, in addition to its potential use as a research method, cognitive mapping is also commonly used as a management consulting technique.

Eden (1992) suggests that cognitive mapping is used to capture individual perspectives, because it is based on the assumption that people interpret data differently and they will, therefore, understand problems in different ways. The method draws on *personal construct theory* (Willment, 2010), which also informs the use of **repertory grid technique** (see Chapter 13), and is based on the assumption that people are actively engaged in constructing models, hypotheses, or representations that enable them to make sense of the world around them. While cognitive maps can be seen as models of cognition, their primary function is as a tool for reflective thinking about a problem that enables steps to be taken towards its solution. Cause maps are a particular version of cognitive mapping that attempt to

Figure 6.2

An example of a part of a cognitive map to show the process of qualitative interviewing

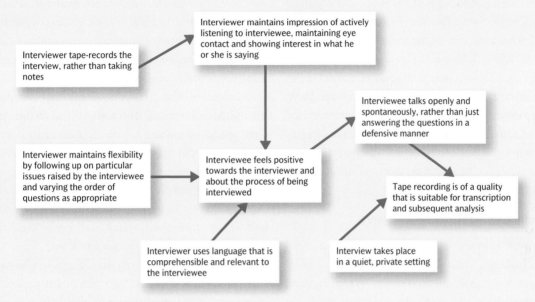

Source: adapted from Eden, Ackermann, and Cropper (1992).

capture arguments and propositions in the form of a hierarchical structure that relates means to ends.

The mapping process involves participants identifying the factors that affect a particular decision-making 'goal'. Ideas or 'concepts' relating to the decision are generated on the basis of either individual or group interviews. The role of the interviewer in this context is to ask questions that explore why concepts are important to the individual and how they are related. This process, known as 'laddering' (Eden, 1988), enables the researcher to understand an individual's construct system. It consists of 'laddering up', asking why a particular construct is important, and 'laddering down' finding out how a particular construct is affected by the particular decision.

These data are then interpreted by the researcher and put into a diagram that reflects the relationship between the concepts. This process results in the construction of a map-like diagram that represents elements of understanding or thinking at a given time. A cognitive map is usually drawn as short pieces of text linked by arrows that show the direction of causality (see Figure 6.1 for a simpli-

fied example). This is intended to make it easy to see how concepts are related to each other and to show the overall structure of assertions, although some cognitive maps place less emphasis on the directional or causal nature of these relationships, focusing instead on the patterns or connections between them. In some cases, individuals are involved in validating their own maps; in others the interpretation of the data into a map is a task undertaken solely by the researcher.

The method is intended not only to enable understanding of an individual's construct system, but also to enable groups of individuals, usually managers, to understand the way that others in the group perceive a problem. The map can thus form the basis for discussion and provide a resource that can help them to form a coherent view in relation to an issue and decide on an appropriate course of action. Maps can, therefore, relate to the thinking processes of individuals, groups, organizations, or even industries, although there is a need for researchers to be clear about the level of analysis they are adopting. An underlying assumption of the approach is that the process of interaction between researcher and research subjects leads to the production of understanding.

There are several software packages on the market that have been developed to support the process of cognitive mapping. One of these is Decision Explorer, developed by Eden and other academics at the universities of Bath and Strathclyde. This enables the display and analysis of maps, and can be used interactively with research subjects or in problem-solving teams. The software, which is produced by a company called Banxia Software, has been used for a variety of academic and management consultancy projects. More information about the software and its potential applications can be found on their website at: http://www.banxia.com.

Feminism and qualitative research

Over the past 20 years or so feminist research has been viewed as making an increasingly important contribution to business and management research. While arguably feminist research has been seen as located largely within the postpositivist traditions (Prasad, 2005), feminists have been drawn to a range or methods that include quantitative as well as qualitative strategies. Some of the early 'women-in-management' research of the 1980s and early 1990s tended to utilize quantitative research techniques to reveal levels of discrimination against women (see, for example, the work of Schein, 1975, 1978), and that tradition can still be found among more critical feminist researchers today (Konrad et al., 2005). It is a tradition that goes back to the earlier part of the twentieth century and the work of Mary Van Kleeck (1924, 1927) who believed that scientific management, properly applied, could be an important aid to women's liberation (Nyland & Rix, 2000; Nyland & Heenan, 2005). Nonetheless, most other feminist traditions, beyond liberal feminism appear to be more drawn to qualitative research and its focus on the voices, perspectives and discursive reflections of women (and men) under study.

Feminist research, in general, has arguably a particularly important role to play in relation to business and management research, which has typically been pursued from a masculinist perspective, i.e., from the assumed viewpoint of men (Hearn & Parkin, 1983; Mills & Tancred, 1992; Bradshaw, 1996). Furthermore, the bias towards a masculine perspective in business and management research may be related to the dominance of quantitative methods, which are regarded as 'hard' or 'masculine', rather than qualitative methods, which are seen as 'soft' and lacking in concreteness (Gherardi & Turner, 1987). However, that has not prevented feminists from drawing on quantitative research to challenge discriminatory practices at all levels.

Nonetheless, some feminists argue that quantitative research faces feminism with a number of challenges. To begin with, the natural science approach, with its emphasis on objectivity, is often evoked against feminist research, with its avowed commitment to improving women's right and opportunities (Eichler & Lapointe, 1985; Hollway, 1989). The criteria of valid knowledge associated with quantitative research also means that women are to be researched in a value-neutral way, when in fact the goals of feminist research should arguably be to conduct research specifically *for* women. Instead, women (along with men) are turned into objects of research, or variables to be controlled and the use of pre-determined categories serves to reinforce the gendered status quo. In the process women's voices can be suppressed through their submergence in a torrent of facts and statistics (Mies, 1993; Maynard, 1998).

By contrast, qualitative research is viewed by many feminists as either more compatible with feminism's central tenets or as more capable of being adapted to those tenets. Thus, in contrast to quantitative research, qualitative research allows: women's voices to be heard; the research process to become a partnership between the researcher and the people she or he is involved with as the subject of the research project; the avoidance of treating women as objects under the control of the researcher's technical procedures; and the emancipatory goals of feminism to be realized (Stanley & Wise, 1983; Kirby & McKenna, 1989).

However, these are not fixed positions associating feminism with qualitative research but rather debates within feminism as to the challenges of matching underlying philosophies and goals with techniques of study (Calas & Smircich, 2005; Konrad et al., 2005). In terms of the quantitative-qualitative divide Prasad, Pringle and Konrad (Prasad et al., 2005) have argued that positivist work can deal with feminist issues where researchers include power relations; commenting that 'such work has been valuable for identifying useful moderators and/or qualitative distinctions in the dynamics affecting high- and low-power identity groups' (p. 16). In a similar vein, Chrobot-Mason, Konrad, and Linnehan (2005) contend that in recent years 'scholars have extended disciplinary understandings of diversity-related concepts by crossing levels of analysis' (p. 237). And Wicks and Bradshaw (2002) have demonstrated how a strategy of mixed methods (mixing quantitative with qualitative methods) helps to throw light on women's experiences of discriminatory organizational cultures.

On the other hand, as we shall see throughout the rest of this book, feminist use of qualitative methods varies across different feminist schools of thought, and are linked to the underlying philosophy of each feminist approach (Calas & Smircich, 2005; Thurlow et al., 2006).

However, feminist research is much less established in the field of business and management than in other social science disciplines. Indeed, some would go so far as to say that business and management research has a tendency towards gender-blindness in terms of the way that research topics are defined (Hearn & Parkin, 1983; Mills and Tancred, 1992; Mills et al., 2007). For example, Mirchandani (1999) observes that much of the research on women's experiences of entrepreneurship focuses on identifying similarities and differences between female and male business-owners, and on providing explanations of these differences. She argues that although this is useful in compensating for the exclusion of women in earlier studies, it does not explain why entrepreneurship is defined and understood only in terms of the behaviour of men. Mirchandani argues that the construction of the category of 'the female entrepreneur' prioritizes gender over other important aspects of identity, such as social stratification, business ownership, organizational structure, and industry, that need to be explored in relation to female and male business-owners. However, in recent years there has been some recognition within business and management research of the need to include gender and diversity as important topics in the study of behaviour at work, however this is still a long way off of taking account of specifically feminist research (Mills & Helms Hatfield, 1998; Mills, 2004). In Canada perhaps

the strongest recognition of the role of gender and feminist concerns was the 1984 report of the *Royal Commission on Equity in Employment* (Abella, 1984) that led to legislation against 'systemic discrimination'. The Commission was chaired by Judge Rosalie Abella and accepted submissions from a number of feminist advocates and women's groups, among others. Although problematic in its implementation, the Abella Report did raise questions about women at work to a national level.

Collaborative and participatory research

Like action research and some kinds of feminist research, collaborative and participatory researchers assume that research should be driven by practical outcomes rather than by theoretical understanding. However, the distinguishing feature of collaborative methods of enquiry is that they assume members of the organization being studied should actively participate in the research process and also benefit from it. Collaborative methods are seen as particularly important in researching groups such as children who would otherwise be at a particular power disadvantage in dealing with researchers. For example, Bolton, Pole, and Mizen (2001) wanted to conduct research into child employment with children as active participants, rather than as passive subjects. Their aim was to explore 'the shape and meaning of child employment in Britain today from the point of view of the children themselves' (2001, p. 510). To do this they offered 70 young workers an opportunity to make a photographic account of their part-time jobs. The children were given disposable cameras and the researchers offered to make two sets of prints, one for them to keep and one for the research. They note that the photographs were composed and selected by the young workers, rather than the researchers, to show what it was like to work and what work meant to them. By giving their research participants a degree of control in taking the photographs and also involving them in the analysis, the researchers were seeking to make the research process more collaborative. Collaborative research can be seen as a form of respondent validation (see Key concept 6.1) by attempting to redistribute power between the researcher and research participants. Park (1999) describes participatory research as focused on disempowered groups that can be helped through research

6.4 Student Experience

Researcher–subject relationships

When Karla began research in her national Parliament she 'emailed the whole staff saying "I am such and such person from such and such university doing such and such and if you have any extra questions, if you want to talk to me about what I do and what it means you can [contact me], and I'm here"'. She promised people that everything would be anonymous, 'that nobody's names would come up'. She basically spelled out that she was wearing three hats 'cause I was doing the research for them—I was an employee and doing research for them, but then I was also doing ethnography for myself, and I guess just me as a person interacting with my colleagues'. As a result she 'got responses from people that were surprised and happy. Like this is the first time something like this has happened in this place'.

that addresses problems related to their welfare in an organized way. The researcher should ideally be someone who is familiar with the community and committed to working towards improving their conditions. This, he argues, is what differentiates participatory researchers from other types of action researchers who are only concerned with solving problems of a job-related nature. This is similar to critical or emancipatory action research (Zuber-Skerritt, 1996), which is a form of collaborative enquiry engaged in by practitioners who want to explore a problem or issue in relation to their own practice.

An important milestone in the development of these research traditions was the publication of a book by Reason and Rowan (1981), which brought together writers from these traditions and argued for the legitimacy of a 'new **paradigm**' of research based on increased participation and collaboration with research subjects. This set of perspectives broadly defined research as a two-way process whereby the researcher becomes involved in the participant's world and the practitioner gets involved in the generation of research outputs. At its most radical this leads to cooperative enquiry, where all those involved are both co-researchers and co-subjects (Reason, 1999).

Collaborative methods of enquiry stem from a desire to challenge the conventional methods whereby knowledge is constructed in the social sciences. This involves challenging the monopoly, traditionally held by universities, over the processes and outcomes of research and offering a more democratic alternative whereby research participants are treated as active agents rather than as passive subjects. It is about doing research 'with people' rather than 'on people' (Heron & Reason, 2000). It also seeks to acknowledge that the motivation to do research is related to our own personal needs for development, change, and learning (Reason & Marshall, 1987) and that research often involves personal growth (see Web Research in focus 6.4 for an illustration).

Key points

- There is disagreement over what precisely qualitative research is.
- Qualitative research does not lend itself to the delineation of a clear set of linear steps.
- It tends to be a more open-ended research strategy than is typically the case with quantitative research.
- Theories and concepts are viewed as outcomes of the research process.
- There is considerable unease about the simple application of the reliability and validity criteria associated with quantitative research to qualitative research. Indeed, some writers prefer to use alternative criteria that have parallels with reliability and validity.

- Action research is an approach in which the researcher and a client collaborate in the diagnosis of a problem and in the development of a solution to the problem based on the diagnosis. It is connected with the method of cognitive mapping.
- Most qualitative researchers reveal a preference for seeing through the eyes of research participants.
- Several writers have depicted qualitative research as having a far greater affinity with a feminist standpoint than quantitative research can exhibit.
- Action research, feminism, and collaborative methods of enquiry have changed the relationship between the researcher and the research subject.

Questions for review

- What are some of the difficulties with providing a general account of the nature of qualitative research?
- Outline some of the traditions of qualitative research.
- What are some of the main research methods associated with qualitative research?

Undertaking qualitative research

- What are the four main reasons for adopting qualitative methods mentioned in the text?

Doing qualitative research

- Does a research question in qualitative research have the same significance and characteristics as in quantitative research?

Some contrasts between quantitative and qualitative research

- 'The difference between quantitative and qualitative research revolves entirely around the concern with numbers in the former and with words in the latter'. How far do you agree with this statement?

Theory and research

- What are some of the differences between quantitative and qualitative approaches to theory?

Concepts in qualitative research

- What is the difference between definitive and sensitizing concepts?

Reliability and validity in qualitative research

- How have some writers adapted the notions of reliability and validity to qualitative research?
- Why have some writers sought alternative criteria for the evaluation of qualitative research?
- Evaluate Lincoln and Guba's criteria.
- What is respondent validation?

The main preoccupations of qualitative researchers

- Outline the main preoccupations of qualitative researchers.
- How do these preoccupations differ from those of quantitative researchers, which were considered in e.g., Chapter 5?

The critique of qualitative research

- What are some of the main criticisms that are frequently levelled at qualitative research?
- To what extent do these criticisms reflect the preoccupations of quantitative research?

Is it always like this?

- Can qualitative research be employed in relation to hypothesis testing?

Researcher–subject relationships

- What is action research?
- How are cognitive maps used in problem solving?
- Is there a role for feminist research in the study of business and management?
- How have collaborative approaches to qualitative research changed the relationship between the researcher and research subjects?

7

Mixed Methods Research: Combining Quantitative and Qualitative Data

Chapter guide

This chapter is concerned with **mixed methods** research—that is, research that combines **quantitative** and **qualitative** data. It shows that, while there are differences between the two data types, there are also many examples of research that transcend the distinction. One way in which this occurs is through research that combines quantitative and qualitative data, and the present chapter is concerned with points of overlap between them. While this may seem a straightforward way of resolving and breaking down the traditional divide between the two types or categories of data, it is not without controversy. Moreover, there may be practical difficulties associated with mixed methods research. This chapter explores:

- Arguments against the combination of quantitative and qualitative data; two kinds of argument are distinguished and are referred to as the embedded methods and paradigm arguments.
- The suggestion that there are two versions of the debate about the possibility of combining quantitative and qualitative research: one that concentrates on methods of research and another that is concerned with **epistemological** issues.
- The different ways in which mixed methods research has been carried out.
- The need to recognize that mixed methods research is not inherently superior to research that employs a single **research strategy**.
- Aspects of qualitative research that can contain elements of the natural science model.
- Aspects of quantitative research that can contain elements of interpretivism.
- The idea that research methods are more independent of epistemological and **ontological** assumptions than is sometimes supposed.
- Ways in which aspects of the quantitative/qualitative contrast sometimes break down.
- Studies in which quantitative and qualitative research are employed in relation to each other, so that qualitative research is used to analyze quantitative research and vice versa.
- The use of quantification in qualitative research.

Introduction

In many respects this chapter is concerned with the degree to which the quantitative/qualitative divide should be regarded as a hard-and-fast one. With this book structured, so far, around the distinction between positivist and postpositivist research strategies it is useful to revisit the distinction between the two main categories of research strategy as they apply to the types of data they use. This points out that while epistemological and ontological commitments may be associated with certain research methods—such as the often-cited links between a natural science epistemology and survey research or between an interpretivist epistemology (for example,

phenomenology) and qualitative interviewing—the connections are not deterministic. In other words, while qualitative interviews may often reveal a predisposition towards or a reflection of an interpretivist and constructionist position, this is not always the case. This means that the connections between the type of data and the research method are largely driven first by epistemological and ontological concerns (see Table 3.2). Thus, we cannot say that the use of a structured interview or self-completion questionnaire necessarily implies a commitment to a natural scientific model or that ethnographic research must mean an interpretivist epistemology.

Instead, we should recognize that the underlying adoption of either a positivist or postpositivist research strategy has implications for how the researcher deals with qualitative, quantitative, and mixed data research in terms of research methods as a consequence of being either positivist or postpositivist in nature. Consequently, research methods are much more free-floating than is sometimes supposed. A method of data collection like participant observation can be employed in such a way that it is in tune with the tenets of constructionism, but equally it can be used in a manner that reveals an objectivist orientation. Also, it is easy to underemphasize the significance of practical considerations in the way in which business research is conducted. Conducting a study of humour and resistance in a factory by mail-in questionnaire may not be totally impossible, but it is unlikely to succeed in terms of yielding valid answers to questions. The term mixed methods research is used as a simple shorthand to stand for research that integrates quantitative and qualitative research within a single project. Of course, there is research that, for example, combines structured interviewing with structured observation or ethnography with semi-structured interviewing. However, these instances of the combination of research methods are associated with just one research strategy.

By mixed methods research we are referring to research that combines research methods that cross the two research strategies. In the earlier edition of this book, we used the term **multi-strategy research** to describe investigations combining quantitative and qualitative research. However, 'mixed methods research' has increasingly become the preferred term and in many ways better expresses the fact that in many cases, using both quantitative and qualitative research should involve a mixing of the research methods involved and not just using them in tandem. In other words, the quantitative and the qualitative data deriving from mixed methods research should be mutually illuminating (Bryman, 2006*a*, 2006*b*). Indeed, mixed methods research has become something of a growth industry since the first edition of this book. Since *Business Research Methods* was first published, there have been numerous discussions of the approach, a handbook on it has been published (Tashakkori & Teddlie, 2003) and a *Journal of Mixed Methods Research* has been established.

In the rest of this chapter, we will examine a variety of ways in which the contrast between quantitative and qualitative data should not be overstated, but instead be situated as being expressed differently depending upon either positivist or postpositivist concerns.

 # The argument against mixed methods research

The argument against mixed methods research tends to be based on either and sometimes both of two kinds of argument:

- the idea that research methods carry epistemological commitments; and
- the idea that quantitative and qualitative research are separate *paradigms*.

These two arguments will now be briefly reviewed.

The embedded methods argument

This first position implies that research methods are ineluctably rooted in epistemological and ontological commitments. Such a view of research methods can be discerned in statements like the following:

> every research tool or procedure is inextricably embedded in commitments to particular versions of the world and to knowing that world. To use a questionnaire, to use an attitude scale, to take the role of participant observer, to select a random sample, to measure rates of population growth, and so on, is to be involved in conceptions of the world which allow these instruments to be used for the purposes conceived. (Hughes, 1990, p. 11)

According to such a position, the decision to employ, for example, participant observation is not simply about how to go about data collection but also a commitment to an epistemological position that is inimical to positivism and that is consistent with interpretivism.

This kind of view of research methods has led some writers to argue that mixed methods research is not feasible or even desirable. An *ethnographer* may collect **questionnaire** data to gain information about a slice of social life that is not amenable to participant observation, but this does not represent an integration of quantitative and qualitative research, because the epistemological positions in which the two methods are grounded constitute irreconcilable views about how social reality should be studied. Smith (1983, pp. 12, 13), for example, argues that each of the two research strategies 'sponsors different procedures and has different epistemological implications', and, therefore, counsels researchers not to 'accept the unfounded assumption that the methods are complementary'. Smith and Heshusius (1986) criticize the integration of research strategies, because it ignores the assumptions underlying research methods and transforms 'qualitative inquiry into a procedural variation of quantitative inquiry' (1986, p. 8).

The main difficulty with the argument that writers like Smith present is that the idea that research methods carry with them fixed epistemological and ontological implications is very difficult to sustain. They are capable of being put to a wide variety of tasks.

The paradigm argument

The paradigm argument was introduced in Chapter 3 in order to categorize some of the ontological and epistemological assumptions that are made in business research. It conceives of positivist and postpositivist research as *paradigms* in which epistemological assumptions, values, and methods are inextricably intertwined and are incompatible between paradigms (e.g., Guba, 1985; Morgan, 1998*b*). Therefore, when researchers combine participant observation with a questionnaire, the only way in which they can truly combine quantitative and qualitative research is within either a positivist or postpositivist paradigm, since paradigms themselves are incommensurable (that is, they are incompatible).

Two versions of the debate about quantitative and qualitative research

There would seem to be two different versions about the nature of quantitative and qualitative research, and these

two different versions have implications in writers' minds about whether or not the two can be combined:

- An epistemological version, as in the embedded methods argument and the paradigm argument, sees quantitative and qualitative research as grounded in incompatible epistemological principles (and ontological ones too, but these tend not to be given as much attention). According to this version of their nature, mixed methods research is not possible.

- A technical version, which is the position taken by most researchers whose work is mentioned in the next section, gives greater prominence to the strengths of the data collection and data analysis techniques with which quantitative and qualitative research are each associated and sees these as capable of being fused. There is a recognition that quantitative and qualitative research are each connected with distinctive epistemological and ontological assumptions, but when the connections are viewed as existing under a broader umbrella of either positivist or postpositivist world views, incommensurability arguments are allayed. That is, there is no inherent incompatibility between methods that utilize either qualitative or quantitative data sources, provided they are each viewed from within the broader positivist-postpositivist paradigm distinction.

The technical version about the nature of quantitative and qualitative research essentially views the utilization of both qualitative and quantitative data sources as potentially compatible (indeed perhaps even complementary). As a result, mixed methods research becomes both feasible and desirable. It is in that spirit that we now turn to a discussion of the ways in which quantitative and qualitative research can be combined.

Approaches to mixed methods research

This section will be structured in terms of a classification Bryman developed many years ago of the different ways in which mixed methods research has been undertaken (Bryman, 1988a, 1992). The classification has been changed slightly from the one presented in his earlier publications. Several other ways of classifying such investigations have been proposed by other authors, and two of these are presented on our website in Thinking deeper 7.1 and 7.2.

The logic of triangulation

The idea of **triangulation**, when applied to the present context, implies that the results of an investigation employing a method associated with one research strategy are cross-checked against the results of using a method associated with the other research strategy. It is an adaptation of the argument by writers like Webb et al. (1966) that confidence in the findings deriving from a study using a quantitative research strategy can be enhanced by using more than one way of measuring a concept. For example, in their longitudinal study of culture in a governmental organization in the United States, Zamanou and Glaser (1994) collected different types of data in order to examine different aspects of organizational reality. By using survey, interview, and observational data, they were able to combine 'the specificity and accuracy of quantitative data with the ability to interpret idiosyncracies and complex perceptions, provided by qualitative analysis' (1994, p. 478). Ratings on the 190 questionnaires were combined with data from the interviews, 76 of which were conducted before and 94 after the introduction of a communication intervention program, which was designed to change the organizational culture. One of the researchers also became a *participant observer* in the organization for a period of two months. Zamanou and Glaser suggested that this triangulated approach enabled the collection of different types of data that related to different cultural elements, from values to material artifacts—something that other cultural researchers have found difficult to achieve.

This use of triangulation places it squarely within the realm of positivism, being an approach to the development of multiple measures in order to improve our confidence in the findings (Webb et al., 1966); some writers have suggested that this kind of triangulation is declining in use. This can be demonstrated by reference to an article that has reviewed the methods used within business and management research. Scandura and Williams (2000) analyzed all articles published in three top-ranking American journals, *Academy of Management Journal*, *Administrative Science Quarterly*, and the *Journal of Management*, over two time periods: 1985–7 and 1995–7. They were particularly interested in tracing changing practices in triangulation of methods and use of different measures of validity. Some 614 articles were coded for the primary research methodologies they employed. The research showed that 'to publish in these three top-tier general management journals, researchers are increasingly employing research strategies and methodological approaches that compromise triangulation' (2000, p. 1259). A further finding indicated that internal, external, and construct validity had also declined during the period. They concluded that 'management research may be moving even further away from rigor', limiting the applicability of findings by failing to triangulate, using various designs in a program of research in order to help counterbalance the strengths and weaknesses of each.

In the Canadian context, Hartt, Yue, Mills, and Helms Mills (2009) conducted a longitudinal content analysis of the proceedings of the Administrative Sciences Association of Canada (ASAC) annual conference. In their study, triangulation was coded as an approach to the research in any given paper 2.73% of the time in 1989, 2.2% in 1999, and further diminished to 1.77% in 2008. This was despite the fact that they coded over 690 individual publications in the conference proceedings and found that 96.5% of the papers fit into a positivistic research strategy category.

 Another illustration of a study that uses a triangulation approach is an investigation by Stiles (2001) into the impact of boards of directors on corporate strategy. Stiles used a multi-method research design, which involved the following methods:

- In-depth semi-structured interviews with 51 main board directors of UK public companies. This was Stiles's primary means of collecting data. In order to develop a grounded understanding of board activities, he sought to allow directors 'to reveal their perceptions' (2001, p. 632). Pilot interviews, using a schedule based on analysis of existing literature, were carried out with five directors, and these were used to develop the final set of topics. Stiles also carried out a number of supplementary interviews with other stakeholders that included a city journalist, a representative from the Consumers' Association, and a number of leading academics.

- A questionnaire survey of 121 company secretaries. Stiles's quantitative element in his research design relied on a questionnaire, which was sent to 900 members of the Institute of Company Secretaries and Administrators. This generated a response rate of 14%. Had this been the main research method upon which the study relied, the low response rate would have called into question the external validity of the findings. However, Stiles points out that questionnaire results are used 'to support the main findings, which emerged from the qualitative data and . . . are meant to be illustrative rather than definitive' (Stiles, 2001, p. 633).

- Four case studies of UK plcs, where several board members were interviewed, and secondary, archival data were collected. Stiles chose four large UK businesses in which to test findings that emerged from data collected using his two preliminary research methods. The cases were chosen because they had strong reputations but had experienced periods of turbulence and change. Stiles claims that 'this buttressing of the original findings through testing in four different research sites affords a further element of triangulation into the study, with the new data from the case testing the validity and generality of the initial findings' (2001, p. 634). Validity was also improved through respondent validation, involving a draft of the findings being sent to the case companies on which individuals were invited to comment.

Stiles's main finding, that multiple perspectives are required in order to understand fully the nature of board activity, owes something to his research approach, which enabled exploration of the strategy-making role of the board and its multifunctional nature. In this research, the use of a triangulation strategy seems to have been planned by the researcher and the two sets of results were broadly consistent. However, researchers may carry out mixed methods research for other purposes, but in the course of doing so discover that they have generated quantita-

tive and qualitative findings on related issues, so that they can treat such overlapping findings as a triangulation exercise. Liff and Steward (2001) provided an example of unplanned triangulation, in that they gathered data about e-gateways through several quantitative and qualitative research methods, but they had not intended the photographs that were taken to be deployed as part of a triangulation exercise. However, their analysis of their data found location and physical layout of the gateways to be significant in reducing barriers to entry and in attracting Internet users. The photographs, therefore, provided an additional source of data through which the researchers were able to corroborate these findings.

Whether planned or unplanned, when a triangulation exercise is undertaken, the possibility of a failure to corroborate findings always exists. This raises the issue of what approach should be taken towards inconsistent results. One approach is to treat one set of results as definitive. However, simply and often arbitrarily favouring one set of findings over another is not an ideal approach to reconciling conflicting findings deriving from a triangulation exercise.

Qualitative research facilitates quantitative research

There are several ways in which qualitative research can be used to guide quantitative research:

- Providing hypotheses. Because of its tendency towards an unstructured, open-ended approach to data collection, qualitative research is often very helpful as a source of hypotheses or hunches that can be subsequently tested using a quantitative research strategy. An example is Prasad's study of computerization in a health-care organization (see Chapter 6). On the basis of her qualitative investigation, which relied on the methods of participant observation and in-depth semi-structured interviewing, Prasad suggests a number of hypotheses, or propositions, that can be drawn in relation to the impact of technological symbolism on organizational-level action. Although Prasad does not say that these should be tested using a quantitative research strategy, it is clear that some of them could form the basis for a quantitative, deductive research project.

- Aiding measurement. The in-depth knowledge of social contexts acquired through qualitative research can be used to inform the design of survey questions for structured interviewing and self-completion questionnaires. In their study of work relationships in telephone call centres, Deery, Iverson, and Walsch (2002) analyzed data from a questionnaire survey of 480 telephone service operators in five call centre locations in Melbourne and Sydney, Australia. The questionnaire was constructed following 'site visits and extensive discussions with focus groups of employees and meetings with shop stewards, team leaders and call centre managers' (2002, p. 481), and this helped the researchers to develop their understanding of the possible negative effects of this kind of work on the psychological well-being of employees. This preliminary, qualitative stage of the research, and the fact that the survey was endorsed both by the company and the union, may have contributed towards the high overall survey response rate of 88%, a further benefit gained from the mixed methods research approach.

Quantitative research facilitates qualitative research

One of the chief ways in which quantitative research can prepare the ground for qualitative research is through the selection of people to be interviewed, or companies to be selected as case studies. For example, Scase and Goffee (1989) used the results of their questionnaire survey of 374 UK managers (see Web Research in focus 4.16) to generate a smaller, representative sample of 80 managers for in-depth interviews. Similarly, in research by Storey et al. (2002) on flexible employment, the postal questionnaire survey of 2700 companies provided a basis for selection of eight case-study firms where the survey data had suggested there was an association between innovation and flexible employment. The case studies were then explored using a qualitative research strategy based on in-depth semi-structured interviewing in order to investigate internal sources of knowledge and expertise within the organization.

Filling in the gaps

This approach to mixed methods research occurs when the researcher cannot rely on either a quantitative or a qualitative method alone and must buttress his or her findings with a method drawn from the other research strategy. Its most typical form is when ethnographers employ structured interviewing or possibly a self-completion questionnaire, because not everything they need to know about is accessible through participant observation. This kind of need can arise for several reasons, such as the need for information that is not accessible to observation or to qualitative interviewing (for example, systematic information about social backgrounds of people in a particular setting), or the difficulty of gaining access to certain groups of people. For example, Hochschild (1989) used quantitative analysis of time use in her study of working couples with children to assess levels of participation in everyday domestic work. This formed the basis for her qualitative exploration based on interviews and observation of the gender strategies that working couples use. Equally, qualitative methods may be used to provide important contextual information that supplements the findings from a larger quantitative study. For example, Zamanou and Glaser (1994) used semi-structured interviews and participant observation in order to help interpret and place in context the results of statistical analyses of the Organizational Culture Scale (ocs), which formed the basis for their questionnaire survey of culture change in a government organization. They state:

> the results of the ocs provided a quantitative description of the culture of the organization, but the study still lacked an exploration of the deeper, more subjective, and less observable layers of culture. Thus qualitative measures (i.e., interviews, observations) were combined with the questionnaire results to illustrate the quantitative findings and to provide an examination of the depth of the culture. (1994, p. 479)

Static and processual features

One of the contrasts suggested by Table 6.1 is that, whereas quantitative research tends to bring out a static picture of social life, qualitative research is more processual. The term 'static' can easily be viewed in a rather negative light. In fact, it is very valuable on many occasions to uncover regularities, and it is often the identification of such regularities that allows a processual analysis to proceed. A mixed methods research approach offers the prospect of being able to combine both elements.

For example, Zamanou and Glaser (1994) wanted to explore the impact of a communication intervention program designed to change the culture of a governmental organization from hierarchical and authoritarian to participative and involved. They argued that the study of organizational culture lends itself to a mixed methods research approach because different methods can be used to capture different cultural elements and processes. In addition, a longitudinal research design can enable understanding of events over time and is, therefore, often used in the study of organizational change (see Web Research in focus 6.5 for an example). The questionnaire survey used by Zamanou and Glaser provided a static picture of the organizational culture prior to the intervention (Time 1) and again after it had ended (Time 2). It was hypothesized that ratings on scales such as teamwork, morale, and involvement would be significantly higher after the intervention than before it. Interviews were then used to explore employees' perceptions of culture in more detail, asking them to describe cultural incidents, events, and stories that had helped to form their perceptions. However, it is not only qualitative research that can incorporate processual analysis. Quantitative diary study research by Stewart (1967) analyzed the way in which 160 managers spent their time during a four-week period in order to discover similarities and differences in their use of time and the reasons for them (see Web Research in focus 10.1). In focusing on managerial activity over a period of time this study provided a dynamic, rather than a static, analysis of what managers actually do.

Research issues and participants' perspectives

Sometimes, researchers want to gather two kinds of data: qualitative data that will allow them to gain access to the perspectives of the people they are studying; and quantitative data that will allow them to explore specific issues in which they are interested. When this occurs, they are seeking to explore an area in both ways, so that they can both adopt an unstructured approach to data collection in which participants' meanings are the focus of attention and investigate a specific set of issues through the more structured approach of quantitative research. An example of this is Milkman's (1997) study of a General Motors car manufacturing plant in the United States.

Milkman was interested in the nature of the labour process in the late twentieth century and whether or not new factory conditions were markedly different for car workers from the negative portrayals of such work in the 1950s and early 1960s (e.g., Blauner, 1964). As such, she was interested in the meaning of industrial work. She employed semi-structured interviews and focus groups with car production workers to elicit data relevant to this aspect of her work. However, in addition she had some specific interests in a 'buyout' plan that the company's management introduced in the mid-1980s after it had initiated a variety of changes to work practices. The plan gave workers the opportunity to give up their jobs for a substantial cash payment. In 1988, Milkman carried out a questionnaire survey of workers who had taken up the company's buyout offer. These workers were surveyed again the following year and in 1991. The reason for the surveys was that Milkman had some very specific interests in the buyout scheme, such as reasons for taking the buyout, how they had fared since leaving General Motors, how they felt about their current employment, and differences between social groups (in particular, different ethnic groups) in current earnings relative to those at General Motors.

The problem of generality

A problem that is often referred to by critics of qualitative research is that the tendency for findings to be presented in an anecdotal fashion is frequently frustrating, since we are given little sense of the relative importance of the themes identified. Silverman (1984, 1985) has argued that some quantification of findings from qualitative research can often help to uncover the generality of the phenomena being described. Of course, generality is a particular focus of the positivist researcher, and given our prior discussion about postpositivism, less of a preoccupation of the part of a researcher adopting a postpositivist perspective.

In addition, the combined use of qualitative and quantitative research methods represents a common pattern in case study research in business and management, used by researchers in order to enhance the generality of their findings. An illustration of this tendency is given in Web Research in focus 7.1, where Kanter (1977) described the diverse range of methods that she used in her case study of a single organization, Indsco Supply Corporation. Even though the fieldwork was undertaken in just one company and the case constituted a focus of interest in its own right, Kanter claimed that its findings are typical of other large corporations. However, it is more than coincidental that she made this claim only after having accounted in some detail for the complex set of methods that were involved in her mixed methods research approach.

Other studies have attempted to counter the criticism of anecdotalism, which is leveled at qualitative research by introducing a quantitative aspect into their analysis. These include Bryman, Stephens, and Campo's (1996) study of leadership in the British police force and Gabriel's (1998) study of organizational culture, both of which calculate the frequency of themes in order to provide a sense of their relative importance. However, Silverman warns that such quantification should reflect research participants' own ways of understanding their social world. If this occurs, the quantification is more consistent with the goals of qualitative research.

Qualitative research may facilitate the interpretation of the relationship between variables

One of the problems that frequently confront quantitative researchers is how to explain relationships between variables. One strategy is to look for what is called an **intervening variable**, which is influenced by the **independent variable** but which in turn has an effect on the **dependent variable**. Thus, if we find a relationship between gender and small business ownership, we might propose that entrepreneurial attitude is one factor behind the relationship implying:

gender → entrepreneurial attitude → small business
ownership

This sequence implies that the variable 'gender' has an impact on how an individual feels about taking on an entrepreneurial role and becoming committed to the ideals associated with it (for example, belief in economic self-advancement, individualism, self-reliance, and a strong work ethic), which in turn has implications for the kinds of choices they make within the labour market. However, an alternative approach might be to seek to explore the relationship between the variables further by conducting a qualitative investigation of the ways in which entrepreneurial work is situated within gendered processes that are embedded within society (Mirchandani, 1999). This would involve challenging the sequence of these variables, drawing attention to the gendered nature of entrepreneurial values.

Truss (2001) argues that more qualitative research is needed in order to increase our understanding of the link between HRM and organizational performance (see Web Research in focus 7.1). She suggests many existing studies rely on a single informant in each organization and focus on financial performance, rather than on a broader range of outcome variables. In contrast, adopting a mixed methods longitudinal research design, Truss was able to explain how Hewlett-Packard's people management philosophy, known as 'The HP Way', was translated into policies by the HR function.

The questionnaire data enabled comparison with other companies, showing, for example, that employees were significantly more positive regarding the effectiveness of recruitment at HP. Overall, employees received more training and development than in the other high-performance companies and appraisals were regularly conducted. However, once the researchers attempted to probe beneath the surface, it emerged that 'The HP Way' was open to quite different interpretations. For example, during the first wave of data collection it was found that, prior to the redundancies in the 1980s, employees had believed that 'The HP Way' meant they would have 'jobs for life'. It was also found that the move towards flexible working was having an adverse effect on staff loyalty. In terms of recruitment and selection, the strength of corporate values expressed in 'The HP Way' had given rise to a rather narrow view of the HP employee, and individuals who did not fit this profile

7.1 Research in Focus

A mixed methods approach to the study of HRM and performance

In her research on the relationship between human resource management (HRM) and performance at Hewlett-Packard, Truss (2001) used a triangulated approach in order to overcome the limitations of research on this topic, which has tended to rely heavily on quantitative methods. She also incorporated a longitudinal element into the research design, by collecting data at two points in time, once in 1994 and again in 1996. Four principal research methods were used on each occasion:

- *Questionnaires*, 400 distributed to a random sample of employees at middle-manager level and below, generating a response rate of 56% in 1994 and 52% in 1996; in order to provide an indicative point of comparison with the questionnaire data, Truss also makes reference to data that were collected from six other high-

performance organizations at the same time and using the same questionnaire instrument, as part of a larger study with which she was involved.
- *Focus groups*, with senior members of the HR department.
- *Semi-structured interviews*, with employees from all levels of the firm.
- *Secondary data*, from documents on topics such as recruitment and selection, training, career management, appraisal, and reward from within the organization.

This approach results in the generation of an extremely in-depth case study from which it is possible to explore 'not only the "rhetoric" of what the HR group was trying to achieve, but also the reality experienced by employees' (Truss, 2001, p. 1128).

---

were unlikely to survive within the company. These findings suggest that changes in the company's environment, which was becoming increasingly competitive and hostile, were having a negative effect on HRM. In conclusion, the research provides only limited support for the view that effective HRM is the key to achieving sustained competitive advantage, instead suggesting that environmental events and conditions play a significant part. Finally, Truss concluded that these findings were the direct result of the qualitative aspect of the study:

> Had we relied on questionnaire data obtained from a single informant (the HR director, as in other studies) and carried out a quantitative analysis linking performance with human resource processes, we would have concluded that this organization was an example of an organization employing 'High Performance Work Practices' to good effect. However, employing a contextualized, case-study method has

enabled us to see below the surface and tap into the reality experienced by employees, which often contrasts sharply with the company rhetoric. (Truss, 2001, p. 1145)

The quantitative research results could thus be seen as somewhat misleading, in that they reflect the organization's rhetorical position rather than the reality experienced by employees. Truss is suggesting that the latter would not have been exposed without the addition of qualitative methods of investigation.

Studying different aspects of a phenomenon

This category of mixed methods research incorporates two forms Bryman has referred to in earlier work as 'the relationship between "macro" and "micro" levels' and 'stages in the research process', but provides a more general formulation (Bryman, 1988a, pp. 147–51). The former draws attention to the tendency to think of quantitative research as most suited to the investigation of 'macro' phenomena (such as social mobility) and qualitative research as better suited to 'micro' ones (such as small group interaction).

In the example shown in Web Research in focus 7.2, Wajcman and Martin (2002) used quantitative methods in the form of a questionnaire survey to explore the career patterns of male and female managers. However, they also carried out qualitative, semi-structured interviews to explore the way that managers made sense of their career patterns in terms of their identity; their choice of methods was, therefore, determined by the particular aspect of career orientation they were interested in.

Table 6.1 (on page 126) also illustrates this distinction. The category 'stages in the research process' draws attention to the possibility that quantitative and qualitative research may be suited to different phases in a study. However, it now seems to us that these are simply aspects of a more general tendency for quantitative and qualitative researchers to examine different aspects of their area of interest.

A further illustration of the use of mixed methods research to explore different aspects of a phenomenon can be found in a study of how people use their time at work conducted by Perlow (1997, 1999), previously encountered in Chapter 6 and Key concept 17.1a and b. Although this study mainly comprised ethnographic methods, which included participant observation and semi-structured interviewing, Perlow also used a time-use diary (see Chapter 10) similar to the one used by Stewart (1967; see Web Key concept in focus 10.1), to record and measure quantitatively the time that software engineers spent on various activities each day. She explains:

> On randomly chosen days, I asked three or four of the twelve software engineers to track their activities from when they woke up until they went to bed. I asked them to wear a digital watch that beeped on the hour and, at each beep, to write down everything that they had done during the previous hour. I encouraged them to write down interactions as they occurred and to use the beeps as an extra reminder to keep track of their activities. (Perlow, 1999, p. 61)

The ethnographic methods were intended to capture the cultural norms and values held by the software engineers, while the time-use diary was specifically directed towards measurement of their time use. Using this combined approach, Perlow was able to build up a picture of *how* the engineers use their work time (using a quantitative strategy) and an understanding of *why* they use their work time in this way (using qualitative methods). In this study, mixed methods research was geared to addressing different kinds of research question. After each tracking log had been completed, Perlow conducted a debriefing interview with each engineer, who explained the patterns of interaction recorded on the log sheets. From this Perlow was able to calculate the total time the engineer spent at work and the proportion of that time spent on interactive versus individual activities. Perlow found that, although 60% of the engineers' time was spent on individual activities, and just over 30% was spent on interactive activities, the time spent alone did not occur in one consecutive block:

> Rather, examination of the sequences of individual and interactive activities revealed that a large proportion of the time spent uninterrupted on individual activities was spent in very short blocks of time, sandwiched between interactive activities. Seventy-five percent of the blocks of time spent uninterrupted on individual activities were one hour or less in length, and, of those blocks of time, 60 percent were half an hour or less in length. (1999, p. 64)

This finding forms the basis for the theoretical conclusions that Perlow was able to draw in relation to the crisis mentality induced by the engineers, work patterns, and the heroic acts that this culture encourages and rewards. In her analysis she was able to illustrate these themes through presentation of the ethnographic research data. However, it is the *quantitative* analysis of time use that provides the initial impetus for the theoretical conclusions that Perlow was able to draw.

This form of mixed methods research entails making decisions about which kinds of research question are best answered using a quantitative research method and

Research in Focus

Combining survey research and qualitative interviewing in a study of managers

Wajcman and Martin (2002) conducted survey research using a questionnaire on male and female managers (470 in total) in six Australian companies. The authors were interested in career orientations and attitudes. They also conducted semi-structured interviews with 136 managers in each company. The survey evidence showed that male and female managers were generally more similar than different in terms of most variables. Thus, contrary to what many people might have anticipated, women's career experiences and orientations were not distinctive. They then examined the qualitative interviews in terms of narratives of identity. Wajcman and Martin found that both male and female managers depicted their careers in 'market' terms (as needing to respond to the requirements of the managerial labour market to develop their skills, experience, and hence career). But, whereas, for men, narratives of career meshed seamlessly with narratives of domestic life, for women there was a disjuncture. Female managers found it much harder to reconcile managerial identities with domestic ones. They needed to opt for one. Thus, choices about career and family are still gendered. This research shows how a mixed methods research approach was able to reveal much more than could have been gleaned through one approach alone by collecting evidence on both career patterns and expectations and identities using research methods suited to each issue area.

which by a qualitative research method, and about how best to interweave the different elements, especially since, as suggested in the context of the discussion about triangulation, the outcomes of mixtures of methods are not always predictable.

Solving a puzzle

The outcomes of research are, as suggested by the last sentence, not always easy to anticipate. Although people sometimes cynically suggest that social scientists find what they want to find or that social scientists just convey the obvious, the capacity of the obvious to provide us with puzzling surprises should never be underestimated. When this occurs, employing a research method associated with the research strategy not initially used can be helpful. One context in which this might occur is when qualitative research is used as a salvage operation, when an anticipated set of results from a quantitative investigation fails to materialize (Weinholtz, Kacer, and Rocklin 1995). Another situation arises when questionnaire response rates are too low to be used as the sole data source upon which to base findings. Stiles (2001), for example,

generated only a 14% response rate from the 900 questionnaires that were sent to members of the Institute of Company Secretaries and Administrators. Interview and case study data provided him with alternative data sources upon which to focus.

Like unplanned triangulation, this category of mixed methods research is more or less impossible to plan for. It essentially provides the quantitative researcher with an alternative either to reconstructing a hypothesis or to filing the results away (and probably never looking at them again) when findings are inconsistent with a hypothesis. It is probably not an option in all cases in which a hypothesis is not confirmed. There may also be instances in which a quantitative study could shed light on puzzling findings drawn from a qualitative investigation.

 # Reflections on mixed methods research

There can be little doubt that mixed methods research is becoming far more common than when one of us first started writing about it (Bryman, 1988a). Two particularly significant factors in prompting this development are:

1. A growing preparedness to think of research methods as techniques of data collection or analysis that are not as encumbered by epistemological and ontological baggage as is sometimes supposed.
2. A softening in the attitude towards quantitative research among feminist researchers, who had previously been highly resistant to its use (see Chapter 6 for a discussion of this point).

Other factors are doubtless relevant, but these two developments do seem especially significant. Yet lingering unease among some practitioners of qualitative research, particularly regarding issues to do with reliability and generalizability of findings, has led to some calls for a consideration of the possible use of quantitative research in tandem with qualitative methods (e.g., Schrøder, 1999). However, it is important to realize that mixed methods research is not intrinsically superior to mono-method or mono-strategy research. It is tempting to think that mixed methods research is more or less inevitably superior to research that relies on a single method on the grounds that more and more varied findings are inevitably 'a good thing'. Indeed, social scientists sometimes display such a view (Bryman, 2006c). However, four points must be borne in mind:

1. Mixed methods research, like mono-method research, must be competently designed and conducted. Poorly conducted research will yield suspect findings no matter how many methods are employed.
2. Just like mono-method or mono-strategy research, mixed methods research must be appropriate to the research questions or research area with which you are concerned. There is no point collecting more data simply on the basis that 'more is better'. Mixed methods research has to be dovetailed to research questions, just as all research methods must be. It is, after all, likely to consume considerably more time and financial resources than research relying on just one method.
3. Any research project has limited resources. Employing mixed methods research may dilute the research effort in any area, since resources would need to be spread.
4. By no means do all researchers have the skills and training to carry out both quantitative and qualitative research, so that their 'trained incapacities' may act as a barrier to integration (Reiss, 1968, p. 351). However, there is a growing recognition of the potential of mixed methods research, so that this point probably carries less weight than it did when Reiss was writing.

In other words, mixed methods research should not be considered as an approach that is universally applicable or as a panacea. It may provide a better understanding of a phenomenon than if just one method had been used. It may also frequently enhance our confidence in our own or others' findings—for example, when a triangulation exercise has been conducted. It may even improve our chances of access to settings to which we might otherwise be excluded; Milkman (1997, p. 192), for example, has suggested in the context of her research on a General Motors factory that the promise that she 'would produce "hard", quantitative data through survey research was what secured [her] access', even though she had no experience in this method. But the general point remains, that mixed methods research, while offering great potential in many instances, is subject to similar constraints and considerations as research relying on a single method or research strategy.

Key points

- While there has been a growth in the amount of mixed methods research, not all writers support its use.
- Objections to mixed methods research tend to be the result of a view that there are epistemological and ontological impediments to the combination of quantitative and qualitative research.
- There are several ways of combining quantitative and qualitative research and of representing mixed methods research.
- The outcomes of combining quantitative and qualitative research can be planned or unplanned.

Questions for review

- What is mixed methods research?

The argument against mixed methods research

- What are the main elements of the embedded methods and paradigm arguments in terms of their implications for the possibility of mixed methods research?

Two versions of the debate about quantitative and qualitative research

- What are the main elements of the technical and epistemological versions of the debate about quantitative and qualitative research? What are the implications of these two versions of the debate for mixed methods research?

Approaches to mixed methods research

- What are the main differences between Hammersley's and Morgan's classifications of mixed methods research?
- What are the chief ways in which quantitative and qualitative research have been combined?
- What is the logic of triangulation?
- Traditionally, qualitative research has been depicted as having a preparatory role in relation to quantitative research. To what extent do the different forms of mixed methods research reflect this view?

Reflections on mixed methods research

- Why has mixed methods research become more prominent?
- Is mixed methods research necessarily superior to single strategy research?

8

Ethics in Business Research

Chapter guide

Ethical issues arise at a variety of stages in business and management research. This chapter deals with the concerns about ethics that might arise in the course of conducting research. The professional bodies concerned with the social sciences have been keen to spell out the ethical issues that can arise, and some of their statements will be reviewed in this chapter. Ethical issues cannot be ignored, in that they relate directly to the integrity of a piece of research and of the disciplines that are involved. This chapter explores:

- Some famous, even infamous, cases in which transgressions of ethical principles have occurred, though it is important not to take the view that ethical concerns arise only in relation to these extreme cases.
- Different stances that can be and have been taken on ethics in business research.
- The significance and operation of four areas in which ethical concerns particularly arise: whether or not harm comes to participants; informed consent; invasion of privacy; and deception.
- Some of the difficulties associated with ethical decision making.

Introduction

Discussions about the ethics of business and management research bring us into a realm in which the role of values in the research process becomes a topic of concern. Ethical issues revolve around such concerns as the following:

- How should we treat the people on whom we conduct research?
- Are there activities in which we should or should not engage in our relations with them?

Questions about ethics in business and management research also bring in the role of government research funding agencies, such as the Canadian Institutes of Health Research (CIHR), the Natural Sciences and Engineering Research Council of Canada (NSERC), and the Social Sciences and Humanities Research Council of Canada (SSHRC), and professional associations, such as the American Academy of Management (AOM), the Administrative Sciences Association of Canada (ASAC), and the Market Research Society (MRS), which have formulated codes of ethics on behalf of their members. State-

ments of professional principles are frequently accessible from the Internet. Some useful codes of ethics for business and management researchers can be found at the following Internet addresses:

- Citizens for Responsible Care and Research: Human Rights Protections: http://www.circare.org/CAindex.htm
- Tri-Council Policy Statement: Ethical Conduct for Research Involving Humans: http://www.pre.ethics.gc.ca/eng/policy-politique/tcps-eptc
- Administrative Sciences Association of Canada (ASAC), *Code of Ethics*: http://www.asac.ca/en/about-asac/code-of-ethics
- Academy of Management (AoM), *Code of Ethical Conduct*: http://www.aomonline.org/aom.asp?ID=24&page_ID=54
- Market Research Society (MRS), *Code of Conduct and Guidelines*: http://www.mrs.org.uk/standards/code-conduct.htm (also includes specific MRS guidelines on qualitative and quantitative research and doing Internet and employee research).

However, it is also useful to look at the way that researchers within the social sciences more generally have dealt with ethical research issues—for example, the Social Research Association (SRA), the British Sociological Association (BSA), the Canadian Sociology and Anthropological Association, the American Psychological Association, and the Canadian Psychological Association. In this chapter, the codes of these professional associations will also be referred to on several occasions:

- Social Research Association (SRA), *Ethical Guidelines*: http://www.the-sra.org.uk/documents/pdfs/ethics03.pdf
- British Sociological Association (BSA), *Statement of Ethical Practice*: http://www.britsoc.co.uk/NR/rdonlyres/468F236C-FFD9-4791-A0BD-4DF73F10BA43/0/StatementofEthicalPractice.doc
- Canadian Sociology and Anthropological Association (CSRA), *Statement of Professional Ethics*: http://www.csaa.ca/structure/Code.htm
- American Sociological Association (ASA), *Code of Ethics*: http://www.asanet.org/about/ethics.cfm
- American Psychological Association (APA), *Ethical Principles and Code of Conduct*: http://www.apa.org/ethics/code/index.aspx
- Canadian Psychological Association (CPA), *Canadian Code of Ethics for Psychologists*: http://www.cpa.ca/cpasite/userfiles/Documents/Canadian%20Code%20of%20Ethics%20for%20Psycho.pdf

 ## Ethics in context

Research ethics in Canada: The Tri-Council policy

In the late 1970s discussion began around the idea of developing a joint set of research ethics guidelines for the Canadian Institutes of Health Research (CIHR), the Natural Sciences and Engineering Research Council of Canada (NSERC), and the Social Sciences and Humanities Research Council of Canada (SSHRC). This eventually led to the establishment, in 1994, of the Tri-Council Working Group, which consulted widely with the academic community in Canada. In 1998 the Working Group issued a policy statement on the ethical conduct of research involving humans. The policy replaced SSHRC's *Ethics Guidelines for Research with Human Subjects* and the former Medical Research Council of Canada (now CIHR) *Guidelines on Research Involving Humans and Guidelines for Research on Somatic Cell Gene Therapy in Humans* (http://www.pre.ethics.gc.ca/eng/policy-politique/tcps-eptc). Under this policy Research Ethics Boards (REBs) were established across Canadian universities to implement the guidelines.

A review of the rationale behind the Tri-Council policy raises many of the issues that will be discussed throughout the chapter. To begin with, the 'moral imperative' guiding the policy is 'respect for human dignity'. The Council recognized the value of research and its potential benefits to individuals and society but argued for the establishment of an 'ethic of research involving human subjects [that] should include two essential components (1) the selection and achievement of morally acceptable ends and (2) the morally acceptable means to those ends'. The first point focused on defining acceptable ends 'in terms of the benefits of research for subjects, for associated groups, and for the advancement of knowledge' (p. i.4). The second point was designed to develop 'ethically appropriate means of conducting research' (p. i.4).

The Council's concerns were translated into a series of ethical principles to ensure respect for human dignity ('from bodily to psychological to cultural integrity') of the subjects of research; the free and informed consent of those being studied; 'high ethical obligations' in the treatment of vulnerable persons; respect for the privacy and confidentiality of subjects; the implementation of research processes based on procedural justice and inclusiveness; careful consideration of the balance between harms and benefits; a minimization of harm and a maximization of benefits.

In the process of developing the guidelines the Council developed a notion of 'minimal risk' whereby research projects can be deemed ethically acceptable if 'potential subjects can reasonably be excepted to encounter no more possible harms than they would encounter [. . .] in those aspects of his or her everyday life that relate to the research' (p. 1.5). Under such conditions 'the research can be regarded as within the range of minimal risk'.

Finally, and of specific interest to discussions on gender and feminist studies at work, the Council pointedly noted that 'women shall not automatically be excluded from research solely on the basis of sex or reproductive capacity' (p. 5.3).

REBs and the Implementation of the Tri-Council policy

In establishing Research Ethics Boards in Canadian Universities the Tri-Council called for the relevant institution to 'mandate the REB to approve, reject, propose modifications to, or terminate any proposed or ongoing research involving human subjects that is conducted within, or by members of, the institution' in accordance with the Council's guidelines used as a minimum standard. This process plays a critical role in Canadian research across the natural sciences, humanities, and social sciences where human subjects are involved.

Today, throughout Canadian universities research on humans is regulated through local research ethics boards (REB) that adjudicate the ethics requirement of each research project. No research project is allowed to proceed until is has been approved by the local REB. In the case of scholars who have been awarded CIHR, NSERC, or SSHRC funding pending ethics review by their university's REB, the appropriate university will release no funds until those scholars have had their research project approved by the REB.

One such REB is the one at Saint Mary's University (SMU), which we will now turn to an example of the functioning of a local REB. While REB's may differ in some of their operations in the medical sciences compared to the social sciences (including business) the one at SMU is fairly typical of the type to which most business students and professors are accountable. At SMU, the Research Ethics Board 'consists primarily of faculty members who work with researchers to apply the Tri-Council Policy Statement on the Ethical Conduct for Research Involving Humans'. It is noted 'compliance with [the Tri-Council] policy is a requirement of the NSERC, the SSHRC and the CIHR for the funding of all research activities of our university involving human subjects' (http://www.smu.ca/academic/reb/). Nonetheless, as at other universities, the Saint Mary's REB requires that 'all research that uses human subjects . . . be submitted . . . for approval regardless of whether it is funded or not by one of the Tri-Council agencies' (http://www.smu.ca/academic/reb/faq.html). However, the requirement to apply to the REB for ethical approval extends beyond faculty research, and includes 'undergraduate and graduate theses, independent research projects, and MRPs' [Master's Research Projects], as well as undergraduate and graduate class projects, and 'librarian research' (http://www.smu.ca/academic/reb/faq.html).

Before embarking on any research project that includes humans as subjects students and professors are required to complete a form that details the research. Forms can typically be found on-line on the university website. At SMU REB forms can be found at: http://www.smu.ca/academic/reb/forms.html.

The type of ethical issues that concern Saint Mary's University REB are typical of the concerns across Canadian universities and are worth pursuing here. To begin with, the SMU REB website reproduces the Tri-Council Policy Statement on minimal risk to show scholars what their research project should normally aim at in terms of compliance with ethical guidelines. The REB then goes on to state that that will 'pay particular attention to studies in which:

- Research procedures induce embarrassment, humiliation, lowered self esteem, discouragement, or other emotional reactions;
- Participants are subject to physical discomfort, threat of physical discomfort, or strenuous physical activity;
- The investigation uses procedures designed to induce participants to act contrary to their wishes or if the research requires deception of the participants;
- The populations studied consist of potentially at risk individuals, (e.g., minors, pregnant women, prisoners, or the mentally handicapped);
- Participants receive any compensation for their participation and if any penalties result if they withdraw from the study or not participate at all;

- Personal information is collected'. (http://www.smu.ca/academic/reb/faq.html)

As we shall see below, these concerns have been at the core of scholarly concerns for decades in the face of well-documented human rights abuses in social and political life and widely publicized cases of alleged ethical transgression in scholarly research in which human subjects were thought to experience harm of some kind in the name of knowledge.

In the primary focus on the well-being of human beings the Tri-Council and REBs exclude some research projects from its remit. Thus, the SMU REB do not require review of the following types of research:

- 'Research about a living individual in the public arena or an artist based exclusively on publicly available information;
- Performance reviews or testing within normal educational requirements;
- Most research involving public policy issues, the writing of modern history, or literary or artistic criticism, even though they may involve living human subjects;
- Research involving a person no longer living (unless you question other people about the deceased individual)'. (http://www.smu. ca/ academic /reb/faq.html)

By way of example, one of the authors, Albert J. Mills, initiated a PH.D. class project to develop a history of the Atlantic Schools of Business (ASB), a scholarly conference that has been held every year in the Atlantic Provinces since 1971. One student undertook to interview people about their perceptions of ASB, while another student undertook an archival study by analyzing the text of conference proceedings. The first student had to submit an REB application while the latter did not.

Sometimes the process can be complex and contested. Amy Warren experienced the following issues when trying to get approval from her university's REB:

'I just recently had to get ethics approval for another qualitative study and the ethics committee was some-what opposed to snowball/network sampling, i.e., they were pushing for us to find a random sample of people. We went back with various quotes/citations that illustrate the importance of network sampling and eventually did get ethics approval. But I think if ethics committees continue to push back in this way qualitative research will die a very quick death, as our ability to get participants will be dependent on access to large lists of people from organizations, whereby the organization can serve as the gatekeeper, this can be problematic and be risky ethically since organizations can them deem which list will be sent the information and technically speaking they could track the IP addresses of anyone who wishes to respond via their work e-mail'.

 ## Broader ethics concerns

Ethics in research are part of broader ethical concerns about the value of human life. A recent example is the debate around the use and value of torture during the George W. Bush administration in the United States (2000–2008). There are those who argue that the goals of the torture (e.g., timely information on terrorist activities) outweigh the suffering inflicted on the individual prisoners involved, while others argue that torture violates broader ethical principles and, in the process, negate those principles (e.g., treating certain people as less than human to uphold the value of human rights) (http://www.worldcantwait.net/ index.php?option=com_content&view=article&id=5646:torture-and-the-need-for-justice-now-its-up-to-you&catid=117:homepage&Itemid=289). This type of debate is echoed in concerns over research ethics, specifically around the issue of how far researchers should be allowed to go to achieve the normally applauded goals of knowledge and other benefits for humankind. As we have seen, the Tri-Council approach is to insist, as far as is possible, that the means should not be incompatible with the ends where those ends involve some form of harm to research subjects.

In terms of research the most notorious examples of abuse can be found in regard to the Nazi use of concentration camp prisoners for medical research. Today, the ethics of using the outcomes of such research are still being debated (http://www.jlaw.com/Articles/NaziMedEx.html). Medical experiments were not the only form of research in the Nazi concentration camps, the development of IBM business machines was part of the research involved in processing large numbers of camp prisoners and the research subsequently benefitted the company (Black, 2001).

Beyond these clearly horrendous cases, debates about ethics have surfaced over the years in the face of well-known publicized cases of alleged ethical transgression in various fields of scholarly research. An example is Dalton's (1959) covert ethnography of unofficial managerial activity. One of the central issues that Dalton addresses in his study is the unofficial use of company resources, including pilfering or corporate theft. There is considerable debate as to whether it was ethical to obtain such data through the method of covert observation. There are also several well-known psychological studies (e.g., Milgram 1963; Haney, Banks, and Zimbardo, 1973) that continue to be widely cited in the field of organizational behaviour, despite the fact that they were based on research designs that would now be widely considered extremely unethical (see Web Research in focus 8.1). However, the problem with this emphasis on notoriety is that it can be taken to imply that ethical concerns reside only in such extreme cases, when in fact the potential for ethical transgression is much more general than this.

The issue of deception is one taken up by the Tri-Council and associated REBs. This does not mean that deception cannot be used in research but the onus is place squarely on the researcher to explain the value of the research and, more importantly, how he or she will avoid doing harm to those being deceived. It is then up to the REB to weigh the potential benefits of the research against any potential harm, with an emphasis on the avoidance of harm. To that end, the REB application form includes a number of safeguards to ensure that deception is carefully identified and justified. The SMU REB form, for example, devotes a section ('G') to deception and asks applicants whether 'the study involves the use of deception' and if so 'describe the deception(s) to be used . . . AND justify its use'. The form also asks applicants whether information

will 'be withheld from participants that might reasonably lead them to decline to participate in the study [and] will the participants be videotaped or audio taped in any manner without their knowledge or consent'. In each case the applicants are asked to explain further where they answer yes to any question, and to provide an outline of 'the process to be used to debrief participants'.

For those students or faculty members whose research involves deception the outcome of their application will depend not only on whether there is obvious risk to the well-being of those under study but also the political process of the REB evaluation where some of the issues may be debatable. It should be noted that deception also violates issues of free and informed consent and the ability of those studied to drop out of the research at any point in the process. The onus is on the research applicant to minimize the appearance of risk and attempt to deal with controversial issues by developing a clear outline of the purposes and safeguards involved in the proposed study. If anything local REBs may tend towards situation ethics where a good case can be made for deception (see Web Key concept 8.1).

Extreme and notorious cases of ethical violation, such as those discussed in Web Research in focus 8.1, tend to be associated with particular research methods, notably disguised observation and the use of deception in experiments. Again, the problem with this association of ethics with certain studies (and methods) is that it implies that ethical concerns reside only or even primarily in some methods but not others. As a result, the impression can be gleaned that other methods, such as questionnaires or overt ethnography, are immune from ethical problems.

In this chapter, not withstanding the fact that research ethics are overseen by the Tri-Council and REBs, we introduce the main issues and debates about ethics. This is because ethics can never simply be relegated to committees and overseers. It is crucial for researchers, be they students or faculty, to be aware of the ethnical principles involved and of the nature of the concerns about ethics in business research. It is only if researchers are aware of the issues involved that they can make informed decisions about the implications of certain choices. If nothing else, you should be aware of the possible outcomes that will be coming your way if you make certain kinds of choice from REB rejection of the proposed course of action to shame or even legal action should your approved research lead to unintended consequences.

Our chief concern lies with the ethical issues that arise in relations between researchers and research participants in the course of an investigation. This focus by no means exhausts the range of ethical issues and dilemmas that arise, such as those that might arise in relation to the funding of business research or how findings are used by non-researchers. However, the ethical issues that arise in the course of doing research are the ones that are most likely to impinge on students. Writers on research ethics adopt different stances concerning the ethical issues that arise in connection with relationships between researchers and research participants.

Ethical principles

Discussions about ethical principles in business research, and perhaps more specifically transgressions of them, tend to revolve around certain issues that recur in different guises. However, they have been usefully broken down by Diener and Crandall (1978) into four main areas, and mirror the types of concerns highlighted in the Tri-Council Policy:

- Whether there is *harm to participants*.
- Whether there is a *lack of informed consent*.
- Whether there is an *invasion of privacy*.
- Whether *deception* is involved.

We will look at each of these in turn, but it should be appreciated that these four principles overlap somewhat. For example, as we indicated above, it is difficult to imagine how the principle of informed consent could be built into an investigation in which research participants were deceived. However, there is no doubt that these four areas form a useful classification of ethical principles in and for business research.

Harm to participants

Research that is likely to harm participants is regarded by most people as unacceptable. But what is harm? Harm can entail a number of facets: physical harm; harm to participants' development or self-esteem; stress; harm to career prospects or future employment; and 'inducing subjects to perform reprehensible acts', as Diener and Crandall (1978, p. 19) put it. In several studies that we have encountered in this book, there has been real or potential harm to participants:

- In Dalton's (1959) study his 'counselling' relationship with the female secretary in exchange for access to valuable personnel files (see Web Research in focus 8.5) was potentially harmful to her, both in terms of the personal relationship and in jeopardizing the security of her employment.
- In Haney, Banks, and Zimbardo's (1973) prison experiments (see Web Research in focus 8.1), several participants experienced severe emotional reactions, including mental breakdown.
- Many of the participants in the Milgram experiment (1963) on obedience to authority (see Web Research in focus 8.1) experienced high levels of stress and anxiety as a consequence of being incited to administer electric shocks. It could also be argued that Milgram's observers were 'inducing subjects to perform reprehensible acts'. Indeed, yet another series of studies in which Milgram was involved placed participants in positions where they were being influenced to steal (Milgram & Shotland, 1973).

The AOM *Code of Ethical Conduct* states that it is the responsibility of the researcher to assess carefully the possibility of harm to research participants, and, to the extent that it is possible, the possibility of harm should be minimized. Similar sentiments are expressed by the MRS's *Code of Conduct*, which advocates that 'the researcher must take all reasonable precautions to ensure that respondents are in no way directly harmed or adversely affected as a result of their participation in a marketing research project'. However, some commentators cast the scope of ethical consideration far wider, suggesting that it is also necessary to consider non-participants in evaluating the risk of harm. Gorard (2002), for example, argues that research outcomes need to take into account the potential users who may constitute a majority of those who are affected by the outcomes (e.g., ensuing policies). This is consistent with recent changes in social research guidelines that extend the definition of what constitutes an ethical issue (see p. 177 for more discussion of these changes).

The issue of harm to participants is further addressed in ethical codes by advocating care over maintaining the confidentiality of records and anonymity of accounts. This means that the identities and records of individuals and organizations should be maintained as confidential. For example, the AOM *Code of Ethical Conduct* recommends that issues relating to confidentiality and anonymity should be negotiated and agreed with potential research participants, and, 'if confidentiality or anonymity is requested, this must be honored'. This injunction also means that care needs to be taken when findings are being published to ensure that individuals and organizations are not identified or identifiable, unless permission has been given for data to be passed on in a form that allows them to be identified. The MRS *Code of Conduct* states that, as a general rule, anonymity must be preserved. If a respondent's identity is to be revealed, '(*a*) the respondent must first have been told to whom the information would be supplied and the purposes for which it will be used, and also (*b*) the researcher must ensure that the information will not be used for any non-research purpose and that the recipient of the information has agreed to conform to the requirements of the Code'.

Nonetheless, the maintenance of confidentiality and anonymity may bring fourth other ethical concerns. One notable example is the case of Dr. Nancy Olivieri. In the early 1990s Olivieri, a hematologist with the University of Toronto, signed a contract with a drug company, Apotex, as a commercial sponsor for a randomized drug trial designed to deal with a potentially fatal blood disorder, called thalassemia. The contract included a confidentiality clause that gave the drug company the right to control the dissemination of information arising out of the drug trails. However, Olivieri became increasingly concerned about the drug being tested because of unexpected risks that had been discovered in the course of the trails. Olivieri wanted to inform patients about the risks but was prevented, under the confidentiality clause, from

doing so. Further, Apotex threatened legal action. Olivieri found herself trapped between contractual requirements and ethical considerations. In the end, she decided to publicize the drug's problems. She was then fired by the university and spent the next decade fighting her case before finally being exonerated and reinstated (Weigand & Mills, 2010; see also http://www.ecclectica.ca /issues /2005/3/ index.asp? Article=2; http://www.caut.ca/uploads/OlivieriInquiryReport.pdf).

In another notable case Russel Ogden, a Master's student at Simon Fraser University (SFU) in Vancouver, found himself in a difficult situation during 1994 when the Vancouver Coroner subpoenaed him. Ogden was being asked to give evidence at a Coroner's inquest by revealing the names of the respondents that he had interviewed for people with AIDS' (http://www.sfu.ca/~palys/ Controversy.htm). Ogden refused and went on to successfully defend his decision in court. However, Ogden was not supported by SFU and ended up suing the university for recovery of his costs. In the end an internal university inquiry agreed to reimburse for legal fees and lost wages; to apologize for SFU's failure to support him; deem appropriate the stand he took in refusing to break confidentiality; and guaranteeing that the university would uphold the issue of confidentiality and support its researchers who found themselves faced with the types of challenge that Ogden faced (http://www.sfu.ca/~palys/ Controversy.htm). Notwithstanding this decision SFU went on to institute a principle of 'limited confidentiality' (see Research in focus 8.1).

In quantitative research, it is often easier to anonymize records and to report findings in a way that does not allow individuals to be identified. However, even in quantitative studies there are sometimes instances where it is virtually impossible to make a company anonymous. The use of pseudonyms is a common recourse, but it may not eliminate entirely the possibility of identification. For example, in the case of Hofstede's (1984) research, although a company pseudonym was used throughout the published study, it was virtually impossible to conceal the company's identity without completely distorting the original data, partly because IBM is such a large and well-known organization. Similarly, although Scott et al. (1956) did not actually name

SFU and the 'Limited Confidentiality' controversy

In 1994, following an internal inquiry into the Ogden case, SFU's University Research Ethics Review Committee instituted a new policy that required researchers to limit confidentiality, arguing that:

> [I]n cases where it can be foreseen that the researchers may not legally be in a position to ensure confidentiality to their subjects, these researchers must be required to provide only limited confidentiality in the wording of the consent form. It was recognized that limited confidentiality might serve to discourage participation of some subjects, and conceivably even prevent the research from taking place at all due to lack of subjects. Nevertheless, it was agreed that causing the researchers to provide limited confidentiality in appropriate cases would protect the subjects, the University, and the researchers (quoted in http://www.sfu.ca/~palys/Controversy.htm).

The following year the university's informed consent form was changed to include the following statement: 'Any information that is obtained during this study will be kept confidential to the full extent permitted by law. . . . It is possible as a result of legal action the researcher may be required to divulge information obtained in the course of this research to a court or other legal body'. (http://www.sfu.ca/~palys/Controversy.htm).

The limited confidentiality principle was challenged in 1997 by two SFU criminologists on the grounds that (1) reference to the limits of the law 'abrogates the ethical responsibility to do everything legally possible to protect research participants from harm' and fails to inform potential informants of the researchers ultimate ethical responsibilities; and (2) it 'infringes academic freedom' (http://www.sfu.ca/~palys/Controversy.htm). Consequently the proposed research projects were held up for 18 months before the researchers were finally supported in their claims and university policy was amended.

In the meantime the Tri-Council Policy was instituted at the national level in Canada and, while not entirely uncontested, appears to agree with the notion that ethics should not be subordinate to law in the last instant, i.e., that universities should not use threat of law as the ultimate arbiter of research ethics.

---

their case-study organization, the details they provided in their analysis about the firm's size, location, history, and activities made it clear to Bacon and Blyton (2001; see Web Research in focus 4.10), and to other researchers, exactly which large steelworks in North Wales they had focused on.

The issues of confidentiality and anonymity raise particular difficulties for many forms of qualitative research, where particular care has to be taken with regard to the possible identification of persons, organizations, and places. The consequences of failing to protect individual anonymity are illustrated by Parker (2000, p. 238; see Chapter 17), who describes how a quote in his report about the managing director was traced to an 'insufficiently anonymized source', whose reputation was damaged as a result of the incident. As the MRS guidelines on employee research note:

Sample sizes in specialised areas may be very small to the point where employees themselves could be identified. If there is a reasonable risk of an employee being identified, due to the sample size of the population or sub-population being covered, the employee should be informed of this risk at the beginning of the interview and given the opportunity to withdraw (p. 11).

The guidelines, therefore, recommend that researchers examine the results of subgroups only in situations where there are 10 or more respondents involved.

The issues of confidentiality and anonymity involve legal as well as ethical considerations. For example, in Cavendish's (1982) study of women factory workers on an assembly line, great care was taken by the researcher

8.1 | Student Experience

Recently, Shelagh Campbell faced a situation not unlike the Ogden case when she was called on to provide information in a legal dispute between the parties she was researching. The situation actually focused on the issue that was an important focal point of her thesis. Her immediate response was to stand in the hall of the university and yell for help. According to Campbell, her thesis supervisor 'helped to calm her down' and called on the resources of the university to assist. She subsequently received support from the university's legal council for a preliminary discovery meeting (i.e., a session where lawyers from either side can ask preliminary questions before the case is heard in court) with the employer's counsel (the issue was a labour relations case).

The problem was compounded because the employer was also Campbell's former employer. The lawyer for Campbell tried to impress upon the situation that it would be detrimental to her thesis if she was called to give testimony against the subjects she was researching. However, this appeared to fall on deaf ears and Campbell was 'tracked to the gym on [her] lunch hour the following day and served with a subpoena in this Supreme Court case'. The parties settled at the eleventh hour, but, as Campbell puts it, 'not before I went down to the court house and sat in the lobby with all these ghosts from my past. [Things] turned out well, however, as I reconnected with folks who had left town and had an excellent meeting with my research subject over coffee'.

to invent names for all the women so that they could not be identified, to protect them from possible victimization by the company. However, Cavendish deliberately left the name of the firm unchanged in order to preserve the realism of the study and to provide 'concrete facts about the factory' (1982, p. vi). However, as Cavendish explains, this proved very naive: 'if the firm was named, here was a risk both to me and to the publisher that the firm might bring a libel action against us' (1982, p. vi). For this reason, after consultation with lawyers, she decided to rewrite the account prior to publication in order to make the firm unidentifiable. This involved changing not only the name of the firm, but also its location, the details of the components manufactured, and the name of the trade union representing the women. In contrast, there are other instances where organizations do consent to be named in publications, for example in Pettigrew's (1985) study of changing culture at Imperial Chemical Industries.

The issues of confidentiality and anonymity also raise particular problems with regard to the secondary analysis of qualitative data (see Chapter 24), since it is very difficult, though by no means impossible, to present field notes and interview transcripts in a way that will prevent people and places from being identified. As Alderson (1998) has suggested, the difficulty is one of being able to ensure that the same safeguards concerning confidentiality can be guaranteed when secondary analysts examine such records as those provided by the original primary researcher.

One of the problems with the harm-to-participants principle is that it is not possible to identify in all circumstances whether or not harm is likely, though that fact should not be taken to mean that there is no point in seeking to protect them. For example, in the prison experiments conducted by Haney, Banks, and Zimbardo (see Web Research in focus 8.1) the extreme reactions of participants surprised the researchers. Arguably they did not anticipate this level of harm to be incurred when they planned the study. This is partly why the AOM *Code of Ethical Conduct* recommends third-party review as a

Tips and Skills

Confidentiality agreements

As part of the process of negotiating access, it is becoming increasingly common for companies to ask their legal departments to prepare a Confidentiality Agreement, which you may be asked to sign on your own behalf, or someone from your university may be asked to sign on behalf of the institution. The main purpose of this is to define what type of information you can have access to and to establish what information you are and are not able to disclose about the company. This usually involves agreeing that you will not pass on information to a third party, particularly that which pertains to commercially sensitive or valuable issues, such as new-product development. In addition, there may be a clause that specifies that the company must have sight of the research once it has been written up, so that it can comment on the findings, particularly if they are going to be published. This legally binding agreement can thus grant a considerable amount of power to the company, and it has the potential to cause considerable difficulties if your research throws up issues that the company would rather were kept out of the public domain. If you are asked to sign a Confidentiality Agreement, before signing it, take it to your supervisor to ask for advice and get it checked by someone who deals with legal issues on behalf of the university. It may be that there is some room for negotiation

in relation to the exact wording of the agreement and the company may be reassured if there is an undertaking that the research will guarantee its anonymity. Thus, when Jean Helms Mills was negotiating with Nova Scotia Power to spend time in the company studying organizational change lawyers for Ernst & Young, the company heading up the Business Process Research change at the time, insisted on a legal agreement. The agreement was to give Ernst & Young control over the content and publication of any outcomes of Helms Mills's research. She refused to sign, citing the fear that her research would be potentially compromised and restricted. In the end, the CEO of the company overrode any legal requirements and allowed her to continue her study of the change process. Although she used the name Power Co to anonymize the company in her previous publications this proved increasingly difficult given the nature of the company and its monopoly situation in power generation in Nova Scotia. Satisfied that her research provided a reasonable and plausible account she decided to use the real company name in her book on *Making Sense of Organizational Change*. In subsequent communications with the then CEO of the company she was informed that the work was a fair account.

means of protecting the interests of research participants, stating: 'research plans involving human participants should be reviewed by an appropriate third party such as a university human subjects committee or a focus group of potential participants'. In addition, the ASA *Code of Ethics* suggests that, if there is any prospect of harm to participants, informed consent, the focus of the next section, is essential: 'Informed consent must be obtained when the risks of research are greater than the risks of everyday life. Where modest risk or harm is anticipated, informed consent must be obtained'.

Lack of informed consent

The issue of informed consent is in many respects the area within business research ethics that is most hotly debated. The bulk of the discussion tends to focus on what is variously called disguised or covert observation. Such

observation can involve covert participant observation (see Key concept 17.1a and b), or simple or contrived observation (see, for example, Web Research in focus 16.3a and 16.3b), in which the researcher's true identity is unknown. The principle means that prospective research participants should be given as much information as might be needed to make an informed decision about whether or not they wish to participate in a study. Covert observation transgresses that principle, because participants are not given the opportunity to refuse to cooperate. They are involved whether they like it or not.

Lack of informed consent is a feature of Research in focus 8.6 and Web Research in focus 8.1. For example, in Dalton's research informed consent is almost entirely absent. Dalton went to great lengths in order to keep the purpose of his research from participants, presumably to maximize his chances of obtaining specific informa-

| 8.2 | **Student Experience** |

Ethical considerations in a student research project

For her PH.D. research, Margaret McKee trained a group of managers and supervisors in an organization. Following the training, everyone was offered a chance to meet one-on-one with her, or one of her colleagues, to discuss the training and their personal goals for putting their training into practice. About half of the 170 people that were trained took Margaret up on the offer to meet. However, senior leaders in the organization were disappointed at what they felt was a low participation rate and wanted to know who had not taken advantage of this opportunity.

When they pressed for names, Margaret had to explain that she couldn't reveal the identities of those who had not agreed to meet. Even though she wasn't collecting any data for her research in the meetings, Margaret felt this aspect of the study should also adhere to the principles of confidentiality and anonymity: 'so that I could cultivate an overall atmosphere of trust with my participants. It wasn't the answer the organization's leaders wanted but, to their credit, when I explained things they did understand my reasoning and let the matter drop'.

---

tion about such things as unofficial use of resources or pilfering. Even those who became key informants, or 'intimates', knew only of Dalton's general interest in 'personnel problems', and great care was taken not to arouse suspicion. Dalton describes his undercover role as similar in indirect actions to that of an espionage agent or spy, although he stresses that his interest was in scientific rather than criminal evidence. The principle of informed consent also entails the implication that, even when people know they are being asked to participate in research, they should be fully informed about the research process. As the AOM *Code of Ethical Conduct* suggests:

> It is the duty of Academy members to preserve and protect the privacy, dignity, well-being, and freedom of research participants. This duty requires both careful research design and informed consent from all participants . . . Informed consent means explaining to potential participants the purposes and nature of the research so they can freely choose whether or not to become involved. Such explanations include warning of possible harm and providing explicit opportunities to refuse to participate and to terminate participation at any time. Because students and em-

ployees are particularly subject to possible coercion, even when unintended, special care must be taken in obtaining their informed consent.

Similarly, the MRS *Code of Conduct* states that informed consent means that respondents should be told, normally at the beginning of the interview, if observation techniques or recording equipment are to be used. Thus, while Milgram's and Haney, Banks, and Zimbardo's experimental subjects (see Web Research in focus 8.1) were volunteers and, therefore, knew they were going to participate in research, there is a lack of informed consent, because they were not given full information about the nature of the research and its possible implications for them.

However, as Homan (1991, p. 73) has observed, implementing the principle of informed consent 'is easier said than done'. At least two major points stand out here:

- It is extremely difficult to present prospective participants with absolutely all the information that might be required to make an informed decision about their involvement. In fact, relatively minor transgressions probably pervade most business research, such as de-

Maintaining anonymity in a small-scale research project

Karla's problem with anonymity was centered on the fact that she was undertaking an ethnographic study in a small parliamentary office of her country's Parliament. She had originally intended to undertake a comparative study at a similar office of another national Parliament but access proved difficult. To disguise the identity of the parliamentary office under study Karla felt that she might have to invent, what she calls, a 'factional' story to protect her sources: 'I'm probably going to have to pretend I've been to two [similar institutions] or even create a third fictional one because they're very small offices and I need to protect my [sources] in every possible way'. This 'factional approach' (i.e., 'a cross between fact and fiction') became more critical when a scandal concerning the research site surfaced in the press and it was revealed that Karla was doing her PH.D. research studies there: now 'everybody knows that my PH.D. research is on [this particular] parliamentary administration, therefore there is no point in hiding . . . trying to claim that it's another public office. I need to use other ways of protection. So [my supervisor] and I have been discussing this concept of factionality and I have been doing some reading on factionality in effect, thinking of like creating a third

space'. Increasingly worried about protecting the identities of the people in her ethnographic study Karla looked at ways of using factionality to present some of her data: 'So, I'm trying to find out if there would be a way that I could create a factional parliamentary office, and therefore blur [the details but] . . . this is tricky. This is like my biggest dilemma at the moment, how to do it, how to write the ethnography in a way that I want, [while avoiding identifying people] 'cause I promised not to do it. [The organization is] too small, too paranoid, and people are too jumpy to start with and now I've got to do my utmost to make sure [of anonymity] . . . I'm thinking of the factionality, I'm thinking of splitting people up . . . [where] one person becomes two people [in my descriptions]'.

As part of the process Karla [not her real name] asked us to anonymize her own name and any other identifying information. We were happy to comply with this request and changed her name to Karla to protect her identity and, equally important, the identities of her respondents. This is also true of Jennifer [the name is also invented] who asked to remain anonymous to protect the identities of the organization and respondents that are the focus of her study.

liberately underestimating the amount of time that an interview is likely to take so that people are not put off being interviewed, and not giving absolutely all the details about one's research for fear of contaminating people's answers to questions.

- In ethnographic research, the researcher is likely to come into contact with a wide range of people, and ensuring that absolutely everyone has the opportu-

nity for informed consent is not practicable, because it would be extremely disruptive in everyday contexts. Also, even when all research participants in a certain setting are aware that the ethnographer is a researcher, it is doubtful whether they are all similarly (let alone identically) informed about the nature of the research. For example, in Lee's (1998) study of women factory workers in Hong Kong and China, she found it difficult to convey her 'version' of what she was doing to her co-workers. This was partly because the academic term 'thesis' did not make sense to them, so the women developed an alternative explanation, which involved the idea that Lee was writing a novel based on her experiences as a worker 'toiling side by side with "real" workers'. Lee explains: 'I had to settle for that definition too . . . ' (1998, p. 173). This example aptly illustrates how it is not always possible for the researcher fully to explain the purposes and nature of the research, and so sometimes a compromise understanding is reached.

In spite of the widespread condemnation of violations of informed consent and the view that covert observation is especially vulnerable to accusations of unethical practice in this regard, studies such as Dalton's (1959) are still regarded as important in providing insight into subversive or illegitimate organizational behaviour. The defense is usually of the 'end-justifies-the-means' kind, which is further discussed below. What is interesting in the context of this discussion is that some ethical codes essentially leave the door ajar for covert observation. The BSA *Statement of Ethical Practice* does suggest that researchers should 'as far as possible' seek to achieve informed consent, but it then goes even further in relation to covert research:

> There are serious ethical dangers in the use of covert research but covert methods may avoid certain problems. For instance, difficulties arise when research participants change their behaviour because they know they are being studied. Researchers may also face problems when access to spheres of social life is closed to social scientists by powerful or secretive interests. However, covert methods violate the principles of informed consent and may invade the privacy of those being studied. Participant or non-participant observation in non-public spaces or experimental manipulation of research participants without their knowledge should be resorted to only where it is impossible to use other methods to obtain essential data. In such studies it is important to safeguard the anonymity of research participants. Ideally,

where informed consent has not been obtained prior to the research it should be obtained post hoc.

While this statement hardly condones the absence of informed consent associated with covert research, it is not unequivocally censorious either. It recognizes that covert research 'may avoid certain problems' and refers, without using the term, to the possibility of reactivity associated with overt observational methods. It also recognizes that covert methods can help to get over the difficulty of gaining access to certain kinds of settings. The passage entails an acknowledgement that informed consent is jeopardized, along with the privacy principle (see below), but implies that covert research can be used 'where it is impossible to use other methods to obtain essential data'. The difficulty here, clearly, is how a researcher is to decide whether or not it is in fact impossible to obtain data other than by covert work. We suspect that, by and large, covert observers typically make their judgements in this connection on the basis of the *anticipated* difficulty of gaining access to a setting or of encountering reactivity problems, rather than as a response to difficulties they have actually experienced. For example, Dalton (1959) has written that it is impossible to get sufficiently close to unofficial managerial activities to access the meanings assigned to them by participants, other than through covert observation. The issue of the circumstances in which violations of ethical principles, like informed consent, are deemed acceptable will reappear in the discussion below.

The principle of informed consent is also bound up to some extent with the issue of harm to participants. Erikson (1967) has suggested that, if the principle is not followed and if participants are harmed as a result of the research, the investigator is more culpable than if they did not know. For example, he writes: 'If we happen to harm people who have agreed to act as subjects, we can at least argue that they knew something of the risks involved . . .' (1967, p. 369). While this might seem like a recipe for seeking a salve for the researcher's conscience, it does point to an important issue—namely, that the business researcher is more likely to be vilified if participants are adversely affected when they were not willing accomplices, than when they were. However, it is debatable whether that means that the researcher is any less culpable for that harm. Erikson implies researchers are less culpable, but this is a potential area for disagreement.

Invasion of privacy

This third area of ethical concern relates to the issue of the degree to which invasions of privacy can be condoned. The right to privacy is a tenet that many of us hold dear, and transgressions of that right in the name of research are not regarded as acceptable. The MRS guidance is clear: 'the objectives of any study do not give researchers a special right to intrude on a respondent's privacy nor to abandon normal respect for an individual's values'. Privacy is very much linked to the notion of informed consent, because, to the degree that informed consent is given on the basis of a detailed understanding of what the research participant's involvement is likely to entail, he or she, in a sense, acknowledges that the right to privacy has been surrendered for that limited domain. Of course, the research participant does not abrogate the right to privacy entirely by providing informed consent. As we have seen, when people agree to be interviewed, they will frequently refuse to answer certain questions on whatever grounds they feel are justified. Often, these refusals will be based on a feeling that certain questions delve into private realms or cover topic areas that they find sensitive and they do not wish to make these public, regardless of the fact that the interview is conducted in private. However, the MRS acknowledges that, although there are some topics that can be judged sensitive to everyone, because of the nature of the subject, it is impossible for the researcher to know beforehand which topics may be sensitive to a particular individual. It, therefore, recommends that the researcher 'treat each case sensitively and individually, giving respondents a genuine opportunity to withdraw'.

Covert methods are usually deemed to be violations of the privacy principle on the grounds that participants are not being given the opportunity to refuse invasions of their privacy. Such methods also mean that they might reveal confidences or information that they would not have revealed if they had known about the status of the confidant as researcher. The issue of privacy is invariably linked to issues of anonymity and confidentiality in the research process, an area that has already been touched on in the context of the question of whether or not harm comes to participants. The BSA *Statement* forges this kind of connection: 'The anonymity and privacy of those who participate in the research process should be respected. Personal information concerning research participants should be kept confidential. In some cases it may be necessary to decide whether it is proper or appropriate to record certain kinds of sensitive information'. Invasion of privacy can also be a particular issue when dealing with certain kinds of data, such as photographs (see Web Research in focus 8.2). However, beyond that, people's personal data are protected under the *Personal Information Protection and Electronic Documents Act* (PIPEDA), which, in 2001, covered the Canadian federally regulated private sector. In 2002 PIPEDA was expanded to include personal health information collected by such bodies and in 2004 was further expanded to cover 'information collected in the course of any commercial activity' in Canada (http://canadaonline.about.com/cs/privacy/a/privacylaw.htm). The subsequent PIPEDA legislation has implications for research, providing a limited exception for personal information that is used for research purposes. The Act 'permits an organization to use of disclose personal information, without the knowledge or consent of the individual; where it is used for statistical, scholarly study or research purposes that cannot be achieved without using the information; the information is used in a manner that will ensure its confidentiality; it is impracticable to obtain consent; and the organization informs the federal Privacy Commissioner of the disclosure or use before the information is disclosed or used' (http://www.longwoods.com/product.php?productid=16401). The exception, however, requires that prior to the collection of data participants be made aware of the uses to which the date will be put. Thus, data collected for one purpose should not be used for other purposes at a later date. Also current data is not 'grandfathered' (i.e., exempt because it was collected prior to the passage of the Act). Its use is also restricted according to the principles of the Act and what respondents reasonably expected when they provided the data in the first place. (http://

www.longwoods.com/product.php?productid=16401). The veracity of the law in regards to scholarly research has yet to be tested but it remains a contested safeguard of privacy that forms part of the context in which research in Canada is conducted.

Raising issues about ensuring anonymity and confidentiality in relation to the recording of information and the maintenance of records relates to all methods of business research. In other words, while covert research may pose certain kinds of problem regarding the invasion of privacy, other methods of business research are implicated in possible difficulties in connection with anonymity and confidentiality.

Deception

Deception occurs when researchers represent their research as something other than what it is. The obedience to authority study by Milgram referred to in Web Research in focus 8.1 involves deception because participants were led to believe they were administering real electric shocks. Another less extreme example is provided by Holliday (1995) in her ethnographic study of small firms (see Web Research in focus 8.3). In pretending to be a student interested in small firms in order to get information about a competitor's product, Holliday was clearly engaged in an element of deception. The AOM *Code of Ethical Conduct* states:

> Deception should be minimized, and, when necessary, the degree and effects must be mitigated as much as possible. Researchers should carefully weigh the gains achieved against the cost in human dignity. To the extent that concealment or deception is necessary, the researcher must provide a full and accurate explanation to participants at the conclusion of the study, including counselling, if appropriate.

Deception in various degrees is probably quite widespread in much research, because researchers often want to limit participants' understanding of what the research is about so that they respond more naturally to the experimental treatment. Indeed, some ethical codes appear to condone the strictly bounded use of deception, in order to preserve the naturalness of the data. For example, in the section on informed consent it was mentioned that the MSR *Code of Conduct* states that respondents should be told at the beginning of an interview if observation techniques or recording equipment are to be used. However, if it is felt that this knowledge might bias the respondent's subsequent behaviour, the respondent may be told about the recording at the *end* of the interview. They should then be given the opportunity to see or hear the relevant section of the record, and, if they so wish, 'the record or relevant section of it must be destroyed or deleted'.

The ethical objection to deception seems to turn on two points. First, it is not a nice thing to do. While the SRA *Guidelines* recognizes that deception is widespread in social interaction, it is hardly desirable. Secondly, there is the question of professional self-interest. If business researchers became known as snoopers who deceived people as a matter of professional course, the image of our work would be adversely affected and we might experience difficulty in gaining financial support and the cooperation of future prospective research participants. As the SRA Guidelines puts it:

> It remains the duty of social researchers and their collaborators, however, not to pursue methods of inquiry that are likely to infringe human values and sensibilities. To do so, whatever the methodological advantages, would be to endanger the reputation of social research and the mutual trust between social researchers and society, which is a prerequisite for much research.

One of the chief problems with the discussion of this aspect of ethics is that deception is, as some writers observe, widespread in business research (see *Ethical transgression is pervasive* section below). As the example from Lee's (1998) research illustrates, it is rarely feasible or desirable to provide participants with a totally complete account of what your research is about. Bulmer (1982), whose stance is predominantly that of a universalist in ethics terms (see below), nonetheless recognizes that there are bound to be instances such as this and deems them justifiable. However, it is very difficult to know where the line should be drawn here and this becomes a contested area as REB's attempt to evaluate projects involving deception.

Stances on ethics

Authors on social research ethics can be characterized in terms of the stances they take on the issue. The following stances can be distinguished:

- Universalism. A universalist stance takes the view that ethical precepts should never be broken. Infractions of ethical principles are wrong in a moral sense and are damaging to social research. This kind of stance can be seen in the writings of Erikson (1967), Dingwall (1980), and Bulmer (1982). Bulmer does, however, point to some forms of what appears to be disguised observation that may be acceptable. One is retrospective covert observation, which occurs when a researcher writes up his or her experiences in social settings in which he or she participated but not as a researcher. An example would be Van Maanen (1991b), who wrote up his experiences as a ride operator in Disneyland many years after he had been employed there in vacation jobs. Even a universalist like Erikson (1967, p. 372) recognizes that it 'would be absurd . . . to insist as a point of ethics that sociologists should always introduce themselves as investigators everywhere they go and should inform every person who figures in their thinking exactly what their research is all about'.
- Situation ethics. Goode (1996) has argued for deception to be considered on a case-by-case basis. In other words, he argues for what Fletcher (1966, p. 31) has called a 'situation ethics', or more specifically 'principled relativism', which can be contrasted with the universalist ethics of some writers. This argument has two ways of being represented:

  1. *The end justifies the means.* Some writers argue that, unless there is some breaking of ethical rules, we would never know about certain social phenomena. Dalton (1959) essentially argues for this position in relation to his study of managers and

the differences between official and unofficial action. Without some kind of disguised observation, this important aspect of organizational life would not have been studied. This is usually linked to the second form of a *situationist* argument in relation to social research ethics.

  2. *No choice.* It is often suggested that we have no choice but to engage in dissimulation on occasions if we want to investigate the issues in which we are interested.

- Ethical transgression is pervasive. It is often observed that virtually all research involves elements that are at least ethically questionable. This occurs whenever participants are not given absolutely all the details on a piece of research, or when there is variation in the amount of knowledge about research. Punch (1994, p. 91), for example, observes that 'some dissimulation is intrinsic to social life and, therefore, to fieldwork'. He quotes Gans (1962, p. 44) in support of this point: 'If the researcher is completely honest with people about his activities, they will try to hide actions and attitudes they consider undesirable, and so will be dishonest. Consequently, the researcher must be dishonest to get honest data'.

- Anything goes (more or less). The writers associated with arguments relating to situation ethics and a recognition of the pervasiveness of ethical transgressions are not arguing for an 'anything-goes' mentality, but for a certain amount of flexibility in ethical decision making. However, Douglas (1976) has argued that the kinds of deception in which social researchers engage are trivial compared to those perpetrated by powerful institutions in modern society (such as the mass media, the police, and industry). His book is an inventory of tactics for deceiving people so that their trust is gained and they reveal themselves to the researcher. Very few researchers subscribe to this stance. Denzin (1968) comes close to an anything-goes stance when he suggests that social researchers are entitled to study anyone in any setting provided the work has a 'scientific' purpose, does not harm participants, and does not deliberately damage the discipline. The harm-to-participants criterion can also be seen in the cases reported in Web Research in focus 8.1.

Other ethical considerations

However, in addition to the four main ethical principles identified by Diener and Crandall (1978), there are other ethical con siderations that need to be taken into account in planning a research project which have been made more prominent as the result of recent changes within the social science research community. These relate to work carried out by research funding bodies such as the Tri-Council (consisting of SSHRC, NSERC and CIHR) in Canada, the Economic and Social Research Council (ESRC) in Britain, and the European Union, which have been active, in recent years, in developing ethical frameworks that apply to all social science researchers, including those in the field of business and management. The Tri-Council's influence on research in Canada was discussed above. In the UK the ESRC *Research Ethics Framework* is the result of discussion and consultation with the social science community and other key stakeholders since 2003, and led to the production of a series of working papers and reports. Although the guidelines apply specifically to research projects funded by these organizations, which will eventually have to show that they have met the requirements set out in the framework in order to receive funding, it is likely that they will also, in due course, affect the awareness of all university social science researchers about ethical matters. These codes and the discussions surrounding their development can be found at:

http://www.respectproject.org/main/index.php
www.esrc.ac.uk/ESRCInfoCentre/opportunities/research_ethics_ framework/index.aspx

Another example of the heightened awareness of ethical issues in university-based research relates to the development of the *Missenden Code* (the *Missenden Code of Practice for Ethics and Accountability*), which aims to address the challenges posed by the increased commercialization of research and shifts in the source of research funding. This code is also available on the Internet at: http://www.missendencentre.co.uk/Ethics_report.pdf

However, rather than being intended as a replacement for the ethics codes developed by professional associations such as those described earlier in this chapter, these frameworks are intended to supplement existing codes and to encourage their further development. Because of this, it is worthwhile reviewing here the main areas that they cover in addition to the four main ethical principles that we have already discussed. These relate to the:

- Impact of data protection legislation.
- Role of reciprocity in determining the relationship between the researcher and research participants.
- Need to declare sources of funding and support that may affect the affiliations of the researcher, causing conflicts of interest.

Data protection

The routine collection and storing of electronic data and use of data-mining techniques has raised new concerns about the confidentiality of information. Questions about the extent to which such information can be used for research purposes that may be different from the reasons for collecting the information in the first place are addressed through making judgements about who owns the data and under what circumstances they are entitled to use it. Data protection is a matter that is regulated by law so, rather than being a matter that requires professional guidance, researchers are obliged to comply with this. The legislation has particular impact on determining how and to what extent personal data may be used for research purposes.

In Canada, as discussed above, the legislation that covers data protection is the Personal Information Protection and Electronics Documents Act (PIPEDA) – see http://www.ccpa-accp.ca/_documents/NotebookEthics/Personal%20Information%20Protection%20and%20Electronics%20Documents%20Act%20PIPEDA.pdf. In the UK the relevant act is the Data Protection Act1988, which came into effect on 1 March 2000. The principles of data protection enshrined in the UK act relate specifically to personal data, which are data that relate to a living individual who can be identified either from the data or from other information in the possession of the data-holder. It includes expressions of opinion as well as factual information. The Data Protection Act 1988 is intended to restrict the processing of this data. Processing includes obtaining, recording, or holding the data or carrying out analytical operations on it. The definition of processing is thus quite broad. In addition to the use of data, processing also refers to disclosure of data, data blocking, and data destruction. The Data Protection Act 1988 states that personal data must:

1. Be processed fairly and lawfully.
2. Be obtained only for one or more specified and lawful purposes and not further processed in any manner incompatible with that purpose or those purposes.
3. Be adequate, relevant, and not excessive in relation to the purpose or purposes for which they are processed.
4. Be accurate and, where necessary, kept up to date.
5. Not be kept longer than necessary.

In addition, the Data Protection Act 1988 states:

- Appropriate technical and organizational measures must be taken to protect against unauthorized or unlawful processing of personal data and against accidental loss or destruction of, or damage to, personal data.
- Personal data shall not be transferred to a country or territory outside the European Economic Area, unless that country or territory ensures an adequate level of protection for the rights and freedoms of data subjects in relation to the processing of personal data.

There is a further category in the Data Protection Act 1988 that relates to sensitive personal data, such as information about a data subject's political or religious beliefs or ethnic origin. This type of data is more rigorously protected and there is greater onus on the researcher to obtain explicit, usually written, consent from data subjects for the processing of this type of personal data. However, the Data Protection Act 1988 does provide for certain exemptions in the case of personal data that are collected for research purposes—namely, that where personal data are processed

for research that is not likely to cause damage or distress to any of the data subjects concerned, they may be kept and further processed at a later stage for other purposes. Additionally, as long as the results of the research are not published in any form that identifies any particular data subject, respondents do not have right of access to the data.

This UK act differs in some details from Canada's PIPEDA but also from those in other European countries. Because the legislation surrounding data protection varies from country to country, the RESPECT project set out to identify some common principles for European researchers to bear in mind when dealing with data protection issues. This involved a group of legal specialists who reviewed the existing EU legislation and came up with a common set of guidelines for researchers to follow in dealing with this issue. These guidelines, which are extremely detailed and run for over 80 pages, can be viewed in full at the following address:

http://www.respectproject.org/data/415data.pdf.

The length and detail of this report highlights the complexity of this issue for which researchers may be advised to take legal advice. However, it is worth highlighting three of the recommendations that the authors of the report make. These include:

- That researchers draft an outline of the processing operations (this is not limited to electronic processing) involved in their use of the data before they start to process it, so they can assess the legality of their usage in advance, rather than perform the operations and then find out afterwards whether or not they are permitted to use the data in this way. This point highlights the potential seriousness of using data unlawfully, for which criminal or administrative sanctions may be applied.
- That researchers should decide who is the controller of the data and thus responsible for its usage, and on the basis of this determine which national legislation applies to their study. This is a particular issue in situations involving a group of researchers working together on a research project but based in different countries. This decision also depends on where the data processing will be carried out.

- That prior to the processing the researcher should define who will be the data subjects and take precautions to respect their rights in relation to the data.

Reciprocity and trust

Ethics codes increasingly emphasize the importance of openness and honesty in communicating information about the research to all interested parties (Bell & Bryman, 2007). Although this issue is related to the ethical principles of informed consent and avoiding deception discussed above, it goes further than these existing principles in placing the responsibility on the researcher for taking action that helps to overcome the power inequalities between themselves and research participants, and for ensuring that the research has benefits for them both. For example, the Tri-Council Policy Statement and the ESRC *Research Ethics Framework* make frequent mention of the need to communicate benefits to research participants. At its most advanced, this incorporates the concept of reciprocity, the idea that the research should be of mutual benefit to researcher and participants and that some form of collaboration or active participation should be built into the research project from the outset. This encourages a view of the research relationship as a mutually beneficial exchange between researcher and participants who see each other as moral beings and enforce on each other adherence to a set of agreed-upon moral norms (Wax, 1982). It also resonates with developments in qualitative research that have sought to reconceptualize researcher–subject relationships (see Chapter 6).

Affiliation and conflicts of interest

In all areas of scientific study it is recognized that affiliations, particularly those related to funding, have the potential to influence the way that research issues are defined and findings presented. The Missenden Code aims to address the challenges posed by the increased commercialization in universities and shifts in the source of research funding. The Missenden Code, which was set up following a number of high-profile ethical controversies (see Thinking deeper 8.7), recommends that universities set up ethics committees to monitor the sources of sponsorship and funding, and to ensure that the source

of funding is acknowledged in any publication. The Missenden Code claims that ethical implications arise when research is financially underwritten by a source that has a vested interest in the results. However, this does not mean that it is automatically biased, rather that it may be perceived to be biased, for example by the media, and, therefore, it is able to be discredited. Moreover, no research is truly independent.

Even if it is not in receipt of funding from commercial sources it is clear that the money must come from somewhere, such as a government source, which will also have interests in funding certain kinds of research and coming up with particular findings. Similarly, in many postgraduate MBA student research projects, the study forms part of a dissertation for a degree, which is at least partly funded by the student's employer. Therefore, the main thing for researchers to be conscious of is the possibility that questions about funding have the potential to affect the credibility of the research and to be explicit and open about the resources that enabled their research in any publication.

 # The difficulties of ethical decision making

The difficulty of drawing the line between ethical and unethical practices can be revealed in several ways. The issue of some members of social settings being aware of the researcher's status and the nature of his or her investment has been mentioned on several occasions. Manuals about interviewing are full of advice about how to entice interviewees to open up about themselves. Researchers using **Likert scales** reword items to identify 'yea sayers' and 'nay sayers'. Interviewers frequently err on the low side when asked how long an interview will take. Women may use their identity as women to influence female interviewees in in-depth interviews to probe into their lives and reveal inner thoughts and feelings, albeit with a commitment to feminist research (Oakley, 1981; Finch, 1984; Freeman, 2000). Qualitative research is frequently very open-ended, and, as a result, research questions are either loose or not specified, so that it is doubtful whether or not ethnographers in particular are able to inform others

8.4 | Student Experience

Bill Murray comments 'as technology is ubiquitous now in the workplace, collecting survey data through online tools has become common. It is inexpensive, quick, and facilitates mass communication with all potential respondents. Yet, I have found that companies are unwilling to provide direct access to employee email information or even group distribution lists; they question what could happen to all of this contact information once release to a third party. In one of my past studies, I was reliant on managers to receive and redistribute my research communications. However, potential respondents became immediately suspect of research communications filtered to them via management, perceiving that the data they provided would first be scanned by managers. Here, both the organization and the research needed to maintain ethical boundaries around privileged information, as well as clearly communicate and reinforce to the survey sample group how these boundaries were being enforced'.

accurately about the nature of their research. Perhaps, too, some interviewees find the questions we ask unsettling or find the cut and thrust of a focus group discussion stressful, especially if they inadvertently reveal more than they might have intended.

There are, in other words, many ways in which there is the potential for deception and, relatedly, lack of informed consent in business research. These instances are, of course, a far cry from the deceptions perpetrated in the research summarized in Research in focus 8.1 and Web Research in focus 8.2, but they point to the difficulty of

arriving at ethically informed decisions. Ethical codes give advice on patently inappropriate practices, though sometimes leaving some room for manoeuvre, as we have seen, but less guidance on marginal areas of ethical decision making. Indeed, guidelines may even be used by research participants *against* the researcher when they seek to limit the boundaries of a fieldworker's investigation (Punch, 1994). Finally, computer technology, and in particular the use of the Internet as a data collection method, has introduced new ethical challenges for researcher that will be discussed in Chapter 25.

✓ *Checklist*

Issues to consider in connection with ethics:

- ☐ Have you read and incorporated into your research the principles that are in line with the Tri-Council Policy Statement?
- ☐ Have you read and incorporated the requirements for doing ethical research in your institution, specifically the requirements of your university's REB?
- ☐ Have you found out whether or not all proposed research needs to be submitted to your university REB?
- ☐ If only certain types of research need to be submitted, have you checked to see whether or not your proposed research is likely to require clearance?

☐ Have you checked to ensure that there is no prospect of any harm coming to participants?

☐ Does your research conform to the principle of informed consent, so that research participants understand:
  - what the research is about?
  - the purposes of the research?
  - who is sponsoring it?
  - the nature of their involvement in the research?
  - how long their participation is going to take?
  - that their participation is voluntary?
  - that they can withdraw from participation in the research at any time?
  - what is going to happen to the data (e.g., how it is going to be kept)?

☐ Are you confident that the privacy of the people involved in your research will not be violated?

☐ Do you appreciate that you should not divulge information or views to your research participants that other research participants have given you?

☐ Have you taken steps to ensure that your research participants will not be deceived about the research and its purposes?

☐ Have you taken steps to ensure that the confidentiality of data relating to your research participants will be maintained?

☐ Once the data have been collected, have you taken steps to ensure that the names of your research participants and the location of your research (such as the name of the organization(s) in which it took place) are not identifiable?

☐ Does your strategy for keeping your data in electronic form comply with data protection legislation?

☐ Once your research has been completed, have you met obligations that were a requirement of doing the research (e.g., submitting a report to an organization that allowed you access)?

 ## *Key points*

This chapter has been concerned with a limited range of issues concerning ethics in business research, in that it has concentrated on ethical concerns that might arise in the context of collecting and analyzing data. In particular we have focused on the importance of the Tri-Council Policy and the work of university Research Ethics Boards. Our concern has mainly been with relations between researchers and research participants but noting that other ethical issues can arise in the course of business research.

- While the codes and guidelines of professional associations provide some guidance, their potency is ambiguous and they often leave the door open for some autonomy with regard to ethical issues.
- The main areas of ethical concern relate to: harm to participants; lack of informed consent; invasion of privacy; and deception.
- Covert observation and certain notorious studies have been particular focuses of concern.
- The boundaries between ethical and unethical practices are not clear-cut.
- Writers on social research ethics have adopted several different stances in relation to the issue.
- While the rights of research participants are the chief focus of ethical principles, concerns about professional self-interest are also of concern.

Questions for review

- Why are ethical issues important in relation to the conduct of business research?
- Outline the different stances on ethics in social research.

Ethics in context

- What is the Tri-Council policy and what does it do?

Ethical principles

- Does 'harm to participants' refer to physical harm alone?
- What are some difficulties with following this ethical principle?
- Why is the issue of informed consent so hotly debated?
- What are some of the difficulties of following this ethical principle?
- Why is the privacy principle important?
- What are some of the implications for research of the Personal Information Protection and Electonic Documents Act (PIPEDA)?
- Why does deception matter?
- How helpful are studies like Milgram's, Zimbardo's, and Dalton's in terms of understanding the operation of ethical principles in business research?

The difficulties of ethical decision making

- How easy is it to conduct ethical research?
- Read the Tri-Council policy statement. How effective is it in guarding against ethical transgressions?
- Were the actions taken by Holliday (1995) and described in Web Research in focus 8.3 ethical? (Explain your viewpoint using the framework provided in this chapter.) Would you have behaved differently in these circumstances? If so, how?

Part Three

Methods

Part Three of this book takes you through four sections that focus on ways of doing research. We have grouped each section roughly around the different senses and thought processes that we draw on to undertake a research project. Those senses and processes include the reasoning, talking, observing, and reading that we use to make sense of a research problem. Naturally many research strategies involve all four processes but we have tried to group each approach according to the primary one used.

In the first section we take you through surveying, examining issues of sampling in Chapter 9, self-completion questionnaires in Chapter 10, asking questions in Chapter 11, and how to use SPSS for Windows in Chapter 12. This section is largely rooted in a positivist approach that privileges a certain form of rational thinking—seeking to answer research questions through a process that is convincing through its objectivity and generalizability. All other sections include approaches that can be rooted in either positivist or postpositivist strategies.

The second section focuses on how research data is generated through asking questions of people. Chapter 13 deals with structured interviewing, where interviewers ask a number of 'respondents' the same series of questions that have relatively contained answers, and often involve some quantification of the data. In Chapter 14 we examine the range of interview techniques used in qualitative research, which usually involve more open-ended questions or, in some cases only a general opening question. Chapter 15 examines the use of focus groups and is located between questioning and observing. We have located it in 'questioning and discussion' because data is primarily generated by discussion questions between participants, however, the role of the researcher can be one of observer and those observations can, in some approaches, form part of the data collection.

The third section moves us to observation, with the more positivist structured observations dealt with in Chapter 16 and the more postpositivist ethnographic observations explored in Chapter 17. In the latter case it should be clear that ethnography often includes interviews and discussions with the people under

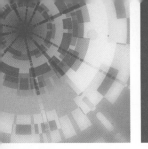

study, as well as 'reading' and analysis of various documentary sources. However, we felt that it is the series of observations—designed to gain insights into what people do as well as say—that characterize ethnographic approaches.

The fourth section deals with the generation of data through the reading of materials. Those materials can be gathered from a variety of sources—from newspapers and the Internet through to those collected in designated archives. In Chapter 18 we deal with content analysis, which is a form of reading that usually looks for and counts themes, which end up as constituting the data that is simultaneously embedded in the text and created from the text. Chapter 19 moves up on to the use of existing analyses of a phenomena (secondary analyses) and statistical data that has been officially collected for a variety of purposes (official statistics). In this case we explore how theoretical insights are drawn from and/or added to using existing data. In Chapter 20 we examine the various approaches that focus on analysis of language, where data is created from reading for such things as what is said and what is not said; what people and events are privileged or marginalized, etc. Chapter 21 moves us to historiography as a method for dealing with history and the past. Clearly some approaches to the study of history centrally involve oral histories (or interviews and discussions with people), however, all approaches to history involve the detailed reading and analysis of a variety of documents. Finally, in Chapter 22 we end the section with a focus on the Internet and the methods used to 'read' and analyze data on the Web.

These various sections and chapters will provide you with a feel for the different ways of doing research, whether from a positivist or postpositivist approach, and their connection to the thought processes and senses that are primarily involved.

9

Sampling

Chapter guide

This chapter, and the three that follow it, are very much concerned with principles and practices associated with social survey research. Sampling principles are not exclusively concerned with survey research; for example, they are relevant to the selection of documents for **content analysis**. However, in this chapter the emphasis will be on sampling in connection with the selection of people who would be asked questions by interview or questionnaire. The chapter explores:

- The related ideas of generalization (also known as external validity) and of a representative sample; the latter allows the researcher to generalize findings from a sample to a population.
- The idea of a probability sample—that is, one in which a random selection process has been employed.
- The main types of probability sample: the simple random sample, the systematic sample, the stratified random sample, and the multi-stage cluster sample.
- The main issues involved in deciding on sample size.
- Different types of non-probability sample, including quota sampling, which is widely used in market research and opinion polls.
- Potential sources of error in survey research.

Introduction

We imagine that many of the readers of this book will be university or college students. At some point in your stay at your university (we will use this term from now on to include colleges) you may have wondered about the attitudes of your fellow students to various matters, or about their behaviour in certain areas, or something about their backgrounds. If you were to decide to examine any or all of these three areas, you might consider conducting **structured interviews** or sending out **questionnaires** in order to find out about their behaviour, attitudes, and backgrounds. You will, of course, have to consider how best to design your interviews or questionnaires, and the issues that are involved in the decisions that need to be made about designing these research instruments and administering them will be the focus of Chapters 10 and 13. However, before getting to that point, you are likely to be confronted with a problem. Let us say that your university is quite large and has around 9000 students. It is extremely unlikely that you will have the time and resources to conduct a survey of all these students. It is unlikely that you would be able to send questionnaires

to all 9000 and even more unlikely that you would be able to interview all of them, since conducting **survey research** by interview is considerably more expensive and time consuming, all things being equal, than by **postal questionnaire** (see Chapter 10). It is almost certain that you will need to **sample** students from the total **population** of students in your university.

The need to sample is one that is almost invariably encountered in **quantitative research**. In this chapter, we will be almost entirely concerned with matters relating to sampling in relation to social survey research involving data collection by structured interview or questionnaire. In social survey research, *sampling* constitutes a key step in the research process, as illustrated in Figure 9.1. However, other methods of quantitative research also involve sampling considerations, as will be seen in Chapters 16 and 18, when we will examine **structured observation** and **content analysis** respectively. The principles of sampling involved are more or less identical in connection with these other methods, but frequently other considerations become apparent as well.

Figure 9.1

Steps in conducting a social survey

But will any old sample suffice? Would it be sufficient to locate yourself in a central position on your campus (if it has one) and then interview the students who come past you and whom you are in a position to interview? Alternatively, would it be sufficient to go around your student union asking people to be interviewed? Or to send questionnaires to everyone on your course?

The answer, of course, depends on whether or not you want to be able to *generalize* your findings to the entire student body in your university. If you do, it is unlikely that any of the three sampling strategies proposed in the previous paragraph would provide you with a **representative sample** of all students in your university. In order to be able to generalize your findings from your sample to the population from which it was selected, the sample must be representative. To discuss these issues in depth, we first need to clarify some basic sampling-related terminology:

- *Population*. The universe of units from which the sample is to be selected. The term 'units' is employed because it is not necessarily people who are being sampled—the researcher may want to sample from a universe of nations, cities, regions, firms, etc. Thus, 'population' has a much broader meaning than the everyday use of the term, whereby it tends to be associated with a nation's entire population.
- *Sample*. The segment of the population that is selected for investigation. It is a subset of the population. The method of selection may be based on a *probability* or a *non-probability* approach (see below).
- *Sampling frame*. The listing of all units in the population from which the sample will be selected.
- *Representative sample*. A sample that reflects the population accurately so that it is a microcosm of the population.
- *Probability sample*. A sample that has been selected using random selection so that each unit in the population has a known chance of being selected. It is generally assumed that a *representative sample* is more likely to be the outcome when this method of selection from the population is employed. The aim of probability sampling is to keep **sampling error** (see below) to a minimum.

- *Non-probability sample.* A sample that has not been selected using a random selection method. Essentially, this implies that some units in the population are more likely to be selected than others.
- *Sampling error.* The difference between a sample and the population from which it is selected, even though a probability sample has been selected.
- *Non-sampling error.* Differences between the population and the sample that arise either from deficiencies in the sampling approach, such as an inadequate sampling frame or **non-response** (see below), or from such problems as poor question wording, poor interviewing, or flawed processing of data.
- *Non-response.* A source of non-sampling error that is particularly likely to happen when individuals are being sampled. It occurs whenever some members of the sample refuse to cooperate, cannot be contacted, or for some reason cannot supply the required data (for example, because of mental incapacity).
- *Census.* The enumeration of an entire population. Thus, if data are collected in relation to all units in a population, rather than in relation to a sample of units of that population, the data are treated as census data.
- The phrase 'the census' typically refers to the complete enumeration of all members of the population of a nation state, i.e., a national census. For example, this form of enumeration occurs once every five years in Canada or once every ten years in the UK. However, in a statistical context, like the term population, the idea of a census has a broader meaning than this.

Why might the strategies for sampling students previously outlined be unlikely to produce a representative sample? There are various reasons, some of which are examined below:

- The first two approaches depend heavily upon the availability of students during the time or times that you search them out. Not all students are likely to be equally available at that time, so the sample will not reflect these students.
- They also depend on the students going to the locations. Not all students will necessarily pass the point

where you locate yourself or go to the student union, or they may vary hugely in the frequency with which they do so. Their movements are likely to reflect such things as where their halls of residence or accommodation are situated, or where their departments are located, or their social habits. Again, to rely on these locations would mean missing out on students who do not frequent them.

- It is possible, indeed likely, that your decisions about which people to approach will be influenced by your judgements about how friendly or cooperative the people concerned are likely to be or by how comfortable you feel about interviewing students of the same (or opposite) gender to yourself, as well as by many other factors.

- The problem with the third strategy is that students on your course by definition take the same subject as each other and, therefore, will not be representative of all students in the university.

In other words, in the case of all of the three sampling approaches, your decisions about whom to sample are influenced too much by personal judgements, by prospective respondents' availability, or by your implicit criteria for inclusion. Such limitations mean that, in the language of survey sampling, your sample will be *biased*. A biased sample is one that does not represent the population from which the sample was selected. As far as possible, bias should be removed from the selection of your sample. In fact, it is incredibly difficult to remove bias altogether and to derive a truly representative sample. What needs to be done is to ensure that steps are taken to keep bias to an absolute minimum.

Three sources of bias can be identified:

- If a non-probability or non-random sampling method is used. If the method used to select the sample is not random, there is a possibility that human judgement will affect the selection process, making some members of the population more likely to be selected than others. This source of bias can be eliminated through the use of probability or random sampling, the procedure for which is described below.

- If the sampling frame is inadequate. If the sampling frame is not comprehensive or is inaccurate or suffers from some other kind of similar deficiency, the sample that is derived cannot represent the population, even if a random/probability sampling method is employed.

- If some sample members refuse to participate or cannot be contacted—in other words, if there is non-response. The problem with non-response is that those who agree to participate may differ in various ways from those who do not agree to participate. Some of the differences may be significant to the research question or questions. If the data are available, it may be possible to check how far, when there is non-response, the resulting sample differs from the population. It is often possible to do this in terms of characteristics such as gender or age, or, in the case of something like a sample of university students, whether the sample's characteristics reflect the entire sample in terms of faculty membership. However, it is usually impossible to determine whether differences exist between the population and the sample after non-response in terms of 'deeper' factors, such as attitudes or patterns of behaviour.

Sampling error

In order to appreciate the significance of **sampling error** for achieving a representative sample, consider Figures 9.2 and 9.6. Imagine we have a population of 200 employees and we want a sample of 50. Imagine, as well, that one of the **variables** that interests us is whether or not employees receive regular performance appraisals from their immediate supervisor and that the population is equally divided between those who do and those who do not. This split is represented by the vertical line that divides the population into two halves (see Figure 9.2). If the sample is **representative** we would expect our sample of 50 to be equally split in terms of this variable (see Figure 9.3). If there is a small amount of **sampling error**, so that we have one employee too many who is not appraised and one too few who is, it will look like Figure 9.4. In Figure 9.5 we see a rather more serious degree of over-representation of employees who do not receive appraisals. This time there are three too

Figure 9.2

Having performance appraisals in a population of 200

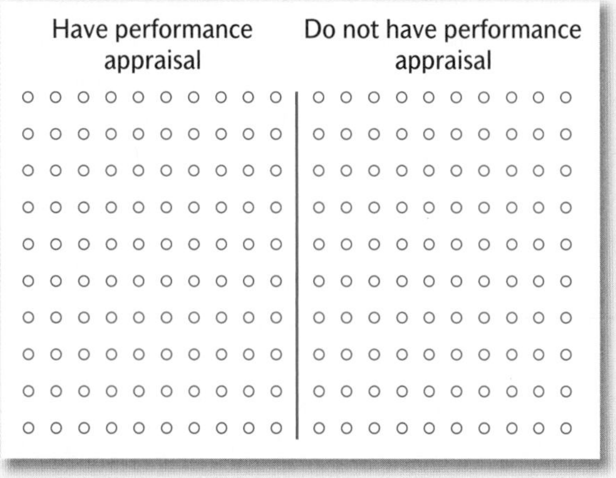

Figure 9.3

A sample with no sampling error

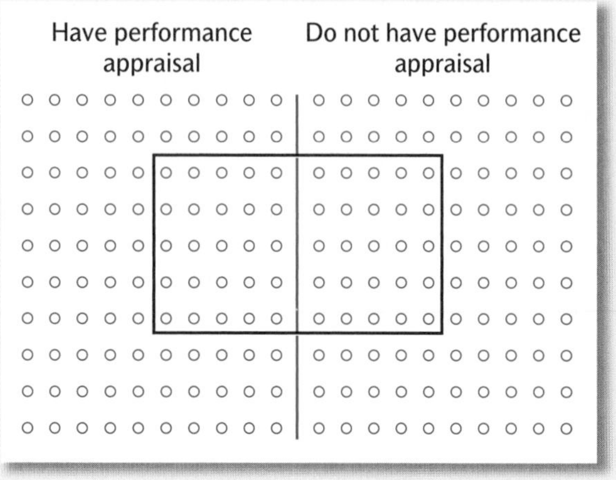

many who are not appraised and three too few who are. In Figure 9.6 we have a very serious over-representation of employees who do not receive performance appraisals,

because there are 35 employees in the sample who are not appraised, which is much larger than the 25 who should be in the sample.

Figure 9.4

A sample with very little sampling error

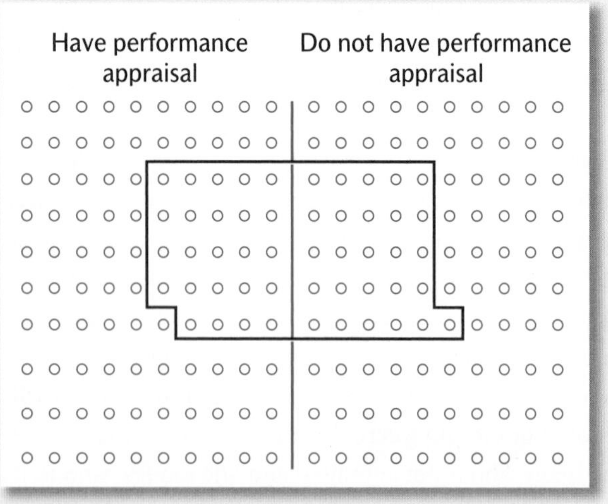

Figure 9.5

A sample with some sampling error

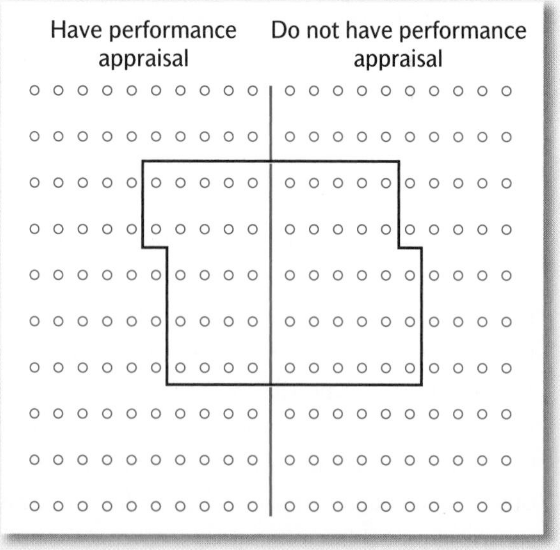

Figure 9.6

A sampling with a lot of sampling error

It is important to appreciate that, as suggested above, probability sampling does not and cannot eliminate sampling error. Even with a well crafted **probability sample**, a degree of sampling error is likely to creep in. However, probability sampling stands a better chance than non-probability sampling of keeping sampling error in check so that it does not end up looking like the outcome illustrated in Figure 9.6. Moreover, probability sampling allows the researcher to employ tests of statistical significance that permit inferences to be made about the sample from which the sample was selected. These will be addressed in Chapter 23.

Types of probability sample

Imagine that we are interested in levels of training, skill development, and learning among employees and the variables that relate to variation in levels of training they have undertaken. We might decide to conduct our research in a single nearby company. This means that our population will all be employees in that company, which, in turn, will mean that we will be able to **generalize** our

findings only to employees of that company. We simply cannot assume that levels of training and their correlates will be the same in other companies. We might decide that we want our research to be conducted only on full-time employees, so that part-time and subcontracted workers are omitted. Imagine, too, that there are 9000 full-time employees in the company.

Simple random sample

The **simple random sample** is the most basic form of probability sample. With random sampling, each unit of the population has an equal probability of inclusion in sample. Imagine that we decide that we have enough money to interview 450 employees at the company. This means that the probability of inclusion in the sample is:

$$\frac{450}{9000} \quad \text{i.e., 1 in 20}$$

This is known as the *sampling fraction* and is expressed as:

$$\frac{n}{N}$$

where *n* is the sample size and *N* is the population size.

The key steps in devising our simple random sample can be represented as follows:

1. Define the population. We have decided that this will be all full-time employees at the company. This is our *N* and in this case is 9000.
2. Select or devise a comprehensive sampling frame. It is likely that the company's personnel department will keep records of all employees and that this will enable us to exclude those who do not meet our criteria for inclusion, i.e., part-time employees and those who work on the premises but are not employees of the company.
3. Decide your sample size (*n*). We have decided that this will be 450.
4. List all the employees in the population and assign them consecutive numbers from 1 to *N*. In our case, this will be 1 to 9000.
5. Using a table of random numbers, or a computer program that can generate random numbers, select *n* (450) different random numbers that lie between 1 and *N* (9000).

6. The employees to which the *n* (450) random numbers refer to constitute the sample.

Two points are striking about this process. First, there is almost no opportunity for human bias to manifest itself. Thus, employees would not be selected on subjective criteria such as whether they looked friendly and approachable. The selection of whom to interview is entirely mechanical. Secondly, the process is not dependent on the employees' availability. They do not have to be working in the interviewer's proximity to be included in the sample. The process of selection is done without their knowledge. It is not until they are contacted by an interviewer that they know that they are part of a **social survey**.

Step 5 mentions the possible use of a table of random numbers. These can be found in the appendices of many statistics books. The tables are made up of columns of five-digit numbers, such as:

09188
90045
73189
75768
54016
08358
28306
53840
91757
89415

The first thing to notice is that, since these are five-digit numbers and the maximum number that we can sample from is 9000, which is a four-digit number, none of the random numbers seems appropriate, except for 09188 and 08358, although the former is larger than the largest possible number. The answer is that we should take just four digits in each number. Let us take the last four digits. This would yield the following:

9188
0045
3189
5768

4016
8358
8306
3840
1757
9415

However, two of the resulting numbers—9188 and 9415—exceed 9000. We cannot have an employee with either of these numbers assigned to him or her. The solution is simple: we ignore these numbers. This means that the employee who has been assigned the number 45 will be the first to be included in the sample; the employee who has been assigned the number 3189 will be next; the employee who has been assigned the number 5768 will be next; and so on.

An alternative but very similar strategy to the one that has been described is to write (or get someone to write for you) a simple computer program that will select *n* random numbers (in our case 450) that lie between 1 and *N* (in our case 9000). As with using a table of random numbers, you may be faced with the possibility of some random numbers turning up more than once. Since you will want to interview the person to whom those recurring random numbers refer on only one occasion, you will want to ignore any random number that recurs. This procedure results in a sample known as a simple random sample *without replacement*. In business research, more or less all simple random samples will be of this kind and so the qualifier 'without replacement' is typically omitted.

Systematic sample

A variation on the simple random sample is the **systematic sample**. With this kind of sample you select units directly from the sampling frame, i.e., without resorting to a table of random numbers.

We know that we are to select 1 employee in 20. With a systematic sample, we would make a random start between 1 and 20 inclusive, possibly by using the last two digits in a table of random numbers. If we did this with the 10 random numbers above, the first relevant one would be 54016, since it is the first one where the last two digits yield a number of 20 or below, in this case 16. This means that the sixteenth employee on our sampling frame is the first to be in our sample. Thereafter, we take every twentieth employee on the list. So the sequence will go:

16, 36, 56, 76, 96, 116, etc.

This approach eliminates the need to assign numbers to employees' names and then to look up names of the employees whose numbers have been drawn by the random selection process. It is important to ensure, however, that there is no inherent ordering of the sampling frame, since this may bias the resulting sample. If there is some ordering to the list, the best solution is to rearrange it.

Stratified random sampling

In our imaginary study of company employees, one of the features that we might want our sample to exhibit is a proportional representation of the different departments in which employees work. It might be that the kind of department an employee works in is viewed as relevant to a wide range of attitudinal features that are relevant to the study of skill development and training. Generating a simple random sample or a **systematic sample** *might* yield such a representation, so that the proportion of employees from the sales and marketing department in the sample is the same as that in the employee population and so on. Thus, if there are 1800 employees in the sales and marketing department, using our sampling fraction of 1 in 20, we would expect to have 90 employees in our sample from this department of the company. However, because of sampling error, it is unlikely that this will occur and that there will be a difference, so that there may be, say, 85 or 93 from this department.

Because it is very likely that the company will include in its records the department in which employees are based, or indeed may have separate **sampling frames** for each department, it will be possible to ensure that employees are accurately represented in terms of their departmental membership. In the language of sampling, this means stratifying the population by a criterion (in this case, departmental membership) and selecting either a simple random sample or a systematic sample from each of the resulting strata. In the present example, if there are five departments we would have five strata, with the numbers in each stratum being one-twentieth of the total for each department, as in Table 9.1, which also shows a hypothetical outcome of using a simple random sample, which results in a distribution of employees across departments that does not mirror the population all that well.

The advantage of **stratified sampling** in a case like this is clear: it ensures that the resulting sample will be distributed in the same way as the population in terms of the stratifying criterion. If you use a simple random or systematic sampling approach, you *may* end up with a distribution like that of the stratified sample, but it is not likely. Two points are relevant here. First, you can conduct stratified sampling sensibly only when it is relatively easy to identify and allocate units to strata. If it is not possible or it would be very difficult to do so, stratified sampling will not be feasible. Secondly, you can use more than one stratifying criterion. Thus, it may be that you would want to stratify by both department and gender and whether or

Table 9.1 The advantages of stratified sampling

Department	Population	Stratified sample	Possible simple random or systematic sample
Sales and marketing	1,800	90	85
Finance and accounts	1,200	60	70
Human resource management and training	1,000	50	60
Technical, research, and new-product development	1,800	90	84
Production	3,200	160	151
TOTAL	9,000	450	450

not employees are above or below a certain salary level or occupational grade. If it is feasible to identify employees in terms of these stratifying criteria, it is possible to use pairs of criteria or several criteria (such as departmental membership plus gender plus occupational level).

Stratified sampling is really feasible only when the relevant information is available. In other words, when data are available that allow the ready identification of members of the population in terms of the stratifying criterion (or criteria), it is sensible to employ this sampling method. But it is unlikely to be economical if the identification of population members for stratification purposes entails a great deal of work because there is no available listing in terms of strata.

Multi-stage cluster sampling

In the example we have been dealing with, employees to be interviewed are located in a single company. Interviewers will have to arrange their interviews with the sampled employees, but, because they are all working on the same premises, they will not be involved in a lot of travel. However, imagine that we wanted a *national* sample of employees. It is likely that interviewers would have to travel the throughout the country to interview the sampled individuals. This would add a great deal to the time and cost of doing the research. This kind of problem occurs whenever the aim is to interview a sample that is to be drawn from a widely dispersed population, such as a national population, or a large region, or even a large city.

One way in which it is possible to deal with this potential problem is to employ **cluster sampling**. With cluster sampling, the primary sampling unit (the first stage of the *sampling procedure*) is not the units of the population to be sampled but groupings of those units. It is these groupings or aggregations of population units that are known as *clusters*. Imagine that we want a nationally representative sample of 5000 employees who are working for the 100 largest publically traded companies in the country (this information is publicly available and could, for example, be generated through the FTSE index in the UK or TSX data in Canada, if size is measured in terms of market capitalization). Using simple random or systematic sampling would yield a widely dispersed sample, which would

result in a great deal of travel for interviewers. One solution might be to sample companies and then employees from each of the sampled companies. A probability sampling method would need to be employed at each stage. Thus, we might randomly sample 10 companies from the entire population of 100 largest companies in the country, thus yielding 10 clusters, and we would then interview 500 randomly selected employees at each of the 10 companies. Web Research in focus 9.1 gives an example of a study that used **cluster sampling**.

This is fine, but there is no guarantee that these 10 companies reflect the diverse range of industrial activities that are engaged in by the population as a whole. One solution to this problem would be to group the 100 largest companies by some standard classification scheme codes and then randomly sample companies from each of the major groups.

Many examples of multi-stage cluster sampling entail stratification. We might, for example, want further to stratify the companies according to whether their headquarters are located in Canada or abroad. To do this we would group companies according to whether their headquarters were based in the country or elsewhere and then select one or two companies from each of the two strata per major industry code.

The advantage of multi-stage cluster sampling should be clear by now: it allows interviewers to be far more concentrated than would be the case if a simple random or stratified sample was selected. The advantages of stratification can be capitalized upon because the clusters can be stratified in terms of strata. However, even when a rigorous sampling strategy is employed, sampling error cannot be avoided, as the example in Research in focus 9.1 illustrates.

The qualities of a probability sample

The reason why probability sampling is such an important procedure in social survey research is that it is possible to make inferences from information about a random sample to the population from which it was selected. In other words, we can generalize findings derived from a sample to the population. This is different from

Tips and Skills

Generalizing from a random sample to the population

Using our imaginary study of training and skill development in a single nearby company, let us say that the sample mean is 6.7 days of training per employee (the average amount of training received in the previous 12 months in the sample). A crucial consideration here is: how confident can we be that the mean number of 6.7 training days is likely to be found in the population, even when probability sampling has been employed? If we take an infinite number of samples from a population, the sample estimates of the mean of the variable under consideration will vary in relation to the population mean. This variation will take the form of a bell-shaped curve known as a normal distribution (see Figure 9.7). The shape of the distribution implies that there is a clustering of sample means at or around the population mean. Half the sample means will be at or below the population mean; the other half will be at or above the population mean. As we move to the left (at or lower than the population mean) or the right (at or higher than the population mean), the curve tails off, implying fewer and fewer samples generating means that depart considerably from the population mean. The variation of sample means around the population mean is the sampling error and is measured using a statistic known as the standard error of the mean. This is an estimate of the amount that a sample mean is likely to differ from the population mean.

This consideration is important, because sampling theory tells us that 68% of all sample means will lie between + or − one standard error from the population mean and that 95% of all sample means will lie between + or − 1.96 standard errors from the population mean. It is this second calculation that is crucial, because it is at least implicitly employed by survey researchers when they report their statistical findings. They typically employ 1.96 standard errors as the crucial criterion in how confident they can be in their findings. Essentially, the criterion implies that you can be 95% certain that the population mean lies within + or − 1.96 sampling errors from the sample mean.

If a sample has been selected according to probability sampling principles, we know that we can be 95% certain that the population mean will lie between the sample mean + or − 1.96 multiplied by the standard error of the mean. This is known as the confidence interval. If the mean number of training days in the previous 12 months in our sample of 450 employees is 6.7 and the standard error of the mean is 1.3, we can be 95% certain that the population mean will lie between:

$$6.7 + (1.96 \times 1.3)$$

Figure 9.7

The distribution of sample means

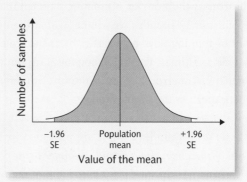

Note: 95% of sample means will lie within the shaded area. SE = standard error of the mean.

and

$$6.7 - (1.96 \times 1.3)$$

i.e., between 9.248 and 4.152.

If the standard error was smaller, the range of possible values of the population mean would be narrower; if the standard error was larger, the range of possible values of the population mean would be wider.

If a stratified sample is selected, the standard error of the mean will be smaller, because the variation between strata is essentially eliminated, because the population will be accurately represented in the sample in terms of the stratification criterion or criteria employed. This consideration demonstrates the way in which stratification injects an extra increment of precision into the probability sampling process, since a possible source of sampling error is eliminated.

By contrast, a cluster sample without stratification exhibits a larger standard error of the mean than a comparable simple random sample. This occurs because a possible source of variability between employees (that is, membership of one department rather than another, which may affect levels of training undertaken) is disregarded. If, for example, some departments have a culture of learning in which a large number of employees were involved, and if these departments were not selected because of the procedure for selecting clusters, an important source of variability would have been omitted. It also implies that the sample mean would be on the low side, but that is another matter.

equivalence sampling, which aims to ensure findings are equivalent between samples rather than representative of the population (see Web Research in focus 9.2). This is not to say that we treat the population data and the sample data as the same. If we take the example of the level of skill development in our sample of 450 employees, which we will treat as the number of training days completed in the previous 12 months, we will know that the mean number of training days undertaken by the sample ($\bar{x}$) can be used to estimate the population mean (μ) but with known margins of error. The mean, or more properly the arithmetic mean, is the simple average.

In order to address this point it is necessary to use some basic statistical ideas. These are presented in Tips and skills '*Generalizing from a random sample to the population*' and can be skipped if just a broad idea of sampling procedures is required.

Sample size

One question about **research methods** that we are asked by students almost more than any other relates to the size of the sample: 'How large should my sample be?' or 'Is my sample large enough?' The decision about sample size is not a straightforward one: it depends on a number of considerations and there is no one definitive answer. This is frequently a source of great disappointment to those who pose such questions. Moreover, most of the time decisions about sample size are affected by considerations of time and cost. Therefore, invariably, decisions about sample size represent a compromise between the constraints of time and cost, the need for precision, and a variety of further considerations that we next address.

Absolute and relative sample size

One of the most basic considerations, and one that is possibly the most surprising, is that, contrary to what you might have expected, it is the *absolute* size of a sample that is important, not its *relative* size. This means that a national probability sample of 1000 individuals in the UK has as much validity as a national probability sample of 1000 individuals in the United States, even though the latter has a much larger population. It also means that

increasing the size of a sample increases the precision of a sample. This means that the 95% confidence interval referred to in Tips and skills '*Generalizing from a random sample to the population*' narrows. However, a large sample cannot *guarantee* precision, so that it is probably better to say that increasing the size of a sample increases the *likely* precision of a sample. This means that, as sample size increases, sampling error decreases. Therefore, an important component of any decision about sample size should be how much sampling error the researcher is prepared to tolerate. The less sampling error one is prepared to tolerate, the larger a sample will need to be. Fowler (1993) warns against a simple acceptance of this criterion. He argues that in practice researchers do not base their decisions about sample size on a single estimate of a variable. Most survey research is concerned to generate a host of estimates, i.e., of the variables that make up the research instrument that is administered. He also observes that it is not normal for survey researchers to be in a position to specify in advance 'a desired level of precision' (Fowler, 1993, p. 34). Furthermore, since sampling error will be only one component of any error entailed in an estimate, the notion of using a desired level of precision as a factor in a decision about sample size is not realistic. Instead, to the extent that this notion does enter into decisions about sample size, it usually does so in a general rather than a calculated way.

Time and cost

Time and cost considerations become very relevant in this context. In the previous paragraph it is clearly being suggested that the larger the sample size the greater the precision (because the amount of sampling error will be less). However, for the most part, up to a sample size of around 1000, the gains in precision are noticeable as the sample size climbs from low figures of 50, 100, 150, and so on upwards. After a certain point, often in the region of 1000, the sharp increases in precision become less pronounced, and, although it does not plateau, there is a slowing-down in the extent to which precision increases (and hence the extent to which the sample error of the mean declines). Considerations of sampling size are likely to be profoundly affected by matters of time and cost at such a **juncture**,

Tips and Skills

Sample size and probability sampling

As we have said in the text, the issue of sample size is the matter that most often concerns students and others. Basically, this is an area where size really does matter (!) as the bigger the sample the more representative it is likely to be (provided the sample is randomly selected), regardless of the size of the population from which it is drawn. However, when doing projects, students clearly need to do their research with very limited resources. You should try to find out from your department or business school if there are any guidelines about whether or not samples of a minimum size are expected. If there are no such guidelines, you will need to conduct your survey in such a way as to maximize the number of interviews you can manage or the number of postal questionnaires you can send out given the amount of time and resources available to you. Also, in many, if not most cases, a truly random approach to sample selection may not be open to you. The crucial point is to be clear about and to justify what you have done. Explain the difficulties that you would have encountered in generating a random sample. Explain why you really could not include any more in your sample of respondents. But, above all, do not make claims about your sample that are not sustainable. Do not claim that it is representative or that you have a random sample when it is clearly not the case that either of these is true. In other words, be frank about what you have done. People will be much more inclined to accept an awareness of the limits of your sample design than claims about a sample that are inherently false. Also, it may be that there are lots of good features about your sample such as the range of people included, the good response rate, and the high level of cooperation you received from the firm. Make sure you play up these positive features at the same time as being honest about its limitations.

since striving for smaller and smaller increments of precision becomes an increasingly uneconomic proposition.

However, considerations about sampling error do not end here. The problem of *non-response* should be borne in mind. Most sample surveys attract a certain amount of non-response. Thus, it is likely that only some of our sample will agree to participate in the research. If it is our aim to ensure as far as possible that 450 employees are interviewed and if we think that there may be a 20% rate of non-response, it may be advisable to sample 540–550 individuals, on the grounds that approximately 90 will be non-respondents. For example, of the 143 survey questionnaires posted to companies in Powell's (1995) research only 40 were returned and of these 36 were usable, making a response rate of 25%. This raises the question of whether or not this sample is significant enough to represent companies in the geographical area of the north-eastern United States that the study claims to represent (see Chapter 10 for further discussion of acceptable response rates). The issue of non-response, and in particular of refusal to participate, is of particular significance, because it has been suggested by some researchers that response rates to surveys are declining in many countries. This implies that there is a growing tendency towards people refusing to participate in survey research. In 1973, an article in the magazine *Business Week* carried an article ominously entitled 'The Public Clams up on Survey Takers'. The magazine asked survey companies about their experiences and found considerable concern about declining **response rates**. Similarly, in Britain, a report from a working party on the Market Research Society's Research and Development Committee in 1975 pointed to similar concerns among market research companies. However, an analysis of this issue by Smith (1995) suggested that, contrary to popular belief, there is no consistent evidence of such a decline. Smith showed that it is difficult to disentangle general trends in response rates from such variables as the subject matter of the research, the type of respondent, and the level of effort expended on improving the number of respondents to individual surveys. The strategies that can improve responses to survey instruments such as structured interviews and postal questionnaires will be examined in Chapter 13.

Heterogeneity of the population

Yet another consideration is the homogeneity and heterogeneity of the population from which the sample is to

Key concept 9.1: What is a response rate?

A response rate is the percentage of a sample that agrees to participate in a study.

be taken. When a sample is very *heterogeneous*, like a sample of a whole country or city, the population is likely to be highly varied. When it is relatively *homogeneous*, such as members of a company or of an occupation, the amount of variation is less. The implication of this is that the greater the heterogeneity of a population, the larger a sample will need to be.

Kind of analysis

Finally, researchers should bear in mind the *kind of analysis* they intend to undertake. A case in point here is the contingency table. A **contingency table** shows the relationship between two variables in tabular form. It shows how variation in one variable relates to variation in another variable. To understand this point, consider our example of employee skill development and learning in the 100 largest national companies. A **contingency table** would show how far the 5000 employees that comprise the sample vary in terms of skill and learning, measured in terms of training received during the previous 12 months. In addition, the table would need to reflect differences between companies that represent the main industrial code sections. However, it is unlikely that the initial criterion of selecting the 100 largest companies would enable all the industrial code sections, such as education, community activities, or fishing, to be represented; therefore, some of the cells of the table would remain empty. In order to overcome this problem, the sample would have to be designed to reflect a much wider range of public and private organizational activity, perhaps by removing the criterion of size of company from the study. This would have a bearing on the number of employees who would be sampled from each company.

 ## Types of non-probability sampling

The term **non-probability sampling** is essentially an umbrella term to capture all forms of sampling that are not

conducted according to the canons of probability sampling outlined above. It is not surprising, therefore, that the term covers a wide range of types of sampling strategy, at least one of which—the **quota sample**—is claimed by some practitioners to be almost as good as a probability sample. Also covered under non-probability sampling is the practice of surveying one individual per organization, often a human resources or senior manager, in order to find out about the organization. In this section we will also cover three main types of non-probability sample: the **convenience sample**, the **snowball sample**, and the **quota sample**.

Convenience sampling

A convenience sample is one that, simply put, is available to the researcher because of its accessibility. Imagine that a researcher who teaches at a university business school is interested in the way that managers deal with ethical issues when making business decisions. The researcher might administer a questionnaire to several classes of students, all of whom are managers taking a part-time MBA degree. The chances are that the researcher will receive all or almost all the questionnaires back, so that there will be a good response rate. The findings may prove quite interesting, but the problem with such a sampling strategy is that it is impossible to generalize the findings, because we do not know of what population this sample is representative. They are simply a group of managers who are available to the researcher. They are almost certainly not representative of managers as a whole—the very fact they are taking this degree program marks them out as different from managers in general.

This is not to suggest that convenience samples should never be used. Let us say that our lecturer/researcher is developing a battery of questions that are designed to measure the ethical decision-making processes used by managers. It is highly desirable to pilot such a research instrument before using it in an investigation, and administering it to a group who are not a part of the main study may be a legitimate way of carrying out some preliminary analysis of such issues as whether or not respondents tend to answer in identical ways to a question, or whether or not one question is often omitted when managers respond to it. In other words, for this kind of purpose, a convenience sample may be acceptable though not ideal. A second kind of context in which it may be at least fairly acceptable to use a convenience sample is when the chance presents itself to gather data from a convenience sample and it represents too good an opportunity to miss. The data will not allow definitive findings to be generated, because of the problem of generalization, but it could provide a springboard for further research or to allow links to be forged with existing findings in an area.

It also should be recognized that convenience sampling probably plays a more prominent role than is sometimes thought. Certainly, in the field of business and management, convenience samples are very common and indeed are more prominent than are samples based on probability sampling (Bryman, 1989*a*, pp. 113–14). Web Research in focus 9.3 provides two examples of the use of convenience samples involving university students. Probability sampling involves a lot of preparation, so it is frequently avoided because of the difficulty and costs involved.

Snowball sampling

In certain respects, snowball sampling is a form of convenience sample, but it is worth distinguishing because it has attracted quite a lot of attention over the years. With this approach to sampling, the researcher makes initial contact with a small group of people who are relevant to the research topic and then uses these to establish contacts with others. Bryman used an approach like this to create a sample of British visitors to Disney theme parks (Bryman, 1999). Another example of snowball sampling is given in the study by Venter, Boshoff, and Maas (2005) (see Web Research in focus 9.4), where this technique was used to identify owner-managers and successors of small- and medium-sized family businesses in South Africa.

A snowball sample is in no sense random, because there is no way of knowing the precise extent of the population from which it would have to be drawn. In other words, there is no accessible sampling frame for the population from which the sample is to be taken, and the difficulty of creating such a sampling frame means that such an approach is the only feasible one. Moreover, even if one could create a sampling frame of strategic decision makers or of British visitors to Disney theme parks, it would almost certainly be inaccurate, because this is a shifting population. People will constantly be coming and ceasing to be associated with the decision-making network, while new theme park visitors are arriving all the time. The problem with snowball sampling is that it is very unlikely that the sample will be representative of the population, though, as we have just suggested, the very notion of a population may be problematic in some circumstances. However, by and large, snowball sampling is used not within a quantitative research strategy, but within a qualitative one: both Franwick's and Bryman's studies were carried out with predominantly qualitative data research frameworks. Concerns about external validity and the ability to generalize often do not loom as large within a qualitative research as they do in a quantitative research one. In qualitative research, the orientation to sampling is more likely to be guided by a preference for **theoretical sampling** than with the kind of statistical sampling that has been the focus of this chapter. There is a much better 'fit' between snowball sampling and the theoretical sampling strategy of qualitative research than with the statistical sampling approach of quantitative research. This is not to suggest that snowball sampling is entirely irrelevant to quantitative research: when the researcher needs to focus upon or to reflect relationships between people, tracing connections through snowball sampling may be a better approach than conventional probability sampling (Coleman, 1958).

Quota sampling

Quota sampling is used intensively in commercial research, such as market research and political opinion polling. The aim of quota sampling is to produce a sample that reflects a population in terms of the relative proportions of people in different categories, such as gender, ethnicity, age groups, socio-economic groups, and region of residence, and in combinations of these categories. However, unlike a stratified sample, the sampling of individuals is not carried out randomly, since the final selection of people is left up to the interviewer.

Once the categories and the number of people to be interviewed within each category (known as *quotas*) have been decided upon, it is then the job of interviewers to select people who fit these categories. The quotas will typically be interrelated. In a manner similar to stratified sampling, the population may be divided into strata in terms of, for example, gender, social class, age, and ethnicity. Census data might be used to identify the number of people who should be in each subgroup. The numbers to be interviewed in each subgroup will reflect the population. Each interviewer will probably seek out individuals who fit several subgroup quotas. Accordingly, an interviewer may know that among the various subgroups of people, he or she must find and interview five Asian, 25–34-year-old, lower-middle-class females in the area in which the interviewer has been asked to work. The interviewer usually asks people who are available to him or her about their characteristics (though gender will presumably be self-evident) in order to determine their suitability for a particular subgroup. Once a subgroup quota (or a combination of subgroup quotas) has been achieved, the interviewer will no longer be concerned to locate individuals for that subgroup.

The choice of respondents is left to the interviewer, subject to the requirement of all quotas being filled, usually within a certain time period. If you have ever been approached on the street by a person toting a clipboard and interview schedule and have been asked about your age, occupation, and so on, before being asked a series of questions about a product or whatever, you have almost certainly encountered an interviewer with a quota sample to fill. Sometimes, he or she will decide not to interview you because you do not meet the criteria required to fill a quota. This may be due to a quota already having been filled or to the criteria for exclusion meaning that a person with a certain characteristic you possess is not required.

A number of criticisms are frequently levelled at quota samples:

- Because the choice of respondent is left to the interviewer, the proponents of probability sampling argue that a quota sample cannot be representative. It may accurately reflect the population in terms of superficial characteristics, as defined by the quotas. How-

ever, in their choice of people to approach, interviewers may be unduly influenced by their perceptions of how friendly people are or by whether the people make eye contact with the interviewer (unlike most of us who look at the ground and shuffle past as quickly as possible because we do not want to be bothered).

- People who are in an interviewer's vicinity at the times he or she conducts interviews, and are, therefore, available to be approached, may not be typical. There is a risk, for example, that people in full-time paid work may be under-represented and that those who are included in the sample are not typical.

- The interviewer is likely to make judgements about certain characteristics in deciding whether or not to approach a person, in particular, judgements about age. Those judgements will sometimes be incorrect—for example, when someone who is eligible to be interviewed, because a quota that he or she fits is unfilled, is not approached because the interviewer makes an incorrect judgement (for example, that the person is older than he or she looks). In such a case, a possible element of bias is being introduced.

- It has also been argued that the widespread use of social class as a quota control can introduce difficulties, because of the problem of ensuring that interviewees are properly assigned to class groupings (Moser & Kalton, 1971).

- It is not permissible to calculate a standard error of the mean from a quota sample, because the non-random method of selection makes it impossible to calculate the range of possible values of a population.

All of this makes the quota sample look a poor bet and there is no doubt that it is not favoured by academic researchers. It does have some arguments in its favour, however:

- It is undoubtedly cheaper and quicker than an interview survey on a comparable probability sample. For example, interviewers do not have to spend a lot of time travelling between interviews.

- Interviewers do not have to keep calling back on people who were not available at the time they were first approached.

Figure 9.8

Four sources of error in social survey research

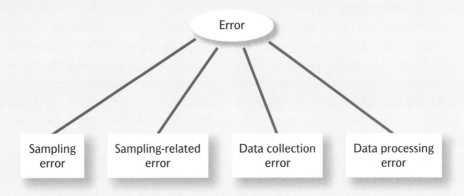

Because calling back is not required, a quota sample is easier to manage. It is not necessary to keep track of people who need to be re-contacted or to keep track of refusals. Refusals occur, of course, but it is not necessary (and indeed it is not possible) to keep a record of which respondents declined to participate.

When speed is of the essence, a quota sample is invaluable when compared to the more cumbersome probability sample. Newspapers frequently need to know how a national sample of voters feels about a certain topic or how they intend to vote at that time. Alternatively, if there is a sudden major news event, such as the terrorist attack on the World Trade Center in New York, the news media may seek a more or less instant picture of the nation's views or responses. Again, a quota sample will be much faster.

As with convenience sampling, it is useful for conducting development work on new measures or on research instruments. It can also be usefully employed in relation to exploratory work from which new theoretical ideas might be generated.

Although the standard error of the mean should not be computed for a quota sample, it frequently is. As Moser and Kalton (1971) observe, some researchers argue that the use of a non-random method in quota sampling should not act as a barrier to such a computation because its significance as a source of error is small when compared to other errors that may arise in surveys (see Figure 9.8). However, they go on to argue that at least with random sampling the researcher can calculate the amount of sampling error and does not have to be concerned about its potential impact.

There is some evidence to suggest that, when compared to random samples, quota samples often result in biases. They under-represent people in lower social strata, people who work in the private sector and manufacturing, and people at the extremes of income levels, and they over-represent women in households with children and people from larger households (Marsh & Scarbrough, 1990; Butcher, 1994). On the other hand, it has to be acknowledged that probability samples are often biased too.

 ## Limits to generalization

One point that is often not fully appreciated is that, even when a sample has been selected using probability sampling, any findings can be generalized only to the population from which that sample was taken. This is an obvious point, but it is easy to think that findings from a study have some kind of broader applicability. If we take our imaginary study of training and skill development among employees of a company, any findings could be generalized only to that company. In other words, you should be very cautious about generalizing to employees at other companies. There are many factors that may imply that the level of training and skill development is higher (or lower) than among company employees as a whole. There may be a higher (or lower) level of skill required in order to do the jobs that the company requires its employees to do, there may be more (or less) money in the company's training budget, there may be more (or less) of a culture of learning at this company, or the company may recruit a higher (or lower) proportion of employees who are already skilled. There could be many additional other factors as well.

Similarly, we should be cautious of over-generalizing in terms of locality. Hence, a frequent criticism made in relation to research on employee motivation relates to the extent to which it can be assumed to be generalizable beyond the extent of the national culture on which the study is based. For example, Herzberg, Mausner, and Snyderman (1959) conducted semi-structured interviews with 203 engineers and accountants in the Pittsburgh area in the United States. Most of the companies that constituted sites for the study were involved in heavy industry, such as steel making or ship building. The population from which the sample was selected consisted of all accountants and engineers who worked for these companies. Respondents were chosen randomly according to certain criteria for stratification, including age, job title, level in the company, and length of service. It is interesting that there is no mention of gender in the study, although we can reasonably assume that, given that this was a study of accountants and engineers in the late 1950s, there is likely to be a male bias to the study. The maximum number of individuals selected for interview in each company was approximately 50. As the authors acknowledge 'the fact that this work was done within a thirty-mile radius around Pittsburgh will inevitably raise questions about the degree to which the findings are applicable in other areas of the country' (1959, p. 31). The findings may also reflect the values of high individualism, self-interest, and

comparatively high masculinity culture that have been identified as characteristic of American national culture (Hofstede, 1984). This is part of the reason there have been so many attempts to replicate the study on other occupational groups and in other localities, including different cultures and nationalities.

However, there could even be a further limit to generalization that is implied by the Herzberg et al. sample. The main study was conducted in the late 1950s. One issue that is rarely discussed in this context, and that is almost impossible to assess, is whether or not there is a time limit on the findings that are generated. Quite aside from the fact that we need to appreciate that the findings cannot (or at least should not) be generalized beyond the Pittsburgh area, is there a point at which we have to say, 'Well, those findings applied to the Pittsburgh area then but things have changed and we can no longer assume that they apply to that or any other locality'? We are, after all, used to thinking that things have changed when there has been some kind of prominent change. To take a simple example: no one would be prepared to assume that the findings of a study in 1980 of university students' budgeting and personal finance habits would apply to students in the early twenty-first century; the past 30 years have seen substantial changes to how students finance their education. However, even when there is no definable or recognizable source of relevant change of this kind, there is nonetheless the possibility (or even likelihood) that findings are specific and time-bound. Such an issue is impossible to resolve without further research (Bryman, 1989b).

 ## Error in survey research

We can think of 'error', a term that has been employed on a number of occasions, as being made up of four main factors (see Figure 9.8):

- Sampling error. This kind of error arises because it is extremely unlikely that one will end up with a truly representative sample, even when probability sampling is employed.
- We can distinguish what might be thought of as sampling-related error. This is error that is subsumed un-

Research in Focus

Sources of sampling and non-sampling error in a survey of the effects of privatization

In a study of the effects of privatization on corporate culture and employee well-being, Cunha and Cooper (2002) describe, first, the difficulties they experienced in obtaining access to companies in Portugal that were going through privatization and, secondly, the impact of a high non-response rate on their research design. Commenting on the first issue, the authors explain, 'we faced a very strong resistance on the part of top management of the companies we contacted, which is understandable considering the "sensitive" [*sic*] political and human resource decisions that were being taken' (2002, p. 27). In relation to the second point, samples were selected by the human resource managers, forming the basis for the questionnaire survey, which was sent directly by the researchers to the employees' home address. The three companies, the samples, and non-response rates were as follows:

- The first was a cement company. It employed approximately 2500 employees and a stratified sample of 750 employees was chosen, in managerial, technical/professional, clerical, and manual jobs; 133 valid responses were obtained (18% response rate).
- The second was a smaller cement company. From a population of 500 a stratified sample of 125 employees was chosen, but no manual workers were included in the sample owing to the low literacy levels among workers. Thirty-five valid responses were received (28% response rate). By occupational level this sample consisted of 22 managers, 11 technical/professional, and 2 clerical employees.
- The third was a paper pulp company with 2800 employees. A stratified sample of 1244 employees was chosen. In this case a longitudinal element was built into the survey— questionnaires were sent in 1994 (before partial privatization) and again in 1996 (after partial privatization). However, the number of employees who responded to both of these surveys was quite small

($n = 545$), so the researchers had to select different kinds of samples that focused on subgroups that were involved in privatization.

This study raises a number of questions in relation to possible sources of sampling error. The fact that samples were chosen by the human resources manager in the company means that they were non-random and thus may have reflected a bias on the part of the individual who was making these choices. The researchers' original aim—to conduct a longitudinal analysis based on surveying employees before and after privatization—had to be modified owing to insufficient access. This meant that the researchers were limited in the extent to which they were able to suggest that changes in corporate culture were caused by privatization.

A further possible source of bias associated with the sampling frame related to the exclusion of manual workers from the survey in the second company, owing to their low levels of literacy. However, it is worth noting that this problem could potentially have been overcome through the use of a structured interview approach instead of a self-administered questionnaire. In addition, we can see from the profile of responses in this company (22 managers, 11 technical/professional, and 2 clerical employees) that this sample consists of significantly more managers than other kinds of employees. Thus, it is extremely likely that the sample does not reflect the actual population. Finally, the high non-response rate in the third company introduced a further source of sample bias (this forced the researchers to find other ways of breaking down the sample in ways that were more statistically meaningful).

The example shows how various sources of sampling and non-sampling error are sometimes closely interrelated. In particular, it illustrates how non-response rates and sampling frames can be affected by the sensitivity of the issue that is being investigated and the consequent willingness of companies and employees to participate in the research.

der the category non-sampling error but which arises from activities or events that are related to the sampling process and are connected with the issue of generalizability or external validity of findings. Examples are an inaccurate sampling frame and non-response.

- There is also error that is connected with the implementation of the research process. We might call this data collection error. This source of error includes such factors as: poor question wording in self-completion questionnaires or structured interviews; poor interviewing techniques; and flaws in the administration of research instruments.

- Finally, there is data processing error. This arises from faulty management of data, in particular, errors in the coding of answers.

- The third and fourth sources of error relate to factors that are not associated with sampling and instead relate much more closely to concerns about the validity of measurement, which was addressed in Chapter 5. An example of the way that non-response can impact upon the external validity and generalizability of findings is shown in Research in focus 9.1. However, the kinds of steps that need to be taken to keep these sources of error to a minimum in the context of social survey research will be addressed in the next three chapters.

Key points

- Probability sampling is a mechanism for reducing bias in the selection of samples.
- Ensure you become familiar with key technical terms in the literature on sampling such as: representative sample; random sample; non-response; population; sampling error; etc.
- Randomly selected samples are important because they permit generalizations to the population and because they have certain known qualities.
- Sampling error decreases as sample size increases.
- Quota samples can provide reasonable alternatives to random samples, but they suffer from some deficiencies.
- Convenience samples may provide interesting data, but it is crucial to be aware of their limitations in terms of generalizability.
- Sampling and sampling-related error are just two sources of error in social survey research.

Questions for review

- What do each of the following terms mean: **population**; **probability sampling**; **non-probability sampling**; **sampling frame**; **representative sample**; and **sampling** and **non-sampling error**?
- What are the goals of sampling?
- What are the main areas of potential bias in sampling?

Sampling error

- What is the significance of sampling error for achieving a **representative sample**?

Types of probability sample

- What is probability sampling and why is it important?
- What are the main types of probability sample?
- How far does a **stratified random sample** offer greater precision than a **simple random** or **systematic sample**?

- If you were conducting an interview survey of around 500 people in Manchester, what type of probability sample would you choose and why?
- A researcher positions herself on a street corner and asks one person in five who walks by to be interviewed: she continues doing this until she has a sample of 250. How likely is she to achieve a representative sample?

The qualities of a probability sample

- A researcher is interested in levels of job satisfaction among manual workers in a firm that is undergoing change. The firm has 1200 manual workers. The researcher selects a simple random sample of 10% of the population. He measures job satisfaction on a **Likert scale** comprising 10 items. A high level of satisfaction is scored 5 and a low level is scored 1. The mean job satisfaction score is 34.3. The standard error of the mean is 8.57. What is the 95% confidence interval?

Sample size

- What factors would you take into account in deciding how large your sample should be when devising a probability sample?
- What is **non-response** and why is it important to the question of whether or not you will end up with a representative sample?

Types of non-probability sampling

- Are non-probability samples useless?
- In what circumstances might you employ **snowball sampling**?
- 'Quota samples are not true random samples, but in terms of generating a representative sample there is little difference between them, and this accounts for their widespread use in market research and opinion polling'. Discuss.

Limits to generalization

- 'The problem of generalization to a population is not just to do with the matter of getting a representative sample'. Discuss.

Error in survey research

- 'Non-sampling error, as its name implies, is concerned with sources of error that are not part of the sampling process'. Discuss.

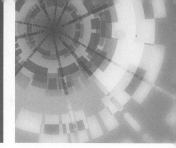

10

Self-Completion Questionnaires

Chapter guide

Questionnaires that are completed by respondents themselves are one of the main instruments for gathering data using a **social survey** design, along with the **structured interview**, which is covered in Chapter 13. Probably the most common form is the **mail** or **postal questionnaire**. The term **self-completion questionnaire** is often used because it is somewhat more inclusive than *mail questionnaire*. This chapter explores:

* The advantages and disadvantages of the questionnaire in comparison to the structured interview.
* How to address the potential problem of poor response rates, which is often a feature of the mail questionnaire.
* How questionnaires should be designed in order to make answering easier for respondents and less prone to error.
* The use of diaries as a form of self-completion questionnaire.

Introduction

The **self-completion questionnaire** is sometimes referred to as a *self-administered questionnaire*. The former term will be followed in this book. With a self-completion questionnaire, respondents answer questions by completing the questionnaire themselves. As a method, the self-completion questionnaire can come in several forms. Probably the most prominent of these forms is the **mail** or **postal questionnaire**, in which, as its name implies, a questionnaire is sent through the mail to the respondent. The survey participant is then usually asked to return the completed questionnaire by mail; an alternative form of return is when respondents are requested to deposit their completed questionnaires in a certain location, such as a box in a supervisor's office in a firm or on the top of a cashier's desk in a restaurant or shop. The self-completion questionnaire also covers forms of administration, such as when a researcher hands out questionnaires to all students in a class and collects them back after they have been completed. However, a slightly different way of administering a self-completion questionnaire was used by Faulkner and Culwin (2005) (see Research in focus 10.2) in their study of patterns of text messaging. A short questionnaire was distributed by students taking a final-year option in Usability Engineering at a London university. The students were asked

to distribute the questionnaires widely but not to other students at the university. One of the students also took a batch of the questionnaires to the mobile phone shop where he worked and asked customers if they wanted to take part—565 usable questionnaires were returned as a result of this method of distribution. 'Self-completion questionnaire' is, therefore, a more inclusive term than 'mail questionnaire', though it is probably true to say that the latter is the most prominent form of the self-completion questionnaire.

In the discussion that follows, when points apply to more or less all forms of self-completion questionnaire, this term will be employed. When points apply specifically or exclusively to questionnaires sent through the mail, the term 'mail questionnaire' will be used.

Evaluating the self-completion questionnaire in relation to the structured interview

In many ways, the self-completion questionnaire and the structured interview are very similar methods of business research. The obvious difference between them is that, with the self-completion questionnaire, there is no interviewer to ask the questions; instead, respondents must read each question themselves and answer the questions themselves. Beyond this obvious, but important, difference, they are remarkably similar. However, because there is no interviewer in the administration of the self-completion questionnaire, the research instrument has to be especially easy to follow and its questions have to be particularly easy to answer. After all, respondents cannot be trained in the way interviewers can be; nor do they know their way around a research instrument in the way a 'lone researcher' might.

As a result, self-completion questionnaires, as compared to structured interviews, tend to:

- Have fewer open questions, since closed ones tend to be easier to answer.
- Have easy-to-follow designs to minimize the risk that the respondent will fail to follow filter questions or will inadvertently omit a question.
- Be shorter to reduce the risk of 'respondent fatigue', since it is easier for a respondent who becomes tired of answering questions in a long questionnaire to throw it out as opposed to terminating an interview.

Advantages of the self-completion questionnaire over the structured interview

Cheaper to administer

Interviewing can be expensive. The cheapness of the self-completion questionnaire is especially advantageous if you have a sample that is geographically widely dispersed. When this is the case, a mail questionnaire will be much cheaper, because of the time and cost of travel for interviewers. This advantage is obviously less pronounced in connection with telephone interviews because of the lower costs of telephone charges relative to travel charges and time spent travelling. But, even in comparison to telephone interviewing, the mail questionnaire enjoys cost advantages.

Quicker to administer

Self-completion questionnaires can be sent out by mail or otherwise distributed in very large quantities at the same time. A thousand questionnaires can be sent out by mail in one batch, but, even with a team of interviewers,

it would take a long time to conduct personal interviews with a sample of that size. However, it is important to keep in mind that the questionnaires do not all come back immediately and that they may take several weeks to be returned. Also, there is usually a need to send out follow-up letters and/or questionnaires to those who fail to return them initially, an issue we will return to below.

Absence of interviewer effects

It was noted in Chapter 8 that various studies have demonstrated that characteristics of interviewers (and respondents) may affect the answers that people give. While the findings from this research are somewhat equivocal in their implications, it has been suggested that such characteristics as ethnicity, gender, and the social background of interviewers may combine to bias the answers that respondents provide. Obviously, since there is no interviewer present when a self-completion questionnaire is being completed, interviewer effects are eliminated. However, this advantage probably has to be regarded fairly cautiously, since a few consistent patterns have emerged over the years from research to suggest what kinds of interviewer characteristics bias answers. Probably of greater importance when considering the presence of an interviewer is the tendency for people to be more likely to exhibit **social desirability bias** when an interviewer is present. Research by Sudman and Bradburn (1982) suggests that mail questionnaires work better than personal interviews when a question carries the possibility of such bias. There is also evidence to suggest that respondents are less likely to under-report activities that induce anxiety or about which they feel sensitive in self-completion questionnaires than in structured interviews (Tourangeau & Smith, 1996).

No interviewer variability

Self-completion questionnaires do not suffer from the problem of interviewers asking questions in a different order or in different ways.

Convenience for respondents

Self-completion questionnaires are more convenient for respondents, because they can complete a questionnaire when they want and at the speed that they want to go.

Disadvantages of the self-completion questionnaire in comparison to the structured interview

Cannot prompt

There is no one present to help respondents if they are having difficulty answering a question. It is always important to ensure that the questions that are asked are clear and unambiguous, but this is especially so with the self-completion questionnaire, since there is no interviewer to help respondents with questions they find difficult to understand and answer. Also, substantial attention must be paid to ensure that the questionnaire is easy to complete; otherwise questions will be inadvertently omitted if instructions are unclear.

Cannot probe

There is no opportunity to probe respondents to elaborate on an answer. Probing can be very important when open-ended questions are being asked. Interviewers are often trained to get more from respondents. However, this problem largely applies to open questions, which are not used a great deal in self-completion questionnaire research.

Cannot ask many questions that are not salient to respondents

Respondents are more likely than in interviews to become tired of answering questions that are not very salient to them, and which they are likely to perceive as boring. Because of the risk of a questionnaire being thrown away in the trash, it is important to avoid including many non-salient questions in a self-completion questionnaire. However, this point suggests that, when a research issue *is* salient to the respondent, a high response rate is feasible (Altschuld & Lower, 1984). This means that, when questions are salient, the self-completion questionnaire may be a good choice for researchers, especially when the much lower cost is taken into account.

Difficulty of asking other kinds of question

In addition to the problem of asking many questions that are not salient to respondents, as previously suggested, it is also important to avoid asking more than a very small number of open questions (because respondents frequently do not want to write a lot). Questions with complex structures, such as filters, should be avoided as much as possible (because respondents often find them difficult to follow).

Questionnaire can be read as a whole

Respondents are able to read the whole questionnaire before answering the first question. When this occurs, none of the questions asked is truly independent of the others. It also means that you cannot be sure that questions have been answered in the correct order. It also means that the problems of question order effects, of the kind discussed in Chapter 13, may occur.

Do not know who answers

With mail questionnaires, you can never be sure that the right person has answered the questionnaire. If a questionnaire is sent to a certain person in a household, it may be that someone else in that household completes the questionnaire. It is also impossible to have any control over the intrusion of non-respondents (such as other members of a household) in the answering of questions. Similarly, if a questionnaire is sent to a manager in a firm, the task may simply be delegated to someone else. This advantage of the structured interview over the mail questionnaire does not apply when the former is administered by telephone, since the same problem applies.

Cannot collect additional data

With an interview, interviewers might be asked to collect snippets of information about the workplace, firm, manager, or whatever. This is not going to be possible in connection with a mail questionnaire, but if self-completion questionnaires are handed out in an organization, it is more feasible to collect such additional data.

Difficult to ask a lot of questions

As mentioned above, because of the possibility of 'respondent fatigue', long questionnaires are rarely feasible. They may even result in a greater tendency for questionnaires not to be answered in the first place.

Not appropriate for some kinds of respondent

Respondents whose literacy is limited or who have a restricted use of the language that the survey is written in, will not be able to answer the questionnaire. In such cases, it often recommended that interviews be employed. However, the second of the mentioned difficulties, the restricted use of the language in which the survey is written, cannot be entirely overcome when interviews are being employed. Nevertheless, such difficulties are typically greater with mail questionnaires.

Greater risk of missing data

Partially answered questionnaires are more likely, because of a lack of prompting or supervision, than is possible in interviews. It is also easier for respondents to actively decide not to answer a question when they are on their own rather than when being asked by an interviewer. For example, questions that appear boring or irrelevant to the respondent might be skipped. If questions are not answered, this creates a problem of *missing data* for the variables that are created.

Lower response rates

One of the most damaging limitations is that surveys by mail questionnaire typically result in lower **response rates** than comparable interview-based studies. The significance of a response rate is that, unless it can be proven that those who do not participate do not differ from those who do, there is likely to be the risk of bias. In other words, if, as is likely, there are differences between participants and refusals, it is probable that the findings relating to the sample will be affected. If a response rate is low, it seems likely that the risk of bias in the findings will be greater.

The problem of low response rates seems to apply particularly to mail questionnaires. This explains why some researchers who use mail questionnaires as a data collection method tend to employ a mixed-methods research design (review Chapter 7 for a discussion of this kind of research). This is because they anticipate the likelihood of a low response rate to the questionnaire survey and, therefore, seek to increase the validity of their research through **triangulation** with other methods. However, there are strategies that can be employed by researchers

to improve self-completion questionnaire response rates. These can sometimes include a small financial incentive. Alternatively, researchers may choose to administer self-completion questionnaires to samples drawn from a population that is more within their control, for example, by sampling from a group of practising managers who are part-time students at the university where the researcher also works. Lucas's (1997) research involved a survey by self-completion questionnaire that was answered by all students to whom it was administered; the only non-respondents were those who were absent from the lecture. When a self-completion questionnaire is employed in this kind of context, it seems less vulnerable to the problem of a low response rate.

Mangione (1995, pp. 60–1) has provided the following classification of bands of response rate to postal questionnaires:

1. over 85% excellent
2. 70–85% very good
3. 60–70% acceptable
4. 50–60% barely acceptable below
5. 50% not acceptable.

Steps to improve response rates to mail questionnaires

Because of the tendency for mail questionnaire surveys to generate lower response rates than comparable structured interview surveys (and the implications this has for the validity of findings), a great deal of thought and research has gone into ways of improving survey response. The following steps are frequently suggested:

- Write a good cover letter explaining the reasons for the research, why it is important, and why the recipient has been selected; mention sponsorship if any, and provide guarantees of confidentiality.
- Mail questionnaires should always be accompanied by a stamped addressed envelope or, at the very least, return postage.
- Follow-up with individuals who do not reply at first, possibly with two or three further mailings. The importance of reminders cannot be overstated—they do

work. Our preferred and recommended approach is to send out a reminder letter to non-respondents two weeks after the initial mailing, reasserting the nature and aims of the survey and suggesting that the person should contact either the researcher or someone else in the research team to obtain a replacement copy of the questionnaire if the initial mailing has been mislaid or lost. Then, two weeks after that, all further non-respondents should be sent another letter along with a further copy of the questionnaire. These reminders have a demonstrable effect on the response rate. Some writers argue for further mailings of reminder letters to non-respondents. If a response rate is worryingly low, such further mailings would certainly be desirable. Some of the tactics used by Fey and Denison (2003) can also be used.

- Unsurprisingly, shorter questionnaires tend to achieve better response rates than longer ones. However, this is not a clear-cut principle, because it is difficult to specify when a questionnaire becomes 'too long'. Also, the evidence suggests that the effect of the length of questionnaires on response rates cannot be separated very easily from the salience of the topic(s) of the research for respondents and from the nature of the sample. Respondents may be highly tolerant of questionnaires that contain many questions on topics that interest them.

- Clear instructions and an attractive layout improve mail questionnaire response rates. Dillman (1983), as part of what he calls the Total Design Method (TDM) for mail questionnaire research, recommends lower case for questions and upper case for closed-ended answers. However, with the growing use of email and the associated rise of 'netiquette', upper case is increasingly associated with shouting, so that this recommendation may become less desirable as this medium of communication spreads.

- Do not allow the questionnaire to appear unnecessarily bulky. Dillman (1983) recommends a booklet format for the questionnaire and using the photocopier to reduce the size of the questionnaire to fit the booklet format. This approach also gives the impression of a more professional approach.

- As with structured interviewing (see Chapter 13), begin with questions that are more likely to be of interest to the respondent. This advice is linked to the issue of salience (see above) but is important for research that may have limited salience for the respondent.

- There is some controversy about how significant for response rates it is to personalize covering letters, by including the respondent's name and address (Baumgartner & Heberlein, 1984). However, one of the features of the TDM approach advocated by Dillman (1983) is that these details are supplied on covering letters and each is individually signed.

- In general, mail questionnaires should have as few open questions as possible, since people are often deterred by the prospect of having to write a lot. In fact, many writers on the subject recommend that open questions be used as little as possible in self-completion questionnaires.

- Providing monetary incentives can be an effective way of increasing the response rate, although it is very unlikely to be an option for most students undertaking project work or research. Incentives are more effective if the money comes with the questionnaire rather than if it is promised once the questionnaire has been returned. Apparently, respondents typically do not cynically take the money and discard the questionnaire! The evidence also suggests that quite small amounts of money have a positive impact on the response rate, but that larger amounts do not necessarily improve the response rate any further.

Some advantages and disadvantages of the self-completion questionnaire, as compared to the structured interview, are illustrated by the example provided in Research in focus 10.1. The WERS study employed a research design that combined both of these methods in order to overcome some of the limitations of each and to represent the perspectives of managers, worker representatives, and employees on a range of employment relations issues. Table 10.1 illustrates their combined use of these methods and provides details of the rates obtained in each case. The main advantage with this triangulated approach is that it enabled a much and more diverse sample to be

Tips and Skills

Response rates

As we have explained, response rates are important because, the lower a response rate, the more questions are likely to be raised about the representativeness of the achieved sample. This is likely, however, to be an issue only with randomly selected samples. With samples that are not selected on the basis of a probability sampling method, it could be argued that the response rate is less of an issue, because the sample would not be representative of a population even if everyone participated! Mail questionnaire surveys, in particular, are often associated with low response rates and, as Mangione's classification illustrates, according to some authorities a response rate of below 50% is not acceptable. On the other hand, many published articles report the results of studies that are well below this level. In an examination of published studies in the field of organizational research in the years 1979–83, Mitchell (1985) found a range of response rates of 30–94%. Bryman (1989a, p. 44) points to two articles in the early 1980s that achieved response rates of 21% and 25%.

Moreover, these articles were published in two of the most highly regarded journals in the field: Academy of Management Journal and Strategic Management Journal. One of the surveys reported by Cunha and Cooper (2002) achieved a sample of just 18%. The point we are making is that if you achieve a low response rate, do not despair. Although writers like Mangione (1995) may regard response rates of 18%, 21%, and 25% as unacceptable (and he may be right about this judgement), a great deal of published research also achieves low response rates. The key point is to recognize and acknowledge the implications of the possible limitations of a low response rate. On the other hand, if your research is based on a convenience sample, ironically it could be argued that a low response rate is less significant. Many students find mail, and other forms of self-completion questionnaire, attractive because of their low cost and quick administration. The point of this discussion is that you should not be put off using such techniques because of the prospect of a low response rate.

---

represented within the financial and temporal constraints of the study.

In a sense, the choice between structured interviews or self-administered questionnaires as a method of data collection is an issue that is primarily about mode of administration. The advantages and disadvantages of mail questionnaires versus other modes of questionnaire administration, including telephone interviewing, email, and Web-based surveys, are summarized in Table 22.1.

 # Designing the self-completion questionnaire

Do not cramp the presentation

Because of the well-known problem of low response rates to the mail questionnaire in particular, it is sometimes considered preferable to make the instrument appear as short as possible in order to deter prospective respondents from not answering. However, this is almost always a mistake. As Dillman (1983) observes, an attractive

---

Table 10.1 Outcomes from the WERS fieldwork 1998 cross-section survey

	Total responses (number)	Response rate (%)	Average duration (minutes)
Management (structured interview)	2,191	80	108
Worker representative (structured interview)	947	82	47
Employee (postal questionnaire)	28,237	64	–

Source: adapted from Cully et al. (1999).

10.1   Research in Focus

Combining the use of structured interviews with self-completion questionnaires

Structured interviews can be used in conjunction with self-completion questionnaires to gain understanding of the perspectives of different groups of participants. The 2004 Workplace Employee Relations Survey (WERS, 2004) is an example of a project that has used different research methods to reach different categories of respondent:

1. The principal method of data collection used is a structured face-to-face interview with the senior member of management at each workplace who deals with industrial relations, employee relations, or personnel matters. These interviews are based on a piloted (or pretested) questionnaire and cover a range of issues such as trade union membership and recognition, patterns of flexible working, training and development, working hours and payment systems, and employee communication. Although the approach is quite structured, the interviewer, who is formally trained, is encouraged to follow up any inconsistent responses within the interview.

2. The second group of respondents included in the **cross-sectional** survey is worker representatives. They are interviewed about the state of employment relations at their workplaces. The researchers explain that, although the majority of questions covered by the survey are factual, the reason for inclusion of worker representatives is the differences in frames of reference. 'For example, a manager may state that the workplace operates a staff suggestion scheme, but a worker representative may think it dormant or non-existent if no-one has made a suggestion for several years' (Cully et al., 1999, p. 7).

3. The third group of respondents is employees. In the 1998 survey up to 25 employees were **randomly** selected from each workplace. This new element to the survey was introduced partly because of a decline in worker representation evident from the 1990 survey. A **mail questionnaire** was sent to each of these employees. The aim of this part of the study was to understand how employees themselves see the employment relationship and to build up a picture of their experience based on their access to training, their participation in workplace decision making, and their interpretation of the psychological contract.

The WERS survey is designed to combine the views of different groups of participants in order to overcome the limitations and partiality of any one group of respondents. The combined use of structured interviews and self-completion questionnaires enables this aim to be achieved, despite the vast scale of the project.

layout is likely to enhance response rates, whereas the kinds of tactics that are sometimes employed to make a questionnaire appear shorter than it really is—such as reducing margins and the space between questions—make it look cramped and thereby unattractive. Also, if questions are too close together, there is a risk that they will be inadvertently omitted.

This is not to say that you should be ridiculously liberal in your use of space, as this does not necessarily provide for an attractive format either and may run the risk of making the questionnaire look bulky. As with so many other issues in business research, a steady course needs to be steered between possible extremes.

Clear presentation

Far more important than making a self-completion questionnaire appear shorter than is the case is to make sure that it has a layout that is easy on the eye, as Dillman

(1983) emphasizes, and that it facilitates the answering of all questions that are relevant to the respondent. Dillman's recommendation of lower case for questions and upper case for **closed** answers is an example of one consideration, but at the very least a variety of print styles (for example, different fonts, print sizes, bold, italics, and capitals) can enhance the appearance, *however, they must be used in a consistent manner*. This last point means that you should ensure that you use one style for general instructions, one for headings, perhaps one for specific instructions (e.g., 'Go to question 7'), one for questions, and one for closed-ended answers. Mixing print styles, so that one style is sometimes used for both general instructions and questions, can be very confusing for respondents.

Vertical or horizontal closed answers?

Keeping in mind that most questions in a self-completion questionnaire are likely to be of the closed kind, one consideration is whether to arrange the fixed answers vertically or horizontally. Very often, the nature of the answers will dictate a vertical arrangement because of their sheer length. Many writers prefer a vertical format whenever possible, because, in some cases where either arrangement is feasible, confusion can arise when a horizontal one is employed (Sudman & Bradburn, 1982). Consider the following:

What do you think of the CEO's performance in his job since he took over the running of this company? (Please tick the appropriate response)
Very good ___ Good ___ Fair ___ Poor ___ Very poor ___

There is a risk that, if the questionnaire is being answered quickly, the required tick will be placed in the wrong space, for example, indicating Good when Fair was the intended response. Also, a vertical format more clearly distinguishes questions from answers. To some extent, these potential problems can be avoided through the judicious use of spacing and print variation, but they represent significant considerations. A further reason why vertical alignments can be superior is that they are probably easier to **code**, especially when pre-codes appear on the questionnaire. Very often, self-completion

---

Tips and Skills

Closed question with a horizontal format

What do you think of the CEO's performance in his job since he took over the running of this company? (*Please tick the appropriate response*)

| Very good ___ | Good ___ | Fair ___ | Poor ___ | Very poor ___ | 5 4 3 2 1 |

Tips and Skills

Closed question with a vertical format

What do you think of the CEO's performance in his job since he took over the running of this company? (*Please tick the appropriate response*)

Very good	____	5
Good	____	4
Fair	____	3
Poor	____	2
Very poor	____	1

Tips and Skills

Formatting a Likert scale

In the next set of questions, you are presented with a statement. You are being asked to indicate your level of agreement or disagreement with each statement by indicating whether you: Strongly Agree (SA), Agree (A), are Undecided (U), Disagree (D), or Strongly Disagree (SD).

Please indicate your level of agreement by circling the appropriate response.

23. My job is like a hobby to me.

    SA   A   U   D   SD

24. My job is usually interesting enough to keep me from getting bored.

    SA   A   U   D   SD

25. It seems that my friends are more interested in their jobs.

    SA   A   U   D   SD

26. I enjoy my work more than my leisure time.

    SA   A   U   D   SD

questionnaires are arranged so that to the right of each question are two columns: one for the column in which data relating to the question will appear in a data matrix; the other for all the pre-codes. The latter allows the appropriate code to be assigned to a respondent's answer by circling it for later entry into the computer. Thus, the choice would be between the formats presented in Tips and skills 'Closed question with a horizontal format' and 'Closed question with a vertical format'. In the second case, not only is there less ambiguity about where a tick is to be placed; the task of **coding** is easier. However, when there is to be a battery of questions with identical answer formats, as in a **Likert scale**, a vertical format will take up too much space. One way of dealing with this kind of questioning is to use abbreviations with an accompanying explanation. An example can be found in Tips and skills 'Formatting a Likert scale'. The four items presented here are taken from an 18-item Likert scale designed to measure job satisfaction (Brayfield & Rothe, 1951).

Identifying response sets in a Likert scale

One of the advantages of using **closed questions** is that they can be pre-coded, thus turning the processing of data for computer analysis into a fairly simple task (see

Chapter 11 for more on this). However, some thought has to go into the scoring of the items of the kind presented in Tips and skills 'Formatting a Likert scale'. We might for example score question 23 as follows:

1. Strongly agree = 5
2. Agree = 4
3. Undecided = 3
4. Disagree = 2
5. Strongly disagree = 1

Thus, a high score for the item (4 or 5) indicates satisfaction with the job and a low score (1 or 2) indicates low job satisfaction. The same applies to question 24. However, when we come to question 25, the picture is different. Here, agreement indicates a lack of job satisfaction. Instead of agreement, it is disagreement that is indicative of job satisfaction. We would have to reverse the coding of this item, so that:

1. Strongly agree = 1
2. Agree = 2
3. Undecided = 3
4. Disagree = 4
5. Strongly disagree = 5

The point of including such items is to identify people who exhibit response sets, like acquiescence (see Chapter 13). If someone were to agree with all 18 items, when some of them indicated *lack* of job satisfaction, it is likely that the respondent was affected by a response set and the answers are unlikely to provide a valid assessment of job satisfaction for that person.

Clear instructions about how to respond

Always be clear about how you want respondents to indicate their replies when answering **closed questions**. Are they supposed to place a check mark or circle or underline the appropriate answer, or are they supposed to delete inappropriate answers? Also, in many cases it is feasible for the respondent to choose more than one answer—is this acceptable to you? If it is not, you should indicate this in your instructions, for example:

(*Please choose the one answer that best represents your views by checking the appropriate box*).

If you do not make this clear and if some respondents choose more than one answer, you will have to treat their replies as if they had not answered. This possibility increases the risk of **missing data** from some respondents.

If it is acceptable to you for more than one category to be chosen, you need to make this clear, for example:

(*Please choose all answers that represent your views by checking the appropriate boxes*).

It is a common error for such instructions to be omitted and for respondents either to be unsure about how to reply or to make inappropriate selections.

Keep question and answers together

This is a simple and obvious, though often transgressed, requirement—namely, that you should never split up a question so that it appears on two separate pages. A common error is to have some space left at the bottom of a page into which the question can be slotted but for the closed answers to appear on the next page. Doing so

carries the risk of the respondent forgetting to answer the question or providing an answer in the wrong group of closed answers (a problem that is especially likely when a series of questions with a common answer format is being used, as with a Likert scale).

Diaries as a form of self-completion questionnaire

When the researcher is specifically interested in precise estimates of different kinds of behaviour, the diary warrants serious consideration, though it is still a relatively under-used method. Unfortunately, the term **diary** has somewhat different meanings in business research (see Key concept 10.1). It is the first of the three meanings—what Elliott (1997) calls the *researcher-driven diary*— that is the focus of attention here, especially in the context of its use in relation to **quantitative research**. When employed in this way, the researcher-driven diary functions in a similar way to the self-completion questionnaire. Equally, it could be said that the researcher-driven diary is an alternative method of data collection to observation. It can be thought of as the equivalent of **structured observation** (see Chapter 16) in the context of research questions that are framed in terms of quantitative research, or of **ethnography** (see Chapter 17) in the context of research questions in terms of qualitative research.

Corti (1993) distinguishes between '*structured diaries*' and '*free text diaries*'. Either may be employed by quantitative researchers. The research on managers and their jobs by Stewart (1967) is an illustration of the structured kind of diary. The diary has the general appearance of a questionnaire with largely closed questions. The kind of diary employed in this research is often referred to as a 'time-use' diary, in that it is designed so that diarists can record the amount of time engaged in certain activities as they are performed, such as time spent travelling, doing paperwork, in committee meetings, and so on. Estimates of the amount

> **Key concept 10.1: What is a research diary?**
>
> A research diary may be a method of data collection, a document for analysis or a log of researcher activities.

of time spent in different activities are often regarded as more accurate, because the events are less subject to memory problems or to the tendency to round up or down. *Structured diaries* are also regarded as more accurate in tracking events as they occur. However, the diary method is more intrusive than answering a questionnaire and it could be argued that it causes changes in behaviour or behavioural awareness of an issue. For example, in their study of psychological contract breach, Conway and Briner (2002) note that their research design may have encouraged respondents to report very minor breaches of the psychological contract that they perhaps otherwise would not have regarded as significant. They conclude that 'it is a matter of debate as to what can be considered as lying inside or outside a psychological contract' (2002, p. 299).

An example of a free-text diary is provided by Huxley et al.'s (2005) study of stress and pressures among mental health social workers. In this study, a diary relating to the previous working week was sent to each of the 237 respondents along with a mail questionnaire. The issues that diarists were invited to cover were based on findings from two focus groups the researchers ran prior to the diary study involving mental health social workers. The diary invited open-ended responses, which were entered into the qualitative software analysis package NVivo, and these were analyzed thematically. One of the advantages of the diary in conjunction with a self-completion questionnaire in this study was that it provided contextual information about factors that had an impact on employee stress, such as the burden of paperwork and bureaucratic procedures, staff shortages and excessive workloads, and constant change and restructuring. This kind of information would probably have been much more difficult to glean from the questionnaires alone.

Using free-text recording of behaviour carries the same kinds of problems as those associated with coding answers to structured interview open questions—namely, the time-consuming nature of the exercise and the increased risks associated with the coding of answers. However, the free-text approach is less likely to be problematic when, as in Huxley et al. (2005), diarists can be instructed on what kind of information to write about, such as that relating to pressures of work, their affective commitment, and job satisfaction. It would be much more difficult to code free-text entries relating to more general questions such as in Stewart's (1967) study of how managers use their time.

Corti (1993) recommends that the person preparing the diary should:

- Provide explicit instructions for diarists.
- Be clear about the time periods within which behaviour is to be recorded, e.g., day, 24 hours, week.
- Provide a model of a completed section of a diary.
- Provide checklists of 'items, events, or behaviour' that can jog people's memories, but the list should not become overwhelming in length or complexity; and
- Include fixed blocks of time or columns showing when the designated activities start and finish (for example, diaries of the kind used by Stewart (1967), which show how managers spend their time).

Advantages and disadvantages of the diary as a method of data collection

The two studies that have been used to illustrate the use of diaries also suggest its potential advantages:

- When fairly precise estimates of the frequency and/or amount of time spent in different forms of behaviour are required, the diary may provide more valid and reliable data than questionnaire data (see Research in focus 10.2).
- When information about the sequencing of different types of behaviour is required, it is likely to perform better than questionnaires or interviews.
- The first two advantages could be used to suggest that structured observation would be just as feasible, but structured observation is probably less appropriate for producing data on behaviour that is personally sensitive, such as work-related gossip. Moreover, although data on such behaviour can be collected by structured interview, it is likely that respondents will be less willing to divulge personal details. If such information were collected by questionnaire, there is a greater risk of recall and rounding problems (see the first point in this list).

10.2   Research in Focus

A diary study of text messaging

Faulkner and Culwin (2005) used a questionnaire and a diary study to explore the uses of text messaging among UK university students. The diary study involved 24 mobile phone users who had also used text messaging. The researchers used a convenience sample made up of students in their mid-20s on a computer studies course at a UK university and the study formed part of their course work. The group was asked to keep diaries of sent and received text messages for a two-week period. 'The study started at midnight on February 15th to avoid the sample being affected by Valentine's Day greetings' (2005, p. 176). The following information was recorded in a structured format:

1. Book number
2. Message number
3. Date
4. Time
5. Send or receive
6. The original message
7. A translation if it was not in English
8. Sender's details
9. Relationship of sender to receiver

Although structured observation could have been used in this study, it would have entailed researchers following users around and waiting for participants to text someone, so a diary study is in this case a more directed method of focusing on one particular type of activity. This study focused on text messages that were predominantly of a personal nature, but text messaging is increasingly being recognized as a method of communication within business where similar research methods could be applied.

On the other hand, diaries may suffer from the following problems:

- They tend to be more expensive than personal interviews (because of the costs associated with recruiting diarists and of checking that diaries are being properly completed).
- Diaries can suffer from a process of attrition, as people decide they have had enough of the task of completing a diary.
- This last point raises the possibility that diarists become less diligent over time about their record keeping.
- There is sometimes failure to record details sufficiently quickly, so that memory recall problems set in.

However, diary researchers argue that the resulting data are more accurate than the equivalent data based on interviews or questionnaires.

Key points

- Many of the recommendations relating to the **self-completion questionnaire** apply equally or almost equally to the **structured interview**, as has been mentioned on several occasions.
- **Closed questions** tend to be used in **survey research** rather than open ones. **Coding** is a particular problem when dealing with answers to **open questions**.
- Structured interviews and self-completion questionnaires both have their respective advantages and disadvantages, but a particular problem with questionnaires sent by mail is that they

frequently produce a low **response rate**. However, steps can be taken to boost response rates for mail questionnaires.

- Presentation of **closed questions** and the general layout constitute important considerations for the self-completion questionnaire.
- The researcher-driven diary was also introduced as a possible alternative to using questionnaires and interviews when the research questions are very specifically concerned with aspects of people's behaviour.

Questions for review

Self-completion questionnaire or postal questionnaire?

- Are the **self-completion questionnaire** and the **mail questionnaire** the same thing?

Evaluating the self-completion questionnaire in relation to the structured interview

- 'The low **response rates** frequently achieved in research with **postal questionnaires** mean that the structured interview is invariably a more suitable choice'. Discuss.
- What steps can be taken to boost mail questionnaire response rates?

Designing the self-completion questionnaire

- Why are self-completion questionnaires usually made up mainly of **closed questions**?
- Why might a vertical format for presenting closed questions be preferable to a horizontal format?

Diaries as a form of self-completion questionnaire

- What are the main kinds of **diary** used in the collection of business research data?
- Are there any circumstances when the diary approach might be preferable to the use of a self-completion questionnaire?

11

Asking Questions

Chapter guide

This chapter is concerned with the considerations that are involved in asking questions that are used in **structured interviews** and **questionnaires** of the kinds discussed in Chapter 10 and also in Chapter 13. Thus in this chapter we consider the asking of questions in both the **self-completion questionnaire** context as well as in the structured interview method. This chapter explores:

* The issues involved in deciding whether or when to use **open** or **closed questions**.
* The different kinds of questions that can be asked in structured interviews and questionnaires.
* Rules to bear in mind when designing questions.
* Vignette questions in which respondents are presented with a scenario and are asked to reflect on the scenario.
* The importance of pilot testing questions.
* The possibility of using questions that have been used in previous **survey research**.

 Introduction

For many people, how to ask questions represents the crux of considerations surrounding the use of survey instruments, such as the structured interview or the self-completion questionnaire. As these other two chapters (namely Chapters 10 and 13) suggest, there is much more to the design and administration of such research instruments than how best to phrase questions. However, there is no doubt that the issue of how questions should be asked is a crucial concern for the survey researcher and consequently this aspect of designing survey instruments has been a major focus of attention over the years and preoccupies many practising researchers.

 Open or closed questions?

One of the most significant considerations for many researchers is whether to ask a question in an open or closed format. The issue of whether to ask a question in an open or closed format is relevant to the design of both structured interview and self-administered questionnaire research.

With an open question respondents are asked a question and can reply however they wish. With a closed question they are presented with a set of fixed alternatives from which they have to choose an appropriate answer. All of the questions in Tips and skills '*Instructions for interviewers in the use of a filter question*' (see Chapter 13) are of the closed kind. So, too, are the Likert-scale items in Web Research in focus 5.1 and 5.2 and Tips and skills '*Closed question with a horizontal format*' and '*Closed question with a vertical format*' (see Chapter 10); these form a particular kind of closed question. What, then, are some of the advantages and limitations of these two types of question format?

Open questions

Open questions present both advantages and disadvantages to the survey researcher, though, as the following discussion suggests, the problems associated with the processing of answers to open questions tend to mean that closed questions are more likely to be used.

Advantages

Although survey researchers typically prefer to use closed questions, open questions do have certain advantages over closed ones, as outlined in the list below:

- Respondents can answer in their own terms. They are not forced to answer in the same terms as those presented to them by the closed answers.
- They allow for unusual or unexpected responses. Replies that the survey researcher may not have contemplated (and that would, therefore, not form the basis for fixed-choice alternatives) are possible.
- The questions do not suggest certain kinds of answer to respondents. Therefore, respondents' levels of knowledge and understanding of issues can be tapped. The salience of issues for respondents can also be explored.
- They are useful for exploring new areas or ones in which the researcher has limited knowledge.
- They are useful for generating fixed-choice format answers. This is a point that we will return to later.

Disadvantages

However, open questions present problems for the survey researcher, as the following list reveals:

- They are time-consuming for interviewers to administer. Interviewees are likely to talk for longer than is usually the case with a comparable closed question.
- Answers have to be 'coded'. This is very time-consuming. For each open question it entails reading through answers, deriving themes that can be employed to form the basis for codes, and then going through the answers again so that the answers can be coded for entry into a computer spreadsheet. The process is essentially identical to that involved in content analysis and is sometimes called post-coding to distinguish it from pre-coding, whereby the researcher designs a coding frame in advance of administering a survey instrument and often includes the pre-codes in the questionnaire (as in Tips and skills 'Processing a closed question'). However, in addition to being time-consuming, post-coding can be an unreliable process, because it can introduce the possibility of variability in the coding of answers and, therefore, of measurement error (and hence lack of validity). This is a form of data processing error (see Figure 9.8).
- They require greater effort from respondents. Respondents are likely to talk for longer than would be the case for a comparable closed question, or, in the case of a self-completion questionnaire, would need to write for much longer. Therefore, it is often suggested that open questions have limited utility in the context of self-completion questionnaires. Because of the greater effort involved, many prospective respondents are likely to be put off by having to write extensively, which may exacerbate the problem of low response rates with mail questionnaires in particular (see Chapter 10).
- There is the possibility in research based on structured interviews of variability between interviewers in the recording of answers. This possibility is likely to arise as a result of the difficulty of writing down verbatim what respondents say to interviewers. The obvious so-

Tips and Skills

Processing a closed question

What do you think of the CEO's performance in his job since he took over the running of this company? (*Please check the appropriate response*)

Very good	____	5
Good	____	4
Fair	____	3
Poor	____	2
Very poor	____	1

lution is to use a tape recorder; however, this may not be practicable, for example, in a noisy environment. Also, the transcription of answers to tape-recorded open questions is immensely time-consuming and adds additional costs to a survey. The problem of transcription is one continually faced by qualitative researchers using semi-structured and unstructured interviews (see Chapter 14).

Closed questions

The advantages and disadvantages of closed questions are in many respects implied in some of the considerations relating to open questions.

Advantages

Closed questions offer the following advantages to researchers:

- It is easy to process answers. For example, the respondent in a self-completion questionnaire or the interviewer using a structured interview schedule will place a check mark or circle an answer for the appropriate response. The appropriate code can then be almost mechanically derived from the selected answer, since the pre-codes are placed to the side of the fixed-choice answers. See Tips and skills '*Processing a closed question*' for an example based on Tips and skills '*Closed question with a vertical format*' (in Chapter 10).

- Closed questions enhance the comparability of answers, making it easier to show the relationship between variables and to make comparisons between respondents or types of respondents. For example, in the research described in Research in focus 11.1, Guest and Dewe (1991) were able to generate a contingency table on the basis of their pre-coding of respondents' answers. Although contingency tables can also be generated by post-coding respondents' answers to open questions, with post-coding there is always a problem of knowing how far respondents' answers that receive a certain code are genuinely comparable. As previously noted, the assignment of codes to people's answers may be unreliable (see the sixth point in Tips and skills

'*Common sources of error in survey research*' in Chapter 13). Checks are necessary to ensure that there is a good deal of agreement between coders and that coders do not change their coding conventions over time. Closed questions essentially avoid this problem.

- Closed questions may clarify the meaning of a question for respondents. Sometimes respondents may not be clear about what a question is getting at and the availability of answers may help to clarify the situation for them.
- Closed questions are easy for interviewers and/or respondents to complete. Precisely because interviewers and respondents are not expected to write extensively and, instead, have to place check marks or circle answers, closed questions are easier and quicker to complete.
- In interviews, closed questions reduce the possibility of variability in the recording of answers in structured interviewing. As noted in Chapter 13, if interviewers do not write down exactly what respondents say to them when answering questions, a source of bias and, hence of invalidity, is in prospect. Closed questions reduce this possibility, though there is still the potential problem that interviewers may have to interpret what is said to them in order to assign answers to a category.

Disadvantages

However, closed questions exhibit certain disadvantages:

- There is a loss of spontaneity in respondents' answers. There is always the possibility that they might come up with interesting replies that are not covered by the fixed answers that are provided. One solution to this possible problem is to ensure that an open question is used to generate the categories. Also, there may be a good case for including a possible response category of 'Other' and to allow respondents to indicate what they mean by this category.
- It can be difficult to make forced-choice answers mutually exclusive. The fixed answers provided to the respondents should not overlap. If they do overlap, respondents will not know which one to choose and so

11.1 Research in Focus

Coding closed questions to create a contingency table

In order to establish whether employees were more strongly committed to their company or their union, Guest and Dewe (1991) selected a sample of 716 workers at random from three electronics plants in the south-east of England as the basis for a self-completion questionnaire survey. Just under half of the sample belonged to a trade union. The questions were developed and piloted specifically for the survey and covered a broad range of issues, including:

Management role. 'How well do the decisions of local management on this site reflect your opinions?' Responses were on a five-point scale from 'very well' to 'I do not expect anything from the management';

Union role. 'How far are the unions successful in properly representing the interests of employees at plant X?' Responses were on a five-point scale from 1 = very successful to 5 = unsuccessful.

The results were used to construct a contingency table (see Table 11.1). This included, on the one hand, employees who perceived both management and unions to represent their interests very well or fairly well (dual identity), and, at the other extreme, employees who perceived that neither management nor unions represented their interests at all (alienated). This showed that the majority of employees did not identify either with the union or with the company.

Table 11.1 A contingency table to show employee identity			
	Union members (%)	Non-unionists (%)	Total sample (%)
Dual identity	16.9	2.5	9.7
Union identity	27.1	1.2	14.2
Management identity	11.1	35.7	23.4
No identity	44.9	60.6	52.8
Of which: Alienated	*8.0*	*22.1*	*15.1*

Source: adapted from Guest and Dewe (1991).

will arbitrarily select one or the other or alternatively may tick both answers. If a respondent were to tick two or more answers when one is required, it would mean that you would have to treat the respondent's answer as missing data, since you would not know which of the ticked answers represented the true one. One of the most frequently encountered forms of this problem can be seen in the following age bands:

18–30
30–40
40–50
50–60
60 and over.

In which band would a 40-year-old position him- or herself?

- It is difficult to make forced-choice answers exhaustive. All possible answers should be offered, although in practice this may be difficult to achieve, since this rule may result in excessively long lists of possible answers. Again, a category of 'Other' may be desirable to provide a wide range of answers.

- There may be variation among respondents in the interpretation of forced-choice answers. There is always a problem when asking a question that certain terms may be interpreted differently by respondents. If this is the case, then validity will be jeopardized. The presence of forced-choice answers can exacerbate this possible problem, because there may be variation in the understanding of key terms in the answers.

- Closed questions may be irritating to respondents when they are not able to find a category that they feel applies to them.

- In interviews, a large number of closed questions may make it difficult to establish rapport, because the respondent and interviewer are less likely to engage with each other in a conversation. The interview is more likely to have an impersonal feel to it. However, because it is difficult to determine the extent to which rapport is a desirable attribute of structured interviewing (see Chapter 13), this is not necessarily too much of a problem.

Types of questions

It is worth keeping in mind that, when you are using a structured interview or self-completion questionnaire, you will probably be asking several different types of questions. There are various ways of classifying these, but here are some prominent types of questions:

- Personal factual questions. These are questions that ask the respondent to provide personal information, such as age, gender, education, employment status, income, and so on. This kind of question also includes questions about behaviour. Such factual questions may have to rely on the respondents' memories, as when they are asked about such things as frequency of individual performance appraisal meetings, how often they visit certain shops, or when they last had any time off work. For example, in the study by Deery, Iverson, and Walsch (2002; see Research in focus 11.3), in addition to being asked to provide demographic details, telephone call centre workers were asked about the number of calls they took on an average day and the average length of calls taken.

- Factual questions about others. Like the previous type of question, this one asks for personal information about others, sometimes in combination with the respondent. An example of such a question would be one about team performance, which would require respondents to consider their own productivity (mea-

sured in terms of such things as daily work rate, frequency of lateness for work, and so on) in conjunction with the productivity of fellow team members. However, a criticism of such research is precisely that it relies on the possibly distorted views of respondents concerning their own and others' behaviour. Like personal factual questions, an element of reliance on memory recall is likely to be present.

- Informant factual questions. Sometimes, we place people who are interviewed or who complete a questionnaire in the position of informants rather than as respondents answering questions about themselves. This kind of question can also be found in such contexts as when people are asked about such things as the size of the firm for which they work, who owns it, whether it employs certain technologies, and whether it has certain specialist functions. Such questions are essentially about characteristics of an entity of which they have knowledge, in this case, a firm. However, informant factual questions may also be concerned with behaviour; for example, in the study by Deery, Iverson, and Walsch (2002; see Research in focus 11.3), telephone call centre employees were asked about the demands placed upon them by customers and priorities of the call centre management.

- Questions about attitudes. Questions about attitudes are very common in both structured interview and self-completion questionnaire research. The Likert scale is one of the most frequently encountered formats for measuring attitudes. Tips and skills '*Response formats for scales*' provides a number of ways of presenting response formats.

- Questions about beliefs. Respondents are frequently asked about their beliefs. Another form of asking questions about beliefs is when respondents are asked whether they believe that certain matters are true or false—for example, a question asking whether or not the respondent believes that Canada is better off as a result of being a member of the Commonwealth. Or a survey about workplace stress might ask respondents to indicate whether or not they believe that the incidence of stress-related absence from work is increasing.

Tips and Skills

Response formats for scales

There are several ways of presenting the response formats for the individual items that make up a scale like a Likert scale. The kind used in Tips and skills '*Formatting a Likert Scale*' (Chapter 10) is an example of a verbal format (see below).

Binary response format

My job is usually interesting enough to keep me from getting bored

    Agree _____ Disagree _____

    (This format is sometimes elaborated to include a 'don't know' response)

Numerical response format

My job is usually interesting enough to keep me from getting bored

    5 4 3 2 1

    (where 5 means Strongly agree and 1 means Strongly disagree)

Verbal format

My job is usually interesting enough to keep me from getting bored

    Strongly agree _____ Agree _____ Undecided _____ Disagree _____ Strongly disagree _____

Bipolar numerical response format

I love my job   7 6 5 4 3 2 1   I hate my job

Frequency format

My job is usually interesting enough to keep me from getting bored

    All of the time _____ Often _____ Fairly often _____ Occasionally _____ None of the time _____

The bipolar numerical response format is used in connection with semantic differential scales. With such scales, the respondent is given lists of pairs of adjectives. Each pair represents opposites (for example, masculine/feminine). A well-known example is the Fiedler (1967) least-preferred co-worker (LPC) scale. With this scale, each leader in a sample of leaders is given a set of between 16 and 25 pairs of adjectives and is asked to describe with whom he or she has least preferred co-working. Examples of the pairs are:

Pleasant	8	7	6	5	4	3	2	1	Unpleasant
Friendly	8	7	6	5	4	3	2	1	Unfriendly
Rejecting	8	7	6	5	4	3	2	1	Accepting
Distant	8	7	6	5	4	3	2	1	Close

Each leader's score on each pair is aggregated to give a total score for that leader. Fiedler argued that leaders who describe their least-preferred co-workers in largely positive terms (pleasant, friendly, accepting, close) were predominantly relationship-oriented; those who described their least-preferred co-workers in largely negative terms (unpleasant, unfriendly, rejecting, distant) were predominantly task-oriented.

- Questions about normative standards and values. Respondents may be asked to indicate what principles of behaviour influence them or they hold dear. The elicitation of such norms of behaviour is likely to have considerable overlap with questions about attitudes and beliefs, since norms and values can be construed as having elements of both.
- Questions about knowledge. Questions can sometimes be employed to 'test' respondents' knowledge in an area. For example, a study of health and safety in the workplace might ask questions about the legal requirements that companies must comply with, in order to test respondents' awareness of these issues.

Most structured interview schedules and self-completion questionnaires will have more than one, and often several, of these types of question. It is important to keep in mind the distinction between different types of questions. There are a number of reasons for this:

- It is useful to keep the distinctions in mind because they force you to clarify in your own mind what you are asking about, although in rather general terms.
- It will help to prevent questions in an inappropriate format. For example, a Likert scale is entirely unsuitable for asking factual questions about behaviour.
- When building scales like a Likert scale, it is best not to mix different types of questions. For example, attitudes and beliefs sound similar and you may be tempted to use the same format for mixing questions about them. However, it is best not to do this and instead to have separate scales for attitudes and beliefs. If you mix them, the questions cannot really be measuring the same thing, thus measurement validity is threatened.

 ## Rules for designing questions

Over the years, numerous rules (and rules of thumb) have been devised to address the 'dos' and 'don'ts' of asking questions. In spite of this, it is one of the easiest areas for making mistakes. There are three simple rules of thumb

as a starting point; beyond that the rules specified below act as a means of avoiding further pitfalls.

General rules of thumb

Always keep in mind your research questions

The questions that you will ask in your self-completion questionnaire or structured interview should always be geared to answering your research questions. This first rule of thumb has at least two implications. First, it means that you should make sure that you ask questions that relate to your research questions. Ensure, in other words, that the questionnaire questions you ask will allow your research questions to be addressed. You do not want to find out at a late stage that you forgot to include some crucial questions, and are now missing important information. Secondly, it means that there is little point in asking questions that do not relate to your research questions. It is also not fair, indeed it is perhaps unethical, to waste your respondents' time answering questions that are of little value.

What do you want to know?

Rule of thumb number two is to decide exactly what it is you want to know. Consider the seemingly harmless question:

> Do you have a car?

What is it that the question is seeking to tap? Is it car ownership? If it is car ownership, the question is inadequate, largely because of the ambiguity of the word 'have'. The question can be interpreted as: personally owning a car; having access to a car in a household; and 'having' a company car or a car for business use. Thus, an answer of 'yes' may or may not be indicative of car ownership. If you want to know whether your respondent owns a car, ask him or her directly about this matter. Similarly, there is nothing wrong with the question:

> How many people does your company employ?

However, this question does not clarify whether you are interested in the workplace, the company, or in the business as a whole—which may include a number of subsidiary companies. In addition, it does not distinguish between full- and part-time workers, or temporary and permanent employees. Hence, if you are interested in knowing how many full-time or full-time equivalent employees there are, then you need to specify this. Similarly, if you are interested only in people who are employed directly by the firm (rather than temporary or contract staff who work on the premises), you need to make this clear in your question.

How would you answer it?

Rule of thumb number three is to place yourself in the position of the respondent, ask yourself the question, and try to work out how you would reply. In doing this, there is at least the possibility that the ambiguity that is inherent in the 'Do you have a car?' question above will become apparent to you. Let us say as well that there is a follow-up question to the previous one:

Have you driven the car this week?

Again, this looks harmless, but if you put yourself in the role of a respondent, it will be apparent that the phrase 'this week' is vague. Does it mean the last seven days or does it mean the week in which the questioning takes place, which will, of course, be affected by such things as whether the question is being asked on a Monday or a Friday? In part, this issue arises because the question designer has not decided what the question is about. Equally, however, a moment's reflection in which you put yourself in the position of the respondent might reveal the difficulty of answering this question.

Taking account of these rules of thumb and the following rules about asking questions may help you to avoid the more obvious pitfalls.

Specific rules when designing questions

Avoid ambiguous terms in questions

Avoid terms such as 'often' and 'regularly' as measures of frequency. They are very ambiguous, because respondents will operate with different frames of reference when employing them. Sometimes their use is unavoidable, but when there is an alternative that allows actual frequency

to be measured, this will nearly always be preferable. So, a question like:

How often do you usually visit the movie theatre?

Very often	_____
Quite often	_____
Not very often	_____
Not at all	_____

suffers from the problem that, with the exception of 'not at all', the terms in the response categories are ambiguous. Instead, try to ask about actual frequency, such as:

How frequently do you usually visit the movie theatre? (*Please check whichever category comes closest to the number of times you visit the movie theatre.*)

More than once a week	_____
Once a week	_____
Two or three times a month	_____
Once a month	_____
A few times a year	_____
Once a year	_____
Less than once a year	_____

Alternatively, you might simply ask respondents about the number of times they have visited the movie theatre in the previous four weeks.

Words like 'colleagues' or 'management' are also ambiguous, because people will have different notions of who their colleagues are or who makes up the management. As previously noted, words like 'have' can also be sources of ambiguity.

It is also important to bear in mind that certain common words, such as 'quality' and 'customer', mean different things to different people. For some, quality is dependent on the purpose of the product, whereas for others it is an absolute measure of the standard of the product. Similarly, some people refer to colleagues from different departments as customers, whereas others take the word to mean those external to the organization who consume the products or services that the firm provides. In such cases, it will be necessary to define what you mean by such terms.

Avoid long questions

It is commonly believed that long questions are undesirable. In a structured interview the interviewee can lose the thread of the question, and in a self-completion questionnaire the respondent may be tempted to omit such questions or to skim them and, therefore, not give them sufficient attention. However, Sudman and Bradburn (1982) have suggested that this advice applies better to attitude questions than to ones that ask about behaviour. They argue that, when the focus is on behaviour, longer questions have certain positive features in interviews—for example, they are more likely to provide memory cues and they facilitate recall because of the time taken to complete the question. However, the general advice is to keep questions short is the main piece of advice to be followed.

Avoid double-barrelled questions

Double-barrelled questions are ones that in fact ask about two things. The problem with this kind of question is that it leaves respondents unsure about how best to respond. Take the question:

> How satisfied are you with pay and conditions in your job?

The problem here is obvious: the respondent may be satisfied with one but not the other. Not only will the respondent be unclear about how to reply, but any answer that is given is unlikely to be a good reflection of the level of satisfaction with pay *and* conditions. Similarly,

> How frequently does your boss give you information concerning your daily work schedule and new developments within the company?

suffers from the same problem. A boss may provide extensive information about the daily work schedule but be totally uninformative about what is going on in the company more generally, so any stipulation of frequency of information is going to be ambiguous and will create uncertainty for respondents.

The same rule applies to fixed-choice answers. For example, the following answer from Schuman and Presser's (1981) study is:

> Work that is pleasant and people are nice to work with.

While there is likely to be symmetry between the two ideas in this answer—pleasant work and nice people—there is no *necessary* correspondence between them. Pleasant work may be important for someone, but he or she may be relatively indifferent to the issue of how pleasant their co-workers are. Further examples of double-barrelled questions are provided in Tips and skills on our website '*Matching question and answers in closed questions*'.

Avoid very general questions

It is easy to ask a very general question when in fact what is wanted is a response to a specific issue. The problem with questions that are very general is that they lack a frame of reference. Thus,

> How satisfied are you with your job?

seems harmless but it lacks specificity. Does it refer to pay, conditions, the nature of the work, or all of these? If there is the possibility of such diverse interpretations, respondents are likely to vary in their interpretations too, and this will be a source of error. One of our favourite general questions comes from Karl Marx's *Enquête Ouvrière* (1880), a questionnaire that was sent to 25,000 French socialists and others (though there is apparently no record of any being returned). The final (one-hundredth) question reads:

> What is the general, physical, intellectual, and moral condition of men and women employed in your trade? (Bottomore & Rubel, 1963, p. 218)

Avoid leading questions

Leading or loaded questions are ones that appear to lead the respondent in a particular direction. Questions of the kind 'Do you agree with the view that . . . ?' fall into this class of question. The obvious problem with such a question is that it is suggesting a particular reply to respondents, although they do have the ability to disagree with any implied answer. Nevertheless, they might feel pushed in a certain direction that they do not naturally incline towards. Such a question as,

> Do you think that corporate directors receive excessive financial compensation?

is likely to make it difficult for some people to answer in a way that indicates they do not believe that corporate directors are overpaid for what they do. But once again, Marx is the source of a favourite leading question:

> If you are paid piece rates, is the quality of the article made a pretext for fraudulent deductions from wages? (Bottomore & Rubel, 1963, p. 215)

Avoid questions that are actually asking two questions

The double-barrelled question is a clear example of the breaking of this rule, but in addition there is the case of a question like:

> When did you last discuss your training needs with your supervisor/line manager?

What if the respondent has never discussed his or her training needs with the line manager? It is better to ask two separate questions:

> Have you ever discussed your training needs with your supervisor/line manager?
> Yes _____
> No _____

> If yes, when did your most recent discussion take place?

Another way in which more than one question can be asked is with a question like:

> How effective have your different job search strategies been?
> Very effective _____
> Fairly effective _____
> Not very effective _____
> Not at all effective _____

The obvious difficulty is that, if the respondent has used more than one job search strategy, his or her estimation of effectiveness will vary for each strategy. A mechanism is needed for assessing the success of each strategy rather than forcing respondents to average out their sense of how successful the various strategies were.

Avoid questions that include negatives

The problem with questions with 'not' or similar formulations in them is that it is easy for the respondent to miss the word when completing a self-completion questionnaire or to miss it when being interviewed. If this occurs, a respondent is likely to answer in the opposite way from the one intended. There are occasions when it is impossible to avoid negatives, but a question like the following should be avoided as much as possible:

> Do you agree with the view that students should not have to take out loans to finance higher education?

Instead, the question should be asked in a positive format. Questions with double negatives should be totally avoided, because it is difficult to know how to respond to them. Oppenheim (1966) gives the following as an example of this kind of question:

> Would you rather not use a non-medicated shampoo?

It is quite difficult to establish what an answer of 'yes' or 'no' would actually mean in response to this question.

Tips and Skills

Common mistakes when asking questions

Over the years, we have read many projects, theses, and dissertations based on structured interviews and self-completion questionnaires. We have noticed that a small number of mistakes are most common. Here is a list of some of them:

1. An excessive use of open questions. Students sometimes include too many open questions. While a resistance to closed questions may be understandable, although not something we necessarily agree with, open questions are likely to reduce your response rate and will cause you analysis problems. Keep the number to an absolute minimum.

2. An excessive use of yes/no questions. Sometimes students include lots of questions that provide just a yes/no form of response. This is usually the result of a lack of critical thinking and preparation. The world rarely fits into a yes/no type of response. Take a question like:

    Are you satisfied with opportunities for promotion in the firm?

    Yes _____   No _____

3. This does not provide for the possibility that respondents will vary in their satisfaction. This question could be rephrased as:

    How satisfied are you with opportunities for promotion in the firm?

    Very satisfied   _____

    Satisfied   _____

    Neither satisfied nor dissatisfied   _____

    Dissatisfied   _____

    Very dissatisfied   _____

4. Failure to give clear instructions on self-completion questionnaires as to how the questions should be answered. Make clear whether you want a check mark, something to be circled or deleted, or whatever mark you are expecting to see. If only one response is required, make sure you so indicate this clearly—for example, 'Check mark the one answer that comes closest to your view'.

5. Allowing respondents to choose more than one answer. Be cautious when allowing respondents to choose more than one answer. Sometimes it is unavoidable, but questions that allow more than one reply are often very difficult, and painful, to analyze.

6. Overlapping, or omitting, answer categories. In spite of the fact that we always warn about the problems of overlapping categories, students still formulate closed answers that are not mutually exclusive. In addition, some categories may be omitted. For example:

    How many times per week do you consult with your line manager?

    1–3 times _____   3–6 times _____   6–9 times _____   More than 10 times _____

7. Not only does the respondent not know where to answer if his or her answer might be 3 or 6; there is no answer for someone who would want to answer 10.

8. Failure to ensure that the answers provided correspond to the question being asked. For example:

    Do you regularly meet with your appraiser for an appraisal interview?

    Never _____   Once a year _____   Twice a year _____   More than twice a year _____

One context in which it is difficult to avoid using questions with negatives is when designing Likert-scale items. Since you are likely to want to identify respondents who exhibit response sets and will, therefore, want to reverse the direction of your question asking (see Chapter 10), the use of negatives will be difficult to avoid.

Avoid technical terms

Use simple, plain language and avoid jargon. Do not ask a question like:

Do you sometimes feel alienated from work?

The problem here is that many respondents will not know what is meant by 'alienated', and furthermore they are likely to have different views of what it means, even if it is a remotely meaningful term to them.

Consider the following question:

The influence of the TUC on management–worker relations has declined in recent years.

Strongly __ Agree __ Undecided __ Disagree __ Strongly__
agree   disagree

The use of acronyms like TUC can be a problem, because some people may be unfamiliar with what they stand for.

Does the respondent have the requisite knowledge?

There is little point in asking respondents lots of questions about matters of which they have no knowledge. It is very doubtful whether or not meaningful data about computer use could be extracted from respondents who have never used or come into direct contact with one.

Make sure that there is symmetry between a closed question and its answers

A common mistake is for a question and its answers to be out of phase with each other. Tips and skills '*Matching question and answers in closed questions*' describes such an instance.

Memory problems

Do not rely too much on stretching people's memories to the extent that the answers for many of them are likely to be inaccurate. It would be nice to have accurate replies to a question about the number of times respondents have visited the movie theatre in the previous 12 months, but it is highly unlikely that most will in fact recall events accurately over such a long space of time (other perhaps than those who have not gone at all or only once or twice in the preceding 12 months). It was for this reason that, in the question regarding movie theatre visits above, the time frame was predominantly just one month.

 # Vignette questions

A form of asking mainly closed questions that has been used in connection with the examination of people's normative standards is the vignette technique. This technique involves presenting respondents with one or more scenarios and then asking them how they would respond when confronted with the circumstances of that scenario. Research in focus 11.2 describes a vignette that was employed in the context of a study of the ethical behaviour of marketing professionals in different situations. The study focused on marketing professionals because, of all the functional areas of business, marketing has been the one most frequently charged with unethical practices.

Four different vignettes were used in this study to tease out respondents' responses to ethical dilemmas of different kinds. Of the two dilemmas presented in Research in focus 11.2, the first is concerned with a conflict of interest (this is where an individual has more than one interest, which, if both are pursued, may lead to personal gain at the expense of the firm); the second dilemma is concerned with a case of false advertising aimed at deception and falsehood. Each dilemma deals with a different aspect of the marketing mix, such as price or promotion. For each vignette, respondents are asked how they would act and responses are recorded on a five-point scale, from 1 = definitely would, to 5 = definitely would not. Many aspects of the issues being tapped by the vignette questions could be accessed through attitude items, such as:

11.2 Research in Focus

Two vignette questions about ethical behaviour

The following vignettes were used by Lund (2000) in a study of marketing professionals. Each of the vignettes reflects a different aspect of the marketing mix (place, promotion, price, and product) and each poses a different kind of ethical dilemma. These vignettes were developed for an earlier study of marketing professionals conducted by Fritzsche (1988); the fact that they have been pre-tested gives us greater confidence in the validity of their use as a measure of ethical behaviour. Two of the four vignettes are presented below.

Vignette 1 [Price]: conflict of interest

Jack Brown is vice-president of marketing for Tangy Spices, a large spice manufacturer. Brown recently joined in a private business venture with Tangy's director of purchasing to import black pepper from India. Brown's private venture is about to sign a five-year contract with Tangy to supply its black pepper needs, but the contract is set at a price of 3 cents per pound above contracts available from other spice importers that provide comparable service and quality. If you were Brown, what are the chances that you would sign the contract?:

Definitely would ( )
Probably would ( )
Neither would nor would not ( )
Probably would not ( )
Definitely would not ( )

Vignette 2 [Promotion]: deceit and falsehood

Dave Smith is developing an advertisement for a new housing development his firm is about to start. The development is located in a low area that has flooded in the past. The company has recently done some work to reduce the danger of flooding in the future. In the preliminary advertisement, Smith has included a statement indicating that the firm has solved the flooding problem. The fact is that if a flood occurs, the homes are still likely to be flooded with up to five feet of water. If you were Smith, what are the chances that you would include the statement in the advertisement?:

Definitely would ( )
Probably would ( )
Neither would nor would not ( )
Probably would not ( )
Definitely would not ( )

Source: Lund (2000, p. 334)

If a senior marketing professional has private business interests that are also related to the business of the firm, he has a duty to declare these interests to other senior executives immediately they arise.

Strongly __ Agree __ Undecided __ Disagree __ Strongly __
agree   disagree

The advantage of the vignette over such an attitude question is that it anchors the choice in a situation and, as such, reduces the possibility of an un-reflective reply. In addition, when the subject matter is a sensitive area (in this case, dealing with ethical behaviour), there is the possibility

that the questions may be seen as threatening by respondents. Respondents may feel that they are being judged by their replies. If the questions are about other people (and imaginary ones at that), this permits a certain amount of distance between the questioning and the respondent and results in a less threatening context. However, it is difficult to believe that respondents will not feel that their replies will at least in part be seen as reflecting on them, even if the questions are not about them as such.

One obvious requirement of the vignette technique is that the scenarios must be believable, so that considerable effort needs to go into the construction of credible situations. Finch (1987) points out two further considerations in relation to this style of questioning. First, it is more or less impossible to establish how far assumptions are being made about the characters in the scenario (such as their ethnicity) and what the significance of those assumptions might be for the validity and comparability of people's replies. Secondly, it is also difficult to establish how far people's answers reflect their own normative views or indeed how they themselves would act when confronted with the kinds of choices revealed in the scenarios. However, in spite of these reservations, the vignette technique warrants serious consideration when the research focus is concerned with an area that lends itself to this style of questioning.

 ## Piloting and pre-testing questions

It is always desirable, if at all possible, to conduct a pilot study before administering a self-completion questionnaire or structured interview schedule to your sample. In fact, the desirability of piloting such instruments is not solely to do with trying to ensure that survey questions operate well; piloting also has a role in ensuring that the research instrument as a whole functions well. Pilot studies may be particularly crucial in relation to research based on the self-completion questionnaire, since there will not be an interviewer present to clear up any confusion.

Also, with interviews, persistent problems may emerge after a few interviews have been carried out and these can then be addressed. However, with self-completion questionnaires, since they are sent or handed out in large numbers, considerable wastage may occur prior to any problems becoming apparent.

Here are some uses of pilot studies in survey research:

- If the main study is going to employ mainly closed questions, open questions can be asked in the pilot to generate the fixed-choice answers. Glock (1988), for example, extols the virtues of conducting qualitative interviews in preparation for a survey for precisely this kind of reason.
- Piloting an interview schedule can provide interviewers with some experience of using it and can infuse them with a greater sense of confidence.

- If everyone (or virtually everyone) who answers a question replies in the same way, the resulting data are unlikely to be of interest because they represent little variability. A pilot study allows such a question to be identified.
- In interview surveys, it may be possible to identify questions that make respondents feel uncomfortable and to detect any tendency for respondents' interest to be lost at certain junctures.
- Questions that seem not to be understood (more likely to be realized in an interview than in a self-completion questionnaire context) or questions that are often not answered should become apparent. The latter problem of questions being skipped may be due to confusing or threatening phrasing, poorly worded instructions, or confusing positioning in the interview schedule or questionnaire. Whatever the cause might be, such missing data are undesirable and a pilot study may be instrumental in identifying the problem.
- Pilot studies allow the researcher to determine the adequacy of instructions to interviewers, or to respondents completing a self-completion questionnaire.
- It may be possible to consider how well the questions flow and whether it is necessary to move some of them around to improve this feature.

The pilot should not be carried out on people who might have been members of the sample that would be employed in the full study. One reason for this is that, if you are seeking to employ **probability sampling**, the selecting-out of a number of members of the **population** or **sample** may affect the *representativeness* of any subsequent sample. If possible, it is best to find a small set of respondents who are comparable to members of the population from which the sample for the full study will be taken.

 ## Using existing questions

One final observation regarding the asking of questions is that you should also consider using questions that have been employed by other researchers for at least part of your **questionnaire** or **interview schedule**. This may

11.3 Research in Focus

Using scales developed by other researchers in a survey of call centre operators

In a study of call centre operators working in the telecommunications industry in Australia, Deery, Iverson, and Walsch (2002) were interested in the possible negative effects of this form of work on the psychological well-being of employees. Specifically, they sought to:

1. identify the factors leading to feelings of emotional exhaustion among operators; and
2. analyze the effects of emotional exhaustion on employee absence.
3. Emotional exhaustion was defined as the extent to which individuals feel emotionally drained from their work. It was predicted that emotional exhaustion would be higher among employees who felt they had a high workload and among those who felt they lacked the skills needed to do the job.

In designing the questionnaire used to test these relationships, Deery et al. (2002) used scales that had been devised by other researchers in earlier studies. These included:

- A five-item scale taken from Wharton (1993) used to measure emotional exhaustion. Item statements included: 'I feel emotionally drained from my work'.
- Emotional expressivity measured by four items adapted from Kring et al. (1994), including, 'I

can't hide the way I'm feeling when talking to customers'.
- Workload and role overload measured by items taken from Caplan et al. (1975), including, 'My job requires me to work very fast'.
- Team leader and team member support measured using items adapted from House (1981), such as, 'My team members are willing to listen to my job-related problems'.

Deery et al. (2002) supplemented these scales with items they developed themselves to measure other variables in the study, such as:

- *Customer interactions*—with the statement, 'I now have more abusive customer calls than I used to have'.
- *Management focus on quality*—using item statements such as, 'I believe senior management are more concerned about the quantity rather than the quality of work'.

The study illustrates how item scales developed by other researchers can be combined with those developed by those conducting the present study to create a questionnaire instrument that is sensitive to the context and relevant to the questions that the research is seeking to address.

---

seem like stealing, and you would be advised to contact the researchers concerned regarding the use of questions they have devised, however, employing existing questions allows you to use questions that have in a sense been piloted for you. If any reliability and validity testing has taken place, you will know about the measurement qualities of the existing questions you use. A further advantage of using existing questions is that they allow you to draw comparisons with other research. This might allow you to

indicate whether change has occurred or whether place makes a difference to findings. At the very least, examining questions used by others might give you some ideas about how best to approach your own questions, even if you decide not to make use of them as they stand. An example of how questions developed by other researchers were used in a study of telephone call centre operators is given in Research in focus 11.3.

Tips and Skills

Getting help in designing questions

When designing questions, as we suggested earlier, try to put yourself in the position of someone who has been asked to answer the questions. This can be difficult, because some (if not all) of the questions may not apply to you, for example, if you are a student doing a survey of managers. However, try to think about how you would reply. This means concentrating not just on the questions themselves but also on the links between the questions. For example, do filter questions work in the way you expect them to? Then try the questions out on some people you know, as in a pilot study. Ask them to be critical and to consider how well the questions connect to each other. Also, look at the questionnaires and structured interview schedules that experienced researchers have devised. They may not have asked questions on your topic, but the way they have asked the questions and the flow of the questions should give you an idea of what to do and what to avoid when designing such instruments.

Checklist

Issues to consider for your structured interview schedule or self-completion questionnaire:

- ☐ Have you devised a clear and comprehensive way of introducing the research to interviewees or questionnaire respondents?
- ☐ Have you considered whether or not there are any existing questions used by other researchers to investigate this topic that could meet your needs?
- ☐ Do the questions allow you to answer all your research questions?
- ☐ Could any questions that are not strictly relevant to your research questions be dropped from the study?
- ☐ Have you tried to put yourself in the position of answering as many of the questions as possible?
- ☐ Have you timed and/or estimated how long it will take to complete the survey or interview?
- ☐ Have you piloted the questionnaire with some appropriate respondents?
- ☐ If it is a structured interview schedule, have you made sure that the instructions to yourself and to anyone else involved in interviewing are clear (e.g., which questions should be answered next with filter questions)?
- ☐ If it is a self-completion questionnaire, have you made sure that the instructions to yourself and to anyone else involved in interviewing are clear (e.g., which questions should be answered next with filter questions)?
- ☐ Are instructions about how to record responses clear (e.g., whether to check mark or circle; whether or not more than one response is allowable)?
- ☐ Have you included as few open questions as possible?
- ☐ Have you allowed respondents to indicate levels of intensity in their replies, so that they are not forced into 'yes' or 'no' answers where intensity of feeling may be more appropriate?
- ☐ Have you ensured that questions and their answers do not span more than one page?
- ☐ Have sociodemographic questions been left until the end of the questionnaire?
- ☐ Are questions relating to the research topic at or very close to the beginning?
- ☐ Have you taken steps to ensure that the questions you are asking really do supply you with the information you need?

☐ Have you taken steps to ensure that there are no:
  • ambiguous terms in questions or closed answers?
  • long questions?
  • double-barrelled questions?
  • very general questions?
  • leading questions?
  • questions that are asking about two or more things?
  • questions that include negatives?
  • questions using technical terms?

☐ Have you made sure that your respondents will have the knowledge to answer your questions?

☐ Is there an appropriate match between your questions and your closed answers?

☐ Do any of your questions rely too much on your respondents' memory?

☐ If you are using a **Likert scale** approach:
  • Have you included some items that can be reverse scored in order to minimize response sets?
  • Have you made sure that the items really do relate to the same underlying cluster of attitudes so that they can be aggregated?

☐ Have you ensured that your closed answers are exhaustive?

☐ Have you ensured that your closed answers do not overlap?

☐ Have you ensured that there is a category of 'other' (or similar category such as 'unsure' or 'neither agree nor disagree') so that respondents are not forced to answer in a way that is not indicative of what they think or do?

Key points

- While open questions undoubtedly have certain advantages, **closed questions** are typically preferable for a survey, because of the ease of asking questions and recording and processing answers.
- This point applies particularly to the **self-completion questionnaire**.
- Open questions of the kind used in qualitative interviewing have a useful role in relation to the formulation of fixed-choice answers and piloting.
- It is crucial to learn the rules of question asking to avoid some of the more obvious pitfalls.
- Remember always to put yourself in the position of the respondent when asking questions and to make sure you will generate data appropriate to your research questions.
- Piloting or pre-testing may clear up problems in question formulation.

Questions for review

Open or closed questions?

- What difficulties do **open questions** present in survey research?
- Why are **closed questions** frequently preferred to open questions in survey research?
- What are the limitations of closed questions?
- How can closed questions be improved?

Types of question

- What are the main types of question that are likely to be used in a **structured interview** or **self-administered questionnaire**?

Rules for designing questions

- What is wrong with each of the following questions?

  What is your annual salary?

  - Below $20,000
  - $20,000–25,000
  - $25,000–30,000
  - $30,000–35,000
  - $35,000–40,000
  - $40,000–45,000
  - $45,000 and over

  Do you ever feel alienated from your work?

  - All the time
  - Often
  - Occasionally
  - Never

  How satisfied are you with the customer services and products provided by this company?

  - Very satisfied
  - Fairly satisfied
  - Neither satisfied nor dissatisfied
  - Fairly dissatisfied
  - Very dissatisfied

Vignette questions

- In what circumstances are vignette questions appropriate?

Piloting and pre-testing questions

- Why is it important to pilot questions?

Using existing questions

- Why might it be useful to use questions devised by others?

Using SPSS for Windows

Chapter guide

In order to implement the techniques that you will find later in Chapter 23, you will need to do one of two things: either learn the underlying formula for each technique and then apply it to your data, or use computer software to analyze your data. The latter is the approach chosen in this book for two main reasons:

- It is closer to the way in which quantitative data analysis is carried out in real research nowadays.
- It helps to equip you with a useful transferable skill.
- You will be learning SPSS for Windows, which is the most widely used package of computer software for doing this kind of analysis. It is relatively straightforward to use. This chapter largely operates in parallel to Chapter 23, so that you can see the links between the techniques learned there and the use of SPSS to implement them.
- We will be continuing to refer to the techniques discussed in Chapter 23 and will continue to use the examples found in this latter chapter.

Introduction

This chapter aims to provide a familiarity with some basic introduce ways of using SPSS to implement the methods aspects of SPSS for Windows, which is possibly the most widely used computer software for the analysis of **quantitative** data for social scientists. SPSS, which was originally short for Statistical Package for the Social Sciences, has been in existence since the mid-1960s and over the years has undergone many revisions, particularly since the arrival of personal computers. The version that was used in preparing this section was Release 14. From this point on, when referring to SPSS for Windows in the text, it will be called simply SPSS. The gym survey used in Chapter 23 will be employed to illustrate SPSS operations and methods of analysis. The aim of this chapter is to introduce ways of using SPSS to implement the methods of analysis discussed later on in Chapter 23. SPSS operations will be presented in **bold**, for example, **Variable Name:** and **Analyze**. Names given to variables in the course of using SPSS will be presented in ***bold italics***, e.g., ***gender*** and ***reasons***. Labels given to values or to variables are also in bold but in a different font, e.g., **reasons for visiting** and **male**. Tips and skills 'Basic operations in SPSS' presents a list summarizing these. One further element in the

presentation is that a right pointing arrow— → —will be used to denote 'click once with the left-hand button of your mouse'. This action is employed to make selections and similar activities.

Getting started in SPSS

Beginning SPSS

To start SPSS, double click on the **spsswin** icon on your computer screen. If there is no icon, → the Start button in the bottom left-hand corner of your screen. From the menu of programs, → SPSS **for Windows**. A menu will appear, from which you should select SPSS **14.0 for Windows**. When SPSS loads, you *may* see an opening dialogue box with the title 'What do you want to do?' and a list of options. Many users prefer to disable this opening box. For our present purposes, it is not important, so → **Cancel**. You will then be viewing the SPSS **Data Editor**. This is made up of two components: **Data View** and **Variable View**. In the following discussion, these two screens are referred to as the **Data Viewer** and the **Variable Viewer**. You move between these two viewers by selecting the appropriate tab

Tips and Skills

Basic operations in SPSS

- The SPSS **Data Editor**. This is the area of SPSS into which data are entered and subsequently edited and defined.
- It is made up of two screens: the **Data Viewer** and the **Variable Viewer**. You move between these two viewers by selecting the appropriate tab at the bottom of the screen.
- The **Data Viewer**. This is the spreadsheet-style matrix into which your data are entered. When you start up SPSS, the **Data Viewer** will be facing you.
- The **Variable Viewer**. This is another spreadsheet, but this one displays information about each of the variables and allows you to change that information. It is the platform from which you provide for each variable such information as: the variable name; a variable label; and value labels (see below).
- **The Output**. When you perform an analysis or produce a diagram (called a 'chart' in SPSS), your output will be deposited here. The **Output Viewer** superimposes itself over the **Data Editor** after an analysis has been performed or a chart generated.
- A **Variable Name**. This is the name that you give to a variable, e.g., *gender*. The name must be no more than eight characters in length. Until you give a variable a name, it will be referred to as *var00001* etc. When the variable has been given a name, it will appear in the column for that variable in the **Data View** window. It is generated from the **Variable Viewer**.
- A **Variable Label**. This is a label that you can give to a variable but which is not restricted to a length of eight characters. Spaces can be used, e.g., **reasons for visiting**. The Label will appear in any output you generate. It is generated from the **Variable Viewer**.
- A **Value Label**. This is a label that you can attach to a code that has been used when entering data for all

types of variables other than interval/ratio variables. Thus, for *var00001*, we would attach the label **male** to 1 and **female** to 2. When you generate output, such as a frequency table or chart, the labels for each value will be presented. This makes the interpretation of output easier. It is generated from the **Variable Viewer**.
- **Missing Values.** When you do not have data for a particular variable when entering data for a case, you must specify how you are denoting missing values for that variable. Missing values are generated from the **Variable Viewer**.
- **Recode**. A procedure that allows codes or numbers to be changed. It is especially helpful when you need to combine groups of people, for example, when producing age bands.
- **Compute**. A procedure that allows you to combine two or more variables to form a new variable.
- **Analyze**. This is the point on the menu bar above the **Data Editor** from which you choose (via a drop-down menu) which method of analysis you want to select. Note that whenever an item on a menu appears with a right-pointing arrowhead after it, this means that, if you select that option, a further menu will follow on.
- **Graphs**. This is the point on the menu bar above the **Data Editor** from which you choose (via a drop-down menu) which chart you want to select.
- **Chart Editor**. When you produce a graph, you can edit it with the **Chart Editor**. To activate this editor, double-click anywhere in the graph. A small chart editor window will appear and your main graph will appear opaque until you exit the Editor. From the Editor, you can make various changes and enhancements to your graph.

at the bottom of the screen. The **Data Viewer** is in the form of a spreadsheet grid into which you enter your data. The columns represent *variables*—in other words, information about characteristics of each person in the gym study example. Until data are entered, each column simply has **var** as its heading. The rows represent *cases*, which can be people (as in the example you will be working through) or any unit of analysis. Each block in the grid is referred to as

a 'cell'. Note also that when the data are in the SPSS spreadsheet, they will look different; for example, 1 will be 1.00.

Entering data in the Data Viewer

To input the data into the **Data Viewer**, make sure that the top left-hand cell in the grid is highlighted (see Plate 12.1). If it is not highlighted, simply click once in that cell. Then, type the appropriate numeric value for that cell—that is,

Plate 12.1

The SPSS Data Viewer

Each column represents a variable

Each row represents a case

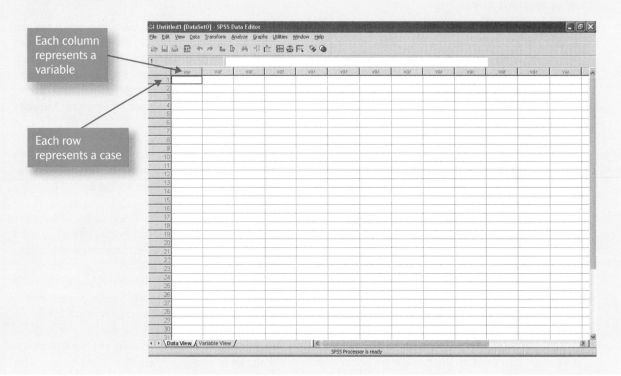

1. This number goes directly into that cell and into the box beneath the toolbar. As an alternative to using the mouse, many people find it easier to use the arrow keys on their keyboard to move from cell to cell. If you make a mistake at any point, simply click once in the cell in question, type in the correct value, and click once more in that cell. When you have finished, you should end up in the bottom right-hand cell of what will be a perfect rectangle of data.

Plate 12.2 shows the **Data Viewer** with the data from the gym survey example entered (though only part of the set of data is visible, in that only the first 22 respondents and 10 of the 12 variables are visible). The first row of data contains the coded answers from the completed questionnaire in Chapter 23 (see Tips and skills 'A completed and processed questionnaire').

In order to proceed further, you will find that SPSS works in the following typical sequence for defining variables and analyzing your data:

1. You make a selection from the menu bar at the top of the screen, e.g., → **Analyze**.
2. From the menu that will appear, make a selection, e.g., **Descriptive Statistics**.
3. This will bring up a *dialog box* into which you will tell SPSS what you are trying to do, e.g., which variables are to be analyzed.

The **Data Viewer** with 'gym study' data entered

4. Very often, you then need to make further specifications concerning what you want and to do this you have to → a button that will bring up what is called, following Bryman and Cramer (2004), a *sub-dialog box*.
5. You then provide the information in the sub-dialog box and then go back to the dialog box. Sometimes, you will need to bring up a further sub-dialog box and then go back to the dialog box.

Plate 12.2

The Data Viewer with 'gym study' data entered

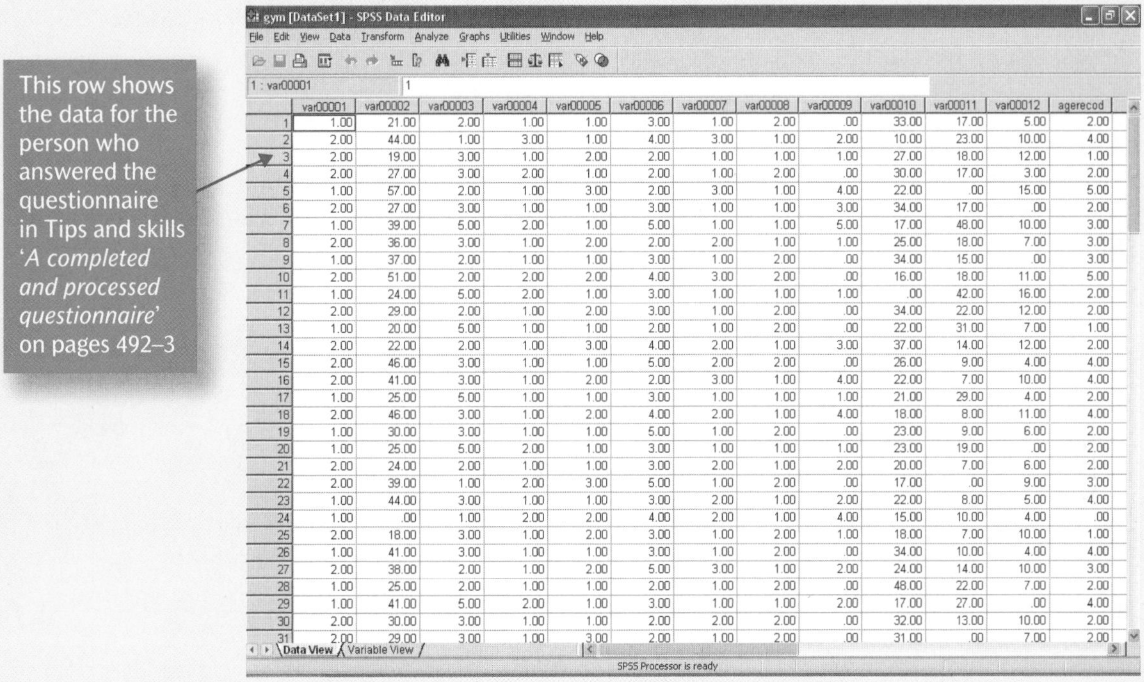
This row shows the data for the person who answered the questionnaire in Tips and skills *'A completed and processed questionnaire'* on pages 492–3
gym [DataSet1] - SPSS Data Editor
File Edit View Data Transform Analyze Graphs Utilities Window Help
1 : var00001
1
Data View
Variable View
SPSS Processor is ready

	var00001	var00002	var00003	var00004	var00005	var00006	var00007	var00008	var00009	var00010	var00011	var00012	agerecod
1	1.00	21.00	2.00	1.00	1.00	3.00	1.00	2.00	.00	33.00	17.00	5.00	2.00
2	2.00	44.00	1.00	3.00	1.00	4.00	3.00	1.00	2.00	10.00	23.00	10.00	4.00
3	2.00	19.00	3.00	1.00	2.00	2.00	1.00	1.00	1.00	27.00	18.00	12.00	1.00
4	2.00	27.00	3.00	2.00	1.00	2.00	1.00	2.00	.00	30.00	17.00	3.00	2.00
5	1.00	57.00	2.00	1.00	3.00	2.00	3.00	1.00	4.00	22.00	.00	15.00	5.00
6	2.00	27.00	3.00	1.00	1.00	3.00	1.00	1.00	3.00	34.00	17.00	.00	2.00
7	1.00	39.00	5.00	2.00	1.00	5.00	1.00	1.00	5.00	17.00	48.00	10.00	3.00
8	2.00	36.00	3.00	1.00	2.00	2.00	2.00	1.00	1.00	25.00	18.00	7.00	3.00
9	1.00	37.00	2.00	1.00	1.00	3.00	1.00	2.00	.00	34.00	15.00	.00	3.00
10	2.00	51.00	2.00	2.00	2.00	4.00	3.00	2.00	.00	16.00	18.00	11.00	5.00
11	1.00	24.00	5.00	2.00	1.00	3.00	1.00	1.00	1.00	.00	42.00	16.00	2.00
12	2.00	29.00	2.00	1.00	2.00	3.00	1.00	2.00	.00	34.00	22.00	12.00	2.00
13	1.00	20.00	5.00	1.00	1.00	2.00	1.00	2.00	.00	22.00	31.00	7.00	1.00
14	2.00	22.00	2.00	1.00	3.00	4.00	2.00	1.00	3.00	37.00	14.00	12.00	2.00
15	2.00	46.00	3.00	1.00	1.00	5.00	2.00	2.00	.00	26.00	9.00	4.00	4.00
16	2.00	41.00	3.00	1.00	2.00	2.00	3.00	1.00	4.00	22.00	7.00	10.00	4.00
17	1.00	25.00	5.00	1.00	1.00	3.00	1.00	1.00	1.00	21.00	29.00	4.00	2.00
18	2.00	46.00	3.00	1.00	2.00	4.00	2.00	1.00	4.00	18.00	8.00	11.00	4.00
19	1.00	30.00	3.00	1.00	1.00	5.00	1.00	2.00	.00	23.00	9.00	6.00	2.00
20	1.00	25.00	5.00	2.00	1.00	3.00	1.00	1.00	1.00	23.00	19.00	.00	2.00
21	2.00	24.00	2.00	1.00	1.00	3.00	2.00	1.00	2.00	20.00	7.00	6.00	2.00
22	2.00	39.00	1.00	2.00	3.00	5.00	1.00	2.00	.00	17.00	.00	9.00	3.00
23	1.00	44.00	3.00	1.00	1.00	3.00	2.00	1.00	2.00	22.00	8.00	5.00	4.00
24	1.00	.00	1.00	2.00	2.00	4.00	2.00	1.00	4.00	15.00	10.00	4.00	.00
25	2.00	18.00	3.00	1.00	2.00	3.00	1.00	2.00	1.00	18.00	7.00	10.00	1.00
26	1.00	41.00	3.00	1.00	1.00	3.00	1.00	2.00	.00	34.00	10.00	4.00	4.00
27	2.00	38.00	2.00	1.00	2.00	5.00	3.00	1.00	2.00	24.00	14.00	10.00	3.00
28	1.00	25.00	2.00	1.00	1.00	2.00	1.00	2.00	.00	48.00	22.00	7.00	2.00
29	1.00	41.00	5.00	2.00	1.00	3.00	1.00	1.00	2.00	17.00	27.00	.00	4.00
30	2.00	30.00	3.00	1.00	1.00	2.00	2.00	2.00	.00	32.00	13.00	10.00	2.00
31	2.00	29.00	3.00	1.00	3.00	2.00	1.00	2.00	.00	31.00	.00	7.00	2.00

When you have finished going through the entire procedure, → **OK**. The toolbar beneath the menu bar allows shortcut access to certain SPSS operations.

Defining variables: variable names, missing values, variable labels, and value labels

Once you have finished entering your data, you need to define your variables. The following steps will allow you to do this:

1. → the **Variable View** tab at the bottom of the **Data Viewer** (this opens the **Variable Viewer** shown in Plate 12.3).
2. To provide a variable name, click on the current variable name (e.g., *var00003*) and type the name you want to give it (e.g., *reasons*). Remember that this name must be no more than eight characters long and you *cannot* use spaces.
3. You next give your variable a more detailed name, known in SPSS as a variable label. To do this, → cell in the **Label** column relating to the variable for which you want to supply a variable label. Then, simply type in the variable label (e.g., **reasons for visiting**).
4. Then you will need to provide 'value labels' for variables that have been given codes. The procedure generally applies to variables that are not interval/ratio variables. The latter, that are numeric variables, do not need to be coded (unless you are grouping them in some way). To assign value labels, → in the **Values** column relating to the variable you are working on. A small button with three dots on it will appear, → the button. The **Value Labels** dialog box will appear (see Plate 12.4). → the box to the right of **Value** and begin to define the value labels. To do this, enter the value (e.g., 1) in the area to the right of **Value** and then the value label (e.g., **relaxation**) in the area to the right of

Plate 12.3

The Variable Viewer

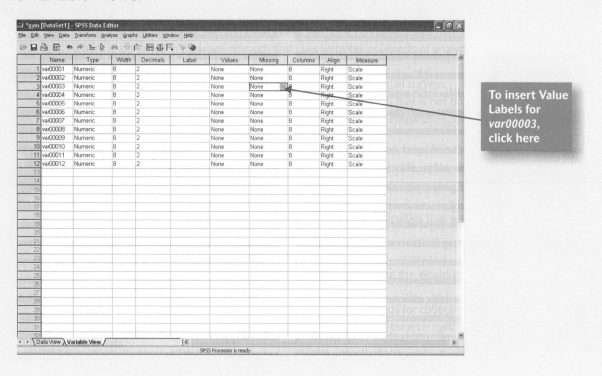

To insert Value Labels for *var00003*, click here

Label. Then → **Add**. Do this for each value. When you have finished → **OK**.

5. You will then need to tell SPSS of the value that you have chosen for each variable to indicate a missing value. In the case of **reasons**, the value is 0 (zero). To assign the missing value, → the cell for this variable in the **Missing** column. Again, → the button that will appear with three dots on it. This will generate the **Missing Values** dialog box (see Plate 12.5). In the **Missing Values** dialog box, enter the missing value (0) below **Discrete missing values:** and then → **OK**.

In order to simplify the following presentation, *reasons* will be the only variable for which a variable label will be defined.

Recoding variables

Sometimes you need to recode variables, for example, when you want to group people. You would need to do this in order to produce a table like Table 23.3 for an interval/ratio variable like *var00002*, which we will give the variable name *age*. SPSS offers two choices: you can recode *age* so that it will be changed in the **Data Viewer**, or you can keep *age* as it is and create a new variable. This latter option is desirable whenever you want to preserve the variable in question as well as create a new one. Since we may want to carry out analyses involving *age* as an interval/ratio variable, we will recode it so that a new variable, which we will call *agegp*, for **age groups**, will be created. The aim of the following operations is to create a new variable, *agegp*, which will comprise five age bands, as in Table 23.3.

Plate 12.4

The Value Labels dialog box

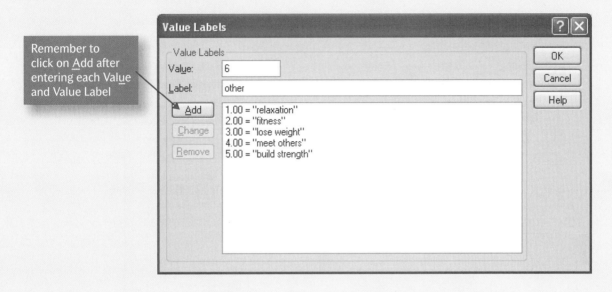

Remember to click on Add after entering each Value and Value Label

Value Labels

Value Labels
Value: 6
Label: other

Add
Change
Remove

1.00 = "relaxation"
2.00 = "fitness"
3.00 = "lose weight"
4.00 = "meet others"
5.00 = "build strength"

OK
Cancel
Help

Plate 12.5

The Missing Values dialog box

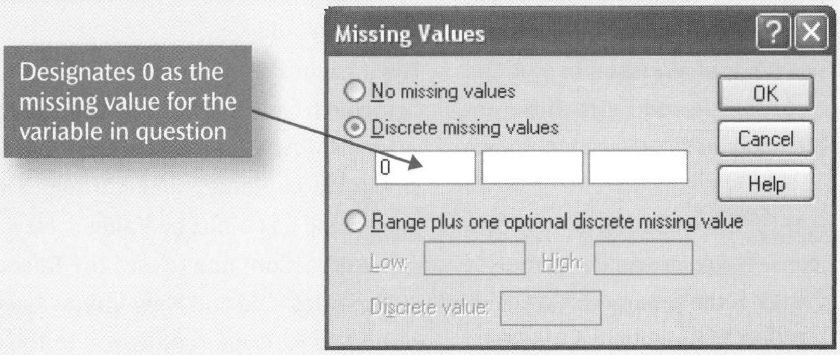

Designates 0 as the missing value for the variable in question

Missing Values

○ No missing values
⦿ Discrete missing values
0

○ Range plus one optional discrete missing value
Low: High:
Discrete value:

OK
Cancel
Help

Plate 12.6

The Recode into Different Variables dialog box

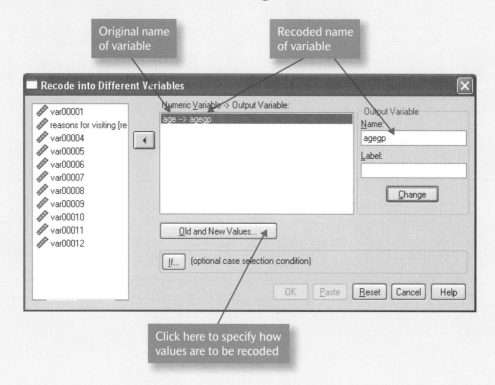

Original name of variable

Recoded name of variable

Click here to specify how values are to be recoded

1. → **Transform** → **Recode** → **Into Different Variables** . . . [opens **Recode into Different Variables** dialog box shown in Plate 12.6]
2. → **age** → ½ button [puts *age* in **Numeric Variable->Output Variable**: box] → box beneath **Output Variable Name**: and type *agegp* → Change [puts *agegp* in the **Numeric Variable->Output Variable**: box] → **Old and New Values** . . . [opens **Recode into Different Variables: Old and New Values** sub-dialog box shown in Plate 12.7]
3. → the circle by **System- or user-missing** and by **System-missing** under **New Value**, if you have missing values for a variable, which is the case for this variable.
4. → circle by **Range, LOWEST through value**: and type **20** in the box → box by **Value** under **New Value** and type **1** → **Add** [the new value will appear in the **Old-> New**: box]

5. → first box by **Range**: and type **21** and in box after **through** type **30** → box by **Value** under **New Value** and type **2** → **Add**
6. → first box by **Range**: and type **31** and in box after **through** type **40** → box by **Value** under **New Value** and type **3** → **Add**
7. → first box by **Range**: and type **41** and in box after **through** type **50** → box by **Value** under **New Value** and type **4** → **Add**
8. → circle by **Range, value through HIGHEST** and type **51** in the box → box by **Value** in **New Value** and type **5** → **Add** → **Continue** [closes the **Recode into Different Variables: Old and New Values** sub-dialog box shown in Plate 12.7 and returns you to the **Recode into Different Variables** shown in Plate 12.6]
9. → **OK**

Plate 12.7

The Recode into Different Variables: Old and New Values sub-dialog box

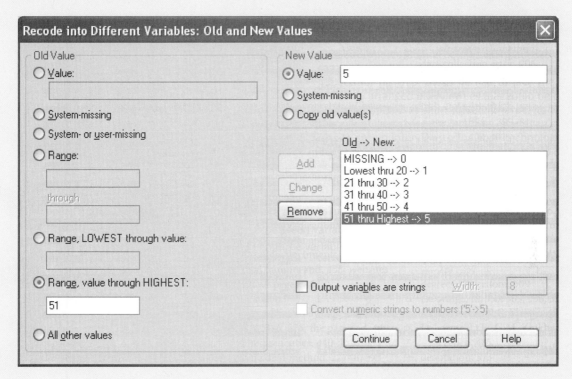

The new variable *agegp* will be created and will appear in the **Data Viewer.** You would then need to generate **value labels** for the five age bands and possibly a **variable label** using the approach described above.

Computing a new variable

A person's total amount of time spent in the gym is made up of three variables: *cardmins, weimins,* and *othmins.* If we add these up, we should arrive at the total number of minutes spent on activities in the gym. In so doing, we will create a new variable *totalmin.* To do this, this procedure should be followed:

1. → **Transform** → **Compute** . . . [opens the **Compute Variable** dialog box shown in Plate 12.8]
2. under **Target Variable**: type *totalmin*

3. from the list of variables at the left, → *cardmins* [puts *cardmins* in box beneath **Numeric Expression:**] → + button; → *weimins* [puts *weimins* after + sign] → + button; → *othmins* [puts *othmins* after + sign]
4. → **OK**

The new variable *totalmin* will be created and will appear in the **Data Editor.**

Now at last, we can begin to analyze the data!

 ## Data analysis with SPSS

Generating a frequency table

To produce a frequency table like the one in Table 23.2:

Plate 12.8

The Compute Variable dialog box

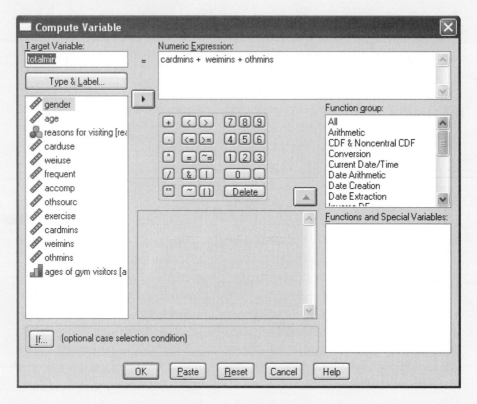

1. → **Analyze** → **Descriptive Statistics** → **Frequencies** . . .[opens the **Frequencies** dialogue box shown in Plate 12.9]
2. → **reasons for visiting** → u button [puts **reasons for visiting** in Variable[s]: box]
3. → **OK**

The table will appear in the **Output Viewer** (see Plate 12.10).

   Note that in the **Frequencies** dialog box, variables that have been assigned labels will appear in terms of their variable labels, but those that have not been assigned labels will appear in terms of their variable names. This is a feature of all dialog boxes produced via **Analyze** and **Graphs** (see below).

Generating a bar chart

To produce a bar chart like the one in Figure 23.2:

1. → **Graphs** → **Bar** . . . [opens **Bar Charts** dialogue box]
2. → **Simple** → **Summaries for groups of cases** → **Define** [opens **Define Simple Bar: Summaries for Groups of Cases** sub-dialog box shown in Plate 12.11]
3. → **reasons for visiting** → ▶ button by **Category Axis** → [**reasons for visiting** will appear in the box] → **N of cases** beneath **Bars Represent** [*if* this has not already been selected, otherwise continue without doing this]
4. → **OK**

Plate 12.9

The Frequencies dialog box

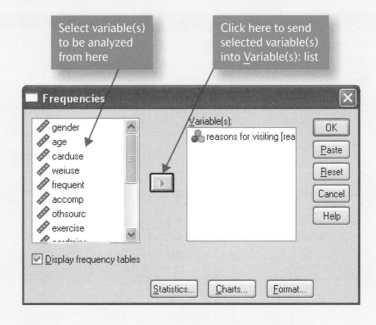

Select variable(s) to be analyzed from here

Click here to send selected variable(s) into Variable(s): list

Generating a pie chart

To produce a pie chart like the one in Figure 23.3:

1. → **Graphs** → **Pie** . . . [opens the **Pie Charts** dialogue box] → **Summaries for groups of cases** → **Define** [opens the **Define Pie: Summaries for Groups of Cases** sub-dialogue box]
2. → **reasons for visiting** → u button by **Define Slices** by: [**reasons for visiting** will appear in the box] → **N of cases** beneath **Slices Represent** [if this has *not* already been selected, otherwise continue without doing this]
3. → **OK**

In order to include percentages, as in Figure 23.3, *double-click* anywhere in the chart in order to bring up the **Chart Editor**. The chart will appear in the **Chart Editor** and the main figure will become opaque. Then → **Elements** and then → **Show Data Labels**. The **Properties**

sub-dialog box will appear (see Plate 12.12). Then to have labels and percentages displayed as in Figure 23.3, rather than frequencies ('counts'), which is the default, place a tick by **Percents** [there should also be a tick by **Text**].

Your chart will be in colour, but, if you only have access to a black and white printer, you can change your pie chart into patterns, which allows the slices to be clearer. This can be done through the **Chart Editor**.

Generating a histogram

In order to generate a histogram for an interval/ratio variable like *age*, → **Graphs** → **Histogram** . . . and then select the relevant variable and place it below **Variable**. This procedure will generate a histogram whose age bands are defined by the software. By double clicking on the diagram, the histogram can be edited using the **Chart Editor**. For example, colours can be changed or patterns inserted.

Plate 12.10

The Output Viewer with Frequency Table

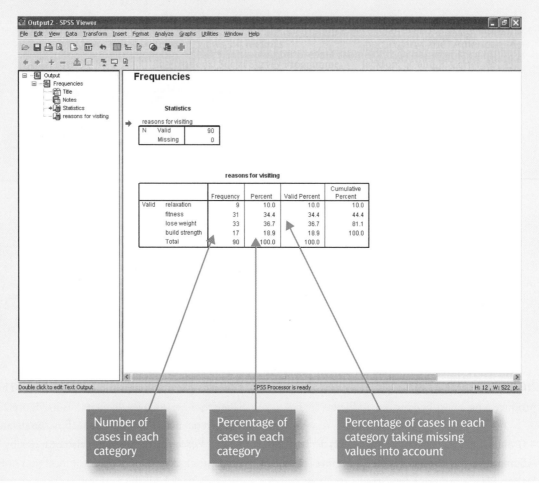

Number of cases in each category

Percentage of cases in each category

Percentage of cases in each category taking missing values into account

Generating the arithmetic mean, median, standard deviation, and range

To produce the mean, median, standard deviation, and the range for an interval/ratio variable like age, the following steps should be followed:

1. → **Analyze** → **Descriptive Statistics** → **Explore . . .** [opens the **Explore** dialog box]
2. → **age** → ▶ button to the left of **Dependent List:** [puts *age* in the **Dependent List**: box] → **Statistics** under **Display** → **OK**

The output will also include the 95% confidence interval for the mean, which is based on the standard error of the mean. The output can be found in Table 12.1. If you select **Plots**, the **Explore: Plots** sub-dialog box will come up and you can elect to generate a histogram. To do this, you will need to select either **Both** or **Plots** under **Display** on the **Explore** dialog box.

Plate 12.11

The Define Simple Bar: Summaries for Groups of Cases sub-dialog box

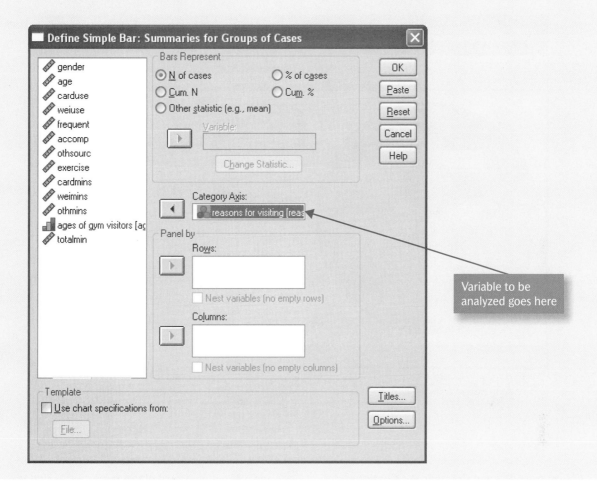

Generating a contingency table, chi-square, and Cramér's *V*

In order to generate a contingency table, like that in Table 23.4, along with a chi-square test and Cramér's V, the following procedure should be followed:

1. → **Analyze** → **Descriptive Statistics** → **Crosstabs** . . . [opens the **Crosstabs** dialog box shown in Plate 12.13]
2. → **reasons for visiting** → ▶ button by **R**<ins>**o**</ins>**w[s]** [**reasons for visiting** will appear in the **R**<ins>**o**</ins>**w[s]:** box] → *gender* → ▶ button by **C**<ins>**o**</ins>**lumn[s]:** [*gender* will appear in the

C<ins>**o**</ins>**lumn[s]:** box] → **Cells** . . . [opens **Crosstabs: Cell Display** sub-dialog box shown in Plate 12.14]
3. Make sure **Observed** in the **Counts** box has been selected. Make sure **Column** under **Percentages** has been selected. If either of these has not been selected, simply click at the relevant point, → **Continue** [closes **Crosstabs: Cell Display** sub-dialog box and returns you to the Crosstabs dialog box shown in Plate 12.13]
4. → **Statistics** . . . [opens the **Crosstabs: Statistics** sub-dialog box shown in Plate 12.15]

Plate 12.12

The Chart Editor and the Properties box for editing a pie chart

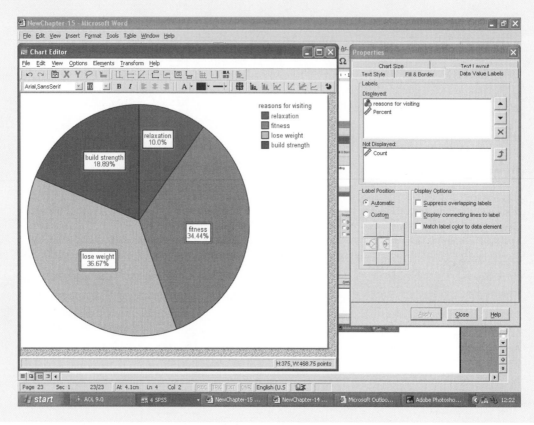

5. → **Chi-square** → **Phi and Cramér's *V*** → **Continue** [closes **Crosstabs: Statistics** sub-dialog box and returns you to the **Crosstabs** dialog box shown in Plate 12.13]

6. → **OK**

The resulting output can be found in Table 12.2.

If you have a table with two dichotomous variables, you would use the same sequence of steps to produce phi.

Generating Pearson's *r* and Spearman's *rho*

To produce Pearson's *r* in order to find the correlations between *age*, *cardmins*, and *weimins*, follow these steps:

1. → **Analyze** → **Correlate** → **Bivariate** . . . [opens **Bivariate Correlations** dialog box shown in Plate 12.16]

2. → **age** → ▶ button → **cardmins** → ▶ button → **weimins** → ▶ button [*age*, *cardmins*, and *weimins* should now be in the **Variables**: box] → **Pearson** [if not already selected] → **OK**

The resulting output is in Table 12.3.

To produce correlations with Spearman's rho, follow the same procedure but instead of selecting **Pearson**, you should → **Spearman** instead.

Generating scatter diagrams

Scatter diagrams, known as *scatterplots* in SPSS, are produced in the following way. Let us say that we want to plot the relationship between *age* and *cardmins*. There is a convention that, if one variable can be identified as likely

Table 12.1 Explore output for age (spss output)

Explore

Case Processing Summary

	Cases					
	Valid		Missing		Total	
	N	Percent	N	Percent	N	Percent
age	89	98.9%	1	1.1%	90	100.0%

Descriptives

			Statistic	Std. Error
age	Mean		33.5955	.94197
	95% Confidence	Lower Bound	31.7235	
	Interval for Mean	Upper Bound	35.4675	
	5% Trimmed Mean		33.3159	
	Median		31.0000	
	Variance		78.971	
	Std. Deviation		8.88656	
	Minimum		18.00	
	Maximum		57.00	
	Range		39.00	
	Interquartile Range		14.00	
	Skewness		.446	.255
	Kurtosis		−.645	.506

to be the independent variable, it should be placed on the *x* axis, that is, the horizontal axis. Since *age* is bound to be the independent variable, we would follow these steps:

1. → **Graphs** → **Scatter/Dot** [opens the **Scatter/Dot** dialog box]
2. → **Simple Scatter** [usually this has been automatically selected] → **Define** [opens the **Simple Scatterplot** sub-dialog box shown in Plate 12.17]
3. → *cardmins* → ▶ button by **Y Axis:** → *age* → ▶ button by **X Axis:** → **OK**.

A default scatter diagram is shown in Figure 12.1. The scatter diagram can then be edited by bringing up the **Chart Editor**. For example, the type and size of the markers can be changed by clicking anywhere in the chart in the **Chart Editor**. This brings up a **Properties** sub-dialog box that allows a variety of changes to the appearance of the diagram, such as colour and the nature of the points on the plot.

Comparing means and eta

To produce a table like Table 23.5, these steps should be followed:

1. → **Analyze** → **Compare Means** → **Means** . . . [opens the **Means** dialog box shown in Plate 12.18]
2. → *cardmins* → ▶ button to the left of **Dependent List:** → **reasons for visiting** → ▶ button to the left of **Independent List:** **Options** . . . [opens the **Means: Options** sub-dialog box]
3. → **Anova table and eta** underneath **Statistics for First Layer** → **Continue** [closes the **Means: Options** sub-

Plate 12.13

The Crosstabs dialog box

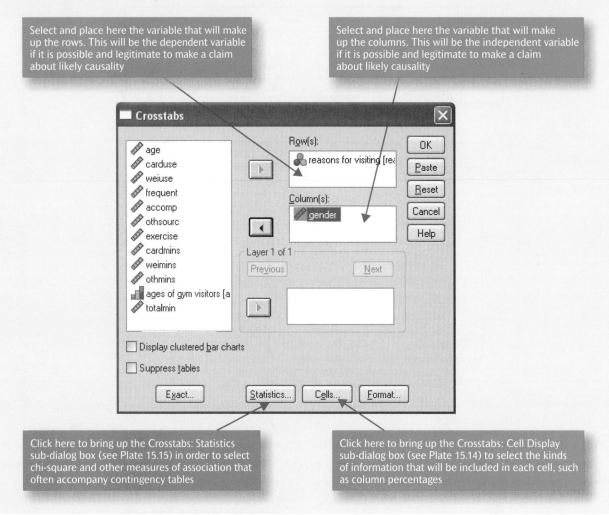

Select and place here the variable that will make up the rows. This will be the dependent variable if it is possible and legitimate to make a claim about likely causality

Select and place here the variable that will make up the columns. This will be the independent variable if it is possible and legitimate to make a claim about likely causality

Click here to bring up the Crosstabs: Statistics sub-dialog box (see Plate 15.15) in order to select chi-square and other measures of association that often accompany contingency tables

Click here to bring up the Crosstabs: Cell Display sub-dialog box (see Plate 15.14) to select the kinds of information that will be included in each cell, such as column percentages

dialog box and returns you to the **Means** dialog box shown in Plate 12.18] → **OK**

Generating a contingency table with three variables

To create a table like that in Table 23.7, you would need to follow these steps:

1. → **Analyze** → **Descriptive Statistics** → **Crosstabs** . . . [opens the **Crosstabs** dialog box shown in Plate 12.13]

2. → *othsourc* → ▶ button by **Row[s]** [**othsourc** will appear in the **Row[s]:** box]

3. → *age3* [this is the name we gave when we created a new variable with *age* recoded into three categories] → ▶ button **by Column[s]:** [*age3* will appear in the **Column[s]:** box] → *gender* → ▶ button beneath **Previous** [*gender* will appear in the box underneath

Plate 12.14

The Crosstabs: Cell Display sub-dialog box

Select this to show the number of cases in each cell in the table

Select to give the percentage of cases of each category of the column variable

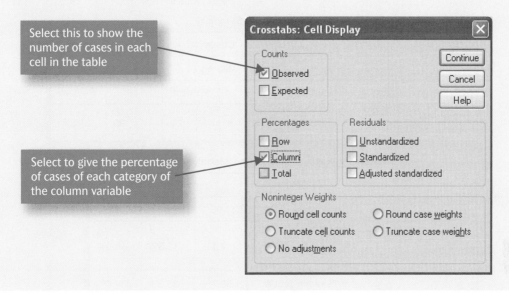

Plate 12.15

The Crosstabs: Statistics sub-dialog box

Select to provide the c² statistic for the contingency table

Select to generate phi and/or Cramér's V

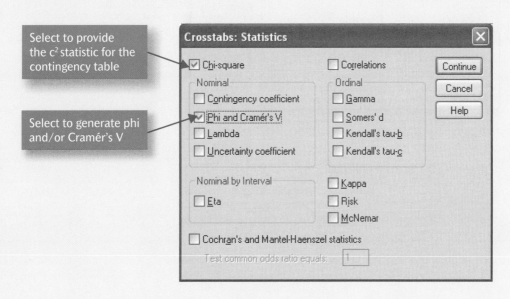

Table 12.2 Contingency table for reasons for visiting by age (SPSS output)

Crosstabs

Case Processing Summary

	Cases					
	Valid		Missing		Total	
	N	Percent	N	Percent	N	Percent
reasons for visiting * gender	90	100.0%	0	.0%	90	100.0%

reasons for visiting * gender Crosstabulation

			gender		Total
			1.00	2.00	
reasons for visiting	relaxation	Count	3	6	9
		% within gender	7.1%	12.5%	10.0%
	fitness	Count	15	16	31
		% within gender	35.7%	33.3%	34.4%
	lose weight	Count	8	25	33
		% within gender	19.0%	52.1%	36.7%
	build strength	Count	16	1	17
		% within gender	38.1%	2.1%	18.9%
Total		Count	42	48	90
		% within gender	100.0%	100.0%	100.0%

Chi-Square Tests

	Value	df	Asymp. Sig. (2-sided)
Pearson Chi-Square	22.726[a]	3	.000
Likelihood Ratio	25.805	3	.000
Linear-by-Linear Association	9.716	1	.002
N of Valid Cases	90		

a. 2 cells (25.0%) have expected count less than 5. The minimum expected count is 4.20.

Interpret the Pearson Chi-Square which is the one whose value is referred to in the text

Table 12.2 *Continued*

Symmetric Measures

		Value	Approx. Sig.
Nominal by Nominal	Phi	.503	.000
	Cramer's V	.503	.000
N of Valid Cases		90	

a. Not assuming the null hypothesis.
b. Using the asymptotic standard error assuming the null hypothesis.

Shows strength of the relationship between the variables

Shows the level of statistical significance of the computed value of Cramér's *V*

Plate 12.16

The Bivariate Correlations dialog box

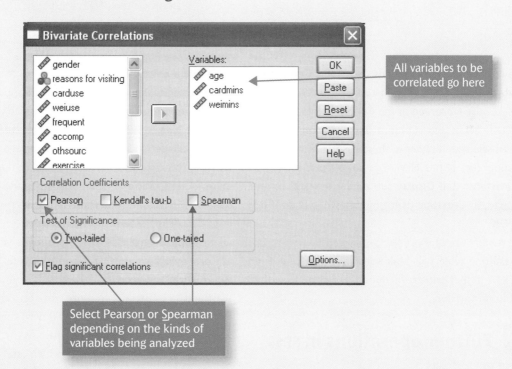

All variables to be correlated go here

Select Pearson or Spearman depending on the kinds of variables being analyzed

Table 12.3 Correlations output for age, weimins, and cardmins (SPSS output)

Correlations

Correlations

		age	cardmins	weimins
age	Pearson Correlation	1	−.109	−.273**
	Sig. (2-tailed)		.311	.010
	N	89	89	89
cardmins	Pearson Correlation	−.109	1	−.161
	Sig. (2-tailed)	.311		.130
	N	89	90	90
weimins	Pearson Correlation	−.273**	−.161	1
	Sig. (2-tailed)	.010	.130	
	N	89	90	90

Correlations of p < 0.05 are 'flagged' with asterisks

**. Correlation is significant at the 0.01 level (2-tailed).

Shows strength of relationship between variables as indicated by Pearson's *r*

Shows level of statistical significance of computed value of Pearson's *r*

Shows number of cases involved in the calculation of a correlation, less any cases for which there are missing values for either or both variables

---

Layer 1 of 1] → **Cells** [opens **Crosstabs: Cell Display** sub-dialog box shown in Plate 12.14]

4. Make sure **Observed** in the **Counts** box has been selected. Make sure **Column** under **Percentages** has been selected. If either of these has not been selected, simply click at the relevant point. → **Continue** [closes **Crosstabs: Cell Display** sub-dialog box and returns you to the **Crosstabs** dialog box shown in Plate 12.13]

5. → **OK**

The resulting table will look somewhat different from Table 23.7 in that *gender* will appear as a row rather than as a column variable.

 Further operations in SPSS

Saving your data

You will need to save your data for future use. To do this, make sure that the **Data Editor** is the active window. Then,

→ File → Save As . . .

The **Save Data As** dialog box will then appear. You will need to provide a name for your data, which will be placed after **File Name:** We called the file 'gym study'. You also need to decide where you are going to save the data, for example, onto a memory stick. To select the destination drive, → **My Computer** in the column to the left and then select the drive and folder into which you want to place your data. Then → **Save**.

Remember that this procedure saves your data *and* any other work you have done on your data, for example, value labels and recoded variables. If you subsequently use the data again and do more work on your data, such as creating a new variable, you will need to save the data again or the new work will be lost. SPSS will give you a choice of renaming your data, in which case you will have two files of data (one with the original data and one with any changes), or keeping the same name, in which case the file will be changed and the existing name retained.

Plate 12.17

The Simple Scatterplot sub-dialog box

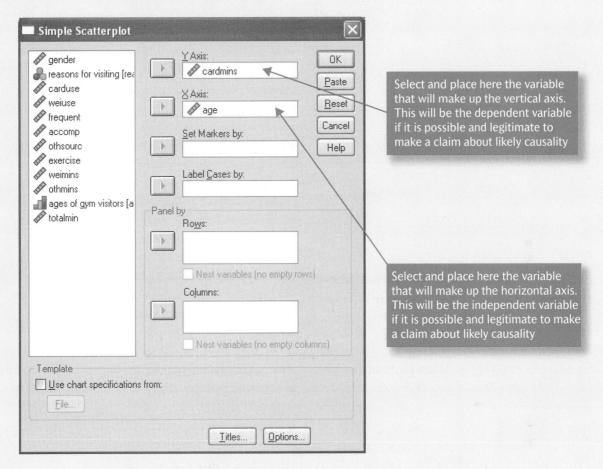

Simple Scatterplot dialog box

Y Axis: cardmins — Select and place here the variable that will make up the vertical axis. This will be the dependent variable if it is possible and legitimate to make a claim about likely causality

X Axis: age — Select and place here the variable that will make up the horizontal axis. This will be the independent variable if it is possible and legitimate to make a claim about likely causality

Retrieving your data

When you want to retrieve the data file you have created,
> → **File** → **Open** . . .

The **Open File** dialog box will appear. You then need to go to the location in which you have deposited your data to retrieve the file containing your data and then → **Open**. A shortcut alternative to this procedure is to → the first button on the toolbar (it looks like an open file), which brings up the **Open File** dialog box.

Printing output

To print all the output in the SPSS **Output Viewer**, make sure that the **Output 1 – SPSS Viewer** is the active window and then
> → **File** → **Print** . . .

The **Print** dialog box will appear and then **OK**. To print just some of your output, hold down the Ctrl button on your keyboard and click once on the parts you want to print. The easiest way to do this is to select all the elements you want in the output summary in the left-hand segment of the **Output Viewer** shown in Plate 12.10. Then

Figure 12.1

Scatter diagram showing relationship between age and cardmins (SPSS output)

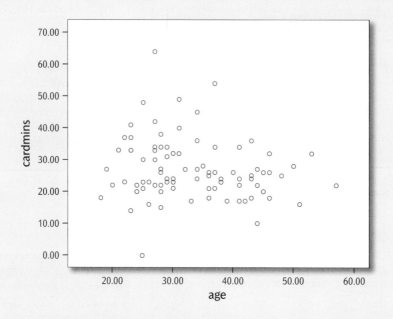

bring up the **Print** dialog box. When the **Print** dialog box appears, make sure **Selection** under **Print Range** has been

selected. The third button on the toolbar (which appears as a printer) provides a shortcut to the **Print** dialog box.

Plate 12.18

The Means dialogue box

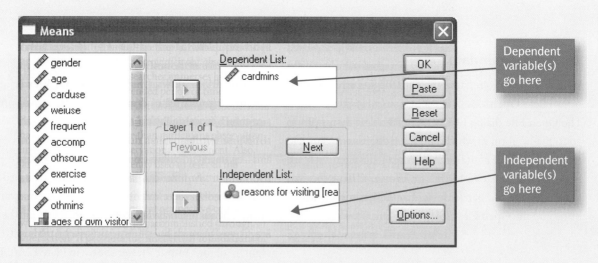

Key points

- spss can be used to implement the techniques discussed later in Chapter 23, but learning new software requires perseverance and at times the results obtained may not seem to be worth the learning process.
- But it is worth it, as it would take you far longer to perform calculations on a sample of around 100 than to learn the software.
- If you find yourself moving into much more advanced techniques, the time saved is even more substantial, particularly with large samples.
- It is better to become familiar with spss before you begin designing your research instruments, so you are aware of difficulties you might have in presenting your data in spss at an early stage.

Questions for review

Getting started in spss

- Outline the differences between: variable names, variable labels, and value labels.
- In what circumstances might you want to recode a variable?
- In what circumstances might you want to create a new variable?

Data analysis with spss

- Using the gym survey data, create:
  - A frequency table for *exercise*.
  - A bar chart and pie chart for *exercise* and compare their usefulness.
  - A histogram for *cardmins*.
  - Measures of central tendency and dispersion for *cardmins*.
  - A contingency table and chi-square test for *exercise* and *gender*.
  - Pearson's r for *age* and *cardmins*.
  - Spearman's rho for *carduse* and *weiuse*.
  - A scatter diagram for *age* and *cardmins*.
  - A comparing means analysis for *totalmin* and **reasons for visiting**.

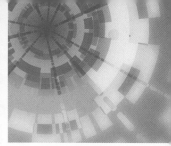

13

Structured
Interviewing

Chapter guide

Once sampling issues have been taken into consideration, the next stage of the survey research process (see Figure 9.1) involves considering whether to administer the questionnaire face to face or to rely on self-completion. This chapter deals with the first option, the **structured interview**.

The structured interview is but one of a variety of forms of research interview, but it is the one that is most commonly employed in survey research. The goal of the structured interview is for the interviewing of respondents to be standardized so that differences between interviews in any research project are minimized. Naturally, this is a reflection of underlying assumptions about the social world, namely a **positivistic** approach. As a result, there are many guidelines about how structured interviewing should be carried out so that variation in the conduct of interviews is small. This chapter explores:

- The reasons why the structured interview is a prominent research method in survey research; this issue entails a consideration of the importance of *standardization* to the process of measurement.
- The different contexts of interviewing, such as the use of more than one interviewer and whether the administration of the interview is in person or by telephone.
- Various prerequisites of structured interviewing, including: establishing rapport with the interviewee; asking questions as they appear on the interview schedule; recording exactly what is said by interviewees; ensuring there are clear instructions on the interview schedule concerning question sequencing and the recording of answers; and keeping to the question order as it appears on the schedule.
- Problems with structured interviewing, including: the influence of the interviewer on respondents and the possibility of systematic bias in answers (known as **response sets**); the feminist critique of structured interview, which raises a distinctive cluster of problems with the method, is also examined.

Introduction

The interview is a common occurrence in social life, because there are many different forms of interviews. There are job interviews, media interviews, social work interviews, police interviews, and appraisal interviews. And then there are research interviews, which represent the kind of interview that will be covered in this chapter and also in Chapter 14. These different kinds of interviews share some common features, such as the eliciting of information by the interviewer from the interviewee and the operation of rules of varying degrees of formality or explicitness concerning the conduct of the interview.

In the business research interview, the aim is for the interviewer to elicit from the interviewee or *respondent*, as he or she is frequently called in **survey research**, dif-

ferent sorts of information: interviewees' own behaviour or that of others, attitudes, norms, beliefs, and values. There are many different types or styles of research interview, but the kind that is primarily employed in positivist research is the structured interview, which is the focus of this chapter. Other kinds of interviews will be briefly mentioned in this chapter but will be discussed in greater detail in later chapters.

The structured interview

The research interview is a prominent data collection method being emphasized in this chapter. The reason why researchers typically prefer structured interviews is

266 Part 3b Methods: Questioning/Discussing

that through the use of the structured interview, standardization of both the asking of questions and the recording of answers is typically employed. Key concept 13.1 examines the virtues of the structured interview from the standpoint of positivist research.

Key concept 13.1: What is a structured interview?

A structured interview entails the administration of an interview schedule by an interviewer. The aim is for all interviewees to be given exactly the same context of questioning. This means that each respondent receives exactly the same interview stimulus as any other.

Reducing error due to interviewer variability

The standardization of both the asking of questions and the recording of answers means that, if the interview is properly executed, variation in people's replies will be due to 'true' or 'real' variation and not due to the interview context. To take a simple illustration, when we ask a question that is supposed to be an indicator of a concept, we want to keep error to a minimum, an issue that was touched on at the end of Chapter 9. We can think of the answers to a question as constituting the values that a variable takes. These values, of course, exhibit variation. This could be the question on skill development and training among employees that was a focus of Chapter 9 at certain points. Employees will vary in the number of training days they receive (see Figure 13.1). However, some respondents may be inaccurately classified in terms of the **variable**. There are a number of possible reasons for this.

Most variables will contain an element of error, so that it is helpful to think of *variation* as made up of two components: true variation and error. In other words: variation = true variation + variation due to error. The aim is to keep the error component to a minimum (see Figure 13.2), since error has an adverse effect on the **validity** of a measure. If the error component is quite high (see Figure 13.3), validity will be jeopardized. The significance for error of standardization in the structured interview is that two sources of variation due to error —the second and fifth in Key concept 13.2—are likely to be less pronounced, since the opportunity for variation in interviewer behaviour in these two areas (asking questions and recording answers) is reduced.

The significance of *standardization* and of, thereby, reducing interviewer variability is this: assuming that there is no problem with an interview question due to such things as confusing terms or ambiguity (an issue that was examined in Chapter 11), we want to be able to say, as far as possible, that the variation that we find is connected with true variation between interviewees and not to variation in the way a question was asked or the

Figure 13.1

A variable

Variation

Tips and Skills

Common sources of error in survey research

1. A poorly worded question.
2. The way the question is asked by the interviewer.
3. Misunderstanding on the part of the interviewee.
4. Memory problems on the part of the interviewee.
5. The way the information is recorded by the interviewer.
6. The way the information is processed, either when answers are coded or when data are entered into the computer.

Figure 13.2

A variable with little error

True variation   Variation due to error

Figure 13.3

A variable with considerable error

True variation   Variation due
to error

answers recorded in the course of the administration of a survey by structured interview. Variability can occur in either of two ways. First, *intra-interviewer variability*, whereby an interviewer is not consistent in the way he or she asks questions and/or records answers. Secondly, when there is more than one interviewer, there may be *inter-interviewer variability*, whereby interviewers are not consistent with each other in the ways they ask questions and/or record answers. Needless to say, these two sources of variability are not mutually exclusive; they can coexist, compounding the problem even further. Given the significance of standardization, it is hardly surprising that some writers prefer to call the structured interview a *standardized interview* (e.g., Oppenheim, 1992) or *standardized survey interview* (e.g., Fowler & Mangione, 1990).

Accuracy and ease of data processing

Like self-completion questionnaires, most structured interviews contain mainly questions that are variously referred to as **closed**, *closed ended*, *pre-coded*, or *fixed choice*. This issue was covered in detail in Chapter 11. However, this type of question has considerable relevance to the current discussion. With the **closed question**, the respondent is given a limited choice of possible answers. In other words, the interviewer provides respondents with two or more possible answers and asks them to select the one or ones that apply. Ideally, this procedure will simply entail the interviewer placing a tick in a box by the answer(s) selected by a respondent or circling the selected answer or using a similar procedure. The advantage of this practice is that the potential for interviewer variability is reduced: there is no problem of whether the interviewer writes down everything that the respondent says or of misinterpretation of the reply given. If an **open** or **open-ended question** is asked, the interviewer may not write down everything said, may embellish what is said, or may misinterpret what is said.

However, the advantages of this type of question in the context of survey research go further than this, as we saw in Chapter 11. One advantage that is particularly significant in the context of the present discussion is that closed questions greatly facilitate the processing of data. When an open question is asked, the answers need to be sifted and **coded** in order for the data to be analyzed **quantitatively**. Not only is this a laborious procedure, particularly if there is a large number of open questions and/or of respondents. It also introduces the potential for another source of error: it is quite likely that error will be introduced as a result of variability in the coding of answers. When open questions are asked, the interviewer is supposed to write down as much of what is said as possible. Answers can, therefore, be in the form of several sentences. These answers have to be examined and then categorized, so that each person's answer can be aggregated with other respondents' answers to a certain question. A number will then be allocated to each category of answer so that the answers can then be entered into a computer database and analyzed quantitatively. This general process is known as coding and was examined in greater detail in Chapter 11.

Coding introduces yet another source of error. First, if the rules for assigning answers to categories, collectively known as the **coding frame**, are flawed, the variation that is observed will not reflect the true variation in interviewees' replies. Secondly, there may be variability in the ways in which answers are categorized. As with interviewing, there can be two sources: *intra-coder variability*, whereby the coder varies over time in the way in which the rules for assigning answers to categories are implemented; and **inter-coder variability**, whereby coders differ from each other in the way in which the rules for assigning answers to categories are implemented. If either (or both) source(s) of variability occur, at least part of the variation in interviewees' replies will not reflect true variation and instead will be caused by error.

The closed question sidesteps this problem neatly, because respondents allocate *themselves* to categories. The coding process is then a simple matter of attaching a different number to each category of answer and of entering the numbers into a computer database. It is not surprising, therefore, that this type of question is often referred to as pre-coded, because decisions about the coding of answers are typically undertaken as part of the design of the schedule—that is, before any respondents have actually been asked questions. There is very little opportunity for interviewers or coders to vary in the recording or the coding of answers. Of course, if some respondents misunderstand any terms in the alternative answers with which they are presented, or if the answers do not adequately cover the appropriate range of possibilities, the question will not provide a valid measure. However, that is a separate issue and one that was dealt with in Chapter 11. The chief point to register about closed questions for the moment is that, when compared to open questions, they reduce one potential source of error *and* are much easier to process for quantitative data analysis.

Relationship of the structured interview to other types of interview

The structured interview is by no means the only type of interview, but it is certainly the main type that is likely to be encountered in survey research and in quantitative research generally. Unfortunately, a host of different terms have been employed by writers on research methodology to distinguish the diverse forms of research interview. Some of the major terms and types of interview are:

- *Structured interview*. See Key concept 13.1.
- *Standardized interview*. See Key concept 13.1.

- *Semi-structured interview*. This is a term that covers a wide range of instances. It typically refers to a context in which the interviewer has a series of questions that are in the general form of an interview schedule but is able to vary the sequence of questions. The questions are frequently somewhat more general in their frame of reference than that typically found in a structured interview schedule. Also, the interviewer usually has some latitude to ask further questions in response to what are seen as significant replies.
- *Unstructured interview*. The interviewer typically has only a list of topics or issues, often called an **interview guide**, that are covered. The style of questioning is usually informal. The phrasing and sequencing of questions will vary from interview to interview.
- *Intensive interview*. This term is employed by Lofland and Lofland (1995) as an alternative term to the **unstructured interview**. Spradley (1979) uses the term **ethnographic** interview to describe a form of interview that is also more or less synonymous with the unstructured interview.
- *Qualitative interview*. For some writers, this term seems to denote an unstructured interview (e.g., Mason, 1996), but more frequently it is a general term that embraces interviews of both the semi-structured and unstructured kind (e.g., Rubin & Rubin, 1995).
- *In-depth interview*. Like the term qualitative interview, this one sometimes refers to an unstructured interview but more often refers to both semi-structured and unstructured interviewing.
- *Focused interview*. This is a term devised by Merton, Fiske, and Kendall (1956) to refer to an interview using predominantly open questions to ask interviewees questions about a specific situation or event that is relevant to them and of interest to the researcher.
- *Focus group*. This is the same as the *focused interview*, but interviewees discuss the specific issue in groups. See Key concept 15.1 for a more detailed definition.
- *Group interview*. Some writers see this term as synonymous with the focus group, but a distinction may be made between the latter and a situation in which members of a group discuss a variety of matters that may be only partially related.

- *Oral history interview*. This is an **unstructured** or **semi-structured interview** in which the respondent is asked to recall events from his or her past and to reflect on them. There is usually a cluster of fairly specific research concerns to do with a particular epoch or event, so there is some resemblance to a focused interview.
- *Life history interview*. This is similar to the *oral history interview*, but the aim of this type of unstructured interview is to glean information on the entire biography of each respondent.

All of the forms of interview outlined above, with the exception of the structured interview and the standardized interview, are primarily used in connection with qualitative research, and it is in that context that they will be encountered again later in this book. They are rarely used in connection with quantitative research and survey research in particular, because the absence of standardization in the asking of questions and recording of answers makes respondents' replies difficult to aggregate and to process. This is not to say that they have no role at all. For example, as we saw in Chapter 11, the unstructured interview can have a useful role in relation to developing the *fixed-choice question*.

 ## Interview contexts

In an archetypal interview, an interviewer stands or sits in front of the respondent asking the latter a series of questions and writing down the answers. However, there are several possible departures from it, although this archetype is the most usual context for an interview.

More than one interviewee

In the case of group interviews or focus groups, there is more than one, and usually quite a few more than one, respondent or interviewee. Nor is this the only context in which more than one person is interviewed. Bell, Taylor, and Thorpe (2001) carried out interviews with two managers in the same company, both of whom had been involved in the implementation of the people-management initiative, Investors in People (IIP). The managers, who had often had different roles in relation to the initiative or been involved with it at different stages of its development, were together able to build a chronological understanding of its implementation. Similarly, in Bryman's research on visitors to Disney theme parks, not just couples but often their children took part in the interview as well (Bryman, 1999). However, it is very unusual for structured interviews to be used in connection with this kind of questioning. In survey research, it is almost always a specific individual who is the object of questioning. Indeed, in survey interviews it is typically advisable to discourage the presence and intrusion of others during the course of the interview. Investigations in which more than one person is being interviewed tend to be exercises in postpositivist qualitative research, though this is not always the case.

More than one interviewer

This is a relatively unusual situation in business research, because of the considerable cost that is involved in having two (or indeed more than two) people to interview someone. Bechhofer, Elliott, and McCrone (1984) describe research in which two people interviewed individuals in a wide range of occupations. However, while their approach achieved a number of benefits for them, their interviewing style was of the unstructured kind that is typically employed in qualitative research, and they argue that the presence of a second interviewer is unlikely to achieve any added value in the context of structured interviewing.

In person or by telephone?

Of course, it is also possible that interviews may be conducted by telephone rather than face to face. While telephone interviewing is quite common in fields like market research, it is less common in business research. In market research opinion has shifted in recent years away from the perception that face to face surveys are more representative than telephone surveys, towards thinking that telephone surveys are either more, or at least, as representative as face to face surveys. This is noteworthy since, as Taylor (1997, p. 429) notes, 'it is not very long since telephone surveys were regarded as a cheap and dirty substitute for face to face interviewing by many survey firms'. See Web Research in focus 13.1 for an example of the use of telephone interviewing. There are several advantages of telephone over personal interviews:

- They are far cheaper and also quicker to administer. This arises because, for personal interviews, interviewers have to spend a great deal of time and money travelling between respondents. This factor will be even more pronounced when a sample is geographically dispersed, a problem that is only partially mitigated for in personal interview surveys by strategies like cluster sampling. Of course, telephone interviews take time and hired interviewers have to be paid, but the cost of conducting a telephone interview will still be lower than a comparable, personal one.

- The telephone interview is easier to supervise than the personal interview. This is a particular advantage when there are several interviewers, since it becomes easier to check on interviewers' transgressions in the asking of questions, such as rephrasing questions or the inappropriate use of probes by the interviewer. In fact, in call centre environments, telephone interviews may be recorded and examined for interviewer consistency.

- Telephone interviewing has a further advantage that is to do with evidence (which is not as clear-cut as one might want) that suggests that, in personal interviews, respondents' replies are sometimes affected by characteristics of the interviewer (for example, class or ethnicity) and indeed by his or her mere presence (implying that the interviewees may reply in ways they feel will be deemed desirable by interviewers). The remoteness of the interviewer in telephone interviewing removes this potential source of bias to a significant extent. The interviewer's personal characteristics cannot be seen and the fact that he or she is not physically present may offset the likelihood of respondents' answers being affected by the interviewer.

Telephone interviewing has certain limitations when compared to the personal interview:

- People who do not own or who are not contactable by telephone obviously cannot be interviewed by telephone. In business research, this characteristic is most likely to be a feature of lower-status employees and, therefore, the potential for sampling bias exists. Lower-income households are more likely not to own

a telephone; also, many people choose unlisted numbers—that is, their telephone numbers do not appear in a telephone directory. Again, these people cannot be interviewed by telephone. One likely solution to this last difficulty is random digit dialing. With this technique, the computer randomly selects telephone numbers within a predefined geographical area. Not only is this a random process that conforms to the rules about probability sampling examined in Chapter 9, it also stands a chance of getting at ex-directory households, though it cannot, of course, gain access to those without a telephone at all. The question of whether response rates are lower with surveys by telephone interview than with surveys by personal interview is unclear, in that there is little consistent evidence on this question, but generally it is believed that telephone surveys achieve lower rates (see Table 22.1).

- Telephone interviewers cannot engage in observation. This means that they are not in a position to respond to signs of puzzlement or unease on the faces of respondents when they are asked a question. In a personal interview, the interviewer may respond to such signs by restating the question or attempting to clarify the meaning of the question, though this has to be handled in a standardized way as far as possible. A further issue relating to the inability of the interviewer to observe is that, sometimes, interviewers may be asked to collect subsidiary information in connection with their visits (for example, whether or not health and safety procedures are made evident at a business premises). Such information cannot be collected when telephone interviews are employed.

- It is frequently the case that specific individuals in households or firms are the targets of an interview. In other words, simply anybody will not do. This requirement is likely to arise from the specifications of the population to be sampled, which means that people in a certain role or position or with particular characteristics are to be interviewed. It is probably more difficult to ascertain by telephone interview whether or not the correct person is replying.

- The telephone interviewer cannot readily employ visual aids such as flash cards from which respondents might be asked to select their replies or to use diagrams or photographs.

Computer-assisted interviewing

In recent years, increasing use has been made of computers in the interviewing process. A large percentage of telephone interviews are conducted with the aid of personal computers, but the reason for their growing use has been that the portability and affordability of 'laptop' computers provides greater opportunity for them to be used in connection with personal interviews. With computer-assisted interviewing (sometimes referred to as computer-assisted personal interviewing [CAPI]), the questions that comprise an interview schedule appear on the screen. As interviewers ask each question, they 'key in' the appropriate reply using a mouse and proceed to the next question. Moreover, this process has the great advantage that, when *filter questions* are asked, so that certain answers may be skipped as a result of a person's reply, the computer can be programmed to 'jump' to the next relevant question. This removes the possibility of interviewers inadvertently asking inappropriate questions or failing to ask ones that should be asked. If the interviewer is out in an organization all day, he or she can either take a disk with the saved data to the research office or transfer the data via email. It is possible that technophobic respondents may be a bit alarmed by their use, but, by and large, the use of computer-assisted interviewing seems destined to grow.

One of us has had personal experience of this technique as a respondent in a market research survey: in this instance the laptop started to beep partway through the interview because the battery was about to expire and needed to be replaced with a back-up. An incident such as this could be disruptive to the flow of an interview and be alarming for technophobic respondents. Finally, the Internet and email communications have introduced a number of further possibilities in terms of the use of computers to facilitate data collection using methods such as interviewing. This issue will be taken up in more detail in Chapter 22, where a detailed comparison of the advantages and disadvantages of face-to-face interviewing, versus other modes of questionnaire delivery, is provided (see Table 22.1).

 ## Conducting interviews

Issues concerning the conduct of interviews are examined here in a very general way. In addition to the matters considered here, there is clearly the important issue of the wording of the interview questions themselves. This area was explored in Chapter 11, since many of the rules of question asking relate to **self-completion questionnaire** techniques like **postal questionnaires** as well as to **structured interviews**. One further general point to make here is that the advice concerning the conduct of interviews provided in this chapter relates to structured interviews. The framework for conducting the kinds of interviewing conducted in qualitative research (such as unstructured and semi-structured interviewing and focus groups) will be handled in later chapters.

Know the schedule

Before interviewing anybody, an interviewer should be fully conversant with the schedule. Even if you are the only person conducting interviews, make sure you know it inside out. Interviewing can be stressful for interviewers and it is possible that under duress standard interview procedures, such as filter questions (see Tips and skills '*Instructions for interviewers in the use of a filter question*'), can cause interviewers to get flustered and miss questions out or even ask the wrong questions. If two or more interviewers are involved, they need to be fully trained to know what is required of them and to be familiar with the interview schedule. Training is especially important in order to reduce the likelihood of interviewer variability in the asking of questions, which is a source of error.

Introducing the research

Prospective respondents have to be provided with a credible rationale for the research in which they are being asked to participate and for giving up their valuable time. This aspect of conducting interview research is of particular significance at a time when response rates to social survey research appear to be declining, though, as noted in Chapter 9, the evidence on this issue is the focus of some disagreement. The introductory rationale may be either spoken by the interviewer or written down. In many cases, respondents may be presented with both modes. It comes in spoken form in such situations as when interviewers make contact with respondents on the street or when they 'cold call' respondents in their homes or at their place of work, in person or by telephone. A written rationale will be required to alert respondents that someone will be contacting them in person or on the telephone to request an interview. Respondents will frequently encounter both forms—for example, when they are sent a letter and then ask the interviewer who turns up to interview them what the research is all about. It is important for the rationale given by telephone to be consistent with the one given by letter, as if respondents pick up inconsistencies they may well be less likely to participate in the survey.

Introductions to research should typically contain the bits of information outlined in Tips and skills '*Topics and issues to include in an introductory statement*'. Since inter-

viewers represent the interface between the research and the respondent, they have an important role in maximizing the response rate for the survey. In addition, the following points should be borne in mind:

- Interviewers should be prepared to keep calling back if interviewees are out or unavailable. This will require taking into account people's likely work and leisure habits—for example, there is no point in calling at home on people who work during the day. In addition, first thing in the morning may not be the best time to contact a busy manager who is likely to be meeting with colleagues and responding to queries.
- Be self-assured that you may get a better response if you presume that people will agree to be interviewed rather than that they will refuse.
- Reassure people that you are not a salesperson. Because of the tactics of certain organizations whose represen-

Tips and Skills

Topics and issues to include in an introductory statement

There are several issues to include in an introductory statement to a prospective interviewee. The following list comprises the principal considerations:

1. Make clear the identity of the person who is contacting the respondent.

2. Identify the auspices under which the research is being conducted—for example, a university or a market research agency.

3. Mention any research funder, or, if you are a student doing an undergraduate or postgraduate dissertation or doing research for a thesis, make this clear.

4. Indicate what the research is about in broad terms and why it is important, and give an indication of the kind of information to be collected.

5. Indicate why the respondent has been selected, e.g., selected by a random process.

6. Provide reassurance about the confidentiality of any information provided.

7. Make it clear that participation is voluntary.

8. Reassure the respondent that he or she will not be identified or be identifiable in any way. This can usually be achieved by pointing out that data are made anonymous when they are entered into the computer and that analysis will be conducted at an aggregate level.

9. Provide the respondent with the opportunity to ask any questions, e.g., provide a contact telephone number if the introduction is in the form of a written statement, or, if in person, simply ask if the respondent has any questions.

These suggestions are also relevant to the covering letter that accompanies mail questionnaires, except that researchers using this method need to remember to include a stamped addressed envelope!

tatives say they are doing market or business research, many people have become very suspicious of people saying they would just like to ask you a few questions.

- Dress in a way that will be acceptable to a wide spectrum of people.
- Make it clear that you will be happy to find a time to suit the respondent.

Rapport

It is frequently suggested that it is important for the interviewer to achieve *rapport* with the respondent. This means that very quickly a relationship must be established that encourages the respondent to want (or at least be prepared) to participate in and complete the interview. Unless an element of rapport can be established, some respondents may initially agree to be interviewed but then decide to terminate their participation because of the length of time the interview is taking or perhaps because of the nature of the questions being asked. While this advice essentially invites the interviewer to be friendly with respondents and to put them at ease, it is important that this quality is not stretched too far. Too much rapport may result in the interview going on too long and the respondent suddenly deciding that too much time is being spent on the activity. Also, the mood of friendliness may result in the respondent answering questions in a way that is designed to please the interviewer. The achievement of rapport between interviewer and respondent is, therefore, a delicate balancing act. Moreover, it is probably somewhat easier to achieve in the context of the face-to-face interview rather than the telephone interview, since in the latter the interviewer is unable to offer obvious visual cues of friendliness like smiling or maintaining good eye contact, which is also frequently regarded as conducive to gaining and maintaining rapport.

Asking questions

It was earlier suggested that one of the aims of the structured interview is to ensure that each respondent is asked exactly the same questions. It was also pointed out that variation in the ways a question is asked is a potential source of error in survey research. The structured interview is meant to reduce the likelihood of this occurring, but it cannot guarantee that this will not occur, because there is always the possibility that interviewers will embellish or otherwise change a question when it is asked. There is considerable evidence that this occurs, even among centres of social research that have a solid reputation for being rigorous in following correct methodological protocol (Bradburn & Sudman, 1979). The problem with such variation in the asking of questions then is that it is likely to engender variation that does not reflect 'true' variation—in other words, error. Consequently, it is important for interviewers to appreciate the importance of keeping exactly to the wording of the questions they are charged with asking.

You might say: 'Does it really matter?' In other words, surely small variations to wording cannot make a significant difference to people's replies? While the impact of variation in wording obviously differs from context to context and is in any case difficult to quantify exactly, experiments in question wording suggest that even small variations in wording can exert an impact on replies (Schuman & Presser, 1981).

Clear instructions

In addition to instructions about the asking of questions, interviewers need instructions about their progress through an interview schedule. An example of the kind of context in which this is likely to occur is in relation to *filter questions*. Filter questions require the interviewer to ask questions of some respondents but not others. For example, the question 'How many days of on-the-job training have you received in the past 12 months?' presumes that the respondent is employed. This option can be reflected in the fixed-choice answers that are provided, so that one of these is a 'not currently employed' alternative. However, a better solution is not to presume anything about respondents' work behaviour but to ask them if they are currently in employment and then to filter out those respondents who are not. A further consideration in relation to this filter question is how many hours or days they are employed for. Tips and skills: '*Instructions for interviewers in the use of a filter question*' provides a simple example in connection with an imaginary study of feedback and job performance. The main point to take from this example is that it requires clear instructions for the interviewer. If such instructions are not provided, there is the risk that either respondents will be asked inappropriate questions (which can be irritating for them) or the interviewer will inadvertently fail to ask a question (which results in missing information).

Question order

In addition to warning interviewers about the importance of not varying the asking of questions and the recording of answers, they should be alerted to the importance of keeping to the order of the questions. For one thing, varying the question order can result in certain questions being accidentally omitted, because the interviewer may forget to ask those that have been leapfrogged during the interview. Also, variation in the order of questions asked may have an impact on how respondents reply, resulting in a source of variability and, therefore, a potential source of error.

Quite a lot of research has been carried out on the general question of question order, but few if any consistent effects on people's responses that derive from asking questions at different points in a questionnaire or interview schedule have been unveiled. Different effects have been demonstrated on various occasions. A study in the United States found that people were less likely to say that their taxes were too high when they had been previously asked whether or not government spending ought to be increased in a number of areas (Schuman & Presser, 1981, p. 32). Apparently, some people perceived an inconsistency between wanting more spending and lower taxes, and adjusted their answers accordingly. However, it is difficult to draw general lessons from such research, at least in part because experiments in question order do not always reveal clear-cut effects of varying the order in which questions are asked, even in cases where effects might legitimately have been expected. There are two general lessons:

- Within a survey, question order should not be varied (unless, of course, question order is the subject of the study!).

- Researchers should be sensitive to the possible implications of the effect of early questions on answers to subsequent questions.

The following rules about question order are sometimes proposed:

- Early questions should be directly related to the topic of the research, about which the respondent has been informed. This removes the possibility that the respondent will be wondering at an early stage in the interview why he or she is being asked apparently irrelevant questions. This means that personal questions about age, social background, and so on should not be asked at the beginning of an interview.

- As far as possible, questions that are more likely to be salient to respondents should be asked early in the interview schedule, so that their interest and attention are more likely to be secured. This suggestion may conflict with the previous one, in that questions specifically about the research topic may not be obviously salient to respondents, but it implies that as far as possible questions relating to the research topic that are more likely to grab their attention should be asked at or close to the start of the interview.

- Potentially embarrassing questions or ones that may be a source of anxiety should be left till later. In fact, research should be designed to ensure that as far as possible respondents are not made uneasy. Nevertheless, with certain topics this effect may be unavoidable.

- With a long schedule or questionnaire, questions should be grouped into sections, since this allows a better flow rather than skipping from one topic to another.

- Within each group of questions, general questions should precede specific ones. Web Research in focus 13.2 provides an illustration of such a sequence.

- A further aspect of the rule that general questions should precede specific ones is that it has been argued that, when a specific question comes before a general one, the aspect of the general question that is covered by the specific one is discounted in the minds of respondents because they feel they have already covered it. Thus, if a question about how people feel about the amount they are paid precedes a general question about job satisfaction, there are grounds for thinking that respondents will discount the issue of pay when responding about job satisfaction.

- During the course of an interview, it sometimes happens that a respondent provides an answer to a question that is to be asked later in the interview. Because of the possibility of a question order effect, when the interviewer arrives at the question that appears already to have been answered, it should be repeated.

However, question order effects remain one of the more frustrating areas of structured interview and questionnaire design, because of the inconsistent evidence that is found and because it is difficult to formulate generalizations or rules from the evidence that does point to their operation.

Probing

Probing is a highly problematic area for researchers employing a structured interview method. It frequently happens in interviews that respondents need help with their answers. One obvious case is where it is evident that they do not understand the question—they may either ask for further information or it is clear from what they say that they are struggling to understand the question or to provide an adequate answer. The second kind of situation the interviewer faces is when the respondent does not provide a sufficiently complete answer and has to be probed for more information. The problem in either situation is obvious: the interviewer's intervention may influence the respondent and the nature of interviewers' interventions may differ. A potential source of **variability** in respondents' replies that does not reflect 'true' variation is introduced—that is, error.

Some general tactics with regard to probes are as follows:

- If further information is required, usually in the context of an open-ended question, standardized probes can be employed, such as 'Could you say a little more about that?' or 'Are there any other reasons why you think that?' or simply 'Mmmm...?'

Tips and Skills

Instructions for interviewers in the use of a filter question

1. Have you received any feedback concerning your job performance during the last 12 months?

   Yes _____

   No _____

   (if No proceed to question 4)

2. (To be asked if interviewee replied Yes to question 1) Who provided you with this feedback?

   (Ask respondent to choose the category that represents the person who most often gives them feedback and to choose one category only.)

   Line manager _____

   Personnel manager _____

   Other _____ (specify) _____

3. How frequently do you receive feedback concerning your job performance? (Ask interviewee to choose the category that comes closest to his or her current experience.)

   Once or twice a week _____

   Once or twice a month _____

   A few times a year _____

   Once or twice a year _____

4. (To be asked if interviewee replied No to question 1) Have you received feedback concerning your job performance at any time during your employment by this organization?

   Yes _____

   No _____

- If the problem is that when presented with a closed question the respondent replies in a way that does not allow the interviewee to select one of the pre-designed answers, the interviewer should repeat the fixed-choice alternatives and make it apparent that the answer needs to be chosen from the ones that have been provided.

- If the interviewer needs to know about something that requires quantification, such as the number of visits to building societies in the last four weeks or the number of building societies in which the respondent has accounts, but the respondent resists this by answering in general terms ('quite often' or 'I usually go to the building society every week'), the interviewer needs to persist with securing a number from the respondent. This will usually entail repeating the question. The interviewer should not try to second-guess a figure on the basis of the respondent's reply and then suggest that figure to him or her, since the latter may be unwilling to demur from the interviewer's suggested figure.

Prompting

Prompting occurs when the interviewer suggests a possible answer to a question to the respondent. The key prerequisite here is that all respondents receive the same prompts. All closed questions entail standardized prompting, because the respondent is provided with a list of possible answers from which to choose. An unacceptable approach to prompting would be to ask an open question and to suggest possible answers only to some respondents, such as those who appear to be struggling to think of an appropriate reply.

During the course of a face-to-face interview, there are several circumstances in which it will be better for the interviewer to use 'flash cards' rather than rely on reading out a series of fixed-choice alternatives. Flash cards display all the answers from which the respondent is to choose and are handed to the respondent at different points of the interview. Three kinds of context in which it might be preferable to employ flash cards rather than to read out the entire set of possible answers are as follows:

- There may be a very long list of possible answers. For example, respondents may be asked which daily newspaper they each read most frequently. To read out a list of newspapers would be tedious and it is probably better to hand the respondent a list of newspapers from which to choose.

- Sometimes, during the course of interviews, respondents are presented with a group of questions to which the same possible answers are attached. An example of this approach is Likert scaling, which is an approach to attitude measurement. A typical strategy entails providing respondents with a series of statements and asking them how far they agree or disagree with the statements.. These are often referred to as items rather than as questions, since strictly speaking the respondent is not being asked a question. It would be excruciatingly dull to read out all seven possible answers ten times. Also, it may be expecting too much of respondents to read out the answers once and then require them to keep the possible answers in their heads for the entire batch of questions to which they apply. A flash card that can be used for the entire batch and to which respondents can constantly refer is one obvious solution.

- Some people are not keen to divulge personal details such as their age or their income. One way of neutralizing the impact of such questioning is to present respondents with age or income bands with a letter or number attached to each band. They can then be asked to say which letter applies to them. This procedure will obviously not be appropriate if the research requires exact ages or incomes.

Leaving the interview

Do not forget common courtesies like thanking respondents for giving their time. However, the period immediately after the interview is one in which some care is necessary in that sometimes respondents try to engage the interviewer in a discussion about the purpose of the interview. Interviewers should resist elaboration beyond their standard statement, because respondents may communicate what they are told to others, which may bias the findings.

Training and supervision

On several occasions, reference has been made to the need for interviewers to be trained. The standard texts on survey research and on interviewing practice tend to be replete with advice on how best to train interviewers.

Such advice is typically directed at contexts in which a researcher hires an interviewer to conduct a large amount of or even all the interviews. It also has considerable importance in research in which several interviewers (who may be either collaborating researchers or hired interviewers) are involved in a study, since the risk of interviewer variability in the asking of questions must be avoided.

For many readers of this book who are planning to do research, such situations are unlikely to be relevant because they will be 'lone' researchers. You may be doing an undergraduate thesis, or an exercise for a research methods course, or you may be a postgraduate conducting research for a Master's thesis or for a PH.D. dissertation. Most people in such a situation will not have the luxury of being able to hire a researcher to do any interviewing (though you may be able to find someone to help you a little). When interviewing on your own, you must train yourself to follow the procedures and advice provided above. This is a very different situation from a large research institute or market research agency, which relies on an army of hired interviewers who carry out the interviews. Whenever people other than the lead researcher are involved in interviewing, they will need training and supervision in the following areas:

- Contacting prospective respondents and providing an introduction to the study.
- Reading out questions as written and following instructions in the interview schedule (for example, in connection with filter questions.
- Appropriate styles of probing.
- Recording exactly what is said.
- Maintaining an interview style that does not bias respondents' answers.

Fowler (1993) cites evidence that suggests that training of less than one full day rarely creates good interviewers.

Supervision of interviewers in relation to these issues can be achieved by:

- Checking individual interviewers' response rates.
- Tape recording at least a sample of interviews.
- Examining completed schedules to determine whether any questions are being left out or if they are being completed properly.
- Call backs on a sample of respondents (usually around 10%) to determine whether or not they were interviewed and to ask about interviewers' conduct.

 ## Other approaches to structured interviewing

A number of other methods or techniques are used in business and management research as part of either the structured or the semi-structured interview. Four main types will be discussed in this section:

- Critical incident method.
- Projective methods, pictorial, and photo elicitation.
- Verbal protocol approach.
- Repertory grid technique.

We have grouped these four methods together here because they can form part of a structured interview. However, they can also form part of a semi-structured interview (see Chapter 14) in a qualitative investigation. They are sometimes used as one part of an interview, in combination with other questions that form part of a more conventional interview schedule, or in other research designs they form the basis for the entire interview. A further use of these methods is to check findings from more conventional quantitative approaches such as structured interviews or questionnaire surveys.

Critical incident method

This method involves asking respondents to describe **critical incidents**, which are defined very broadly by Flanagan (1954) as any observable human activity where the consequences are sufficiently clear as to leave the observer with a definite idea as to their likely effects. The term is derived from the analysis of near-disaster situations, where a version of the technique can be used to build up a picture of the events that contribute to a potential disaster and to develop a plan of action for dealing with them. The most common use of critical incident method involves interviewing respondents about particular types of event or behaviour in order to develop an understanding of their sequence and their significance to the individual.

One of the earliest and most well-known illustrations of this method in management research is the study by Herzberg, Mausner, and Snyderman (1959). The authors explain: 'We decided to ask people to tell us stories about times when they felt exceptionally good or bad about their jobs. We decided that from these stories we could discover the kinds of situations leading to negative or positive attitudes toward the job and the effects of these attitudes' (1959, p. 17). Their initial interview strategy was followed up by a series of probe questions that filled in missing information in the spontaneously told accounts. **Content analysis** (see Chapter 18) was then used to focus on exploring the essential features of the critical incident in order to reveal the values that they reflected. A more recent example of the use of critical incident method is found in the study of self-managing work teams described in Research in focus 13.1.

Projective methods, pictorial, and photo elicitation

Projective methods classically involve the presentation of ambiguous stimuli to individuals, which are interpreted by the researcher to reveal underlying characteristics of the individual concerned. A common example is the Rorschach inkblot test, where respondents are asked to describe random inkblots. Analysis relies on expert psychological interpretation of the way that respondents have described the inkblots and this is suggested to be indicative of their dominant channels of thinking. Another form of projective analysis involves the 'sentence completion test', where the individual is asked to complete a number of unfinished sentences; this technique has been

13.1 Research in Focus

An example of the critical incident method

Urch, Druskat, and Wheeler (2003) used the critical incident technique in interviews with self-managing work team leaders and team members as part of a mixed-method case study. Their research site was a Fortune 500 durable consumer goods manufacturing plant in the mid-western United States with 3500 employees that had introduced self-managing work teams five years previously. The critical incident interview technique involved 'asking interviewees to alternate between describing incidents on the job in which they felt effective and incidents in which they felt ineffective' (2003, p. 440). The role of the interviewer in this context is to 'obtain detailed descriptions of events while remaining as unobtrusive as possible in order to avoid leading interviewees' (2003, p. 440). The questions consisted of the following:

- What led up to the event?
- Who did and said what to whom?
- What happened next?
- What were you thinking and feeling at that moment?
- What was the outcome?

To enhance the validity and reliability of the critical incident interviews, events were limited to those that had happened within approximately the last year. The kinds of events that respondents recalled included specific team meetings, production or equipment changes, and times when production goals were met or times when they were not met due to adverse conditions.

used in the context of recruitment and selection, often as an assessment centre exercise.

One of the best-known examples of the use of **projective techniques** in management research involves the study by McClelland (1961) of leadership and the need for individual achievement. Informed by experimental psychology and the psychoanalytic insights of Freud, McClelland's study involved stimulating the achievement motive in a group of subjects. He then sought to elicit their 'spontaneous thoughts' and fantasies in order to determine the effect of achievement motivation. The subjects were male college students who were told that they were going to be tested to determine their intelligence and leadership ability; it was assumed that this would arouse a desire in the subjects to do well. After the 'tests' were completed, subjects were asked to write short, five-minute stories suggested by pictures that flashed onto a screen for a few seconds. 'The pictures represented a variety of life situations centering particularly around work' (1961, p. 40). The stories were compared with those that had been written by a control group under normal conditions. The experimental group was found to refer more often in their stories to ideas related to achievement. From this, McClelland concluded that, if someone 'in writing his stories consistently uses achievement-related ideas of the same kind as those elicited in everyone under achievement "pressure", then he would appear to be someone with a "bias", a "concern", or a "need" for achievement' (1961, p. 43). This led him to develop a score for the need for achievement, defined as the number of achievement-related ideas in stories written by an individual under normal conditions.

 A more recent example of projective methods can also be found in advertising research (see Web Research in focus 13.3). Using a range of methods including collage, storytelling, sentence completion, and word associations, the authors of this study sought to investigate the nature of consumer desire among students in three countries. However, the use of projective methods is relatively uncommon in business and management research. They have largely been superseded by the use of visual techniques to stimulate creative thinking, problem solving, and to explore feelings, emotions, and values. For example, Stiles

(2004) asked members of UK and North American business schools to express how they saw their organization's identity by drawing pictures (see Research in focus 13.2). The use of *photo elicitation* can also be seen as an adaptation of projective methods.

Verbal protocol approach

This technique builds on the work of Newell and Simon (1972) in the area of human problem solving and has since been used in relation to a number of topics that are relevant to business and management researchers. The approach involves asking respondents to 'think aloud' while they are performing a task. The idea is to elicit the respondent's thought processes while they are making a decision or judgement or solving a problem. The subject's account of what they are doing and why is usually recorded and transcribed and then content analyzed using a coding scheme that is used to discern different categories of thinking.

Repertory grid technique

Repertory grid technique is based on Kelly's (1955) personal construct theory and it is used to identify the *interpretative* processes whereby an individual constructs meaning in relation to his or her social context. The theory portrays the individual as a scientist, striving to make sense of his or her environment in order to predict and cope with future events. Kelly claimed that sensemaking occurs through an individual's personal *construct* system, which provides an order for dealing with incoming information. This system is composed of a series of interlinked and hierarchically related constructs, which are the bipolar sorting mechanisms that distinguish between similarity and dissimilarity for a given event. In order to make sense of an event, the individual must assign information to either one pole of the construct or the other. The researcher's task, therefore, involves identifying the constructs that people use to make

> **Key concept 13.2: What is photo elicitation?**
>
> This method involves integrating photographs into the interview by asking the respondent questions about photographs that the researcher has taken of the research setting.

13.2   Research in Focus

Using pictorial exercises in a study of business school identity

Stiles (2004) used pictorial methods in a study of strategy in UK and North American business schools. The first stage of the research involved asking individual interviewees to imagine their organization as having a personality and then asking them to draw a picture of what that personality looks like. The second stage of the research involved flashing these drawings to members of a focus group who are invited to reach a consensus in choosing five pictures, ranging from an unfavourable depiction of the organization, to neutral, through to a favourable one. 'The group then produces a composite free-drawn personality image of its own' (2004, p. 130). The focus group discussion was videotaped and transcribed. The importance of the pictures stems from the discussion that respondents had around their selection decisions, which revealed insights into the way academics perceived the management styles associated with their organizations and leaders. Stiles notes that although this study was conducted in a business school setting, it could equally be applied in relation to a variety of other organizational settings. Stiles concludes that the pictorial exercises revealed constructs that were not identified using verbal research instruments, thus introducing the possibility that images are useful in revealing more latent perceptions.

---

sense of their world and seeking to understand the way in which a person's thought processes are conditioned by events that they anticipate.

The first stage in developing a repertory grid involves the researcher, sometimes together with the participant, identifying a number of (usually between 6 and 12) *elements*, which are terms or categories that are deemed relevant to the subject of study—they may be persons, events, or objects. These elements are then written on cards and presented to the respondent, typically in groups of three. The researcher then asks questions that encourage respondents to express how they see the relationship between these elements, such as: 'In what way are two similar?' or 'How does one differ?' The process is then repeated with another three cards, until eventually a picture is built up about how the person construes his or her particular context. This procedure, which is known as the *sequential triadic method*, enables the elements to be sorted. These data can then be entered into the grid, which relates elements to the constructs that underlie the individual's rationale for sorting decisions, and the respondent is asked to rank each element in relation to each construct, using a five- or seven-point scale, as illustrated in Figure 13.4.

Repertory grids have been used in the study of strategic management and decision making, and in studies of recruitment, personnel management, and other areas of organizational behaviour. For example, a study conducted by Neil Anderson (1990) explored how the technique could be used in employee selection to assess the task reactions of applicants in a recruitment situation. In this study, it was used to focus on the job-person match for a marketing manager position. An example of a completed grid for a marketing manager applicant, which has been adapted and simplified for our purposes of illustration, is provided in Figure 13.4. The grid illustrates 10 elicited constructs relating to five elements, which in this case are 'present job', 'disliked past job', 'liked past job', 'neutral past job', and 'ideal job'. The participant was presented with these elements in triads and asked to identify two that were alike and to explain what differentiated them from the third element. This process resulted in the generation of a series of constructs, such as 'career opportunities', which the participant used to relate one kind of job to another. The participant was then asked to indicate the preferred pole for each of the constructs he or she had identified, so 'career opportunities' was identified as pre-

Figure 13.4

An example of a repertory grid designed to elicit an applicant's perceptions of preferred job tasks

Construct—emergent pole (1)	Present job	Disliked past job	Elements Liked past job	Neutral past job	Ideal job	Construct—contrast pole (5)
1. Career opportunities*	4	5	2	3	1	No career opportunities
2. Close supervision	4	2	4	3	5	Discretionary*
3. Changeable*	2	5	2	4	1	Fixed
4. Challenging*	1	5	2	4	1	Not challenging
5. Innovative*	2	4	2	3	2	Repetitive
6. Deskbound	5	1	5	4	5	Mobile*
7. No leadership responsibility	4	5	4	2	4	Leadership responsibilities*
8. Administrative work	4	1	4	3	5	Planning work*
9. Enjoyed variety*	2	5	1	3	1	Monotonous/repetitive
10. 'Standing still'	2	2	5	3	5	Career development*

* Denotes preferred pole

Source: adapted from N. Anderson (1990)

ferred to 'no career opportunities'. Finally, the applicant was asked to assess each element against each construct using a five-point scale, with 1 = 'emergent pole' and 5 = 'contrast pole'. As Figure 13.4 illustrates, this managerial applicant has ranked the elements 'ideal job' and 'disliked past job' at opposite ends of these poles, as might be expected. Once the grid is completed, analysis can be either interpretative or statistical in nature. Anderson's use of the technique involved feedback of the results of the analysis to each participant as a basis for counselling and discussion. However, as you will probably by now have gathered, one of the difficulties with using repertory grids is that the technique is quite complex, both for the researcher to use and for the respondent to complete. Some researchers, therefore, suggest that the primary value of repertory grid technique derives from its use as a tool for enabling in-depth discussion and thinking about a topic.

A qualitative application of the repertory grid technique can be found in the study of recruiters' perceptions of job applicants conducted by Kristof-Brown (2000; see

Research in focus 13.3). In this study, semi-structured interviews were used to determine what the recruiters thought about each applicant, but the data generated were analyzed quantitatively in order to gain an impression of the relative importance of each characteristic. This study illustrates a further important aspect of the technique, which is that it requires that participants base their responses on a common set of stimuli. The use of videotaped interviews in this study of recruiters' selection of job applicants meant that all participants were basing their responses on exactly the same set of interviews.

In sum, the repertory grid technique has been used as a supplement and as an alternative to structured interviewing, both as a basis for qualitative exploration and analysis and as a device for generating data that can be statistically analyzed using quantitative methods. For an illustration of some of the potential applications of the repertory grid interview in management and business research you might want to consult the following website: http://www.enquirewithin.co.nz/.

13.3   Research in Focus

An example of the use of repertory grid technique

Kristof-Brown (2000) carried out a study using repertory grid technique to assess whether recruiters form perceptions of an applicant based on:

- the match between the person and the requirements of a specific job; or
- the match between the applicant and the broader organizational attributes.

In the first part of the study, 31 recruiters from four consulting organizations participated in the study. The repertory grid method was chosen because it allowed recruiters to articulate their own criteria for evaluating applicants. The recruiters watched a video recording flashing a series of short mock interviews with job applicants, who were also MBA students, and then they reviewed the applicants' curriculum vitae. This allowed recruiters to view applicants' verbal and non-verbal behaviour, appearance, and interpersonal skills in a realistic setting. After they had watched the video, individual interviews were carried out with each recruiter.

Each person was presented with the details of three randomly selected applicants, and questioned about the degree to which each one matched (a) the job, and (b) the organization. For example, the researcher might ask: 'Comparing applicants four, five, and two, which of these people is the best fit with your company?' After having identified the best-fitting applicant in terms of the person and the job, recruiters were then asked to describe the characteristics of the applicant that had led them to make this choice. The process of presenting three applicants at a time to recruiters was repeated until all applicants had been evaluated and this information could be represented in the form of a repertory grid.

The researchers then coded the data from the interviews to generate a list of 119 characteristics of applicants, which were judged by five independent raters for similarity, resulting in the eventual generation of 62 applicant characteristics. The coders then analyzed the responses from each interview to generate frequency data, including the number and type of characteristics that were reported by each recruiter. The study thus combined qualitative data collection with quantitative analysis of data that were generated using the repertory grid technique.

Problems with structured interviewing

While the **structured interview** is a commonly used method of business research, certain problems associated with it have been identified over the years. These problems are not unique to the structured interview, in that they can also be attributed to similar methods, such as the **self-completion questionnaire** in **survey research** or even **semi-structured interviewing**, often used in **qualitative research**. However, it is common for the structured interview to be a seen as a focus for the identification of certain limitations that are briefly examined below.

Characteristics of interviewers

There is evidence that interviewers' attributes can have an impact on respondents' replies, but, unfortunately, the literature on this issue does not lend itself to definitive generalizations. In large part, this ambiguity in the broader implications of experiments relating to the effects of interviewer characteristics is due to several problems, such as: the problem of disentangling the effects of interviewers' different attributes from each other ('race', gender, socio-economic status); the interaction between the characteristics of interviewers and the characteristics of respondents; and the interaction between any effects observed and the topic of the interview. Nonetheless, there is some evidence that effects due to characteristics of interviewers are evident.

The ethnicity of interviewers is one area that has attracted some attention. Schuman and Presser (1981) cite a study that asked respondents to nominate two or three of their favourite actors or entertainers. Respondents were much more likely to mention black actors or entertainers when interviewed by black interviewers than when interviewed by white ones. Schuman and Converse (1971) interviewed 619 black Detroiters shortly after Martin Luther King's assassination in 1968. The researchers found significant differences between black and white interviewers in approximately one-quarter of the questions asked.

Although this proportion is quite disturbing, the fact that the majority of questions appear to have been largely unaffected does not offer substantial confidence that a consistent biasing factor has being uncovered. Similarly inconclusive findings tend to occur in relation to experiments with other sets of characteristics of interviewers. These remarks are not meant to play down the potential significance of interviewers' characteristics for measurement error, but to draw attention to the limitations concerning the evidence of interviewer based effects. We simply need to be aware that almost certainly the characteristics of interviewers do have an impact on respondents' replies but that the extent and nature of the impact are not clear, likely varying from context to context.

Response sets

Some writers have suggested that the **structured interview** is particularly prone to the operation among respondents of what Webb et al. call '**response sets**', which they define as 'irrelevant but lawful sources of variance' (Webb et al.,1966, p. 19). This form of response bias is especially relevant to **multiple-indicator measures** (see Chapter 5), where respondents reply to a battery of related questions or items, of the kind found in a **Likert scale**. The idea of a response set implies that people respond to the series of questions in a consistent way but one that is irrelevant to the concept being measured. Two of the most prominent types of response set are known as the 'acquiescence' (also known as 'yea saying' and 'nay saying' effect) and the '**social desirability**' effect.

Acquiescence

Acquiescence refers to a tendency for some people consistently to agree or disagree with a set of questions or items. This problem could arise with multiple-item measures in which none of the item measure statements is written in a way that implies an opposite stance. This could be seen as a potential source of bias in this multiple-item measure. A wording that would imply an opposite stance might help to weed out those respondents who were replying within the framework of an acquiescence response set.

Social desirability

The **social desirability** effect refers to evidence that some respondents' answers to questions are related to their perception of the social desirability of those answers. An answer that is perceived to be socially desirable is more likely to be endorsed than one that is not. In order to try to prevent social desirability bias, Jackson (2001) framed the questions in a way that was intended to enable the respondents to distance themselves from their responses, by imagining what a peer might do rather than having to state what they would do. It was expected that this would reduce the likelihood that individuals would respond in a way that they anticipate will be more acceptable.

In so far as these forms of response error go undetected, they represent sources of error in the measurement of concepts. However, while some writers have proposed outright condemnation of social research on the basis of evidence of response sets (e.g., Phillips, 1973), it is important not to get carried away with such findings. We cannot be sure how prevalent these effects are, and to some extent awareness of them has led to measures to limit their impact on data (for example, by weeding out cases obviously affected by them) or by instructing interviewers to limit the possible impact of the social desirability effect by not becoming overly friendly with respondents and by not being judgmental about their replies.

The problem of meaning

A critique of survey interview data and findings gleaned from similar techniques was developed by social scientists influenced by **phenomenological** and other **interpretivist** ideas of the kinds touched on in Chapter 3 (Cicourel, 1964,

1982; Filmer et al., 1972; Briggs, 1986; Mishler, 1986). This critique revolves around what is commonly referred to as the 'problem of meaning'. The kernel of the argument is that when humans communicate they do so in a way that not only draws on commonly held meanings but also simultaneously creates meanings. 'Meaning' in this sense is something that is worked at and achieved—it is not simply pre-given. Considering the problem of meaning in structured interviewing draws attention to the notion that survey researchers presume that interviewer and respondent share the same meanings of terms employed in the interview questions and answers. In fact, the problem of meaning implies that the possibility that interviewer and respondent may not be sharing the same meaning systems is simply sidestepped in structured interview research. The problem of meaning is, therefore, resolved by ignoring it.

The feminist critique

The feminist critique of structured interviewing is difficult to disentangle from the critique launched against positivist research in general. However, for many feminist social researchers the structured interview symbolized more readily than other methods the limitations of quantitative research, partly because of its prevalence but also partly because of its nature. By 'its nature' is meant the fact that the structured interview epitomizes the asymmetrical relationship between researcher and subject that is seen as an ingredient of positivist research: the researcher extracts information from the research subject and gives nothing in return. For example, standard textbook advice of the kind provided in this chapter implies that rapport is useful to the interviewer but he or she should guard against becoming too familiar. This means that questions asked by respondents (for example, about the research or about the topic of the research) should be politely but firmly rebuffed and too much familiarity should be avoided because the respondents' subsequent answers may be biased.

This is perfectly valid and appropriate advice from the vantage point of the canons of structured interviewing with its quest for standardization and for valid and reliable data. However, from the perspective of feminism, when women interview women, a wedge is hammered between them that, in conjunction with the implication of a hierarchical relationship between the interviewer and respondent, is incompatible with its values. An impression of exploitation is created, but exploitation of women is precisely what feminist social science seeks to fight against. Hence Cotterill (1992) claims the methods that feminists adopt are crucially important in developing an understanding of women that relies on breaking down the artificial split between the researcher and the researched. According to Oakley (1981), this entails the interviewer investing her own personal identity in the research relationship, by answering questions, giving support, and sharing knowledge and experience in a way that can lead to long-term friendships with interviewees. Oakley's point is that to act according to the canons of textbook practice would be impossible for a feminist in such a situation. It was this kind of critique of structured interviewing, and indeed of positivist research in general, that ushered in a period in which a great many feminist social researchers found qualitative, indeed postpositivist, research more compatible with their goals and norms. In terms of interviewing, this trend resulted in a preference for forms of interviewing such as unstructured and semi-structured interviewing and focus groups. These will be the focus of later chapters.

Key points

- The **structured interview** is a research instrument that is used to standardize the asking and often the recording of answers in order to keep interviewer-related error to a minimum.
- It can be administered in person or over the telephone.
- It is important to keep to the wording and order of questions when conducting **social survey research** by structured interview.

- While there is some evidence that interviewers' characteristics can influence respondents' replies, the findings of experiments on this issue are somewhat equivocal.
- **Response sets** can be damaging to data derived from structured interviews and steps need to be taken to identify respondents exhibiting them.
- The structured interview symbolizes the characteristics of **quantitative** research that feminist researchers find distasteful: in particular, the lack of reciprocity and the taint of exploitation.

Questions for review

The structured interview

- Why is it important in interviewing for survey research to keep interviewer **variability** to a minimum?
- How successful is the structured interview in reducing interviewer variability?
- Why might a survey researcher prefer to use a structured rather than an unstructured interview approach for gathering data?
- Why do structured interview schedules typically include mainly closed questions?

Interview contexts

- Are there any circumstances in which it might be preferable to conduct structured interviews with more than one interviewer?
- 'Given the lower cost of telephone interviews as against personal interviews, the former are generally preferable'. Discuss.

Conducting interviews

- Prepare an opening statement for a study of manual workers in a firm in which access has already been achieved.
- To what extent is rapport an important ingredient of structured interviewing?
- How strong is the evidence that question order can significantly affect answers?
- How strong is the evidence that interviewers' characteristics can significantly affect answers?
- What is the difference between probing and prompting? How important are they and what dangers are lurking with their use?

Other approaches to structured interviewing

- What is the critical incident method and how has it been applied in business and management research?
- Make a list of the projective methods that could be used in a study of organizational culture and consider how they might be applied.
- How might repertory grids be used in qualitative analysis?

Problems with structured interviewing

- What are response sets and why are they potentially important?
- What are the main issues that lie behind the critique of structured interviewing by feminist researchers?

14

Interviewing in Qualitative Research

Chapter guide

This chapter is concerned with the interview in **qualitative** research, specifically **unstructured** and **semi-structured** as opposed to **structured interviews** discussed in Chapter 13. The chapter explores:

- The differences between structured interviewing and qualitative interviewing.
- The main characteristics of and differences between unstructured and semi-structured interviewing; this entails a recognition that the two terms refer to extremes and that in practice a wide range of interviews with differing degrees of structure lie between the extremes.
- How to devise and use an interview guide for semi-structured interviewing.
- The different kinds of question that can be asked in an interview guide.
- The importance of tape recording and **transcribing** qualitative interviews.
- Approaches to sampling in studies using qualitative interviews.
- The significance of qualitative interviewing in feminist research.
- The advantages and disadvantages of qualitative interviewing relative to **participant observation**.

Introduction

The interview is probably the most widely employed method in qualitative research. This is likely due to the fact that it is a fairly flexible method. It can, as will be discussed in Chapter 17, be used as part of ethnographic studies but also in case studies, discourse analysis and narrative analysis (Chapter 20) and as a stand alone method. However, as we shall show, the process of interviewing, transcribing, and analysis of the transcriptions can be time consuming and quite a skill, requiring attention to detail and careful thought about the potential focus and outcomes.

Differences between the structured interview and qualitative research interviews

Qualitative interviewing is usually very different from interviewing in quantitative research in a number of ways:

- The approach tends to be much less structured in qualitative research. In quantitative research, the approach is structured to maximize the reliability and validity of measurement of key concepts. It is also more structured because the researcher has a clearly specified set of research questions that are to be investigated. The

structured interview is designed to answer these questions. Instead, in qualitative research, there is an emphasis on greater generality in the formulation of initial research ideas and on interviewees' own perspectives.

- In qualitative interviewing, there is much greater interest in the interviewee's point of view; in quantitative research, the interview reflects the researcher's concerns. This contrast is a direct outcome of the previous one. For example, Ram (1994) describes his qualitative interviewing style as owing little to the 'textbook' approach, which 'exhorts the interviewer to remain aloof while seeking to extract information from the respondent' (1994, p. 32), as it would have been 'absurd and counter-productive' to assume this degree of social distance from family and friends whom he had known for years.

- In qualitative interviewing, 'rambling' or going off at tangents is often encouraged—it gives insight into what the interviewee sees as relevant and important; in quantitative research, it is usually regarded as a nuisance and discouraged.

- In qualitative interviewing, interviewers can depart significantly from any schedule or guide that is being used. They can ask new questions that follow up interviewees' replies and can vary the order of questions and even the wording of questions. In quantitative research, none of

14.1   Student Experience

Things can go wrong with interviews

It is often the simple things that can go wrong. Take the situation of Melissa. As part of her undergraduate Research Methods course she conducted several interviews. However, when she came to transcribe the interviews she found that there were points in the tape where she could not hear what the person said. Based on this experience she now recommends to other students that they should 'go to the place where the interview is being held and make sure it's quiet in the room'. Otherwise 'if you test [the recorder elsewhere], it could be different than in a smaller room where it echoes more and the sounds are kind of bouncing off the walls and it could have a very different effect. So, not only testing the equipment, but testing it in the environment where the interview's being conducted, that would be helpful as well'.

This is advice is echoed by Mary Runté who, in answer to the question 'What can go wrong with interviews?' answers 'What can't go wrong?':

I had the standard 'forgot the batteries' mistake. Quite funny (in retrospect) as the interviewee ran around his office helping me look for batteries. Did break the ice, at least.

And there were other mistakes I made along the way. On one occasion I left the interview guide in the car. On another occasion there were various interruptions because the interviewee's kid was there, but this couldn't be avoided although it was fun weeding out the kid stuff from the grownup stuff on the transcript!

The funniest thing that happened to me was showing up for the interview (set up by email through a snowball sample) and finding out that the person didn't speak English (They assumed because my last name looks French that I was bilingual.). Finally, I had a participant hit on me during the interview. It was a woman. She kept reaching out and stroking my cheek.

For Jennifer one of the key problems of interviewing is dealing with self-identity management. She feels that in interview situations the self-identity issues: 'definitely plays out . . . For example, I'm quite sensitive about . . . all kinds of power relations. . . [These affected a] situation where I interviewed a person who was in a management position and I wasn't prepared for that and then I started to act in a very stupid way. So it definitely plays out, yes'.

She felt that her first interview could have gone better if she had prepared herself by, among other things, thinking about her own personality and how she would 'feel' in the interview situation: 'I think that the problem with me was probably that I was too nervous, that I was like [that] at least in the beginning'. And she had the sense that her nervousness may have affected her first interview: 'It was with a guy who . . . [was] in a really good position in the company and I was kind of . . . I don't know . . . intimidated by that. And it ended up that I didn't . . . ask all the questions that I wanted to ask maybe, but then later on I kind of relaxed'.

Her advice to those about to embark on interviews is not only to think about the type of questions you will ask but how you will ask them and how you will potentially deal with and feel about the answers: 'I felt that I don't have the nerve in me to go there and ask these people all this personal stuff. That was maybe the thing that I felt a little bit . . . and I was thinking about "What do they expect from me?" and I'm very sure that I did show [my nervousness] in the way I was acting. For example [when I thought about] interviewing the management, I [thought] that they would think "Why does she ask about our own identities instead of . . . asking about the company's [identity]?" I felt a little bit at unease with that'. Jennifer's biggest piece of advice on interviewing is to think through the issues of your identity work before you start the process and find a way of dealing with the potential personality issues that may arise by identifying them in advance.

these things should be done, because they will compromise the standardization of the interview process and hence the reliability and validity of measurement.

- As a result, qualitative interviewing tends to be flexible (see Web Research in focus 14.1 for an example), responding to the direction in which interviewees take the interview and perhaps adjusting the emphases in the research as a result of significant issues that emerge in the course of interviews. By contrast, structured interviews are typically inflexible, because of the need to standardize the way in which each interviewee is dealt with.

- In qualitative interviewing, the researcher wants rich, detailed answers; in quantitative research the interview is supposed to generate answers that can be coded and processed quickly.

- In qualitative interviewing, the interviewee may be interviewed on more than one and sometimes even several occasions. In quantitative research, unless the research is longitudinal in character, the person will be interviewed on one occasion only.

Unstructured and semi-structured interviewing

However, qualitative interviewing varies a great deal in the approach taken by the interviewer. The two major types were mentioned at the beginning of the chapter:

- The almost totally unstructured interview. Here the researcher uses at most a brief set of prompts to deal with a certain range of topics. There may be just a single question that the interviewer asks and the interviewee is then allowed to respond freely, with the interviewer simply responding to points that seem worthy of being followed up. Unstructured interviewing tends to be very similar in character to a conversation. Cox, Wilcock, and Aung (2007, p. 78), for example, in their study of stakeholder decisions and corporate social responsibility, describe the use of in-depth interviews as a 'non-threatening conversation based on the existential-phenomenological method' (see also Colwell, Beckman, &

Cunningham, 2007; Reay, Germann, Hinings, Golden-Biddle, & Casebeer, 2008). See Research in focus 14.1 for an illustration of an unstructured interview style.

- A semi-structured interview. The researcher has a list of questions on fairly specific topics to be covered, often referred to as an interview guide, but the interviewee has a great deal of leeway in how to reply. Questions may not follow on exactly in the way outlined on the schedule. Questions that are not included in the guide may be asked as the interviewer picks up on things said by interviewees. But, by and large, all the questions will be asked and a similar wording will be used from interviewee to interviewee. For example, Foran and Driscoll (2008) carried out semi-structured interviews with people known to be generous donors to charitable organizations. The interviews covered a range of issues around the primary theme of motivation to donate, and asked questions about the types of reasons why people give money to charities. They also asked questions that would help them to pin point 'lessons underlying [the] stories' (p. 41). Data were then coded by thematic units and placed into one of two categories: 'motivation' and 'underlying theme'. From this the researchers were able to develop, what they called, a 'motivational hierarchy' (p. 40). They concluded that 'the difference in generosity between givers will be explained by the two primary motivations of "gratitude" and "helping" others' (p. 45).

In Mary Runté's case the issue was more about the beginning of the process; what needs to be thought about before you begin your interviews:

> I was discussing with a colleague—a trained [quantitative] researcher who wants to now do interviews—about whether to give the questions to the participant ahead of time. He prefers to do so because it would help them 'prepare' and give more thought-out answers. I prefer not to give them ahead of time. In part this is because I don't really ask the questions as they appear on the interview guide, but more because the last thing I want is the 'prepared' answer where you just get the party line. I want the spontaneous, almost visceral reaction to a question. I think that this reflects the difference in our

An example of unstructured interviewing

Wallace (2009) discusses the problem of doing a 'non-directive', or unstructured, interview. She interviewed 13 female Chartered Accountants (CA) at various stages of their career. Wallace was interested in the women's decision-making throughout their careers and how this might provide an (existential-feminist) understanding of the career trajectory of women in accounting. Wallace started off with the view that the women were 'narrators with stories to tell and a voice of their own' and that the interview should be a collaborative effort between her and the interviewees. Nonetheless, as she notes, she felt that she had to balance each interview between allowing the interviewees to find their voice while ensuring that her own interest in women CAs' career trajectory was also discussed. Thus, she reflects, she could not

and did not want to shape the outcome of the interviews in advance so began each with a 'grand tour question designed to provide the participants with the opportunity to tell their own story about their career and career choices "on their own terms"' (p. 69). To ensure that some of her questions were answered about what shaped each woman's decisions, Wallace developed several secondary questions based on her own personal and professional experience in the accounting industry. She found that she rarely needed to draw on the secondary questions as each respondent provided a rich account of her life. However, she reflects that 'the phenomenon of anticipating and answering unvoiced questions may be a result of [the women's] professional training' (2009, p. 69).

training as mine was obviously critical and qualitative and his was the Industrial-Organizational Psychology 'give them a survey and run the numbers' type.

In both cases, the interview process is *flexible*. Also, the emphasis must be on how the interviewee frames and understands issues and events—that is, what the interviewee views as important in explaining and understanding events, patterns, and forms of behaviour. Thus, Leidner (1993) describes the interviewing she carried out in a McDonald's restaurant as involving a degree of structure, but adds that the interviews also 'allowed room to pursue topics of particular interest to the workers' (1993, p. 238). Milkman (1997), in her study of auto workers at General Motors, describes how in the second stage of her research she interviewed a total of 30 buyout takers and workers, using a 'very general interview guide', trying to be as casual as she could, and never discouraging anyone from going off on tangents. Most interviews were with individuals. However, in a few cases workers invited their friends from the plant as well. Milkman claims that 'these turned out to be among the best interviews, since they developed a group dynamic in which my presence often became marginal' (1997, p. 198). In an interview study

of secretarial work involving almost 500 office workers, Pringle (1988) followed an oral history format. She explains: We did not restrict the subject matter to work. Initially people were asked to start by talking about a typical day . . . Over time, our interests shifted or became more focused on the relation between different parts of their lives, on home and family, and their views on a range of political and social issues, and on their notions of a "good boss" and "good secretary"'. (1988, p. 270)

Once again, we must remember that qualitative research is *not* quantitative research with the numbers missing. The kinds of interviewing carried out in qualitative research are typical also of **life history** and **oral history** interviewing (see Key concept 14.1).

The two different types of interviews in qualitative research are extremes and there is quite a lot of variability between them, but most qualitative interviews are close to one type or the other. In neither case does the interviewer slavishly follow a schedule, as is done in quantitative research interviewing; but in semi-structured interviews the interviewer does follow a script to a certain extent. The choice of whether to veer towards one type rather than the other is likely to be affected by a variety of factors:

14.2 # Student Experience

The challenge of interviews

Interviews can be challenging in a number of ways. For Margaret McKee, it was how to make sense of the unexpected:

> As part of my doctoral research, I conducted in-depth interviews with a group of individuals who had taken part in a leadership training initiative. I wanted to explore their experiences of participating in the training and implementing their learning on the job. Since the training had been done in waves, I interviewed people anywhere from three to twelve months after their training's completion. In my first couple of interviews, people had real difficulty recalling what they had learned, even though they were quite able to talk about what they had done in terms of training implementation. I remember leaving those first few interviews feeling deflated about the success of the training and even a little panicked that the interviews weren't eliciting the kinds of responses I had hoped for. When I finally finished all the interviews and started analyzing my data, I saw that this pattern existed across my interviews. It struck me then that this was an interesting and perfectly reasonable finding. My training participants remembered what was most important to them—that is their training goals—and not necessarily what I thought was important. It taught me that it is important to trust in the interview process and my participants, and not to be too concerned with my own ideas and expectations.

- If it is important to the researcher to gain a genuine understanding of the world views of members of a social setting or of people sharing common attributes, an unstructured interviewing approach may be preferable. With a more unstructured approach, the researcher is less likely to come at participants' worldviews with presuppositions or expectations and is more likely to see things as the participants see them.

- If the researcher is beginning the investigation with a fairly clear focus, rather than a very general notion of wanting to do research on a topic, it is likely that the interviews will be semi-structured ones, so that the more specific issues can be addressed. More structure is also likely to be imposed when the researcher has a clear idea of how the data will be analyzed. In the case of using interviews to generate data about critical incidents (see Web Research in focus 14.2), a set of subject themes can be used to guide respondents who are asked to recall examples of specific events that illustrate each theme.

- If more than one person is to carry out the fieldwork, in order to ensure a modicum of comparability of interviewing style, it is likely that semi-structured interviewing will be preferred.

- If you are doing multiple-case-study research, you are likely to find that you will need some structure in order to ensure cross-case comparability. Certainly, all Bryman's qualitative research on different kinds of organization has entailed semi-structured interviewing and it is not a coincidence that this is because most of it has been multiple-case-study research (e.g., Bryman, Haslam, & Webb, 1994; Bryman, Gillingwater, & McGuinness, 1996).

In business and management research there are some additional considerations that relate to qualitative interviewing. Interviewing managers often raises specific issues; the status and power held, particularly at a senior level, mean that gaining access to this group of people can be extremely difficult, and arranging a mutually convenient time in which to conduct an interview, which may last several hours, even more so. Given the number of outside requests for information and assistance that most managers receive, it is particularly important

Tips and Skills

Where to conduct an interview?

Finding a quiet, private space in which to conduct an interview uninterrupted can be one of the most difficult tasks for the qualitative researcher. Many organizations will struggle to find you a spare room that is not being used and is even remotely suitable. Think carefully before agreeing to interview someone in their own office; are there likely to be frequent telephone calls or interruptions that make the interview difficult? Also, traffic, aircraft, or machinery can contribute to background noise that can make the tape-recorded speech inaudible. It is a good idea to spend some time in the room prior to the interview; do a speech recording to test the acoustics of the room and carefully position the furniture; if there is noise from outside the room, think about closing doors or windows. Similarly, you may wish to turn off a noisy heater. Position the microphone as near to your interviewees as possible and make sure that they are unlikely to knock it. You will, of course, need to balance these issues against the comfort and convenience of your interviewee (it would not be feasible to insist on having all the windows closed in a hot factory in the middle of summer!). But do not be afraid to explain what you need in order to conduct the interview, even though you may have to be prepared to compromise when it comes to actually getting it.

Key concept 14.1a: The life history interview

invites the subject to look back in detail across his or her entire life course (Palmer, 2010); a kind of unstructured interview covering the totality of an individual's life.

Key concept 14.1b: The oral history interview

is usually somewhat more specific in tone in that the subject is asked to reflect upon specific events or periods in the past. Like life histories, it is sometimes combined with other sources, such as documents.

to structure a request for interview in a way that is most likely to lead to a favourable response. A request for interview may be made either by letter or by telephone. Healey and Rawlinson (1993) recommend a dual approach: first make a telephone call, 'fishing' for a named person who is most likely to be appropriate for the interview, then follow this up with an introductory letter. In the letter, it may be appropriate to enclose a short outline of the nature and purpose of the project and an indication of how the findings might be useful to the respondent.

If the research is supported by a high-profile sponsoring organization (e.g., a company or university business school) it may be worth enclosing a letter from a senior person within this organization endorsing the aims of the research. Finally, a telephone call made a few days after receipt of the letter can provide an opportunity for the researcher to deal with any queries the manager may have. The most important thing to remember, however, is that 'polite persistence' is often crucial (Healey & Rawlinson, 1993).

Interviewing within organizations also involves encroaching on an individual's work time and in some cases it may not be possible to take people away from their work during the hours of their employment. Managers may be unwilling to grant lower-level employees the time away from productive activity that is needed to conduct an interview, or there may simply be no one available to cover their duties. When employees are paid on an hourly basis, this becomes a particularly important issue. For example, in her research into work roles in restaurants, Elaine Hall (1993) wanted to interview a sample of the servers (waiters and waitresses) who worked in the five selected restaurants. To do this, she had to approach servers on duty to schedule individual interviews for off-duty times, usually before or after their work shift. This relied on servers' willingness to devote an hour of their unpaid time to this task.

However, sometimes managers demonstrate a willingness to enable the interview process despite the cost implications. For example, Carroll, Mills, and Helms Mills (2008) found that a number of call centre managers were willing to allow on-site interviewing of employees despite the fact that this involved a cost to the company in lost time.

Tips and Skills

Multiple interviewers

Bechhofer, Elliott, and McCrone (1984) claim there are certain advantages to having more than one interviewer to interview each respondent. In their study, this nearly always meant having two interviewers but in one instance three interviewers were involved. They explain: 'After the customary introductory pleasantries and opening remarks, one person would take up the interview, making only brief notes as it went on. The other would take extensive notes, carefully observe the reactions of the respondent and the other interviewer, nod sagely from time to time, or grunt in the way of interviewers. The "passive" interviewer could thus assess the overall development of the interview, keep an eye on topics to be covered, and await the appropriate moment to take over' (Bechhofer, Elliott, McCrone, 1984, p. 97). The passive interviewer could intervene at any point at which they felt an issue needed to be probed further or when they felt the questioning needed a change of direction. It was also possible for the two interviewers to debate a point between themselves, as a means of drawing the interviewee into the discussion, but with less risk of antagonizing them than if they were the focus of the debate. Finally, the use of two interviewers enables the incorporation of different styles of questioning, as one interviewer can play the 'hard' role in asking difficult questions while the other can play a softer, more supportive one.

The use of multiple interviewers also contributed to a more informal atmosphere, akin to a discussion between three people rather than an exchange between two persons. However, they acknowledge that some respondents might find talking to two interviewers intimidating and that it might be inappropriate for some social groups. They claim it works best 'in what one might call "collegial" situations; a small group carrying out an investigation, doing the interviewing themselves and in constant touch with each other' (1984, p. 98). There are also disadvantages in terms of the time cost involved in having two interviewers attending each interview. They further highlight the importance of sensitivity; both interviewers need to be sensitive to each other, and to be able to read each others' conversational cues and respond to them.

Similarly Carroll et al. (2008) felt that the presence of two interviewers—Carroll and Helms Mills—provided the team the ability to hear different things in the interview setting and to respond accordingly by asking particular follow-up questions. Carroll's direct experience in the industry was felt to help cue her to certain facets of the conversation that an outsider may not have understood. On the other hand, it was felt that she may have been too close to some of the facets and thus not examined what was being said as closely as she might. Also, Helms Mills had some experience 20 years earlier in the nascent call centre world of Air Canada but was new to the now developed call centre industry. While missing some of the nuances it was thought that she was able to pick up things that Carroll may have otherwise missed.

In this particular case Carroll, a former call centre manager herself, was able to draw on her past contacts to gain access to selected call centres to conduct research.

Similarly, Bell et al. (2001) were able to conduct a group interview with employees in one plant because the section manager and his team agreed to cease production for a period of time, in order to allow the interview to take place. However, this is not to suggest that it is only the interviewer who benefits from the interview process. Some interviewees, particularly senior managers, may welcome the opportunity to off-load issues and concerns or think through a problem in a structured way, particularly if they are able to see a copy of the transcript afterwards. In these instances the interview is very much a two-way process, with both parties gaining something beneficial from it.

Preparing an interview guide

The idea of an interview guide is much less specific than the notion of a structured interview schedule. In fact, the term can be employed to refer to the brief list of memory prompts of areas to be covered that is often employed in unstructured interviewing or to the somewhat more structured list of issues to be addressed or questions to be asked in semi-structured interviewing. Moreover, an interview guide does not necessarily have to comprise written words; instead it can take the form of a series of visual prompts related to a subject (see Web Research in focus 14.3). Researchers may offer to provide a copy of the interview guide or schedule to interested readers on request. This can help to strengthen the dependability of the research (see Chapter 5). What is crucial is that the questioning allows interviewers to glean the ways in which research participants view their social world and that there is flexibility in the conduct of the interviews. The latter is as much if not more to do with the conduct of the interview than with the nature of the interview guide as such.

In preparing for qualitative interviews, Lofland and Lofland (1995, p. 78) suggest asking yourself the question, 'Just what about this thing is puzzling me?' This can be applied to each of the research questions you have generated or it may be a mechanism for generating some research questions. They suggest that your puzzlement can be stimulated by various activities: random thoughts in different contexts, which are then written down as quickly as possible; discussions with colleagues, friends, and relatives; and, of course, the existing literature on the topic. The formulation of the research question(s) should not be so specific that alternative avenues of enquiry that might arise during the collection of field work data are

closed off. Such premature closure of your research focus would be inconsistent with the process of qualitative research (see Figure 6.1), with the emphasis on the world view of the people you will be interviewing, and with the approaches to qualitative data analysis like grounded theory that emphasize the importance of not starting out with too many preconceptions (see Chapter 24). Gradually, an order and structure will begin to emerge in your meanderings around your research question(s) and will form the basis for your interview guide.

You should also consider, 'What do I need to know in order to answer each of the research questions I'm interested in?' This means trying to get an appreciation of what the interviewee sees as significant and important in relation to each of your topic areas. Thus, your questioning will need to cover the areas that you need but from the perspective of your interviewees. This means that, even though qualitative research is predominantly unstructured, it is rarely so unstructured that the researcher cannot at least specify a research focus.

Some basic elements in the preparation of your interview guide will be:

Tips and Skills

Criteria of a successful interviewer

Kvale (1996) has proposed a very useful list of 10 criteria of a successful interviewer:

- *Knowledgeable*. Is thoroughly familiar with the focus of the interview; pilot interviews of the kind used in survey interviewing can be useful here.
- *Structuring*. Gives purpose for interview; rounds it off; asks whether interviewee has questions.
- *Clear*. Asks simple, easy, short questions; no jargon.
- *Gentle*. Lets people finish; gives them time to think; tolerates pauses.
- *Sensitive*. Listens attentively to what is said and how it is said; is empathetic in dealing with the interviewee.
- *Open*. Responds to what is important to interviewee and is flexible.
- *Steering*. Knows what he or she wants to find out.
- *Critical*. Is prepared to challenge what is said, for example, dealing with inconsistencies in interviewees' replies.

- *Remembering*. Relates what is said to what has previously been said.
- *Interpreting*. Clarifies and extends meanings of interviewees' statements, but without imposing meaning on them.

To Kvale's list we would add the following:

- *Balanced*. Does not talk too much, which may make the interviewee passive, and does not talk too little, which may result in the interviewee feeling he or she is not talking along the right lines.
- *Ethically sensitive*. Is sensitive to the ethical dimension of interviewing, ensuring the interviewee appreciates what the research is about, its purposes, and that his or her answers will be treated confidentially.

- Create a certain amount of order on the topic areas, so that your questions about them flow reasonably well, but be prepared to alter the order of questions during the actual interview.
- Formulate interview questions or topics in a way that will help you to answer your research questions (but try not to make them too specific).
- Try to use a language that is comprehensible and relevant to the people you are interviewing; just as in interviewing in quantitative research, do not ask leading questions.
- Remember to ensure that you ask or record 'facesheet' information of a general kind (name, age, gender, etc.) and a specific kind (position in company, number of years employed, number of years involved in a group, etc.), because such information is useful for contextualizing people's answers.

There are some practical details to attend to before the interview:

- Make sure you are familiar with the setting in which the interviewee works or lives or engages in the behaviour of interest to you. This will help you to understand what he or she is saying in the interviewee's own terms.
- Get hold of a good tape recorder and microphone. Qualitative researchers nearly always tape-record and then transcribe their interviews. This procedure is important for the detailed analysis required in qualitative research and to ensure that the interviewees' answers are captured in their own terms. If you are taking notes, it is easy to lose the phrases and language used. Also, because the interviewer is supposed not to be following a strictly formulated schedule of questions of the kind used in structured interviewing, he or she will need to be responsive to the interviewee's answers so that it is possible to follow them up. A good microphone is highly desirable, because many interviews are let down by poor recording.
- Make sure as far as possible that the interview takes place in a setting that is quiet (so there is no or little outside noise that might affect the quality of the tape recording) and private (so the interviewee does not have to worry about being overheard).
- Prepare yourself for the interview by cultivating as many of the criteria of a quality interviewer suggested by Kvale (1996) (see Tips and skills '*Criteria of a successful interviewer*') as possible.

 After the interview, make notes about:

- How the interview went (was interviewee talkative, cooperative, nervous, well-dressed/scruffy, etc.?).
- Where the interview took place.
- Any other feelings about the interview (did it open up new avenues of interest?).
- The setting (busy/quiet, many/few other people in the vicinity, new/old buildings, use of computers).

These various guidelines suggest the series of steps in formulating questions for an interview guide in qualitative research presented in Figure 14.1.

Kinds of question

The kinds of question asked in qualitative interviews are highly variable. Kvale (1996) has suggested nine different kinds of questions. Most interviews will contain virtually all of them, although interviews that rely on lists of topics are likely to follow a somewhat looser format. Kvale's nine types of question are as follows:

- Introducing questions. 'Please tell me about when your interest in X first began?'; 'Have you ever . . . ?'; 'Why did you go to . . . ?'
- Follow-up questions. Getting the interviewee to elaborate his or her answer, such as 'Could you say some more about that?'; 'What do you mean by that . . . ?'; 'Can you give me an example . . . ?'
- Probing questions. Following up what has been said through direct questioning.
- Specifying questions. 'What did you do then?'; 'How did X react to what you said?'
- Direct questions. 'Do you find it easy to keep smiling when serving customers?'; 'Are you happy with the amount of on-the-job training you have received?'

Figure 14.1

Formulating questions for an interview guide

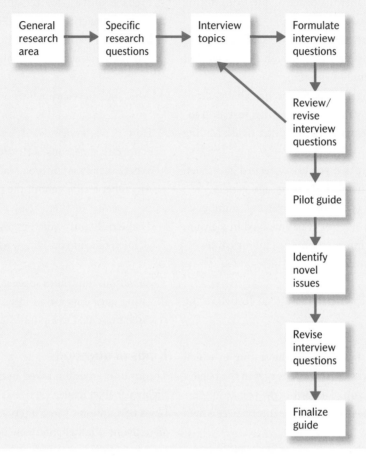

Such questions are perhaps best left until towards the end of the interview, in order not to influence the direction of the interview too much.

- Indirect questions. 'What do most people round here think of the ways that management treats its staff?', perhaps followed up by 'Is that the way you feel too?', in order to get at the individual's own view.
- Structuring questions. 'I would now like to move on to a different topic'.
- Silence. Allow pauses to signal that you want to give the interviewee the opportunity to reflect and amplify an answer.
- Interpreting questions. 'Do you mean that your leadership role has had to change from one of encouraging others to a more directive one?'; 'Is it fair to say that you don't mind being friendly towards customers

most of the time, but when they are unpleasant or demanding you find it more difficult?'

As this list suggests, one of the main ingredients of the interview is listening—being very attentive to what the interviewee is saying or even not saying. It means that the interviewer is active without being too intrusive—a difficult balance. But it also means that, just because the interview is being tape-recorded (the generally recommended practice whenever it is feasible), the interviewer cannot take things easy. In fact, an interviewer must be very attuned and responsive to what the interviewee is saying and doing. This is also important because something like body language may indicate that the interviewee is becoming uneasy or anxious about a line of questioning. An ethically sensitive interviewer will not want to place undue pressure on the

Tips and Skills

Interviewees and distance

Sometimes you may need to contact interviewees who are a long way from you—perhaps even abroad. While interviewing in qualitative research is usually of the face-to-face kind, time and money restrictions may mean that you will need to interview such people in a less personal context. There are two possibilities. One is telephone interviewing. The cost of a telephone interview is much less than the cost involved in travelling long distances. Such interviewing is touched on in the context of the structured interview in Chapter 13. Another possibility is the on-line interview in which the interview is con-ducted by email. This method is described in Chapter 22. With the advance of different technologies other options are opening up. When, or example, Salvador Barragan planned to interview senior women executives in Mexico for his PH.D. thesis he had to face the problem of hastily arranged interviewees that could be cancelled and rescheduled at short notice. In order to fit in with the schedules of busy executives, Barragan's solution was to set up interviews using SKYPE technology that allows people to talk (and even see each other) over long distances using the Internet.

person he or she is talking to and will need to be prepared to cut short that line of questioning if it is clearly a source of concern.

Remember as well that in interviews you are going to ask about different kinds of things, such as:

- Values. Of the interviewee, of group, of organization.
- Beliefs. Of interviewee, of others, of group.
- Behaviour. Of interviewee, of others.
- Formal and informal roles. Of interviewee, of others.
- Relationships. Of the interviewee, of others.
- Places and locales.
- Emotions. Particularly of the interviewee, but also, possibly, of others.
- Encounters.
- Stories.

Try to vary the questioning in terms of types of question (as suggested by Kvale's nine types, which were outlined above) and the types of phenomena you ask about. Finally, you must think about how to end interviews satisfactorily, making sure that your interviewees have had a chance to comment fully on the topic concerned and giving them the opportunity to raise any issues that they think you have overlooked in your questions. The closing moments of an interview also provide an opportunity to include a final 'catch-all' question. Journalists sometimes refer to this as the 'doorknob question', since it is asked at the end, when rapport has been established and the interviewee has relaxed into the situation. This type of closing question tends to be directive—for example, 'If you were advising the organization on this subject, what are the main changes or improvements that you would recommend?' or 'From your experience in this area, what advice would you offer to other managers facing similar problems?' This encourages the interviewee to comment on specific issues and to put forward a personal opinion.

Using an interview guide: An example

Research in focus 14.2 is taken from an interview from Bryman's (1999) study of visitors to Disney theme parks. The study was briefly mentioned in Chapter 9 as an example of a snowball sampling procedure. The interviews were concerned to elicit visitors' interpretations of the parks that had been visited. The interview is with a man who was in his sixties and his wife who was two years younger. They had visited Walt Disney World in Orlando, Florida, and were very enthusiastic about their visit.

The sequence begins with the interviewer asking what would be considered a 'direct question' in terms of the list of nine question types suggested by Kvale (1996) and outlined above. The replies are very bland and do little more than reflect the interviewees' positive feelings about their visit to Disney World. The wife acknowledges this when she says 'but I need to say more than that, don't I?'. Interviewees frequently know that they are expected to be expansive in their answers. This sequence occurred around halfway through the interview, so the interviewees were primed by then into realizing that more details were expected. There is almost a tinge of embarrassment that the answer has

Student Experience

Learning how to interview

Mikael, who is in the early stages of his PH.D. program, wants to study change in the Information Technology industry. Although he is still in the process of learning about the wide spectrum of different qualitative methods, he already feels that he would like to interview practitioners active in the target industry to gain a perception of the environment as told by its actors. He had used semi-structured interviews for his Master's thesis and enjoyed the experience. He had wanted to know more 'about the decision-making [process] from the people involved' in the industry and because of their 'diverse background, or diverse positions, I really didn't feel that . . . a survey approach would have been the most effective way [to gather] information'. Nonetheless, inexperienced in qualitative research, when he 'analyzed the interviews [he] struggled with that part of the research. I thought it would be easy to identify themes from interviews. When you've been there yourself, you listen to the people, you've written up all the interviews. However, there's such a large amount of text that without a tool other than Notepad, I felt kind of lost . . . You have to take more distance from the actual statements [and], see what the underlying perhaps answers are . . . not really what is said but what the message really is'. Learning from his experiences Mikael reflects that it was a 'really good decision' to leave himself 'the option to state follow-up questions if certain things come up; not just to stick to the preformulated structure, because I noticed that the order of the questions wasn't always optimal. . . . So it was really a good experience to know what to do the next time, if one does this kind of interviews because I felt it hard to keep up a natural discussion with a discussion-based interview which was structured'. For his future doctoral work he plans to 'get enough domain knowledge and credibility from the construction IT people to really get to speak their language so to say

before I start with the interviews so I know what questions to ask and how to ask them so that I don't come off as ignorant, or just asking completely wrong questions for what's really important'. Another concern of Mikael's was to ensure that he is clear on being able to explain and defend how he came up with the interview questions and how he came to the conclusions that follow: 'it would be perhaps good to make some kind of a diary to record thinking as you go along; [to] have some kind of . . . evidence later on [about] how it all came about. [Also] to observe one's own development during the program and the courses, to look how perception . . . one's perception and knowledge about these kinds of things develops so [as to gain] confidence [in oneself and the research process]'.

Karen felt that through the experience of doing qualitative interviewing she acquired a new and potentially transferable skill. 'I learned a lot through [the interviews that I did] about how to . . . probe and to get what you want out of it. . . . You [can] so easily just go into an interview and . . . sit there and listen to what they're saying and then you . . . [go] out and think, "Actually they didn't give me anything [that] I wanted. They just talked at me." But you need to balance that with not actually telling them what you want to know, but just sort of . . . guiding them towards [it] so that you can achieve the objectives that you've got . . . That's another sort of skill that I wouldn't say I've managed to learn . . . completely, but I think it's . . . something that you pick up and you can get better at through doing this sort of research. . . . Since then I've done quite a lot of sort of client-based consultancy projects . . . and I think [this is] definitely one of the main skills [I applied there] . . . Having [it] clear in your own mind what you want to get . . . and asking the questions in a way that can get what you want without leading people to tell you . . . what you want to hear'.

been so brief and unilluminating. The husband's answer is more expansive but not particularly enlightening.

There then follows the first of two important prompts by the interviewer. The husband's response is more interesting in that he now begins to answer in terms of the possibility that black people were under-represented in attractions like the American Adventure, which tells the story of America through tableaux and films via a debate between two audio-animatronic figures: Mark Twain and Benjamin Franklin. The second prompt yields further useful reflection, this time carrying the implication that Third World countries are under-represented in the World Showcase in the Epcot Center. The couple are clearly aware that it is the prompting that has made them provide these reflections when they say: 'Well thinking about it now, because I hadn't really given this any consideration before you started asking about it' and 'Well, like you, I hadn't thought of it like that before'. This is the whole point of prompting—to get the interviewee to think more about the topic and to provide the opportunity for a more detailed response. It is not a leading question, since the interviewees were not being asked, 'Do you think that the Disney company fails to recognize the significance of Black history (or ignores the Third World) in its presentation of different cultures?' There is no doubt that it is the prompts that elicit the more interesting replies, but that is precisely their role.

Tape recording and transcription

The point has already been made on several occasions that, in qualitative research, the interview is usually tape-recorded and transcribed whenever possible (see Tips and skills *'Why you should record and transcribe interviews'*). Qualitative researchers are frequently interested not just in what people say but also in the way that they say it. If this aspect is to be fully woven into an analysis, it is necessary for a complete account of the series of exchanges in an interview to be available. Also, because the interviewer is supposed to be highly alert to what is being said—following up interesting points made, prompting and probing where necessary, drawing attention to any inconsistencies in the interviewee's answers—it is best if he or she is not distracted by having to concentrate on getting down notes on what is said.

As with just about everything in conducting business research, there is a cost (other than the financial cost of tape recorders), in that the use of a tape recorder may disconcert respondents, who become self-conscious or alarmed at the prospect of their words being preserved. Most people accede to the request for the interview to be tape-recorded, though it is not uncommon for a small number to refuse (see, for example, Rafaeli et al., 1997). When faced with refusal, you should still go ahead with the interview, as it is highly likely that useful information will still be forthcoming. For example, Prasad (1993; see Chapter 6) recounts that, in the few instances where employees at Paragon indicated discomfort with being recorded, she took notes during the interview and wrote these up after the session. The summary notes were then shown to the interviewee, who evaluated their accuracy. This advice also applies to cases of tape recorder malfunction. Among those who do agree to be tape-recorded, there will be some who will not get over their alarm at being confronted with a microphone. As a result, some interviews may not be as interesting as you might have hoped. In qualitative research, there is often quite a large amount of variation in the amount of time that interviews take. For example, in Milkman's (1997) study of technological change at General Motors the length of the interviews ranged from between 45 minutes and four hours. Similarly, Marshall's (1995) research into women managers involved interviews with women managers that lasted between one and a half and two hours. It should not be assumed that shorter interviews are necessarily inferior to longer ones, but very short ones that are a product of interviewee non-cooperation or anxiety about being tape-recorded are likely to be less useful. In the extreme, when an interview has produced very little of significance, it may not be worth the time and cost of transcription. Thankfully, such occasions are relatively unusual. If people do agree to be interviewed, they usually do so in a cooperative way and loosen up after initial anxiety about the microphone. As a result, even short interviews are often quite revealing.

The problem with transcribing interviews is that it is very time consuming. Pettigrew (1985) notes that his interviews at Imperial Chemical Industries (ICI) produced around 500 hours of tape-recorded information for analysis, which were either completely transcribed or coded

14.2   Research in Focus

Part of the transcript of a semi-structured interview

Interviewer   OK. What were your views or feelings about the presentation of different cultures, as shown in, for example, Jungle Cruise or It's a Small World at the Magic Kingdom or in World Showcase at Epcot?

Wife   Well, I thought the different countries at Epcot were wonderful, but I need to say more than that, don't I?

Husband   They were very good and some were better than others, but that was down to the host countries themselves really, as I suppose each of the countries represented would have been responsible for their own part, so that's nothing to do with Disney, I wouldn't have thought. I mean some of the landmarks were hard to recognize for what they were supposed to be, but some were very well done. Britain was OK, but there was only a pub and a Welsh shop there really, whereas some of the other pavilions, as I think they were called, were good ambassadors for the countries they represented. China, for example, had an excellent 360 degree film showing parts of China and I found that very interesting.

Interviewer   Did you think there was anything lacking about the content?

Husband   Well I did notice that there weren't many black people at World Showcase, particularly the American Adventure. Now whether we were there on an unusual day in that respect I don't know, but we saw plenty of black Americans in the Magic Kingdom and other places, but very few if any in that World Showcase. And there was certainly little mention of Black history in the American Adventure presentation, so maybe they felt alienated by that, I don't know, but they were noticeable by their absence.

Interviewer   So did you think there were any special emphases?

Husband   Well thinking about it now, because I hadn't really given this any consideration before you started asking about it, but thinking about it now, it was only really representative of the developed world, you know, Britain, America, Japan, world leaders many of them in technology, and there was nothing of the Third World there. Maybe that's their own fault, maybe they were asked to participate and didn't, but now that I think about it, that does come to me. What do you think, love?

Wife   Well, like you, I hadn't thought of it like that before, but I agree with you.

---

onto 8 by 5-inch cards according to predetermined and emergent categories. Similarly, in their study of traders and managers in four investment banks, Willman et al. (2002) interviewed 118 traders and trader-managers and 10 senior managers. Interviews averaged one hour in duration and they were all taped and transcripts were produced. It is best to allow around five to six hours for transcription for every hour of speech. Also, transcription yields vast amounts of (electronic and/or paper) pages, which you will need to wade through when analyzing the data. Prasad (1993) reports that her 34 interviews on computerization (see Chapter 6) generated nearly 800 pages of interview transcripts that needed to be analyzed, in addition to over 1800 pages of field notes from observations. Wallace's (2009, p.

69) interviews with 13 women generated 22 hours of tape and some 321 pages of material. It is clear, therefore, that, while transcription has the advantage of keeping intact the interviewee's (and interviewer's) words, it does so by piling up the amount of text to be analyzed. It is no wonder that writers like Lofland and Lofland (1995) advise that the analysis of qualitative data is not left until all the interviews have been completed and transcribed. To procrastinate may give the researcher the impression that he or she faces a monumental task. Also, there are good grounds for making analysis an ongoing activity, because it allows the researcher to be more aware of emerging themes that he or she may want to ask about in a more direct way in later interviews. The preference for ongoing analysis is also very

Tips and Skills

Why you should record and transcribe interviews

With approaches that entail detailed attention to language, such as conversation analysis and discourse analysis (see Chapter 20), the recording of conversations and interviews is to all intents and purposes mandatory. However, researchers who use qualitative interviews and focus groups (see Chapter 15) also tend to record and then transcribe interviews. Heritage (1984, p. 238) suggests that the procedure of recording and transcribing interviews has the following advantages:

- It helps to correct the natural limitations of our memories and of the intuitive glosses that we might place on what people say in interviews.
- It allows more thorough examination of what people say.
- It permits repeated examinations of the interviewees' answers.
- It opens up the data to public scrutiny by other researchers, who can evaluate the analysis that is carried out by the original researchers of the data (that is, a secondary analysis).
- It, therefore, helps to counter accusations that an analysis might have been influenced by a researcher's values or biases.

- It allows the data to be reused in other ways from those intended by the original researcher, for example, in the light of new theoretical ideas or analytic strategies.

However, it has to be recognized that the procedure is very time consuming. It also requires good equipment, usually in the form of a good-quality tape recorder and microphone, but also, where applicable, a transcription machine (when using micro tapes) or translation software when using digital recorders. Transcription can also very quickly result in a daunting set of electronic and/or paper pages. Also, recording equipment may be off putting for interviewees.

It is also worth bearing in mind that in Bryman's experience, focus group research, which is the subject of Chapter 15, can be difficult to transcribe. This is because people in the discussions often talk over each other, in spite of warnings by the moderator not to do so. Even a high-quality microphone will not readily deal with this issue. One possibility is to video-record, as well as audio-record. However, this is likely to be beyond the means of most students and also requires a very suitable environment for the focus group. The possible problems of transcription should be borne in mind if you are considering using a focus group.

much recommended by proponents of approaches to qualitative data analysis like grounded theory (see Chapter 24).

It is easy to take the view that transcription is a relatively unproblematic translation of the spoken into the written word. However, given the reliance on transcripts in qualitative research based on interviews, the issue should not be taken lightly. The first question to consider is whether to do the transcription yourself, or use secretarial assistance. Transcribers need to be trained in much the same way that interviewers do. Moreover, even among experienced transcribers, errors can creep in. For example, Spender (1989) describes how, of the 34 interviews in his sample, 25 were transcribed. During the exploratory stages of the research this was done by assistants. However, this proved unsatisfactory, as 'There are important data in the respondent's intonations, hesitations, etc. which need to be available'. He concluded that 'The recording can help to recapture the actual data, which is neither the recording, nor the tran-

script, but the researcher's experience of the interview in its own context' (1989, p. 82). Poland (1995) has provided some fascinating examples of mistakes in transcription that can be the result of many different factors (mishearing, fatigue, carelessness). For example, one transcript contained the following passage:

> I think unless we want to become like other countries, where people have, you know, democratic freedoms . . .

But the actual words on the audiotape were:

> I think unless we want to become like other countries, where people have no democratic freedoms . . .
> (Poland, 1995, p. 294)

Steps clearly need to be taken to check on the quality of transcription.

Tips and Skills

Conventions when using direct quotes from an interview

When transcribing an interview it is important to have in mind what kind of approach you will take to your analysis. For example, in his interviews with visitors to Disney theme parks Bryman (1999; see Research in focus 14.2) was primarily interested in the interviewees' interpretations of what they had seen. To that end, he focused on what they said rather than how they said it. McGowan (1999), on the other hand, was also particularly interested in the way that people expressed their views (on elder care). With that in mind she transcribed each pause and the use of fillers, such as 'um,' 'er,' etc. This helped McGowan to identity a difference in the overall responses between men and women, with the men being more hesitant (longer pauses) and less certain (more fillers) than the women in talking about elder care.

Regardless of approach it is likely safer to have the interview completely transcribed, complete with pauses and fillers. This will provide the researcher with more options in the analysis stage (but will be more timely). It is also important that the written text reproduces exactly what the interviewee said, word for word. For this reason, if there are parts of the interview that you can't hear properly on the tape recording, don't be tempted to guess or make them up, instead indicate in your transcript that there is a missing word or phrase, for example by using the convention {???}. This helps to give the reader confidence in your data collection process. However, people rarely speak in fully formed sentences, they often repeat themselves and they may have verbal 'tics' in the form of a common word or phrase that is repeated either through habit or just because they like it! So when it comes to writing up your research, when you will probably wish to quote directly from the interview transcripts, you may want to edit out some of these digressions for the sake of length and ease of understanding. However, you must make sure that you do not paraphrase the words of the speaker and then claim these as the actual words that were spoken because this is misleading and there is always the possibility that someone reading your work might suspect that people did not really speak in such a fluent way. The use of certain conventions when quoting from an interview transcript helps to overcome these problems:

- Use quotation marks to indicate that this is a direct quote or indicate this by consistently setting quotes so they stand out from the main body text, for example by indenting them or by using a different font, in a similar way to how you would quote at length from a book. This makes it immediately apparent to the reader that this is a direct quote and it enables you to differentiate between your presentation of the data and your analysis of it.

- If it is appropriate in relation to ethical considerations (see Chapter 8), indicate who is speaking in the quote, either introducing the speaker before the quote by saying something like 'As John put it', or 'Anne explained her reasons for this:', or attribute the quote to the interviewee immediately afterwards, for example by writing their pseudonym or [Interviewee 1] in square brackets.

- If you wish to quote the first sentence from a section of speech and then a sentence or two further on from the transcript, use the convention of three consecutive dots to indicate the break point (e.g., It was said . . . by many people.)

- If an interviewee omits a word from a sentence which is a grammatical omission or if the interviewee refers to a subject in a way that does not make its meaning clear and you need to provide the reader with more contextual information so that they can understand the quote, use the convention of brackets or square brackets in which you insert the words you have added (e.g., 'It is [Interviewee #4's] firm opinion that . . . .')

- Finally, one of the most difficult things about presenting interview data as part of your analysis is that it can take some effort and perseverance to create a smooth flow to the text because of the switches between your 'voice', as the researcher, and the 'voices' of the interviewees, which can make the text seem quite fragmented. For this reason it is important to introduce direct quotes before you present them and then take a sentence or two of your analysis to explain in your own words how you have interpreted them. In this way you construct a narrative that guides the reader through your data and shows why you have chosen the particular quotes you have as illustrative of particular themes or concepts.

These conventions are applied in the example that follows, which is taken from an article that reports the findings from an interview study of Irish women entering the labour force. As this study involved interviewing the women on more than one occasion, the authors also included specification of whether this was the first or second interview at the end of each quote.

Grace still hopes to move out of retail work and plans to start a bed and breakfast business:

> I am aiming (to) leave the retailing industry completely . . . and I work in (an area of Dublin) which is logistically quite far from where I live and people say to me 'would you not get a transfer' . . . and I say why would I transfer from the devil to the deep blue sea. I'd want to move into something completely different . . . I'd hate to think that was my only a mbition to get the company to move me to a different store. (First interview)

> [From: Collins, G., & Wickham, J. (2004). Inclusion or exploitation: Irish women enter the labour force. *Gender, Work and Organization, 11* (1), 26–46.]

You may have noticed by now that the Student experience features in this book apply similar conventions when quoting directly the students we interviewed for the book, in part so you can see how interview data are presented.

Tips and Skills

Transcribing sections of an interview

Some interviews or at least large portions of them are sometimes not very useful, perhaps because interviewees are reticent or their answers are not as relevant to your research topic as you had hoped. There seems little point in transcribing material that you know is unlikely to be fruitful. It may be that, for many of your interviews, it would be better to listen to them closely first, at least once or more usually twice, and then transcribe only those portions that you think are useful or relevant. However, this may mean that you miss certain things or that you have to go back to the tapes at a later stage in your analysis to try to find something that emerges as significant only later on.

14.4 Student Experience

To transcribe or not to transcribe?

The students that we talked to on this issue were mixed. Mary Runté summed things up in comparison with her researcher husband Robert:

> Robert is a firm believer in the 'transcribe them yourself' school. He feels that this gives you a greater intimacy with the data, you can connect with the emotion of the subject as you transcribe to give more substance to the real meaning of the words. I belong to the 'pay someone else' school. I find that if I transcribe them myself there is such a gap between the interview and transcription and analysis that I lose touch with the research question. I have a great transcriptionist so I can do the interview, pass off the tape/file and have it back within a couple of days. I can then engage in a more iterative process by absorbing both the transcript and my recall of the interview before I am off to the next one.

Similarly, Janet Bell Crawford 'absolutely did not transcribe the interviews [she] conducted' arguing that 'professional transcription services can do it a lot faster allowing me time to focus on other research activities':

> I would digitally record the interview (or focus group) and upload the file to the transcriber's server. A couple of days later they would send me a file that I could import into content analysis software (I used NVivo). Before importing, I would listen to the interview (focus group) recording with the transcription to double-check it for accuracy. Sometimes terms, language or acronyms are used that the transcriber is unfamiliar with. Overall, I didn't consider transcribing a competency that I

needed to learn. One note, however, not all transcription services are created equal. For example, if your interviews include people with accents, make sure that the service has transcribers who can work with accents'.

Terry Weatherbee, on the other hand, used a professional transcription service for one project because he was 'new to interviews and transcription'. The decision 'was simply time-driven, and an acknowledgment of his inability to type efficiently'. However, next time around, he decided to transcribe the interviews himself:

in order to 'get the feel' of the interview responses. Also allowed me to match my notes to the transcriptions. I was doing [my] cyber aggression research and I discovered that it was not just what the respondents said, but how they said it, and the body language and emotions that went with the responses. This provided additional valuable information when it came to analysis. I suspect, depending on the subject area of the research, that at times this may not be important, but in my case it was. While I found the professional transcription was 'exact', fast, and correct—it did not provide the same 'feel' for the data that doing it myself did.

Trish and Marcelle both cite costs (they didn't have the funds to hire transcribers) and empathy (the need to 'hear' their interviewees) as reasons for undertaking their own transcriptions. Trish wanted to 'hear what people said—not just read it', while Marcelle wanted to listen to the responses rather than simply hear them, thus pick up on the non-verbals such as change in tone of voice, rate of speech, pauses, etc. that may provide deeper insight than the verbal. Bill sayss that for him the audio version of interviews identified moments of learning (errors) that occurred during the interviews; these moments where then used to improve my interviewing skills for future research.

Finally, Margaret McKee hired someone to do the transcriptions for her dissertation study:

My reasons were mainly pragmatic. I was completing this part of my research project under time constraints, and so I wanted to transcribe my interviews as I was conducting new ones, rather than wait and do the transcription all at the end. I'm not that fast a typist and I found it quite difficult to listen to the tapes at a reasonable speed and still be able to capture what was being said. Since I had digital copies of the tapes, I decided that if I had them transcribed I could still listen to the tapes and immerse myself in the data that way. Once I had my transcribed copies and I listened to the tapes and read the documents on my computer screen. I could then easily correct any small errors that had been made by my transcriber, and also review sections that she had found difficult or confusing because of background noise or use of unfamiliar terms. While I know there is a great benefit in transcribing the tapes yourself, I felt this was a good compromise arrangement for me.

14.5 | Student Experience

For Amy Warren, one of the biggest issues she encountered with interviews was that: 'Often people tell you things that are their true answers to the question once you turn your recorder off and then it is clearly "off the record" so you can't report what they said … this can be frustrating but does test your ethics. Also, the informed consent form throws some people off. Often times they see this as a formal legal document and it can intimidate them from participating, not because of the explanation of the study but how it is presented in the form'.

Tips and Skills

Translating interviews into English

If you are interviewing people whose primary language is not English but another language in which you the interviewer are fluent, you may decide to interview respondents in their primary language, so that their ability to communicate effectively is not impaired by having to speak in a language with which they are less familiar. You should first transcribe the interviews in the language spoken during the interview and then translate the transcript into English so that you can analyze the data in the language that you will be using when you come to write up your research. Differences in the meaning of words between the two languages may mean that the translation process leads to some distortion of the data. To overcome this, you may wish to back-translate the transcript into the primary language and then compare the back-translation with the original version, noting any discrepancies. However, it should be noted that this is bound to be a time-consuming process, so it needs to be borne in mind when deciding how many interviews to do.

14.6 | Student Experience

How many interviews in a student research project?

The answer to this question depends on many things, including the nature of the research project for the level of study involved. For example, for some undergraduate research methods courses students may only be, where required, expected to do a handful of interviews—more for the experience than the viability of the research project. However, at graduate level, particularly with a D.B.A. or PH.D., the number of people interviewed can be an issue that the student needs to make a decision about and be able to justify the decision taken. Using a snowball process where she interviewed one person and then asked that person who they would recommend, Peggy Wallace interviewed 13 women. She wanted to see what can be learned from women's career choices—how they made them, what influenced their decisions—to understand why fewer women than men make it to partner level in the accounting industry. As each career trajectory is different, Wallace knew that her sample would not be representative so much as indicative of the way that some people make decisions. We could learn from the decision process rather than the content of the decisions themselves. To that end, she had in mind 10 to 20 interviews. By the thirteenth interview she began to feel that she was already hearing what others had already described. She had reached saturation, i.e., a point where no new data appeared to be forthcoming (Wallace, 2009). Similarly, Scott MacMillan's study of existentialism at work reached a similar point of saturation after he had interviewed around 12 different people (MacMillan, 2009).

Learning from others in her PH.D. program, Doreen MacAulay decided to do 16 interviews for her qualitative study of public servant identity. Her decision was based on the availability of individuals and a reasonable expectation based on previous thesis work of others on how many would be required for theoretical saturation.

14.7 | Student Experience

Stratified sampling in a student's research project

Amy Thurlow was interested in people's sense of change in two different organizations. It was not a comparative analysis but she felt that she needed sufficient numbers of people from each organization and at different levels. Thus, she interviewed '3 CEOs, 9 senior managers, 12 middle managers and 11 front-line staff people. Two of the managers and two of the staff people were actually former employees who had left the organizations, in some cases voluntarily, and in others as a result of layoffs' (Thurlow, 2007, pp. 100–101). Interviews were conducted at the participants' workplace or by telephone. Twenty of the interviewees were recruited from organization 'A' (a community college system) and 15 came from organization 'B' (a hospital). In the latter case Thurlow also took care to speak to a roughly equal number of people from each of the two former hospitals that had merged to form organization 'B'. Similarly, with the college system, Thurlow ensured that she had participants from both rural and urban campuses, and who were either new employees or had served with the institution for 10 or more years: 'Individual participants were selected for the study as they represented voices from a variety of locations within the organization and reflected differing degrees of organizational power'. The number of interviews at each site was determined by the point at which Thurlow felt confident that she had gathered the dominant and any alternative language of change which had emerged as meaningful within the organization. To determine this point she relied on the principle of 'theoretical saturation' (Glaser & Strauss, 1967):

> When the narratives of change which emerged during the interviews ceased to provide new interpretations of

change and language and served to reinforce or repeat narratives that had already emerged, I determined that theoretical saturation had been achieved. At [organization 'B'] theoretical saturation occurred slightly more quickly than at the College site, mainly because the ways in which individuals made sense of the language of change in relation to different sites of power in the organization was very consistent.

Thurlow conducted several more interviews at organization 'A' (20 in total) because it had more physical sites and a larger number of employees.

To ensure that she heard from those more directly involved in 'the production or dissemination of the language of change at both sites', Thurlow included individuals who were 'officially designated with roles in the change initiative by their organizations'. These designated change agents were all familiar with the language of change introduced by the organization, and likely as not would have insight into the language used throughout the organization 'either in response or resistance to the change'. Finally, to manage the scope of the thesis, Thurlow 'decided to limit participation in the research to employees of these two organizations, as opposed to other stakeholder groups' (e.g., students, patients, government officials, physicians, or members of external accreditation bodies). Thurlow (2007, pp. 100–101) reflected that, 'although these stakeholder groups all represent significant influences on the power relations exercised within the organization, the logistics of managing research with this many groups would have compromised the in-depth nature the research process'.

Flexibility in the interview

One further point to bear in mind is that you need to be generally flexible in your approach to interviewing in qualitative research. This advice is not just to do with needing to be responsive to what interviewees say to you and following up interesting points that they make. Such flexibility is important and is an important reminder that, with semi-structured interviewing, you should not turn the interview into a kind of structured interview but with open questions. Flexibility is important in such areas as varying the order of questions, following up leads, and clearing up inconsistencies in answers. Flexibility is important in other respects, such as coping with audio-recording equipment breakdown and refusals by interviewees to allow a recording to take place. A further element is that interviewers often find that, as soon as they switch off their tape recorders, the interviewee continues to ruminate on the topic of interest and frequently will say more interesting things than in the interview. It is usually not feasible to switch the machine back on again, so try to take some notes, either while the person is talking or as soon as possible after the interview. Such 'unsolicited accounts' can often be the source of revealing information or views (Hammersley & Atkinson, 1995).

 ## Sampling

Many, if not most, of the issues raised in connection with sampling in ethnographic research apply more or less equally to sampling in qualitative interviewing. Very often, the lack of transparency that is sometimes a feature of qualitative research (referred to in Chapter 6) is particularly apparent in relation to sampling. It is sometimes more or less impossible to discern from researchers to account from their methods either how their interviewees were selected or how many there were of them. Often, qualitative researchers are clear that their samples are convenience or opportunistic ones, and, on other occasions, the reader suspects that this is the case. This may be due to a belief that, because it aims to generate an in-depth analysis, issues of representativeness are less important in qualitative research than they are in quantitative research. For her study of woman managers, Marshall (1984) made a number of decisions to limit certain potential influencing factors. First, to interview in and around London, to reduce the significance of whether or not managers were geographically mobile; second, to impose an upper age limit of 45 years, to reduce the potential differences between generations; third, to contact several people in each company to provide a guide to the influence of the company; and

fourth, to restrict the number of personnel managers in the sample, to avoid weighting her sample towards this 'traditional stronghold of female employment' (1984, p. 115). Sometimes, convenience samples may be the result of restrictions placed on the researcher. For example, when members of an organization select interviewees rather than giving the researcher a free rein to do so.

Another example of opportunistic sampling is provided by Jackall (1988), who went into several large organizations in order to study how bureaucracy shapes moral consciousness. Analysis of the occupational ethics of corporate managers was based on core data of 143 intensive, semi-structured interviews with managers at every level of the organization. This formed the basis for selection of a smaller stratified group of 12 managers who were reinterviewed several times and asked to interpret materials that Jackall was collecting. However, as the study progressed Jackall realized that an investigation of organizational morality should also explore managerial dissenters, or 'whistleblowers'—individuals who had taken stands against their organizations on grounds that they defined as moral. Between 1982 and 1988, Jackall conducted case studies of these dissenters, interviewing 18 'whistleblowers' and reviewing large amounts of documentary evidence. In order to explore managerial morality further, he then presented these cases to the stratified group of 12 managers, and asked them 'to assess the dissenters' actions and motives by their own standards' (1988, p. 206).

Snowball sampling is sometimes used to contact groups of people for whom there is no sampling frame. This approach was employed in Bryman's study of visitors to Disney theme parks and by Marshall (1984), who asked women managers to suggest other potential interviewees. Pettigrew and McNulty (1995) also describe their in-depth interview research into part-time board members of top UK firms as based on a 'snowball effect'. Pilot-study interviews with 20 board members were used to get access to other prominent directors in the overall population. Pettigrew and McNulty's research approach is guided by the assumption that access to elites is best achieved through other elite members.

Sometimes, a probability sampling approach is employed. The research on organizational dress by Rafaeli et al. (1997) employed such an approach. The authors

Table 14.1   A stratified interview sample

Interviewees by occupation	Number	%
Top and middle management	54	22
Lower management	22	9
Administrative	18	7.5
Supervisory	9	3.5
Personal assistant	3	1.5
Secretary (1 boss)	67	27.5
Secretary (2+ bosses)	29	12
Word processor/typist	22	9
Clerical assistant	20	8
Total	244	100

Source: adapted from Pringle (1988).

write: 'First, we identified a stratified random sample of 20 people from the population of full-time, permanent administrative employees in the organization' (1997, pp. 13–14). The stratifying criteria were administrative section and hierarchical level. A similar kind of sampling strategy occurs when a sample of interviewees is taken (sometimes randomly, sometimes by ensuring a 'spread' in terms of stratifying criteria) from a much larger sample generated for social survey purposes. This approach allows the researcher to sample purposively (if not randomly) and so ensure a wide range of characteristics of interviewees. Pringle (1988) also used this approach in a study of power relations and secretarial work. This study involved interviews with secretarial students and with a range of workers, both secretarial and non-secretarial, in a variety of Australian workplaces. The first stage of this process involved groups of three secretarial students who were interviewed for 20–30 minutes about their course. A smaller sample ($n = 30$) were interviewed again near the end of their course and then followed into the workforce. Fifteen were interviewed, a third time, individually, at home and asked to reflect on the value of their course. The second stage of interviews was carried out in a representative range of workplaces. 'Of 244 interviews 72 were with employees in the public sector, 32 with unions, 92 with large corporations and 44 with small companies, agencies

and partnerships' (Pringle, 1988, p. 268). A breakdown of interviewees by occupation is given in Table 14.1.

In addition, a theoretical sampling approach might be employed (see Key concept 17.4 and Figure 17.2). This approach entails sampling interviewees until your categories achieve theoretical saturation (see Key concept 17.5) and selecting further interviewees on the basis of your emerging theoretical focus. The approach is supposed to be an iterative one—that is, one in which there is a movement backwards and forwards between sampling and theoretical reflection—but it may be that the researcher feels that his or her categories achieve theoretical saturation at a relatively early stage. For example, for their research on organization dress, Rafaeli et al. (1997) initially employed a stratified random sampling approach, but then evaluated their data 'after completing interviews with the 20 individuals selected and concluded that, because we had reached theoretical saturation (Glaser & Strauss 1967), no additional interviews were necessary' (1997, p. 14). A sampling approach that is more in tune with Glaser and Strauss's (1967) idea of theoretical sampling is provided by Gephart (1993) in his account of a study of disaster sensemaking (see Research in focus 14.3).

The chief virtue of theoretical sampling is that the emphasis is upon using theoretical reflection on data as the guide to whether or not more data are needed. It, therefore, places a premium on theorizing rather than on the statistical adequacy of a sample, which may be a limited guide to sample selection in many instances.

Feminist research and interviewing in qualitative research

Unstructured and semi-structured interviewing have become extremely prominent methods of data gathering within a feminist research framework. In part, this is a reflection of the preference for qualitative research among feminist researchers, but it also reflects a view that the kind of interview with which qualitative research is associated allows many of the goals of feminist research to be realized. Indeed, the view has been expressed that, 'Whilst several brave women in the 1980s defended quantitative methods, it is nonetheless still the case that not just qualitative methods, but the in-depth face-to-face interview has become the paradigmatic "feminist method"' (Kelly, Burton, & Regan, 1994, p. 34). This comment is enlightening because it implies that it is not simply that qualitative research is seen by many writers and researchers as more consistent with a feminist position than quantitative research, but that specifically qualitative interviewing is seen as especially appropriate. The point that is being made here is not necessarily that such interviewing is somehow more in tune with feminist values than, say, ethnography (especially since it is often an ingredient of ethnographic research). Instead, it could be that the intensive and time-consuming nature of ethnography means that, although it has great potential as an approach to feminist research (see Chapter 17), qualitative interviewing is often preferred because it is usually less invasive in these respects.

However, it is specifically interviewing of the kind conducted in qualitative research that is seen as having potential for a feminist approach, not the structured interview with which survey research is associated. Why might one type of interview be consistent with a sensitivity to feminism and the other not? In a frequently cited article, Oakley outlines the following points about the standard survey interview:

- It is a one-way process—the interviewer extracts information or views from the interviewee.
- The interviewer offers nothing in return for the extraction of information. For example, interviewers using a structured interview do not offer information or their own views if asked. Indeed, they are typically advised not to do such things because of worries about contaminating their respondents' answers.
- The interviewer-interviewee relationship is a form of hierarchical or power relationship. Interviewers arrogate to themselves the right to ask questions, implicitly placing their interviewees in a position of subservience or inferiority.
- The element of power is also revealed by the fact that the structured interview seeks out information from the perspective of the researcher.
- Because of these points, the standard survey interview is inconsistent with feminism when women interview other women. This view arises because it is seen as indefensible for women to 'use' other women in these ways.

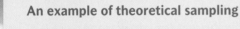

14.3 Research in Focus

An example of theoretical sampling

Gephart (1993) developed a theoretical sample in his study of disaster sense making, by deciding on analytic grounds which data to collect and analyze based on his emerging theory (see Research in focus 21.6 for a more detailed account of this study). Sampling was determined by three main considerations.

- *Persons and documents*. Gephart chose to focus on the testimony and remarks of (1) the assistant district manager and district manager from the company; (2) a pipeline crew member; and (3) the government energy board members and its attorneys. This analytic choice was made because

these three parties represented the main cultural groups involved in the enquiry.

- Key issues. Ethnographic observation sensitized Gephart to the actors' concern with making sense of the disaster and determining who was responsible for the fire and related events. He then worked with the literature to review the theory of sense making and used this concept to develop further his analysis.
- Limits. Sampling was also partly determined by Gephart's inability to gain access to publicly inaccessible settings. This meant that certain issues such as power and politics could not be addressed.

Janet Bell Crawford found it difficult to balance a positivist approach to interviewing with what she saw as the aims of feminist research:

> Upon reflection of the interviews I've conducted, mainly with executive level individuals, my greatest challenges have been to remain impartial and to get beyond social desirability bias and organizational rhetoric or scripts. In terms of remaining impartial, as a research interviewer I am not there to challenge or question the opinions or perspectives of the interviewee. This can be particularly challenging when the content of the interview contains a topic, for example women and leadership, that could potentially expose sexist attitudes and beliefs or viewpoints that act as a basis for discriminatory actions toward women. Having the knowledge that comes from studying the literature in a particular area can make it difficult to resist turning the interview into a conversation of ideas.

> If at the end of the interview I'm asked questions about the area, I'm more than happy to share. My second challenge is getting beyond the organizational rhetoric. I find some executives are so well rehearsed in their role that getting beyond company-speak or a summary of company policy is difficult. I might try asking the same question in a variety of ways but media savvy executives tend not to go beyond the image of the company that they want to portray. I find asking quantitative questions, for example, 'How many women are on the executive management team?', with follow-up questions, for 'Why do you think there are so few women on the executive management team?', helps. Yes, interviewing executives can be challenge but it can also be a great experience getting time with people who run companies and observing how they handle interviews and how they talk about their organization. It certainly makes reading the business section more interesting.

Instead of this framework for conducting interviews, feminist researchers advocate one that establishes:

- A high level of rapport between interviewer and interviewee.
- A high degree of reciprocity on the part of the interviewer.
- The perspective of the women being interviewed.
- A non-hierarchical relationship.

In connection with the reciprocity that she advocates, Oakley noted, for example, that, in her research on the transition to motherhood, she was frequently asked questions by her respondents. She argues that it was ethically indefensible for a feminist not to answer when confronted with questions of a certain kind. For Oakley, therefore, the qualitative interview was viewed as a means of resolving the dilemmas that she encountered as a feminist interviewing other women. However, as noted in previous chapters, while this broad adherence to a set of principles for interviewing in feminist research continues, it has been tempered by a greater recognition of the possible value of quantitative research.

An interesting dilemma that is perhaps not so easily resolved is the question of what feminist researchers should do when their own 'understandings and interpretations of women's accounts would either not be shared by some of them [i.e., the research participants], and/or represent a form of challenge or threat to their perceptions, choices and coping strategies' (Kelly, Burton, & Regan, 1994, p. 37). It is the first type of situation that will be examined, at least in part, because, while it is of particular significance to feminist researchers, its implications are somewhat broader. It raises the tricky question of how far the commitment of seeing through the eyes of the people you study can and/or should be stretched. Two examples are relevant here. Reinharz (1992, pp. 28–9) cites the case of an American study by Andersen (1981), who interviewed 20 'corporate wives', who came across as happy with their lot and were supportive of feminism only in relation to employment discrimination. Andersen interpreted their responses to her questions as indicative of 'false consciousness'—in other words, she did not really believe her interviewees. When Andersen wrote an article on her findings, the women wrote a letter rejecting her account, affirming that women can be fulfilled as wives and mothers. A similar situation confronted Millen (1997) when she interviewed 32 British female scientists using 'semi-structured, in-depth individual interviewing' (1997, p. 4.6). As Millen puts it:

> There was a tension between my interpretation of their reported experience as sex-based, and the meaning the participants themselves tended to attribute to their experience, since the majority of respondents did not analyse these experiences in terms of patriarchy or sex–gender systems, but considered them to be individualised, or as 'just something that had to be coped with'. . . . From my external, academically privileged vantage point, it is clear that sexism pervades these professions, and that men are assumed from the start by other scientists to be competent scientists of status whilst women have to prove themselves, overcome the barrier of their difference before they are accepted. These women, on the other hand, did not generally view their interactions in terms of gendered social systems. There is therefore a tension between their characterisation of their experience and my interpretation of it. . . . (1997, pp. 5.6, 5.9)

Three interesting issues are thrown up by these two accounts. First, how can such a situation arise? This is an issue that pervades qualitative research that makes claims to reveal social reality as viewed by members of the setting in question. If researchers are genuinely seeing through others' eyes, the 'tension' to which Millen refers should not arise. However, it clearly can and does, and this strongly suggests that qualitative researchers are more affected by their own perspectives and research questions when collecting and analyzing data than might be expected from textbook accounts of the research process. Secondly, there is the question of how to handle such a 'tension'—that is, how do you reconcile the two accounts? Andersen's (1981) solution to the tension she encountered was to reinterpret her findings in terms of the conditions that engender the contentment she uncovered. Thirdly, given that feminist research is often concerned with wider political goals of emancipation, a tension between participants' world views and the researcher's position raises moral questions about the appropriateness of imposing an interpretation that is not shared by research participants themselves. Such an imposition could hardly be regarded as consistent with the principle of a non-hierarchical relationship in the interview situation.

Therefore, while qualitative interviewing has become a highly popular research method for feminist researchers because of its malleability into a form that can support the principles of feminism, interesting questions are raised in terms of the relationship between researchers' and participants' accounts. Such questions have a significance generally for the conduct of qualitative research.

Qualitative interviewing versus participant observation

The aim of this section is to compare the merits and limitations of interviewing in qualitative research with those of participant observation. These are probably the two most prominent methods of data collection in qualitative research, so there is some virtue in assessing their strengths, a debate that was first begun many years ago (Becker & Geer, 1957a, 1957b, Trow, 1957). In this section, interviewing is being compared to participant observation rather than ethnography, because the latter invariably entails a significant amount of interviewing. So, too, does participant observation, but in this discussion we will be following the principle that we will outline in Key concept 17.1—namely, that the term will be employed to refer to the specifically observational activities in which the participant observer engages. As noted in Key concept 17.1, the term 'ethnography' is being reserved for the wide range of data collection activities in which ethnographers engage—one of which is participant observation—along with the written account that is a product of those activities.

Advantages of participant observation in comparison to qualitative interviewing: Seeing through others' eyes

As noted in Chapters 3 and 6, this is one of the main tenets of qualitative research, but, on the face of it, the participant observer would seem to be better placed for gaining a foothold on social reality in this way. The researcher's prolonged immersion in a social setting would seem to make him or her better equipped to see as others see. The participant observer is in much closer contact with people for a longer period of time; also, he or she participates in many of the same kinds of activity as the members of the social setting being studied. Research that relies on interviewing alone is likely to entail much more fleeting contacts, though in qualitative research interviews can last many hours and re-interviewing is not unusual.

Learning the native language

Becker and Geer (1957a) argued that the participant observer is in the same position as a social anthropologist visiting a distant land, in that, in order to understand a culture, the language must be learned. However, it is not simply the formal language that must be understood in the case of the kinds of business research in which a participant observer in a complex organization engages. It is also very often the 'argot'—the special uses of words and slang that are important to penetrate that culture. Such an understanding is arrived at through the observation of language use.

The taken for granted

Although much important information can be obtained through interviews, some kinds of data cannot be captured through this particular research method. The interview relies primarily on verbal behaviour and as such matters that interviewees take for granted are less likely to surface than in participant observation, where implicit features in social life are more likely to be revealed as a result of the observer's continued presence and because of the ability to observe behaviour rather than just rely on what is said. For example, few interviewees will be able accurately to recollect the dynamics of a meeting involving several people—they may remember parts of what was said, and the nature of the problem under discussion, but are unlikely to recollect how decisions evolved as part of a social process (Whyte, 1953), so for this researchers must continue to rely on observation.

Deviant and hidden activities

Much of what we know about patterns of resistance at work, industrial sabotage, and other criminal or deviant activity within organizations has been gleaned from participant observation. For example, Linstead's (1985) account of the practical jokes, general kidding, and games played by bakery workers was obtained through participant observation. Similarly, Collinson's (1988) analysis of humour in the context of a male-dominated workplace relied partly on non-participant observation to obtain data about the daily jibes, socialization rituals, and initiation ceremonies that characterized daily life on the shop floor at Slavs. These are areas that insiders are likely to be reluctant to talk about in an interview context alone. Understanding is again likely to come through prolonged interaction. Ethnographers conducting participant observation are more likely to place themselves in situations in which their continued involvement allows them gradually to infiltrate such social worlds and to insinuate themselves into the lives of people who might be sensitive to outsiders.

Sensitivity to context

The participant observer's extensive contact with a social setting allows the context of people's behaviour to be mapped out fully. The participant observer interacts with people in a variety of situations and possibly roles, so that the links between behaviour and context can be forged.

Encountering the unexpected and flexibility

It may be that, because of the unstructured nature of participant observation, it is more likely to uncover unexpected topics or issues. Except with the most unstructured forms of interview, the interview process is likely to entail some degree of closure as the interview guide is put together, which may blinker the researcher slightly. Also, participant observation may be more flexible because of the tendency for interviewers to instill an element of comparability (and hence a modicum of structure) in their questioning of different people. Ditton's (1977) decision at a very late stage in the data collection process to focus on pilferage in the bakery in which he was a participant observer is an example of this feature.

Naturalistic emphasis

Participant observation has the potential to come closer to a naturalistic emphasis, because the qualitative researcher confronts members of a social setting in their natural environments. Interviewing, because of its nature as a disruption of members' normal flow of events, even when it is at its most informal, is less amenable to this feature. It is unsurprising, therefore, that, when referring to naturalism as a tradition in qualitative research, Gubrium and Holstein (1997) largely refer to studies in which participant observation was a prominent component (e.g., Whyte, 1955).

Advantages of qualitative interviewing in comparison to participant observation

Issues resistant to observation

It is likely that there is a wide range of issues that are simply not amenable to observation, so that asking people about them represents the only viable means of finding out about them within a qualitative research strategy. For example, in Bell's (2001) research on payment systems in the chemical industry it was not really possible to explore the systems and rules whereby payments were made by observing shop floor practices, although the latter was very useful in gaining an understanding of the cultural context in which

payment systems were located. For most workers, payment is an issue that surfaces through consideration of issues that relate to the 'effort-bargain' and this understanding was more readily accessed through interviews. MacMillan (2009) could hardly observe people's existential angst no more than Wallace (2009) was privy to women's thought processes about their careers over a lifetime.

Reconstruction of events

Qualitative research frequently entails the reconstruction of events by asking interviewees to think back over how a certain series of events unfolded in relation to a current situation. An example is Pettigrew's (1985) research on Imperial Chemicals Industries (ICI), which entailed interviewing about contemporaneous events but also included 'retrospective interviewing', as Pettigrew defined it (see Web Research in focus 4.9). This reconstruction of events is something that cannot be accomplished through participant observation alone.

Ethical considerations

There are certain areas that could be observed—albeit indirectly through hidden hardware like a microphone—but would raise ethical considerations. For example, Ditton (1977) never disclosed to his fellow workers in the bakery that he was interested in pilferage, although he did seek to protect their anonymity, by omitting names and changing other irrelevant facts in the published study. He goes on to claim that he could not have disclosed his interest in pilferage, partly because he did not decide to concentrate on this subject until some time after the conclusion of the study. However, in this case, participant observation does raise ethical issues relating to the observation of criminal activity and the extent to which the researcher actively participates in it.

Reactive effects

The question of reactive effects is by no means a straightforward matter. As with structured observation (see Chapter 17), it might be anticipated that the presence of a participant observer would result in reactive effects (see Key concept 16.3). People's knowledge of the fact that they are being observed may make them behave less naturally.

However, participant observers, like researchers using structured observation, typically find that people become accustomed to their presence and begin to behave more naturally the longer they are around. Indeed, members of social settings sometimes express surprise when participant observers announce their imminent departure when they are on the verge of disengagement. Interviewers clearly do not suffer from the same kind of problem, but it could be argued that the unnatural character of the interview encounter can also be regarded as a context within which reactive effects may emerge. Participant observation also suffers from the related problem of observers disturbing the very situation being studied, because conversations and interactions will occur in conjunction with the observer that otherwise would not happen. This is by no means an easy issue to resolve and it seems likely that both participant observation and qualitative interviewing set in motion reactive effects but of different kinds.

Less intrusive in people's lives

Participant observation can be very intrusive in people's lives in that the observer is likely to take up a lot more of their time than in an interview. Interviews in qualitative research can sometimes be very long and re-interviewing is not uncommon, but the impact on people's time will probably be less than having to take observers into account on a regular basis, though it is likely that this feature will vary from situation to situation. Participant observation is likely to be especially intrusive in terms of the amount of people's time taken up when it is in organizational settings. In work organizations, there is a risk that the rhythms of work lives will be disrupted.

Longitudinal research easier

One of the advantages of participant observation is that it is inherently longitudinal in character because the observer is present in a social setting for a period of time. As a result, change and connections between events can be observed. However, there are limits to the amount of time that participant observers can devote to being away from their normal routines. Consequently, participant observation does not usually extend much beyond two to three years in duration. When participant observation is being

conducted into an area of research that is episodic rather than requiring continued observation, a longer time period may be feasible. Pettigrew's (1985) research at ICI combined interviewing in late 1975, 1976, and early 1977, the latter parts of 1980 and early 1981, and again in 1982, with his interventions into the company as a consultant. During that period 134 people were interviewed from the ICI corporate headquarters and the four divisions under study. Several of these individuals were interviewed more than once and the total number of research interviews amounted to 175. Kanter (1977) employed a similar strategy combining consultant activity with research over a five-year period. Web Research in focus 14.4 gives an example of a longitudinal telephone interview study which, although it took place over a shorter six-month time period, traced a period of dramatic change following the closure of a car plant that marked the loss of the last remaining British-owned car manufacturer. In sum, interviewing can be carried out within a longitudinal research design somewhat more easily because repeat interviews may be easier to organize than repeat visits to participant observers' research settings, though the latter is not impossible. Following up interviewees on several occasions is likely to be easier than returning to research sites on a regular basis.

Greater breadth of coverage

In participant observation, the researcher is invariably constrained in his or her interactions and observations to a fairly restricted range of people, incidents, and localities. Participant observation in a large organization, for example, is likely to mean that knowledge of that organization beyond the confines of the department or section in which the observation is carried out is not likely to be very extensive. Interviewing can allow access to a wider variety of people and situations.

Specific focus

As noted in Chapter 6, qualitative research sometimes begins with a specific focus, and indeed Silverman (1993) has been critical of the notion that it should be regarded as an open-ended form of research. Qualitative interviewing would seem to be better suited to such a situation, since the interview can be directed at that focus and its associated research questions. Thus, the research by Bryman et al. on the police had a very specific research focus in line with its Home Office funding—namely, conceptualizations of leadership among police officers (Bryman, Stephens, & Campo, 1996). The bulk of the data gathering was in two police forces and entailed the interviewing of police officers at all levels using a semi-structured interview guide. As it had such a clear focus, it was more appropriate to conduct the research by interview rather than participant observation, since issues to do with leadership notions may not crop up on a regular basis, which would make observation a very extravagant method of data collection.

Overview

When Becker and Geer (1957*a*, p. 28) proclaimed over 40 years ago that the 'most complete form of the sociological datum . . . is the form in which the participant observer gathers it', Trow (1957, p. 33) reprimanded them for making such a universal claim and argued that 'the problem under investigation properly dictates the methods of investigation'. The latter view is very much the one taken in this book. Research methods are appropriate to researching some issues and areas but not others. The discussion of the merits and limitations of participant observation and qualitative interviews is meant simply to draw attention to some of the considerations that might be taken into account if there is a genuine opportunity to use one or the other in a study.

Equally, and to repeat an earlier point, the comparison is a somewhat artificial exercise, because participant observation is usually carried out as part of ethnographic research and as such it is usually accompanied by interviewing as well as other methods. In other words, participant observers frequently buttress their observations with methods of data collection that allow them access to important areas that are not amenable to observation. However, the aim of the comparison was to provide a kind of balance sheet in considering the strengths and limitations of a reliance on either participant observation or qualitative interview alone. Its aim is to draw attention to some of the factors that might be taken into account in deciding how to plan a study and even how to evaluate existing research.

Checklist

Issues to consider for your qualitative interview:

☐ Have you devised a clear and comprehensive/informative way of introducing the research to interviewees?

☐ Does your interview guide clearly relate to your research questions?

☐ Have you piloted the guide with some appropriate respondents?

☐ Have you thought about what you will do if your interviewee does not turn up for the interview?

☐ Does the guide contain a good mixture of different kinds of questions, such as probing, specifying, and direct questions?

☐ Have you ensured that interviews will allow novel or unexpected themes and issues to arise?

☐ Is your language in the questions clear, comprehensible, and free of unnecessary jargon?

☐ Are your questions relevant to the people you are proposing to interview?

☐ Does your interview guide include requests for information about the interviewee, such as his or her age, work experience, position in the firm?

☐ Have your questions been designed to elicit reflective discussions, so that interviewees are not tempted to answer in 'yes' or 'no' terms?

☐ Do your questions offer a real prospect of seeing the world from your interviewees' point of view rather than imposing your own frame of reference on them?

☐ Are you familiar with the setting(s) in which the interviews will take place?

☐ Are you thoroughly familiar with and have you tested your recording equipment?

☐ Have you thought about how you will present yourself in the interview, such as how you will be dressed?

☐ Have you thought about how you will go about putting into operation the skills that make a good interviewer?

Key points

- Interviewing in qualitative research is typically of the unstructured or semi-structured kind.
- In qualitative research, interviewing may be the sole method in an investigation or may be used as part of an ethnographic study, or indeed in tandem with another qualitative method.
- Qualitative interviewing is meant to be flexible and to seek out the world views of research participants.
- If an interview guide is employed, it should not be too structured in its application and should allow some flexibility in the asking of questions.
- The qualitative interview should be tape-recorded and then transcribed.
- As with ethnographic research, investigations using qualitative interviews tend not to employ random sampling to select participants.
- The qualitative interview has become an extremely popular method of data collection in feminist studies.
- Whether to use participant observation or qualitative interviews depends in large part on their relative suitability to the research questions being addressed. However, it must also be borne in mind that participant observers invariably conduct some interviews in the course of their investigations.

Questions for review

Differences between the structured interview and qualitative research interviews
- How does qualitative interviewing differ from structured interviewing?

Unstructured and semi-structured interviewing
- What are the differences between unstructured and semi-structured interviewing?
- Could semi-structured interviewing stand in the way of flexibility in qualitative research?
- What are the differences between life history and oral history interviews?
- What kinds of consideration need to be borne in mind when preparing an interview guide?
- What kinds of question might be asked in an interview guide?
- What kinds of skill does the interviewer need to develop in qualitative interviewing?
- Why is it important to tape-record and transcribe qualitative interviews?

Sampling
- Compare theoretical sampling and snowball sampling.

Feminist research and interviewing in qualitative research
- Why has the qualitative interview become such a prominent research method for feminist researchers?
- What dilemmas might be posed for feminist researchers using qualitative interviewing?

Qualitative interviewing versus participant observation
- Outline the relative advantages and disadvantages of qualitative interviewing and participant observation.
- Does one method seem more in tune with the preoccupations of qualitative researchers than the other?

15

Focus Groups

Chapter guide

The focus group method is an interview with several people on a specific topic or issue. This chapter explores:

- The possible reasons for preferring **focus group** interviews to individual interviews of the kind discussed in the previous chapter.
- The role of focus groups in market and public relations research.
- How focus groups should be conducted in terms of such features as the need for tape recording, the number and size of groups, how participants can be selected, and how direct the questioning should be.
- The significance of interaction between participants in focus group discussions.
- The suggestion that the focus group method fits particularly well with a feminist research approach.
- Some practical difficulties with focus group sessions, such as the possible loss of control over proceedings and the potential for unwanted group effects.

Introduction

We are used to thinking of the interview as something that involves an interviewer and one interviewee. Most textbooks reinforce this perception by concentrating on individual interviews. The focus group technique is a method of interviewing that involves more than one, usually at least four, interviewees. Essentially it is a group interview. Some authors draw a distinction between the focus group and the group interview techniques. Three reasons are sometimes put forward to suggest a distinction:

- Focus groups typically emphasize a specific theme or topic that is explored in depth, whereas group interviews are often more broad in focus.
- Sometimes group interviews are carried out so that the researcher is able to save time and money by carrying out interviews with a number of individuals simultaneously. However, focus groups are not carried out for this reason.
- The focus group practitioner is invariably interested in the ways in which individuals discuss a certain issue as members of a group, rather than simply as individuals.

In other words, with a focus group the researcher will be interested in such things as how people respond to each other's views and build up a view out of the interaction that takes place within the group.

However, the distinction between the focus group method and the group interview is by no means clear-cut and the two terms are frequently employed interchangeably. Nonetheless, the definition proposed in Key concept 15.1 provides a starting point.

Most focus group researchers undertake their work within the traditions of qualitative research. This means that they are explicitly concerned with revealing how the group participants view the issues with which they are confronted. Therefore, the researcher will aim to provide a fairly unstructured setting for the extraction of their views and perspectives. The person who runs the focus group session is usually called the **moderator** or **facilitator** and he or she will be expected to guide the session but not to be too intrusive.

Another general point about the *focus group method* is that, although it has been used for many years in market research to test reactions to products and to advertising initiatives, it has more recently been developed for a wider variety of purposes. The field of public relations has a strong history of using focus groups, and consequently they are now used by politicians, not only quantitatively

Key concept 15.1: What is the focus group method?

The focus group method is a form of group interview in which there are several participants, in addition to a moderator/facilitator. There is an emphasis upon both a tightly defined topic and the interaction within the group.

to predict the outcome of an election, but also qualitatively to shape their policies and images. Cowley (2000) reports that one politician used focus group research to determine that he should be filmed only from one side of his face, and he should be made to look older in order to increase voter support. Focus groups are used by filmmakers to determine the end of a major film run, by art entrepreneurs to determine what paintings will sell, and by CEOs to test corporate communications. However, the popularization of the focus group method may have disadvantages for business and management researchers. For example, Blackburn and Stokes (2000) in their study of small businesses suggest that it was more difficult to convince research audiences of the significance of their focus group research, partly because of the proliferation of the use of focus groups by political parties. Similarly, Cowley (2000) suggests that, in order to distinguish research based on 'strategic qualitative market research focus groups' from research that is done by those who simply decide 'they can run' focus groups, despite their lack of experience, a professional code of conduct is needed. However, it must be remembered that, while the use of focus groups is gaining in popularity at the moment, it is by no means a new technique, as it has a long-established use in various forms of social research.

 ## Uses of focus groups

What are the uses of the focus group method? In many ways its uses are bound up with the uses of qualitative research in general, but, over and above these, the following points can be highlighted:

- The original idea for the focus group—the focused interview—was that people who were known to have had a certain experience could be interviewed in a

relatively unstructured way about that experience. The bulk of the discussion by Merton et al. (1956) of the notion of the focused interview was in terms of individual interviews, but their book also considered the extension of the method into group interview contexts. Subsequently, the focus group has become a popular method for researchers examining the ways in which individuals, in conjunction with one another, construe the general topics in which the researcher is interested. In management and business, early use of the focus group technique was also seen as a way of helping individuals to define problems and work together to identify potential solutions (Hutt, 1979). The dynamics of group discussion could lead individuals to define business problems in new and innovative ways and stimulate creative ideas for their solution.

- The technique allows the researcher to develop an understanding about why people feel the way they do. In a normal individual interview the interviewee is often asked about his or her reasons for holding a particular view, but the focus group approach offers the opportunity of allowing people to probe each other's reasons for holding a certain view. This can be more interesting than the sometimes predictable question-followed-by-answer approach of normal interviews. For one thing, an individual may answer in a certain way during a focus group, but, as he or she listens to others' answers, he or she may want to qualify or modify a view; or alternatively may want to voice agreement to something that he or she probably would not have thought of without the opportunity of hearing the views of others. These possibilities mean that focus groups may also be very helpful in the elicitation of a wide variety of views in relation to a particular issue.

- In focus groups, participants are able to highlight issues in relation to a topic that they deem to be important and significant. This is clearly an aim of individual interviews too, but, because the moderator has to relinquish a certain amount of control to the participants, the issues that concern them can surface. This is clearly an important consideration in the context of qualitative research, since the viewpoints of the people being studied are often the point of the research.

- In conventional one-to-one interviewing, interviewees are rarely challenged; they might say things that are inconsistent with earlier replies or that patently could not be true, but we are often reluctant to point out such inconsistencies. In the context of a focus group, individuals will often argue with each other and challenge each other's views. This process of arguing means that the researcher may stand a chance of ending up with more realistic accounts of what people think, because they are forced to think about and possibly revise their views.

- The focus group offers the researcher the opportunity to study the ways in which individuals collectively make sense of a phenomenon and construct meanings around it. It is a central tenet of theoretical positions, like symbolic interactionism, that the processes of coming to terms with (that is, understanding) social phenomena are not undertaken by individuals in isolation from each other. Instead, this occurs in interaction and discussion with others. In this sense, therefore, focus groups reflect the processes through which meaning is constructed in everyday life and to that extent can be regarded as more naturalistic than individual interviews (Wilkinson, 1998).

As we mentioned in the introduction, focus groups have been used extensively in market research for many years where the method is used for such purposes as testing responses to new products and advertising initiatives. Focus groups typically involve groups of 6 to 12 consumers, who are brought together to discuss their reactions to new products, packaging, advertisements, or promotions. In fact there is a large literature within market research concerning the practices that are associated with focus group research and their implementation (e.g., Calder, 1977).

However, the use of focus group methods in market research has attracted its fair share of controversy. Some researchers have suggested that it is a weaker method than, say, experiments or surveys (to name two other research approaches that are common in market research). The most frequently mentioned problem is the perceived lack of generalizability, results are not always a reliable indicator of the reactions of the wider population.

Criticism is also made of the unsystematic nature of the sample, which is not as rigorous as **probability sampling** (see Chapter 9). For example, Sudman and Blair (1999, p. 272) have suggested that, although the focus group method is an excellent tool for gaining insight about markets, 'it should be evident that a group of 10 or so people chosen haphazardly at a single location cannot be expected to reflect the total population of consumers'. A further difficulty stems from the lack of realism associated with focus groups. Participants may be given written or verbal descriptions of a product, or an artist's sketch, but this bears little relation to the real-life experience of choosing a product in a competitive context. Criticisms also stem from problems of **reliability**. This relates to the role of the moderator and the suggestion that there can be variation in the interpretation of **transcripts**. Fern (2001) has provided a rebuttal of these criticisms by arguing that the **generalizability** of focus group findings, as with other research methods, depends on the scale of the **sample**— a two-group study may have limited generalizability but 32-group study is another matter. He also defends the reliability of focus groups, suggesting that representativeness can be achieved by stratifying the population and in drawing **random samples** from each stratum. Fern suggests that greater **reliability** can be gained by using different moderators with different backgrounds (e.g., male and female) to conduct group discussions on a relevant topic (e.g., gender). The results from each group can then be compared for consistency of interpretation. Overall, however, what seems puzzling is that market researchers are attempting to defend their use of focus group methods in terms of quantitative rather than qualitative criteria; this is mainly because they are being criticized in terms of quantitative criteria.

 ## Conducting focus groups

There are a number of practical aspects of the conduct of focus group research that require some discussion.

Recording and transcription

As with interviewing for qualitative research, the focus group session will work best if it is recorded and subsequently transcribed. The following reasons are often used to explain this preference:

- One reason is the simple difficulty of writing down not only exactly what people say but also who says it. In an individual interview you might be able to ask the respondent to hold on while you write something down, but to do this in the context of an interview involving several people would be extremely disruptive.
- The researcher will be interested in who expresses views within the group, such as whether certain individuals seem to act as opinion leaders or dominate the discussion. This also means that there is an interest in ranges of opinions within groups; for example, in a session, does most of the range of opinion derive from just one or two people or from most of the people in the group?
- A major reason for conducting focus group research is the fact that it is possible to study the processes through which meaning is collectively constructed within each session (see above). It would be very difficult to do this by taking notes, because of the need to keep track of who says what (see also previous point). If this element is lost, the dynamics of the focus group session would also be lost, and a major rationale for doing focus group interviews rather than individual ones would be undermined.
- Like all qualitative researchers, the focus group practitioner will be interested in not just what people say but how they say it, for example, the particular language that they employ. There is every chance that the nuances of language will be lost if the researcher has to rely on notes.

It should be kept in mind that transcribing focus group sessions is more complicated and more time consuming than transcribing traditional interview recordings. This is because you need to take account of *who* is talking in the session, as well as what is said. This is sometimes difficult, since people's voices are not always easy to distinguish. Also, people sometimes talk over each other, which can make transcription even more difficult. In addition, it is extremely important to ensure that you equip yourself with a very high-quality microphone, which is capable of picking up voices, some of which may be quite faint, from many directions. Focus group transcripts always seem to have more missing bits owing to lack of audibility than transcripts from conventional interviews.

A recent development in market research has involved the introduction of virtual focus groups (see Research in focus 15.1), who interact with each other via computer. This overcomes some of the problems associated with recording what goes on in focus groups, but it also raises some problems as well.

How many groups?

How many groups do you need? There is a good deal of variation in the numbers of focus groups that are used in any particular study, with the norm being somewhere between 12 and 15.

Clearly, it is unlikely that just one group will meet the needs of the researcher, since there is always the possibility that the responses are particular to that one group. Obviously, time and resources will be a factor, but there are strong arguments for saying that too many groups will be a waste of time. Calder (1977) proposes that, when the moderator reaches the point that he or she is able to anticipate fairly accurately what the next group is going to say, then there are probably enough groups already. This notion is very similar to the **theoretical saturation** criterion. In other words, once your major analytic categories have been saturated, there seems little point in continuing, and so it would be appropriate to bring data collection to a halt. For their study of audience discussion programs, Livingstone and Lunt (1994, p. 181) used this criterion: 'The number of focus groups was determined by continuing until comments and patterns began to repeat and little new material was generated'. When this point of theoretical saturation is reached, as an alternative to terminating data collection, there may be a case for moving on to an extension of the issues that have been raised in the focus group sessions that have been carried out.

One factor that may affect the number of groups is whether the researcher feels that the kinds and range of views are likely to be affected by socio-demographic

15.1 Research in Focus

Virtual focus groups

Recent developments in market research have enabled the computerization of focus group interaction, whereby group members interact with each other using specially designed software rather than using a moderator. Kiely (1998) describes this process as typically involving participants assembled in a room where there are networked computers. They type in their ideas about a given subject onto their own screen, where they see only the ideas that they type. A large screen at the front of the room then displays all the participants' comments simultaneously and anonymously. Kiely (1998) suggests this process makes it easier for each group member to have an equal voice and more difficult for one person to dominate the discussion. The technology also makes it possible to reduce the time it takes to run a focus group, as all members of the group are able to express their ideas simultaneously rather than serially. As they see the ideas of others on the main screen, individuals are able to build on the ideas already expressed. However, focus group members do report feeling more anonymous within the encounter and, therefore, that it is less satisfactory. Recent advances in computer graphics have also enabled innovations like virtual shopping, which is used within market research focus groups to simulate the atmosphere of an actual retail store on a computer screen (Burke, 1996). Within this virtual environment, focus group members are able to view shelves stocked with a range of products, examine the packaging, and decide whether or not they would purchase them.

The Internet has opened up opportunities for focus groups to be held entirely virtually—group members need not be in the same room with one another, or even in the same country. The main features of online focus groups will be discussed in depth in Chapter 22. One of the main differences between online and in-person focus groups is that in online groups the questions are usually more structured, since they are written in full-sentence form in advance so they can be displayed on-screen (Sweet, 2001). This just leaves the moderator to interject additional probes into the dialogue as it develops. Sweet recommends that 40–45 questions be used within a typical 90-minute group discussion. He also notes that one of the advantages of online focus groups is that participants do not have to travel to a venue in order to attend the meeting. This can be helpful in reducing the number of no-shows due to things like traffic problems and bad weather. He also recommends that moderators have fast and accurate keyboard skills so they are able to keep up with the discussion. Moderators should also be familiar with the social conventions associated with online venues such as chat rooms.

Reid and Reid (2005) conducted an experimental study comparing the effectiveness of in-person focus groups with those that relied on computer-mediated discussion. They found that although a greater number of contributions were made by the in-person focus group participants (this is explained by the time it takes to type being longer than the time it takes to talk), proportionally more ideas and answers were generated within the computer-mediated groups. However, participants were more satisfied with the face-to-face method of communication, more appreciative of other participants' feelings, and found it easier to follow the discussion in the in-person groups.

factors such as age, gender, class, and so on. Many focus group researchers like to use stratifying criteria like these to ensure that groups with a wide range of features will be included. If this is done, a larger number of groups may be required to reflect the criteria. In connection with the research described in Web Research in focus 15.1, Blackburn and Stokes (2000) explain that the composition of the groups was stratified according to business

Tips and Skills

Transcribing focus group interviews

Earlier in the book, we provided the practical tip that it may be that it is not always desirable or feasible to transcribe the whole of the interview. The same applies to focus group research, which is often more difficult and time consuming to transcribe than personal interview recordings because of the number of speakers who are involved. The suggestions we made in Chapter 14 in relation to transcribing sections of an interview therefore apply equally well to focus group recordings.

and personal criteria, including gender. A range of business sectors was represented within the focus groups, including manufacturing, construction, and services. Small businesses were defined quite broadly in terms of certain revenue parameters—from a minimum of £50,000 to a maximum of £3,000,000 (at the time of the study, this would represent a range of approximately $110,195–$6,600,000 in Canadian dollars). However, it may be that high levels of diversity are not anticipated in connection with some topics, in which case a large number of groups could represent an unnecessary expense.

One further point to keep in mind when considering the number of groups is that more groups will increase the complexity of your analysis. For example, Schlesinger et al. (1992, p. 29) report that the 14 tape-recorded sessions they organized produced over 1400 pages of transcription. This pile of paper was accumulated from discussions in each group of an average of one hour for each of the four screenings that session participants were shown. Although this means that the sessions were longer than is normally the case, it does demonstrate that the amount of data to analyze can be very large, even though a total of 14 sessions may not sound a lot to someone unfamiliar with the workings of the method.

Size of groups

How large should groups be? Morgan (1998a) suggests that the typical group size is 6 to 10 members, although in their study of small business owner-managers Blackburn and Stokes (2000) found that discussion in groups of more than eight was difficult to manage, so, as the research progressed, they scaled down the number of participants who were invited on each occasion. One major problem faced by focus group practitioners is people who agree to participate but who do not turn up on the day. It is almost impossible to control for 'no-shows' other than consciously over-recruiting, a strategy that is sometimes recommended (e.g., Wilkinson, 1999a, p. 188).

In their research into small businesses, Blackburn and Stokes (2000) found that recruiting business owners to attend a group discussion at a pre-set date and venue away from their business context proved to be a time-consuming process (see Web Research in focus 15.1). The acceptance rate to invitations was as low as 1 to 10 and the exercise of ensuring attendance involved a great number of telephone calls to ensure a broad spread of participants. However, after participants had attended one focus group and had got to know each other and exchanged business cards, they were more likely to attend a second time, as they were keen

Tips and Skills

Number of focus groups

Focus groups take a long time to arrange and it takes a long time to transcribe the recordings that are made. It is likely that students will not be able to include as many focus group sessions for projects or dissertations as the studies cited in this chapter. You will, therefore, need to make do with a smaller number of groups in most instances. Make sure you are able to justify the number of groups you have chosen and why your data are still significant.

to hear how each other's businesses were developing. Overall the researchers found it very difficult to predict the 'no-show' rate. This meant that the size of their focus groups varied considerably, from 3 to 10 (see Table 15.1). Blackburn and Stokes (2000) acknowledge that there were likely to be quite different dynamics in the different sized groups; in particular, in the smaller groups greater demands were made on each participant to contribute more.

Almost the opposite problem was faced by Milkman (1997) in her study of auto factory workers at the General Motors plant in New Jersey. Milkman and her colleague conducted three focus group discussions at the plant: two with production workers and one with skilled trades workers. Each discussion was held in a conference room inside the plant during regular working hours, lasted around two hours, and was tape-recorded and transcribed. Workers were selected randomly from the plant roster and they were paid their normal wage for the time spent in discussion. This, according to Milkman, 'ensured perfect attendance', but it also 'underscored the project's official status' (1997, p. 195). She suspects that this made some participants suspicious and less inclined to speak freely.

Morgan (1998a) recommends smaller groups when participants are likely to have a lot to say on the research topic. This is likely to occur when participants are very involved in or emotionally preoccupied with the topic. He also suggests smaller groups when topics are controversial or complex and when gleaning participants' personal accounts is a major goal. Morgan recommends larger groups when involvement with a topic is likely to be low or when the researcher wants 'to hear numerous brief suggestions' (1998a, p. 75). However, we are not convinced that larger groups are necessarily superior for topics in which participants have little involvement, since it may be more difficult to stimulate discussion in such a context. Larger groups may make it even more difficult if people are rather diffident about talking about a topic about which they know little or have little experience. This was a potential problem in Blackburn and Stokes's (2000) study, where external information, such as government proposals on late payment legislation, formed the basis for discussion. However, in these instances, the researchers found that participants relied more heavily on their own personal experiences and provided detailed accounts of payment practices in their industry.

Level of moderator involvement

How involved should the moderator/facilitator be? In qualitative research, the aim is to get at the perspectives of those being studied. Consequently, the approach should not be intrusive and structured. Therefore, there is a tendency for researchers to use a fairly small number of very general questions to guide the focus group session. Moreover, there is a further tendency for moderators to allow quite a lot of latitude to participants, so that the discussion can range fairly widely. Tips and skills *Extract from a focus group discussion showing no moderator involvement* provides an example of this. In this instance, three quite different opinions emerge in relation to the issue of succession planning without any moderator prompting. Obviously, if the discussion goes off at a total tangent, it may be necessary to refocus the participants' attention, but even then it may be necessary to be careful, because what may appear to be digressions may in fact reveal something of interest to

Location	Number of participants in each focus group			
	Sept. 1997	Mar. 1998	Nov. 1998	Mar. 1999
Reading	10	5	6	6
London	8	3	6	5
Kidderminster	7	7	3	6
Manchester	5	5	5	7
Glasgow/Hartlepool	6	6	–	–
TOTAL	36	26	26	30

Table 15.1 Location and attendees from five focus groups

Source: adapted from Blackburn and Stokes (2000).

Tips and Skills

Extract from a focus group discussion showing no moderator involvement

Michael: . . . —talking about your family taking over the business—that's something I wouldn't do with my family because I don't think they've got the fire. I just don't think my daughters have got the same fire as I've got.

Mike: You're forcing them down a particular channel—there are so many things they can do . . . I think that they may or may not have the right qualities to do that—they may wish to go out and do other things . . . plus you might think that in giving them a thriving business you're spoiling them so I just think this whole family business thing is an absolute can of worms.

Gary: If they're in it already though it's a different situation.

Mike: . . . Well I accept that . . . my exit strategy is that at some point I've got to sell the business and I think the management team realize that. So they know when we're discussing share options there's only one point—you know we were discussing what's the point in owning shares in a private business—there is only one point when it is worth it and that's when the business is sold. So what it is, is when the business is sold they get a share of the benefit—so that's the sort of logic there.

(Blackburn & Stokes, 2000, p. 60)

the group participants. The advantage of allowing a fairly free rein to the discussion is that the researcher stands a better chance of getting access to what individuals see as important or interesting. On the other hand, too much totally irrelevant discussion may prove too unproductive, especially in the commercial environment of market research. It is not surprising, therefore, that, as Wilkinson (1999a) observes, some writers on focus groups perceive the possibility that participants come to take over the running of a session from the moderator as a problem and offer advice on how to reassert control (e.g., Krueger, 1988).

One way in which the moderator may need to be involved is in responding to specific points that are of potential interest to the research questions but that are not picked up by other participants. In Tips and skills '*Extract from a focus group discussion showing some moderator involvement*', which is taken from the study of small business owner-managers (Blackburn & Stokes, 2000), the moderator provides a prompt to guide the discussion of planned business succession to find out if any of the participants have taken advice on this issue. This encourages the group to share their experiences.

Tips and Skills

Extract from a focus group discussion showing some moderator involvement

Moderator: Has anyone other than Gary taken advice on exit routes?

Lilian: We took advice when we made our plan in the first place about moving ourselves away from the front end of the business. How we geared our pension schemes . . .

Mike: I've taken advice and their advice was you need to be bigger . . . to make the amount of

money you need to actually walk away from it . . . I'm in the process of doing that . . . .

Marina: We started this actually about two years ago and we have taken advice and put plans into place. I do believe it is very important to have those plans and the correct ones. They always advise you to get bigger and you have to be a certain size . . . .

(Blackburn & Stokes, 2000, p. 59)

Clearly, the moderator has to straddle two positions: allowing the discussion to flow freely and intervening to bring out especially salient issues, particularly when group participants do not do so. This is not an easy co-nundrum to resolve and each tactic— intervention and nonintervention—carries risks. The best advice is to err on the side of minimal intervention—other than to start the group on a fresh set of issues—but to intervene when the group is struggling in its discussions or when it has not alighted on something that is said in the course of the session that appears significant for the research topic.

Selecting participants

So who should participate in a focus group? This depends on who will find the topic relevant and who can represent specific occupational or organizational groupings that have an interest in the topic concerned. Usually a wide range of organizational members or stakeholders from different organizations is required, but they are organized into separate groups in terms of stratifying criteria, such as age, gender, occupation, profession, hierarchical position within the organization, or length of service. Participants for each group can then be selected randomly or through some kind of snowball sampling method. The aim is to establish whether or not there is any systematic variation in the ways in which different groups discuss a matter.

A further issue in relation to the selection of group participants is whether to select people who are unknown to each other (for example, members of the same profes-sional association or employees from different divisions within the same organization) or to use natural group-ings (for example, co-workers or students on the same course). Some researchers prefer to exclude people who know each other on the grounds that pre-existing styles of interaction or status differences may contaminate the session. Not all writers accept this rule of thumb. Some prefer to select natural groups whenever possible. For ex-ample, in marketing research, companies like Procter & Gamble tend to go back repeatedly to the same pool from which they draw focus groups (Kiely, 1998).

However, opting for a strategy of recruiting peo-ple entirely from natural groups is not always feasible, because of difficulties of securing participation. For example, it is not always feasible to remove a number of employees from work activity at the same time, in which case other strategies of selection may have to be used. Morgan (1998a) suggests that one problem with using natural groups is that people who know each other well are likely to operate with taken-for-granted assumptions that they feel do not need to be brought to the fore. He suggests that, if it is important for the researcher to bring out such assumptions, groups of strangers are likely to work better. On the other hand, if the focus group is in-tended to explore collective understandings or shared meanings held within a work group, this can be achieved more readily by using participants who are all members of the same group.

Asking questions

An issue that is close to the question of the degree of in-volvement on the part of the moderator is the matter of how far there should be a set of questions that must be addressed. This issue is very similar to the considerations about how unstructured an interview should be in qualita-tive interviewing (see Chapter 14). Some researchers prefer to use just one or two very general questions to stimulate discussion, with the moderator intervening as necessary along the lines outlined above. However, other research-ers prefer to inject somewhat more structure into the or-ganization of the focus group sessions. A clear example of this is the research on small business owner-managers, in which moderators worked with a topic agenda with times allocated to the discussion of each topic (see Figure 15.1). Initial questions were designed to generate initial reactions in a relatively open-ended way, to put the owner-managers at ease and to get them talking as soon as possible in an in-formal manner. Then the moderator moved the discussion on to the substantive issues of the trading climate; chal-lenges in the business environment, government policies, and business succession and exit strategies. Such a general approach to questioning, which is fairly common in focus group research, allows the researcher to navigate the chan-nel between, on the one side, addressing the research ques-tions and ensuring comparability between sessions, and, on the other side, allowing participants to raise issues they see as significant and in their own terms.

Figure 15.1

An example of a topic agenda for a small business owner-manager focus group

Topic Agenda

1. **Introduction (15 mins.)**
   Introduce the research team and roles
   Aim and format of the focus group
   Conventions (confidentiality, speak one at a time, recordings, everybody's views, open debate, report of proceedings)
   Personal introduction of participants and their businesses

2. **Discussion Topics**
   i) *Current trading climate* (15 mins.)
      (e.g., comparative order levels)
   ii) *Main challenges in the business environment* (20 mins.)
      (e.g., exchange rates, recruitment, raising money)
   iii) *Government policies and small firms* (20 mins.)
      (e.g., the minimum wage, entry into the Euro)
   iv) *Topical issues* (20 mins.)
      (e.g., business succession and exit strategies)

3. **Summing Up**
   Thanks for participation and report back
   Invite back to next event in 6 months
   Reimburse expenses

4. **Lunch**
   Sandwiches and drinks
   Close

Clearly, there are different questioning strategies and approaches to moderating focus group sessions. Most seem to lie somewhere in between the rather open-ended approach employed by Cunha and Cunha (2004) (see Web Research in focus 15.2) and the somewhat more structured one used by Blackburn and Stokes (2000) (see Web Research in focus 15.1). There is probably no one best way and the style of questioning and moderating is likely to be affected by various factors, such as the nature of the research topic (for example, is it one that the researcher already knows a lot about, in which case a modicum of structure is feasible) and levels of interest and/or knowledge among participants in the research (for example, a low level of participant interest may require a somewhat more structured approach).

Whichever strategy of questioning is employed, the focus group researcher should generally be prepared to allow at least some discussion that departs from the interview guide, since such debate may provide new and unexpected insights. A more structured approach to questioning might inhibit such spontaneity, but it is unlikely to remove it altogether.

 ## Group interaction in focus group sessions

Kitzinger (1994) has observed that reports of focus group research frequently do not take into account interaction within the group. This is surprising, because it is precisely the operation of social interaction and its forms and impact that would seem to distinguish the focus group session from the individual interview. Yet, as Kitzinger (1994) observes, very few publications based on focus group research cite or draw inferences from patterns of interaction within the group. Wilkinson reviewed over 200 studies based on focus groups published between 1946 and 1996. She concluded: 'Focus group data is most commonly presented as if it were one-to-one interview data, with interactions between group participants rarely reported, let alone analyzed' (1998, p. 112).

Interactions between focus group participants may either be complementary or argumentative (Kitzinger, 1994). The former brings out the elements of the social world that provide participants' own frameworks of understanding so that agreement emerges in people's minds. In the example in Tips and skills *Extract from a focus group discussion showing some moderator involvement*', the first part of the discussion demonstrates broad agreement between Michael and Mike about the issues involved in handing over the business to a family member, with Mike building on the preceding remarks made by Michael. This complementary interaction is then interrupted by Gary, who suggests that this depends on whether or not the family member is actively involved in the day-to-day running of the business. This more argumentative interaction leads Mike to revert to an alternative exit strategy—one that relies ultimately on selling the business.

However, as Kitzinger (1994) suggests, arguments in focus groups can be equally revealing. She suggests that moderators can play an important role in identifying differences of opinion and exploring with participants the factors that may lie behind them. Disagreement can provide participants with the opportunity to revise their opinions or to think more about the reasons why they hold the view that they do. As Kitzinger (1994) argues, drawing attention to patterns of interaction within focus groups allows the researcher to determine how group participants view the issues with which they are confronted in their own terms. The posing of questions by, and agreement and disagreement among, participants helps to bring out their own stances on these issues. The resolution of disagreements also helps to force participants to express the grounds on which they hold particular views.

The focus group as a feminist method

The use of focus groups by feminist researchers has grown considerably in recent years, and Wilkinson (1998, 1999*b*) has argued that it has great potential in this regard. Three aspects of the method stand out in terms of their compatibility with the ethics and politics of feminism:

- Focus group research is less artificial than many other methods, because, in emphasizing group interaction, which is a normal part of social life, it does not suffer from the problem of gleaning information in an unnatural situation. Moreover, the tendency of many focus group researchers to recruit participants from naturally occurring groups underpins the lower level of artificiality of the method, since people are able to discuss in situations that are quite normal for them. As a result, there is greater opportunity to derive understandings that chime with the 'lived experience' of women. However, not all writers accept the contention that focus groups are more naturalistic than individual interviews. Even when natural groups are used, gathering people to discuss a certain topic (such as a television advertisement) is not inherently naturalistic, because the social setting is to a significant extent contrived (Morrison, 1998, pp. 154–5). Indeed, completing questionnaires or being interviewed may appear more natural, because such instruments are fairly commonplace, whereas being asked to discuss in a group an issue not necessarily of one's choosing is less so.

- Feminist researchers have expressed a preference for methods that avoid decontextualization—that is, that successfully study the individual within a social context. The tendency for most methods to treat the individual as a separate entity devoid of a social context is disliked by many feminist researchers, who prefer to analyze 'the self as relational or as socially constructed' (Wilkinson, 1999*b*, pp. 229–30). Because the individual is very much part of a group in the focus group method, this tendency towards decontextualization is avoided.

15.2 **Research in Focus**

Using focus groups in a study of female entrepreneurs

In a qualitative analysis of female entrepreneurs' accounts of their role, Buttner (2001) used the focus group method to explore the leadership and management style of women entrepreneurs in their own organizations. Although the study was exploratory, 'designed to capture the women's "voice" as they spoke about their role in their businesses' (2001, p. 258), a structured interview protocol was used. One hundred and twenty-nine women entrepreneurs from 12 research sites across the United States participated in the focus groups and the results were videotaped and transcribed. One of the interesting things about the way that the data in this study were analyzed and presented is that the frequency of comments was recorded in addition to the content. In reporting the results of the focus groups, in addition to using direct quotes of the focus group participants, Buttner (2001) also records the number or proportion of the women in her sample who made comments about a particular issue. This helps to add strength to her argument and is an example of how qualitative researchers sometimes undertake a limited amount of quantification of their data (an issue discussed in more depth in Chapter 7).

● As we have seen in previous chapters, feminist researchers are suspicious of research methods that are exploitative and create a power relationship between the female researcher and the female respondent. Wilkinson observes that the risk of this occurring is greatly reduced, because focus group participants are able to take over much of the direction of the session from the moderator. Indeed, they may even subvert the goals of the session in ways that could be of considerable interest to the moderator. As a result, participants' points of view are much more likely to be revealed than in a traditional interview.

Wilkinson does not argue that focus groups or indeed any method can be described as inherently feminist. Instead, she argues that, because of these three features and when employed with sensitivity towards feminist concerns, the focus group method has considerable potential as a tool of feminist research.

The kinds of argument put forward regarding the fit between the focus group method and feminist research have been extended to suggest they may have a further role in allowing the voices of highly marginalized groups of women to surface. Madriz (2000, p. 843) argues that, for a group like lower socio-economic class women of colour, focus groups constitute a relatively rare opportunity for them to 'empower themselves by making sense of their experience of vulnerability and subjugation'. Research in focus 15.2 provides an example of some research that uses focus groups to study women, although this study does not claim to be feminist research, and it involves studying women who are relatively powerful (running successful businesses and employing other staff) rather than powerless. However, Buttner's (2001) use of focus group methods could be seen as supportive of the feminist emphasis on methods that seek to avoid decontextualizing research subjects, since her study is interested in developing understanding of women entrepreneurs in a relational context, based on earlier research into gender that suggests women's identities are based on an ability to make and maintain relationships with others. Focus groups could, therefore, be seen as a way for female entrepreneurs to make sense of their relationships with employees, suppliers, and clients through talking to other women who had similar experiences.

 ## Limitations of focus groups

Focus groups clearly have considerable potential for research questions in which the processes through which meaning is jointly constructed is likely to be of particular interest. Indeed, it may be that, even when this is not a prominent emphasis, the use of the focus group method may be appropriate and even advantageous, since it allows participants' perspectives—an important feature of much qualitative research (see Chapter 6)—to be revealed in ways that are different from individual interviews (for example, through discussion, participants' questions, arguments, and so on). It also offers considerable potential for feminist researchers. What, then, might be its chief limitations?:

- The researcher probably has less control over proceedings than with the individual interview. As we have seen, by no means all writers on focus groups perceive this as a disadvantage and indeed feminist researchers often see it as an advantage. However, the question of control raises issues for researchers of how far they can allow a focus group to 'take over' the running of proceedings. There is clearly a delicate balance to be taken into account over how involved moderators should be and how far a set of prompts or questions should influence the conduct of a focus group, as some of the earlier discussions have suggested. What is not clear is the degree to which it is appropriate to surrender control of a focus group to its participants, especially when there is a reasonably explicit set of research questions to be answered, as is commonly the case, for example, in funded research.
- The data are difficult to analyze. A huge amount of data can be very quickly produced. Developing a strategy of analysis that incorporates both themes in what people say and patterns of interaction is not easy. Also, as previously pointed out, focus group recordings are particularly prone to inaudible elements, which affects transcription.
- They are difficult to organize. Not only do you have to secure the agreement of people to participate in your study; you also need to persuade them to turn up at a particular time. Small inducements, such as payment of expenses or provision of lunch, are sometimes made to induce participation, but nonetheless it is common for people not to turn up.
- The recordings are probably more time consuming to transcribe than equivalent recordings of individual in-

terviews, because of variations in voice pitch and the need to take account of who says what.
- There are possible problems of group effects. This includes the obvious problem of dealing with reticent speakers and with those who hog the stage! In this respect, they are a bit like tutorials. Krueger (1998) suggests in relation to the problem of overly prominent participants that the moderator should make clear to the speaker and other group participants that other people's views are definitely required; for example, he suggests saying something like, 'That's one point of view. Does anyone have another point of view?' (1998, p. 59). As for those who do not speak very much, it is recommended that they are actively encouraged to say something. Also, as the well-known Asch experiments showed (see Web Research in focus 15.3), an emerging group view may mean that a perfectly legitimate perspective held by just one individual may be suppressed. There is also evidence that, as a group comes to share a certain point of view group members come to think uncritically about it and to develop almost irrational attachments to it (Janis, 1982). It is not known how far such group effects have an adverse impact on focus group findings, but it is clear that they cannot be entirely ignored. In this context, it would be interesting to know how far agreement among focus group participants is more frequently encountered than disagreement (we have a hunch that it is), since the effects to which both Asch and Janis referred would lead us to expect more agreement than disagreement in focus group discussions.
- Madriz (2000) proposes that there are circumstances when focus groups may not be appropriate, because of their potential for causing discomfort among participants. When such discomfort might arise, individual interviews are likely to be preferable. Situations in which unease might be occasioned are: when intimate details of private lives need to be revealed; when participants may not be comfortable in each other's presence (for example, bringing together people in a hierarchical relationship to each other); and when participants are likely to disagree profoundly with each other.

Checklist

Issues to consider for your focus group:

- [ ] Have you devised a clear and comprehensive way of introducing the research to participants?
- [ ] Do the questions or topics you have devised allow you to answer all your research questions?
- [ ] Have you piloted the guide with some appropriate respondents?
- [ ] Have you devised a strategy for encouraging respondents to turn up for the focus group meeting?
- [ ] Have you thought about what you will do if some participants do not turn up for the session?
- [ ] Have you ensured that interviews will allow novel or unexpected themes and issues to arise?
- [ ] Is your language in the questions clear and comprehensible?
- [ ] Are your questions relevant to the people who are participating in the focus groups?
- [ ] Have your questions been designed to elicit reflective discussions so that participants are not tempted to answer in 'yes' or 'no' terms?
- [ ] Have your questions been designed to encourage group interaction and discussion?
- [ ] Do your questions offer a real prospect of seeing the world from your interviewees' point of view rather than imposing your own frame of reference on them?
- [ ] Are you familiar with the setting(s) in which the interview will take place?
- [ ] Are you thoroughly familiar with and have you tested your recording or audio-visual equipment?
- [ ] Have you thought about how you will present yourself in the session, such as how you will be dressed?
- [ ] Have you devised a strategy for dealing with silences?
- [ ] Have you devised a strategy for dealing with participants who are reluctant to speak?
- [ ] Have you devised a strategy for dealing with participants who speak too much and hog the discussion?
- [ ] Do you have a strategy for how far you are going to intervene in the **focus group** discussion?
- [ ] Do you have a strategy for dealing with the focus group if the discussion goes off at a tangent?
- [ ] Have you tested out any aids that you are going to present to focus group participants (e.g., visual aids, segments of film, case studies)?

Key points

- The focus group is a group interview that is concerned with exploring a certain topic.
- The **moderator** generally tries to provide a relatively free rein to the discussion. However, there may be contexts in which it is necessary to ask fairly specific questions, especially when cross-group comparability is an issue.
- There is concern with the joint production of meaning.
- Focus group discussions need to be recorded and **transcribed**.
- There are several issues concerning the recruitment of focus group participants—in particular, whether to use natural groupings or to employ stratifying criteria.
- Group interaction is an important component of discussions.
- Some writers view focus groups as well-suited to a feminist standpoint.

Questions for review

- Why might it be useful to distinguish between a focus group and a group interview?

Uses of focus groups

- What advantages might the focus group method offer in contrast to an individual qualitative interview?

Conducting focus groups

- How involved should the moderator be?
- Why is it necessary to tape-record and transcribe focus group sessions?
- Are there any circumstances in which it might be a good idea to select participants who know each other?
- What might be the advantages and disadvantages of using an interview guide in focus group sessions?

Group interaction in focus group sessions

- Why might it be important to treat group interaction as an important issue when analyzing focus group data?

The focus group as a feminist method

- Evaluate the argument that the focus group can be viewed as a feminist method.
- To what extent are focus groups a naturalistic approach to data collection?

Limitations of focus groups

- Does the potential for the loss of control over proceedings and group effects damage the potential utility of the focus group as a method?
- How far do the greater problems of transcription and difficulty of analysis undermine the potential of focus groups?

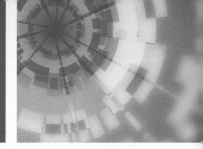

16

Structured Observation

Chapter guide

Structured observation attracted a large amount of attention in business and management research during the 1970s and early 1980s. However, in more recent years it has been less commonly employed as a research method. It entails the direct observation of behaviour and the recording of that behaviour in terms of categories that have been devised prior to the start of data collection. This chapter explores:

- The limitations of survey research for the study of behaviour.
- The different forms of observation in business research.
- The potential of structured observation for the study of behaviour.
- How to devise an observation schedule.
- Different strategies for observing behaviour in structured observation.
- Sampling issues in structured observation research.
- Issues of reliability and validity in structured observation;
- Field stimulations, whereby the researcher actively intervenes in social life and records what happens as a consequence of the intervention, as a form of structured observation.
- Some criticisms of structured observation.

Introduction

Structured observation is a method for systematically observing the behaviour of individuals in terms of a schedule of categories. It is a technique in which the researcher uses explicitly formulated rules for the observation and recording of behaviour. One of its main advantages is that it allows behaviour to be observed directly, unlike in survey research, which only allows behaviour to be inferred. In survey research, respondents frequently report their behaviour, but there are good reasons for thinking that such reports may not be entirely accurate. Structured observation offers a possible solution in that it entails the direct observation of behaviour. Interest in structured observation within business and management stemmed initially from the fact that it was seen as having the potential to provide researchers with far greater insight into the issue of what managers actually do. In this respect it was seen by many as providing an alternative to the diary study method (see Chapter 10) used by Stewart (1967).

Problems with survey research on behaviour

Chapters 9–11 have dealt with several different aspects of survey research. Through outlining procedures associated with the social survey, certain problems with the techniques with which it is typically associated have been identified. For example, in the field of leadership research, which relies a great deal on questionnaire measures, researchers have relied heavily on the responses of subordinates and what they say leaders do, rather than what leaders actually do (the two are often used interchangeably). To some extent the deficiencies associated with the survey are recognized by researchers, who have developed ways of dealing with them or at least of offsetting their impact to some degree. When survey techniques, such as the structured interview or the self-completion questionnaire, are used in connection with the study of respondents' behaviour, certain characteristic difficulties are encountered, some of which have been touched on in earlier chapters. Tips and skills *Problems with using*

Tips and Skills

Problems with using social survey research to investigate behaviour

- *Problem of meaning*. People may vary in their interpretations of key terms in a question.
- *Problem of omission*. When answering the question, respondents may inadvertently omit key terms in the question.
- *Problem of memory*. They may misremember aspects of the occurrence of certain forms of behaviour.
- *Social desirability effect*. They may exhibit a tendency towards replying in ways that are meant to be consistent with their perceptions of the desirability of certain kinds of answer.
- *Question threat*. Some questions may appear threatening and result in a failure to provide an honest reply.
- *Interviewer characteristics*. Aspects of the interviewer may influence the answers provided.
- *Gap between stated and actual behaviour*. How people say they are likely to behave and how they actually behave may be inconsistent.

social survey research to investigate behaviour' identifies some of the difficulties entailed in using survey methods to research behaviour. The list is certainly not exhaustive, but it does capture some of the main elements.

So why not observe behaviour?

An obvious solution to the problems identified is to observe people's behaviour directly rather than to rely on research instruments like questionnaires to elicit such information. In this chapter, we are going to outline a method called **structured observation** (see Key concept 16.1), also often called **systematic observation**.

It has been implied that structured observation can be viewed as an alternative to survey methods of research. After all, in view of the various problems identified in Tips and skills '*Problems with using social survey research to investigate behaviour*', it would seem an obvious solution to observe people instead. However, structured observation has not attracted a large following and, instead, tends to be in use in certain specific research areas, such as in educational research, where it is used to study the behaviour of school teachers and pupils and the interaction between them.

Central to any structured observation study will be the **observation schedule** or *coding scheme*. This guide specifies the categories of behaviour that are to be observed and how behaviour should be allocated to those categories. It is best to illustrate what this involves by looking at examples. One of the best-known studies to have used structured

observation is Mintzberg's (1973) study of managerial work. Mintzberg studied five chief executives, each for one week, as they went about their normal business day, took phone calls, attended scheduled and unscheduled meetings, scanned mail, received visitors, and walked around buildings. The detailed nature of his investigation restricted the amount of **quantitative** data that could be generated but it also enabled more detailed analysis of the kind of work that managers do. The activity categories used in the study were: desk work, tours, unscheduled meetings, scheduled meetings, and telephone calls (see Research in focus 16.1).

Structured data were collected using three records:

- Chronology record. Described activity patterns, noting the time, nature, and duration of the activity.
- Mail record. Described each piece of incoming/outgoing mail and the action that was taken in order to respond to it.
- Contact record. Described each verbal contact, noting the participants and where it took place.

In Mintzberg's coding scheme, time, and activities were coded separately, so that the distribution of clock

> **Key concept 16.1: What is structured observation?**
>
> Structured observation, often also called systematic observation, is a technique in which the researcher uses explicitly formulated rules for the observation and recording of behaviour.

16.1 Research in Focus

Mintzberg's categories of basic activities involved in managerial work

Mintzberg (1973) identified five categories into which the activities of managerial work could be placed. They are listed below:

- Scheduled meeting. A prearranged face-to-face meeting involving the manager and one or more other participants is defined as scheduled.
- Unscheduled meeting. A meeting is defined as unscheduled if it is arranged quickly, as when someone just 'drops in'.

- Desk work. This refers to the time the manager spends at his or her desk, processing mail, scheduling activities, writing letters, or communicating with the secretary.
- Call. This category refers to telephone calls.
- Tour. This refers to a chance meeting in the hall, or to the 'promenades' taken by the manager to observe activity and to deliver information.

---

time might overlap an activity or vice versa. For example, 'tours' of the work site and 'desk work' included time spent talking. Almost 40% of activities were meetings; this accounted for 70% of the managers' work time. From such data a number of features could be derived. Mintzberg's main conclusions were that managerial work is highly fragmented, varied, and brief, and that managers have a need for instant communication on which to base further verbal contact and action. These findings ran contrary to the traditional view that was dominant at the time, which suggested that managerial activity was planned and rational. Research in focus 16.2 gives two examples of studies that involve a replication of Mintzberg's methods.

It is interesting to think about how a scheme like this might be employed in connection with higher education teaching and in particular in tutorials and seminars. In the following imaginary scheme, the focus is on the tutor. The categories might be:

Tutor:
1. Asking question addressed to group.
2. Asking question addressed to individual.
3. Responding to question asked by member of group.
4. Responding to comment by member of group.
5. Discussing topic.
6. Making arrangements.
7. Silence.

Student(s):
8. Asking question.
9. Responding to question from tutor.
10. Responding to comment from tutor.
11. Responding to question from another student.
12. Responding to comment from another student.
13. Talking about arrangements.

We might want to code what is happening every five seconds. The coding sheet for a five-minute period in the tutorial might look like Figure 16.1. We might try to relate the amount of time that the tutor is engaged in particular activities to such things as: number of students in the group; layout of the room; subject discipline; gender of tutor; age of tutor; and so on.

The observation schedule

Devising a schedule for the recording of observations is clearly a crucial step in the structured observation project. The considerations that go into this phase are very similar to those involved in producing a structured interview schedule. The following considerations are worth taking into account:

- A clear focus is necessary. There are two aspects to this point. First, it should be clear to the observer exactly

16.2 Research in Focus

Structured observation of managerial work

Mintzberg's (1973) research was highly influential and led to several other studies that replicated and extended his study of what managers do in their day-to-day work. In part, these later studies are an attempt to address two of the criticisms that have been made of Mintzberg's study: not actually reflecting the variation between different kinds of managerial work and not relating managerial work to managerial and organizational efficiency and effectiveness.

The first example, by Martinko and Gardner (1990), extends the research question that informs Mintzberg's study from 'How do senior managers spend their work time?' to 'How does senior managers' use of work time affect their performance?' Their sample consisted of 41 school principals. This group of managers was selected because they have a relatively high level of autonomy in their work (and, therefore, an ability to influence organizational performance). Also, because they are a relatively homogenous group, their performance levels can be more easily compared. The observations were conducted mainly by doctoral students who attended a two-day training session in which they were taught the principles of structured observation. Minute-by-minute observation led to the production of written protocols that recorded managerial events, the time they started and ended, and their purpose. The mean number of observations was 6.7 days per principal. The sample was stratified into high- and moderate-performing managers, based on the assumption that the performance of the principal would be reflected by the performance of the school. Although the research confirmed Mintzberg's earlier finding that managerial work is brief, varied, fragmented, and interpersonal, there was no evidence to suggest that managerial behaviour was related to performance level. In other words, there was no significant difference in the behaviours of highly effective and less effective managers

in terms of how they organized their daily activities. It is interesting to note that the researchers deliberately excluded low-performing managers from their sample because they had anticipated difficulties in securing the cooperation of individuals who had been labelled as low performers. However, it may have been that a comparison of high- and low-performing managers would have revealed greater differences between principals in terms of the time spent on events and the number of events that were associated with certain activities.

O'Gorman, Bourke, and Murray (2005) also used Mintzberg's (1973) observational study of managerial work as the basis for their investigation into managerial work in small growth-oriented businesses. A purposive sample of 10 owner-managers of small high-growth manufacturing companies was selected based on their participation in growth seminars at the Department of Business Studies at Trinity College in Dublin, Ireland. The CEOs were all male and their businesses represented the printing, construction, chemicals, pharmaceuticals, and agricultural-food sectors. The researchers describe their observational method as follows: 'two days were spent with the CEO, during the Spring and Summer of 1992. . . . Using a chronological record, based on the data-recording format used by Mintzberg, the daily activities of each CEO were recorded' (O'Gorman, Bourke, & Murray, 2005, p. 9). In addition, two other types of activity were recorded: the first recorded CEOs' attendance at social functions related to the business, and the second classified the type of functional duty being performed in each activity (production, research and development, sales and marketing, market research, finance, engineering, legal affairs, distribution, personnel, and general management). They found that managerial work in these organizations was even more fragmented than for the managers in Mintzberg's study.

Figure 16.1

Coding sheet for imaginary study of university tutors

3	3	3	3	10	10	10	10	10	10	10	10
10	10	10	10	10	10	7	7	7	8	8	8
8	8	8	8	8	8	8	8	11	11	11	11
11	11	11	11	11	11	11	11	11	11	11	11
7	7	7	7	7	4	4	4	4	4	4	1

Note: Each cell represents a 5-second interval and each row is 1 minute.

Numeric codes in each cell correspond to the categories described in the schedule in the text.

who or what (and possibly both) is to be observed. For example, if people are the focus of attention, the observer needs to know precisely who is to be observed. Also, the observer needs to know which if any aspects of the setting are to be observed and recorded. The second sense in which a clear focus is necessary is that the research problem needs to be clearly stated so that the observer knows which of the many things going on in any setting are to be recorded.

- As with the production of a closed question for a structured interview schedule or self-completion questionnaire, the forms taken by any category of behaviour must be both mutually exclusive (i.e., not overlap) and inclusive. Taking the earlier example of coding behaviour in a university tutorial, we might conceivably run into a problem of the 12 categories not being exhaustive if a student knocks on the tutor's door and quickly asks him or her a question (for example, perhaps about the tutorial topic if the student is from another of the tutor's groups). An observer unfamiliar with the ways of university life might well be unsure about whether this behaviour needs to be coded in terms of the 12 categories and whether the coding should be temporarily suspended. Perhaps the best approach would be to have another category of behaviour to be coded what we might term 'interrup-

tion'. It is often desirable for a certain amount of unstructured observation to take place prior to the construction of the observation schedule and for there to be some trialing of it so that possible problems (e.g., a lack of inclusiveness) can be anticipated.

The recording system must be easy to operate. Complex systems with large numbers of types of behaviour will be undesirable. In a similar way to interviewers using a structured interview schedule, observers need to be trained, but even with training it is easy for an observer to become confused when faced with too many options.

One possible problem with some observation schedules is that they may require a certain amount of interpretation on the part of the observer. For example, it might be difficult to distinguish in any meaningful sense between an unscheduled meeting and a discussion with two or three colleagues that takes place in a corridor, apart from the fact that in the first instance the participants are more likely to be seated! To the extent that it may be difficult to distinguish between the two, a certain amount of interpretation on the part of the observer may be required. If such interpretation is required, there would need to be clear guidelines for the observer and considerable experience would be required (see Web Research in focus 16.1 for an illustration of a study in which a good deal of interpretation seems to have been necessary).

Strategies for observing behaviour

There are different ways of conceptualizing how behaviour should be recorded:

- We can record in terms of incidents. This means waiting for something to happen and then recording what follows from it. Essentially, this is what Mintzberg (1973) did, as the following account of his method illustrates: 'The researcher observes the manager as he performs his work. Each observed event (a verbal contact or a piece of incoming or outgoing mail) is categorized by the researcher in a number of ways (for example, duration, participants, purpose) . . . .' (1973, p. 231). In this study, the categories, or activity codes, are developed either during the observation or shortly after it takes place, rather than beforehand. Only after the observation has taken place did Mintzberg begin to draw connections between the activities in order to develop his final activity codes. Similarly, a newspaper story several years ago reported that someone placed a ladder over a pavement and then observed whether people preferred to go under the ladder or to risk life and limb in the face of oncoming traffic. A considerable number preferred the latter option, confirming the persistence of superstitious beliefs in an apparently secular society. Once again, an incident (someone approaching the ladder) triggered the observation. Webb et al. (1966) would regard this as an example of contrived observation, because the researchers fabricated the situation. The discussion later in this chapter of field stimulations further illustrates of this kind of research.
- We can observe and record in terms of short periods of time, observing one individual for a couple of minutes and then returning at structured intervals to conduct further observations. This can help to ensure the generalizability of what goes on in the setting. For example,

if a manager holds regular meetings each day at 4 p.m., three observations, each lasting 20 minutes, conducted in the morning, at lunchtime, and in the afternoon, will ensure a more representative sample of activities than would one observation lasting an hour from 4–5 p.m.

- We can observe and record observations for quite long periods of time, with the observer watching and recording more or less continuously. For example, the study of job characteristics by Jenkins et al. (1975), which entailed the observation of each worker on two occasions but for an hour on each occasion (see Web Research in focus 16.1): 'The observation hour was structured so that the observer spent 10 min becoming oriented to the job, 30 min observing specific job actions, and 20 min rating the job in situ. The observers then typically spent an additional 15 min away from the job completing the observation instrument' (Jenkins et al., 1975, p. 174). This last study is an example of what Martin and Bateson (1986) refer to as 'continuous recording', whereby the observer observes for extended periods, thus allowing the frequency and duration of forms of behaviour to be measured. They contrast this approach with time sampling, described below.

- Time sampling is a further approach to the observation of behaviour. An example here would be a study of schools known as the ORACLE (Observational Research and Classroom Learning Evaluation) project (Galton et al., 1980). In this research, eight children (four of each gender) in each class in which the observations took place were observed for around four minutes but on 10 separate occasions. A mechanical device made a noise every 25 seconds and on each occasion this occurred the observer made a note of what the teacher or pupils were doing in terms of the observation schedule. The sampling of time periods was random.

Sampling

Just like survey research, structured observation requires decisions to be made concerning sampling. Mintzberg's study was somewhat unusual in that it relied on a very small sample of only five individuals—a decision that he explains was forced partly by practical constraints, as the research was done for his doctoral dissertation. This meant that 'the time of only one researcher was available, and that for only 12 months or so' (Mintzberg, 1973, p. 237). However, with structured observation it is more usual not only to sample a larger number of people, but also to incorporate several other sampling issues as well.

Sampling people

When people are being sampled, considerations very similar to those encountered in Chapter 9 in respect of probability sampling become most important. This means that the observer will ideally want to sample on a random basis. In the study of job characteristics (see Web Research in focus 16.1), the individuals who were observed at work were randomly selected (Jenkins et al., 1975). However, structured observation can also be based on non-probability sampling such as in the example in Research in focus 16.3.

Sampling in terms of time

As implied by the idea of time sampling (see above), it is often necessary to ensure that, if certain individuals are sampled on more than one occasion, they are not always observed at the same time of the day. This means that, if particular individuals are selected randomly for observation on several different occasions for short periods, it is desirable for the observation periods to be randomly selected. For example, it would not be desirable for a certain manager working in his office to always be observed at the end of the day. He or she may be tired and this would give a false impression of that manager's behaviour.

Further sampling considerations

The sampling procedures mentioned so far conform to probability sampling principles, because it is feasible to construct a sampling frame for individuals. However, this is not always possible for different kinds of reasons. Studies in public areas, like the research on superstition mentioned above, do not permit random sampling, because we cannot very easily construct a sampling frame of people walking along a street. Similarly, it is not feasible to construct a sampling frame of interactions—for example, of meetings between managers and their subordinates. The problem with doing structured observation research on such a topic is that it does not lend itself to the specification of a sampling frame, and, therefore, the researcher's ability to generate a probability sample is curtailed.

As suggested in Chapter 9, considerations relating to **probability sampling** largely concern the external validity of findings. Such concerns are not necessarily totally addressed by resorting to probability sampling, however. For example, if a **structured observation** study is conducted over a relatively short span of time, issues concerning the *representativeness* of the findings are likely to arise. Consequently, consideration has to be given to the question of the timing of observation. Furthermore, how are the sites in which structured observation is to take place selected? Can we assume that they are themselves representative? Clearly, a random sampling procedure for the selection of organizations may offer us some level of reassurance. However, given the difficulty of securing access to settings such as schools and business organizations, it is likely that the organizations to which access is secured may not be representative of the population of appropriate ones.

A further set of distinctions between types of sampling in structured observation have been drawn by Martin and Bateson (1986) between:

- Ad libitum sampling. Whereby the observer records whatever is happening at the time.
- Focal sampling. In which a specific individual is observed for a set period of time; the observer records all examples of whatever forms of behaviour are of interest in terms of a schedule.
- Scan sampling. Whereby an entire group of individuals is scanned at regular intervals and the behaviour of all of them is recorded at that time. This sampling strategy allows only one or two types of behaviour to be observed and recorded.
- Behaviour sampling. Whereby an entire group is watched and the observer records who was involved in a particular kind of behaviour.

16.3 Research in Focus

Structured observation with a sample of one

Louhiala-Salminen (2002) observed a Finnish business manager who works in a multinational corporation for one day to identify the features that characterize the discourse in a multinational corporation. The aim of the study 'was to describe the discourse activities of a professional who is a non-native speaker of English and uses English "as a business lingua franca"' (2002, p. 215). Most of the day was recorded using audio tapes and an observation protocol was used to make notes about the nature of the activity, including type of communication and language used. Louhiala-Salminen undertook the observation between 9 a.m. and 4 p.m., and followed the manager all day except for one 20-minute meeting which entailed confidential information. The manager stayed at work for a further 90 minutes after the observation ended 'catching up with some planning and writing which he was not able to do in the day' (2002, p. 217). On the day after the observation, the manager, his superior, and subordinates were interviewed to seek clarification of events the previous day and to gain background information about the manager's education, experience, and attitudes towards language, communication, and culture.

One of the issues this study had to deal with is the impact of technology on managerial time use, specifically the use of email as a communication medium as opposed to writing letters or making telephone calls. The researcher explains: 'The written documents that the manager read or wrote during the day were e-mail messages. Because of the large number of the messages (about 150 altogether) it would have been impossible to have copies of all without seriously disturbing the normal flow of work. Therefore about one third of the e-mail messages were printed as examples' (2002, p. 214). Louhiala-Salminen notes the crucial role of email in structuring the events of the working day. The manager spent the first two hours of his day working through the 95 emails that had arrived for him during the previous two days when he had been out of the office, and the majority of subsequent interactions were initiated by email messages. The study also highlights the blurred boundaries between different kinds of activity: 'Throughout the day spoken and written communication were totally intertwined, there was hardly any activity in either mode where the other would not be present as well; many of the phone calls were to confirm an issue in an e-mail message, e-mail messages referred to phone calls, and they were constantly discussed in face-to-face communication with colleagues' (2002, p. 217).

This study is also interesting in terms of reactive effects (see Key concept 16.3). When discussing the nature of the observation and in particular the low number of direct spoken encounters, which Louhiala-Salminen found puzzling given the open-plan nature of the office, the manager suggested that more people would have stopped to talk to him had the researcher not been sitting near his desk. Finally, although this study involved the structured observation of just one manager for one day, it is intended to form part of a bigger international comparative study across four different countries once the research design and data collection methods have been tested. One of the things that Louhiala-Salminen discovered from the study was that because of the hectic pace of work involving different communication media, the observation protocol was too detailed to be completed during the observation. She suggests that a video recording would make analysis of simultaneous and interconnected activities easier.

Most structured observation research seems to employ focal sampling, such as: Mintzberg's (1973) study, and the research by Martinko and Gardner (1990) as well as O'Gorman, Bourke, and Murray's (2005) study (see Research in focus 16.2), in addition to Jenkins et al.'s research (1975; see Web Research in focus 16.1).

Issues of reliability and validity

One researcher has concluded that, when compared to interviews and questionnaires, structured observation: 'Provides (a) more reliable information about events; (b) greater precision regarding their timing, duration, and frequency; (c) greater accuracy in the time ordering of variables; and (d) more accurate and economical reconstructions of large-scale social episodes' (McCall, 1984, p. 277). This is a very strong endorsement for structured observation, but, as McCall notes, there are several issues of reliability and validity that confront practitioners of the method. Some of these issues are similar to those faced by researchers when seeking to develop measures in business research in general (see Chapter 5) and by survey research in particular. However, there are certain concerns specific to structured observation.

Reliability

Practitioners of structured observation have been concerned with the degree of inter-observer consistency. Essentially, this issue entails considering the degree to which two or more observers of the same behaviour agree in terms of their coding of that behaviour on the observation schedule—that is, inter-observer consistency. The main statistic for assessing this component of reliability is called kappa (also known as Cohen's kappa; see Key concept 16.2).

A second consideration in relation to reliability is the degree of consistency of the application of the observation schedule over time—that is, *intra-observer consistency*. This is clearly a difficult notion, because people can and often have to behave in different ways on different occasions and in different contexts. Assessing the consistency of observation ratings across all possibilities is clearly difficult. The procedures for assessing this aspect of reliability are broadly similar to those applied to the issue of inter-observer consistency. The Jenkins et al. (1975) research addressed the issue of inter-observer consistency over time and found that the measures fared even worse in this respect.

It is clearly not an easy matter to achieve reliability in structured observation. This is an important point, because validity presupposes reliability (see Chapter 5). Reliability may be difficult to achieve on occasions, because of factors such as observer fatigue or lapses in attention. Nevertheless, we should not exaggerate this point, because some studies have been able to achieve high levels of reliability for many of their measures, and indeed two critics of structured observation have written that 'there is no doubt that observers can be trained to use complex coding schedules with considerable reliability' (Delamont & Hamilton, 1984, p. 32).

> **Key concept 16.2: What is Cohen's kappa?**
>
> Cohen's kappa is a measure of the degree of agreement over the coding of items by two people. A coefficient of 0.75 or above is considered very good; between 0.6 and 0.75, it is considered good; and between 0.4 and 0.6, it is regarded as fair.

Validity

Measurement validity concerns whether or not a measure is measuring what it is supposed to measure. The validity of any measure will be affected by:

- whether or not the measure reflects the concept it has been designed to measure (see Chapter 5); and
- error that arises from the implementation of the measure in the research process (see Chapter 13).

The first of these issues simply means that in structured observation it is necessary to pay attention to the same kinds of issues concerning the checking of validity (e.g., assessing face validity, concurrent validity, and so on) that are encountered in research based on interviews and questionnaires. The second aspect of validity—error in implementation—relates to two matters in particular:

- Is the observation instrument administered as it is supposed to be? This is the equivalent of ensuring that interviewers using a structured interview schedule follow the research instrument and its instructions exactly as they are supposed to. If there is variability between observers or over time, the measure will be unreliable and, therefore, cannot be valid. Ensuring that observers have as complete an understanding as possible of how the observation schedule should be implemented is, therefore, crucial.

- Do people change their behaviour because they know they are being observed? This is an instance of what is known as the 'reactive effect' (see Key concept 16.3). After all, if people adjust the way they behave because they know they are being observed, their behaviour would have to be considered atypical. As a result, we could hardly regard the results of structured observation research as indicative of what happens in reality. As McCall (1984) notes, there is evidence that a reactive effect occurs in structured observation, but that research participants become accustomed to being observed, so that the researcher essentially becomes less intrusive the longer he or she is present. Moreover, it should be kept in mind that often people's awareness of the observer's presence is offset by other factors. For example, managers have many tasks to accomplish that reflect the demands of the organization, so that the observer's ability to make a big impact on behaviour may be lessened by the requirements of the situation.

> ### Key concept 16.3: What is the reactive effect?
>
> Webb et al. wrote about the 'reactive measurement effect', by which they meant that 'the research subject's knowledge that he is participating in a scholarly search may confound the investigator's data' (1966, p. 13).

Other forms of structured observation

Field stimulation

Salancik (1979) has used the term 'field stimulation' to describe a form of observation research that shares many of structured observation's characteristics. Although he classifies field stimulations as a qualitative method, they are in fact better thought of as often operating with a positivist research strategy, since the researcher typically seeks to quantify the outcomes of his or her interventions. In terms of the classification offered in Key concept 16.2, it is in fact 'contrived observation'. A field stimulation is a study in which the researcher directly intervenes in and/or manipulates a natural setting in order to observe what happens as a consequence of that intervention. However, unlike most structured observations, in a field stimulation participants do

not know they are being studied, which makes it a form of unobtrusive observation as defined by Webb et al. (1966). In business and management, consumer researchers use field stimulations to study the behaviour of retail store staff using the 'mystery shopper' technique. An example of the use of this technique in the study of travel agents' recommendations is given in Web Research in focus 16.3.

While such research provides some quite striking findings and gets around the problem of **reactivity** by not alerting research participants to the fact that they are being observed, ethical concerns are sometimes raised, such as the use of deception. Moreover, the extent to which an observation schedule can be employed is inevitably limited (unless the researcher is carrying a hidden camera, as some 'mystery shoppers' have done), because excessive use will potentially alert those being studied to the research. All that can usually be done is to engage in limited coding at the time of the interaction, paying particular attention to the nature of the effect of the intervention, or to document the interaction immediately after the observation has taken place, as the Hudson et al. (2001) research in Web Research in focus 16.3 did.

Organizational simulation

An alternative method for observing behaviour in which participants are made aware of the fact that they are being studied involves the organizational simulation. A simulation involves representing a situation by creating an artificial setting in which individual or group behaviour can be observed. An example of an organizational simulation is provided in Web Research in focus 16.4. In a sense, a simulation is similar to a laboratory experiment (see Chapter 4), except that it does not seek to control participants' activities as much as in an experimental research design. Simulations can thus give participants much greater freedom to act according to their judgement and to make decisions and their actions become the focus of observation. McEnery and Blanchard (1999) used an adapted version of the Looking Glass simulation (see Web Research in focus 16.4) to examine the reliability and validity of assessor, peer, and self-ratings of management skills. The sample comprised 261 business undergraduate students in a university in the Midwest of the United States. The 'president' of Looking Glass was elected by class vote after a nomination speech. The president then collaborated with other participants to determine who would play which role. Once this was decided, participants were each provided with an annual report and various memos and reports to accompany individual roles.

The simulations were conducted in university laboratories that resembled organizational conference rooms and students were expected to dress as though they were business professionals. The students were assessed by graduate students and faculty volunteers, who observed and rated them according to a behavioural checklist, which included items such as 'delegating: matches tasks with people effectively' and 'listening: gives feedback, does not interrupt, used a variety of listening skills and techniques'. After the simulation, the students completed a self-rating checklist to rate their own managerial skills. Each student was also assessed by a peer, a peer who had been working with that student. The study found that the highest evaluation of managerial skill was made by the students' peers, whereas the lowest evaluations were made by the assessors. The study suggested this was because assessors were more likely to be objective because they did not know the students and because they had received more training.

Simulations create large amounts of data in a relatively short period of time, thereby overcoming some of the difficulties of cost and access typically associated with business and management research. They also enable access to issues that may not be amenable to observation in real life, such as problem solving or decision making. Moreover, simulation enables the researcher to create and alter the situation in order to examine the effect of an intervention. If the effects of such interventions are studied in 'real' organizations, research is likely to take a considerable length of time. However, simulations are also subject to the charge of artificiality. For example, by ensuring that participants dress as business professionals, as McEnery and Blanchard (1999) did in their study, there is no certainty that they will see themselves as business professionals (rather than undergraduate students) and act accordingly.

 ## Criticisms of structured observation

Although it is not very extensively used in business and management research, structured observation has, in the

past, been quite controversial. Certain criticisms have been implied in some of the previous discussion of reliability and validity issues, as well as in connection with the issue of generalizability. However, certain other areas of criticism warrant further discussion.

- There is a risk of imposing a potentially inappropriate or irrelevant framework on the setting being observed. This point is similar to the problem of the closed question in questionnaires. This risk is especially great if the researchers have little knowledge concerning the setting prior to the research. One solution is for the structured observation to be preceded by a period of unstructured observation, so that appropriate variables and categories can be specified.

- Because it concentrates upon directly observable behaviour, structured observation is rarely able to get at intentions behind behaviour. Sometimes, when intentions are of concern, they are imputed by observers. Thus, in Mintzberg's basic activity categories of managerial behaviour it is not entirely clear what the difference is between an 'unscheduled meeting' and a 'tour' that involves a chance meeting. Essentially, the problem is that structured observation does not readily allow the observer to get a grasp of the meaning of behaviour.

- There is a tendency for structured observation to generate lots of bits of data. The problem here concerns trying to piece them together to produce an overall picture, or trying to find general themes that link the fragments of data together. It becomes difficult, in other words, to see a bigger picture that lies behind the segments of behaviour that structured observation typically uncovers. It has been suggested, for example, that the tendency for structured observation studies of managers at work to find little evidence of planning in their everyday work (e.g., Mintzberg, 1973) is due to the tendency for the method to fragment a manager's activities into discrete parts. As a result, something like planning, which may be an element in many managerial activities, becomes obscured from view (Snyder & Glueck, 1980).

- It is often suggested that structured observation neglects the context within which behaviour takes place. For example, Martinko and Gardner (1990) found that some of Mintzberg's categories of basic activity were represented differently among school principals, rather than general managers, and, in particular, the amount of time spent on unscheduled meetings was much greater. Of course, were data about the context in which behaviour takes place collected, this criticism would have little weight, but the tendency of structured observation researchers to concentrate on overt behaviour tends to highlight this criticism.

On the other hand . . .

It is clear from the previous section that there are undeniable limitations to structured observation. However, it also has to be remembered that, when overt behaviour is the focus of analysis and perhaps issues of meaning are less salient, structured observation is almost certainly more accurate and effective than getting people to report on their behaviour through questionnaires. It may also be that structured observation is a method that works best when accompanied by other methods. Since it can rarely provide reasons for observed patterns of behaviour, if it is accompanied by another method that can probe reasons, it is of greater utility.

In laboratory experiments in fields like social psychology and medical research, observation with varying degrees of structure is quite commonplace, but in business and management research, with the exception of Mintzberg's classic study, structured observation has not been that frequently used. Perhaps one major reason is that, although interviews and questionnaires are limited in terms of their capacity to tap behaviour accurately, as noted above, they do offer the opportunity to reveal information about both behaviour *and* attitudes and social backgrounds. In other words, they are more flexible and offer the prospect of being able to uncover a variety of correlates of behaviour (albeit reported behaviour), such as social background factors. They can also ask questions about attitudes and investigate explanations that people proffer for their behaviour. As a result, researchers using questionnaires are able to gain information about some factors that may lie behind the patterns of behaviour they uncover. Also, not all forms of behaviour are liable to be accessible to structured observation and it is likely that survey research or researcher-driven diaries are the only likely means of gaining access to them. However, greater use of structured observation may result in a greater capability to use the method, so that reliable measures might emerge.

Checklist

Structured observation research:
- ☐ Have you clearly defined your research questions?
- ☐ Is the **sample** to be observed relevant to your research questions?
- ☐ Can you justify your sampling approach?
- ☐ Does your **observation schedule** indicate precisely which kinds of behaviour are to be observed?
- ☐ Have your observation categories been designed so that there is no need for the observer to interpret what is going on?
- ☐ Have you made sure that the categories of behaviour do not overlap?
- ☐ Do all the different categories of behaviour allow you to answer your research questions?
- ☐ Have you pilot tested your observation schedule?
- ☐ Are the coding instructions clear?
- ☐ Are the categories of behaviour inclusive?
- ☐ Is it easy to log the behaviour as it is happening?

Key points

- **Structured observation** is an approach to the study of behaviour that is an alternative to survey-based measures.
- It comprises explicit rules for the recording of behaviour.

- Structured observation has tended to be used in relation to a rather narrow range of forms of behaviour, such as that of managers.
- It shares with survey research many common problems concerning reliability, **validity**, and **generalizability**.
- **Reactive effects** have to be taken into account but should not be exaggerated.
- **Field stimulations** represent a form of **structured observation** but suffer from difficulties concerning ethics.
- Problems with structured observation revolve around the difficulty of imputing meaning and ensuring that a relevant framework for recording behaviour is being employed.

Questions for review

Problems with survey research on behaviour

- What are the chief limitations of **survey research** with regard to the study of behaviour?

So why not observe behaviour?

- What are the chief characteristics of **structured observation**?
- To what extent does it provide a superior approach to the study of behaviour than **questionnaires** or **structured interviews**?

The observation schedule

- What is an observation schedule?
- 'An observation schedule is much like a self-completion questionnaire or structured interview except that it does not entail asking questions'. Discuss.
- Devise an **observation schedule** of your own for observing an area of social interaction in which you are regularly involved. Ask people with whom you normally interact in those situations how well they think it fits what goes on. Have you missed anything?

Strategies for observing behaviour

- What are the main ways in which behaviour can be recorded in structured observation?

Sampling

- Identify some of the main sampling strategies in structured observation.

Issues of reliability and validity

- How far do considerations of reliability and validity in structured observation mirror those encountered in relation to the asking of questions in structured interviews and self-completion questionnaires?
- What is the reactive effect and why might it be important in relation to structured observation research?

Other forms of structured observation

- What are **field stimulations** and what ethical concerns are posed by them?
- What are the advantages and disadvantages of simulation as a form of structured observation?

Criticisms of structured observation

- 'The chief problem with structured observation is that it does not allow us access to the intentions that lie behind behaviour'. Discuss.
- How far do you agree with the view that structured observation works best when used in conjunction with other research methods?

17

Ethnography and Participant Observation

Chapter guide

Ethnography and **participant observation** involve the extended involvement of the researcher in the social life of those he or she studies (see Web Key concept 17.1). However, the former term is also frequently taken to refer to the written output of that research. This chapter explores:

* The problems of gaining access to different settings and some suggestions about how they might be overcome.
* The issue of whether or not a covert role is practicable and acceptable.
* The role of key informants and gatekeepers for the ethnographer.
* The different kinds of roles that ethnographers can assume in the course of their fieldwork.
* Sampling strategies in ethnography, in particular *theoretical sampling*, which is associated with the grounded theory approach to qualitative data analysis, which will be examined in Chapter 21.
* The role of **field notes** in ethnography and the variety of forms they can assume.
* Bringing ethnography to an end.

Introduction

Discussions about the merits and limitations of participant observation have been a fairly standard ingredient in textbooks on business research for many years. However, for some time, writers on research methods have increasingly preferred to write about ethnography rather than participant observation. It is difficult to date the point at which this change of terminology (though it is more than just this) occurred, but sometime in the 1970s ethnography began to become the preferred term. Prior to that, ethnography was primarily associated with social anthropological research, whereby the investigator visits a (usually) foreign land, gains access to a group (for example, a tribe or village), spends a considerable amount of time (often many years) with that group with the aim of uncovering its culture, watches and listens to what people say and do, engages people in conversations to probe specific issues of interest, takes copious field notes, and returns home to write up the fruits of his or her labours.

Ethnography could be viewed as a simple process of joining a group, watching what goes on, making some notes, and writing it all up. In fact, ethnography is nowhere nearly as straightforward as this implies. This chapter will outline some of the main decision areas that confront ethnographers, along with some of the many contingencies they face. However, it is not easy to generalize about the ethnographic research process in such a way as to provide definitive recommendations about research practice. The diversity of experiences that confront ethnographers and the variety of ways in which they deal with them does not readily permit clear-cut generalizations. The following comment on ethnography makes this point well:

> Every field situation *is* different and initial luck in meeting good informants, being in the right place at the right time and striking the right note in relationships may be just as important as skill in technique. Indeed, many successful episodes in the field do come about through good luck as much as through sophisticated planning, and many unsuccessful episodes are due as much to bad luck as to bad judgement. (Sarsby, 1984, p. 96)

Organizational ethnography

Ethnography has also become a 'label of choice' for researchers working in professional and applied fields, who have discovered and adapted ethnographic methods to suit their own purposes. Among these are business researchers who have imported the methods and many of the conventions of ethnography into the study of organizational settings. Rosen (1991) understands organizational ethnography to be distinctive because it is concerned with social relations that are related to certain goal-directed activities. He suggests that the rules, strategies, and meanings within a structured work situation are different from those that affect other areas of social life. An ethnographic approach implies intense researcher involvement in the day-to-day running of an organization, in order for the researcher to be able to understand it from an insider's point of view. In order to become immersed in other people's realities, organizational ethnographers, like their anthropological predecessors, engage in fieldwork that tends to commit them to a period of time spent in the organization, or a long stay 'in the field'.

Indeed many of these early studies draw attention to the similarities between ethnography and participant observation (see Key concept 17.1 for an explanation of the relationship between these terms). Industrial sociologists working out of the Chicago School (Adelman, 2010) were followed by a group of writers who studied UK-based work organizations and relied heavily on the traditional ethnographic method of participant observation. These studies, which sometimes involved taking jobs in the research sites, included:

- Roy (1958), who spent two months working as a machine operator in the 'clicking room' of a factory in Chicago. The same factory was later used as a research setting by Burawoy (1979), who also worked as a machine operator for 10 months in the same plant.
- Lupton (1963), who became a participant-observer in Manchester factories in order to explore the processes of work group influence on production levels.
- Lupton compared an engineering plant in which 'fiddles' were prevalent with a clothing factory where these practices were absent.
- Beynon (1975), who over a period of five years, studied the Ford Motor Company's Halewood assembly plant in Liverpool to produce an account of factory life that described the process whereby people became shop stewards, the way they understood the job, and

the kinds of pressures they experienced. This study also involved understanding the experience of people who worked on the assembly lines and the way they made sense of industrial politics.

However, since the 1980s the popularity of organizational culture as a concept has meant that ethnographic methods have enjoyed something of a revival within business and management research in Europe, and to a lesser extent in the United States (see for example the work of Pratt (2000)), but has still to become popular in Canada (Hartt, Yue, Helms Mills, & Mills, 2009; Kim, Kumar, & Murphy, 2008; Paré, Bourdeau, Marsan, Shuraida, & Nach, 2007; Serenko, Cocosila, & Turel, 2008). Ethnography, which denotes the practice of writing (*graphy*) about people and cultures (*ethno*), has provided researchers with an obvious method for understanding work organizations as cultural entities. Studies that focus on the construction of cultural norms, expressions of organizational values, and patterns of workplace behaviour include:

- Kunda's (1992) study of the fictitiously named high-technology company 'Lyndsville Tech' in Silicon Valley, in the United States.
- Watson's (1994*a*) account of managerial identity in a UK-based telecommunications firm.
- Casey's (1995) exploration of new-product development workers in an American-based multinational corporation.

Key concept 17.1a: What is ethnography?

Ethnography, like participant observation, is a research method in which the researcher immerses himself or herself in a social setting for an extended period of time, observing behaviour, listening to what is said in conversation both between others and with the fieldworker, and asking questions.

Key concept 17.1b: What is participant observation?

Participant observation is a research strategy that is highly similar to ethnography but in this book will refer specifically to the observational aspect of ethnography.

Tips and Skills

Micro-ethnography

If you are doing research for an undergraduate project or Master's thesis, it is unlikely that you will be able to conduct a full-scale ethnography, because this will almost certainly involve you spending a considerable period of time in an organizational setting. Nevertheless, it may be possible for you to carry out a form of microethnography (Wolcott, 1995). This involves focusing on a particular aspect of an organizational culture, such as the way the organization has implemented TQM, and showing how the culture is reflected through this managerial initiative. A shorter period of time (from a couple of weeks to a few months) could be spent in the organization—on either a full-time or a part-time basis—to achieve this more closely defined cultural understanding.

- Delbridge's (1998) study of the impact of new manufacturing techniques on worker experiences in a Japanese-owned consumer electronics plant, 'Nippon CTV', and a European-owned automotive components supplier, 'Valleyco'.
- Helms Mills's (2003) study of the relationship between sensemaking and organizational change at Nova Scotia Power between 1986 and 2000. Helms Mills spent two different periods at the company, in 1990 and 1993.
- Gephart's (2010; 1988) pioneering development of ethnostatistics and its application to the process of university ranking in Canada (2004; Helms Mills, Weatherbee, & Colwell, 2006). (See Key concept 17.2).

 ## Access

One of the key and yet most difficult steps in ethnography is gaining access to a social setting that is relevant to the research problem in which you are interested. The way in which access is approached differs according to whether the setting is a relatively open one or a relatively closed one (Bell, 1969). The majority of organizational ethnography is done in predominantly closed or non-public settings of various kinds, such as factories or offices. The negotiation of access involves gaining permission to enter these privately managed spaces or situations. Gaining access to organizations can initially be a very formal process involving a lengthy sequence of letter writing and meetings, in order to deal with managerial concerns about your goals. However, the distinction between open and closed settings is not a hard-and-fast one. Organizations also have a highly public character, made visible through marketing and public relations activities.

Buchanan, Boddy, and McCalman (1988) suggest that researchers should adopt an opportunistic approach towards field work in organizations, balancing what is desirable against what is possible. 'The research timetable must therefore take into account the possibility that access will not be automatic and instant, but may take weeks and months of meetings and correspondence to achieve' (1988, p. 56). As Van Maanen and Kolb (1985, p. 11) observe: 'gaining access to most organizations is not a matter to be taken lightly but one that involves some combination of strategic planning, hard work and dumb luck'. Sometimes, ethnographers will be able to have their paths smoothed by individuals who act as both sponsor and gatekeeper. Some of the most influential organizational research relationships are those made with senior management, who may act as 'gatekeepers' to the research setting. Gaining access is also sometimes seen as a process of exchange whereby the organizational ethnographer cannot expect to get something out, in the form of data, without giving something in return, often in the form of their physical, mental, or emotional labour.

In selecting a particular social setting to act as a case study in which to conduct an ethnographic investigation,

Key concept 17.2: What is ethnostatistics?

Ethnostatistics, developed by Bob Gephart of the University of Alberta, uses the methods of ethnography to gain an understanding of how certain groups develop, use, and interpret statistics.

17.1 | Student Experience

Using participant observation in a small-scale research project

When Karla originally began her ethnographic studies she was located in a 'researcher's room' in the library of her national Parliament, with little to no one to talk to and little to observe (see Student experience '*Access issues and data collection*' in Chapter 6). However, she eventually was given a series of research tasks to perform and was able to become more of a participant observer. She made it clear to every one that her primary purpose for being at the research site was as a Ph.D. student engaged in research, and that she wore three hats—researcher, employee, and colleague—and this helped her to make contact with people (see Student experience '*Researcher-subject relationships*' in Chapter 6). However, her dual or triple role eventually got to her and she began to feel burned out: 'it's really exhausting to be with people, especially when you have to wear the double hat. [It's] like, I'm your colleague but I'm also writing notes about what you just said in a minute when I go to the toilet or something like that. But it's a bit like being on stage all the time, but you're not expecting that double role. I found it very laboursome. I guess it depends on what kind of person you are. You have to work sort of very hard 'cause they need to like you and kind of include you into the community for you to be able to be there. So you've got to be very likeable and sociable and in kind of chit chat mode all the time and on top of that you've got to . . .

observe from another angle . . . what's going on here. And I find it extremely tiring. I was exhausted every evening'. Reflecting on the kind of advice she would give other students to prepare for this eventuality, Karla comments that this 'very personal, very strenuous working process is something that you cannot be prepared for. But you should at least try to think about it . . . Even if you've got the happiest workplace in the world, you'll still end up exhausted because you've got to do this double work every day. [It is] constant. Maybe everyone's not as anal with themselves as I am and I ended up feeling like I never did enough of talking with people that you know I should have walked around more and I should have just gone in . . . but it's socially very demanding as well because you've got to be able and prepared to go into situations and introduce yourself to people and explain yourself to people and that was also something that I wasn't prepared [for]. I mean I had thought about all this but I never expected it to be as much as it then was and the amount of having to tell them your story . . . . There were days when I could not come out of my room, when I could not bring myself to do it. I was just sitting there thinking, I can't face you, I don't want to . . . think. And then there were days when I would spend so much time with some of them that I would [feel that this] too is part of the process of doing ethnography'.

the researcher may employ several criteria. These criteria should be determined by the general research area in which he or she is interested. Very often a number of potential cases (and sometimes very many) will be relevant to your research problem. Hence, during his year of par-

ticipant observation at ZTC Ryland, Watson (1994*a*) used to joke with managers about the fact that he had chosen the company for the study because of its convenient location, just a 20-minute walk from his house. The other reason he gave for choosing the company as a research site was because management had been involved in a succession of change initiatives associated with the development of a 'strong' corporate culture. These policies had been informed by the advice of consultants who were academics, providing Watson with potential insight into the processes whereby managerial ideas about culture building were transferred into practice.

You may also choose a certain case because of its 'fit' with your research questions, but there are no guarantees of success, as Van Maanen and Kolb's remark suggests. Sometimes, sheer perseverance pays off. Leidner (1993) was determined that one of the organizations in which she conducted ethnographic research on the routinization of service work should be McDonald's. She writes:

> I knew from the beginning that I wanted one of the case studies to be of McDonald's. The company was a pioneer and exemplar of routinized interaction, and since it was locally based, it seemed like the perfect place to start. McDonald's had other ideas, however, and only after tenacious pestering and persuasion did I overcome corporate employees' polite demurrals, couched in terms of protecting proprietary information and the company's image. (Leidner, 1993, pp. 234–5)

This kind of determination is necessary for any instance in which you want to study a specific organization, where rejection is likely to require a complete rethink. However, with many research questions, several potential cases are likely to meet your criteria.

For Jean Helms Mills serendipity played a role. During the completion of her Master's degree in Behaviour in Organizations, at Lancaster University in the UK, she found herself back home in Halifax, waiting at a bus stop when she bumped into an old acquaintance. Discussion of her Master's thesis and the need to gain access to a company to study their organizational culture prompted the acquaintance to contact her company, Nova Scotia Power, which was undergoing a culture change and needed someone to audit the outcome. This chance meeting led to a longitudinal study of Nova Scotia Power as the company moved from organizational culture to Business Process Reengineering and Helms Mills moved from a Master's to a PH.D. program (Helms Mills, 2003).

Organizational researchers have developed a range of tactics, many of which may seem rather unsystematic in tone, but they are worth drawing attention to:

- Use friends, contacts, colleagues, academics to help you gain access; provided the organization is relevant to your research question, the route should not matter.
- Try to get the support of someone within the organization who will act as your champion. This person may be prepared to vouch for you and the value of your research. Such people are placed in the role of 'sponsors'.
- Usually you will need to get access through top management/senior executives. Even though you may secure a certain level of agreement lower down the hierarchy, you will usually need clearance from them. Such senior people act as 'gatekeepers'.
- Offer something in return (e.g., a report). This helps to create a sense of being trustworthy. However, this strategy also carries risks, in that it may turn you into a cheap consultant and may invite restrictions on your activities, such as insistence on seeing what you write or restrictions on who is willing to talk to you. For example, Milkman (1997) in her study of General Motors (see Web Research in focus 17.1) found that, although her research approach gained her legitimacy in the eyes of management, it stimulated skepticism and lack of trust among the workers.
- Provide a clear explanation of your aims and methods and be prepared to deal with concerns. Suggest a meeting at which you can deal with worries and provide an explanation of what you intend to do in terms that can readily be understood by others.
- Be prepared to negotiate—you will want complete access but it is unlikely you will be given a carte blanche. Milkman (1997) describes how, in negotiating access to the General Motors automobile assembly plant, the promise to produce 'hard', quantitative data to management, through survey research, was what eventually secured the researcher's access to the plant even though she had no previous experience in designing

Student Experience

Gaining research access through family, friends, and acquaintances

In setting up a small-scale research project it is important to make use of whatever practical resources and personal contacts are available to you, providing that you are working within ethical guidelines (see Chapter 8). When Wendy Carroll and her colleagues (Carroll & Helms Mills, 2005; Carroll, Mills, & Helms Mills, 2006; Carroll, Mills, & Helms Mills, 2008) wanted to study identity work and resistance in the call centre industry she drew on a number of contacts that she had made over the years as a former call centre manager. Similarly, Amy Thurlow (Thurlow, 2007; Thurlow & Helms Mills, 2005, 2009) drew on former contacts in the community college system and hospitals where she previously worked as a change agent prior to starting her Ph.D. program. Amy was interested in how the use of language shapes people's acceptance of organizational change.

Jennifer fared less well. Her original idea was to undertake an ethnographic study of an organization undergoing a merger: 'when I started I basically wanted to do . . . ethnography. I wanted to have interviews and then I wanted to have observations also . . . I tried to negotiate access for that but I guess I didn't have too much experience. I don't think I was the best negotiator either but I got access for interviews and that was relatively easy, but then . . . they were also quite strict with [the] number of interviews I [could do]'. Reflecting on her lack of success in gaining access to undertake an ethnographic study, Jennifer felt that maybe 'there could have been several things I could have done'. She wondered if perhaps she may have fared better if she had been 'more experienced and more skilled so it could have

maybe gone better, but maybe, in terms of ethnography, I was proposing maybe too much at the beginning, like maybe they didn't know me yet so well and that could have been one thing because then they reacted very harshly that "no you can come and do your interviews, but that's about it"'. At the initial meeting with the person who had to grant research access to the company Jennifer did not mentioned ethnography per se but rather suggested 'for example, coming to meetings and maybe . . . spending some time in the company and something like that'. Although it was not a particularly sensitive organization, such as a call centre, Jennifer felt that perhaps her failure to gain ethnographic access was because she had not sufficiently confided in the person she was in contact with. That person 'was quite strong minded and quite protective about the organization. And she was also very proud of the organization and . . . maybe didn't want me to come and look at things too much'. As Jennifer's story suggests, gaining access to a company can involve the skillful development of strategies to convince the 'gate-keeper' that your study is relevant and worthwhile and will be of limited cost to the company. However, even with the best will in the world some companies are very reluctant to allow people to observe their activities regardless of motive. So the moral of the story is prepare to 'sell' your research aims to an organizational 'gate-keeper' (stressing relevance, interest, potential outcomes, anonymity, limited cost, etc.), but also be prepared to be turned away. In Jennifer's case she decided that access to interviews was much better than nothing and adjusted her research strategy accordingly.

or conducting surveys! Similarly, Helms Mills (2003) had to promise Nova Scotia executives a survey of employee attitudes to culture change in exchange for broader access to the company to undertake a qualitative, in-depth study of the organization's culture.

- Be reasonably honest about the amount of people's time you are likely to take up. This is a question you will almost certainly be asked if you are seeking access to commercial organizations and, probably, many not-for-profit ones too.

'Hanging around' is another common access strategy. As a strategy, it typically entails either loitering in an area until you are noticed or gradually becoming incorporated into or asking to join a group. For example, as well as interviewing shop stewards who represented assembly-line workers and a selection of workers from each of the four main production departments, Beynon spent a day each week at the Ford plant, observing and listening to the shop stewards 'as they negotiated, argued and discussed issues amongst themselves and with their members' (1975, p. 13). He describes how he 'sat at tables in the canteens and at benches around the coffee-vending machines at break times' and 'talked with workers as they queued up for their dinner, for buses or to clock their cards at the beginning and the end of every day' (1975, p. 13). Similarly, Casey, in her study of a group of professional workers at the multinational 'Hephaestus' Corporation, tells how she 'spent a great deal of time lingering around individual people' (1995, p. 201). Similarly, Parker (2000, p. 236) describes how he spent time waiting 'outside managers' offices, often for long periods of time, and wandering around the factory or offices' just to collect small details or fragments of data. The example given in Web Research in focus 17.2 uses the technique of shadowing which could form part of an ethnographic study.

Sometimes, as research relationships evolve, they come to a point where a degree of informal interaction becomes significant in developing insider status. For example, Heyes, whose research took place inside a chemical plant, lists the many social aspects of organizational life in which he was eventually involved, including 'general conversation, banter, smoke breaks' and rituals such as 'the take-away meals which were consumed on the weekend night-shift' (1997, p. 69).

As these anecdotes suggest, gaining access to social settings is a crucial first step in ethnographic research, in that, without access, your research plans will be halted in their tracks. As Ram (1994) illustrates in his study of employment relations in small firms (see Web Research in focus 17.3), attention to cultural context and local norms and values can be very important considerations when seeking access to closed settings. Gender can also be an important dynamic when negotiating access to many male-dominated organizational settings (see Web Research in focus 17.4). In sum, gaining access is often fraught with difficulties. Therefore, this discussion of access strategies can be only a starting point in knowing what kinds of approach can be considered.

Opportunities for access, however, can also arise from studying contexts with which the researcher is already involved as a complete participant, for example through being employed in the organization they intend to study. Spradley and McCurdy (1972) suggest that the ethnographer's own place of work may even have special advantages as a research site, such as ease of access and already formed relationships with key informants. This may make the time needed to conduct the research shorter. However, this ethnographic approach is not without its own difficulties as the more familiar you are with a social situation, the less you may be able to recognize the tacit cultural rules that are at work. Alvesson (2003) uses the term self-ethnography to refer to a particular type of ethnographic study based on settings which the researcher is highly familiar with, such as universities, which he argues offer particular advantages in terms of gaining research access, understanding the culture, and managing the time demands associated with qualitative research. Brannick and Coghlan (2007) also refer to this as 'insider research', which they suggest is related to **action research**, which was discussed in Chapter 6.

Overt versus covert?

One way to ease the access problem is to assume a covert role—in other words, not to disclose the fact that you are a researcher. This strategy obviates the need to negotiate access to organizations or to explain why you want to intrude into people's lives and make them objects of study. As we will see, seeking access is a highly fraught business and the adoption of a covert role removes some of these difficulties (see Web Key concept 17.1).

Covert ethnography is relatively uncommon within studies of management and business. An exception is Dalton's (1959) classic study of managers, *Men Who Manage*, which focused on the gap between official and unofficial action. Dalton describes how, in setting up access, he made no formal approach to the top management of any of the four firms he studied in the heavily industrialized area of 'Mobile Acres' in the United States. He relied instead on his status as an employee in two of the firms he studied and relied primarily on the method of covert participant observation. Describing some of the difficulties associated with his covert research role, Dalton draws attention to the problem of 'knowing too much', describing how his situation became more sensitive as he acquired more unofficial information about practices such as 'pilfering' (employee theft of materials).

Dalton describes his work role as giving him 'great freedom of movement and wide contacts' (1959, p. 278) within the firm. However, it is not clear from his accounts of the research process to what extent people in the firms actually knew what he was doing. Dalton draws attention to the importance of 'intimates', trusted individuals who gave information and aid to the research process. This circle of individuals had shown over a period of about three years that 'they could be counted on not to jeopardize the study' (Dalton, 1964, p. 66) and did not pry too much into the information that he was getting from others. As far as these intimates were concerned, therefore, it is not clear to what extent they encountered his research role as truly covert.

In another classic study, Donald Roy (1958) was similarly oblique with his co-workers about why he was working at the factory. Working under the pseudonym 'Danelly', he describes how workers knew that he had been attending 'college' but 'the specific course of study remained somewhat obscure' (1958, p. 164) to them. In answer to the question 'Why are you working here?', Roy

stressed the importance of working 'lots of overtime' and this, according to Roy, seemed to 'suffice' for the workers.

However, the overt versus covert distinction is not without problems. For example, while an ethnographer may seek access through an overt route, there may be many people with whom he or she comes into contact who will not be aware of the ethnographer's status as a researcher. Also, some ethnographers move between the two roles (see Web Research in focus 17.5).

Ethnographers are far more likely to be in an overt role than a covert one. Some of the reasons for this situation are extremely practical. For example, Freeman (2000) explains that being white and American made it impossible for her to adopt a covert role in her study of data entry workers in Barbados, and company production demands and limited space made it impossible for her to work on an unpaid temporary basis. However, as discussed above, the reasons for the preference of most ethnographers for an overt role are to do with ethical considerations. Due to the ethical problems that beset covert research (and indeed some of the practical difficulties), the bulk of the discussion of access issues that follows will focus upon ethnographers seeking to employ an overt role.

Pratt (2000), on the other hand, adopted, what he refers to as, 'semiovert participant observation' (p. 460). This involved joining the studied organization—in his case the Amway Corporation—and letting co-workers know of his 'dual role as an employee and researcher' (p. 460). The covert element refers to the fact that Pratt was able to observe and note a number of activities without making it clear at any given point that he was studying those activities. In particular Pratt came to focus on the way that the organization managed the way that employees managed their identities, i.e., they did not attempt to manage identities directly but through the processes that employees used to make sense of themselves and others.

In a similar way Delbridge's (1998) ethnography of British workers' experiences of Japanese management techniques involved a 'position as observer of, and participant in, the social settings of the research [in which] the research was known to the majority of those with whom [he] came in contact' (p. 17).

Both Pratt and Delbridge argue that much of the research work involved the development of trust with co-workers by telling them they were researchers and by working alongside them.

Ongoing access

But access does not finish when you have made contact and gained an entrée to the group. You still need access to people. Simply because you have gained access to an organization does not mean that you will have an easy passage through it. Securing access is in many ways an ongoing activity, which takes considerable effort and time. This is likely to prove a particular problem in closed contexts like organizations, as Delbridge (1998) so effectively illustrates when describing his attempts to become integrated as a worker on the shop floor of a factory sited in a small Welsh valley community. At first, 'I stood out like a sore thumb, I was even noticed and looked at in the street'. However, 'my actual participation in the tasks which faced the workers helped to break down the barriers and several people approached me over the weeks and told me that when they actually saw me sitting there alongside them day after day they began to have some respect for what I was doing' (1998, p. 19).

Even so, there are various concerns that group members may have and these will affect the level of ongoing access that you are able to achieve:

- People will have suspicions about you, perhaps seeing you as an instrument of top management (it is very common for members of organizations to believe that researchers are placed there to check up on them or even to mistake them for other people). For example, Roethlisberger and Dickson (1939) describe how one of the interviewers in the Hawthorne studies was mistaken for a rate setter:

> There was a buzz of conversation and the men seemed to be working at great speed. Suddenly there was a sharp hissing sound. The conversation died away, and there was a noticeable slowing up in the work pace. The interviewer later discovered from an acquaintance in the department that he had been mistaken for a rate setter. One of the workmen, who acted as a lookout, had stepped on a valve releasing compressed air, a prearranged signal for slowing down. (1939, p. 386)

- Another example is provided by Freeman (2000), who found that her research access was halted because of fears that she was a corporate spy, sent by a competitor organization to poach members of the workforce.
- They will worry that what they say or do may get back to bosses or to colleagues. Van Maanen (1991a) notes from his research on the police that, when conducting ethnographic research among officers, you are likely to observe activities that may be deeply discrediting and even illegal. Your credibility among police officers will be determined by your reactions to situations and events that are known to be difficult for individuals.
- If they have these worries, they may go along with your research but in fact sabotage it, engaging in deceptions, misinformation, and not allowing access to 'back regions' (Goffman, 1956).

There are four things you can do to smooth the path of ongoing access:

- Play up your credentials—past work and experience; your knowledge of the organization and/or its sector; understanding of their problems—and be prepared for tests of either competence or credibility. An example of this is provided by Perlow (1997), who claims that a critical factor in gaining the support of engineers at the Ditto corporation was that she came from the Massachusetts Institute of Technology (MIT), as 'there is no institution that the engineers we studied hold in higher regard' (1997, p. 142).
- Pass tests—be non-judgemental when things are said to you about informal activities or about the organization; make sure information given to you does not get back to others, whether bosses or peers. Parker (2000) describes how, when at the end of his field work he submitted his report to management, an uncompli-

mentary comment about the Managing Director was traced back to an insufficiently anonymized source. Parker subsequently came in for a humiliating grilling from three of the company directors. He claims that this event probably damaged the manager's reputation in the organization, and his trust in him.

- You may need a role—if your research involves quite a lot of participant observation, the role will be related to your position within the organization (see Web Research in focus 17.1). Otherwise, you will need to construct a 'front', as Ditton (1977; see Web Research in focus 17.5) did when referring to 'his studies'. This will involve thinking about your dress and your explanations about what you are doing there, and possibly helping out occasionally with work or offering advice. Make sure you have thought about ways in which people's suspicions can be allayed and be consistent and do not behave ambiguously or inconsistently.
- Be prepared for changes in circumstances that may affect your access, such as changes of senior management.

Key informants

One aspect of having sponsors or gatekeepers who smooth access for the ethnographer is that they may become key informants in the course of the subsequent field work. The ethnographer relies a lot on informants, but certain informants may become particularly important to the research. They often develop an appreciation of the research and direct the ethnographer to situations, events, or people likely to be helpful to the progress of the investigation.

An interesting example is provided by Kanter (1977), who describes the relationships she developed with a small group of people with whom she worked closely at Indsco Corporation. 'These people were largely in functions where they were well placed to see a large number of people in a large number of levels . . . .They could tell me about the history of the company and a variety of experiences in the organization as well as provide information about the issues in their own careers. I could also use them to check out stories I gathered elsewhere' (1977, p. 336). Similarly, Collinson (1992b) describes how being a man research-

ing equal opportunities sometimes resulted in research respondents withholding cooperation. He describes how the identification of key women informants, who were prepared to assist the 'young lad from the university', was crucial in providing him with 'insider' information. One female trade unionist in particular provided extensive help with the project. Working together, Collinson developed 'a much closer and mutually supportive working relationship than would usually be the case between researcher and respondents' (1992b, p. 115). This provided him with 'deeper insight into the difficulties faced by women in employment and within the trade union movement' (1992b, p. 115) and greater understanding of the problems of managing work and home.

In sum, key informants can clearly be of great help to the ethnographer and frequently provide a support that helps with the stress of field work. However, it also needs to be borne in mind that they carry risks in that the ethnographer may develop an undue reliance on the key informant, and, rather than seeing social reality through the eyes of members of the social setting, the researcher is seeing social reality through the eyes of the *key informant*.

In addition, the ethnographer will encounter many other people who will also act as informants. Their accounts may be solicited or unsolicited (Hammersley & Atkinson, 1995). Some researchers prefer the latter, because of its greater spontaneity and naturalism. Very often, research participants develop a sense of the kinds of events the ethnographer wants to see or encounters that it would be beneficial to be present at. Such unsolicited sources of information are highly attractive to the ethnographer because of their relative spontaneity, although, as Hammersley and Atkinson (1995, pp. 130–1) observe, they may on occasion be staged for the ethnographer's benefit. Solicited accounts can occur in two ways: by interview (see Chapter 14) or by casual questioning during conversations (though in ethnographic research the boundary between an interview and a conversation is by no means clear-cut, as Burgess (1984) makes clear). When the ethnographer needs specific information concerning an issue that is not amenable to direct observation or that is not cropping up during 'natural' conversations, solicited accounts are likely to be the only way forward.

Roles for ethnographers

Related to the issue of ongoing access (or relationships in the field, as it is sometimes called) is the question of the kind of role the ethnographer adopts in relation to the social setting and its members. Several schemes have been devised by writers on research methods to describe the various roles that can be and have been adopted by ethnographers. One of the most widely cited schemes is Gold's (1958) classification of participant observer roles, which can be arrayed on a continuum of degrees of involvement with and detachment from members of the social setting (see Figure 17.1). There are four roles:

- Complete participant. According to Gold, the complete participant is a fully functioning member of the social setting and his or her true identity is not known to members. As such, the complete participant is a covert observer, like Roy (1958) and Dalton (1959).
- Participant-as-observer. This role is the same as the complete participant one, but members of the social setting are aware of the researcher's status as a researcher. The ethnographer is engaged in regular interaction with people and participates in their daily lives and is open about their research. In organizational ethnography this frequently involves taking up either paid or unpaid employment in the research setting, as did Pratt (2000) in his study of Amway, Delbridge (1998) in his study of contemporary manufacturing under

TQM, and Sharpe (1997) in her study of Japanese work practices in a UK-based car manufacturing plant.
- Observer-as-participant. In this role, the researcher is mainly an interviewer. There is some observation but very little of it involves any participation. Many of the studies covered in Chapter 14 are of this type. Prasad's (1993) study of the effects of computerization of work, described in Chapter 6, also fits into this category, as her research relied on structured periods of observation during which she would watch the staff at work and document these observations, only helping out occasionally on the reception desk when it was particularly busy.
- Complete observer. The researcher does not interact with people. According to Gold, people do not have to take the researcher into account. This kind of role relies on forms of observation that are unobtrusive in character. For example, in studies at the Western Electric Company's Hawthorne plant, investigators spent a total of six months observing the informal social relationships between operators in the Bank Wiring Observation Room. Investigations involved an observer, who maintained a role as 'disinterested spectator' with the aim of observing and describing what was going on. Observation involved certain general rules: the investigator should not give orders or answer any questions that necessitated the assumption of authority; he should not enter voluntarily into any argument and generally should remain as non-committal as possible; he should not force himself into any conversation or

Figure 17.1

Gold's classification of participant observer roles

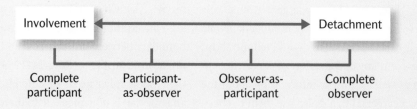

appear anxious to overhear; he should never violate confidences or give information to supervisors; and he should not by his manner of speech or behaviour 'set himself off from the group' (Roethlisberger & Dickson, 1939, pp. 388–9).

However, most writers would take the view that, since ethnography entails immersion in a social setting and fairly prolonged involvement, the complete observer role should not be considered as participant observation or ethnography at all, since participation is likely to be more or less entirely missing. Some writers might also question whether research based on the observer-as-participant role can genuinely be regarded as ethnography, but, since it is likely that certain situations are unlikely to be amenable to the immersion that is a key ingredient of the method, it could be argued that to dismiss it totally as an approach to ethnography is rather restrictive. It is significant in this context that Gold referred to the four roles in relation to conducting 'fieldwork', which has the potential for a broader meaning than either participant observation or ethnography.

Each role carries its own advantages and risks. The issues concerning being a complete participant were covered in Web Key concept 17.1. According to Gold, the participant-as-observer role carries the risk of over-identification and hence of '**going native**' (see Key concept 17.3), but offers the opportunity to get close to people. Gold argues that the observer-as-participant role carries the risk of not understanding the social setting and people in it sufficiently and, therefore, of making incorrect inferences. The complete observer role shares with complete participation the removal of the possible problem of reactivity, but it carries even fur-

ther risks than the observer-as-participant role of failing to understand situations.

Gans (1968) has devised a classification of participant observer roles, but he views these as roles that will coexist in any project. In other words, the three roles he outlines will be employed at different times in the course of ethnographic research and for different purposes. The three roles are:

- Total participant. In which the ethnographer is completely involved in a certain situation and has to resume a researcher stance once the situation has unfolded and then write down notes.
- Researcher-participant. Whereby the ethnographer participates in a situation but is only semi-involved, so that he or she can function fully as a researcher in the course of the situation;
- Total researcher. Which entails observation without involvement in the situation, as in attendance at a public meeting or watching what is going on in a bar; when in this role, the researcher does not participate in the flow of events.

The advantage of Gans's classification is that, like Gold's, it reflects degrees of involvement and detachment, but has the advantage that it deals only with overt observation and recognizes that ethnographers do not typically adopt a single role throughout their dealings. For example, looking at the research process described by Ram (1994; see Web Research in focus 17.3), it is clear that in one sense Ram was a total participant, running the firm, speaking Punjabi, and having first-hand experience of the clothing industry. However, in relation to the women shop floor machinists, he was a total researcher, unable, because of the customary regulation of gender relationships in Asian society, to participate in the flow of events.

Table 17.1 outlines some of the working roles that organizational ethnographers take on in order to secure access to closed settings. However, it is evident from the table and the organizational ethnographies referred to in this chapter that more than one role may be involved in a particular setting. Examples of working roles are given in Web Research in focus 17.1.

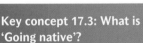

Key concept 17.3: What is 'Going native'?

'Going native' refers to a situation where an ethnographer loses his or her sense of being a researcher and become wrapped up in the world view of the people being studied. The prolonged immersion of ethnographers in the lives of the people they study, coupled with the commitment to seeing the social world through their eyes, lie behind the risk and actuality of going native.

Table 17.1 Three roles for organizational ethnographers

	Ethnographer's role		
	Consultant	**Apprentice**	**Confidant**
Characteristics	Competent, knowledgeable, professional	Naïve, unthreatening, personable	Mature, attentive, trustworthy
	A credible outsider who secures the trust of management	A younger person who can make him or herself useful within the organization	An impartial outsider who is able to listen to people's problems
	Exchange of access for knowledge or information, often in the form of a written report or verbal presentation	Exchange of access for productive labour	Exchange of access for psycho-social support or therapy
Examples	Ram (1994)	Dalton (1959)	Collinson (1992)
	Watson (1994*a*)	Casey (1995)	Crang (1994)
	Holliday (1995)	Perlow (1997)	Holliday (1995)
	Parker (2000)	Freeman (2000)	Sharpe (1997
		Parker (2000)	Delbridge (1998)
			Fletcher (2002)

Clearly these three organizational roles are overlapping and more than one may be adopted in a particular setting. They are also likely to change over time as the fieldwork progresses. It is arguably the case that, even if it were possible to adopt a single ethnographic role over the entire course of a project, it is likely that it would be undesirable, because there would be a lack of flexibility in handling situations and people, and risks of excessive involvement (and hence going native) or detachment would loom large. This is a criticism that was levelled at Beynon (1975) in his ethnographic study of *Working for Ford*. The issue of the kind of role(s) the ethnographer adopts is, therefore, of considerable significance, because it has implications for field relationships in the various situations that are encountered (Altamirano-Jimenez, 2010).

Active or passive?

A further issue that is raised about any situation in which the ethnographer participates is the degree to which he or she should be or can be an active or a passive participant (Van Maanen, 1978). Even when the ethnographer is in an observer-as-participant role, there may be contexts in which either participation is unavoidable or a compulsion to join in a limited way may be felt. For example, Fine's

Tips and Skills

Being a participant observer in a familiar situation

It is easy to gain the impression that, in order to become a participant observer, you need to gain access to an organization to which you do not belong as a member. However, it may be that you already have access to an organizational setting that could provide the basis for a more modest study using the method of participant observation. Several examples of this are provided by Spradley and McCurdy (1972), who encouraged their undergraduate students to engage in participant observation in organizations with which they were already familiar. This could include a place of work where you work either full- or part-time, or an organization where you are a volunteer or social member, such as a church group or the Canadian Forces Reserve. The important thing to remember is that, if you are studying a cultural scene with which you are familiar, it is even more important to develop a high degree of self-awareness so that you don't take what you see for granted.

(1996) research on the work of chefs in restaurants was carried out largely by semi-structured interview. In spite of his limited participation, he found himself involved in washing up in the kitchens to help out during busy periods. Sometimes ethnographers may feel they have no choice but to get involved, because a failure to participate actively might indicate to members of the social setting a lack of commitment and lead to a loss of credibility. Another example is provided by Holliday (1995), who describes how in smaller organizations active work-role participation is more likely to be expected of the ethnographer than in larger companies where there is more space to 'hang around'. She describes how at FranTech she was given 'a variety of jobs, from typing and answering the telephone to "managerial" tasks such as auditing the production schedule and writing procedures for the BS5750' (Holliday, 1995, p. 27). Similarly Ram (1994; see Web Research in focus 17.3), in his study of family-owned and -managed firms in Britain's West Midlands clothing industry, talks about helping with social security queries, housing issues, passport problems, advising on higher education, and even tying turbans while in the field. However, the pressure to get involved raises ethical considerations, as the ethnographer may be asked to participate in an activity that involves a degree of deception or even illegal activity (see Chapter 8 for more on ethical considerations).

 ## Sampling

The sampling of informants in ethnographic research is often a combination of convenience sampling and snowball sampling (see Chapter 9 for an explanation of these terms). Much of the time ethnographers are forced to gather information from whatever sources are available to them. Very often they face opposition or at least indifference to their research and are relieved to glean information or views from whoever is prepared to divulge such details. For example, Dalton refers to the importance of 'conversational interviewing' as the basis for his data collection strategy. These are not interviews in the usual sense, but a series of broken and incomplete conversations that, when written up, may, according to Dalton, be 'tied together as one statement' (1959, p.

280). Conversational interviews are characterized by being precipitated by events. In some instances, these were prompted by Dalton, who asked managers at the end of an important meeting an open-ended question like 'How did things go?', but in others they were simply the result of overheard exchanges in shops or offices.

Ethnographers who take on a role that is closer to the observer-as-participant one rely somewhat more on formally asking for names of others who might be relevant and who could be contacted. For example, Marshall (1984) describes how, in order to identify her sample of 30 women managers, she would first make a contact within a particular company (sometimes a woman manager and sometimes a helpful member of the personnel department) and then ask him or her to suggest other potential interviewees.

In other instances, greater emphasis may be placed on how representative interviewees are of the overall population, using a *stratified sampling* approach. Casey (1995) describes how she interviewed 60 people during her research at the Hephaestus Corporation, in an effort to gain a wide sample of occupation, rank, tenure, and demographic features such as gender, race, ethnicity, and regional origin. She goes on to describe how interviewees came from a variety of occupational groupings, including engineers, computer professionals, scientists, technical analysts, financial analysts, administrators, managers, and manufacturing workers. Finally, some individuals were chosen on the basis of their strategic importance within the team or division, including the vice president, a union representative, a new entry employee, and a returned retiree.

Whichever of the two strategies is adopted, the question is raised as to the degree to which either can result in a **representative sample** of informants. **Probability sampling** is almost never used in **ethnographic research** and is even rarely employed in **qualitative research** based on interviews. In many cases, it is not feasible to conduct a probability sampling exercise because of the constraints of ongoing fieldwork and also because it can be difficult and often impossible to map 'the population' from which a **random sample** might be taken—that is, to create a **sampling frame**. Instead, ethnographers have to ensure that they gain access to as wide a range of individuals relevant to the research question as possible, so that many different perspectives and ranges of activity are the focus of attention.

Theoretical sampling

An alternative strategy is theoretical sampling (see Key concept 17.4), advocated by Glaser and Strauss (1967) and Strauss and Corbin (1998) in the context of an approach to qualitative data analysis they developed known as grounded theory. In Glaser and Strauss's view, because of its reliance on statistical rather than theoretical criteria, probability sampling is not appropriate to qualitative research. Theoretical sampling is meant to be an alternative strategy. As they put it: 'Theoretical sampling is done in order to discover categories and their properties and to suggest the interrelationships into a theory. Statistical sampling is done to obtain accurate evidence on distributions of people among categories to be used in descriptions and verifications' (Glaser and Strauss, 1967, p. 62).

Figure 17.2 outlines the main steps in theoretical sampling. The reference in Web Key concept 17.2 to 'places, people, or events' reminds us that, in ethnographic research, it is not just people who are being sampled but events and contexts as well (see below).

In grounded theory, you carry on collecting data (observing, interviewing, collecting documents) until you have achieved **theoretical saturation** (see Key concept 17.5). This means that: successive interviews/observations have both formed the basis for the creation of a category and confirmed its importance; there is no need to continue with data collection in relation to that category or cluster of categories; instead, the researcher should move on and generate hypotheses out of the categories that are building up and then move on to collecting data

> **Key concept 17.4: What is theoretical sampling?**
>
> Theoretical sampling 'is the process of data collection for generating theory whereby the analyst jointly collects, codes, and analyzes his data and decides what data to collect next and where to find them, in order to develop her theory as it emerges' (Glaser & Strauss, 1967, p. 45).

in relation to these hypotheses. Proponents of **grounded theory** argue that there is a great deal of redundancy in statistical sampling. For example, committing yourself to interviewing x per cent of an organization's members may mean that you end up wasting time and resources because you could have confirmed the significance of a concept and/or its connections with other concepts by using a much smaller sample. Instead, grounded theory advocates that you sample in terms of what is

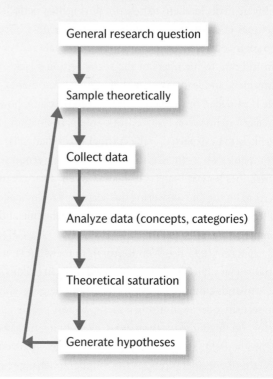

Figure 17.2

The process of theoretical sampling

> **Key concept 17.5: What is theoretical saturation?**
>
> Theoretical saturation refers to a process of continuing to sample theoretically until a category has been saturated with data, i.e., 'until (a) no new or relevant data seem to be emerging regarding a category; (b) the category is well developed in terms of its properties and dimensions demonstrating variation; and (c) the relationships among categories are well established and validated' (Strauss & Corbin, 1998, p. 212).

relevant to and meaningful for your theory. The key is to ensure you sample so as to test your emerging theoretical ideas.

The ideas of **theoretical sampling** and **theoretical saturation** will be encountered again when grounded theory is examined in greater detail in Chapter 21.

Not just people

As was pointed out in the last section, in ethnographic research sampling is not just about people but also about other things. Hammersley and Atkinson (1995) mention time and context as units that need to be considered in the context of sampling. Attending to time means that the ethnographer must make sure that people or events are observed at different times of the day and different days of the week. To do otherwise risks drawing inferences about certain people's behaviour or about events that are valid only for mornings or for weekdays rather than weekends. It is impossible to be an ethnographer all the time for several reasons: need to take time out to write up notes; other commitments (work or domestic); and body imperatives (eating, sleeping, and so on). When the group in question operates a different cycle from the ethnographer's normal regime (such as night shifts in a factory or hospital), the requirement to time sample may necessitate a considerable change of habit. Delbridge (1998), for example, describes how tired he felt after a day making windscreen wipers or circuit boards for televisions. In addition, he explains that 'there was real pressure and intensity during the fieldwork, particularly during the early stages when I was negotiating my informal access and acceptance into the group. I developed a nervous tic in my cheek during the first two weeks, something I have never experienced before or since' (1998, p. 19).

It can also be important to sample in terms of *context*. People's behaviour is influenced by contextual factors, so that it is important to ensure that such behaviour is observed in a variety of locations. For example, in his study of masculinity and workplace culture in a lorry-making factory in the north-west of England, Collinson (1992*a*) draws attention to the ways in which shop floor workers resist managerial control by spending time chatting and joking. By spending time with workers during lunch

and unofficial breaks, in the toilet, the canteen, on the car park, on the works' bus, in the pub, and occasionally in people's homes, Collinson was able to explore these cultural practices in far more detail than if he had confined his study and himself to observing practices within formal workplace settings.

 ## Field notes

Because of the frailties of human memory, ethnographers have to take notes based on their observations. These should be fairly detailed summaries of events and behaviour and the researcher's initial reflections on them. The notes need to specify key dimensions of whatever is observed or heard. There are some general principles:

- Write down field notes, however brief, as quickly as possible after seeing or hearing something interesting.
- Write up full field notes at the very latest at the end of the day and include such details as location, who is involved, what prompted the exchange or whatever, date and time of the day, etc.
- Nowadays, people may prefer to use a tape recorder to record initial notes, but this may create a problem of needing to transcribe a lot of speech.
- Notes must be vivid and clear—you should not have to ask at a later date, 'What did I mean by that?'
- You need to take copious notes, so, if in doubt, write it down. The notes may be of different types (see below).

Obviously, it can be very useful to take your notes down straight away—that is, as soon as something interesting happens. However, wandering around with a notebook and pencil in hand and scribbling notes down on a continuous basis runs the risk of making people self-conscious. It may be necessary, therefore, to develop strategies of taking small amounts of time out, though hopefully without generating the anxieties Ditton (1977) appears to have occasioned (see Web Research in focus 17.5).

To some extent, strategies for taking field notes will be affected by the degree to which the ethnographer enters the field with clearly delineated research questions.

Tips and Skills

Global ethnography

One of the defining features of a classic approach to ethnography is the way that the researcher concentrates on the specific social processes within one particular community. This means that there is a tendency to overlook the context within which that particular community operates. This is particularly important in organizational ethnography because the culture of a particular workgroup or company can only be understood in relation to the cultural context in which it is located. Moreover, it is often difficult to set boundaries around the particular community that is being studied, especially in cases where the organization being studied is part of a multinational corporation. Traditionally, these boundaries were determined by place—the ethnographer travelled to the place where the community was located and studied what they found there. However, organizations are increasingly distributed over a wide geographical area, and this too makes it difficult to determine the focus of study. However, Burawoy et al. (2000) describe the emergence of a new form of ethnographic research that departs from this convention. Global ethnography instead focuses on the way that particular cultures are affected by globalization, leading to the dissolution of traditional ways of working. The global ethnographer seeks to gain insight into the lived experience of globalization through the study of such diverse groups as job-hopping Irish software engineers or Indian nurses working in the United States. This shift in emphasis opens up significant opportunities for organizational ethnographers to study such things as the effects of advances in telecommunications and information technologies on working practices and to explore how work has become less dependent on physical location. Global ethnography thus extends the tradition of ethnographic studies of industrial and large bureaucratic organizations that was started by writers like Beynon (1975) and continued by Casey (1995), who study social settings with relatively fixed boundaries.

As noted in Chapter 6, most **qualitative research** adopts a general approach of beginning with general research questions (as specifically implied by Figure 6.1), but there is considerable variation in the degree to which this is the case. Obviously, when there is some specificity to a research question, ethnographers have to orientate their observations to that research focus, but at the same time maintain a fairly open mind so that the element of flexibility, that is such a strength of a qualitative research strategy, is not eroded. Ditton (see Web Research in focus 17.5) provides an illustration of a very open-ended approach when he writes that his research 'was not set up to answer any empirical questions' (1977, p. 11).

Similarly, Kunda (1992) describes how he was swamped with information, partly because he did not seek to define his focus of study. His interest in any event that was occurring at the time led to the generation of a vast quantity of data. During his year in the field he 'generated thousands of pages of fieldnotes and interview transcripts (produced each day from the fragmented notes hastily scribbled during and between events and interviews), collections of archival material, computer output, newsletters, papers, memos, brochures, posters, textbooks, and assorted leftovers' (1992, p. 237). This period of open-endedness usually cannot last long, because there is the temptation to try to record the details of absolutely everything, which can be very trying. Usually the ethnographer will begin to narrow down the focus of his or her research and to match observations to the emerging research focus. Hence, Parker (2000, p. 239) describes how, as each case study progressed, he began to focus on certain key issues and ideas that began to guide his interviews and observation. This was partly a result of feeling the need to develop a framework that could enable him to cope with the 'huge quantity of ideas' and 'incoherent impressions' that he had generated. This approach is implied by the sequence suggested by Figure 6.1.

For most ethnographers, the main equipment with which they will need to supply themselves in the course of observation will be a notepad and pen (see e.g., Armstrong 1993, p. 28). A tape recorder can be another useful addition to one's hardware, but, as suggested above, it is likely to increase radically the amount of transcription and is possibly more obtrusive than writing notes. Most ethnographers re-

| 17.3 | # Student Experience |

Writing field notes

Shelagh Campbell found her field notes to be helpful in a number of ways. In undertaking focus groups, as part of a broad study of professional identity (Campbell & Haiven, 2008; Campbell & Mills, 2007), she found that occasionally the transcriber of the audio files would mix up the labels for the text, and attribute the wrong comments to a person:

My own field notes helped to keep this straight, particularly if I was not recording verbatim, but making commentary-type notes as I went along. Writing these up in detail as a summary of impressions about each speaker right after the sessions helped to keep the material fresh and aided in completeness and corrections, as sometimes it took weeks to get the text files back from transcription. Body language notes were most useful in focus groups as these enabled me to write more detail than otherwise possible in a regular interview, where some subjects actively read my notes upside down. In a focus group the dis-

cussion centres on participants and I am more often ignored.

Field notes also helped me to record the details of a setting, and ambient issues and the circumstances around the interview that gave important context to the data. This was particularly important when I had been referred to a contact from an earlier interview. Noting the dates between meetings, the rapidity of response to the second request to meet, and the issues surrounding the relationship between the two parties ensured I considered these contextual factors. (In one case the first person was preparing to leave the country on a sabbatical for six months and was keen to have his leads followed up quickly; the second person was a very close friend and likewise about to undertake a significant outside commitment that would preclude comment on some issues of a political nature. Six months from now I will have forgotten these details if not for field notes.)

Tips and Skills

Recording field notes

Ethnographic field notes are traditionally handwritten and kept in a notebook or 'diary'. This medium for the recording of data has a number of advantages, not the least that it is flexible and discrete, the diary can be taken most places (including the toilet!), and it can be slipped out of the way into a pocket when not required. However, the main disadvantage with a handwritten diary is that at the end of the fieldwork you will be left with a huge quantity of notes (possibly not in very clear

handwriting) and, if you want to analyze the data with the aid of CAQDAS (Computer-assisted qualitative data analysis; see Chapter 24) or even if you intend to quote extensively from your field notes in your dissertation, you will have to undertake the laborious and time-consuming task of typing them into word-processed form. In any case, the advantages and disadvantages of both methods for recording field notes should be considered carefully.

port that after a period of time they become less obtrusive to participants in social settings, who become familiar with their presence (e.g., Atkinson 1981, p. 128). Speaking into a tape recorder may rekindle an awareness of the ethnographer's presence. Also, in shops, offices, and factories it may be difficult to use, without the availability of an interview room, because of the impact of extraneous noise.

Photography can be an additional source of data, which helps to stir the ethnographer's memory or be built into the research design in a way which accords visual images equal status to written and spoken forms of data (see Key concept 17.6). Photographs, for example, can provide a graphic illustration of the organizational architecture, which is suggested to be influential in determining methods of organizational control and techniques of employee surveillance. Photography can also provide powerful illustration of organizational symbolism, enabling representation of logos, uniforms, and other visual artifacts, which can be interpreted as aspects of the organizational culture (Pondy et al., 1983). However, it is unlikely that photography will be suitable for all kinds of research; it may be less appropriate for researching more abstract organizational issues, such as strategy or structure, which have fewer obvious physical manifestations.

> **Key concept 17.6: What is visual ethnography?**
>
> Visual ethnography refers to the use of such things as photography, video, and hypermedia as methods of data collection in ethnographic research; it can also include the analysis of visual images.

Types of field notes

Some writers have found it useful to classify the types of field notes that are generated in the process of conducting ethnographic research. The following classification is based on the similar categories suggested by Lofland and Lofland (1995), and Sanjek (1990):

- Mental notes. Particularly useful when it is inappropriate to be seen taking notes.
- Jotted notes (also called scratch notes). Very brief notes written down on pieces of paper or in small notebooks to jog one's memory about events that should be writ-

ten up later. Lofland and Lofland (1995, p. 90) refer to these as being made up of 'little phrases, quotes, key words, and the like'. They need to be jotted down inconspicuously, preferably out of sight, since detailed note taking in front of people may make them self-conscious. Crang (1994) refers to his use of scratch notes in his study of waiting staff in a restaurant (see Web Research in focus 17.6).

- Full field notes. As soon as possible make detailed notes, which will be your main data source. They should be written at the end of the day or sooner if possible. Write as promptly and as fully as possible. Write down information about events, people, conversations, etc. Write down initial ideas about interpretation. Record impressions and feelings.

It is worth adding that field notes are often to do with the ethnographer as well as the social setting being observed. It is frequently in field notes that the ethnographer's presence is evident. For example, when Holliday (1995) describes the emotions associated with her fieldwork experience, she draws attention to her prevailing fear of incompetence, her concern about being liked, and her anxiety about whether or not to disagree with or challenge people. Precisely because they record the quotidian as observed and experienced by ethnographers, it is here that they come to the surface. In the finished work—the ethnography in the sense of a written account of a group and its culture—the ethnographer is frequently written out of the picture (Van Maanen, 1988). A major difference here is that field notes are invariably for personal consumption (Coffey, 1999), whereas the written ethnography is for public consumption and has to be presented as a definitive account of the social setting and culture in question. To keep on allowing the ethnographer to surface in the text risks conveying a sense of the account as an artifice rather than an authoritative chronicle. This issue will be addressed in further detail in Chapter 25.

 ## The end

Knowing when to stop is not an easy or straightforward matter in ethnography. Because of its unstructured nature and the absence of specific hypotheses to be tested (other than those that might emerge during data collection and analysis), there is a tendency for ethnographic research to lack a sense of an obvious end-point. Traditions within anthropology have dictated that long-term continuous fieldwork should usually consist of a period of 12 months, so as to enable the study of a culture through a full seasonal cycle of activity (Davies, 1999). These conventions apply to a lesser extent within organizational ethnography, where a 'long stay' in the field is still seen as crucial to securing 'insider' status. At some point, however, ethnographic research does come to an end. In organizational research it is likely that a deadline for data collection will be negotiated at the outset. Buchanan, Boddy, and McCalman (1988) recommend that leaving the research site, or 'getting out', is handled in such a way as to leave the door open to the possibility of future research or fieldwork visits. At this stage it is useful to confirm the conclusion of the research in writing, thanking staff for their cooperation. Sometimes, the rhythms of the ethnographer's occupational career or personal and family life will necessitate withdrawal from the field, or research funding commitments will bring fieldwork to a close. Such factors include: the end of a period of sabbatical leave; the need to write up and submit a doctoral thesis by a certain date; or funding for research drawing to a close.

Moreover, ethnographic research can be highly stressful for many reasons: the nature of the topic, which places the fieldworker in stressful situations; the marginality of the researcher in the social setting and the need constantly to manage a front; and the prolonged absence from one's normal life that is often necessary. The ethnographer may feel that he or she has simply had enough. A further possibility that may start to bring about moves to bring fieldwork to a close is that the ethnographer may begin to feel that the research questions on which he or she has decided to concentrate are answered, so that there are no new data worth generating. The ethnographer may even feel a strong sense of *déjà vu* towards the end of data collection. Altheide (1980, p. 310) has written that his decision to leave the various news organizations in which he had conducted ethnographic research was often motivated by 'the recurrence of familiar situations and the feeling that little worthwhile was being revealed'. In the language of grounded theory, all the researcher's categories are thoroughly *saturated*, although Glaser and Strauss's approach would invite you to be certain that there are no new questions to be asked of the area you are investigating, or no new comparisons to be made.

The reasons for bringing ethnographic research to a close can involve a wide range of factors from the personal to matters of research design. Whatever the reason, disengagement has to be *managed*. For one thing, this means that promises must be kept, so that, if you promised a report to an organization as a condition of entry, that promise should not be forgotten. It also means that ethnographers must provide good explanations for their departure. Members of a social setting always know that the researcher is a temporary fixture, but over a long period of time, and especially if there was genuine participation in activities within that setting, people may forget that the ethnographer's presence is finite. The farewells have to be managed and in an orderly fashion.

Also, the ethnographer's *ethical* commitments must not be forgotten, such as the need to ensure that persons and settings are anonymized. It is common practice within organizational ethnography to change the name of a company in order to protect the anonymity of the organization, as well as the names of individuals who participated in the study—even place names and locations may be changed. For example, Dalton (1959) protected the anonymity of his 'intimates' or informants by changing the place names and locations associated with the study. He also declined to disclose the nature of his formal work roles at Milo and Fruhling, as he felt this would endanger the exposure of 'intimates' to their superiors. Whatever happens, it is wise to reach an agreement with senior members of the organization before disclosing the identity of an organization, and it may be less threatening for senior managers and employers to offer anonymity as an explicit aspect of the access agreement.

Autoethnography

One of the ways in which more reflexive, narrative forms of ethnographic writing have been cultivated is through the emerging cross-disciplinary genre of autoethnography (Marechal, 2010). This relates to the interest of anthropologists in autoanthropology (Strathern, 1987), which is an autobiographical form of research that is concerned with researching settings where the cultural backgrounds of the observer and observed are shared. Autoethnography involves the writing of a highly personalized text in which the personal is related to the cultural and the political in a way that claims the conventions associated with literary writing. However, it is difficult to summarize what autoethnography is about, precisely because its purpose is to challenge the conventions of social scientific writing by blurring the boundaries of genre that separate art and science, a practice that has come to be known as 'genre bending'. An example of this is a book by Ellis (2004) entitled *The ethnographic I: A methodological novel about teaching and doing autoethnography*, which uses a fictitious account of her teaching a graduate course on autoethnography as the basis for discussion of doing and writing autoethnography. This involves blending the highly personalized accounts of her own and her students' lives with methodological discussions in a way that has come to be labelled as 'creative non-fiction'.

Crucial to the autoethnographic style of writing is the focus on 'creating a palpable emotional experience' (Holman Jones, 2005, p. 767) for the reader so that they experience the narrative 'as if it were happening to them' (Ellis, 2004, p. 116). Although the import of autoethnography into the study of management and business has been relatively slow since the work of Goodall (1994) there have been a few more recent examples, including Watson (2000); Katila and Merilainen (1999, 2002); Bruni and Gherardi (2002); Hearn (2004); Brewis (2004); and Friedman, Dyke, and Murphy (2007). In the latter case Friedman was interested to understand how expatriates adjust to and 'master' their new culture. To that end, Friedman, a Canadian, drew on her own experiences of working in Hong Kong. Through this method she, and her colleagues, were able to theorize that 'success in the new environment is dependent on the expatriate's ability to adjust and master the new culture . . . [but] that culture shock needs to be reconceptualized as a discontinuous process [with] . . . cultural acceptance [playing] a critical role in expatriate adjustment' (p. 67). Brewis (2004) was perhaps the first to develop a **poststructuralist** approach to authoethnography by courageously applying Foucault's (1988) 'techniques of the self' to her own life. She set out to make sense of a series of recent events that had happened to her 'and to explore the implications of the subsequent changes [she had] made to [her] way of being-

in-the-world'. The outcome was an assessment of her identity 'as an over-achieving adherent of the Protestant ethic [that had] resulted in significant costs [including] . . . two breakdowns' (p. 24). Pioneering feminist autoethnicity within management and organization studies is the work of Katila and Merilainen, who contend that 'placing the self in the centre of research—that is, seeing self both as the subject and the object of the research—can be a meaningful and fruitful research strategy when dealing with the gendered practices of academic work' (2002, p. 185). Through a study of organizational life at their own university department where they were PH.D. students, Katila and Merilainen argue that they 'were able to highlight the gendered nature of academic life in general, and the difficulties women face in constructing their professional identity in particular' (2002, p. 197):

> By doing research on our own community and using ourselves as research instruments we have highlighted the fluid boundaries between the object and subject of research . . . We have shown how individual and experiences and emotions are always partly collective and how individual actions are constrained and controlled by organizational rules. We have argued that through our personal experience we gain access to collective organizational reality. (2002, p. 197)

 ## Can there be a feminist ethnography?

In this final section we will review some of the central debates within feminist research within the social sciences and business research and relate them to the ethnographic tradition. However, it must be noted that it remains relatively unusual in business and management research for ethnography to be conducted in a way that involves applying a gender perspective with the aim of promoting the interests of women. Hence, in business and management research, there are several examples of ethnographies done by women and of women's work (e.g., Cavendish, 1982; Westwood, 1984; and Pollert, 1981; see Web Research in focus 17.7), but—Katila and Merilainen's work notwithstanding— there are very few ethnographic studies that are informed by feminist tenets of the kind outlined in Chapter 6. However, it is our view that feminist research could inform innovative research in this area by helping to expose the gendered nature of management and organizations (Runté & Mills, 2004). This would help to counterbalance the tendency for organizational ethnographers to interpret male-dominated settings from their point of view as a male researcher, using their own gender to reinforce the authenticity of their account (see Web Research in focus 17.4).

The title of this section is taken from a widely cited article by Judith Stacey (1988). It is a rebuttal of the view that there is and/or can be a distinctively feminist ethnography that combines the distinctive strengths of ethnography with a feminist position. Reinharz (1992) sees feminist ethnography as significant in terms of feminism, because:

- It documents women's lives and activities, which were previously largely seen as marginal and subsidiary to men's.
- It understands women from their perspective, so that the tendency that 'trivializes females' activities and thoughts, or interprets them from the standpoint of men in the society or of the male researcher' (1992, p. 52) is militated against.
- It understands women in context.

However, such commitments and practices go only part of the way. Of great significance to feminist researchers is the question of whether or not the research allows for a non-exploitative relationship between researcher and researched. One of the main elements of such a strategy is that the ethnographer does not treat the relationship as a one-way process of extracting information from others, but actually provides something in return. However, Stacey (1988) argues, on the basis of her fieldwork experience, that the various situations she encountered as a feminist ethnographer placed her:

> in situations of inauthenticity, dissimilitude, and potential, perhaps inevitable, betrayal situations that I now believe are inherent in fieldwork method. For no matter how welcome, even enjoyable the fieldworker's presence may appear to 'natives', fieldwork represents an intrusion and intervention into a system of relationships, a system of relationships that the researcher is far freer to leave. (1988, p. 23)

Stacey also argues that, when the research is written up, it is the feminist ethnographer's interpretations and judgments that come through and have authority.

However, Reinharz (1992, pp. 74–5) argues that, although ethnographic fieldwork relationships may sometimes *seem* manipulative, a clear undercurrent of reciprocity often lies beneath them. The researcher, in other words, may offer help or advice to her research participants, or she may be exhibiting reciprocity by giving a public airing to normally marginalized voices (although the ethnographer is always the mouthpiece for such voices and may be imposing a particular 'spin' on them). Moreover, it seems extreme to abandon feminist ethnography on the grounds that the ethnographer cannot fulfill all possible obligations simultaneously. Indeed, this would be a recipe for the abandonment of all research, feminist or otherwise. What is also crucial is *transparency*——transparency in the feminist ethnographer's dealings with the women she studies and transparency in the account of the research process. Nonetheless, it is clear that the question of whether there is or can be a feminist ethnography is a matter of ongoing debate.

Key points

- Ethnography is a term that refers to both a method and the written product of research based on that method.
- The ethnographer is typically a participant observer who also uses non-observational methods and sources such as interviewing and documents.
- The ethnographer may adopt an overt or a covert role, but the latter carries ethical difficulties.
- The negotiation of access to a social setting can be a lengthy process. It may depend on establishing an exchange relationship.

- Key informants frequently play an important role for the ethnographer, but care is needed to ensure that their impact on the direction of research is not excessive.
- There are several different ways of classifying the kinds of role that the ethnographer may assume. These are not necessarily mutually exclusive.
- Sampling considerations differ from those addressed in the context of quantitative research, in that issues of representativeness are emphasized less.
- Field notes are important for prompting the ethnographer's memory.
- Ethnostatistics is an interesting branch of ethnography that focuses on making sense of how the development, analysis, and dissemination of statistics as knowledge occurs.
- Autoethnography is an approach to ethnography that puts the researcher's own self at the centre of the study and explores the interface between self as object and subject in the research process.

Questions for review

- Is it possible to distinguish ethnography and participant observation?
- How does participant observation differ from structured observation?

Organizational ethnography

- To what extent do participant observation and ethnography rely solely on observation?
- What distinguishes organizational ethnography from other forms of ethnography?

Access

- 'Covert ethnography obviates the need to gain access to inaccessible settings and therefore has much to recommend it'. Discuss.
- Examine some articles in business and management journals in which ethnography and participant observation figure strongly. Was the researcher in an overt or a covert role? How was access achieved?
- Does the problem of access finish once access to a chosen setting has been achieved?
- What might be the role of key informants in ethnographic research? Is there anything to be concerned about when using them?

Roles for ethnographers

- Compare Gold's and Gans's schemes for classifying participant observer roles.
- What is meant by 'going native'?
- Should ethnographers be active or passive in the settings in which they conduct research?

Sampling

- What is snowball sampling?
- What is theoretical sampling?
- How crucial is the idea of theoretical saturation to theoretical sampling?

Field notes

- Why are field notes important for ethnographers?
- Why is it useful to distinguish between different types of field notes?

The end

- How do you decide when to complete the data collection phase in ethnographic research?

Autoethnography

- What are some of the main characteristics of autoethnography?
- What are the strengths and weaknesses of autoethnography as a social scientific method?

Can there be a feminist ethnography?

- What are the main ingredients of feminist ethnography?

18

Content Analysis

Chapter guide

Content analysis is a widely used method by both **positivist** and **postpositivist**, **quantitative** and **qualitative** researchers. However, for that very reason, definitions of **content analysis** are often contested and, like case study research (see Chapter 4), a strong association with quantification of data has led many researchers to view content analysis as a positivist technique. However, as we shall show in this chapter, there is a shared view of content analysis as a systematic analysis of **texts** (which may be printed or visual) designed to determine the presence, association, and meaning of images, words, phrases, concepts, and/or themes. Through the systematic focus on images and/or words, content analysis is used to reveal the structure of a text (either written or visual) and the relationship between its intended and unintended message(s). In the process it simultaneously generates data (e.g., information on the structure of the text) and provides the systematic framework for data analysis (e.g., a search for themes; the predominance of certain images, etc.). This chapter explores:

- The kinds of research question to which content analysis is suited.
- The difference between positivist and postpositivist content analysis.
- How to approach the sampling of documents to be analyzed.
- What kinds of features of documents or texts are counted.
- How to go about *coding*, which is probably the central and most distinctive stage of doing a content analysis.
- The advantages and disadvantages of content analysis.

Introduction

Imagine that you are interested in the amount and nature of the interest shown by the mass media, such as newspapers, in a business news item such as the collapse of Enron and WorldCom and the impact this has had on corporate accountability and ethical behaviour. You might ask such questions as:

- When did news items on this topic first begin to appear?
- Which newspapers were fastest in generating an interest in the topic?
- Which newspapers have shown the greatest interest in the topic?
- At what point did media interest begin to wane?
- Have journalists' stances on the topic changed, for example, in terms of their support for business accountants and consultants, such as Arthur Andersen,

or in calling for increased government regulation of corporate behaviour?

If you want to know the answers to research questions such as these, you are likely to need to use content analysis to answer them. But which strategy should you adopt (see Chapter 3)?

From a positivist perspective you may focus on issues of objectivity, seeking to understand the facts of the case. Berelson (1952, p. 18), in a classic example, refers to content analysis as 'a research technique for the objective, systematic and quantitative description of the manifest content of communication'. Similarly, Holsti (1969, p. 14) describes content analysis as 'any technique for making inferences by objectively and systematically identifying specified characteristics of messages'.

A **postpositivist** perspective, on the other hand, may focus more on the meaning of the texts. Thus, according to Stan (2010, pp. 225–226):

> Content analysis is a tool of qualitative research used to determine the presence and meaning of concepts, terms, or words in one or more pieces of recorded communication. This systematic and replicable technique allows for compressing many words of text into fewer content categories based on explicit rules of coding in order to allow researchers to make inferences about the author (individuals, groups, organizations, or institutions), the audience, their culture and time.

All three definitions—by Barelson (1952), Holsti (1969), and Stan (2010)—share a common description of content analysis as systematic but they disagree on the extent to which the material can be treated as real (and thus objective). If we examine these two concepts we will see how **positivist** and **postpositivist** approaches differ and what the implications are for **content analysis**.

In the definitions of Barelson (1952) and Holsti (1969) objectivity is similar to the entity discussed in regard to an observation schedule (see Chapter 16), rules are clearly specified in advance for the assignment of the raw material (such as newspaper stories) to categories. Objectivity, in this sense, resides in the fact that there is transparency in the procedures for assigning the raw material to categories so that the analyst's personal biases intrude as little as possible in the process. The content analyst is simply applying the rules in question. From this perspective, being systematic means that the application of the rules is done in a consistent manner so that bias is again suppressed. As a result of these two factors, anyone could employ the rules and, hopefully, come up with the same results. The process of analysis is one that means that the results are not an extension of the analyst and his or her personal biases. The rules in question may, of course, reflect the researcher's interests and concerns and, therefore, these might be a product of subjective bias, but the key point is that, once formulated, the rules can be (or should be capable of being) applied without the intrusion of bias.

Berelson's definition also makes reference to 'quantitative description'. Here content analysis is firmly rooted in a (positivist) **quantitative research** strategy, in that the aim is to produce quantitative accounts of the raw material in terms of the categories specified by the rules. The feature of quantification adds to the general sense of the systematic and objective application of neutral rules, so that it becomes possible to say with some certainty, and in a systematic way, that, for example, national newspapers carried far more coverage of a particular issue than local newspapers.

Another element in Berelson's definition is striking, especially when juxtaposed against Holsti's. First, Berelson refers to '*manifest content*'. This means that content analysis is concerned with uncovering the apparent content of the item in question: what it is clearly about. Holsti makes no such reference, alluding only to 'specified characteristics'. The latter essentially opens the door to conducting an analysis in terms of what we might term '*latent content*'—that is, with meanings that lie beneath the superficial indicators of content. Uncovering such latent content means interpreting meanings that lie beneath the surface, such as whether the impression is given that the author construes the Enron scandal as an issue solely of concern to American shareholders and accountancy practices, or as having a broader set of implications for business practice and corporate accountability across the globe. A related distinction is sometimes made between an emphasis on the linguistic structure of the text (in particular, counting certain words) and an emphasis on themes within the text, which entails searching for certain ideas within the text (Beardsworth, 1980).

As we can see, the work of Holsti (1969) begins to move us in the direction of searches for the underlying meaning of texts, right through to analysis of interpretations of those meanings in context (i.e., how given terms were likely understood at the time in which they were written). For example, Dye and Mills's (2011) study of Pan American Airways, over time, found that everyday conversation about the relationships between men and women were understood differently in different time periods. In the 1950s the phrase 'female employee' needs to be understood against a background in which the notion of family life was a dominant theme that shaped the way that women's employment was judged—usually as temporary and a threat to the family. Whereas the term took on a different meaning in the 1980s, and was more understood relative to the types of job that women could be expected to perform.

While it might be expected that the more *objectivist* (positivist) strategies tend towards quantitative analysis and the *subjectivist* (postpositivist) strategies tend towards qualitative analysis the distinction is not particularly helpful when dealing with content analysis (see Key concept 18.1). It is the case that positivist researchers are more likely to use quantitative analysis in content analysis texts: 'counting the frequency with which specific words or themes appear in the texts and then [conducting] statistical analyses on those frequencies' (Esterberg, 2002, p. 171): see, for example, Stuart's (2006, p. 18) study of 'the supply management of 50 companies using reported supplier-buyer project specific initiatives' and Das and Das's (2009) study of gender stereotyping in contemporary Indian magazine fiction.

However, not all positivist studies based on content analysis involve statistical analyses (see, for example, Scherrer-Rathje & Boyle, 2008), nor do postpositivist studies avoid some form of quantification. As Esterberg (2002, p. 171) points out 'sometimes simple counting is useful. For example, if you want to know how often men and women appear in textbooks, you might simply count how many photos there are of each'. This approach was used by Mills and Helms Hatfield (1998), for example, to assess how business textbooks in North America portray women and people of colour. Their finding was that not only are women depicted far less than men but are shown as marginal to the workplace (e.g., imaged as shoppers and housewives). People of colour, until recently, were virtually non-existent in the pages of American and Canadian business textbooks (Mills & Helms Hatfield, 1998). Helms Mills (2003, p. 183) conducted a similar content analysis of the annual reports of Nova Scotia Power, examining the relative use of images of women and people of colour (see Figure 18.1).

Returning to Berelson's definition we find the term 'communication', which differs from Holsti's reference to 'messages'. Berelson's (1952) book was concerned with communication research, a field that has been especially concerned with newspapers, television, and other mass media. Holsti refers somewhat more generally to 'messages', which raises the prospect of a quite wide applicability of content analysis beyond the specific boundaries of the mass media and mass communications. Content analysis becomes applicable to many different forms of unstructured information, such as transcripts of semi- and unstructured interviews (e.g., Bryman, Stephens, & Campo, 1996), textbooks (Weatherbee & Dye, 2005), magazines (Das & Das, 2009), and case studies of organizations (Lightstone & Driscoll, 2008). Nor is it necessary for the medium being analyzed to be in a written form. Research has been conducted on:

- The visual images (as well as the text) of company annual reports to explore how these reflect organizational beliefs about customers (Dougherty & Kunda, 1990; see Research in focus 21.5), or reveal the portrayal of women and people of color in the United States (Tinker & Neimark, 1987) and in Europe (Benschop & Meihuizen, 2002).
- Motivational videos featuring management guru Frederick Herzberg giving a live lecture to managers (Jackson & Carter, 1998).
- The pictures drawn by managers to express their views about organizational change (Broussine & Vince, 1996).
- The interview transcripts produced as a part of a research project (Scherrer-Rathje & Boyle, 2008).

However, there is little doubt that the main use of content analysis has been to examine mass media items, as well as texts and documents that are either produced by the organization, such as annual reports, or written about it, such as articles in the business press. For example, O'Connell and Mills (2003) examined the way that the media made sense of the Westray Mine disaster. Bettman and Weitz (1983) examined letters to stockholders from the annual reports of 181 companies in four industries. A good year (1972) and a bad year (1974) were compared, based on GNP and stock market performance. In this regard, content analysis is one of a number of approaches to the examina-

Key concept 18.1: What is content analysis?

Content analysis is a systematic analysis of texts (which may be printed or visual) to determine the presence, association, and meaning of images, words, phrases, concepts, and/or themes.

tion of texts that have been developed over the years (see Key concept 18.1). In 1997 Insch, Moore, and Murphy suggested that content analysis was not very popular in business and management because researchers were unsure how to use it. However, a recent study by Hartt et al. (2009) found that content analysis was a method in use by researchers across 7 of the 20 divisions of the Administrative Sciences Association of Canada (ASAC). Nonetheless, it is worthwhile revisiting Insch et al.'s (1997) call for the development and outlining of a step-by-step process of content analysis that will help researchers to better understand content analysis. It is the intention of this chapter

to provide a framework through which systematic content analysis can be conducted.

 # Three forms of content analysis

Brewerton and Millward (2001, pp. 151–153) provide a useful contrast between three forms of content analysis: quantitative, qualitative, and structural.

Qualitative content analysis

This approach is usually subjectivist, fairly unspecific, and less structured in the process of interpretation of selected material. Emphasis is on meaning more than quantification. Classification of material initially arises from the research question and the researcher's topic guide but the process is open to the addition of concept codes following closer examination of the overall data. Coded

---

18.1 | Student Experience

Making sense of content

Salvador Barragan used content analysis as a preliminary step to analyze both the images on the covers of two Mexican business magazines and the main topics advertized on those covers of all the issues of 2007. For the images, he found that the majority were pictures of male executives, with a handful of female executives in just three issues. For the topics, he categorized the theme of the topic by counting all the topics on each cover. The topics were either 'gender neutral' or focused on masculine characteristics in regards to the 'man' in charge of top companies. Just one issue contained topics about powerful women in business:

> The advantages of this content analysis was that after reviewing one year of two different business magazines you can of-

fer a picture of both images (pictures) and topics to have a sense of these magazines and the audience they try to reach. However, one disadvantage is that you don't get a deeper analysis that may reveal more subtle gendered issues. Then, in order to complement the methodology—using a Critical Sense-making framework, I had to analyze the discourse of some of the topics on the covers to see how they covey more masculine attributes to describe the top male executives (and in some cases the females), the cultural and contextual aspects of the Mexican 'masculine' culture, and how these artifacts (magazines) contain cues that managers or would be managers use to make sense of their 'masculine' managerial identity.

Figure 18.1

Images of women and people of colour in the Annual Reports of Nova Scotia Power, 1989–96*

Annual Report	Number of male images	Number of female images (% of all images*)		Number of white images	Number of images of people of colour (% of all images*)	
1989–90	62	13	(18%)	61	1	(1.5%)
1990–1	25	3	(11%)	28	0	(0%)
1992	31	9	(22.5%)	37	3	(7.5%)
1993	19	2	(9.5%)	21	0	(0%)
1994	29	9	(24%)	37	1	(2.5%)
1995	22	18	(45%)	34	6	(15%)
1996	14	6	(30%)	18	2	(10%)

Note: * Percentage adjusted to the nearest 0.5.
Source: Jean Helms Mills, *Making Sense of Organizational Change*, Routledge, 2003, p. 183.

segments can include such things as particular sentences, phrases, long exchanges between people and ideas, and useful quotations that can later me used to illustrate the outcome (or themes) of the content analysis.

Quantitative content analysis

This approach is more often aimed at producing numerical values (including frequencies, rankings, or ratings) of the material that the analysis in focused on so that they can then be statistically analyzed.

In the initial stage of the process the material to be analyzed is selected based on the type of research question being asked. Then units of analysis (or coding unit) are selected, i.e., discrete bits of information that will be assigned to categories at a later stage. These bits of information can be words, themes, characters, items, time spent on a topic (e.g., how much media attention is given over to a particular subject), etc. At one end of the spectrum the counting of words is fairly simple, e.g., the number of times an article refers to a manager as either he or she. But this can be problematic with some words because the process of counting leaves little room for meaning and the context in which the word is used. For example, an article may use the word 'she' more than 'he' when discussing managers, which can suggest some type of equity in the use of the term manager. However, if the article is

about the problem of female as opposed to male managers there are very different implications. Themes are more complex to code because they involve a greater degree of (realist) interpretation in the identification process. Thus, to pursue a thematic content analysis the quantitative researcher 'needs to develop a coding frame [consisting] of a set of categories into which instances will be allocated' (p. 152). In such cases the categories need to be both exhaustive (i.e., all instances are assigned to a category) and exclusive (i.e., assigned to only a single category).

To ensure the objectivity of the analysis a reliability check may be established by way of the use of more than one coder. This is followed by an assessment of, what is called, inter-rater reliability (the extent to which coders ratings are similar) through statistical tests of agreement such as **Cohen's kappa**. Lajili and Zéghal's (2005, pp. 129, 131) study of risk management in TSE 300 Canadian companies, for example, undertook a content analysis of company annual reports. A 'graduate student familiar with content analysis procedures was instructed to code the risk information in the annual reports and identify the categories. . . . [Then] to increase the reliability of such content analysis, two more knowledgeable coders [Lajili and Zéghal] verified the graduate student's scoring worksheet'.

As might be expected, the final stage of quantitative content analysis involves some form of quantification of the material such as the frequency with which a particular coded element occurs in the studied text. Evaluation of the content along an ordinal dimension can increase the scope for statistical analysis; ranking can be used where a number of instances are being analyzed, and, in some cases, rating scales might be a possibility.

Structural content analysis

This type of content analysis is used to develop 'a representation of the relationships between elements' in the studied materials (p. 153). Thus, it is deemed appropriate for studying complex systems, and is useful for investigating decision-making, 'belief systems and social representations' (p. 153). In the process it draws on aspects of both (positivist) quantitative and qualitative content analysis and in some ways is similar to cognitive mapping (see Web Research in focus 6.3). A key issue involves defining the rules 'governing the relationship between response categories' and these 'relational rules will vary depending on the research aims' but are linked to issues of co-variation and potential causality.

Further discussion on this approach to content analysis is dealt with in Chapter 6 under cognitive mapping. For ease of discussion the rest of this chapter will focus on the difference between positivist and postpositivist content analysis.

What are the research questions?

As we indicated above, postpositivist research tends to involve a fluid and iterative approach to content analysis. Some initial categorization will occur, such as, for example, factors that constitute the 'gendered substructure' of an organization, i.e., elements of a workplace such as division of labour, symbols, interactions within and across jobs that might be though to influence the relative job opportunities of women (Acker, 1992). However, in the process of studying those initial categories others may arise, such as particular discourses of 'family', 'competition', and 'women's liberation', that may serve to better explain how a gendered substructure works in action (Dye & Mills, 2005, 2011). Here, more than anything,

the research question helps to shape the rules of analysis; including what is focused on such as particular elements (e.g., symbols), words (e.g., masculine, feminine), themes (e.g., warfare), relationships (e.g., between male and female employees), and the iterative process itself—what is likely to emerge (e.g., the role of masculinity). Thus, for example, when Mills and Helms Mills (2006) undertook a content analysis of Air Canada's early years (1937–41) to assess the impact of gender on hiring practices what emerged was not simply the relative number of male (93%) to female employees (less than 7%) but the influence of the different masculinities that helped shape whether and what type of women were hired.

As with most quantitative research, it is necessary to specify the research questions precisely, as these will guide both the selection of the media to be content analyzed and the **coding schedule**. If the research questions are not clearly articulated, there is a risk that inappropriate media will be analyzed or that the coding schedule will miss out key dimensions. Most content analysis is likely to entail several research questions. For example, the aim of Harris's (2001) study was to investigate the way the word 'courage' was used in the business community. In itself this is not very specific and hardly directs you to a clear specification of the media to be examined or the development of a coding schedule. However, to achieve this aim Harris sought to content analyze stories in certain newspapers that were about courage in order to compare a definition of courage derived from the literature with the way the word 'courage' is used in the community (especially in business, commerce, and government). This gave rise to other, more specific research questions, including:

- Is it possible to categorize the types of courage event described in the newspaper stories?
- What tools, if any, are said to have helped people show courage?
- Are obstacles identified in accounts of courage, and, if so, what are they?
- Are aspects of the accounts linked to specific professions or sectors of activity?
- Is courage used to describe dispositions, actions, or a virtue?

Such questions seem to revolve around the questions of: who (gets reported); what (gets reported); where (does the issue get reported); location (of coverage within the items analyzed); how much (gets reported); and why (does the issue get reported).

As with much content analysis, the researchers were just as interested in omissions in coverage as in what *does* get reported. For example, details about the profession, qualifications, and beliefs of the courageous person were frequently omitted. Such omissions are in themselves potentially interesting, as they may reveal what is and is not important to reporters and their editors.

Another kind of issue that is frequently encountered in content analysis is: 'How far does the amount of coverage of the issue change over time?' This kind of research question or problem is particularly asked by researchers who are keen to note trends in coverage to demonstrate ebbs and flows in interest. An example of this kind of research is a study by Barley, Meyer, and Gash (1988) which used content analysis to assess whether or not members of two distinct subcultures, business and management academics and practitioners, had influenced each other's interpretations. Content analysis focused on 192 articles published on the subject of organizational culture between 1975 and 1984. This time span was chosen to reflect changes in discussion of organizational culture at a time when understanding of this topic in the business and management field was still emerging. Content analysis focused on changes in the language used by the two groups to frame this particular issue. The research showed that, although in the mid-1970s academics and practitioners conceptualized organizational culture quite differently, by the mid-1980s academics had moved towards greater appreciation of the practitioners' point of view while practitioners' interpretations were little influenced by academics.

 # Selecting a sample

There are several phases in the selection of a sample for content analysis. Because it is a method that can be applied to many kinds of document, the case of applying it to the mass media will be explored here. However, the basic principles have a broader relevance to a wide range of applications of content analysis.

Sampling media

Many studies of the mass media entail the specification of a research problem in the form of 'the representation

---

18.2	**Student Experience**

Brad Long reports that he: 'had one foray into content analysis. The key for me was to have a clear theoretical framework to underpin the analysis; in my case, institutional theory and legitimacy. Once I had some understanding of the different forms that legitimacy can take, I analyzed codes of ethics to find evidence of which form they were aimed at establishing. This "thematic"'approach examined via words the meanings being conveyed by the codes of ethics to determine whether they were promoting moral or strategic legitimacy, and hence why they were written in the first place. Another important feature of the analysis was multi-coding, as both myself and my co-author independently reviewed the same codes of ethics to answer a specific series of questions. In the end, content analysis proved useful to empirically highlight how the content of several codes of ethics were largely written as codes of (mis) conduct, articulating a series of behaviours to avoid so as to not increase company risk, but not articulating a set of guidelines aimed at promoting consideration of the ethical implications (i.e., impact on stakeholders) of one's behaviour'.

of X in the mass media'. The X may be trade unions, human resources management, or women and leadership. But which mass media might one choose to focus upon? Will it be newspapers or television or radio or magazines, or whatever? And, if focusing on newspapers, will it be all newspapers or only regional newspapers? And, if both regional and national newspapers will it be all of them and will it include Sunday papers? And will it include free newspapers? And if newspapers, will all news items be candidates for analysis, for example, would feature articles and letters to the editor be included? And if newspapers, will newspapers from more than one country be included? When Das and Das (2009) reviewed Indian magazines to see how they portrayed women and men they faced several issues, not least of which was language issues. They settled on a sample of stories from magazines in Malayalam, Tamil, and English. Malayalam was chosen 'primarily because Kerala, where the language is spoken, is a state with a strong matrilineal heritage' (p. 68); Tamil was chosen because 'it is the most widely spoken south Indian language and across a number of other countries', and also because it has 'a literary tradition that can be traced back to at least the third century BC' (p. 69); and English was chosen because English-language 'magazines in India primarily target the more educated, upwardly mobile and Westernized middle-class men and women' (p. 69). Deciding to go for breadth of coverage, Das and Das (2009) undertook content analysis of over 800 stories from 32 magazines in three different languages, which, they believe, 'is the most extensive study of its kind both in India and outside the country, in terms of sample size, breadth of sample, and number of languages considered' (p. 65).

Typically, researchers will opt for one or possibly two of the mass media and may sample within that type or types. In the research described in Web Research in focus 18.1, Harris (2001) chose to focus on just four daily newspapers over one year, 1996, which is just as well since the author was able to locate a large number of appropriate items (news items containing one or more of the words 'courage', 'courageous', or 'courageously'), 610 in total. However, the study also incorporated a cross-cultural element by sampling one newspaper from Australia, the UK, the United States, and China. However, other media that typically have a smaller, more carefully selected audience can also form the focus for content analysis. For example, Barley, Meyer, and Gash (1988) conducted content analysis on items from business and management journals. Although these periodicals cannot be classified as mass media in the conventional sense, as the average peer-reviewed journal article is read by only a handful of people, these journals do represent a highly influential medium for the subcultural groups that Barley and his colleagues were concerned to investigate.

Sampling dates

Sometimes, the decision about dates is more or less dictated by the occurrence of a phenomenon. For example, the timing of representation of the Enron scandal will have been more or less dictated by the speed of the American government's investigation into the company's downfall and its accounting practices. One could hardly examine the issue fully prior to this investigation, though there may be an important consideration in deciding at what point the content analysis should cease, since discussions about Enron and what it means for other businesses could continue for some time after the cessation of the investigation and may entail a reappraisal as a result of subsequent events, such as the demise of Andersen Consulting. Walker, Thiengtham, and Lin's (2005) study of the performance of airplane manufacturers following aviation disasters did, however, include the events of the September 11th attacks on New York and Washington. They collected data published by the U.S. National Transportation Safety Board (NTSB) on aviation disasters for the period 1935 to 2003 (the year they presumably began the study). They also collected data on daily stock price returns for publically traded American airlines from the Center for Research in Security Prices (CRSP). They then used event study methodology to measure the abnormal stock price performance of airlines and airplane manufacturers. There findings were that, while aviation disasters do have a negative impact on the stock performance of airlines some have a great impact and some a very limited impact. They speculate that this might be due to the unusually detrimental impact of the September 11th attacks on stock price performance and the location of the disaster (e.g., those outside of the United States are more limited in their liability compared to those that occur within the United States).

With a research question that entails an ongoing general phenomenon, such as the representation of courage in managerial decision making or the cultural values of companies, the matter of dates is more open. Rowe et al.'s (2003) study of the impact of *Fortune* magazine on performance expectations, for example, selected a sample of the magazine for the years 1986–1991. Their reasoning was that 1986 was the fifth year of *Fortune*'s publication of its annual Survey of Corporate Reputation, and thus respondents and investors alike were familiar with the survey.

The principles of **probability sampling** outlined in Chapter 9 can readily be adapted for sampling dates, for example, generating a **systematic sample** of dates by randomly selecting one day of the week and then selecting every *n*th day thereafter. Alternatively, Monday newspapers could provide the first set of newspapers for inclusion, followed by Tuesday the following week, Wednesday the week after, and so on.

One important factor is whether the focus will be on an issue that entails keeping track of representation as it happens, in which case the researcher may begin at any time and the key decision becomes when to stop, or whether or not it is necessary to go backwards in time to select media from one or more time periods in the past. For example,

18.3 | Student Experience

For his dissertation, Jim Grant used a qualitative, analytic software called ATLAS.ti in the coding process. The software enables the researcher to code directly on an electronic version of the documents.

According to Jim, there are significant benefits and costs realized by this method.

Benefits:

- When complete the researcher has a searchable electronic data base record of the content analysis. The database can be used as a teaching tool, a tool for later qualitative analysis, to create more complete definitions and descriptions of the factors, and as a method for ensuring greater validity and reliability of the resulting data.

While researchers may have a relatively extensive and comprehensive coding form to begin analysis, they may also discover factors that are consistent with their theory but not revealed in existing empirical study. ATLAS.ti provides spreadsheet output of the coding record for each case examined. The spreadsheet may be used in the quantitative analytic software with relatively limited modification.

Costs:

- Because of the great temptation to code extensively and to allow new codes to emerge in the process, the researcher may find the method adds considerable time compared to the traditional methods.
- The method requires the purchase of software that may be new to the researcher and, therefore, require additional preparation. In addition, the use of software increases the complexity and cost of training an assistant. However, the software may be used initially to explore the research materials before a coding sheet is created for the assistant. Adding this step provides the benefit of the additional consideration of the material available through the use of qualitative software as well as the relatively low cost of employing a research assistant.

if Kabanoff, Waldersee, and Cohen (1995) had wanted to examine whether or not there had been a marked change in the way that companies represent their cultural values through annual reports and other documents (see Web Research in focus 18.2), they would obviously have needed to examine the reports, magazines, and newsletters of years prior to 1986. They might have taken comparable samples from 10 and 20 years earlier, had the companies been in existence for this long, and perhaps even beyond. Similarly, because the topic of organizational culture had attracted 'only sporadic interest before the late 1970s', Barley, Meyer, and Gash (1988, p. 32) stipulated that content analysis should be carried out only on articles, written in English, that appeared in periodicals or collections of readings published after January 1975. The researchers' own informed judgement of interest in this topic thus determined their decision as to how far back to go in their sampling of the journals. Moreover, content analysis of texts was seen by the authors to be a more favourable method for studying the way that concepts of organizational culture have changed over time because journal articles are preserved at the point in time when they were written. This makes them less prone to retrospective construction than other, observational methods that could have been used to capture the author's point of view.

What is to be counted?

Obviously, decisions about what should be counted in the course of a content analysis are bound to be profoundly affected by the nature of the research questions under consideration. Content analysis offers the prospect of different kinds of 'units of analysis' being considered. The following kinds of units of analysis are frequently encountered and can be used as guides to the kinds of objects that might be the focus of attention. However, what you would actually want or need to count will be significantly dictated by your research question and your methodological strategy (see Chapter 3).

Significant actors

Particularly in the context of mass media news reporting, the main figures in any news item and their characteristics

are often important items to code. These considerations are likely to result in such persons as the following being recorded in the course of a content analysis:

- What kind of person has produced the item (e.g., general or specialist news reporter)? (see O'Connell & Mills, 2003).
- Who is or are the main focus of the item (e.g., senior executive of an organization, manager, politician, or employee representative)? (see Rowe et al., 2003).
- Who provides alternative voices (e.g., consumer representative, official from a professional association, or employee)? (see Mills & Helms Hatfield, 1998).
- What was the context for the item (e.g., publication of financial results, major organizational event, or disaster)? (see Walker et al., 2005).

In the case of the content analysis of managerial courage (see Web Research in focus 18.1), the significant actors included:

- The courage event or events described in the newspaper story.
- The type of newspaper item (e.g., long or short general article, biography or obituary, book review, etc.) in which the courage event was reported.
- The details of the actor associated with the courageous act or action in the item (e.g., personal details, status, and the kinds of obstacles he or she faced and the tools he or she used to help him or her to take courageous action).

The chief objective in recording such details is to map the main protagonists in news reporting in an area and to begin to reveal some of the mechanics involved in the production of information for public consumption.

Words

While it may seem a dull and time-consuming activity, counting the frequency with which certain words occur is sometimes undertaken in content analysis. Deciding what the unit of analysis will be, whether word, phrase, or sentence, is an important consideration in content analysis research. For example, Helms Mills (2003) examined the changing focus on certain words (e.g., environment, profitability) as the company she studied moved from a culture change program to Business Process Reengineering. In Kabanoff, Waldersee, and Cohen's (1995) study (see Web Research in focus 18.2), the focus was on the sentence and a total of 40,593 sentences were analyzed.

Such a large sample would be difficult to contemplate using manual analysis and so the authors used computer-aided content analysis (see Web Key concept 18.1). Gephart (1993; see Research in focus 21.6) also used data analysis software to assist his qualitative study of accounts of a pipeline disaster, taking the phrase, rather than the word, to be the unit of analysis. In Bettman and Weitz's (1983) study of corporate annual reports, the unit of analysis was defined as a phrase or sentence in which there is some sort of causal reasoning about a performance outcome. The use of some words rather than others can often be of some significance because they have the potential to reveal the interpretative frameworks used by different subcultural groupings. For example, Barley, Meyer, and Gash (1988) proposed that practitioner-oriented papers on organizational culture would use words associated with rational organizing strategies. In order to test their proposition they calculated the percentage of a paper's paragraphs that contained words associated with bureaucracy, such as 'hierarchy', and words associated with structural differentiation, such as 'departments' or 'divisions'. Similarly, they suggested practitioner-oriented papers would make more references to external forces and environmental uncertainty that posed a threat to corporate performance. Words associated with this discourse included 'changing technology', 'foreign competition', 'fluctuating interests', and 'Japanese management'.

Subjects and themes

Frequently in a content analysis the researcher will want to code text in terms of certain subjects and themes. Essentially, what is being sought is a categorization of the

> **Key concept 18.1: What is computer-assisted content analysis?**
>
> A computer-assisted approach to content analysis automatically searches and codes terms or phrases within the text. Since a great deal of text, including newspaper and journal articles is now commonly available in digital electronic format, it is quite straightforward to use these documents as the basis for computer-assisted quantitative analysis.

Tips and Skills

Making content analysis more efficient

The main disadvantages associated with content analysis arise from the fact that it can be very labour intensive. Franzosi (1995), therefore, suggests several strategies for making it more efficient. The first involves identifying the different parts or the schemata that is associated with the genre of text that is being analyzed. For example, newspaper articles have a schema that comprises a summary and a story, containing 'background' (history and context) and 'episode' (main events and consequences). He suggests that the time and cost of content analysis can be reduced by excluding parts of the article that contain summary and background information. 'The longer an event lasts, the more likely that the "background" section of the articles dealing with an event become increasingly repetitive. The percentage of new material in each article is thus likely to decrease with the temporal position of the article in the sequence of articles that report an event' (1995, p. 159). Franzosi also suggests that a Taylorist approach to coding can help to make it more efficient. In this several coders read the same article with each of them coding a specific type of information, such as keywords, within a limited set of coding categories. However, he acknowledges that such a Taylorist approach would not be suitable for more complex thematic analyses. His final strategy for increasing the efficiency of content analysis entails a focus on sampling, not just of the time period of interest and the data sources (e.g., newspapers) to be used, but also of the articles that are going to be coded and the kinds of information coded within each article. Postpositivist researchers would also find the Taylorist approach too restricting in allowing the emergence of themes and understandings.

phenomenon or phenomena of interest. In the study by Barley, Meyer, and Gash (1988), the researchers further posited that academically oriented articles would exhibit a number of key themes. In addition, words associated with the causal framework employed in the papers that were written for a practitioner audience would be 'conspicuously absent'. While categorizations of specific words are often relatively straightforward, when the process of coding is thematic, a more interpretative approach needs to be taken. At this point, the analyst is searching not just for manifest content but latent content as well. It becomes necessary to probe beneath the surface in order to ask deeper questions about what is happening. One theme that cut across all the papers was the justification of organizational culture as an alternative paradigm for understanding organizational phenomena. Hence they found that, 'although the precise nature of the alternative varied from article to article, the perception that culture offered a radical departure from traditional organizational theory was nearly invariant' (1988, p. 44). Like the practitioner-oriented articles, academic articles also viewed organizational culture as a source of social integration, but, unlike the articles aimed at practitioners, they did not seek to portray culture as a force for social control. The researchers, therefore, sought to classify academically oriented articles according to the percentage of paragraphs that contained sentences which expressed gain or loss of control through culture. They speculated that articles written for an academic audience from a functionalist perspective would see culture as a means of gaining control, but that very few of the articles would see culture as leading to loss of control because this would not fit with the academics' anthropologically informed paradigm. To test the model, the three researchers, therefore, coded all 192 of the articles according to these indicators and arrived at a final score that comprised a percentage average of the three individual ratings. Their analysis showed that, although practitioners and academics initially saw culture quite differently, over time academics changed their understanding of organizational culture to incorporate the practitioner's point of view, even though practitioners' understanding of culture was little influenced by the academic viewpoint. In Dye and Mills's (2011) study

of the gendered substructure of Pan American Airways they focused on emergent themes that addressed issues of gender. Eventually it became clear to the researchers that emergent themes differed over time and appeared to form part of larger discourses such as family values (in the 1950s), women's liberation (in the 1970s) and, increasingly, competition (through the 1980s). These discourses, revealed through a number of related themes, could be seen as organizing principles in the assignment of work to female employees. In a related vein, drawing on fantasy theme analysis, Wood and de Paula (2008) examined 'texts, phrases, images, performances, and discourse in general' in selected Brazilian business magazines to understand (citing Jackson, 2001) 'how and why certain types of messages excite widespread public attention on sporadic and cyclical bases' (p. 192): a 'fantasy theme is manifest within a group by a word, sentence, or statement according to which past facts, future events, or things dislocated in space and time are interpreted' (p. 192).

Dispositions

A further level of interpretation is likely to be entailed when the researcher seeks to demonstrate a disposition in the texts being analyzed. For example, it may be that the researcher wants to establish whether the journalists, in the reporting of an issue in the news media, are favourably inclined or hostile towards an aspect of it (O'Connell & Mills, 2003), such as their stances on the practice of paying chief executives large financial bonuses. McQuarrie (2005) was directly interested in how business textbook authors discussed the 'Hawthorne Studies' and whether, in terms of the information imparted, they differed in their accounts. They did! Alternatively, the researcher may be interested in the views of a news article reader, rather than the writer. This was the case with Rowe et al.'s study (2003). In a study by Chen and Meindl (1991), the authors wanted to discern the image formed by news article readers about the owner of the airline People Express, entrepreneur Donald Burr. Each item was coded in terms of whether the reader had interpreted the editorial commentary on the leader's image in a way that was positive or negative. In many cases, it was necessary to infer whether the editorial commentary was implicitly positive or negative on the basis of image themes. For example, positive image themes were defined by the authors to include 'motivation', that is, Burr as an individual who is motivated, ambitious, and energetic, whereas the theme 'overdone' was interpreted by the authors as a negative image, characterized by descriptions of the leader as over-zealous, idealistic, and lacking in realism. Such an analysis entails establishing whether a judgemental stance can be discerned in the items being coded and, if so, what the nature of the judgement is.

 # Coding

As much of the foregoing discussion has implied, coding is a crucial stage in the process of doing a content analysis. There are two main elements to a content analysis coding scheme: designing a coding schedule and designing a coding manual. To illustrate its use, imagine a student who is interested in newspaper reports of employment tribunal hearings dealing with sex, race, or disability discrimination in the workplace and reported in a national daily newspaper over a three-month period. The student chooses to focus on the reporting of the employment tribunal hearing and the outcomes of the hearing. To simplify the issue, the following variables might be considered:

1. Nature of the claim (e.g., denial of promotion).
2. Gender of the complainant.
3. Ethnicity of the complainant.
4. Occupation of the complainant.
5. Age of the complainant.
6. Marital status of the complainant.
7. Nature of the employer's business.
8. Number of employees.
9. Outcome of tribunal (case sustained/not sustained; nature of award).
10. Position of the news item.
11. Number of words in the item.

Analysis would enable the student to record information about the kinds of sex, race, or disability discrimination issues that employment tribunals deal with and also to look for patterns in the characteristics of complainants and employers. The content analysis could, thereby, provide valuable insight, for example, into the way that gendered managerial structures, cultures, and organizational practices are reproduced. Content analysts would normally be interested in a much larger number of variables than this, but a simple illustration like this can be helpful to show the kinds of variables that might be considered. But it is important to note here that post-positivist and positivist researchers may differ in their use of terms such as variables or even coding. Where the postpositivist researcher uses the word coding it is more likely a shorthand way of talking about organizing aspects of the content, whereas a positivist researcher may imbue the term with more scientific meaning. Similarly, the postpositivist will likely not use the term 'variable' but rather speak in terms of socially constructed categories. While the positivist may ultimately be interested in testing the relationships between variables the postpositivist is more likely to be interested in how socially constructed categories come to influence behaviour and how that relationship is maintained and changed over time. For example, when Day et al. (2009) researched the moderating impact of job control and team efficacy on workplace risks they used 'gender' as one of 13 'study variables'. This is aimed at ensuring that the study controls for such things as the potential differences between men and women and the impact of those differences on workplace stress. The concern is not with women (or men) but rather the potential impact of gender as a variable. However, in the process, the underlying assumption is that men and women are essentially different, with women sharing similar characteristics that are different from the shared characteristics of men. Benschop and Meihuizen (2002), on the other hand, in their focus on representations of women in annual reports saw the idea of women (and of men) as socially constructed and thus as problematic concepts. In counting the relative number of times women appeared in the images of annual reports (compared to men) they were centrally focused on how gender differences are produced and reproduced, rather than accepting that women are a fixed category of human being.

Figure 18.2

Coding schedule

No.	Information about the actor	Code	No.	Features of courage displayed, sought, or observed	Code
i.	Gender of actor		viii.	Word used to describe courage	
ii.	Age of actor		ix.	Tools mentioned	
iii.	Qualifications		x.	Obstacles mentioned	
iv.	Profession		xi.	Involves choice between personal values and corporate values	
v.	Place		xii.	Involves defence of corporate/ organizational values or vision	
vi.	Rank		xiii.	Involves choice between personal advantage and corporate/community good	
vii.	Evidence of being a risk-taker		xiv.	Courage refers to the action or to disposition of actor or to a virtue	

Source: adapted from Harris (2001).

Coding schedule

The coding schedule is a form into which all the data relating to an item being coded will be entered. Figure 18.2 provides an example of a coding schedule based on the study of managerial courage and decision making described in Web Research in focus 18.1. The schedule is very much a simplification in order to facilitate the discussion of the principles of coding in content analysis and of the construction of a coding schedule in particular.

Each of the Roman numerals in Figure 18.2 relates to a specific dimension that is being coded, for example, 'i' relates to the dimension 'gender' of the actor, and depending on the methodological strategy being followed, this may serve as a variable (positivist) or a problematic social category (postpositivist). The blank **cells** on the coding form are the places where codes are written. A new coding schedule form would be used for each media item coded. The codes can then be transferred to a computer data file for analysis with a software package like SPSS (see Chapter 12).

Coding manual

A coding manual is usually developed where the research will rely on two or more researchers. This is more likely to be the case with positivist research but not exclusively and some postpositivist researchers may also want to achieve some consistency across raters where a team of people is involved in the project. Postpositivist researchers, in their search for meaning and understanding, will have more open questions that allow for greater flexibility. Questions on gender, for example, might ask the researcher to look for different forms of masculinity, femininity, and sexual orientation to find out what types of gender characteristics are privileged by an organization in its corporate material. These types of categories will be dependent on the types of research question being asked. Positivist researchers are more likely to develop fairly narrow categories to prepare the way for statistical analysis at a later stage. For clarity, our discussion on coding manuals, below, examples a largely positivist approach to content analysis.

On the face of it, the coding schedule in Figure 18.2 seems very bare and does not appear to provide much information about what is to be done or where. This is where the coding manual comes in. The coding manual, sometimes referred to as the content analysis dictionary, is a statement of instructions to coders that specifies the categories that will be used to classify the text based on a set of written rules that define how the text will be classified. It provides: a list of all the dimensions; the different categories subsumed under each dimension; the letters or numbers (i.e., codes) that correspond to each category; and guidance on what each dimension is concerned with; the definitions or rules to be used in assigning words to categories; and any factors that should be taken into account in deciding how to allocate any particular code to each dimension. The coding manual enables the message content to be coded in a consistent manner. The coding categories for each dimension need to be mutually exclusive and exhaustive so that there is no sense of overlap. There are a number of off-the-shelf content analysis dictionaries (e.g., Harvard VI Psychosocial Dictionaries) that are often used as a starting point from which the researcher himself or herself constructs a coding manual that relates to the particular research project.

For example, in his study of managerial courage and managerial decision making, Harris (2001) constructed a coding manual to define the features of courage that he was looking for in the newspaper stories. Figure 18.3 provides a simplified version of the coding manual that corresponds to the coding schedule developed by Harris in this study (see Figure 18.2). The coding manual includes all the dimensions that would be employed in the coding process, indications of guidance for coders, and the lists of categories that were created for each dimension. The coding manual includes instructions for classification of information about the actor in addition to categories for various features of the courage referred to in the newspaper article, how it was displayed, sought, or observed. The coding schedule and manual permit only one obstacle or

tool to be recorded in relation to a particular phrase or sentence in a newspaper article. However, if a phrase contains two or more obstacles or tools, the coder may break down the phrase and code a single word or a few words at a time.

The coding manual is crucial, because it provides coders with complete listings of all categories for each dimension they are coding and guidance about how to interpret the dimensions. At this stage, decisions must be made regarding the treatment of words that have more than one meaning. For example, Harris (2001) had to filter out items that were referring to 'Courage' as a brand of beer or its brewer from those that were dealing with courage as a quality or personal trait. It is on the basis of these lists and guidance that a coding schedule of the kind presented in Figure 18.2 will be completed. Even if you are a lone researcher, such as a student conducting a content analysis for a dissertation or thesis, it is important to spend a lot of time providing yourself with instructions about how to code. While you may not face the problem of inter-coder reliability, the issue of intra-coder reliability is still significant for you and you will probably need to use the coding manual to keep reminding yourself of your rules for coding the data.

Figure 18.4 illustrates how a fictitious example of a news item that presents an act of courage might be coded according to Harris's coding manual. The news story, published in the UK newspaper *The Guardian*, focuses on a 35-year-old female entrepreneur and small business-owner who is described as having acted courageously in taking the decision to turn down a contract with a major distributor and retailer because of concerns, which were subsequently proved correct, about the tactics being used to undermine the competition. The coding of the incident would then appear as in Figure 18.4 and, for a *positivist* researcher, the data would be entered into a computer program like SPSS as follows:

2 35 1 6 14 4 2 1 4 4 3 1 2 1

Each newspaper item that mentions the word 'courage' would create a row of data with an identical structure.

A postpositivist researcher would have a more open approach to coding and allow for interpretive elements, but may use some of the elements of the coding manual

Figure 18.3

Coding manual

Information about the actor	Features of courage displayed, sought, or observed
i. Gender of actor Male (1); Female (2); Unknown (3)	**viii. Word used to describe courage** Courage/ous/ly (1); Moral courage (2); Brave/ry (3); Dare/ing (4); Moral fibre (5); Strong will (6); Persevere/nce (7)
ii. Age of actor (at the time the event occurred) Record age in years (0 if unknown)	**ix. Tools mentioned (activities, circumstances, or events that facilitated the courage)** Bind (1) = made a public statement so as to make it harder to avoid the intended action Devil's advocate (2) = a person specifically designated to put contrary views Example (3) = e.g., 'seeing what A did gave me courage' Horror (4) = can't allow it to continue, sheer enormity (to the actor) of what is proposed/happening meant that major obstacles had to be overcome Others (5) = support expressed by others who may not necessarily be being courageous themselves Vision (6) = clear focus Faith (7) = inspiration or belief in a higher force
iii. Qualifications (only include if unambiguous) Degree/professional (1); Trade (2); Unknown (3)	**x. Obstacles mentioned (something faced or overcome, a difficulty, concern, temptation, or hurdle)** Easy path (1) = temptation to avoid the hard work Name calling (2) = personal abuse directed at the actor Physical threat (3) = violence or threat of violence to actor, family, etc. Commercial risk (4) = includes potential financial consequences Unpopular (5) = what is planned is unpleasant or trenchantly opposed
iv. Profession (only include if unambigious) Law (1); Medicine (2); Engineering (3); Accounting (4); Journalism (5); Other (6); Not clear or combined (7)	**xi. Involves choice between personal values and corporate values** Yes, personal values chosen (1); Yes, corporate and community values chosen (2); Unknown (3)
v. Place in which the event occurred Use 2-letter ISO country code (see Web Research in focus 18.7 for some examples); if many, code as World (−1)	**xii. Involves defence of corporate/organizational values or vision** Yes (1); No (2)
vi. Rank (only include if unambiguous) Minister and ranking opposition, US senator (1); Member of Parliament (2); Manager (3); Company owner (4); Board member (5); Self-employed (6); Corporate professional, e.g., engineer or lawyer (7); other (8)	**xiii. Involves choice between personal advantage and corporate/community good** Yes, personal advantage chosen (1); Yes, corporate and community good chosen (2); Unknown (3)
vii. Evidence of being a risk-taker (evidence in the item apart from courage event of the actor being a risk-taker) Yes (1); No (2)	**xiv. Courage refers to the action or to disposition of actor or to a virtue** The word 'courage' is used to describe an act or action, or some other outcome—*a courageous act, acted courageously, acted with courage* (1); Courage is attributed to the actor in relation to the act(s)—*to show courage, to be courageous* (2); Courage is mentioned without attribution to either act or person *e.g., reference to a disembodied virtue* (3)

Source: adapted from Harris (2001).

18.4 Student Experience

Coding Troubles

Donna Boone Parsons thought that content analysis would be fun:

I mean, the quantitative version of CA is a very precise kind of thing. I read the book (literally, there is one) that spells out exactly how it is to be done. It is a very defined methodology. However, I tried to stretch it a bit past what it is intended to do. Instead of doing simple counts and, therefore, using very descriptive statistics to analyze the data, I tried to measure most variables on a five-point scale in an effort to generate data that could be analyzed with parametric techniques.

It took five (yes, that's right—five) tries to get a useable code book. I thought my descriptions of the variables and the scales with which they were to be measured made a lot of sense. Obviously, however, they only made sense to me. The first time I did a pre-test with my coders, the inter-rater reliability was about .20. Through five iterations, I re-defined and refined all my variables and I just dropped some outright. I compressed the rating scale on most variables from five points to three. Even after all of that, my IRR was barely acceptable. All of that was a nightmare because I was using family business succession stories from popular magazines, and I only had a limited number of stories to begin with. Every time I had to do a pre-test again, I used up some possible stories, further limiting my number. My coders were both very educated professionals who were very familiar with the popular family business literature. In short, I was asking them to measure distinctions that just weren't measurable in that way. (I was trying to measure qualitative data quantitatively)—how positivist of me!

My coders and I estimated how much time the coding was going to take. After 5 pre-tests, we thought our estimate was going to be pretty accurate. As it turned out, it took about 4 times longer than we estimated.

And . . . here's the best part. After all of that, I put all of my lovely numbers in SPSS and, voila! . . . NOTHING. It showed nothing. Even after [my supervisor] manipulated [the data], there was nothing. So, I wrote a wonderful paper that took 20 pages to say, 'I got nothin'. Strangely, it was rejected by the conference to which it was submitted.

So, it was a great experience, and I learned a lot about CA [content analysis], but I think I will stick to qualitative text analysis.

(described in Figure 18.4) to identify how some categories are used and discussed by a textbook, newspaper or other document.

Potential pitfalls in devising coding schemes

There are several potential dangers in devising a content analysis coding scheme and they are very similar to the kinds of consideration that are involved in the design of structured interview and structured observation schedules:

- Discrete dimensions. Make sure that your dimensions are entirely separate; in other words, there should be no conceptual or empirical overlap between them. For

Figure 18.4

Completed coding schedule

No.	Information about the actor	Code	No.	Features of courage displayed, sought, or observed	Code
i.	Gender of actor	2	viii.	Word used to describe courage	1
ii.	Age of actor	35	ix.	Tools mentioned	4
iii.	Qualifications	1	x.	Obstacles mentioned	4
iv.	Profession	6	xi.	Involves choice between personal values and corporate values	3
v.	Place	14	xii.	Involves defence of corporate/ organizational values or vision	1
vi.	Rank	4	xiii.	Involves choice between personal advantage and corporate/community good	2
vii.	Evidence of being a risk-taker	2	xiv.	Courage refers to the action or to disposition of actor or to a virtue	1

Source: adapted from Harris (2001).

example, coding manual rules may be needed to distinguish between 'management' positions (such as the administrators of a firm) and 'management' actions (like the management of innovation).

- Mutually exclusive categories. Make sure that there is no overlap in the categories supplied for each dimension. If the categories are not mutually exclusive, coders will be unsure about how to code each item.
- Exhaustive. For each dimension, all possible categories should be available to coders.
- Clear instructions. Coders should be clear about how to interpret what each dimension is about and what factors to take into account when assigning codes to each category. Sometimes, these will have to be very elaborate. Coders should have little or no discretion in how to allocate codes to units of analysis.
- Be clear about the unit of analysis. For example, in Harris's (2001) study of courage and managerial decision making, more than one courage event per media

item can be recorded. The coding schedule needs to be clear in distinguishing between the media item (for example, a newspaper article) and the event being coded. In practice, a researcher is interested in both but needs to keep the distinction in mind.

In order to be able to enhance the quality of a coding scheme, it is highly advisable to pilot early versions of the scheme, as Todd, McKeen, and Gallupe (1995) did (see Web Research in focus 18.3). Piloting will help to identify difficulties in applying the coding scheme, such as uncertainty about which category to employ when considering a certain dimension or discovering that no code was available to cover a particular case. Piloting will also help to identify any evidence that one category of a dimension tends to subsume an extremely large percentage of items. If this occurs, it may be necessary to consider breaking that category down so that it allows greater discrimination between the items being analyzed.

The reliability of coding is a further potential area of concern. Coding must be done in a consistent manner. As with structured observation, coding must be consistent between coders (*inter-coder reliability*) and each coder must be consistent over time (**intra-coder reliability**). An important part of piloting the coding scheme will be testing for consistency between coders and, if time permits, intra-coder reliability. However, coding may not be consistent and the extent of inter-coder reliability may vary depending on the type of content that is being analyzed (see Web Research in focus 18.4 for an example).

Advantages of content analysis

Kabanoff, Waldersee, and Cohen (1995) suggest that content analysis offers an important method for the cultural study of organizations because it enables researchers to analyze organizational values, traces of which can be observed in organizational documents. Moreover, by measuring the frequency with which values occur, researchers are able to discern their importance. Content analysis has several further advantages, which are outlined below:

- Content analysis is a very transparent research method. The coding scheme and the sampling procedures can be clearly set out so that replications and follow-up studies are feasible.
- It can allow a certain amount of longitudinal analysis with relative ease. Several of the studies referred to above allow the researcher to track changes in frequency over time (Barley, Meyer, & Gash, 1988; Chen & Meindl, 1991; Kabanoff, Waldersee, & Cohen, 1995; Todd, McKeen, & Gallupe, 1995; Helms Mills, 2002, 2003; Mills, 2004, 2006). For example, Kabanoff et al.'s research entailed an analysis of organizational values over a four-year time period, Todd et al. (1995) examined information systems job advertisements over a 20-year period (see Web Research in focus 18.3), while Web Research in focus 18.5 gives an example of a content analysis that spanned an even longer time period. Similarly, in the example of employment tribunal hearings concerning sex, 'race', or disability discrimination, a tem-

poral analysis could be introduced through comparison of employment tribunal reporting in newspapers during two different time periods, such as the 1960s and the 2000s. Changes in emphasis could thus be examined.

- Content analysis is often referred to favourably as an unobtrusive method, a term devised by Webb et al. (1966) to refer to a method that does not entail participants in a study having to take the researcher into account. It is, therefore, a nonreactive method (see Key concept 16.3). However, this point has to be treated with a little caution. It is certainly the case that, when the focus of a content analysis is upon things such as newspaper articles or television programs, there is no reactive effect. Newspaper articles are obviously not written in the knowledge that a content analysis may one day be carried out on them. Hence Harris (2001) suggests that the content analysis of secondary data such as newspaper articles is particularly useful when researching sensitive issues such as the ethical behaviour of managers, because the method overcomes the problematic tendency of individuals to deny socially undesirable traits and only to admit to socially desirable ones (see Chapter 13 on social desirability as a source of error). On the other hand, if the content analysis is being conducted on documents, such as interview transcripts or ethnographies (e.g., Hodson, 1996; see Web Research in focus 18.6), while the process of content analysis does not itself introduce a reactive effect, the documents may have at least partly been influenced by such an effect.

- It is a highly flexible method. It can be applied to a wide variety of kinds of unstructured information. While content analysis in the social sciences is primarily associated with the analysis of mass media outputs, in business and management research it has a much broader applicability than this. Web Research in focus 18.6 presents an illustration of a rather unusual but nonetheless interesting application of content analysis.

- Content analysis can allow information to be generated about social groups that are difficult to gain access to. For example, most of our knowledge of the social backgrounds of elite groups, such as company directors, derives from content analyses of such publications as *Who's Who* and *Burke's Peerage and Gentry* (Bryman, 1974).

18.1 Research in Focus

A content analysis spanning 72 years

One of this book's authors, Albert J. Mills, undertook a study of the gendering of British Airways overtime to find out how organizational cultures develop, maintain, and change in terms of discriminatory practices over time. Based on the long-standing feminist distinction between 'sex' as physiological characteristics and 'gender' as the cultural outcome of factors regularly associated with 'sex' (Oakley, 1972), Mills (2006) was interested in the relationship between organizational culture and gender. Namely, how do organizational cultures contribute to the social construction of certain (often discriminatory) images of 'women' and 'men'? To that end, he searched for an organization that had been in business at least 50 years (as a reasonable time frame to explore an established culture), had some public association with gendered images of men and women (the airline industry was a good example), was widely known, was the subject of written histories, and had an accessible archive (to follow events over time). The result was a focus on British Airways from the time of its inception in 1919 to 1991 when Mills began undertaking the study.

At the British Airways Archive Collection in London Mills was faced with a wealth of material, including memoranda, letters, annual reports, corporate advertisements, and in-house newsletters—even films. Prior to accessing the archive he began reading a number of histories of British Airways and its predecessor airlines. This allowed him to get something of a feel for the airline, the people involved, critical events and, most importantly, how historians and others characterized the men and women who worked for the airline. This reading provided a useful road map for the archived material and encouraged Mills to attempt to read through the materials in some chronological order. It also provided some clues as to hiring practices over time and varying images of preferred masculinities and femininities.

From a postpositivist perspective Mills did not view the various materials as simple representations of reality but rather socially constructed notions of people and events of the time. Nor did Mills view the company's history as linear and progressive. But both issues presented early problems in the selection and collection of material. He solved the problem by a methodological device that he developed for the project and subsequent projects involving events over time—the juncture, which refers 'to a concurrence of events in time in which a series of images, impressions, and experiences come together, giving the appearance of a coherent whole that influences how an organization is understood' (Mills, 2010, p. 509). Using this as a major guideline, Mills then went through material to first get a sense of the employment of women over time. This generated eight major hiring practices that Mills then used to search for when the practice began, when it ended, and what major people and events were associated with each time period. Mills's eight junctures consisted of the following periods:

1. The development of an all-male organization (1919–1924).
2. The introduction and growth of female employment (1924–1939).
3. The war years and the rapid expansion of female employment (1940–1954).
4. The consolidation and normalization of female employment (1946–1960).
5. The eroticization of female labour (1960–1974).
6. Equity struggles (1974–1981).
7. The development and consolidation of professionalized female labour (1982–1991).
8. The emergence of a new juncture focused on female management and leadership (1991–) (Mills, 2010, p. 519).

18.2 Research in Focus

A content analysis of newspaper articles about HRM

Mazza and Alvarez (2000) were interested in the role of the popular press in the production and legitimation of management ideas and practices. To explore this further they conducted a content analysis of articles on Human Resource Management (HRM) published in leading newspapers and magazines in Italy. Focusing on the time period from 1988 to 1996, data were collected from articles on HRM in two periodicals selected on the basis of their wide diffusion (circulation). Articles were selected by searching for keywords related to HRM in the CD-ROM databases of the two publications. Next, the selected articles were read to see if they dealt with HRM issues. The articles were then analyzed using a predominantly qualitative approach, rather than using a coding scheme.

In order to assess the level of interaction between academic literature and press coverage of management ideas, they also measured the frequency of articles on HRM in leading academic journals such as *Administrative Science Quarterly*, as well as in more practitioner-oriented publications, such as *Harvard Business Review*, using the ABI/INFORM database (see Chapter 2). They observe that the number of HRM-related articles in the selected popular press sources during the period 1988–94 grew, declining thereafter but peaking again in 1996. They speculate that the timing of this popularity may be related to a generalized concern about political corruption in Italy, noting that the articles about HRM were paralleled by discussion of business ethics, which is presented as a solution to the problem of corruption.

Although this study used a qualitative approach to content analysis, rather than one designed to ensure consistency and replicability through the application of explicit coding criteria, we can learn from the method of sampling and of recording changes over time used in Mazza and Alvarez's study, which could be a model for content analyses of the diffusion of other business and management ideas, such as total quality management, knowledge management, or business process reengineering.

In some ways this echoes the work of Mary Runté, who analyzed North American HR journals for what they had to say about work-family conflict. Runté collected information on the extent to which selected HR journals discussed work, family, and work-family conflict. She examined the use of these terms throughout the various texts to see how the authors characterized each of the terms. Through her analysis she identified a dominant trend that privileged the notion of 'work' over 'family' and which tended to characterize 'family' according to traditional notions of the nuclear, heterosexual family. Her research findings allowed her to conclude that debates around work–family conflict were premised on a competing discourse of work and family, where work was privileged over family and, despite rhetoric to the contrary, encouraged traditional families to fit in more with the demands of work (Runté, 2005; Runté & Mills, 2002, 2004).

Disadvantages of content analysis

Like all research techniques, content analysis suffers from certain limitations, which are described below:

- A content analysis can only be as good as the documents on which the practitioner works. John Scott (1990) recommends assessing documents in terms of such criteria as: authenticity (that the document is what it purports to be); credibility (whether there are grounds for thinking that the contents of the document have been or are distorted in some way); and representativeness (whether or not the documents examined are representative of all possible relevant documents, as if certain kinds of document are unavailable or no longer exist generalizability will be jeopardized). These kinds of consideration will be especially important to bear in mind when a content analysis is being conducted on documents like company reports or internal memoranda. These issues will be explored in further detail in Chapter 21.

- It is almost impossible to devise coding manuals that do not entail some interpretation on the part of coders. Coders must draw upon their everyday knowledge as participants in a common culture in order to be able to code the material with which they are confronted (Cicourel, 1964; Garfinkel, 1967). To the extent that this occurs, it is questionable whether or not it is justifiable to assume a correspondence of interpretation between the persons responsible for producing the documents being analyzed and the coders (Beardsworth, 1980).

- Particular problems are likely to arise when the aim is to impute latent rather than manifest content. In searching for traditional markers of organizational leadership, as in Chen and Meindl's study (1991), or inferring organizational values (see Web Research in focus 18.2), the potential for invalid inference being made is magnified.

- It is difficult to ascertain the answers to 'why?' questions through content analysis. For example, Barley, Meyer, and Gash (1988) found that over the course of nearly a decade academically oriented papers on the subject of organizational culture gradually adopted or accommodated practitioners' concerns. Why? Although the authors provide a number of speculative answers to these questions, content analysis alone cannot provide the answers. As they claim, 'the convergence may have resulted because academics were subtly influenced to adopt a more managerial agenda in order to secure valued resources and a larger audience for their work, but given the nature of the data, other explanations are equally plausible' (1988, p. 55). Hence, the authors claim that to establish the motives for the convergence would require interviewing the paper authors 'and studying networks of citations to determine who influenced whom' (1988, p. 55). Similarly, although Mazza and Alvarez (2000) were able to identify two peaks in the popularity of articles about HRM in the Italian popular press, they could only speculate as to the reasons for this (see Research in focus 18.2).

- Content analytic studies are sometimes accused of being atheoretical. This is more charged at positivist than postpositivist accounts, which, by their very nature, are rooted in well-developed and necessarily transparent theoretical perspective. In terms of positivist accounts, it is easy to see why an atheoretical approach might arise. The emphasis in content analysis on measurement can easily and unwittingly result in an accent being placed on what is measurable rather than on what is theoretically significant or important. However, content analysis is not necessarily atheoretical. For example, Barley et al. (1988) place their findings about academic and practitioner subcultures in the context of a political perspective of knowledge creation and diffusion, suggesting that the research interests of academics are ultimately defined by the interests of practitioners who influence the research process, through exercising constraints on funds, sites, and objectives. Similarly, Hodson's (1996) content analysis of workplace ethnographies was underpinned by theoretical ideas deriving from the work of influential writers such as Blauner (1964) and Edwards (1979) concerning developments in modes of workplace organization and their impacts on workers' experiences.

✓ *Checklist*

Doing content analysis

- ☐ Are you clear which methodological approach you are going to take? (see Chapter 3)
- ☐ Are you familiar with the demands of requirements of the approach you are taking? (e.g., if your are taking a poststructuralist approach is your content analysis ultimately consistent with poststructuralism?)
- ☐ Have you clearly defined your research questions?
- ☐ Is the population of documents to be content analyzed relevant to your research questions?
- ☐ Can you justify your sampling approach?

☐ Have you made sure that your dimensions do not overlap?
☐ Have you made sure that the categories used for each of your dimensions do not overlap?
☐ Do all the dimensions allow you to answer your research questions?
☐ Have you piloted your coding schedule?
☐ Are the coding instructions clear?
☐ If your research is based on the mass media, can you justify the time span of your coverage?
☐ Are you clear about the unit of analysis?

Key points

- Content analysis is a method that is appropriate to quantitative and qualitative, positivist and postpositivist researchers but you need to be clear which approach you are taking in advance.
- It is crucial to be clear about your research questions in order to be certain about your units of analysis and what exactly is to be analyzed.
- You also need to be clear about if or what is to be counted.
- The coding schedule and coding manual are crucial stages in the preparation for a positivist content analysis but can serve as useful sensemaking guides for postpositivist approaches.

Questions for review

- What are the main differences between positivist and postpositivist approaches to content analysis?
- To what kinds of documents and media can content analysis be applied?
- What is the difference between manifest and latent content? What are the implications of the distinction for content analysis?

Three forms of content analysis
- What are the main characteristics of the three forms of content analysis?

What are the research questions?
- Where and why are precise research questions especially crucial in content analysis?
- With what general kinds of research questions is content analysis concerned?

Selecting a sample
- What special sampling issues does content analysis pose?

What is to be counted?
- What kinds of things might be counted in the course of doing a content analysis?
- To what extent do you need to infer latent content when you go beyond counting words?

Coding
- Why is coding so crucial to positivist content analysis?
- What is the difference between a coding schedule and a coding manual?
- What potential pitfalls need to be guarded against when devising coding schedules and manuals?

Advantages of content analysis
- 'One of the most significant virtues of content analysis is its immense flexibility in that it can be applied to a wide variety of documents'. Discuss.

Disadvantages of content analysis
- To what extent does the need for coders to interpret meaning undermine content analysis?
- How far are content analysis studies atheoretical?

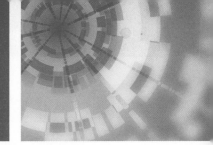

19

Secondary Analysis and Official Statistics

Chapter guide

This chapter explores the possibilities associated with the analysis of data that have been collected by others. There are two main types discussed in this chapter:

- **The secondary analysis** of data collected, either for commercial or research purposes, by other people.
- The secondary analysis of **official statistics**—that is, statistics collected by government departments in the course of their work or specifically for statistical purposes.

This chapter explores:

- The advantages and disadvantages of carrying out secondary analysis of data collected by other researchers, particularly given that many such data sets are based on large, high-quality investigations that are invariably beyond the means of students.
- How to obtain such data sets.
- The potential of official statistics in terms of their **reliability** and **validity**.
- The growing recognition of the potential of official statistics after a period of neglect as a result of criticisms levelled at them.
- The notion that official statistics are a form of **unobtrusive method**—that is, a method that is not prone to a reaction on the part of those being studied to the fact that they are research participants.

Introduction

Many of the techniques we have covered so far—survey research by questionnaire or structured interview, structured observation, and content analysis—can be extremely time consuming and expensive to conduct. Students in particular may have neither the time nor the financial resources to conduct very extensive research. Yet we know that large amounts of quantitative data about business and management are collected by social scientists, market intelligence firms, professional associations, and others. Some of this information, such as that produced by market research organizations, can be expensive. However, many organizations, most notably government departments and their various representatives, collect data that are presented in statistical form and that may be usable without charge by students and university researchers. Would it not be a good idea to analyze such data rather than collect new data? This would be advantageous for managers and employees, in that they would not be bothered by interviewers and by questionnaires arriving in the mail or their email inbox.

This is where **secondary analysis** comes in. Secondary analysis offers this kind of opportunity. Key concept 19.1 contains a brief definition of secondary analysis and raises one or two basic points about what it involves. As the opening paragraph suggests, we will in this chapter be concerned with two kinds of issue:

- The secondary analysis of data that have been collected by other researchers.
- The secondary analysis of data that have been collected by other organizations in the course of their business.

In business and management, secondary analysis is of increasing interest to researchers. Traditionally, economists have been focused upon the analysis of secondary data and they have drawn conclusions about how it relates to the world of business. However, since the 1960s, more researchers, particularly those from an industrial relations background, have begun to take greater interest in the analysis of large-scale workplace survey data. Part of the reason for this relates to the availability of large panel style data sets such as the Workplace Employee Relations Survey (WERS) in the UK or the Workplace and Employee Survey (WES) administered by Statistics Canada, both of which considerably opened up the potential for secondary analysis of work-related issues, largely because of its breadth and scope. Moreover, their experience of designing survey research has informed the way that these data were collected and used, by bringing insights from a more **qualitative** case study-based tradition to bear on the design and development of large-scale surveys and ensuring that the right kinds of question continue to be asked (Marginson, 1998).

> **Key concept 19.1: What is secondary analysis?**
>
> Secondary analysis is the analysis of data by researchers who will probably not have been involved in the collection of those data, for purposes that, in all likelihood, were not envisaged by those responsible for the data collection. Secondary analysis may entail the analysis of either quantitative or qualitative data.

Other researchers' data

There are several reasons why secondary analysis should be considered a serious alternative to collecting new data. These advantages of secondary analysis have been covered by Dale, Arber, and Proctor (1988), from which we have borrowed most of the following observations. When considering the various advantages of secondary analysis, we have in mind the particular needs of the lone student conducting a small research project as an undergraduate or perhaps a more substantial piece of work as a postgraduate. However, this emphasis should definitely not be taken to imply that secondary analysis is only appropriate or relevant to students. Quite the contrary: secondary analysis should be considered by all business researchers. However, secondary data need not necessarily be collected by other researchers; instead it may be collected by a company or another type of organization for its own purposes (see Research in focus 19.1). It is

---

19.1 Research in Focus

Secondary analysis of data collected by a business

Sørensen's (2004) study of the racial composition of workplaces was based on secondary data that he obtained from a large multidivisional financial services organization. Access to the personnel records was provided on the condition that no identifying information about the firm would be revealed (see discussion of anonymity in Chapter 8). Analysis focused on groups of newly hired staff in retail branches of the company, where interaction between employees was considered to be more likely. 'These data selection rules resulted in a data set covering 1,673 employees from 263 district branches' (Sørensen, 2004, p. 643). Sørensen explains that 'a distinct advantage of this dataset is that it contains the demographic characteristics not only of the focal employees who are tracked from the time of hire, but also of all other employees at the branch, regardless of the date of hire. I can therefore continuously measure the demographic composition of the branches from the time a sampled employee is hired into the branch until the time of exit or censoring' (Sørensen, 2004, p. 643). The use of a quantitative case study design enabled a longitudinal element to be designed into the study (see Chapter 4), as the dataset contained information about the exact point at which employees joined and left the company over the time period under investigation, January 1, 1996–May 31, 1999. This enabled Sørensen to explore changes in turnover rates over time. The results of this analysis revealed that employees were more likely to leave the organization if the number of employees of the same racial grouping as themselves declined during the time that they worked there.

also possible for secondary analysis to be used in combination with the collection of primary data. This can enable a comparative element to be incorporated into the research design. However, we have one other reason for emphasizing the prospects of secondary analysis for students that is simply based on our personal experience, in that they tend to assume that any research they carry out has to entail the collection of primary data. Provided secondary analysis does not conflict with the guidelines students are given regarding projects they are asked to complete, we feel there is a strong case for students considering the use of secondary analysis because it allows them to spend more time searching the literature, designing their research questions, and analyzing and interpreting their data.

Advantages of secondary analysis

Secondary analysis offers numerous benefits to students carrying out a research project. These are outlined below.

- Cost and time. As noted at the outset, secondary analysis offers the prospect of having access to good-quality data, such as that available from Statistics Canada, for a tiny fraction of the resources involved in carrying out a data collection exercise yourself.
- High-quality data. Many of the data sets that are employed most frequently for secondary analysis are of extremely high quality. By this we mean several things. First, the sampling procedures have been rigorous, in most cases resulting in samples that are as close to being representative as reasonably possible. While the organizations responsible for these studies suffer the same problems of survey non-response as anybody else, well-established procedures are usually in place for following up non-respondents, thus keeping this problem to a minimum. Secondly, the samples are often national samples or at least cover a wide variety of regions. In addition, some data sets enable cross-national comparison (see Research in focus 19.2). The degree of geographical spread and the sample size of such data sets are invariably attained only in research that attracts quite substantial resources. It is certainly inconceivable that student projects could

even get close to the coverage that such data sets attain. Thirdly, many data sets have been generated by highly experienced researchers and, in the case of some of the large data sets, like the WERS in the UK or the WES in Canada, the data have been gathered by research organizations that have developed structures and control procedures to check on the quality of the emerging data.

- Opportunity for longitudinal analysis. Partly linked to the last point is the fact that secondary analysis can offer the opportunity for longitudinal research, which, as noted in Chapter 4, is rather rare in business and management research because of the time and cost involved. Sometimes, as with the WERS and the WES, a panel design has been employed and it is possible to chart trends and connections over time. Such data are sometimes analyzed cross-sectionally, but there are obviously opportunities for longitudinal analysis as well. Moreover, with data sets where similar data are collected over time, usually because certain interview questions are recycled each year, trends (such as changes in working time or shifting patterns of employment) can be identified over time. With such data sets, respondents differ from year to year, so that causal inferences over time cannot be readily established, but nonetheless it is still possible to gauge trends. For example, the 2006 study by Schweitzer and Duxbury using WES data (see Web Research in focus 19.2) allowed the authors to build a profile of Canadian teleworkers based upon data collected over a number of years.
- Subgroup or subset analysis. When large samples are the source of data there is the opportunity to study what can often be quite sizeable subgroups of individuals or subsets of questions. Very often, in order to study specialized categories of individuals, small, localized studies are the only feasible way forward because of costs. However, large data sets can frequently yield quite large nationally representative samples of specialized categories of individuals, such as workers in a particular industry or occupation, or with a particular set of personal characteristics. These can form the basis for representative sampling of individuals. Similarly, when a large-scale survey covers several

19.2 Research in Focus

Cross-national comparison of work orientations: An example of a secondary data set

The International Social Survey Programme (ISSP) has conducted two surveys focusing on the topic of work orientations, first in 1989 and again in 1997. Participating countries in the 1997 survey included: Bangladesh, Bulgaria, Canada, Cyprus, the Czech Republic, Denmark, France, Germany, Great Britain, Hungary, Israel, Italy, Japan, the Netherlands, New Zealand, Norway, the Philippines, Poland, Portugal, Russia, Slovenia, Spain, Sweden, Switzerland, and the United States. As in 1989, the survey, which uses oral interviews and self-completion questionnaires, focused on respondents' general attitudes towards work and leisure, work organization, and work content. Opinions were elicited on such issues as: respondents' preferences for more work or more leisure time, the value of work in general, and the relative importance to respondents of factors such as job security, high income, opportunities for advancement, job interest, independence, and value to others. Other questions focused on what factors should determine how to pay two people doing the same kind of work, the effects the introduction of new technologies (computers, robots, etc.) would have on the workplace, attitudes about self-employment, size of the workplace, public- versus private-sector employment, and full-time versus part-time work. Respondents were also asked how easy or difficult it would be to find an acceptable job, how they felt about their present job, and how they viewed their working conditions (for example, if they came home exhausted from work, the amount of stress and possible danger on the job, working hours, place of work, whether their status was temporary or permanent, how their present job made use of their skills, and how they acquired these skills). Additional questions sought information on relations in the workplace between management and employees, and among workers, how satisfied respondents were with their job, how they felt about their organization, how many days they had been absent (excluding vacation) from work in the last six months, how likely it was that they would try to find a new job within the next 12 months, and how much they worried about the possibility of losing their job. A special group of questions focused on respondents who were not currently employed. Demographic variables include: age, sex, education, marital status, personal and family income, employment status, household size and composition, occupation, religion and church attendance, social class, union membership, political party, voting history, size of community, region, and ethnicity.

topic areas, analysis may involve focusing on a smaller subset of questions that are covered by the survey. For example, Addison and Belfield (2000) were interested in the effects of European works councils on organizational performance and employee attitudes. They, therefore, analyzed the responses from just one question in the 1998 WERS, which related to the status of these new institutional arrangements.

• Opportunity for cross-cultural analysis. Cross-cultural research has considerable appeal at a time when social scientists are more attuned to the processes associated with globalization and to cultural differences. It is easy to forget that many findings should not be taken to apply to countries other than the one in which the research was conducted. However, cross-cultural research presents barriers to the social scientist. There are obvious barriers to do with the cost and practical difficulties of doing research in a different country, especially when language and cultural differences are likely to be significant. The secondary analysis of comparable data from two or more countries provides one possible model for conducting cross-cultural research.

The International Social Survey Programme (ISSP) is explicitly concerned with bringing together findings from existing social science surveys from different countries and contexts. An example of the kind of cross-cultural analysis the program has produced is given in Research in focus 19.2. Another example to illustrate how data from more than one country can be compared is a study by Coutrot (1998), in which he compared the industrial relations systems of France and Britain through statistical analysis of two broadly similar data sets: WERS 1990 and Relations Professionnelles et Négociations d'Entreprise (REPONSE) 1992 (a large-scale survey that covers similar issues to WERS and is based on interviews with managers and employee representatives in France). However, in order for a cross-cultural analysis to be conducted, some coordination is necessary so that the questions asked are comparable. Differences between countries in the definitions used and the criteria for inclusion can make this difficult, as the example relating to the use of official statistics, given by Davies (2001; see Research in focus 19.4), illustrates.

- More time for data analysis. Precisely because data collection is time consuming, the analysis of data is often squeezed. It is easy to think of the data collection as the difficult phase and to consider the analysis of data to be relatively straightforward. This may not be the case. Figuring out what to make of your data is not simple and requires considerable thought and often a willingness to consider learning about unfamiliar techniques of data analysis. While secondary analysis invariably entails a lot of data management, partly so that you can get to know the data and partly so that you can get it into a form that you need (see below), and this phase should not be underestimated, the fact that you are freed from having to collect fresh data means that

19.3 Research in Focus

Teleworking arrangements in Canada using WES secondary data

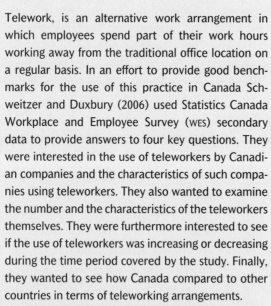

Telework, is an alternative work arrangement in which employees spend part of their work hours working away from the traditional office location on a regular basis. In an effort to provide good benchmarks for the use of this practice in Canada Schweitzer and Duxbury (2006) used Statistics Canada Workplace and Employee Survey (WES) secondary data to provide answers to four key questions. They were interested in the use of teleworkers by Canadian companies and the characteristics of such companies using teleworkers. They also wanted to examine the number and the characteristics of the teleworkers themselves. They were furthermore interested to see if the use of teleworkers was increasing or decreasing during the time period covered by the study. Finally, they wanted to see how Canada compared to other countries in terms of teleworking arrangements.

The data the researchers used was collected in 1999 and 2001 from over 20,000 employees and 6300 workplaces by Statistics Canada. These data allowed Schweitzer and Duxbury to build a profile of Canadian teleworkers. They found that they were well paid and well educated. These workers were also satisfied with their jobs, received on-the-job training and likely to have been promoted by their employer. Their findings did not support the popular notion that such teleworkers were engaged in 'sweatshop' type work. The authors also highlight the fact that telework in Canada does not seem to be growing in popularity, despite the fact that its use is considerably higher than in the United States or in Europe. They suggest that this might be because so much of the telework they identified occurs in companies that do not explicitly identify with having telework policies and programs. The authors conclude that their findings may well represent what they term 'guerrilla telework', essentially highlighting informal arrangements and utilization of telework, rather than formal institutionalized ways of adopting such flexible work practices.

19.4 Research in Focus

Difficulties in making cross-cultural comparisons using official statistics

Davies (2001) carried out an international comparison of labour disputes and strike action in 23 OECD countries between 1990 and 1999 using statistical data collected at a national level. However, the article is careful to point out the limitations of such an analysis for the following reasons:

- Voluntary notification. In most of the countries governments rely on employers notifying them of any disputes, which they are then able to confirm through media reports.
- Fail to measure full effects. None of the countries records the full effects of stoppages at work—for example, measured in terms of lost working time in companies that are not involved in the dispute but are unable to work because of a shortage of materials caused by the strike.
- Different thresholds for inclusion. The countries differ in the criteria they use to determine when a stoppage is entered into the statistics. In the UK, for example, disputes involving fewer than 10 employees or lasting less than one day are excluded from the recorded figures. In some countries, the thresholds for inclusion are particularly high. For example, in the United States records include only disputes involving more than 1000 workers. This can make comparison of strike rates between countries particularly problematic.
- Exclusion of certain industrial sectors. Some of the countries exclude the effects of disputes in certain sectors— for example, Portugal omits public-sector and general strikes.

- Changes in the way figures are recorded. For example, France has changed the way it records lost working days, thus making it difficult to make comparison over time.
- Indirectly involved workers. There are differences between the countries in their attempts to record those workers who are indirectly involved in a stoppage but who are unable to work because others at their workplace are on strike. Half of the countries, including France, the Netherlands, and New Zealand, attempt to include these workers in the statistics, but the other half, including Italy and Japan, do not.
- Dispute rates affected by small number of very large strikes. Some countries can appear to have very high labour dispute rates in one particular year because of one strike involving a large number of workers. In France, for example, there was a strike in 1995 involving the whole public sector. Some of these difficulties can be overcome by making comparisons over several years.

These differences lead some countries, such as the United States or Japan, to record a lower number of working days lost through labour disputes than say the UK or Germany, simply because of the different methods used for compiling statistics in the individual countries. This means that cross-cultural comparisons using nationally collected statistics need to be made with a degree of caution.

your approach to the analysis of data can be more considered than it might otherwise have been.

- Reanalysis may offer new interpretations. It is easy to take the view that, once a set of data has been analyzed, the data have in some sense been drained of further insight. In other words, what could be gained by going

over the same data that someone else has analyzed? In fact, data can be analyzed in so many different ways that it is very unusual for the range of possible analyses to be exhausted. A secondary analyst may decide to consider the impact of a certain variable on the relationships between variables of interest. Such a possibility may not have been envisaged by the initial researchers. Secondly, the arrival of new theoretical ideas may suggest analyses that could not have been conceived of by the original researchers. In other words, the arrival of such new theoretical directions may prompt a reconsideration of the relevance of the data. Thirdly, an alternative method of quantitative data analysis may be employed and offer the prospect of a rather different interpretation of the data. Fourthly (and related to the last point), new methods of quantitative data analysis, such as meta-analysis are continuously emerging. As awareness of such techniques spreads, and their potential relevance is recognized, researchers become interested in applying them to new data sets.

- The wider obligations of the business researcher. For all types of business research, research participants give up some of their time, usually for no reward. It is not unreasonable that the participants should expect that the data that they participate in generating should be used to their fullest extent. However, much business research is chronically under-analyzed. Primary researchers may feel they want to analyze only data relating to central research questions, or lose interest as a new set of research questions arise. Making data available for secondary analysis enhances the possibility that fuller use will be made of data.

Limitations of secondary analysis

The following list of benefits of secondary analysis sounds almost too good to be true. In fact, there are not very many limitations, but the following warrant some attention:

- Lack of familiarity with data. When you collect your own data, when the data set is generated, it is hardly surprising that you are very familiar with the structure and contours of your data. However, with data collected by others, a period of familiarization is necessary. You have to come to grips with the range of variables, the ways in which the variables have been coded, and various aspects of the organization of the data. The period of familiarization can be quite substantial with large complex data sets and should not be underestimated.

- Complexity of the data. Some of the best-known data sets that are employed for secondary analysis, such as the WES, are very large in the sense of having large numbers of both respondents and variables. Sometimes, the sheer volume of data can present problems with the management of the information at hand, and, again, a period of acclimatization may be required. Also, some of the most prominent data sets that have been employed for secondary analysis are known as hierarchical data sets, such as the WERS. The difficulty here is that the data are collected and presented at the level of both the organization and the individual, as well as other levels. The secondary analyst must decide which level of analysis is going to be employed. If the decision is to analyze individual-level data, the individual-level data must then be extracted from the data set. Different data will apply to each level. Thus, at the organizational level, the WERS provides data on such variables as number of employees and level of ownership, while, at the individual level, data on age, qualifications, and salary level can be found. For example, Hoque (2003) was interested in the impact of Investors in People (IIP) accreditation regarding workplace-training practice. He used data from the 1998 WERS managers' survey to extract organization-level data to build up a profile of workplaces that have IIP accreditation. However, in order to evaluate the impact of IIP accreditation on training practice, Hoque relied on individual-level data, in the form of data about training activity taken from the survey of employees. These included questions about the number of days spent on training that were paid for or organized by the employer and whether or not the employee had, in the previous 12 months, discussed their training needs with their supervisor. He used these data to draw conclusions at the level of the organization, and to make comparisons of the effectiveness of training practice in accredited versus non-accredited workplaces.

- No control over data quality. The point has been made on several occasions that secondary analysis offers the opportunity for students and others to examine data of far higher quality than they could collect themselves. However, this point applies mainly to data sets from a regulated source such as Statistics Canada. While the quality of data should never be taken for granted, in the case of such data sets it is reasonably assured, though that is not to say that the data will necessarily meet all of a prospective secondary analyst's needs, since they may not have been collected on an aspect of a topic that would have been of considerable interest. Moreover, with other data sets, somewhat more caution may be necessary in connection with assessment of data quality. This may be of particular concern when using data that are the result of commercially commissioned research, as is the case in market research or when using surveys that have been conducted in-house by a company that wants, for example, to measure the effectiveness of its HRM strategy.

- Absence of key variables. Because secondary analysis entails the analysis of data collected by others for their own purposes, it may be that one or more key variables may not be present. You may, for example, want to examine whether or not a relationship between two variables holds when one or more other variables are taken into account. Such an analysis is known as multivariate analysis, an area that will be touched on in Chapter 23. The inability to examine the significance or otherwise of a theoretically important variable can be frustrating and can arise when, for example, a theoretical approach that has emerged since the collection of the data suggests its importance. This is also a drawback in meta-analysis, sometimes making it difficult for researchers to generate unambiguous conclusions as a result of the analysis (see Research in focus 19.5). Obviously, when researchers collect primary data themselves, the prospect of this happening should be less pronounced.

 ## Official statistics

The use and analysis of official statistics for purposes of business research have been subject to controversy for many years. Agencies of the government, in the course of their business, are required to keep a running record of their areas of activity. When these records are aggregated, they form the official statistics in an area of activity. As an example, in Great Britain, the Employment Service collects data that form the basis for the level of unemployment (also known as the 'claimant count'). This is just one, as it happens, high profile, set of statistics that can be subsumed under the general category of 'official statistics'. Such statistics are frequently the cause of headlines in the mass media—for example, if there has been a sharp increase in the level of unemployment. But they also seem to offer considerable potential for business and management researchers. We could imagine such official statistics offering the researcher certain advantages over some other forms of quantitative data, such as data based on surveys.

- The data have already been collected. Therefore, as with other kinds of secondary analysis of data (see above), considerable time and expense may be saved. Also, the data may not be based on samples, so that a complete picture can be obtained.
- Since the people, who are the source of the data, are not being asked questions that are part of a research project, the problem of reactivity will be much less pronounced than when data are collected by interview or questionnaire.
- There is the prospect of analyzing the data both cross-sectionally and longitudinally. When analyzing the data cross-sectionally, we could examine employment rates (in addition to unemployment rates) in terms of such standard variables as social class, income, ethnicity, age, gender, and region. Such analyses allow us to search for the factors that are associated with employment. Also, we can analyze the data over time. Precisely because the data are compiled over many years, it is possible to chart trends over time and perhaps to relate these to wider social changes.
- There is the prospect as well of cross-cultural analysis, since the official statistics from different nation states can be compared for a specific area of activity.

However, readers who recall the discussion of *convergent validity* introduced in Chapter 1 will already be on their guard. The official statistics concerned with an area of social life like employment can be very mislead-

19.5 Research in Focus

A meta-analysis of the relationship between rewards and intrinsic motivation

Deci, Koestner, and Ryan (2001) conducted a meta-analysis of reward effects on intrinsic motivation in educational settings such as classrooms. They began by calculating the effects of rewards—whether verbal or tangible—on the intrinsic motivation of students in educational settings. The authors examined 128 experiments published between 1971 and 1996. Their concept of reward included verbal rewards or positive feedback as well as tangible rewards, such as money or prizes that are given to students to reinforce their motivation to learn. The researchers speculated that rewards could be used to affect student motivation in a way that was either informational or controlling. The meta-analysis tested the following hypotheses:

1. Controlling positive feedback would lead to less intrinsic motivation than informational positive feedback.
2. Tangible rewards will decrease intrinsic motivation.

The results were analyzed in two separate meta-analyses by separating studies into those that examined verbal versus those that examined tangible rewards. The tangible reward studies were further subdivided into four groups according to whether they were:

- Contingent on working on a task.
- *Not* contingent on working on a task.
- Contingent on finishing a task.
- Contingent on a specified level of task performance.

The research found that verbal rewards tend to have an enhancing effect on intrinsic motivation, although they are more likely to have a negative effect if the interpersonal context within which they are administered is controlling rather than informational. On the other hand, the meta-analysis showed that tangible rewards significantly undermined intrinsic motivation, particularly among children. This led them to conclude that rewards substantially undermine intrinsic interest.

This conclusion contradicted the findings from an earlier meta-analytic study on the same subject (Cameron & Pierce, 1994), which found that negative effects of reward occur only under certain conditions, and, when appropriately arranged, rewards could actually be used to enhance intrinsic motivation and performance. These competing meta-analyses have thus become the focus of fierce intellectual debate, critics comparing their analysis to 'putting a beautiful dessert (peaches and ice cream drizzled with raspberry sauce and a dollop of whipped cream) into an industrial blender and liquefying the entire concoction' (Cameron, 2001, p. 31). Much of the debate relates to the way that studies are categorized so their findings can be meaningfully compared. Criticisms are also levelled at the way studies are selected for inclusion in the analysis, for example: How long is the period of time for the meta-analysis and are only published studies considered, or does the analysis include unpublished studies, such as doctoral dissertations?

A further reason for the fierceness of the debate relates to the relationship between educational research and policy. One of the aims of this meta-analysis was to produce a definitive statement about the relationship between rewards and intrinsic motivation that could be used to inform current educational practice. Hence, Deci et al. relate their findings to a wider agenda by stating 'it is an injustice to the integrity of our teachers and students to simply advocate that educators focus on the use of rewards to control behaviour rather than grapple with the deeper issues of (a) why many students are not interested in learning within our educational system and (b) how intrinsic motivation and self regulation can be promoted among these students' (2001, p. 50). Similar issues about the role of meta-analysis in creating such a link between research and practice apply in the field of management and business.

ing, because they record only those individuals who are processed by the agencies that have the responsibility for compiling the statistics. In addition, the process whereby official statistics are generated involves an element of interpretation. In the case of labour disputes, for example, this means that a substantial number of disputes are likely to go unrecorded as a result either of not being reported or of not being recognized as a labour dispute according to the criteria used by the agency. Of course, the example of labour disputes cannot be regarded as alone in this regard. To push the point even further, the deficiencies of official statistics also extend to the recording of levels of employment and unemployment. For example, the 'claimant count', which is used to gain a picture each month of the level of unemployment in Great Britian, may misrepresent the 'real' level of unemployment: people who are unemployed but who do not claim benefits or whose claim is disallowed will not be counted in the statistics, while those who form part of the claimant count but who work in part of what is known as the 'underground' economy (and who therefore are not really unemployed) *will* be included in the unemployment statistics.

A great deal of national and cross-national official statistical information can be obtained via Internet sources. The Statistics Canada website is a portal to official statistics, reflecting the economy, population, and society at national and local level, summary stories, and detailed data releases, in many cases, free of charge. There are also tutorials that aid in understanding statistics and how data were collected. The website address for Statistics Canada is:

http://www.statcan.gc.ca/start-debut-eng.html

Reliability and validity

Issues of reliability and validity seem to loom large in these considerations. Reliability seems to be jeopardized because definitions and policies regarding the phenomena to be counted vary over time, as the example of the different definitions of labour disputes used by Organisation for Economic Co-operation and Development (OECD) nations given by Davies (2001) effectively illustrates (see Research in focus 19.4). The problem concerning the reliability of such statistics is that variations over time in levels of labour disputes may be due not to variations in the level of workplace conflict but to variations in the likelihood of expending resources to record these events. Also, there may be changes over time in the definitions of labour dispute or in the propensity of employers to report disputes to government. Such changes will clearly affect the degree to which fluctuations in the rate of occurrence of labour disputes reflect 'real' fluctuations in the rate of incidence. To the extent that such issues are present, the reliability of the data will be adversely affected and, as a result, validity will be similarly impaired.

Also, the problems with official statistics extend to the examination of the variables with which the rate of occurrence is associated. For example, it might be assumed that, if an examination of differences in labour disputes demonstrates that the rate varies by sector—for example, with industries such as manufacturing and transport having consistently high strike rates whereas sectors like agriculture have very low ones—this implies that the industrial sector is related to labour militancy leading to strike action. There are two problems with drawing such an inference. First, there is an analytic difficulty known as the **ecological fallacy** (see Key concept 19.2). Secondly, even if we could ignore the problem of the ecological fallacy (which we cannot), we would still be faced with an issue that is related to the matter of validity. Variations between industrial sectors may be a product of factors other than the difference in their propensity to take strike action. Instead, the variations may be due to such factors as: variations in the average rates of pay and the terms and conditions of employment in different industrial sectors; likelihood of employers in different industrial sectors to report a dispute; differences in the number of employees working in these sectors; variation in the average number of people employed by organizations in different sectors; differences in the level of union membership and union activity; and variations in the effectiveness of formal communication systems.

> **Key concepts 19.2: What is the ecological fallacy?**
>
> The ecological fallacy is the error of assuming that inferences about individuals or organizations can be made from findings relating to aggregate data.

Condemning and resurrecting official statistics

Criticism of the use of various kinds of official statistics in the social sciences has drawn attention to these problems. Instead, it was recommended that researchers should turn their attention to the investigation of the organizational processes that produce the various deficiencies identified by the various writers. The effect of this view was to relegate official statistics to the sidelines of business research so that it became an object of research interest rather than a potential source of data, although research based on official statistics continued in certain quarters. It would also be wrong to think that critique was the sole reason for the neglect of official statistics during this period. The fact that official statistics, because they are a sideline for many state agencies, are invariably not tailored to the needs of business and management researchers can be considered a further limitation. In other words, it may be that the definitions of apparently similar or identical terms (such as labour disputes or working at home) employed by those responsible for compiling official statistics may not be compatible with the definitions employed by business and management researchers. However, others have argued that the flaws in many of the official statistics are probably no worse than the errors that occur in much measurement deriving from methods like social surveys based on questionnaires and structured interviews (Bulmer, 1980). Indeed, some forms of official statistics are probably very accurate by almost any set of criteria, such as population census data.

A further criticism of the rejection of various forms of official statistics is that it seems to imply that quantitative data compiled by business researchers are somehow error free or at least superior. However, as we have seen in previous chapters, while business and management researchers do their best to reduce the amount of error in their measurement of key concepts (such as through the standardization of the asking of questions and the recording of answers in survey research), it is not the case that the various measures that are derived are free of error. All social measurement is prone to error; what is crucial is taking steps to keep that error to a minimum. Therefore, to reject official statistics because they contain errors is misleading if, in fact, all measurement in business research contains errors.

It is clear that the wholesale rejection of official statistics by many researchers has been tempered. While there is widespread recognition and acknowledgement that problems remain with certain forms of official statistics, each set of statistics has to be evaluated for the purposes of business and management research on its own merits.

Official statistics as a form of unobtrusive measure

One of the most compelling and frequently cited cases for the continued use of official statistics is that they can be considered a form of unobtrusive measure, although nowadays many writers prefer to use the term 'unobtrusive method' (Lee, 2000). This term is derived from the notion of 'unobtrusive measure' coined by Webb et al. (1966). In a highly influential book, Webb et al. argued that social researchers are excessively reliant on measures of social phenomena deriving from methods of data collection that are prone to reactivity. This means that, whenever people know that they are participating in a study (which is invariably the case with methods of data collection such as structured interviewing, self-completion questionnaire, and structured observation), a component of their replies or behaviour is likely to be influenced by their knowledge that they are being investigated. In other words, their answers to questions or the behaviour they exhibit may not be typical. In such cases, unobtrusive measures are especially useful.

What are unobtrusive measures?

An unobtrusive measure is 'any method of observation that directly removes the observer from the set of interactions or events being studied' (Denzin 1970). Webb et al. (1966) distinguished four main types.

- Physical traces. These are the 'signs left behind by a group' and include such things as graffiti and garbage.
- Archive materials. This category includes statistics collected by governmental and non-governmental organizations, diaries, the mass media, and historical records.
- Simple observation. This refers to 'situations in which the observer has no control over the behavior or sign in question, and plays an unobserved, passive, and

nonintrusive role in the research situation' (Webb et al., 1966, p. 112).

- Contrived observation. This is the same as simple observation, but the observer either actively varies the setting in some way (but without jeopardizing the unobtrusive quality of the observation) or employs hidden hardware to record observations, such as video cameras.

Official statistics would be subsumed under Category 2, as would content analysis of media of the kind described in Chapter 18. However, this would not be the case in a content analysis in which the material being content analyzed derives from studies in which the data were generated in an obtrusive fashion. Structured observation of the kind covered in Chapter 16 will typically not fall into Categories 3 and 4, because the observer is usually known to those being observed.

It is important to realize that Webb et al. (1966) were not intending that **unobtrusive methods** should supplant conventional methods. Instead, they argued that the problem they were identifying was the almost exclusive reliance upon methods that were likely to be affected by **reactivity**. Webb et al. argued for greater '**triangulation**' in social research, whereby conventional (reactive) and unobtrusive (non-reactive) methods would be employed together. For example, they wrote that they were providing an inventory of unobtrusive methods, 'because they demonstrate ways in which the investigator may shore up reactive infirmities of the interview and questionnaire' (1966, p. 174).

It is worth noting that unobtrusive methods or measures encapsulate at least two kinds of ways of thinking about the process of capturing data. First, many so-called unobtrusive measures are in fact *sources* of data, such as graffiti, diaries, media articles, and official statistics. Such sources require analysis in order to be rendered interesting to a business school audience. Secondly, it includes *methods* of data collection, such as simple and contrived observation. While the data generated by such methods of data collection also require analysis, the data have to be produced by the methods. The data are not simply out there awaiting analysis in the way in which diaries or newspaper articles are (although, of course, a great deal of detective work is often necessary to unearth such sources). This means that neither of the terms 'unobtrusive methods' or 'unobtrusive measures' captures the variety of forms terribly well. A further disadvantage of the term 'unobtrusive measure' is that it seems to imply a connection to **quantitative** research alone, whereas certain approaches employed by **qualitative** researchers may qualify as unobtrusive methods.

As noted, official statistics fit fairly squarely in the second of the four types of *unobtrusive measures* outlined above. This second grouping covers a very wide range of sources of data, which includes statistics generated by organizations that are not agencies of the state. This is a useful reminder that potentially interesting statistical data are frequently compiled by a wide range of organizations, such as market research agencies. There may be greater potential for searching out and mining statistical data produced by organizations that are relatively independent of the state.

Key points

- **Secondary analysis** of existing data offers the prospect of being able to explore research questions of interest to you without having to go through the process of collecting the data yourself.
- Very often, secondary analysis offers the opportunity of being able to employ high-quality data sets that are based on large reasonably **representative samples**.
- Secondary analysis presents few disadvantages.
- The analysis of **official statistics** may be thought of as a special form of secondary analysis but one that is more controversial because of the unease about the **reliability** and **validity** of certain types of official data, especially those relating to unemployment and labour disputes.
- Some forms of official statistics are much less prone to errors, but there remains the possible problem of divergences of definition between compilers of such data and business researchers.

- Official statistics represent a form of **unobtrusive method** and enjoy certain advantages (especially lack of **reactivity**) because of that.

Questions for review

- What is **secondary analysis**?

Other researchers' data

- Outline the main advantages and limitations of secondary analysis of other researchers' data.
- Does the possibility of conducting a secondary analysis apply only to quantitative data produced by other researchers?
- What is **meta-analysis** and why is it of particular interest to researchers in business and management?

Official statistics

- Why have many business researchers been skeptical about the use of official statistics for research purposes?
- How justified is their skepticism?
- What reliability and validity issues do official statistics pose?
- What are unobtrusive methods or measures? What is the chief advantage of such methods?

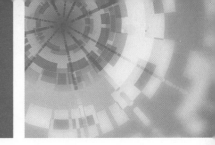

20

Language in Qualitative Research

Chapter guide

This chapter is concerned with approaches to the examination of language, including **conversation analysis** and **discourse analysis.** For the practitioners of these approaches, language is an object of interest in its own right and not simply a resource through which research participants communicate with researchers. The chapter explores:

- Fine-grained approaches to analysis, including conversation and discourse analysis, that focus in detail on the way that language is used, especially in conversation and dialogue.
- Analytical approaches that explore the use of specific literary devices, including narrative and rhetoric, to create meaning in social situations through the use of language.
- Approaches that seek to contextualize the use of language by analyzing the historical and social circumstances in which it is produced by treating texts (see Chapter 21 for a definition) as interrelated to each other and dependent on context.

Introduction

Language is bound to be of importance for organizational researchers. It is after all through language that we ask people questions in interviews and through which the questions are answered. Language is also central to the structuring of organizations, if only because people in work organizations rely so heavily on talk—in meetings, on the telephone, in the cafeteria—in order to accomplish their everyday business. It is through language that people in organizations exchange information, skills, services, and resources and make sense of their situation through interaction with each other. Furthermore, within managerial work a remarkably high emphasis is placed on verbal interaction, as findings from various research studies have suggested. For example, Mintzberg's (1973) classic study reports that verbal contacts, face to face and on the telephone, accounted for 75% of senior managers' time and 67% of their activities (see Chapter 21 for a more detailed explanation of Mintzberg's study). Other studies have shown that between 57% and 89% of managerial time is spent in verbal interaction (Boden, 1994). The role of the organizational researcher who focuses on language is to explore the nature of the relationship between language and action in these instances.

What is crucial about the approaches discussed in this chapter is that, unlike traditional views of the role of language in business research, they treat language as a topic rather than as a resource. This means that language is treated as significantly more than a medium through which the business of research is conducted (such as asking questions in interviews). It becomes a focus of attention in its own right. This implies that language is not just seen as reflective of what goes on in an organization; instead language and organization become one and the same. This means, for example, that, as soon as managers in a public-sector organization start to talk of their client groups as 'customers', a whole new way of defining the organization's purpose and activities is introduced.

Fine-grained approaches

The first part of this chapter examines two fine-grained approaches that treat language as their central focal points—conversation analysis (CA) and discourse analysis (DA). Fine-grained approaches focus on language in use, in conversation, or dialogue, and seek to examine talk in order to understand its organizing properties, in other words, the rules and structures that determine what people say in a given interaction. Both CA and DA are predominantly concerned with capturing and analyzing language as it is used in a particular moment rather than over a period of time. While CA and DA do not exhaust the range of possibilities for studying language as a topic, they do represent two of the most prominent fine-grained approaches. Each has evolved a technical vocabulary and set of techniques. The first part of this chapter will outline some of the basic elements of each of them and draw attention to some contrasting features.

Conversation analysis

The roots of CA lie in ethnomethodology, a sociological position developed in the United States under the general tutelage of Harold Garfinkel and Harvey Sacks, though it is the latter with whom CA is most associated. Ethnomethodology takes as its basic focus of attention 'practical, commonsense reasoning' in everyday life and as such is fundamentally concerned with the notion of social life as an accomplishment. Social order is not seen as a pre-existing force constraining individual action, but as something that is worked at and accomplished through interaction. Contrary to what its name implies, ethnomethodology is not a research methodology; it is the study of the methods employed in everyday life though which social order is accomplished.

Two ideas are particularly central to ethnomethodology and find clear expression in CA: **indexicality** and **reflexivity**. The former means that the meaning of an act, which in CA essentially means spoken words or utterances, including pauses and sounds, depends upon the context in which it is used. Reflexivity means that spoken words are constitutive of the social world in which they are located; in other words, the principle of reflexivity in ethnomethodology means that talk is not a 'mere' representation of the social world, so that it does much more than just stand for something else. In these ways, ethnomethodology fits fairly squarely with two aspects of qualitative research: the predilection for a contextual understanding of action (see Chapter 6) and an **ontological** position associated with **constructionism** (see Chapter 3).

In the years following its initial introduction into sociology, ethnomethodological research split into two camps. One entailed drawing on traditional social research methods, albeit in perhaps a somewhat altered form, and on ethnography in particular (e.g., Cicourel, 1968). The other, which is mainly associated with Sacks and his coworkers (e.g., Sacks, Schegloff, & Jefferson, 1974), sought to conduct fine-grained analyses of talk in naturally occurring situations. Moreover, it is not just talk in itself that is the object of interest but talk as it occurs in and through social interaction. CA concerns itself with the organization of such talk in the context of interaction (see Key concept 20.1). In order to conduct such investigations, a premium was placed on the recording of naturally occurring conversations and their transcription for the purpose of intensive analysis of the sequences of interaction revealed in the subsequent transcripts. As such, CA is a multifaceted approach: part theory, part method of data acquisition, part method of analysis. The predilection for the analysis of talk gleaned from naturally occurring situations suggests that CA chimes with another preoccupation among qualitative researchers—namely, a commitment to **naturalism** (see Key concept 4.3).

As the definition in Key concept 20.1 and the preceding discussion suggest, CA takes from ethnomethodology a concern with the production of social order through and in the course of social interaction, but takes conversation as the basic form through which that social order is achieved. The element of indexicality is also evident, in that practitioners of CA argue that the meaning of words is contextually grounded, while the commitment to reflexivity is revealed in the view that talk is constitutive of the social context in which it occurs.

Conversation analysts have developed a variety of procedures for the study of talk in interaction. Psathas (1995, p. 1) has described them as 'rigorous, systematic procedures' that can 'provide reproducible results'. Such a framework smacks of the commitment to the *codification* of procedures that generate valid, reliable, and replicable findings that are a feature of **quantitative** research. It is not surprising, therefore, that CA is sometimes described as having a **positivist** orientation. For example, the emphasis on context in CA

> ### Key concept 20.1: What is conversation analysis?
>
> **Conversation analysis** (CA) is the fine-grained analysis of talk as it occurs in interaction in naturally occurring situations. Analysis is concerned with uncovering the underlying structures of talk in interaction and as such with the achievement of order through interaction.

is somewhat at variance with the way in which contextual understanding is normally conceptualized in **postpositivist** qualitative research. For CA practitioners, context refers to the specific here-and-now context of immediately preceding talk, whereas for most postpositivist qualitative researchers it has a much wider set of resonances, which has to do with an appreciation of such things as the culture of the group within which action occurs. In other words, action is to be understood in terms of the values, beliefs, and typical modes of behaviour of that group. This is precisely the kind of attribution from which CA practitioners are keen to refrain. It is no wonder, therefore, that writers like Gubrium and Holstein (1997) treat it as a separate tradition within qualitative research while Silverman (1993) finds it difficult to fit CA into broad descriptions of the nature of qualitative research.

Even though organizations are important contexts for talk and interaction, CA has rarely focused directly on the management of business and work organizations. However, although they have not tended to focus on work organizations per se, conversation analysts have studied talk in a number of other formal institutional settings, such as television news interviews, courtroom trials, and clinical interaction, which share similarities with the settings of business and management. Boden (1994) uses CA to explore how talk influences organizational structures. She highlights the importance of formal and informal meetings, which she sees as involving sequences of talk that enable people to transmit information, make decisions, and sort out misunderstandings. She suggests CA can provide a means of understanding these interactional contexts, by looking at the way talk is organized in meetings. A further example of CA in management meetings is provided by Gibson (2005), who analyzes the effects of hierarchical and horizontal networks on managers' participation shifts (see Web Research in focus 20.1).

 Heritage (1984, 1987) and Grandy (2010) have proposed that CA is governed by four basic assumptions:

- Order is 'produced by those who engage in social action' (Grandy, 2010, p. 238). This means, according to Grandy, that 'ordered patterns of interaction are determined by the individuals who are engaged in social

action' (p. 238). This assumption directs the CA researcher to be open to unique patterns of orderliness.

- Talk is structured. Talk comprises invariant patterns—that is, it is structured. Participants are implicitly aware of the rules that underpin these patterns. As a result, conversation analysts eschew attempts to infer the motivations of speakers from what they say or to ascribe their talk to personal characteristics. Such information is unnecessary, since the conversation analyst is oriented to the underlying structures of action, as revealed in talk.

- Talk is forged contextually. Action is revealed in talk and as such talk must be analyzed in terms of its context. This means that we must seek to understand what someone says in terms of the talk that has preceded it and that, therefore, talk is viewed as exhibiting patterned sequences. Order, in this case, is both context sensitive (i.e., 'subject to its own order') and context free (i.e., the underlying rules and structures are not determined by individual characteristics)—see Grandy (2010, p. 238).

- Analysis is grounded in data. Conversation analysts shun prior theoretical schemes and instead argue that characteristics of talk and of the constitutive nature of social order in each empirical instance must be induced out of data. Heritage (1987, p. 258) has written: 'It is assumed that social actions work in detail and hence that the specific details of interaction cannot simply be ignored as insignificant without damaging the prospects for coherent and effective analyses'. As Grandy (2010, p. 238) puts it, 'It is the task of the researcher to discover, describe, and analyze the produced orderliness of talk-in-interaction. Once the rules and structures of social action are determined, formal terms can be employed to capture the ordered patterns of interaction'. These assumptions represent a manifesto for the emphasis on fine-grained details (including length of pauses, prolongation of sounds, and so on) that is the hallmark of CA.

As the fourth of the three assumptions associated with CA indicates, the approach requires the analyst to produce detailed transcripts of natural conversation that includes all the pauses, interruptions, and intonations used by speakers. Some of the basic notational symbols employed in CA are listed below:

- A figure in parentheses is used to indicate the length of a period of silence, usually measured in tenths of one second. Thus, (0.3) signals three-tenths of a second of silence.
- Punctuation marks, such as an exclamation mark, are used to capture characteristics of speech delivery rather than grammatical notation.
- Italics are indicative of an emphasis in the speaker's delivery of a word.
- A hyphen represents a cut-off of a prior word or syllable, which may arise because a speaker is interrupted by someone else.
- Brackets indicate the point at which simultaneous speech overlaps, for example when more than one speaker talks at the same time.
- A colon in the middle of a word indicates that the sound that occurs directly before the colon is prolonged (e.g., we:ll). More than one colon means further prolongation (e.g., : : : :).
- .hh h's preceded by a dot indicate an intake of breath. If no dot is present, it means breathing out.
- (.) Indicates a very slight pause.

The attention to detail in CA is very striking and represents a clear difference from the way in which talk is normally treated by social researchers in their transcription conventions when analyzing qualitative interviews. It has sometimes been suggested that CA fails to capture body movements, but in recent times the use of video recordings, as in the analysis of the public lectures of management gurus by Greatbatch and Clark (2003; see Web Research in focus 20.2), has supplemented its tool kit of methods (e.g., Heath, 1997). Attention to fine details is thus an essential ingredient of CA work. Pauses and emphases are not to be regarded as incidental or of little significance in terms of what the speaker is trying to achieve; instead, they are part of 'the specific details of interaction [that] cannot simply be ignored as insignificant', as Heritage (1987, p. 248) puts it.

The gradual accumulation of detailed analyses of talk in interaction has resulted in recognition of recurring features in the way that talk is organized. These features can be regarded as tools that can be applied to sequences of conversation. One of the most basic ideas in CA is the notion that one of the ways in which order is achieved in everyday conversation is through turn taking. This is a particularly important tool of CA, because it illustrates that talk depends on shared **codes**. If such codes did not exist, there would not be smooth transitions in conversation. In other words, there must be codes for indicating the ends of utterances.

One of the ways in which turn taking is revealed is through the examination of **adjacency pairs**. The idea of the adjacency pair draws attention to the well-attested tendency for some kinds of activity as revealed in talk to involve two linked phases: a question followed by an answer; an invitation followed by a response (accept/decline); or a greeting followed by a returned greeting. The first phase invariably implies that the other part of the adjacency pair will be forthcoming—for example, that an invitation will be responded to. The second phase is of interest to the conversation analyst not just because it becomes a springboard for a response in its own right, but because compliance with the putative normative structure of the pairing indicates an appreciation of how one is supposed to respond to the initial phase. In this way, 'intersubjective understandings' are continuously reinforced (Heritage, 1987, pp. 259–60). This is not to imply that the second phase will *always* follow the first; indeed, the response to a failure to comply with the expected response is itself the focus of attention by conversation analysts.

A further tool employed in CA is the account. The important feature to note about the treatment of accounts in CA is that they are analyzed in context—that is, the form that they assume is handled as being occasioned by the speech act that precedes it. Moreover, in CA, accounts are not unusual phenomena to be deployed when things go wrong but are intrinsic to talk in a variety of situations. It is striking that many accounts are, in essence, simply a description or expression of a state of affairs. However, this review of CA can only scratch the surface of an approach that has developed a highly sophisticated way of studying talk in interaction.

The insistence of conversation analysts that it is important to locate understanding in terms of sequences of

20.1   Research in Focus

A conversation analysis of the gendered nature of management talk

McGowan (2003) used CA to reveal ways in which 'managerial talk sustains and resists gendered discourses and codes of conduct'; to show how discursive microprocesses construct gendered understandings; and to surface 'the deeply embedded taken-for-granted nature of those understandings and discourse' (p. 132).

To that end, McGowan (2003) conducted in-depth interviews with 12 female and 4 male managers from a variety of industries in Southern Ontario. The interviews were all taped and the transcription notation of those tapes followed the work of Atkinson and Heritage (1984). The following examples indicate how CA notation is used in transcribing tapes.

In an interview with a male respondent (referred to as 'Tony' for the sake of anonymity) McGowan comments that he offered a detailed description of 'how "leaders" should conduct themselves in the workplace' (2003, p. 133):

> (627) The image I have of a leader is that the leader is supposed to be the
> (628) one the strong one, the strong person with his feet on the ground
> (629) and you know NO MATTER what the storms that rage about, you're
> (630) on stable ground and that's . . . That's the image that you try to create.

McGowan notes that Tony's image of the ideal leader is based on two metaphors: 'the image' and 'the storm'. In expanding on this, McGowan points out that Tony introduces the notion of 'the image' on line 627 and describes the aspects of the metaphor on lines 628 to 630. From McGowan's reading of this, Tony is talking about the constant need to create an image of the good manager. When he talks about 'the storm' (line 629) he is referring to a particular image of the leader as strong (line 628). In the process he talks in a gender way about the strong leader as 'his' (line 628) quality but also something that characterizes Tony himself (line 627).

The gendered notion of the leader as exhibiting a particular type of strength that is associated with men is reproduced by a female respondent—Laurie:

> (848) . . . I haven't ever consciously thought about that
>
> …
>
> (858) . . . it is part of my job to sort of shoulder all of that and in turn
> (859) not pass on any of my own angsts if that's what it is. Yeah, I
> (860) haven't . . .you're right I haven't thought about it but indeed that's
> (861) it . . . yeah . . . (*unintelligible*) Well, sure, I would, I would consider
> (862) it unprofessional.
>
> …
>
> (877)   …..……………………………………………
> that uh I should somehow
> (878) be able to compartmentalize my life and when I'm here, the job that
> (879) I do. I guess it's . . . I guess my-my image of what managers should
> (880) be I mean I don't want to see, I don't want to see, really . . . I
> (881) shouldn't – that doesn't seem right. I was going to say I don't want to
> (882) see my boss sort of falling apart over an issue.
>
> …
>
> (895) ………….But I don't, I don't think anybody has imposed that
> (896) idea on me, I think it's just something I, just a image I have and
> (897) maybe it's, maybe it starts out because when you start working,
> (898) you're young and and the managers tend to be older. Maybe,

(899) maybe you see them as as sli-, you know, they should be slightly

(900) less human (laughs) than uh, than you. I don't know so there is an

(901) element of me that expects that if you work at some level you

(902) should swallow a lot of things of that kind that are going on and

(903) keep going. (McGowan, 2003, p. 136)

Commenting on Laurie's talk, McGowan points out that she appears to share Tony's view of 'gendered images of strength and the separation of public and private mark her discourse . . . and she chooses not to talk about family caregiving in the workplace' (p. 136). Thus, in line 879 Laurie seems to draw on the traditional male notion of management as her own (referring to "my-my image"). Far from recognizing this traditional image as male-associated or imposed on the workplace (lines 895–896), Laurie views the image as one that arises naturally from her own early experiences of work (lines 897–903).

The notion of leadership as exhibitions of a particular type of (male-associated) strength is but one of several elements pursued by McGowan in her detailed conversation analysis. Through this process McGowan (2003, p. 141) is able to conclude that: 'managers sometimes understand why they behave [in a certain] way but more often are unable to articulate the factors that influence their behaviours. Comments such as "I don't know" (Sharon, line 457) and "I haven't every consciously thought about it" (Laurie, line 848) surface the taken-for-granted nature of the gendered discourses and behaviours that operate within organizations'.

talk, and, therefore, to avoid making extraneous inferences about the meanings of that talk, marks CA as representing a somewhat different approach from much qualitative research. As we have seen in previous chapters, qualitative researchers often claim (perhaps erroneously from the perspective of CA) that they seek to achieve understanding from the perspective of those being studied. Conversation analysts claim to do this only in so far as that understanding can be revealed in the specific contexts of talk. To import elements that are not specifically grounded in the here and now of what has just been said during a conversation risks the implanting of understanding that is not grounded in participants' own terms (Schegloff, 1997). Boden (1994), for example, points out that her concern is not automatically with 'typical' variables such as age, race, class, or gender, nor does she assume organizational structure or size as an important starting point for analysis. The status of the speaker is not assumed to dictate the talk; instead the point of interest for her as a conversation analyst is on how 'aspects of biography and social structure are made relevant in particular talk settings' (1994, p. 77).

Two points seem relevant here. First, this is a somewhat limiting stance, in that it means that the attribution of motives and meanings as a result of an in-depth understanding of a culture is illegitimate. While an interpretative understanding of social action carries risks on misunderstanding, an approach that prohibits such speculation is potentially restrictive. Secondly, CA is contextual in that it locates understanding in the sequences of talk. However, for the participants of an exchange, much of their talk is informed by their mutual knowledge of contexts. The analyst is restricted from taking those additional components of the context into account if they are not specifically part of the organization of talk. Again, this admonition seems to restrict the analyst more than is desirable in many circumstances and to consign CA to a range of research questions that are amenable solely to the location of meaning in talk alone. On the other hand, CA reduces the risk about making unwarranted speculations about what is happening in social interaction and has contributed much to our understanding of the accomplishment of social order, which is one of the classic concerns of social theory.

Discourse analysis

Unlike CA, DA is an approach to language that can be applied to forms of communication other than talk. As such,

Key concept 20.2: What is discourse analysis?

Discourse analysis is normally applied to both naturally occurring and contrived forms of talk and to texts, and 'emphasizes the way versions of the world, of society, events and inner psychological worlds are produced in discourse' (1997, p. 146).

it can be and has been applied to other types of texts, such as company mission statements, websites, email messages, or a video recording of the interactions of respondents (see Kelsey & Siegel, 1996), and in this respect it is more flexible than CA. Moreover, in DA there is much less of an emphasis on naturally occurring talk, so that talk in research interviews can be a legitimate target for analysis. However, DA should not be treated totally in opposition to CA, since it incorporates insights from it.

Unlike CA, which by and large reveals a uniformity based on an orthodoxy associated with certain classic statements concerning its core practices (e.g., Sacks, Schegloff, & Jefferson, 1974), there are several different approaches that are labelled as DA (Jacques, 2010; Potter, 1997). The version that is to be discussed in this section is one that is associated with such writers as Potter (1997), Potter and Wetherell (1987, 1994), Billig (1992), and Gilbert and Mulkay (1984). It is to be differentiated from **critical discourse analysis** (CDA), which is associated with writers like Fairclough (1992, 1995, 2003), Hardy (2001), and Phillips and Hardy (2002), which will be dealt with later in this chapter. The version of DA that we are concerned with here (see Key concept 20.2) has been described as exhibiting two distinctive features at the level of epistemology and ontology (Potter, 1997).

- It is anti-realist, in other words, it denies that there is an external reality awaiting a definitive portrayal by the researcher and it, therefore, disavows the notion that any researcher can arrive at a privileged account of the aspect of the social world being investigated. Some discourse analysts, however, adopt a stance that is closer to a realist position, but most seem to be anti-realist in orientation.
- It is constructionist, in other words, the emphasis is placed on the versions of reality propounded by mem-

bers of the social setting being investigated and on the fashioning of that reality through their renditions of it (see Key concept 3.7). More specifically, the constructionist emphasis entails a recognition that discourse involves a selection from many viable renditions and that in the process a particular depiction of reality is built up.

Thus, discourse is not simply a neutral device for imparting meaning. People seek to accomplish things when they talk or when they write; DA is concerned with the strategies they employ in trying to create different kinds of effect. McGowan (1999), for example, used discourse analysis on interviews with managers who were involved in balancing work and elder care concerns, 'to identify issues of empowerment and constraint in the managerial "role"; and the discrepancies between the advice offered to others about balancing work and elder care and the lived experience of the managers' (p. 12). In addition, DA shares with CA a preference for locating contextual understanding in terms of the situational specifics of talk. As Potter (1997, p. 158) puts it, discourse analysts prefer to avoid making reference in their analyses to what he refers to as 'ethnographic particulars' and argues that instead they prefer 'to see things as things that are worked up, attended to and made relevant in interaction rather than being external determinants'. However, DA practitioners are less wedded to this principle than conversation analysts, in that the former sometimes show a greater preparedness to make reference to 'ethnographic particulars'.

Discourse analysts resist the idea of a codification of their practices and, indeed, argue that such a codification is probably impossible. Instead, they prefer to see their style of research as an 'analytic mentality' and as such as 'a craft skill, more like bike riding or chicken sexing than following the recipe for a mild Chicken Rogan Josh' (Potter 1997, pp. 147–8). One useful point of departure for DA research that has been suggested by Gill (1996), following Widdicombe (1993), is to treat the way that something is said as being 'a solution to a problem' (1993, p. 97, quoted in Gill, 1996, p. 146). She also suggests adopting a posture of 'sceptical reading' (Gill, 2000). This means searching for a purpose lurking behind the ways that something is said or presented.

Three studies are useful to illustrate the use of DA. The first study by Orlikowski and Yates (1994; see Web Research in focus 20.3) shows how a group of distributed knowledge workers seek to develop a common computer language almost entirely through email communication; the second study by Ball and Wilson (2000; see Web Research in focus 20.4) provides an illustration of how the notion of interpretative repertoires can be used to explore power and control in organizations; finally, in the study of company websites by Coupland (2005; see Web Research in focus 20.5), discourse analysis is applied to understanding the way that constructions of corporate social responsibility are made plausible and legitimate in the context of company websites.

A further element to be sensitive to is that, as Gill (1996), following Billig (1991), suggests, what is said is always a way of *not* saying something else. In other words, either total silence on a topic, or formulating an argument in a conversation or article in one way rather than in another way, is a crucial component of seeing discourse as a solution to a problem. For example, Orlikowski and Yates (1994) found that some genres of communicative practice were used hardly at all by the knowledge workers in their project. As they explain, 'the absence of genres from a repertoire is also particularly revealing about what forms of interacting are not valued or salient to a community. We searched for something resembling the business letter genre . . . we found only four examples (0.3 percent) in the entire dataset' (Orlikowski & Yates, 1994, p. 561). This leads them to conclude that 'it appears that in this community—in which professional ties were strong and informality was the norm—and for this type of work—extended, complex, and documented negotiations among peers—letters were not seen as appropriate or effective types of written communication' (Orlikowski & Yates, 1994, p. 561).

Potter and Wetherell (1994) suggest that there are two tendencies within DA, although they acknowledge that the distinction is somewhat artificial. One is the identification of 'the general resources that are used to construct discourse and enable the performance of particular actions' (1994, pp. 48–9), which is concerned with identifying **interpretative repertoires**. The other is concerned to

identify 'the detailed procedures through which versions are constructed and made to look factual' (1994, p. 49). We will now explore these two strands of DA.

In order to illustrate the idea of an interpretative repertoire, a study of computer-based performance monitoring in two UK financial service organizations will be referred to (see Web Research in focus 20.4). Another example of the use of repertoires can be seen in the study by Coupland (2005) of corporate social responsibility on the Web. This research is outlined in Web Research in focus 20.5.

Ball and Wilson (2000) found significant differences between their two case-study organizations in the way that language was used to make sense of computer-based performance monitoring. From this they identify four interpretative repertoires that reflect the ways that individuals make sense of power relations within the organization:

- The empowerment repertoire. Informants' talk that contains themes of 'self management', 'proactivity', 'choice', and 'freedom'. This is illustrated by one manager who positions himself in these terms, stating:

  > Extract 1: ' . . . you empower people, people start throwing out ideas and actually manage themselves, and that's worked, we think, quite well in our area . . . .' (Ball & Wilson, 2000, p. 551).

- The 'life in work' repertoire. This comprises a set of patterns that construe work as 'objective', 'neutral', and 'egalitarian', so that a manager may be seen, for example, as treating 'everybody as equal'.
- The 'legitimate authority' repertoire. Typified by themes of 'discipline', 'rules', 'negative instruction', and 'inflexibility'. Ball and Wilson suggest that managers who claim a position based on legitimate authority repertoire tend to emphasize their access to, and control over, the computer-based performance monitoring statistics.
- The 'power through experience' repertoire. This is concerned with the knowledge and understanding that is needed to do the job; it can be mobilized as a form

of resistance by showing how some managers do not have the experience to be able to manage. For example:

> Extract 10: 'I was an inputter, and I've done grade two and now I'm a grade three (supervisor). I know, from scratch, so it's easier for me so I can relate to the grade ones and the grade twos, because I've been there and I've done it, so I'm in a good position I would say' (Ball & Wilson, 2000, p. 555).

Ball and Wilson locate these interpretative repertoires as mechanisms whereby disciplinary power is exercised over individuals. However, they also suggest that, though 'troubling' (Wetherell, 1998), individuals are able to exercise resistance to the *dominant discourse* through their conversation. Resistance is, thereby, generated through *reciprocal positioning*; this is when individuals position themselves so that, even though they use the terms associated with the dominant discourse, they do so in a way that enables them to position themselves in opposition to it. Another form of resistance is generated by *alternative positioning*, whereby an individual positions himself or herself in terms of a discourse that represents an alternative to the dominant one (see also Wicks, 1996).

The notion of the interpretative repertoire is interesting because it brings out the idea that belief and action take place within templates that guide and influence the writer or speaker. Orlikowski and Yates (1994) use the notion of genre in conjunction with the concept of repertoire to highlight the idea that organizational communication is structured in particular ways (see Web Research in focus 20.3). They explain, 'just as identifying a symphony orchestra's repertoire of symphonic works sheds light on the orchestra's established musical practices, identifying a community's repertoire of genres provides information about its established communicative practices and, hence, how it organizes some of its activities' (Orlikowski & Yates, 1994, p. 542).

However, the interpretative repertoires identified by Coupland (2005) and Ball and Wilson (2000) by no means exhaust the range of possibilities of analysis, as the advantages of the notion of interpretative repertoires stem primarily from its flexibility in accounting for a diverse range of social practices. Hence, Potter, and Wetherell (1987) suggest that repertoires are available to people with many different social group memberships. They also point out that there is no need to attempt to find consensus with regard to repertoires—because they are used to perform different sorts of accounting tasks, individuals are able to draw upon a variety of repertoires in different situations. Finally, they emphasize that 'the concept of repertoire is but one component in a systematic approach to the study of discourse' (Potter & Wetherell, 1987, p. 157), one that in a few years' time may be developed further or even discarded.

In discourse analytic research there is also an emphasis on the resources that are employed in conveying allegedly factual knowledge or what Potter and Wetherell (1994) might describe as *quantification rhetoric*, by which is meant the ways in which numerical and non-numerical statements are made to support or refute arguments. Instead, the texts largely consist of general statements, claims, and conclusions. This is interesting given the importance of quantification in everyday life and, in part, in the tendency for many social scientists to make use of this strategy themselves (John, 1992).

A number of further characteristics apply to DA. Some of the most important are presented in the list that follows:

- Reading the detail. Discourse analysts incorporate the CA preference for attention to the details of discourse.
- Looking for rhetorical detail. Attention to rhetorical detail entails a sensitivity to the ways in which arguments are constructed.
- Looking for accountability. Discourse analysts draw on CA practitioners' interest in and approach to accounts. From the point of view of both CA and DA, discourse can, and should, be regarded as accounts. For DA practitioners, the search for accountability entails attending to the details through which these accounts are constructed.
- Cross-referencing discourse studies. Potter and Wetherell suggest that reading other discourse studies is itself an important activity. First, it helps to sharpen the

analytic mentality at the heart of DA. Secondly, other studies often provide insights that are suggestive for one's own data.

As this discussion of DA has emphasized on several occasions, DA draws on insights from CA. Particularly when analyzing strings of talk, DA draws on conversation analytic insights into the ways in which interaction is realized in and through talk in interaction, but it is more flexible than CA in terms of the kinds of texts that are analyzed, including various kinds of documents and research interviews, in addition to naturally occurring conversation in their work. The CA injunction to focus on the talk itself and the ways in which intersubjective meaning is accomplished in sequences of talk are also incorporated into DA. DA, however, permits the intrusion of understandings of what is going on that are not specific to the immediacy of previous utterances to a greater extent than CA. For their part, discourse analysts object to the restriction that this injunction imposes, because it means that conversation analysts 'rarely raise their eyes from the next turn in the conversation, and, further, this is not an entire conversation or sizeable slice of social life but usually a tiny fragment' (Wetherell, 1998, p. 402). Thus, for discourse analysts, phenomena like interpretative repertoires are very much part of the context within which talk occurs, whereas in CA they are inadmissible evidence. But it is here that we see the dilemma for the discourse analyst, for, in seeking to admit a broader sense of context (such as attention to interpretative repertoires in operation) while wanting to stick close to the conversation analysts' distaste for ethnographic particulars, they are faced with the uncertainty of just how far to go in allowing the inclusion of conversationally extraneous factors.

Hence, fine-grained approaches such as CA and DA have been criticized for being too narrow in focus or not sufficiently sensitive to context. The anti-realist inclination of many DA practitioners has been a source of controversy, because the emphasis on representational practices through discourses sidelines any notion of a pre-existing material reality that can constrain individual agency. Reality becomes little more than that which is constituted in and through discourse. This lack of attention to a mate-

rial reality that lies behind and underpins discourse has proved too abstracted for some social researchers and theorists. This is an issue that will be returned to at the end of this chapter when we examine critical discourse analysis. The main point to note at this stage is that while many DA practitioners are anti-realist, an alternative realist or critical realist position in relation to discourse is also feasible.

 ## Narrative analysis

Narrative analysis is an approach to the elicitation and analysis of language that is sensitive to the sense of temporal sequence that people, as tellers of stories about their lives or events around them, detect in their lives and surrounding episodes and inject into their accounts. Proponents of narrative analysis argue that most approaches to the collection and analysis of data neglect the fact that people perceive their lives in terms of continuity and process, and that attempts to understand social life that are not attuned to this feature neglect the perspective of those being studied. Life history research (see Key concept 14.1) is an obvious location for the application of a narrative analysis, but its use can be much broader than this. Mishler (1986, p. 77), for example, has argued for greater interest in 'elicited personal narratives'. In his view, and that of many others, the answers that people provide, in particular in qualitative interviews, can be viewed as stories that are potential fodder for a narrative analysis. In other words, narrative analysis relates not just to the life span but also to accounts relating to episodes and to the interconnections between them. Some researchers apply narrative analysis to interview accounts (e.g., Riessman, 1993), others deliberately ask people to recount stories (e.g., Miller, 2000), and yet others use such things as company annual reports to assess the use of narratives (Kelly, 1994). A further type of qualitative analysis that is related to narrative analysis involves dramatism (see Web Research in focus 20.6).

Coffey and Atkinson (1996) argue that a narrative should be viewed in terms of the functions that the narrative serves for the teller. The aim of narrative interviews is to elicit interviewees' reconstructed accounts of connections between events and between events and contexts.

A narrative analysis will then entail a seeking out of the forms and functions of narrative. Miller (2000) proposes that narrative interviews in life story or biographical research are far more concerned with eliciting the interviewee's perspective as revealed in the telling of the story of his or her life or family than with the facts of that life. There is a concern with how that perspective changes in relation to different contexts. The interviewer is very much a part of the process, in that he or she is fully implicated in the construction of the story for the interviewee (Boje, 2010).

Narrative analysis has made inroads into management research in recent years (Boje, 2001, 2010; Boudens, 2005; Czarniawska-Joerges, 1998, 2004; Reissner, 2005). For the management researcher, narrative analysis can prove extremely helpful in providing a springboard for understanding what Weick (1995) has termed 'organizational **sensemaking**'. In one of the best known studies using a narrative approach, Boje (1991) analyzes the types and uses of stories in an office supply firm based on his participant observation in the organization and interviews with key actors. Stories became a common focus of attention when researchers became interested in organizational culture in the 1980s and this interest in organizational stories has continued, but they have tended to form just one of a number of aspects of culture in which researchers have been interested (for example, rituals and mission statements). Thus, Boje (1991) provides an example of a strategic planning session in which during a fairly brief interlude a number of stories are recounted that serve the function of conveying to participants that printing was a different enterprise at the time of the stories in question from the current situation (see also Boje 2001, pp. 118–21). For the CEO, the story helps participants to make sense of their current situation and conveys a sense of things being better now than they were in the past at the time that the less than desirable features relating to printing orders pertained. In the process, the CEO is able to gain a certain amount of political advantage by portraying the current context in a more favourable light. The example in Web Research in focus 20.7 illustrates how narrative analysts focus on the identification of particular narrative styles that are commonly found within organizations.

The significance of narrative for understanding the internal politics of organizations is further indicated by the study referred to in Web Research in focus 20.8. As Brown notes, in relation to this study, one of the advantages of narrative analysis in a context such as this is that it conveys a clear sense of an organization as an arena in which a variety of perspectives and viewpoints coexist, rather than a monolithic entity with a single voice. However, as Brown notes, his rendition of the three narratives of the implementation is itself a narrative. As such, it is either a compelling one or one that fails to convince us. This point presages the kind of issue that will receive more treatment in Chapter 25. In this sense, all research, when it is written up, entails a narrative analysis because the researcher/author always has a story to tell about his or her data.

Rhetorical analysis

Related to narrative analysis is an approach that focuses on the importance of rhetorical devices as a means of communication and persuasion within management and organization. This includes analysis of classic rhetorical devices, such as argumentation, as well as various literary devices, including tropes such as metaphor, synecdoche, metonymy, and irony (Czarniawska-Joerges, 2004; Morgan, 1996). Rhetoric and tropes are argued to be an unavoidable feature of organizational life (Oswick, Putnam, & Keenoy, 2004). For example, Suddaby and Greenwood (2005) analyzed the role of rhetoric in the legitimization of change in the merger to two radically different organizations: an accounting and a law firm. Rhetorical analysis has also been used to critique management fashions and management gurus by exploring how language is used to communicate ideas to global audiences (Jackson, 2001; see Web Research in focus 20.2). Rhetorical analysis is also applied in the study of leadership, as another organizational context in which language is targeted at large audiences. For example, the study by Hartog and Verburg (1997) in Web Research in focus 20.12 analyzed the message, style, and delivery of charismatic business leaders' speeches, identifying several classic rhetorical devices.

This study highlights the importance of rhetorical devices in provoking identification and commitment among

20.2 Research in Focus

Rhetorical strategies of legitimacy

Following the takeover of a law firm by a large accounting firm, Suddaby and Greenwood (2005) examined the rhetorical strategies involved in jurisdictional struggles between opponents and proponents of the new organizational form that emerged. The new organizational form involved the creation of multidisciplinary partnerships (MDPs) that was largely supported by the industry's large accounting firms and professional associations and largely opposed by a range of law firms and professional associations.

In the end, those in favour of the new MDPs mostly prevailed.

Suddaby and Greenwood (2005) set out to understand how new institutional logic takes hold through a period of dramatic change and contestation. To that end, they undertook a detailed analysis of the transcripts of two American commissions established in 1998 to look into the proposed merger. The transcripts consisted of 800 pages of testimony and reports from numerous individuals and organizations from across the relevant fields.

The first stage of the research involved content analysis focused on 'the manifest content', or 'those elements that are physically present' (p. 42). Here they used NUD*IST computer software, to read through transcripts from the data set and identify major players in the debate and their explicit arguments supporting or opposing MDPs (pp. 42–43). In the second stage they focused on the latent content to capture 'the "deep structure" or implicit categories of meaning' (p. 44). Through this process Suddaby and Greenwood (2005) identified six main rhetorical strategies aimed at effecting or resisting change:

- *Ontological*. Here opponents of MDPs drew on an underlying theme of what can or cannot naturally co-exist. Fully integrated MDPs, they argued, are

an illegitimate organizational form because of the incompatibility of audits with the practice of law. One prominent opponent of MDPs contended that there was an inherent conflict in the provision of audit and legal services.
- *Historical*. Here resistance to change was based on 'appeal to history and tradition'(p. 52). In this case the rhetoric appeared to accept change while arguing for 'evolutionary or path-dependent change' that is effect puts the breaks on the proposed MDPs as too radical and too soon.
- *Teleological*. This strategy involves arguments based of a 'divine purpose' or 'final cause', such as the need to implement MDPs to ensure the survival of the accounting industry (p. 54).
- *Cosmological*. From this perspective MDPs are supported as an outcome of the inevitability 'of forces beyond the agency of immediate actors and audiences. Such arguments describe MDPs as a natural process of evolution or consequence of globalization' (p. 55).
- *Value based*. 'A final type of theorization of change relies on an emphasis of values [that] appeals to normative authority drawn from wider belief systems. This approach often involves ethical evaluations of the relative "goodness" or "evil" of a proposed change [and] openly appeals, directly or indirectly, to emotion' (p. 56).

Suddaby and Greenwood (2005, p. 58) concluded that, while 'rhetoric was an important component of an overall strategy to legitimate MDPs [but the outcome also] required significant financial and political resources'. Additionally, 'the MDP debate was eventually overshadowed by external events, particularly the collapse of Enron and the revelation of accounting abuses at WorldCom'.

---

listeners. It suggests that how a leader's message is framed, through the use of metaphors, rhythm, contrasts, and lists, is as important as what the speech is about in gaining commitment from followers. These 'tools for framing' define the form and construction of the message by providing vivid images for the audience. According to Hartog and Verburg (1997), they include the following:

- *Contrast.* Where a subject is described in terms of its opposite in order to reinforce a point. For example, in Anita Roddick's speech she states:

> 3. Remember, corporations are invented. They are human institutions, not species found in nature. (Hartog & Verburg, 1997, p. 367)

- List. This is usually composed of three parts, this being the minimum number to show that there is a group of items without adding too many elements that would make the list excessive. Here is an example, in the first sentence of a speech given by Jan Timmer:

> 6. That together we are strong, together we can make progress and that our destiny really is in our own hands. That we no longer say they ought to do something but that we continue to say after today we are going to do something. That will restore the Philips-image. That will make Philips again a very nice place to work in. That will make Philips a company we can all be proud of. (Hartog & Verburg, 1997, p. 368)

> This is analyzed as:

1. Together we are strong.
2. Together we can make progress.
3. Our destiny really is in our own hands.

- Headline-punchline/puzzle-solution. In this instance the speaker creates the opportunity to present a punchline or solution by first presenting a headline or puzzle. This is illustrated using an excerpt from a speech given by Anita Roddick:

> 9. I came from an Italian immigrant family. At ten years of age, when my father died, my mother and us four kids worked in a large

café. There were no family holidays, there were no family diversions, except for the weekly cinema, it was work! It was a livelihood. It was an extension of our home, our kitchen. Courtships flourished in that café, marriages formed, friendships connected, the eye was delighted, the music from the jukebox spoke personally to everyone and your heart was in the workplace. It taught me a huge lesson, you can bring your heart to work with you. It taught me business was not financial science, it is about trading, buying and selling. It is about creating a product or service so good that people will pay a higher price for that. (Hartog & Verburg, 1997, p. 369)

According to Hartog and Verburg, the story of Roddick's youth provides the puzzle from which she constructs a solution: 'it taught me . . . you can bring your heart to work with you'.

- Position taking. The speaker begins by giving a fairly neutral description of a state of affairs and then he or she strongly agrees or disagrees with it. In a speech by Matthew Barrett he takes a position regarding the state of the Canadian economy, stating:

> 10. As the weeks since October 30 have passed one by one, my optimism has slowly waned. What I hear are seductive voices calling us back to 'jobs and the economy'. Even the incoming premier of Quebec is saying as much. And the polls suggest the public agrees. I *don't* agree. (Hartog & Verburg, 1997, p. 370)

- Pursuit, repetition, alliteration. The speaker may actively pursue audience reactions by repeating or otherwise stressing a point, for example by saying 'I repeat . . .'. For example, in the speech given by Jan Timmer he uses repetition in the delivery of his three part list:

1. *That will* restore the Philips-image.
2. *That will* make Philips again a very nice place to work in.

3. *That will* make Philips a company we can all be proud of. (Hartog & Verburg, 1997, p. 370)

Rhetorical analysis enables a focus on the persuasive acts that help to engender identification and foster co-operation within a group. For example, in the study by Swales and Rogers (1995) of corporate mission statements, the researchers were especially interested in the way that mission statements were rhetorically designed to ensure maximum employee 'buy-in' and identification with the company. However, they note that mission statements operate at a general and ambiguous level and deal mainly with abstractions. From the mission statements they analyze, they observe that there is an almost total absence of 'support' in the form of examples, quotations, or statistics. Swales and Rogers (1995, p. 227) note that verb forms used within the mission statements are predominantly present, imperative (e.g., 'return to underwriting profit'), or purpose infinitive (e.g., 'to provide a caring environment . . .'; 'to be the safest carrier'). The rhetorical devices that we have described in this section provide an important means whereby organizational researchers are able to explore and systematically analyze this use of language. (Web Research in focus 20.6 and 20.10 provide some further examples of a rhetorical approach).

Context-sensitive approaches

The accusations levelled at fine-grained approaches, as too narrowly focused on language in use and insufficiently related to social and historical context, lead to consideration of approaches that seek to take into account to a greater extent factors that influence how language is produced, disseminated, and consumed. The approaches of narrative and rhetorical analysis can be considered to be more focused on the way that social reality is shaped through language. They can thus be characterized as meso-level approaches (Alvesson & Karreman, 2000), being more sensitive to the context in which language is produced, concerned with finding generalizable patterns and going beyond the detail of the text to a greater extent than fine-grained approaches. However, there is

a further group that Grant et al. (2004) describe as 'context-sensitive approaches', which take account of factors beyond the text itself. The most influential of these, in organizational research at least, is critical discourse analysis (CDA). The section that follows will introduce the theoretical approaches that underpin CDA and outline the basic framework and key concepts that CDA practitioners employ.

Critical discourse analysis

Critical discourse analysis emphasizes the role of language as a power resource that is related to ideology and sociocultural change. While the inspiration is drawn from the work of Foucault (1974, 1977, 1978), there are other variants that are rooted in the work of Fairclough (2005), and of Mumby and Claire (1997).

Foucault's (1974, 1977, 1978) approach sought to uncover the representational properties of discourse as a vehicle for the exercise of power based on the construction of disciplinary practices that enable the construction of the self-disciplining subject. The notion of discourse is, therefore, defined more broadly than in fine-grained approaches, as this summary by Phillips and Hardy illustrates:

> We define a discourse as an interrelated set of texts, and the practices of their production, dissemination, and reception, that brings an object into being (Parker 1992) . . . In other words, social reality is produced and made real through discourses, and social interactions cannot be fully understood without reference to the discourses that give them meaning. As discourse analysts, then, our task is to explore the relationship between discourse and reality. (Phillips and Hardy, 2002, p. 3)

As the final part of this quote indicates, some practitioners of critical discourse analysis are more receptive to the idea of a pre-existing material reality that constrains individual agency, and in particular to the **epistemology** of critical realism (see Key concept 3.4), arguing that discourses should be examined in relation to social structures, including the power relationships that are responsible for occasioning them (Reed, 2000). Discourse is thus conceived as a 'generative mechanism' rather than as a self-referential sphere in which nothing of significance exists outside it. This is the approach taken by Fairclough (2005).

However, this approach can be seen in contrast to a number of other approaches to critical discourse analysis that place more stress on the role of language in constructing social realities (Mumby & Claire, 1997). Thurlow and Helms Mills (2009), for example, while focusing on 'talk' in constructing understandings of change also attempt to take account of the social-psychological properties through which sense is made of talk.

Fairclough (2005) argues that a version of critical discourse analysis (CDA) based on critical realism (see Key concept 3.4) is of particular value to organization studies, especially in relation to the study of organizational change. Fairclough is skeptical of the anti-realist assumptions of some discourse analysts who reject objectivist conceptions of organization as social structure in favour of seeing it as 'an interactive accomplishment' (2005, p. 917), according to a constructionist perspective (see Chapter 3). He quotes Mumby and Clair (1997) as typical of the latter position in saying 'we suggest that organizations exist only in so far as their members create them through discourse' (1997, p. 181).

Instead, Fairclough recommends an approach that centres on the tension between organizational discourse and organizational structure. Therefore, a **critical realist** approach to discourse analysis involves not just analyzing the discourse per se but also its relationship to non-discoursal elements. This is particularly important in relation to the study of organizational change because, 'while change in discourse is a part of organizational change, and organizational change can often be understood partly in terms of the constructive effects of discourse on organizations, organizational change is not simply change in discourse' (2005, p. 931). Fairclough identifies four sets of organizational research issues that a critical realist approach to discourse analysis can address:

- Emergence. Founded on the notion that 'new' organizational discourses emerge 'through "reweaving" relations between existing discourses' (2005, p. 932).

- Hegemony. Focusing on how particular discourses become hegemonic in particular organizations and on 'how discourse figures within the strategies pursued by groups of social agents to change organizations in particular directions' (2005, p. 933).
- Recontextualization. Involving identification of the principles through which 'external' discourses are internalized within particular organizations.
- Operationalization. Focusing on how discourses are operationalized, transformed into new ways of acting and interacting, inculcated into new ways of being, or materialized within organizations.

The approaches by Fairclough, Mumby and Claire, as well as Philips and Hardy discussed above are variants of what has become known as CDA, a version of Foucauldian analysis which has proved useful for analyzing organizational events and outcomes. Whereas the sweep of Foucault's work is more societal (e.g., in its focus on such phenomena as madness, sexuality, punishment) and historical (i.e., examining the constitution of selected phenomena across different time periods, or epistemes), CDA tends to be more narrowly focused on 'organizations' in more-or-less contemporary time spans (see, for example, Thomas & Davies, 2005; Vaara & Tienari, 2010). Studies that draw on critical discourse analysis to analyze the relationship between organizational and societal phenomena over time include (Durepos, Helms Mills, & Mills, 2008; Hartt, Mills, Helms Mills, & Durepos, 2009; Mills, 2006).

In an organizational context, one of the things that CDA practitioners seek to trace is how discourses are constructed and maintained in relation to certain phenomena, such as discriminatory practices (Mills & Helms Mills, 2006); work-family initiatives (Hurst, 1995); HRM or globalization (see Web Thinking deeper 20.1); or trends on business education (Neu & Mahaffey, 1991; Skipton & Foster, 1995). Analysis seeks to reveal the meaning of a particular phenomenon by exploring how:

- The discourse came to have a particular meaning today when 40 or 50 years ago it may have had none or a quite different meaning.
- The discourse draws on and influences other discourses.

20.1 # Student Experience

And then there is language

In qualitative research a focus on 'language' usually refers to methods for understanding the contexts and meaning systems in which our own language is expressed. However, it is well to remind ourselves that different languages can also play a part in the problems of interpretation. This is what Lotta found when constructing and analyzing her survey data. Her university, Hanken (also known as the Swedish School of Economics), provides a university education in Swedish for the Swedish minority in Finland—in much the same way as some universities operate in Canada such as St. Anne's in Nova Scotia, for example. However, at the doctoral level many of the courses are taught in English and Lotta had an English (as a first language) supervisor. Her Web survey data, however, were aimed at Finnish and Swedish speaking employees of Finnish companies. She did all the follow-up interviews in Finnish. Nonetheless, as she observed, the 'language issue . . . was quite interesting, because I did all the interviews in Finnish, and both my supervisors are native English speakers [and] the UK and Finland are different in this. The use and the concepts are different. So that was a challenge . . . I have to then sort of be aware of this. [I began by developing] the questions pretty well in English and then I did the translations. And now also with the results I'm just sort of translating them [back into English]'. Reflecting on the process Lotta felt that 'to have as few translations as possible, because you lose something [especially] if it's a constructed term; if it is the correct translation'. She also noted that 'reading' the process involved in the interviews can also be language and culturally specific. When discussing her interviews with people from Nordic countries, and some from Australia, she found that the latter saw some form of 'a gender objective' in the interactions, while the Australians she spoke to saw strategic interactions rather than gender. Thus, the problem of language is further compounded when the research project relies on more than one language.

- The discourse is constructed through texts (such as academic articles or journalistic writing).
- The discourse gives meaning to social life and makes certain activities possible, desirable, or inevitable.
- Particular actors draw on the discourse to legitimate their positions and actions. (Phillips & Hardy, 2002, p. 8)

As the second point in the above list indicates, discourses are conceived of as drawing on and influencing other discourses, so for example the discourse of globalization might affect discourses on new technology, free trade and liberalism, or corporate social responsibility.

However, this is not always a complementary process, as in some cases discourses compete with each other for dominance in what is termed *dialogical struggle* (Keenoy et al., 1997). An example of this can be seen in the analysis by Dye and Mills (2010) that traces changing gendered discourses in Pan American Airways (PAA) from the 1950s to the 1970s. While examining various practices involving the hiring and imaging of women (using Acker's 1992 notion of gendered substructure), Dye and Mills found evidence of strong organizing principles in the form of gendered discourses. In the 1950s PAA's workplace practices were heavily influenced by a discourse of traditional family roles, with employees judged in terms of the roles they were expected to play in familial situations. Thus, managers were cast as father figures who decided the direction of the 'PAA family' and women were cast as support staff but also, in the case of young women, as potential wives and mothers (with a limited future in the workplace). However, in the 1970s there was evidence not only of a newer discourse (of 'competition') but also a competing discourse (of women's liberation). The effect of the former was that female potential was judged (using masculine standards) according to their ability to perform particular tasks. The latter had the effect of providing countervailing views of women and men that allowed the space for resistance and challenge to dominant norms. Another example of how the temporal evolution of discourses can be traced analytically is provided in Web Thinking deeper 20.1 in relation to globalization. CDA thus involves exploring why some meanings become privileged or taken for granted and others become marginalized. In other words, discourse does not just provide an account of what goes on in organizations; it is also a process whereby meaning is created. This involves asking 'who uses language, how, why and when' (Van Dijk, 1997, p. 2).

Analysis of a particular *discursive event* is usually carried out according to a 'three dimensional' framework, which proceeds as follows:

- Examination of the actual content, structure, and meaning of the text under scrutiny (the text dimension).
- Examination of the form of discursive interaction used to communicate meaning and beliefs (the discursive practice dimension).
- Consideration of the social context in which the discursive event is taking place (the social practice dimension). (Grant et al., 2004, p. 11)

A further key concept within CDA is the notion of *intertextuality*, which draws attention to the notion of discourse as existing beyond the level of any particular discursive event on which analysis is focused. The notion of intertextuality thus enables a focus on the social and historical context in which discourse is embedded.

Overview

Language has until relatively recently rarely been a primary focus of management research (Hartt, Yue, Helms Mills, & Mills, 2009). One of the reasons for this may relate to the preference for action rather than talk: 'dialogue, discussion and debate are usually portrayed as being of secondary importance to action' (Grant, Keenoy, and Oswick, 1998, p. 5). However, in recent years there has been a considerable expansion in management and business research studies that use some sort of approach to the analysis of language which, as Grant, Keenoy, and Oswick point out, is perhaps not surprising because the importance of language in understanding organizations is hard to underestimate since it plays such a significant part in 'constructing, situating, facilitating and communicating the diverse cultural, institutional, political and socio-economic parameters of "organizational being"' (Grant, Keenoy, and Oswick, 1998, p. 12). In Canada, studies that focus on language constitute a relative small and new aspect of research but seem to be growing. In a study of the Administrative Sciences Association of Canada proceedings Hartt et al. (2009) found an increasing use of content analysis, discourse analysis, and conversation analysis.

Many of the recent studies refer to their analysis of language using the term discourse. However, the extensive use of this term brings its own problems, because what different researchers understand the term discourse to mean varies considerably, and so does their approach to analysis. There is thus a danger, noted by Alvesson and Karreman (2000), that the term 'discourse analysis' is too broad to be meaningful, authors treating the term as though it has a clear and broadly agreed-upon meaning which, just from reading this chapter, you will be able to see it does not. Hence, 'discourse sometimes comes close to standing for everything, and thus nothing' (Alvesson & Karreman, 2000, p. 1128). However, the important thing to remember is that understanding how language is used is viewed by some researchers as crucial to understanding the social world, and the approaches examined in this chapter provide some tools through which language can be explored as a focus of attention in its own right.

Key points

- The approaches examined in this chapter take the position that language is itself a focus of interest, and not just a medium through which research participants communicate with each other or with researchers.
- Fine-grained approaches such as CA and DA focus in detail on the organizing properties of language and the rules and structures that determine what people say in a given interaction.
- CA is a highly detailed approach to the analysis of naturally occurring conversation and dialogue that uses systematic rules to reveal the underlying structures of language.
- DA is an anti-realist, **constructionist** approach for the analysis of language that conceives of discourse as a means of conveying meaning.
- **Narrative analysis** is an approach to the elicitation and analysis of language that is sensitive to the stories that people tell about their lives or events around them.
- *Rhetorical analysis* examines the use of persuasive forms of language that help to engender identification and foster cooperation within a group, focusing on the importance of rhetorical devices in this process.
- CDA conceives of a discourse as an interrelated set of **texts** and sees discourses as drawing on and influencing other discourses.
- CDA emphasizes the role of language as a power resource that is related to ideology and sociocultural change.

Questions for review

- In what ways do fine-grained approaches to language differ from context-sensitive approaches?

Conversation analysis
- What three basic assumptions underpin the CA practitioner's approach?
- Why are notational symbols employed in CA?

Discourse analysis
- What is the significance of saying that DA is anti-realist and **constructionist**?
- What is an **interpretative repertoire**?

Narrative analysis
- What might be the main purpose of seeking to uncover organizational stories?
- How is it that the writing up of research is in itself a process of narrative construction?

Rhetorical analysis
- List some of the main areas of business and management where rhetorical analysis has been applied and explain why rhetorical analysis is useful in understanding them.

Context-sensitive approaches
- What are the main criticisms made of fine-grained approaches?

Critical discourse analysis
- What key questions might a CDA practitioner ask in seeking to reveal the meaning of TQM discourses?
- Why is the notion of *intertextuality* important to CDA practitioners?

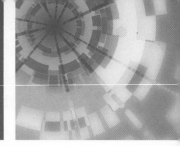

21

Historiography and the Past in Business Studies

Chapter guide

This chapter discusses the significance and the methods of studying the past in business studies. In particular it examines the study of history, or **historiography**; the ways that the past is conceptualized within different research **paradigms** and the implications for making sense of business. The chapters explores:

- The use of the past in management and organization studies.
- The call for a historic turn in business studies.
- The contribution of business and management history to business studies.
- Different approaches to historiography or studies of the past.
- Sources or 'traces' of the past for business studies.

Introduction

In business studies there has been considerable discussion over the past two decades about the role of the past, history, and appropriate methods of study. Debates have been influenced by developments within political economy, philosophy, history, and business studies itself.

Historical influences on business studies

The Marxist influence

The influence of Marxist historiography (i.e., historical materialism, see Key concept 21.1) on political economy (Miliband, 1970; Laxer, 1973) and history (Hobsbawm, 1994; Thompson, 1964) appeared in business studies in the UK (Clegg, 1975; Clegg & Dunkerley, 1980) and the United States (Benson, 1977; Braverman, 1974) in the late 1970s—constituting, what Burrell and Morgan (1979) termed, a radical structuralist paradigm (see Chapter 3). This led to a number of studies of the historical contexts in which management theory developed, including Acker and van Houten's (1974) re-analysis of the sociohistoric context of the Hawthorne Studies. This type of research was developed through various groups of radical researchers, including those grouped around an annual 'Labour Process' conference (Kieser, 1994; Goldman, 1994). Founded in 1983, the annual Labour Process conferences brought together economists, sociologists, and those working in business schools to study, among other things, the relationships between management thought and the changing 'arrangements of production . . . and the evolution of labour organization' (Smith, 2009). In 1999 the first international Critical Management Studies (CMS) conference in the UK, and the CMS Interest Group of the Academy of Management included researchers from the Marxist tradition, along with feminists, radical ecologists, and postmodernists. The latter group was composed of those who were influenced by the work of Foucault (1979, 1980*b*), Lyotard (1984), Derrida (1978, 1984), and other French philosophers (Best & Kellner, 1997).

The postmodernist influence

Beginning in the mid-1960s a number of French postmodernist philosophers began to challenge orthodox views of knowledge, specifically how knowledge is constituted

---

Key concept 21.1: What is historical materialism?

Historical materialism is a method of analysis developed by Karl Marx to make sense of the dynamic of human change over time; focusing on the interactions between socio-economic relationships (termed 'class' relations), the dominant means of production (e.g., the tools and materials involved in the process), and the ideological (e.g., the church, media, education) and political (e.g., the armed forces, government, law) support systems that maintain class privilege in the constitution of a particular mode of production (e.g., feudalism, capitalism, communism).

(i.e., the ontological status of knowledge). In the process they cast doubt on the constitution of the past and, ultimately, of history itself. Jean-Francois Lyotard (1984), for instance, contended that knowledge (e.g., what we understand about social life and our role in it) is organized through 'grand narratives' that link current existence to past and future events. This perspective on knowledge challenged not only the positivist notion of the progressive nature of social life but also the Marxist idea of history as the unfolding of class struggle towards a utopian communist stage of human existence. Jacques Derrida (1978) pointed to the constitutive role of language in knowledge, contending that far from reflecting reality language creates (a sense of) reality. Thus, arguably, the past is not reproduced but rather produced through language. Michel Foucault (1965, 1972), more than anyone within this tradition, challenged not only understandings of the role of the past but the practice and discipline of history itself. Foucault theorized the past as contextual and history as discontinuous; viewing knowledge as discursive. Basically, this means that at any given time knowledge will be rooted in a particular group of discourses (powerful ideas that are reinforced in practice). Those discourses can be traced back to particular sets of inter-relationships and practices and the context in which they are generated and maintained. Foucault argues that various discourses come to reinforce aspects of one another to constitute a given discursive formation (or collection of dominant mutually reinforcing discourses). This discursive formation can be said to constitute an episteme, or era, which shapes not only the way that people understand the conditions of life but also the possibilities for expression of and challenge to existing knowledge.

Through studies of mental illness (1965) and punishment (1979) over time Foucault showed how the changing contexts of discursive formations led to different epochs of knowledge—stressing that history is not continuous, progressive, or linear. From this perspective the writing of history (or History) is also seen as discursive—complete with its own discourse.

From roughly the mid-1980s postmodernist theory began to make an impact on business studies in Europe (Burrell, 1988; Morgan & Knights, 1991; Alvesson, 1995)

and, to a lesser extent in North America (Calás & Smircich, 1996; Boje et al., 1996), although there have been few empirical accounts focused on the past or history.

The influence of writing genres

Within the discipline of history itself, the work of White (1973, 1985) challenged much of the orthodoxy of positivist and Marxist historiography in the claim that history was a form of fiction rather than a science. White's argument rested on at least two key contentions: (a) the past consists of innumerable, disparate elements that, by definition, cannot be brought back or reproduced; (b) attempts to reproduce the past are limited by a number of processes that are akin to fiction in the choices the historian has to make in terms of which elements to focus on and which narrative style to use to order the elements. White argues that the historian makes choices about the many stories (histories) to tell by selecting some elements of the past and ignoring others; the historian's interpretation is compounded by the fact that he or she is faced with 'traces' (documents, memories, etc.) that are themselves selected interpretations of the past; and finally, in constructing a history, much like the novelist, the historian is constrained by a limited number of writing genres for telling a story.

Genres of historical writing

White (1973) argues that history is 'emplotted' through the use of well established forms of expression (or 'tropes'). What this means is that history is not so much captured in the 'facts' that are presented to the reader (e.g., details of the French Revolution) as the way the 'facts' are assembled into a narrative. White (1973) contends that the historian only has a limited number of tropes at hand and it is the chosen tropes that constitute the history being told, contributing to the way that the story's plot (or 'emplotment'). Those tropes include metaphor (which helps us to understand one term by reference to another: 'the manager's style was Machiavellian'); metonymy (the substitution of a certain word with an attribute, e.g., 'suits' for business people); synecdoche (a noun where the part represents the whole or vice versa, e.g., 'the hired hands' to represent the worker); and irony (expression of meaning through reference to its opposite, e.g., 'her female abilities were as good as a man's'). These tropes, according to White (1973) are linked to an equally limited range of narrative forms that include romance (a focus on the heroic qualities of an individual, e.g., a history of Nova Scotia Power that focuses on the 'transformational role' of CEO Louis Comeau more than the details of the company's many other developments); tragedy (a focus on the impact of fate on events, usually with a bad ending, e.g., the use of the theory of the life cycle to discuss events in a company in its death phase, see Kimberly and Miles, 1980); comedy (a focus on human beings as part of a greater organic whole, not subject to fate so much as resolving things through harmonious relations, e.g., a history that focuses on a company's survival due to its people working together to overcome adversity); and satire (focuses on absurdity and questions such things as the role individual attributes, the fates, and harmony in the resolve of organizational problems, e.g., a history that focuses on such things as chaos and decision making (Cohen, March, & Olsen, 1972), the social construction of a sense of organization (Vaughan, 1996) or the influence of discursive fields (Foucault, 1972)). More often than not certain tropes are likely associated with certain narrative forms such as metaphor with romance (to emphasize the hero or heroine's character: e.g., 'she has the kindness of Mother Teresa'); metonymy with tragedy (to evoke certain images, e.g., 'they failed because of corporate neglect'); synecdoche with comedy (to see the individual in the collective and the collective in the individual, e.g., 'he is a good organizational citizen'); and irony with satire (to express skepticism, e.g., 'the company could have succeeded but for the lack of adequate funds, technological know-how, and good leadership but also an inability to make sense of what was going wrong').

With its challenge to dominant positivist and Marxist accounts, White's work proved unpopular for a time within history, especially in his native United States (Green, 2007). However, White's approach has proven popular in the long run among newer generations of historians in the field of history (Jenkins, 1994) but also business studies (Rowlinson, 2004a; Czarniawska-Joerges, 2004).

Outside of business and corporate history, views of the role of history in business studies have varied dramatically over time. In the United States, for example, there were three major tendencies in regard to history and management theory—one was associated with the *Society for the Advancement of Management* (SAM, formerly the Taylor Society); another was associated with the *Academy of Management* (AOM); and a third was more loosely linked with a small but important group of European émigrés. The first group emerged from the former Taylor Society and focused on the development of an objectivist, scientific management that was informed by experiment and other attempts to develop scientific methods. In so far as history was difficult to control and quantify it did not generally form part of the scientific endeavor of SAM and others in the field of Scientific Management. From this perspective the manager was viewed as the recipient of scientific management.

The second group tended to view management as a philosophy and set out to recruit like-minded scholars to join with them in an alternative to SAM, to be called the Academy of Management (Wrege, 1986). While not central to the writing of these management scholars, history was utilized from time to time in the textbooks of the founding AOM group to provide perspective on the development of the field. The third group was more disparate and consisted of former leftist American philosophers and political scientists who used history to reflect on and locate the development of management and management theory. James Burnham was the most prominent of the American political scientists, while Peter Drucker and Herbert Marcuse were the more prominent of the émigré group. In their different ways Burham (1941), a former Trotskyist, and Drucker (1939, 1942), an escapee from Nazi Europe, documented the historical trajectory of management and the idea of the manager. Marcuse (1941, 1964, 1970), a former member of the leftist Frankfurt School (disbanded by the Nazis in the early 1930s, see Held, 1980), drew on historical analysis to develop accounts of the impact of capitalism and bureaucracy on personality and sense of self.

Things changed quite dramatically in the post-war era and the onset of the Cold War (Cooke, 1999; Mills &

Helms Hatfield, 1998; Kelley et al., 2006), and history and the social context of management theorizing were very much pushed into the background. One cause was a considerable shift in management and organizational theorizing to **behavioralism** (Robin, 2001)—a methodological approach modelled after the natural sciences that 'seeks to examine the behaviour, actions, and acts of *individuals*—rather than the characteristics of institutions such as legislatives, executives, and judiciaries—and groups in different social settings and explain this behaviour as it relates to [organizations]' (see http://en.wikipedia.org/wiki/Behavioralism). This trend was shaped by wartime government needs and expenditures that carried through the first half of the post-war era (Robin, 2001; Khurana, 2007) but its central focus on quantifiable data and the individual moved management theory away from history and philosophy.

The context of the Cold War also arguably had an influence on the move away from history in management theory (Cooke, 2006; Grant & Mills, 2006; Landau, 2006), with an atmosphere of fear and suspicion that discouraged scholars from dealing with or even discussing broad social issues (Schrecker, 1986; Lazarsfeld & Thielens, 1958).

In this immediate post-war era the Academy of Management moved towards behavioralism and away from philosophy and history (Wrege, 1986; Wren, 1979; Grant & Mills, 2006); Burnham's work—now centrally within political science—became largely focused on polemics against communism; leftists like Marcuse received little or no attention (Cooke, 1999) in management theory; and the work of Drucker was more often used in mainstream management theory as support for empirical rather than philosophical accounts (McLaren et al., 2009).

Nonetheless, there continued to be influential examples of the value of history in business studies. Lyndall Urwick (1938, 1963), the co-founder of the *Administrative Sciences Quarterly* (ASQ), continued to publish historical accounts of the development of management theory well into the 1960s, and the work of Alfred Chandler (1962, 1977) introduced new generations of management theorists to the value of historical analysis. Within the Academy of Management a division of Management History, established at the beginning of the 1970s, encouraged management theorists to take history into account. The division included Claude George (1972) and Daniel Wren (1979)—who went on to write widely used textbooks on the history of management thought, and Arthur ('Art') Bedeian (1984) and Charles Wrege (1986) who serve as the unofficial historians of the AOM: all four served as Divisional Chairs of Management History and Bedeian also served as President of the AOM in 1989. In Canada a Business History Division of the *Administrative Sciences Association of Canada* (ASAC) was established in the late 1980s to serve a similar purpose to that of the AOM's Management History Division and, more recently (in the mid-2000s), the *Atlantic Schools of Business* (ASB) began to include *Business History* as an 'area of interest'. In the UK the *British Academy of Management* (BAM) has yet to establish a history division but, nonetheless, in line with other associations—AOM (Wrege, 1986), ASAC (Austin, 1998, 2000*b*), and ASB (Haddon & Mills, 2008; Long et al., 2008)—BAM (McKiernan, 2008) has developed a history of the association.

The early 1980s saw the development of a widespread interest in the phenomenon of organizational culture that helped to shift interest to some of the less structural and rational elements of organizational thinking (Weick, 1985) and opened the door for considerations of the role of the past in organizational theorizing in general (Clegg, 1981; Mills, 1988) and organizational culture in particular (Dellheim, 1986; Rowlinson & Procter, 1999).

The early 1990s saw the beginning of a concerted call for 'the reintegration of historical analyses into organization theory' (Frost, 1994), which included a speech by Alfred Kieser to the 1993 Paris conference of the European Group for Organization Studies (EGOS): a version of the speech was later reproduced in *Organization Science* (Kieser, 1994). Kieser, a former editor of the journal *Organization Studies*, had made his own contribution to historical analysis in organization theory in high-profile articles in leading management journals (Kieser, 1987; Kieser, 1989).

The call for a 'historic turn' in management and organizational studies continued steadily into the twenty-first century and culminated in several notable events and publications. In the United States Wren's (1994) management history textbook was in its fourth edition and, in Canada, Barbara Austin and her colleagues were developing studies of such things as the role of ASAC and management theory (1994, 1995, 1998); management education and development in Canada (Sharma & Steier, 1990); strategy formation over time (Arnold & Brown, 1986; Austin & Mintzberg, 1996); the early development of marketing thought in Canada (Jones, 1992), and investment opportunities over time (Korkie & Turtle, 1998). New calls for an historic turn developed from the work of Michael Rowlinson and others, particularly in the UK (Cooke, 1999; Rowlinson, 2004b; Cooke & Kothari, 2001) but also Canada (Mills & Helms Hatfield, 1998), the United States (Jacques, 1996), and other parts of Europe (Üsdiken & Kieser, 2004), and beyond (Landau, 2006).

The call for the historic turn in management and organization studies

In this section we review the arguments for a reintegration of historical analyses into business studies.

Kieser (1994) argues that despite the earlier importance of history to organization studies it has now 'become extremely rare' for organizational researchers to draw on historical analysis (p. 609). Here he makes four main arguments (an illustration of all four points can be seen in the work of Helms Mills, 2003, see Research in Focus 21.1):

1. *In order to understand contemporary institutions it important to know something of their historical development (p. 609).*

    A recent example of this approach is Khurana's (2007) study of the role of management in the United States today. His starting point is a focus on the professional status of management in the United States and the role of the business school in the process. He is interested the influence of 'the manager' on modern society in terms of 'knowledge and normative claims and their uses in claiming professional prerogatives' (p. 10) that serve to legitimize management

as an institution. In particular, he is interested in the influence of the business school in the creation of the idea of the modern manager. However, as Khurana (2007) explains, the manager is more than just the sum total of a collection of specific roles, but is a culturally defined phenomenon. Similarly, the business school is an institution whose functioning and influence is a taken-for-granted aspect of public life, and one whose development is strongly associated with the rise of the modern manager:

> Grasping the nature of business education is therefore essential for our understanding of the functioning of management in the American economy and American society today, and of how the institution of management can be not only critically evaluated but also, if deemed necessary, reshaped to make way for a better fit with overall social aspirations. (Khurana, 2007, pp. 5–6)

Drawing on **New Institutional Theory** (NIT; see Key concept 21.2), Khurana (2007) argues that to understand the role of institutions it is important to study their origins (and development over time). It 'is essential to examine an institution's birth—its emergence out of an interaction with the larger society and culture, the evolution of its internal dynamics, and the interface between the two. . . . The key here is to show organizations responding to particular problems posed by history' (Khurana, 2007, pp. 14–15). Khurana (2007, p. 18) contends that while NIT 'recognizes the importance of such links and interactions, it has not always paid enough attention to the emergence and development of institutions in their historical fields as well as in their organizational fields'. He goes on to argue:

> To understand this crucial aspect of an institution, then, requires a deep familiarity with the social context of the period of its founding and development, and with the debates to which a set of institutional entrepreneurs were engaged, as well as an understanding of why it is that particular

stances gained acceptance from resource providers. (Khurana, 2007, p. 18)

2. *Through historical analysis we can reduce the ideological biases that are embedded in 'current "fashionable" trends in organization theory and practice' (p. 610).*

Kieser's (1997) own work on 'rhetoric and myth in management fashion' details how management theory can as much reflect popular currents of thought as attempts to retain an objectivist focus (see also Abrahamson, 1996; Jackson, 2001; Chaulk & Sexty, 2002). Studies of the development of management theory in context have also revealed the problem of ideological bias. Mills, Kelley, and Cooke's (2002) historical analyses of leadership studies, for example, suggest that Lewin, Lippitt, and White's (1939) classic leadership archetypes (democratic, autocratic, laissez-faire) were influenced by the political climate in which they were developed (i.e., the onset of the Second World War and the classification of the political systems of the various protagonists), and that the changed characteristics of those archetypes in the post-war era (White & Lippitt, 1972) were influenced by the Cold War climate in which they were revised. Similar analyses of the work of Maslow have documented the gendered and cultural biases in his work and the historical contexts in which those biases surfaced (Cullen, 1997; Dye et al., 2005; Cooke et al., 2005).

3. *Through historical analyses we can 'interpret existing organizational structures not as determined by [objective] laws but as the result of decisions in past choice opportunities', whether intentional or implicit (p. 611).*

Here the work of Henry Mintzberg and his colleagues is illustrative. Through a number of studies Mintzberg has examined the development of strategy over time to reveal that not all strategies are consciously developed but often arise out of a combination of spoken and unspoken assumptions that can be detected as 'a pattern in a stream of action, whether the pattern is an intended outcome or 'realized despite, or in the absence of intentions' (Mintzberg et al., 1986, p. 4).

In an historical analysis of American hospital administration Arndt and Bigelow (2005) revealed that extant portrayals of 'men rather than women as the appropriate practitioners' (p. 233) masks the fact that the occupation had originated and developed as a female-dominated occupation. The current gendered structured was not the outcome of objective assessments of the relative merits of male and female administrators but was rooted in historical change at the turn of the twentieth century. Basically, the intervention of the male-dominated medical professional associations, to establish 'a jurisdiction, body of knowledge, and educational requirements . . . created a male sex boundary' (p. 233) and drove women from the position:

> Rhetorical use of gender created a male image of the generic practitioner and the occupation, while an internal boundary segregated women within the occupation (p. 233).

4. *'By confronting theories of organizational changes with historical development, these theories can be subjected to a more radical test than they have to pass when merely being confronted with data on short-run changes' (p. 612).*

Through an historical analysis of the realized strategies employed by McGill University over time (1829–1980), Mintzberg and Rose (2003) called into question a number of the 'fundamental premises of strategic management' (p. 270). What they discovered was that 'amidst continual change in detail, there was remarkable stability in the aggregate, and nothing resembling quantum or revolutionary change in strategy ever occurred' (p. 270). And they conclude:

> To the extent that this describes their strategic behaviour, so much that has been written about strategic management, with its focus on the planners, the chief executive as 'architect' of strategy, and the management of change as driven from the 'top', becomes questionable. Certainly all the hype about turnaround and revolution needs to

be reconsidered in such contexts. Perhaps these companies change best from the inside out, at their own pace, rather than from the top down, frenetically (p. 289).

In a related observation they argue that today's 'claims about change in society, renewal, turbulence, and so on' may be over-rated because 'the fact is that some things are always changing in society while others remain rather stable' (p. 288).

Towards the very end of the twentieth century there developed two related, but very different, calls for an historic turn in business studies: one followed in the tradition of Keiser (Leblebici & Sherer, 2008; Üsdiken & Kieser, 2004) and another came from a group of critical management scholars who questioned not only the need for an historic turn in business studies but also a critical assessment of the methods of historical (and organizational) analysis (Booth & Rowlinson, 2006; Jacques, 2006). We shall return to this critical call for the historic turn when we consider the methods of studying history and the past. In this next section we will look at some of the ways that business scholars have drawn on studies of history and the past to make sense of current business practice and knowledge.

 ## History and the past in business studies

Business scholars have dealt with the past in a number of ways but often without direct reference to history or methods of historical study (i.e., historiography, see Key concept 21.3).

A review of the *Canadian Journal of Administrative Sciences* (CJAS) since 2000 is useful for illustrating some of the various ways that business scholars have deal with the past. At least five trends are evident: *tracking* (Mintzberg & Rose, 2003; see also Arnold & Brown, 1986; Austin & Mintzberg, 1996); *longitudinal study* (Delios & Ensign, 2000); *evolutionary analysis* (Baum et al., 2004; see also Korkie & Turtle, 1998); *junctures* (Mills & Helms Mills, 2006); and *historical analysis* (McQuarrie, 2005; Sexty, 2000; Sexty, 2008; see also Arnold & Brown, 1986; Austin, 1998; Jones, 1992; and Sharma & Steier, 1990). The list is not exhaustive but it illustrates some of the various ways that the past is conceptualized and explored as an issue in business studies.

Tracking. Mintzberg et al. have adopted an approach to the study of strategy by which they define a particular phenomenon and then track its appearance (or lack of appearance) over time. Austin and Mintzberg (1996) describes the methodology as one 'that has been applied to several organizations in Canada . . . [And] is based on the definition of strategy as not only intended, but also as *realized* (pattern in action), in order to contrast *deliberate* strategies that are formulated (intended strategies that were realized, i.e., plans manifested in patterns of action) with *emergent* ones that formed (patterns realized in the absence of, or despite intended strategies . . .)' (pp. 46–47). They used this method to track the strategies of a '"quintessentially Canadian company", Dominion Textile Inc., through most of its history, from 1873 to 1990' (p. 46). The study involved 'traces of action taken by the organization', that included examination of company 'shareholders, directors, and executive committee *Minute*

Key concept 21.2: What is New Institutional Theory (NIT)?

New Institutional Theory (NIT) seeks to explain the process of institutionalization (i.e., how certain organizations, or groups of organizations, become—over time—institutions, or socially legitimated and accepted bodies) and its influence on organizational structure and behaviour. As such it is focused on explaining such things as legitimacy, conformity, and the coherence of behaviour and structure across a range of organizations.

Key concept 21.3: What is historiography?

Historiography is the study of historical method. It involves an examination of how history is conceived (e.g., whether it utilizes a materialist or a poststructuralist epistemology), written (e.g., the types of tropes and narrative form used), and analyzed (e.g., does the historian frame the 'historical traces' in terms of a grand narrative or a lower case history approach, i.e., collecting data without any preconceived notions).

21.1   Research in Focus

Studying organizational culture over time: Lessons for organizational research

The work of Helms Mills (2003) illustrates each of the four points raised by Kieser.

1. *Understand contemporary institutions through their historical development*. In her study of Nova Scotia Power (see Research in focus 1.1) Helms Mills was asked by the company to report on the 'success' of an ongoing culture change in the early 1990s. Her attempt to define 'success' led her to an examination of the sense that managers (and employees) made of 'organizational culture'. Developing a longitudinal study of the company, and drawing on Weick's (1995) **sensemaking** frame, Helms Mills traced the development of change at Nova Scotia Power over the period 1985–2000. What she found was that in the mid-1980s senior management adopted a culture change program in response to a new leader who, as head of a Crown Corporation, was faced with political pressure to please the voters (by keeping down costs); business pressures to be more customer oriented; social pressures to be more environmentally responsible (the Green movement was beginning to have an impact); and internal pressure to be more responsive to employees (a workplace survey had indicated low morale throughout the company). Dealing with these different pressures the company adopted a set of key values that valued the employees, the customers, the province, and the environment.

   Through analysis of the context in which the original culture change had been adopted Helms Mills (2003) viewed the question of 'success' as related to the sensemaking frame and how employees and managers had made sense of the culture change program. In the event that made it difficult to assess the 'success' of the change program except in terms of how well the sense of the program had been enacted, i.e., be-

lieved and accepted by a critical mass of managers and employees.

2. *Ideological biases and current trends*. As we have seen from Helms Mills's (2003) study of Nova Scotia Power, analysis of the structuring and culture of an organization can look very different when subjected to historical analysis. When she explored the reasons why senior management adopted a culture change program to address their needs she found that they were influenced by the fact that culture change was at the height of popularity throughout North American business education and practice (Kieser, 1997), and that, in particular, it was a growing trend throughout the industry and in the local region (Atlantic Canada). In other words, management's decision making was not influenced by data or empirical evidence so much as the popularity and widespread acceptance of organizational culture change.

3. *Interpreting existing structures as the outcome of past decisions rather than objective laws*. When Nova Scotia Power was privatized in the early 1990s they made a shift from culture change and adopted Business Process Reengineering (BPR) as a method of change. In doing so senior management presented the change as an extension of the culture change program—the development of 'the efficiency phase' of the ongoing culture change program. However, as Helms Mills (2003) demonstrates, the decision to introduce BPR needs to be understood in terms of the context of privatization and prior decision choices. There was never mention of an efficiency phase or the use of BPR in the earlier culture change. Instead, the focus was on valuing employees, customers, voters (it was a crown corporatation), and the environment. With the privatization of the company in the early 1990s a new emphasis was introduced that valued the shareholders, and valued them above other constituents. The decision

to introduce BPR was more of a political than a scientific decision.

4. *Confronting theories of organizational change with historical development.* By studying Nova Scotia Power over time Helms Mills (2006) identified a corporate trend towards serial change, as they moved from employee survey techniques (1984), culture change (1985–1990), BPR (1991–1993), to strategic business units (1995–2000), to Balanced Score Card (2001–). Helms Mills (2003; 2006) contends that the changes form a pattern of response to current trends across industry rather than a concerted effort to apply scientific management techniques

Books', newspaper articles ('from the 1870s onwards'); *The Canadian Textile Journal*; and interviews with current and past executives of the company (p. 47). One of the outcomes of the study was the observation that the company can be seen as going through three different eras, 'each interrupted by a crisis that bumped the company up to a faster pace of evolution when management realized that their view of the environment was based on schemas that were historical and not current' (p. 60).

Similar studies have tracked the strategies of Pacific Western Airlines from 1945 to 1984 (Arnold & Brown, 1986); and McGill University (Mintzberg & Rose, 2003) to shed light on how companies formulate and change strategies over time.

Longitudinal study. Strictly speaking longitudinal study differs from most studies of the past in that the initial orientation is future occurrences. Instead of tracing events, i.e., people's actions or phenomena that have already occurred, longitudinal study is a method designed to observe things as they occur over a lengthy period of time into the future. In this way the researcher or research team do not have to rely on particular documentation or the memories of people, both of which may be faulty. The basic idea is to make a series of observations that are repeated at selected points over time. By its very nature this research method involves a considerable time commitment that usually puts it beyond the requirements of student dissertations (including PH.D. theses) but also researchers who rely on published results to build a career. However, as discussed in Chapter 4, some researchers cir-

cumvent the time frame by tracing some elements back in time. Jean Helms Mills took this approach to her study of Nova Scotia Power. She began the study for a Master's degree in 1990–1991, spending time analyzing an ongoing culture change program. She continued her study of the change process when she started her PH.D. thesis work in late 1993, and followed events in the company of the next seven years (successfully defending her thesis in 2000). However, in order to gain an understanding of the context in which the initial culture change began she also engaged in retrospective of the study, using archived materials and interviews. Thus, the study ended up tracking the company from the employment of a new CEO in the early 1980s through to 2000.

Delios and Ensign (2000) is one of the few business studies published in CJAS that make claim to a 'longitudinal' approach, examining 'longitudinal aspects of Japanese foreign direct investment in Canada' (p. 38). However, strictly speaking, the otherwise very useful and interesting study fits more into studies of events that were already in the past prior to the onset of the study. In their development of 'a descriptive analysis of entry and exit rates and on an econometric analysis of the determinants of subsidiary survival and exit' (p. 38), Delios and Ensign (2000, p. 41) analyzed 'observations derived from the 1986 and 1994 editions of Japanese Investments Overseas, a Japanese language publication', consisting of data from annual surveys of 'general managers of all Japanese subsidiaries of which the parent (10% equity interest minimum) is listed on the Tokyo, Osaka, or Nagoya stock exchanges or is a major unlisted firm'.

Evolutionary analysis. Analysis of evolutionary processes runs through several different approaches to study of the past. It is a metaphor that has influenced business studies from the early days of the establishment of the business school in the United Sates (Khurana, 2007) and runs through various historical accounts of management and organizations (Wren, 1994; Kieser, 1989; Weatherbee, 2009). Indeed, the domain statement of the Management History Division of the Academy of Management speaks of a focus on 'pragmatic investigations into the historical evolution of management thought and action' (http://www.aomonline.org/aom.asp?id=18#). It does not necessarily constitute a different method so much as an epistemological focus that shapes the direction and analysis of the research outcome, and can range from suggest anything from an established to a preordained direction that organizations follow (Weatherbee, 2009). Delios and Ensign (2000, pp. 38–39), for example, in their analysis of Japanese foreign direct investment in Canada, justify their longitudinal approach in the argument that it 'is becoming increasingly apparent in the literature on FDI (foreign direct investment), there is an evolutionary component to firm's and a country's FDI that need to be understood through the study of longitudinal patterns'. Similarly, in their 'tracking' of Dominion Textile Austin and Mintzberg (1996, p. 46) argue that 'following the evolution of this company is much like following the evolution of Canadian business in general'.

Baum, Rowley, and Shipilov (2004), on the other hand, drawing on 'evolutionary dynamics' (Baum & Singh, 1994), push the metaphor further, making it a more central element of their analysis. In their study of Canadian capital markets they set out to analyze the 'evolution of its clique substructure over time' (p. 314), with a clique defined as 'a distinct region within the overarching network in which as set of actors forms a cohesive subgroup, characterized by: (a) closeness of subgroup members; (b) dense interconnection within the group; and (c) sparse connection to actors outside the group' (p. 314). Using data 'drawn from the Record of New Issues (Financial Data Group)' (p. 307), Baum et al. (2004,

p. 321) concluded that their analysis of 'the evolution of syndicate networks' underlying clique substructure provided support for the idea that small-world networks are characterized by relatively stable groups of densely interconnected actors that are sparsely linked to one another'. And they call for further research into 'the emergence and evolution of small-world networks' (p. 323). Similarly, in an earlier study, of the Canadian Opportunity Set, 1967–1993, Korkie and Turtle (1998) set out to analyze 'the evolution of asset risks over time' (p. 213).

History as/at junctures. The growing interest in critical management studies (i.e., feminism, poststructuralism, postcolonialism, Marxism, etc.) in recent years (see Chapter 3) has been accompanied by the development and/or refinement of a range of appropriate methods, including critical discourse analysis and narrative analysis (see Chapter 20); critical hermeneutics (see below); and the notion of junctures. In the latter case Mills and Helms Mills (2006) use the idea of junctures to explore the role of masculinity in the development of discriminatory practices in Air Canada over time. Developed by Mills (1994a, 2006, 2010) to deal with organizational change over time, juncture refers to 'a concurrence of events in time in which a series of images, impressions, and experiences come together, giving the appearance of a coherent whole that influences how an organization is understood' (Mills, 2010, p. 509).

The idea of junctures is related to the Foucauldian notion of episteme, or a form of knowledge that characterizes a particular era (Foucault, 1980a), and to the Annales School's notion of mentalities, where a certain mind set can be seen as embedded in a particular set of practices (see Web Key concept 21.6). Mills and Helms Mills (2006) draw on this method to follow the development of different forms of masculinity over time to assess how they influence the dominant think of the organization at any given point. Their aim is to identify how certain (discriminatory) practices develop, are maintained but also how they change over time.

In the early 1990s Albert J. Mills began a study of a single organization—British Airways (BA)—to identify the role of organizational culture in the development, maintenance, and changing character of discriminatory practices. In the course of the research he noted several things, including the fact that the hiring and promotion of women by BA did not follow a linear or progressive path. He also noted that attitudes to the hiring and promotion of women changed dramatically over time, and again not in a linear or progressive fashion. For example, in the late 1930s women were publically ridiculed by the airline when they applied for work as flight attendants; were seen as equal to men in the mid-1940s; and hired, albeit on an 'experimental basis', and treated as sex objects in the 1960s. To deal with and explain the role of changing mentalities and gender discrimination, Mills developed the notion of junctures—to represent a dominant mindset at given point. He then set out to track the different junctures through a focus on company hiring and promotion practices in regard to women. In the process he identified eight separate junctures:

1. The development of an all-male organization (1919–24).
2. The introduction and growth of female employment within BA (1924–39).
3. The war years and the rapid expansion of female employment (1940–45).
4. The consolidation and 'normalization' of female employment (1946–1960).
5. The eroticization of female labour (1960–74).
6. The organization as the site of equity struggles (1974–81).
7. The development and consolidation of professionalized female labour (1981–91).
8. The emergence of a new juncture focused on female management and leadership (1991–). (Mills, 1994*b*)

Through extensive archival research of company documents; interviews with current and retired employees; and analysis of numerous written histories of the airline and of the socio-political context in which it operated, Mills then set out to identify some of the key factors that lead to key changes in peoples' thinking about gender, including widespread (e.g., warfare) and organizational (e.g., changes in leadership) shocks; mimetic isomorphism (i.e., the copying of established practices elsewhere;

resistance (e.g., internal trade union activities; and the advent of the women's liberation movement in the 1960s).

The past as History. While Mills and Helms Mills (2006) relate their notion of junction to a form of doing history few of the other studies discussed in this section relate their approach to an explicit discussion of history or methods of history (Mintzberg & Rose (2003) is the other exception). McQuarrie (2005) is one of several CJAS papers that focus directly on history and its representation in business studies. McQuarrie's study focuses on how the past is presented in Canadian Management and Organizational Behaviour textbooks. In particular she examines the presentation of the Hawthorne Studies. She uses her analysis to point out some of the problems of historical representation in management texts. Sexty (2000) also deals with the issue of representations of history, in his study of how business history has been reflected in Canadian postage stamps over the past 100 years (see also Sexty, 2008).

Perhaps the most consistent and coherent attempt to inject history into business studies in Canada can be found in the work of Austin, who began to make an impact with her histories of the Administrative Sciences Association of Canada (1994, 1995, 1998, 2000*b*), culminating in an edited work on 'the history of business education in Canada' (Austin, 2000*a*). As she notes in the introduction, 'Canadian historians have frequently reflected upon the importance of professional disciplines like law, engineering, or education, but they have displayed scant interest in management as an academic subject' (p. 3), her edited book thus set out to rectify that situation. Interestingly enough Khurana (2007) makes a similar point about management education in the United States and, like Khurana, Austin focuses on the role of professionalization. This is largely achieved through a focus on 'the *evolution* of Canadian business schools' (p. 4, emphasis added), and indeed almost all authors in the edited collection make reference to the study of the evolution of their business school.

While the book does not make reference to **historiography** per se Austin (2000*a*, p. 5) points out that the 'authors' approach the subject with diverse viewpoints and methodologies'. These include several descriptive accounts developed out of historical 'traces' and include the essays by Austin (2000*b*), Boothman (2000*a*, 2000*b*), Gillies and Dickinson (2000), Harvey (2000), and Ogden and Driscoll (2000). Three refer to their approach as a 'case study' or 'case history' (Daub & Buchan, 2000; Jones & Lane, 2000; Sawyer, 2000)—although in the latter study Sawyer adds that his is a 'case study based upon a mixture of documented history, personnel recollections, and subjective impressions' (p. 163). Sexty and Pecore (2000) draw on Mintzberg's method of tracking, while Ellis and McCutcheon (2000) use oral history—referencing an earlier work (Ellis & McCutcheon, 1996), for a fuller explication of the approach (see Chapter 14 for discussion of oral history and Web Research in focus 21.7).

Other approaches to the study of the past

As discussed earlier, there are various other methods used in the study of the past including narrative analysis, critical discourse analysis, and critical hermeneutics. Each has been used by a growing number of researchers in business studies to make sense of the past.

Narrative analysis

Is an approach to the elicitation and analysis of language that is sensitive to the sense of temporal sequence that people, as tellers of stories about their lives or events around them, detect in their lives and surrounding episodes and inject into their accounts' (see p. 419). As such it lends itself to the development and/or analysis of historical accounts. This approach is evident in a number of business studies across disciplines, including studies of the role of narratives in military history and lessons for management (Ahistrom et al., 2009); an examination of the narratives of management historians (i.e., Wren & Bedeian, 2009) to understand 'outstanding academic leadership in the field of management history' (Abraham et al., 2009, p. 9); an exploration of how managers use historical narratives (i.e., narratives of history) to 'affect strategy-making' (Brunninge, 2009, p. 8); the role of time (Ericson, 2006) and historicism (Novicevic et al., 2008) in narrative accounts of strategic management (see Web Research in focus 21.3); historical reviews of narrative writing in marketing (Witkowski & Jones, 2008; Jones,

1992); accounting (Lee & Humphrey, 2006); and Industrial Relations (Roberts, 2006); and studies of the role of narratives and organizational change over time (McCollom, 1991).

Critical discourse analysis (CDA)

Following the work of Foucault (1972, 1979) and his unique approach to history and historiography, a number of poststructuralist (Phillips & Hardy, 2002) and critical realist (Fairclough, 1995) scholars have developed methods of analyzing discourse in organization and management practice. Ironically, for the most part, such studies have not involved historical analysis despite their Foucauldian origins, but there have been a growing number in the past five years. These studies include: Ruef and Harness's (2009) analysis of slavery and management practices in the late Roman Republic and the American antebellum South; Storberg-Walker and Bierema's (2008) analysis of the historical development of Human Resources Development knowledge; Dar's (2008) review of the impact of modernity on understandings of health management; Walker's (2006) study of current trends in accounting history; McLaren et al.'s (2009) exploration of management discourse; and the dissemination of the work of management guru Peter Drucker; Hartt et al.'s (2009a) study of the impact of Pan America Airways on the discourse of the Cold War; Grant and Mills's (2006) analysis of the impact of the Cold War on the development of management theory; and Taylor and Freer's (2002) examination of how stakeholders in a nuclear power generating organization developed a particular history to 'perform preferred ideological narratives' (p. 563; see Web Research in focus, 21.9).

Critical hermeneutics

Linked to the analysis of text, critical hermeneutics is a useful method for archival research that has begun to attract poststructuralist, feminist, and other postpositivist researchers (Phillips & Brown, 1993; Forster, 1994; Phillips & Hardy, 2002; Mills & Helms Mills, 2006), including those with a particular interest in historical analysis (Prasad, 2002; Prasad & Mir, 2002; Hartt et al., 2009b; McLaren et al., 2009).

Hermeneutics refers to an approach that was originally devised in relation to the understanding or interpretation of texts, and of theological texts in particular. It has been influential in the general formulation of **interpretivism** as an **epistemology** (see Chapter 3). That influence has been generally more notable in Europe than in North America (Kinsella, 2006) although some of the more prominent work in business studies has come from the United States (Prasad, 2002; Prasad & Mir, 2002) and Canada (Phillips & Brown, 1993; Phillips & Hardy, 2002).

According to Kinsella (2006) hermeneutics can be seen as consisting of five elements. It is an approach that: (1) Seeks understanding through attempting 'to clarify the interpretive conditions in which understanding takes place'; (2) Recognizes the situated location of interpretation by taking into account the 'insights' that the knower brings to his or her study and the active role they play in the process of interpretation; (3) Stresses the role of language and history in shaping interpretations and as 'conditions and limitations of understanding'; (4) Views inquiry as conversation in so far as the art of interpretation is seen as a form of translation of the sociohistorical context of the text and of the researcher, with both levels of interpretation (past and present locations) being surfaced; and (5) Is comfortable with ambiguity by avoiding the temptation to provide a single reading of the text but rather sets out to 'restore life to [the text's] original difficulty'.

At the heart of hermeneutics is an attempt to come to terms with the past, with history and with sociocontext. In the words of Gadamer (1996, p. 307, cited in Kinsella, 2006) 'Part of real understanding is that we regain the concepts of a historical past in such a way that they also include our own comprehension of them' (p. 374). But at the same time, we must go beyond this historical past. For the process of understanding to take place a *fusion of horizons* [i.e., merger of the views of text and interpreter] needs to occur'.

Building on this process, 'critical hermeneutics seeks to unveil hidden meanings that serve the interests of the socially and politically powerful . . . . Through this analysis, the critical-hermeneutic researcher can locate the text as a tool "of the ongoing maintenance of asymmetric relations that characterize a particular organization"' (Prasad & Mir, 2002, p. 96). Prasad and Mir's (2002) research ref-

erences the work of Phillips and Brown (1993), who for studied the corporate image in advertisements of a Canadian company that produces synthetic crude oil. Phillips and Brown employed a large database of magazine and newspaper articles relating to the company, which also supplied the authors with additional documentary materials. Their approach entailed the examination of the advertisements in terms of three 'moments':

- The social-historical moment. Which involves 'an examination of the producer of the text, its intentional recipient, its referent in the world [i.e., what it refers to], and the context in which the text is produced, transmitted, and received' (1993, p. 1558).
- The formal moment. That involves 'a formal analysis of the structural and conventional aspects of the text' (1993, p. 1563). This means that the texts must be examined in terms of the constituent parts of each text and the writing conventions employed. This phase can involve the use of any of several techniques, such as semiotics or discourse analysis (see Chapter 20). Phillips and Brown used the former of these.
- The interpretation-reinterpretation moment. That 'involves the interpretation of the results of the first two moments' (1993, p. 1567); in other words, they are synthesized.

Through this strategy, Phillips and Brown show the ways in which the corporate image advertisements constitute an attempt to mobilize support for the company's activities from government (and from among the public, who were unlikely to be familiar with the company) at a time of intense competition for funding, and to ward off environmental legislation. The approach has points of affinity with the idea of the active audience (see below and Web Research in focus 21.15), in that there is an emphasis on the reception of texts and as such the notion that there may be a plurality of interpretations of them.

Paradigmatic approaches to history and the critical call for the historic turn

In proposing a call for an historic turn in business studies Kieser's (1994) identified several barriers, including a growing preference in business studies for scientific methods (e.g., 'experiments or interviews', p. 609) and a stress on the general, rather than the unique, characteristics of organizations. Perhaps more critical were perceptions of history as 'myopic fact-collect[ing] without a method' (p. 612); involving 'a high degree of arbitrariness' (p. 617) and a tailoring of 'facts to fit a preconceived theory' (p. 617); a research strategy that is 'especially susceptible to ideologies' (p. 617); and associated with 'inductively generated theories' where causal mechanisms are either absent, implicit or used in an ad hoc manner' (p. 618).

Rejecting much of Kieser's case for history, Goldman (1994) made a number of critical points. He began by dismissing much of the claim for the importance or 'pragmatic' value of history, before exposing the weaknesses in the historical method itself. Beginning with a defence of scientific methods (of 'direct observation, interviewing, [and] survey research'), Goldman (1994, pp. 621–622) argues that such methods are useful 'modes of assessing the fit between concepts and empirical experience'. He then goes on to point out the theoretically underdeveloped state of organizational theory as an important reason for not being receptive to historical analysis. He argues that organizational scholars are limited by the time in which they exist, the requirements of scientific study to stay within the bounds of what is testable and or controllable, and not move too far beyond the immediate context in which behaviour is located, and the absence of 'mature organizational theory, agreed-upon propositions about how organizations work, and how organizations and organizational configurations relate to larger social contexts' (p. 621). Goldman (1994) then dismisses history as a method for enriching studies of organization, arguing that its various limitations serve to exacerbate rather than enhance understanding: 'without agreed-upon theory that transcends time and place, history becomes data, not explanation' (p. 621). Worse still historical accounts differ greatly in regard to 'variables' and research methodologies; 'history analysis cannot truly free [research] from ideology [because] history carries its own intellectual baggage' (p. 622); and historical data add more, not less, forms of bias that arise from 'those distortions that originate either from creators of the documents and artifacts we use from those persons who subsequently collect, catalog, or interpret them' (p. 622).

In defence of historical analysis, Kieser (1994) argues that on the issue of selective biases regarding historical facts, 'a selection cannot be avoided because the historical material in inexhaustible'. Furthermore, the selection 'as well as the interpretation of events is always in danger of reflecting the ideologies of the researcher' (p. 619). He answers several other critiques of historical method by problematizing each issue as mirroring the problems of organizational science. Kieser (1994, p. 618) contends that critiques of *inductivism* not only overlook 'the fact that all general propositions have been generated inductively [but also neglect] that it is not possible to clearly distinguish hypotheses that contain causal mechanisms from those that do not'. He dismisses charges that historians can select facts to fit a particular general model, arguing that in any research endeavour 'one can never be sure that the researcher is not leaving out important facts that contradict it. It is also very unlikely that any two researchers would select the same historical data and interpret these data in the same way in order to prove the model' (p. 617). On ideology, Keiser argues that beyond history organizational analyses are also 'susceptible to ideologies' (p. 617). The answer is not to dismiss the historical method but rather to minimize the problem through a 'critical examination of historical sources' (p. 619), concluding that 'theory building may be biased through the 'unsystematic nature of the sample' but, on the other hand, a theory-induced bias in selecting and interpreting historical source is minimized' (p. 619).

The Kieser-Goldman debate is interesting because it raises a number of questions not only about the importance of the reintegration of history into business studies but also the nature of historical analysis. Many of the issues and the underlying *positivist* nature of the debate were taken up in a new call for critical management and organizational methods of history by Booth and Rowlinson in 2006.

The Booth-Rowlinson 'Agenda'. The call for a more critical historic turn in management and organizational theory was made by way of an introduction to the launch of the journal *Management & Organizational History* in

2006. Introducing the new journal Booth and Rowlinson outline 'an agenda' not only for the need for the historic turn in business studies but also for 'more critical and ethical reflections' (p. 7). In the process their agenda serves to surface and summarize a number of paradigmatic differences that have marked the field over the past decade or so. Those differences are explored in relationship to the nature of the historic turn, historical methods and styles of writing, and philosophies of history and historical theorists.

The 'historic turn'. Drawing on Üsdiken and Kieser's (2004) notion of different positions on historical integration, Booth and Rowlinson (2006, p. 8) view their approach as *reorientationalist*, which 'involves a thoroughgoing critique of existing theories of organization for their ahistorical orientation' (p. 8). This stands in sharp contrast to a *supplementarist* position, which 'adheres to the view of organization theory as social scientistic, and merely adds history as another contextual variable, alongside other variables such as national cultures'. This approach can be seen in some of the history projects referred to above, where researchers view history as an otherwise important dimension of the scientific study of organizations (see for example Boothman, 2000*a*, 2000*b*; Gillies & Dickinson, 2000; Harvey, 2000; and Ogden and Driscoll 2000). It also stands in sharp contrast to the integrationist position, favoured by Üsdiken and Kieser, which 'seeks to enrich organization theory by developing links with the humanities, including history, literary theory and philosophy, without completely abandoning a social scientistic orientation' (p. 8).

Booth and Rowlinson develop their critical interrogation of organization theory in the argument that 'the approach to problems in business school social science is "universalist and presentist"' (p. 6). The former refers to the view that 'contemporary organization theory applies to organizational phenomena in all societies at all times', while the latter refers to research that is reported as if 'it occurred in a decontextualized extended present' (p. 6):

> Presentism contradicts universalism to the extent that the present is often assumed to be a period of unprecedented change, heralding the dawning of a new age. But this is usually done without proper consideration of possible historical precedents. It is largely a rhetorical device for privileging an unbounded, extended present .... (p. 6)

Universalism and presentism can be seen as important outcomes of a search in the social sciences for general and abstracted laws that, in the process 'cut itself off from history' (p. 6).

They go on to argue that calls 'for more historical awareness are often aligned with critical management studies, including claims that business schools have been cut off from humanistic thinking; that business school faculty have 'been allowed to escape from "any real sensitivity to the issue raised by the humanities, including history"', and that 'an "historical perspective" can "provide a critically reflective version of the good society"' (p. 7). Thus, they conclude, the historic turn should also involve 'more critical and ethical reflection' (p. 7).

Historical methods and styles of writing. Booth and Rowlinson (2006, p. 8) contend that beyond simply calling for the alignment of historical facts with organizational theory (the supplementary position), the 'historic turn in management and organization theory raises questions about methods and appropriate styles of writing for more historically oriented research'. They argue that much of what counts as historical analyses in business studies—whether by non-historians or historians (including business historians)—does not require the accompaniment of methodological justification: at its best 'the copious notes detailing the location of sources in the archives are usually seen as sufficient methodological justification in their own right' (p. 9). This can be compared with the requirements of 'social science research in general, and for qualitative researchers in particular [where] it is expected that there will be a detailed methodological justification of the research conducted' (p. 9). Thus, continue Booth and Rowlinson (2006, p. 9), 'we would therefore expect the historic turn to lead to greater reflection on the historical methods appropriate for studying organizations'.

Philosophies of history and historical theorists. Finally, at least for our purposes, Booth and Rowlinson (2006) draw attention to the different approaches to the study of history and the implications for business studies. They argue (2006, p. 10) that 'if there is to be methodological reflection and experimentation in historical writing, then this will involve further engagement with the philosophy of history and historical theorists such as Hayden White (1973, 1987), Michel Foucault (1970, 1972), Paul Ricoeur (1984), David Carr (1986), and Deirdre McCloskey (1994)'.

Three paradigms of organizational history

In an earlier account Rowlinson (2004b, p. 8) outlined three 'arguments for an historical perspective in organization studies [—] factual, narrative, and archaeo-genealogical'.

The factual approach

Can be seen as aligned with positivism in the argument that 'if organization studies were to take account of the facts revealed by history then a number of erroneous assumptions would be undermined' (p. 8). From this framework history is viewed as 'a repository of facts which, so long as historians properly interpret them, can conveniently confirm or refute preferred or non-preferred theoretical positions in organization studies' (p. 10). This approach can also be seen as aligned to the supplementary position on history and organization theory discussed above. Examples of the factual approach would include the work of Arnold and Brown (1986), Austin (1998, 2000a, 2000b), Baum et al. (2004), Delios and Ensign (2000), Jones 1992, Korkie and Turtle (1998), Sexty (2000, 2008), and Sharma and Steier (1990).

The narrative approach

So called because it focuses on the role of narrative in the social construction of historical accounts. Here the argument is that History is not so much the skillfully crafted recounting of real, or factual, events from the past so much as a well-crafted story about the past that is constructed by the historian through the careful use of narrative. As we have seen earlier, White (1973, 1985, 1987) exemplifies this type of work in his contention that 'all history is the study, not of past events that are gone for ever from perception, but rather of the "traces" of those events distilled into documents and monuments on one side, and the praxis of present social formations on the other. These "traces" are the raw materials of the historian's discourse, rather than the events themselves' (White, 1987, p. 102, cited in Rowlinson 2004b, p. 10). The work of White (1995) 'has shifted the emphasis away from seeing archival research as the historian's craft towards a view that it is the conventions and customs of writing that constitute the craft of history (Rowlinson, 2004b, p. 11). Nonetheless, his approach to History 'is informed by a programmatic, if ironic commitment to the return to narrative as one of its enabling presuppositions' (Rowlinson, 2004b, p. 11).

Beyond the work of White other examples of this kind of approach to history in business studies would include the work of Rowlinson (2004a, 2004b, 2006), Durepos (2009), Mills and Durepos (2010), and Novicevic, Harvey, Buckley, and Adams (2008). We would not include those studies that focus on narratives but do not question the factual or underlying realism of historical facts; seeing narratives as either expressing or misrepresenting historical facts (see for example Jones, 1992; Lee & Humphrey, 2006; McCollom, 1991; Roberts, 2006; Witkowski & Jones, 2008).

The archaeo-genealogical approach

Is derived from the work of Foucault and his various attempts to deconstruct the present through analyses of the past. In, what he called, his archaeological phase Foucault explored 'in language the sedimented evidence of the assumptions; the values; the common sense through which, for instance, a phenomenon such as madness could have one set of meanings in one era and a contradictory set of meanings in another' (Jacques, 2010, p. 305). In his later genealogical phase Foucault examined 'the conditions under which the different ways of interpreting and evaluating ourselves have come to exist. The purpose of the genealogical method is to analyze and excavate the taken-for-granted' assumptions that define the present (Poutanen & Kovalainen, 2010, p. 263). As Rostis (2010, p. 418) puts it, 'the problematization of the present is at the core of genealogy'. This process of problematization arises through a process of defamilarization of the taken for granted through a rejection of 'linear histories of knowledge that emerge from a single origin' (Rostis, 2010, p. 418). In effect it sets out to reframe 'the conduct of historical analysis to understand how it has transpired that the present has come to be accepted as inevitable or natural' (Rostis, 2010, p. 418).

In contrast to the traditional historian who presents historical events as 'linked together into a rational, linear progression from an origin toward the current order of things . . . the genealogist seeks to demonstrate that the present is not the product of an inevitable series of events' (Rostis, 2010, pp. 416–417). Arguably, genealogy differs from traditional histories in three significant ways. First, it 'does not portray the present as the inevitable outcome of a select series of past events. . . . [Second, it seeks] to understand how the present has come to be defined and understood in its current form' (Rostis, 2010, p. 416). Third, the genealogist departs from the traditional historian in her or his understanding of archival research. Foucault (1978), for example, argues that an 'archive' refers not to 'the mass of texts which have been collected at a given period, or chanced to have survived oblivion from this period' but rather to 'a set of rules which at a given period and for a definite society' structure the conditions in and through which knowledge is produced (quoted in McHoul & Grace, 2003, p. 30). Nonetheless, 'there is a point where the activity in *doing* archival research is remarkably similar in appearance, and that similarity is in the use and accessing of documents and other artifacts, which have been, in the traditional sense, archived . . . The difference lies in the treatment of the documents' (Mills & Helms Mills, 2011, in press). As McHoul and Grace (2003, p. 31, cited in Mills & Helms Mills, 2011, in press) explain, while much of Foucauldian or genealogical analysis involves the use of 'meticulous and detailed textual documentation, this documentation is not, in itself what Foucault means by "archive". The documentation and its arrangement by the historian only exists to reveal the archive: the conditions (the "set of rules") by which it is possible to "know" something at a specific historical point and by which this knowledge changes'.

Genealogical research has generated numerous studies in the field of business research but, as Rowlinson (2004*b*,

p. 13) contends, few of these accounts have involved any form of archival research (either in the narrow or broader sense of the word). Exceptions include Jacques's (1996) account of the trajectory of 'management knowledge from the 19th to 21st centuries'. It would also include the work of Cooke (Cooke, 1999; Cooke, 2006; Cooke et al., 2005), Dar (2008), McLaren et al. (2009), Hartt, Mills, Helms Mills, and Durepos (2009), Mills (2006), Mills and Helms Mills (2006), Prasad and Mire (2002), Ruef and Harness (2009), Storberg-Walker and Bierema (2008), and Taylor and Freer (2002).

 ## Towards an ANTi-History

More recently Durepos and Mills (Durepos, 2006; Durepos, 2009; Mills and Durepos, 2010) have attempted to fuse different theoretical insights on history and knowledge of the past to create an approach that 'sets out to simultaneously represent and destabilize selected past events with the ultimate aim of pluralizing history' (Mills & Durepos, 2010, p. 26). It is an approach that fuses together insights from the sociology of knowledge—particularly the work of Mannheim (1968) and Marx (1846, 1971), poststructuralist historiography—especially the work of Foucault (1972, 1973, 1979), and Jenkins (1994, 2003), the poststructuralist historiographic accounts of White (1973, 1985, 1987), and the actor network theory (ANT) accounts of Latour and colleagues (Law, 1994; Latour & Woolgar, 1986; Latour, 1987, 2005; Callon & Law, 1982). The aim is to 'develop a historiography that is capable of dealing with the past as "available" through innumerable traces whose construction lends itself to equally innumerable histories' (Mills & Durepos, 2010, p. 26). It is a method that 'encourages the development (or reassembling) of historical analyses, not simply to represent the past but also to reveal alternative readings (or histories) that surface that which is marginalized, hidden, suppressed' (p. 26). Thus, it is argued, that through this process 'histories are revealed as useful guides to human action at the same time that they are destabilized by an understanding that they are reassembled for current action rather than grounded in fact' (p. 26). Hence the term ANTi-History (ANT signifies a link to actor network theory) is designed to suggest that approaches to the past need to surface the value of 'learning from the past' for destabilizing the present while avoiding the traps of assuming that there is only one history or that history consists of concrete facts waiting to be uncovered (rather than constructed) by the historian. An outline of the method is provided in Research in focus 21.2.

Sources or 'traces' of the past for business studies

Historians seek out a number of 'traces' or sources to develop an understanding of a particular historical account. Those traces include a fairly heterogeneous set of sources, such as letters, memos, diaries, autobiographies, internal

---

21.2 Research in Focus

Sketching the method of ANTi-History*

In developing a new approach to the study of history Gabrielle Durepos (2009) outlines a series of steps that collectively inform an approach that she calls ANTi-History. Each step can also be seen as useful in its own right as a (postpositivist) method for studying history. ANTi-History is a method that:

1. *Focuses on the constitution of the past as an outcome of the socio-politics of actor networks.* Here, drawing on actor network theory (ANT), sociopolitics is understood as the engagement of actors in endless interest work, translation, and enrollment of other actors to enlist them into their cause. Actor networks are the outcome of successful sociopolitics, where the interests of a group of actors have become aligned and durable. Knowledge—of the present and of the past—is constituted in and through the socio-politics of actor networks. In studies of Pan American Airways Durepos et al. (Durepos, 2009; Durepos et al., 2008c) view histories of the airline not as more or less factual accounts of the real story but the outcomes of actor-networks. To that end, Durepos et al. set out to understand how the histories were constituted.

2. *Does not begin by assuming what it is that the researcher wishes to explain or imposing a plot.* The researcher problematizes the *a priori* by avoiding preconceptions that serve to order the traces of the past and impose a plot. Instead the researcher allows his or her self to be lead by actor-networks. This is based on the assumption that knowledge of the past is performed through an actor's effort to define and characterize it. Durepos et al.'s (2008a, 2008b, 2008c) study of Pan American Airways (Pan Am) did not begin with assumptions about the reasons, motives, or drives behind the development of Pan Am but rather treated explanations of events as the outcome of sociopolitics and the development of various actor networks.

3. *Maps the socio-past by following a series of socio-politics of actor-networks, to understand how they construct their past.* This stems from the view that the past is already gone and since 'nothing ever repeats itself exactly' (Jenkins, 2003, p. 23) the historian's task for constructing history is always one of (re)assembly. Durepos et al. (Durepos, 2009; Durepos et al., 2008c) used this approach to trace the development of a particular history of Pan American Airways by following the interactions of a series of actors to produce that history.

4. *Privileges the voice of the actors over that of the historian and privileges the empirical over the theoretical when (re)assembling the traces of the socio-past.* Following Marx, ANTi-History aspires to 'not explain practice from the idea but explains the formation of ideas from the material practice' (Marx, 1983, p. 182). Following Mannheim (1953, 1985), ANTi-History assumes that distinct ways of knowing the past by actor-networks grows out of existing social conditions in which the actor-network is a participant. As Latour (2005, p. 9) notes, 'the actors' objection to their social explanations

offer the best proof that those explanations are right'. Thus, in following the actor-networks that constitute a socio-past, the researcher who uses ANTi-History is encouraged to privilege the voice of the actors over that of her own. She lets the actor-networks speak louder than her own voice (which has been shaped by academic conventions that offer specific insight offer specific insight on her epistemological and methodological grounding). The researcher lets her empirical analysis be guided by the socio-political engagements or associations of actor-networks to understand them on their own terms.

5. *Views actor-networks as materially heterogeneous.* Drawing on the work of Latour (2006) and other actor-network theorists, it is assumed that the past is constituted of materially heterogeneous (non-human and humans) actor-networks. This is 'not simply about bringing "nature" back into the historical picture so much as attempting to decipher the interrelationship between human and non-human worlds' (Gunn, 2006, pp. 187–188). Law's (1994) study of actor-networks in a scientific laboratory, for example, explores the role of computers as material things that require human being to interact—through the technology—with other humans who, although not present, constructed the language and design of computer science. Thus, the ANTi-Historian seeks to understand the various roles of human and non-human actors in the constitution of an actor-network.

6. *History is viewed as an effect of the interest driven socio-politics of actor-networks.* Thus, the craft of history is understood through the socio-politics of actor-networks and suggests that the socio-past can be plural and political (Jenkins, 1991, 1995; Joyce, 2007). Networks where knowledge of the past is constructed are comprised of many interacting actors, including historians, her traces, the archive, documents, telephones, pencils, the computer, paper, ink, the archivist, academic books, popular books, newspapers, authors, academics, and academic conventions, etc. History

or knowledge of the past is an effect of the extreme alignment of these actor-networks. Thus, when the heterogeneous actors making up a network have become aligned in their interpretation and knowledge of the past, history is possible.

7. *Sees 'history' as a punctuated actor or a black box.* ANTi-History stresses that an interpretation of knowledge of the past or history can only be possible when all of the actors involved in its creation have aligned both their interests and their various interpretations of the past. All of the actors that constitute a history, of which a non-exhaustive list includes, traces, archives, historians, publishing houses, computers, the Internet, must not only be enrolled onto a network but must act in extreme alignment thus, as one actor. ANT theorists refer to this process as a punctuated actor or a 'black box' (Whitley, 1972). Thus, ANTi-History draws on ANT to suggest that history is a punctuated actor, which conceals the series of relations and socio-politics of actor-networks that has enabled its formation.

8. *Explores the conditions for the favourable dispersion of a 'punctuated history'.* It is suggested that histories or knowledge of the past disperse and gain legitimacy to the degree that their content is plausible, accepted, and, shared by a collective. Drawing on ANT, ANTi-History seeks to understand the conditions that allow for the dispersion and absorption of a 'history' through the socio-politics of actor-networks.

9. *Acknowledge and expose the potential instrumentality of historical accounts.* As has been suggested, ANTi-History assumes that the process of constructing history, its punctuation as well as its dispersion can be understood through the interest driven socio-politics of actor-networks. Since the socio-politics of actor-networks are understood as enacted with the goal of exerting influence, are purposive, as well as exerted towards achieving a desired use or end, and 'history as a punctuated actor' is understood as an effect of actor-networks, then embedded in ANTi-History is the

assumption that 'history' is purposive and potentially instrumental. By tracing the socio-politics of the actor-networks involved in the construction of history, we can ask questions such as which actors were involved in the history's creation, on whose terms was the history created, who benefits, and, who is marginalized from a particular interpretation of history? By following the socio-politics of actor-networks, the ANTi-History researcher can expose the interests the actor-networks that were involved in the construction of a history.

10. *Makes transparent the socio-political conditions of the creation of history.* This means that histories must render transparent the socio-politics of the actor-networks that were involved in the construction of the history. As has been suggested, the punctuation of a history leads to the concealment of the socio-politics and the series of relations that allowed for the emergence of the history and its punctuation. Thus, a history grows out of the so-cio-politics of an actor-network but then goes on to hide those socio-politics. ANTi-History suggests that those socio-politics and techniques of power must be written into the history to show the history as a socially constructed, ordered, political, and, situated (ideological, spatial, temporal) product.

Durepos ends with a summary of implications for the researcher. These include that the researcher who uses ANTi-History (1) is understood as positioned and situated spatially, temporally, and ideologically; (2) is understood as a punctuated actor-network; (3) is engaged in constructing histories that are effects of the interplay of the situated researcher and her traces; (4) (re)assembles history reflexively; and (5) is enrolled by the actor-network associated with the history for which she is engaged in (re)assembling, and she conducts interest work with the hope of enrolling alternative actors onto the actor-network she is (re)assembling.

*The title and much of the text is taken from Durepos (2009).

---

reports, newspapers, magazines, and photographs. By and large these documents have not been produced at the request of a business researcher—instead, they 'out there' waiting to be assembled and analyzed. Not that it is an easy process. It is often time consuming to track down and access the sources.

The search for documents relevant to historical and other research can often be a frustrating and highly protracted process. Moreover, as we saw above, considerable interpretative skill is required to ascertain the meaning of the materials that have been uncovered.

Documents have already been encountered in this book, albeit in a variety of contexts or guises. For example, the kinds of source upon which content analysis is often carried out are documents, such as newspaper articles. However, the emphasis in this chapter will be upon the use of documents in historical research. In discussing the different kinds of documents used in the social sciences generally, John Scott (1990) has usefully distinguished between **personal documents** and official documents, and has further classified the latter in terms of private as opposed to state documents. These distinctions will be employed in much of the discussion that follows. A further set of important distinctions made by Scott relate to the criteria for assessing the quality of documents. He suggests (1990, p. 6) four criteria:

- Authenticity. Is the evidence genuine and of unquestionable origin?
- Credibility. Is the evidence free from error and distortion?
- Representativeness. Is the evidence typical of its kind, and, if not, is the extent of its untypicality known?
- Meaning. Is the evidence clear and comprehensible?

This is an extremely rigorous set of criteria against which documents might be gauged, and frequent reference to them will be made in the following discussion. The way that

Student Experience

Judging historical sources

Cindy came across the problem of author credibility when undertaking a research topic for her major in History at Mount Saint Vincent University. The program focused on the War of 1812 and Cindy was drawn to a study of Laura Secord: 'I thought it would be an interesting topic because she [was] a female historical figure which is interesting'. However, Cindy initially found that it 'was very difficult to find information [because] there wasn't that much documentation about [Secord] specifically. [There] really wasn't that much information'. She started off 'going to the libraries' and accessing every book she could find on Laura Secord. When she exhausted that important source of information she then turned to the Internet to find out more: '[In] order to dig down, to find out what you really need, you need to look a little bit further, and sometimes it can be overwhelming'. Drawing on an earlier course on the methods of history, Cindy was aware that there can be problems with sources, and this can be particularly the case with the Internet: '[You] have to look at [the] credibility of all the sources to make sure that they're

useable and they're appropriate for what your thesis is going to determine so yeah, I think that that's a challenge—sometimes you think you have too much and you really have to narrow down what exactly [you are] going to . . . what exactly am [you are] proving and what can [you] use to prove that?' To address the issue of credibility Cindy questioned such things as the qualifications the authors whose sources she referenced: 'anybody can go on . . . the Internet and write a document about Laura Secord or about anything for that matter so I think that you have to find out what credentials the author has, who the publisher is of the [source], and also find out if [they have been peer reviewed]'. Interestingly enough because of the questionable credibility of some of the sources (i.e., as to their historical 'accuracy'), Cindy ended up changing her topic to a study of the way that Laura Second had been depicted in history; using such things as children's story books and 'the Canadian Heritage Advertisements on Canadian television' to analyze how certain people like Secord become written about as historic figures.

---

historian's 'read' and adapt this criteria will vary across different approaches (clarity of 'meaning', for example, will mean different things to a factual compared to narrative historian), but they are nonetheless useful as broad guidelines.

Personal documents
Diaries, letters, and autobiographies

Diaries and letters kept for reasons other than research purposes tend to be used extensively by historians but less by those studying the past in business studies.

However, there is some scope for them to be used in the study of management, as Research in focus 21.3 illustrates. In this example, Grey's (1996) analysis of managerialism is based on the work of Simone Weil. In addition to his analysis of Weil's academic writings, Grey draws on Weil's published diaries, which document her experiences as a factory worker, arguing that these experiences were significant in informing her view of management as a form of oppression.

Another example of the use of personal documents in historical organizational research is given in Research

21.3   Research in Focus

The diary of a French factory worker

The diaries and letters of Simone Weil (1909–43), a French philosopher and social-political writer, are used by Grey (1996) to gain insight into her conceptualization of management as a form of oppression. Grey suggests that Weil's views about management derive in part from her experiences as a factory worker. Quoting from her Factory Journal (Weil 1987), in which she records her experiences of working at the Alsthom electrical plant in Paris, a metal-working factory, and at Renault, Grey shows how these experiences shaped her view that mechanized work was degrading to the individual. He further argues that 'Weil's experience of factory work showed her that the condition of oppression was in part an outcome of the ways in which workers themselves were actors in the reproduction of their own servility' (1996, p. 604). In other words, it was her view that managerial oppression relies on employees being willing to submit themselves to managerial control and being active in maintaining and reinforcing this oppression.

in focus 21.4. In this study, Bloor (2002) analyzed oral history tapes and transcripts from interviews carried out with Welsh miners in the 1970s. As Bloor comments, the main interest of these documents for the researcher 'lies in the fact that they describe events from the partisan standpoint of lived experience. They are thus a record of a local culture and of situated communal understandings of events' (2002, p. 93). Personal documents can also be used to trace the history of an organization through the letters and diaries of its founders and other members of the organization (Plowman, 2010). For example, the company archives of the chocolate manufacturer Cadbury are held at the Birmingham, UK, factory. The archives include diaries and letters documenting more than 100 years of history of the family firm (Rowlinson, 2002; Dellheim, 1987). Many of these documents are held in private collections, making research access potentially difficult. However, the emergence of alternative forms of communication has undoubtedly limited the use of letters as a source of data and it is likely that the emergence of email will mean that the role of letters as a potential source of documentary data will continue to decline.

Whereas letters are a form of communication with other people, diarists invariably write for themselves. However, when they are written for wider consumption, diaries are difficult to distinguish from another kind of personal document—the autobiography. Like letters and diaries, autobiographies can be written at the behest of the researcher, particularly in connection with life history studies (see Key concept 14.1 for a full explanation of the **life history method**). However, commercially published autobiographical sources can also be used for research purposes. For example, Dye et al. (2005) found Maslow's diaries an important source for assessing both the trajectory of his thinking in context and over time. In this case, Maslow's diaries were likely not written for publication but were published in their existing raw form sometime following his death (see Lowry, 1979a, 1979b).

However, the widespread distinction between biographies and autobiographies can sometimes break down. Walt Disney provides a case in point. As Bryman (1995) has shown, Disney provided, in short articles he authored and in articles written by others, many snippets about his life. The first biography of Disney, written by his daughter, Diane Disney Miller (1956), would almost certainly have been fed information by its subject. Moreover, several writers have noted the 'sameness' about subsequent biographies. This feature can be attributed to the tight control by the Disney Archive, which is itself controlled by the Walt Disney Corporation. It is from the primary materials of this archive (letters, notes of meetings, and

21.4 # Research in Focus

Using oral histories in a historical study of safety risks in mining

In a study of industrial injury and safety threats in the coal-mining industry, Bloor (2002) used the oral history archive in the South Wales Miners' Library, focusing on 176 taped oral history interviews conducted in 1973–4 (see Key concept 18.4 for a definition of oral history interviews). He explains, 'the tapes describe experiences of pit and community going back before the First World War, and in some cases going back to the end of the 19th century' (Bloor, 2002, p. 92). Bloor analyzed the transcripts and untranscribed tapes for references to 'accidents' and 'disasters', photocopying relevant sections of the

transcripts and transcribing relevant sections of the untranscribed tapes. He was interested in the way that miners acted as enforcers of pit safety regulations and the role of the workforce's representatives, 'workmen inspectors', in reducing safety threats in pits between 1900 and 1947. Bloor argues that these documents have relevance for health and safety at work today by showing that collective health behaviour is driven by class struggle against management and government, whom the workers did not trust to ensure their own safety.

so on) that biographies would be fashioned. As a result, while Walt Disney never wrote an autobiography in the conventional meaning of the term, his hand and subsequently that of the company can be seen in the biographies that have been written.

When we evaluate personal documents, the *authenticity* criterion is clearly of considerable importance. Is the purported author of the letter or diary the real author? In the case of autobiographies, this has become a growing problem in recent years as a result of the increasing use of 'ghost' writers by the famous, but also in the development of 'official' accounts of the role of selected people in the founding of a company. Durepos and colleagues (Durepos et al., 2008b; Durepos & Mills, 2009; Durepos et al., 2008c), for example, have detailed the problems of establishing who was the 'founder' of Pan American Airlines and what role he played in subsequent developments. While official accounts and histories of Pan American talk specifically about Juan Trippe and his 'pioneering role' (see, for example, Bender & Altschul, 1982; Daley, 1980; Josephson, 1944) there is some conflicting evidence in the archives and elsewhere, suggesting that Hap Arnold and a group of army officers played a key role in the establishment of the airline (Durepos & Mills, 2009).

The same is potentially true of other documents. Turning to the issue of *credibility*, John Scott (1990) observes that there are at least two major concerns with respect to personal documents: the factual accuracy of reports, and whether or not they report the true feelings of the writer. Scott recommends a strategy of healthy skepticism regarding the sincerity with which the writer reports his or her true feelings. Famous business people such as Richard Branson and Conrad Black are likely to be fully aware that their letters or diaries will be of considerable interest to others and may, therefore, have one eye firmly fixed on the degree to which they really reveal themselves in their writings, or alternatively ensure that they convey a 'front' that they want to project. Authorized biographies and autobiographies have to be treated with similar caution, since they can frequently be exercises in reputation building.

Representativeness is an additional concern for these materials. Surviving historical documents are relatively few in number and they have been preserved only in relation to the most influential of companies, such as Cadbury, British Airways, Unilever, Air Canada, or the Ford Foundation. Therefore, such historical documents are likely to be biased in terms of the organizations they represent. A further problem is the selective survival of documents like letters. Why do any survive at all and what proportion are damaged, lost, or thrown away? The question of *meaning* is often rendered problematic by such things as damage to letters and diaries, and the use by authors of abbreviations or codes that are difficult to decipher.

Visual objects

Organizations are significant producers of visual objects, including photographic, video, and artwork images. These tend to constitute an important part of an organization's image and identity, and they are often publicly accessible and widely disseminated, for example through websites, advertising, or newspaper reports. There is thus considerable potential for organizational researchers to incorporate visual documentary methods into their data collection process. In recent years there has been more interest in business and management research in the analysis of visual objects. One of the main types of visual objects that can be used either as a main or a supplementary data source alongside written or spoken words are photographs. An example of the analysis of photographs that are naturally occurring (i.e., produced for a specific organizational purpose other than business research) can be seen in research by Dougherty and Kunda (1990); in this study, photographs found in company annual reports formed the basis of analysis (see Research in focus 21.5). See also Tinker and Neimark's (1987) study of the annual reports of General Motors (GM) over time. They undertook a detailed analysis of the use of photographs (as well as text) in GM's annual reports to see how they portrayed men and women, and black and white people. What they found was a portrait of business life that was overwhelmingly white and masculine; favoring certain forms of masculinity (business leadership, professionalism, etc.); associating certain qualities of leadership and professionalism with whiteness and masculinity; and, in the process, marginalizing other qualities (e.g., caring) and characteristics of being non-white and feminine.

Marketing and advertising research also makes use of photographs as a source of data. Peñaloza (2000) looked at the way that the cultural meaning of the American West was produced through the activities of a cattle trade show. She suggests that the rich imagery of the American West, reflected by such examples as Marlboro cigarettes, Wrangler jeans, and Jeep Cherokees, is represented through the trade show where animals are bought and sold, but also where the culture of the American West is enacted and celebrated. In addition to participant observation and in-depth interviewing, her ethnographic study incorporated 550 photographs taken at the shows over a six-year period. These were mainly photographs of the events—including cattle sales, breed shows, and rodeos. As a visible record of people and activities, the photographs helped Peñaloza to build up a profile of the race/ethnicity and sex of attendees at particular events and of the type of activities that were involved in the show.

However, the photograph must not be taken at its face value when used as a research source; it is also necessary to have considerable additional knowledge of the social context to probe beneath the surface. Glossy photographs of happy, smiling employees in corporate brochures or newsletters, for example, might suggest that there is a gap between the photographic image of the company and the underlying reality as experienced at a day-to-day level. Scott sees the issue of *representativeness* as a particular problem for the analyst of photographs. As he suggests, the photographs that survive the passage of time—for example, in archives—are very unlikely to be representative. They are likely to have been subject to all sorts of hazards, such as damage and selective retention. Sensitivity to what is not photographed can reveal the 'mentality' of the person(s) behind the camera. What is clear is that the question of representativeness is much more fundamental than the issue of what survives, because it points to the way in which the selective survival of photographs may be constitutive of a reality that business owners and managers seek to fashion. As an example, in his study of British Airway Mills (1995, 1996) found that photographs in company materials (e.g., internal newsletters, annual reports, etc.) were interesting not only for what they included but what they did not include. Throughout the first 20 years of

21.5 **Research in Focus**

Using photographs to capture organizational beliefs about customers

In seeking to develop a longitudinal and comparative research design for the study of organizational beliefs about customers, Dougherty and Kunda (1990) chose to focus on company annual reports because they were comparable across organizations and could be studied over time, thereby incorporating a longitudinal element into the study. They looked in particular at the photographs of customers found in the reports, which revealed 'aspects of an organization's theory of its customers in a nonverbalized yet substantive way' (1990, p. 187). The study was limited to firms in the computer equipment manufacturing sector and annual reports from the five largest of these—IBM, Burroughs, Digital (DEC), Data General (DG), and Honeywell. Dougherty and Kunda analyzed 425 photographs from the annual reports of these companies between 1975 and 1984. A major task for the researchers was to develop categories for the analysis of the data. After several weeks of scrutiny and discussion they decided on two broad descriptive dimensions. These related to the nature of

1. *the customer organization*—how many people are shown in the photograph, what are they like, e.g., sex, hierarchical position, what tasks are they undertaking?
2. *the relationship with customers*—where and how does the product fit into the customer's activities?

The photographs were categorized according to these dimensions to reveal the unique views of customers held across the firms. For example, in relation to the task theme, which conveys what the organization believes their customers do, the photographs illustrate how hospital, bank, and aircraft manufacturing customers are viewed differently by the five firms.

For example, in relation to the hospital customer, Dougherty and Kunda illustrate how DEC's photographs emphasize the importance of the task and its social contribution, combined with an emphasis on the high degree of technological sophistication that is involved. A typical image is therefore of a tense, dramatic moment in a hospital operating room. In contrast, both IBM and Burroughs use photographs to portray the more ordinary, repetitive aspects of hospital work; showing a relaxed, simple check-up in the case of IBM, and featuring information processing in the image portrayed by Burroughs. People are thus 'adjuncts to the task of information processing; data going into or coming out of the equipment dominate the scene' (1990, p. 193).

Moreover, Dougherty and Kunda show how many of these perceptions of customers remained consistent over the 10-year period, despite changes in users of computing products. They suggest that beliefs about customers are significant because they can affect an organization's ability to adapt to its environment. However, perhaps the more significant contribution made by this study lies in its methods; as the authors themselves acknowledge: 'We hope our findings at least suggest that much can be learned from the contrast of seemingly innocent photographs and the self conscious tales they tell' (1990, p. 204).

the airline's operation there were very few pictures of female employees but numerous pictures of male employees. In the immediate post-World War II era, there was a rapid increase in the use of photographs of female employees but, in contrast to those of male employees, they were largely decorative (i.e., focused on female beauty and appearance).

Public documents

The government is the source of a great deal of information of potential significance for business researchers. It produces a large amount of statistical information, some of which was touched on in Chapter 19. In addition to such quantitative data, the government is the source of a lot of textual material of potential interest, such as Acts of Parliament and official reports.

An interesting use of official documents is Turner's (1994) employment of the reports of public inquiries into three disasters, one of which—the fire at the Summerland Leisure Centre in Douglas on the Isle of Man, in 1973—is a particular emphasis in his discussion. The report was published in 1974. Turner was primarily interested in the preconditions of the fire—the factors that were deemed by the inquiry to have led to the fire itself and to the way in which the handling of the incident produced such disastrous consequences (50 deaths). In his initial analysis, which was based on a grounded theory approach, Turner aimed to produce a theoretical account of the fire's preconditions. Turner describes the process for this and the other two public inquiry reports he examined as one of slowly going through the details of the report. He describes the process as follows:

> I asked, for each paragraph, what names or 'labels for ideas' I needed in order to identify those elements, events or notions which were of interest to me in my broad and initially very unfocused concern to develop a theory of disaster preconditions. I then recorded each name or concept label on the top of a 5 inch by 8 inch card, together with a note of the source paragraph, and added further paragraph references to the card as I encountered additional instances of the concept identified. (1994, p. 198)

He ended up with 182 of these cards, which provided the raw materials for building his theoretical model. Similar sources were employed by Weick (1990) in his study of the Tenerife plane crash in 1977, in that he used an official report of the Spanish Ministry of Transport and Communication and a further report by the United States-based Airline Pilots Association.

A further example of this kind of study is provided by Gephart (1993), who based his analysis on naturally occurring retrospective and archival qualitative data, including public inquiry transcripts and proceedings, newspaper reports, and corporate and government documents (see Research in focus 21.5). This type of analysis, which uses publicly available data to analyze critical events or disasters, has been referred to as 'organizational post mortem' research (Orton, 1997), and there are an increasing number of research studies in business and management that use this approach. Other examples include Vaughan's (1990) analysis of the space shuttle *Challenger* tragedy in 1986 and Orton's (1997) study of three critical events in the history of the American intelligence community. In the former, Vaughan used documents gathered by the Presidential Commission and reports and transcripts that related to the disaster; she also interviewed journalists and people responsible for regulating safety at NASA. Orton, instead, relied on organizational and presidential libraries, in particular the Ford Library, which contained over fourteen million original documents from the Ford Administration. Familiarizing oneself with these kinds of research materials can be an extremely time-consuming activity, mainly because of the vastness and detail of documents associated with official events and inquiries, and this needs to be taken into account when planning to use such materials as a potential source of data.

In terms of John Scott's (1990) four criteria, such materials can certainly be seen as authentic and as having meaning (in the sense of being clear and comprehensible to the researcher), but the two other standards require somewhat greater consideration. The question of credibility raises the issue of whether or not the documentary source is biased. In other words, such documents can be interesting precisely because of the biases they reveal. Equally, this point suggests that caution is necessary in attempting to treat them as depictions of reality. The issue of representativeness is complicated in that materials like these are in a sense unique and it is precisely their official or quasi-official character that makes them interesting in their own right. There is also, of course, the question of whether or not the case itself is representative, but in the context of qualitative research this is not a meaningful question, because no case can be representative in a statistical sense. The issue is one of establishing a cogent theoretical account and possibly examining that account in other contexts. Turner (1994), in fact, examined three disasters and noted many common factors that were associated with behaviour in crisis situations.

Research in Focus

Using public documents to analyze an organizational disaster

Gephart (1993) employed what he describes as a 'textual approach', using a variety of retrospective archival material in a way that treats researchers' observations and written documents as 'texts'. Two kinds of data were collected:

1. Naturally occurring retrospective and archival qualitative data, including public inquiry **transcripts** and proceedings, newspaper reports, and corporate and government documents.
2. Self-generated texts, including field notes describing inquiry events.

These texts were analyzed in order to trace the life history of the focal event—a pipeline disaster—from the perspectives of a range of participants. The study sought to address the following research questions in the public inquiry context:

- What concepts and terms, or vocabularies, are used by organizational members in sensemaking about disasters?
- How do people use risk and blame concepts in disaster sensemaking?
- How are **sensemaking** practices used in the interpretation of disasters?
- What role do collective and individual interpretative schemes play in disaster sensemaking?

The pipeline accident occurred in 1985 on the Western Pipe Lines system in Canada. A fireball erupted during attempts to control a leak of natural gas liquids and two employees of the company died of burns. There followed a public inquiry in which the federal government energy board took evidence about the causes and consequences of the disaster. The public inquiry provided Gephart with a focus for his investigation through the series of texts that attempted to make sense of the disaster and tried publicly to attribute responsibility and blame.

Gephart attended the public inquiry throughout, informally interviewing managers, lawyers, and safety managers who were also attending the inquiry. This ethnographic aspect of his data collection resulted in 500 pages of field notes. These were combined with the other, naturally occurring, data used in the study, such as the official proceedings of the inquiry, and used to compile two electronically held databases:

1. A word processor database containing all the information from the transcripts, company documents, field notes, newspaper articles, and official report.
2. A textual database from the entire text of the inquiry proceedings.

Analysis, using a computer-based text retrieval program, focused on creating 'textual exhibits' 'that tell the story of the disaster and the inquiry using actual segments of text'; this enabled Gephart in his analysis to 'remain close to the raw data' and to illustrate its richness (1993, p. 1483). A set of key words was then developed to reflect the way that participants saw concepts of risk, blame, and responsibility.

It was then possible to retrieve 'every occurrence of the key words in the data' using the textual analysis software and to show these frequencies speaker by speaker. Gephart claims that the textual approach offers a way of uncovering practices and processes that generate and sustain organizational interpretations of events. The use of archival materials enables the longitudinal study of events that are in this case complemented by the collection of primary, ethnographic data.

Organizational documents

This is a very heterogeneous group of sources that is of particular importance to the business and management researcher, not least because of the vast quantity of documentary information that is available within most organizations. Some of these documents are in the public domain, such as annual reports, mission statements, reports to shareholders, transcripts of chief executives' speeches, press releases, advertisements, and public relations material in printed form and on the Internet. Other documents are not (or may not be) in the public domain, such as company newsletters, organizational charts, external consultancy reports, minutes of meetings, memos, internal and external correspondence, manuals for new recruits, policy statements, company regulations, and so on. Such materials can provide the researcher with valuable background information about the company. They are, therefore, often used by organizational ethnographers and historians as part of their investigations. Similarly, in case-study research, documents can be used to build up a description of the organization and its history. Because documents can offer at least partial insights into past managerial decisions and actions, they can also be useful in building up a 'timeline', particularly in processual studies of organizational change (see Chapter 6).

However, the difficulty of gaining access to some organizations means that some researchers have to rely on public domain documents alone. Even if the researcher is an insider who has gained access to an organization, it may well be that certain documents that are not in the public domain will not be available to him or her. For his study of ICI, Pettigrew (see Web Research in focus 4.17) was allowed access to company archives, so that, in addition to interviewing, he was allowed to examine 'materials on company strategy and personnel policy, documents relating to the birth and development of various company OD (organizational development) groups, files documenting the natural history of key organizational changes, and information on the recruitment and training of internal OD consultants, and the use made of external OD consultants' (1985, p. 41). Such information can be very important for

researchers conducting case studies of organizations using such methods as participant observation or (as in Pettigrew's case) **qualitative interviews**. Other writers have relied more or less exclusively on documents. For example, in Turner's (1994) study of large-scale disasters, his analysis relied entirely on the detailed accounts of action provided by the public inquiry records and these formed the basis for his own written notes, which constituted his data documents.

Such documents need to be evaluated using Scott's four criteria. As with the materials considered in the previous section, documents deriving from private sources like companies are likely to be authentic and meaningful, in the sense of being clear and comprehensible to the researcher, though this is not to suggest that the analyst of documents should be complacent. Issues of credibility and representativeness are likely to exercise the analyst of documents somewhat more. For instance, organizational documents that are in the public domain, such as company annual reports, may not be an accurate representation of how different organizational actors perceive the situations in which they are involved.

People who write organizational documents, such as managers, are likely to have a particular point of view that they want to get across. An interesting illustration of this simple observation is provided by a study of company documentation by Forster (1994). In the course of a study of career development issues in a major British retail company (referred to as TC), Forster carried out an extensive analysis of company documentation relating primarily to HRM issues, as well as **interviews** and a **questionnaire** survey. Because he was able to interview many of the authors of the documents about what they had written, 'both the accuracy of the documents and their authorship could be validated by the individuals who had produced them' (1994, p. 155). In other words, the authenticity of the documents was confirmed and it would seem that credibility was verified as well. However, Forster also tells us that the documents showed up divergent interpretations among different groupings of key events and processes.

One of the clearest themes to emerge was the apparently incompatible interpretations of the same events and processes among the three subgroups within the company—senior executives, HQ personnel staff and regional personnel managers. . . . These documents were not produced deliberately to distort or obscure events or processes being described, but their effect was to do precisely this (1994, p. 160).

In other words, members of the different groupings expressed through the documents certain perspectives that reflected their positions in the organization. Consequently, although authors of the documents could confirm the content of those documents, the latter could not be regarded as 'free from error and distortion', as John Scott puts it. Therefore, documents cannot be regarded as providing objective accounts of a state of affairs. They have to be interrogated and examined in the context of other sources of data. As Forster's case suggests, the different stances that are taken up by the authors of documents can be used as a platform for developing insights into the processes and factors that lie behind divergence. In this instance, the documents are interesting in bringing out the role and significance of subcultures within the organization.

Issues of representativeness are likely to loom large in most contexts of this kind. Did Forster have access to a totally comprehensive set of documents? It could be that some had been destroyed or that he was not allowed access to certain documents that were regarded as sensitive. Finally gaining access to confidential or potentially sensitive documents within an organization, such as personnel files, as Dalton (1959) did (see Chapter 17), raises particular ethical issues, which have been discussed in Chapter 8.

 ## Mass media outputs

Newspapers, magazines, television program, films, and other mass media are potential sources for historical analysis in business and management study. Of course, we have encountered these kinds of source before when exploring content analysis in Chapter 18. An example is a study by Chen and Meindl (1991) that analyzed articles in the popular press about Donald Burr, an entrepreneur who in 1980 started the low-cost American airline, People Express. The study relied exclusively on articles

about Burr that were published in the popular press. Typically, such analysis entails searching for themes in the sources that are examined. Chen and Meindl (1991) focused on the journalists' descriptions of Burr (i.e., the writers rather than readers of the text) and screened each article sentence by sentence for words, phrases, or clauses that metaphorically described Burr's personality, his behaviours, or his impact. They had a number of (student) respondents read the various texts and develop descriptions of Burr. The findings demonstrated the influence of the business press in constructing particular images of organizational leaders as the respondents consistently reproduced similar images of Burr that were dominant throughout the journal articles.

Authenticity issues are sometimes difficult to ascertain in the case of mass media outputs. While the outputs can usually be deemed to be genuine, the authorship of articles is often unclear (for example, editorials, some magazine articles), so that it is difficult to know if the account can be relied upon as being written by someone in a position to provide an accurate version.

Credibility is also frequently an issue, but in fact it is often the uncovering of error or distortion that is the objective of the analysis. For example, Jackson and Carter (1998) have explored the constitution of management gurus through the analysis of a BBC management video featuring Frederick Herzberg giving a live lecture to an audience of UK managers on his Motivation-Hygiene theory. They compare this video with an earlier transmission of the lecture, which was shown on normal television in 1973, under the title 'Jumping for the Jelly Beans'.

Comparison of the two versions reveals a number of differences between them; notably, in the video version a section subtitled 'KITA' (Herzberg's acronym for 'Kick in the Arse'), containing some offensive references including a joke about rape, has been edited out of the lecture.

Jackson and Carter suggest that the reason for this careful editing relates to the need to maintain Herzberg's credibility as a management guru, ensuring that his image remains intact despite the fact that the editing distorts the presentation of his ideas.

Representativeness is rarely an issue for analyses of newspaper or magazine articles, since the corpus from which a sample has been drawn is usually ascertainable, especially when a wide range of newspapers is employed.

Finally, the evidence is usually clear and comprehensible but may require considerable awareness of contextual factors relating to the organization or company, such as information about share prices, movements of key personnel, and merger speculation.

Virtual outputs

There is one final type of document that ought to be mentioned—the documents that appear on the Internet. This is an area that is rapidly growing among business researchers because of the vastness of the Internet and its growing accessibility, which make it a likely source of documents for historical analysis. Coupland's (2005) analysis of the websites of four multinational oil producing and refining organizations (see Web Research in focus 20.8) provides one example involving the analysis of virtual documents. Similarly, Orlikowski and Yates (1994) analyzed archived email messages relating to the development of a common computing language over a two-year time period (see Web Research in focus 20.6).

There is clearly huge potential with the Internet as a source of documents, but John Scott's criteria need to be kept in mind. First, authenticity: anyone could set up a website, so that information and advice may be given by someone who is not an authority. Secondly, credibility: we need to be aware of possible distortions. For example, if we were studying advice about the purchase of shares, it is known that websites have been set up encouraging people to buy or sell particular stocks held by the website authors, so that the prices of stocks can be manipulated. Thirdly, given the constant flux of the Internet, it is doubtful that we could ever know how representative websites on a certain topic are. An important consideration related to this issue stems from the dynamic nature of the content of websites that may be updated on a weekly or even daily basis. It is particularly important, therefore, not only to record the date on which a website was consulted, but also to print out the relevant content in case it changes. Indeed, these changes may be important to the analysis; for example, Coupland's (2005) study monitored oil company

websites for discourses of corporate social responsibility over a six-month period, noting any major changes in the discourse in this time period. Finally, websites are notorious for a kind of webspeak, so that it may be difficult to comprehend what is being said without considerable insider knowledge. As the use of computers and in particular the Internet as a source of data is undoubtedly increasing, we will be returning to these issues and discussing them further in Chapter 22.

The world as text

There is one word that we have done our best to avoid using in the chapter so far—**text**. The word 'text' is frequently employed as a synonym for a term like 'written document'. We have clearly strayed from this association, in that photographs and films have been touched upon. But, in relatively recent times, the word 'text' has been applied to an increasingly wide range of phenomena, so that theme parks, landscapes, heritage attractions, technologies, and a wide range of other objects are treated as texts out of which a 'reading' can be fashioned (e.g., Grint & Woolgar, 1997). Thus, in Barthes's (1972) influential collection of essays, objects as varied as wrestling matches, Citroën cars, and strip tease acts are submitted to readings. In a sense, therefore, just about everything can be treated as a text and perhaps as a document. Research in focus 21.6 provides an example of textual analysis in management and business. In this study Gephart (1993) treats both the written documents and his own ethnographic field notes as texts, analyzing them both using the same methods. The aim using this approach is 'to account for how a given text is made meaningful to readers', seeking 'to uncover the general conventions, interests and cultural practices' (1993, p. 1468) that enable meaning to be created. This approach is based on two assumptions: first, that the texts have the interpretations of their creators embedded in them and, second, that a text acquires meaning through 'its embeddedness in a multiplicity of discourses and texts' (1993, p. 1469). Gephart thus seeks to interpret the meaning of texts in relation to events, both of which constitute aspects of culture.

Readers and audiences—active or passive?

A further important issue about texts and their nature is whether or not audiences/readers are active interpreters of what they see or hear. Do they passively derive the meanings that authors or designers infuse into their texts, or do they resist those meanings and arrive at resistant readings, or do they arrive at a middle point that incorporates both passive and active elements? Much research on this issue suggests that audiences frequently come up with alternative readings to those that were intended by authors or designers, as the example given in Web Research in focus 21.15 illustrates. Although the idea of the 'active audience' has not gone unchallenged (e.g., McGuigan, 1992), the stream of research has been very influential and has placed a question mark over the readings of texts by social scientists. This means that we have to be cautious in concluding that the interpretations offered by social scientists of texts are going to be the same as those of another social scientist, or as those of the readers or audiences of these outputs. The business researcher is always providing his or her own 'spin' on the texts that are analyzed. The same is true of all social science data: the conclusions you derive from historical analysis (or other forms of analysis) are always going to be a reflection of your own personal interpretation. However, the main point being made for the present is that caution is required when reading writers' renditions of texts of all kinds.

Key points

- In North America management and organization theory have moved a considerable way from studies of history and the past since World War Two.

- Since the early 1990s there have been increasing calls for an historic turn—or 'reintegration' of history—in management and organization studies.

- Over the past two decades there has been an increasing number of studies involving historical analysis, including various studies of organizational culture, institutionalization, discursive fields, population ecology, labour processes, actor networks, and path dependency.

- Recent studies of the past/history in business studies have included longitudinal study, critical hermeneutics, critical discourse analysis, evolutionary analysis, tracking, narrative analysis, and various approaches to history.

- Three major positions on the historic turn have been identified: *supplementarist*, *integrationist*, and *reorientationalist*. While the integrationist position characterized the initial call for an historic turn the reorientationalist position characterized a newer call for a critical historical turn.

- Three paradigmatic approaches to history in business studies have also been identified: *factual*, *narrative*, and **archaeo-genealogical**.

- The reorientationalist call for an historic turn in business studies includes a critique of presentism and universalism; and an alignment with critical management studies that includes critical reflections on ethics, historical method, writing styles, and philosophies of history.

- One of the responses to the reorientationalist call has been the development of a new approach to historiography—ANTi-History—that builds on insights from the Sociology of Knowledge, **poststructuralist historiography**, and **actor-network theory**.

- Historical research draws on a variety of archived and other sources, including personal, public, and organizational documents, as well as mass media and virtual outlets.

- Criteria for evaluating the quality of documents include *authenticity*, credibility, *representativeness*, and meaning. The relevance of these criteria varies somewhat according to the kind of document being assessed and the paradigmatic tradition of the historian and other researchers into the past.

Questions for review

Background to the development of a call for an historic turn in business studies

- Discuss some of the causes for the move from historical analysis in management and organizational analysis in North America since the advent of World War Two.
- Detail and evaluate some of the events that are said to have contributed to the call for the historic turn in management and organization studies.

The call for a reintegration of history into business studies

- Critically discuss the case for and against the reintegration of history in business studies.

History and the past in business studies

- Briefly outline three different approaches to study of the past.
- Compare and contrast the *integrationist* and *reorientationalist* positions on history in business studies.
- What are the main differences between the **narrative** and **archaeological approaches** to history?

Towards an ANTi-History

- Chose three insights from ANTi-**History** (as outlined in Research in focus 21.2) and outline how you would apply them to an historical analysis of some aspect of business studies.

Personal documents

- What is meant by a document?
- What are John Scott's four criteria for assessing documents?
- Outline the different kinds of personal documents.
- How do they fare in terms of John Scott's criteria?
- What might be the role of personal documents in relation to the life history or biographical method?
- What uses can photographs have in business research?

Public documents

- What do the studies by Gephart and Turner suggest in terms of the potential for business researchers to use official documents?
- How do such documents fare in terms of John Scott's criteria?

Organizational documents

- What kinds of documents might be obtained from organizational sources?
- How do such documents fare in terms of John Scott's criteria?

Mass media outputs

- What kinds of documents are mass media outputs?
- How do such documents fare in terms of John Scott's criteria?

Virtual outputs

- Do Internet documents and other virtual outputs raise special problems in terms of assessing them from the point of view of John Scott's criteria?

The world as text

- Can anything be treated as a text?
- What is the significance of audiences in connection with textual readings by academics?

22

Internet Research Methods

Chapter guide

This chapter is concerned with the ways in which the Internet can be used in research. Most readers will be familiar with using the Internet as a means of searching for material on companies or on topics for essays and various other uses. It can be very valuable for such purposes, but this kind of activity is not the focus of this chapter. Instead, we are concerned with the ways in which Internet websites can be used as objects of analysis in their own right and with the ways that the Internet can be used as a means of collecting data, much like the mail and the telephone.

 # Introduction

There can be little doubting that the Internet and online communication have proliferated since the early 1990s and it would be surprising if this boom did not have implications for business research methods. In May 2001, the UK-based newspaper *The Times* reported that the number of households using the Internet had increased to 10 million from 6 million in the previous year. Use of the Internet is particularly high among university students, many of whom have been brought up with technology and for whom it is a very natural medium. A survey of Internet use among American college students found particularly high rates of use in comparison with the population at large, with 86% of students being compared with 59% of the population (Jones, 2002). Nearly 80% of university students felt that the Internet had had a positive impact on their college experience. The situation in Canada is likely to be similar to that found in the United States.

Given this background, it is plausible that many students will be drawn to the Internet as an environment within which to conduct business research. The Internet offers several opportunities in this regard and in this chapter we will focus on:

• World Wide Websites or pages as objects of analysis.
• Ethnographic study of the Internet.
• Qualitative research using online focus groups.
• Qualitative research using online personal interviews.
• Online social surveys.

The ongoing and burgeoning nature of the Internet and online communication makes it difficult to characterize this field and its impact on business research as well as its conduct in any straightforward and simple way. In this chapter, we will be concerned with the following areas of e-research:

1. World Wide Web sites or pages as objects of analysis.
2. Using the World Wide Web or online communications as a means of collecting data from individuals and organizations.

In addition, we will address some of the broader implications and ramifications of the Internet for conducting business research.

While the choice of these two areas of online research and their classification is rather arbitrary and tend to shade into each other somewhat, they provide the basis for a reasonably comprehensive overview in the face of a highly fluid field. This chapter does not consider the use of the Internet as an information resource or as a means of finding references. The Internet is a vast information resource and has too many possible forms to be covered in a single chapter. Moreover, we advise caution about the use of such materials; while the Internet is a cornucopia of data and advice, it also contains a great deal of misleading and downright incorrect information. Healthy skepticism should guide your searches.

 ## Websites or web pages as objects of analysis

Websites and web pages are potential sources of data in their own right and can be regarded as potential opportunities for both quantitative and qualitative content analysis of the kind discussed in Chapter 18. As an example, Aldridge (1998) examined both written consumer guides to personal finance published in the UK and several Internet websites. Through an analysis of such documents Aldridge extracted a number of themes that he saw as part of the 'promotional culture' in which we live. Examples of such themes are:

1. The necessity for members of the public to assume responsibility for their personal finances, particularly in the light of the reductions in welfare provision.
2. The depiction of the professional-client relationship as unthreatening and as one in which the client might legitimately ask informed questions.

However, there are clearly difficulties with using websites as sources of data in this way. Some considerations relating to the use of websites as data include:

- You will need to find the websites relating to your research questions. This is likely to mean searching the Web using a search engine such as Google. However, any search engine provides access to only a portion of the Web. This is why Dorsey, Steeves, and Porras (2004) used several search engines to find websites that promote ecologically sensitive tourism (see Research in focus 22.1), and even then there is evidence that the combined use of several search engines will allow access to only just under a half of the total population of websites (Ho, Baber, & Khondker, 2002). While this means that the use of several search engines is highly desirable when seeking out appropriate websites, it has to be recognized that not only will they allow access to just a portion of the available websites but also they may be a biased sample.
- Related to this point, seeking out websites on a topic can only be as good as the keywords that are employed in the search process. The researcher has to be very patient to try as many relevant keywords as possible (and combinations of them—known as Boolean searches) and may be advised to ask other people (librarians, supervisors, etc.) if the most appropriate ones are being used.

- New websites are continually appearing and others disappearing. Researchers basing their investigations on websites need to recognize that their analyses may be based on websites that no longer exist and that new ones may have appeared since data collection was terminated.
- Websites themselves are also continually changing, so that an analysis may be based upon at least some websites that have been quite considerably updated.

Most researchers who use documents as the basis for their work have to confront the issue that it is difficult to determine the universe or population from which they are sampling. Therefore, the problems identified here are not entirely unique to websites. However, the rapid growth and speed of change in the Web accentuate these kinds of problems for business researchers, who are likely to feel that the experience is like trying to hit a target that not only continually moves but is in a constant state of metamorphosis. The crucial issue is to be sensitive to the limitations of the use of websites as material that can be content analyzed, as well as to the opportunities they offer, especially in marketing research (see Research in focus 22.2). Employing both printed and website materials, as Aldridge (1998) did, has the potential to bring out interesting contrasts in such sources and can also provide the basis for cross-validating sources.

In addition, it is important to bear in mind the quality criteria recommended by John Scott (1990) in connection with documents. He suggests (1990, p. 6) the following four criteria:

- Authenticity. Is the evidence genuine and of unquestionable origin?
- Credibility. Is the evidence free from error and distortion?
- Representativeness. Is the evidence typical of its kind, and, if not, is the extent of its untypical nature known?
- Meaning. Is the evidence clear and comprehensible?

Scott's suggestions invite us to consider why a website is constructed. Why is it there at all? Is it there for commercial reasons? Does it have an axe to grind? In other

22.1 Research in Focus

Conducting an analysis of websites

Dorsey, Steeves, and Porras (2004) note that a growing interest in environmental issues in the West has been associated with a growth in 'ecotourism' and in cultural tourism. The former term denotes tourism to remote areas that are ecologically sensitive; cultural tourism reflects an interest in people and their cultures in relation to their ecosystems. They argue that the Internet has played a significant role in promoting these newer forms of tourism, and were interested in the ways in which they are promoted on websites. Using several search engines, they searched for such websites. They emerged with seven websites that met their criteria for inclusion: well-established companies; a claim to offer 'sustainable' tours; culture is emphasized for at least some of the tours; developing societies were the main destinations; plenty and a variety of information, including photographs; and varied destinations advertised.

Dorsey et al. (2004) submitted the websites to a detailed narrative analysis guided by two research questions. First, do the companies advertising these tours on their websites do so in a manner consistent with the discourse of ecotourism and sustainable development? Secondly, does the online strategy of advertising these tours differ from traditional forms? Regarding the first research question, the research-

ers found that only two of the seven websites represented their tours in a manner consistent with the discourse of ecotourism and sustainable development. The others missed key elements of the discourse. Moreover, the authors found that most websites 'do not discuss the principles of sustainability and only rarely refer to the environmental dynamics of the communities and landscapes that are visited' (Dorsey, Steeves, & Porras, 2004, p. 774). In the case of the second research question, the researchers found that there was little difference between online advertising of such tourism and what had been found by previous researchers who had examined the advertising of ecotourism in traditional media.

This is a study that has produced some interesting findings from an examination of websites. It provides useful findings for tourism researchers and for those with an interest in advertising and in the marketing of tourist destinations. It also provides an interesting use of previous findings, as reported in books and journals: the researchers did not conduct their own investigation of the advertising of ecotourism in traditional media in order to forge a comparison with their own findings regarding online advertising because they were able to employ previous findings generated by other researchers to do so.

Tips and Skills

Referring to websites

There is a growing practice in academic work that, when referring to websites, you should include the date you consulted them. Indeed, some referencing styles (e.g., APA) make this an explicit requirement. This convention is very much associated with the fact that websites often disappear and frequently change, so that, if subsequent researchers want to follow up your findings, or even to check on them, they may find that they are no longer there or that they have changed. Citing the date you consulted the website may help to relieve any anxieties about someone not finding a website you have referred to or finding it has changed. This does mean, however, that you will have to keep a running record of the dates you consulted the websites to which you refer.

22.2 Research in Focus

Determinants of consumers' attitudes towards corporate websites

The increasing prominence of the Internet as a device for communication, marketing, and distribution has meant that many companies today are concerned with the design of attractive and entertaining websites that appeal to potential consumers and create strong brand identity. Consequently, market researchers are interested in examining the determinants of consumer attitudes towards corporate websites and in exploring patterns of site visiting and usage. Here are three examples of the kind of research that is undertaken to find out about this.

An experiment into the effects of including entertaining and/or interactive content on brand evaluations was carried out by Raney, Arpan, Pashupati, and Brill (2003). The study involved research participants visiting and evaluating the websites of four major automotive manufacturers. All the sites included video and audio advertisements related to the product and one of the sites also contained a 'mini movie', a marketing strategy pioneered by the luxury car-maker BMW, which commissioned well-known filmmakers to produce short feature films featuring its products. Based on a sample of 87 individuals recruited from undergraduate communication courses at a large university in the southeastern United States, each participant was involved in five testing sessions of approximately 45 minutes. The participants used a laptop computer with wireless Internet connection that was opened to a home page specifically designed for the research that directed them to each of the websites and enabled them to complete the web survey. The study found that entertaining website content did seem to enhance perception of brands and this could be interpreted as an indirect predictor of purchase intent.

Supphellen and Nysveen (2001) were concerned with what makes consumers revisit the sites of particular companies. Taking the SAS airline company as a case study, they hypothesized that brand loyalty is a powerful determinant of intentions to revisit a company website. They tested this using a paper-based survey study of 198 passengers at Oslo airport who had visited the SAS website. The results showed that brand loyalty affects attitudes towards and intentions to revisit the site: 'customers with affective bonds to the company will tend to seek out the websites, even though the site as such is not superior to sites for other companies' (2001, p. 350). This implies that brand loyalty is still developed through traditional channels, such as TV or radio. The authors advise that companies should, therefore, be wary about transferring resources from traditional media to the Internet, and websites should thus be seen as a vehicle for strengthening the brand rather than establishing it.

A third experimental study by Coyle and Thorson (2001) examined interactivity and vividness in commercial websites. The 68 participants in the study explored four websites that were designed specifically for the study to see if vividness (indicated by if there was audio and animation) and interactivity (measured by the number of choices and if there was a clickable image) resulted in more positive and enduring attitudes towards the site. Participants were tested in groups of up to three persons and were given three minutes to explore each website. They then completed an attitudinal measurement questionnaire that used a seven-point Likert scale. The order in which the websites were explored was randomized. As the websites were designed specifically for the study, the degree of vividness and interactivity could be manipulated. The study found that participants who saw sites with high levels of vividness developed stronger attitudes towards the sites and this helped to create more enduring attitudes. However, no effect on attitudes was found for interactivity.

It is interesting that two of the three studies mentioned here used an experimental design, studies of computer usage being relatively conducive to the creation of controlled conditions.

words, we should be no less skeptical about websites than about any other kind of document.

 ## Using websites to collect data from individuals

In this section we examine research methods that use of either the Web or online communications, such as email, as a platform for collecting data from individuals. Presently, the bulk of the discussion concerned with this issue has emphasized four main areas:

1. Ethnography of the Internet.
2. Qualitative research using online focus groups.
3. Qualitative research using online personal interviews.
4. Online social surveys.

These types of Internet-based research methods do not exhaust the full range of possibilities but they do represent recurring emphases in the emerging literature on this subject. All of them offer certain advantages over their traditional counterparts because:

- They are usually more economical in terms of time and money.
- They can reach large numbers of people very easily.
- Distance is not a problem, since the research participant need only be accessible by computer—it does not matter if he or she is in the same building or across the world.
- Data can be collected and collated very quickly.

The main general disadvantages tend to revolve around the following issues:

- Access to the Internet is still not universal, so that for certain people it is likely to be inaccessible.
- Invitations to take part in research may be viewed as just another nuisance email.
- There is loss of the personal touch owing to lack of rapport between interviewer and interviewee, including the inability to pick up visual or auditory cues.

- There are concerns among research participants about confidentiality of replies given ongoing anxiety about fraud and hackers.

More specific balance sheets of advantages and disadvantages relating to some of the individual e-research methods will be covered below.

There are two crucial distinctions that should be borne in mind when examining Internet-based research methods:

1. There is a distinction between *web-based* and *communication-based* methods. The former is a research method whereby data are collected through the Web—for example, a questionnaire that forms a web page and that the respondent then completes. A communication-based research method is one where email or a similar communication medium is the platform from which the data collection instrument is launched.
2. There is a distinction between **synchronous** and **asynchronous** methods of data collection. Synchronous data collection occurs in real time. An example would be an interview in which an online interviewer asks a question and the respondent, who is also online, replies immediately, as in a chat room. An asynchronous method is not in real time so that there is no immediate response from the respondent, who is unlikely to be online at the same time as the interviewer (or, if the respondent is online, he or she is extremely unlikely to be in a position to reply immediately). An example would be an interview question posed by the interviewer in an email that is opened and answered by the respondent some time later, perhaps days or weeks later.

With these distinctions in mind we can now move on to examine the four main forms of online research methods previously identified. However, one final point to note before concluding this section is that the issues discussed above can also be used to collect data from organizations as well as from individuals.

Virtual ethnography

Ethnography may not seem to be an obvious method for collecting data on Internet use. The popular image of the ethnographer is that of someone who visits places or locations, and, particularly in the context of business research, organizations. The Internet seems to go against the grain of ethnography, in that it seems a decidedly placeless space. In fact, as Hine (2000) has observed, conceiving of the Internet as a place—a cyberspace—has been one strategy for an ethnographic study of the Internet, and it is just a short journey from this idea to the examination of communities in the form of online communities or virtual communities. In this way, our concepts of place and space that are constitutive of the way in which we operate in the real world are grafted onto the Internet and its use. A further issue is that, as noted in Chapter 17, ethnography entails participant observation, but in cyberspace what is the ethnographer observing and in what is he or she participating?

Markham's (1998) approach to an ethnography of life on the Internet involved interviews. The interviews followed a period of 'lurking' (reading but not participating) in computer-mediated communication forums like chat rooms and multi-user domains. The interviews allowed synchronous questioning and answering; in other words, the asking and answering of questions were in real time, rather than the kind of questioning and answering that might occur via email, where a question might be answered several hours or days later. She used an **interview guide**, and the interviews lasted between one hour and over four hours. Such interviews are a very real challenge for both interviewer and interviewee, because neither party can pick up on visual cues (for example, puzzlement, anxiety) or auditory cues (sighs, groans).

One of Markham's interests lay in the reality or otherwise of online experiences. This can be seen in the following brief online interview sequence (Markham's pseudonym is Annette):

> *Annette*: 'How real are your experiences in the Internet?'
> *Sherie*: 'How real are experiences off the Internet?' (Markham, 1998, p. 115)

In fact, Markham notes how her notion of 'real' was different from that of her interviewees. For Markham 'real' or 'in real life' carried a connotation of genuineness or authenticity, but for her interviewees it was more to do with distinguishing experiences that occur off-line. Indeed, Markham increasingly felt that her interviewees were questioning the validity of the dichotomous distinction between the real and the non-real, so far as online interaction was concerned. However, it is likely that these distinctions between life online and life off-line will become less significant as younger people who are growing up with the Internet conduct large portions of their lives online. This development would have considerable implications for business researchers, since for many research participants the online world may become very naturalistic.

An interesting question about this research is: In what sense is it an ethnography? At one level, Markham was simply an interviewer who used a **semi-structured interview** guide to elicit information and the world view of her correspondents. At another level, she was indeed a participant in and observer of life online, although the life that she was participating in and observing was very much a product of her promptings, no matter how open the questions she asked were and no matter how willing she was to allow her interviewees leeway in what they wanted to discuss. In much the same way that her interviewees were questioning the nature of reality, Markham's investigation invites us to question the nature of ethnography so far as research on the Internet is concerned.

Kendall (1999) was probably closer to the traditional concept of the ethnographer in that she describes her research as comprising three years of online participant observation in a multi-user domain, as well as face-to-face interviews and attendance at face-to-face gatherings. Such research is probably closer to the conventional notion of ethnographic research in its use of several methods of data collection and a sense of participation in the lives of those being studied, as well as interviewing them.

A further example of the use of ethnography in relation to the study of online worlds can be found in Web Research in focus 22.1, which shows how the study of online discussion groups can be revealing about enthusiasms in our era of consumerism and brands.

Miller and Slater's (2000) ethnography of Internet use takes an approach that is more similar to traditional ethnography than Markham's (see Research in focus 22.3). Its location in a particular place (Trinidad), its use of several methods of gathering data, and its commitment to observation (for example, in cybercafés) are, for many people, closer to the traditional meanings of ethnography. As the authors put it: 'For us an ethnography does include participating, which may mean going on a chat line for the eight hours that informants will remain online, or participating in a room full of people playing networked Quake . . . .' (Miller & Slater, 2000, p. 22).

One of Miller and Slater's chief interests lay in the state of e-commerce in Trinidad. They found a situation in which there was considerable uncertainty at the time about how far to get into this business medium. There was recognition that the Internet should provide more than a means of advertising wares but little agreement beyond that. Thus, the clothing firms they studied rec-ognized that the Internet could provide more than just a catalogue on a monitor screen, but the nature of any kind of alternative or additional interface represented an area of some uncertainty. Generally, however, Trinidadian consumers did little of their purchasing of goods on the Internet.

A feature that is striking about all these studies from the point of view of anyone familiar with organizational behaviour research on technology is the way in which it treats the Internet as a technology as a 'given'. Recent thinking on technology and work has preferred to view technologies as texts that have 'interpretive flexibility' (Grint & Woolgar, 1997). This notion means that the researcher needs to approach any technology through an examination of both the principles inscribed into it and how it is interpreted by users. Such a position is very much associated with the notion that suggests that the audiences of **texts** need to be the focus of attention as much as the texts themselves. Taking this position, Hine (2000,

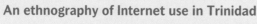

22.3 **Research in Focus**

An ethnography of Internet use in Trinidad

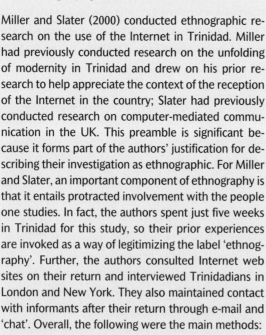

Miller and Slater (2000) conducted ethnographic research on the use of the Internet in Trinidad. Miller had previously conducted research on the unfolding of modernity in Trinidad and drew on his prior research to help appreciate the context of the reception of the Internet in the country; Slater had previously conducted research on computer-mediated communication in the UK. This preamble is significant because it forms part of the authors' justification for describing their investigation as ethnographic. For Miller and Slater, an important component of ethnography is that it entails protracted involvement with the people one studies. In fact, the authors spent just five weeks in Trinidad for this study, so their prior experiences are invoked as a way of legitimizing the label 'ethnography'. Further, the authors consulted Internet web sites on their return and interviewed Trinidadians in London and New York. They also maintained contact with informants after their return through e-mail and 'chat'. Overall, the following were the main methods:

1. interviews 'largely devoted to the study of the political economy of the Internet, including businesses, the isps [Internet service providers] and government officers' (2000, p. 22);
2. hanging around 'in cybercafes watching people go online and chatting with them. We also interviewed them more formally' (2000, p. 22);
3. an exploration with friends of how the Internet had become intertwined with their lives;
4. a house-to-house survey in the same four areas in which Miller had previously conducted a similar nvestigation to ascertain levels of Internet usage;
5. in-depth interviews with some of those contacted through the survey.

Like Markham, Miller and Slater found that the worlds of the Internet and of everyday life beyond the Internet are highly intertwined.

p. 9) locates the Internet 'as a product of culture: a technology that was produced by particular people with contextually situated goals and priorities. It is also a technology which is shaped by the ways in which it is marketed, taught and used'.

Hine describes her approach as one of 'virtual ethnography' (see Research in focus 22.4), which has a dual meaning: it is at once an ethnography of being online—that is, of the virtual—but it is also a virtual ethnography, that is, not quite an ethnography in any of the term's conventional settings. In particular, a virtual ethnography requires getting away from the idea that an ethnography is of or in a place in any traditional sense. It is also an ethnography of a domain that infiltrates other spaces and times of its participants, so that its boundedness is problematic to participants and analysts alike. Regarding the issue of the interpretative flexibility of the Internet, Hine shows that there was some general agreement about its purposes as a technology. However, these purposes were not inscribed or

embedded in the technology in the way that a technological determinist position might imply, but they had arisen in the course of the use of the Internet. Moreover, Hine argues that the nature and capacities of the Internet have not become totally stabilized in the minds of participants and that gradual increments of change are likely in response to particular needs and purposes of participants.

Studies like these are invite us to consider the nature of the Internet as a domain for investigation, but they also ask us to consider the nature and the adaptiveness of our research methods. In the examples discussed in this section, the question of what is and is not ethnography is given a layer of complexity that adds to the considerations about this issue referred to in Chapter 17. But these studies are also cases of using Internet-based research methods to investigate Internet use. Future online ethnographic investigations of issues unrelated to the Internet will give a clearer indication of the possibilities that the method offers.

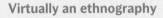

22.4 Research in Focus

Virtually an ethnography

Hine's (2000) research was concerned with the trial in 1997 in Boston of a British nanny (Louise Woodward) for the murder of the child in her charge, as well as the aftermath of the trial. While not an area relevant in any direct way to business and management research, Hine's research is relevant as an approach that could be adapted to such a substantive focus. Hine's data collection strategy included: searching out websites concerned with the case, which attracted a great deal of Internet interest; contacting web authors by e-mail and asking a series of questions about their intentions, familiarity with the Web, experiences, and so on; examining communication in newsgroups in which 10 or more postings about the case had been made and posting a message in those groups; and contact with the official site that campaigned for Louise Woodward. In contacting web developers and newsgroup participants, Hine writes:

> I introduced myself as a researcher in communications who was looking at the specific case of

Louise Woodward on the Internet. I explained that I was concerned with how people got interested in the case, where they got their information from, and what they thought of the quality of information on newsgroups and web pages. . . . I offered people a promise of confidentiality and the chance to check my own credentials through my web site. (2000, p. 78)

Hine did not receive a very good response to the newsgroup postings, which may reflect a tendency noticed by other researchers for newsgroup, MUD, listserv, and other participants to be sceptical about the use of their cyberdomains for research and suspicious about researchers who contact them. In her examination of newsgroup communication, Hine employed an approach that was heavily influenced by discourse analysis (see Chapter 20)—for example, by showing the discursive moves through which participants sought to construe the authenticity or factual nature of their information.

Qualitative research using online focus groups

There is a crucial distinction between synchronous and asynchronous online focus groups. With the former, the focus group is in real time, so that contributions are made more or less immediately after previous contributions (whether from the moderator or other participants) among a group of participants, all of whom are simultaneously online. Contributions can be responded to as soon as they are typed (and with some forms of software, the contributions can be seen as they are being typed). As Mann and Stewart (2000) observe, because several participants can type in a response to a contribution at the same time, the conventions regarding turn taking in conversations are largely left aside.

With asynchronous groups, focus group exchanges are not in real time. Email is one form of asynchronous communication that is sometimes used (see Research in focus 22.5 for an example). For example, the moderator might ask a question and then send the email containing it to focus group participants. The latter will be able to reply to the moderator and to other group members at some time in the future. Such groups get around the time zone problem and are probably easier than synchronous groups for participants who are not skilled at using the keyboard.

One of the advantages of both types of online focus groups stems from the possibility of using a 'captive population' of people who are already communicating with each other, unlike face-to-face focus groups that are brought together for the purpose of the focus group meeting. This means researchers are often able to take advantage of pre-existing social groups of people who are already communicating with one another online (Stewart & Williams, 2005). Online focus groups also enable geographical distances to be overcome. International focus groups can enable cross-cultural discussions at a relatively low cost. However, setting up a time and place for synchronous online focus group discussions between international participants may be problematic because of time zone differences, making it hard to find a time that is convenient to everyone (Stewart & Williams, 2005).

Conferencing software is used for synchronous groups and is often used for asynchronous groups as well. This may mean that **focus group** participants will require access to the software, which can be undesirable if the soft-

22.5 Research in Focus

An asynchronous focus group study

Adriaenssens and Cadman (1999) report their experiences of conducting a market research exercise to explore the launch of an online share-trading platform in the UK. Participants were in two groups: one group of active shareholders (20 participants) and a second group of passive shareholders (10 participants). They were identified through the MORI Financial Services database as 'upmarket shareholders who were also Internet users' (1999, p. 418–19). The participants who were identified were very geographically spread, so online focus groups were ideal. Questions were e-mailed to participants in five phases with a deadline for returning replies, which were then copied anonymously to the rest of the participants. The questions were sent in the body of the e-mail, rather than as attachments, to solve problems of software incompatibility. After each phase, a summary document was produced and circulated to participants for comment, thus injecting a form of respondent validation into the project. The researchers found it difficult to ensure that participants kept to the deadlines, which in fact were rather tight, although it was felt that having a schedule of deadlines that was kept to as far as possible was helpful in preventing drop-outs. The researchers felt that the group of active shareholders was too large to manage and suggest groups of no more than 10 participants.

ware needs to be loaded onto their computers. Participants may not feel confident about loading the software and there may be compatibility problems with particular machines and operating systems.

Selecting participants for online focus groups is potentially difficult, not least because they must normally have access to the necessary hardware and software. One possibility is to use **questionnaires** as a springboard for identifying possible participants, while another possibility is to contact them by email, this being a relatively quick and economical way of contacting a large number of possible participants. For their study of virtual communities concerned with consumption issues Evans et al. (2001) used a combination of questionnaires (both paper and online) and focus groups made up of respondents to the questionnaires that had indicated a willingness to take further part in the research. The British focus groups were of the face-to-face kind, but, in addition, international respondents to the questionnaire, who were prepared to be further involved in the research, participated in an online focus group. Other sources of participants for online focus groups might involve postings on appropriate special interest websites or on special interest bulletin boards or chat rooms.

The required number of participants is affected by the question of whether the online focus group is being conducted synchronously or asynchronously. Mann and Stewart (2000) suggest that, with the former type, the group should not be too large, because it can make it difficult for some people to participate, possibly because of limited keyboard skills, and they recommend groups of between six and eight participants. Also, moderating the session can be more difficult with a large number. In asynchronous mode, such problems do not exist and very large groups can be accommodated—certainly much larger ones than could be envisaged in a face-to-face context, although Adriaenssens and Cadman (1999) suggest that large groups can present research management problems.

Before starting the focus group, moderators are advised to send out a welcome message introducing the research and setting out the ground rules for the ongoing discussion. There is evidence that participants respond

more positively if the researchers reveal something about themselves (Curasi, 2001). This can be done in the opening message or by creating links to personal websites.

One problem with the asynchronous focus group is that moderators cannot be available online 24 hours a day, although it is not inconceivable that moderators could have a shift system to deal with this limitation. This lack of continuous availability means that emails or postings may be sent and responded to without any ability of the moderator to intervene or participate. This feature may not be a problem, but perhaps could become so if offensive messages were being sent or if it meant that the discussion was going off at a complete tangent. Further, because focus group sessions in asynchronous mode may go on for a long time, perhaps several days or even weeks, there is a greater likelihood of participants dropping out of the study. A further problem arises from response rates, which may be lower than for face-to-face focus groups (Stewart & Williams, 2005). Even though it is relatively easy for the researcher to contact a large number of possible respondents using email, the response rates of those wishing to participate in an online focus group has been found to be quite low (between 5% and 20%). Further reservations have been expressed about the lack of nonverbal data obtained from online focus groups, such as facial expression.

Online focus groups are unlikely to replace their face-to-face counterparts. Instead, they are likely to be employed in connection with certain kinds of research topic and/or sample. As regards to the latter, dispersed or inaccessible people are especially relevant to online focus group research. As Sweet (2001) points out, relevant topics are likely to be ones involving sensitive issues and ones concerned with Internet use—for example, the study discussed in Research in focus 22.5 and studies like O'Connor and Madge (2001).

The discussion in Tips and skills '*Advantages and disadvantages of online focus groups and personal interviews compared to face-to-face interviews in qualitative research*' is combined with online personal interviews, which are the subject of the next section, since most of the elements in the balance sheet of advantages and disadvantages are the same.

Qualitative research using online personal interviews

The issues involved in conducting online personal interviews for qualitative research are essentially the same as those to do with conducting online focus groups. In particular, the researcher must decide whether the interviews should take place in synchronous or asynchronous mode. The factors involved in deciding which to use are also largely the same, although issues to do with variable typing speed or computer-related knowledge among focus group participants will not apply.

Although online interviews run the risk, when compared with face-to-face interviews, that the respondent is somewhat more likely to drop out of the exchange (especially in asynchronous mode, since the interviews can sometimes be very protracted), Mann and Stewart (2000, pp. 138–9) suggest that in fact a relationship of mutual trust can be built up. This kind of relationship can make it easier for a longer-term commitment to the interview to be maintained, but also makes it easier for the researcher to go back to his or her interviewees for further information or reflections, something that might be difficult to do with the face-to-face personal interview. The authors also suggest that it is important for interviewers to keep sending messages to respondents to reassure them that their written utterances are helpful and significant, especially since interviewing through the Internet is still an unfamiliar experience for most people.

A further issue for the online personal interviewer to consider is whether to send all the questions at once or to interview on a question followed by reply basis. The problem with the first tactic is that respondents may read all the questions and then reply only to those that they feel interested in or to which they feel they can make a genuine contribution, so asking one question at a time is likely to be more reliable.

There is evidence that prospective interviewees are more likely to agree to participate if their agreement is solicited prior to sending them questions and if the re-

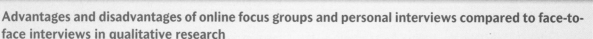

Tips and Skills

Advantages and disadvantages of online focus groups and personal interviews compared to face-to-face interviews in qualitative research

Here is a summary of the main advantages and disadvantages of both online focus groups and personal interviews when compared to their face-to-face counterparts. The two methods are combined because the list of advantages and disadvantages applies more or less equally well to both of them.

Advantages
- Online interviews and focus groups are inexpensive to conduct compared with comparable face-to-face equivalents. They are likely to take longer, however, especially when conducted asynchronously.
- Interviewees or focus group participants who would otherwise normally be inaccessible (for example, because they are located in another country) or hard to involve in research (for example, very senior executives, people with almost no time for participation) can more easily be involved.
- Large numbers of possible online focus group participants can be contacted by email.

- Interviewees and focus group participants are able to re-read what they (and, in the case of focus groups, others) have previously written in their replies.
- People participating in the research may be better able to fit the interviews into their own time.
- People participating in the research do not have to make additional allowances for the time spent travelling to a focus group session.
- The interviews do not have to be audio-recorded, thus eliminating interviewee apprehension about speaking and being recorded.
- There is no need for transcription. This represents an enormous advantage because of the time and cost involved in getting recorded interview sessions transcribed.
- As a result of the previous point, the interview transcripts can be more or less immediately entered into computer-assisted qualitative data analysis software.
- The **transcripts** of the interviews are more likely to be accurate, because the problems that may arise from

mishearing or not hearing at all what is said do not arise. This is a particular advantage with focus group discussions, because it can be difficult to establish who is speaking and impossible to distinguish what is said when participants speak at the same time.

- Focus group participants can employ pseudonyms so that their identity can be more easily concealed from others in the group. This can make it easier for participants to discuss potentially embarrassing issues or to divulge potentially unpopular views. The ability to discuss sensitive issues generally may be greater in electronic than face to face focus groups.
- In focus groups, shy or quiet participants may find it easier to have their perspectives heard.
- Equally, in focus groups overbearing participants are less likely to predominate, but in synchronous groups variations in keyboard skills may mitigate slightly against equal participation.
- Participants are less likely to be influenced by characteristics like the age, ethnicity, or appearance (and possibly even gender if pseudonyms are used) of other participants in a focus group.
- Similarly, interviewees and focus group participants are much less likely to be affected by characteristics of interviewers or moderators, so that interviewer bias is less likely.
- When interviewees and participants are online at home, they are essentially being provided with an 'anonymous, safe and non-threatening environment' (O'Connor & Madge, 2002, p. 11.2), which may be especially helpful to vulnerable groups.
- Similarly, researchers are not confronted with the potentially uncomfortable experience of having to invade other people's homes or workplaces, which can sometimes be unsafe environments.

Disadvantages
- Only people with access to online facilities and/or who find them relatively straightforward are likely to be in a position to participate.
- It can be more difficult for the interviewer to establish rapport and to engage with interviewees. However, when the topic is of interest to participants, this may not be a great problem.
- It can be difficult in asynchronous interviews to retain over a longer term any rapport that has been built up.

- Probing is more difficult though not impossible. Curasi (2001) reports some success in eliciting further information from respondents, but it is easier for interviewees to ignore or forget about the requests for further information or for expansion on answers given.
- Asynchronous interviews may take a very long time to complete, depending on cooperativeness.
- With asynchronous interviews, there may be a greater tendency for interviewees to discontinue their participation than is likely to be the case with face-to-face interviews.
- There is less spontaneity of response, since interviewees can reflect on their answers to a much greater extent than is possible in a face-to-face situation. However, this can be construed as an advantage in some respects, since interviewees are likely to give more considered replies (though some commentators see the ability to provide more considered replies an advantage, see Adriaenssens & Cadman, 1999).
- There may be a tendency for non-response to be higher in online personal interviews and from possible online focus group participants.
- The researcher cannot be certain that the people who are interviewed are who they say they are (although this issue may apply on occasion to face-to-face interviews as well).
- In synchronous focus groups, variations in keyboard skills may make equal levels of participation difficult.
- Online interviews and focus groups from home require considerable commitment from interviewees and participants if they have to install software onto their computers and remain online for extended periods of time, thereby incurring expense (though it is possible to offer remuneration for such costs) .
- The interviewer/moderator may not be aware that the interviewee/participant is distracted by something and in such circumstances will continue to ask questions as if he or she had the person's full attention.
- Online connections may be lost, so research participants need to know what to do in case of such an eventuality.
- Interviewers cannot capitalize on body language or other forms of non-verbal data that might suggest puzzlement, or in the case of focus groups a thwarted desire to contribute to the discussion.

Sources: Clapper and Massey (1996); Adriaenssens and Cadman (1999); Tse (1999); Mann and Stewart (2000); Curasi (2001); O'Connor and Madge (2001); Sweet (2001).

searcher uses some form of self-disclosure, such as directing the person being contacted to the researcher's website, which contains personal information, particularly information that might be relevant to the research issue (Curasi, 2001; O'Connor & Madge, 2001). The argument for obtaining prior agreement from interviewees before sending them questions to be answered is that unsolicited emails, often referred to as 'spamming', are regarded as a nuisance among online users and receiving them can result in an immediate refusal to take the message seriously.

Curasi (2001) conducted a comparison in which 24 online interviews carried out through email correspondence (and, therefore, asynchronous) were contrasted with 24 parallel face-to-face interviews. The interviews were concerned with shopping on the Internet. She found the following:

- Face-to-face interviewers are better able than online interviewers to maintain rapport with respondents.
- Greater commitment and motivation are required for completing an online interview, but, because of this, replies are often more detailed and considered than with face-to-face interviews.
- Online interviewers are less able to have an impact on whether the interview is successful or not because they are more remote.
- Online interviewees' answers tend to be more considered and grammatically correct because they have more time to ponder their answers and because they can tidy them up before sending them. Whether this is a positive feature is debatable: there is the obvious advantage of a 'clean' transcript, but there may be some loss of spontaneity.
- Follow-up probes can be carried out in online interviews, as well as in face-to-face ones.

On the other hand, Curasi also found that the worst interviews in terms of the amount of detail forthcoming were from online interviews. It may be that this and the other differences are to do with the fact that, whereas a qualitative face-to-face interview is *spoken*, the parallel online interview is *typed*. The full significance of this difference in the nature of the respondent's mode of answering has not been fully appreciated.

It is very clear from many of the discussions about online interviews by email that a significant problem for many interviewers is that of keeping respondents involved in the interview when questions are being sent one or two at a time. Respondents tend to lose momentum or interest. However, Kivits (2005) has shown that re-contacting interviewees on regular occasions and adopting an accessible and understanding style can not only help to maintain momentum for many interviewees but also bring some who have lost interest or forgotten to reply back into the research.

Thus far, most of the discussion of online personal interviewing assumes that the exchange is conducted entirely in a textual context (particularly by email). However, the webcam offers further possibilities for synchronous online personal interviews. Such a development makes the online interview similar to a telephone interview, in that it is mediated by a technology, but also similar to an in-person interview, since those involved in the exchange are able to see each other. However, one of the main advantages of the online interview would be lost, in that the respondent's answers would need to be transcribed, as in traditional **qualitative** interviewing.

The possibilities associated with conducting online focus groups have probably attracted greater attention than online personal interviews, perhaps because the potential advantages are greater with the former. For example, with focus groups, a great deal of time and administration can be saved by online focus groups, whereas there is less comparable saving with online personal interviews unless a great deal of travel is involved.

 # Online social surveys

There has been a considerable growth in the number of surveys being administered online. It is questionable whether the research instruments should be regarded as structured interviews (see Chapter 13) or as self-completion questionnaires (see Chapter 10)—in a sense they are both. So far as online social surveys are concerned, there is a crucial distinction between surveys administered by email (email surveys) and surveys administered via the Web (Web surveys). In the case of the former, the questionnaire is sent via email to a respondent, whereas, with a Web survey, the respondent is directed to a website in order to answer a questionnaire. Sheehan and Hoy (1999) suggest that there has been a tendency for email surveys to be employed in relation to internally similar groups, whereas Web surveys have been used to study large, heterogeneous groups.

Email surveys

With email surveys it is important to distinguish between embedded and attached questionnaires sent by email. In the case of the embedded questionnaire, the questions are to be found in the body of the email. There may be an introduction to the questionnaire followed by some division between the introduction from the questionnaire itself. Respondents have to indicate their replies using simple notations, such as an 'x', or perhaps they may be asked to delete alternatives that do not apply. If questions are open-ended, they are asked to type in their answers. They then simply need to select the reply button to return their completed questionnaires to the researcher. In the case of an attached questionnaire, the questionnaire arrives as an attachment to an email that introduces it. As with the embedded questionnaire, respondents must select and/or type their answers. To return the questionnaire, it must be attached to a reply email, although respondents may also be given the opportunity to fax or send the completed questionnaire by mail to the researcher (Sheehan & Hoy, 1999).

The chief advantage of the **embedded** questionnaire is that it is easier for the respondent to return to the researcher and requires less computer expertise. Knowing how to read and then return an attachment requires a certain familiarity with handling online communication that may not be universally applicable. Also, the recipients' operating systems or software may present problems with reading attachments, while many respondents may refuse to open the attachment because of concerns about a virus. On the other hand, the limited formatting that is possible with most email software, such as using bold, variations in font size, indenting, and other features, makes the appearance of embedded questionnaires rather dull and featureless, although this limitation is rapidly changing.

Furthermore, it is slightly easier for the respondent to type material into an attachment that uses well-known software like Microsoft Word, since, if the questionnaire is embedded in an email, the alignment of questions and answers may be lost.

Dommeyer and Moriarty (2000) compared the two forms of email survey in connection with an attitude study. The attached questionnaire was given a much wider range of embellishments in terms of appearance than was possible with the embedded one. Before conducting the survey, undergraduate students were asked about the relative appearance of the two formats. The attached questionnaire was deemed to be better looking, easier to complete, clearer in appearance, and better organized. The two formats were then administered to two random samples of students, all of whom were active email users. The researchers found a much higher response rate with the embedded than with the attached questionnaire (37% versus 8%), but there was little difference in terms of speed of response or whether questions were more likely to be omitted with one format rather than the other. Although Dommeyer and Moriarty (2000, p. 48) conclude that 'the attached email survey presents too many obstacles to the potential respondent', it is important to appreciate that this study was conducted during what were still early days in the life of online surveys. It may be that, as prospective respondents become more adept at using online communication methods and as viruses become less of a threat (for example, as virus-checking software becomes more widespread in use), the concerns that led to the lower response rate for the attached questionnaire will be less pronounced. Also, the researchers do not appear to have established a prior contact with the students before sending out the questionnaires; it may be that the reaction to such an approach, which is frowned upon in the online community, may have been more negative in the case of the attached questionnaire format.

Web surveys

Web surveys operate by inviting prospective respondents to visit a website at which the questionnaire can be found and completed online. The Web survey has an important advantage over the email survey in that it can use a much wider variety of embellishments in terms of appearance.

Plate 22.1 presents part of the questionnaire from the gym survey from Chapter 23 in a Web survey format and answered in the same way as in Tips and skills '*A completed and processed questionnaire*' (see Chapter 23). Common features include 'radio buttons' (in which respondents makes a choice between closed-question answers by clicking on a circle in which a dot appears, see question 8 in Plate 22.1) and pull-down menus of possible answers (see Plate 22.2). There are also greater possibilities in terms of the use of colour. With open questions, the respondent is invited to type directly into a boxed area (for example, question 2 in Plate 22.1).

However, the advantages of the Web survey are not just to do with appearance. The questionnaire can be designed so that, when there is a filter question (for example, 'if yes go to question 12, if no go to question 14'), it skips automatically to the next appropriate question. The questionnaire can also be programmed so that only one question ever appears on the screen or so that the respondent cannot scroll down and look at all questions in advance. Finally, respondents' answers can be automatically programmed to download into a database, thus eliminating the task of coding a large number of questionnaires. One of the chief prob-

lems with the Web survey is that, in order to produce the attractive text and all the other features, the researcher will either have to be highly sophisticated in the use of HTML or will need to use one of a growing number of software packages that are designed to produce questionnaires with all the features that have been described. However, some of these difficulties are mitigated through the use of websites, such as SurveyMonkey (http://www.surveymonkey.com) that offers survey design, hosting, and reportage facilities. Alan Bryman has also employed Survey Galaxy (http://www.surveygalaxy.com/) in a study of social policy researchers (Becker, Bryman, & Sempik, 2006). With commercial websites such as these, you can design your questionnaire online and then create a web address to which respondents can be directed in order to complete it. There is a fee for using this software. The fee will be affected by the number of respondents who complete the questionnaire and the length of time that the questionnaire is active. Each respondent's replies are logged and the entire data set can be retrieved once you decide the data collection phase is complete. This means that there is no coding of replies and entering of data into your software. Not only does this save time, it also reduces the likelihood of errors in the processing of data.

Plate 22.1

Gym survey in Web survey format

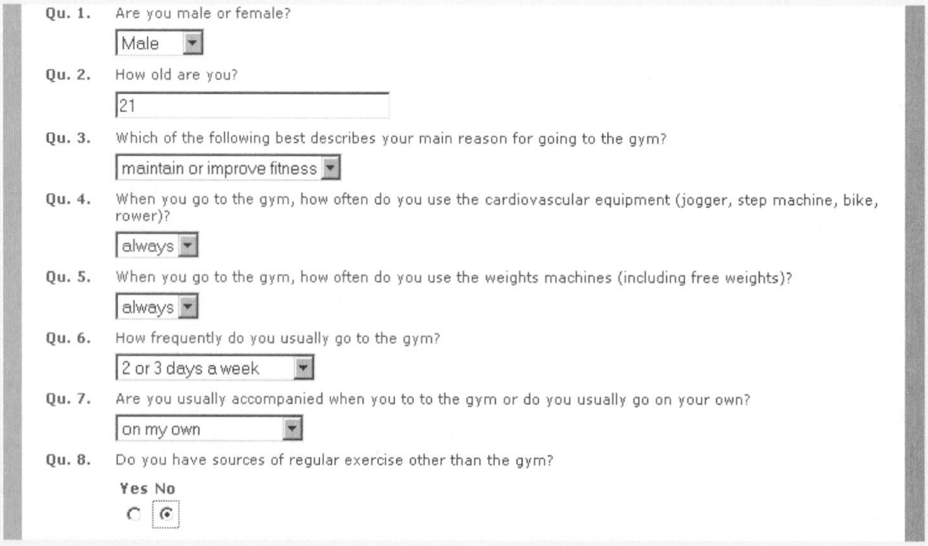

Plate 22.2

A pull-down menu

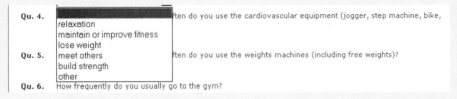

Qu. 4.   [relaxation] ften do you use the cardiovascular equipment (jogger, step machine, bike,
           relaxation
           maintain or improve fitness
           lose weight
Qu. 5.   meet others   ften do you use the weights machines (including free weights)?
           build strength
           other
Qu. 6.   How frequently do you usually go to the gym?

Potential respondents need to be directed to the website containing the questionnaire. Research in focus 22.6 provides an example of the kind of approach that might be used. Where there are possible problems to do with restricting who may answer the questionnaire, it may be necessary to set up a password system to filter out people for whom the questionnaire is not appropriate.

Sampling issues

Anyone who has read Chapter 9 must be wondering how the sampling principles described there might apply to online surveys. A major issue and limitation is that not everyone in any nation is online and has the technical ability to handle questionnaires online in either email or web formats. Certain other features of online communications make the issue more problematic:

- Many people have more than one email address.
- Many people use more than one Internet Service Provider (ISP).
- A household may have one computer but several users.
- Internet-users are a biased sample of the population, in that they tend to be better educated, wealthier, younger, and not representative in ethnic terms (Couper, 2000).
- Few sampling frames exist of the general online population and most of these are likely to be expensive to acquire, since they are controlled by ISPs or may be confidential.

Such issues make the possibilities of conducting online surveys using **probability sampling** principles difficult to envisage. This is not to say that online surveys should

22.6   Research in Focus

Combining ways of responding to electronic surveys

In 2009 Yue et al. studied the impact of a communications issues training program upon managers. Their study involved the nationwide (Canada) surveying of management employees of a federal government department. This government department was in the process of delivering communications training workshops to managerial employees. This one-shot self-report survey research design was constructed to offer some feedback to the organization concerning the training. Individuals were surveyed through a number of formats and in both official languages. Survey completion was through either an Internet-based survey instrument, a printed, completed and faxed PDF or Microsoft Word document (which could also be emailed to a secure off-site server), or to respond using the telephone. Of the potential 881 respondents, 199 individuals answered the survey. Most of them (168 individuals) made use of the online Internet-based survey option, while 31 respondents emailed their surveys. While the organization was especially concerned to ensure that the researchers offered the maximum possible flexibility for methods of survey response, none of the respondents used the telephone nor the fax-based options.

not be considered. Indeed, for researchers in the field of business and management, there may be more opportunities than for researchers in other areas. For example, in many organizations, most if not all non-trades workers are likely to be online and to be familiar with the details of using email and the Internet. Thus surveys of samples of online populations can be conducted using essentially the same probability sampling procedures. Similarly, surveys of members of commercially relevant online groups can be conducted using these principles. Smith (1997) conducted a survey of Web presence providers (people or organizations that are involved in creating and maintaining Web content). She acquired her sample from a directory of providers, which acted as her **sampling frame**. A further example of the use of a directory to generate a **probability sample** can be found in Research in focus 22.7.

As Couper (2000) notes regarding **surveys** of **populations** using **probability sampling** procedures:

> Intra-organizational surveys and those directed at users of the Internet were among the first to adopt this new survey technology. These restricted populations typically have no coverage problems . . . or very high rates of coverage. Student surveys are a particular example of this approach that are growing in popularity. (2000, p. 485)

The main problem with sampling strategies and Web survey questionnaires (although the same applies to the respondents to their paper-based questionnaire too), relates to the representativeness of the sample. On the other hand, given that we have so little knowledge and understanding of online behaviour and attitudes relating to online issues, it could reasonably be argued that some information about these areas is a lot better than none at all, provided the limitations of the findings in terms of their generalizability are appreciated.

A further issue in relation to sampling and **sampling**-related **error** is the matter of **non-response**. There is growing evidence that online surveys typically generate lower response rates than mail questionnaire surveys (Tse, 1998; Sheehan, 2001). In the early years, in the late 1980s, response rates for email surveys were quite encouraging (Sheehan & Hoy, 1999), but since the mid-1990s they have been declining and are at lower levels than those for most mail questionnaires (Sheehan, 2001), though there are clear exceptions to this tendency (for example, see Research in focus 22.7). Two factors may account for this decline: the novelty of email surveys in the early years and a growing negativity towards unsolicited emails among online communities. However, response rates can be boosted by following two simple strategies:

22.7 Research in Focus

Sampling for an online survey

Cobanoglu, Ward, and Moreo (2001) report the results of a study in which three different modes of survey administration were used: post, fax, and online. The questionnaires were administered to 300 hospitality professors in the USA, who had been randomly sampled from the online directory of the Council on Hotel, Restaurant, and Institutional Education. The sampling was carried out only from those who had an email address. The 300 professors were randomly assigned to one of the three modes of survey administration.

The authors write:

For the web-based survey, an email message was sent to the professors along with a cover letter and the website address. The respondents were informed that they could request a paper copy of the survey should they have problems accessing the survey online. A unique website address was created for each respondent . . . (2001, p. 447)

Compared with the postal administration of the questionnaire, the online administration achieved a higher response rate (26% versus 44%) and a faster response speed, and was cheaper.

Tips and Skills

Using Internet surveys to supplement traditional mail questionnaire surveys

There is a growing tendency for researchers who conduct mail questionnaire surveys to offer their respondents the opportunity to complete their questionnaires online (Couper, 2000). This can be done by indicating in the covering letter that goes out with the mail questionnaire that they can have the questionnaire emailed to them, or, if the questionnaire is accessible via the Web, they can be directed to the web address. The advantage of doing this is that some of the samples of respondents may feel more comfortable completing the questionnaire online because of the long periods of time they spend online and the removal of the need to return the paper survey. There is the question of whether or not the mode of administration (mail versus online) influences the kinds of response received. This is an issue that is likely to attract research in the future.

1. Contact prospective respondents before sending them a questionnaire. This is regarded as basic 'netiquette'.
2. As with mail questionnaire surveys, follow up non-respondents at least once.

The case for the first of these two strategies in boosting response rates is not entirely clear (Sheehan, 2001), but seems to be generally advisable.

Tips and skills '*Advantages and disadvantages of online surveys compared to mail questionnaire surveys*' summarizes the main factors to take into account when comparing online surveys with mail questionnaire surveys.

Overview

Online surveys are still in early stages of development, but they have considerable potential. There is evidence that having a Web survey or even an email option can boost response rates to mail questionnaires (Yun & Trumbo, 2000). Several problems have been identified with Web and email surveys, but it is too early to dismiss them because methodologists are only beginning to come to grips with this approach to survey research and may gradually develop ways of overcoming the limitations that are being identified. Moreover, as we have pointed out, for certain kinds of populations and as more and more people and organizations go online, some of the sampling-related problems will diminish. As Yun and Trumbo (2000) observe: 'the electronic-only survey is advisable when resources are limited and the target population suits an electronic survey'.

It is also worth making the obvious point that, when conducting an online survey, you should bear in mind the principles about sampling, interview design, and question construction that were posed earlier in the section of the book dedicated to surveying. While online surveys are distinctive in certain ways, they require the same rigorous considerations that go into the design of conventional surveys that are conducted by mail questionnaire or by personal or telephone interview.

 ## Ethical considerations in Internet research

Conducting research by using the Internet as a method of data collection raises specific ethical issues that are only now starting to be widely discussed and debated. Some of these are related to the vast array of environments in which these new forms of communication and possibilities for research occur, including weblogs, listservs, or discussion groups, email, chat rooms, instant messaging, and newsgroups. The behaviour of Internet users is governed by 'netiquette', the conventions of politeness or definitions of acceptable behaviour that are recognized by online communities, as well as by service providers' acceptable use policies and by data protection legislation. Anyone contemplating using the Internet as a method of data collection should start by familiarizing themselves with these and by considering the general ethical principles discussed in Chapter 8. However, this section is concerned with the specific ethical issues raised by Internet research.

Tips and Skills

Advantages and disadvantages of online surveys compared to mail questionnaire surveys

This box summarizes the main advantages and disadvantages of online surveys compared to mail questionnaire surveys. The tally of advantages and disadvantages in connection with online surveys relates to both email and Web surveys. It should also be made clear that by and large online surveys and mail questionnaires suffer from one disadvantage relative to personal and telephone interviews—namely, that the researcher can never be certain that the person answering questions is who the researcher believes him or her to be.

Advantages

1. Low cost. Even though mail questionnaire surveys are cheap to administer, there is evidence that email surveys are cheaper. This is in part due to the cost of postage, paper, envelopes, and the time taken to stuff covering letters and questionnaires into envelopes with mail questionnaire surveys. However, with Web surveys there may be start-up costs associated with the software needed to produce the questionnaire.

2. Faster response. Online surveys tend to be returned considerably faster than mail questionnaires.

3. Attractive formats. With Web surveys, there is the opportunity to use a wide variety of stylistic formats for presenting questionnaires and **closed-question** answers. Also, automatic skipping when using filter questions and the possibility of immediate downloading of questionnaire replies into a database make this kind of survey quite attractive for researchers.

4. Mixed administration. They can be combined with mail questionnaire surveys so that respondents have the option of replying by post or online. Moreover, the mode of reply does not seem to make a significant difference to the kinds of replies generated (see Research in focus 22.7).

5. Unrestricted geographical range. There are no constraints in terms of geographical coverage. The same might be said of mail questionnaire surveys, but the problems of sending respondents stamped addressed envelopes that can be used in their own countries is overcome.

6. Fewer unanswered questions. There is evidence that online questionnaires are completed with fewer unanswered questions than mail questionnaires, resulting in less missing data. However, there is also evidence of little difference between the two modes of administering surveys.

7. Better response to open questions. To the extent that open questions are used, they tend to be more likely to be answered online and to result in more detailed replies.

Disadvantages

1. Low response rate. Typically, response rates to online surveys are lower than those for comparable mail questionnaire surveys.

2. Restricted to online populations. Only people who are available online can reasonably be expected to participate in an online survey. This restriction may gradually ease over time, but, since the online population differs in significant ways from the non-online population, it is likely to remain a difficulty. On the other hand, if online populations are the focus of interest, this disadvantage is not a substantial problem.

3. Requires motivation. As online survey respondents must be online to answer the questionnaire, if they are having to pay for the connection and perhaps are tying up their telephone lines, they may need a higher level of motivation than mail questionnaire respondents. This suggests that the solicitation to participate must be especially persuasive.

4. Confidentiality and anonymity issues. It is normal for survey researchers to indicate that respondents' replies will be confidential and that they will be anonymous. The same suggestions can and should be made with respect to online surveys. However, with email surveys, since the recipient must return the questionnaire either embedded within the message or as an attachment, respondents may find it difficult to believe that their replies really are confidential and will be treated anonymously. In this respect, Web surveys may have an advantage over email surveys.

5. Multiple replies. With Web surveys, there is a risk that some people may mischievously complete the questionnaire more than once. There is much less risk of this with email surveys.

Sources: Schaeffer and Dillman (1998); Tse (1998); Kent and Lee (1999); Sheehan and Hoy (1999); Cobanoglu, Ward, and Moreo (2001).

Table 22.1 The strengths of email and Web-based surveys in relation to face-to-face interview, telephone interview, and postal questionnaire surveys

Issues to consider	Mode of survey administration				
	Face-to-face interview	Telephone interview	Postal questionnaire	Email	Web
Resource issues					
Is the cost of the mode of administration relatively low?	✓	✓✓	✓✓✓	✓✓✓	✓ (unless access to low-cost software)
Is the speed of the mode of administration relatively fast?	✓	✓✓✓	✓✓✓	✓✓✓	✓✓✓
Is the cost of handling a dispersed sample relatively low?	✓ (✓✓ if clustered)	✓✓✓	✓✓✓	✓✓✓	✓✓✓
Does the researcher require little technical expertise for devising a questionnaire?	✓✓✓	✓✓✓	✓✓✓	✓✓	✓
Sampling-related issues					
Does the mode of administration tend to produce a good response rate?	✓✓✓	✓✓	✓	✓	✓
Is the researcher able to control who responds (i.e., the person at whom it is targeted is the person who answers)?	✓✓✓	✓✓✓	✓✓	✓✓	✓✓
Is the mode of administration accessible to all sample members?	✓✓✓	✓✓	✓✓	✓ (because of need for respondents to be accessible online)	✓ (because of need for respondents to be accessible online)
Questionnaire issues					
Is the mode of administration suitable for long questionnaires?	✓✓✓	✓✓	✓✓	✓✓	✓
Is the mode of administration suitable for complex questions?	✓✓✓	✓	✓✓	✓✓	✓✓
Is the mode of administration suitable for open questions?	✓✓✓	✓✓	✓	✓✓	✓✓
Is the mode of administration suitable for filter questions?	✓✓✓ (especially if CAPI used)	✓✓✓ (especially if CATI used)	✓	✓	✓✓✓ if allows jumping ✓
Does the mode of administration allow control over order questions are answered?	✓✓✓	✓✓✓	✓	✓	✓✓✓
Is the mode of administration suitable for sensitive questions?	✓	✓✓	✓✓✓	✓✓✓	✓✓
Is the mode of administration less likely to result in non-response to some questions?	✓✓✓	✓✓✓	✓✓	✓✓	✓✓✓
Does the mode of administration allow the use of visual aids?	✓✓✓	✓	✓✓✓	✓✓	
Answering context issues					
Does the mode of administration give respondents the opportunity to consult others for information?	✓✓	✓	✓✓✓	✓✓✓	✓✓✓

Does the mode of administration minimize the impact of interviewers' characteristics (gender, class, ethnicity)?	✓	✓✓	✓✓✓	✓✓✓	✓✓✓
Does the mode of administration minimize the impact of the social desirability effect?	✓	✓✓	✓✓✓	✓✓✓	✓✓✓
Does the mode of administration allow control over the intrusion of others in answering questions?	✓✓✓	✓✓	✓	✓	✓
Does the mode of administration minimize need for respondents to have certain skills to answer questions?	✓✓✓	✓✓✓	✓✓	✓ (because of need to have online skills)	✓ (because of need to have online skills)
Does the mode of administration enable respondents to be probed?	✓✓✓	✓✓✓	✓	✓✓	✓

Notes: Number of ticks indicates the strength of the mode of administration of a questionnaire in relation to each issue. More ticks correspond to more advantages in relation to each issue. A single tick implies that the mode of administering a questionnaire does not fare well in terms of the issue in question. Three ticks imply that it does very well, but two ticks imply that it is acceptable. This table has been influenced by the authors' own experiences and by Dillman (1978) and Czaja and Blair (1996).
CAPI is computer-assisted personal interviewing; CATI is computer-assisted telephone interviewing.

The Association of Internet Researchers (AOIR, 2002) recommends that researchers start by considering the ethical expectations established by the venue. For instance, is there a posted site policy that notifies users that the site is public and specifies the limits to privacy? Or are there mechanisms that users can employ to indicate that their exchanges are private? The more the venue is acknowledged to be public the less obligation there is on the researcher to protect the confidentiality and anonymity of individuals using the venue, or to seek their informed consent. However, the distinction between public and private space on the Internet is blurred and contested. Hewson et al. (2003) suggest that data that have been deliberately and voluntarily made available in the public Internet domain, such as newsgroups, can be used by researchers without the need for informed consent provided anonymity of individuals is protected. However, other researchers (Hudson & Bruckman, 2004) found that, although certain Internet venues might be considered by some to be public spaces, entering chat rooms and recording the conversation for research purposes provoked an extremely hostile response from chat room users (see Research in focus 22.8). Barnes (2004) identifies five types of Internet message each presenting slightly different ethical concerns for anonymity, confidentiality, and informed consent:

- Messages exchanged in online public discussion lists. A typical forum for these would be discussion or newsgroups. Although most group members see their messages as public, Barnes (2004) found that some consider them as private, despite having been sent statements upon joining the group indicating the public nature of the space. Barnes (2004) recommends as a general principle that the ideas of individuals who share their ideas on public lists should be attributed to their authors in the same way as you would attribute something they had written in a printed text under traditional copyright law. However, it is a good idea to check the welcoming messages of public discussion lists for guidance on how to approach the ethics of citing email messages. Some discussion groups state that researchers must notify the group in advance of any research being undertaken. Barnes advises that when researching any Internet group it is a good idea to contact them in advance and ask for permission to observe them.
- Messages exchanged in private discussions between individuals and on private lists. Barnes (2004) suggests in this situation the names of the lists and participants should never be revealed. To further protect individual identities she recommends that messages are combined, all headers and signatures are removed, references to

22.8 · Research in Focus

Chat room users' responses to being studied

Hudson and Bruckman (2004) designed an experiment to understand how potential participants react to being invited to participate in an online study. This involved entering a number of online moderated chat rooms and informing the participants that they were recording them and then recording how they responded. They downloaded a list of available chat rooms on 'ICQ Chat' each evening at 9:50 p.m. Dividing the chat rooms by size from very small (2–4 participants) to large (30 or more participants), they then randomly selected 16 chat rooms from each set, then subdivided these into groups of four. Each group of four chat rooms was sent a different message as follows:

No Message – the researchers entered the chat room using the nickname 'Chat Study' and said nothing;

Recording Message – the researchers entered the chat room as 'Chat Study' and announced that they were recording the chat room for a study;

Opt Out Message – the researchers entered the chat room in the same way as above but posted a message giving the participants the option not to be recorded;

Opt In Message – the researchers entered the chat room in the same way as before but gave participants the option to volunteer to be recorded.

Based on a sample of 525 chat rooms studied over a two-week period, Hudson and Bruckman found that posting a message about the study resulted in significant hostility, greatly increasing the likelihood of researchers being kicked out of the chat room by the moderator. Moreover, the likelihood of being kicked out of a chat room decreased as the number of participants in the chat room increased. The reasons given for being kicked out included referring to the study as 'spamming' (unwanted electronic communication often involving some form of commercial advertising), objection to being studied, general requests to leave, and insults. When given a chance to opt in, only four of the 766 potential respondents actually did so. Hence, even when the option of fully informed consent was given, chat room participants still objected to being studied. The researchers conclude that 'these results suggest that obtaining consent for studying online chat rooms is impracticable' (Hudson and Bruckman 2004, p. 135). This example highlights the potential ethical difficulties in intruding on a pre-existing Internet communication venue for research purposes, even if it is considered to be a public space.

---

the exact type of forum being studied are not made, and behaviour is described in general terms in a composite personality type rather than by referring to specific messages that could be traced to particular individuals.

- Personal messages sent to the researcher. In Barnes's (2004) research these were sent on to her by a contact who had already deleted the names and email addresses of the original sender, but in any case she suggests that headers and signatures are removed to protect the authors' anonymity.

- Messages re-posed and passed around the Internet. This includes messages that people forward on to other people and discussion lists because they think they are interesting. They can contain the name of the original author or be distributed as anonymous email. If they are distributed anonymously, Barnes (2004) believes it is worth trying to find the original author so they can be properly credited in research publication. She advises emailing the author and asking for permission to use the message.

- Messages generated by computer programs. This refers to messages generated by natural language computer programs that form the basis for interaction with people.

22.9   Research in Focus

Ethical issues in a virtual ethnography of change in the NHS

There have also been some attempts to highlight the ethical considerations associated with particular kinds of Internet research such as virtual ethnography. Smith (2004) was interested in organizational change and the role played by professionals in the NHS. While she was in the process of doing her research she came across a listserv that was being used by British general practitioners (GPs) as a forum to discuss their feelings about the proposed reforms to the British health-care system and their likely effects. She explains, 'essentially, I had stumbled on a "setting" in which GPs were "talking" among themselves about the significance of the proposed health care reforms for them as individuals, for the wider profession and generally about the future of general practice in Britain' (2004, p. 225). The geographically dispersed nature of GPs' work meant that the list provided a unique opportunity for them to interact with each other. Smith argues that one of the advantages of such virtual methods is that they provide the opportunity to conduct research with virtually no observer effects. Therefore, her strategy was covert because, she explains, 'I anticipated difficulties in informing participants about my research without intruding in the ongoing interaction to an unacceptable extent' (200, p.: 232) and feared that this might also arouse hostility because of the way she observed 'spam' messages were received unfavourably. For 15 months she 'participated' in the list by receiving and reading messages daily without explicitly stating or explaining her presence to the majority of the listserv's members. A further difficulty in seeking informed consent arose from the nature of the list as an unmoderated forum; therefore there was no gatekeeper to whom she could address her request. Added to this, the membership of the list of around 500 members was in constant flux, so any single request for consent would have been impossible.

Hence 'the only appropriate way to gain informed consent would be to repeatedly post requests to the entire list. Through my previous exposure to the list, however, I knew that such behavior was clearly out of line with accepted practice in this domain' (2004, p. 233).

However, as Smith explains, 'I am aware that in making the decision not to expound my presence on the list, I may face considerable ethical critique. My research appears analogous with the notion of "covert" research so demonized in the usual discussions of research ethics' (2004, p. 225). One of the ways in which she justifies this is through discussion of the features of her study that distinguish it from other studies of virtual interaction. She notes how her study examined interaction between participants who were not engaged in the kind of 'fantasy interaction' associated with sexual or social virtual interaction. Therefore, Smith argues, her participants were not taking the opportunity to 'engage in behavior with which they would not be comfortable engaging as part of their "real" lives' (2004, p. 228). A further ethical justification of her research arises from the extent to which participants saw the list as a public rather than a private space. Hence, the warning posted to each member on subscription and at monthly intervals states 'MEMBERS ARE ADVISED TO CONSIDER COMMENTS POSTED TO LISTX TO BE IN THE PUBLIC DOMAIN' (2004, p. 229, capitalization in original). In addition, list members receive guidelines on the copyright implications of email messages which state that comments posted to public lists are comparable to sending letters to a newspaper editor. Smith suggests that this provides justification for her 'electronic eavesdropping' since the ethical guidelines she was working to suggested that it was 'not necessary to explicitly seek permission for recording and analyzing publicly posted messages' because this is 'akin to conducting research in a marketplace, library or other public area, where observers are not necessarily expected to obtain informed consent from all present' (2004, p. 230).

A final ethical issue arising from the study concerns the principle of anonymity. Initially, Smith assumed she should protect the identity of participants when reporting her research findings, but through her involvement in the list she became aware that 'participants might wish to be "credited" for their postings' (2004: 234) because of the reaction when journalists used list messages without crediting the authors. However, despite this she felt that because she had not sought informed consent from all list members it would be wrong to do this.

There may also be specific ethical considerations associated with certain types of research, such as virtual ethnography (see Research in focus 22.9).

A further ethical issue relates to the principle of protecting research participants from harm (see Chapter 8) and the related issues of individual anonymity and confidentiality. Complete protection of anonymity is suggested by Stewart and Williams (2005) to be almost impossible in Internet research, since in computer-mediated communication information about the origin of a computer-generated message, revealed for instance in the header, is very difficult to remove. It is also more difficult to guarantee confidentiality because the data are often accessible to other participants. In a similar vein, DeLorme, Zinkhan, and French (2001) suggest that the Internet raises particular ethical concerns for qualitative researchers arising from the difficulty of knowing who has access to information. For example, a message posted on an Internet discussion group can be accessed by anyone who has a computer and an Internet connection. In addition, some Internet environments enable 'lurkers', people who listen to what is going on without making themselves identifiable. This makes it difficult for researchers to protect the confidentiality of data that they collect. A further concern arises from the potential for individuals to present a 'fake' identity during online interaction. If a research participant does this, it has implications for the validity of the data (see Chapter 5), but there is also potential for the researcher to deceive participants in the expectation that this will encourage them to respond more openly, for example by pretending to be a man when conducting a focus group with all-male participants. This is thus a form of covert research which raises particular ethical issues due to the lack of informed consent, as discussed in Chapter 8.

These concerns have led some researchers to suggest that there is a need for an ethics code for Internet research. DeLorme, Zinkhan, and French (2001) surveyed qualitative researchers to find out whether or not they felt there was a need for an ethics code for qualitative researchers using the Internet and, if so, what kinds of issues should it cover. A majority of respondents thought that there should be an ethics code for qualitative Internet research. When asked what their reasons were for believing this, researchers expressed a rationale based on principles, driven by a professional view of what constitutes good research, and a practical rationale, based on the belief that dishonest practices will discourage Internet users from taking part in future online studies and undermine the reputation of legitimate researchers who use the Internet. DeLorme, Zinkhan, and French (2001) suggest that ethics codes designed by professional associations such as those discussed in Chapter 8 need to be revised to include an addendum that deals with these issues. However, the debates about the ethics of Internet research and the development of guidelines for researchers are ongoing, and even though traditional ethical guidelines may need to be revised to reflect the ethical issues raised by Internet research, researchers should continue to be guided by the ethical principles discussed in Chapter 8.

Key points

- The growth in the use of the Internet offers significant opportunities for business researchers in allowing them access to a large and growing body of people.
- Many research methods covered elsewhere in this book can be adapted to online investigations.
- There is a distinction between research that uses websites as objects of analysis and research that uses the Internet to collect data from others.
- Online surveys may be of two major types: Web surveys and email surveys.
- Most of the same considerations that go into designing research that is not online apply to e-research.
- Both quantitative and qualitative research can be adapted to e-research.

Questions for review

Websites or web pages as objects of analysis

- In what ways might the analysis of websites pose particular difficulties that are less likely to be encountered in the analysis of non-electronic documents?

Using websites to collect data from individuals

- What are the chief ways of collecting data from individuals using the World Wide Web and online communications?
- What advantages do they have over traditional research methods for collecting such data?
- What disadvantages do they have in comparison to traditional research methods for collecting such data?
- What is the difference between Web-based and communication-based research methods?

Virtual ethnography

- How does **ethnography** need to be adapted in order to collect data on the use of the Internet?
- Does the study of the impact of the Internet necessarily mean that we end up as technological determinists?
- Are ethnographies of the Internet really ethnographic?

Qualitative research using online focus groups

- What is the significance of the distinction between **synchronous** and **asynchronous** focus groups?
- How different is the role of the moderator in online, as against face to face, focus groups?

Qualitative research using online personal interviews

- Can online personal interviews really be personal interviews?
- To what extent does the absence of direct contact mean that the online interview cannot be a true interview?

Online social surveys

- What is the significance of the distinction between email and Web surveys?
- Are there any special circumstances in which **embedded email** questionnaires will be more likely to be effective than attached questionnaires?
- Do sampling problems render online **social surveys** too problematic to warrant serious consideration?
- Are response rates in online surveys worse or better than in traditional surveys?

Ethical considerations in Internet research

- What ethical issues are raised by using the Internet as a method of data collection?

Part Four

Completion

Having taken you through how to get started on a research project (Part One), helped you understand and develop a research strategy (Part Two), and provided you with a range of methodological choices and the know-how to apply them (Part Three). In Part Four we literally complete the process by showing you how to undertake quantitative analysis (Chapter 23), qualitative analysis (Chapter 24) and, importantly, how to write up (and even get published) your research project.

23

Quantitative Data Analysis

Chapter guide

In this chapter, some of the basic but nonetheless most frequently used methods for analyzing **quantitative** data will be presented. In order to illustrate the use of the methods of data analysis, a small and imaginary set of data based on attendance at a gym is used. It represents the kind of small research project that would be feasible for most students doing undergraduate research projects for an honor's thesis or similar exercise. The chapter explores:

- The importance of *not* leaving considerations of how you will analyze your quantitative data until after you have collected all your data; you should be aware of the ways in which you would like to analyze your data from the earliest stage of your research.
- The distinctions between the different kinds of **variables** that can be generated in quantitative research; knowing how to distinguish types of variables is crucial so that you appreciate which methods of analysis can be applied when you examine variables and relationships between them.
- Methods for analyzing a single variable at a time (*univariate analysis*).
- Methods for analyzing relationships between variables (*bivariate analysis*).
- The analysis of relationships between three variables (**multivariate analysis**).

Introduction

In this chapter we will examine some very basic techniques for analyzing quantitative data. You may recall that in Chapter 12 we explored some of the features and ways to use SPSS for Windows in order to work with quantitative data using a computer. We did so early on in order to get you thinking about what you would need to do in order to analyze a quantitative data set. Thus, this chapter is, therefore, not so much about how to perform certain statistical tests, but rather what the implications and meanings of the results can tell us about our data. We suggest that you frequently refer back to Chapter 12 as you consider the information in this chapter. Just as in the earlier chapter regarding using SPSS, formulae that underpin the techniques to be discussed in this chapter will not be presented, since the necessary calculations can easily be carried out by using the computer program. Naturally, two chapters simply cannot do justice to these topics and readers are advised to move as soon as possible on to books that provide more detailed and advanced treatments (e.g., Bryman & Cramer, 2004).

Before beginning this discussion and illustration of techniques, we would like to give you advance warning

of one of the biggest mistakes that people make about quantitative data analysis: 'I don't have to concern myself with how I'm going to analyze my survey data until after I've collected my data. I'll leave thinking about it till then, because it doesn't impinge on how I collect my data'.

This is a common error that arises because quantitative data analysis looks like a distinct phase that occurs after the data have been collected (see for example Figure 5.1, in which the analysis of quantitative data is depicted as a late step in quantitative research). Quantitative data analysis is indeed something that occurs typically at a late stage in the overall process and is also a distinct stage.

However, this does not mean that you should not be considering how you will analyze your data until such a late stage in your research project. In fact, you should be fully aware of what techniques you will apply at a fairly early stage—for example, when you are designing your **questionnaire**, **observation schedule**, **coding frame**, or whatever. The two main reasons for this are as follows:

- You cannot apply just any technique to any variable. Techniques have to be appropriately matched to the types of variables that you have created through your research. This means that you must be fully aware of the ways in which different types of variable are classified and the resulting implications of the properties of variables.

- Both the size and nature of your sample are likely to impose limitations on the kinds of techniques you can use.

In other words, you need to be aware that decisions that you make at quite an early stage in the research process, such as the kinds of data you collect and the size of your sample, will have implications for the sorts of analysis that you will be able to conduct.

 # A small research project

The discussion of quantitative data analysis will be based upon an imaginary piece of research carried out by an undergraduate marketing student for an Honour's thesis. The student in question is interested in the role of the sport and leisure industry and in particular, because of her own enthusiasm for leisure clubs and gyms, with the ways in which such venues are used and people's reasons for joining them. She has read an article that suggests that participant involvement in adult fitness programs is associated with their attitudinal loyalty, comprising investment of time and money, social pressure from significant others, and internalization or commitment to the fitness regime (Park, 1996). She intends to use this theory as a framework for her findings. The student is also interested in issues relating to gender and body image and she suspects that men and women will differ in their reasons for going to a gym and the kinds of activities in which they engage while at the gym. Her final issue of interest relates to the importance of age in determining gym involvement. In particular, she has discovered that previous research has shown that older people generally tend to show higher levels of attitudinal loyalty to recreational activities and she wants to find out if this finding also applies to involvement in leisure clubs and gyms.

She secures the agreement of a gym close to her home to contact a sample of its members by mail. The gym has 1200 members and she decides to take a simple **random** **sample** of 10% of the membership (i.e., 120 members). She mails out questionnaires to members of the sample with a covering letter testifying to the gym's support of her research and the prior approval of the Research Ethics Board (REB) of her educational institution. One thing she wants to know is how much time people spend on each of the three main classes of activity in the gym: cardiovascular equipment, weights equipment, and exercises. She defines each class of activity carefully in the covering letter and asks members of the sample to keep a note of how long they spend on each of the three activities on their next visit. They are then requested to return the questionnaires to her in a prepaid reply envelope. She ends up with a sample of 90 questionnaires—a response rate of 75%.

Part of the questionnaire is presented in Tips and skills '*Part of a questionnaire used in study of gym users*'. The entire questionnaire runs 4 pages long, but only 12 of the questions are provided here. Many of the questions (1, 3, 4, 5, 6, 7, 8, and 9) are pre-coded and the student simply has to circle the code to the far right of the question under the column 'code'. With the remainder of the questions, specific figures are requested and she simply transfers the relevant figure to the code column. An example of a questionnaire that has been completed by a respondent and coded by the student is presented in Tips and skills '*A completed and processed questionnaire*'.

Missing data

The data for all 90 respondents are presented in Tips and skills '*Gym survey data*'. Each of the 12 questions is known for the time being as a variable number (var00001, etc.). Each variable number corresponds to the question number in Tips and skills '*Part of a questionnaire used in study of gym users*' (i.e., var00001 is question 1, var00002 is question 2, etc.). An important issue arises in the management of data as to how to handle 'missing data'. **Missing** data situations occur when respondents fail to reply to a question—either by accident or because they do not want to answer the question. Thus, in the Gym Survey data, respondent 24 has failed to answer question 2, which is concerned with age. This has been coded as a zero (0) and it will be important to ensure that the computer software is notified of this fact, since it needs

Tips and Skills

Part of a questionnaire used in study of gym users

Questionnaire   Code

1. Are you male or female (please tick)?

    Male _____   Female _____   1   2

2. How old are you?   _____ years

3. Which of the following best describes your main reason for going to the gym? (please tick one only)

    Relaxation   _____   1

    Maintain or improve fitness   _____   2

    Lose weight   _____   3

    Meet others   _____   4

    Build strength   _____   5

    Other (please specify)   _____   6

4. When you go to the gym, how often do you use the cardiovascular equipment (jogger, step machine, bike, rower)? (please tick)

    Always   _____   1

    Usually   _____   2

    Rarely   _____   3

    Never   _____   4

5. When you go to the gym, how often do you use the weights machines (including free weights)? (please tick)

    Always   _____   1

    Usually   _____   2

    Rarely   _____   3

    Never   _____   4

6. How frequently do you usually go to the gym? (please tick)

    Every day   _____   1

    4–6 days a week   _____   2

    2 or 3 days a week   _____   3

    Once a week   _____   4

    2 or 3 times a month   _____   5

    Once a month   _____   6

    Less than once a month   _____   7

7. Are you usually accompanied when you go to the gym or do you usually go on your own? (please tick one only)

    On my own   _____   1

    With a friend   _____   2

    With a partner/spouse   _____   3

8. Do you have sources of regular exercise other than the gym?

Yes ____ No ____   1 2

If you have answered No to this question, please proceed to question 10

9. If you have replied Yes to question 9, please indicate the main source of regular exercise in the last 6 months from this list. (please tick one only)

Sport	____	1
Cycling on the road	____	2
Jogging	____	3
Long walks	____	4
Other (please specify)	____	5

10. During your last visit to the gym, how many minutes did you spend on the cardiovascular equipment (jogger, step machine, bike, rower)?

____ minutes

11. During your last visit to the gym, how many minutes did you spend on the weights machines (including free weights)?

____ minutes

12. During your last visit to the gym, how many minutes did you spend on other activities (e.g., stretching exercises)?

____ minutes

Tips and Skills

A completed and processed questionnaire

Questionnaire   Code

1. Are you male or female (please tick)?

Male _✓_ Female ____   ① 2

2. How old are you?   21 years   21

3. Which of the following best describes your main reason for going to the gym? (please tick one only)

Relaxation		1
Maintain or improve fitness	✓	②
Lose weight	____	3
Meet others	____	4
Build strength	____	5
Other (please specify)	____	6

4. When you go to the gym, how often do you use the cardiovascular equipment (jogger, step machine, bike, rower)? (please tick)

Always	✓	①
Usually	____	2
Rarely	____	3

Never ____ 4

5. When you go to the gym, how often do you use the weights machines (including free weights)? (please tick)

Always ✓ ①
Usually ____ 2
Rarely ____ 3
Never ____ 4

6. How frequently do you usually go to the gym? (please tick)

Every day ____ 1
4–6 days a week 2
2 or 3 days a week ✓ ③
Once a week ____ 4
2 or 3 times a month ____ 5
Once a month ____ 6
Less than once a month ____ 7

7. Are you usually accompanied when you go to the gym or do you usually go on your own? (please tick one only)

On my own ✓ ①
With a friend ____ 2
With a partner/spouse ____ 3

8. Do you have sources of regular exercise other than the gym?

Yes ✓ No ____ 1 ②

If you have answered No to this question, please proceed to question 10

9. If you have replied Yes to question 9, please indicate the main source of regular exercise in the last 6 months from this list. (please tick one only)

Sport ____ 1
Cycling on the road ____ 2
Jogging ____ 3
Long walks ____ 4
Other (please specify) ____ 5

10. During your last visit to the gym, how many minutes did you spend on the cardiovascular equipment (jogger, step machine, bike, rower)?

33 minutes 33

11. During your last visit to the gym, how many minutes did you spend on the weights machines (including free weights)?

17 minutes 17

12. During your last visit to the gym, how many minutes did you spend on other activities (e.g., stretching exercises)?

5 minutes 5

to be taken into account during the analysis. Also, question 9 has a large number of zeros, because many people did not answer it, because they have been filtered out by the previous question (i.e., they do not have other sources of regular exercise). These have also been coded as zero to denote missing data, though strictly speaking their failure to reply is more indicative of the question not being applicable to them. Note also, that there are zeros for var00010, var00011, and var00012. However, these do not denote missing data but that the respondent spends zero minutes on the activity in question. Everyone has answered questions 10, 11, and 12, so there are in fact no missing data for these variables. If there had been missing data, it would be necessary to code missing data with a number that could not also be a true figure. For example, nobody has spent 99 minutes on these activities, so this might be an appropriate number as it is easy to remember and could not be read by the computer as anything other than missing data.

 ## Types of variable

One of the things that might strike you when you look at the questions is that the kinds of information that you receive varies by question. Some of the questions call for answers in terms of real numbers: questions 2, 10, 11, and 12. Questions 1 and 8 yield either/or answers and are therefore in the form of dichotomies. The rest of the questions take the form of lists of categories, but there are differences between these too. Some of the questions are in terms of answers that are rank ordered: questions 4, 5, and 6. Thus we can say in the case of question 6 that the category 'every day' implies greater frequency than '4–6 days a week', which in turn implies greater frequency than '2 or 3 days a week', and so on. However, in the case of questions 3, 7, and 9, the categories are not capable of being rank ordered. We cannot say in the case of question 3 that 'relaxation' is more of something than 'maintain or improve fitness' or 'lose weight'.

These considerations lead to a classification of the different types of variables that are generated in the course of research. The four main types are:

- Interval/ratio variables. These are variables where the distances between the categories are identical across the range of categories. In the case of variables var00010 to var00011, the distance between the categories is one minute. Thus, a person may spend 32 minutes on cardiovascular equipment, which is one

minute more than someone who spends 31 minutes on this equipment. That difference is the same as the difference between someone who spends 8 minutes and another who spends 9 minutes on the equipment. This is the 'highest' level of measurement and a very wide range of techniques of analysis can be applied to interval/ratio variables. There is, in fact, a distinction between interval and ratio variables, in that the latter are interval variables with a fixed zero point. However, since most ratio variables exhibit this quality in business research (e.g., income, age, number of employees, revenue), they are not being distinguished here.

- Ordinal variables. These are variables whose categories can be rank ordered (as in the case of interval/ratio variables) but the distances between the categories are not equal across the range. Thus, in the case of question 6, the difference between the category 'every day' and '4–6 days a week' is not the same as the difference between '4–6 days a week' and '2 or 3 days a week', and so on. Nonetheless, we can say that 'every day' is more frequent than '4–6 days a week', which is more frequent than '2 or 3 days a week', etc. You should also bear in mind that, if you subsequently group an interval/ratio variable like var00002, which refers to people's ages, into categories (e.g., 20 and under; 21–30; 31–40; 41–50; 51 and over), you are transforming it into an ordinal variable.

- Categorical variables. These variables, also known as nominal variables, comprise categories that cannot be rank ordered. As noted previously, we cannot say in the case of question 3 that 'relaxation' is more of something than 'maintain or improve fitness' or 'lose weight'.

- Dichotomous variables. These variables contain data that have only two categories (e.g., sex). Their position in relation to the other types is slightly ambiguous, as they have only one interval. They, therefore, can be considered as having attributes of the other three types of variable. They look as though they are categorical variables, but because they have only one interval they are sometimes treated as ordinal variables. However, it is probably safest to treat them for most purposes as if they were ordinary categorical variables.

Tips and skills

Gym survey data

var00001	var00002	var00003	var00004	var00005	var00006	var00007	var00008	var00009	var00010	var00011	var00012
1	21	2	1	1	3	1	2	0	33	17	5
2	44	1	3	1	4	3	1	2	10	23	10
2	19	3	1	2	2	1	1	1	27	18	12
2	27	3	2	1	2	1	2	0	30	17	3
1	57	2	1	3	2	3	1	4	22	0	15
2	27	3	1	1	3	1	1	3	34	17	0
1	39	5	2	1	5	1	1	5	17	48	10
2	36	3	1	2	2	2	1	1	25	18	7
1	37	2	1	1	3	1	2	0	34	15	0
2	51	2	2	2	4	3	2	0	16	18	11
1	24	5	2	1	3	1	1	1	0	42	16
2	29	2	1	2	3	1	2	0	34	22	12
1	20	5	1	1	2	1	2	0	22	31	7
2	22	2	1	3	4	2	1	3	37	14	12
2	46	3	1	1	5	2	2	0	26	9	4
2	41	3	1	2	2	3	1	4	22	7	10
1	25	5	1	1	3	1	1	1	21	29	4
2	46	3	1	2	4	2	1	4	18	8	11
1	30	3	1	1	5	1	2	0	23	9	6
1	25	5	2	1	3	1	1	1	23	19	0
2	24	2	1	1	3	2	1	2	20	7	6
2	39	1	2	3	5	1	2	0	17	0	9
1	44	3	1	1	3	2	1	2	22	8	5
1	0	1	2	2	4	2	1	4	15	10	4
2	18	3	1	2	3	1	2	1	18	7	10
1	41	3	1	1	3	1	2	0	34	10	4
2	38	2	1	2	5	3	1	2	24	14	10
1	25	2	1	1	2	1	2	0	48	22	7
1	41	5	2	1	3	1	1	2	17	27	0
2	30	3	1	1	2	2	2	0	32	13	10
2	29	3	1	3	2	1	2	0	31	0	7
2	42	1	2	2	4	2	1	4	17	14	6
1	31	2	1	1	2	1	2	0	49	21	2
2	25	3	1	1	2	3	2	0	30	17	15
1	46	3	1	1	3	1	1	3	32	10	5
1	24	5	2	1	4	1	1	2	0	36	11
2	34	3	1	1	3	2	1	4	27	14	12
2	50	2	1	2	2	3	2	0	28	8	6
1	28	5	1	1	3	2	1	1	26	22	8
2	30	3	1	1	2	1	1	4	21	9	12
1	27	2	1	1	2	1	1	3	64	15	8
2	27	2	1	2	4	2	1	4	22	10	7
1	36	5	1	1	3	2	2	0	21	24	0

var00001	var00002	var00003	var00004	var00005	var00006	var00007	var00008	var00009	var00010	var00011	var00012
2	43	3	1	1	4	1	2	0	25	13	8
1	34	2	1	1	3	2	1	1	45	15	6
2	27	3	1	1	2	1	1	4	33	10	9
2	38	2	1	3	4	2	2	0	23	0	16
1	28	2	1	1	3	3	1	2	38	13	5
1	44	5	1	1	2	1	2	0	27	19	7
2	31	3	1	2	3	2	2	0	32	11	5
2	23	2	1	1	4	2	1	1	33	18	8
1	45	3	1	1	3	1	1	2	26	10	7
2	34	3	1	2	2	3	2	0	36	8	12
1	27	3	1	1	2	3	1	3	42	13	6
2	40	3	1	1	2	2	1	4	26	9	10
2	24	2	1	1	2	1	1	2	22	10	9
1	37	2	1	1	5	2	2	0	21	11	0
1	22	5	1	1	4	1	1	1	23	17	6
2	31	3	1	2	3	1	1	4	40	16	12
1	37	2	1	1	2	3	2	0	54	12	3
2	33	1	2	2	4	2	2	0	17	10	5
1	23	5	1	1	3	1	1	1	41	27	8
1	28	3	1	1	3	3	2	0	27	11	8
2	29	2	1	2	5	2	1	2	24	9	9
2	43	3	1	1	2	1	2	0	36	17	12
1	28	5	1	1	3	1	1	1	22	15	4
1	48	2	1	1	5	1	1	4	25	11	7
2	32	2	2	2	4	2	2	0	27	13	11
1	28	5	1	1	2	2	2	0	15	23	7
2	23	2	1	1	5	1	1	4	14	11	5
2	43	2	1	2	5	1	2	0	18	7	3
1	28	2	1	1	4	3	1	2	34	18	8
2	23	3	1	1	2	1	2	0	37	17	17
2	36	1	2	2	4	2	1	4	18	12	4
1	50	2	1	1	3	1	1	2	28	14	3
1	37	3	1	1	2	2	2	0	26	14	9
2	41	3	1	1	2	1	1	4	24	11	4
1	26	5	2	1	5	1	1	1	23	19	8
2	28	3	1	1	4	1	2	0	27	12	4
2	35	2	1	1	3	1	1	1	28	14	0
1	28	5	1	1	2	1	1	2	20	24	12
2	36	2	1	1	3	2	2	0	26	9	14
2	29	3	1	1	4	1	1	4	23	13	4
1	34	1	2	2	4	2	1	0	24	12	3
1	53	2	1	1	3	3	1	1	32	17	6
2	30	3	1	1	4	1	2	0	24	10	9
1	43	2	1	1	2	1	1	2	24	14	10
2	26	5	2	1	4	1	1	1	16	23	7
2	44	1	1	1	4	2	2	0	27	18	6
1	45	1	2	2	3	3	2	0	20	14	5

The four main types of variable and illustrations of them from the gym survey are provided in Table 23.1.

Multiple-indicator (or multiple-item) **measures** of concepts, like **Likert scales**, produce, strictly speaking, ordinal variables. However, many writers argue that they can be treated as though they produce interval/ratio variables, because of the relatively large number of categories they generate. For a brief discussion of this issue, see Bryman and Cramer, who distinguish between 'true' interval/ratio variables and those produced by multiple-indicator measures (2004, pp. 71–3).

Figure 23.1 provides guidance about how to identify variables of each type.

 # Univariate analysis

Univariate analysis refers to the analysis of one variable at a time. In this section, the most common approaches will be outlined.

Frequency tables

A frequency table provides the number of people and the percentage belonging to each of the categories for the variable in question. It can be used in relation to all of the different types of variable. An example of a frequency table is provided for var00003 in Table 23.2. Notice that nobody chose two of the possible choices of answer—'meet others' and 'other'—so these are not included in the table. The table shows, for example, that 33 members of the sample go the gym to lose weight and that they represent 37% (percentages are often rounded up and down in frequency tables) of the entire sample. The procedure for generating a frequency table with SPSS is described in Chapter 12.

If an **interval/ratio variable** (like people's ages) is to be presented in a frequency table format, it is invariably the case that the categories will need to be grouped. When grouping in this way, take care to ensure that the categories you create do not overlap (for example, like this: 20–30, 30–40, 40–50, etc.). An example of a frequency table for an interval/ratio variable is shown in Table 23.3, which provides a frequency table for var00002, which reports the ages of those visiting the gym. If we do not group people in terms of age ranges, there would be 34 different categories, which is far too many to be meaningful at a glance. By creating five categories, the distribution of ages is easier to comprehend. Notice that the sample totals 89 and that the percentages are based

Table 23.1 Types of variable

Type	Description	Examples in gym study	Variable Name in SPSS (see Chapter 12)
Interval/ratio	Variables where the distances between the categories are identical across the range	var00002	age
		var00010	cardmins
		var00011	weimins
		var00012	othmins
Ordinal	Variables whose categories can be rank ordered but the distances between the categories are not equal across the range	var00004	carduse
		var00005	weiuse
		var00006	frequent
Categorical	Variables whose categories cannot be rank ordered; also known as nominal	var00003	reasons
		var00007	accomp
		var00009	exercise
Dichotomous	Variables containing data that have only two categories	var00001	gender
		var00008	othsourc

Figure 23.1

Deciding how to categorize a variable

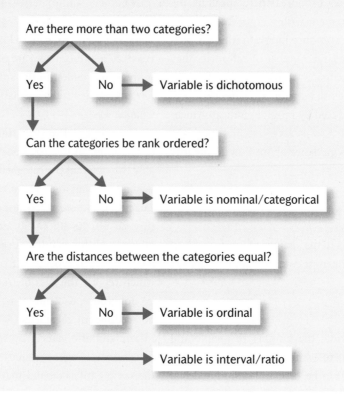

on a total of 89 rather than 90. This is because this variable contains one missing value (respondent 24). Recall that the procedure for grouping respondents using SPSS is also described in Chapter 12.

Diagrams

Diagrams are among the most frequently used methods of displaying quantitative data. Their chief advantage is that they are relatively easy to interpret and understand. If you are working with categorical or ordinal variables, the bar chart and the pie chart are two of the easiest methods to use. A bar chart of the same data presented in Table 23.2 is presented in Figure 23.2. Each bar represents the number of people falling in each category. This figure was produced with SPSS for Windows as in Chapter 12.

Another way of displaying the same data is through a pie chart, like the one in Figure 23.3. This also shows the relative size of the different categories but brings out as well the size of each slice relative to the total sample. The percentage that each slice represents of the whole sample is also given in this diagram, which was also produced with SPSS for Windows.

If you are displaying an interval/ratio variable, like var00002, a *histogram* is likely to be employed. Figure 23.4, which is also generated by SPSS for Windows, uses the same data and categories as Table 23.3. As with the bar chart, the bars represent the relative size of each of the age bands. However, note that, with the histogram, there is no space between the bars, whereas there is a space between the bars of a bar chart. Histograms are produced for interval/ratio variables, whereas bar charts are produced for categorical and ordinal variables. We have already discussed the procedure for generating a histogram with SPSS in the earlier chapter.

Table 23.2 Frequency table showing reasons for visiting the gym		
Reason	*n*	%
Relaxation	9	10
Maintain or improve fitness	31	34
Lose weight	33	37
Build strength	17	19
TOTAL	90	100

Table 23.3 Frequency table showing ages of gym members		
Age	*n*	%
20 and under	3	3
21–30	39	44
31–40	23	26
41–50	21	24
51 and over	3	3
TOTAL	89	100

Measures of central tendency

Measures of central tendency encapsulate in one number a value that is typical for a distribution of values. In effect, we are seeking out an average for a distribution, but, in quantitative data analysis, three different forms of average are recognized.

- Arithmetic mean. This is the average as we commonly understand it in everyday use—that is, we add up all the values in a distribution and then divide by the number of values. Thus, the arithmetic mean (or more simply the mean) for var00002 is 33.6, meaning that the average age of gym visitors is nearly 34 years of age. The mean should be employed only in relation to interval/ratio variables, though it is not uncommon to see it being used for ordinal variables as well.
- Median. This is the mid-point in a distribution of values. Whereas the mean is vulnerable to outliers (extreme values at either end of the distribution), which will exert considerable upwards or downwards pressure on the mean, by taking the mid-point of a distribution, the median is not affected in this way. The median is found by arranging all of the values in a distribution from the smallest to the largest and then finding the middle point. If there is an even number of values, the median is calculated by taking the mean of the two middle numbers of the distribution. In the case of var00002,

Figure 23.2

Bar chart showing main reasons for visiting the gym (SPSS output)

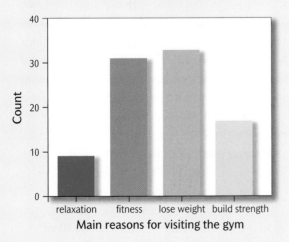

Figure 23.3

Pie chart showing main reasons for visiting the gym (SPSS output)

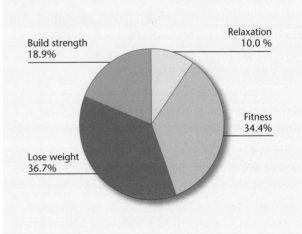

Figure 23.4

Histogram showing the ages of gym visitors (SPSS output)

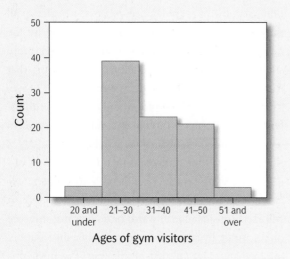

the median is 31. This is slightly lower than the mean in part because some considerably older members (especially respondents 5 and 10) inflate the mean slightly. The median can be employed in relation to both interval/ratio and ordinal variables.

- Mode. This is the value that occurs most frequently in a distribution. The mode for var00002 is 28. The mode can be employed in relation to all types of variable.

We have discussed the procedures for generating the mean, median, and mode with SPSS in Chapter 12.

Measures of dispersion

The amount of variation in a sample can be just as interesting as providing estimates of the typical value of a distribution. For one thing, it becomes possible to draw contrasts between comparable distributions of values. For example, is there more or less variability in the amount of time spent on cardiovascular equipment as compared to weights machines?

The most obvious way of measuring dispersion is by the *range*. This is simply the difference between the maximum and the minimum value in a distribution of values associated with an interval/ratio variable. In our example, we find that the range for the two types of equipment is 64 minutes for the cardiovascular equipment and 48 minutes for the weights machines. This suggests that there is more variability in the amount of time spent on the former. However, like the mean, the range is influenced by **outliers**, such as respondent 60 in the case of var00010.

Another **measure of dispersion** is the **standard deviation**, which is essentially the average amount of variation around the mean. Although the calculation is somewhat more complicated than this, the standard deviation is calculated by taking the difference between each value in a distribution and the mean and then dividing the total of the differences by the number of values. The standard deviation for var00010 is 9.9 minutes and for var00011 it is 8 minutes. Thus, not only is the average amount of time spent on the cardiovascular equipment higher than for the weights equipment; the standard deviation is greater too. The standard deviation is also affected by outliers, but, unlike the range, their impact is offset by dividing by the number of values in the distribution. See the chapter on using SPSS for Windows to recall how to generate standard deviation values for data sets.

 ## Bivariate analysis

Bivariate analysis is concerned with the analysis of two variables at a time in order to uncover whether or not the two variables are related. When we are exploring relationships between variables, this means searching for evidence that the variation in one variable coincides with variation in another variable. A variety of techniques are available for examining relationships, but their use depends on the nature of the two variables being analyzed. Figure 23.5 offers a convenient portrayal of the main types of bivariate analysis according to the types of variable involved.

Relationships not causality

An important point to bear in mind about all of the methods for analyzing relationships between variables is that it is precisely relationships that they uncover. As was noted in Chapter 4 in relation to cross-sectional designs, this means that you cannot infer that one variable causes another. Indeed, there are cases when what appears to be a causal influence working in one direction actually works in the other way.

Sometimes, we may feel *confident* that we can infer a causal direction when a relationship between two variables is discerned—for example, if we find that age and voting behaviour are related. It is impossible for the way people vote to influence their age, so, if we do find the two variables to be related, we can infer with complete confidence that age is the **independent variable**. It is not uncommon for researchers, when analyzing their data, to draw inferences about *causal direction* based on their assumptions about the likely causal direction among related variables. Although such inferences may be based on sound reasoning, they can only be inferences and there is the possibility that the real pattern of causal direction is the opposite of that which is anticipated.

Contingency tables

Contingency tables are probably the most flexible of all methods of analyzing relationships in that they can be used in relation to any pair of variables, though they are not the most efficient method for some pairs, which is the reason why the method is not recommended in all of the cells in Figure 23.5. A contingency table is like a frequency table but it allows two variables to be simultaneously analyzed so that relationships between the two variables can be examined. It is normal for contingency tables to include percentages, since these make the tables easier to interpret. Table 23.4 examines the relationship between two variables from the gym survey: gender and reasons for visiting

Figure 23.5

Methods of bivariate analysis

	Nominal	Ordinal	Interval/ratio	Dichotomous
Nominal	Contingency table + chi-square (χ^2) + Cramér's *V*	Contingency table + chi-square (χ^2) + Cramér's *V*	Contingency table + chi-square (χ^2) + Cramér's *V*. If the interval/ratio variable can be identified as the dependent variable, compare means + eta	Contingency table + chi-square (χ^2) + Cramér's *V*
Ordinal	Contingency table + chi-square (χ^2) + Cramér's *V*	Spearman's rho (ρ)	Spearman's rho (ρ)	Spearman's rho (ρ)
Interval/ratio	Contingency table + chi-square (χ^2) + Cramér's *V*. If the interval/ratio variable can be identified as the dependent variable, compare means + eta	Spearman's rho (ρ)	Pearson's *r*	Spearman's rho (ρ)
Dichotomous	Contingency table + chi-square (χ^2) + Cramér's *V*	Spearman's rho (ρ)	Spearman's rho (ρ)	phi (ϕ)

the gym. The percentages are column percentages—that is, they calculate the number in each cell as a percentage of the total number in that column. Thus, to take the top left-hand cell, the three men who go to the gym for relaxation are 7% of all 42 men in the sample. Users of contingency tables often present the presumed independent variable (if one can in fact be presumed) as the column variable and the presumed dependent variable as the rows variable. In this case, we are presuming that gender influences reasons for going to the gym. In fact, we know that going to the gym cannot influence gender. In such circumstances, it is column rather than row percentages that will be required. Chapter 12 has covered the generation of contingency tables using SPSS.

Contingency tables are generated so that patterns of association can be searched for. In this case, we can see clear gender differences in reasons for visiting the gym. As our student anticipated, females are much more likely than men to go to the gym to lose weight. They are also somewhat more likely to go to the gym for relaxation. By contrast, men are much more likely to go to the gym to build strength. There is little difference between the two genders in terms of fitness as a reason.

Pearson's *r*

Pearson's *r* is a method for examining relationships between interval/ratio variables. The main features of this method are:

- The coefficient will almost certainly lie between 0 (zero or no relationship between the two variables) and 1 (a perfect relationship)—this indicates the strength of a relationship.
- The closer the coefficient is to 1, the stronger the relationship; the closer it is to 0, the weaker the relationship.
- The coefficient will be either positive or negative—this indicates the direction of a relationship.

To illustrate these features consider Tips and skills '*Imaginary data from five variables to show different types of relationship*', which gives imaginary data for five variables, and the *scatter diagrams* in Figures 23.6–23.9,

Table 23.4 Contingency table showing the relationship between gender and reasons for visiting the gym

Reasons	Male		Female	
	No.	%	No.	%
Relaxation	3	7	6	13
Fitness	15	36	16	33
Lose weight	8	19	25	52
Build strength	16	38	1	2
TOTAL	42		48	

Note: $x^2 = 22.726$ $p < 0.0001$.

which look at the relationship between pairs of interval/ratio variables. The scatter diagram for variables 1 and 2 is presented in Figure 23.6 and shows a perfect **positive relationship**, which would have a Pearson's *r* **correlation** of 1. This means that, as one variable increases, the other variable increases by the same amount and that no other variable is related to either of them. If the correlation was below 1, it would mean that variable 1 is related to at least one other variable as well as to variable 2.

The scatter diagram for variables 2 and 3 (see Figure 23.7) shows a perfect **negative relationship**, which would have a Pearson's *r* correlation of −1. This means that, as one variable increases, the other variable decreases and that no other variable is related to either of them.

If there was no or virtually no correlation between the variables, there would be no apparent pattern to the markers in the scatter diagram. This is the case with the relationship between variables 2 and 5. The correlation is virtually zero at −0.041. This means that the variation in each variable is associated with other variables than the ones present in this analysis. Figure 23.8 shows the appropriate scatter diagram.

If a relationship is strong, a clear patterning to the variables will be evident. This is the case with variables 2 and 4, whose scatter diagram appears in Figure 23.9. There is clearly a **positive relationship** and in fact the Pearson's *r* value is +0.88 (usually, *positive correlations* are presented without the + sign). This means that the variation in the two variables is very closely connected,

Figure 23.6

Scatter diagram showing a perfect positive relationship

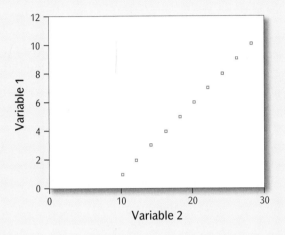

but that there is some influence of other variables in the extent to which they vary.

Going back to the gym survey, we find that the correlation between age (var00002) and the amount of time spent on weights equipment (var00011) is −0.27, imply-ing a weak negative relationship. This suggests that there is a tendency such that, the older a person is, the less likely he or she is to spend much time on such equipment, but that other variables clearly influence the amount of time spent on this activity.

In order to be able to use Pearson's r, the relationship between the two variables must be broadly *linear*—that is, when plotted on a scatter diagram, the values of the two variables approximate to a straight line (even though they may be scattered, as in Figure 23.9) and do not curve. Therefore, plotting a scatter diagram before using Pearson's r is important, in order to determine that the nature of the relationship between a pair of variables does not violate the assumption that the two variables have a somewhat linear relationship.

When you square a value of Pearson's r (i.e., multiply the value by itself), you can derive a further useful statistic called the *coefficient of determination*. This statistic expresses how much of the variation in one variable is due to the other variable. Thus, if r is −0.27, r^2 is 0.0729. We can then express this as a percentage by multiplying r^2 by 100. The product of these calculations is 7%. This means that just 7% of the variation in the use of cardiovascular equipment is accounted for by age. The *coefficient of determination* is a useful adjunct to the interpretation of correlation information.

Tips and Skills

Imaginary data from five variables to show different types of relationship

Variables				
1	2	3	4	5
1	10	50	7	9
2	12	45	13	23
3	14	40	18	7
4	16	35	14	15
5	18	30	16	6
6	20	25	23	22
7	22	20	19	12
8	24	15	24	8
9	26	10	22	18
10	28	5	24	10

Figure 23.7

Scatter diagram showing a perfect negative relationship

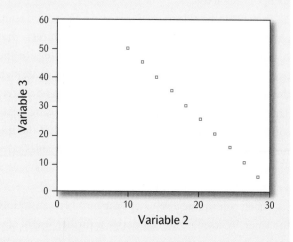

Figure 23.8

Scatter diagram showing two variables that are not related

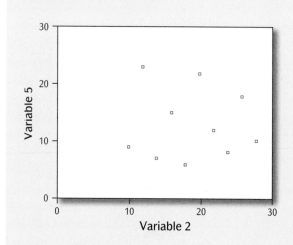

The procedure for generating Pearson's *r* with spss, complete with instructions on how to produce scatter diagrams, is described in Chapter 12.

Spearman's rho

Spearman's rho, which is often represented with the Greek letter ρ, is designed for the use of pairs of ordinal variables, but is also used, as suggested by Figure 23.5, when one variable is ordinal and the other is interval/ ratio. It is exactly the same as Pearson's *r* in terms of the outcome of calculating it, in that the computed value of rho will be either positive or negative and will vary between 0 and 1. If we look at the gym study, there are three ordinal variables: var00004, var00005, and var00006 (see Table 23.1). If we use Spearman's rho to calculate the correlation between the first two variables, we find that the correlation between var00004 and var00005—frequency of use of the cardiovascular and weights equipment—is low at 0.2. A slightly stronger relationship is found between var00006 (frequency of going to the gym) and var00010 (amount of time spent on the cardiovascular equipment), which is 0.4. Note that the latter variable is an interval/ ratio variable. When confronted with a situation in which

Figure 23.9

Scatter diagram showing a strong positive relationship

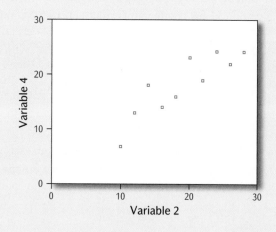

we want to calculate the correlation between an ordinal and an interval/ratio variable, we cannot use Pearson's *r*, because both variables must be at the interval/ratio level of measurement. Instead, we must use Spearman's rho (see Figure 23.5). Spearman's rho can also be calculated by SPSS.

Phi and Cramér's *V*

Phi (φ) and Cramér's *V* are two closely related statistics. The phi coefficient is used for the analysis of the relationship between two dichotomous variables. Like Pearson's *r*, it results in a computed statistic that varies between 0 and + or −1. The correlation between var00001 (gender) and var00008 (other sources of regular exercise) is 0.24, implying that males are somewhat more likely than females to have other sources of regular exercise, though the relationship is weak.

Cramér's *V* uses a similar formula to phi and can be employed with categorical variables (see Figure 23.5). However, this statistic can only be a positive value, so that it can give solely give an indication only of the strength of the relationship between two variables, not of the direction. The value of Cramér's *V* associated with the analysis presented in Table 23.4 is 0.50. This suggests a moderate relationship between the two variables. Cramér's *V* is usually reported along with a contingency table and a chi-square test (see below). It is not normally presented on its own. The procedure for generating phi and Cramér's *V* with SPSS was described in Chapter 12.

Comparing means and eta

If you need to examine the relationship between an interval/ratio variable and a categorical variable, and if the latter can be relatively unambiguously identified as the independent variable, a potentially fruitful approach is to compare the means of the interval/ratio variable for each subgroup of the categorical variable. As an example, consider Table 23.5, which presents the mean number of minutes spent on cardiovascular equipment (var00010) for each of the four categories of reasons for going to the gym (var00003). The means suggest that people who go to the gym for fitness or to lose weight spend considerably more time on this equipment than people who go to the gym to relax or to build strength.

This procedure is often accompanied by a test of association between variables called **eta**. This statistic expresses the level of association between the two variables and, like Cramér's *V*, will always be positive. The level of eta for the data in Table 23.5 is 0.48. This suggests a moderate relationship between the two variables. Eta-squared expresses the amount of variation in the interval/ratio variable that is due to the categorical variable. In the case of this example, eta-squared is 22%. Eta is a very flexible method for exploring the relationship between two variables, because it can be employed when one variable is categorical and the other interval/ratio. Also, it does not make the assumption that the relationship between variables is linear. The procedure for comparing means and for generating eta with SPSS has been detailed in Chapter 12.

 ## Multivariate analysis

Multivariate analysis entails the simultaneous analysis of three or more variables. This is quite an advanced topic and it is recommended that readers examine a text book on quantitative data analysis for an exposition of techniques (e.g., Bryman & Cramer, 2004). There are three main contexts within which multivariate analysis might be employed.

Could the relationship be spurious?

In order for a relationship between two variables to be established, not only must there be evidence that there is a relationship but the relationship must be shown to be non-spurious. A spurious relationship exists when there appears to be a relationship between two variables, but the relationship is not real: it is being produced because each variable is itself related to a third variable. For example, if we find a relationship in a firm between employees' levels of organizational commitment and job satisfaction, we might ask: could the relationship be an artifact of the leadership style of respondents' immediate managers (see Figure 23.10)? The more committed people are to their organization, the more job satisfaction they are likely to exhibit. However, whether leaders are considerate to their subordinates or not is likely to influence both organizational commitment and job satisfaction. If leadership style were found to be producing the apparent relationship between organizational commitment and job satisfaction, we would conclude that the relationship is spurious. An

Table 23.5 Comparing subgroup means: time spent on cardiovascular equipment by reasons for going to the gym

Time	Reasons				
	Relaxation	Fitness	Lose weight	Build strength	Total
Mean number of minutes spent on cardiovascular equipment	18.33	30.55	28.36	19.65	26.47
n	9	31	33	17	90

interesting possible case of a spurious relationship was highlighted in a very short report in the UK newspaper *The Times* (October, 1, 1999, p. 2) concerning some medical findings. The article noted that there is evidence to suggest that women on hormone replacement therapy (HRT) have lower levels of heart disease than those not on this form of therapy. The article cites Swedish findings that suggest that the relationship may be due to the fact that women who choose to start the therapy are 'thinner, richer and healthier' than those who do not. These background factors would seem to affect both the likelihood of taking HRT and the likelihood of getting heart disease. A further illustration in connection with a health-related issue comes from another Times article (Hawkes, 2003), which reports a relationship among men between frequency of shaving and likelihood of a heart attack or stroke. The reason appears to be that each of the variables (frequency of shaving and vulnerability to a heart attack or stroke) is affected by lifestyle and hormonal factors.

Could there be an intervening variable?

Suppose that, unlike the previous examples, we do not find that the relationship is spurious; we might ask why there is a relationship between two variables. For example, there have been several studies that have explored the relationship between an organization's market orientation and its business performance. However, the mixed nature of the findings to have emerged from these studies led Piercy, Harris, and Lane (2002) to suggest that there is a more complex relationship between these two variables than previous studies have assumed. In particular, they speculated that higher levels of market orientation are associated with higher levels of employee motivation, satisfaction, and commitment, which in turn leads to enhanced organizational performance. Employee attitudes are thus an intervening variable:

market → employee → organizational
orientation attitudes performance

Figure 23.10

A spurious relationship

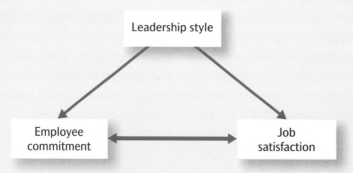

An intervening variable allows us to answer questions about the bivariate relationship between variables. It suggests that the relationship between the two variables is not a direct one, since the impact of market orientation on organizational performance is viewed as occurring via employee attitudes.

Could a third variable moderate the relationship?

We might ask a question like: does the relationship between two variables hold for men but not for women? If it does, then the relationship is said to be moderated by gender. We might ask in the gym study, for example, if the relationship between age and if visitors have other sources of regular exercise (var00008) is moderated by gender. This would imply that, if we find a pattern relating age to other sources of exercise, that pattern will vary by gender. Table 23.6 shows the relationship between age and other sources of exercise. In this table, age has been broken down into just three age bands to make the table easier to read. The table suggests that the 31–40 age group is less likely to have other sources of regular exercise than the 30 and under and 41 and over age groups. However, Table 23.7, which breaks the relationship down by gender, suggests that the pattern for males and females is somewhat different. Among males, the pattern shown in Table 23.6 is very pronounced, but for females the likelihood of having other sources of exercise declines with gender. It would seem that the relationship between age and other sources of exercise is moderated by gender. This example illustrates the way in which contingency tables can be employed for multivariate analysis. However, there is a wide variety of other techniques (Bryman & Cramer, 2004; Chapter 10).

 ## Statistical significance

One difficulty with working on data deriving from a sample is that there is often the lingering worry that, even though you have employed a probability sampling procedure (as in the gym survey), your findings will not be generalizable to the population from which the sample was drawn. As we saw in Chapter 9, there is always the possibility that sampling error (difference between the population and the sample that you have selected) has occurred, even when probability sampling procedures have been followed. If this happens, the sample will be unrepresentative of the wider population and, therefore, any findings will be invalid. To make matters worse, there is no feasible way of finding out whether or not they do in fact apply to the population! What you can do is provide an indication of how confident you can be in your findings. This is one of the purposes of the concept of statistical significance and the various tests for it.

We need to know how confident we can be that our findings can be generalized to the **population** from which that sample was selected. Since we cannot be absolutely certain that a finding based on a sample will also be found in the population, we need a technique that allows us to establish how confident we can be that the finding exists in the population and what risk we are taking in inferring that the finding exists in the population. These two elements—confidence and risk—lie at the heart of **tests of statistical significance** (see Key concept 23.1). However, it is important to appreciate that tests of statistical significance can be employed only in relation to samples that have been drawn using probability sampling.

In Chapter 9 (see Tips and skills '*Generalizing from a random sample to the population*'), in the context of the discussion of the **standard error of the mean**, we began to get an appreciation of the ideas behind **statistical significance**. For example, we know that the mean age of the gym sample is 33.6. Using the concept of the standard error of the mean, we can calculate that we can be 95% confident that the population's mean lies between 31.72 and

Table 23.6 Contingency table showing the relationship between age and whether or not gym visitors have other sources of regular exercise (percentages)

Other source of exercise	Age		
	30 and under	31–40	41 and over
Other source	64	43	58
No other source	36	57	42
n	42	23	24

Table 23.7 Contingency table showing the relationship between age and whether or not gym visitors have other sources of regular exercise for males and females (percentages)

Other source of exercise	Gender					
	Male			Female		
	30 and under	31–40	41 and over	30 and under	31–40	41 and over
Other source	70	33	75	59	50	42
No other source	30	67	25	41	50	58
n	20	9	12	22	14	12

35.47. This suggests that we can broadly determine the degree of confidence that we can have in a sample mean.

In the rest of this section, we will look at the tests that are available for determining the degree of confidence we can have in our findings when we explore relationships between variables. All of the tests have a common structure:

- Set up a **null hypothesis**. A null hypothesis stipulates that two variables are not related in the population—for example, that there is no relationship between gender and visiting the gym in the population from which the sample was selected.
- Establish the **level of statistical significance** that you find acceptable. This is essentially a measure of the degree of risk that you might reject the null hypothesis (implying that there actually is a relationship in the population) when instead you should support it (implying that there is no relationship in the population). Levels of statistical significance are expressed as probability levels—that is, the probability of rejecting the null hypothesis when you should be confirming it. See Key concept 23.2 on this issue. The convention among most business researchers is that the maximum level of statistical significance that is acceptable is $p < 0.05$, which implies that there are fewer than 5 chances in 100 that you could have a sample

that shows a relationship when there is not one in the population.

- Determine the statistical significance of your findings (i.e., use a statistical test like chi-square, see below).
- If your findings are statistically significant at the 0.05 level—so that the risk of getting a relationship as strong as the one you have found, when there is no relationship in the population, is no higher than 5 in 100—you would reject the null hypothesis. Therefore, you are implying that the results are unlikely to have occurred by chance.

There are in fact two types of error that can be made when inferring statistical significance. These errors are known as Type I and Type II errors (see Figure 23.11). A Type I error occurs when you reject the null hypothesis when it should in fact be confirmed. This means that your results have arisen by chance and you are falsely concluding that there is a relationship in the population when there is not one. The use of a $p < 0.05$ level of significance means that we are more likely to make a Type I error than when we use a $p < 0.01$ level of significance. This is because with 0.01 there is less chance of falsely rejecting the null hypothesis. However, in doing so, you increase the chance of making a Type II error (accepting the null hypothesis when

Key concept 23.1: What is a test of statistical significance?

A test of statistical significance offers an estimate of how confident we can be that the results deriving from a study based on a randomly selected sample are generalizable to the population from which the sample was drawn.

Key concept 23.2: What is the level of statistical significance?

This is the level of risk that you are prepared to take that you are inferring that there is a relationship between two variables in the population from which the sample was taken when in fact no such relationship exists.

you should reject it). This is because you are more likely to confirm the null hypothesis when the significance level is 0.01 (1 in 100) than when it is 0.05 (1 in 20). This example highlights the relationship between Type I and Type II errors; namely that you cannot reduce the likelihood of incurring one type of error without causing subsequent possible increases in the other.

The chi-square test

The chi-square (x^2) test is applied to contingency tables like Table 23.4. It allows us to establish how confident we can be that there is a relationship between the two variables in the population. The test works by calculating for each cell in the table an expected frequency or value—that is, one that would occur on the basis of chance alone. The chi-square value, which in Table 23.4 is 22.726, is calculated by calculating the differences between the actual and expected values for each cell in the table and then adding up those differences (it is slightly more complicated than this, but the details need not concern us here). The chi-square value means nothing on its own and can be meaningfully interpreted only in relation to its associated level of statistical significance, which in this case is $p < 0.0001$. This means that there is only one chance in 10,000 of rejecting the null hypothesis (that is, inferring that there is a relationship in the population when there is no such relationship in the population). You could be extremely confident that there is a relationship between gender and reasons for visiting the gym among all gym members, since the chance that you have obtained a sample that shows a relationship when there is no relationship among all gym members is 1 in 10,000.

Whether or not a chi-square value achieves statistical significance depends not just on its magnitude but also on the number of categories of the two variables being analyzed. This latter issue is governed by what is known as the '*degrees of freedom*' associated with the table. The number of degrees of freedom is governed by the simple formula:

Number of degrees = (number of columns −1)
of freedom   (number of rows −1).

In the case of Table 23.5, this will be (2 −1) (4 −1), that is, 3. In other words, the chi-square value that is arrived at is

affected by the size of the table, and this is taken into account when deciding whether the chi-square value is statistically significant or not. The procedure for chi-square in conjunction with a contingency table with SPSS is described in Chapter 12.

Correlation and statistical significance

Examining the statistical significance of a computed correlation coefficient, which is based on a randomly selected sample, provides information about the likelihood that the coefficient will be found in the population from which the sample was taken. Thus, if we find a correlation of −0.62, what is the likelihood that a relationship of at least that size exists in the population? This tells us if the relationship could have arisen by chance.

If the correlation coefficient r is −0.62 and the significance level is $p < 0.05$, we can reject the null hypothesis that there is no relationship in the population. We can infer that there are only 5 chances in 100 that a correlation of at least −0.62 could have arisen by chance alone. You *could* have 1 of the 5 samples in 100 that shows a relationship when there is not one in the population, but the *degree of risk* is reasonably small. If, say, it was found that $r = -0.62$ and $p < 0.1$, there could be as many as 10 chances in 100 that there is no correlation in the population. This would *not* be an acceptable level of risk for most purposes. It would mean that in as many as 1 sample in 10 we might find a correlation of −0.62 or above when there is not a correlation in the population. If $r = -0.62$ and $p < 0.001$, there is only 1 chance in 1,000 that no correlation exists in the population. There would be a very low level of risk if you inferred that the correlation had not arisen by chance.

Whether a correlation coefficient is statistically significant or not will be affected by two factors:

* the size of the computed coefficient; and
* the size of the sample.

This second factor may appear surprising. Basically, the larger a sample, the more likely it is that a computed correlation coefficient will be found to be statistically significant. Thus, even though the correlation between age and the amount of time spent on weights machines in the gym

Figure 23.11

Type I and Type II errors

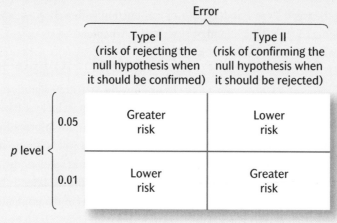

survey was found to be just −0.27, which is a fairly weak relationship, it is statistically significant at the p < 0.01 level. This means that there is only 1 chance in 100 that there is no relationship in the population. Because the question of whether or not a correlation coefficient is statistically significant depends so much on the sample size, it is important to realize that you should always examine both the correlation coefficient and the significance level. You should not examine one at the expense of the other.

This treatment of correlation and statistical significance applies to both Pearson's *r* and Spearman's rho. A similar interpretation can also be applied to phi and Cramér's *V*. SPSS automatically produces information regarding statistical significance when Pearson's *r*, Spearman's rho, phi, and Cramér's *V* are generated.

Comparing means and statistical significance

A test of statistical significance can also be applied to the comparison of means that was carried out in Table 23.5.

This procedure entails treating the total amount of variation in the dependent variable—amount of time spent on cardiovascular equipment—as made up of two types: variation within the four subgroups that make up the independent variable, and variation between them. The latter is often called the explained variance and the former the error variance. A test of statistical significance for the comparison of means entails relating the two types of variance to form what is known as the F statistic. This statistic expresses the amount of explained variance in relation to the amount of error variance. In the case of the data in Table 23.5, the resulting F statistic is statistically significant at the $p < 0.001$ level. This finding suggests that there is only 1 chance in 1,000 that there is no relationship between the two variables among all gym members. SPSS produces information regarding the F statistic and its statistical significance if the procedures described in Chapter 12 are followed.

Checklist

Doing and writing up quantitative data analysis:

- [ ] Have you answered your research questions?
- [ ] Have you made sure that you have presented only analyses that are relevant to your research questions?

☐ Have you made sure that you have taken into account the nature of the **variable**(s) being analyzed when using a particular technique (i.e., whether **categorical**, **ordinal**, **interval/ratio**, or **dichotomous**)?

☐ Have you used the most appropriate and powerful techniques for answering your research questions?

☐ If your **sample** has *not* been randomly selected, have you made sure that you have not made *inferences* about a **population** (or at least, if you have done so, have you outlined the limitations of making such an inference?)?

☐ If your data are based on a **cross-sectional design**, have you resisted making unsustainable inferences about **causality**?

☐ Have you remembered to **code** any **missing data**?

☐ Have you commented on all the analyses you present?

☐ Have you gone beyond **univariate analysis** and conducted at least some **bivariate analyses**?

☐ If you have used a **Likert scale** with reversed items, have you remembered to reverse the coding of them?

Key points

- You need to think about your data analysis before you begin designing your research instruments.
- Techniques of data analysis are applicable to some types of variable and not others. You need to know the difference between categorical, ordinal, interval/ratio, and dichotomous variables.
- You need to think about the kinds of data you are collecting and the implications your decisions will have for the sorts of techniques you will be able to employ.
- Become familiar with computer software like SPSS before you begin designing your research instruments, because it is advisable to be aware at an early stage of difficulties you might have in presenting your data in SPSS.
- Make sure you are thoroughly familiar with the techniques introduced in this chapter and when you can and cannot use them.
- The basic message, then, is not to leave these considerations until your data have been collected, tempting though it may be.
- Do not confuse **statistical significance** with substantive significance.

Questions for review

- At what stage should you begin to think about the kinds of data analysis you need to conduct?
- What are missing data and why do they arise?

Types of variable

- What are the differences between the four types of variable outlined in this chapter: interval/ratio; ordinal; categorical; and dichotomous?
- Why is it important to be able to distinguish between the four types of variable?
- Imagine the kinds of answers you would receive if you administered the following four questions in an interview survey. What kind of variable would each question generate: dichotomous; categorical; ordinal; or interval/ratio?

    1. Do you enjoy going shopping? Yes ___ No ___
    2. How many times have you shopped in the last month? Please write in the number of occasions below.

3. For which kinds of items do you most enjoy shopping? Please tick one only.
   Clothes (including shoes)   ____
   Food   ____
   Things for the house   ____
   Presents   ____
   Entertainment (CDs, videos, etc.) ____

4. How important is it to you to buy clothes with designer labels?
   Very important   ____
   Fairly important   ____
   Not very important   ____
   Not at all important ____

Univariate analysis

* What is an outlier and why might one have an adverse effect on the mean and the range?
* In conjunction with which measure of central tendency would you expect to report the standard deviation: the mean; the median; or the mode?

Bivariate analysis

* Can you infer causality from bivariate analysis?
* Why are percentages crucial when presenting contingency tables?
* In what circumstances would you use each of the following: Pearson's r; Spearman's rho; phi; Cramér's V; eta?

Multivariate analysis

* What is a spurious relationship?
* What is an intervening variable?
* What does it mean to say that a relationship is moderated?

Statistical significance

* What does statistical significance mean and how does it differ from substantive significance?
* What is a significance level?
* What does the chi-square test achieve?
* What does it mean to say that a correlation of 0.42 is statistically significant at $p < 0.05$?

24

Qualitative Data Analysis

Chapter guide

In previous chapters (20 and 21) we examined *poststructuralist* approaches to qualitative research that help to frame data collection and *analysis*. The approaches we examined included **critical discourse analysis**, **critical hermeneutics**, poststructuralist **historiography**, and ANTi-**History**, as well as **poststructuralist** approaches to **narrative analysis** and **ethnography**. Basically, we argued that the theoretical frameworks involved provided the basis for data collection that was linked to a particular form of analysis. For example, by using **critical discourse analysis** researchers set out to collect data on the existence (or absence) or powerful discourses and their influence on those involved. At the level of data collection the researcher may end up with, what appears to be, a multitude of statements about various things. However, data analysis is usually helped because the collected statements (and/or observations) were framed to provide clues to the existence of certain discourses. Thus, at the level of data analysis the research begins to comb the statements/observations for strands or traces of knowledge that—when cumulative across a number of statements/observations—appear to constitute a discourse or discursive field. Although the process of interpretation is never quite that easy this roughly describes the process involved and the relationship between the theoretical framework, data, and analysis.

However, as we have discussed in Chapters 2, 3, and 6, not all qualitative research falls under the category of **postpositivist** research, and some **qualitative** approaches have very different start (and end) points. In this chapter we are going to look at two main approaches, **analytic induction** and classic **grounded theory**, that lie more within a **positivist** framework. These approaches to **quantitative** data, deriving from interviews and or **participant observation**, typically generate a large corpus of unstructured textual material, they are not straightforward to analyze. Moreover, unlike quantitative data analysis, clear-cut rules about how qualitative data analysis should be carried out have not been developed. In this chapter, some general approaches to selective positivist qualitative data analysis will be examined, along with **coding**, which is the main feature of most of these approaches. The chapter explores:

- *Analytic induction* as a general strategy of qualitative data analysis.
- *Grounded theory* as a general strategy of qualitative data analysis. This is probably the most prominent of the general approaches to qualitative data analysis. The chapter examines its main features, processes, and outcomes, along with some of the criticisms that are sometimes levelled at the approach.
- *Coding* as a key process in grounded theory and in approaches to qualitative data analysis more generally. It is the focus of an extended discussion in terms of what it entails and some of the limitations of a reliance on coding; the criticism that is sometimes made of coding in relation to qualitative data—namely, that it tends to fragment data.
- The idea of *narrative analysis* is introduced as an approach to data analysis that is gaining a growing following and that does not result in data fragmentation; the possibility of conducting a secondary analysis of other researchers' qualitative data.

Introduction

One of the main difficulties with qualitative research is that it very rapidly generates a large, cumbersome database because of its reliance on prose in the form of such media as field notes, interview transcripts, or documents. Miles (1979) has described qualitative data as an 'attractive nuisance', because of the attractiveness of its richness but the difficulty of finding analytic paths through that richness. The researcher must guard against being captivated by the richness of the data collected, so that there is a failure to give the data wider significance for the business and management community. For example, the data generated from the study of an unusual organization like, say, a tattoo parlour, is not enough to make a contribution to the study of business. The rich and unique data is not enough in itself: Grandy and Wicks, however, managed to use their data on tattoo parlours to throw new light on organizational culture (Wicks & Grandy, 2007) and strategy (Grandy & Wicks, 2008).

Yet, finding a path through the thicket of prose that makes up your data is not an easy matter and is baffling to many researchers confronting such data for the first time. 'What do I do with it now?' is a common refrain. In large part, this is because, unlike the analysis of quantitative data, there are few well-established and widely accepted rules for the analysis of qualitative data. Thus, for various methodological reasons (discussed earlier), qualitative research has not reached the degree of codification of analytic procedures that characterizes quantitative re-

| 24.1 | ## Student Experience |

Generating large amounts of rich data

Tom found that in one key respect his experience of doing a research project did tally with what he'd been led to expect from his reading—the tendency for qualitative research to generate large amounts of textual data that were difficult to analyze systematically: 'All textbooks say, don't they, that inexperienced researchers are likely to collect too much data and then not be able to process it all or analyze it all properly and it's true! [laughs] It's true! I certainly . . . found it hard to process the amount of stuff that I'd collected'.

Beata had a similar experience. She had already conducted 56 interviews prior to collecting data specifically for her thesis, through a further 25 interviews. When the interviews were transcribed and her notes written up she faced 1000 pages of material. The sheer magnitude of the material and the task ahead was daunting:

I guess I'm still in a phase where it's difficult to express all this, but I think . . . I've been surprised by how difficult it was to do the analysis. I love doing interviews and I love asking people questions and you get to know people and you actually have the right to ask them things you're interested in. So I've enjoyed doing the interviews, and that probably has influenced why I did interviews and not perhaps used other methods. I did the interviews and then I went on maternity leave and I was really looking forward to coming back and jumping into all this data and seeing how all these things . . . and discourses would emerge. And it has taken quite a lot of energy from me I think and that was a surprise. But on the other hand, . . . I've enjoyed it and you really get to challenge yourself and I learned quite a lot by using an abductive [approach] . . . I don't see any other way of doing this than using an abductive approach than going back and forth to make sense of this.

search. Many writers would argue that this is not necessarily desirable anyway (see Bryman & Burgess, 1994*b* on this point). What *can* be provided are broad guidelines (Okely, 1994), and that is the focus of this chapter.

This chapter has three main sections:

- General strategies of qualitative data analysis. In this section, we consider two approaches to data analysis—analytic induction and grounded theory.
- Basic operations in qualitative data analysis. This section focuses on the steps, considerations, and problems that are associated with coding.
- Computers in qualitative analysis. In this section we focus on the use of computers in qualitative analysis.

General strategies of qualitative data analysis

This section considers two strategies of analysis—analytic induction and grounded theory. They are probably the most frequently cited approaches in the realm of positivist qualitative approaches, though others do exist (e.g., Williams, 1976; Hycner, 1985). By a general strategy of qualitative data analysis, we simply mean a framework that is meant to guide the analysis of data. As we will see, one of the ways in which qualitative and quantitative data analysis sometimes differ is that, with the latter, analysis invariably occurs after your data have been collected. However, as noted in Chapter 3, general approaches like grounded theory (and analytic induction) are often described as iterative—that is, there is a repetitive interplay between the collection and analysis of data. This means that analysis starts after some of the data have been collected and the implications of that analysis then shape the next steps in the data collection process. Consequently, while grounded theory and analytic induction are described as strategies of analysis, they can also be viewed as strategies for the collection of data as well.

Analytic induction

The main steps in analytic induction are outlined in Figure 24.1. Analytic induction (see Key concept 24.1) begins with a rough definition of a research question, proceeds to

a hypothetical explanation of that question, and then continues onto the collection of data (examination of cases). If a case that is inconsistent with the hypothesis is encountered, the analyst either redefines the hypothesis so as to exclude the deviant or negative case or reformulates the hypothesis and proceeds with further data collection. If the latter path is chosen, if a further deviant case is found, the analyst must choose again between reformulation or redefinition. An example of analytic induction used in a study of corporate ecological responsiveness is given in Research in focus 24.1.

As this brief outline suggests, analytic induction is an extremely rigorous method of analysis, because encountering a single case that is inconsistent with a **hypothesis** is sufficient to necessitate further data collection or a reformulation of the hypothesis, and the selection of cases must be sufficiently diverse as to have adequately challenged the theory (see also Goerzen (1999), who uses an analytic inductive approach to examine the relationship between social and economic performance). This is reflected by Bansal and Roth's (2000) inclusion of Japanese companies in their sample, in order to test their model of corporate ecological responsiveness in a different cultural context (see Research in focus 24.1). Nor should the alternative of reformulating the hypothetical explanation be regarded as a soft option. The rigours of analytic induction have not endeared the approach to qualitative researchers, and most of the examples used in textbooks to illustrate **analytic induction** derive from the 1940s and early 1950s (Bryman & Burgess, 1994*a*, p. 4); Bansal and Roth's (2000) work is unusual in being a relatively recent example.

Two further problems with analytic induction are worth noting. First, the final explanations that analytic induction arrives at specify the conditions that are *sufficient* for the phenomenon occurring but rarely specify the *necessary* conditions. This means that analytic induction may find

> **Key concept 24.1: What is analytic induction?**
>
> Analytic induction is an approach to the analysis of data in which the researcher seeks universal explanations of phenomena by pursuing the collection of data until no cases that are inconsistent with a hypothetical explanation (deviant or negative cases) of a phenomenon are found.

Figure 24.1

The process of analytic induction

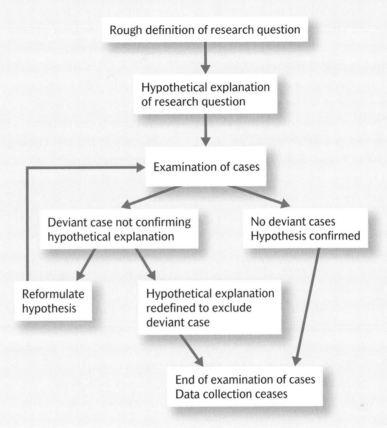

out why companies with certain characteristics or in certain circumstances become ecologically responsive but it does not allow us to say why those particular companies became more responsive, rather than others in the same situation with the same characteristics. Secondly, it does not provide useful guidelines (unlike grounded theory) as to how many cases need to be investigated before the absence of negative cases and the validity of the hypothetical explanation (whether reformulated or not) can be confirmed. Zimmerman (1991), suggests one way forward in combining an inductive, with a **deductive** and *aductive* approach.

Grounded theory

Grounded theory (see Key concept 24.2) has become one of the more widely used frameworks for analyzing qualitative data. The book that is the chief wellspring of the

approach, *The Discovery of Grounded Theory: Strategies for Qualitative Research* by Barney G. Glaser and Anselm L. Strauss (published in 1967), is one of the most widely cited books in the social sciences. However, providing a definitive account of the approach is by no means a straightforward matter, for the following reasons.

- Glaser and Strauss developed grounded theory along different paths after the publication of the above book. Glaser felt that the approach to grounded theory that Strauss was promoting (most notably in Strauss, 1987, and Strauss & Corbin, 1990) was too prescriptive and emphasized too much the development of concepts rather than of theories (Glaser, 1992). However, because of the greater prominence of Strauss's writings, his version is largely the one followed in the exposition below.

There is, however, considerable controversy about what grounded theory is and entails (Charmaz, 2000).

- Straussian grounded theory has changed a great deal over the years. This is revealed in a constant addition to the tool chest of analytic devices that is revealed in his writings.
- Some writers have suggested that grounded theory is honoured more in the breach than in the observance, implying that claims are often made that grounded theory has been used but that evidence of this being the case is at best uncertain (Bryman, 1988a, pp. 85, 91; Locke, 1996; Charmaz, 2000; Vincze, 2010). Sometimes the term is employed simply to imply that the analyst has grounded his or her theory in data. Grounded theory is more than this and refers to a set of procedures that are described below. Referencing academic publications is often part of a tactic of persuading readers of the legitimacy of one's work (Gilbert, 1977) and this process can be discerned in the citation of grounded theory. For example, references to grounded theory can be found across a range of very different business studies disciplines, including gender studies (Bradshaw et al., 2005); health care management (Casebeer et al., 2006); management science (Cox & Aung, 2005); organizational theory (Grandy & Wicks, 2003); technology and innovative management (Isabelle & Heslop, 2006); information systems (Jamieson et al., 2007; Wu & Alagheband, 2008); and management (Suddaby, 2006). Alternatively, researchers sometimes appear to have used just one or two features of grounded theory but refer to their having used the approach without qualification (Locke, 1996).

Against such a background, writing about the essential ingredients of grounded theory is not an easy matter. It is not going to be possible to describe here grounded theory in all its facets; instead, its main features will be outlined. In order to organize the exposition, we find it helpful to distinguish between *tools* and *outcomes* in grounded theory.

Tools of grounded theory

Some of the tools of grounded theory have been referred to in previous chapters. Their location is indicated in the list that follows:

- Theoretical sampling. See Key concept 17.4.
- Coding. The key process in grounded theory, whereby data are broken down into component parts, which are given names. It begins soon after the collection of initial data. As Charmaz (2000, p. 515) puts it: 'We grounded theorists code our emerging data as we collect it. . . . Unlike quantitative research that requires data to fit into *preconceived* standardized codes, the researcher's interpretations of data shape his or her emergent codes in grounded theory' (emphasis in original). In grounded theory, different types or levels of coding are recognized.
- Theoretical saturation. See Key concept 17.5. Theoretical saturation is a process that relates to two phases in grounded theory: the coding of data (implying that you reach a point where there is no further point in reviewing your data to see how well they fit with your concepts or categories) and the collection of data (implying that, once a concept or category has been developed, you may wish to continue collecting data to determine its nature and operation but then reach a point where new data are no longer illuminating the concept).
- Constant comparison. An aspect of grounded theory that was prominent in Glaser and Strauss (1967) and that is often referred to as a significant phase by practitioners, but that seems to be an implicit, rather than an explicit, element in more recent writings. It refers to a process of maintaining a close connection between data and conceptualization, so that the correspondence between concepts and categories with their indicators is not lost. More specifically, attention to the procedure of constant comparison enjoins the researcher constantly to compare phenomena being coded under a certain category so that a theoretical elaboration of that category can begin to emerge. Glaser and Strauss advised writing a memo (see below) on the category after a few phenomena had been coded. It also entails being sensitive to contrasts between the categories that are emerging.

Charmaz (1983, p. 186) explains: 'Codes . . . serve as shorthand devices to *label, separate, compile,* and *organize*

An example of the use of analytic induction

The aim of Bansal and Roth's (2000) research was to develop a robust model of the motives for corporate ecological responsiveness, or 'greening'. They chose an analytic induction approach because it enabled them to accommodate existing theories of corporate greening. This allowed them to begin by reviewing the literature in order to develop a set of hypotheses and then to move back and forth between data collection and theory generation.

From the data they developed a preliminary model of corporate ecological responsiveness as driven by legislation, stakeholder pressures, economic opportunities, and ethical motives. To test this model, data were collected from 53 firms in the UK and Japan. Theoretical sampling was used to select the case studies from sectors that faced a wide range of ecological issues. These included:

- food retailers – chosen because they were facing issues relating to the location of sites, the distribution of products, packaging, labelling, and recycling;
- subsidiaries of the British-based multinational P&O – chosen to assess the importance of internal organizational structure and culture in motivating a corporate environmental policy;
- auto manufacturers – a sample of five firms based in the UK;
- oil companies – involved in the extraction or refining of oil in the UK;
- Japan-based companies – a sample of 10 companies chosen in order to challenge the emerging theory in a different cultural context.

Data sources included:

- interviews – a selection of key informants within the firms, chosen for their knowledge of the ecological initiatives of their firms;
- participant observation – of training seminars where environmental issues were discussed;
- public and private documents – including a newspaper search of the Reuters and Data Star databases, company accounts, annual reports, and corporate environmental reports.

Analysis involved an iterative process of collecting data from these sources, coding, developing, or refining emerging ideas, relating them to existing theory, and selecting further data for the next phase of analysis. Analysis focused on understanding why companies engaged in ecologically responsible initiatives. Three basic motives for ecological responsiveness were found:

1. competitiveness;
2. legitimation;
3. ecological responsibility.

Motives were also affected by three contextual dimensions, which influenced the dominant motivation of a firm. This led to the development of an advanced theoretical model that took the relationship between motives and context into account. By assessing the relationship between motives and context, Bansal and Roth suggest that it is possible to predict the kinds of ecological initiatives that firms will adopt.

The main weakness of the model, however, stems from the fact that Bansal and Roth were attempting to uncover a firm's motivations only after they had made the decision to act. This means that the research is subject to bias associated with retrospective accounts.

data' (emphases in original). Coding is a somewhat different process from coding in relation to quantitative data, such as survey data. With the latter, coding is more or less solely a way of managing data, whereas in grounded theory, and indeed in approaches to qualitative data analysis that do not subscribe to the approach, it is an important

Key concept 24.3: What is grounded theory?

Grounded theory has been defined by Strauss and Corbin (1998, p. 12) as 'theory that was derived from data, systematically gathered and analyzed through the research process'.

first step in the generation of theory. Coding in grounded theory is also somewhat more tentative than in relation to the generation of quantitative data, where there is a tendency to think in terms of data and codes as very fixed. Coding in qualitative data analysis tends to be in a constant state of potential revision and fluidity. The data are treated as potential indicators of concepts and the indicators are *constantly compared* (see under '*Tools of grounded theory*') to see which concepts they best fit with. As Strauss (1987, p. 25) put it: 'Many indicators (behavioral actions/events) are examined comparatively by the analyst who then "codes" them, naming them as indicators of a class of events/behavioral actions'.

Strauss and Corbin (1990), drawing on their grounded theory approach, distinguish between three types of coding practice:

- Open coding. 'the process of breaking down, examining, comparing, conceptualizing and categorizing data' (1990, p. 61); this process of coding yields concepts, which are later to be grouped and turned into categories (see also Price, 2010*a*).
- Axial coding. 'a set of procedures whereby data are put back together in new ways after open coding, by making connections between categories' (1990, p. 96). This is done by linking codes to contexts, to consequences, to patterns of interaction, and to causes (see also Wicks, 2010).
- Selective coding. 'the procedure of selecting the core category, systematically relating it to other categories, validating those relationships, and filling in categories that need further refinement and development' (1990, p. 116). A core category is the central issue or focus around which all other categories are integrated. It is what Strauss and Corbin call the storyline that frames your account (see also Price, 2010*b*).

The three types of coding are really different levels of coding and each relates to a different point in the elaboration of categories in grounded theory.

24.2 Research in Focus

Developing categories using concept cards

Prasad (1993) used techniques of grounded theory to analyze the vast quantity of field notes and interview transcripts that were generated by her study (see Chapter 16 for a detailed account of this research). Using concept cards to identify important concepts in the data, she accumulated incidents, events, or pieces of conversation – elements – that related to a particular theme and put them together under a meaningful label on a concept card (see Figure 22.2). The initial aim of labels was to find a level of abstraction that was high enough to avoid creating a separate card for every element observed but low

enough to ensure that the concept accurately represented the phenomenon.

Maintaining the concept cards was an iterative process that began early in the research process. New concepts were generated and further elements were added to the cards as more data were collected. Prasad then scanned the concept cards for relationships among elements on the same and different cards. She states that this led to the development of 'a new set of second order cards that helped me make connections between certain symbolic representations of computerization and areas of organizational action' (1993, p. 1411).

Outcomes of grounded theory

The following are the products of different phases of grounded theory:

- Concept(s). Refers to labels given to discrete phenomena; concepts are referred to as the 'building blocks of theory' (Strauss & Corbin, 1998, p. 101). The value of concepts is determined by their usefulness or utility. One criterion for deciding if a concept is useful is that it will typically be found frequently and members of the organization under study will be able to recognize it and relate it to their experiences. Concepts are produced through open coding. Concepts can be recorded using concept cards (see Research in focus 24.2), through which incidents in the data can be recorded. An example of a concept card is provided in Figure 24.2.
- Category, categories. A concept that has been elaborated so that it is regarded as representing real-world phenomena. As noted in Key concept 17.5, a category may subsume two or more concepts. As such, categories are at a higher level of abstraction than concepts. A category may become a core category around which the other categories pivot. The number of core categories may, in fact, be relatively few. For example, Martin and Turner (1986) give an example of one study in which from a large data set and an initial 100 concepts, fewer than 40 of these proved to be very useful and only 19 provided the basis for the final analysis.
- Properties. Attributes or aspects of a category.
- Hypotheses. Initial hunches about relationships between concepts.
- Theory. According to Strauss and Corbin (1998, p. 22), 'a set of well-developed categories . . . that are systematically related through statements of relationship to form a theoretical framework that explains some relevant social . . . or other phenomenon'. Since the inception of grounded theory, writings have pointed to two types or levels of theory: substantive theory and formal theory. The former relates to theory in a certain empirical instance or substantive area, such as occupational socialization. A formal theory is at a higher level of abstraction and has a wider range of applicability to several substantive areas, such as socialization in a number of spheres, suggesting that higher-level processes are at work. The generation of formal theory requires data collection in contrasting settings.

The different elements are portrayed in Figure 24.3. As with all diagrams, this is a representation, and it is particularly so in the case of grounded theory, because the existence of different versions of the approach does not readily permit a more definitive rendition. Also, it is difficult to get across diagrammatically the iterative nature of grounded theory—in particular its commitment to the idea that data collection and analysis occur in parallel. This is partly achieved in the diagram through the presence of arrows pointing in both directions in relation to certain steps. The figure implies the following:

- The researcher begins with a general research question (step 1).
- Relevant people and/or incidents are theoretically sampled (step 2).
- Relevant data are collected (step 3).
- Data are coded (step 4), which may at the level of open coding generate concepts (step 4a).
- There is a constant movement backwards and forwards between the first four steps, so that early coding suggests the need for new data, which results in the need to sample theoretically, and so on.
- Through a constant comparison of indicators and concepts (step 5) categories are generated (step 5b). The crucial issue is to ensure that there is a fit between indicators and concepts.
- Categories are saturated during the coding process (step 6).
- Relationships between categories are explored (step 7) in such a way that hypotheses about connections between categories emerge (step 7a).
- Further data are collected via theoretical sampling (steps 8 and 9).
- The collection of data is likely to be governed by the theoretical saturation principle (step 10) and by the testing of the emerging hypotheses (step 11), which leads to the specification of substantive theory (step 11a).

Figure 24.2

An example of part of a concept card to show the symbolism of organizational turmoil related to work computerization

Data source	Organization member	Incident, quotation, opinion, event
Field notes No. 7, p. 3	Project manager	Discussing possible resistance to computers: 'Yes . . . we have got to pull out all our weapons to fight this thing out. But until we win . . . It's going to mean confusion.'
Interview No. 8, p. 23	Receptionist	Describing the first two weeks of computerization: 'What I hated was the anger and well, the confusion. It was almost like my divorce all over again . . . blaming each other and mistakes every minute.'
Field notes No. 33, p. 24	Nurse supervisor	Official memo to trainers: 'We need to be well prepared for the next few weeks of chaos. Even the people you work with will not seem the same any more.'
Interview No. 24, pp. 8–9	Senior manager	'I finally know what army generals feel like . . . that's exactly what it was like. Fighting people all the time . . . the girls, the nurses, Joe, and the big brass at Paragon . . . and not knowing where the next attack would come from.'

Source: adapted from Prasad (1993).

- The substantive theory is explored using grounded theory processes in relation to different settings from that in which it was generated (step 12), so that formal theory may be generated (step 12a). A formal theory will relate to more abstract categories, which are not specifically related to the research area in question.

Step 12 is relatively unusual in grounded theory, because researchers typically concentrate on a certain setting. One way in which formal theory can be generated is through the use of existing theory and research in comparable settings.

Concepts and categories are perhaps the key elements in grounded theory. Indeed, it is sometimes suggested that, as a qualitative data analysis strategy, it works better for generating categories than theory. In part, this may be because studies purporting to use the approach often generate grounded *concepts* rather than grounded theory as such. Concepts and categories are nonetheless at the heart of the approach, and key processes such as **coding**, **theoretical sampling**, and **theoretical saturation** are designed to guide their generation.

Memos

One aid to the generation of concepts and categories is the memo. Memos in grounded theory are notes that researchers might write for themselves and for those with whom they work concerning such elements of grounded theory as coding or concepts. They serve as reminders about what is meant by the terms being used and provide the building blocks for a certain amount of reflection. Memos are potentially very helpful to researchers in helping them to crystallize ideas and not to lose track of their thinking on various topics (see Research in focus 24.3).

Finding examples of grounded theory that reveal all its facets and stages is very difficult, and it is unsurpris-

Figure 24.3

Processes and outcomes in grounded theory

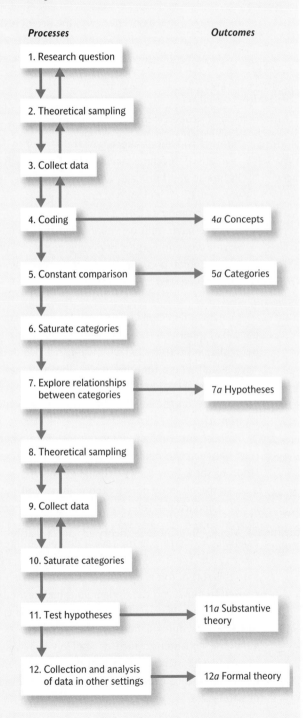

Processes	Outcomes
1. Research question	
2. Theoretical sampling	
3. Collect data	
4. Coding	4a Concepts
5. Constant comparison	5a Categories
6. Saturate categories	
7. Explore relationships between categories	7a Hypotheses
8. Theoretical sampling	
9. Collect data	
10. Saturate categories	
11. Test hypotheses	11a Substantive theory
12. Collection and analysis of data in other settings	12a Formal theory

ing that many expositions of grounded theory fall back on the original illustrations provided in Glaser and Strauss (1967). Many studies show some of its ingredients but not others. For example, Prasad's (1994) study of technological change (see Chapter 6; Research in focus 24.2 and Figure 24.2) certainly incorporates some of the features of a grounded theory approach, such as the use of concept cards to keep a record of coding, enabling a series of 'second-order' or core categories to be generated. However, other tools of grounded theory, such as memos, were not used as part of this study. Similarly, although Gersick (1994) claims to have used a grounded theory approach in her study of the effects of time on organizational adaptation, her coding was based partly on themes that she was interested in prior to data collection, in addition to those that emerged during the interviews. Gersick's approach thus relied on isolating and coding statements from the interview transcripts that related to time and identifying themes among them.

Criticisms of grounded theory

In spite of the frequency with which it is cited and the frequent lip service paid to it, grounded theory is not without its limitations, including the following:

- Bulmer (1979) has questioned whether or not, as prescribed by the advocates of grounded theory, researchers can suspend their awareness of relevant theories or concepts until a quite late stage in the process of analysis. Business researchers are typically sensitive to the conceptual armoury of their disciplines and it seems unlikely that this awareness can be put aside. Indeed, nowadays it is rarely accepted that theory-neutral observation is feasible. In other words, it is generally agreed that what we 'see' when we conduct research is conditioned by many factors, one of which is what we already know about the social world being studied (in terms both of social scientific conceptualizations and as members of society). Also, many writers might take the view that it is desirable that researchers are sensitive to existing conceptualizations, so that their investigations are focused and can build upon the work of others.

Research in Focus

A memo

In the course of research into the bus industry that Bryman carried out with colleagues in the early 1990s (Bryman, Gillingwater, and McGuinness, 1996), the researchers noticed that the managers they interviewed frequently referred to the notion that their companies had inherited features that derived from the running of those companies before deregulation. They often referred to the idea of inheriting characteristics that held them back in trying to meet the competitive environment they faced in the 1990s. As such, inheritance is what Strauss (1987) calls an in vivo code (one that derives from the language of people in the social context being studied), rather than what he calls sociologically constructed codes, which are labels employing the analyst's own terminology. The following memo outlines the concept of inheritance, provides some illustrative quotations, and suggests some properties of the concept.

Memo for Inheritance

Inheritance: many of our interviewees suggest that they have inherited certain company traits and traditions from the period prior to deregulation (i.e., pre-1985). It is a term that many of them themselves employed to denote company attributes that are not of their choosing but have survived from the pre-deregulation period. The key point about inheritance is that the inherited elements are seen by our interviewees as hindering their ability to respond to the changing environment of the post-deregulation era.

Inherited features include:

- expensive and often inappropriate fleets of vehicles and depots;
- the survival of attitudes and behaviour patterns, particularly among bus drivers, which are seen as inappropriate to the new environment (for example, lack of concern for customer service) and which hinder service innovation;

- high wage rates associated with the pre-deregulation era; means that new competitors can enter the market while paying drivers lower wages.

Sample comments:

We *inherited* a very high cost structure because of deregulation. 75% of our staff were paid in terms of conditions affected by [rates prior to deregulation]. (Commercial Director, Company B).

I suppose another major weakness is that we are very tied by conditions and practices we've *inherited*. (Commercial Director, Company G).

We have what we've *inherited* and we now have a massive surplus of double decks . . . We have to go on operating those. (Managing Director, Company B).

Managing Director of Company E said the company had inherited staff who were steeped in pre-deregulation attitudes, which meant that 'we don't have a staff where the message is "the customer is number one". We don't have a staff where that is emblazoned on the hearts and minds of everyone, far from it.'

Prepost-deregulation: interviewees make a contrast between the periods before and after deregulation to show how they've changed. This shows in a sense the absence of inherited features and their possible impact; can refer to how the impact of possibly inherited features was negated or offset. For example, X referring to the recent end of the three-week strike: 'there was no way we were going to give in to this sort of thing, this sort of blackmail. We just refused to move and the trade unions had never experienced that. It was all part of the change in culture following deregulation . . .'

Inheriting constraints: such as staff on high wage rates and with inappropriate attitudes.

Inheriting surplus capacity: such as too many buses or wrong size.

24.2

Student Experience

Becoming grounded

Anne used a 'classic version' of grounded theory in her study of 'how consumers construct their images' of companies. She was interested in 'image construction and how earlier images influence . . . how [a] company is perceived today. So those earlier images, held in memory, or actually activated on certain occasions, also became the interpretation framework for image construction in the present'. She began by using an inductive approach to the gathering of data through a number of interviews. However, at the analysis stage she first tried narrative analysis but felt that this wasn't working because 'the text didn't take narrative form'. She then tried discourse analysis but felt that 'it left out quite a lot' and did not capture 'the process kind of phenomena' (i.e., how people develop and process imagery). Thus, she explored the grounded theory approach but the exploration was to last a half a year as she studied the method: 'So when I finally started to read about grounded theory, I could immediately say that this is how I want to do this. And this sort of provides . . . me the structure for the analysis. Anyhow, it's very inductive in the beginning and when you . . . find a core category, which I found quite quickly not easily . . . but you know I saw it quite quickly, then you can focus on your core category. So it worked very well in this situation where I didn't know at all, what [the data suggested]'. In the process of identifying a grounded theory approach Anne considered the work of Strauss and Corbin but felt that their approach required her 'to have preconceived ideas too early' that it 'wasn't that inductive'. However, she was drawn to the 'classic version' of grounded theory that allowed her to 'understand from the consumers' perspective' by not forcing data into categories at too early a stage.

- Related to this first point is that, in many circumstances, researchers are required to spell out the possible implications of their planned investigation. For example, a lecturer making a bid for research funding or a student applying for funding for postgraduate research is usually required to demonstrate how his or her research will build upon what is already known or to demonstrate that he or she has a reasonably tightly defined research question, something which is also frequently disdained in grounded theory.

- There are practical difficulties with grounded theory. The time taken to transcribe tape recordings of interviews, for example, can make it difficult for researchers, especially when they have tight deadlines, to carry out a genuine grounded theory analysis with its constant interplay of data collection and conceptualization.

- It is somewhat doubtful whether grounded theory in many instances really results in theory. As previously suggested, it provides a rigorous approach to the generation of concepts, but it is often difficult to see what theory, in the sense of an explanation of something, is being put forward. Moreover, in spite of the frequent lip service paid to the generation of formal theory, most grounded theories are substantive in character; in other words, they pertain to the specific social phenomenon being researched and not to a broader range of phenomena (though, of course, they may have such broader applicability).

- In spite of the large amount written on grounded theory, but perhaps because of the many subtle changes in its presentation, it is still vague on certain points, such as the difference between concepts and categories. For example, while Strauss and Corbin (1998, p. 73) refer to theoretical sampling as 'sampling on the basis of emerging *concepts*' (emphasis added), Charmaz (2000, p. 519) writes that it is used to 'develop our emerging *categories*' (emphasis added). The term 'categories' is increasingly being employed rather than concepts, but such inconsistent use of key terms is not helpful to people trying to understand the overall process.

- Grounded theory is very much associated with an approach to data analysis that invites researchers to fragment their data by coding the data into discrete chunks. However, in the eyes of some writers, this kind of activity results in a loss of a sense of context and of narrative flow (Coffey & Atkinson, 1996), a point to which we will return below.

- The presence of competing accounts of the ingredients of grounded theory does not make it easy to characterize it or to establish how to use it. This situation has been made even more problematic by Charmaz's (2000) suggestion that most grounded theory is objectivist and that an alternative, constructionist (she calls it constructivist) approach is preferable. She argues that the grounded theory associated with Glaser, Strauss, and Corbin is objectivist in that it aims to uncover a reality that is external to social actors. She offers an alternative, constructionist version that 'assumes that people create and maintain meaningful worlds through dialectical processes of conferring meaning on their realities and acting within them . . . . Thus, social reality does not exist independent of human action' (Charmaz, 2000, p. 521). Such a position stands in contrast to earlier grounded theory texts that 'imply that categories and concepts inhere within the data, awaiting the researcher's discovery. . . . Instead, a constructivist approach recognizes that the categories, concepts, and theoretical level of an analysis emerge from the researcher's interaction within the field and questions about the data' (Charmaz, 2000, p. 522). One difficulty here is that the two meanings of constructionism referred to in Web Key concept 3.16 seem to be conflated. The first quotation refers to constructionism as an ontological position in relating to social

objects and categories; the second is a reference to constructionism in relation to the nature of knowledge of the social world. It is certainly fair to suggest that Glaser, Strauss, and Corbin, in their various writings, neglect the role of the researcher in the generation of knowledge, but it is not clear that they are indifferent to the notion that social reality exists independently of social actors. Strauss was, after all, the lead of the study referred to on the now classic study of the hospital as a negotiated order, which was used as an illustration of constructionism (Strauss et al., 1973). However, there is little doubt that there is considerable confusion currently about the nature of grounded theory. According to Partington (2000), there is little evidence of the successful application of Strauss and Corbin's (1990) grounded theory within management and business research. This is partly because of the greater difficulty in following this more prescriptive, proceduralized approach, which contrasts sharply with Glaser and Strauss's (1967) earlier emphasis on the development of insight based on open-minded sensitivity.

Nonetheless, grounded theory probably represents one of the most influential general strategies for conducting qualitative data analysis, though how far the approach is followed varies from study to study. Locke (2001) argues that grounded theory is particularly well suited to organizational research. She suggests that it is particularly good at the following:

- Capturing complexity. Grounded theory is good at capturing the complexity of contexts as action unfolds.
- Linking with practice. It frequently facilitates an appreciation among organizational members of their situations. Such understanding can provide a helpful springboard for organizational action.
- Facilitating theoretical work in substantive areas that have not been well researched by others. As new forms of organizational or technological change emerge and become prominent in the business world, grounded theory is ideal for an open-ended research strategy that can then be employed for the generation of theory out of the resulting data.

- Putting life into well-established fields. Grounded theory can provide the basis for an alternative view of well-established fields, like group effectiveness and leadership, through its open-ended approach to data collection followed by a rigorous approach to theoretical work.

In addition, many of grounded theory's core processes, such as coding, memos, and the very idea of allowing theoretical ideas to emerge out of one's data, have been hugely influential. Indeed, it is striking that one of the main developments in qualitative data analysis in recent years—computer-assisted qualitative data analysis—has implicitly promoted many of these processes, because the software programs have often been written with grounded theory in mind (Richards & Richards, 1994; Lonkila, 1995).

 ## More on coding

Coding is the starting point for most forms of qualitative data analysis, including ethnography (see Research in focus 24.4 for an example). The principles involved have been well developed by writers on grounded theory and others. Some of the considerations in developing codes, some of which are derived from Lofland and Lofland (1995), are as follows:

24.4 Research in Focus

An example of ethnographic coding

Delbridge (1998) describes the process of analyzing the hundreds of pages of handwritten field notes that described day-to-day events on the shop floor of Valleyco and Nippon CTV as extremely challenging: 'Once the field notes were completed, I read through the first set from Valleyco and began to pick out themes which emerged from these notes. At first this consisted of noting any type of event, interaction or comment that occurred more than once. After generating a very long list of such instances, I then grouped these around a set of tentative themes that had begun to emerge. In the first round of reviewing the data, I identified about 150 key events or notes from my first month at Valleyco and labelled these under one or more of the nine themes. I then grouped the second month's notes from Valleyco within these themes and added to or amended the themes to cope with additional instances. I repeated these iterative loops on a weekly basis for the Nippon CTV notes until I have centred on thirteen issues which came from the data' (1998, p. 22).

The 13 labels were:

QLTY: denoting systems of quality management
SYS: the manufacturing system at the plants
RELS: data regarding formal and informal relationships between actors
UNTY: denoting issues of uncertainty and informality in the workplace
CONT: issues of control and surveillance
WORK: workers, their roles, and experiences
COMM: communication issues and practices
MGT: managers, their roles, and perspectives
ACCOMM: issues of accommodation, indulgence, and resistance
UNION: the role of unions in the workplace
RES: issues pertaining to the research process
COFACT: factual data on the companies involved
JAP: data relating specifically to Japan and the Japanese.

It is interesting to note that, in starting to identify themes based on events, interactions, or comments that occurred 'more than once', Delbridge was attempting to make an initial judgement about the significance of the data based on frequency. However, it is not that unusual for qualitative researchers to engage in some kind of quantitative assessment of qualitative data, as Chapter 7 illustrates.

- Of what general category is this item of data an instance?
- What does this item of data represent?
- What is this item of data about?
- Of what topic is this item of data an instance?
- What question about a topic does this item of data suggest?
- What sort of answer to a question about a topic does this item of data imply?
- What is happening here?
- What are people doing?
- What do people say they are doing?
- What kind of event is going on?

Steps and considerations in coding

The following steps and considerations need to be borne in mind in preparation for and during coding:

- Code as soon as possible. It is well worth coding as you go along, as grounded theory suggests. This may sharpen your understanding of your data and help with theoretical sampling. Also, it may help to alleviate the feeling of being swamped by your data, which may happen if you defer analysis entirely until the end of the data collection period. At the very least, you should ensure that, if your data collection involves recording interviews, you begin transcription at a relatively early stage.
- Read through your initial set of transcripts, field notes, documents, etc. without taking any notes or considering an interpretation; perhaps at the end jot down a few general notes about what struck you as especially interesting, important, or significant.
- Do it again. Read through your data again, but this time begin to make marginal notes about significant remarks or observations. Make as many as possible. Initially, they will be very basic—perhaps key words used by your respondents, names that you give to themes in the data. When you do this you are coding—generating an index of terms that will help you to interpret and theorize in relation to your data.
- Review your codes. Begin to review your codes, possibly in relation to your transcripts. Are you using

two or more words or phrases to describe the same phenomenon? If so, remove one of them. Do some of your codes relate to concepts and categories in the existing literature? If so, might it be sensible to use these instead? Can you see any connections between the codes? Is there some evidence that respondents believe that one thing tends to be associated with or caused by something else? If so, how do you characterize and, therefore, code these connections?

- Consider more general theoretical ideas in relation to codes and data. At this point, you should be beginning to generate some general theoretical ideas about your data. Try to outline connections between concepts and categories you are developing. Consider in more detail how they relate to the existing literature. Develop hypotheses about the linkages you are making and go back to your data to see if they can be confirmed.
- Remember that any one item or slice of data can and often should be coded in more than one way.
- Do not worry about generating what seem to be too many codes—at least in the early stages of your analysis; some will be fruitful and others will not—the important thing is to be as inventive and imaginative as possible; you can worry about tidying things up later.
- Keep coding in perspective. Do not equate coding with analysis. It is part of your analysis, albeit an important one. It is a mechanism for thinking about the meaning of your data and for reducing the vast amount of data that you are facing (Huberman & Miles, 1994). Miles and Huberman (1984) have developed several techniques for the display of data that have been coded through content analysis as a way of overcoming the difficulty of representing the complexity of qualitative analysis. One of the most important of these is the matrix format, which identifies constructs along one axis and occurrences along the other. This technique introduces an element of quantification into the qualitative analysis by drawing attention to the frequency of occurrences in the data. Another data display mechanism described by Gersick (1994) in her study of a new business venture is the timeline; this is used to represent the company's history, including major events and decisions, the time period over which they were

implemented, and the eventual outcome of the actions. Whatever data display techniques you use, you must still interpret your findings. This means attending to issues like the significance of your coded material for the lives of the people you are studying, forging interconnections between codes, and reflecting on the overall importance of your findings for the research questions and the research literature that have driven your data collection.

Turning data into fragments

The coding of such materials as interview transcripts has typically entailed writing marginal notes on them and gradually refining those notes into codes. In this way, portions of transcripts become seen as belonging to certain names or labels. In the past, this process was accompanied by cutting and pasting in the literal sense of using scissors and paste. It entailed cutting up one's transcripts into files of chunks of data, with each file representing a code. The process of cutting and pasting is useful for data retrieval, though it is always important to make sure that you have ways of identifying the origins of the chunk of text (for example, name, position, date). Word processing programs allow this to be done in a way that does not rely on your DIY skills so much through the use of the 'find' function. Nowadays CAQDAS software is increasingly being used to perform these tasks (see below).

There is no one correct approach to coding your data. As suggested above, grounded theory conceives of different types of code. Coffey and Atkinson (1996) point to different levels of coding. These levels can be related to the passage from an interview that was previously encountered in Chapter 14 about the study of visitors to Disney theme parks. Tips and skills 'Coded text from the Disney project' shows some coded text from the Disney project, illustrating three coding levels.

- First there is a very basic coding, which, in the passage in Tips and skills 'Coded text from the Disney project', could be in terms of liking or disliking the Disney theme parks. However, such a coding scheme is

unlikely to get us very far from an analytical vantage point.

- A second level comprises much more awareness of the content of what is said. Themes reflect much more the language the interviewee uses. We see much more the kinds of issues with which the interviewee is concerned. Examples might be 'developed world', 'black people', and 'black history'.

- A third level moves slightly away from a close association with what the respondent says and towards a concern with broad analytic themes. This is the way that the passage in Tips and skills 'Coded text from the Disney project' has been coded. Here the passage has been coded in terms of such features as whether a response is uncritically enthusiastic ('uncritical enthusiasm') or is not critical of the Disney Corporation ('not critical of Disney'); reveals comments made about typical visitors ('visitors' ethnicity'); and makes critical comments ('aesthetic critique'; 'ethnicity critique'; 'nationality critique'). Interestingly, the passage also reveals the potential for a code employed by Coffey and Atkinson (1996, pp. 43–5) in relation to one of their examples—namely, the use of a 'contrastive rhetoric'. This occurs when a person makes a point about something by comparing it to something else. This feature occurs when the husband makes a point about the representation of British culture, which in fact he regards as poor, by comparing it to that of China, which he regards as good. The poor showing of Britain is brought out by comparing it in a negative light to China. However, this coding category was not employed in relation to this research.

As Coffey and Atkinson (1996) observe, following Strauss and Corbin's account (1990) of grounded theory, codes should not be thought of purely as mechanisms for the fragmentation and retrieval of text. In other words, they can do more than simply manage the data you have gathered. For example, if we ask about the properties and interconnections between codes, we may begin to see that some of them may be dimensions of a broader phenomenon. For example, 'ethnicity critique' came to be seen as a dimension of 'ideology critique', along with 'class critique' and 'gender critique'. In this way, we can begin to map the more general or formal properties of concepts that are being developed.

Problems with coding

One of the most commonly mentioned criticisms of the coding approach to qualitative data analysis is the possible problem of losing the context of what is said. By plucking chunks of text out of the context within which they appeared, such as a particular interview transcript, the social setting can be lost.

A second criticism of coding is that it results in a fragmentation of data, so that the narrative flow of what people say is lost (Coffey & Atkinson, 1996). Sensitivity to this issue has been heightened by a growing interest in narrative analysis since the late 1980s (see Chapter 20). Riessman became concerned about the fragmentation of data that occurs as a result of coding themes when she came to analyze data she had collected through structured interviews on divorce and gender. She writes:

> Some [interviewees] developed long accounts of what had happened in their marriages to justify their divorces. I did not realize these were narratives until I struggled to code them. Applying traditional qualitative methods, I searched the texts for common thematic elements. But some individuals knotted together several themes into long accounts that had coherence and sequence, defying easy categorization. I found myself not wanting to fragment the long accounts into distinct thematic categories. There seemed to be a common structure beneath talk about a variety of topics. While I coded one interview, a respondent provided language for my trouble. As I have thought about it since, it was a 'click moment' in my biography as a narrative researcher. (1993, p. vi)

Riessman's account is interesting because it suggests several possibilities: that the coding method of qualitative data analysis fragments data; that some forms of data may be unsuitable for the coding method; and that researchers can turn **narrative analysis** on themselves, since what

she provides in this passage is precisely a narrative. Interest in narrative analysis certainly shows signs of growing, and in large part this trend parallels the revival of interest in the **life history** approach (see Key concept 14.1). Nonetheless, the coding method is unlikely to become less prominent, because of several factors: its widespread acceptance in the research community; not all analysts are interested in research questions that lend themselves to the elicitation of narratives; the influence of grounded theory and its associated techniques; and the growing use and acceptance of computer software for qualitative data analysis, which frequently invites a coding approach.

Regardless of which analytical strategy you employ, what you must not do is simply say: 'this is what my subjects said and did—isn't that incredibly interesting?' It may be reasonably interesting, but your work can acquire significance only when you theorize in relation to it. Many researchers are wary of this. They worry that, in the process of interpretation and theorizing, they may fail to do justice to what they have seen and heard; that they may contaminate their subjects' words and behaviour. This is a risk, but it has to be balanced against the fact that your findings acquire significance in our intellectual community only when you have reflected on, interpreted, and theorized your data. You are not there as a mere mouthpiece.

 ## Secondary analysis of qualitative data

One final point to bear in mind is that this discussion of qualitative data analysis may have been presumed to be solely concerned with the analysis of data in which the analyst has played a part in collecting. However, in recent

> **Key concept 24.4: What is abductive analysis?**
>
> Abductive analysis is 'the process of forming a possible explanation involving an imaginative effort to understand on the past of beings acting and learning in the world. It is a practical reasoning mode whose purpose is to invent and propose ideas and explanations that account for surprises and unmet expectations' (Locke, 2010, p. 1).

Interpreting and theorizing qualitative data

One of the problems faced by Beata in the analysis stage was in deciding how to deal with the 56 interviews that she had completed prior to undertaking her doctoral studies (see Chapter 3, Student experience, '*Gaining research access through workplace contacts*'). Her biggest concern was how to treat these interviews as data: 'I'm more a bit afraid of the critique I might get and how I can support my arguments. [I am not afraid of the critique from my supervisor] but more of when I hand in my thesis and the process after that perhaps and being able to defend my thesis'. One of the ways that she decided to deal with her concerns was to be very open about the process she adopted, to explain the background to the earlier 56 interviews and their relationship to the 25 new interviews that were completed as a more direct part of her doctoral research: 'So one thing that I have done, because I'm very open about how I've done all this, [is that] I start the whole thing by having a table with these interviews and I say I have all this fifty-six interviews here in Organization A and then I write these [up as] HR—I call them HR Interviews—and then I have the other interviews and then I call them Re-

search Interviews, so the reader can already see for what purposes I did these. So I hope I will be forgiven'. Beata also dealt with the 'HR Interviews' through a process of abduction (see Key Concept 24.4):

> I did not go into this subject with any very strong pre-conceptualizations about what I would find—I was very open minded. And as I see it with my perspective, I could have . . . taken a more critical perspective and gone into this process and looked at power relations and gender issues . . . . But I was quite analytical and then my attempt has been to find something in an abductive way, not inductive, but [a] more abductive way to find something to produce a more critical account in the discussion.

She did this by concentrating on the original ('HR') interviews and then asking her newer ('Research') interviewees questions about the type of information that was emerging. In this way she began to develop her hunches about how people responded to change in the IT industry.

years, secondary analysis of qualitative data has become a growing focus of discussion and interest. While the secondary analysis of quantitative data has been on the research agenda for many years (see Chapter 19), similar use of qualitative data has only recently come to the fore. The general idea of secondary analysis was addressed in Key concept 19.1.

There is no obvious reason why qualitative data cannot be the focus of secondary analysis, though it is undoubtedly the case that such data do present certain prob-

lems that are not fully shared by quantitative data. Bloor's study in Research in focus 21.4 provides an example involving the secondary analysis of oral history interviews. The possible grounds for conducting a secondary analysis are more or less the same as those associated with quantitative data (see Chapter 19). With such considerations in mind, ESDS Qualidata, an archival resource centre, was created in the UK in 1994. The centre is not a repository for qualitative data (unlike the Data Archive, which does house quantitative data); instead, it is concerned with 'locating, assessing and documenting qualitative data and arranging their deposit in suitable public archive repositories' (Corti et al., 1995). It has a very useful website:

http://www.qualidata.essex.ac.uk

and its online catalogue—Qualicat—can be searched at the following address:

http://www.qualidata.essex.ac.uk/search/qualicat.asp

In Canada a useful website for qualitative (as well as quantitative) data sources is:

http://www.collectionscanada.gc.ca/

A useful guide to social sciences resources data in different countries, including Canada and the United States, is:

http://www.socsciresearch.com/r6.html

An example involving secondary analysis of qualitative data is provided by Savage (2005), who analyzed field notes that had been collected by Goldthorpe et al. in the *Affluent Worker* studies in the early 1960s, which he accessed through the Qualidata Archive. Savage argues that although a huge amount of qualitative data was generated through the *Affluent Worker* studies, very little of this part of the research made its way into publication. Instead the researchers focused on aspects of their data that could be quantified and consistently coded and 'a huge amount of evocative material was "left on the cutting room floor"' (Savage, 2005, p. 932). Savage (2005) uses the field notes, which contain many verbatim quotes from respondent interviews, to argue that re-reading the field notes with a contemporary understanding of issues of money, power, and status indicates that the respondents had different understandings of class from Goldthorpe et al. which the researchers did not pick up on and this difference of understanding affected how the data was interpreted.

Nonetheless, it is important to acknowledge there are certain difficulties with the reuse of qualitative data, such as the difficulty of making settings and people anonymous

and the ethical problems involved in such reuse associated with promises of confidentiality. Also, Hammersley (1997) has suggested that reuse of qualitative data may be hindered by the secondary analyst's lack of an insider's understanding of the social context within which the data were produced. This possible difficulty may hinder the interpretation of data but would seem to be more of a problem with ethnographic field notes than with interview transcripts. Such problems even seem to afflict researchers revisiting their own data many years after the original research had been carried out (Mauthner et al., 1998, p. 742). There are also distinctive ethical issues deriving from the fact that the original researcher(s) may not have obtained the consent of research participants for the analysis of data by others. This is a particular problem with qualitative data in view of the fact that it invariably contains detailed accounts of contexts and people that can make it difficult to conceal the identities of institutions and individuals in the presentation of raw data (as opposed to publications in which such concealment is usually feasible). Nonetheless, in spite of certain practical difficulties, secondary analysis offers rich opportunities not least because the tendency for qualitative researchers to generate large and unwieldy sets of data means that much of the material remains under explored.

 ## Computer-assisted qualitative data analysis

One of the most significant developments in qualitative research in the past 25 years is the emergence of computer software that can assist in the use of qualitative data analysis. This software is often referred to as computer-assisted (or computer-aided) qualitative analysis software (CAQDAS)—a term and abbreviation coined by Lee and Fielding (1991). CAQDAS removes many, if not most, of the clerical tasks associated with the manual coding and retrieving of data. There is no industry leader among the different programs (in the sense that SPSS holds that position among quantitative data analysis software) and in this section we review six of the better known/more used CAQDAS in the field, including ATLAS.ti, Kwalitan, MAXQDA 2007, NVivo, HyperRESEARCH, and TAMS. The first four work only on Windows while TAMS works on Macintosh OS X and HyperRESEARCH works on both PC and Macintosh operating systems.

Most of these programs are variations on the code-and-retrieve theme. This means that they allow the analyst to code text while working at the computer and to retrieve the coded text. Thus, if we code a large number of interviews, we can retrieve all those sequences of text to which a code (or combination of codes) was attached. This means that the computer takes over manual tasks associated with the coding process. Typically, the analyst would: go through a set of data marking sequences of text in terms of codes (coding); and for each code, collect together all sequences of text coded in a particular way (retrieving).

The computer takes over the physical task of writing marginal codes, making photocopies of transcripts or field notes, cutting out all chunks of text relating to a code, and pasting them together. CAQDAS does not automatically do these things: the analyst must still interpret his or her data, then code, and then retrieve the data, but the computer takes over the manual labour involved (wielding scissors and pasting small pieces of paper together, for example).

Is CAQDAS like quantitative data analysis software?

One of the comments often made about CAQDAS is that it does not and cannot help with decisions about the coding of textual materials or about the interpretation of findings (Sprokkereef et al., 1995; Weitzman & Miles, 1995). However, this situation is little different (if at all) from quantitative data analysis software. In quantitative research, the investigator sets out the crucial concepts and ideas in advance rather than generating them out of his or her data. Also, it would be wrong to represent the use of quantitative data analysis software like SPSS as purely mechanical: once the analyses have been performed, it is still necessary to interpret them. Indeed, the choice of variables to be analyzed and the techniques of analysis to be employed are themselves areas in which a considerable amount of interpretive expertise is required. Creativity is required by both forms of software.

A Review of Six Popular CAQDAS

Each of the following programs differs in the structuring of its system of data management and coding; the degree to which it allows the input of different media; and, system requirements (with ATLAS.ti, Kwalitan, MAXQDA 2007, and NVivo requiring a Windows environment and HyperRESEARCH and TAMS requiring Macintosh OS X). Thus, the choice of any one program will depend on at least three things: (1) operating system (Macintosh or PC); (2) the extent to which different data sources are involved (e.g., from text only to the inclusion of audio files, video, etc.); and (3) methodological strategy (i.e., positivist, postpositivist, mixed methods, etc.). In the latter case, while most programs are more geared to traditional form of grounded theory (and, in some cases, mixed methods) they will allow for some exploration of postpositivist qualitative research. Most programs come with a free download to allow the researcher to test the program before purchase. The download sites and/or further information is provided after each program:

ATLAS.ti

This program supports the 'interpretation and analysis of a variety of data sources, including text, audio and images. Data can be coded, searched, retrieved, codes defined, related codes or documents grouped together, conceptual diagrams of the emerging understanding of the data created, memos written, and tables of numerical data abstracted and exported to statistical software such as SPSS' (Bassett, 2010a, p. 182).

A primary element of the program is a tool called the Hermeneutic Unit (HU), which allows the researcher to bundle together 'all relevant data sources, codes, conceptual linkages, memos, and comments. [Data] . . . are imported into the software and organized, managed, coded, and analyzed in the HU'. (p. 182).

In ATLAS.ti 'data files are referred to as primary documents (PDs) [and each file is] numbered according to the order in which it is imported' (p. 182). Then 'data must be coded to access further functions of the software' (p. 182). According to Bassett (2010, p. 183) 'there are at least two types of codes that organize the data': data management codes and conceptual codes. The former are usually derived from sociodemographic variables (e.g., retiree, male) and describe the characteristics of a PD. The latter 'assign meaning drawn from the data (inductive) or from theory (deductive) . . . Segments of a PD (e.g., lines of text, portions of a photograph, seconds of an audio file, or frames of a video) are assigned to multiple conceptual codes' (Bassett, 2010, p. 183). In terms of researcher commentary, ATLAS.ti allows the researcher to add comments, memos, etc. and use them to generate new insights, comparisons, themes, and relationships between codes.

In a case study of the use of Outcomes Management System (OMS) data in the health-care field Patel and Riley (2007) used ATLAS.ti—grouping PDs according to case (e.g., type of staff, service setting). 'Following coding . . . reports displaying sections of text assigned to specific codes were generated and read to further the fragmenting of codes. . . . The authors' reported an iterative and cyclical process of coding, memo development, reports, and further reading of PDs to deepen the case study analysis' (Bassett, 2010, p. 184).

Bassett (2010, p. 184) comments that in ATLAS.ti codes 'are not linked to any other code until the researcher specifically creates the relationship, differing from many other software where hierarchical relationships between codes are encouraged. Codes and themes can be easily interrogated in ATLAS.ti, enhancing analysis and the construction of theory'.

According to Wikipedia 'ATLAS.ti is used by researchers and practitioners in a wide variety of fields including anthropology, arts, architecture, criminology, economics, educational sciences, engineering, ethnological studies, and management studies' (http://en.wikipedia.org/wiki/Atlas.ti).

Users' corner. A review of user comments on the Web suggest that ATLAS.ti's strength is as a network tool that can help the researcher who is interested in the links between codes or the links within texts. For example, it can pick up contradictions between statements and in the process help to generate new insights. Arguably, it is also good at allowing the researcher to work in various different ways with the data while also allowing him or her to move quickly through coded data for particular themes. And it is arguably also useful for examining data in context (see http://forums.qsrinternational.com/index.php?showtopic=211).

Further information can be found at: http://www.atlasti.com

Kwalitan

Kwalitan was developed in the late 1980s to specifically aid the process of grounded theory research (Peters, 2010) but its uses can be extended to other qualitative analysis. In Kwalitan all 'original data that have to be analyzed (interviews, documents, observation protocols) and all data that are generated by the researcher during the analysis process (e.g., memos, codes, word lists) are stored in one single file, referred to as the project. Inside the project, the data are ordered in work files (for different groups of respondents or for different types of data), documents (the interviews of the observation protocols), and segments' (Peters, 2010, p. 187). Although mainly focused on text analysis, Kwalitan can handle some graphic input and '(short) audio or video fragments' (p. 187). The program is structured to deal with, what is identified as, four levels of analysis: words (e.g., the spoken words of an interviewee or textual words in documents); codes (devised by the researcher); concepts (developed by the researcher); reflections (on the research process, as found in comments, memos, etc.). Peters (2010, p. 189) contends that 'one of the strengths of Kwalitan . . . [is that] it can be applied to a variety of research traditions'.

Users' corner. Kwalitan is 'designed to assist in the development of grounded theories, enables hierarchical coding and the navigation of data with Boolean searches' (http://www.restore.ac.uk/lboro/research/software/caqdas.php#kwalitan). It 'takes care of an efficient storage of the data and offers several features to analyze the qualitative material, like coding, retrieving, categorization of codes, overviews of codes or words in the text, keywords in context and writing memos' (http://shanti.virginia.edu/tools/384).

Further information can be found at: http://www.kwalitan.nl.

MAXQDA 2007

MAXQDA 2007 is geared to textually based qualitative research (Humble, 2010): unlike ATLAS.ti and Kwalitan, MAXQDA 2007 cannot handle other media (e.g., video, audio, etc.). However, like Kwalitan, MAXQDA 2007 saves all study documents into a single file called a project. According to Humble (2010, p. 192), 'MAXQDA 2007 user interface results in easy organization of and access to multiple textually based data sources. This program also has numerous options for finely tuned coding, data management, visual data analysis, and visual presentation of findings'.

Users' corner. Users have referred to the program as intuitive; providing the ability to turn insights into 'descriptive and theoretical codes, analytical models in the form of hierarchical code system'; facilitates the conducting of 'different kinds of qualitative or texts analysis simultaneously'; and 'well-suited for integrating ethnographic and epidemiological methods' (http://www.maxqda.com/about/comments).

Further information can be found at: http://www.maxqda.com/.

NVivo

NVivo is seen as the main rival to ATLAS.ti but most comparisons suggest that, in the last analysis, their individual strengths and weaknesses should be judged against the researcher's particular needs and requirements (Lewis, 2004). Like ATLAS.ti, NVivo 'facilitates the use of a variety of data sources, including text documents, portable document format (PDF), and audio, video, and image files' (Bassett, 2010b, p. 192). In this system 'data sources are coded to nodes [that] represent and bear the label of a code, category, or concept, and includes the relevant references to the document sources' (p. 192). NVivo allows for the development of various nodes, including free nodes (i.e., stand alone); tree nodes (i.e., those that involve 'hierarchically linked codes, concepts, and categories), case nodes (i.e., data grouped according to specific entities), and relationship nodes (i.e., the connection of items in a case study) (p. 192). Various notations, researcher observations, and memos can be captured in the annotations and memos functions of the program. Searches and retrievals can be done through either a Boolean (and, or, not) or 'a proximatory (near, preceding, surrounding) search' (Bassett, 2010b, p. 193). An early example of the application of NVivo to a qualitative research project can be found in Jakobsen and McLaughlin's (2004) study of an ecosystem management project.

Users' corner. User's have commented that 'NVivo's strength is its search tool'; it's matrix tables provide a 'quick cut at the data so you can see if patterns are emerging between the different groups in your study or across different themes'; the ability to insert hyperlinks 'within a document in NVIVO to another document or to a precise point in a document'; its facilitation of writing 'journal or memos directly in NVIVO and have links to text that support the argument [being] constructed—a technique that 'is also valuable when using NVIVO to analyze literature reviews'; invaluable at 'searching and producing resources to write up from'; and 'great for comparative work across say, different types of respondent at the end of the coding process'. (http://forums.qsrinternational.com/index.php?showtopic=211)

Further information is available at: http://www.qsrinternational.com.

HyperRESEARCH

HyperRESEARCH is a software programs that 'enables strong coding and retrieval as well as the generation and testing of theories' (Hurworth & Shrimpton, 2007, p. 191). It is 'founded on a case-base approach so that data is tackled the way it was collected' (p. 191); it can deal with various media, including text, graphics, and video sources; and it 'allows researchers from several projects, or the same project to merge their data' (p. 191).

According to one review, the program has an 'unusual database structure [in which] each project is a 'study'. Within the study you can have up to 900 cases although HyperRESEARCH examines one 'case' at a time. The researcher determines what a case will represent—so it could be an individual, a site, a community, a classroom, a time period or a focus group (Hurworth & Shrimpton, 2007, p. 192). The program also facilitates memoing, as well as theory generation and testing.

Users' corner. Reviewers have called it intuitive in a way that allows the researcher to 'focus more on the research rather than on trying to fathom the program' (Hurworth & Shrimpton, 2007, p. 191). However, some drawbacks have been noted, including the fact that word files have to be converted to text files in order to enter them into the program; entered segments cannot be modified but have to be deleted and reentered where changes are needed; it cannot run several projects simultaneously; it is not possible to create hyperlinks between anything other than code and data segments; and video clips have to be cut into relatively small (5–10 minutes) segments (Hurworth & Shrimpton, 2007, p. 192).

Further information can be found at: http://www.researchware.com/.

TAMS

TAMS Analyzer (TA) differs from other programs in that it is a free, open source, tool that runs on both Macintosh and Linux operating systems. It allows the researcher 'to import documents, field notes, or interview transcripts and quickly code them by clicking on codes from [his or her generated] list or by creating new tags on the fly' (Warters, 2005, p. 321). The researcher can 'extract coded passages based on various criteria, recode found sets of data, and perform many other useful analytic and management tasks' (p. 321) in order to simply gather 'relevant text or audio/video exemplars for use in writing up a project, or [to] . . . output sophisticated concept maps exploring the relationship between different nodes in [the] data' (p. 321). The system is built around three basic code types: I(1) global descriptors that 'describe entire documents (i.e., this file in an interview)'; (2) sectional descriptors 'that describe a section of a file (i.e., this is John talking)'; and (3) data codes that identify themes or concepts in varying passages of text (Warters, 2005, p. 321).

The program allows the researcher to 'develop hierarchies of codes [that can be colour coded]' and to 'nest and overlap tags [that provide] the user with lots of freedom in terms of the length and types of passages that get marked up for retrieval and analysis. Teams are also supported via an inter-rater reliability test routine using **Cohen's kappa** and the ability to "sign" tags according to who has applied them' (Warters, 2005, pp. 321–322).

Users' corner. According to Warters (2005, pp. 325–326), one drawback with TAMS is that that the documentation is 'currently scatted across quite a number of different files that have been unevenly revised'. Nonetheless, his overall impression was that TAMS Analyzer 'is a powerful and flexible program that permits the casual user to get started coding

passages of text quickly, simply by converting their source documents to text files and pointing the program at them and developing some codes. At the same time, it enables larger or more complex projects and more sophisticated users to customize and manipulate a broad range of document types and content formats' (Warters, 2005, p. 327).

Further information can be found at: http://tux.educ.kent.edu/mweinste/tams/.

Lack of universal agreement about the utility of CAQDAS

Unlike quantitative data analysis, in which the use of computer software is both widely accepted and to all intents and purposes a necessity, among qualitative data analysts its use is by no means universally embraced. There are several concerns:

- Some writers are concerned that the ease with which coded text can be quantified, either within qualitative data analysis packages or by importing coded information into quantitative data analysis packages like SPSS, will mean that the temptation to quantify findings will prove irresistible to many researchers. As a result, there is a concern that qualitative research will then be colonized by the reliability and validity criteria of quantitative research (Hesse-Biber, 1995).

- It has been suggested that CAQDAS reinforces and even exaggerates the tendency for the code and retrieve process that underpins most approaches to qualitative data analysis to result in a fragmentation of the textual materials on which researchers work (Weaver & Atkinson, 1994). As a result, the narrative flow of interview transcripts and events recorded in field notes may be lost.

- It has also been suggested that the fragmentation process of coding text into chunks that are then retrieved and put together into groups of related fragments risks decontextualizing data (Buston, 1997; Fielding & Lee, 1998, p. 74). Having an awareness of context is crucial to many qualitative researchers and the prospect of this element being sidelined is not an attractive one.

- Catterall and Maclaran (1997) have argued on the basis of their experience that CAQDAS is not very suitable for focus group data because the code and retrieve function tends to result in a loss of the communication process that goes on when this method is used. Many writers view the interaction that occurs in focus groups as an important feature of the method (Kitzinger, 1994).

- Stanley and Temple (1995) have suggested that most of the coding and retrieval features that someone is likely to need in the course of conducting qualitative data analysis are achievable through powerful word-processing software. They show how this can be accomplished using Word for Windows. The key point here is that the advantage of using such software is that it does not require a lengthy period of getting acquainted with the mechanics of its operations. Also, of course, if someone already has the necessary word-processing software, the possible cost of a CAQDAS program is rendered unnecessary.
- Researchers working in teams may experience difficulties in coordinating the coding of text when different people are involved in this activity (Sprokkereef et al., 1995).
- Coffey et al. (1996) have argued that the style of qualitative data analysis enshrined in most CAQDAS software (particularly the more prominent ones) is resulting in the emergence of a new orthodoxy. This arises because these programs presume and are predicated on a certain style of analysis—one based on coding and retrieving text—that owes a great deal to grounded theory. Coffey et al. argue that the emergence of a new orthodoxy is inconsistent with the growing flirtation with a variety of representational modes in qualitative research, partly as a result of the influence of postmodernism (see Chapter 7 for a discussion of these considerations).

On the other hand, several writers have sought to extol the virtues of such packages on a variety of grounds:

- Most obviously, CAQDAS can make the coding and retrieval process faster and more efficient.
- It has been suggested that new opportunities are offered. For example, Mangabeira (1995) has argued on the basis of her experience with a program called The Ethnograph that her ability to relate her coded text to what are often referred to as 'facesheet variables' (sociodemographic and personal information, such as age, title of job, number of years in school education) offered new opportuni-

ties in the process of analyzing her data. Thus, CAQDAS may be helpful in the development of explanations.

- It is sometimes suggested that CAQDAS enhances the transparency of the process of conducting qualitative data analysis. It is often noted that the ways in which qualitative data are analyzed are unclear in reports of findings (Bryman & Burgess, 1994b). CAQDAS may force researchers to be more explicit and reflective about the process of analysis.
- CAQDAS, like NVivo, invites the analyst to think about codes that are developed in terms of 'trees' of interrelated ideas. This can be a useful feature, in that it urges the analyst to consider possible connections between codes.
- Writers like Silverman (1985) have commented on the tendency towards anecdotalism in much qualitative research—that is, the tendency to use quotations from interview transcripts or field notes but with little sense of the prevalence of the phenomenon they are supposed to exemplify. CAQDAS invariably offers the opportunity to count such things as the frequency with which a form of behaviour occurred or a viewpoint was expressed in interviews. However, as previously noted, some qualitative researchers perceive risks in the opportunity offered for quantification of findings.

To use or not to use CAQDAS? If you have a very small data set, it is probably not worth the time and trouble navigating your way around new software. On the other hand, if you think you may use it on a future occasion, taking the time and trouble may be worth it. If you do not have easy access to CAQDAS, it is likely to be too expensive for your personal purchase, though various sites do outline student and educational discounts. It is also worth bearing in mind that learning new software does provide you with useful skills that may be transferable on a future occasion. And, as we have seen in our reviews of leading programs, some software packages have develop their capabilities that take care of at least some of the concerns expressed by postpositivist researchers. By and large, we feel it is worthwhile, but you need to bear in mind some of the factors mentioned above in deciding whether or not to use it. Where possible download free trial versions and do a user search on the Web to get a feel for the potential strengths and weaknesses.

Key points

- The collection of **qualitative** data frequently results in the accumulation of a large volume of information.
- Qualitative data analysis is not governed by codified rules in the same way as quantitative data analysis.
- There are different approaches to qualitative data analysis, of which **grounded theory** is one of the more prominent.
- **Coding** is a key process in most qualitative data analysis strategies, but it is sometimes accused of fragmenting and decontextualizing text.
- **Secondary analysis** of qualitative data is becoming a more prominent activity than in the past.
- CAQDAS does not and cannot help with decisions about how to code qualitative data or how to interpret findings.
- CAQDAS can make many if not most of the clerical tasks associated with the manual coding and retrieving of data easier and faster.
- If you have a very small data set, it is probably not worth the time and trouble navigating your way around a new software program.
- If you have a larger data set, or are intending to use the software skills that you acquire on other research projects in the future, CAQDAS can be an invaluable tool.

Questions for review

- What is meant by suggesting that qualitative data are an 'attractive nuisance'?

General strategies of qualitative data analysis

- What are the main ingredients of **analytic induction**?
- What makes it a rigorous method?
- What are the main ingredients of grounded theory?
- What is the role of coding in grounded theory and what are the different types of coding?
- What is the role of memos in grounded theory?
- Charmaz has written that theoretical sampling 'represents a defining property of grounded theory' (2000, p. 519). Why do you think she feels this to be the case?
- What are some of the main criticisms of grounded theory?

More on coding

- Is coding associated solely with grounded theory?
- What are the main steps in coding?
- To what extent does coding result in excessive fragmentation of data?
- To what extent does narrative analysis provide an alternative to data fragmentation?

Secondary analysis of qualitative data

- How feasible is it for researchers to analyze qualitative data collected by another researcher?
- What are the main points of difference between CAQDAS and quantitative data analysis software like SPSS?
- Why is CAQDAS controversial?
- To what extent does CAQDAS help with qualitative data analysis?
- What three major factors shape a researcher's decision on which program to use?

25

Writing Up Business Research

Chapter guide

It is easy to forget that one of the main stages in any research project, regardless of its size, is that it has to be written up. Not only is this how you will convey your findings, but being aware of the significance of writing is crucial, because your audience must be persuaded about the credibility and importance of your research. This chapter presents some of the characteristics of the writing up of business research, including writing up a student research project. The chapter explores:

- Why writing, and especially good writing, is important to business research.
- How to write up your research for a dissertation project.
- How **quantitative** and **qualitative** research are composed, using examples.
- The influence and implications of *postmodernism* for writing.
- Key issues raised by discussions about the writing of **ethnography**, an area where discussions about different ways of writing have been especially prominent.

Introduction

The aim of this chapter is to examine some of the strategies that are employed in writing up business research. As well as providing students with some practical advice on writing up a student research project, we will explore the question of whether or not quantitative and qualitative research reveal divergent approaches. As we will see, the similarities are frequently more striking and apparent than the differences. However, the main point of this chapter is to extract some principles of good practice that can be developed and incorporated into your own writing. This is an important issue, since many people find writing up research more difficult than carrying it out. On the other hand, many people treat the writing up stage as relatively unproblematic. But no matter how well research is conducted, others (that is, your readers) have to be convinced about the credibility of the knowledge claims you are making. Good writing is, therefore, very much to do with developing your style so that it is persuasive and convincing. Flat, lifeless, uncertain writing does not have the power to persuade and convince. In exploring these issues, we will touch on rhetorical strategies in the writing of business research (see Key concept 25.1). As Atkinson (1990, p. 2) has observed in relation to social research, 'the conventions of text and rhetoric are among the ways in which reality is constructed'. This chapter will review some of the ways in which business research is written up in a way that will provide some basic ideas about structuring your own written work if you have to produce something like a dissertation.

We often encounter the term rhetoric in a negative context, such as 'mere rhetoric' or the opposition of 'rhetoric and reality'. However, rhetoric is an essential ingredient of writing, because when we write our aim is to convince others about the credibility of our knowledge claims. To suggest that rhetoric should somehow be suppressed makes little sense, since it is in fact a basic feature of writing. The examination of rhetorical strategies in written texts based on business research is concerned with the identification of the techniques in those texts that are designed to convince and persuade. An interesting and useful example of the way that rhetoric is used to influence debate can be found in a study by Suddaby and Greenwood (2005) who describe the role of rhetoric

> **Key concept 25.1: What is rhetoric?**
>
> Rhetoric is the study of the ways in which attempts to convince or persuade an audience are formulated.

in legitimating wide sweeping institutional change in the North American accounting industry in the late 1990s.

Writing up your research project

It is easy to neglect the writing stage of your work because of the difficulties that you often encounter in getting your research underway. But—obvious though this point is—your dissertation has to be written. Your findings must be conveyed to an audience, something that all of us who carry out research have to face. The first bit of advice is:

Start early

It is easy to take the view that the writing up of your research findings is something that you can think about after you have collected and analyzed your data. There is, of course, a grain of truth in this view, in that you could hardly write up your findings until you know what they are, which is something that you can know only once you have gathered and analyzed your data. However, there are good reasons for beginning writing early on, since you might want to start thinking about such issues as how best to present and justify the research questions that are driving your research or how to structure the theoretical and research literature that will have been used to frame your research questions. Students often tend to underestimate the time that it will take to write up their research so it is a good idea to allow plenty of time for this, especially if you are expecting your supervisor to read and comment on an early draft since you will also need to allow them a reasonable amount of time for this. A further reason why it is advisable to begin writing earlier rather than later is an entirely practical one: many people find it difficult to get started and employ (probably unwittingly)

25.1 | Student Experience

The benefits of writing up early

Tom and Karen both found that there were advantages to having completed writing up their dissertations early so they were able to come back to it after a break before the deadline and make further changes. Tom said, 'The deadline was to hand it in by the end of August, but I had a holiday at the beginning of August and I was going to move house, so I knew I had to finish by the end of July because otherwise it was going to be nightmare. And that was quite good because it meant I finished, went off on holiday, then I . . . just let it sort of settle for a couple of weeks and . . . when I came back I was able to look at it with a fresh eye and give it a final kind of tidy up and tweak'.

Karen found that starting her research project early was an advantage in helping her to see her argument more clearly:

I wanted to give it a lot of time to . . . think about all the different issues . . . I did one draft . . . and then just left it for four months and then came back to it, which I think was a definite benefit because then I came back to it with fresh eyes and . . . I'd had a couple of thoughts . . . about different things . . . it was . . . one of those things that was just constantly at the back of my mind. . . . And I think that's definitely the best way to do it because I had so many friends who sort of rushed it in the last two weeks and I think then you lose all of the . . . conceptual thinking and . . . [the ability to think] more broadly about . . . the topic . . . and you just get a bit bogged down in all the detail.

procrastination strategies to put off the inevitable. This tendency can result in the writing being left until the last minute and consequently being rushed. Writing under this kind of pressure is not ideal. How you represent your findings and conclusions is a crucial stage in the research process. If you do not provide a convincing account of your research, you will not do justice to it.

Sometimes the student's choice is restricted by the supervisory process. Some supervisors, for example, may require that the student develop a 'research proposal' that spells out the why, what, and how of the research thesis. That can range from one to three chapters depending on the demands of the particular graduate program and/or the methodological direction of the supervisor. At Saint Mary's University, for example, **postpositivist** research supervisors tend to require an introductory chapter that lays out the purpose, direction, and methodology of the thesis in the first 'introduction' chapter, while **positivist** researchers tend to require at least three chapters to constitute the formal proposal. The variance in requirement, however, is only partially linked to the methodological differences of the supervisors.

Be persuasive

This point is crucial. Writing up your research is not simply a matter of reporting your findings and drawing some conclusions. Writing up your research will contain many other features, such as referring to the literature on which you drew, explaining how you did your research, and outlining how you conducted your analysis. But above all, you must be persuasive. This means that you must convince your readers of the credibility of your conclusions. Simply saying, 'This is what I found; isn't it interesting?' is not enough. You must persuade your readers that your findings and conclusion are significant and that they are plausible.

Get feedback

Try to get as much feedback on your writing as possible and respond positively to the points anyone makes about what they read. Your supervisor is likely to be the main source of feedback, but institutions vary in what supervisors are allowed to comment on. Provide your supervisor with drafts of your work to the fullest extent that

regulations will allow. Give him or her plenty of time to provide feedback. There will be others like you who will want your supervisor to comment on their work, and, if he or she feels rushed, the comments may be less helpful. Also, you could ask others on the same degree program to read your drafts and comment on them. They may ask you to do the same. Their comments may be very useful, but, by and large, your supervisor's comments are the main ones you should seek out.

Avoid sexist, racist, and disablist language

Remember that your writing should be free of sexist, racist, and disablist language. Several organizations provide very good general and specific advice about this issue, including the Ontario Institute for Studies in Education (OISE) division of the University of Toronto theses guide and the University of Calgary's online style guidelines. See, respectively:

> http://www.ro.oise.utoronto.ca/OISE_Theses_Guide
> .pdf
> http://www.ucalgary.ca/news/styleguide#inclusive

See also the respective sites of the British Sociological Association:

> www.britsoc.org.uk/about/antisex.htm
> www.britsoc.org.uk/about/antirace.htm
> www.britsoc.org.uk/about/ablist.htm

Structure your writing

It may be that you have to write a thesis of around 10,000 to 15,000 words for your undergraduate degree, and anything from 60,000 to 100,000 words for a graduate dissertation. How might it be structured? The following is typical of the structure of a dissertation but bear in mind that this may vary depending on the methodological approach taken (see below).

Title page

You should examine your institution's rules about what should be entered here.

Acknowledgements

You might want to acknowledge the help of various people, such as gatekeepers who gave you access to an organization, people who have read your drafts and provided you with feedback, or your supervisor for his or her advice.

List of contents

Your institution may have recommendations or prescriptions about the form this should take.

An abstract

A brief summary of your dissertation. Not all institutions require this component, so check on whether it is required. Journal articles usually have abstracts, so you can draw on these for guidance on how to approach this task.

Introduction

- You should explain what you are writing about and why it is important. Saying simply that it interests you because of a long-standing personal interest is not enough.
- You might indicate in general terms the theoretical approach or perspective you will be using and why.
- You should also at this point outline your research questions. Regardless of which research strategy you have adopted (see Chapter 3) you should clearly spell out your research questions. The reader will then know what it is you are trying to understand, why it is important to understand the issue at hand (e.g., because it deals with a gap in the literature, contradicts existing theory, etc.), how you have formulated the problem; and how you set about studying it. This will allow the reader to judge the rest of the dissertation and how convincingly you have researched the stated issue.
- The opening sentence or sentences are often the most difficult of all. Becker (1986) advises strongly against opening sentences that he describes as 'vacuous' and 'evasive'. He gives the example of 'This study deals with the problem of careers', and adds that this kind of sentence employs 'a typically evasive manoeuvre, pointing to something without saying anything, or anything much, about it. What about careers?' (Becker, 1986, p. 51). He suggests that such evasiveness often occurs be-

cause of concerns about giving away the plot. In fact, he argues, it is much better to give readers a quick and clear indication of what is going to be meted out to them and where it is going.

Literature review

More detailed advice on how to go about writing this chapter of your dissertation is given in Chapter 2.

Research methods

The term 'research methods' is meant here as a kind of catch-all for several issues that need to be outlined: your research design; your sampling approach; how access was achieved, if relevant; the procedures you used (such as, if you used a mailed-out or an online survey, did you follow up non-respondents); the nature of your questionnaire, interview schedule, participant observation role, observation schedule, coding frame, or whatever (in positivist research these will usually appear in an appendix, but you should comment on such things as your style of questioning or observation and why you asked the things you did); problems of non-response; note taking; issues of ongoing access and cooperation; coding matters; and how you proceeded with your analysis. When discussing each of these issues, you should describe and defend the choices that you made, such as why you used a mailed-out survey rather than a structured interview approach, or why you focused upon a particular population for sampling purposes.

Results

In this chapter you present the bulk of your findings. If you intend to have a separate Discussion chapter, it is likely that the results will be presented with little commentary in terms of the literature or the implications of your findings. If there will be no Discussion chapter, you will need to provide some reflections on the significance of your findings for your research questions and for the literature. Bear these points in mind:

- Whichever approach you take, remember not to include all your results. You should present and discuss only those findings that relate to your research questions. This requirement may mean a rather painful process of leaving out many findings, but it is necessary, so that the thread of your argument is not lost.

- Your writing should point to particularly salient aspects of the tables, graphs, textual passages and quotes, or other forms of analysis you present. Do not just summarize what a table shows; you should direct the reader to the component or components of it that are especially striking from the point of view of your research questions. Try to ask yourself what story you want the table to convey and try to relay that story to your readers.

- Another 'sin' to be avoided is simply presenting a graph or table or a section of the transcript of a semi-structured interview or focus group session without any comment whatsoever, because the reader is left wondering why you think the finding is important.

- When reporting quantitative findings, it is quite a good idea to vary wherever possible the method of presenting results—for example, provide a mixture of diagrams and tables. However, you must remember the lessons of Chapter 23 concerning the methods of analysis that are appropriate to different types of variable.

- A particular problem that can arise with qualitative research is that students find it difficult to leave out large parts of their data. As one experienced qualitative researcher has put it: 'The major problem we face in qualitative inquiry is not to get data, but to get rid of it!' (Wolcott, 1990, p. 18). He goes on to say that the 'critical task in qualitative research is not to accumulate all the data you can, but to 'can' (i.e., get rid of) most of the data you accumulate' (Wolcott, 1990, p. 35). You simply have to recognize that much of the rich data you accumulate will have to be jettisoned. If you do not do this, any sense of an argument in your work is likely to be lost. There is also the risk that your account of your findings will appear too descriptive and lack an analytical edge. This is why it is important to use research questions as a focus and to orient the presentation of your findings to them.

- If you are writing a thesis, for example for a Master's or a Doctorate, it is likely that you will have more than one and possibly several chapters in which you present your results. Cryer (1996) recommends showing

at the beginning of each chapter the particular issues that are being examined in the chapter. You should indicate which research question or questions are being addressed in the chapter and provide some signposts about what will be included in the chapter. In the conclusion of the chapter, you should make clear what your results have shown and draw out any links that might be made with the next results chapter.

Discussion

In the Discussion, you reflect on the implications of your findings for the research questions that have driven your research. In other words, how do your results illuminate your research questions? If you have specified hypotheses, the discussion will revolve around whether the hypotheses have been confirmed or not, and, if not, you might speculate about some possible reasons for and the implications of their refutation.

Conclusion

The main points here are as follows:

- A Conclusion is not the same as a summary. However, it is frequently useful to bring out in the opening paragraph of the Conclusion your argument thus far. This will mean relating your findings and your discussion of them to your research questions. Thus, your brief summary should be a means of hammering home to your readers the significance of what you have done. However, the Conclusion should do more than merely summarize.

- You should make clear the implications of your findings for your research questions.

- You should suggest some ways in which your findings have implications for theories relating to your area of interest.

- You might also suggest some ways in which your findings have implications for practice in the field of business and management.

- You might draw attention to any limitations of your research with the benefit of hindsight, but it is probably best not to overdo this element and provide examiners with too much ammunition that might be used against you!

It is important to propose areas of further research that are suggested by your findings.

Two things to avoid are engaging in speculations that take you too far away from your data, or that cannot be substantiated by the data, and introducing issues or ideas that have not previously been brought up.

Appendices

In your appendices you might want to include such things as your questionnaire, coding frame, or observation schedule, letters sent to sample members, and letters sent to and received from gatekeepers where the cooperation of an organization was required.

References

Include here all references cited in the text. For the format of the References section you should follow whichever approach is prescribed by your department.

Finally

Remember to fulfill any obligations you entered into, such as supplying a copy of your dissertation, if, for example, your access to an organization was predicated on providing one, and maintaining the confidentiality of information supplied and the anonymity of your informants and other research participants.

Writing convincingly by reading your audience

A research project is (at least in theory) written up for different audiences—from your course professor, project or thesis supervisor, through to an examiner or examination committee and onward to journal reviewers, editors, and potential journal readers or the readers of other media (e.g., government agencies, practitioners, and newspaper and magazine readers). At each level your research project or thesis has to be well written and convincing. As we will demonstrate below, the two go hand in hand.

Supervisors and Examiners

Every required research project has to get past an academic supervisor, be they the course professor or a specifically designated research supervisor or examiner who is an expert in your field of study. At this level you need to be able to demonstrate to the supervisor that you were capable of undertaking a project of research.

Undergraduate level

By the time you have completed your project or dissertation you should have a clear idea of what your supervisor is looking for. Amanda, Cindy, and Mellissa, for example, knew that the requirement of their undergraduate research methods course was to undertake a small research project that utilized a choice of a survey, a focus group, or a series of interviews. They knew that they had to develop a research question or questions that could be appropriately studied using one of the three assignment choices of method. They also understood that they were required to show some knowledge of the method used: its application, its strengths, and limitations. Thus, when it came to the writing up of the research project the students in the research methods course at Mount Saint Vincent University needed to write convincingly about the method they

---

Tips and Skills

Proofreading your dissertation

Before submitting your dissertation make sure that it is spell-checked and check it for grammatical and punctuation errors. There are many useful guides and handbooks that can be used for this purpose. It may also be useful to ask someone else, such as a friend or family member, to proofread your work in case there are errors that you have missed. As well as being an important presentational issue, this will affect the ease with which your written work can be read and understood. It, therefore, has the potential to significantly affect the quality of your dissertation.

used, how and why they chose that method (from a choice of three methods), how they developed an appropriate research question (or questions) and how this led to the chosen research method; how they applied the method and what, if anything, they learned about the strengths and limitations of the method. It should be noted that, at this level, the research 'findings' are less important than the application of the chosen method. Therefore, the student needs to convince the supervisor that he or she has a good grasp of the method.

At the level of a course project or an undergraduate thesis academic advisors are not expecting the findings to be convincing enough to be published in a scholarly journal (although occasionally this does happen—see for example Parker & Grandy, 2009). This is due to the limited nature of the research project in terms of time and other resources. The supervisor is more likely to judge the extent to which the findings can be connected to the methods used. Here the student needs to convince the supervisor that the findings have been arrived at through the coherent application of appropriate methods, rather than through speculation, hunches, guesswork, or other forms of anecdotal accounts.

Graduate level

At the graduate level the findings take on an increasingly important role, with the expectation that the results are adequately researched and of sufficient interest to practitioners and communities of scholars to be published. This is particularly true at the doctoral level where the expectation is that the thesis, either in whole or in part, will be capable of generating publishable materials (i.e., a scholarly book or journal articles). Thus, at the graduate level, more weight is given to the relationship between the methods used and the findings that are generated. Usually, especially with doctorates, the thesis is examined by an academic expert in the subject area to be examined, who is normally someone outside of the university in which the thesis is to be examined. In Britain, the United States, and Canada this person is usually referred to as the 'external examiner', while in Finland he or she is called 'the Opponent'. In Finland two 'Pre-readers' (who are also external to the university) examine the thesis prior to the official, public defence, where the

Opponent questions the student. In the UK the doctoral defence normally involves the addition of an 'internal examiner', who—as the title suggests—is recruited from inside the student's university and is also an expert in the area of study to be examined. In the United States and Canada the 'external examiner' is usually part of an 'examination committee' that includes the supervisor and two to three other faculty members from inside the university. The examination committee of the Sobey Ph.D. in Management (at Saint Mary's University), for example, consists of the student's supervisor, one other member of the Management Department, and two other faculty members who are external to the department. Prior to the defence this same group of people, minus the external examiner, constitute what is called the supervisory committee. Committee members are recruited for their expertise in one or more aspects of the thesis. For example, where a student is using a mixed methods approach the committee may consist of at least one person versed in quantitative methods and one versed in qualitative methods as well as faculty who are experts in the specific area of study. The experience of Dr. Amy Thurlow, a successful Sobey Ph.D. graduate, provides a good example. Amy's thesis was focused on organizational change and she was interested in investigating it from a post-structuralist perspective (that included critical discourse analysis and critical sensemaking). With that in mind she approached Jean Helms Mills, a faculty member well known for her published work on organizational change and critical sensemaking. One of this book's authors, Albert J. Mills, was recruited to her supervisory committee because of his knowledge of critical discourse analysis. Sara Malton, a professor from the university's English Department, was recruited because of her interest in culture and poststructuralism, and a third member of the Management Department, Elden Wiebe, was recruited to the committee because of his interest in narrative analysis and organizational change. For her defence the committee identified Professor Bill Cooke, an expert in postpositivist approaches to organizational change, as the external examiner.

What this all means is that the graduate student, in the first instance, needs to write the thesis in a way that is convincing to one or more examiners. That can mean writing convincingly for people with relatively disparate views and opinions. In the normal course of a PH.D. development and examination, an examination committee, regardless of whether it consists wholly of quantitative or quantitative researchers, will have some differences of opinion that has to be overcome. Thus, the student, in cooperation with his or her supervisor, will need to write convincingly for the thesis to pass the concerns of different faculty members.

Getting published: Editors, reviewers, and readers

Assuming that your thesis has been successfully passed/defended you may want to publish the findings in practitioner or a scholarly journal. This is where you need to take into account the audience that you are appealing to.

The practitioner audience

If, for example, you are writing for a practitioner audience the challenge will be two-fold: (1) to emphasize the practical outcomes of your findings (i.e., to show how your findings can be utilized to improve some aspect of business practice); and (2) to write in a clear, jargon-free style that will make sense to a broad audience. A good example of a practitioner magazine is the Sobey Business School's e-journal *The Workplace Review*, which sets out to deal with 'day-to-day workplace challenges' by translating current research into everyday language (http://sobey.smu.ca/workplacereview). More recent articles include 'Fire on the line: A stakeholder analysis of a telecommunication outage' (Rixon & Furey, 2009) that draws lessons from a fire at Bell Aliant in Newfoundland for company accountability to stakeholders; 'Finding space to breathe: Balancing control and freedom in all centres' (Murray & Helms Mills, 2009) that examines human resources practices in call centres and makes recommendations for improvements; and 'The relevance of the market concept' (Blotnicky, 2009), which examines the importance for businesses of adopting a marketing orientation. In this latter case the argument is laid out in a clear and direct introduction:

> For nearly 50 years, marketers have focused on the importance of adopting a marketing orientation

in order to achieve the greatest success in business. However, some experts have questioned whether or not the marketing orientation is a panacea. The current study utilized survey research to contact 21 of the Atlantic Canada Top 101 firms to find out if they adopted a marketing orientation, and whether or not it was related to the success they enjoyed in their industrial sectors. . . . The results from the top 101 firms interviewed indicated the firms were either not marketing oriented, or just barely marketing oriented, despite their success. Also, counter to previous research in the field, environmental constraints seemed to have little impact at all on marketing orientation or organizational performance. (Blotnicky, 2009, p. 3)

Here we see in a clear and precise fashion Blotnicky (2009) spells out the problem at hand (i.e., the relationship between marketing orientation and organizational performance), the fact that it is controversial (i.e., has 'been questioned'), the way she attempts to throw light on the issue (i.e., through a survey), and some of the findings (i.e., that marketing orientation is only vaguely associated with organizational performance).

The scholarly audience

Writing for a scholarly journal raises other particular issues. To begin with you need to review the following elements of your thesis/study:

1. The broad discipline or disciplines that your thesis fits under (e.g., accounting, organizational behaviour, marketing).
2. The theoretical orientation (i.e., **positivist** or **postpositivist**).
3. The research strategy adopted (**qualitative/quantitative/mixed methods**; see Chapter 3).
4. Any particular theoretical orientation that forms an important part of your research strategy (e.g., **grounded theory**, **interpretivism**);
5. Any particular methodological orientation (e.g., **analytic induction**, **ethnography**, **narrative analysis**) that forms an important part of your research strategy).

6. The general (e.g., organizational behaviour) and specific area(s) of research (e.g., motivation theory) that your study/thesis contributes to.

Identifying each of these factors will help you to identify the type of journal that is more likely to publish your work. To start with the more obvious issue, most journals are focused on a specific discipline within business studies. There are, for example, journals specifically for accounting (e.g., *Accounting and Business Research*); human resource management (*Human Resource Management Review*); history (*Management & Organizational History*); organizational behaviour (*Journal of Organizational Behaviour*); and a host of other disciplines and sub-disciplines. In some cases there are more specialized journals that are country (e.g., *Accountancy in Canada*) or theme (e.g., *Culture and Organization*) specific. There are other journals that are rooted in a particular paradigmatic approach to research, such as *Organization* or *Tamara*, and those that are focused on social issues, such as *Gender, Work & Organization*. Still other journals attempt to be relatively inclusive of a range of disciplines and sub-disciplines: the *Academy of Management Review*, the *Administrative Sciences Quarterly*, and the *Academy of Management Journal* are examples. And there are a few journals that attempt to be multi-disciplinary, such as the *Canadian Journal of Administrative Sciences*.

In each of the various journals in business studies the editor will be looking for articles that fit with the particular 'aims and scope' of their particular journal. Thus, the first thing you should do is to look for journals that seem to publish articles that are in line with your own work. There are five simple tips:

1. Look through the references of your own study/thesis and note the types of journals associated with the work you cite.
2. Do a library/online search for journals that appear to fit with your interests and check its aims and scope, which are usually published at the front or the back of the journal and/or on the journal's website. Sometimes the journal refers specifically to its 'aims and scope' (e.g., *Organization*), while other times the information is contained in 'notes to contributors' (e.g., *Administrative Sciences Quarterly*) or in other guides to potential authors.
3. Take a look at the editor and editorial board members of a journal to gain an impression of the type of research they do. They are the gatekeepers who will decide whether your article will be published or not.
4. Look through several recent issues of selected journals for articles that deal with the types of issue that your work is trying to address or comment on.
5. Pay particular attention to the style guide of the journal. Again, this is normally found towards the front or the back of the journal and/or on the journal's website, and appears under such headers as 'Style Guide for Authors' (e.g., *The Academy of Management Journal*), 'manuscript style' (e.g., *Canadian Journal of Administrative Sciences*), and 'notes for contributors' (e.g., *Gender, Work & Organization*).

These tips will not only help you to identify the range of journals that you are aiming to publish in but also give you a number of important clues as to the style of writing that is required and the likely audience that you are writing for (see also Tips and Skills on '*Conventions of writing for journal publication*'). For example, if your work is quantitative and largely framed within a positivist approach then some journals will not be an appropriate venue for your research. It may be appropriate for journals such as *The Academy of Management Journal* but not *Culture and Organization* (which rarely publishes statistical data) or *Organization* (which largely published critical postpositivist work).

 # Comparing quantitative and qualitative research articles: Two examples

In the following section two research-based articles that have been published in journals are examined to detect some helpful features. One is based on quantitative research and the other on qualitative research.

Tips and Skills

Conventions of writing for journal publication

An attempt to make the tacit rules of publishing more explicit is attempted by Cummings and Frost (1995) in an edited collection entitled *Publishing in the Organizational Sciences*, in which contributors speak from a variety of perspectives, as writers, reviewers, editors, and readers, incorporating viewpoints from newcomers and established scholars, about how the publishing process works.

One of the most revealing chapters by Daft (1995) is the somewhat bluntly titled 'Why I Recommended that Your Manuscript be Rejected and What You can Do about It', which is written from the perspective of the reviewer. Drawing upon his own experiences of writing papers and submitting them to journals, Daft argues that 'the journal review process is central to each scholar's growth and development' and is comprised of a series of highs and lows. Some reviews, he explains, 'were absolutely devastating. The reviewers seemed determined to be destructive, hurtful, and narrow-minded', whereas others were helpful and encouraging, their 'constructive criticism' improving his work 'dramatically' (1995, p. 165). One of the reasons for sharing views and experiences of the review process is thus because of the enormous impact it can have on the writer. However, Daft suggests that 'reviewing is more subjective than objective', admitting that 'subtle, intangible cues' concerning writing style, tone, and method of theory building 'often cause me to like or dislike the paper, and hence to support or not support the paper for revision or publication' (1995, p. 165). He goes on to list 11 common manuscript problems based on analysis of 111 of his own reviews of manuscripts which assumed a traditional theory-based, hypothesis testing approach that were submitted to the American journals *Administrative Science Quarterly* and *Academy of Management Journal*. The common types of problems identified were:

- No theory, this involves a lack of explanation of the relationships among variables: 'without a theory, there is nothing to pull the study together, nothing to justify why the variables should be studied' (1995, p. 167).
- Concepts and operationalization not in alignment, this problem occurs when the research design does not reflect the variables under study, sometimes because of differences in level of analysis, or because indicators of a variable rather than the variable itself are measured. An example of this might involve using fluctuations in the number of employees in an organization as a measure of organizational change.
- Insufficient definition of theory, this occurs when authors do not explain what their concepts mean, since enacting a definition is often a part of theory development;
- Insufficient rationale for design, this problem arises when manuscripts fail to explain the procedures or methods used in the study, such as sample size, response rates, in sufficient detail.
- Macrostructure regarding the organization and flow, this refers to whether or not the various parts of the paper, such as theory section, methods, conclusions, fit together into a coherent whole. Problems arise when manuscripts contain measures in the results section that are not referred to in the theory section or when conclusions are reached that are not related to the paper's research questions.
- Amateur style and tone, indications of amateurism, according to Daft (1995, p. 170) include 'frequent use of underlining or exclamation marks' or exaggerating the importance of the research topic in order to make the case for publication or tearing down the work of others to justify the author's own study rather than showing how it builds on previous work.
- Inadequate research design, this involves the inappropriate use of methods that cannot address the research question posed by the study, such as use of an undergraduate student sample to analyze the selection of business strategies by corporate executives, as undergraduate students have little or no experience of strategy selection. These often constitute a fatal problem that cannot be put right after the study has been conducted.
- Not relevant to the field: some papers were inappropriate for the type of journal they were submitted to and would have been better placed in another discipline (although Daft suspects that some of them have already been rejected from another discipline and are trying for publication in another area). It is also harder to get published in a topic area where a large number of studies have already been published because 'the case for publication is easier if the topic is new, fresh and poorly understood rather than mature and overstudied' (1995, p. 172).

- Overengineering, sometimes authors concentrate so much on the methodology that it becomes an end in itself, at the expense of making a theoretical contribution.
- Conclusions not in alignment, this problem involves manuscripts where conclusions are too short or lack sufficient interpretation of the findings, as well as manuscripts that generalize far beyond the data; 'the important thing is to use the conclusion section to fully develop the theoretical contribution and to point out the new understanding from the study' (1995, p. 173).
- Cutting up the data, this problem occurred when a paper under review for one journal overlapped with another paper by the same authors under review for another journal, sometimes with slight modifications. As Daft explains, 'this did not happen often, but when it did the impression on me was terrible' (1995, p. 173).

Daft suggests that papers based on qualitative research studies are prone to similar shortcomings as quantitative papers, especially in relation to lack of theory and misalignment of concepts and operationalization. Qualitative papers were rejected 'not because referees did not like qualitative research, but because the investigators had not used the manuscript to build theory' (1995, p. 174).

He then goes on to suggest seven ways of overcoming these common problems, or what you can do about having your manuscript rejected. His suggestions are:

- Tell a story, think of each variable in the research as a character and explain how the characters interact with each other. This will give meaning to the observed relationships between variables.
- Discuss fully your procedures and thought processes, be open about weaknesses and limitations because it gives reviewers confidence that you are not hiding something.
- Concentrate on the macrostructure, make sure that all sections of the paper are coordinated and flow logically from one to another.
- Find the operational base of your research and stick to it, think of the research design as the core of an empirical paper, to which the theory, results, and discussion correspond.
- Listen to your reviewers, use the feedback they provide to revise the manuscript and keep in mind that sometimes a paper is just not that good and you may have to accept that it is unpublishable and use it as a learning experience.
- Allow the manuscript to ripen naturally, it takes time to write a good paper and most manuscripts go through many revisions before they are ready to be submitted to a journal. Use feedback from colleagues to develop your manuscript prior to submission.
- Don't exaggerate, it is better to be cautious in your argument than to overstate your claims. Avoid statements like 'these findings prove' and instead say 'these findings suggest'.

Although these guidelines are offered to researchers who are trying to publish their work in prestigious academic journals, some of the advice is also relevant to students who are writing up a research project. In our experience, students writing up a research project can tend to overstate claims in the way described by Daft and sometimes feel that admitting the limitations of the study is likely to give them a lower mark when actually it can improve it. This discussion may also help students and other readers to get a sense of the rigorousness of the peer review process that is employed by many journals and of the humiliations that their lecturers and supervisors frequently have to endure at the hands of their colleagues.

An example of quantitative research

To illustrate some of the characteristics of the way quantitative research is written up for academic journals, we will take an article by Armstrong-Strassen and Schlosser (2008). We are not suggesting that this article is somehow exemplary or representative, but rather that it exhibits some features that are often regarded as desirable qualities in terms of presentation and structure. However, it does have the distinction of being awarded the 2008 'Verity International Award for Overall Outstanding Paper in Management' published in the *Canadian Journal of Administrative Sciences*. The article reports on the findings of a survey questionnaire of two Canadian federal government departments on the issue of downsizing. The article was accepted for publication in Canada's leading journal in the field of business and administrative studies: the *Canadian Journal of Administrative Sciences* (CJAS). The vast majority of published articles in academic journals entail the blind refereeing of articles submitted. This means that an article will be read by two or three peers who comment on the article. They will give the editors their assessment of its merits and hence whether it is worthy of publication. Most articles submitted are rejected. With highly prestigious journals, it is common for in excess of 90% of articles to be rejected. It is unusual for an article to be accepted on its first submission. Usually, the referees will suggest areas that need revising and the author (or authors) is expected to respond to that feedback. Revised versions of articles are usually sent back to the referees for further comment and this process may result in the author having to revise the draft yet again. It may even result in rejection. Therefore, an article like Armstrong-Strassen and Schlosser's is not just the culmination of a research process, but is also the outcome of a feedback and review process. The fact that it has been accepted for publication, when many others have been rejected, testifies to its merits as having met the standards of the journal. That is not to say it is perfect, but the refereeing process is an indication that it does possess certain crucial qualities.

The article has the following components, aside from the abstract:

1. Introduction.
2. Theory and hypotheses.
3. Methods.
4. Results.
5. Discussion.

Introduction

Right at the beginning of the introduction, the opening sentences attempt to grab our attention, to give a clear indication of where the article's focus lies, and to provide an indication of the significance and importance of the subject of study for practitioners, policy makers, and academics. This is what the authors write:

Researchers are taking an increasing interest in positive workplace attitudes and behaviours as predictors of organizational outcomes (Luthans & Youssef, 2007; Youssef & Luthans, 2007). Emerging from the field of positive psychology (see Seligman & Csikszentmihalyi, 2000), positive organizational behaviour (POB) is defined as 'the study and application of positively-oriented human resource strengths and psychological capacities that can be measured, developed, and effectively managed for performance improvement in today's workplace' (Luthans, 2002*b*, p. 59). Although practitioners and consultants in the business field have long been interested in how to promote positive attitudes and behaviours, only recently has academic research considered the strategic ramifications of POB for organizations (e.g., Wooten & Crane, 2004; Youssef & Luthans, 2007).' (Armstrong-Strassen & Schlossser, 2008, pp. 93–94)

The authors use the opening paragraph to achieve three things. Let us look at what each sentence does:

- The first sentence locates the article's focus as addressing an important aspect of business and management research that is currently the focus of growing interest, namely, a link between positive workplace attitudes and behaviours and organizational outcomes.
- The second sentence clearly locates and defines the authors' theoretical framework within Positive Organizational Behaviour (POB).
- The third sentence goes on to suggest that POB is of interest to practitioners, consultants and, more recently, scholarly researchers.

Having defined and established the importance of POB, Armstrong-Strassen and Schlosser (2008, p. 94) lay out the focus of their article as a contribution to the literature on POB and downsizing:

Bakker and Schaufeli (2008) cautioned that the make a substantive contribution to organizational science, POB will need to show the added value of the positive over the negative. Research on organizational downsizing has been dominated by a focus on the nega-tive consequences of downsizing for the organization and its remaining employees—the layoff survivors (e.g., Armstrong-Strassen 1993; Brockner & Wiesen-feld, 1993; Campbell-Jamison et al., 2001; Jalajas & Bommer, 1996; Kalimo, 2003; Luthans & Sommer, 1999; Virik et al., 2007). We aim to show that a POB approach can be applied within the context of orga-nizational downsizing and can contribute to our un-derstanding of the responses of layoff survivors over time. Although organizational downsizing is a nega-tive experience for many layoff survivors, some fare better than others (Armstrong-Strassen, 1994). A POB perspective would attribute this, in part, to their posi-tive approach to downsizing.

Having drawn attention to the potential significance of POB, in the second paragraph Armstrong-Strassen and Schlosser outline the focus and contribution of their study to the POB and downsizing literatures:

- The first sentence skillfully draws attention to an im-portant critique of POB (the need to show its applica-tion in negative contexts) so that the authors can then show how they address the problem and, thus, make a unique contribution to the literature.
- The second sentence introduces the research lit-erature on downsizing to suggest an area where POB could be tested in a situation that is usually perceived as negative; it also provides a working definition—'layoff survivors'—for employees who retain their jobs in downsizing situations; and it references the earlier work of Armstrong-Strassen to suggest that she has also made a contribution to the field of down-sizing.
- The third sentence outlines the focus and contribution of the study by linking together POB, an important cri-tique of POB, and downsizing.
- The fourth and fifth sentences work together to stress the potentially contradictory perceptions of layoff sur-vivors in situations of downsizing (once again earlier work of Armstrong-Strassen is referenced to indicate her previous contribution to the field).

Theory and hypotheses

Armstrong-Strassen and Schlosser (2008) deal with theory and hypothesizing under a section heading called 'Conceptual Model'. They start off by clearly indicating that they:

> integrated POB concepts with Lasarus and Folkman's (1984) process model of stress and coping to exam-ine how managers reacted to the downsizing of their organization over a two-and-a-half year period. Ac-cording to Lazuras and Folkman, how people cope with a potentially stressful event or situation such as downsizing is influenced by the resources available to them. Our conceptual model (see Figure 1) focused on positive resources, that is generalized optimism and future success expectancy (a domain-specific form of optimism), and positive coping behaviour. (Armstrong-Strassen & Schlossser, 2008, p. 94)

In the opening paragraph of this section the authors introduce their model (building of Lazuras and Folkman) and some key concepts (resources, generalized optimism, and future success expectancy). Each of these items is subsequently laid out and explained in the rest of the section (see, for example, their graphic depiction of the model, or 'Figure 1' which is reproduced in this chapter as Figure 25.1). Resources are referred to as psychological and/or environmental factors that a person can draw on for support and inspiration (pp. 94–95); 'optimism refers to generalized expectations that good things will happen, even in the face of adversary' (p. 95) and its importance in this case is because it has 'been identified as an import-ant resource in both the survivor and POB literatures' (p. 95); future success expectancy refers to 'the expectancy of future career and performance success' (p. 95). Based on a review of the POM and downsizing literatures, Arm-strong-Strassen and Schlosser (2008, pp. 95–96) go on to develop four hypotheses for theory generation:

- Hypothesis 1. 'Generalized optimism assessed prior to organizational downsizing relates positively to surviv-ors' "future success expectancy" during the downsiz-ing' (p. 95).

- Hypothesis 2. 'Generalized optimism measured prior to organizational downsizing relates positively to the use of "positive thinking" as a coping strategy during downsizing' (p. 96).
- Hypothesis 3. 'Expectations for future success measured during downsizing mediates the positive influence of generalized optimism on the following outcomes, measured approximately one year following downsizing: expectations for future success, perceived coping effectiveness, job performance, and job satisfaction' (p. 96).
- Hypothesis 4. 'Positive thinking coping (measure during organizational downsizing) mediates the positive relationship between generalized optimism (measured prior to downsizing) and expectations of future success, perceived coping effectiveness, job performance,

and job satisfaction (measured one year following downsizing)' (p. 96).

These four hypotheses suggest a possible relationship between positive thinking (i.e., generalized optimism), coping strategies in times of downsizing, job performance, and job satisfaction.

Methods

In this section, the authors outline the methods that were used in conducting the research and provide details about how they collected and analyzed the data. This involved several elements and each is spelled out clearly in turn using the following sub-headings:

Organizational context. Here we are informed that data 'were collected from two Canadian federal government

Figure 25.1

Conceptualized framework showing hypothesized relationships

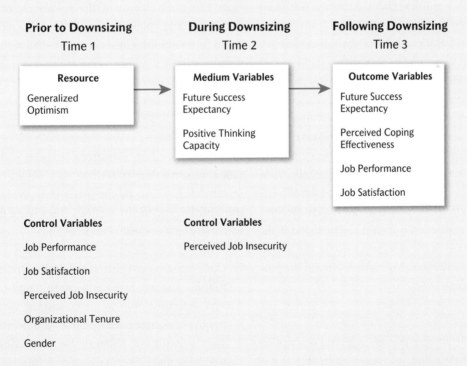

Source: Marjorie Armstrong-Strassen and Francine Schlosser, 'Taking a Positive Approach to Organizational Downsizing', *Canadian Journal of Administrative Sciences*, 2008:94.

departments that were targeted for a 20% or more reduction of their workforce' (p. 96). We are also informed that data were collected prior to downsizing (referred to as time period 1 or 'T1'); a period of 1½ years during the downsizing ('T2'; and 1 year after the completion of the downsizing ('T3') (p. 96)

Participants and Procedure. The data were collected by means of a **questionnaire** distributed by way of a 'disproportional **random sampling**' (see Chapter 9) to 'ensure adequate representation' (p. 96) across 11 different regions of Canada.

Measures. Here the authors are careful to specify the variety of measures they used and why. These included a '5-point **Likert** response format' (see Chapters 5 and 13); three items from the Life Orientation Test-Revised (LOT-R) to test for generalized optimism; six items from the Revised Generalized Expectancy of Success Scale (GESS-R); various items from the Positive Thinking Coping subscale to assess positive thinking coping and perceived coping effectiveness; and five items from the Job Diagnostic Survey (see Chapter 5) to measure job satisfaction (p. 98).

In terms of a 'control **variable**' Armstrong-Stratten and Schlosser drew on three items adapted from the Job Insecurity Scale. 'Demographic variables included job classification, education, and marital status' (p. 98).

Data analysis. Finally, the authors' report that they used paired *t*-tests to determine whether there was a significant change in those variables that were assessed over time. [They also] used correlations to assess the **bivariate** relationships [see Chapter 23] and conducted hierarchical regressions to test [their] hypotheses' (p. 98). They also 'conducted a Sobel test (Sobel, 1982) to assess the significance of the mediation effect of expected future success' (p. 98).

This detailed exposition helps the reader to judge the range and usefulness of the measures used for the overall research project and helps to build confidence in the process and the findings.

Results

In this section, the authors provide a general description and discussion of their findings, illustrated by way of five separate tables. Pointing to their various measures, analyses of the data, and the levels of statistical significance found

in each case (see Chapter 23) Armstrong-Strassen and Schlosser are able to convincingly argue that there was support for all four hypotheses, although this was not as strong in the case of some of the mediations in hypothesis 3.

We would note here that the style of argument throughout this section follows a somewhat fragmentary style (or statistical-ese) where the authors attempt to convince other (quantitative) researchers that their findings are linked to a specific statistical measurement:

> After controlling for the demographic variables, perceived job insecurity and T1 job performance, generalized optimism explained significant variance in the change in job performance (Table 4). For job satisfaction, where T1 job satisfaction was included in the regressions, generalized optimism did not contribute to a significant increase in the variance accounted for in the change in job satisfaction (Table 5). (Armstrong-Strassen and Schlosser, 2008, pp. 100–101)

This form of writing style is generally expected in quantitative analysis as part of the evidencing of statistical knowledge and application, which help to secure confidence in the results. However, as we shall see in the next section, it is often an important requirement to conclude with more of a narrative or story telling style as the authors stress the importance of their findings.

Conclusion

In this final section, Armstrong-Strassen and Schlosser (2008) return to the issues that have been driving their investigation. These are the issues they presented in the introduction and theory sections. They begin this section with a strong statement of their findings:

> Our results suggest that generalized optimism is a valuable resource in times of stress. Survivors who were optimistic prior to the downsizing were more positive about their future career and performance success during and following the downsizing. They were also more likely to employ a positive thinking coping strategy than were there less optimistic counterparts. In the postdownsizing period, they

were more likely to report they had coped effectively with the downsizing than were their less optimistic counterparts. Generalized optimism also positively predicted postdownsizing job performance, even after controlling for predownsizing job performance. It appears that generalized optimism has several personal and organizational benefits during and following organizational downsizing. (p. 102)

They go on to claim that their 'study differs from most others in the literature on layoff survivors' because rather 'than focusing on the negative aspects of organizational downsizing [they] took a positive approach and incorporated concepts from POB literature into a well-established and researched theoretical framework' (p. 102). This brief statement serves to stress the unique contribution of the study while also linking it to well-established research.

The article ends with a section on 'limitations and future research', where the authors can once again be authoritative (and thus convincing) by assuring the readers that they are aware of some of the limitations of their study but that these do not overwhelm the strength of their findings.

Lessons

What lessons can be learned from Armstrong-Strassen and Schlosser's article? To some extent, these have been alluded to in the course of the above exposition, but they are worth spelling out:

- There is a clear attempt to grab the reader's attention with strong opening statements, which also act as a signpost to what the article is about.
- The authors spell out clearly the rationale of their research. This entails pointing to the significance of Positive Organizational Behaviour as a framework for analysis of the relationship between generalized optimism and the ability to survive (and perhaps even thrive) in the wake of organizational downsizing.
- The research questions are spelled out in a very specific way. In fact, the authors present hypotheses that are a highly specific form of research question. As noted in Chapter 5, by no means all quantitative research

is driven by hypotheses, even though outlines of the nature of quantitative research often imply that it is. Nonetheless, Armstrong-Strassen and Schlosser chose to frame their research questions in this form.
- The research methods employed, the nature of the data, the measurement of concepts, the sampling, and the approaches to the analysis of the data are clearly and explicitly summarized.
- The presentation of the findings is oriented very specifically to the questions that drive the research.
- The discussion returns to the research questions and spells out the implications of the findings for them and for the theories examined earlier on in the paper. This is an important element. It is easy to forget that you should think of the research process as closing a circle in which you must return unambiguously to your research questions. There is no point inserting extraneous findings if they do not illuminate your research questions. Digressions of this kind can be confusing to readers, who might be inclined to wonder about the significance of the extraneous findings. In this section there is an attempt to consider the limitations of the study, in addition to its strengths, and to identify possibilities for further research. In addition, because business and management are an applied field of research, it is also common at this stage to draw attention to practical implications that arise from the study.

We also see that there is a clear sequential process moving from the formulation of the research questions through the exposition of the nature of the data and the presentation of the findings to the conclusions. Each stage is linked to and follows on from its predecessor (but see Web Thinking deeper 25.2). The structure used by Armstrong-Strassen and Schlosser is based on a common one employed in the writing up of quantitative research for academic journals in business and management. Sometimes, there is a separate Theory section that appears between the Introduction and the Data sections. Another variation is that issues of measurement and analysis appear in separate sections from the one dealing with research methods.

Rhetorical strategy in quantitative research

The rhetorical strategies used by quantitative researchers include the following:

- There is a tendency to remove the researcher from the text as an active ingredient of the research process in order to convey an impression of the objective nature of the findings—that is, as part of an external reality that is independent of the researcher (Gusfield, 1976). Woolgar (1988) refers to this as an externalizing device.
- The researcher surfaces in the text only to demonstrate his or her ingenuity in overcoming obstacles (Bazerman, 1987; Bryman, 1998).
- Key figures in the field are routinely cited to bestow credibility on the research (McCloskey, 1985).
- The research process is presented as a linear one to convey an air of inevitability about the findings arrived at (Gusfield, 1976).
- Relatively strict rules are followed about what should be reported in published research and how it should be reported (Bazerman, 1987).
- The use of a management metaphor is common in the presentation of findings in which the researcher is depicted as ingeniously 'designing' research, 'controlling' variables, 'managing' data, and 'generating' tables (Bryman, 1998, p. 146). See Shapiro (1985–6) and Richardson (1990) on this point.

Note that the first two are somewhat inconsistent. There is some evidence that disciplines within the social sciences differ in respect of their use of an impersonal style of writing. But it may well also be that it sometimes depends on what the writer is trying to do; for example, sometimes getting across a sense of one's cunning in overcoming practical difficulties can be just as useful as giving a sense of the external nature of the findings. Therefore, sometimes the style of presentation may vary somewhat.

An example of qualitative research

Now we will look at an example of a journal article based on qualitative research. This time it is by Roy Suddaby and Royston Greenwood and was published in the *Administrative Sciences Quarterly*. Again, we are not suggesting that the article is exemplary or representative, but that it exhibits some features that are often regarded as desirable qualities in terms of presentation and structure. Interestingly, given our discussion of rhetoric, the article focuses 'on the role of rhetoric in legitimizing profound institutional change' in the North American accountancy and legal services fields (Suddaby & Greenwood, 2005, p. 35).

The structure runs as follows:

1. Introduction.
2. Review of the literature.
3. Methods.
4. Data analysis.
5. Results.
6. Theorization.
7. Discussion and conclusions.

What is immediately striking about the structure is that it is not dissimilar to Armstrong-Strassen and Schlosser's (2008). Nor should this be all that surprising. After all, a structure that runs:

Introduction → Literature review → Research design/ methods → Results → Discussion → Conclusions

is not obviously associated with one research strategy rather than the other. One difference from quantitative research articles is that the presentation of the results and the discussion of them are frequently rather more interwoven in qualitative research articles. We will see this in the case of Suddaby and Greenwood's article. As with Armstrong-Strassen and Schlosser's article, we will examine the writing in terms of the article's structure.

Introduction

In this article the authors rely on a 150-word abstract to identify the focal element of the study—the purchase of a law firm by a Big Five accounting firm, the jurisdictional struggle that ensued, and the implications for organizational change, and the research process involved—which included a description 'of the role of rhetoric'; an analysis of 'the discursive struggle' involved; observation of 'rhetorical strategies'; and identification of 'theorizations of change. (Suddaby & Greenwood, 2005, p. 35). This takes us to the heart of what the subject matter of the paper and what we can learn in terms of organizational change. It is sufficiently interesting and novel to gain the reader's attention; the promise of a way of understanding organizational change through a focus on rhetorical strategies of legitimacy. Nonetheless, the authors also feel that the paper has an important contribution to make to the literature on New Institutional Theory (see Chapter 21) and they use the introduction to spell this out. In the process they end the abstract with a note of thanks to 'three anonymous reviewers' and four leading scholars in the field of organizational theory: 'Paul Hirsch, Lynne Zucker, Dick Scott, [and] Martin Kilduff . . . for helpful and patient comments on earlier drafts of [the] paper' (Suddaby & Greenwood, 2005, p. 35). We would note three things here. First, it is a very useful exercise to get someone who is knowledgeable in your area of study to read through your manuscript before you send it off to a journal. That way you can gain valuable feedback that will improve the way the paper reads. Second, where possible (not all journals facilitate the process), it is important to acknowledge those who have commented on your work, including the anonymous reviewers. Third, if you are fortunate enough, as were Suddaby and Greenwood, to have well-known people comment on your paper then mentioning their names adds to the credibility of the paper: interestingly enough, with the exception of Hirsch, three of the named people are also cited in the paper. (Suddaby and Greenwood are themselves well-known in their own right but even in their case, regardless of intent, reference to four leading scholars adds credibility to the arguments made. See Reinharz (1988) on the use of asides in published work).

In the introduction the authors make four points to (1) set up the key ingredients of their overall argument; and (2) build their theoretical case:

1. That 'the question of where new organizational forms comes from . . . remains largely unresolved' (p. 35).
2. A 'key task in explaining how new forms are created is understanding how affected interests seek to contest them' (p. 35).

3. That '"neo-institutional theory" [or NIT] offers a way forward as a theoretical framework for dealing with the issues noted in the other two points (p. 35).

All three points are succinctly stated in the first paragraph:

Where do new organizational forms come from? Despite broad acknowledgement of the central importance of this question for organization theory (e.g., Hannan and Freeman, 1986; Romanelli, 1991; Daft and Lewin, 1993; Aldrich, 1999), the question remains largely unresolved. For early social theorists, the key to understanding the emergence of new organizational forms rested in understanding broader processes of institutional change (Durkheim, 1933; Weber, 1978) or the process by which alternative models of collective action are contested. Because nascent forms inevitably trigger social conflict (Eisenstadt, 1980), a key task in explaining how new forms are created is understanding how affected interests seek to contest them (Rao and Singh, 1999). Despite its early premise of isomorphism, neo-institutional theory offers considerable promise in answering the question of how affected actors seek to attach or deny legitimacy to new organizational forms'. (Suddaby & Greenwood, 2005, p. 35)

4. That NIT contributes 'three foundational elements to explain how new organizational forms emerge [: legitimacy, institutional logics, and rhetoric]' (Suddaby & Greenwood, 2005, p. 35).

This fourth point is made throughout the second paragraph, and sets up the three elements of the authors' theoretical framework:

Institutional theory has developed three foundational elements to explain how new organizational forms emerge. The first is a growing knowledge of legitimacy, which is a key component of institutional change. New technology (Hargadon and Douglas, 2001), new organizational practices (Kostova and Roth, 2002), even new industries (Leblebici et al., 1991) clearly depend on mechanisms by which alternatives, often in spite of their technical superiority, are perceived as less 'desirable, proper or appropriate' (Suchman, 1995: 574). A second stream of research links institutional change to dramatic shifts in institutional logics that underpin actors' frame-works for reason and belief (Friedland and Alford, 1991; Ruef and Scott, 1998; Rao, Morrill, and Zald, 2000; Lounsbury, 2001). From this perspective, institutional change is the result of shifts in the underlying logic by which legitimacy is assessed. A final nascent theme in institutional theory suggests that the strategic use of persuasive language, or rhetoric, is the means by which shifts in institutional logic are secured. (Suddaby & Greenwood, 2005, p. 35)

In the third and fourth paragraphs the authors skillfully pull together all the stated points to (1) develop a their model; and (2) apply it to the identified gap in the literature, namely, how shift in institutional logics occur and how knowledge of this will help us to understand institutional change:

These three elements provide the beginnings of a model of new-form creation in which language is used to achieve shifts in logic within organizational fields. Shifts in logic alter the criteria used to assess the legitimacy of organizational forms, enabling new forms to emerge and survive. Profound change, such as the establishment of a new organizational form, is therefore the product of sustained symbolic work in which actors construct 'legitimating accounts' (Creed, Scully, and Austin, 2002) linking innovations to cultural views (Meyer and Rowan, 1977). This emerging perspective offers a distinctly political view of institutional change in which entrepreneurs skillfully interpret and exploit contradictions embedded in dominant institutional logics to further their self-interest (Fligstein, 1997; Seo and Creed, 2002). New organizational forms, from this point of view, are the ongoing consequence of negotiations and contests over which logic, and thus the criteria by which organizational legitimacy is assessed, will dominate. (Suddaby & Greenwood, 2005, pp. 35–36)

We know little, however, about the means by which shifts in logics occur. More specifically, we lack accounts of the process by which the assumptions that define institutional logics are contested and changed. How are symbolic resources used to persuade a community of actors to accept profound institutional change in the absence of objective information? This study addresses this question by examining a contest over a new organizational form in the professions, multidisciplinary practices (MDPs), organizations that comprise multiple professions, primarily lawyers, accountants, and management consultants. In 1997, the very largest accounting firms extended their version of MDPs to include lawyers and sparked an intense conflict between the professions of accounting and law. Combining multiple professions in a single firm represented a controversial rupture of jurisdictional boundaries (Abbott, 1988, 1995) and was a significant departure from the institutionalized norm that a single profession should control and populate professional organizations. Our analysis focuses explicitly on the arguments and language used to connect competing conceptions of the new organizational form to broader templates about the nature of professions and their role in society. We offer three insights. First, we deepen understanding of how cognitive legitimacy develops by demonstrating how rhetoric can be used to expose and manipulate dominant and subordinate institutional logics and create the impetus for institutional change. Second, we demonstrate how rhetoric can facilitate or oppose a new form by connecting the innovation to broadly stated theories of change. Finally, we add to our understanding of professions and professional organizations by describing a process by which contradictory notions of professionalism were contested in the debate over multidisciplinary practices. (Suddaby & Greenwood, 2005, p. 36)

We can see how, in the last paragraph, the authors reintegrate the case study (highlighted in the abstract) with the theoretical framework outlined in the introduction.

Review of the literature

Having set up the three central elements of their 'model', the authors then review each in turn, being careful to ensure that they (1) connect with the relevant literature; and (2) link that literature to the central focus of institutional change. They begin with a summary statement to direct the reader to the main points they will be making:

> Our overall theoretical argument is based on three observations. First, new organizational forms do not routinely emerge to fill latent resource opportunities. They have to acquire legitimacy (Aldrich and Fiol, 1994). Second, the criterion for legitimacy is encoded within institutional logics. Therefore, legitimating an organizational form that does not fit a prevailing logic involves modifying or displacing that logic in order to establish new legitimacy criteria. Finally, we argue that this is achieved primarily through the use of rhetoric. (Suddaby & Greenwood, 2005, pp. 36–37)

These points having been flagged, the authors take us through, in turn, a discussion of legitimacy, institutional logics, and rhetoric, ending with a restatement of the direction of the paper: 'These studies provide a useful theoretical connection between rhetoric and the emergence of new organizational forms' (Suddaby & Greenwood, 2005, p. 41).

Methods

This section covers not only the methods used but also a discussion of the context in which the case study occurred (i.e., the take over of a law firm by a large accounting firm). Although the authors do not spell it out the organizational context (or 'institutional fields', see Chapter 20) in which the take over took place is an essential part of the method of NIT. This allows them to introduce the fact that the take over was the focus of considerable inquiry involving an American Bar Association (ABA) Commission to Study Multidisciplinary Practice, and the Securities and Exchange Commission Public Hearings on Auditor Independence.

Making sure to stress the central importance of these two commissions of inquiry, the authors make clear that their 'primary data consist of the transcripts of testimony pro- vided by witnesses to these two commissions' (Suddaby & Greenwood, 2005, p. 42). They then go on to stress the significance (i.e., **trustworthiness**) of the data, not only because of its importance to the eventual outcome but also because the of the size or extent of the data involving 266 witnesses (including leading members of the legal and accounting professions, or 'key actors') and 1300 pages of testimony (p. 42). In addition a table (labelled 1a and 1b) is used to indicate the range of industry experts that gave testimony across the main professions involved (see Table 25.1).

However, it is in a section called 'data analysis' where the authors spell out the type of methods they used. Basically they analyzed the data using, what they call, 'a modified version of content analysis':

> Iterating between the data and theories of rhetoric, our analysis occurred in two stages. The first stage focused on the manifest content, or 'those elements that are physically present' (Berg, 2004: 269). Using NUD*IST computer software, we read through transcripts from the data set and identified major players in the debate and their explicit arguments supporting or opposing MDPs . . . The second stage of analysis focused on the latent content of the data. Here we were concerned with capturing the 'deep structure' or implicit categories of meaning (Berg, 2004). (Suddaby & Greenwood, 2005, pp. 42–43)

We might note here that Suddaby and Greenwood are following a qualitative approach to content analysis (see Chapter 18) and, in the process, use a Computer Assisted Qualitative Data Analysis Software (CAQDAS) program to assist them (see Chapter 24). Nonetheless, the authors note in the margin of the paper that it was 'an anonymous reviewer [who helped them] with the appropriate language and conceptual sources to better describe [their] methodology' (p. 42). Such is the uncertainty in

Table 25.1a Participants in the American Bar Association's Commission on Multidisciplinary Practice Public Hearings, by Type and Critical Position

	Professionl Associations (N = 56)								
	Provessional Associations in Law								
Stance	International	ABA sub-comittees	Other national (US) groups	Bar Associations			Accounting	Other	
				State	Regional	Local			
Pro	8	8	0	1	2	3	3	8	
Con	6	5	3	7	1	1	0	0	

	Other Categories of Participants (N = 89)								
	Academics		Consumer/Interest Groups	Gov't/ Judiciary	Big Five	Law Firms		Corporations	
	Accounting	Law				Big	Small	Big	Small
Pro	2	5	40	0	5	6	4	2	7
Con	0	3	0	5	0	2	7	1	0

Table 25.1b Participants in the U.S. Securities and Exchange Commission's Public Hearings on Auditor Independence, by Type and Critical Position (N = 93)

Stance	Professional Associations		Academic		Accounting Firms		Corporations		Interest Groups
	Law	Accounting	Accounting	Other	Big 5	Other	Big	Small	
Pro	0	14	5	0	5	3	17	2	1
Con	0	8	5	3	0	0	6	7	2

Source: Roy Suddaby and Ryston Greenwood, *Rhetorical Strategies of Legitimacy*, vol. 50, March 2005: 35-67.

some quarters of academia about the nature of qualitative research and the need for special terms to describe qualitative methods. This would rarely happen in regard to quantitative research and says something about being very clear about your methodological approach (and its nomenclature) when sending a paper to a journal.

Suddaby and Greenwood (2005) then go into detailed explanation of how they coded the data in the second stage, and to be fully clear they provide a detailed table of how they coded the data (see Table 25.2). The authors then demonstrate how the coding led them to identify five 'theorizations of change (teleological, historical, cosmological, ontological, and value-based)' (p. 35) that organizational members adopt, with dramatically different outcomes for the organizations involved.

Results

It is relatively unusual for a qualitative paper to have a section called 'results'. This is often because the 'findings' are seen as (1) an outcome of the researcher's interpretive processes; and (2) because of the nature of qualitative (especially postpositivist) research, are incorporated throughout the various sections. For instance, Suddaby and Greenwood (2005) discussed an element (the institutional field) of the case study in the introduction and in the methods section; they discussed the discovery of different theorizations of change (or institutional logics) in the data analysis section. They then used the results section to develop detailed discussion of each of the identified theorizations of change and show how they worked (both individually and in contestation with each other) to maintain or change institutional logics. In short, describing 'how one element of rhetoric, institutional vocabularies, were used to construct legitimacy by drawing on different logics of professionalism' (Suddaby & Greenwood, 2005, pp. 50–51).

Discussion and Conclusion

In the final section the authors combine discussion with the conclusion to: (1) restate the key findings; (2) re-engage with the literature to show their particular contribution and how it throws new light on the field; (3) suggest the use-value of the knowledge produced by the study; and (4) to discuss potential limitations of the study. Thus, they argue that important contributions of the study includes refocusing 'institutional analysis on meaning systems' (p. 60); connecting 'rhetoric with the deliberate manipulation of institutional logics' (p. 61); pointing 'out the rhetorical underpinnings of legitimating institutional change' (p. 62); and raising 'a key question of causality in the relationship between symbolic and material action' (p. 62). Above all, Suddaby and Greenwood (2005, p. 62) conclude that their study 'points to the importance of renewing interest in Berger and Luckmann's (1966, p. 64) early observation that 'institutions are built upon language'. This last point serves to signify the link between Suddaby and Greenwood's (2005) study and that of the original NIT theorists.

For theorists and practitioners alike Suddaby and Greenwood's study suggests that 'new organizational forms are enabled by shifts in logic, in which previously subordinate elements of a prevailing logic are made evident. Rhetoric, applied to the contradictions inherent in a prevailing logic, is the means by which such shifts are achieved or resisted [through . . .] institutional vocabularies and theorizations of change' (Suddaby & Greenwood, 2005, p. 59). This reference to use-value provides a much needed legitimacy to the paper by meeting underlying expectations of the practice-based nature of business studies and also dealing with potential doubts about the value of qualitative and postpositivist research for the field.

Finally, as with the Armstrong-Strassen and Schlosser paper, Suddaby and Greenwood (2005, pp. 62–63) end by pointing to the limitation of their own study, pointing out that their 'study is one in which, ultimately, change was inconclusive. We need to compare the role of rhetoric in successful and unsuccessful cases of change so as to understand its relative significance and whether its probabilities of success are enhanced when accompanied by particular other dynamics'. However, while this statement serves to show that the researchers are aware of the limitations of their approach it comes at the end of a discussion that details the important *theoretical* contribution that the paper makes to the field.

Lessons

As with Armstrong-Strassen and Schlosser's article, it is useful to review some of the lessons learned from this examination of Suddaby and Greenwood's article:

- Just like the illustration of quantitative research writing, there are strong opening sentences, which attract our attention and give a clear indication of the nature and content of the article.
- The rationale of the research is clearly identified. To a large extent, this revolves around noting the limitations of existing (NIT) literature that does not adequately explain change or deal with issues of language use.
- Research questions are specified but they are somewhat more open-ended than in Armstrong-Strassen and Schlosser's article, which is in keeping with the general orientation of qualitative researchers. The research questions revolve around different layers of language use in the process of organizational changes.
- The research methods are outlined and an indication is given of the approach to analysis. The sections in which these issues are discussed demonstrates greater transparency than is sometimes the case with articles reporting qualitative research.
- The presentation of main themes is geared to the broad research questions that motivated the researchers' interest in institutional change. However, those sections also represent a major opportunity for the idea of the role of rhetorical strategies in institutional change to be articulated. The inductive nature of qualitative research means that the concepts and theories that are generated from an investigation must be clearly identified and discussed, as in this case.
- The discussion section allows concepts and theories to be developed into a more general framework, or 'model' in this case, which is used to characterize the present study in the context of other qualitative studies of institutional change.
- The implications elucidate in a more or less specific way the significance of these results for practitioners as well as theorists, thereby addressing a requirement that is specifically made of business and management

researchers to highlight the practical relevance of research findings.

Postmodernism and its implications for writing

Postmodernism is an extremely difficult idea to pin down. In one sense, it can be seen as a form of sensitivity—a way of seeing and understanding that results in a questioning of the taken-for-granted. It questions the very notion of the dispassionate social scientist seeking to uncover a pregiven external reality. Instead, postmodernists view the social scientist's account as only one among many ways of rendering social reality to audiences. The social world itself is viewed as a context out of which many accounts can be hewn. As a result, 'knowledge' of the social world is relative; any account is just one of many possible ways of rendering social reality. As Rosenau (1992, p. 8) puts it, postmodernists 'offer "readings" not "observations", "interpretations" not "findings" . . . .'.

Postmodernism defined

As noted above, postmodernism is extremely difficult to pin down. Part of the problem is that as an approach, postmodernism is at least two things. One, is that it is an attempt to come to grips with the nature of modern society and culture. The other, which is the more relevant aspect for this book, is that it represents a way of thinking about and representing the nature of the social sciences and their claims to knowledge. In particular, it is a distinctive sensitivity regarding the representation of social scientific findings.

Postmodernists tend to be deeply suspicious of notions that imply that it is possible to arrive at a definitive version of any reality. Reports of findings are viewed as versions of an external reality, so that the key issue becomes one of the plausibility of those versions rather than whether they are right or wrong in any absolute sense. Typically, writers of a postmodernist persuasion have less to say about data collection issues than about the writing and representation of social science findings, though it is probably the case that they are more sympathetic to qualitative than quantitative research (Alvesson, 2002). Indeed, postmodernists have probably been most influential in qualitative research when discussing the nature of ethnographic accounts and questioning the ethnographer's implicit claim that he or she has provided a definitive account of a society. This thinking can be discerned in Van Maanen's (1988) implicit critique of 'realist tales', as he called them (see Key concept 25.2).

For postmodernists, there can be no sense of an objective reality out there waiting to be revealed to and uncovered by social scientists. That reality is always going to be accessed through narratives in the form of research reports that provide representations. With this shift in orientation came an interest in the language employed in research reports, like written ethnographies, to reveal the devices researchers use to convey the definitiveness of their findings (Delamont & Atkinson, 2004). Postmodernists tend to emphasize the notion of **reflexivity** (see Key concepts 25.2 and 25.3), which posits the significance of the researcher for the research process and consequently the tentativeness of any findings presented in a research report (since the researcher is always implicated in his or her findings). As this account of postmodernism implies, postmodernists tend to be deeply suspicious of any view of research that implies

Key concept 25.2: What is reflexivity?

Reflexivity, as defined by ethnomethodologists, refers to the way in which speech and action are constitutive of the social world in which they are located. For business researchers, the term means that they should be reflective about the implications of their methods, values, biases, and decisions for the knowledge of the social world they generate.

Key concept 25.3a: What is methodological reflexivity?

Methodological reflexivity stems from an objectivist view of ontology, which holds that social phenomena exist independently of social actors.

Key concept 25.3b: What is deconstructive reflexivity?

Deconstructive reflexivity arises from a constructionist ontological view, which presupposes that social phenomena are produced through social interactions involving social actors.

that there are or can be accepted foundations to knowledge, as is suggested by positivists (see Key concept 3.2).

Postmodernism is a deeply disruptive stance on social and business research, in that it problematizes and questions our capacity ever to know anything. Views vary on postmodernism's current appeal. Matthewman and Hoey (2006) depict its influence as having waned to a significant extent, while Bloland (2005) argues that it has had an impact on thinking in many fields in higher education and that this is especially noticeable among those who do not identify themselves as postmodernists.

One of the effects of the impact of postmodernism since the 1980s has been a growing interest in the writing of social science. For postmodernists, reporting findings in a journal article provides merely one version of the social reality that was investigated (for examples of this type of approach see *Tamara: Journal for Critical Organization Inquiry*). Postmodernists mistrust the knowledge claims that are frequently boldly made when findings are reported and instead they adopt an attitude of investigating the bases and forms of those knowledge claims and the language that is used to represent them. This has led to what is described as a linguistic turn within the social sciences (see Key concept 25.4). While the writing of all types of social science is potentially in the postmodernist's firing line, it has been the kinds of text produced by ethnographers that have been a particular focus of attention. This focus has led to a particular interest in the claims to ethnographic authority that are inscribed into *ethnographic* texts (Clifford, 1983). The ethnographic text 'presumes a world out there (the real) that can be captured by a "knowing" author through the careful transcription and analysis of field materials (interviews, notes, etc.)' (Denzin, 1994, p. 296). Postmodernism problematizes such accounts and their authority to represent a reality because there 'can never be a final, accurate representation of what was meant or said, only different textual representations of different experiences' (Denzin, 1994, p. 296).

However, it would be wrong to depict the growing attention being focused on ethnographic writing as exclusively a product of postmodernism. Atkinson and Coffey (1995) have argued that there are other intellectual trends in the social sciences that have stimulated this interest. Writers in the area of theory and research known as the social studies of science have been concerned with the limitations of accepted distinctions between rhetoric and logic and between the observer and the observed (e.g., Gilbert & Mulkay, 1984). The problematizing of these distinctions, along with doubts about the possibility of a neutral language through which the natural and social worlds can be revealed, opened the door for an evaluation of scientific and social scientific writing. Some illustrations of these analyses can be discerned in Web Thinking deeper 25.3. Atkinson and Coffey also point to the antipathy within feminism towards the image of the neutral 'observer-author' who assumes a privileged stance in relation to members of the social setting being studied. This stance is regarded as revealing a position of domination of the observer-author over the observed that is inconsistent with the goals of feminism (see Chapter 6 for an elaboration of this general point). This concern has led to an interest in the ways in which privilege is conveyed in ethnographic texts and how voices, particularly of marginal groups, are suppressed.

The concerns within these and other traditions (including postmodernism) have led to experiments in writing ethnography (Richardson, 1994) that involve the identity of the ethnographer being written into the

---

Key concept 25.3c: What is epistemic reflexivity?

Epistemic reflexivity seeks out new modes of engagement with research subjects that are more amenable to the co-creation of knowledge through the adoption of more participatory approaches. Unlike deconstructive reflexivity, epistemic reflexivity retains the hope that truth can be attained through consensus with research subjects.

Key concept 25.4: What is linguistic turn?

The linguistic turn is based on the idea that language shapes our understanding of the world. Moreover, because knowledge is constructed through language, and language can never create an object representation of external reality, meaning is uncontrollable and undiscoverable.

text (see Web Research in focus 25.1). An example is the use of a 'dialogic' form of writing that seeks to raise the profile of the multiplicity of voices that can be heard in the course of fieldwork. As Lincoln and Denzin (1994, p. 584) put it: 'Slowly it dawns on us that there may . . . be . . . not one 'voice', but polyvocality; not one story, but many tales, dramas, pieces of fiction, fables, memories, histories, autobiographies, poems, and other texts to inform our sense of lifeways, to extend our understandings of the Other . . .'. This postmodern preference for seeking out multiple voices and for turning the ethnographer into a 'bit player' reflects the mistrust among postmodernists of 'meta-narratives'—that is, positions or grand accounts that implicitly make claims about absolute truths and that, therefore, rule out the possibility of alternative versions of reality. On the other hand, 'mini-narratives, micro-narratives, local narratives are just stories that make no truth claims and are, therefore, more acceptable to post-modernists' (Rosenau, 1992, p. xiii).

Postmodernism has also encouraged a growing **reflexivity** (see Key concept 25.2) in considerations about the writing of business and management research (see Key concept 25.3) stimulated by the debates about the writing of ethnography. This reflexivity can be discerned in the way in which many ethnographers have turned inwards to examine the truth claims inscribed in their own classic texts, which is the focus of the next section. In the end, what postmodernism leaves us with is an acute sense of uncertainty. It raises the issue of how we can ever know or capture the social reality that belongs to others and in so doing it points to an unresolvable tension that will not go away and that is further revealed in the issues raised in the next section, because, to quote Lincoln and Denzin (1994, p. 582) again: 'On the one hand there is the concern for validity, or certainty in the text as a form of isomorphism and authenticity. On the other hand there is the sure and certain knowledge that all texts are socially, historically, politically, and culturally located. We, like the texts we write, can never be transcendent'. At the same time, of course, such a view renders problematic the very idea of what knowledge is or comprises. In the process it draws our attention to the powerful role played by language and discourse in the construction of identities and knowledge.

Writing ethnography

The term 'ethnography', as noted in Chapter 17, is interesting, because it refers to both a method of business research and the finished product of ethnographic research. In other words, it is both something that is carried out in doing research and something one reads. Thus, writing seems to be at the heart of the ethnographic enterprise. In recent years, the production of ethnographic texts has become a focus of interest in its own right. This means that there has been a growth of interest not just in how ethnography is carried out in the field but also in the rhetorical conventions employed in the production of ethnographic texts.

Ethnographic texts are designed to convince readers of the reality of the events and situations described, and the plausibility of the analyst's explanations. The ethnographic text must not simply present a set of findings: it must provide an 'authoritative' account of the group or culture in question. In other words, the ethnographer must convince us that he or she has arrived at an account of social reality that has strong claims to truth.

The ethnographic text is permeated by stylistic and **rhetorical** devices whereby the reader is persuaded to enter into a shared framework of facts and interpretations, observations and reflections. Just like the scientific paper and the kind of approach to writing found in reporting quantitative business research, the ethnographer typically works within a writing strategy that is imbued with realism. This simply means that the researcher presents an authoritative, dispassionate account that represents an external, objective reality. In this respect, there is very little difference between the writing styles of quantitative and qualitative researchers. Van Maanen (1988) calls ethnography texts that conform to these characteristics realist tales. These are the most common type of ethnographic writing, though he distinguishes other types. However, the form that this realism takes differs. Van Maanen distinguishes four characteristics of realist tales: experiential authority; typical forms; the native's point of view; and interpretative omnipotence. **Realist** tales are particularly prevalent in business and management research writing (see Research in focus 25.1).

25.1   Research in Focus

Realism in organizational ethnography

Many organizational ethnographies tend to be written as realist tales (see Key concept 25.2) and narrated dispassionately in order to reinforce the authenticity of the account. Typically, the author is absent from the text, or is a minor character in the story, and methods are revealed only at the end, in the form of a 'confessional' chapter or appendix, where the ethnographer 'reveals his hand' (Watson, 1994*a*) by disclosing personal details about the fieldwork experience. However, this is not to say that organizational ethnographers are unaware of the representational difficulties caused by such an approach to writing. Consider, for example, the first few sentences of the methodological appendix that is provided by Kunda (1992) in the book *Engineering Culture: Control and Commitment in a High-Tech Corporation*.

This study belongs to the genre known as 'ethnographic realism'. This identification says much about presentational style, little about the actual research process. The descriptive style of this genre presents an author functioning more or less as a fly on the wall in the course of his sojourn in the field—an objective, unseen observer following well-defined procedures for data collection and verification. It requires no great insight, however, to recognize that ethnographic realism is a distortion of convenience. Fieldwork, as all who have engaged in it will testify, is an intensely personal and subjective process, and there are probably at least as many 'methods' as there are fieldworkers (Kunda, 1992, p. 229).

Kunda (1992) questions the extent to which the ethnographer is an objective observer, suggesting instead that he or she experiences organizational life from a situated position as an insider. He implies that it is therefore impossible for ethnographers to distance themselves from the fieldwork experience. However, despite this recognition of the need for greater 'reflexivity' within organizational ethnography, only a few organizational ethnographies are actually written in the first person, with the researcher as a main character who is telling the story. Even in cases when this does occur, the main character narrative tends to be located peripherally, in the appendices or footnotes of an article or book (Hatch, 1996), such as Kunda himself has done.

Experiential authority

Just as in much quantitative research writing, the author disappears from view. We are told what members of a group say and do, and they are the only people directly visible in the text. The author provides a narrative in which he or she is no longer to be seen. As a result, an impression is conveyed that the findings presented are what any reasonable, similarly placed researcher would have found. As readers, we have to accept that this is what the ethnographer saw and heard while working as a participant observer or whatever. The personal subjectivity of the author/ethnographer is essentially played down by this strategy. The possibility that the fieldworker may have his or her own biases or may have become too involved with the people being studied is suppressed. To this end, when writing up the results of their ethnographic work, authors play up their academic credentials and qualifications, their previous experience, and so on. All this enhances the degree to which the author's account can be relied upon. The author/ethnographer can then appear as a reliable witness.

A further element of experiential authority is that, when describing their methods, ethnographers invariably make a great deal of the intensiveness of the research that they carried out—they spent so many months in the field, had conversations and interviews with countless individuals, worked hard to establish rapport, and so on. These features are also added to by drawing the reader's attention to such hardships as the inconvenience of the fieldwork—the danger, the poor food, the disruptive effect on normal life, the feelings of isolation and loneliness, and so on.

Also worth mentioning are the extensive quotations from conversations and interviews that invariably form part of the ethnographic report. These are also obviously important ingredients of the author's use of evidence to support points. However, they are a mechanism for establishing the credibility of the report in that they demonstrate the author's ability to encourage people to talk and so demonstrate that he or she achieved rapport with them. The copious descriptive details—of places, patterns of behaviour, contexts, and so on—can also be viewed as a means of piling on the sense of the author being an ideally placed witness for all the findings that have been uncovered.

Typical forms

The author often writes about typical forms of institutions or of patterns of behaviour. What is happening here is that the author is generalizing about a number of recurring features of the group in question to create a typical form that that feature takes. He or she may use examples based on particular incidents or people, but basically the emphasis is upon the general. For example, in Watson's (1994a) conclusion to his ethnographic study of managers in a UK telecommunications company, which was cited several times in Chapter 17, we encounter the following statement:

> The image which has taken shape is one of management as essentially and inherently a social and moral activity; one whose greatest successes in efficiently and effectively producing goods and services is likely to come through building organisational patterns, cultures and understandings based on relationships of mutual trust and shared obligation among people involved with the organisation. (1994a, p. 223)

The study is thus meant to portray managers in general, and individuals are important only in so far as they represent such general tendencies.

The native's point of view

The point has been made several times that one of the distinguishing features of much qualitative research is the commitment to seeing through the eyes of the people being studied. This is an important feature for qualitative researchers, because it is part of a strategy of getting at the meaning of social reality from the perspective of those being studied. However, it also represents an important element in creating a sense of authoritativeness on the part of the ethnographer. After all, claiming that he or she takes the native's point of view and sees through their eyes means that he or she is in an excellent position to speak authoritatively about the group in question. The very fact that the ethnographer has taken the native's point of view testifies to the fact that he or she is well placed to write definitively about the group in question. Realist tales frequently include numerous references to the steps taken by the ethnographer to get close to the people studied and his or her success in this regard. Thus, in her study of Afro-Caribbean women working in high-tech informatics (see Chapter 17), Freeman (2000) writes about the small group of six women at Multitext who became the focus of more intense, long-term data collection:

> After many Sunday lunches, picnics, church services, birthday celebrations, and family outings, I got to know these few women better, seeing them not only as workers but also as members of families, as partners in complex relationships, as mothers, as daughters, as co-workers, and as friends. We spent time together in my rented flat, and in their wood and 'wall house' homes, cooking and eating meals together, sometimes watching videos as we talked. I persuaded them, on rare occasions, to picnic at the beach, and they took me to their churches and fetes and on special outings—to the circus, to the calypso contests, and to national sites enjoyed by tourists and locals alike. Sometimes we went shopping, and sometimes we bought ice cream after work. (2000, p. 17)

Interpretative omnipotence

When writing up an ethnography in the realist style, the author rarely presents possible alternative interpretations of an event or pattern of behaviour. Instead, the phenomenon in question is presented as having a single meaning or significance, which the fieldworker alone has cracked. Indeed, the evidence provided is carefully marshalled to support the singular interpretation that is placed on the event or pattern of behaviour. We are presented with an inevitability. It seems obvious or inevitable that someone would draw the inferences that the author has drawn when faced with such clear-cut evidence.

These four characteristics of realist tales imply that what the researcher did qua researcher is only one part of creating a sense of having figured out the nature of a culture. It is also very much to do with how the researcher represents what he or she did through writing about ethnography. For the postmodernist position, any realist tale is merely one 'spin'—that is, one version—that can be or has been formulated in relation to the culture in question.

Ways of writing differently

Van Maanen (1996) has suggested that 'in these textually sophisticated times, few argue that a research report is anything more (or, certainly, anything less) than a blurring of the boundaries between narrative and literary framework- or paradigm-dependent document, crafted and shaped within the rules and conventions of a particular research community, some articulated (and written in the back of research journals) and some tacitly understood' (1996, p. 376). Ways of writing in business and management thus involve following such conventions of style and structure as we have tried to make explicit in this chapter, through our analysis of a published quantitative example (Armstrong-Strassen & Schlosser, 2008) and a qualitative example (Suddaby & Greenwood, 2005). However, this should not be taken to mean that we are wholly in favour of strictly maintaining these conventions, but rather we think it is helpful to students who are starting to write a dissertation project to try to decipher them as a first step in the process of learning the craft of academic writing. Becoming aware of these conventions can also be helpful to students in reading and understanding the work of others because these two activities are so closely related. Understanding the conventions of academic writing can also be the first step towards challenging them, since it is easier and probably safer to do this from the vantage point of having some idea of what

they are and how they work, rather than from a position of relative ignorance. Czarniawska (1999) has argued that management and business researchers need to rethink the way that they think and write and to master the art of persuasion as opposed to the presentation of 'facts'. This involves a blurring of the boundaries between narrative and literary theory and the social sciences. Writing is, she argues, the main activity of organizational researchers and, as such, it is in the interests of the writers as well as the readers that it is as 'good' as possible, although there is by no means agreement as to what 'good' writing is actually like. The art of writing is also important in relating management theory to practice, in part because it is through writing and being read that researchers remain in contact with management practice (Weatherbee et al., 2008). She goes on to suggest that certain conventions about how management and organization theory is written have arisen during the relatively short life of this field of inquiry, which all writers who wish to contribute to this field must either struggle with or against. These rules constitute management and organizational theory as a genre with boundaries that are regulated (see Thinking deeper 25.11). This may have resulted in what Czarniawska (1999) sees as unhelpfully rigid constraints of genre that can lead to stagnation of a discipline wherein it has the potential to become dull and self-centered. These concerns correspond to broader calls within the social sciences for a more engaging and compelling style of qualitative research writing (Goodall, 2000) that has led to the emergence of new genres such as autoethnography (see Chapter 17).

Czarniawska (1999) suggests that organizational theory texts are recognized as scientific because of the devices that they use to indicate logical reasoning based on logical propositions. However, she argues that closer examination of the texts reveals that they, in fact, incorporate aspects of narrative in their production, by employing literary devices such as storytelling, trope, rhetoric, and metaphor (see also McLaren et al., 2009; McLaren & Mills, 2008; Mills & Helms Hatfield, 1998). To illustrate, Czarniawska takes the example of detective stories, as a subgenre with which she compares organization studies. She argues that detective stories and organization studies both have a preference for a realist style of writing based on an interest in social life, and both are built around problem solving. The central characters, the detective and the researcher/consultant, are often invisible narrators of the story who are called in to investigate a situation and provide a solution without being part of it. Although both detective stories and organization studies are 'supposed to build on analytical logic and employ deduction or induction', Czarniawska argues that 'in practice, formal logic is rare in both' (1999, p. 81).

Other management and organizational researchers and writers have also challenged the conventions of logico-scientific writing that define the business and management field, arguing that the style of writing that authors wanting to publish in the leading journals are required to adopt has become too abstruse and difficult even for academics themselves to understand (Grey, 2005). Although these comments are directed principally at the way that critical management studies are written, many of these points have a resonance that extends beyond this particular academic grouping. As Grey, in a paper written with Sinclair (2006, p. 447), confesses: 'I am increasingly bored and irritated by critical writing on organizations and management. I suppose that I used to think that such writing was necessarily complicated because it dealt with complicated ideas. But now I think that the complexity of expression often conceals what are quite simple ideas'. He goes on to say that he used to think that it was his own fault that he found this writing so complicated and difficult to understand, explaining 'I used to think that I was stupid if I didn't understand papers—now I see it as at least partially a deficiency in the way they are written. If someone who has been involved in this stuff for two decades doesn't get it, then could there be something wrong with the way it is expressed?' (Grey & Sinclair, 2006, p. 447). Our experience in talking with students doing a research project suggests that many of them experience similar doubts to Grey when they are reading the literature and struggling to understand it. Students can also feel intimidated by the thought that they are expected to write in a similar way to this in their dissertation. Knowing that there are some academics out there who admit to finding some styles of scientific writing dull, pretentious, and even intimidating might give students greater confidence in themselves as readers and writers, and some encouragement to try to find different ways of writing.

 ## *Checklist*

Issues to consider for writing up a piece of research:

- ☐ Have you clearly specified your research questions?
- ☐ Have you clearly indicated how the literature you have read relates to your research questions?
- ☐ Is your discussion of the literature critical and organized so that it is not just a summary of what you have read?
- ☐ Have you clearly outlined your research design and your research methods, including:
  1. Why you chose a particular research design?
  2. Why you chose a particular research method?
  3. How you selected your research participants?
  4. If there were any issues to do with cooperation (e.g., response rates)?
  5. Why you implemented your research in a particular way (e.g., how the interview questions relate to your research questions, why you observed participants in particular situations, why your focus group guide asked the questions in a particular way and order)?
  6. If your research required access to an organization, how and on what basis was agreement for access forthcoming?
  7. Steps you took to ensure that your research was ethically responsible?
  8. How you analyzed your data?

9. Any difficulties you encountered in the implementation of your research approach?

☐ Have you presented your data in a manner that relates to your research questions?

☐ Does your discussion of your findings show how they relate to your research questions?

☐ Does your discussion of your findings show how they shed light on the literature that you presented?

☐ Are the interpretations of your data that you offer fully supported with tables, figures, or segments from transcripts?

☐ If you have presented tables and/or figures, are they properly labelled with a title and number?

☐ If you have presented tables and/or figures, are they commented upon in your discussion?

☐ Do your conclusions clearly allow the reader to establish what your research contributes to the literature?

☐ Have you explained the limitations of your study?

☐ Do your conclusions consist solely of a summary of your findings? If they do, rewrite them!

☐ Do your conclusions make clear the answers to your research questions?

☐ Does your presentation of the findings and the discussion allow a clear argument and narrative to be presented to the reader?

☐ Have you broken up the text in each chapter with appropriate subheadings?

☐ Does your writing avoid sexist, racist, and disablist language?

☐ Have you included all appendices that you might need to provide (e.g., interview schedule, letters requesting access, communications with research participants)?

☐ Have you checked that your list of references includes all the items referred to in your text?

☐ Have you checked that your list of references follows precisely the style that your institution requires?

☐ Have you followed your supervisor's suggestions when he or she has commented on your draft chapters?

☐ Have you got people other than your supervisor to read your draft chapters for you?

☐ Have you checked to ensure that there is not excessive use of jargon?

☐ Do you provide clear signposts in the course of writing, so that readers are clear about what to expect next and why it is there?

☐ Have you ensured that your institution's requirements for submitting projects are fully met in terms of such issues as word count (so that it is neither too long nor too short) and whether or not an abstract and table of contents are required?

☐ Have you ensured that you do not quote excessively when presenting the literature?

☐ Have you fully acknowledged the work of others so that you cannot be accused of plagiarism?

☐ Is there a good correspondence between the title of your project and its contents?

☐ Have you acknowledged the help of others where this is appropriate (e.g., your supervisor, people who may have helped with interviews, people who read your drafts)?

Key points

- Good writing is probably just as important as good research practice. Indeed, it is probably better thought of as a part of good research practice.
- Clear structure and statement of your research questions are important components of writing up research.
- Be sensitive to the ways in which writers seek to persuade us of their points of view.

- The study of rhetoric and writing strategies generally teaches us that the writings of scientists and social scientists do more than simply report findings. They are designed to convince and to persuade.
- The emphasis on rhetoric is not meant to imply that there is no external social reality; it merely suggests that our understanding of that reality is profoundly influenced by the ways it is represented by writers.
- Postmodernism and other traditions have exerted a particular influence on this last point.
- The basic structure of and the rhetorical strategies employed in most quantitative and qualitative research articles are broadly similar.
- We need to get away from the idea that rhetoric and the desire to persuade others of the validity of our work are somehow bad things. They are not. We all want to get our points across and to persuade our readers that we have got things right. The question is—do we do it well? Do we make the best possible case? We all have to persuade others that we have got the right angle on things; the trick is to do it well. So when you write an essay or dissertation, do bear in mind the significance of your writing strategy.

Questions for review

- Why is it important to consider the ways in which business research is written?

Writing quantitative research: An example
- Read an article based on quantitative research in an American business and management journal (e.g., the *Academy of Management Journal*). How far does it exhibit the same characteristics as Armstrong-Strassen and Schlosser's article?
- What is meant by rhetorical strategy? Why might rhetorical strategies be important in relation to the writing up of business research?
- Do Armstrong-Strassen and Schlosser employ an empiricist repertoire?

Writing qualitative research: An example
- Read an article based on qualitative research in a European business and management journal (e.g., the *Journal of Management Studies*). How far does it exhibit the same characteristics as Suddaby and Greenwood's article?
- How far is the structure of Suddaby and Greenwood's article different from Armstrong-Strassen and Schlosser's?

Postmodernism and its implications for writing
- Why has postmodernism produced a growth of interest in writing business research?
- What is reflexivity?
- What is the linguistic turn?

Writing ethnography
- How far is it true to say that ethnographic writing is typically imbued with realism?
- What forms of ethnographic writing other than realist tales can be found?
- What are the main characteristics of realist tales?

Ways of writing differently
- What are the implications of the linguistic turn for business and management writing?

Glossary

Abduction or Abductive analysis The process of forming a possible explanation involving an imaginative effort to understand on the past of beings acting and learning in the world. It is a practical reasoning mode whose purpose is to invent and propose ideas and explanations that account for surprises and unmet expectations' (Locke, 2010, p. 1).

Action research An approach in which the action researcher and a client collaborate in the diagnosis of a problem and in the development of a solution based on the diagnosis.

***Ad libitum* sampling** A sampling approach in structured observation whereby whatever is happening at the moment that observation is due to occur is recorded.

Adjacency pair The tendency for certain kinds of activity in talk to be characterized by linked phases.

Analytic induction An approach to the analysis of qualitative data in which the researcher seeks universal explanations of phenomena by pursuing the collection of data until no cases that are inconsistent with a hypothetical explanation (deviant or negative cases) of a phenomenon are found.

ANTi-History An approach to the study of the past and of history in the production and dissemination of knowledge. Developed by Durepos and Mills, ANTi-History draws on Actor Network Theory, poststructuralist historiography and the Sociology of Knowledge, to simultaneously represent and destabilize selected past events with the ultimate aim of pluralizing history.

Archaeological approach to the past An approach which characterizes an earlier phase of the work of Foucault and involves exploration 'in language the sedimented evidence of the assumptions; the values; the common sense through which, for instance, a phenomenon such as madness could have one set of meanings in one era and a contradictory set of meanings in another' (Jacques, 2010, p. 305).

Arithmetic mean Also known simply as the *mean*, this is the everyday average—namely, the total of a distribution of values divided by the number of values.

Asynchronous online interview or focus group Online interviews may be asynchronous or *synchronous*. In the case of the former, the transactions between participants are not in real time, so that there may be long spaces of time between interviewers' questions and participants' replies, and in the case of focus groups, between participants' contributions to the discussion.

Attached email survey A survey in which respondents are sent a questionnaire, which is received as an email attachment. Compare with *embedded email survey*.

Behaviour sampling A sampling approach in *structured observation* whereby an entire group is watched and the observer records who was involved in a particular kind of behaviour.

Behavioralism A methodological approach modelled after the natural sciences that focuses on the behaviour of individuals and the way it can be shaped to achieve more efficient (organizational) outcomes.

Biographical method See *life history method*.

Bivariate analysis The examination of the relationship between two variables, as in *contingency tables* or correlation.

Boolean search Is a search which makes use of one or more of the four common Boolean operators (AND, OR, NOT, ADJ). These connectors allow for a narrowed and specified search requiring:
- All the terms specified through the use of the operator AND (e.g., internal AND reliability).
- Either or both terms or phrases through the use of the operator OR (e.g., firm OR company).
- The elimination of results through the use of the operator NOT (e.g., research NOT medical).
- The specified sequence in order through the operator ADJ (e.g., focus ADJ group).\

CAQDAS An abbreviation of *c*omputer-*a*ssisted (or -*a*ided) *q*ualitative *d*ata *a*nalysis *s*oftware.

Case study A *research design* that entails the detailed and intensive analysis of a single case. The term is sometimes extended to include the study of just two or three cases for comparative purposes.

Causality A concern with establishing causal connections between variables, rather than mere *relationships* between them.

Cell The point in a table, such as a *contingency table*, where the rows and columns intersect.

Census   The enumeration of an entire *population*. Unlike a *sample*, which comprises a count of *some* units in a population, a census relates to *all* units in a population. Thus, if a *postal questionnaire* is mailed to every person in a town or to all members of a profession, the research should be characterized as a census.

Chi-square test   Chi-square ($\chi 2$) is a test of *statistical significance*, which is typically employed to establish how confident we can be that the findings displayed in a *contingency table* can be generalized from a *probability sample* to a *population*.

Closed question   A question employed in an *interview schedule* or *self-completion questionnaire* that presents the respondent with a set of possible answers to choose from. Also called *fixed-choice question* and *pre-coded question*.

Cluster sample   A sampling procedure in which at an initial stage the researcher samples areas (i.e., clusters) and then samples units from these clusters, usually using a *probability sampling* method.

Code, coding   In *quantitative research*, codes act as tags that are placed on data about people or other units of analysis. The aim is to assign the data relating to each *variable* to groups, each of which is considered to be a category of the variable in question. Numbers are then assigned to each category to allow the information to be processed by the computer. In *qualitative research*, coding is the process whereby data are broken down into component parts, which are given names.

Coding frame   A listing of the codes used in relation to the analysis of data. In relation to answers to a structured interview schedule or questionnaire, the coding frame will delineate the categories used in connection with each question. It is particularly crucial in relation to the coding of *open questions*. With *closed questions*, the coding frame is essentially incorporated into the pre-given answers, hence the frequent use of the term *pre-coded question* to describe such questions.

Coding manual   In *content analysis*, this is the statement of instructions to coders that outlines all the possible categories for each dimension being coded.

Coding schedule   In *content analysis*, this is the form onto which all the data relating to an item being coded will be entered.

Cognitive mapping   A method used to map the thought processes and decision-making sequences used by an individual or a group to solve a problem.

Cohen's kappa   See kappa.

Collaborative enquiry   A tradition founded on the assumption that the people who are the focus of study should be fully involved in the research process at all stages, from the identification of aims to the writing-up of findings. The tradition stems from a desire to challenge the conventional methods whereby knowledge is constructed in the social sciences and to dismantle the assumed authority of the researcher, and for this reason it is sometimes referred to as 'new paradigm' research or cooperative enquiry.

Comparative design   A *research design* that entails the comparison of two or more cases in order to illuminate existing theory or generate theoretical insights as a result of contrasting findings uncovered through the comparison.

Concept   A name given to a category that organizes observations and ideas by virtue of their possessing common features.

Concurrent validity   One of the main approaches to establishing *measurement validity*. It entails relating a measure to a criterion on which cases (e.g., people) are known to differ and that is relevant to the *concept* in question.

Connotation   A term used in *semiotics* to refer to the principal and most manifest meaning of a *sign*. Compare with *denotation*.

Constant   An attribute in terms of which cases do not differ. Compare with *variable*.

Constructionism, constructionist   An *ontological* position (often also referred to as *constructivism*) that asserts that social phenomena and their meanings are continually being accomplished by social actors. It is antithetical to *objectivism* and *essentialism*.

Constructivism   See *constructionism*.

Content analysis   is a systematic analysis of texts (which may be printed or visual) to either quantify content in terms of predetermined categories (as in qualitative analysis) or determine the presence, association, and meaning of images, words, phrases, concepts, and/or themes (as in qualitative analysis).

Contingency table   A table, comprising rows and columns, that shows the *relationship* between two *variables*. Usually, at least one of the variables is a *nominal variable*. Each cell in the table shows the frequency of occurrence of that intersection of categories of each of the two variables and usually a percentage.

Continuous recording   A procedure in *structured observation*, whereby observation occurs for extended periods, so that the frequency and duration of certain types of behaviour can be carefully recorded.

Convenience sample   A sample that is selected because of its availability to the researcher. It is a form of *non-probability sample*.

Conversation analysis   The fine-grained analysis of talk as it occurs in interaction in naturally occurring situations. The talk is recorded and *transcribed* so that the detailed analyses can be carried out. The analysis is concerned with uncovering the underlying structures of talk in interaction and as such with the achievement of order through interaction. Conversation analysis is grounded in *ethnomethodology*.

Correlation   An approach to the analysis of relationships between *interval/ratio variables* and/or *ordinal variables* that seeks to assess the strength and direction of the relationship between the variables concerned. *Pearson's r* and *Spearman's rho* are both methods for assessing the level of correlation between variables.

Covert research   A term frequently used in connection with *ethnographic* research in which the researcher does not reveal his or her true identity. Such research violates the ethical principle of *informed consent*.

Cramér's V   A method for assessing the strength of the relationship between two variables, at least one of which must have more than two categories.

Critical incident method   A technique that usually relies on *structured interviewing* to elicit from respondents an account of key events or specific kinds of behaviour (critical incidents) and their consequences. Analysis involves interpretation of critical incidents so as to identify common patterns of behaviour.

Critical Discourse Analysis   (CDA) Draws largely from the work of Foucault in its focus of the relationship between dominant ideas and interrelated practices that are experienced as 'knowledge'. CDA studies the influence of discourse on the creation of powerful notions of reality and the people involved.

Critical hermeneutics   Builds on hermeneutics but seeks to unveil hidden meanings that 'serve the interests of the socially and politically powerful . . . . Through this analysis, the critical-hermeneutic researcher can locate the text as a tool 'of the ongoing maintenance of asymmetric relations that characterize a particular organization' (Prasad & Mir, 2002, p. 96).

Critical sensemaking   Is an approach, developed by Jean Helms Mills and Albert J. Mills, that builds on Weick's sensemaking framework to deal with issues of power, structure, and context. They ground the notion of socio-psychological process in Foucauldian discourse analysis (power/knowledge),

Mills' rules theory (structure), and Unger's formative context (context).

Critical realism   A *realist* epistemology that asserts that the study of the social world should be concerned with the identification of the structures that generate that world. Critical realism is critical because its practitioners aim to identify structures in order to change them, so that inequalities and injustices may be counteracted. Unlike a *positivist* epistemology, critical realism accepts that the structures that are identified may not be amenable to the senses. Thus, whereas *positivism* is *empiricist*, critical realism is not.

Cross-sectional design   A *research design* that entails the collection of data on more than one case (usually quite a lot more than one) and at a single point in time in order to collect a body of quantitative or quantifiable data in connection with two or more variables (usually many more than two), which are then examined to detect patterns of association.

Deductive   An approach to the relationship between theory and research in which the latter is conducted with reference to hypotheses and ideas inferred from the former. Compare with *inductive*.

Denotation   A term used in *semiotics* to refer to the meanings of a sign associated with the social context within which it operates that are supplementary to and less immediately apparent than its *connotation*.

Diary   A term that, in the context of social research methods, can mean different things. Three types of diary can be distinguished: diaries written or completed at the behest of a researcher; personal diaries that can be analyzed as a *personal document*, but that were produced spontaneously; and diaries written by social researchers as a log of their activities and reflections.

Dependent variable   A *variable* that is causally influenced by another variable (i.e., an *independent variable*).

Dichotomous variable   A *variable* with just two categories.

Dimension   Refers to an aspect of a *concept*.

Discourse analysis   An approach to the analysis of talk and other forms of discourse that emphasizes the ways in which versions of reality are accomplished through language.

Distribution of values   A term used to refer to the entire data relating to a *variable*. Thus, the ages of members of a *sample* represent the distribution of values for that variable for that sample.

Ecological fallacy   The error of assuming that inferences about individuals can be made from findings relating to aggregate data.

Ecological validity   A concern with the question of whether or not social scientific findings are applicable to people's everyday, natural social settings.

Embedded email survey   A social survey in which respondents are sent an email that contains a *questionnaire*. Compare with *attached email survey*.

Empiricism   An approach to the study of reality that suggests that only knowledge gained through experience and the senses is acceptable.

Emplotment   refers to the way that historical accounts (or narratives) are constructed through various combinations of tropes, or styles of story telling (including metaphor, metonymy, synecdoche, and irony), and narrative forms (including Romance, Comedy, Tragedy, and Satire).

Epistemology, epistemological   A theory of knowledge. It is particularly employed in this book to refer to a stance on what should pass as acceptable knowledge. See *positivism*, *realism*, and *interpretivism*.

Essentialism   A position that has close affinities with naive *realism*. Essentialism suggests that objects have essences that denote their authentic nature. Compare with *constructionism*.

Eta   A test of the strength of the *relationship* between two *variables*. The *independent variable* must be *a nominal variable* and the *dependent variable* must be an *interval variable* or *ratio variable*. The resulting level of correlation will always be positive.

Ethnographic content analysis   See *qualitative content analysis*.

Ethnography, ethnographer   Like *participant observation*, a research method in which the researcher immerses him- or herself in a social setting for an extended period of time, observing behaviour, listening to what is said in conversations both between others and with the fieldworker, and asking questions. However, the term has a more inclusive sense than participant observation, which seems to emphasize the observational component. Also, the term 'an ethnography' is frequently used to refer to the written output of ethnographic research.

Ethnomethodology   A sociological perspective concerned with the way in which social order is accomplished through talk and interaction. It provides the intellectual foundations of *conversation analysis*.

Ethnostatistics   Developed by Bob Gephart of the University of Alberta, uses the methods of ethnography to gain an understanding of how certain groups develop, use and interpret statistics.

European Foundation for Quality Management (EFQM)   a not-for-profit organization that has developed a business excellence model for implementing high quality performance strategies.

Evaluation research   Research that is concerned with the evaluation of real-life interventions in the social world.

Evolutionary analysis   An approach to studying organizational events over time through a focus on the way a selected process or event develops (or evolves) over time.

Experiment   A *research design* that rules out alternative explanations of findings deriving from it (i.e., possesses *internal validity*) by having at least (*a*) an experimental group, which is exposed to a treatment, and a control group, which is not exposed to a treatment, and (*b*) *random assignment* to the two groups.

External validity   A concern with the question of whether or not the results of a study can be generalized beyond the specific research context in which it was conducted.

Face validity   A concern with whether or not an *indicator* appears to reflect the content of the *concept* in question.

Facilitator   See *moderator*.

Factor analysis   A statistical technique used for large numbers of *variables* to establish whether there is a tendency for groups of them to be inter-related. It is often used with *multiple-indicator measures* to see if the *indicators* tend to bunch to form one or more groups of indicators. These groups of indicators are called factors and must then be given a name.

Field notes   A detailed chronicle by an *ethnographer* of events, conversations, and behaviour, and the researcher's initial reflections on them.

Field stimulation   A study in which the researcher directly intervenes in and/or manipulates a natural setting in order to observe what happens as a consequence of that intervention.

Frequency table   A table that displays the number and/or percentage of units (e.g., people) in different categories of a variable.

Focal sampling   A sampling approach in structured observation whereby a sampled individual is observed for a set period of time. The observer records all examples of whatever forms of behaviour are of interest.

Focus group   A form of group interview in which: there are several participants (in addition to the *moderator–facilitator*); there is an emphasis in the questioning on a particular fairly tightly defined topic; and the emphasis is upon interaction within the group and the joint construction of meaning.

Genealogical approach to the past   refers to a later phase in the work of Foucault, and involved the examination of 'the conditions under which the different ways of interpreting and evaluating ourselves have come to exist. The purpose of the genealogical method is to analyze and excavate the taken-for-granted' assumptions that define the present (Poutanen & Kovalainen, 2010, p. 263).

Generalization, generalizability   A concern with the *external validity* of research findings.

Going native   refers to a situation where an ethnographer loses his or her sense of being a researcher and become wrapped up in the world-view of the people being studied. The prolonged immersion of ethnographers in the lives of the people they study, coupled with the commitment to seeing the social world through their eyes, lie behind the risk and actuality of going native.

Grounded theory   An approach to the analysis of qualitative data that aims to generate theory out of research data by achieving a close fit between the two.

Grounded theory coding   Entails reviewing transcripts and/or field notes and giving labels (names) to component parts that seem to be of potential theoretical significance and/or that appear to be particularly salient within the social worlds of those being studied.

Hawthorne effect   See *reactivity*, *reactive effect*.

Hermeneutics   A term drawn from theology, which, when imported into the social sciences, is concerned with the theory and method of the interpretation of human action. It emphasizes the need to understand from the perspective of the social actor.

Historical materialism   A method of analysis developed by Karl Marx to make sense of the dynamic of human change over time; focusing on the interactions between socio-economic relationships (termed 'class' relations), the dominant means of production (e.g., the tools and materials involved in the process), and the ideological (e.g., the church, media, education) and political (e.g., the armed forces, government, law) support systems that maintain class privilege in the constitution of a particular mode of production (e.g., feudalism, capitalism, communism).

Historiography   Is the study of historical method. It involves an examination of how history is conceived (e.g., whether it utilizes a materialist or a poststructuralist epistemology), written (e.g., the types of tropes and narrative form used), and analyzed (e.g., does the historian frame the 'historical traces' in terms of a grand narrative or a lower case history approach i.e., collecting data without any preconceived notions).

Hypothesis   An informed speculation, which is set up to be tested, about the possible relationship between two or more variables.

Independent variable   A *variable* that has a causal impact on another variable (i.e., a *dependent variable*).

Index   See *scale*.

Indexicality   Refers to the meaning of an act which in conversation analysis means spoken words or utterances, including pauses and sounds, that are in a particular context, i.e., understandings of the words, utterances etc. depend on the context in which they are used.

Indicator   A measure that is employed to refer to a *concept* when no direct measure is available.

Inductive   An approach to the relationship between theory and research in which the former is generated out of the latter. Compare with *deductive*.

Informed consent   A key principle in social research ethics. It implies that prospective research participants should be given as much information as might be needed to make an informed decision about whether or not they wish to participate in a study.

Inter-coder reliability   The degree to which two or more individuals agree about the *coding* of an item. Inter-coder reliability is likely to be an issue in *content analysis*, *structured observation*, and when *coding* answers to *open questions* in research based on *questionnaires* or *structured interviews*.

Internal reliability   The degree to which the indicators that make up a *scale* are consistent.

Internal validity   A concern with the question of whether or not a finding that incorporates a causal relationship between two or more variables is sound.

Internet survey   A very general term used to include any survey conducted online. As such, it includes the *Web survey* and the *attached email survey* and the *embedded email survey*.

Interpretative repertoire   A collection of linguistic resources that are drawn upon in order to characterize and assess actions and events.

Interpretivism   An *epistemological* position that requires the social scientist to grasp the subjective meaning of social action.

Interval variable   A *variable* where the distances between the categories are identical across its range of categories.

Intervening variable   A *variable* that is affected by another variable and that in turn has a causal impact on another variable. Taking an intervening variable into account often facilitates the understanding of the relationship between two variables.

Interview guide   A rather vague term that is used to refer to the brief list of memory prompts of areas to be covered that is often employed in *unstructured interviewing* or to the somewhat more structured list of issues to be addressed or questions to be asked in *semi-structured interviewing*.

Interview schedule   A collection of questions designed to be asked by an interviewer. An interview schedule is always used in a *structured interview*.

Intra-coder reliability   The degree to which an individual differs over time in the *coding* of an item. Intra-coder reliability is likely to be an issue in *content analysis*, *structured observation*, and when *coding* answers to *open questions* in research based on *questionnaires* or *structured interviews*.

Juncture   Refers to a heuristic for studying organizational change over time, which avoids the idea of linear or progressive events, developments or histories. It documents dominant mentalities that out a particular era in the life or an organization and seeks to explain how it develops, is maintained but is also changed over time. A juncture is defined as 'a concurrence of events in time in which a series of images, impressions, and experiences come together, giving the appearance of a coherent whole that influences how an organization is understood' (Mills, 2010, p. 509).

Kappa (or Cohen's kappa)   Cohen's kappa is a measure of the degree of agreement over the coding of items by two people. A coefficient of 0.75 or above is considered very good; between 0.6 and 0.75, it is considered good; and between 0.4 and 0.6, it is regarded as fair.

Key informant   Someone who offers the researcher, usually in the context of conducting an *ethnography*, perceptive information about the social setting, important events, and individuals.

Level of statistical significance   This is the level of risk that you are prepared to take that you are inferring that there is a relationship between two variables in the population from which the sample was taken when in fact no such relationship exists.

Life history interview   Similar to the *oral history interview*, but the aim of this type of unstructured interview is to glean information on the entire biography of each respondent.

Life history method   Also often referred to as the *biographical method*, this method emphasizes the inner experience of the individual and its connection with changing events and phases throughout the life course. The method usually entails *life history interviews* and the use of *personal documents* as data.

Likert scale   A widely used format developed by Rensis Likert for asking attitude questions. Respondents are typically asked their degree of agreement with a series of statements that together form a *multiple-indicator* or *-item* measure. The scale is deemed then to measure the intensity with which respondents feel about an issue.

Longitudinal research   is a method designed to observe things as they occur over a lengthy period of time into the future. In this way the researcher or research team do not have to rely on particular documentation or the memories of people—both of which may be faulty. The basic idea is to make a series of observations that are repeated at selected points over time.

Mail questionnaire   Traditionally, this term has been synonymous with the *postal questionnaire*, but, with the arrival of email-based questionnaires (see *embedded email survey* and *attached email survey*), many writers prefer to refer to postal rather than mail questionnaires.

Mean   See *arithmetic mean*.

Measure of central tendency   A statistic, like the *arithmetic mean*, *median*, or *mode*, which summarizes a *distribution of values*.

Measure of dispersion   A statistic, like the *range* or *standard deviation*, which summarizes the amount of variation in a *distribution of values*.

Measurement validity   The degree to which a measure of a concept truly reflects that concept. See also *face validity* and *concurrent validity*.

Median   The mid-point in a *distribution of values*.

Meta-analysis   A method for determining the overall effect of the relationship between variables by drawing together the findings from more than one, and often many more research studies. This is typically achieved through quantitative measurement and the use of statistical procedures.

Meta-ethnography is a method that is used to achieve interpretive synthesis of qualitative research and other secondary sources, thus providing a counterpart to meta-analysis in quantitative research.

Missing data Data relating to a case that are not available, for example, when a respondent in *survey* research does not answer a question. These are referred to as 'missing values' in SPSS.

Mixed methods research A term that is increasingly employed to describe research that combines the use of both quantitative and qualitative research. The term can be employed to describe research that combines just quantitative research methods or that combines just qualitative research methods. However, in recent times, it has taken on this more specific meaning of combining quantitative and qualitative research methods.

Mode The value that occurs most frequently in a *distribution of values*.

Moderated relationship A *relationship* between two *variables* is said to be moderated when it holds for one category of a third variable but not for another category or other categories.

Moderator The person who guides the questioning of a *focus group*. Also called a *facilitator*.

Multiple-indicator measure A measure that employs more than one *indicator* to measure a *concept*.

Multi-strategy research A term used to describe research that combines *quantitative* and *qualitative research*.

Multivariate analysis The examination of relationships between three or more *variables*.

Narrative analysis An approach to the elicitation and analysis of data that is sensitive to the sense of temporal se quence that people, as tellers of stories about their lives or events around them, detect in their lives and surrounding episodes and inject into their accounts. However, the approach is not exclusive to a focus on life histories.

Naturalism A confusing term that has at least three distinct meanings: a commitment to adopting the principles of natural scientific method; being true to the nature of the phenomenon being investigated; and a style of research that seeks to minimize the intrusion of artificial methods of data collection.

Negative relationship A *relationship* between two *variables*, whereby as one increases the other decreases.

New institutional theory (also known as new institutionalism or neoinstitutionalism) seeks to explain the process of institutionalization (i.e., how certain organizations, or groups of organizations, become, over time, institutions, or socially legitimated and accepted bodies) and its influence on organizational structure and behaviour. As such it is focused on explaining such things as legitimacy, conformity, and the coherence of behaviour and structure across a range of organizations

Nominal variable Also known as a *categorical variable*, this is a variable that comprises categories that cannot be rank ordered.

Non-manipulable variable A *variable* that cannot readily be manipulated either for practical or for ethical reasons and that, therefore, cannot be employed in an *experiment*.

Non-probability sample A sample that has not been selected using a random sampling method. Essentially, this implies that some units in the population are more likely to be selected than others.

Non-response A source of *non-sampling error* that occurs whenever some members of a sample refuse to cooperate, cannot be contacted, or for some reason cannot supply the required data.

Non-sampling error Differences between the *population* and the *sample* that arise either from deficiencies in the sampling approach, such as an inadequate *sampling frame* or *non-response*, or from such problems as poor question wording, poor interviewing, or flawed processing of data.

Null hypothesis A *hypothesis* of no relationship between two variables.

Objectivism An *ontological* position that asserts that social phenomena and their meanings have an existence that is independent of social actors. Compare with *constructionism*.

Observation schedule A device used in *structured observation* that specifies the categories of behaviour that are to be observed and how behaviour should be allocated to those categories.

Official statistics Statistics compiled by or on behalf of state agencies in the course of conducting their business.

Ontology, ontological A theory of the nature of social entities. See *objectivism* and *inductivism*.

Open question A question employed in an *interview schedule* or *self-completion questionnaire* that does not present the respondent with a set of possible answers to choose from. Compare with *closed question*.

Operational definition   The definition of a *concept* in terms of the operations to be carried out when measuring it.

Operationism, operationalism   A doctrine, mainly associated with a version of physics, that emphasizes the search for *operational definitions* of *concepts*.

Oral history interview   A largely *unstructured interview* in which the respondent is asked to recall events from his or her past and to reflect on them.

Ordinal variable   A variable whose categories can be rank ordered (as in the case of *interval* and *ratio variables*), but the distances between the categories are not equal across the range.

Outlier   An extreme value in a distribution of values. If a *variable* has an extreme value—either very high or very low—the *arithmetic mean* or the *range* will be distorted by it.

Paradigm   A term deriving from the history of science, where it was used to describe a cluster of beliefs and dictates that for scientists in a particular discipline influence what should be studied, how research should be done, and how results should be interpreted.

Participant observation   Research in which the researcher immerses him- or herself in a social setting for an extended period of time, observing behaviour, listening to what is said in conversations both between others and with the fieldworker, and asking questions. Participant observation usually includes interviewing key informants and studying documents, and as such is difficult to distinguish from *ethnography*. In this book, participant observation is employed to refer to the specifically observational aspect of ethnography.

Pearson's r   A measure of the strength and direction of the relationship between two *interval/ratio variables*.

Personal documents   Documents such as *diaries*, letters, and autobiographies that are not written for an official purpose. They provide first-person accounts of the writer's life and events within it.

Phenomenology   A philosophy that is concerned with the question of how individuals make sense of the world around them and how in particular the philosopher should bracket out preconceptions concerning his or her grasp of that world.

Phi   A method for assessing the strength and direction of the relationship between two *dichotomous variables*.

Population   The universe of units from which a *sample* is to be selected.

Positive relationship   A *relationship* between two *variables*, whereby as one increases the other increases as well.

Positivism   An *epistemological* position that advocates the application of the methods of the natural sciences to the study of social reality and beyond.

Postal questionnaire   A form of *self-completion questionnaire* that is sent to respondents and usually returned by them by non-electronic mail.

Postmodernism   A position that displays a distaste for master narratives and for a *realist* orientation. In the context of research methodology, postmodernists display a preference for qualitative methods and a concern with the modes of representation of research findings.

Postpositivism   Is a disparate number of 'intellectual traditions' that share a common rejection of fundamental tenets of positivism—especially the insistence on emulating the natural sciences in the study of human society, and its characterization as a unified scientific community or practice.

Pre-coded question   Another name for a *closed question*. The term is often preferred, because such a question removes the need for the application of a *coding frame* to the question after it has been answered. This is because the range of answers has been predetermined and a numerical *code* will have been pre-assigned to each possible answer. The term is particularly appropriate when the codes appear on the *questionnaire* or *interview schedule*.

Probability sample   A sample that has been selected using *random sampling* and in which each unit in the population has a known probability of being selected.

Projective techniques   A method involving the presentation of ambiguous stimuli to individuals, which are interpreted by the researcher to reveal the underlying characteristics of the individual.

Qualitative content analysis   An approach to documents that emphasizes the role of the investigator in the construction of the meaning of and in texts. There is an emphasis on allowing categories to emerge out of data and on recognizing the significance for understanding the meaning of the context in which an item being analyzed (and the categories derived from it) appeared.

Qualitative research   Qualitative research usually emphasizes words rather than quantification in the collection and analysis of data. As a *research strategy* it is *inductivist*, *constructivist*, and *interpretivist*, but qualitative researchers do not always subscribe to all three of these features. Compare with *quantitative research*.

Quantitative research   Quantitative research usually emphasizes quantification in the collection and analysis of data. As a *research strategy* it is *deductivist* and *objectivist* and incorporates a natural science model of the research process (in particular, one influenced by *positivism*), but quantitative researchers do not always subscribe to all three of these features. Compare with *qualitative research*.

Quasi-experiment   A *research design* that is close to being an experiment but that does not meet the requirements fully and therefore does not exhibit complete *internal validity*.

Questionnaire   A collection of questions administered to respondents. When used on its own, the term usually denotes a *self-completion questionnaire*.

Quota sample   A *sample* that non-randomly samples a *population* in terms of the relative proportions of people in different categories. It is a type of *non-probability sample*.

Random assignment   A term used in connection with *experiments* to refer to the random allocation of research participants to the experimental group and the control group.

Random sampling   Sampling whereby the inclusion of a unit of a *population* occurs entirely by chance.

Random Selection   Is the process whereby probability sampling is ensured. In fundamental terms, each case within a population is given an equal and known chance of being selected.

Range   The difference between the maximum and the minimum value in a *distribution of values* associated with an *interval* or *ratio variable*.

Ratio variable   An *interval variable* with a true zero point.

Reactivity, reactive effect   A term used to describe the response of research participants to the fact that they know they are being studied, also sometimes referred to as the Hawthorne effect. Reactivity is deemed to result in untypical behaviour.

Realism   An epistemological position that acknowledges a reality independent of the senses that is accessible to the researcher's tools and theoretical speculations. It implies that the categories created by scientists refer to real objects in the natural or social worlds. See also *critical realism*.

Reflexivity   A term used in research methodology to refer to a reflectiveness among social researchers about the implications for the knowledge of the social world they generate of their methods, values, biases, decisions, and mere presence in the very situations they investigate.

Relationship   An association between two variables whereby the variation in one variable coincides with variation in another variable.

Reliability   The degree to which a measure of a concept is stable.

Repertory grid technique   A method for mapping the relationship between constructs used by an individual or a group of individuals to construct meaning. The method results in the production of a diagrammatic matrix representing the various constructs and elements involved in analyzing this relationship, i.e., the repertory grid.

Replication, replicability   The degree to which the results of a study can be reproduced. See also *internal reliability*.

Representative sample   A *sample* that reflects the population accurately, so that it is a microcosm of the *population*.

Research design   This term is employed in this book to refer to a framework for the collection and analysis of data. A choice of research design reflects decisions about the priority being given to a range of dimensions of the research process (such as *causality* and *generalization*).

Research strategy   A term used in this book to refer to a general orientation to the conduct of social research (see *quantitative research* and *qualitative research*).

Respondent validation   Sometimes called *member validation*, this is a process whereby a researcher provides the people on whom he or she has conducted research with an account of his or her findings and requests feedback on that account.

Response rate   Is the proportion of invited participants or respondents who choose to take part in research compared to the total number of those who were invited to do so. This is typically expressed as a percentage (e.g., 75% of those approached to take part in a survey actually chose to do so).

Response set   The tendency among some respondents to *multiple-indicator measures* to reply in the same way to each constituent item.

Rhetoric   A concern with the ways in which appeals to convince or persuade are devised.

Rhetorical analysis is the study of rhetoric and its impact, specifically the influence of language on the structuring of social action and outcomes.

Sample   The segment of the population that is selected for research. It is a subset of the *population*. The method of selection may be based on *probability sampling* or *non-probability sampling*.

Sampling error   Differences between a *random sample* and the *population* from which it is selected.

Sampling frame   The listing of all units in the *population* from which a *sample* is selected.

Scale   A term that is usually used interchangeably with *index* to refer to a *multiple-indicator measure* in which the score a person gives for each component *indicator* is used to provide a composite score for that person.

Scan sampling   A sampling approach in *structured observation* whereby an entire group of individuals is scanned at regular intervals and the behaviour of all of them is recorded at each occasion.

Secondary analysis   The analysis of data by researchers who will probably not have been involved in the collection of those data for purposes that may not have been envisaged by those responsible for the data collection. Secondary analysis may entail the analysis of either quantitative data or qualitative data.

Self-administered questionnaire   See *self-completion questionnaire*.

Self-completion questionnaire   A *questionnaire* that the respondent answers without the aid of an interviewer. Sometimes called a *self-administered questionnaire*.

Semiotics   The study/science of *signs*. An approach to the analysis of documents and other phenomena that emphasizes the importance of seeki ng out the deeper meaning of those phenomena. A semiotic approach is concerned to uncover the processes of meaning production and how signs are designed to have an effect upon actual and prospective consumers of those signs.

Semi-structured interview   A term that covers a wide range of types. It typically refers to a context in which the interviewer has a series of questions that are in the general form of an *interview guide* but is able to vary the sequence of questions. The questions are frequently somewhat more general in their frame of reference from that typically found in a *structured interview* schedule. Also, the interviewer usually has some latitude to ask further questions in response to what are seen as significant replies.

Sensemaking   A heuristic, developed by Karl Weick, consisting of seven socio-psychological properties, for studying the way that people develop a sense of organization: the seven properties consist of: retrospection; identity construction; social cues; social group influences (social sensemaking); dominant senses of organizational reality (ongoing sensemaking); enactment; and plausibility (see also critical sensemaking).

Sensitizing concept   A term devised by Blumer to refer to a preference for treating a *concept* as a guide in an investigation, so that it points in a general way to what is relevant or important. This position contrasts with the idea of an *operational definition*, in which the meaning of a concept is fixed in advance of carrying out an investigation.

Sign   A term employed in *semiotics*. A sign is made up of a signifier (the manifestation of a sign) and the signified (that idea or deeper meaning to which the signifier refers).

Simple observation   The passive and unobtrusive observation of behaviour.

Simple random sample   A *sample* in which each unit has been selected entirely by chance. Each unit of the *population* has a known and equal probability of inclusion in the sample.

Snowball sample   A *non-probability sample* in which the researcher makes initial contact with a small group of people who are relevant to the research topic and then uses these to establish contacts with others.

Social survey   See *survey research*.

Social desirability bias   A distortion of data that is caused by respondents' attempts to construct an account that conforms to a socially acceptable model of belief or behaviour.

Spearman's rho (ρ)   A measure of the strength and direction of the *relationship* between two *ordinal variables*.

SPSS   Originally short for Statistical Package for the Social Sciences, SPSS is a widely used computer program that allows quantitative data to be managed and analyzed.

Spurious relationship   A *relationship* between two *variables* is said to be spurious if it is being produced by the impact of a third variable on each of the two variables that form the spurious relationship. When the third variable is controlled, the relationship disappears.

Standard deviation   A measure of dispersion around the mean.

Standard error of the mean   An estimate of the amount that a sample mean is likely to differ from the population mean.

Statistical inference   See *statistical significance (test of)*.

Statistical significance (test of)   Allows the analyst to estimate how confident he or she can be that the results deriving from a study based on a randomly selected *sample* are generalizable to the *population* from which the sample was drawn. Such a test does not allow the researcher to infer that the findings are of substantive importance. The *chi-square test* is an example of this kind of test. The process of using a test of statistical significance to generalize from a sample to a population is known as *statistical inference*.

Stratified random sample   A *sample* in which units are *randomly sampled* from a *population* that has been divided into categories (strata).

Structured interview   A research interview in which all respondents are asked exactly the same questions in the same order with the aid of a formal *interview schedule*.

Structured observation   Often also called *systematic observation*, structured observation is a technique in which the researcher employs explicitly formulated rules for the observation and recording of behaviour. The rules inform observers about what they should look for and how they should record behaviour.

Survey research   A *cross-sectional design* in relation to which data are collected predominantly by *self-completion questionnaire* or by *structured interview* on more than one case (usually quite a lot more than one) and at a single point in time in order to collect a body of quantitative or quantifiable data in connection with two or more *variables* (usually many more than two) which are then examined to detect patterns of *relationship*.

Symbolic interactionism   A theoretical perspective in sociology and social psychology that views social interaction as taking place in terms of the meanings actors attach to action and things.

Synchronous online interview or focus group   Online interviews may be asynchronous or synchronous. In the case of the latter, the transactions between participants are in real time, so that there will be only brief time lapses between interviewers' questions and participants' replies, and, in the case of focus groups, between participants' contributions to the discussion.

Systematic observation   See *structured observation*.

Systematic sample   A *probability sampling* method in which units are selected from a *sampling frame* according to fixed intervals, such as every fifth unit.

Taylorism   Named after Frederick Taylor, Taylorism refers to the use of Taylor's 'scientific' approach to the study of job design. He called his approach 'scientific management'. The method involves systematic study of the types of efforts and energies required to most efficiently carry out a specific task. In his classic study of the shovelling of pig iron, Taylor studied the various ways that men shovelled pig iron to determine the most efficient form of carrying out the task. He then trained workers in the new, effective ways of carrying out the task. In the process Taylor demonstrated that 'scientifically' redesigned jobs could lead to much higher levels of productivity. The wide scale use of such techniques became known as 'Taylorism' and was popular for a time not only in the United States, but also Fascist Italy and the Soviet Union.

Text   A term that is used either in the conventional sense of a written work or in more recent years to refer to a wide range of phenomena. For example, in arriving at a *thick description*, Geertz refers to treating culture as a text.

Theoretical sampling   'is the process of data collection for generating theory whereby the analyst jointly collects, codes, and analyzes his data and decides what data to collect next and where to find them, in order to develop her theory as it emerges' (Glaser & Strauss, 1967, p. 45).

Theoretical saturation   refers to a process of continuing to sample theoretically until a category has been saturated with data, i.e., 'until (*a*) no new or relevant data seem to be emerging regarding a category, (*b*) the category is well developed in terms of its properties and dimensions demonstrating variation, and (*c*) the relationships among categories are well established and validated' (Strauss & Corbin, 1998, p. 212).

Thick description   A term devised by Geertz to refer to detailed accounts of a social setting that can form the basis for the creation of general statements about a culture and its significance in people's social lives.

Time sampling   A sampling method in *structured observation*, which entails using a criterion for deciding when observation will occur.

Tracking   Is an approach developed by Mintzberg and his colleagues to study strategy over time. It involves defining a particular phenomenon and then tracking its appearance (or lack of appearance) over time.

Transcription, transcript   The written translation of a tape-recorded *interview* or *focus group* session.

Triangulation   The use of more than one method or source of data in the study of a social phenomenon so that findings may be cross-checked.

Trustworthiness   A set of criteria advocated by some writers for assessing the quality of *qualitative research*.

Turn taking   The notion from *conversation analysis* that order in everyday conversation is achieved through orderly taking of turns in conversations.

Univariate analysis   The analysis of a single *variable* at a time.

Unobtrusive methods   Methods that do not entail the awareness among research participants that they are being studied and that are therefore not subject to *reactivity*.

Unstructured interview   An interview in which the interviewer typically only has a list of topics or issues, often called an *interview guide*, that are typically covered. The style of questioning is usually very informal. The phrasing and sequencing of questions will vary from interview to interview.

Validity   A concern with the integrity of the conclusions that are generated from a piece of research. There are different aspects of validity. See, in particular, *measurement validity*, *internal validity*, *external validity*, and *ecological validity*. When used on its own, *validity* is usually taken to refer to *measurement validity*.

Variable   An attribute in terms of which cases vary. See also *dependent variable* and *independent variable*. Compare with *constant*.

Verbal protocol approach   A method that involves asking respondents to think aloud while they are performing a task in order to capture their thought processes while they are making a decision or judgment or solving a problem.

Visual ethnography   Refers to the use of such things as photography, video, and hypermedia as methods of data collection in ethnographic research; it can also include the analysis of visual images.

Web survey   A *social survey* conducted so that respondents complete a *questionnaire* via a website.

References

Abella, R.S. (1984). *Equity in employment: A royal commission report*. Ottawa, ON: Ministry of Supply and Services Canada.

Abbott, A. (1988). *The System of Professions*. Chicago: University of Chicago Press.

———. (1995). Things of boundaries. *Social Research, 62*, 857–881.

Acker, J. (1992). Gendering organizational theory. In A.J. Mills & P. Tancred (Eds), *Gendering organizational analysis* (pp. 248–260). Newbury Park, CA: Sage.

Acker, J., & van Houten, D.R. (1974). Differential recruitment and control: The sex structuring of organizations. *Administrative Science Quarterly, 9*, 152–163.

Addison, J.T., & Belfield, C.R. (2000). The impact of financial participation and employee involvement on financial performance: A reiteration using the 1998 WERS. *Scottish Journal of Political Economy, 47*(5), 571–583.

Adelman, C. (2010). The Chicago school. In A.J. Mills, G. Durepos, & E. Weibe (Eds), *Sage encyclopedia of case study research* (Vol. 1, pp. 140–144). Thousand Oaks, CA: Sage.

Adler, N. (1983). A typology of management studies involving culture. *Journal of International Business Studies, Fall*, 29–47.

Adriaenssens, C., & Cadman, L. (1999). An adaptation of moderated e-mail focus groups to assess the potential of a new online (Internet) financial services offer in the UK. *Journal of the Market Research Society, 41*, 417–424.

Alderson, P. (1998). Confidentiality and consent in qualitative research. *Network: Newsletter of the British Sociological Association, 69*, 6–7.

Aldrich, H.E. (1972). Technology and organizational structure: A re-examination of the findings of the Aston Group. *Administrative Science Quarterly, 17*(1), 26–43.

Aldrich, H.E., & Fiol, C.M. (1994). Fools rush in? The institutional context of industry creation. *Academy of Management Review, 19*(4), 645–670.

Aldridge, A. (1998). Reproducing the value of professional expertise in post-traditional culture: Financial advice and the creation of the client. *Cultural Values, 2*, 445–462.

Allaire, Y., & Firsirotu, M. (1984). Theories of organizational culture. *Organization Studies, 5*, 193–226.

Altamirano-Jimenez, I. (2010). Going native. In A.J. Mills, G. Durepos, & E. Wiebe (Eds), *Sage encyclopedia of case study research* (Vol. 1, pp. 424–427). Thousand Oaks, CA: Sage.

Altheide, D.L. (1980). Leaving the newsroom. In W. Shaffir, R.A. Stebbins & A. Turowetz (Eds), *Fieldwork experience: Qualitative approaches to social Research*. New York, NY: St Martin's Press.

Altschuld, J.W., & Lower, M.A. (1984). Improving mailed questionnaires: Analysis of a 96 percent return rate. In D.C. Lockhart (Ed.), *Making effective use of mailed questionnaires*. San Francisco, CA: Jossey-Bass.

Alvesson, M. (2002). *Postmodernism and social research*. Buckingham: Open University Press.

Alvesson, M., & Karreman, D. (2000). Varieties of discourse: On the study of organization through discourse analysis. *Human Relations, 53*(9), 1125–1149.

Al Zaman, A., & Lightstone, K. (2008). Reassessing Canadian hedging practices. In C. Wilson (Ed.), *Proceedings of the Annual Conference of the Administrative Sciences Association of Canada* (Vol. 29, pp. 15–31). Halifax, NS: ASAC.

Andersen, M. (1981). Corporate wives: Longing for liberation or satisfied with the status quo? *Urban Life, 10*, 311–327.

Argyris, C., Putnam, R., & Smith, D.M. (1985). *Action science*. San Francisco, CA: Jossey-Bass.

Armstrong, G. (1993). Like that Desmond Morris? In D. Hobbs & T. May (Eds), *Interpreting the field: Accounts of ethnography*. Oxford: Clarendon Press.

Armstrong-Stassen, M. (1994). Coping with transition: A study of layoff survivors. *Journal of Organizational Behavior, 15*, 597–621.

Armstrong-Strassen, M., & Schlossser F. (2008). Taking a positive approach to organizational downsizing. *Canadian Journal of Administrative Sciences, 25*(2), 93–106.

Arndt, M., & Bigelow, B. (2005). Professionalizing and Masculinizing a Female Occupation: The Reconceptualization of Hospital Administration in the Early 1900s. *Administrative Science Quarterly, 50*, 233–261.

Aronson, E., & Carlsmith, J.M. (1968). Experimentation in social psychology. In G. Lindzey & E. Aronson (Eds), *The handbook of social psychology*. Reading, MA: Addison-Wesley.

Atkinson, P. (1981). *The clinical experience*. Farnborough, UK: Gower.

———. (1990). *The ethnographic imagination: Textual constructions of society*. London, UK: Routledge.

Atkinson, P., & Coffey, A. (1995). Realism and its discontents: The crisis of cultural representation in ethnographic texts. In B. Adam & S. Allen (Eds), *Theorising culture*. London: UCL Press.

Austin, B. (2000). The Administrative Sciences Association of Canada, 1957–1999. In B. Austin (Ed.), *Capitalizing Knowledge*. Toronto, ON: University of Toronto Press.

Austin, B., & Mintzberg, H. (1996). Mirroring Canadian Industrial Policy. Strategy Formation at Dominion Textile from 1873 to 1990. Canadian Journal of Administrative Sciences, 13, 46–64.

Bacon, N., & Blyton, P. (2001). Management practices and

employee attitudes: A longitudinal study spanning fifty years. *Sociological Review, 49*(2), 254–274.

Bakker, A.B., & Schaufeli, W.B. (2008). Positive organizational behavior: Engaged employees in flourishing organizations. *Journal of Organizational Behavior, 29*, 147–154.

Bakker, J.I. (Hans). (2010). Theory, role of. In A.J. Mills, G. Durepos, & E. Wiebe (Eds), *Sage encyclopedia of case study research* (Vol. 1, pp. 930–932). Thousand Oaks, CA: Sage.

Ball, K., & Wilson, D.C. (2000). Power, control and computer-based performance monitoring: Repertoires, resistance and subjectivities. *Organization Studies, 21*(3), 539–565.

Bansal, P., & Roth, K. (2000). Why companies go green: A model of ecological responsiveness. *Academy of Management Journal, 43*(4), 717–736.

Barber, K. (Ed.) (2004). *Canadian Oxford Dictionary* (2nd ed.). Don Mills, ON: Oxford.

Barley, S., Meyer, G., & Gash, D. (1988). Cultures of culture: Academics, practitioners and the pragmatics of normative control. *Administrative Science Quarterly, 33*, 24–60.

Barnes, S. (2004). Issues of attribution and identification in online social research. In M.D. Johns, S-L.S. Chen, & G.J. Hall (Eds), *Online social research.* New York, NY: Peter Lang.

Barnett, R. (1994). Editorial. *Studies in Higher Education, 19*(2). 123–124.

Baron, S., Vincent G., & Beaulieu, S. (2008, May). *Typologie de la filiére de l'environnment au Québec.* Paper presented at the Annual Conference of the Administrative Sciences Association of Canada (ASAC). Halifax, ON.

Bartunek, J.M., Bobko, P., & Venkatraman, N. (1993). Toward innovation and diversity in management research methods. *Academy of Management Journal, 36*(6), 1362–1373.

Bassett, B.R. (2010). Computer-based analysis of qualitative data: ATLAS.ti. In A.J. Mills, G. Durepos, & E. Wiebe (Eds), *Sage encyclopedia of case study research.* Thousand Oaks, CA: Sage.

Baum, J.A.C., Rowley, T.J., & Shipilov, A.J. (2004). The small world of Canadian capital markets: Statistical mechanics of investment bank syndicate networks, 1952–1989. *Canadian Journal of Administrative Sciences, 21*, 307–325.

Baumgartner, R.M., & Heberlein, T.A. (1984). Applying attitude theories to the return of mailed questionnaires. In D.C. Lockhart (Ed.), *Making effective use of mailed questionnaires.* San Francisco, CA: Jossey-Bass.

Bazerman, C. (1987). Codifying the social scientific style: The APA publication manual as a behaviorist rhetoric. In J.S. Nelson, A. Megill, & D.N. McClosky (Eds), *The rhetoric of the human sciences.* Madison, WI: University of Wisconsin Press.

Bechhofer, F., Elliott, B., & Mccrone, D. (1984). Safety in numbers: On the use of multiple interviewers. *Sociology, 18*, 97–100.

Becker, H.S (1986). *Writing for social scientists: How to start and finish your thesis, book, or article.* Chicago, IL: University of Chicago Press.

Becker, H. S., & Geer, B. (1957a). Participant observation and interviewing: A comparison. *Human Organization, 16*, 28–32.

Becker, S., Bryman, A., & Sempik, J. (2006). Defining 'quality' in social policy research. Lavenham: Social Policy Association: http://www.social-policy.com/documents/spaquality06.pdf

Bell, C. (1969). A note on participant observation. *Sociology, 3*, 417–18.

Bell, C., & Newby, H. (1977). *Doing sociological research.* London, UK: George Allen & Unwin.

Bell, C., & Roberts, H. (1984). *Social researching: Politics, problems, practice.* London, UK: Routledge & Kegan Paul.

Bell, E. (2001). The social time of organizational payment systems. *Time & Society, 10*(1), 45–62.

Bell, E. & Bryman, A. (2007). Ethical codes and management research: A comparative content analysis. *British Journal of Management, 18*(1).

Bell, E., Taylor, S., & Thorpe, R. (2001). Investors in people and the standardization of professional knowledge in personnel management, *Management Learning, 32*(2), 201–219.

Bell, E.L. & Nkomo, S. (1992). Re-visioning women managers' lives. In A.J. Mills & P. Tancred (Eds), *Gendering Organizational Analysis* (pp. 235–47). Newbury Park, CA: Sage.

Benschop, Y., & H.E. Meihuizen. (2002). Reporting gender: Representations of gender in financial and annual reports. In I. Aaltio & A.J. Mills (Eds), *Gender, identity and the culture of organizations* (pp. 160–184). London, UK: Routledge.

Berelson, B. (1952). *Content analysis in communication research.* New York, NY: Free Press.

Berg, B.L. (1989). *Qualitative research methods.* Boston, MA: Allyn and Bacon.

Bettman, J., & Weitz, B. (1983). Attributions in the board room: Causal reasoning in corporate annual reports. *Administrative Science Quarterly, 28*, 165–83.

Beynon, H. (1975). *Working for Ford* (2nd ed.). Harmondsworth, UK: Penguin.

Bhaskar, R. (1975). *A realist theory of science.* Leeds: Leeds Books.

Billig, M. (1991). *Ideology and opinions: Studies in rhetorical psychology.* Cambridge, UK: Cambridge University Press.

Black, E. (2001). *IBM and the Holocaust: The strategic alliance Between Nazi Germany and America's most powerful corporation.* New York, NY: Crown.

Blackburn, R., & Stokes, D. (2000). Breaking down the barriers: Using focus groups to research small and medium-sized enterprises. *International Small Business Journal, 19*(1), 44–67.

Blauner, R. (1964). *Alienation and freedom.* Chicago, IL: University of Chicago Press.

Bloland, H.G. (2005). Whatever happened to postmodernism in higher education? *Journal of Higher Education, 76*, 121–150.

Bloor, M. (1978). On the analysis of observational data: A discussion of the worth and uses of inductive techniques and respondent validation. *Sociology, 12*, 545–552.

Blotnicky, K.A. (2009). The relevance of the marketing concept. *The Workplace Review, 3*(1), 3–12.

Blumer, H. (1954). What is wrong with social theory? *American Sociological Review, 19*, 3–10.

———. (1956). Sociological analysis and the variable. *American Sociological Review, 21*, 683–690.

Boden, D. (1994). *The business of talk: Organizations in action.* Cambridge, UK: Polity.

Boje, D. (1991). The storytelling organization: A study of performance in an office supply Firm. *Administrative Science Quarterly, 36*, 106–126.

———. (1995). Stories of the storytelling organization: A postmodern analysis of Disney as Tamara-Land. *The Academy of Management Journal, 38*(4), 997–1035.

———. (2001). *Narrative methods for organizational and communication research.* Thousand Oaks, CA: Sage.

———. (2010). Narrative analysis. In A.J. Mills, G. Durepos, & E. Wiebe (Eds), *Sage encyclopedia of case study research* (Vol. II, 591–594). Thousand Oaks, CA: Sage.

Bolton, A., Pole, C., & Mizen, P. (2001). Picture this: Researching child workers. *Sociology, 35*(2), 501–518.

Bottomore, T.B., & Rubel, M. (1963). Karl Marx: Selected writings in sociology and social philosophy. Harmondsworth, UK: Penguin.

Boudens, C.J. (2005). The story of work: A narrative analysis of workplace emotion. *Organisation Studies, 26*, 1285–1306.

Bozec, Y., & Bozec, R. (2007). Ownership concentration and corporate governance practices: Substitution or expropriation effects? *Canadian Journal of Administrative Sciences / Revue Canadienne des Sciences de l'Administration, 24*(3), 182–195.

Bradburn, N.A., & Sudman, S. (1979). *Improving interview method and questionnaire design.* San Francisco, CA: Jossey-Bass.

Bradshaw, P. (1996). Women as constituent directors: Rereading current texts using a feminist-postmodernist approach. In D.M. Boje, R.P. Gephart, & T.J. Thatchenkery (Eds), *Postmodern management and organization theory* (pp. 95–125). Beverly Hills, CA: Sage.

Bradshaw, P., Ingilis, S., & Fredette, C. (2005). A new model of diversity: Learning from nonprofit boardrooms. *Proceeding of the 2005 Administrative Sciences Association of Canada, Gender & Diversity in Organizations Division*, Toronto, May 28–31, 26:11, 12–24.

Brannick, T. & Coghlan, D. (2007). In defense of being native: The case for insider academic research. *Organizational Research Methods, 10*(1), 59–74.

Brayfield, A., & Rothe, H. (1951). An index of job satisfaction. *Journal of Applied Psychology, 35*, 307–11.

Brewerton, P. & Millward, L. (2001). *Organizational research methods.* London, UK: Sage.

Brewis, J. (2004). Refusing to be 'me'. In R. Thomas, A.J. Mills & J. Helms Mills (Eds), *Identity politics at work. Resisting gender, gendering resistance* (pp. 23–39). London, UK: Routledge.

Bridgman, P.W. (1927). *The logic of modern physics.* New York, NY: Macmillan.

Briggs, C.L. (1986). *Learning how to ask: A sociolinguistic appraisal of the role of the interview in social science research.* Cambridge, MA: Cambridge University Press.

Brockner, J., & Wiesenfeld, B. (1993). Living on the edge (of social and organizational psychology): The effects of job lay-offs on those who remain. In J.K. Murnighan (Ed.), *Social psychology in organizations: Advances in theory and research* (pp. 119–140). Englewood Cliffs, NJ: Prentice-Hall.

Brotheridge, C.M. (1999). Unwrapping the black box: A test of why emotional labour may lead to emotional exhaustion. In D. Miller (Ed.), *Proceedings of the Administrative Sciences Association of Canada, Halifax* (pp. 11–20). Saint John, NB: ASAC.

Broussine, M., & Vince, R. (1996). Working with metaphor towards organizational change. In C. Oswick & D. Grant (Eds), *Organization development: Metaphorical explanations.* London, UK: Pitman Publishing.

Bruni, A. & Gherardi, S. (2002). En-gendering differences, transgressing the bounderies, coping with the dual presence. In I. Aaltio & A.J. Mills (Eds), *Gender, identity and the culture of organizations* (pp. 21–38). London, UK: Routledge.

Bryman, A. (1988a). *Quantity and quality in social research.* London, UK: Routledge.

———. (1988b). *Doing research in organizations.* London, UK: Routledge.

———. (1989a). *Research methods and organization studies.* London, UK: Routledge.

———. (1989b). The value of re-studies in sociology: The case of clergy and ministers, 1971 to 1985. *Sociology, 23*, 31–54.

———. (1992). Quantitative and qualitative research: Further reflections on their integration. In J. Brannen (Ed.), *Mixing methods: Qualitative and quantitative research.* Aldershot, UK: Avebury.

———. (1998). Quantitative and qualitative research strategies in knowing the social world. In T. May & M. Williams (Eds), *Knowing the Social World* (pp. 138–156). Buckingham: Open University Press.

———. (1999). Global Disney. In P. Taylor & D. Slater (Eds), *The American century.* Oxford, UK: Blackwell.

———. (2006a). Integrating quantitative and qualitative research. *Qualitative Research, 6*, 97–113.

———. (2006b). Paradigm peace and the implications for quality. *International Journal of Social Research Methodology, 9*, 111–126.

Bryman, A., Bell, E., Mills, A.J., & Yue, A.R. (2010). *Business Research Methods.* Toronto, ON: Oxford University Press.

——— & ———. (1994a). Developments in qualitative data Analysis: An introduction. In A. Bryman & R.G. Burgess (Eds), *Analyzing qualitative data.* London, UK: Routledge.

Bryman, A., & Burgess, R.G. (1994b). Reflections on qualitative data analysis. In A. Bryman & R.G. Burgess (Eds), *Analyzing qualitative data.* London, UK: Routledge.

Bryman, A., & Cramer, D. (2004). *Quantitative data analysis with SPSS 12 and 13: A guide for social scientists.* London, UK: Routledge.

Bryman, A., Gillingwater, D., & Mcguinness, I. (1996). Industry culture and strategic response: The case of the British bus industry. *Studies in Cultures, Organizations and Societies, 2,* 191–208.

Bryman, A., Haslam, C., & Webb, A. (1994). Performance appraisal in UK universities: A case of procedural compliance? *Assessment and Evaluation in Higher Education, 19,* 175–188.

Bryman, A., Stephens, M., & Campo, C. (1996). The importance of context: Qualitative research and the study of leadership. *Leadership Quarterly, 7,* 353–370.

Buchanan, D.A., Boddy, D., & McCalman, J. (1988). Getting in, getting out and getting back. In A. Bryman (Ed.), *Doing research in organizations.* London, UK: Routledge.

Bulmer, M. (1979). Concepts in the analysis of qualitative data. *Sociological Review, 27,* 651–77.

———. (1982). The merits and demerits of covert participant observation. In M. Bulmer (Ed.), *Social research ethics.* London, UK: Macmillan.

———. (1984). Facts, concepts, theories and problems. In M. Bulmer (Ed.), *Social research methods.* London, UK: Macmillan.

———. (1980). Why don't sociologists make more use of official statistics? *Sociology, 14,* 505–23.

Bunce, D., & West, M. (1996). Stress management and innovation interventions at work. *Human Relations, 49*(2), 209–232.

Burawoy, M. (1979). *Manufacturing consent.* Chicago, IL: University of Chicago Press.

Burgess, R.G. (1984). *In the field.* London, UK: Allen & Unwin.

Burke, R.R. (1996). Virtual shopping: Breakthrough in marketing research. *Harvard Business Review, 74*(2), 120–131.

Burrell, G., & Morgan, G. (1979). *Sociological paradigms and organizational analysis.* London, UK: Heinemann.

Buston, K. (1997). NUD*IST in action: Its use and its usefulness in a study of chronic illness in young people. *Sociological Research Online, 2,* www.socresonline.org.uk/socresonline/2/3/6.html

Butcher, B. (1994). Sampling methods—An overview and review. *Survey Methods Centre Newsletter, 15,* 4–8.

Butterfield, K., Treviño, L., & Weaver, G. (2000). Moral awareness in business organizations: Influences of issue-related and social context factors. *Human Relations, 53*(7), 981–1018.

Buttner, E.H. (2001). Examining female entrepreneurs management style: An application of a relational Frame. *Journal of Business Ethics, 29,* 253–269.

Cable, D., & Graham, M. (2000). The determinants of job seekers' reputation perceptions. *Journal of Organizational Behavior, 21,* 929–947.

Calas, M., & Smircich, L. (2005). From the 'woman's point of view' ten years later: Towards a feminist organization studies. In S. Clegg, C. Hardy, T. Lawrence, & W. Nord (Eds), *The Sage Handbook of Organization Studies.* London, UK: Sage.

Calder, B.J. (1977). Focus groups and the nature of qualitative marketing research. *Journal of Marketing Research, 14,* 353–364.

Cameron, J. (2001). Negative effects of reward on intrinsic motivation: A limited phenomenon: Comment on Deci, Koestner, & Ryan (2001). *Review of Educational Research, 71*(1), 29–42.

Cameron, J., & Pierce, W. (1994). Reinforcement, reward and intrinsic motivation: A meta-analysis. *Review of Educational Research, 64,* 363–423.

Campbell, D.T. (1957). Factors relevant to the validity of experiments in social settings. *Psychological Bulletin, 54,* 297–312.

Campbell, S., & Mills, A.J. (2007). *Mind the gap: Labour process meets sensemaking in the re/creation of identity at work.* Paper presented at the 5th International Conference on Critical Management Studies, Machester, UK.

Campbell, S., & Haiven, L. (2008). *Struggles on the frontier of control over professional identity: Leading cases from Canada.* Paper presented at the International Labour Process Conference, Dublin.

Campbell-Jamison, F., Worrall, L., & Cooper, C. (2001). Downsizing in Britain and its effects on survivors and their organizations. *Anxiety, Stress, and Coping, 14,* 35–58.

Caplan, R., Cobb, S., French, J., Harrison, R., & Pinneau, S. (1975). *Job demands and worker health.* Washington, DC: US Department of Health, Education and Welfare.

Carroll, W.R., & Helms Mills, J. (2005, May). *Identity and resistance in call centres: Toward a critical sensemaking approach.* Paper presented at the Annual Conference of the Administrative Sciences Association of Canada, Toronto, ON.

Carroll, W.R., Mills, A.J., & Helms Mills, J. (2006, August). *Managing power and resistance: Making critical sense of call centre management.* Paper presented at the Critical Management Studies Interest Group of the Academy of Management annual meeting, Atlanta, GA.

———, ———, & ———. (2008). Managing identity and resistance: Making critical sense of call centre management. *Gestion 2000 (Belgian Journal of Management), 25*(6), 57–82.

Casebeer, A., Reay, T., & Pablo, A. (2006). Organizational response to broad public policy: Multiple level actions, interactions and reactions. *Proceeding of the 2006 Administrative Sciences Association of Canada, Health Care Management Division, Banff, June 3–6 27 (28),* 14–33.

Casey, C. (1995). *Work, Self and Society: After Industrialism.* London, UK: Routledge.

Catterall, M., & Maclaran, P. (1997). Focus group data and qualitative analysis programs: Coding the moving picture as well as snapshots. *Sociological Research Online, 2,* www.socresonline.org.uk/socresonline/2/1/6.html

Cavendish, R. (1982). *Women on the Line.* London, UK: Routledge & Kegan Paul.

Charmaz, K. (2000). Grounded theory: Objectivist and constructivist methods. In N.K. Denzin & Y.S. Lincoln (Eds), *Handbook of qualitative research* (2nd ed.). Thousand Oaks, CA: Sage.

Chaudhry, B., Wang, J., Wu, S., Maglione, M., Mojica, W., Roth, E., Morton, S.C., & Shekelle, P.G. (2006). Systematic review: impact of health information technology on quality, efficiency, and costs of medical care. *Annals of Internal Medicine, 144*(10), 742–752.

Chen, C.C., & Meindl, J.R. (1991). The construction of leadership images in the popular press: The case of Donald Burr and People Express. *Administrative Science Quarterly, 36,* 521–51.

Chrobot-Mason, D., Konrad, A.M., & Linnehan, F. (2005). Measures for Quantitative Diversity Scholarship, in Konrad, A.M., Prasad, P., & Pringle, J.K. (Eds), *Handbook of Workplace Diversity* (pp. 237–270). Thousand Oaks, CA: Sage.

Cicourel, A.V. (1964). *Method and measurement in sociology.* New York, NY: Free Press.

———. (1968). *The social organization of juvenile justice.* New York, NY: Wiley.

———. (1982). Interviews, surveys, and the problem of ecological validity. *American Sociologist, 17,* 11–20.

Clapper, D.L., & Massey, A.P. (1996). Electronic focus groups: A framework for exploration. *Information and Management, 30,* 43–50.

Clifford, J. (1983). On ethnographic authority. *Representations, 1,* 118–146.

Cobanoglu, C., Ward, B., & Moreo, P.J. (2001). A comparison of mail, fax and web-based survey methods. *International Journal of Market Research, 43,* 441–452.

Coffey, A. (1999). *The ethnographic self: Fieldwork and the representation of reality.* London, UK: Sage.

Coffey, A., & Atkinson, P. (1995). *Ethnography: Principles in practice* (2nd ed.). London, UK: Routledge.

———, & ———. (1996). *Making sense of qualitative data: Complementary research strategies.* Thousand Oaks, CA: Sage.

Coffey, A., Holbrook, B., & Atkinson, P. (1996). Qualitative data analysis: technologies and representations. *Sociological Research Online, 2,* www.socresonline.org.uk/socresonline/1/1/4.html

Coghlan, D. (2001). Insider action research projects: Implications for practising managers. *Management Learning, 32*(1), 49–60.

Coleman, J. S. (1958). Relational Analysis: The study of social organization with survey methods. *Human Organization, 16,* 28–36.

Collins, G., & Wickham, J. (2004). Inclusion or exploitation: Irish women enter the labour force. *Gender, Work and Organization, 11*(1), 26–46.

Collinson, D. (1988). Engineering humour: Masculinity, joking and conflict in shop floor relations. *Organisation Studies, 9*(2), 181–199.

———. (1992a). *Managing the shopfloor: Subjectivity, masculinity and workplace culture.* Berlin: DeGruyter.

———. (1992b). Researching recruitment: Qualitative methods and sex discrimination. In R. Burgess (Ed.), *Studies in qualitative methodology* (Vol. 3). London, UK: JAI Press.

Colwell, A., Beckman, T., & Cunningham, P. (2007). Corporate social responsibility in emerging markets: The Chilean experience. *Proceeding of the Administrative Sciences Association of Canada, Social Responsibility Interest Group, Ottawa, June 2–5, 28,* 155–171.

Conger, J.A., & Kanungo, R.N. (1998). *Charismatic leadership in organizations.* Thousand Oaks, CA: Sage.

Conway, N., & Briner, R. (2002). A daily diary study of affective responses to psychological contract breach and exceeded promises. *Journal of Organizational Behaviour, 23,* 287–302.

Cook, T.D., & Campbell, D.T. (1979). *Quasi-experimentation: Design and analysis for field settings.* Boston, MA: Houghton Mifflin.

Cooke, B. (1999). Writing the left out of management theory: The historiography of the management of change. *Organization, 6*(1), 81–105.

———. (2006). The Cold War origin of action research as managerialist cooptation. *Human Relations, 59*(5), 665–693.

Cooper, D.R., & Schindler, P.S. (2006). *Business research methods.* New York, NY: McGraw-Hill Irwin.

Corbin, J., & Strauss, A. (1998). *Basics of qualitative research: techniques and procedures for developing grounded theory.* Thousand Oaks, CA: Sage.

Corman, S.R., & Poole, M.S. (Eds). (2000). *Perspectives on organizational communication.* New York, NY: The Guildford Press.

Corti, L. (1993). Using diaries in social research. *Social Research Update, 2.*

Corti, L., Foster, J., & Thompson, P. (1995). Archiving qualitative research data. *Social Research Update, 10.*

Cotterill, P. (1992). Interviewing women: Issues of friendship, vulnerability, and power. *Women's Studies International Forum, 15*(5–6), 593–606.

Couper, M.P. (2000). Web surveys: A review of issues and approaches. *Public Opinion Quarterly, 64,* 464–494.

Coupland, C. (2005). Corporate social responsibility on the Web. *Journal of Business Ethics, 62,* 355–366.

Coutrot, T. (1998). How do institutional frameworks affect industrial relations outcomes? A micro-statistical comparison of France and Britain. *European Journal of Industrial Relations, 4*(2), 177–205.

Cowley, J.C. (2000). Strategic qualitative focus group research: Define and articulate our skills or we will be replaced by others. *International Journal of Market Research, 42*(1), 17–38.

Cox, D., & Aung, M. (2005). Using tripartite paradigm modeling to understand enterprise value. *Proceeding of the 2005 Administrative Sciences Association of Canada, Management Science Division, Toronto, May 28–31 26* (2), 202–213.

Cox, D., Wilcock, A., & Aung, M. (2007). Beyond Babel: Measuring social responsibility using tripartite paradigm framework and narratives. *Proceeding of 2007 the Administrative Sciences Association of Canada, Social Responsibility Interest Group, Ottawa, June 2–5, 28,* 73–87.

Coyle, J.R., & Thorson, E. (2001). 'The effects of progressive levels of interactivity and vividness in web marketing sites', Journal of Advertising, 30(3), 65–77.

Crang, P. (1994). It's showtime: On the workplace geographies of display in a restaurant in Southeast England. *Environment and Planning D: Society and Space, 12*, 675–704.

Creed, W.E., Scully, M.A., and Austin, J.R. (2002) Clothes make the person? The tailoring of legitimating accounts and the social construction of identity. *Organization Science, 13*, 475–496.

Cryer, P. (1996). *The research student's guide to success.* Buckingham, UK: Open University Press.

Cully, M., Woodland, S., O'Reilly, A., & Dix, G. (1999). *Britain at work: As depicted by the 1998 Workplace Employee Relations Survey.* London, UK: Routledge.

Cummings, L.L., & Frost, P.J. (1995). *Publishing in the organizational sciences.* London: Sage.

Cunha, M.P., & Cunha, R.C. (2004). The dialectics of human resource management in Cuba. *International Journal of Human Resource Management, 15*(7), 1280–92.

Cunha, R.C., & Cooper, C.L. (2002). Does privatization affect corporate culture and employee wellbeing? *Journal of Managerial Psychology, 17*(1), 21–49.

Curasi, C.F. (2001). A critical exploration of face-to-face interviewing vs. computer-mediated interviewing. *International Journal of Market Research, 43*, 361–375.

Czarniawska, B. (1999). *Writing management: Organization theory as a literary genre.* Oxford, UK: Oxford University Press.

Czarniawska-Joerges, B.(1998). *A narrative approach in organization studies.* Thousand Oaks, CA: Sage.

———. (2004). *Narratives in social science research.* Thousand Oaks, CA: Sage.

Daft, R. (1995). Why I recommended that your manuscript be rejected and what you can do about it. In L.L. Cummings, & P.J. Frost (Eds), *Publishing in the organizational sciences.* London, UK: Sage.

Daft, R., & Lewin, A. (1993). Where are the theories for new organizational forms? *Organization Science, 4*, i–iv.

Dale, A., Arber, S., & Proctor, M. (1988). *Doing secondary analysis.* London, UK: Unwin Hyman.

Dalton, M. (1959). *Men who manage: Fusion of feeling and theory in administration.* New York, NY: Wiley.

———. (1964). Preconceptions and methods in men who manage. In P. Hammond (Ed.), *Sociologists at work.* New York, NY: Basic Books.

Das, H., & Das, M. (2009). Gender stereotyping in contemporary Indian magazine fiction. *Asian Studies Review, 33*(March), 63–82.

Davies, C.A. (1999). *Reflexive ethnography: A guide to researching selves and others.* London, UK: Routledge.

Davies, J. (2001). International comparisons of labour disputes in 1999. *Labour Market Trends, 4*, 195–201.

Day, A., Sibley, A., Tallon, J.M., & Ackroyd-Stolarz, S. (2009). Workplace risks and stressors as predictors of burnout: The moderating impact of job control and team efficacy. *Canadian Journal of Administrative Sciences, 26*(1), 7–22.

De Beauvoir, S. (1952). *The second sex.* New York, NY: Alfred A Knopf, Inc.

Deci, E.L., Koestner, R., & Ryan, R. (2001). Extrinsic rewards and intrinsic motivation in education: Reconsidered once again. *Review of Educational Research, 71*(1), 1–27.

Deery, S., Iverson, R., & Walsch, J. (2002). Work relationships in telephone call centres: Understanding emotional exhaustion and employee withdrawal. *Journal of Management Studies, 39*(4), 471–496.

Delamont, S., and Atkinson, P. (2004), Qualitative Research and the Postmodern Turn. In C. Hardy and A. Bryman (Eds), *Handbook of data analysis.* London, UK: Sage.

Delamont, S., & Hamilton, D. (1984). Revisiting classroom research: A continuing cautionary tale. In S. Delamont (Ed.), *Readings on interaction in the classroom.* London, UK: Methuen.

Delbridge, R.(1998). *Life on the line in contemporary manufacturing.* Oxford: Oxford University Press.

Delios, A., & Ensign, P.C. (2000). A subnational analysis of Japanese direct investment in Canada. *Canadian Journal of Administrative Sciences, 17*, 38–51.

DeLorme, D.E., Zinkhan, G.M., & French, W. (2001). Ethics and the internet: Issues associated with qualitative research. *Journal of Business Ethics, 33*, 271–86.

Denzin, N. (1968). On the ethics of disguised observation. *Social Problems, 15*, 502–504.

———. (1970). *The research act in sociology.* Chicago, IL: Aldine.

Denzin, N. (1994). Evaluating qualitative research in the poststructural moment: The lessons James Joyce teaches us. *International Journal of Qualitative Studies in Education, 7*, 295–308.

Denzin, N.K., & Lincoln, Y.S. (2000). *Handbook of qualitative research* (2nd ed.). Thousand Oaks, CA: Sage.

Diener, E., & Crandall, R. (1978). *Ethics in social and behavioral research.* Chicago, IL: University of Chicago Press.

Dillman, D.A. (1983). Mail and other self-administered questionnaires. In P.H. Rossi, J.D. Wright, & A.B. Anderson (Eds), *Handbook of Survey Research.* Orlando, FL: Academic Press.

Dingwall, R. (1980). Ethics and ethnography. *Sociological Review, 28*, 871–891.

Ditton, J. (1977). *Part-time crime: An ethnography of fiddling and pilferage.* London, UK: Macmillan.

Dommeyer, C.J., & Moriarty, E. (2000). Comparison of two forms of an e-mail survey: Embedded vs attached. *International Journal of Market Research, 42*, 39–50.

Donaldson, L. (1985). *In defence of organization theory.* Cambridge, MA: Cambridge University Press.

———. (1996). *For positivist organization theory.* Thousand Oaks, CA: Sage.

Dong-Young, K., Kumar, V., & Murphy, S.A. (2008). European foundation for quality management (EFQM) business excellence model: A literature review and future research agenda. In B.S. Deo (Ed.), *Proceedings of the Annual Conference of the Administrative Sciences Association of Canada, Production and Operations Management Division.* Halifax, NS: ASAC.

Dorsey, E.R., Steeves, H.L., & Porras, L.E. (2004). Advertising ecotourism on the Internet: Commodifying environment and culture. *New Media and Society, 6,* 753–779.

Dougherty, D., & Kunda, G. (1990). Photograph analysis: A method to capture organizational belief systems. In P. Gagliardi (Ed.), *Symbols and artifacts: Views of the corporate landscape.* Berlin: DeGruyter.

Douglas, J.D. (1976). *Investigative social research: Individual and team field research.* Beverly Hills, CA: Sage.

Durepos, G. (2009). *Anti-history: Toward an historiographical approach to (re)assembling knowledge of the past* (Unpublished doctoral dissertation). Saint Mary's University, Halifax, NS.

Durepos, G., Helms Mills, J., & Mills, A.J. (2008a). Flights of fancy: Myth, monopoly and the making of Pan American Airways. *Journal of Management History, 14*(2), 116–127.

———, ———, & ———. (2008b). The Pan American Dream and the myth of the pioneer. In M. Kostera (Ed.), *Organizational Epics and Sagas: Tales of Organizations* (pp. 131–143). London, UK: Routledge.

———, ———, & ———. (2008c). Tales in the manufacture of knowledge: Writing a company history of Pan American World Airways, *Management & Organizational History, 3*(1), 63–80.

Durkheim, E. (1938). *The rules of sociological method* (S.A. Solavay & J.H. Mueller, Trans). New York, NY: Free Press. (Original work published 1895)

Dye, K., & Mills, A.J. (2005). Engaging Acker: Toward an understanding of the gendered organization. In B. Sharma (Ed.), *Proceedings of the 35th annual meeting of the Atlantic Schools of Business, Halifax* (pp. 89–97).

———, & ———. (2011). Pleading the fifth: Refocussing Acker's gendered substructure through the lens of organizational logic. *Equal Opportunities International* (in press).

Dyer, W.G., & Wilkins, A.L. (1991). Better stories, not better constructs, to generate better theory: A rejoinder to Eisenhardt. *Academy of Management Review, 16,* 613–619.

Easterby-Smith, M., Thorpe, R., & Lowe, A. (1993). *Management research: An introduction.* London, UK: Sage.

Eden, C. (1988). Cognitive mapping: A review. *European Journal of Operational Research, 36,* 1–13.

Eden, C. (1992). On the status of cognitive maps. *Journal of Management Studies, 29*(3), 261–265.

Eden, C., & Huxham, C. (1996). Action research for management research. *British Journal of Management, 7*(1), 75–86.

Edwards, P., Collinson, M., & Rees, C. (1998). The determinants of employee responses to total quality management: Six case studies. *Organization Studies, 19*(3), 449–475.

Edwards, R. (1979). *Contested terrain.* New York, NY: Basic Books.

Eichler, M., & Lapointe, J. (1985). *On the Treatment of the Sexes in Research.* Ottawa, ON: Social Sciences and Humanities

Eisenhardt, K.M. (1989). Building theories from case study research. *Academy of Management Review, 14,* 532–550.

Eisenstadt, S.N. (1980) Cultural orientations, institutional entrepreneurs and social change: Comparative analyses of traditional civilizations. *American Journal of Sociology, 85,* 840–69.

Elliott, H. (1997). The use of diaries in sociological research on health experience. *Sociological Research Online, 2,* www.socresonline.org.uk/socresonline/2/2/7.html

Ellis, C. (2004). *The ethnographic I: A methodological novel about teaching and doing autoethnography.* Walnut Creek, CA: AltaMira.

Ellis, R., & McCutcheon, J. (2000). The evolution of management education in a small Canadian university: The School of Business and Economics at Wilfrid Laurier University. In B. Austin (Ed.), *Capitalizing knowledge.* Toronto: University of Toronto Press.

Erikson, K.T. (1967). A comment on disguised observation in sociology. *Social Problems, 14,* 366–373.

Esterberg, K.G. (2002). *Qualitative methods in social research.* Boston, MA: McGraw-Hill.

Evans, M., Wedande, G., Ralston, L., & van't Hul, S. (2001). Consumer interaction in the virtual era: Some qualitative insights. *Qualitative Market Research, 4,* 150–159.

Fairclough, N. (1992). *Discourse and social change.* Cambridge, UK: Polity Press.

———. (1995). *Critical discourse analysis: The critical study of language.* New York, NY: Longman.

———. (2003). *Analysing discourse: Textual analysis for social research.* London, UK: Routledge.

Faulkner, X., & Culwin, F. (2005). When fingers do the talking: A study of text messaging. *Interacting with Computers, 17,* 167–185.

Felstead, A., Gallie, D., & Green, F. (2002). *Work skills in Britain.* Nottingham, UK: DFES Publications.

Fern, E.F. (2001). *Advanced focus group research.* Thousand Oaks, CA: Sage.

Fey, C.F., & Denison, D.R. (2003). Organizational culture and effectiveness: Can American theory be applied in Russia? *Organization Science, 14*(6), 686–706.

Fiedler, E.E. (1967). *A theory of leadership effectiveness.* New York, NY: McGraw-Hill.

Fielding, N., & Lee, R.M. (1998). *Computer analysis and qualitative research.* London, UK: Sage.

Filmer, P., Phillipson, M., Silverman, D., & Walsh, D. (1972). *New directions in sociological theory.* London, UK: Collier-Macmillan.

Finch, J. (1984). 'It's great to have someone to talk to': The ethics and politics of interviewing women. In C. Bell & H. Roberts (Eds), *Social researching: Politics, problems, practice.* London, UK: Routledge & Kegan Paul.

———. (1987). The vignette technique in survey research. *Sociology, 21,* 105–114.

Fine, G.A. (1996). Justifying work: Occupational rhetorics as resources in kitchen restaurants. *Administrative Science Quarterly, 41,* 90–115.

Fischer, E., & Arnold, S.J. (1994). Sex, gender identity, gender role attitudes, and consumer behavior. *Psychology and Marketing, 11*(2), 163–182.

Flanagan, J.C. (1954). The critical incident technique. *Psychological Bulletin, 1*, 327–358.

Fletcher, J. (1966). *Situation Ethics*. London, UK: SCM Press.

Foran, S.J., & Driscoll, C. (2008). Rethinking motivations for charitable giving. *Proceeding of the 2008 Administrative Sciences Association of Canada, Social Responsibility Interest Group, Halifax, May 24–27, 29*, 37–54.

Forster, N. (1994). The analysis of company documentation. In C. Cassell & G. Symon (Eds), *Qualitative methods in organizational research*. London: Sage.

Foucault, M. (1974). *The order of things: An archaeology of the human sciences*. New York, NY: Vintage.

———. (1977). *The history of sexuality* (Vol. 1). New York, NY: Vintage Books.

———. (1978). *Discipline and punish: The birth of the prison*. New York, NY: Vintage Books.

———. (1988). Technologies of the self. In L.M. Martin, H. Gutman, & P.H. Hutton (Eds), *Technologies of the Self* (pp. 16–49). Amherst, MA: University of Massachusetts Press.

Fowler, F. J. (1993). *Survey research methods* (2nd ed.). Newbury Park, CA: Sage.

Fowler, F.J., & Mangione, T.W. (1990). *Standardized survey interviewing: Minimizing interviewer-related error*. Beverly Hills, CA: Sage.

Franzosi, R. (1995). Computer-assisted content-analysis of newspapers: Can we make an expensive research tool more efficient? *Quantity and Quality, 29*(2), 157–72.

Freeman, C. (2000). *High tech and high heels in the global economy: Women, work and pink-collar identities in the Caribbean*. Durham, NC: Duke University Press.

Frege, C.M. (2005). Varieties of industrial relations research: Take-over, convergence or divergence? *British Journal of Industrial Relations, 43*(2), 179–207.

Friedland, R., & Alford, R.R. (1991) Bringing society back in: Symbols, practices and institutional contradictions. In W.W. Powell and P.J. DiMaggio (Eds.), *The New Institutionalism in Organizational Analysis* (pp. 232–263). Chicago, IL: University of Chicago Press.

Friedman, P.A., Dyke, L.S., & Murphy, S.A. (2007). Making sense of nonesense in Hong Kong. *Proceeding of the 2007 Administrative Sciences Association of Canada, International Business Division*, Ottawa, 2–5 June 28(8), 68–83.

Fritzsche, D.J. (1988). An examination of marketing ethics: Role of the decision maker, consequences of the decision, management position, and sex of the respondent. *Journal of Macromarketing, 8*, 29–39.

Gabriel, Y. (1998). The use of stories. In G. Symon & C. Cassell (Eds), *Qualitative methods and analysis in organizational research: A practical guide*. Thousand Oaks, CA: Sage.

Gallupe, R.B., Dennis, A.R., Cooper, W.H., Valacich, J.S., Bastianutti, L.M., & Nunamaker, J.F. (1992). Electronic brainstorming and group size. *Academy of Management Journal, 35*, 350–369.

Galton, M., Simon, B., & Croll, P. (1980). *Inside the primary classroom*. London, UK: Routledge & Kegan Paul.

Gans, H.J. (1962). *The urban villagers*. New York, NY: Free Press.

———. The participant-observer as human being: Observations on the personal aspects of field work. In H.S. Becker (Ed.), *Institutions and the person: Papers presented to Everett C. Hughes*. Chicago, IL: Aldine.

Garfinkel, H. (1967). *Studies in ethnomethodology*. Englewood Cliffs, NJ: Prentice-Hall.

Geertz, C. (1973a). Thick description: Toward an interpretive theory of culture. In C. Geertz, *The interpretation of cultures*. New York, NY: Basic Books.

Gephart, R.P. (1988). *Ethnostatistics: Qualitative foundations for quantitative research*. Newbury Park, CA: Sage.

———. (1993). The textual approach: Risk and blame in disaster sensemaking. *Academy of Management Journal, 36*(6), 1465–1514.

———. (1997). Hazardous measures: An interpretive textual analysis of quantitative sensemaking during crisis. *Journal of Organizational Behavior, 18*, 583–622.

———. (2010). Ethnostatistics. In A.J. Mills, G. Durepos, & E. Weibe (Eds), *Sage encyclopedia of case study research* (Vol. I, 353–355). Thousand Oaks, CA: Sage.

Gersick, C.J. (1994). Pacing strategic change: The case of a new venture. *Academy of Management Journal, 37*(1), 9–45.

Gherardi, S., & Turner, B. (1987). Real men don't collect soft data. *Quaderno, 13*, Department of Social Policy: University of Trento.

Ghobadian, A., & Gallear, D. (1997). TQM and organization size. *International Journal of Operations and Production Management, 17*(2), 121–63.

Gibbons, M., Limoges, C., Nowotny, H., Schwartzman, S., Scott, P., & Trow, M. (1994). *The new production of knowledge*. London: Sage.

Gibson, D.R. (2005). Taking turns and talking ties: Networks and conversational interaction. *American Journal of Sociology, 110*(6), 1561–1597.

Gilbert, G.N. (1977). Referencing as persuasion. *Social Studies of Science, 7*, 113–122.

Gilbert, G.N., & Mulkay, M. (1984). *Opening Pandora's box: A sociological analysis of scientists' discourse*. Cambridge, UK: Cambridge University Press.

Gill, R. (1996). Discourse Analysis: Practical Implementation. In J.T. Richardson (Ed.), *Handbook of qualitative research methods for psychology and the social sciences*. Leicester, UK: BPS Books.

———. (2000) *Discourse analysis*. In M.W. Bauer & G. Gaskell (Eds.) *Qualitative research with text, image and sound*. London, UK: Sage.

Glaser, B.G., & Strauss, A.L. (1967). *The discovery of grounded theory: Strategies for qualitative research*. New York, NY: Aldine.

Glock, C.Y. (1988). Reflections on doing survey research. In H.J. O'Gorman (Ed.), *Surveying social life*. Middletown, CT: Wesleyan University Press.

Goerzen, A.R.(1999). The relationship between social and economic performance. *Proceeding of the 1999 Administrative*

Sciences Association of Canada, Organizational Behaviour Division, Saint John, NB, 20 (8), 49–59.

Goffman, E. (1956). *The presentation of self in everyday life.* New York, NY: Doubleday.

Gold, R.L. (1958). Roles in sociological fieldwork. *Social Forces, 36,* 217–223.

Goldman, P. (1994). Searching for history in organizational theory: Comment on Kieser. *Organization Science, 5,* 621–623.

Goldthorpe, J.H., Lockwood, D., Bechhofer, F., & Platt, J. (1968). *The affluent worker: Industrial attitudes and behaviour.* Cambridge: Cambridge University Press.

Goodall, H.L. (1994). *Casing the promised land: The autobiography of an organizational detective as cultural ethnographer.* Carbondale, IL: Southern Illinois University Press.

———. (2000). *Writing the new ethnography.* Walnut Creek, CA: AltaMira Press.

Goode, E. (1996). The ethics of deception in social research: A case study. *Qualitative Sociology, 19,* 11–33.

Gorard, S. (2002). Ethics and equity: Pursuing the perspective of non-participants. *Social Research Update, 39.*

Grandy, G. (2010). Conversation analysis. In A.J. Mills, G. Durepos, & E. Weibe (Eds), *Sage encyclopedia of case study research* (Vol. I, 238–241). Thousand Oaks, CA: Sage.

Grandy, G., & Wicks, D. (2003). What culture(s) exists in the tatooing collectivity? An exploration of socialization and cultural identities. *Proceeding of the 2003 Administrative Sciences Association of Canada, Organizational Theory Division, Halifax, June 14–17, 24* (22), 29–40.

———, & ———. (2008). Competitive advantage as a legitimacy-creating process. *Qualitative research in organizations and management: An international journal, 3*(1), 21–41.

Grant, D., Hardy, C., Oswick, C., & Putnam, L.L. (2004). Introduction: Organizational discourse: Exploring the field. In D. Grant, C. Hardy, C. Oswick, & L.L. Putnam (Eds), *The sage handbook of organizational discourse.* London, UK: Sage.

Grant, D., Keenoy, T., & Oswick, C. (1998). *Discourse and organization.* London, UK: Sage.

Greatbatch, D., & Clark, T. (2003). Displaying group cohesiveness: Humour and laughter in the public lectures of management gurus. *Human Relations, 56*(12), 1515–1544.

Greenberg, J., Baron, R.A., Sales, C.A., & Owen, F.A.(1996). *Behavior in organizations* (Canadian Edn). Scarborough, ON: Prentice Hall.

Grey, C., & Sinclair, A. (2006). Writing differently. *Organization, 13*(3), 443–453.

Griffin, R.W., Ebert, R.J., & Starke, F.A. (2002). *Business* (4th Canadian Edn). Toronto, ON: Prentice Hall.

Grint, K. (2000). *The arts of leadership.* Oxford, UK: Oxford University Press.

Grinyer, P.J., & Yasai-Ardekani, M., (1980) Dimensions of organizational structure: A critical replication. *Academy of Management Journal, 23,* 405–421.

Guba, E.G., (1985). The context of emergent paradigm research. In Y.S. Lincoln (Ed.), *Organization theory and inquiry: The paradigm revolution.* Beverly Hills, CA: Sage.

Guba, E.G., & Lincoln, Y.S. (1989). *Fourth Generation Evaluation.* Newbury Park, CA: Sage.

———, & ———. (1994). Competing Paradigms in Qualitative Research. In Denzin, N.K. & Lincoln, Y.S. (Eds), *Handbook of Qualitative Research* (pp. 105–117). Thousand Oaks, CA: Sage.

Gubrium, J.F., & Holstein, J.A. (1997). *The new language of qualitative method.* New York, NY: Oxford University Press.

Guest, D.E., & Dewe, P. (1991). Company or trade union? Which wins worker's allegiance? A study of commitment in the UK electronics industry. *British Journal of Industrial Relations, 29*(1), 73–96.

Gulli, C., Kohler, N., & Patriquin, M. (2009). *The great university cheating scandal.* Macleans.ca 2007 [cited 12 March 2009]. Available from http://www.macleans.ca/homepage/magazine/article.jsp?Content=20070209_174847_6984.

Gummesson, E. (2000). *Qualitative methods in management research.* London, UK: Sage.

Gusfield, J. (1976). The literary rhetoric of science: Comedy and pathos in drinking driving research. *American Sociological Review, 41,* 16–34.

Hackman, J., & Oldham, G. (1976). Motivation through the design of work: Test of a theory. *Organizational Behavior and Human Performance, 16*(2), 250–279.

———, & ———. (1980). *Work redesign.* Reading, MA: Addison-Wesley.

Hair, J.F., Babin, B., Money, A.H., & Samouel, P. (2003*). Essentials of business research methods.* Hoboken, NJ: John Wiley & Sons, Inc.

Halfpenny, P. (1979). The analysis of qualitative data. *Sociological Review, 27,* 799–825.

Hall, E. (1993). Smiling, deferring and flirting: Doing gender by giving good service. *Work and Occupations, 20*(4), 452–471.

Hammersley, M. (1992a). By what criteria should ethnographic research be judged? In M. Hammersley (Ed.), *What's wrong with ethnography?* London, UK: Routledge.

———. (1992b). Deconstructing the qualitative–quantitative divide. In M. Hammersley (Ed.), *What's wrong with ethnography?* London, UK: Routledge.

———. (1997). Qualitative data archiving: Some reflections on its prospects and problems. *Sociology, 31,* 131–142.

Hammersley, M., & Atkinson, P. (1995). *Ethnography: Principles in practice* (2nd ed.). London, UK: Routledge.

Hammond, P. (1964). *Sociologists at work.* New York, NY: Basic Books.

Haney, C., Banks, C., & Zimbardo, P. (1973). Interpersonal dynamics in a simulated prison. *International Journal of Criminology and Penology, 1,* 69–97.

Hantrais, L. (1996). Comparative research methods. *Social Research Update, 13.*

Hardy, C. (2001). Researching organizational discourse. *International Studies of Management and Organization, 31*(3), 25–47.

Hargadon, A.B. & Douglas, Y. (2001). When innovations meet

institutions: Edison and the design of the electric light. *Administrative Science Quarterly, 46*, 476–501.

Harris, H. (2001). Content analysis of secondary data: A study of courage in managerial decision making. *Journal of Business Ethics, 34*(3–4), 191–208.

Hartog, D.N., & Verburg, R.M. (1997). Charisma and rhetoric: Communicative techniques of international business leaders. *Leadership Quarterly, 8*(4), 355–391.

Hartt, C., Yue, A.R., Helms Mills J., & Mills, A.J. (2009). Method and disciplinary convention in the Administrative Sciences Association of Canada, 1978–2008: Implications for teaching and research. *Proceedings of the annual conference of the Atlantic Schools of Business conference*, Moncton, NB.

Haslam, C., & Bryman, A. (1994). The research dissemination minefield. In C. Haslam & A. Bryman (Eds), *Social scientists meet the media*. London: Routledge.

Hawkes, N. (2003, February 1). Close shaves beat death by a whisker. *The Times*, p. 6.

Healey, M.J., & Rawlinson, M.B. (1993). Interviewing business owners and managers: A review of methods and techniques. *Geoforum, 24*(3), 339–355.

Hearn, J. (2004). Personal resistance through persistence to organizational resistance through distance. In R. Thomas, A.J. Mills & J. Helms Mills (Eds), *Identity Politics At Work: Resisting Gender, Gendering Resistance* (pp. 40–63). London, UK: Routledge.

Hearn, J., & Parkin, P.W. (1983). Gender and organizations: A selective review and a critique of a neglected area. *Organization Studies, 4*(3), 219–242.

Helms Mills, J. (2000). *Sensemaking and the management of change: A longitudinal study of organisational change in Nova Scotia Power Department* (Doctoral dissertation). Behaviour in Organizations, Lancaster University.

———. (2002). Employment practices and the gendering of Air Canada's culture during its Trans Canada Airlines Days. *Culture and Organization, 8*(2), 117–128.

———. (2003). *Making Sense of Organizational Change*. London, Routledge.

Helms Mills, J., Weatherbee, T.G., & Colwell, S.C. (2004). An ethnostatistical study of how Canadian business schools use accreditation and media rankings as sensemaking devices. *Best Paper Proceedings of the Academy of Management annual conference*. New Orleans, LA.

———, ———, & ———. (2006). Ethnostatistics and sensemaking: Making sense of business school rankings. *Organizational Research Methods, 9*(4), 1–25.

Heritage, J. (1984). *Garfinkel and ethnomethodology*. Cambridge, MA: Polity.

———. (1987). *Ethnomethodology*. In *Giddens*, A., Turner, J. (Eds), *Social theory today* (pp. 224–72). Cambridge: Polity Press.

Herschovis, M.S., Turner, N., Barling, J., Inness, M., Leblanc, M.M., Arnold, K.A., Dupré, K.E., & Sivnathan, N. (2007). Predicting workplace aggression: A meta-analysis. *Journal of Applied Psychology, 92*(1), 228–238.

Herzberg, F., Mausner, B., & Snyderman, B.B. (1959). *The motivation to work* (2nd ed.). New York, NY: Wiley.

Hesse-Biber, S. (1995). Unleashing Frankenstein's monster? The use of computers in qualitative research. *Studies in Qualitative Methodology, 5*, 25–41.

Hewson, C., Yule, P., Laurent, D., & Vogel, C. (2003). *Internet research methods: A practical guide for the social and behavioural sciences*. London, UK: Sage.

Hilton, G. (1972). Causal inference analysis: A seductive process. *Administrative Science Quarterly, 17*(1), 44–54.

Hine, V. (2000). Virtual Ethnography. London: Sage.

Hinings, C.R., Ranson, S., & Bryman, A. (1976). Churches as organizations. In D.S. Pugh & C.R. Hinings (Eds), *Organizational structure: Extensions and replications, The Aston Programme II*. Farnborough, UK: Saxon House.

Hochschild, A.R. (1983). *The managed heart*. Berkeley and Los Angeles, CA: University of California Press.

———. (1989). *The second shift: Working parents and the revolution at home*. New York, NY: Viking.

Hodson, R. (1996). Dignity in the workplace under participative management. *American Sociological Review, 61*, 719–738.

Hofstede, G. (1984). *Culture's consequences: International differences in work related values*. Beverly Hills, CA: Sage.

Holdaway, E.A., Newberry, J.F., Hickson, D.J., & Heron, R.P. (1975). Dimensions of structure in complex societies: The educational sector. *Administrative Science Quarterly, 20*, 37–58.

Holliday, R. (1995). *Investigating small firms: Nice work?* London, UK: Routledge.

Hollway, W. (1989). *Subjectivity and method in psychology: Gender, meaning and science*. London, UK: Sage.

Holman Jones, S. (2005). Autoethnography: Making the personal political. In N.K. Denzin & Y.S. Lincoln (Eds), *Handbook of qualitative research* (3rd ed.). London, UK: Sage.

Holsti, O.R. (1969). *Content analysis for the social sciences and humanities*. Reading, MA: Addison-Wesley.

Homan, R. (1991). *The ethics of social research*. London, UK: Longman.

Hoque, K. (2003). All in all, it's just another plaque on the wall: The incidence and impact of the investors in people standard. *Journal of Management Studies, 40*(2), 543–571.

House, J. (1981). *Work stress and social support*. Reading, MA: Addison-Wesley.

Howell, J.M., & Frost, P.J. (1989). A laboratory study of charismatic leadership. *Organizational Behavior and Human Decision Processes, 43*, 243–269.

Huberman, A.M., & Miles, M.B. (1994). Data management and analysis methods. In N.K. Denzin, & Y.S. Lincoln (Eds), *Handbook of qualitative research*. Thousand Oaks: CA: Sage.

Hudson, J.M., & Bruckman, A.S. (2004). 'Go away': Participant objections to being studied and the ethics of chatroom research. *The Information Society, 20*, 127–139.

Hudson, S., Snaith, T., Miller, G., & Hudson, P. (2001). Distribution channels in the travel industry: Using mystery shoppers to understand the influence of travel agency recommendations. *Journal of Travel Research, 40*, 148–154.

Hughes, J.A. (1990). *The Philosophy of Social Research* (2nd ed.). Harlow, UK: Longman.

Humble, Å.M. (2010). Computer-based analysis of qualitative data: MAXQDA 2007. In A.J. Mills, G. Durepos, & E. Wiebe (Eds), *Sage encyclopedia of case study research*. Thousand Oaks, CA: Sage.

Hurst, D. (1995). Improving on extant theories of change in organizational interpretive schemes: The case of work/family initiatives. *Proceeding of the 1995 Administrative Sciences Association of Canada, Organization Theory Division*, Windsor, 3–6 June 16(13), 48–57.

Hurworth, R., & Shrimpton, B. (2007). Review of hyperresearch 2.7 for qualitative data analysis and hypertranscribe 1.0 for transcribing audio and video files. *Qualitative Research Journal, 6*(2), 191–201.

Hutt, R.W. (1979). The focus group interview: A technique for counseling small business clients. *Journal of Small Business Management, 17*(1), 15–20.

Huxley, P., Evans, S., Gately, C., Webber, M., Mears, A., Pajak, S., . . . Catona, C. (2005). Stress and pressures in mental health social work: The worker speaks. *British Journal of Social Work, 35*, 1063–1079.

Hycner, R.H. (1985). Some guidelines for the phenomenological analysis of interview data. *Human Studies, 8*, 279–303.

Insch, G., Moore, J., & Murphy, L. (1997). Content analysis in leadership research: Examples, procedures and suggestions for future use. *Leadership Quarterly, 8*(1), 1–25.

Isabelle, D.A., & Heslop, L.A. (2006). The business of international scientific collaborations: How is Canada perceived? *Proceeding of the 2006 Administrative Sciences Association of Canada, technology & inovative management division*, Banff, 3–6 June 27 (25), 110–123.

Jackall, R. (1988). *Moral mazes: The world of the corporate manager*. Oxford, UK: Oxford University Press.

Jackson, B. (2001). *Management gurus and management fashions*. London, UK: Routledge.

Jackson, N., & Carter, P. (1991). In defence of paradigm incommensurability. *Organization Studies, 12*(1), 109–127.

Jacques, S.R. (2010). Discourse Analysis. In A.J. Mills, G. Durepos, & E. Wiebe (Eds), *Sage encyclopedia of case study research* (Vol. 1, pp. 304–308). Thousand Oaks, CA: Sage.

Jakobsen, C.H., & McLaughlin, W.J. (2004). Communication in ecosystem management: A case study of cross-disciplinary integration in the assessment of the Interior Columbia Basin Ecosystem Management Project. *Environmental Management, 33*, 591–605.

Jalajas, D.S., & Bommer, M. (1996). The effect of downsizing on the behaviors and motivations of survivors. *Organization Development Journal, 14*(2), 45–54.

Jamieson, C., Grant, G., Gonsalves, S., & Vedmani, V. (2007). Characteristics and expectations of ES-induced technological change in a higher education setting. *Proceeding of the 2007 Administrative Sciences Association of Canada, Information Systems*, Ottawa, June 2–5, 28 (4), 34–51.

Janis, I.L. (1982). *Groupthink: Psychological studies of policy decisions and fiascos* (2nd ed.). Boston, MA: Houghton-Mifflin.

Jenkins, G.D., Nader, D.A., Lawler, E.E., & Cammann, C. (1975). Standardized observations: An approach to measuring the nature of jobs. *Journal of Applied Psychology, 60*, 171–181.

John, I.D. (1992). Statistics as rhetoric in psychology. *Australian Psychologist, 27*, 144–149.

Johns, G., Xie, J., & Fang, Y. (1992). Mediating and moderating effects in job design. *Journal of Management, 18*(4), 657–676.

Johnson, P., & Duberley, J. (2000). *Understanding Management Research*. London, UK: Sage.

———. & ———. (2003). Reflexivity in management research. *Journal of Management Studies, 40*(5), 1279–1303.

Jones, G. (1983). Life history methodology. In G. Morgan (Ed.), *Beyond method: Strategies for social research*. London, UK: Sage.

Kabanoff, B., Waldersee, R., & Cohen, M. (1995). Espoused values and organizational change themes. *Academy of Management Journal, 38*(4), 1075–1104.

Kalimo, R., Taris, T.W., & Schauf eli, W.B. (2003). The effects of past and anticipated future downsizing on survivor well-being: An equity perspective. *Journal of Occupational Health Psychology, 8*, 91–109.

Kanter, R.M. (1977). *Men and women of the corporation*. New York, NY: Basic Books.

Katila, S., & Merilainen, S. (1999). A serious researcher or just another nice girl? Doing gender in a male-dominated scientific community. *Gender, Work & Organization, 6*(3), 163–173.

———, & ———. (2002). Self in research: Hopelessly entangled in the gendered organizational culture. In I. Aaltio & A.J. Mills (Eds), *Gender, identity and the culture of organizations* (pp. 185–200). London, UK: Routledge.

Keenoy, T., Oswick, C., & Grant, D. (1997). Organizational discourses: Text and context. *Organization, 2*, 147–158.

Kelley, E.S., Mills, A.J., & Cooke, B. (2006). Management as a Cold War phenomenon? *Human Relations, 59*(5), 603–610.

Kelly, L. (1994). A narrative model: Interpreting strategy through annual reports. *Proceeding of the 1994 Administrative Sciences Association of Canada, Policy Division*, Halifax, 25–28 June 15(6), 50–59.

Kelly, L., Burton, S., & Regan, L. (1994). Researching women's lives or studying women's oppression? Reflections on what constitutes feminist research. In M. Maynard and J. Purvis (Eds), *Researching women's lives from a feminist perspective*. London, UK: Taylor & Francis.

Kelsey, B.L., & Siegel, J.P.(1996). The dynamics of multicultural groups: Ethnicity as a determinant of leadership. *Proceeding of the 1996 Administrative Sciences Association of Canada, organizational behaviour division*, Montreal, 25–28 June 17(5), 59–68.

Kendall, L. (1999). Recontextualizing 'cyberspace': Methodological considerations for on-line research. In S. Jones (Ed.), *Doing internet research: Critical issues and methods for examining the net.* Thousand Oaks, CA: Sage.

Kent, R., & Lee, M. (1999). Using the internet for market research: A study of private trading on the internet. *Journal of the Market Research Society, 41,* 377–85.

Khoury, N., Savor, M., & Toffoli, R. (2006). Le couverture des risques financiers par les PME Québécoises, *Canadian Journal of Administrative Science, 23*(1), 67–80.

Khurana, R. (2007). *From higher aims to hired hands. The social transformation of American business schools and the unfulfilled promise of management as a profession.* Princeton: Princeton University Press.

Kiely, T. (1998). Wired focus groups. *Harvard Business Review, 1,* 12–16.

Kim, D.Y., Kumar, V., & Murphy, S.A. (2008). European Foundation for Quality Management (EFQM) Business Excellence Model: A literature review and future research agenda. *Proceeding of the 2008 Administrative Sciences Association of Canada, Production and Operations Management,* Halifax, 24–27 May, 31–48.

Kinsella, E.A. (2006). Hermeneutics and critical hermeneutics: Exploring possibilities within the art of interpretation. *Forum Qualitative Sozialforschung / Forum: Qualitative Social Research, 7,* http://nbn-resolving.de/urn:nbn:de:0114-fqs0603190.

Kirby, S.L., & McKenna, K. (1989). *Experience, research, social change: Methods from the margins.* Toronto, ON: Garamond.

Kirk, J., & Miller, M.L. (1986). *Reliability and validity in qualitative research.* Newbury Park, CA: Sage.

Kitchenham, A.D. (2010). Mixed methods in case study research. In Mills, A.J., Durepos, G., & Weibe, E. (Eds), *Sage encyclopedia of case study research.* Thousand Oaks, CA: Sage.

Kitzinger, J. (1994). The methodology of focus groups: The importance of interaction between research participants. *Sociology of Health and Illness, 16,* 103–21.

Kivits, J. (2005). Online interviewing and the research relationship. In C. Hine (Ed.), *Virtual methods: Issues in social research on the internet.* Oxford: Berg.

Knight, K., & Latreille, P. (2000). Discipline, dismissals and complaints to employment tribunals. *British Journal of Industrial Relations, 38*(4), 533–555.

Knights, D., & McCabe, D. (1997). How would you measure something like that?: Quality in a retail bank. *Journal of Management Studies, 34*(3), 371–388.

Konrad, A.M., Prasad, P., & Pringle, J.K. (Eds). (2005). *Handbook of workplace diversity.* London, UK: Sage.

Korkie, B., & Turtle, H. (1998). The Canadian investment opportunity set, 1967–1993. *Canadian Journal of Administrative Sciences, 15,* 213–229.

Kostova, T., and Roth, K. (2002). Adoption of an organizational practice by subsidiaries of multinational corporations: Institutional and relational effects. *Academy of Management Journal, 45,* 215–33.

Kring, A.M., Smith, D., & Neale, J. (1994). Individual differences in dispositional expressiveness: Development and validation of the emotional expressivity scale. *Journal of Personality and Social Psychology, 66,* 934–949.

Kristof-Brown, A. (2000). Perceived applicant fit: Distinguishing between recruiters' perceptions of person–job and person–organization fit. *Personnel Psychology, 53,* 643–671.

Krueger, R.A. (1998). *Moderating focus groups.* Thousand Oaks, CA: Sage.

Kunda, G. (1992). *Engineering culture: Control and commitment in a high-tech corporation.* Philadelphia, PA: Temple University Press.

Kvale, S. (1996). *InterViews: An introduction to qualitative research interviewing.* Thousand Oaks, CA: Sage.

Lajili, K., & Zéghal, D. (2005). A content analysis of risk management disclosures in Canadian annual reports. *Canadian Journal of Administrative Sciences, 22*(2), 125–142.

Lapiere, R.T. (1934). Attitudes vs. actions. *Social Forces, 13,* 230–237.

Latour, B. (1987). *Science in action: How to follow scientists and engineers through society.* Cambridge, MA: Harvard University Press.

Law, J. (1994). *Organizing modernity.* Oxford: Blackwell Publishers.

Lawrence, P.R., & Lorsch, J.W. (1967). *Organization and environment.* Boston: Addison Wesley.

Lazarsfeld, P. (1958). Evidence and inference in social research. *Daedalus, 87,* 99–130.

Lazarus, R.S., & Folkman, S. (1984). *Stress, appraisal, and coping.* New York, NY: Springer.

Leblebici, H., Salancik, G.R., Copay, A., and King, T. (1991). Institutional change and the transformation of the U.S. radio broadcasting industry. *Administrative Science Quarterly, 36,* 333–6.

Lecompte, M.D., & Goetz, J.P. (1982). Problems of reliability and validity in ethnographic research. *Review of Educational Research, 52,* 31–60.

Lee, C.K. (1998). *Gender and the South China miracle: Two worlds of factory women.* Berkeley and Los Angeles, CA: University of California Press.

Lee, R.M. (2000). *Unobtrusive methods in social research.* Buckingham: Open University Press.

Leidner, R. (1993). *Fast food, fast talk: Service work and the routinization of everyday life.* Berkeley and Los Angeles, CA: University of California Press.

Lewin, K., Lippitt, R., & White, R.K. (1939). Patterns of aggressive behavior in experimentally created 'social climates'. *Journal of Social Psychology, 10,* 271–299.

Lewis, R.B. (2004). Nvivo 2.0 and Atlas.ti 5.0: Comparative review of two popular qualitative data-analysis programs. *Field Methods, 16*(4), 439–469.

Liff, S., & Steward, F. (2001). Community e-gateways: Locating networks and learning for social inclusion. *Information, Communication and Society, 4*(3), 317–340

Lightstone, K., & Driscoll, C. (2008). Disclosing elements of disclosure: A test of legitimacy theory and company ethics. *Canadian Journal of Administrative Science, 25*(1), 7–21.

Lincoln, Y.S., & Guba, E. (1985). *Naturalistic inquiry*. Beverly Hills, CA: Sage.

Linstead, S. (1985). Jokers wild: The importance of humour and the maintenance of organizational culture. *Sociological Review, 33*(4), 741–767.

———. (1993). From postmodern anthropology to deconstructive ethnography. *Human Relations, 46*(1), 97–120.

Livingstone, S., & Lunt, P. (1994). *Talk on television: Audience participation and public debate*. London, UK: Routledge.

Locke, K. (1996). Rewriting the discovery of grounded theory after 25 years? *Journal of Management Inquiry, 5*, 239–245.

———. (2001). *Grounded theory in management research*. London, UK: Sage.

———. (2010) Abduction. In A.J. Mills, G. Durepos, & E. Wiebe (Eds), *Sage encyclopedia of case study research*. Thousand Oaks, CA: Sage.

Lofland, J., & Lofland, L. (1995). *Analyzing social settings: A guide to qualitative observation and analysis* (3rd ed.). Belmont, CA: Wadsworth.

Long, B., & Morris, E. (2008). *Beyond Corporate Board Representation: Understanding the Experience of Female Directors in Canada*. Workplace Review, July, 10–14. Retrieved from http://www.smu.ca/academic/sobey/workplacereview/jul2008/WPR_jul%2008.pdf

Lonkila, M. (1995). Grounded theory as an emergent paradigm for computer-assisted qualitative data analysis. In U. Kelle (Ed.), *Computer-aided qualitative data analysis*. London, UK: Sage.

Louhiala-Salminen, L. (2002). The fly's perspective: Discourse in the daily routine of a business manager. *English for Specific Purposes, 21*, 211–231.

Lounsbury, M. (2001) Institutional sources of practice variation: Staffing college and university recycling programs. *Administrative Science Quarterly, 46*, 29–56.

Lucas, R. (1997). Youth, gender and part-time work: Students in the labour process. *Work, Employment and Society, 11*, 595–614.

Lund, D. (2000). An empirical examination of marketing professionals' ethical behaviour in differing situations. *Journal of Business Ethics, 24*, 331–342.

Lupton, T. (1963). *On the shopfloor*. Oxford, UK: Pergamon Press.

Luthans, F. (2002b). Positive organizational behavior: Developing and managing psychological strengths. *Academy of Management Executive, 16*, 57–72.

Luthans, F., & Sommer, S.M. (1999). The impact of downsizing on workplace attitudes. *Group & Organization Management, 24*, 46–70.

Luthans, F., & Youssef, C.M. (2007). Emerging positive organizational behavior. *Journal of Management, 33*, 321–349.

McCall, M.J. (1984). Structured field observation. *Annual Review of Sociology, 10*, 263–282.

McClaren, P.G., Durepos, G., & Mills, A.J. (2009). Disseminating Drucker: Knowledge, Tropes and the North American management textbook. *Journal of Management History, 15*(4), 388–403.

McClaren, P.G., & Mills, A.J. (2008). A Product of 'His' Time? Exploring the Construct Of Managers in the Cold War Era. *Journal of Management History, 14*(4), 386–403.

McClelland, D.C. (1961). *The achieving society*. Princeton, NJ: Van Nostrand.

McClosky, D.N. (1985). *The rhetoric of economics*. Brighton, UK: Wheatsheaf.

McCracken, G.D. (1988). *The long interview*. Newbury Park, CA: Sage.

McDonald, G. (2000). Cross-cultural methodological issues in ethical research. *Journal of Business Ethics, 27*, 89–104.

McEnery, J., & Blanchard, P. (1999). Validity of multiple ratings of business student performance in a management simulation. *Human Resource Development Quarterly, 10*(2), 155–172.

McGowan, R. (1999). Managers balancing work and elder care advice versus experience: Empowerment and constraint. *Proceeding of the 1999 Administrative Sciences Association of Canada, Women in Management Division*, Saint John, NB, June 12–15, *20*(11), 12–21.

———. (2003). Organizational discourse: How managerial talk sustains and resists gendered organizational understandings. *Proceeding of the 2003 Administrative Sciences Association of Canada, Gender & Diversity in Organizations Division*, Halifax, 14–17 June, 132–142.

McKay, R.B. (2001). Changing role of women in education: Dialectic and duality of the organizational power ethos. *Canadian Journal of Administrative Science, 18*(3), 79–191.

McLeod, E.A., & Helms Mills, J. (2009). The story behind the water in Walkerton, Ontario. In E. Raufflet & A.J. Mills (Eds), *The dark side: Critical cases on the downside of business*. Sheffield: Greenleaf Publishing.

Macmillan, S. (2009). *Understanding the pieces of a life: An existential approach to the meaning of work* (Unpublished doctoral dissertation). Saint Mary's University, Halifax, NS.

Macquarrie, C. (2010). Theoretical saturation. In A.J. Mills, G. Durepos, & E. Wiebe (Eds), *Sage encyclopedia of case study research* (Vol. 2, pp. 927–929). Thousand Oaks, CA: Sage.

Mcquarrie, F.A.E. (2005). How the past is present(ed), A comparison of information on the Hawthorne studies in Canadian management and organizational behaviour textbooks. *Canadian Journal of Administrative Sciences, 22*(3), 230–242.

Madriz, M. (2000). Focus groups in feminist research. In N.K. Denzin & Y.S. Lincoln (Eds). *Handbook of qualitative research* (2nd ed.). Thousand Oaks, CA: Sage.

Mangabeira, W. (1995). Qualitative analysis and microcomputer software: Some reflections on a new trend in sociological research. *Studies in Qualitative Methodology, 5*, 43–61.

Mangione, T.W. (1995). *Mail surveys: Improving the quality*. Thousand Oaks, CA: Sage.

Mann, C., & Stewart, F. (2000). *Internet communication and qualitative research: A handbook for researching online*. London, UK: Sage.

Marechal, G. (2010). Autoethnography. In A.J. Mills, G. Durepos, & E. Wiebe (Eds), *Sage encyclopedia of case study research* (Vol. 1, pp. 43–45). Thousand Oaks, CA: Sage.

Marginson, P. (1998). The survey tradition in British industrial relations research: An assessment of the contribution of large-scale workplace and enterprise surveys. *British Journal of Industrial Relations, 36*(3), 361–388.

Markham, A. (1998). *Life online: Researching the real experience in virtual space*. London and Walnut Creek, CA: AltaMira Press.

Marsden, R. (1982). Industrial relations: A critique of empiricism. *Sociology, 16*(2), 232–250.

Marsh, C. (1982). *The survey method: The contribution of surveys to sociological explanation*. London, UK: Allen & Unwin.

Marsh, C., & Scarbrough, E. (1990). Testing nine hypotheses about quota sampling. *Journal of the Market Research Society, 32*, 485–506.

Marshall, J. (1984). *Women managers: Travellers in a male world*. Chichester, UK: Wiley.

———. (1995). *Women managers moving on: Exploring career and life choices*. London, UK: Routledge.

Martin, J. (2002). *Organizational Culture: Mapping the Terrain*. Thousand Oaks, CA: Sage.

Martin, P., & Bateson, P. (1986). *Measuring behaviour: An introductory guide*. Cambridge, UK: Cambridge University Press.

Martinko, M.J., & Gardner, W.L. (1990). Structured observation of managerial work: A replication and synthesis. *Journal of Management Studies, 27*(3), 329–357.

Mason, J. (1994). Linking qualitative and quantitative data analysis. In A. Bryman & R.G. Burgess (Eds), *Analyzing qualitative data*. London, UK: Routledge.

Martin, P.Y., & Turner, B.A. (1986). Grounded theory and organizational research. *Journal of Applied Behavioral Science, 22*(2), 141–157.

Matthewman, S., & Hoey, D. (2006). What happened to postmodernism? *Sociology, 40*, 529–547.

Mauthner, N.S., Parry, O., & Backett-Milburn, K. (1998). The data are out there, or are they? Implications for archiving and revisiting qualitative data. *Sociology, 32*, 733–745.

Mayer, T. (2009). *The plagiarism charges against Ward Churchill*. Retrieved from www.wardchurchill.net/files/mayer_on_plagiarism_charges_0607.pdf.

Maynard, M. (1998). Feminists' knowledge and the knowledge of feminisms: Epistemology, theory, methodology and method. In T. May & M. Williams (Eds), *Knowing the social world*. Buckingham, UK: Open University Press.

Mazutis, D., & Crossan, M. (2008). Strategic leadership and innovation: A multi-level perspective. In W.G. Rowe (Ed.), *Proceedings of the Annual Conference of the Administrative Sciences of Canada, Strategy Division*. Halifax, ASAC.

Mazza, C., & Alvarez, J.L. (1998). Haute couture and prêt-à-porter: The popular press and the diffusion of management practices. *Organization Studies, 21*(3), 567–588.

Merton, R. K. (1967). *On Theoretical Sociology*. New York, NY: Free Press.

Merton, R.K., Fiske, M., & Kendall, P.L. (1956). *The focused interview: A manual of problems and procedures*. New York, NY: Free Press.

Mies, M. (1993). Towards a methodology for feminist research. In M. Hammersley (Ed.), *Social research: Philosophy, politics and practice*. London, UK: Sage.

Miles, M.B. (1979). Qualitative data as an attractive nuisance. *Administrative Science Quarterly, 24*, 590–601.

Miles, M.B & Huberman, A.M. (1984). *Qualitative data analysis: A sourcebook of new methods*. London, UK: Sage.

Milgram, S. (1963). A behavioral study of obedience. *Journal of Abnormal and Social Psychology, 67*, 371–378.

———. (1974). *Obedience to authority*. London, UK: Tavistock.

Milgram, S., & Shotland, L. (1973). *Television and antisocial behavior: Field experiments*. New York, NY: Academic Press.

Milkman, R. (1997). *Farewell to the factory: Auto workers in the late twentieth century*. Berkeley and Los Angeles, CA: University of California Press.

Millen, D. (1997). Some methodological and epistemological issues raised by doing feminist research on non-feminist women. *Sociological Research Online, 2*, www.socresonline.org.uk/socresonline/2/3/3.html

Miller, D. (1990). *The Icarus paradox : how exceptional companies bring about their own downfall : New lessons in the dynamics of corporate success, decline, and renewal*. New York, NY: HarperCollins.

Miller, D., & Slater, D. (2000). *The internet: An ethnographic approach*. Oxford, UK: Berg.

Miller, R.L. (2000). *Researching life stories and family histories*. London, UK: Sage.

Mills, A.J. (2004). Feminist organizational analysis and the business textbook. In D.E. Hodgson, & C. Carter (Eds), *Management knowledge and the new employee* (pp. 30–48). London, UK: Ashgate.

———. (2006). *Sex, strategy and the stratosphere: Airlines and the gendering of organizational culture*. London, UK: Palgrave Macmillan.

———. (2008). Getting critical about sensemaking. In D. Barry, & H. Hansen (Eds), *The sage handbook of new approaches to organization studies*. London, UK: Sage.

———. (2010). Juncture. In A.J. Mills, G. Durepos, & E. Weibe (Eds), *Sage encyclopedia of case study research*. Thousands Oaks, CA: Sage.

Mills, A.J., Durepos, G., & Wiebe, E. (2010). *Sage encyclopedia of case study research*. Thousand Oaks, CA, Sage.

Mills, A.J., & Helms Mills, J.(1998). From imperialism to globalization: Internationalization and the management text. In S.R. Clegg, E. Ibarra, & L. Bueno (Eds), *Theories of the management process: Making sense through difference* (pp. 37–67). Thousand Oaks, CA: Sage.

———, & ———. (2004). When plausibility fails: Towards a critical sensemaking approach to resistance. In R. Thomas, A.J. Mills, & J. Helms Mills (Eds), *Identity politics at work: Resisting gender and gendered resistance* (pp. 141–159). London, UK: Routledge.

———, & ———. (2006). Masculinity and the making of Trans-Canada Air Lines, 1937–1940: A feminist poststructuralist account. *Canadian Journal of Administrative Sciences, 23*(1), 34–44.

Mills, A.J., Helms Mills, J., Bratton, J., & Foreshaw, C. (2007). *Organizational behaviour in a global context.* Peterborough, ON: Broadview Press.

Mills, A.J., Kelley, E., & Cooke, B. (2002). Management theory in context: Exploring the influence of the Cold War. In G. Spraakman (Ed.), *Proceedings of the Business History Division of the Administrative Sciences Association of Canada.* Winnipeg.

Mills, A.J., Simmons, T., & Helms Mills, J. (2005). *Reading organization theory: A critical approach to the study of organizational behaviour and structure* (3rd ed.). Toronto, ON: Garamond Press.

Mills, A.J., & Tancred, P. (1992). *Gendering organizational analysis.* Newbury Park, CA: Sage.

Mintzberg, H. (1973). *The Nature of Managerial Work.* New York, NY: Harper & Row.

———. (1987). The strategy concept II: Another look at why organizations need strategies. *California Management Review, 30*, 25–32.

Mintzberg, H., Brunet, J.P., & Waters, J.A. (1986). Does planning impede strategic thinking? Tracking the strategies of Air Canada from 1937 to 1976. In R. Lamb, & P. Shrivastava (Eds), *Advances in strategic management* (pp. 3–41). Greenwich, CT: JAI Press.

Mintzberg, H., & Rose, J. (2003). Strategic management upside down: Tracking strategies at McGill University from 1829 to 1980. *Canadian Journal of Administrative Sciences, 20*, 270–290.

Mirchandani, K. (1999). Feminist insight on gendered work: New directions in research on women and entrepreneurship. *Gender, Work and Organization, 6*(4), 224–235.

Mishler, E.g., (1986). *Research interviewing: Context and narrative.* Cambridge, MA: Harvard University Press.

Mitchell, J.C. (1983). Case and situation analysis. *Sociological Review, 31*, 186–211.

Mitchell, T. (1985). An evaluation of the validity of correlational research conducted in organizations. *Academy of Management Review, 10*(2), 192–205.

Morgan, D.L. (1998a). *Planning focus groups.* Thousand Oaks, CA: Sage.

———, (1998b). Practical strategies for combining qualitative and quantitative methods: Applications for health research. *Qualitative Health Research, 8*, 362–376.

Morgan, G. (1996). *Images of Organization* (2nd ed.). Thousand Oaks, CA: Sage.

Morrison, D.E. (1998). *The search for a method: Focus groups and the development of mass communication research.* Luton, UK: University of Luton Press.

Moser, C.A., & Kalton, G. (1971). *Survey methods in social investigation.* London, UK: Heinemann.

Mullen, J.E. (2004). Investigating factors that influence individual safety behaviour at work. *Journal of Safety Research, 35*, 275–285.

Mumby, D., & Clair, R. (1997). Organizational discourse. In T.A. Van Dijk (Ed.), *Discourse as social interaction: Discourse studies* (Vol. 2: A Multidisciplinary Introduction). Newbury Park, CA: Sage.

Murray, W.H., & Helms Mills, J. (2009). Finding space to breathe: Balancing control and freedom in call centres. *The Workplace Review, 3*(1), 22–27.

Neu, D., & Mahaffey, T. (1991). Alternative directions in the philosophy of management education. *Proceeding of the 1991 Administrative Sciences Association of Canada, Management Education Division,* St. Catherines, May 30–June 2, *12*(4), 15–22.

Newell, A., & Simon, H.A. (1972). *Human problem solving.* Englewood Cliffs, NJ: Prentice Hall.

Noblit, G.W., & Hare, R.D. (1988). *Meta-ethnography: Synthesizing qualitative studies.* Newbury Park, CA: Sage.

Nyland, C., & Heenan, T. (2005). Mary van Kleek, Taylorism and the control of management knowledge. *Management Decision, 43*(10), 1358–1374.

Nyland, C., & Rix, M. (2000). Mary van Kleek, Lillian Gilbreth and the women's bureau study of gendered labor law. *Journal of Management History, 6*(7).

Oakley, A. (1972). *Sex, gender and society.* London, UK: Temple Smith.

———. (1981). Interviewing women: A contradiction in terms. In H. Roberts (Ed.), *Doing Feminist Research.* London, UK: Routledge & Kegan Paul.

O'Connell, C., & Mills, A.J. (2003). Making sense of bad news: The media, sensemaking and organizational crisis. *Canadian Journal of Communication, 8*(3), 323–339.

O'Connor, H., & Madge, C. (2001). Cyber-mothers: Online synchronous interviewing using conferencing software. *Sociological Research Online, 2*, www.socresonline.org.uk/5/4/oconnor.html

O'Gorman, C., Bourke, S., & Murray, J.A. (2005). The nature of managerial work in small growth-oriented businesses. *Small Business Economics, 25*, 1–16.

Okely, J. (1994). Thinking through fieldwork. In A. Bryman, & R.G. Burgess (Eds), *Analyzing qualitative data.* London, UK: Routledge.

Orlikowski, W.J., & Yates, J. (1994). Genre Repertoire: The structuring of communicative practices in organizations. *Administrative Science Quarterly, 39*, 541–574.

Orton, J.D. (1997). From inductive to iterative grounded theory: Zipping the gap between process theory and process data. *Scandinavian Journal of Management, 13*(4), 419–438.

Oswick, C., Putnam, L. & Keenoy, T. (2004). Tropes, discourse and organizing. In D. Grant, C. Hardy, C. Oswick, & L. Putnam (Eds), *Handbook of organizational discourse.* London, UK: Sage.

Ouadahi, J. (2008). A qualitative anaysis of factors associated with users acceptance and rejection of a new workplace information system in the public sector: A conceptual Model. *Canadian Journal of Administrative Science, 25*(3), 201–213.

Palmer, A.D. (2010). Life History. In A.J. Mills, G. Durepos, & E. Weibe (Eds), *Sage encyclopedia of case study research* (Vol. 1, pp. 527–530). Thousand Oaks, CA: Sage.

Paré, G., Bourdeau, S., Marsan, J., Shuraida, S., & Nach, H. (2007). Re-examining the causal structure of information technology impact research: Some preliminary evidence. *Proceeding of the 2007 Administrative Sciences Association of Canada, Information Systems Division,* Ottawa, 2–5 June: 161–176.

Park, P. (1999). People, knowledge, and change in participatory research. *Management Learning, 30*(2), 141–157.

Park, S.H. (1996). Relationships between involvement and attitudinal loyalty constructs in adult fitness programmes. *Journal of Leisure Research, 28*(4), 233–50.

Parker, D., & Grandy, G. (2009). Looking to the past to understand the present: Organizational change in varsity. *Qualitative Research in Organizations and Management, 4*(3), 231–254.

Parker, I. (1992). *Discourse dynamics.* (London, UK: Routledge).

Parker, M. (2000). *Organizational culture and identity.* London, UK: Sage.

Parsons, D.B., & Mills, A.J. (2008). It's in the paper! Gendered order, change, and the role of the in-house magazine—Rotary International, 1985-2007. *Proceedings of the 24th Colloquium of the European Group for Organization Studies (EGOS),* Amsterdam, July 10–12.

Partington, D. (2000). Building grounded theories of management action. *British Journal of Management, 11,* 91–102.

Patel, V.N., & Riley, A.W. (2007). Linking data to decision-making: Applying qualitative data analysis methods and software to identify mechanisms for using outcomes data. *Journal of Behavioural Health Sciences & Research, 34,* 459–474.

Peñaloza, L. (2000). The commodification of the American west: Marketers' production of cultural meanings at the trade show. *Journal of Marketing, 64,* 82–109.

Peräkylä, A. (1997). Reliability and validity in research based on transcripts. In D. Silverman (Ed.), *Qualitative research: Theory, method and practice.* London, UK: Sage.

Perlow, L.A. (1995). *The time famine: The unintended consequences of the way time is used at work* (Unpublished doctoral thesis). Cambridge, MA: MIT.

———. (1999). Time famine: Toward a sociology of work time. *Administrative Science Quarterly, 44,* 57–81.

Peters, V. (2010). Computer-based analysis of qualitative data: kwalitan. In In A.J. Mills, G. Durepos, & E. Weibe (Eds), *Sage encyclopedia of case study research* (Vol. 1, pp. 527–530). Thousand Oaks, CA: Sage.

Pettigrew, A. (1985). *The awakening giant: Continuity and change in imperial chemical industries.* Oxford, UK: Blackwell.

———. (1990). Longitudinal field research on change: Theory and practice. *Organization Science, 1*(3), 267–292.

———. (1997). What is a processual analysis? *Scandinavian Journal of Management, 13,* 337–348.

Pettigrew, A., & McNulty, T. (1995). Power and influence in and around the boardroom. *Human Relations, 48*(8), 845–873.

Phillips, D.L. (1973). *Abandoning method.* San Francisco, CA: Jossey-Bass.

Phillips, N., & Brown, J.L. (1993). Analyzing communications in and around organizations: A critical hermeneutic approach. *Academy of Management Journal, 36,* 1547–1576.

Phillips, N. & Hardy, C. (2002) *Discourse analysis: Investigating processes of social construction.* Thousand Oaks, CA: Sage.

Piekkari, R., Welch, C., & Paavilainen, E. (2009). The case study as disciplinary convention: Evidence from international business journals. *Organizational Research Methods, 12*(3), 567–589.

Piercy, N.F., Harris, L.C., & Lane, N. (2002). Market orientation and retail operatives' expectations. *Journal of Business Research, 55,* 261–273.

Podsakoff, P.M., & Dalton, D.R. (1987). Research methodology in organizational studies. *Journal of Management, 13,* 419–44.

Poland, B.D. (1995). Transcription quality as an aspect of rigor in qualitative research. *Qualitative Inquiry, 1,* 290–310.

Pollert, A. (1981). *Girls, wives, factory lives.* London, UK: Macmillan.

———. (1985). *Unequal Opportunities: Racial Discrimination and the Youth Training Scheme.* [Pamphlet] Birmingham, UK: TURC Publishing.

Pondy, L., Frost, P., Morgan, G., & Dandridge, T. (1983). *Organizational symbolism.* London, UK: JAI Press.

Potter, J. (1997). Discourse analysis as a way of analysing naturally occurring talk. In D. Silverman (Ed.), *Qualitative research: Theory, method and practice.* London, UK: Sage.

Potter, J., & Wetherell, M. (1987). *Discourse and social psychology: Beyond attitudes and behaviour.* London, UK: Sage.

———, & ———. (1994). Analyzing discourse. In A. Bryman & R.G. Burgess (Eds). *Analyzing qualitative data.* London, UK: Routledge.

Powell, T.C. (1995). Total quality management as competitive advantage: A review and empirical study. *Strategic Management Journal, 16,* 15–37.

Prasad, A., & Mir, R. (2002). Digging deep for meaning: A critical hermeneutic analysis of CEO letters to shareholders in the oil industry. *Journal of Business Communication, 39,* 92–116.

Prasad, A., & Prasad, P. (2002). The coming of age of interpretive organizational research. *Organizational Research Methods, 5,* 4–11.

Prasad, P. (1993). Symbolic processes in the implementation of technological change: A symbolic interactionist study of work computerization. *Academy of Management Journal, 36*(6), 1400–1429.

———. (2005). *Crafting Qualitative Research. Working in the Postpositivist Traditions.* Armonk, NY: M.E. Sharpe.

Prasad, P., Pringle, J.K., & Konrad, A.M. (2005). Examining the contours of workplace diversity. In A.M. Konrad, P. Prasad,

& J.K. Pringle (Eds), *Handbook of workplace diversity* (pp.1–22). Thousand Oaks, CA: Sage.

Pratt, M.G. (2000). The good, the bad, and the ambivalent: Managing identification among Amway distributors. *Administrative Science Quarterly, 45*(3), 456–493.

Price, J.M. (2010a). Open coding. In A.J. Mills, G. Durepos, & E. Weibe (Eds), *Sage encyclopedia of case study research* (Vol. 1, pp. 527–530). Thousand Oaks, CA: Sage.

———. (2010b). Selective coding. In A.J. Mills, G. Durepos, & E. Weibe (Eds), *Sage encyclopedia of case study research.* Thousand Oaks, CA: Sage.

Pringle, R. (1988). *Secretaries talk: Sexuality, power and work.* London, UK: Verso.

Psathas, G. (1995). *Conversation analysis: The study of talk-in-interaction.* Thousand Oaks, CA: Sage.

Pugh, D.S., Hickson, D.J., Hinings, C.R., & Turner, C. (1968). Dimensions of organization structure. *Administrative Science Quarterly, 13*, 65–105.

Punch, M. (1994). Politics and ethics in qualitative research. In N.K. Denzin & Y.S. Lincoln (Eds), *Handbook of qualitative research.* Thousand Oaks, CA: Sage.

Putler, D.S., Li, T., & Liu, Y. (2007). The value of household life cycle variables in consumer expenditure research: An empirical examination. *Canadian Journal of Administrative Sciences / Revue Canadienne des Sciences de l'Administration, 24*(4), 284–299.

Rafaeli, A., Dutton, J., Harquail, C.V., & Mackie-Lewis, S. (1997). Navigating by attire: The use of dress by female administrative employees. *Academy of Management Journal, 40*, 9–45.

Ram, M. (1994). *Managing to survive: Working lives in small firms.* Oxford, UK: Blackwell.

Ramirez, I., & Bartunek, J. (1989). The multiple realities and experiences of internal organization development in healthcare. *Journal of Organizational Change Management, 2*(1), 40–57.

Raney, A.A., Arpan, L.M., Pashupati, K., & Brill, D.A. (2003). At the movies, on the web: An investigation of the effects of entertaining and interactive web content on site and brand evaluations. *Journal of Interactive Marketing, 17*(4), 38–53.

Rao, H., & Singh, J. (1999) Types of variation in organizational populations: The speciation of new organizational forms. In J.A. Baum & B. McKelvey (Eds), *Variations in Organizational Science* (pp. 63–77). Thousand Oaks, CA: Sage.

Reason, P. (1999). Integrating action and reflection through cooperative inquiry. *Management Learning, 30*(2), 207–226.

Reason, P., & Marshall, J. (1987). Research as personal process. In D. Boud & V. Griffin (Eds), *Appreciating adult learning.* London, UK: Kogan Page.

Reason, P., & Rowan, J. (Eds) (1981). *Human inquiry.* Chichester, UK: John Wiley.

Reay, T., Germann, K., Hinings, C.R., Golden-Biddle, K., & Casebeer, A. (2008). Building a foundation for organizational learning: Innovation in primary health care.

Proceeding of the Administrative Sciences Association of Canada, Health Care Management Division, Halifax, 24–27, *28,* 1–14.

Reed, M. (1985). *Redirections in organizational analysis.* London: Tavistock.

Reid, D.J., & Reid, F.J. (2005). Online focus groups: An in-depth comparison of computer-mediated and conventional focus group discussions. *International Journal of Market Research, 47*(2), 131–162.

Reinharz, S. (1988). Feminist Distrust: Problems of Context and Content in Sociological Work. In D.N. Berg & K.K Smith (Eds), *The Self in Social Inquiry.* Newbury Park, CA: Sage.

———. (1992). *Feminist methods in social research.* New York, NY: Oxford University Press.

Reiss, A.J. (1968). Stuff and nonsense about social surveys and participant observation. In H.S. Becker, B. Geer, D. Riesman, & R.S. Weiss (Eds), *Institutions and the person: Papers in memory of Everett C. Hughes.* Chicago, IL: Aldine.

Reissner, S.C. (2005). Learning and innovation: A narrative analysis. *Journal of Organizational Change Management, 18*(5), 482–494.

Rhodes, C., & Brown, A.D. (2005). Narrative, organizations and research. *International Journal of Management Research, 7*(3), 167–188.

Richards, L., & Richards, T. (1994). From filing cabinet to computer. In A. Bryman & R.G. Burgess (Eds), *Analyzing qualitative data.* London, UK: Routledge.

Richardson, L. (1990). Narrative and sociology. *Journal of Contemporary Ethnography, 19*, 116–135.

———. (1994), 'Writing: A Method of Inquiry', in N.K. Denzin and Y.S. Lincoln (Eds), *Handbook of Qualitative Research* (Thousand Oaks, Calif.: Sage).

Riessman, C.K. (1993). *Narrative analysis.* Newbury Park, CA: Sage.

Rixon, D., & Furey, M. (2009). Fire on the line: A stakeholder analysis of a telecommunication outage. The *Workplace Review, 3*(1), 13–21.

Roethlisberger, F.J., & Dickson, W.J. (1939). Management and the worker: An account of a research programme conducted by the Western Electric Company. *Hawthorne Works,* Cambridge, MA: Harvard University Press.

Roine, R., Ohinmaa, A., & Hailey, D. (2001). Assessing telemedicine: A systematic review of the literature. *Canadian Medical Association Journal, 165*(6), 765–777.

Romanelli, E. (1991) The evolution of new organizational forms. *Annual Review of Sociology, 17*, 79–103.

Rorty, R. (1979). *Philosophy and the mirror of nature.* Princeton, NJ: Princeton University Press.

Rose, M. (1978). *Industrial Behaviour.* Harmondsworth, UK: Penguin.

Rose-Anderssen, C., Baldwin, J., & Ridgway, K. (2010). Focus group interviews—The effects of communicative interactions on meaning construction in group discussions. *Qualitative Research in Organizations and Management,* Vol. 5(2), 196–215.

Rosen, M. (1991). Coming to terms with the field: Understanding and doing organizational ethnography. *Journal of Management Studies, 28*(1), 1–24.

Rosenau, P.M. (1992). Post-modernism and the social sciences: Insights, inroads, and intrusions. Princeton, NJ: Princeton University Press.

Rostis, A. (2010). Genealogy. In A.J. Mills, G. Durepos, & E. Wiebe (Eds), *The sage encyclopedia of case study research*. Thousand Oaks, CA: Sage.

Rostis, A., & Helms Mills, J. (2009). Critical incident: Organizational behaviour and the response to Hurricane Katrina. *Proceedings of the Case Track of the Administrative Sciences Association of Canada*, annual meeting, June.

Rousseau, D. (1985). Issues of level in organizational research: Multi-level and cross-Level perspectives. In L. Cummings & B. Staw (Eds), *Research in organizational behaviour* (Vol. 7). London, UK: JAI Press.

Rowe, W.G., Harris, I.C., Cannella, J., Albert, A., & Francolini, T. (2003). In search of meaning: Does the fortune reputation survey alter performance expectations? *Canadian Journal of Administrative Sciences, 20*(3), 187–195.

Rowlinson, M. (2002). Public history review essay. Cadbury World. *Labour History Review, 67*, 101–119.

———. (2004a). Historical analysis of company documents. In C. Cassell & G. Symon (Eds), *Essential guide to qualitative methods in organizational research*. London, Sage.

———. (2004b). Historical perspectives in organization studies: Factual, narrative, and archeo-genealogical. In D.E. Hodgson & C. Carter (Eds), *Management knowledge and the new employee*. Burlington, VT: Ashgate.

Roy, D. (1958). Banana time: Job satisfaction and informal interaction. *Human Organisation, 18*, 156–168.

Rubin, H.J., & Rubin, I.S. (1995). *Qualitative Interviewing: The art of hearing data*. Thousand Oaks, CA: Sage.

Ruef, M., & Scott, W.R. A multidimensional model of organizational legitimacy: Hospital survival in changing institutional environments. *Administrative Science Quarterly, 43*(4), 877–904.

Runté, M. (2005). *Labour and birth stories: A feminist post-structural reading of the discourse of work-family interaction* (Doctoral dissertation). Department of Management, Sobey School of Business: Saint Mary's University, Halifax, NS.

Runté, M., & Mills, A.J. (2002). The discourse of work–family conflict: A critique. (G. Miller Ed.). *Proceedings of the Gender and Diversity in Organization Division of the annual meeting of the Administrative Sciences Association of Canada*, Winnipeg, May 25–28.

———, & ———. (2002). Time after time: A feminist post-structuralist critique of the discourse of work–family conflict. *Proceedings of the Standing Conference on Organizational Symbolism*, Budapest, July.

———, & ———. (2004). Paying the toll: A feminist post-structural critique of the discourse bridging work and family. *Culture and Organization, 10*(3), 237–249.

Sackmann, S.A. (1992). Culture and subcultures: An analysis of organizational knowledge. *Administrative Science Quarterly, 37*(3), 363–399.

Sacks, H., Schegloff, E.A., & Jefferson, G. (1974). 'A simplest systematics for the organization of turn-taking in conversation. *Language, 50*, 696–735.

Salancik, G.R. (1979). Field stimulations for organizational behavior research. *Administrative Science Quarterly, 24*, 638–649.

Sarsby, J. (1984). The fieldwork experience. In R.F. Ellen (Ed.). *Ethnographic research: A guide to general conduct*. London, UK: Academic Press.

Sanjek, R. (1990). A vocabulary for fieldnotes. In R. Sanjek (Ed.), *Fieldnotes: The making of anthropology*. Ithaca, NY: Cornell University Press.

Savage, M. (2005). Working-class identities in the 1960s: Revisiting the affluent worker study. *Sociology, 39*(5), 929–46.

Scandura, T.A., & Williams, E.A. (2000). Research methodology in management: current practices, trends and implications for future research. *Academy of Management Journal, 43*(6), 1248–1264.

Scase, R., & Goffee, R. (1989). *Reluctant managers: Their work and lifestyles*. London, UK: Routledge.

Schegloff, E.A. (1997). Whose text? Whose context? *Discourse and Society, 8*, 165–187.

Schein, E.H. (1985). *Organizational Culture and Leadership*. San Francisco, CA: Jossey-Bass.

———. (1990). Organizational Culture. *American Psychologist, 45*(2), 109–119.

———. (1991). What is Culture?. In P.J. Frost, L.F. Moore, M.R. Louis, C.C. Lundberg, & J. Martin (Eds), *Reframing organizational culture* (pp. 243–253). Newbury Park, CA: Sage.

———. (1992). *Organizational Culture and Leadership*. San Francisco, CA: Jossey–Bass.

———. (2000). Sense and nonesense about culture and climate. In N.M. Ashkanasy, C.P. Wilderom, & M.F. Peterson (Eds), *Handbook of organizational culture & climate* (pp. xxiii–xxx). Thousand Oaks, CA: Sage.

Schein, V.E. (1975). Relationships between sex role stereotypes and requisite management characteristics among female managers. *Journal of Applied Psychology, 60*, 340–344.

———. (1978). Sex-role stereotyping, ability and performance: Prior research and new direction, *Personnel Psychology, 31*, 259–268.

Scherrer-Rathje, M., & Boyle, T.A. (2008). An end-user perspective of ERP flexibility. *Proceedings of the 2008 Administrative Sciences Association of Canada, Production and Operations Management Division*, Halifax, May 24–27, *29*(7), 83–98.

Schlesinger, P., Dobash, R.E., Dobash, R.P., & Weaver, C.K. (1992). *Women viewing violence*. London, UK: British Film Institute.

Schoonhoven, C.B. (1981). Problems with contingency theory: Testing assumptions hidden within the language of contingency theory. *Administrative Science Quarterly, 26*, 349–377.

Schrøder, K.C. (1999). The best of both worlds? Media audience research between rival paradigms. In P. Alasuutari (Ed.), *Rethinking the media audience*. London, UK: Sage.

Schuman, H., & Converse, J. (1971). The effects of black and white interviewers on black responses in 1968. *Public Opinion Quarterly, 35*, 44–68.

Schuman, H., & Presser, S. (1981). *Questions and answers in attitude surveys: Experiments on question form, wording, and context*. San Diego, CA: Academic Press.

Schutte, N., Toppinnen, S., Kalimo, R., & Schaufeli, W. (2000). The factorial validity of the Maslach Burnout Inventory–General Survey (MBI–GS) across occupational groups and nations. *Journal of Occupational and Organizational Psychology, 73*(1), 53–67.

Schutz, A. (1962). *Collected papers, I. The problem of social reality*. The Hague, The Netherlands: Martinus Nijhof.

Schweitzer, L., & Duxbury, L. (2006). Benchmarking the use of telework arrangements in Canada. *Canadian Journal of Administrative Science, 23*(2), 105–117.

Scott, A. (1994). *Willing slaves?: British workers under HRM*. Cambridge, UK: Cambridge University Press.

Scott, J. (1990). *A matter of record*. Cambridge: Polity.

Scott, W., Banks, J., Halsey, A., & Lupton, T. (1956). *Technical change and industrial relations*. Liverpool: Liverpool University Press.

Seale, C. (1999). *The quality of qualitative research*. London, UK: Sage.

Seligman, M.E., & Csikszentrnihalyi, M. (2000). Positive psychology: An introduction. *American Psychologist, 55*, 5–14.

Serenko, A., Cocosila, M., & Turel, O. (2008). The state and evolution of information systems research in Canada: A sociometric analysis. *Canadian Journal of Administrative Science, 25*(4), 279–294.

Sexty, R. (2008). cjas: Recollections of its origins and challenges. *Canadian Journal of Administrative Sciences / Revue Canadienne des Sciences de l'Administration, 25*(4), 269–270.

Sexty, R., & Pecore, G. (2000). Tracking history and strategy at Memorial's Faculty of Business. In B. Austin (Ed.), *Capitalizing knowledge*. Toronto: U of T Press.

Shaffir, W.B., and Stebbins, R.A. (1991). *Experiencing Fieldwork: An Inside View of Qualitative Research*. Newbury Park, CA: Sage.

Shapiro, M. (1985–6). Metaphor in the philosophy of the social sciences. *Cultural Critique, 2*, 191–214.

Sharpe, D. (1997). Managerial control strategies and subcultural processes. In S. Sackmann (Ed.), *Cultural complexity in organizations*. London, UK: Sage.

Sheehan, K., & Hoy, M.G. (1999). Using e-mail to survey internet users in the United States: Methodology and assessment. *Journal of Computer-Mediated Communication, 4*, www.ascusc.org/jcmc/vol4/issue3/sheehan.html

Shenoy, S. (1981). Organization structure and context: A replication of the Aston Study in India. In D.J. Hickson & C.J. McMillan (Eds), *Organisation and nation: The Aston programme IV* (pp. 113–154). Farnborough, UK: Gower.

Shrivastava, P. (1987). *Bhopal: Anatomy of a crisis*. Cambridge, MA: Ballinger.

Silverman, D. (1984). Going private: Ceremonial forms in a private oncology Clinic. *Sociology, 18*, 191–204.

Silverman, D. (1985). *Qualitative methodology and sociology: Describing the social world*. Aldershot, UK: Gower.

———. (1993). *Interpreting qualitative data: Methods for analysing qualitative data*. London, UK: Sage.

———. (2000). *Doing qualitative research: A practical handbook*. London, UK: Sage.

———. (2005). *Doing qualitative research*. London, Sage.

Skipton, M., & D. Foster.(1995). The unchanging classroom: A design for disciplined subjects rather than for subject disciplines. *Proceeding of the 1995 Administrative Sciences Association of Canada, Organization Theory Division*, Windsor, 3–6 June, *16*(10), 56–64.

Skipton, M.D., & Furey, M. (2008). Introduction to Business in Society: Course design for a more relevant first course in a business program. In L. Bauer & A. Faseruk (Eds), *Proceedings of the 38th Atlantic Schools of Business Conference*, Memorial University of Newfoundland, St. Johns, Oct. 17–19. St. John's, NL: Atlantic Schools of Business.

Sloan, A.P., Jr. (1963). *My years with General Motors*. New York, NY: Doubleday.

Smircich, L. (1983). Concepts of culture and organizational analysis. *Administrative Science Quarterly, 28*, 339–358.

Smith, C. (2009). The short overview of the labour process perspective and history of the International Labour Process Conference. International Labour Process conference.

Smith, C.B. (1997). Casting the net: Surveying an internet population. *Journal of Computer-Mediated Communication, 3*, www.ascusc.org/jcmc/vol3/issue1/yun.html.

Smith, J.K. (1983). Quantitative versus qualitative research: An attempt to clarify the issue, *Educational Researcher, 12*, 6–13.

Smith, J.K., & Heshusius, L. (1986). Closing down the conversation: The end of the quantitative–qualitative debate among educational enquirers. *Educational Researcher, 15*, 4–12.

Smith, K. Clegg (2004). 'Electronic eavesdropping': The ethical issues involved in conducting a virtual ethnography. In M.D. Johns, S-L.S. Chen, & G.J. Hall (Eds), *Online social research*. New York: Peter Lang.

Smith, T.W. (1995). Trends in non-response rates. *International Journal of Public Opinion Research, 7*, 157–171.

Snyder, N., & Glueck, W.F. (1980). 'How managers plan: The analysis of managers' activities. *Long Range Planning, 13*, 70–76.

Sørensen, J.B. (2004). The organizational demography of racial employment segregation. *American Journal of Sociology, 110*(3), 626–671.

Spector, B. (2008). The business of blacklisting. *Canadian Journal of Administrative Sciences / Revue Canadienne des Sciences de l'Administration, 25*(2), 121–133.

Spender, J. (1989). *Industry recipes: An enquiry into the nature and sources of managerial judgement*. Oxford, UK: Blackwell.

Spradley, J.P. (1979). *The ethnographic interview*. New York, NY: Holt, Rinehart & Winston.

Spradley, J.P., & McCurdy, D. (1972). *The cultural experience.* Chicago, IL: Science Research Associates.

Sprokkereef, A., Larkin, E., Pole, C.J., & Burgess, R.G. (1995). The data, the team, and the ethnograph. *Studies in Qualitative Methodology, 5,* 81–103.

Stacey, J. (1988). Can there be a feminist ethnography? *Women's International Studies Forum, 11,* 21–27.

Stake, R.E. (1995). *The art of case study research.* Thousand Oaks, CA: Sage.

Stanley, L., & Temple, B. (1995). Doing the business? Evaluating software packages to aid the analysis of qualitative data sets. *Studies in Qualitative Methodology, 5,* 169–197.

Stanley, L., & Wise, S. (1983). *Breaking out: Feminist consciousness and feminist research.* London, UK: Routledge & Kegan Paul.

Starbuck, W.H. (1981). A trip to view the elephants and rattlesnakes in the Garden of Aston. In A.H. van de Ven & W.F. Joyce (Eds), *Perspectives on organization design and behaviour.* New York: Wiley.

Statistics Canada. *Ethnic Diversity Survey.* Statistics Canada (2003). [cited 29 September.] Available from http://www.statcan.ca/Daily/English/030929/d030929a.htm.

Stewart, K. & Williams, M. (2005). Researching online populations: The use of online focus groups for social research. *Qualitative Research, 5*(4), 395– 416.

Stewart, R. (1967). *Managers and their jobs.* London, UK: Macmillan.

Stiles, P. (2001). The impact of the board on strategy: An empirical examination. *Journal of Management Studies, 38*(5), 627–650.

Storey, J., Quintas, P., Taylor, P., & Fowle, W. (2002). Flexible employment contracts and their implications for product and process innovation. *International Journal of Human Resource Management, 13*(1), 1–18.

Strathern, M. (1987). The limits of auto-anthropology. In A. Jackson (Ed.). *Anthropology at home.* London, UK: Tavistock.

Strauss, A. (1987). *Qualitative analysis for social scientists.* New York, NY: Cambridge University Press.

Strauss, A., & Corbin, J. (1990). *Basics of qualitative research: Grounded theory procedures and techniques.* Newbury Park, CA: Sage.

———, & ———. (1998). *Basics of qualitative research: Grounded theory procedures and techniques.* Thousand Oaks, CA: Sage.

Strauss, A., Schatzman, L., Ehrlich, D., Bucher, R., & Sabshin, M. (1963). The hospital and its negotiated order. In E. Friedson (Ed.), *The Hospital in Modern Society.* New York, NY: Macmillan.

Stuart, I. (2006). Lean supply, collaborative supplier relations and supplier alliances: Strategic advantage of illusory gains? *Proceedings of the 2006 Administrative Sciences Association of Canada, Production and Operations Management Division,* Banff, 3–6 June, 27(7), 18–35.

Suddaby, R. (2006). From the editors: what grounded theory is not. *Academy of Management Journal, 49*(4), 633–642.

Suddaby, R., & Greenwood, R. (2005). Rhetorical strategies of legitimacy. *Administrative Science Quarterly, 50*(1), 35–67.

Sudman, S., & Blair, E. (1999). Sampling in the twenty-first century. *Journal of the Academy of Marketing Science, 27*(2), 269–77.

Sudman, S., & Bradburn, N.M. (1982). *Asking Questions: A practical guide to questionnaire design.* San Francisco, CA: Jossey-Bass.

Suchman, M.C. (1995). Managing legitimacy: Strategic and institutional approaches. *Academy of Management Review, 20,* 571–611.

Supphellen, M., & Nysveen, H. (2001). Drivers of intention to revisit the websites of well-known companies. *International Journal of Market Research, 43*(3), 341–352.

Swales, J.M., & Rogers, P.S. (1995). Discourse and the projection of corporate culture: The mission-statement. *Discourse and Society, 6*(2), 223–242.

Sweet, C. (2001). Designing and conducting virtual focus groups. *Qualitative Market Research, 4,* 130–135.

Tashakkori, A., & Teddlie, C. (2003). *Handbook of mixed methods in social and behavioral research.* Thousand Oaks, CA: Sage

Taylor, H. (1997). The very different methods used to conduct telephone surveys of the public. *Journal of the Market Research Society, 39*(3), 421–432.

Terkel, S. (1974). *Working.* Harmondsworth: Penguin.

Thomas, R., & Davies, A. (2005). Theorizing the micro-politics of resistance: New public management and managerial identities in the UK Public Services. *Organization Studies, 26*(5), 683–706.

Thurlow, A. (2007). *Meaningful change: Making sense of the discourse of the language of change* (Doctoral dissertation), Sobey School of Business, Department. Of Management, Saint. Mary's University, Halifax, NS.

Thurlow, A., & Helms Mills, J. (2005). Language, power and identity in organizational change. In B. Sharma (Ed.), *Proceeding of the 35th annual meeting of the Atlantic Schools of Business* (pp. 122–130), September 29–October 1, Halifax, Nova Scotia.

———, & ———. (2009). Change, talk and sensemaking. *Journal of Organizational Change Management, 22*(5), 459–479.

Thurlow, A., Mills, A.J., & Helms Mills, J. (2006). Feminist qualitative research and workplace diversity. In A.M. Konrad, P. Pradas, & J.K. Pringle (Eds), *Handbook of workplace diversity* (pp. 217–236). London, UK: Dage.

Tinker, T., & Neimark, M. (1987). The role of annual reports in gender and class contradictions at General Motors: 1917–76. *Accounting, Organizations and Society, 12*(1), 71–88.

Todd, P.A., McKeen, J.D., & Gallupe, R.B. (1995). The evolution of is job skills: A content analysis of is job advertisements from 1970 to 1990. *MIS Quarterly, 19*(1), 1–27.

Tourangeau, R., & Smith, T.W. (1996). Asking sensitive questions: The impact of data collection mode, question format, and question context. *Public Opinion Quarterly, 60,* 275–304.

Tranfield, D., Denyer, D., & Smart, P. (2003). Towards a methodology for developing evidence-informed management knowledge by means of systematic review. *British Journal of Management, 14*, 207–222.

Tranfield, D., & Starkey, K. (1998). The nature, social organisation and promotion of management research: Towards policy. *British Journal of Management, 9*, 341–353.

Trow, M. (1957). Comment on participant observation and interviewing: A comparison. *Human Organization, 16*, 33–5.

Truss, C. (2001). Complexities and controversies in linking HRM with organizational outcomes. *Journal of Management Studies, 38*(8), 1121–1149.

Tse, A.C.D. (1999). Conducting electronic focus group discussions among Chinese respondents. *Journal of the Market Research Society, 41*, 407–415.

Turner, B.A. (1994). Causes of disaster: Sloppy management. *British Journal of Management, 5*, 215–219.

Urch Duskat, V., & Wheeler, J.V. (2003). Managing from the boundary: The effective leadership of self-managing work teams. *Academy of Management Journal, 46*(4), 435–457.

Üsdiken, B., & Kieser, A. (2004). Introduction: History in organization studies. *Business History, 46*, 321–330.

Usunier, J.C. (1998). *International & cross-cultural management research*. London, UK: Sage.

Vaara, E., & Tienari, J. (Eds) (2010). *Sage encyclopedia of case study research* (Vol. 1). Thousand Oaks, CA: Sage.

Van Dijk, T.A. (1997). Discourse as interaction in society. In T.A. Van Dijk (Ed.). *Discourse as social interaction: Discourse Studies Vol. 2 – A Multidisciplinary Introduction*. Newbury Park, CA: Sage.

Van Kleeck, M. (1924). The social meaning of good management, *Bulletin of the Taylor Society & the Society of Industrial Engineers, 11*(6), December.

———. (1927). Financial incentives: An inseparable part of the task of management – discussion, *Bulletin of the Taylor Society and the Society of Industrial Engineers,* June.

Van Maanen, J. (1978). On watching the watchers. In P. Manning & J. Van Maanen (Eds), *Policing: The view from the street*. Santa Monica, CA: Goodyear.

———. (1988). *Tales of the Field*. Chicago, IL: The University of Chicago Press.

———. (1991a). Playing back the tape: Early days in the field. In W.B. Shaffir & R.A. Stebbins (Eds), *Experiencing fieldwork: An inside view of qualitative research*. Newbury Park, CA: Sage.

———. (1991b). The smile factory: Work at Disneyland. In P.J. Frost, L.F. Moore, M.R. Louis, C.C. Lundberg, & J. Martin (Eds), *Reframing Organizational Culture*. Newbury Park, CA: Sage.

———. (1996). On the matter of voice. *Journal of Management Inquiry, 5*(4), 375–381.

Van Maanen, J., & Kolb, D. (1985). The professional apprentice: Observations on fieldwork roles in two organizational settings. *Research in the Sociology of Organizations, 4*, 1–33.

Vaughan, D. (1990). Autonomy, independence and social Control: NASA and the Space Shuttle Challenger. *Administrative Science Quarterly, 35*, 225–257.

———. (1996). *The Challenger Launch Decision*. Chicago, IL: University of Chicago Press.

Venter, E., Boshoff, C., & Maas, G. (2005). The influence of successor related factors on the succession process in small and medium-sized family businesses. *Family Business Review, 18*(4), 283–303.

Vincze, Z. (2010). Grounded theory. In A.J. Mills, G. Durepos, & E. Weibe (Eds), *Sage encyclopedia of case study research*. Thousand Oaks, CA: Sage.

Virick, M., Lilly, J.D., & Casper, W.J. (2007). Doing more with less: An analysis of work life balance among layoff survivors. *Career Development International, 12*, 463–80.

von Wright, G.H. (1971). *Explanation and understanding*. London: Routledge.

Wagar, T. (1997). Factors affecting permanent workforce reduction: Evidence from large Canadian organizations. *Canadian Journal of Administrative Sciences, 14*(3), 303–314.

Wajcman, J., & Martin, B. (2002). Narratives of identity in modern management: The corrosion of identity difference? *Sociology, 36*, 985–1002.

Walker, T.J., Thiengtham, D.J., & Lin, M.Y. (2005). On the performance of airlines and airplane manufacturers following aviation disasters. *Canadian Journal of Administrative Sciences, 22*(1), 21–34.

Wallace, P. (2007). *Stories within stories: The career stories of women chartered accountants. A multi-layered analysis of career choice using Beauvoir's feminist existentialism as the lens* (Doctoral dissertation). Department of Management, Sobey School of Business, Saint Mary's University, Halifax, NS.

———. (2009a). Career stories of women professional accountants: Examining the personal narratives of career using Simone de Beauvoir's feminist existentialist philosophy as a theoretical framework. *Qualitative Research in Organizations and Management: An International Journal, 4*(1), 62–84.

———. (2009b). Why do women leave public accounting firms before reaching the partnership level? Stories told by women provide different answers to this same old question. *Canadian Journal of Administrative Science, 26*(3), 179–196.

Walsh, D. (1972). Sociology and the social world. In P. Filmer, M. Phillipson, D. Silverman, & D. Walsh (Eds), *New directions in sociological theory*. London: Collier-Macmillan.

Warren, A.M. (2009). An investigation of mandatory retirement: A qualitative and quantitative examination. *Management*. Halifax, NS: Saint Mary's University.

Warters, B. (2005). Software review: Review of TAMS analyzer (Macintosh version). *Field Methods, 17*(3), 321–328.

Watson, T. (1994a). *In search of management: Culture, chaos and control in managerial work*. London, UK: Routledge.

Watson, T. (1994b). Managing, crafting and researching: Words, skill and imagination in shaping management research. *British Journal of Management, 5S*: S77–87.

Watson, T.J. (2000). Ethnographic fiction science: Making sense of managerial work and organizational research processes with Caroline and Terry. *Organization, 7*(3), 489–510.

Wax, M.L. (1982). Research reciprocity rather than informed consent in fieldwork. In J.E. Sieber (Ed.), *The ethics of social research: Fieldwork, regulation and publication.* New York, NY: Springer-Verlag.

Weatherbee, T.G., & Dye, K.E. (2005). Stuck in time: The de-centering of the textbook in higher education. In B. Sharma (Ed.), *Proceedings of the 35th annual meeting of the Atlantic Schools of Business* (pp. 211–222).

Weatherbee, T.G., Dye, K.E., & Mills, A.J. (2008). There's nothing as good as a practical theory: The paradox of management education. *Management and Organizational History, 3*(2), 147–159.

Weaver, A., & Atkinson, P. (1994). *Microcomputing and qualitative data analysis.* Aldershot, UK: Avebury.

Webb, E.J., Campbell, D.T., Schwartz, R.D., & Sechrest, L. (1966). *Unobtrusive measures: Nonreactive measures in the social sciences.* Chicago, IL: Rand McNally.

Weber, M. (1947). *The theory of social and economic organization* (A.R. Henderson & T. Parsons, Trans.). London, UK: Free Press.

———. (1967). *The protestant ethic and the spirit of capitalism.* (T. Parsons, Trans.). London, UK: Allen & Unwin.

———. (1978). *Economy and Society* (G. Roth & C. Wittich, Trans). Berkeley, CA: University of California Press.

Weick, K.E. (1990). The vulnerable system: An analysis of the Tenerife Air Disaster. *Journal of Management, 16*(3), 571–593.

———. (1993). The collapse of sensemaking in organizations: The Mann Gulch disaster. *Administrative Science Quarterly, 38*, 628–652.

———. (1995). *Sensemaking in Organizations.* London, UK: Sage.

———. (1996). Drop your tools: An allegory for organizational study. *Administrative Science Quarterly, 41*, 301–313.

———. (2001). *Making Sense of the Organization.* Oxford, UK: Blackwell.

Weick, K.E., Sutcliffe, K., & Obstfeld, D. (2005). Organizing and the Process of Sensemaking. *Organization Science, 16*(4). 409–421.

Weigand, H., & Mills, A.J. (2010). The Olivieri case: The relationship between clinical research and corporate responsibility. A take of ethics, greed, and organizational conflict. Case presented at the Dark Side' case writing competition at the Academy of Management annual meeting, Montreal [Competition finalist].

Weinholtz, D., Kacer, B., & Rocklin, T. (1995). Salvaging quantitative research with qualitative data. *Qualitative Health Research, 5*, 388–397.

Weitzman, E.A., & Miles, M.B. (1995). *Computer programs for qualitative data analysis.* Thousand Oaks, CA: Sage.

Wesson, M, Clinton, R.N., Limon, J.E., McIntosh, M.K. & Radelet, M.L. (2009). *Report of the Investigative Committee of the Standing Committee on Reseacrh Misconduct at the University of Colorado at Bolder concerning Allegations of Academic Misconduct against Professor Ward Churchill.* University of Colorado at Bolder 2006 [cited 13 March 2009]. Available from http://www.colorado.edu/news/reports/churchill/churchillreport051606.html.

Westwood, S. (1984). *All day every day: Factory, family, women's lives.* London, UK: Pluto Press.

Wetherell, M. (1998). Positioning and interpretative repertoires: Conversation analysis and post-structuralism in dialogue. *Discourse and Society, 9*, 387–412.

Wharton, A. (1993). The affective consequences of service work. *Work and Occupations, 20*, 205–232.

White, H. (1985). *Tropics of discourse: Essays in cultural criticism.* Baltimore, MD: Johns Hopkins University Press.

Whittington, R. (1989). *Corporate Strategies in Recession and Recovery.* London, UK: Unwin Hyman.

Whyte, W.F. (1953). Interviewing for organizational research. *Human Organization, 12*(2), 15–22.

———. (1955). *Street corner society* (2nd ed.). Chicago, IL: University of Chicago Press.

Wicks, D. (1996). Individual agency and compliance: A critical examination of embedded assumptions of subordinate volition in theories of organization. *Proceeding of the 1996 Administrative Sciences Association of Canada, Organizational Behaviour Division,* Montreal, 25–28 June, *17*(5), 170–179

———. (2010). Axial coding. In A.J. Mills, G. Durepos, & E. Weibe (Eds), *Sage encyclopedia of case study research.* Thousand Oaks, CA: Sage.

Wicks, D., & Bradshaw, P. (2002). Gendered value foundations that reproduce discrimination and inhibit organizational change. In I. Aaltio & A.J. Mills (Eds), *Gender, identity and the culture of organizations* (pp. 137–159). London, UK: Routledge.

Wicks, D., & Grandy, G. (2007). What cultures exist in the tattooing collectivity? Ambiguity, membership and participation. *Culture and Organization, 13*(4), 349–363.

Widdicombe, S. (1993). Autobiography and change: Rhetoric and authenticity of Gothic style. In E. Burman & I. Parker (Eds), *Discourse analytic research: Readings and repertoires of text.* London, UK: Routledge.

Wilkinson, S. (1998). Focus groups in feminist research: Power, interaction, and the co-production of meaning. *Women's Studies International Forum, 21*, 111–125.

———. (1999a). Focus group methodology: A review. *International Journal of Social Research Methodology, 1*, 181–203.

———. (1999b). Focus groups: A feminist method. *Psychology of Women Quarterly, 23*, 221–244.

Williams, R. (1976). Symbolic interactionism: Fusion of theory and research. In D.C. Thorns (Ed.), *New directions in sociology.* London, UK: David & Charles.

Willman, P., Renton-O'Creevy, M., Nicholson, N., & Soane, E. (2002). Traders, managers and loss aversion in investment banking: A field study. *Accounting, Organizations and Society, 27*, 85–98.

Willment, J.A. (2010). Cognitive mapping. In A.J. Mills, G.

Durepos & E. Weibe (Eds), *Sage encyclopedia of case study research* (pp. 161–162). Thousand Oaks, CA: Sage.

Willmott, H. (1990). Beyond paradigmatic closure in organisational enquiry. In J. Hassard & D. Pym (Eds), *The theory and philosophy of organizations*. London: Routledge.

Wilson, F. (1995). *Organizational Behaviour and Gender*. London, UK: McGraw Hill.

Winter, R. (1989). *Learning from experience: Principles and practice in action-research*. London, UK: Falmer.

Wolcott, H.F. (1990). *Writing up qualitative research*. Newbury Park, CA: Sage.

———. (1995). Making a study more ethnographic. In J. Van Maanen (Ed.), *Representation in ethnography*. London, UK: Sage.

Wolfram Cox, J., & Hassard, J. (2009). Triangulation. In A.J. Mills, G. Durepos, & E. Weibe (Eds), *Sage encyclopedia of case study research*. Thousand Oaks, CA: Sage.

Wood, T.J., & De Paula, A.P. (2008). Pop-management literature: Popular business press and management culture in Brazil. *Canadian Journal of Administrative Sciences, 25*(3), 185–200.

Woolgar, S. (1988). *Science: The very idea*. Chichester, UK: Ellis Horwood.

Wooten, L.P., & Crane, P. (2004). Generating dynamic capabilities through a humanistic work ideology. *American Behavioral Scientist, 47*, 848–866.

Wu, S., & Alagheband, F.K. (2008). The construction of acrual e-negotiation protocols: A preliminary study. *Proceeding of the 2008 Administrative Sciences Association of Canada, Information Systems Division*, Halifax, 24–27 May, *29*(4), 239–241.

Yin, R.K. (1984). *Case study research: Design and methods*. Beverly Hills, CA: Sage.

———. (2003). *Applications of case study research* (2nd ed.). Thousand Oaks, CA: Sage.

Youssef, C.M., & Luthans, F. (2007). Positive organizational behavior in the workplace: The impact of hope, optimism, and resilience. *Journal of Management, 33*, 774–800.

Yue, A.R. (2009). Validity. In A.J. Mills, G. Durepos, & E. Weibe (Eds), *Sage encyclopedia of case study research*. Thousand Oaks, CA: Sage.

Yue, A.R., McKee, M., Kelloway, E.K., & Jamieson, R. (2009). Training for issues management: Measuring the impact on manager learning, efficacy and commitment. Presentation at the 2009 Academy of Management Conference, Chicago, IL. Yue, A.R., & Mills, A.J. (2008). Making sense out of bad faith: Sartre, weick & existential sensemaking in organizational analysis. *Tamara: Journal of Critical Postmodern Organization Science, 7*(1), 66–80.

Yun, G.W., & Trumbo, C.W. (2000). Comparative response to a survey executed by post, e-mail, and web form. *Journal of Computer-Mediated Communication, 6*, www.ascusc.org/jcmc/vol6/issue1/yun.html.

Zamanou, S., & Glaser, S.R. (1994). Moving toward participation and involvement. *Group and Organization Management, 19*(4), 475–502.

Zerbe, W., Dobni, D. & Harel, G.H. (1998). Promoting employee service behaviour: The role of perceptions of human resource management practices and service culture. *Canadian Journal of Administrative Sciences, 15*(2), 165–179

Zikic, J., & Richardson, J. (2007). Unlocking the careers of business professionals following job loss: sensemaking and career exploration of older workers. *Canadian Journal of Administrative Science, 24*(1), 58–73.

Zimmerman, B. (1991). Of patterns, theories and strategic processes. *Proceeding of the 1991 Administrative Sciences Association of Canada, Policy Division*, Niagara Falls, May 30–June 2, *12*(9), 75–83.

Zuber-Skerritt, O. (1996). *New directions in action research*. London, UK: Falmer.

Index